P9-DYZ-954

International Directory of

COMPANY HISTORIES

International Directory of
COMPANY
HISTORIES

VOLUME 87

Editor

Jay P. Pederson

ST. JAMES PRESS

An imprint of Thomson Gale, a part of The Thomson Corporation

THOMSON

GALE

Detroit • New York • San Francisco • New Haven, Conn. • Waterville, Maine • London

THOMSON
GALE

International Directory of Company Histories, Volume 87
Jay P. Pederson, Editor

Project Editor
Miranda H. Ferrara

Editorial
Virgil Burton, Donna Craft, Louise Gagné, Peggy Geeseman, Julie Gough, Linda Hall, Sonya Hill, Keith Jones, Lynn Pearce, Holly Selden, Justine Ventimiglia

Production Technology Specialist
Mike Weaver

Imaging and Multimedia
Lezlie Light

Composition and Electronic Prepress
Gary Leach, Evi Seoud

Manufacturing
Rhonda Dover

Product Management
David Forman

LIBRARY OF CONGRESS CATALOG NUMBER 89-190943

ISBN-13: 978-1-55862-591-4   ISBN-10: 1-55862-591-7

This title is also available as an e-book
ISBN-13: 978-1-4144-2971-7   ISBN-10: 1-4144-2971-1

BRITISH LIBRARY CATALOGUING IN PUBLICATION DATA

International directory of company histories, Vol. 87
I. Jay P. Pederson
33.87409

Printed in the United States of America
10 9 8 7 6 5 4 3 2 1

Contents

Preface

The St. James Press series *The International Directory of Company Histories* (*IDCH*) is intended for reference use by students, business people, librarians, historians, economists, investors, job candidates, and others who seek to learn more about the historical development of the world's most important companies. To date, *IDCH* has covered over 8,600 companies in 87 volumes.

INCLUSION CRITERIA

Most companies chosen for inclusion in *IDCH* have achieved a minimum of US$25 million in annual sales and are leading influences in their industries or geographical locations. Companies may be publicly held, private, or nonprofit. State-owned companies that are important in their industries and that may operate much like public or private companies also are included. Wholly owned subsidiaries and divisions are profiled if they meet the requirements for inclusion. Entries on companies that have had major changes since they were last profiled may be selected for updating.

The *IDCH* series highlights 10% private and nonprofit companies, and features updated entries on approximately 35 companies per volume.

ENTRY FORMAT

Each entry begins with the company's legal name; the address of its headquarters; its telephone, toll-free, and fax numbers; and its web site. A statement of public, private, state, or parent ownership follows. A company with a legal name in both English and the language of its headquarters country is listed by the English name, with the native-language name in parentheses.

The company's founding or earliest incorporation date, the number of employees, and the most recent available sales figures follow. Sales figures are given in local currencies with equivalents in U.S. dollars. For some private companies, sales figures are estimates and indicated by the abbreviation *est.* The entry lists the exchanges on which the company's stock is traded and its ticker symbol, as well as the company's NAIC codes.

Entries generally contain a *Company Perspectives* box which provides a short summary of the company's mission, goals, and ideals; a *Key Dates* box highlighting milestones in the company's history; lists of *Principal Subsidiaries, Principal Divisions, Principal Operating Units, Principal Competitors*; and articles for *Further Reading*.

American spelling is used throughout *IDCH*, and the word "billion" is used in its U.S. sense of one thousand million.

Users of the *IDCH* series will notice some changes to the look of the series starting with Volume 77. The pages have been redesigned for better clarity and ease of use; the standards for entry content, however, have not changed.

SOURCES

Entries have been compiled from publicly accessible sources both in print and on the Internet such as general and academic periodicals, books, and annual reports, as well as material supplied by the companies themselves.

CUMULATIVE INDEXES

IDCH contains three indexes: the **Index to Companies**, which provides an alphabetical index to companies discussed in the text as well as to companies profiled, the **Index to Industries**, which allows researchers to locate companies by their principal industry, and the **Geographic Index**, which lists companies alphabetically by the country of their headquarters. The indexes are cumulative and specific instructions for using them are found immediately preceding each index.

SUGGESTIONS WELCOME

Comments and suggestions from users of *IDCH* on any aspect of the product as well as suggestions for companies to be included or updated are cordially invited. Please write:

The Editor
International Directory of Company Histories
St. James Press
27500 Drake Rd.
Farmington Hills, Michigan 48331-3535

St. James Press does not endorse any of the companies or products mentioned in this series. Companies appearing in the *International Directory of Company Histories* were selected without reference to their wishes and have in no way endorsed their entries.

Notes on Contributors

M. L. Cohen
Novelist, business writer, and researcher living in Paris.

Jeffrey L. Covell
Seattle-based writer.

Ed Dinger
Writer and editor based in Bronx, New York.

Jodi Essey-Stapleton
Writer based in Illinois.

Robert Halasz
Former editor in chief of *World Progress* and *Funk & Wagnalls New Encyclopedia Yearbook*; author, *The U.S. Marines* (Millbrook Press, 1993).

Frederick C. Ingram
Writer based in South Carolina.

Kathleen Peippo
Minneapolis-based writer.

Nelson Rhodes
Editor, writer, and consultant in the Chicago area.

Carrie Rothburd
Writer and editor specializing in corporate profiles, academic texts, and academic journal articles.

David E. Salamie
Part-owner of InfoWorks Development Group, a reference publication development and editorial services company.

Ted Sylvester
Photographer, writer, and editor of the environmental journal *From the Ground Up*.

Mary Tradii
Colorado-based writer.

Frank Uhle
Ann Arbor-based writer; movie projectionist, disc jockey, and staff member of *Psychotronic Video* magazine.

A. Woodward
Wisconsin-based writer.

List of Abbreviations

¥ Japanese yen
£ United Kingdom pound
$ United States dollar

A

AB Aktiebolag (Finland, Sweden)
AB Oy Aktiebolag Osakeyhtiot (Finland)
A.E. Anonimos Eteria (Greece)
AED Emirati dirham
AG Aktiengesellschaft (Austria, Germany, Switzerland, Liechtenstein)
aG auf Gegenseitigkeit (Austria, Germany)
A.m.b.a. Andelsselskab med begraenset ansvar (Denmark)
A.O. Anonim Ortaklari/Ortakligi (Turkey)
ApS Amparteselskab (Denmark)
ARS Argentine peso
A.S. Anonim Sirketi (Turkey)
A/S Aksjeselskap (Norway)
A/S Aktieselskab (Denmark, Sweden)
Ay Avoinyhtio (Finland)
ATS Austrian shilling
AUD Australian dollar
ApS Amparteselskab (Denmark)
Ay Avoinyhtio (Finland)

B

B.A. Buttengewone Aansprakeiijkheid (Netherlands)
BEF Belgian franc

BHD Bahraini dinar
Bhd. Berhad (Malaysia, Brunei)
BRL Brazilian real
B.V. Besloten Vennootschap (Belgium, Netherlands)

C

C.A. Compania Anonima (Ecuador, Venezuela)
CAD Canadian dollar
C. de R.L. Compania de Responsabilidad Limitada (Spain)
CEO Chief Executive Officer
CFO Chief Financial Officer
CHF Swiss franc
Cia. Companhia (Brazil, Portugal)
Cia. Compania (Latin America (except Brazil), Spain)
Cia. Compagnia (Italy)
Cie. Compagnie (Belgium, France, Luxembourg, Netherlands)
CIO Chief Information Officer
CLP Chilean peso
CNY Chinese yuan
Co. Company
COO Chief Operating Officer
Coop. Cooperative
COP Colombian peso
Corp. Corporation
C. por A. Compania por Acciones (Dominican Republic)
CPT Cuideachta Phoibi Theoranta (Republic of Ireland)

CRL Companhia a Responsabilidao Limitida (Portugal, Spain)
C.V. Commanditaire Vennootschap (Netherlands, Belgium)
CZK Czech koruna

D

D&B Dunn & Bradstreet
DEM German deutsche mark
Div. Division (United States)
DKK Danish krone
DZD Algerian dinar

E

EC Exempt Company (Arab countries)
Edms. Bpk. Eiendoms Beperk (South Africa)
EEK Estonian Kroon
eG eingetragene Genossenschaft (Germany)
EGMBH Eingetragene Genossenschaft mit beschraenkter Haftung (Austria, Germany)
EGP Egyptian pound
Ek For Ekonomisk Forening (Sweden)
EP Empresa Portuguesa (Portugal)
E.P.E. Etema Pemorismenis Evthynis (Greece)
ESOP Employee Stock Options and Ownership
ESP Spanish peseta
Et(s). Etablissement(s) (Belgium,

France, Luxembourg)
eV eingetragener Verein (Germany)
EUR euro

F
FIM Finnish markka
FRF French franc

G
G.I.E. Groupement d'Interet Economique (France)
gGmbH gemeinnutzige Gesellschaft mit beschraenkter Haftung (Austria, Germany, Switzerland)
G.I.E. Groupement d'Interet Economique (France)
GmbH Gesellschaft mit beschraenkter Haftung (Austria, Germany, Switzerland)
GRD Greek drachma
GWA Gewerbte Amt (Austria, Germany)

H
HB Handelsbolag (Sweden)
HF Hlutafelag (Iceland)
HKD Hong Kong dollar
HUF Hungarian forint

I
IDR Indonesian rupiah
IEP Irish pound
ILS new Israeli shekel
Inc. Incorporated (United States, Canada)
INR Indian rupee
IPO Initial Public Offering
I/S Interesentselskap (Norway)
I/S Interessentselskab (Denmark)
ISK Icelandic krona
ITL Italian lira

J
JMD Jamaican dollar
JOD Jordanian dinar

K
KB Kommanditbolag (Sweden)
Kft Korlatolt Felelossegu Tarsasag (Hungary)
KG Kommanditgesellschaft (Austria, Germany, Switzerland)
KGaA Kommanditgesellschaft auf Aktien (Austria, Germany, Switzerland)

KK Kabushiki Kaisha (Japan)
KPW North Korean won
KRW South Korean won
K/S Kommanditselskab (Denmark)
K/S Kommandittselskap (Norway)
KWD Kuwaiti dinar
Ky Kommandiitiyhtio (Finland)

L
LBO Leveraged Buyout
Lda. Limitada (Spain)
L.L.C. Limited Liability Company (Arab countries, Egypt, Greece, United States)
L.L.P. Limited Partnership (United States)
L.P. Limited Partnership (Canada, South Africa, United Kingdom, United States)
Ltd. Limited
Ltda. Limitada (Brazil, Portugal)
Ltee. Limitee (Canada, France)
LUF Luxembourg franc

M
mbH mit beschraenkter Haftung (Austria, Germany)
Mij. Maatschappij (Netherlands)
MUR Mauritian rupee
MXN Mexican peso
MYR Malaysian ringgit

N
N.A. National Association (United States)
NGN Nigerian naira
NLG Netherlands guilder
NOK Norwegian krone
N.V. Naamloze Vennootschap (Belgium, Netherlands)
NZD New Zealand dollar

O
OAO Otkrytoe Aktsionernoe Obshchestve (Russia)
OHG Offene Handelsgesellschaft (Austria, Germany, Switzerland)
OMR Omani rial
OOO Obschestvo s Ogranichennoi Otvetstvennostiu (Russia)
OOUR Osnova Organizacija Udruzenog Rada (Yugoslavia)

Oy Osakeyhtiot (Finland)

P
P.C. Private Corp. (United States)
PHP Philippine peso
PKR Pakistani rupee
P/L Part Lag (Norway)
PLC Public Limited Co. (United Kingdom, Ireland)
P.L.L.C. Professional Limited Liability Corporation (United States)
PLN Polish zloty
P.T. Perusahaan/Perseroan Terbatas (Indonesia)
PTE Portuguese escudo
Pte. Private (Singapore)
Pty. Proprietary (Australia, South Africa, United Kingdom)
Pvt. Private (India, Zimbabwe)
PVBA Personen Vennootschap met Beperkte Aansprakelijkheid (Belgium)

Q
QAR Qatar riyal

R
REIT Real Estate Investment Trust
RMB Chinese renminbi
Rt Reszvenytarsasag (Hungary)
RUB Russian ruble

S
S&P Standard & Poor's
S.A. Société Anonyme (Arab countries, Belgium, France, Jordan, Luxembourg, Switzerland)
S.A. Sociedad Anónima (Latin America [except Brazil], Spain, Mexico)
S.A. Sociedades Anônimas (Brazil, Portugal)
SAA Societe Anonyme Arabienne (Arab countries)
S.A.C. Sociedad Anonima Comercial (Latin America [except Brazil])
S.A.C.I. Sociedad Anonima Comercial e Industrial (Latin America [except Brazil])
S.A.C.I.y.F. Sociedad Anonima Comercial e Industrial y Financiera (Latin America [except Brazil])

S.A. de C.V. Sociedad Anonima de Capital Variable Mexico)

SAK Societe Anonyme Kuweitienne (Arab countries)

SAL Societe Anonyme Libanaise (Arab countries)

SAO Societe Anonyme Omanienne (Arab countries)

SAQ Societe Anonyme Qatarienne (Arab countries)

SAR Saudi riyal

S.A.R.L. Sociedade Anonima de Responsabilidade Limitada (Brazil, Portugal)

S.A.R.L. Société &agrave: Responsabilité Limitée (France, Belgium, Luxembourg)

S.A.S. Societ&aacute: in Accomandita Semplice (Italy)

S.A.S. Societe Anonyme Syrienne (Arab countries)

S.C. Societe en Commandite (Belgium, France, Luxembourg)

S.C.A. Societe Cooperativa Agricole (France, Italy, Luxembourg)

S.C.I. Sociedad Cooperativa Ilimitada (Spain)

S.C.L. Sociedad Cooperativa Limitada (Spain)

S.C.R.L. Societe Cooperative a Responsabilite Limitee (Belgium)

Sdn. Bhd. Sendirian Berhad (Malaysia)

SEK Swedish krona

SGD Singapore dollar

Sdn. Bhd. Sendirian Berhad (Malaysia)

S.L. Sociedad Limitada (Latin America (except Brazil), Portugal, Spain)

S/L Salgslag (Norway)

S.N.C. Société en Nom Collectif (France)

Soc. Sociedad (Latin America (except Brazil), Spain)

Soc. Sociedade (Brazil, Portugal)

Soc. Societa (Italy)

S.p.A. Societ&agrave: per Azioni (Italy)

Sp. z.o.o. Spólka z ograniczona odpowiedzialnoscia (Poland)

S.R.L. Sociedad de Responsabilidad Limitada (Spain, Mexico, Latin America [except Brazil])

S.R.L. Societ&agrave: a Responsabilit&agrave: Limitata (Italy)

S.R.O. Spolecnost s Rucenim Omezenym (Czechoslovakia

S.S.K. Sherkate Sahami Khass (Iran)

Ste. Societe (France, Belgium, Luxembourg, Switzerland)

Ste. Cve. Societe Cooperative(Belgium)

S.V. Samemwerkende Vennootschap (Belgium)

S.Z.R.L. Societe Zairoise a Responsabilite Limitee (Zaire)

T

THB Thai baht

TND Tunisian dinar

TRL Turkish lira

TWD new Taiwan dollar

U

U.A. Uitgesloten Aansporakeiijkheid (Netherlands)

u.p.a. utan personligt ansvar (Sweden)

V

VAG Verein der Arbeitgeber (Austria, Germany)

VEB Venezuelan bolivar

VERTR Vertriebs (Austria, Germany)

VND Vietnamese dong

V.O.f. Vennootschap onder firma (Netherlands)

VVAG Versicherungsverein auf Gegenseitigkeit (Austria, Germany)

W–Z

WA Wettelika Aansprakalikhaed (Netherlands)

WLL With Limited Liability (Bahrain, Kuwait, Qatar, Saudi Arabia)

YK Yugen Kaisha (Japan)

ZAO Zakrytoe Aktsionernoe Obshchestve (Russia)

ZAR South African rand

ZMK Zambian kwacha

ACCION International

---

56 Roland Street
Boston, Massachusetts 02129
U.S.A.
Telephone: (617) 625-7000
Fax: (617) 625-7020
Web site: http://www.accion.org

Private Company
Incorporated: 1965
Employees: 125
Sales: $25.14 million (2005)
NAIC: 522298 All Other Non-Depository Credit Intermediation; 523999 Miscellaneous Financial Investment Activities; 561499 All Other Business Support Services

■■■

ACCION International is a nonprofit organization that finances, through partner lending organizations, small, short-term loans sought by poor people starting their own businesses. They pay interest rates that reflect the cost of lending only. ACCION's partners and affiliates operate in more than 20 countries in Latin America, the Caribbean, Asia, and sub-Saharan Africa. A subsidiary, ACCION USA, active in nine states, is the largest microlender in the United States. ACCION also provides technical assistance to improve business operations and efficiency and loan guarantees to help access commercial capital.

HELPING PEOPLE HELP THEMSELVES: 1961–72

ACCION International was founded in 1961 by Joseph Blatchford, an idealistic law student who had just completed a goodwill tennis tour of 30 Latin American cities. He returned haunted by the images of Latin America's urban poor living in crowded shantytowns without elementary sanitary facilities. Blatchford and his law school friends raised $90,000 from U.S. companies to start a new kind of organization: a community development effort intended to help the poor help themselves. ACCION was adopted as an acronym for Americans for Community Cooperation in Other Nations.

That summer, Blatchford and 30 volunteers flew to Venezuela. They were soon living and working with local residents to identify the most pressing community needs. The volunteers and residents installed electricity and sewer lines, started training and nutrition programs, and built schools and community centers. By the end of 1964, when the volunteers completed this pilot program, turning it over to Venezuelans, they and local residents had initiated 5,015 self-help projects affecting 200,000 persons, and had stimulated investments amounting to $476,000, including contributions of material and the value of volunteer labor. Although unskilled and often illiterate, the people in these communities had completed such projects as laying water mains and building schools, roads, community centers, and an array of small industries, gaining training, experience, and confidence as they worked. In Caracas, ACCION helped start a cooperative bakery, which became self-supporting by selling its goods through a super-

COMPANY PERSPECTIVES

The mission of ACCION International is to give people the tools they need to work their way out of poverty. By providing "micro" loans and business training to poor women and men who start their own businesses, ACCION's partner lending organizations help people work their own way up the economic ladder, with dignity and pride. With capital, people can grow their own businesses. They can earn enough to afford basics like running water, better food and school for their children.

In a world where three billion people live on less than $2 a day, it is not enough to help 1,000 or even 100,000 individuals. Our goal is to bring microfinance to tens of millions of people—enough to help change the world. We know that there will never be enough donations to do this. That's why ACCION has created an anti-poverty strategy that is permanent and self-sustaining.

market chain. A construction company organized in a new model city built ten homes, employing 27 workers.

Blatchford recruited a board of directors headed by Donald M. Kendall, president of PepsiCo Inc., and including ten other corporate executives, one of them Rodman C. Rockefeller. Now incorporated and with headquarters in New York City (although it later moved to the Boston area), ACCION International chose Brazil for its next stage of operations. By 1970 the organization also had entered Peru, aiding Lima businesses ranging from dressmaking to burials. Soon after, it extended its activities to Colombia. By this time ACCION had a staff of 32, supported by 127 private businesses and banks. During the 1960s and early 1970s the organization placed over 1,000 volunteers and contributed more than $9 million to development in some of the poorest communities of Latin America.

Blatchford left ACCION in 1969 to become head of the Peace Corps. He was succeeded as executive director by Terry Holcombe. During the next few years, he and other ACCION leaders became increasingly aware that their projects did not address the major cause of urban poverty in Latin America: lack of economic opportunity. "We began to sense that a school or a water system didn't necessarily have long-term impact," said Holcombe. "We were simply reorganizing the resources that a community already had within it, rather

than increasing their resources." ACCION felt that it could harness the energy of the unemployed, many of whom had started their own small enterprises. No effort was too humble: they wove belts, banged out pots, and sold potatoes. Yet they had no way to grow larger because, lacking funds to buy supplies, they often had to borrow from informal lenders at rates as high as 10 percent a day.

FOCUS ON MICROLENDING FROM 1973

In 1973, ACCION's staff in Recife, Brazil, began issuing small loans at commercial interest rates to what it called "microenterprises." The organization believes these first loans launched the field of microcredit. Within four years, ACCION provided 885 loans, helping to create or stabilize 1,386 new jobs and finding—the group believed—a way to generate new wealth for the working poor of Latin America. These loans were far from charity; in the late 1980s, for example, ACCION's affiliates were charging from 2.5 to 8 percent interest per month. Nevertheless, they were available, required little or no paperwork, and were repaid at a rate of 97 percent. The interest each borrower paid helped cover the cost of lending to another, convincing ACCION that microlending had the potential to transform the economic landscape of Latin America. The ability to cover its costs, aided by ACCION's new loan guarantee fund, the Bridge Fund, enabled the organization's partners to reach many more microentrepreneurs. Between 1989 and 1995, the amount of money lent by ACCION's Latin American Network increased more than twentyfold.

During the 1980s, ACCION helped start microlending programs in 14 Latin American countries. In the beginning, financial institutions affiliated with ACCION offered collectively guaranteed "solidarity loans" to groups of five people. Although collectively responsible for making payments, the members received a tiny amount allocated individually, allowing them personally to establish a credit history that would qualify them for further loans. Over time, a growing number of ACCION affiliates came to see limitations in this model. Since businesses financed by group members grew at different rates, the more successful entrepreneurs were not able to borrow as much as they wanted, while the less successful found they were guaranteeing loans for others. The time spent holding group meetings limited the amount available to individual businesses. Perhaps most significantly, group members no longer felt the need for collective guarantees once they had developed personal credit histories through their loan payments. Successful clients were also demanding more capital and other financial products, but governments were reluctant to grant banking licenses to microfinance institutions.

As a result of these limitations, ACCION's micro-credit network, though greatly enlarged in size, was still reaching less than 2 percent of the microentrepreneurs in need of its services. In response, ACCION helped create BancoSol, the world's first commercial bank dedicated solely to microenterprise. Founded in Bolivia in 1992, BancoSol was established to serve the poor, with its clients typically market vendors, sandal makers, and seamstresses. Two years later, ACCION helped Ban-coSol sell certificates of deposit in the United States that were, in effect, typically backed only by the word of a vendor plying the streets of La Paz. According to the organization, "For the first time, the world's premier financial institutions invested in microenterprise, not out of charity, but because it was good business." By 2005, 15 ACCION-affiliated organizations were regulated financial institutions.

Among ACCION's lending partners, Mexico's Fin-anciera Compartamos stood out as the largest microfi-nance institution in Latin America. The two formed a strategic alliance to help Compartamos transform itself into a regulated financial institution. By 2005, Compar-tamos was present in 26 Mexican states and also had 16 branches in Mexico City. Over 95 percent of its clients lived in the rural areas of Mexico, and 95 percent of its 453,131 active clients were women.

Another notable partner was Banco de la Microem-presa S.A. (Mibanco), founded in 1998 as Peru's first for-profit, fully regulated commercial bank dedicated to microenterprise. Mibanco's majority shareholder and operative manager was Comunitaria del Perú, a private nonprofit community development organization founded in 1982 with assistance from ACCION, whose Gateway Fund became an investor in Mibanco.

In 2000 ACCION International began working in partnership with microlending organizations in sub-Saharan Africa, its first such initiative outside the Americas. By 2005 it was providing technical assistance to microlenders in Angola, Benin, Mozambique, Nigeria, Tanzania, Uganda, and Zimbabwe. In that year it began work in Asia for the first time when it teamed with Unitus to establish the Unitus-ACCION Alliance for India.

MICROLENDING IN THE UNITED STATES FROM 1991

Concerned about growing income inequality and unemployment in the United States, ACCION brought its microlending model home. Like microentrepreneurs abroad, small business owners in the United States faced many significant barriers to financing: no credit history, a bad credit background, or loan requirements too small for a bank to handle profitably. New York City's borough of Brooklyn was the first to get a U.S. AC-CION office, in 1991. Many of the people helped were Hispanics, such as Ulvada Alvarado, a Mexican im-migrant and single mother of four who rose in less than a decade from taco street vendor to owner of four restaurants, with the help of six loans totaling $23,000, all of them at 16 percent annual interest, less than many Americans paid on their credit cards. By 1997, this program had 344 active borrowers who had taken out a total of $1.4 million in loans. In 1996 ACCION New York became the first microcredit organization to sell a package of loans to an investor. In 1999 revenue from interest and fees paid 45 percent of the organization's operating costs, with the remainder covered by grants.

ACCION Texas began in 1994 by making loans in San Antonio, armed with a $50,000 grant and $125,000 to lend. In 2004 it was operating offices in eight Texas cities and had lent in more than 200 com-munities in the state. By midyear 2004 the organization had booked 5,678 loans totaling $29.46 million to 3,460 small business owners. The average loan that year was $7,256, and the average interest rate only 12 percent annually. ACCION Texas was losing money on the loans but was making up the deficit in grants and donations, often from banks meeting their Community Reinvestment Act requirements.

ACCION's U.S. initiative was renamed ACCION USA in 2000, when there were offices in Atlanta, Miami, and New England, and licensees in California,

Illinois, New Mexico, New York, and Texas. ACCION USA and its licensees made up the U.S. ACCION Network, the largest microlending network in the country. By the end of 2003, the U.S. ACCION Network had lent more than $90 million to more than 10,000 low-income entrepreneurs in over 30 cities and towns across these nine states. First loans were as low as $500. The average loan in 2006, when ACCION USA had 1,031 active clients at year-end, was $5,197.

ACCION INTERNATIONAL IN 2005

ACCION, in 2005, had 27 loosely affiliated members in 22 countries and direct investments in ten. Besides its Boston headquarters, the organization had offices in Washington, D.C.; Bogotá, Colombia; and Bangalore, India. Its partner programs were continuing to work with poor, self-employed women and men who relied on microenterprise as their main source of income. Its borrowers abroad were among their regions' poorest people at the time of their loan. They usually had no collateral, might not be able to read or write, and might not have enough capital to open for business every day. Some 65 percent were women.

Because of the poverty of its clients, ACCION was sending loan officers to meet potential borrowers in their places of work. ACCION's character based lending approach allowed these officers to go beyond the numbers and consider such intangibles as references from customers and neighbors and their own gut feelings about a microentrepreneur's drive to succeed in order to develop a more complete picture of a potential borrower than a traditional credit score. Borrowers either applied for loans individually or, if they lacked material collateral or a cosigner, to team up with a few other borrowers. First loans were as low as $100 in Latin America. Borrowers who repaid their loans on time were eligible for increasingly larger loans in a process called stepped lending.

Several of ACCION International's partners had transformed themselves from nonprofit, charity-dependent organizations to banks or other regulated financial institutions. The three largest—Ecuador's Banco Solidario, Mexico's Financiera Compartamos, and Peru's Mibanco—each were reaching more than

100,000 poor and low-income microentrepreneurs. ACCION International also had helped Haiti's Sogebank, Ecuador's Banco del Pichincha, and Brazil's Banco ABN-AMRO Real begin lending to the self-employed.

In the United States, ACCION USA was working with low- and moderate-income borrowers who had their own businesses but were economically marginalized and had no access to commercial business loans. They were typically unable to afford formal business training, receive peer support, or form their own business contacts. They often relied on their microbusinesses for half or more of their family income and generally had business assets of less than $5,000. Many had no personal or business credit or had bad credit prior to receiving an ACCION loan. Some were storefront owners with small but well established businesses; others were single mothers on public assistance. Accion USA borrowers in 2005 were 87 percent minority and 52 percent Hispanic. Some 35 percent were women.

Robert Halasz

PRINCIPAL SUBSIDIARIES

ACCION USA.

FURTHER READING

Duggan, Patrice, "Do-Gooders Who Really Do Good," *Forbes,* January 10, 1987, pp. 117–18.

Eaton, Leslie, "Minor Loans Giving Major Help," *New York Times,* July 11, 1998, pp. B1, B5.

Farnsworth, Clyde H., "Micro-Loans to the World's Poorest," *New York Times,* February 21, 1988, Sec. 3, pp. 1, 10.

Hendricks, David, "Accion Texas Gets Proof of Its Impact," *San Antonio Express-News,* August 28, 2004.

"A Lending Hand," *Business Week,* February 28, 2000.

McLaughlin, Kathleen, "Wealthy Venezuela Is Getting Wealthier, but Finds Reasons for Concern," *New York Times,* January 28, 1966, p. 70.

"A 'Peace Corps' for Latin Slums," *Business Week,* January 17, 1970, p. 48.

"A Survey of Microfinance," *Economist,* November 5, 2005, Microfinance supplement, pp. 7–8.

Acindar Industria Argentina de Aceros S.A.

Estanislao Zeballos 2739
Beccar, Buenos Aires 1643AG
Argentina
Telephone: (54 11) 4719-8500
Fax: (54 11) 4719-8501
Web site: http://www.acindar.com.ar

Public Company
Incorporated: 1942
Employees: 2,628
Sales: ARS 2.78 billion ($911.48 million) (2006)
Stock Exchanges: Buenos Aires
Ticker Symbol: ACIN
NAIC: 331111 Iron and Steel Mills; 331221 Cold-Rolled Steel Shape Manufacturing; 331222 Steel Wire Drawing; 332111 Iron and Steel Forging; 332116 Metal Stamping

■ ■ ■

Acindar Industria Argentina de Aceros S.A. is Argentina's oldest and second largest steel producer and the leader in the field of non-flat steel products (products other than sheets and strips), offering more than 200 of such products for agriculture, industry, and construction. The company's steel mill converts iron ore and other minerals to sponge iron by the direct reduction process, then converts the iron into molten steel in electric furnaces. The raw steel is then fashioned by casting and rolling into such products as bars, wires, cables, mesh, screens, and structural products.

ACINDAR'S STRUGGLE FOR INDEPENDENCE: 1942–78

Argentina had no steel producer when World War II broke out, and as the war continued, the economy was seriously affected by the supply shortage, especially of rods used in construction. Faced with the situation, Arthur Acevedo, an engineer, enlisted the companies Acevedo y Shaw and Compañia de Construcciones Civiles de Aguirre y Aragón in conversations about establishing a plant for the production of steel. Acindar was incorporated in 1942 for this purpose.

Most of the equipment had to be imported from Chile and transported over the Andes Mountains. Other scrapped articles, such as parts from old locomotives and tractors, were returned to service since replacements were impossible to obtain. A small Siemens Martin furnace was installed in the plant, located in Rosario, and steel production began in 1944. Two years later, the Chilean investors in the company were bought out by Argentines, and in 1948 Acindar made its initial public offering of stock in the Bolsa de Comercio, the Buenos Aires stock exchange. By 1951, when the company produced 100,000 metric tons of steel, a bigger plant was needed, and in that year a new mill opened in Villa Constitución, Santa Fe.

During the ensuing years the company added a foundry (Acinfer) to produce steel rails for railroads, a factory (Acinplast) for plastic pipes, and a company (Armetal) to stamp pieces for the auto industry. In 1962 Acindar joined with a member company of West Germany's Thyssen group to establish Marathon

COMPANY PERSPECTIVES
■

Vision: To exceed the expectations of our customers. To contribute to the personal development of our people. To increase the profitability of our investors. To develop sustainable relationships with our suppliers. To collaborate with the welfare of our community.

Argentina S.A., a firm dedicated to producing special steels. Acindar bought out its partner ten years later.

The Argentina government had established, after World War II, a larger steelmaking enterprise known by its acronym, Somisa. This enterprise, unlike Acindar, was fully integrated, meaning that it was engaged in all processes of steelmaking, from obtaining iron ore to turning out all finished steel products. Acindar was not allowed to expand its activities and engage in full competition with Somisa until 1975, when a federal decree finally authorized the company to integrate its production operations. In 1978 Acindar opened new installations, including its own port for bringing in minerals, a plant for converting iron ore into sponge iron by means of the direct reduction process, followed by conversion to molten steel in three electric furnaces, and then to semifinished products by two continuous casting units.

With integrated facilities for making steel, including its own port facilities, Acindar could import its own iron ore for conversion into sponge iron and no longer was as dependent on others for scrap iron, not easily available in Argentina. The company's direct reduction process relied on natural gas, readily available in Argentina, rather than coking coal, which had to be imported. In addition, Acindar no longer depended on Somisa for semifinished products such as billets (squarish pieces of steel) to turn into its own finished steel products. By 1980 it was producing more than 500,000 metric tons of steel per year. The quality of its steel improved noticeably with a feedstock of imported iron pellets.

TWO DIFFICULT DECADES:
1980–2000

In 1981 Acindar absorbed three smaller steel producers: Gurmendi S.A., Genaro Grasso S.A., and Santa Rosa S.A., issuing one-third of its shares in payment to the stockholders of these companies. Weak domestic demand, competition from state-owned enterprises, and the fall of international prices because of overproduction, were some of the reasons that steelmaking was being concentrated into fewer hands. The eight plants of the amalgamated group were quickly reduced to four in three locations. The acquisition buttressed Acindar's domination of the non-flat steel market in Argentina, which reached about 70 percent of the total. It was the national leader in profiles, wires, cables, and steel bars and rolls for concrete, and it was the chief exporter in the steel sector.

This expansion involved taking on a heavy load of debt, which reached $740 million at the end of 1981, when the Argentine economy was buckling under the impact of a world economic recession. Repeated peso devaluations, hyperinflation, and the disastrous Falkland Islands war followed. Yet Acindar continued to turn a profit until 1985, when, for perhaps the first time, it fell into the red and the value of its shares of common stock nosedived. By this time, the company was the private sector's largest debtor, with $370 million in commercial bank loans in which more than 70 banks were involved. Arrears in interest payments, amounting to $60 million, dated back to 1982. A restructuring agreement was reached in early 1987. Soon after, Acindar made a deal to buy back $56 million of its debt at 25 cents on the dollar, and in 1988 it was able to issue a fully underwritten equity offer.

As the Argentine economy weakened yet again in the late 1980s and once more experienced hyperinflation, it made more sense for Acindar, which was still heavily in debt, to look abroad rather than at home for sales and profit. Shortly after Carlos Menem took office as president of Argentina in 1989, the government adopted an economic policy that stabilized the peso at a level relative to the dollar that made exports of Acindar's steel uncompetitive. Menem's government also privatized many state-owned companies, including Somisa, which became Siderar S.A.I.C., and this proved useful to Acindar, since the newly privatized company decided to eliminate its production of non-flat rolled steel, allowing Acindar to consolidate its virtual monopoly of that market subsector. (It also held the 10 percent of the market for hot rolled flat products not held by Siderar.)

The restructuring of the steel industry reduced the labor force by almost half between 1989 and 1994. Acindar was one of the companies that took a tough line. In 1991, it broke agreements with the metalworkers' union by obliging machine operators to be responsible for the maintenance of their own equipment. After a work slowdown at Villa Constitución, which had lost $60 million the previous year, and unsuccessful labor-management negotiations, the

KEY DATES

1942: Foundation of Acindar, Argentina's first steel producer.

1948: Acindar becomes a public company, its shares traded on the Buenos Aires stock exchange.

1978: Acindar becomes fully integrated, capable of converting iron ore to finished steel products.

1981: Acindar raises its debt level by acquiring three smaller steelmakers.

2000: After two difficult decades and much red ink, Acindar sells stock to a Brazilian company.

2003: Acindar returns to profitability and agrees to restructure its debt.

company fired all 3,000 of the plant's unionized workers, leading to a temporary shutdown. By the end of 1992 the company workforce had been trimmed to 4,500, compared to 8,000 in 1988.

Acindar reversed its heavy loss in fiscal 1991 (the year ended June 30, 1991) and earned a slim profit in fiscal 1992. The liberalized economy was picking up steam, and Acindar impressed foreign investors as one of the lowest cost and most efficient producers of non-flat steel products in the world, characterized by rising productivity and superior technology. Its products were grouped in three areas: carbon steel; specialty steel, used mainly by the industrial sector; and finished products, primarily for construction and agriculture.

RECOVERY UNDER NEW OWNERSHIP

Yet, with a debt of about $400 million still hanging over its head, Acindar was poorly equipped to weather Argentina's deep recession of the late 1990s, which continued into 2001 and resulted in the collapse of the peso. The crisis had devastating effects on construction, auto production, and farming and ranching, which accounted for the greater part of Acindar's sales, and the company fell into the red in fiscal 1999, losing even more money the next year. Accordingly, the Acevedo family sold some of its stake in late 2000 to Belgo Companhia Siderúrgica S.A. (Belgo-Mineira), a Brazilian steelmaker. Associated transactions resulted in shared control of the enterprise between the two partners, who held 40 percent of the enterprise. The rest was held by public investors, except for 8 percent in the hands of the International Finance Corporation, an affiliate of the World Bank. By this time Belgo-Mineira was one of six

companies in an industrial holding company that was merging with France's Usinor to form the Arcelor group, the world's largest steelmaker.

A few months later, Belgo-Mineira purchased securities convertible into common stock shares, raising its stake in Acindar to about 30 percent. Then it subsequently bought the remaining stake held by the Acevedo family, and by these actions held more than 70 percent of Acindar by early 2004. The company had defaulted on about $220 million of debt in November 2001, but had paid back some of that amount over the next two years. With the Argentine economy in strong recovery, Acindar was again profitable, earning about $207 million in 2003, when it ended at least four consecutive years of losses. It also had reached agreement with its creditors for the restructuring of the remainder of its debt. Acindar was producing steel to the limits of its installed capacity. Moreover, there were areas of synergy between its activities and those of Belgo-Mineira, especially in distribution. The two had created Abemex, a Rosario-based firm, to sell their products outside the Mercosur area of southern South America.

Arturo Acevedo remained Acindar's chairman of the board even after selling the family shares to Belgo-Mineira. Interviewed for the Buenos Aires daily *La Nación* in 2006, he expressed concern over rising prices and possible shortages in meeting the company's high consumption of electrical energy and its chief feedstock, natural gas. He said that the company was investing $150 million in a project to augment production capacity by 250,000 metric tons a year. During the year, the company raised $83.2 million by selling its two plants for the production of steel pipes and its cold formed profiles business. Acindar also took a half-share in an insurance and leasing joint venture, Acindar Pymes S.G. R., and paid out $34.2 million on its restructured debt. It ended the year with a handsome profit of ARS 604 million (about $198 million), its fourth consecutive annual profit, on net sales of ARS 2.78 billion ($911.48 million).

Production rose to 1.44 million metric tons of molten steel, all produced at Villa Constitución. Production of steel plates came to 1.43 million metric tons, and that of steel rods, at La Tablada, a suburb of Buenos Aires, to 173,662 metric tons. The company was also turning out such products as bars, rods, wires, and cables. It was also producing industrial bars in Jandira, São Paulo, Brazil. Other facilities provided services such as bending and cutting bars and rods for customers. Exports, which accounted for 30 percent of sales a few years earlier, represented only 13 percent of sales because of strong domestic demand. Total debt came to $450 million. Belgo-Mineira owned 66 percent of Acindar's shares. Pension and retirement funds held 15 percent and public investors 19 percent.

Robert Halasz

PRINCIPAL SUBSIDIARIES

Acindar Agroindustrial S.A.; Acindar do Brasil S.A. Ltda. (Brazil); Acindar Pymes S.G.R. (50%); Acindar Uruguay I.A.A.S.A.; CDSA S.A.; Comercial Bagual Ltda.; Elmec S.A.; Performa S.A.

PRINCIPAL COMPETITORS

Siderar S.A.I.C.

FURTHER READING

"Acindar: A Private Enterprise That Meets the Challenges of Time," *Euromoney,* May 1993, pp. 124–25.

Brittos, Alejandro, "Eslabones de hierro," *Mercado,* July 2001, pp. 70–72.

"El crecimiento de Acindar," *Mercado,* June 19, 1980, pp. 34–36.

Dalmasso, Juan Pablo, "Carrera de acero," *AméricaEconomía,* January 30–February 19, 2004, pp.30–32.

Etchemendy, Sebastian, "Constructing Reform Coalitions: The Politics of Compensations in Argentina's Economic Liberalization," *Latin American Politics and Society,* Fall 2001, pp. 16–19.

Evans, Judith, "Argentina Discovers the Bailout," *Euromoney,* September 1988, pp. 266, 269.

Ferrarese, Laura, "Para el titular de la firma siderurgica controlada por la brasileña Belgo Mineira, la situación económica se encuentra en un delicado equilibrio," *La Nación,* October 1, 2006.

Garcia, Luis F., "La acción del mes," *Mercado,* May 16, 1985, pp. 46–48.

Kepp, Michael, "Argentina Enters Acindar Rift," *American Metal Market,* May 3, 1991, pp. 4, 10.

Mendes de Paula, Germano, "The Marriage of Acindar & Belgo-Mineira," *Steel Times International,* March 2001, p. 50.

Moyano, Julio, *The Argentine Economy,* Buenos Aires: J. Moyano Construcciones, 1997, pp. 534–35.

"El primer millón de Acindar," *Mercado,* December 9, 1982, pp. 20–22, 24.

"La unión hace el acero," *Mercado,* December 31, 1981, pp. 35–38.

Wong, Wallin, "Case of Acindar Carries Hope, Caution," *Wall Street Journal,* October 22, 2003.

Al Habtoor Group L.L.C.

PO Box 25444
Al Habtoor Group Building
Sheikh Zayed Road
Dubai,
United Arab Emirates
Telephone: (+971 04) 3431111
Fax: (+971 04) 3431140
Web site: http://www.habtoor.com

Private Company
Incorporated: 1971
Employees: 6,000
Sales: $3.3 billion (2006 est.)
NAIC: 541330 Engineering Services; 441110 New Car
Dealers; 532111 Passenger Cars Rental; 551112 Of-
fices of Other Holding Companies

∎ ∎ ∎

Al Habtoor Group L.L.C. is the holding company behind the United Arab Emirates' largest construction and engineering company, which operates under the name Al Habtoor Engineering Enterprises. The company has been a major contractor in Dubai since the late 1970s and has been responsible for many of that city's largest and most well-known landmarks. The company's projects include the massive "seven-star" Burj Al Arab hotel complex, as well as most of the Dubai airport, and the Abu Dhabi airport. Al Habtoor is also one of the top construction and engineering firms in the Middle East, with projects in Qatar, Abu Dhabi, Bahrain, Egypt, and Jordan. While construction was the

group's original business, and remains its largest operation, Al Habtoor has long established diversified holdings including automotive sales through Al Habtoor Motors, which holds concessions for Aston Martin, Bentley, Bugatti, and Mitsubishi; the company also operates a motor leasing subsidiary, Diamondlease. Al Habtoor owns and manages the Metropolitan hotel brand, including seven hotels in Dubai and Jordan, through subsidiary Habtoor Hospitality L.L.C. Al Habtoor Real Estate controls a number of prime Dubai properties, such as the vast complex encompassing Al Habtoor Residence, Habtoor House, the Metropolitan Hotel, and Metroplex–the Entertainment & Leisure Complex. Other Al Habtoor properties under construction include the Al Habtoor Grand Office Tower at Dubai Marina; Emirates Oasis, a complex of 90 luxury villas; and Al Wasl Village, featuring 26 townhouses in the Jumeirah district.

The small Al Habtoor Publishing Division exists largely as the publisher of *Al Shindagah* magazine, the outspoken journal that serves as the mouthpiece for chairman and founder Khalaf Al Habtoor's vision of Middle Eastern politics. Son Mohammed Al Habtoor serves as the group's managing director. Al Habtoor remains a private company, with sales estimated at $3.3 billion in the middle of the first decade of the 2000s.

FOUNDING A DUBAI CONSTRUCTION GIANT IN 1970

The Al Habtoor family was originally one of many involved in Dubai's pearl trade. For most of the port city's history, pearling had been the small village's main industry. Following a crisis in the local pearl industry after the introduction of Japanese cultured pearls in the 1930s, however, the pearling market had gone into a long decline, and the Al Habtoor family's fortunes remained modest. Yet Khalaf Al Habtoor's father had greater ambitions for his son, and introduced the boy to then ruler Sheikh Rashid bin Saeed Al Maktoum at the evening *majlis,* the weekly town meeting held by the royal family. Khalaf Al Habtoor soon became friends with Al Maktoum's youngest son, Mohammed, and Al Habtoor became a fixture at the royal palace.

Into the 1960s, the Al Maktoum family had begun developing ambitious plans to redevelop the city, largely abandoned by the British government in the waning years of the empire's control of the region, into a major deepwater port, as well as important tourist destination. In 1967, the government launched construction of Port Rashid, a 16-berth deepwater harbor capable of accommodating even the largest of the world's oceangoing vessels and oil tankers. The discovery of oil in Dubai further stimulated the city's construction boom, as Dubai reinvented itself as an independent, sovereign state.

The boom in construction provided a new source of employment for Dubai's natives, and Khalaf Al Habtoor began working at a construction firm at the age of 15, while still in high school. Before long, Al Habtoor had risen through the ranks, becoming the firm's youngest manager. By the end of the 1960s, Al Habtoor had recognized that the movement toward the creation of the United Arab Emirates would create a new boom phase in the region's construction market. Backed by his intimate relationship with the royal family, Al Habtoor decided to go into business on his own, founding Al Habtoor Engineering Enterprises in 1970.

Al Habtoor started out with just 100 employees, and initially focused on the city's housing market, completing several residential homes. Yet Al Habtoor had higher ambitions, and soon had completed his first movie theater. His continued relationship with the royal family—and his penchant for self-promotion displayed at the *majlis,* and later in the pages of his *Al Shindagah*

magazine—enabled him to begin competing for larger projects. By 1977, Sheikh Al Maktoum had awarded Al Habtoor the contract to build the country's second hospital. The contract called for the hospital to be completed in 36 weeks. Instead, Al Habtoor completed the project in just 30 weeks. As a result, the sheikh gave Al Habtoor the contracts to build three more hospitals, as well as the headquarters building for the country's department of health.

Into the 1980s, Al Habtoor was awarded another high-profile contract, that of building a four-star hotel complex on the outskirts of the city, an important part in Sheikh Maktoum's goal of transforming Dubai into the region's primary tourism destination. Government contracts continued to play a prominent role in Al Habtoor's growth, and into the next century, the company completed nearly 35 major projects for the state. The company's success in Dubai also enabled expansion elsewhere in the region. In 1980, the company launched construction of Gulf University, in Bahrain. The company also entered Jordan, with the construction of the Zarqa'a Ma'een Spa/Ashtar Hotel complex, starting in 1982.

DIVERSIFYING BUSINESS IN 1983

With growth at his construction and engineering business well underway, Al Habtoor sought new avenues for expansion of his holdings in the 1980s. Automotive sales attracted Al Habtoor's attention, and in 1983 he established Al Habtoor Motors, based on an exclusive contract to sell Mitsubishi trucks, 4x4s, and other automobiles in Dubai. The rising wealth associated with Dubai's oil-based economy, coupled with the United Arab Emirates' highly liberal tax and investment policies, attracted a growing number of the world's wealthy, which in turn led Al Habtoor to expand its own range of automotive concessions. As such, the company became the exclusive dealer for three of the world's top luxury automobile brands, Aston Martin, Bentley, and Bugatti.

Hotel operation represented another growth area for Al Habtoor's holdings. The company owned just one hotel through the 1980s, then launched construction of a second hotel, the Metropolitan Beach Resort, on the then deserted Jumeirah Beach. The growth of that area, following the government's decision to invest massively in that section of the city, gave Al Habtoor a piece of some of the world's most expensive real estate at the end of the 20th century.

The family's hotel operations also helped introduce the next generation into the company, when son Mohammed Al Habtoor, who had studied hotel manage-

That business built a fleet of more than 2,000 vehicles, offering prestige automobiles, including Rolls-Royce, Bentley, BMW, Mercedes, and others, as well as a fleet of chauffeur-driven vehicles.

KEY DATES

1970: Khalaf Al Habtoor founds construction and engineering business in Dubai.

1977: Company wins contract to build second Dubai hospital.

1983: Automobile sales subsidiary Al Habtoor Motors is formed.

1996: Company launches automotive leasing subsidiary Diamondlease.

1999: Al Habtoor acquires Monkey Island Hotel on Thames River in England.

2000: Company enters Lebanon with acquisition of Metropolitan Palace Hotel.

2007: Al Habtoor wins contract to build Landmark tower on Abu Dhabi island.

INTERNATIONAL FOCUS IN THE NEW CENTURY

Increasingly, Al Habtoor sought to expand its operations, and especially its core construction and engineering business, beyond Dubai. The company began competing for contracts elsewhere in the region, successfully entering the Abu Dhabi and Bahrain markets, then winning contracts as far away as Egypt and Jordan. The company hoped to fuel its expansion, as well as resolve potential future succession conflicts, by listing its stock on the United Arab Emirates stock exchange. Yet the exchange's restrictive nature, especially toward the region's large, family-owned conglomerates such as Al Habtoor, prevented the company from making its public offering for the near future.

Instead, the company focused on winning construction contracts and expanding its hotel operations. In 1999, the company bought the Monkey Island Hotel, located on an island in the Thames River. Closer to home, the company looked toward Lebanon following the withdrawal of Israeli troops from the south Lebanese border in 2000. Al Habtoor took the decision to enter that country's hotel market, acquiring a 183-room hotel renamed as the Metropolitan Palace Hotel. The company also began construction of the Habtoor Grand Hotel Convention Centre & Spa Beirut, featuring Beirut's tallest building amid a complex totaling more than 115,000 square meters, which opened in 2005. Also in Beirut the company launched construction of a theme park, Habtoorland. In all, Al Habtoor invested some $400 million in Lebanon, before the outbreak of the August 2006 war cast a pall over the country's tourism sector.

ment in the United States during the 1980s, returned to Dubai. Yet the younger Al Habtoor found himself forced to work his way from the ground up, starting his career as a porter at the original Metropolitan Hotel. Later, Khalaf Al Habtoor fired his son, twice, for making decisions without consulting him first. Nonetheless, the younger Al Habtoor rapidly ascended the company's ranks, taking over the managing director's position from his father in the 2000s. Another son, Rashid, joined the family business in 1990, but left after only three years to found his own construction company.

Other, less profit-driven Al Habtoor operations were developed at the beginning of the 1990s. In 1991, the company founded the Emirates International School. The first of its kind in the United Arab Emirates, the new school provided a kindergarten to high school education tailored to the needs of the internationally focused local population as well as the fast-growing expatriate community in Dubai. On a more personal scale, Khalaf Al Habtoor, who had developed a reputation for his outspoken nature, founded a new company, Al Habtoor Publishing, in 1993. That company launched a new magazine, *Al Shindagah,* which served as a corporate magazine, showcasing the company's varied high-profile construction projects, such as the massive Burj Al Arab hotel complex launched in 1994. The magazine also served as Khalaf Al Habtoor's mouthpiece for his often highly critical views of the West and Middle Eastern politics.

In another diversification move, Al Habtoor expanded its automotive business in the mid-1990s, adding a new leasing subsidiary, Diamondlease, in 1996.

The United Arab Emirates remained the group's bread-and-butter market into the second half of the decade. In 2005, the company won in its joint venture bid with Aljaber Engineering for the primary contract to build the Dubai Tower. The company completed construction of its Metropolitan Suites complex, marking the company's entry into the fast-growing furnished apartment market in Dubai. In early 2007, the company had scored another high-profile contract, to build the Landmark tower on Abu Dhabi island. Yet Al Habtoor had not renounced its further international expansion, acknowledging plans to enter the European market in the new century.

M. L. Cohen

PRINCIPAL SUBSIDIARIES

Al Habtoor Engineering Enterprises; Al Habtoor Motors; Al Habtoor Publishing; Al Habtoor Real Estate; Diamondlease; Emirates International School; Habtoor Hospitality L.L.C.

PRINCIPAL COMPETITORS

Dubai World; Arabtec Construction; Arabian Construction Company; Al-Hamad Contracting Company; Saudi Oger; Dubai Contracting Company; Al Naboodah General Enterprises Holding Company L.L.C.; Al-Shafar General Contracting.

FURTHER READING

"Al Habtoor Group Fine Tunes Its Plans to Expand Operations in Lebanon," *Asia Africa Intelligence Wire,* January 4, 2005.

"Al Habtoor Lands Deal to Build Island Landmark," *MEED Middle East Economic Digest,* February 16, 2007, p. 25.

"Al Habtoor Plans to Enter Furnished Apartment Sector," *Gulf News,* September 5, 2006.

Dean, Richard, "The Making of Mohammed Al Habtoor," *Forbes,* June 2, 2004.

Pendleton, Devon, "Gulf Goliath," *Forbes,* March 26, 2007, p. 172.

"Pulling Ahead of the Pack: The Biggest Contractor in the Federation Is Poised to Grow Even Bigger in 2007," *MEED Middle East Economic Digest,* January 26, 2007, p. 36.

Alpargatas S.A.I.C.

Azari 841
Buenos Aires, C.F. 1267
Argentina
Telephone: (54 11) 4303-0041
Fax: (54 11) 4303-0049
Web site: http://www.argentina.com.ar

Public Company
Incorporated: 1885 as S.A. Fábrica Argentina de Alpargatas
Employees: 4,000
Sales: ARS 490.2 million ($160.72 million) (2006)
Stock Exchanges: Bolsa de Comercio de Buenos Aires
Ticker Symbol: ALPA
NAIC: 313111 Yarn Spinning Mills; 313311 Broadwoven Fabric Finishing Mills; 314129 Other Household Textile Product Mills; 314912 Canvas and Related Product Mills; 314991 Rope, Cordage, and Twine Mills; 315225 Men's and Boys' Cut and Sew Work Clothing Manufacturing; 316211 Rubber and Plastics Footwear Manufacturing; 339920 Sporting and Athletic Goods Manufacturing

■ ■ ■

Alpargatas S.A.I.C., one of Argentina's oldest continuing business enterprises, is the nation's leader in the field of footwear and textiles. Best known for its Topper line of sneakers, the company makes and markets other casual footwear and manufactures athletic footwear for other parties. The textile division turns out denim for jeans and a variety of other fabrics, including fabrics used in its footwear. It also manufactures and markets a broad range of household textiles and work clothing. The retail division sells Alpargatas products in various store formats. In spite of these wide-ranging activities, two areas dominate sales: Topper athletic footwear and sports apparel, and denim for jeans. Alpargatas was close to ruin during Argentina's late 1990s economic crisis but has returned to profitability.

THE FIRST CENTURY: 1885–1985

Alpargata is a Spanish word, derived from Arabic, to describe a traditional Egyptian sandal that was made more durable by the Romans, who passed it on to Spain, where it was fastened around the ankle with strings rather than a strap. By the time it reached Argentina, the top was made of canvas and the sole of braided jute or hemp. Many artisanal workshops in Buenos Aires turned out this slipperlike article in the second half of the 19th century before Juan Etchegaray, a Basque, teamed with Robert Fraser, a Scot whose family firm made textile machinery, to mechanize production of Etchegaray's model in 1883. Additional capital came from Ashworth & Co., a Manchester manufacturer of cotton textiles, which also raised money from other British investors and obtained jute from Burma. The business was incorporated in 1885.

Alpargatas extended its operations to Uruguay in 1890 and began producing textiles in 1892, when the first looms for making canvas arrived in Argentina. In 1907 the enterprise that later became São Paulo Alpargatas S.A. arrived in Brazil, with the Argentine company taking a small stake in return for its privileges and

COMPANY PERSPECTIVES

Our mission is to be a regional business providing top quality footwear and fabrics for its customers.

Our goal is to become a business leader by promoting sustained growth in sales and profits, creating economic value both for shareholders and employees, and serve our customers, suppliers, and community.

patents. Alpargatas shares were first traded on the Bolsa de Comercio, the Buenos Aires stock exchange, in 1913. With the aid of Ashworth & Co., Alpargatas obtained substantial loans from such elite financial institutions as London's Baring Brothers & Co., New York's First National City Bank, and, in Buenos Aires, the Banco de Londres.

Alpargatas was especially profitable in the 1920s, when its sales soared to record levels. In 1923 operations commenced at the first cotton spinning mill in Argentina, which met one-quarter of its demand for thread. After that it began using cotton waste to make flannel, rags, and cleaning cloths. The company opened a fabric plant in Buenos Aires in 1928. Five years later, it began making shoes with soles of vulcanized rubber, also in Buenos Aires. During the 1930s it began producing fabrics for tires and, later, plastic shoes, stamped cloths, and clothing. Its growth coincided with the expansion of the domestic market and was also aided by a government policy of import substitution.

In 1950 Alpargatas built a larger plant, in Florencio Varela in the province of Buenos Aires, for athletic footwear, rubber boots, and reinforced work shoes. Its brands—Rueda, Luna, Boyero, Far West—were popularized throughout Argentina. The Flecha line of casual footwear was introduced in 1962. Three years later, Alpargatas opened a cotton ginning factory in Saenz Peña, Chaco. Denim production began in 1968. In 1972 Alpargatas began making footwear in Planta Aguilares, Tucumán; initiated cloth dyeing at the Florencio Valera plant, and started producing children's shoes and clothing under the Pampero label, later also adopted for work clothing. Other Alpargatas plants were located in the provinces of Formosa (cotton ginning) and Córdoba (for weaving palm fiber). Topper footwear and sportswear made their debuts in 1975, when the company also introduced Media Naranja cleaning cloths. In that year Alpargatas ranked 11th among reporting Argentine

enterprises in terms of sales. In terms of profits, it was doing even better, ranking sixth.

Members of the Fraser family were long in charge of Alpargatas. Ashworth & Co., originally the firm's sales agent and exclusive distributor, cut its ties to the firm at some point. Leng Roberts, a banker who owned Banco Roberts and an insurance company, La Buenos Aires Cia. de Seguros S.A., gradually became the principal shareholder. He made his influence felt directly or through other family members with the surnames Lockwood and Oxenford. Eduardo Oxenford was the head of the firm during the late 1970s and the 1980s. The surname Clutterbuck was also prominent in management until the 21st century.

Alpargatas opened another textile plant near Catamarca in 1978, at a cost of $58 million, to produce cotton and cotton/polyester textiles. This facility was distant both from Argentina's cotton fields and its prime market, Buenos Aires, but it benefited from tax credits and conformed to the company's policy of scattering production plants throughout northern and central Argentina.

Also that year, Alpargatas started producing bedspreads, blankets, sheets, and towels under the Palette label in the province of San Luis.

The early 1980s saw continued expansion, although the shares in São Paulo Alpargatas were sold. Alpargatas opened a plant in Bella Vista, Corrientes, for denim in 1981, and the following year completed an addition to the Catamarca plant for Topper footwear soles injected with PVC (polyvinyl chloride), plus another small facility in San Luis principally dedicated to shoe uppers of canvas. It completed a factory in Santa Rosa, La Pampa, for footwear with polyurethane-injected soles. While footwear was directed almost entirely inside Argentina, Alpargatas was making efforts to export its textiles, consisting chiefly of heavy grades of corduroy and denim. In all, some 10,000 workers were employed in 14 plants that occupied 250,000 square meters of floor space in six provinces and the city of Buenos Aires.

The company had also diversified into fields unrelated to its core businesses, such as sugar refining, petroleum exploration, and banking and insurance. In 1979, for example, it took the majority share in Alpesca S.A., a new seafood enterprise with six ships in two ports and shore facilities for fileting fresh and frozen fish. This joint venture, with Spanish partners, which yielded sales of about $10 million in 1985, was only one of 20 subsidiaries under the Alpargatas umbrella at the time, not including Banco Francés y Río de la Plata, in which it held a 24 percent share.

KEY DATES

1885: Alpargatas is incorporated to make the slipperlike footwear known by this name.

1913: Alpargatas becomes a public company.

1968: Denim production begins.

1975: The company begins making Topper footwear and sportswear.

1985: Now a conglomerate, Alpargatas has 14 factories and 20 subsidiaries.

1992: Alpargatas dominates the national market for blue denim and casual and athletic footwear.

1995: The company creates a retail division to market its products.

1999: U.S. investment funds take over Alpargatas by assuming most of its heavy debt.

2005: Alpargatas returns to profitability, with Topper leading the way.

STRUGGLING TO SURVIVE: 1985–2004

This expansion, at an estimated cost of $160 million over a decade, proved unwise and unsustainable. Petroleum exploration, for example, emerged as a venture requiring much more capital than the company could provide, even though it had a partner in Shell Argentina. By 1985, the centennial of Alpargatas's incorporation, the company had slipped to 30th place in revenues, and in that year it lost almost $30 million, despite dismissing 1,000 workers in 1984 and imposing a 30 percent pay cut on its managers. Its stock price dropped ninefold in a single month. In order to meet payments on its debt, which was absorbing one-fifth of its revenues, Alpargatas took out a $15 million, five-year loan from the World Bank's International Finance Corporation (IFC) affiliate and a $20 million, ten-year one from a government-owned institution, Banco de la Nación. Moreover, JP Morgan and Citibank led a $98 million, 30-bank buyback of the company's debt. In 1988 Alpargatas sold preferred shares to the IFC and three private sector financial institutions for $21 million.

Chastened by its setbacks, company executives directed their efforts toward earning more money through exports, which in 1988 reached about $70 million, or 22 percent of total sales. Frozen fish exports from Alpesca accounted for a significant amount, as did sales abroad of the textile division's blue denim and clothing. Alpargatas earned about $15 million during the year. Also in 1988, the company opened a plant in

Uruguay, its second in that country, for the manufacture of alpargatas made with jute soles. Within Argentina, Topper was doing well, and sneakers made and marketed for Nike Inc. under a licensing agreement were a smashing success. By 1992, Alpargatas also controlled 70 percent of the market for blue denim in Argentina and nearly half of the market for casual and athletic footwear. Denim accounted for almost half of the textile division's production and included orders to supply brands such as Lee, Levi's, Wrangler, Calvin Klein, Gloria Vanderbilt, and Guess in Argentina. Denim was also being exported to the United States for brands such as Levi Strauss's Britannia and J.C. Penney's Provee.

In spite of these promising results, and its sale, in 1991, of its stakes in Banco Francés and La Buenos Aires for $42 million, plus its entry into the American Depositary Receipts market in New York, Alpargatas was not able to improve its financial position. In addition, the adoption of free market economics by the new administration of President Carlos Menem exposed the company to competition from inexpensive Brazilian fabrics and Chinese shoes. Despite an increase in sales and the dismissal of 1,000 employees, it lost $16 million in 1991. By the end of the year, the company had sold one of the four Alpesca processing plants and put three of its ships up for sale.

Alpargatas also had been roiled by the departure of its top three executives: one by retirement; another, Eduardo Oxenford, by sudden death; and the third, Rodolfo Clutterbuck, by kidnapping. (A Lockwood had previously, in the 1970s, been kidnapped by leftist guerrillas and released only after paying a sizable ransom.) In any case, a banker told Jonathan Friedland of the *Wall Street Journal,* the company "was run like a Soviet ministry." According to Friedland, "Running a successful business in Argentina traditionally had less to do with making things well than taking advantage of tax and credit subsidies, lobbying for stiff tariffs and coping with frequent devaluations.... And Alpargatas CEOs were often ex-ministers, recruited more for political clout than business acumen." In early 1992 about half of all company shares were held by some 20,000 public investors, of which 12 percent were foreign, generally institutional. Members of the board of directors represented three groups of investors, including Roberts S.A. de Inversiones, which (in 1995) held 15 percent of the shares.

Two U.S. corporations decided to ride to Alpargatas's rescue in 1994. Nike entered into a manufacturing joint venture that gave Alpargatas access to its partner's advanced shoe manufacture technology and also gave the joint venture marketing rights to the huge Brazilian market through 1999. Greenwood Mills Inc., a major producer of denim, purchased a 20 percent stake in the textile subsidiary, Alpargatas Textil S.A., for $18 million and provided technical support to rehabilitate the Catamarca factory, which Friedland characterized as "a filthy plant full of battered machines." Alpargatas was still a formidable enterprise, with 9,700 employees and 16 production sites. It held half of the denim market in Argentina, 42 percent of the market share in athletic footwear, and 35 percent in casual footwear. In 1995, Alpargatas created a retail division by opening a Factory Outlet store on the grounds of its Barracas plant in Buenos Aires.

Still, as Argentina's economy sank into recession in the late 1990s, Alpargatas could not stem continuing losses, partly because of falling domestic demand and partly because of the burden of making interest payments on its debt, which by 1999 had ballooned to $638 million, mostly owed to banks. Common stock was selling for a nickel a share when trading was suspended. A debt restructuring left 88 percent of the company in the hands of creditors. By the end of the year the main shareholders were the U.S.-based private equity investment funds Newbridge Latin America and Farallon Capital Management LLC. There were a few bright spots: Converse Inc. and Fila Holding S.p.A. had signed licensing agreements with Alpargatas, with Converse even expanding the scope of the agreement to take in other South American countries, including Brazil. Even so, after hitting bottom in 2001 (when it sold its stake in Alpesca), Alpargatas was only in fifth place in its business sector in 2002. Only 4,000 workers were still employed by the company, and the shoe division was turning out only a million pairs a year, just enough to meet current orders.

RECOVERY IN 2005–06

By 2005, however, Alpargatas, like Argentina itself, was in much better health. The company escaped from red ink that year, earning about $13 million, after losing about $12 million in 2004. It had returned to its traditional place as the leader in the footwear and textiles sector. Topper sneakers were leading the way, accounting for some 60 percent of the company's revenues and selling 5.8 million pairs during the year. A million pairs of the classic alpargata were also sold. By the end of the year, Alpargatas's debt of about $280 million, mostly held by the public-owned Banco de la Nación, had been considerably reduced.

Nostalgia proved the key to Topper's surprising advance. Company footwear executives found that middle-aged Argentines retained an emotional tie to the basic white canvas sneaker that tennis star Guillermo

Vilas wore in the 1970s, when he was, for a time, almost unbeatable on the clay courts that Argentine players favor. People a decade younger also remembered the sneaker fondly, associating it with rock 'n' roll, Rolling Stones concerts, and the garb of their youth. Moreover, the economic crisis had accustomed them to rejecting the hyped and expensive products of the big international firms in favor of the homegrown (a phenomenon that marketers tagged with the buzz word "authenticity"). Alpargatas advertised the product with the slogan "You've changed, too," but when this proved unsuccessful, switched to "Everything is in play." By 2006 Topper was also marketing seven models for soccer, always a mania in Argentina, and lines for basketball, tennis, running, rugby, golf, and volleyball.

Topper articles accounted for more than half of Alpargatas's revenues in 2005, with footwear alone accounting for almost an even half. Denim for jeans was the company's other main production activity, accounting for about 28 percent of company sales. Retail sales came to 10 percent of the company total, which was 27 percent higher than the 2004 figure.

Alpargatas still retained its 11 factories—seven for footwear, four for textiles—although production appeared to be well below capacity. Topper was making sneakers with uppers of leather as well as cloth and soles of vulcanized rubber, PVC-injected, and cemented. It was also producing sportswear. Casual footwear included the classic alpargata, rubber boots, and children's shoes, and came in the Pampero, Flecha, Rueda, Bull, and Tracy brands, among others. The division was also making athletic footwear for others, including adidas, for which it was making vulcanized-rubber models, and Nike. The textile division was producing denim, stretch cotton flat fabrics, and cotton/polyester blended fabrics (canvas, serge, gabardine, and others); cleaning textile products such as floor and dish cloths and kitchen towels under the Media Naranja and Rueda brands; home products such as sheets, bedspreads, and towels under the Palette and Horizons labels; and durable work clothing such as shirts, overalls, reinforced shoes, and heavy-duty gloves under the Pampero trademark. The retail division consisted of Topper Stores, Alpargatas Directos, and Alpargatas Básicos, the latter at discount prices. In 2004 there were 25 stores, not counting temporary ones established at vacation centers, sporting events, and expositions. Five more opened in 2005, including Topper outlets in two seaside resorts and the elegant Buenos Aires neighborhood of Palermo Viejo.

The following year was even better. Alpargatas raised its net revenues by about 20 percent and its operating profit by about two-thirds. Topper brand merchandise accounted for more than half of all revenue. Some 6.5 million pairs of Topper shoes were sold, and 1.6 million pairs of alpargatas. Alpargatas produced ARS 12 million (nearly $14 million) of footwear for Nike and adidas, and at the end of the year began turning out Reebok sneakers with vulcanized soles as well. Denim and jeanswear accounted for 26 percent of company revenue, with 91 percent of sales coming from the Argentine market. Retail operations accounted for 9 percent of revenue.

Robert Halasz

PRINCIPAL SUBSIDIARIES

Alpalina S.A.; Alpargatas Calzados S.A.; Alpargatas Textil S.A.; Calzado Catamarca S.A.; Confecciones Textiles S.A.; Textil Catamarca S.A.

PRINCIPAL DIVISIONS

Footwear; Retail; Textiles.

PRINCIPAL COMPETITORS

Manufacturas de Fibras Sintéticas; Santista Textil Argentina S.A.

FURTHER READING

"Alpargatas," *LatinFinance,* December 1992, pp. 33–34.

"Alpargatas camina rápido," *Mercado,* March 15, 1984, pp. 35–36.

"Alpargartas pone punto final a su reestructuración financiera," *El Cronista,* December 29, 2000.

Bodmer, Virginia F., "A World-Class Textile Manufacturer," *ITS Textile Leader,* Autumn 1995, pp. 70–72, 74.

Díaz Fuentes, Antonio, "Alpargatas en alta mar," *Mercado,* January 3, 1980, pp. 41–43.

———, "Alpargatas llega a Catamarca," *Mercado,* August 26, 1976, pp. 29–32.

Estenssoro, María Eugenia, "Momendo de decisión," *Mercado,* October 1992, pp. 29–30, 32.

Friedland, Jonathan, "Reforms Reshape Argentina Shoe Maker," *Wall Street Journal,* April 24, 1996, p. A10.

García, Luis F., "Un camino menos sinuoso," *Mercado,* April 30, 1986, pp. 138–40.

———, "Jeans para el mundo," *Mercado,* May 26, 1988, pp. 99–100.

Lara Serrano, Rodrigo, "Denme una zapatilla de lona y moveré el mundo," *AméricaEconomía,* March 3–16, 2006, pp. 32–35.

Murphy, Helen, "Argentina's Alpargatas Coming In from Dark," September 23, 1999.

Peagan, Norman, "Corporate Argentina Faces Shake-Out," *Euromoney,* March 1992, p. 63.

Sguiglia, Eduardo, *El club de los poderosos,* Buenos Aires: Editorial Planeta, 1990, pp. 35–38.

ALTANA AG

Am Pilgerrain 15
Bad Homburg, D-61352
Germany
Telephone: (+49) 06172 17 12 0
Fax: (+49) 06172 17 12 365
Web site: http://www.altana.com

Public Company
Incorporated: 1977
Employees: 13,276
Sales: EUR 3.27 billion ($4.19 billion) (2005)
Stock Exchanges: Frankfurt
Ticker Symbol: ALTG
NAIC: 325412 Pharmaceutical Preparation Manufacturing; 325510 Paint and Coating Manufacturing; 325910 Printing Ink Manufacturing

■ ■ ■

ALTANA AG (Altana) is the holding company for Altana Chemie, a world-leading producer of specialty chemicals, including inks, coatings, sealing and casting compounds, electrical insulation materials, and resins and other additives. The sale of Altana's pharmaceuticals division, to Nycomed in October 2006, raised EUR 4.5 billion ($5.7 billion) for the holding company and refocused its operations on its smaller, but fast-growing chemicals business. Altana Chemie itself operates through four main divisions. Additives & Instruments includes additive maker BYK-Chemie, wax additives producer BYK-Cera, and BYK-Gardner, a maker of instruments. Coatings & Sealants produces specialty coatings for the packaging and other industries, such as internal and external coatings for cans, as well as sealing and casting compounds. Electrical Insulation includes the group's wire enamels and related resins and compounds. The last division, Effect Pigments, includes the group's production of metallic effects and pearlescent pigments and other specialty inks, and operates under subsidiary Eckart GmbH, acquired in 2005.

Each of Altana's divisions are among the world leaders in their markets. Altana Chemie generated EUR 907 million ($1.2 billion) in sales in 2005, as part of Altana AG's total revenues of EUR 3.27 billion in 2005. Europe remains Altana's largest market, accounting for approximately half of the company's revenues. Altogether, international sales generated 84 percent of Altana Chemie's sales. Additives - Instruments produced 40 percent of sales, while Electrical Insulation added 32 percent. The consolidation of Eckart, expected to add more than EUR 300 million per year to the group's revenues, would produce roughly one-third of the company's sales in 2006. Altana AG is listed on the Frankfurt Stock Exchange. Susanne Klatten, a member of Germany's wealthy Quandt family, is the company's largest shareholder.

ORIGINS IN THE 19TH CENTURY

Altana was created as part of the breakup of the Varta AG conglomerate in 1977. The new company took over Varta's chemicals, pharmaceuticals, food, and cosmetics operations. Yet Altana traces its own history back to 1873, when Dr. Heinrich Byk founded a chemicals factory in Berlin. Byk began producing chemicals for both

COMPANY PERSPECTIVES

Our values and our know-how have made us into what we are and show how ALTANA is different from other companies. In the past years ALTANA has enjoyed increasing success as an international and innovative company in the fields of pharmaceuticals and specialty chemicals.

industrial and commercial markets, and over the following decades evolved into the basis of the later Altana Chemie's Additives & Instruments division. At the same time, Byk's company also began developing pharmaceuticals. This led to the development of euphyllin, used to treat bronchial ailments.

Byk died in 1915. By then, Byk had developed a close working relationship with the Gulden family, which operated the paint company Leibziger Farbwerke. In 1917, the Byk business was merged with the Gulden family operation, and changed its name to BYK-Guldenwerke Chemische Fabrik AG. The merged company continued to grow through the 1920s, expanding its range of chemical operations to include cold asphalt in 1929. In 1931, the company bought Ernst Lomberg-Photochemische Produkte, a company originally founded in 1892. The company added the Lomberg name to its own following the acquisition. The company's coatings business took off in 1935, when it launched the first in the longstanding Anti-Terra line of wetting and dispersing additives.

The war years nearly ended the company's existence, however. Following the outbreak of the war, BYK's business suffered greatly, and only the intervention of Günther Quandt, chairman of the future Varta AG, saved the company. In 1941, Quandt bought up majority control of the BYK chemicals business. Nonetheless, bombing raids through the end of the war succeeded in destroying some 90 percent of BYK's headquarters and production facilities.

Following the war, BYK moved its headquarters to Constance, in what became West Germany, and, renamed as BYK-Gulden, relaunched production. The postwar period saw a dramatic rise in the Quandt family's holdings, despite Günther Quandt's 18-month internment as a "mitläufer" (Quandt's ex-wife married Joseph Goebbels in 1931; Quandt and his two sons all became members of the Nazi party in the 1930s, and Quandt's main businesses made use of slave labor during the war). When Günther Quandt died in 1954, his

sons Herbert and Harald took over at the head of the family's holdings. Over the next two decades, the Quandt family's operations, which officially adopted the name Varta AG only in 1973, swelled to a conglomerate of more than 200 companies involved in a wide range of industries.

BYK-Gulden also grew strongly during this period. The company moved its headquarters to Wesel in 1962, where it built new, larger production facilities for its own steadily diversifying product line. The company also began developing international operations, notably establishing an additives production subsidiary in the United States in 1964. Also during the 1960s, other members of the future Altana joined the Varta group, including Rhenania GmbH, acquired in 1969, which produced coatings for can and foil packaging. During this time, BYK-Gulden merged its additives business with the pharmaceuticals operations of Mallinckrodt Inc., creating the joint venture BYK-Mallinckrodt Chemische Produkte GmbH.

EMERGING FROM THE VARTA BREAKUP IN 1977

Into the late 1970s, however, the Quandt family had decided to refocus Varta around the production of batteries. In 1977, therefore, the group was broken up into three new companies. Majority control of each company was then turned over to different members of the Quandt family. As such, Susanne Klatten, granddaughter of Günther Quandt, became majority shareholder in the new Altana, regrouping Varta's pharmaceuticals, chemicals, food (or dietetics, specializing in infant formulas), and various other holdings. Most of these companies were sold off by the end of the 1970s.

The BYK operations, together with the group's pharmaceuticals business, played the major role in Altana's development over the next decade. The company had continued to find success with its drug development, with such strong-selling products as Riopan, an ulcer treatment, introduced in 1954, and Ebrantil, a high blood pressure medication, released in 1976. In 1979, BYK-Gulden built a new production site in Singen that specialized in the development of new active substances. This effort later led to the development of the group's blockbuster drug, Pantoprazole, a treatment for gastrointestinal disorders that became a huge international success for the company following its launch in 1994.

BYK also continued to expand its chemicals side, launching a subsidiary in Japan in 1980, and moving its U.S. operations to a larger facility in Connecticut in 1981. The company also established chemicals subsidiar-

---

KEY DATES

∎

1873: Heinrich Byk founds chemicals factory in Berlin.

1907: Company achieves first pharmaceuticals success with euphyllin, for treatment of respiratory problems.

1917: Byk merges with Leibziger Farbwerke and becomes BYK-Gulden.

1931: Company acquires Ernst Lomberg Photochemische Produkte.

1941: Günther Quandt buys BYK-Gulden, which is placed in Varta AG conglomerate.

1946: BYK-Gulden moves headquarters to Constance, Germany.

1962: BYK-Gulden moves headquarters and production to Wesel.

1964: Company establishes subsidiary in the United States.

1977: Breakup of Varta creates new company, Altana, with chemicals, pharmaceuticals, food, and other holdings.

1979: Altana launches production of active substances in Singen.

1980: Altana launches subsidiary in Japan.

1986: Company acquires Labotron, a maker of additive measuring instruments, and creates dedicated chemicals division, Altana Chemie.

1989: Altana acquires Gardner Lab in the United States; enters production of wire enamels with purchase of Dr. Wiedeking in Germany.

1992: Company acquires wire enamels specialist Deatech of Italy.

1995: Altana restructures around core of chemicals and pharmaceuticals; acquires DS Chemie of Bremen, Germany.

1997: Altana launches production in Shunde, China.

2001: Altana acquires Italy's Syntel SpA.

2003: Company restructures operations, creating two companies, Altana Chemie AG and Altana Pharma AG.

2005: Company announces plan to sell Altana Pharma and refocus around Altana Chemie; acquires Eckart GmbH and adds production of metallic-effects pigments and metallic printing inks.

2006: Company sells Altana Pharma Nycomed for EUR 4.5 billion; acquires Rad-Cure Corporation.

---

ies in France. In 1984, the BYK-Mallinckrodt joint venture was abandoned and a new company, BYK-Chemie GmbH, was established as Altana's fully owned additives subsidiary. The following year, BYK-Chemie expanded through the purchase of a stake in Labotron, an additive measuring instruments manufacturer in Gerestsried, Germany. Altana acquired full control of Labotron in 1986.

These acquisitions paved the way toward the creation of a new dedicated chemicals division, called Altana Chemie, in 1986. The new division grouped BYK's operations in the United States, Japan, and France together with BYK-Gardner and the coatings operation, Rhenania. By then, Altana had added a new business area, through its purchase of software developer DAT in 1985.

The company's chemical division continued to grow through the end of the decade, notably through the purchase of instruments producer Gardner Lab in the United States in 1989. That company was placed under BYK-Labotron, which took on the new name of BYK-Gardner. The company also expanded its chemicals operations into a new product category, through the acquisition of Dr. Wiedeking, based in Kempen, Germany. The Wiedeking company was one of the leading European specialist producers of wire enamels for the electrical industry. The company boosted its new enamels division again in 1992, when it acquired Italy's Deatech.

BECOMING A FOCUSED CHEMICALS BUSINESS

Altana Chemie's product diversification continued into the 1990s, as it entered the wax additives sector through the purchase of Cera Chemie BV, based in the Netherlands. The company next boosted its packaging coatings wing, buying the French operations of Rhenacoat.

The worldwide success of Pantoprazole, and the strong growth of the Altana Chemie division, led Altana to restructure its operations in 1995. In that year, the company sold its dietetics and software divisions, regrouping around a core of pharmaceuticals and chemicals.

The chemicals division maintained its steady growth through the 1990s. Acquisitions remained an important part of Altana Chemie's expansion through the decade and into the mid-2000s. In 1995, for example, the company acquired DS-Chemie, based in Bremen, Germany, which produced sealing compounds. The following year, Altana Chemie added Spain's La Artistica, another sealing compound producer, and the United States' PD George Company. The chemicals division also expanded its operations deeper into the Asia-Pacific region, adding sales offices in China, Taiwan, and Malaysia. By 1997, Altana Chemie had launched production in the Chinese mainland, creating Shunde-Rhenacoat, based in Shunde, to produce special coatings for the packaging market.

Altana also deepened its penetration of the electrical sector, buying Italy's Camattini, and Tongling Siva Insulating Materials, in China, in 1998. The company then boosted its sealants operations, taking over Germany-based Terra Lacke in 2000. The company further developed its Chinese presence through the creation of BYK-Chemie Tongling in 2001. In that year, the company also acquired Italy's Syntel SpA, a wire enamels producer, which was subsequently merged into Deatech in 2003.

By then, Altana Chemie had regrouped into three primary business units, namely Additives & Instruments, Coatings & Sealants, and Electrical Insulation. Following that reorganization, the company formally changed the name of its chemicals operations to Altana Chemie AG, while its pharmaceuticals businesses were regrouped under the newly named Altana Pharma AG.

Altana Chemie maintained its steady expansion into the mid-2000s. In 2003, the company bought Beck Electrical Insulation and Beck India, the former based in Hamburg, Germany, the latter in Pune, India. The following year, the company opened its fourth manufacturing site in China, launching Altana Electrical Insulation Zhuhai. The group had also been developing a new sophisticated additives technology, using nanotechnology to develop barriers to prevent gas diffusion in plastic. This effort came to fruition in 2004, with the launch of the industry's first nano-additives in 2004.

The year 2005 represented a turning point for Altana Chemie. In August of that year, the group reached an agreement to acquire Furth, Germany-based Eckart GmbH. The addition of Eckart enabled Altana to enter an entirely new product segment, that of metallic-effect pigments and metallic printing inks. The purchase, completed in October 2005, also added more than EUR 300 million to the division's revenues, enabling it to top the EUR 1 billion mark for the first time.

The Eckart purchase also led holding company Altana AG to announce its decision to redevelop its two primary divisions as independently operating companies. This proved a prelude, however, to the company's announcement in 2006 that it intended to sell its pharmaceuticals division and instead refocus around a new core of specialty chemicals manufacturing. Part of the motivation behind this change of strategy was Altana Pharma's relatively shallow new drug pipeline and its over-reliance on Pantoprazole. Yet that drug's patent was set to expire by 2009. With only limited prospects for a new blockbuster in its lineup, Altana AG decided the time was right to narrow its focus. In October 2006, the company announced that it had agreed to sell Altana Pharma to Nycomed, in a deal worth EUR 4.5 billion.

In the meantime, Altana had taken steps to boost its chemicals operations, and particularly its new inks division. In March 2006, the company agreed to buy Rad-Cure Corporation, which specialized in the manufacture of overprint UV coatings, as well as adhesives for the packaging sector. This purchase followed on the acquisition of another prominent inks and pigment group, Kelstar. The newly refocused Altana had emerged as a global leader in each of its specialty chemicals markets.

M. L. Cohen

PRINCIPAL SUBSIDIARIES

ALTANA Chemie AG; ALTANA Electrical Insulation Co. Ltd. (China); ALTANA Inc. (U.S.A.); Beck Electrical Insulation GmbH; Beck India Ltd.; BYK-Chemie (Tongling) Co. Ltd. (China); BYK-Chemie Asia Pacific Pte. Ltd. (Singapore); BYK-Chemie GmbH; BYK-Chemie Japan KK; BYK-Chemie USA Inc.; BYK-Gardner GmbH; BYK-Gardner USA; DS-Chemie GmbH; ECKART America L.P.; ECKART GmbH & Co. KG; Kelstar International Inc. (U.S.A.); Rhenania Coatings GmbH; Shunde-Rhenacoat Coating Co. Ltd. (China); Terra Lacke GmbH; The P.D. George Company (U.S.A.); Tongling City (China); Tongling SIVA Insulating Materials Co. Ltd.; Zydus ALTANA Healthcare Private Ltd. (India).

PRINCIPAL DIVISIONS

Additives & Instruments; Coatings & Sealants; Electrical Insulation; Effect Pigments.

PRINCIPAL COMPETITORS

Sun Chemical Corp.; Liksin Corp.; Environments Inks Encoding; Belcar S.A.; Kohl and Madden Inc.; Flint Group; Toyo Ink Manufacturing Company Ltd.; Sakata Inx Corp.; Tokyo Ohka Kogyo Company Ltd.; SICPA S.A.

FURTHER READING

"Altana Chemie Acquires Kelstar International," *Ink World,* December 2005, p. 12.

"Altana Chemie Acquires Rad-Cure Corporation," *Ink World,* March 2006, p. 12.

"Altana to Buy Brazilian Resins," *Chemical Week,* January 25, 2006, p. 4.

D'Amore, Nick, "More Changes for Altana," *Med Ad News,* September 2005, p. 36.

Dorey, Emma, "Nycomed Buys Altana Pharma," *Chemistry and Industry,* October 2, 2006, p. 6.

Savastano, David, "Altana Chemie Makes Major Gains in Ink, Coatings Markets," *Ink World,* May 2006, p. 18.

Walsh, Kerri, "Altana Lists on the New York Stock Exchange," *Chemical Week,* May 29, 2002, p. 27.

Wassener, Bettina, "The Strong Hand of a Shy Billionairess," *Business Week,* December 5, 2005, p. 32.

Young, Ian, "Altana Plans to Spin Off Chemicals; Acquires Pigments Maker," *Chemical Week,* August 10, 2005, p. 8.

AmeriCares

AmeriCares Foundation, Inc.

———— ■ ————

88 Hamilton Avenue
Stamford, Connecticut 06902
U.S.A.
Telephone: (203) 658-9500
Toll Free: (800) 486-4357
Fax: (203) 327-5200
Web site: http://www.americares.org

Nonprofit Company
Incorporated: 1979 as Americares Foundation, Inc.
Employees: 55
Operating Revenues: $1.32 billion (2006)
NAIC: 624230 Emergency and Other Relief Services

■ ■ ■

AmeriCares Foundation, Inc., is one of the top disaster-relief and humanitarian-aid organizations in the world. The majority of the Connecticut-based nonprofit's activities support permanent, ongoing healthcare programs in more than 50 countries, but the organization is best known for being the first on the ground when a major disaster strikes anywhere on the planet. With only a small number of paid employees, AmeriCares operates on the energy of hundreds of volunteers; the donations of medicines, medical supplies, and other relief materials from pharmaceutical companies and other corporations; and annual cash contributions from more than 150,000 individual and corporate donors. The group constantly collects donated supplies and stores them in two warehouses, one in the United States and one in Europe. When a need arises, it charters the cheapest and most appropriate means of air or sea transport and delivers the goods for distribution by one of many of its local partners on the ground, which include the International Federation of the Red Cross/ Red Crescent, the Order of Malta, and Mother Teresa's Missionaries of Charity. AmeriCares' key domestic programs include Camp AmeriKids, AmeriCares Free Clinics, Inc., and AmeriCares HomeFront.

LEVERAGING CONNECTIONS IN THE EARLY YEARS

When 55-year-old Robert C. Macauley officially established Americares in 1979, he was no stranger to helping the needy. In 1968, he founded the Shoeshine Boys Foundation, a charitable organization that operated in Saigon, Vietnam, and by the war's end had established 14 homes and given help to over 2,500 Vietnamese war orphans. On April 4, 1975, just weeks before the fall of Saigon, a U.S. jet carrying 243 war orphans bound for adoption in the U.S. crashed into the jungle outside Tan Son Nhut, killing a third of the children and critically injuring many more. When the Pentagon said it could not get help to the crash site for 11 days, Macauley sprung into action. As a private citizen, he arranged to have a Pan American Airlines 747 diverted from Guam to rescue the children and fly them to San Francisco. The $50 million paper mill that he founded a few years earlier, Virginia Fibre Corporation, was still deeply in debt, so when Pan Am sent the $251,000 bill for the jet, Macauley was forced to hock his house to the bank to cover the expense.

The year 1981 brought the fledgling nonprofit, tax-exempt Americares Foundation its first real mission.

Macauley, who is not a Catholic, was summoned to a private meeting in Rome with Pope John Paul II. The pope asked Macauley if he could find a way to get some medicines, clothing, and other supplies into Poland, the pope's native country, which at the time was under martial law. In March 1982, Americares airlifted drugs and supplies into Poland valued at $2.4 million. The Roman Catholic Church handled distribution and a representative from Americares filmed the operation from beginning to end. The organization's inaugural relief operation established Americares' hallmark recipe for future success: leverage Macauley's business and personal connections to secure donated relief supplies, money, and volunteer time, while keeping costs low and maintaining tight control over distribution.

Macauley was well connected. He was born in Connecticut and attended Andover Academy and Yale University, where he studied international affairs. He had been a classmate and friend since kindergarten of George H. W. Bush, the 41st president of the United States. Macauley's newly chartered organization's list of sponsors included ambassadors and corporate executives as well as Christian and Jewish religious leaders. Zbigniew Brzezinski, the Polish-born national security adviser to former President Jimmy Carter, signed on as honorary chairman of the board of directors. When approaching the nation's top drug and medical supply companies for handouts, Macauley later recounted, "Either I knew someone on their boards or I knew someone who did." Macauley kept organizational costs down by working without compensation, often with weekend help from his wife, Leila, and son, Robert, Jr.

In August 1982, Americares cosponsored a $1 million shipment of medical supplies to Lebanon, another country torn by civil conflict. The distribution of supplies locally was handled by the Knights of Malta and marked the beginning of a long-term relationship between the two organizations. Founded in 1050 to aid the wounded and to battle Muslims during the Crusades, the devoutly Roman Catholic Sovereign

Military Order of Malta, known as the Knights of Malta, is the world's only recognized sovereign nation without territory. In 1982, it had over 10,000 members and ambassadors in 40 countries. Affiliation with the Order of Malta meant that medical aid could be moved through diplomatic "pouches" into target countries without going through customs. Before 1982 was over, Americares had airlifted and transported by ship another $2 million worth of medical supplies to Poland, and had also provided humanitarian relief work in India.

In 1983, Americares and the Knights of Malta started shipping medical supplies to Central America. Prescott Bush, Jr., brother of then vice-president George H. W. Bush, and former Treasury Secretary William E. Simon, both Americares board members, helped Macauley raise funds and obtain free medicine for the effort. Americares expanded its work in southwest Asia in 1983 when it began sending medical supplies to Afghan refugees in Pakistan who had been uprooted by fighting between the Soviet-backed Afghan government and insurgents.

In May 1984, the organization was given the President's Volunteer Action Award for International Humanitarianism from President Ronald Reagan. In August, Americares facilitated the flight of seven wounded Afghan rebels to the United States for treatment, and by November, had delivered about $5 million in medical supplies to the Afghan rebels. By December 1984, Americares had sent over $14 million in medical aid to Central America, primarily to the two countries where U.S.-backed governments were battling rebel insurgencies. About $10 million in aid went to hospitals and clinics in El Salvador and $3.4 million to Guatemala. At the time, all officials denied that Americares and the Knights had any political involvement in the region. For the year, the organization shipped $20 million in supplies on a budget of only $600,000. The group had only one paid employee, a secretary/bookkeeper.

EXPANDING THE MISSION
1985–1992

In 1985, Americares sent food, medicine, and other relief supplies to Ethiopia and Sudan, where more than one million people had already died from famine. In the same year, Americares and the Knights of Malta in the Philippines began a partnership to support hospitals, clinics, homes for the elderly, and orphanages throughout the country. In May 1985, Americares, the Knights, and the Christian Broadcasting Company announced they were teaming up to send an additional $20 million of humanitarian aid to El Salvador, Guatemala, and Honduras. An earthquake in Mexico

KEY DATES

1975: Robert Macauley's bold actions help rescue Vietnamese war orphans injured in a jungle plane crash.

1979: Macauley founds Americares in New Canaan, Connecticut.

1981: Pope John Paul II gives the group its first mission: deliver medical aid to strife-torn Poland.

1990: A foundation relief plane is first U.S. flight to land in Iran since 1979–80 hostage crisis.

1993: *Money* rates AmeriCares the Best Charity in America.

1997: AmeriCares flies the first-ever private relief mission into North Korea.

2002: With Macauley's health declining, organization hires its first president and chief executive officer.

2003: Foundation headquarters moves to Stamford, Connecticut.

2006: The *Chronicle of Philanthropy* ranks AmeriCares third best-funded charity in the nation.

City in September followed by a volcanic eruption in Colombia also brought relief efforts to the area from the organization.

The April 26, 1986, Chernobyl nuclear accident in the Soviet Union prompted Americares to send milk products, iodine tablets, and other aid to Poland, Belarus, and Ukraine to alleviate problems created by radioactive fallout. The organization responded to an October earthquake in El Salvador with its largest disaster relief operation to date, and during the course of the year expanded its ongoing Central American relief efforts to Nicaragua and Panama. It was at about this time that the organization changed the typography in its name from Americares to AmeriCares. In June 1987, Macauley was referred to in the media as a "one-man Red Cross." His organization had, since its birth, distributed $140 million worth of medicine and supplies around the world.

In April 1988, AmeriCares launched its HomeFront division. HomeFront's main task was to organize and coordinate an annual one-day volunteer-driven project that provided free home repairs for people with special needs. The first HomeFront event drew 300 volunteers and took place in South Norwalk, Connecticut. AmeriCares responded to a December 7 earthquake in

Armenia with a December 23 airlift of emergency aid, which was accompanied by John E. "Jeb" Bush, son of president-elect George H. W. Bush. In 1989, Doctors To All Peoples was formed by AmeriCares to set up a clinic in the Armenian capital of Yerevan and to facilitate the medical care and rehabilitation of December earthquake victims in hospitals in New York and Connecticut.

Following a devastating earthquake in June 1990, an AmeriCares-sponsored cargo jet containing a medical team and 40 tons of supplies became the first shipment of U.S. aid accepted by Iran since the hostage crisis of 1979–80, when 52 Americans were held at the U.S. Embassy in Tehran for 444 days. When the invasion of Kuwait by Iraq in August and the run-up to the 1991 Gulf War caused thousands in the region to flee their homes, AmeriCares sent food, water, and medicine to refugee camps in Iran, Turkey, and Jordan. In December, the group became the first American charity to send supplies to relieve widespread shortages in the Soviet Union and pledged to deliver one million tons of food and medicine.

In March 1991, the private relief group airlifted medical supplies, and medical personnel from the White House staff and the Mayo Clinic, into Kuwait City, just days after that city was liberated from Iraqi occupation by a U.S.-led multinational military force. In May, an AmeriCares medical team was forced to abandon a health clinic in a refugee camp for Kurds in Iran after being harassed and receiving death threats from armed Iranian guards. In April 1992, AmeriCares' annual HomeFront project drew over 4,000 volunteers in 15 communities. By November, the group had sent three shipments of aid to combat starvation in refugee camps along the Kenya-Somalia border, as well as supplies to clinics in Mogadishu, Somalia.

NAMED "BEST CHARITY IN AMERICA," 1993

In 1993, AmeriCares began sending monthly shipments to American Near East Refugee Aid (ANERA), which distributed the hospital supplies, medicines, nutritional supplements, hygiene items, and school supplies to Palestinians in the West Bank and Gaza. At the time, AmeriCares was operating long-term programs in approximately 80 countries around the world. In December, *Money* rated AmeriCares, with its paid staff of only 45 people, the Best Charity in America, citing the fact that 99.1 percent of the $100.6 million it raised in 1992 was spent on services, not administrative costs. The year ended with former First Lady Barbara Bush acting as ambassador-at-large for AmeriCares on a mission that delivered humanitarian aid to war refugee camps in Croatia.

AmeriCares continued to earn its worldwide reputation for being the first disaster relief organization on the ground in May 1994, when it sent emergency supplies to Tanzania to aid Rwandans fleeing a three-week-old civil war between rival Hutu and Tutsi clans. In November, the organization opened the first AmeriCares Free Clinic, a state-of-the-art primary care facility that served the community of Norwalk, Connecticut. On January 10, 1995, AmeriCares became the first international relief agency to airlift humanitarian supplies into war-torn Chechnya. The organization created Camp AmeriKids in 1995 to provide an outdoor camping experience for inner-city children from New York, New Jersey, and Connecticut who were affected by HIV/AIDS.

In April 1996, the ninth annual HomeFront project drew 10,000 volunteers in New York and Connecticut. In June, AmeriCares organized a campaign to assist more than 70 African American parishes that had lost their churches to arson since January 1995. The group used two anonymous $1 million donations to purchase tents and pianos and a donated DC-8 flight to deliver the cargo to any of the churches that requested help. International efforts continued with help going to flood victims in China and Cambodia, and more than $1.4 million of medicines and medical supplies to aid 100,000 Tibetan refugees in China.

In January 1997, the second AmeriCares Free Clinic opened in Danbury, Connecticut. The big story of 1997 was the group's humanitarian aid to North Korea, where an estimated five million people faced starvation caused by drought, flooding, and crop failures since 1995. In September, the group's chartered cargo plane, carrying medical personnel, medicine, and medical equipment, was the first civilian American plane to land in Pyongyang since 1949. By the end of 1997, the foundation had delivered more than $1.68 billion worth of donated medicine and relief supplies, and had long-term aid programs in 109 countries.

In April 1998, AmeriCares delivered medicines and supplies to Albanians in strife-torn Kosovo through Mother Teresa's order, the Missionaries of Charity. The shipment was one of many that AmeriCares had delivered over the years, with help from the Order of Malta, to the Missionaries of Charity in Albania, India, South and Central America, parts of Africa, and the Middle East. On April 28, an AmeriCares-sponsored airlift carried the first U.S. humanitarian supplies to land in Iraq since economic sanctions were imposed by the United Nations on the country for its 1990 invasion of Kuwait. The medical and nutritional supplies were distributed to 22 clinics by the Iraqi Red Crescent Society. By November, AmeriCares had sent 12 airlifts to survivors of Hurricane Mitch in Guatemala, Honduras, and Nicaragua.

In a year of typical activity, AmeriCares in 1999 sent aid to earthquake victims in Colombia, Turkey, and Taiwan; to flood victims in Venezuela; and to war refugees in Kosovo. In February, the group delivered $3.3 million in medical supplies to the Palestinian Authority and dedicated the shipment to the memory of King Hussein of Jordan.

SERVICING A WORLDWIDE NETWORK IN 2000

During the course of 2000, a toxic-waste spill in Kentucky; flooding in Mozambique, Cambodia, and Vietnam; a cyclone in Madagascar; drought in Ethiopia and Armenia; and continuing conflict in the Middle East all initiated emergency aid shipments from AmeriCares. In addition to responding to disasters, in February 2000, the organization began an ongoing partnership with the Giao Diem Humanitarian Foundation to sponsor mobile health clinics, hospitals, orphanages, and elementary schools throughout Vietnam. In March, AmeriCares began providing ongoing assistance to Mongolia through Fraternité Notre Dame for the operation of a soup kitchen, shelter, orphanage, and hospital. In October, the organization expanded its partnership with ANERA with a grant of $14 million in medical aid to Lebanon and the establishment of an ongoing program of yearly shipments.

As 2001 began, AmeriCares had delivered disaster relief in some form to 137 nations and had established ongoing programs in many of the same countries. Consequently, when an earthquake struck Peru in June 2001, 11 tons of medical supplies were already en route by sea from Miami as part of a long-term humanitarian aid campaign. In 2001, the group responded to major earthquakes in India and El Salvador, famine in North Korea, severe medicine and medical supply shortages in Bulgaria, Kyrgyzstan, and Uzbekistan, and civil conflict in Congo, all places with ongoing programs. AmeriCares responded within hours of the September 11 attack on the World Trade Center, sending four helicopters loaded with medical supplies and personnel to lower Manhattan.

In 2002, AmeriCares began a medical aid partnership with the Bulgarian Red Cross in Bulgaria and the Asociatia Speranta Pentru Sanatate (Hope for Health) in Romania, a provider of medical and social services to children infected with HIV. With the founder and chairman of the board, 78-year-old Robert Macauley, in declining health, the organization hired Duncan Edwards, former Headmaster at Brunswick School in Greenwich, Connecticut, as president and chief executive officer in January. Edwards would be responsible for overseeing the daily operations at AmeriCares as well as programs, communications, and development. By May, war in Afghanistan had prompted two airlifts of medical supplies and blankets for distribution to hospitals, clinics, and orphanages by Help the Afghan Children. In October, Edwards was replaced by Curtis R. Welling, a former investment banker. In December, the organization launched a major relief effort to deliver medicines and nutritional supplies to Ethiopia and southern Africa, where 20 million people had already died from AIDS and famine.

In April 2003, just weeks after the start of war in Iraq, AmeriCares passed the $3 billion mark in aid delivered since its founding when the group's shipment of emergency medical supplies arrived in Kirkuk, Iraq. The delivery, as well as another to Baghdad in May, also marked the first humanitarian aid from a U.S. nongovernmental organization to arrive in either city after the U.S. military had declared victory. AmeriCares had actually prepositioned medicines and supplies in Turkey and Jordan in the run-up to the March 23 coalition invasion of Iraq. By the end of the year, the group had delivered over $8.3 million of aid by air and truck into Iraq, with most of the supplies originating from its warehouse in Amsterdam. In October, AmeriCares moved its headquarters from elegant downtown New Canaan to an industrial pocket of Stamford, Connecticut. The new facility had cheaper rent and allowed for a larger office and warehouse to be located on the same site.

TAPPING INTO THE INTERNET IN 2005

In May 2004, AmeriCares began a series of shipments of emergency medical aid to Sudanese refugees in northeastern Chad that were seeking safety from a brutal civil conflict in Darfur. Closer to home, starting in August, the organization responded to four hurricanes in six weeks, sending aid to Florida, Alabama, Haiti, Jamaica, Grenada, and the Cayman Islands. AmeriCares, which had become the major provider of essential medicines for the entire Darfur region, was finally able to send supplies directly into Darfur in October. In November, the *Chronicle of Philanthropy* ranked the foundation, with $695 million in contributions from individuals, foundations, and corporations in fiscal 2003, as the nation's sixth largest nonprofit recipient of private donations. In December, AmeriCares received a gift of $50 million worth of antibiotics from Purdue

Pharma, the largest single donation in the organization's history. As the year came to a close, the group's focus turned to supplying emergency relief to victims of very powerful tsunamis that struck Sri Lanka, Indonesia, and India on December 26.

AmeriCares continued its major tsunami relief effort in January 2005 with additional airlifts to Sri Lanka, where it established an office in the capital city of Colombo and shifted its focus to long-term relief. The public's response to the disaster was unprecedented. On March 31, 2005, with $40 million in donations in hand, AmeriCares stopped accepting contributions to its Tsunami Relief Fund (TRF). The source of the funds also showed, for the first time, the significant power of the Internet. In a matter of months, AmeriCares' TRF had received $12.7 million from over 75,000 web donations. When Hurricane Katrina hit the Gulf Coast in August, in the worst natural disaster in modern U.S. history, AmeriCares responded with $8.1 million in relief supplies to Louisiana, Mississippi, and Alabama in a three-month emergency response effort. After an October earthquake in Pakistan that claimed over 70,000 lives, the organization sent a series of relief shipments to its local partner, Islamic Relief, and opened a 15-bed field hospital in the village of Bana in early December.

In 2006, AmeriCares sent three airlifts of essential medicines and relief supplies to Sudanese refugees in February and March, and a fourth shipment in April to restock clinics operated by Save the Children. The AmeriCares Indonesian office, set up following the tsunami disaster, was able to respond quickly with emergency supplies when an earthquake struck Java in May. The organization continued its recovery efforts in quake-ravaged areas of Pakistan with shipments of medicines and relief supplies, and in October opened the first of 20 rural health centers in a partnership with the World Health Organization. The *Chronicle of Philanthropy* ranked AmeriCares third in the nation, trailing the Salvation Army and the American Cancer Society, in its 2006 edition of the "Philanthropy 400," which rates charities based on the amount of support they raise from individuals, foundations, and corporations.

As 2007 began, the organization had distributed more than $6 billion in aid to more than 137 countries since its founding. Historically, it could boast that every $100 it raised in cash enabled it to distribute $3,000 in emergency relief, a record that made it one of the most efficient organizations in the nonprofit industry. AmeriCares' incredibly well-connected and compassionate founder, Robert Macauley, was no longer involved in day-to-day operations but the organization he founded, based on delivering the greatest amount of aid to the people most in need for the least amount of money, was still growing and maintaining its reputation as one of the premier charities in the world.

Ted Sylvester

PRINCIPAL COMPETITORS

The American Red Cross; World Vision International, Inc.; The Salvation Army; American Cancer Society, Inc.; Feed the Children, Inc.; Food For The Poor, Inc.

FURTHER READING

"AmeriCares Started with a Favor for the Pope: Medical Relief Agency Known, Criticized for Airlifts That Become Media Circuses," *Richmond Times-Dispatch,* December 20, 1992.

"AmeriCares to Build 20 Rural Health Centres in Quake Hit Areas," *Baluchistan Times,* May 22, 2006.

"AmeriCares to Help North Korea from Worst Drought in 80 Years," *PrimeZone Media Network,* August 7, 2001.

Cappiello, Janet L., "AmeriCares Forced to Abandon Medical Clinic for Kurds," *Associated Press,* May 7, 1991.

Christoffersen, John, "AmeriCares Founder Gambled for Good," *Associated Press Newswires,* November 29, 2003.

Greene, Donna, "Solo Effort That Led to Worldwide Relief," *New York Times,* April 27, 1997.

Greer, William R., "Seven Afghan Rebels Are Flown to U.S. for Care," *New York Times,* November 5, 1984.

Holtz, Jeff, "Quick Response by Two State-Based Groups," *New York Times,* January 9, 2005.

Kampeas, Ron, "First Airlift to Iraq by U.S. Organization," *Associated Press Newswires,* April 22, 1998.

Lecker, Alan K., "Editorial: Time for Charity to Answer Claims," *Austin American-Statesman,* January 7, 1991.

Lenhart, Jennifer, "'Our Hearts Were Heavy': Bushes Return from Aid Trip to Guatemala," *Houston Chronicle,* October 3, 1994.

"Letter to the Editor: 'Expired' Drugs Save Millions of Lives," *Wall Street Journal,* March 12, 1993.

MacFarquhar, Neil, "First U.S. Aid Shipment Arrives for Iran Quake Victims," *Associated Press,* June 24, 1990.

McGuire, Craig, "Organization Case Study: AmeriCares Spreads Relief by Spreading Message," *PR Week US,* November 1, 2004.

Nathans Spiro, Leah, "Stepping into a Role Without Missing a Beat," *New York Times,* November 3, 2002.

"Overt U.S. Operations," *Wall Street Journal,* December 26, 1986.

"Philanthropy; Antibiotics Valued at $50M Donated to AmeriCares," *Biotech Business Week,* January 24, 2005.

"Profile: Bob Macauley of AmeriCares Is Profiled on 'Who We Admire Series' for His Humanitarian Work with People Around the World," *NBC News: Today,* November 19, 2003.

Schwartz, Karen, "Tents to Replace Burned Churches," *Associated Press,* June 27, 1996.

Sherrid, Pamela, "Leverage: Robert Macauley's Charitable Operations," *Forbes,* May 6, 1985.

Sternberg, Steve, "Charity Drug Shipments Get Clean Bill of Health," *USA Today,* August 16, 1999.

Teltsch, Kathleen, "Rushing Medicine to Crisis Areas," *New York Times,* December 19, 1982.

Welling, Curtis R., "Humanitarian Assistance After Military," *Congressional Testimony by Federal Document Clearing House,* May 13, 2003.

Apple Corps Ltd.

‒■‒

27 Ovington Square
London SW3 1LJ,
United Kingdom
Telephone: (+44-020) 7761-9600
Fax: (+44-020) 7225-0661
Web site: http://thebeatles.com; http://www.
    applecorps.com

Private Company
Incorporated: 1968
Employees: 16
Sales: $10.5 million (2006 est.)
NAIC: 533110 Lessors of Nonfinancial Intangible Assets
    (Except Copyrighted Works)

■ ■ ■

Apple Corps Ltd. is a music and trademark licensing company that represents The Beatles, arguably rock and roll music's most celebrated band. The firm initially dabbled in a wide range of activities including music publishing, record production, films, electronics, and retailing, but now concentrates solely on exploiting the legacy of The Beatles. Apple receives a portion of the proceeds from sales of Beatles recordings, videos including *Yellow Submarine* and *The Beatles Anthology,* and from licensing the group's image and logo for use on T-shirts, calendars, and other items. The company is jointly owned by Paul McCartney, Ringo Starr, Yoko Ono Lennon, and the estate of George Harrison.

ORIGINS

The story of Apple Corps Ltd. is also the story of The Beatles: John Lennon, Paul McCartney, George Harrison, and Ringo Starr. The four young men from Liverpool (with Pete Best on drums prior to Starr) began playing together as teens in the late 1950s, honing their craft at venues including the local Cavern Club and seedy bars in Hamburg, Germany. In December 1961 they signed a management contract with 27-year-old Liverpool record shop manager Brian Epstein, who would act as their adviser, secure them bookings, and try to win them a record contract. He subsequently formed a company called NEMS Enterprises, Ltd. (named for his family's North End Rd. Music Stores), which paid the group salaries and living expenses while taking a 25 percent commission on all of their earnings except songwriting.

In May 1963 a partnership called The Beatles Ltd. was formed, owned jointly by the four band members (now including Starr), to manage their non-songwriting income. Earnings from musical compositions (primarily by Lennon and McCartney) would be handled by another new firm, Northern Songs Music Publishing, which was headed by former singer Dick James. By this time the group had signed with Parlophone Records, an imprint of industry giant EMI, and begun releasing a string of hit singles.

Over the next several years The Beatles' catchy songs and engaging, irreverent personalities took them to the top of the world's pop music charts and box-office rankings (both for concert performances and such films as *A Hard Day's Night* and *Help*), while their

KEY DATES

1968: The Beatles found Apple Corps Ltd. as a music, record, film, and retail company.

1969: New York lawyer Allen Klein takes control of firm and begins to cut costs.

1970: The Beatles break up and litigation ensues.

1973: With the departure of Klein, Neil Aspinall is named to head firm.

1975: Beatles' split is finalized; Apple label and recording studio are shut down.

1981: First lawsuit against Apple Computer is settled.

1989: Lawsuit against EMI is resolved; Apple wins creative control of group's catalog.

1995: *The Beatles Anthology* documentary airs, and new CD sets are released.

1996: Firm receives $26.5 million to end second suit against Apple Computer.

2007: Royalty dispute with EMI is settled, opening way for Beatles downloads; trademark lawsuit with Apple, Inc., ends; Jeff Jones is named to replace Aspinall.

income landed them in England's highest tax bracket, then notoriously close to 90 percent. Unhappy with the amount of money the government was taking, they began looking for strategic investments to help reduce their tax burden. In April 1967 a new entity called The Beatles & Co. was created as the first step in a thorough business realignment, though the process was sidetracked by the August death of manager Epstein, after which control of NEMS shifted to his brother Clive.

In the latter half of 1967 the group's new business structure continued to take shape, with a company called Apple Music Publishing established to sign promising songwriters, taking half of their royalties in exchange for tracking earnings and promoting tunes to performers and radio. The name "Apple" had been suggested by McCartney, after a painting by surrealist artist René Magritte.

Though initially set up as a tax shelter, Apple was quickly infected by the creative spirit of The Beatles and evolved into something more ambitious and offbeat. After a second company was formed with Greek inventor John Alexis "Magic Alex" Mardas (Fiftyshapes, Ltd., later Apple Electronics), on December 7, 1967, a shop called The Apple Boutique was opened on Baker Street

in London, with inventory that ranged from records and books to jewelry, clothes, psychedelic posters, and inflatable furniture.

The following month an umbrella company called Apple Corps Ltd. was officially established with the four Beatles as its co-owners, absorbing the operations of the 1963 partnership The Beatles Ltd. Apple would also own 80 percent of The Beatles & Co., with 5 percent stakes of the latter retained by each group member. The new structure would allow the bulk of their income to be taxed at the lower corporate rate.

By February Apple Corps Ltd. had been organized into five divisions, one being The Beatles musical group and the other four comprising Merchandising (Retail and Wholesale), Music (Publishing and Records), Electronics, and Films. The firm also announced plans for separate publicity, management, and arts foundation units, though these were never set up. Heading the enterprise would be Beatles road manager Neil Aspinall, who had studied accounting before taking a full-time job with the group in 1962. The company's distinctive Granny Smith apple logo (shown cut in half on the reverse side of record labels) was soon registered in 47 countries, and quickly became an indelible part of The Beatles' visual legacy.

APPLE RECORDS: 1968

The most active of the company's business units would be Apple Records, which was run by 33-year-old Ron Kass, former head of the U.K. branch of Liberty Records. Distribution would be handled by Capitol in North America and EMI in the United Kingdom and foreign territories. While Beatles records would henceforth appear on Apple, the group remained officially signed to EMI and Capitol through 1976.

To house the rapidly growing firm, in July 1968 a five-story townhouse at the fashionable address of 3 Savile Row was purchased. It was soon renovated with cream-colored walls and green carpets, with a staff kitchen on the fourth floor and a recording studio under construction in the basement by Magic Alex. The Beatles' high profile and their public encouragement of submissions resulted in a deluge of demonstration tapes, sheet music, film scripts, and more, while legions of fans, hippies, and freeloaders from around the world began arriving at 3 Savile Row hoping to catch a glimpse of their idols, or at least a handout.

Meanwhile, suffering from a poor location, esoteric and overpriced goods, and rampant theft, on July 30 the money-losing Apple Boutique was abruptly closed and its entire stock given away to the public. During its brief existence the shop reportedly lost $400,000.

A few weeks later the first four Apple single records were released, with The Beatles' epic "Hey Jude" and Mary Hopkin's McCartney-produced "Those Were the Days" quickly reaching the top of the U.K. charts and the top ten in the United States. In November the first Apple album, George Harrison's experimental film soundtrack *Wonderwall Music,* was released, which was followed by the double-disc, individually numbered *The Beatles* (popularly known as "The White Album") and the Lennon/Yoko Ono experimental collaboration *Two Virgins,* whose nude cover photos of the pair caused distribution problems and controversy. The fall had also seen the release of the animated film *Yellow Submarine,* for which Apple received onscreen credit, though the project had been started several years prior to the company's formation.

At the start of 1969 Magic Alex's recording studio was completed but found to be totally unworkable, its designer proving to have more imagination than technical ability. The Beatles were engaged in filming a television special about the recording of their next album, and when they decided to abandon the sterile confines of film studio Twickenham for Savile Row, mobile equipment from EMI had to be trucked over. The latter would come in handy when the group filmed an impromptu public performance (its last one ever) on the chilly Apple roof on January 30, 1969.

ALLEN KLEIN TAKES CHARGE: SPRING 1969

The free-wheeling character of Apple would change forever when its owners decided to turn the chaotic, money-hemorrhaging enterprise over to a new leader in early 1969. Allen Klein was a New York lawyer who had been involved with the music industry since the early 1960s and had managed such performers as Sam Cooke and The Rolling Stones, winning a reputation for being hard-nosed along the way. After seeking an audience with The Beatles he won over first Lennon, then Harrison and Starr, convincing them he could boost their earnings. McCartney was suspicious of Klein's motives and also preferred his new father-in-law, Lee Eastman, a more refined New York entertainment lawyer, and did not sign the March 1969 agreement making Klein The Beatles' manager and head of Apple in exchange for a 20 percent commission.

Klein's initial efforts to buy out both NEMS (to which the group still paid 25 percent of its earnings) and the now-public Northern Songs failed, but he successfully renegotiated The Beatles' contract with EMI to boost their royalty rate by more than 50 percent, and soon launched a purge of Apple in which about a third of its 50 employees were fired or quit, many of them

executives. Several units were gutted including Apple Music Publishing, whose once promising work was taken over by Essex Music in exchange for a royalty cut, and Apple Films, which had bought the rights to J. R. R. Tolkein's *Lord of the Rings* books though producing little of note, with the completely unprofitable Apple Electronics also shut down. After these moves original company head Neil Aspinall was left with little to do, and at McCartney's urging he began spending his days assembling a collection of all known film footage of The Beatles.

In September 1969 The Beatles' new *Abbey Road* album was released, the last the group would make as a unit. With Beatles solo discs beginning to appear, the still unreleased sessions recorded earlier in the year were handed over to American producer Phil Spector for reworking, while the television film shot at the same time was edited into a feature, *Let It Be.* Released the following spring by United Artists, the title song would also be the name of the group's final album and single release.

Tension that had been brewing between The Beatles began to boil over after Klein's arrival, and in April 1970 McCartney announced he was quitting the group, filing suit a few months later to dissolve their partnership. Apple's annual revenues for the band's last year together were £4.3 million, with a profit of £1.4 million reported.

In spite of the group's split Apple continued to function, in 1971 cosponsoring George Harrison's New York benefit for Pakistani relief and opening a new $1.5 million recording studio in the basement of 3 Savile Row, which was soon receiving heavy use. Apple Records also continued to release music ranging from rock to jazz to Indian classical, and having hit singles with Mary Hopkin and the Beatlesque rock group Badfinger. In 1972, however, Hopkin and Badfinger both left for other labels.

DEPARTURE OF KLEIN IN 1973; RECORD LABEL WINDS DOWN

On March 31, 1973, Allen Klein's management contract with the group expired, and soon afterward Neil Aspinall again took charge of Apple with the blessing of all four Beatles. Offices that had been established in Los Angeles and New York were shut down, with the files from the latter transferred directly to Lennon's apartment. Apple Records was running in low gear, with all of its remaining artists released from their contracts save Yoko Ono and Ravi Shankar. Apple Films continued to be active, however, with such projects as the Ringo-produced *Son of Dracula.* In the fall the company filed suit against Klein, alleging mismanagement.

In January 1975 The Beatles' last legal ties were officially severed, their income (and Apple's) having been handled by a court-appointed receiver since 1971. On May 6 Apple Records ceased operations (though the label was used for a few months afterward for Beatles solo discs), and by the end of the month all of the firm's employees were gone save Aspinall and a half-dozen accounting and legal affairs staffers. The company also closed its still profitable recording studio, and its staff moved to smaller quarters across the street.

In early 1976 all non-Beatles Apple records were deleted and Beatles albums began appearing on EMI and Capitol in the various territories. The group's contract with EMI had expired in February, though EMI/Capitol continued to own the rights to previously released Beatles material. In October Apple's Savile Row building was sold, after which it stood empty for five years before being gutted and rebuilt due to structural instability, attributed in part to Magic Alex's unauthorized modifications to the basement.

Aspinall and his staff were busy sorting out the tangled legal wreckage left in the wake of The Beatles' breakup and Allen Klein's four-year tenure, while examining old contracts to see whether all monies had been paid and determining what the company actually owned rights to. In October 1977 a back-and-forth legal battle with Klein was settled with Apple agreeing to pay him $4.5 million. He was later convicted of tax fraud for selling thousands of Apple albums designated as promotional copies, however, and served a short jail term. During the year a new Beatles record, *Live at the Hollywood Bowl,* was released, the first album of previously unreleased material by the group since its breakup and the first in nearly a decade to appear without an Apple label.

On December 8, 1980, as he returned home with his wife Yoko Ono from a New York recording studio, John Lennon was murdered by a deranged Beatles fan. Afterward Lennon's one-quarter share of Apple passed to Ono, with whom he had recorded a new album for Geffen Records.

SETTLING FIRST LAWSUIT AGAINST APPLE COMPUTER

In 1981 Apple Corps settled a trademark infringement suit against a small California firm called Apple Computer. The company received $80,000, with the computer maker allowed use of the name if it stayed out of the music business. Revenues hit a peak of £6 million in 1982, but over the next several years slipped below

£2 million annually while net earnings began to fall into the red for the first time.

Aspinall and Apple had by this time earned a reputation for conservative stewardship of The Beatles' legacy, preferring to let the group's work speak for itself and refusing to cheapen its image with media overexposure or garish merchandise. It frequently resorted to legal action to defend these interests, and in early 1986 won a total of $10 million from the producers of a stage and film musical called *Beatlemania,* which had used the group's identity without permission. The next year Apple sued footwear maker Nike over its use of The Beatles song "Revolution" in television ads. Though approved by Michael Jackson, the owner of Northern Songs' catalog, and licensed for $250,000 from Capitol Records, the ads were later dropped.

In 1987 Beatles music began appearing for the first time on compact disc, and two years later a complicated ten-year dispute with EMI over the issues related to The Beatles' back catalog was finally settled out of court, with Apple reportedly winning creative control over the recordings and EMI retaining ownership of the master tapes. Future Beatles albums would once again sport the familiar Apple label.

In 1991 the company began reissuing long out-of-print music by such recording acts as Badfinger and Mary Hopkin, while the revived Apple Films released a documentary about The Beatles' first trip to the United States, which included most of their famed *Ed Sullivan Show* appearances. A new unit, Apple Productions, was also created to assemble a definitive video history of the group, drawing on the material Aspinall had gathered two decades earlier.

In October the company settled a second lawsuit against Apple Computer with the California firm agreeing to pay $26.5 million. The suit had been launched several years earlier because of the computer maker's addition of a musical digital interface (MIDI) feature to its machines.

In 1993 Apple Corps' music publishing earnings surged when pop diva Mariah Carey had a smash hit with an old Badfinger song, "Without You," though it split the proceeds with Warner Music Publishing per a Klein-era agreement with predecessor Essex Music.

In 1994, for the first time in nearly two decades, a collection of previously unheard Beatles music was released. *The Beatles at the Beeb* consisted of live-in-studio performances recorded by the British Broadcasting Corporation during the group's heyday. It would go on to sell over nine million copies worldwide. The resurgent Apple also moved into new space, this time a four-story building on Ovington Square.

ANTHOLOGY A HIT IN 1995

In the fall of 1995 The Beatles returned to the limelight with the broadcast of *The Beatles Anthology* video series on television in more than 40 countries. The project was hugely profitable, with the U.S. rights alone bringing $20 million and worldwide TV income estimated at $75 million. A compelling blend of vintage footage and new interviews (with Lennon speaking via archival tapes), it touched off a new wave of Beatlemania that caused sales of the band's music and merchandise to skyrocket. The series was accompanied by three double-CD sets that presented unreleased songs and alternate versions of existing ones, as well as the first new Beatles recording in 26 years, "Free As a Bird," which became a hit single. Featuring the three surviving band members accompanying a 1977 Lennon work tape, it would be the first Beatles recording that Apple could claim full ownership of. The company also launched a clothing line called Apple Organics that featured Beatles and Apple images, which were promoted via inserts in the new albums. The clothing and related items would be marketed by new worldwide merchandising partner Sony Signatures. The Beatles' back catalog was selling an estimated one million albums per year, with total record and music publishing earnings put at $12 million.

In the fall of 1996 an expanded version of the *Anthology* TV series was released on home video, becoming one of the year's top sellers, and in 1999 the film *Yellow Submarine* was reissued in theaters and on home video, accompanied by an enhanced version of the original soundtrack album. Apple received a sizable cut of the proceeds from both. The following year a new Beatles hits album titled *1* was also issued, which would eventually sell more than 26 million copies worldwide.

On November 29, 2001, the 58-year-old George Harrison, who had survived a knife attack by a mentally ill intruder at his home, died of cancer. His interest in Apple subsequently passed to his widow Olivia and son Dhani.

In 2006 Apple's earnings were boosted by the album *Love,* a musical collage "mash-up" of various Beatles songs and outtakes that had been concocted by longtime producer George Martin and his son Giles for a Las Vegas Cirque du Soleil production. Apple also received a licensing fee from the show.

The Beatles' catalog had sold a total of more than 600 million albums worldwide. Though the closely held firm revealed few financial details, it had reported a loss of $956,000 for 2005, while also making payments to McCartney, Starr, Ono, and Olivia Harrison for "promotional services" of $2.2 million each.

By this time, the firm was once again in the midst of lawsuits against both Apple Computer and EMI. The former had found tremendous success with its iPod portable music player, and when it began selling music downloads on the Internet in 2003 via the iTunes Music Store, Apple Corps had sued. In late 2005 the firm also went after EMI for $59.2 million in unpaid royalties, dating to the period from 1994 to 1999, when efforts to mediate the dispute broke down.

In early 2007 Apple, Inc., (as the computer maker was now known) agreed to settle the firm's claim for an undisclosed amount put by some observers at $50 to $100 million, receiving full control of the Apple name which would henceforth be licensed back to Apple Corps. The EMI suit was resolved a few weeks later for an undisclosed amount as well, which cleared the way for The Beatles' catalog to be sold as downloadable files, preparation for which was revealed in court documents. Rumors were soon rampant that Beatles songs would be available on iTunes or that a special "Beatles Edition" iPod would be released.

In April 2007 45-year Beatles employee Neil Aspinall announced he was leaving the company to pursue new ventures, reportedly having clashed with Apple's board about allowing digital downloads. The 65-year-old "fifth Beatle" would be replaced by former Sony Executive Vice-President Jeff Jones, who had helped reissue the catalogs of Bob Dylan and Miles Davis, among others. The company's annual earnings were estimated at more than $10 million.

Nearly 40 years after British music icons The Beatles founded Apple Corps Ltd. to manage their business interests, the firm continued to serve as custodian of the group's legacy, carefully supervising the rerelease of its music and films, as well as sales of related merchandise. Interest in the "Fab Four" showed no signs of abating, and the firm was readying itself for a new wave of interest when their music was made available for download.

Frank Uhle

PRINCIPAL SUBSIDIARIES

Apple Films Ltd.; Apple Publishers Ltd.; Python Music Ltd.; Subafilms Ltd.; Apple Corps, Inc. (U.S.A.).

PRINCIPAL COMPETITORS

Elvis Presley Enterprises, Inc.; Musidor, B.V.; CMG Worldwide, Inc.

FURTHER READING

"Apple Computer Settles Lawsuit with Apple Corps," *Wall Street Journal,* October 11, 1991, p. B8.

"Aspinall Quits Apple Corps After Decades with Beatles," *Wall Street Journal Europe,* April 11, 2007.

Brandle, Lars, "Apple Corps Sues EMI over Beatles Royalties," *Billboard,* December 16, 2005.

DiLello, Richard, *The Longest Cocktail Party,* Chicago: Playboy Press Books, 1972.

Evangelista, Benny, "Apple vs. Apple," *San Francisco Chronicle,* September 13, 2003, p. B1.

Goodman, Chris, "Beatles Take Bigger Bite Out of Apple," *Daily Express,* April 22, 2007.

Granados, Stefan, *Those Were The Days—An Unofficial History of The Beatles' Apple Organization 1967–2002,* London: Cherry Red Books, 2002.

Harrington, Richard, "$10 Million to Beatles," *Washington Post,* June 5, 1986, p. C1.

Morris, Chris, "Beatles Work It Out with Capitol-EMI," *Billboard,* November 18, 1989, p. 9.

Newcomb, Peter, and Robert LaFranco, "All You Need Is Love … and Royalties," *Forbes,* September 25, 1995, p. 130.

Prashad, Sharda, "Assetscore," *Toronto Star,* April 2, 2006, p. A18.

Quinn, Jennifer, "A Long and Winding Road for Beatles' Record Company–Turned Corporate Watchdog," *Associated Press Newswires,* March 31, 2006.

Robertson, Jordan, "Apple, Beatles End Trademark Issues Over 'Apple' Name, Logos, but Still No Word on Downloads," *Associated Press Newswires,* February 5, 2007.

Schmitt, Richard B., "Sour Apples: Beatles Sue Computer Firm in Trademark Flap," *Wall Street Journal,* February 22, 1989.

Shepard, Richard F., "Beatles Broaden Role in Business," *New York Times,* May 15, 1968, p. 40.

Siegmann, Ken, "Apple Settles Lawsuit with Beatles Company," *San Francisco Chronicle,* October 12, 1991, p. B1.

White, Adam, and Brian Mulligan, "A Dead Apple in London," *Billboard,* May 10, 1975.

Applied Signal
Technology, Inc.

■

400 West California Avenue
Sunnyvale, California 94086
U.S.A.
Telephone: (408) 749-1888
Fax: (408) 738-1928
Web site: http://www.appsig.com

Public Company
Incorporated: 1984 as Applied Signal Technology, Inc.
Employees: 700
Sales: $161.91 million (2006)
Stock Exchanges: NASDAQ
Ticker Symbol: APSG
NAIC: 334220 Radio and Television Broadcasting and Wireless Communications Equipment Manufacturing; 334290 Other Communication Equipment Manufacturing; 334418 Printed Circuit Assembly (Electronic Assembly) Manufacturing; 334419 Other Electronic Component Manufacturing; 541512 Computer Systems Design Services

■ ■ ■

Applied Signal Technology, Inc., produces digital signal processing equipment for intelligence agencies and the military. The company also offers engineering services. Applied Signal Technology operates from ten locations across the United States, including a central manufacturing facility.

Originally specializing in COMINT, or communications intelligence, Applied Signal Technology has expanded into electronic intelligence (ELINT), or detec-

tion and analysis of signals from enemy radars and weapons systems, and measurement and signature intelligence (MASINT), which monitors nuclear materials and weapon movements. Applied Signal Technology has developed a specialty in low size, weight, and power (SWAP) electronics.

FORMATION IN 1984

Applied Signal Technology, Inc., was formed 1984 by Gary Yancey and John Treichler, who were former employees of electronic reconnaissance system manufacturer ARGOSystems, Inc. (which was later acquired by The Boeing Company). These two would hold top positions at the company for some time—Treichler as Applied Signal Technology's senior scientist and later chief technology officer, Yancey as president, chairman, and CEO; there were also two other founders. Yancey, originally from Oregon, had earned a master's degree in electrical engineering at San Jose State University before starting his career at defense contractor GTE Sylvania, Inc.

Applied Signal Technology was incorporated in California and headquartered in Sunnyvale in Silicon Valley. Its first business was performing research studies and producing signal intelligence hardware for U.S. government agencies. It later began creating highly customized software solutions. First year sales were reportedly $80,000.

COMMERCIAL ATTEMPTS

Revenues were $11.9 million by fiscal 1988 and they continued to grow dramatically, reaching $50.9 million in fiscal 1992. Net profit grew from $600,000 to $3.4 million over the same period. By this time Applied Signal Technology had 400 employees.

Applied Signal Technology made the *Inc.* 500 list of fastest-growing U.S. private companies in 1991, as cofounder Gary Yancey was named "Entrepreneur of the Year" by Ernst & Young. In the same year the company opened offices in Jessup, Maryland, near such intelligence community clients as the National Security Agency. In addition to supplying engineering support, the East Coast staffers were active in the design of PC-based signal processors.

The rapid rise was not without its growing pains. Yancey later revealed to San Jose's *Business Journal* that the company had to scramble for cash in 1990 in spite of a doubling of revenues that year.

1993 INITIAL PUBLIC OFFERING

The company went public on the NASDAQ in March 1993. Its initial public offering raised about $13 million.

The slowdown in government spending following the end of the Cold War had Applied Signal Technology, like many other contractors, looking to make up lost revenues by developing products for the commercial market, such as tools to help cell phone companies fight fraud, for example.

Applied Signal Technology created a Commercial Telecommunications Division and a Military Reconnaissance Division in the fall of 1994. In the mid-1990s, the government still accounted for 98 percent of revenues, which were $67.7 million in 1995; net income slipped 71 percent in that year to $904,000. Until this point, Applied Signal Technology had dealt mostly with the intelligence community, including the National Security Agency, Department of Energy, and Drug Enforcement Agency. U.S. armed forces, however, were beginning to draw on the company's telecommunications surveillance technology. A portion of the company's equipment was approved for export to other friendly governments.

The company increased its space in Maryland fivefold in 1996 by leasing 30,000 square feet of a new office building in Annapolis Junction. It was also preparing to more than double the size of its 215,000-square-foot Silicon Valley campus. This site, once occupied by Libby's Canning Co., featured a historical landmark: a water tower shaped like a giant can of fruit cocktail.

By 1997, revenues were $96.7 million and the company had more than 600 employees. In a bid to attract increasingly scarce tech talent, in 1998 Applied Signal Technology opened offices in Salt Lake City and Portland. By this time, it also had a location in the Washington, D.C., suburb of Herndon, Virginia. Ample training opportunities and tuition reimbursement were other ways for the company to keep turnover low. The corporate culture was said to be egalitarian and hard-working.

Two subsidiaries were established in 2000: Transcendent Technologies focused on bandwidth management tools, while eNetSecure supplied products to protect companies' telecommunications networks. Both of these would be quietly reabsorbed into the company after a year or so, however. In the meantime, eNetSecure released ICEMON, an intrusion detection system.

POST–SEPTEMBER 11, 2001

After 16 consecutive years of growth, revenues slipped 9 percent in fiscal 2000 to $104.6 million. Still, the emphasis remained on government work. Poor results led to layoffs and plant closings; world events, however, would soon produce unprecedented demand for the company's technology. CEO Gary Yancey told a California business journal that orders rose more than 30 percent within a couple of weeks of the September 11, 2001, terrorist attacks on the United States (9/11). Many of Applied Signal Technology's products were designed for precisely the kind of communications surveillance called for in the homeland security mission. Investors took immediate notice, sending the stock price up 50 percent within three days. Over the next four years, it would rise to nearly five times pre-9/11 levels.

Applied Signal Technology was unique among its competitors in that it had not been swallowed up in previous waves of industry consolidation. The company felt this made it more flexible than most of its rivals, most of whom had become divisions of large defense contractors.

KEY DATES

1984: Company is founded in Silicon Valley by former ARGOSystems employees.
1992: Revenues exceed $50 million.
1993: Initial public offering on the NASDAQ raises $13 million.
1998: Revenues reach $110 million.
1999: Satellite offices open in Portland and Salt Lake City.
2001: September 11 terrorist attacks on the United States result in increased orders, soaring share price.
2005: Defense electronics company Dynamics Technology Inc. is acquired for $30 million; R&D center opens in Allen, Texas.

The signal intelligence marketplace continued to evolve, following technologies introduced by the telecommunications industry. New cellular networks, Wi-Fi, and voice-over Internet protocol kept the company busy.

It was also entering other new realms of signal intelligence. In fiscal 2004, the company began investing in electronic intelligence (ELINT), or gathering of signals related to radars and weapons systems. Applied Signal Technology bought another defense electronics firm, Dynamics Technology Inc. (DTI) of Torrance, California, in 2005. The price was $30 million. DTI had 110 employees and offices in California and Virginia.

Applied Signal Technology had developed a specialty in low size, weight, and power (SWAP) electronics. In October 2005, the company opened an R&D center in Allen, Texas, to develop and test these modular, scalable devices, which could be used on a variety of platforms, including UAVs (unmanned aerial vehicles).

Hiring adequate numbers of capable technical staffers continued to be a priority. The Salt Lake satellite office had doubled in size in the previous few years, to 70 employees, and the company was leasing additional space there.

Frederick C. Ingram

PRINCIPAL COMPETITORS

BAE Systems plc; The Boeing Company; L-3 Communications Holdings Inc.; Lockheed Martin Corporation; Raytheon Corporation.

FURTHER READING

"Applied Signal Lands U.K. Deal," *Defense Week,* October 5, 1998.

"Applied Signal Stock Soars; President Says He Doesn't Know Why," *Aerospace Daily,* February 2, 1996, p. 167.

"Applied Signal Technology," *Going Public: The IPO Reporter,* March 15, 1993.

"Applied Signal Technology Acquires Dynamics Technology," *C4I News,* July 21, 2005.

"Applied Signal Technology, Inc.: A Leader in Advanced Signal Processing Technology," *EDN,* June 18, 1997, p. 182.

"Applied Signal to Acquire Dynamics Technology," *Silicon Valley/San Jose Business Journal,* May 24, 2005.

"Applied Signal to Double Size of Salt Lake City Office," *Enterprise* (Salt Lake City), September 6, 2004, p. 5.

Brandel, Mary, "Rising in Riches; IT Salaries Are Rising by Double Digits Again, As Companies Pander to Workers Who Are Much Wiser About Their Worth and Bolder with Their Demands," *Computerworld,* September 4, 2000, p. 48.

Caldwell, Douglas E., "High-Tech's 'Back-Door' Man; Security Expert's Firm Keeps Companies from Getting Hacked Off," *Silicon Valley/San Jose Business Journal,* February 2, 2001.

"CEO Interview: Gary Yancey; Applied Signal Technology, Inc.," *Wall Street Transcript,* January 10, 2000.

"CEO Interview: Gary L. Yancey; Applied Signal Technology, Inc.," *Wall Street Transcript,* April 12, 2004.

"CEO Interview: Gary L. Yancey, Brian Offi; Applied Signal Technology," *Wall Street Transcript,* CEO Supplement, September 7, 1998.

"Company Interview: Gary Yancey; Applied Signal Technology, Inc.," *Wall Street Transcript,* Suntrust Robinson Humphrey Conference, April 2005.

"Corporate Profile: Applied Signal Technology, Inc.; Products for Signal Acquisition and Processing," *EDN,* Products Ed., December 13, 1993, p. 78.

Hostetler, Michele, "Gary Yancey: Handling Runaway Jeeps and Cash-Flow Scares No Problem," *Business Journal* (San Jose), March 6, 1995, p. 12.

Hostetler, Michele, and Gary Marsh, "Upside of Downsizing: Defense Firm Applied Signal Growing," *Business Journal* (San Jose), January 16, 1995, pp. 1, 18.

"Intelligence Systems Provider Looks to OTS Products," *Defense Electronics,* December 1992, p. 29.

Jones, Timothy, "Big Planet/Scary Planet—ENetSecure's ICEMON—A Big Brother Intrusion Detection System Sans All That Newspeak," *Teleconnect,* March 1, 2001, p. 20.

Lee, Dan, "Applied Signal CEO Sells Shares," *San Jose Mercury News,* January 31, 2005.

Lott, Daniel, "Anne Arundel Sees First New Office Building in Three Years with Tenant Demand for Area Office Space Stronger Than Anticipated," *Daily Record* (Baltimore), August 13, 1996, p. 1.

Marcial, Gene G., "More Phones to Tap?" *Business Week,* September 2, 2002, p. 107.

Marsh, Gary, "Applied Will Occupy Five New Buildings," *Business Journal* (San Jose), January 16, 1995, p. 18.

McKinzie, B., "Applied Signal to Open Salt Lake City Office," *Enterprise* (Salt Lake City), October 5, 1998, p. 1.

McMillan, Dan, "Silicon Valley Firm to Open Engineering Office," *Business Journal—Portland,* October 2, 1998, p. 15.

Orman, Neil, and Timothy Roberts, "Valley Likely Defense Player," *Silicon Valley/San Jose Business Journal,* September 24, 2001.

Velocci, Anthony L., "Applied Signal Shows There Are Niches of Growth," *Aviation Week & Space Technology,* May 26, 2003, p. 14.

Wall, Robert, "Army Moves Ahead on UAV-Based SIGINT," *Aviation Week & Space Technology,* September 3, 2001, p. 88.

Atkinson Candy Company

1608 Frank Avenue
Lufkin, Texas 75904
U.S.A.
Telephone: (936) 639-2333
Fax: (936) 639-2337
Web site: http://www.atkinsoncandy.com

Private Company
Incorporated: 1938
Employees: 260
Sales: $30 million (2006 est.)
NAIC: 311340 Nonchocolate Confectionery Manufacturing

■ ■ ■

Among the top suppliers of Halloween candy in the nation, Atkinson Candy Company is a third-generation family-owned and family-run business that manufactures nonchocolate candies using founder Basil E. Atkinson, Sr.'s original recipes. The company also owns Judson-Atkinson Candy Company, which manufactures jelly beans and other soft-inside candies. It sells its confections domestically and exports them to the Caribbean, Mexico, Micronesia, and Guam. The company does not warehouse its products, but produces and ships on demand.

FAMILY CANDY BUSINESS MAKES A NAME FOR ITSELF IN THE SOUTH

Basil E. Atkinson founded Atkinson Candy Company in 1932 in the small city of Lufkin in east Texas. Having been laid off as a lathe operator at the local foundry, Lufkin Industries, Atkinson scraped up some cash, borrowed a truck, and with his wife and two young sons, drove the two-day, 120-mile trip to Houston to buy candy and tobacco. The family slept in the car, and Atkinson began his new career selling candy and tobacco to small mom-and-pop stores on the drive back home to Lufkin where he opened a wholesale distribution business.

When one of Atkinson's manufacturers in Jacksonville, Texas, began to compete with him by selling directly to some of Atkinson's customers, Atkinson decided he could make his own sweets cheaper and better. He started out making peppermint sticks, coconut haystacks, and peanut patties, and by 1938, he was manufacturing candy in a 3,000-square-foot facility on Lufkin's Cotton Square. Mabel Atkinson, his wife, also played a role in the business, packing and wrapping the candies by hand. By the late 1930s, the company was making its version of a southern specialty, called chicken bones, presumably because it resembled "a piece of fried chicken."

Both of Atkinson's sons, Joseph and Basil E., Jr., accompanied their father on his sales rounds in his truck and worked in the factory in the early days. According to Eric Atkinson in the *Houston Chronicle*, the candy business was then "all a good-boy thing and relied heavily on how nice you were, how wide your smile was, [how good your BS was,] and the level of service you gave.... You'd say, 'Would you favor me with an order today?'"

Basil E. Atkinson, Jr., completed college and went on to Southwestern Medical School. From 1957 to 1967, he practiced medicine privately in Lufkin, Texas, while remaining active in the family business. When he quit medicine to join the family business full time, many of his former patients became his clients. Joseph Atkinson also worked in the business, and was responsible for inventing many of the machines used to manufacture Atkinson's candies. When his father was about to shut down the candy-making side of business to focus exclusively on wholesale in 1938, Joseph Atkinson's inventions helped to make the company profitable again.

By the 1950s, the company was growing rapidly and expanding beyond the South. J. Powell Wear, the company's first vice-president in charge of sales and marketing, went to trade shows where he introduced the company's products to a national audience and, in short order, put together Atkinson's national brokerage network. In 1954, when Atkinson Candy decided to sell the peanut butter–filled hard candy covered in toasted coconut known as "chicken bones" outside the state of Texas, it named the candy Chick-O-Stick because another company already had rights to the name Chicken Bones.

In 1961, with the company still growing steadily, Atkinson Candy Company built a new production facility. In the years to come, it expanded upon that facility several times.

NEW MARKETING TACTICS AND NEW CANDY LINES

The third generation of the Atkinson family came on board in the 1970s. Basil "Eric" Atkinson III did not intend to work for the family business. Having majored in economics at the University of Texas in 1978, he began his work life as a systems consultant. When he approached his grandfather, Basil E., Sr., for a job in 1979, the founder of Atkinson Candy told him, "I can pay you this much. There's plenty to do. Just get out there and do it," according to Eric Atkinson in a *Houston Chronicle* article. The young Atkinson did and

eventually found his place in sales and marketing, working side by side with J. Powell Wear.

Through the late 1970s, the company's regional and national sales relied primarily upon count goods and took place through distributors, but times were changing in the marketplace. Retailers were consolidating, and brokers were having a profound impact on how candy makers did business, first through grocery stores and then through mass merchandisers. Although Atkinson Candy Company continued to sell count goods, it began primarily to market its candies in bags.

The company also expanded its lines with Basil E. Atkinson, Jr.'s 1983 purchase of Judson Candy Co., a San Antonio, Texas-based candy-making institution founded in 1899 that "made the best sour cherry balls in the world," according to Eric Atkinson. Judson's manufacturing plant in Alamo City also made chewy pralines, soft-centered candies, such as jelly beans, orange fruit slices, and marshmallow peanuts or circus peanuts, a "quirky" piece of candy described by Eric Atkinson in a 2006 *Austin Chronicle* article as looking "like a peanut but [tasting] like a banana."

J. W. Judson originally bought the company in 1910 and built a new factory on the old Judson Ranch. During the 1930s, he added a starch department and began to make the company's signature candies with jelly and creme centers, such as fruit drops and slices, jelly beans and Easter eggs. When he started to experiment with making a tarter jelly bean, he wound up inventing the sour ball. Judson's sons purchased the company in 1941 and then sold it to Pearl Brewing Co. in 1965.

Basil E., Jr., and two of his daughters moved to San Antonio to run the renamed Judson-Atkinson Candy Co. Joseph Atkinson became president of Atkinson Candy in late 1992 and remained in that role until 2000. Eric Atkinson stayed in Lufkin and became national sales manager of Atkinson Candy, and in this capacity, he marketed the company's candies as far and wide as possible. Company sales increased 22 percent during his first year at Atkinson. In 1990, the Southern Association of Wholesale Distributors honored him with its "Candy Man of the Year" award for his efforts.

Throughout the 1990s Atkinson Candy held its own in competition with the candy giants. According to Atkinson in a 2006 *Austin Chronicle* article, the company has "relied on quality and [its] reputation to get [it] through the tough times," but the industry as a whole had its ups and downs. In 1991, when the price and lack of sugar almost put the company out of business, the company decided not to move manufacturing operations to Canada or Mexico to take advantage of cost-savings in labor and sugar. This decision proved to

KEY DATES

1932: Basil E. (B. E.) Atkinson, Sr., founds Atkinson Candy Company to distribute candies and tobacco.
1938: Atkinson starts to manufacture his own candies.
1961: The company erects a new facility.
1983: Dr. Basil E. Atkinson, Jr., purchases Judson Candy Company.
1992: Joseph Atkinson becomes president of the company.
2000: Dr. Basil E. Atkinson becomes chief executive and Eric Atkinson becomes president.
2002: The company acquires the Long Boy candy line from American Candy Company.
2006: Atkinson Candy opens The Candy Kitchen.

be one that Eric Atkinson later regretted. He called it a "poor decision" in a 2006 *Houston Chronicle* article.

2000–06: CONTINUING PROSPERITY DESPITE RISING SUGAR PRICES

By 1999, the company was using nine million pounds of sugar and toasting three million pounds of peanuts a year for its product line that consisted of about 70 items. In 2000, under the direction of Basil E. Atkinson, Jr., as chief executive and Eric Atkinson as president, the company began operating 18-hour days in response to demand. However, beginning in the late 1990s, sugar prices and shortages again had an ongoing impact on Atkinson Candy Company. Florida hurricane-damaged crops in 2004 led to a drop in sugarcane production from four million tons in 2003 to 3.3 million in 2004. By 2004, a pound of refined sugar cost 23.5 cents in the United States, more than twice the world price of 10.9 cents.

When Hurricanes Katrina and Rita hit in 2005, the situation worsened further. Thousands of acres of ready-to-harvest sugarcane were damaged, and operations at two sugar refineries temporarily ceased, leading to an increase in the domestic price of sugar from 28 to 40 cents or more per pound. World price for sugar at the time was 14.8 cents per pound. To take the pressure off, the government temporarily increased sugar imports and released sugar beet reserves into the market.

Despite all this, Atkinson Candy Company continued to prosper. Between 2001 and 2005, the company experienced 10 percent annual growth. It acquired the Long Boy line from American Candy Company in 2002. The company, which placed a strong emphasis on customer service, attributed its success in large part to "getting the product where it needs to be, in the proper quantities and when it needs to be there.... [W]hen one of our customers needs an answer, we respond with speed. Our goal is to answer any questions the customer may have while they are still on the phone."

By the middle of the first decade of the 2000s, the company was focused on "three categories for new product development," according to Atkinson: internal development, strategic partnerships, and acquisitions. As an example of the first category of activity, it introduced Pic-O-Sito, a Chick-O-Stick spiced up with chiles, and Chocolate Long Boys, as well as miniatures of these two items. In 2006, it introduced sugar-free Chick-O-Sticks, Peanut Butter Bars, and Mint Twists. It also added larger-sized Peanut Butter Bars, and began selling combo packs of its candies, as well as developing candies to target the Hispanic palate.

With sugar prices still increasing and difficulty getting enough sugar from domestic suppliers, Atkinson and other candy manufacturers criticized the federal government's policy of limiting sugar imports and restricting how much sugar could be sold domestically in the interests of propping up U.S. sugar prices and protecting domestic producers. They pointed to a Commerce Department study of February 2006 that showed that the confectionery industry lost nearly three jobs between 1997 and 2002 for every sugar-producing job saved through U.S. control of sugar prices.

Those hardest hit by the 30 percent jump in sugar costs were small confectioners and bakers who do not buy sugar on the futures market. For Atkinson Candy, which used 30,000 to 40,000 pounds of sugar each day, or between 11 to 14 million pounds of sugar by 2006, "[a] day without sugar ... is like a day without air," according to Eric Atkinson in the *Contra Costa Times*. The company tried to bring in two trucks of cheaper Mexican sugar after its distributor proved unable to deliver sugar three times in October 2005, but the plan proved prohibitive because of cost.

The company continued to struggle with increased sugar costs throughout 2006. Trying to preserve market share, it passed on only half of its increased sugar costs to its customers. With about 90 percent of its sales outside the state of Texas and a steady rate of growth of 5 percent, the company experienced its second consecutive year of record sales. Also in 2006, Atkinson opened a retail store, called The Candy Kitchen, in Lufkin, which carried the full line of Atkinson's candy as well as specialty made-to-order and seasonal gift items. Murals on the exterior of the store give passersby the illusion of peering into the factory to watch the candy-making in process, while in-store videos provide live monitoring of the workers in the factory.

Although the company opted to pursue its American Institute of Baking certification mid-decade to become a bona fide food production facility and to replace some of its original equipment with state-of-the-art technology, for Eric Atkinson, it was "still a matter of old-fashioned pride that we make the highest-quality candy we can. We still make it the way we made it in the '30s and '40s." Nevertheless, as the fourth generation prepared to come on board starting in the summer of 2007, the company was exploring moving some of its operations to South America.

Carrie Rothburd

PRINCIPAL SUBSIDIARIES

Judson-Atkinson Candy Company.

FURTHER READING

Doering, Christopher, "Candy Makers Frustrated by High U.S. Sugar Costs," *Houston Chronicle,* April 26, 2006.

Jennings, Diane, "After 70 Years, It's Still a Treat, Texas Company to Sell Chick-O-Sticks," *Dallas Morning News,* October 28, 2001.

Kientz, Renee, "Candy Calling: Little Plant in Lufkin Still Cranks Out Sweet Memories," *Houston Chronicle,* November 5, 2000, p. 1.

Lorek, L. A., "Family Owned Factory; Business Sweetens; Judson-Atkinson Candy Plant Still Making Sour Balls and Jelly Beans on Northeast Side," *San Antonio Express-News,* May 29, 2002, p. 1E.

McLeod, Gerald E., "Day Trips." *Austin Chronicle,* October 20, 2006.

"Sugar Prices Up in Hurricanes' Wake," *Contra Costa Times,* November 15, 2005.

B.R. Guest Inc.

206 Spring Street
New York, New York 10012
U.S.A.
Telephone: (212) 529-0900
Fax: (212) 653-0099
Web site: http://www.brguestrestaurants.com

Private Company
Founded: 1987
Sales: $125 million (2006 est.)
NAIC: 722110 Full-Service Restaurants

■■■

Based in New York City, B.R. Guest Inc. operates about 16 fine-dining restaurants, located mostly in Manhattan. While the company's name is whimsical, it also reflects a commitment to pampering its customers. Hospitality and not overly expensive "accessible" food are the hallmarks of the company's restaurants. On the one hand, other than the three-star Fiamma Osteria, an Italian restaurant in Manhattan's Soho district, B.R. Guest eateries do not try to offer an especially adventurous dining experience, generally waiting a year before joining the latest trend. *New York* magazine once called the company's founder the "king of the one-star restaurant world." On the other hand, the restaurants maintain well-stocked wine cellars, able to provide $250 bottles of wine to diners in the mood to splurge. The restaurants also tend to be large, seating around 300 people, and are designed by hot architects. B.R. Guest takes advantage of its buying power to gain access to the best fish, meat,

and produce at lower prices, and in this way is able to keep down prices. The company's approach has proven to be a winning formula in New York City, where restaurants open and close at an alarming rate.

B.R. Guest restaurants pursue a variety of cuisines. Concentrating on seafood are the Atlantic Grill, Blue Fin, Ocean Grill, and Blue Water Grill in Manhattan, as well as Blue Water Grill Chicago in Dearborn, Illinois. Modern Mexican dishes are the focus of the three Manhattan Dos Caminos restaurants. Located on the Upper West Side of Manhattan, Isabella's offers contemporary American cuisine, and Vento Trattoria, located in the old meatpacking district close to Greenwich Village, serves Italian food and includes the Level V bar in the basement. The company's pan-Asian entry, Ruby Foo's, is found at Times Square as well as the Upper West Side. B.R. Guest also operates Fiamma Trattoria at the MGM Grand in Las Vegas, Nevada. In addition, the company has teamed up with chef David Burke to develop a steakhouse concept, David Burke's Primehouse, located in the James Chicago Hotel.

FOUNDER IN ROLE OF TGI FRIDAY'S MANAGER: 1976

B.R. Guest was founded by its president, Stephen P. Hanson. He was born and raised in New Rochelle, north of New York City, the son of Betty Hanson, who was an executive in the garment industry working for designer Anne Klein and eventually launched her own sportswear company. His father, a gregarious salesman for the Anne Klein line, was also a fixture on Seventh Avenue, the heart of the nation's fashion industry. The dinner table each night was like a college seminar on marketing. From his mother Hanson learned how to be a hard-nosed businessperson, but from his father how to schmooze, attributes that would come in handy as a restaurateur. While attending college at New York University in the early 1970s, Hanson worked as a maître d' at Alan Stillman's original T.G.I. Friday's in Manhattan. Upon graduation in 1976 he became manager and worked closely with Stillman, gaining more valuable lessons for his future endeavors. "Alan said there were three things we sold here: food, liquor and sex," Hanson told *Nation's Restaurant News* in 1999. "Now we don't mean sex in a bad way, but I still manage and teach my staff the same thing: You have to have sexiness in your restaurants."

Hanson soon drifted away from the restaurant trade, however. He became partners with some college friends, took over the 18,000-square-foot Cookie's Steak House in a New Rochelle mall and turned it into a discotheque named Peachtree's. It was the era of *Saturday Night Fever* and Peachtree's became one of the most popular discos in New York City's outlying areas. While enjoying his time as a 25-year-old disco owner, Hanson prepared for the future, earning a license in commodities trading. Before the disco craze ended, he sold the nightclub and became a commodities broker. He made and lost millions trading in gold and silver, and again found something to take away from the experience. "I learned about leveraging as a commodities trader and I learned about incorrect levels of leveraging and correct levels of leverage," he told *Nation's Restaurant News*. As a result, when he began opening restaurants, Hanson was highly disciplined in the way he approached debt.

Hanson then joined the sportswear company his mother had established, heading production. Once more, a new profession would pay off later when he turned his attention to restaurants. He learned the importance of knowing your customers' wants and then consistently delivering. "You don't build a market and earn their trust, just to disappoint them next season with some loud color or wild style no one understands," he explained to *Nation's Restaurant News*. In keeping with this philosophy, Hanson's restaurants shied away from being daring out of a sense of ego.

FIRST RESTAURANT OPENING: 1987

Hanson's mother died in 1984 from breast cancer and the family business began to lose its edge, as Calvin Klein, Donna Karan, and others proved more adept at leveraging their celebrity to gain market share. Hanson finally turned his attention to the restaurant business. In 1987 he opened the Coconut Grill, a family-friendly 150-seat American regional bistro, on Manhattan's Upper East Side. It became so popular so quickly that a year later Hanson was able to open a second restaurant on the Upper West Side, the Mediterranean-inspired Isabella's.

Because the New York City economy struggled in the early 1990s, five years passed before Hanson opened his third restaurant. Then in October 1993 Hanson along with partners Joy Weber, a commercial casting director, and talent agent J. Michael Bloom, opened Park Avalon, which focused on seafood, located at Park Avenue South close to 18th Street. With three restaurants to run, Hanson experienced some uncertainty on how to proceed and wrote a letter to famed Chicago restaurateur Richard Melman, founder of Lettuce Entertain You, seeking advice. Melman invited Hanson to visit with him in Chicago. Hanson claimed that the half-day meeting was a major influence on his career and provided a much needed spark. "When I look back on that meeting," Melman told *Nation's Restaurant News*, "I think all he needed was a little direction and guidance, not that much tutoring really. He just wanted a sense of how to structure things going forward." Hanson also became aware of the appropriateness of the Lettuce Entertain You name; while humorous it also served as what Hanson considered a perfect mission statement for a hospitality company. Hanson searched for a comparable name to make his own statement, resulting in "B.R. Guest."

In the mid-1990s Hanson sensed there was an opening in the New York restaurant scene for high-quality seafood restaurants. To fill this niche, in 1996 Hanson opened his fourth restaurant, Blue Water Grill, located west of Union Square in the marble lobby of a former bank, next door to the trendy Union Square Café. The following year he added Ocean Grill on the Upper West Side, and then in 1998 opened Atlantic

KEY DATES

1987: Steve Hanson opens Coconut Grill.
1993: Park Avalon opens.
1996: Blue Water Grill opens.
2002: First haute cuisine restaurant, Fiamma, opens.
2004: B.R. Guest enters Las Vegas market.
2006: David Burke's Primehouse opens in Chicago.

Grill on the Upper East Side. With three major seafood restaurants in the fold, Hanson achieved buying power, and as one of the leading seafood buyers in the city he had the clout to demand first choice and better prices.

By the end of 1998 B.R. Guest was serving about 35,000 meals a week, leading to sales of more than $40 million for the year and producing annual returns of about 35 percent for Hanson and his partners. As a result, Hanson had no difficulty in attracting new investors. For his seventh restaurant, Hanson turned to the popular pan-Asian cuisine concept. Spending $3.5 million he opened the highly theatrical Ruby Foo's on the Upper West Side. The ornate interior, designed by acclaimed New York architect David Rockwell, included "a startling red-lacquered wall of Asian artifacts," in the words of *New York* magazine. Once again, Hanson proved that he knew what his market wanted. Ruby Foo's was soon overflowing with diners and Hanson was soon making plans to transfer the concept to Times Square, where a second Ruby Foo's opened in 2000, its theatrical persona a perfect fit on Broadway.

In the late 1990s Hanson was also thinking about expanding beyond New York City and transferring his concepts to other parts of the country. He was reportedly talking with venture capital firms, pursuing the possibility of taking B.R. Guest public as a way to secure the necessary funding for expansion. Hanson was patient and willing to bide his time, however. For example, he secured property on Hudson Street in the meatpacking district but was willing to sit on it until he deemed the neighborhood was ready. Hanson was also forging partnerships with hotels. His next restaurant, opened in 2001, was Blue Fin, housed in the trendy W Hotel, owned by Starwood Hotels. Hanson also forged an alliance with the James Hotels, these relationships providing a way for B.R. Guest to easily expand nationally. While he nurtured these channels he also continued to till the very fertile ground that Manhattan had to offer. At the same time, he closed his first restaurant, Coconut Grill, which was sacrificed after the landlord tripled the rent.

OPENING OF FIAMMA: 2002

In 2002 B.R. Guest made its first attempt at chef-driven haute cuisine, opening Fiamma (Italian for "flame") in the Soho district with chef/partner Michael White. It was located in a three-level townhouse, offering a number of differently decorated dining rooms. Hanson next turned his attention to Mexican food, looking to fulfill a growing interest for upscale Mexican restaurants. The result was Dos Caminos, which opened in Midtown at 50th Street and Third Avenue in 2003. A smaller Dos Caminos eatery soon followed in Soho. In 2003 systemwide sales for B.R. Guest reached $91 million.

After warehousing the space on Hudson Street for several years, Hanson was finally ready to act. In May 2004 he opened the 380-seat Vento Trattoria Italian restaurant, essentially a sister concept to Fiamma but offering more casual fare. It also featured exposed brick walls and wooden beams as well as an outdoor café. In the basement B.R. Guest opened the Level V lounge and dance club, able to seat another 140. The year 2004 also saw B.R. Guest's first restaurant opening outside of New York City when Fiamma Trattoria Las Vegas opened in the MGM Grand to strong reviews.

In addition to opening restaurants, Hanson also harbored an interest in the hotel trade. Teaming up with Danny Errico, founder of Equinox Fitness, in early 2004 he opened the James Hotel in Scottsdale, Arizona. It was supposed to establish a toehold for B.R. Guest in the boutique hotel field, pioneered by the Morgans Hotel Group and exploited by Starwood Hotels. While Hanson may have had a feel for the pulse of restaurant-goers, he did not do as well as a hotelier. The James Hotel, supposed to be an "urban resort," was in reality a $25 million surface renovation of a structure that had once been a Holiday Inn, Clarion, and Doubletree hotel, which the partners had purchased out of bankruptcy. Work was still being done when the first guests checked in. Yet even after the remodeling was complete, the reviews were less than flattering. One reviewer called it "slicked-up and tricked-out" and derisively called it Jimmy instead of the James. In 2006 the property was sold to Morgans.

While Hanson was experiencing problems in Arizona, he also suffered his first major setback in the Manhattan restaurant trade. He closed Park Avalon after a decade in operation and reopened it as Barca 18, Hanson's attempt to do with Spanish cuisine what had worked so well with pan-Asian, Italian, and Mexican fare. It received mixed reviews, the *New York Times*'s Frank Bruni concluding in his assessment, "You ultimately don't know what to make of it. Maybe that's because it doesn't know what to make of itself." Reviews had never been the most important factor in the success of a B.R. Guest restaurant, diners were the ultimate arbiter, but when they failed to support the restaurant, it closed in 2006. B.R. Guest fared better with the opening of a third Manhattan Dos Caminos in 2006, this outlet located on Park Avenue South between 26th and 27th Streets.

When the James opened a hotel in Chicago in 2006, Hanson and B.R. Guest's involvement was limited to the in-house restaurant. A year earlier B.R. Guest had entered the Chicago market through the opening of a second Blue Water Grill, located in Dearborn, Illinois. Next the company joined forces with celebrity chef David Burke to develop a steakhouse concept. The result was David Burke's Primehouse which opened in the James in Chicago. In addition to possibly opening restaurants in future James hotels, B.R. Guest also teamed up with Barry Sternich and Starwood Capital group, creator of the W Hotels brand, to develop what they called an eco-friendly dining concept that would be part of a new luxury, eco-friendly global hotel brand called "1" Hotel and Residences, the first scheduled to open in Seattle in late 2008. A "1" hotel was planned for Paris, France, as well, perhaps offering B.R. Guest an opportunity to play on an international stage.

Ed Dinger

PRINCIPAL OPERATING UNITS

Atlantic Grill; Blue Fin; Blue Water Grill Chicago; Blue Water Grill New York; David Burke's Primehouse; Dos Caminos Park; Dos Caminos Soho; Dos Caminos Third Avenue; Fiamma Las Vegas; Fiamma New York; Isabella's; Ocean Grill; Ruby Foo's Times Square; Ruby Foo's Uptown; Vento.

PRINCIPAL COMPETITORS

Myriad Restaurant Group, Inc.; Palm Management Corp.; Patina Restaurant Group LLC.

FURTHER READING

Barrier, Brooke, "Viva Las Vegas: N.Y.'s B.R. Guest Right at Home in Desert," *Nation's Restaurant News,* September 29, 2003, p. 45.

"B.R. Guest … Really," *Nation's Restaurant News,* October 18, 2004, p. 30.

Gordon, Meryl, "Steve Hanson Wants You to Be Happy," *New York,* March 1999, p. 36.

Kamen, Robin, "Steve Hanson Discovers Secret of Menu Cloning," *Crain's New York Business,* May 15, 2000, p. 102.

Kanter, Larry, "Ruby Foo's Restaurateur Orders Expansion," *Crain's New York Business,* September 27, 1999, p. 12.

Kramer, Louise, "Hanson Chews Up the Competition," *Crain's New York Business,* November 25, 2002, p. 3.

Prewitt, Milford, "Steve Hanson," *Nation's Restaurant News,* January 1999, p. 102.

Baird & Warner Holding Company

120 South LaSalle Street
Chicago, Illinois 60603
U.S.A.
Telephone: (312) 368-1855
Toll Free: (800) 644-1855
Fax: (312) 368-1490
Web site: http://www.bairdwarner.com

Private Company
Founded: 1855 as Lucius D. Olmsted
Employees: 2,200
Sales: $170 million (2005 est.)
NAIC: 531210 Offices of Real Estate Agents and
    Brokers

■ ■ ■

Baird & Warner Holding Company is the parent company of Chicago's Baird & Warner real estate agency, the oldest independent broker in the United States and largest in Illinois. The company does more than $6 billion in gross transactions each year. With 1,800 sales associates, it serves over 300 communities in the Chicago area through 30 branch offices. In addition to bringing together home buyers and sellers, Baird & Warner provides a variety of other services. It offers a full range of financial services, including a variety of mortgages and construction loans, and title services. Baird & Warner Home Services connects clients with reputable maintenance, improvement, and decorating providers. The company's relocation services unit helps clients moving into a new community to make the

transition, whether within the Chicago area or elsewhere. Baird & Warner is headed by the fifth generation of the Baird family.

FOUNDED IN 1855

Baird & Warner was founded in 1855 by Lucius D. Olmsted. The son of a Yale University professor, Olmsted came to Chicago at the age of 21, forsaking literary pursuits according to his obituary in the *Chicago Tribune* to pursue a business career in the fast-growing town of Chicago. He found work as a clerk at a dry goods store, T.B. Carter & Company. He soon became head clerk and bought a partnership in the business. In 1855 he sold his stake and went into business for himself, establishing a real estate loan company in the T.B. Carter & Company building. He made his first loan in March of that year, $5,000 to Edward Casey & Brothers, the first known transaction in the history of Baird & Warner.

With Chicago expanding rapidly, the business thrived, and Olmsted soon needed trustworthy help. He convinced a childhood friend, Lyman Baird, to leave his job in the office of the treasurer at Yale to join him in 1857. Three years later, in January 1860, Baird became a copartner in what became known as L.D. Olmsted & Company. Together they began investing heavily in Chicago real estate, the bulk of the funds coming from New York and Connecticut insurance companies. The partnership lasted little more than two years, however. Early in 1862 Olmsted took ill and after three or four weeks returned to the East to convalesce at his father-in-law's house in Springfield, Massachusetts, but his condi-

COMPANY PERSPECTIVES

Founded in 1855, Baird & Warner is the largest independent real estate broker in Illinois and the oldest in the country.

tion took a turn for the worse and two weeks later he died at the age of 35.

After Olmsted's death Baird brought in another New Haven man to serve as his partner, Francis Bradley, and the firm assumed the name of Baird & Bradley. A former bank teller and cashier, Bradley had been working as an auditor for the Rock Island Railroad in Chicago since 1857. The firm at this point expanded beyond lending, becoming involved in property management and insurance sales. By this time, the country was mired in the Civil War, which provided Baird & Bradley with an opportunity to help companies set up factories to supply the Union's military needs.

Following the war, Chicago's population continued to soar, approaching 300,000 by the end of the decade, a threefold increase over the course of the decade. Chicago suffered a major setback when a large portion of the city was destroyed by the great fire of October 1871. Baird & Bradley played a key role in Chicago's recovery because the firm's safe was able to survive the fire intact, which could not be said for the rest of the offices. The courthouse's public real estate records were also destroyed, and the city came to rely on Baird & Bradley's paperwork to re-create property titles and boundaries. The firm was also instrumental in Chicago's recovery by raising $140 million over the next ten years from East Coast investors to rebuild the city.

A new generation of the Baird family became involved in the business in 1878 when 19-year-old Wyllys Warner Baird joined his father. He was just a year old when he moved to Chicago with his family, grew up in the city, and received his education there. He started out as an office boy and made partner in 1887. In that same year, Lyman Baird's 36-year-old brother-in-law, George L. Warner, was also named junior partner. Born in New Haven, he had come to Chicago in 1868, and worked as a shipping clerk at a grocery wholesaler before joining Baird & Bradley in 1883. The new partners were dispatched to live in other parts of Chicago to bring in business, with Wyllys setting up residence on the North Side and Warner in the Hyde Park suburb. By this point Chicago's population had reached 850,000.

The 78-year-old Bradley died in 1892. Lyman Baird became consulting partner, as the younger members of the firm reorganized as Baird & Warner in 1893. That same year brought the World's Fair to Chicago, officially called the World's Columbia Exposition of 1893. One of the many innovations that emerged from the fair, including the first Ferris wheel, was the elevated railroad system that had been created to transport fairgoers from downtown Chicago to "The Great White City" where the exposition was held. Afterward the public demanded more elevated lines and Baird & Warner was hired to acquire property and right-of-ways for several of the traction companies. The firm also became involved in the new suburbs that were created because of the expansion of the railways. In 1897 the firm opened its first branch office, established near the end of the North Side elevated line. In addition to houses, Baird & Lyman also increased its property management business as large numbers of apartment buildings were constructed in the city.

In 1903 Wyllys Baird was named president. Lyman Baird died in 1908 and five years later Warner passed away as well. By this time, a third generation of the Baird family had joined the company, Warner Green Baird, who took over the building management department in 1911. His training had been in engineering, and he worked for Illinois Malleable Iron Co. for three years after graduating from Cornell University.

The firm retained the Baird & Warner name and continued to grow. A second branch office, in Rogers Park, was opened in 1917. Following a recession in 1919 after World War I, the economy boomed across the country, and Baird & Warner prospered as well. It became involved in the development and management of cooperative apartments and office buildings in the city. A fourth branch office opened in Evanston in 1921. Two years later Baird & Warner was incorporated, a move made to increase the firm's ability to borrow money in order to meet the large demand for mortgages and construction loans. The change in ownership structure would also prove beneficial when Baird & Warner soon faced the most difficult period in its history.

DEATH OF WYLLYS BAIRD: 1928

In April 1928 Wyllys Baird suffered a stroke while in Florida. He returned to Chicago and appeared to be recovering when his condition suddenly worsened and he died in June at the age of 68. Warner Baird took over as president and bought back shares of stock in the firm his father had awarded to nonfamily members. With that matter settled he would soon be faced with a far great challenge, the Great Depression that enveloped the

KEY DATES

1855: Lucius D. Olmsted forms Chicago real estate company.
1862: Firm becomes Baird & Bradley.
1893: Firm is reorganized as Baird & Warner.
1903: Wyllys Baird is named president.
1928: Warner Baird becomes president after father's death.
1963: John Baird succeeds father as president.
1979: Baird & Warner Real Estate and Investment Trust lost to Carl Icahn in proxy fight.
1991: Stephen Baird becomes fifth-generation president.
2000: Home Services division is formed.

country after the stock market crash of 1929. Baird & Warner gained some protection because of its corporate status, but the emphasis at this time was on sheer survival. Funds dried up as did the demand for mortgages, but because a large number of mortgage defaults resulted in properties being seized Baird & Warner was able to increase its property management business, serving life insurance companies that took possession of apartment hotels and other buildings. For a few years in the early 1930s, property management provided most of the firm's income. Three more branch offices were opened in 1933 to manage these properties around the city. After the federal government made money available for single-family homes through the Federal Housing Administration, real estate sales improved in the late 1930s and Baird & Warner converted the building management branches into sales offices.

While the United States' entry in World War II in December 1941 spurred the economy due to military spending, Baird & Warner suffered because of a lack of new construction in Chicago. That would change after the war when a housing boom coincided with a baby boom and a surging economy. The end of the war also saw the arrival of members of the fourth generation of the Baird family, who had been called away to serve in the military. In 1946, John Wyllys Baird, a holder of a Harvard MBA, joined the business. A year later he was joined by Warner Green Baird, Jr., who held a law degree from Northwestern University. During the postwar years, Baird & Warner took advantage of the measures the government took to alleviate the housing crunch. Rent controls were lifted by the Housing and Rent Act of 1947, spurring apartment building, and the

firm began providing a large number of construction loans for apartment buildings. In the 1950s Baird & Warner teamed up with insurance companies and other investors in building shopping centers in the Chicago suburbs, where it also opened offices to become involved in the residential home business. In addition, Baird & Warner became one of the first real estate firms to participate in urban renewal projects.

In 1963 John Baird succeeded his father as president while his brother became vice-president and secretary, although the elder Baird remained very much involved, serving as chairman of the board. John Baird soon found himself a controversial figure in Chicago real estate when in the mid-1960s he became a vocal supporter of fair housing initiatives that sought to eliminate the mechanisms used to keep minorities from moving into white neighborhoods. He made headlines in 1965 when he resigned from the Chicago Real Estate Board, which his family had been instrumental in founding in the 1880s, because the organization was supporting the Property Owner's Coordinating Committee, a group that espoused housing discrimination. While his stance cost Baird & Warner some business in the short term, John Baird's beliefs were borne out when new housing legislation was passed later in the decade outlawing the practices he found so abhorrent.

In the 1970s John Baird played an important role in the preservation and restoration of Chicago's historic neighborhoods, and the firm participated in the redevelopment of the Printers Row area, one of the first loft initiatives in the city. Also, in 1971 the firm formed the Baird & Warner Real Estate and Investment Trust (REIT) to raise capital for an increasing demand from industrial, office, and housing developers. The REIT was strong enough to withstand the recession of the early 1970s, and later in the decade it caught the attention of New York corporate raider Carl Icahn. He won a proxy fight over the company in 1979 and renamed it Baywater Realty & Investment Trust, a tribute to the neighborhood where he grew up.

In 1980 a fifth generation of the Baird family joined the firm, John Baird's son Stephen W. Baird. Also a Harvard graduate, the younger Baird took a position in the shopping center division. Two years later he launched the firm's real estate securities division. In 1983 Warner Baird finally turned over the chairmanship to his son John. He died a year later at the age of 98.

After more than a decade of grooming, Steve Baird succeeded his father as president in 1991, and like his father before him, John Baird retained the chairmanship while the next generation assumed day-to-day control. Maintaining something of a family tradition Steve Baird graduated from Harvard and came to the family business after studying something unrelated to real estate, graduating with a degree in psychology while taking a minor in art history. He took charge of a company with sales of $1.5 billion. It served northern Illinois's residential real estate market with 35 offices and more than 700 brokers, and the property management unit managed 35 buildings containing a total of 2,500 apartments. The firm also established a ten-person office in Denver and considered opening an office in Milwaukee. However, a drop in oil prices adversely affected the Denver real estate market, and Baird & Warner lost a significant amount of money on a development deal in the city. To make matters worse the economy soured as did the real estate market around the country.

To weather the storm, Baird & Warner pulled out of some development projects and restructured others, while also narrowing the firm's focus. More emphasis was placed on the residential sales group, which in 1995 posted the best year in its history with more than $2 billion in sales. A year later Baird & Warner joined forces with Christie's Great Estates, an offshoot of the famous Christie's fine arts auction house, to market expensive homes, exceeding $500,000, in the Chicago area. With the housing market booming, Baird & Warner began adding related services. To focus even more attention on residential sales, two major units were sold in the late 1990s: the commercial mortgage business, which took the name Baird & Warner Real Estate Capital, and the property management division, taking the name BW Phillips.

NEW CENTURY: ADDING SERVICES

As Baird & Warner entered its third century, it had to adapt to a rapidly consolidating industry and contend with large national firms that were rolling up small independent real estate brokerages at a steady clip. In order to remain competitive Baird & Warner had to continue to add what it offered residential customers and become adept at cross-selling. In 2000 the firm launched its home services division to connect home-buyers to contractors, movers, and other service providers. "Nowadays," Steve Baird told Crain's Chicago Business in 2003, "a customer may buy four or five services from us, where 25 years ago, they only bought one. Today, we're looking at increasing our marketshare by offering more services."

Baird & Warner celebrated its 150th birthday in 2005, and despite his 90 years of age, John Baird continued to take the train into work four days a week. The company remained very much an independent firm and the Baird family made it clear they had no interest in selling, although Steve Baird received an occasional inquiry. Sales volumes had grown to more than $6.2 billion, compared to the $1.4 billion when Steve Baird took the reins in 1991, and annual revenues totaled $170 million. Baird believed that continued growth was a must, and that standing still was the beginning of a company's decline. In order to fuel expansion the firm began thinking of franchising to open new offices rather than incur the expense of building from the ground up. Baird & Warner was a strong brand in the Chicago area and, should it pursue franchising, might well begin yet another phase in its storied history, becoming a regional powerhouse.

Ed Dinger

PRINCIPAL SUBSIDIARIES

Baird & Warner Financial Services; Baird & Warner Home Services; Baird & Warner Title Services; Baird & Warner Relocation Services.

PRINCIPAL COMPETITORS

Coldwell Banker Real Estate Corporation; Century 21 Real Estate LLC; Re/Max International, Inc.

FURTHER READING

"Celebrating 150," Chicago: Baird & Warner Holding Company, 2005.

"Death of an Estimable Citizen," *Chicago Tribune*, March 15, 1862.

Donovan, Deborah, "The John Baird Story," *Daily Herald* (Arlington Heights, Ill.), September 13, 1996, p 1.

Klein, Sarah A., "Baird; Real Estate, Chicago (John Baird and His Generation Run Business)," *Crain's Chicago Business*, October 17, 2005, p. 85.

Richardson, Patricia, "Father-Son Team Scores Big at Home," *Crain's Chicago Business*, June 2, 2003, p. A113.

Umberger, Mary, "Baird & Warner Weighs Franchising," *Chicago Tribune*, May 1, 2005.

"Warner G. Baird, 98; Guided Realty Company," *Chicago Tribune*, February 9, 1984, p. B18.

"Wyllys W. Baird, Pioneer Realty Dealer, Is Dead," *Chicago Daily Tribune*, June 17, 1928, p. 12.

Ballistic Recovery Systems, Inc.

300 Airport Road
South St. Paul, Minnesota 55075
U.S.A.
Telephone: (651) 457-7491
Fax: (651) 457-8651
Web site: http://www.brsparachutes.com

Public Company
Incorporated: 1980
Employees: 75
Sales: $9.19 million (2006)
Stock Exchanges: NASDAQ
Ticker Symbol: BRSI.OB
NAIC: 336413 Other Aircraft Part and Auxiliary Equipment Manufacturing; 541710 Research and Development in the Physical, Engineering, and Life Sciences

∎ ∎ ∎

Ballistic Recovery Systems, Inc., (BRS) makes parachutes for saving entire planes in the event of engine failure or other emergency. BRS's whole-plane parachutes are standard equipment on the few hundred Cirrus Design aircraft being produced every year and are available as options on other makes. Retrofits are available for such popular models as the Cessna 152, 172, and 182; the company started making recovery chutes for ultralights. BRS has also been developing chutes for heavier, faster planes.

ORIGINS

Ballistic Recovery Systems, Inc., was formed in 1980 by Boris Popov of Minnesota. Five years earlier Popov had fallen 400 feet into a lake after his hang glider collapsed. The spill shook a few fillings loose, and got him thinking about the possibility of softening such falls with a parachute.

BRS, based in South St. Paul, initially focused on the ultralight market and brought out its first product in 1982. The system Popov ultimately came up with worked like this: in event of emergency, the pilot pulled a lever to trigger a huge parachute deployed by a solid-fuel rocket.

Recreational aircraft represented a small niche, and the company did not exceed $2 million in annual revenues until progressing to systems for factory-built planes.

One of BRS's favorite metrics, though, was the number of times its products saved lives. The first of these came on August 7, 1983, when an ultralight flown by Colorado's Jay Tipton was rescued by a BRS parachute. The save was all the more dramatic as it occurred in front of Tipton's wife and young daughter.

PUBLIC IN 1986

BRS underwent an initial public offering (IPO) in 1986 to raise money to develop products for general aviation use. The IPO and a secondary offering a few years later together raised more than $2 million.

BRS founder Boris Popov stepped down from the CEO position in 1989, a classic case of the visionary

COMPANY PERSPECTIVES

Like seat belts and airbags, the BRS whole-airframe parachute is a safety system that is fast becoming standard equipment on modern aircraft. BRS believes there are now only two types of pilots in the world: those who embrace the concept of having a whole-airplane parachute system ... and those who will.

entrepreneur making way for more professional management to take the company to the next level. However, Popov soon came back as president, feeling his replacements were not sufficiently committed to developing a general aviation product. One of BRS's directors and investors, real estate developer Darrel D. Brandt, provided a loan to continue development and served as acting chief executive for four years beginning in 1991.

Until the early 1990s, BRS's market remained largely limited to operators of ultralights or home-built kit planes that required the warning "EXPERIMENTAL" to be printed on the fuselage. In 1993, after several years of effort, the company won the first Federal Aviation Administration (FAA) approval to build whole-plane parachutes for a certified (factory-built) aircraft, the ubiquitous Cessna 150/152 series. The first of these, dubbed the GARD-150 (later BRS-150), was delivered to a customer the next year.

With thousands of Cessnas in the fleet, many of them at the hands of novice pilots at flight schools, it seemed like a sure bet. The company planned to sell 20,000 units, President and CEO Mark Thomas later told a Minneapolis business journal. However, in the years it took to bring the product to market, the little Cessna 152 fell out of favor among flight schools, which had begun a mass transition to four-place aircraft. It took BRS a decade to sell even a dozen of the chutes for the 152.

The company's research efforts attracted support from the aerospace establishment. In 1994, the National Aeronautics and Space Administration began providing it grants to study lightweight parachute materials. A couple of years later, Alliant Techsystems hired BRS to make a recovery parachute for a UAV (unmanned aerial vehicle) it was making.

PARTNERSHIP WITH CIRRUS DESIGN

In 1994, BRS entered what would be its most significant business relationship for some time to come.

In that year, it agreed to produce a recovery system for a new plane being developed by the Cirrus Design Corporation of Duluth, Minnesota.

Cirrus made BRS parachutes standard equipment on its new Cirrus SR20 light plane in 1998, and a BRS system was also included as standard equipment in the next generation Cirrus aircraft, the SR22, which was certified in November 2000. A second manufacturer, OMF Aircraft, began making BRS systems available as original equipment on its planes in 2003.

Sales were up to $1.5 million by the fiscal year ended September 30, 2000, and were climbing rapidly on the success of Cirrus, which was quickly emerging as the largest producer of single-engine piston-powered aircraft in the United States. The company's net income rose from $78,715 that year to $599,010 as sales increased 60 percent to $2.4 million.

THINKING BIGGER AFTER 2000

In the 1990s, there was a shift toward using larger aircraft in flight instruction, reducing the market for BRS-equipped Cessna 150s and 152s. BRS obtained a certificate for parachute systems for the Cessna 172 in 2002 and the Cessna 182 Skylane in 2004. By this time, there were about 1,500 Cirrus Design aircraft plying the skies, each of them equipped with a BRS chute.

The company had a new president and CEO in 2004, Larry E. Williams, formerly an executive with Phoenix's AmSafe Aviation, a leading manufacturer of aviation restraints.

BRS's annual sales were about $7 million a year by this point. The concept was winning recognition kudos from the mainstream aerospace community. BRS received a Laureate Award from *Aviation Week & Space Technology* magazine in 2005.

25TH ANNIVERSARY IN 2005

BRS had many reasons to celebrate during its 25th anniversary year. It had sold nearly 20,000 whole-plane parachute systems and saved nearly 200 lives. Cirrus Design, which had made the whole-plane parachute system a central selling point of its aircraft, was also having record results. Cirrus Design raised its shareholding in BRS to 15.3 percent in February 2005. BRS eked out a pretax profit of $45,577 in the fiscal year ended September 30, 2006, after losing $1.8 million before taxes in fiscal 2005. Revenues rose 13 percent to $9.2 million.

In September 2005, BRS acquired the Tijuana, Mexico, factory of Paranetics Technology, Inc. The buy

<table>
<tr><td>

KEY DATES

1980: Ballistic Recovery Systems (BRS) formed to produce rescue parachutes for ultralights.
1983: First life is saved by a BRS product.
1986: BRS goes public to raise funds to develop a general aviation product.
1993: BRS wins first Federal Aviation Administration approval to build whole-plane parachutes for a certified aircraft, a Cessna.
1998: Cirrus Design makes BRS parachutes standard equipment on its new aircraft.
2005: Tijuana plant is acquired from Paranetics Technology.
2007: BRS tests Next Generation Parachute System, designed for larger aircraft.

</td></tr>
</table>

added new parachute product lines with annual sales of about $1.5 million. The company hoped to find nonaviation cut-and-sew work to perform at this facility. In 2007, BRS agreed to manufacture parachute products on behalf of Spain's CIMSA Ingenieria de Sistemas SA, a leading maker of military parachutes.

A number of light sport aircraft (LSA) manufacturers, including Germany's Flight Design GmbH, announced they were including BRS systems in their designs. (LSAs operated under less stringent FAA requirements than general aviation craft.) BRS was also entering another emerging product category, very light jets, via Toronto's Diamond Aircraft, which was preparing to offer BRS chutes in its forthcoming D-Jet model. After several years of development efforts, BRS had begun testing its Next Generation Parachute System, designed to handle larger and faster planes.

By 2007, BRS had produced more than 25,000 parachute systems; more than 3,000 of them were installed on certified aircraft. The company's handiwork was credited with saving at least 200 lives. A decade after its only U.S. rival (Second Chantz) had left the business, BRS still had the whole-airframe parachute market largely to itself, though there were a couple of European competitors.

Frederick C. Ingram

PRINCIPAL SUBSIDIARIES

BRS de Mexico S.A. de C.V.

PRINCIPAL COMPETITORS

Airborne Systems, Ltd.; Bostik Industries, LLC; Parasport c.i.p. S.L.; Stratos 07 s.r.o.

FURTHER READING

"Ballistic Recovery Systems Inc.—Records Saves Number 135, 136, 137 & 138; Rare Incident Is #2 for the Same Pilot/Aircraft," *Market News Publishing*, July 19, 2001.

"Ballistic Recovery Systems Inc.—Refurbished and Renewed Cessna 150s with Parachute Systems—Coming to Flight Schools," *Market News Publishing*, June 11, 2001.

"Ballistic Recovery Systems Inc.—Ventures Award Given to BRS—As One of Minnesota's Best-Performing Public Companies," *Market News Publishing*, May 31, 2001.

Byrne, Gerry, "Life-Saving Chutes to Rescue Jet Planes," *New Scientist*, April 24, 2004, p. 25.

"Company Interview: Robert Nelson, Larry E. Williams; Ballistic Recovery Systems, Inc.," *Wall Street Transcript*, March 28, 2006.

"Company Offers Softer Landing for Smaller Aircraft in Distress," *New York Times*, December 25, 2004, p. A20.

Davis, Riccardo A., "St. Paul, Minn.–Based Company Makes Parachutes for Recreational Planes," *Knight-Ridder/Tribune Business News*, March 11, 1998.

Divine, Mary, "Business Owner Flying High," *Saint Paul Pioneer Press*, April 8, 2005.

Goyer, Robert, "Chute: What the Whole-Airplane Recovery Parachute System Is Doing for Safety," *Flying*, December 2004, http://www.flyingmag.com/article.asp?section_id=13&article_id=510&page_number=1.

Higgins, Amy, and Sherri Koucky, "First Time's a Charm—Parachute Floats Plane to Safety," *Machine Design*, January 9, 2003, p. 44.

Murray, Charles J., "Rocket-Deployed 'Chute Saves Small Planes," *Design News*, April 24, 1989, p. 132.

Sarsfield, Kate, "Ballistic Recovery to Expand Parachute System Application," *Flight International*, November 10, 1999, p. 31.

———, "BRS Parachutes in Shares-for-Sales Deal," *Flight International*, September 29, 1999, p. 22.

———, "BRS to Offer Parachute System for Cessna 150," *Flight International*, November 21, 2000, p. 31.

———, "Diamond to Offer D-Jet Parachute; Austrian Manufacturer Works on Recovery System Option for High-Gross Weight Version of Single-Engined Aircraft," *Flight International*, June 29, 2004, p. 17.

Tellijohn, Andrew, "BRS Reflects on Lessons Learned," *CityBusiness* (Minneapolis), June 9, 2000, p. 11.

———, "BRS Revisits Cessna," *CityBusiness* (Minneapolis), October 6, 2000, p. 11.

———, "Companies Target Technology Investment to Boost Business," *CityBusiness* (Minneapolis), May 12, 2000, p. 15.

————, "Companies Weather the Seasons with Preparation," *CityBusiness* (Minneapolis), August 11, 2000, p. 11.

————, "Diary: Companies Review Year's Goals and Growth," *CityBusiness* (Minneapolis), February 9, 2001, p. 10.

————, "Firms Take on Promotion," *CityBusiness* (Minneapolis), July 14, 2000, p. 11.

————, "Leaders Divvy Up Duties," *CityBusiness* (Minneapolis), November 10, 2000, p. 13.

————, "Parachute Maker Lands NASA Grant; $60,000 Funds Test of Chutes in Business Jets," *CityBusiness* (Minneapolis), October 5, 2001, p. 3.

Wieffering, Eric J., "A Lifesaver," *Corporate Report-Minnesota,* December 1993, pp. 16+.

Youngblood, Dick, "Coming In on a Chute and a Prayer; Boris Popov Adapted His Parachute System to Light Aircraft. He's Made Some Money—and Saved Some Lives," *Star Tribune* (Minneapolis), August 29, 2004, p. 3D.

BIOLASE®

Biolase Technology, Inc.

4 Cromwell
Irvine, California 92618-1816
U.S.A.
Telephone: (949) 361-1200
Fax: (949) 273-6677
Web site: http://www.biolase.com

Public Company
Incorporated: 1984 as Societe Endo Technic, SA
Employees: 199
Sales: $69.7 million (2006)
Stock Exchanges: NASDAQ
Ticker Symbol: BLTI
NAIC: 339114 Dental Equipment and Supplies Manufacturing; 335999 All Other Miscellaneous Electrical Equipment and Component Manu facturing

■■■

Biolase Technology, Inc., develops and markets laser products for the dental and medical markets. Biolase holds a commanding lead in the dental laser market through its Waterlase system, which performs various types of hard- and soft-tissue dental procedures with less pain and faster recovery times than procedures performed with conventional high-speed drills and other traditional dental instruments. The Waterlase MD, the second generation of the company's Waterlase system, sells for approximately $70,000. The company also markets LaserSmile, a laser system originally developed for tooth-whitening procedures that is approved to treat periodontal disease. LaserSmile sells for approximately $23,000. Biolase also has received approval from U.S. regulators to market its Oculase MD laser system for general ophthalmic soft-tissue surgical indications. Biolase markets its products in more than 45 countries through subsidiary companies located in Europe, Australia, and New Zealand.

ORIGINS

As with most pioneering achievements, Biolase's flagship Waterlase device did not achieve dominance in the dental laser market overnight. The technology that underpinned the company's financial growth in the early 21st century was the product of years of work, work begun nearly 6,000 miles away from Biolase's Irvine, California, headquarters and 15 years before Waterlase generated its first stream of revenue. The journey, both in time and distance, represented the evolution of Waterlase and described the link between Biolase and its predecessor, Societe Endo Technic, S.A.

Societe Endo Technic was founded in 1984, starting out as a small, research-and-development firm based in Marseille, France. The company began experimental work on various endodontic (related to root canal therapy) and laser products, eventually developing a semiautomated root canal handpiece known as the "Canal Finder System." As the development of the Canal Finder System was underway, a move across the Atlantic took place. In 1986, Societe Endo Technic created a Massachusetts-based subsidiary, Endo Technic Corporation, to serve as its sales arm in the United States. The next year, the parent company followed its

COMPANY PERSPECTIVES

Biolase's products are designed to elevate the worldwide standard of medical and dental care. The company addresses the tissue heating problem of traditional laser systems on hard tissue cutting procedures by developing its innovative Target Tissue CoolingT system (TTCT). This breakthrough should allow for the advanced use of lasers in many medical areas and holds tremendous potential for the dental, orthopedic, cosmetic, dermatological, and neurosurgical markets.

subsidiary, relocating to the United States after all the assets of Endo Technic Corp. were transferred to a California-based subsidiary, Societe Endo Technic, Inc. Before the year was through, Pamplona Capital Corp., a company created to raise capital and pursue acquisitions, purchased 77 percent of the Societe Endo Technic enterprise, taking control over the Canal Finder System and various other endodontic products. Pamplona Capital changed its name several times during the ensuing years before settling on Biolase Technology, Inc., as its corporate title in 1994, by which time the company had shelved the Canal Finder System as its principal product and had begun moving toward developing the Waterlase.

During its first seven years in business, the company's signal achievement was the Canal Finder System. For the next seven years, research-and-development efforts picked up pace, at least in terms of the number of new dental lasers that were released, culminating in the debut of the Waterlase. In 1991, the company completed development of "Laser-35," a 25-watt, Nd:YAG (neodymium: yttrium, aluminum, garnet) dental laser system. Deliveries of Laser-35 commenced in early 1992, quickly followed by the development of the next generation of the company's dental lasers. In early 1993, development was completed of another Nd:YAG laser, "Nylad," a system available in various wattages that began shipping in mid-1993. As deliveries of Nylad began, the company completed development of "Elmer," a six-watt, Er,Cr:YSGG (erbium, chromium: yttrium, scandium, gallium, garnet) dental laser. Elmer's design incorporated proprietary technology that was applied to the Biolase's new hydrokinetic, tissue-cutting system, the Millennium, the original name of Waterlase. Design of the Millennium, an Er:YSGG (erbium: yttrium, scandium, gallium,

garnet) dental laser, began in 1995 and was concluded in late 1996, giving Biolase what would prove to be its first genuine market success.

INTRODUCTION OF WATERLASE: 1998

The U.S. Food and Drug Administration (FDA) approved Waterlase for the treatment of hard tissue in October 1998, one month before Jeffrey W. Jones was appointed president and chief executive officer of Biolase and given the task of turning the company's hydrokinetic, tissue-cutting system into a commercial success. Jones joined Biolase after spending a dozen years working for a number of privately held companies, including HGM Medical Laser Systems, a producer of medical lasers used in ophthalmologic, dental, and aesthetic applications. His task at Biolase, though daunting, was made easier by the remarkable advantages of Waterlase when compared to traditional high-speed dental drills. Dental drills, aside from producing unsettling sounds that racked the nerves of any patient, caused pain because of the friction produced from the grinding action of the drill against tooth enamel. Waterlase, by contrast, did not produce any friction, eliminating the need for painkilling shots. The threatening whine and grind of a dental drill was replaced with an innocuous popping sound, a muffled crackling described as similar to the sound of popcorn popping.

At the heart of Waterlase's pain-free technology was the use of water, Biolase's groundbreaking hydrokinetic, tissue-cutting system. The machine emitted a laser beam fired into a stream of water, not the tissue itself. The laser accelerated water molecules to 2,000 miles-per-hour, creating laser-powered particles that removed enamel and dentin for cavity preparation, cleaning, cooling, and washing the targeted area at the same time. "It's basically a microexplosion," the company's head of research and clinical development said in a March 31, 2003, interview with *Forbes*. The device heralded the beginning of a new era in dentistry, giving Jones a product to target the 140,000 dental offices in the United States, an estimated $1.4 billion market, and the 400,000 dentists practicing worldwide. Aside from educating dentists about the wonders of the new technology, Jones's greatest challenge in realizing the commercial potential of Waterlase was the machine's one shortcoming: cost. Waterlase trounced conventional dental drills in all areas except for price point, retailing for more than 30 times the amount of a high-speed drill, which proved to be a barrier to its market penetration during its first few years of availability. Waterlase sold for $50,000, or it could be leased for roughly $1,000 per month, a hefty price compared to the $1,000 to $1,500 fetched by conventional drills.

KEY DATES

1984: Biolase is founded as Marseille, France-based Societe Endo Technic, S.A.
1987: Societe Endo Technic moves its headquarters to California.
1994: Biolase Technology, Inc., name is adopted.
1995: Development of Waterlase system begins.
1998: Waterlase gains approval from the U.S. Food and Drug Administration.
2004: Waterlase MD is released.
2006: Biolase moves to Irvine, California, and launches Biolase University, a certification training and education program for dentists.

Armed with a remarkable, potentially revolutionary product, Jones geared Biolase for the release of Waterlase after gaining FDA approval in late 1998. The first few years of the machine's availability produced both encouraging news and reflected the difficulties of marketing a device that was exponentially more expensive than the devices it intended to supplant. At first, Jones relied primarily on word of mouth within the dental community to promote Waterlase, a marketing effort later augmented by Biolase's participation in trade shows and sponsorship of seminars. Between 1999 and 2002, as word spread about Biolase's hydrokinetic, tissue-cutting system, sales more than quadrupled to $29.2 million, making Waterlase the best-selling dental laser in the United States. Swelling revenue totals were offset, however, by substantial annual losses during the period, as the company endured years in the red. Biolase posted a net loss of $10.3 million in 1998, followed by a $4.7 million loss in 1999, a $3.7 million loss in 2000, and a $400,000 loss in 2001. The company's fortunes improved in 2002, however, when Biolase posted its first annual profit, recording $2.6 million in net income.

With its financial performance improving, Biolase took steps to build on its momentum. By the end of 2002, the company had sold roughly 1,500 Waterlase systems, enough to make it the market leader among dental laser makers, but the total represented only a small fraction of the overall dental market. The company needed greater penetration of the market, and in 2002 several positive developments pointed to a potential increase in business. In January, the FDA cleared Waterlase for root canal procedures. The following month, the regulatory agency cleared Waterlase for bone surgery. One year later, in February 2003, Waterlase gained approval to treat root canal complications.

Waterlase's greater suitability for various dental procedures, the company hoped, would promote sales, but it did not wait for customers to come to it. Biolase adopted a proactive stance, forming the World Clinical Laser Institute in 2002 to educate and train practitioners and researchers in laser dentistry. Further marketing assistance was secured via acquisition, specifically the purchase in mid-2003 of all the laser-related assets of American Medical Technologies. American Medical, which had developed the world's first dental laser in 1988, sold a portfolio of dental laser patents, intellectual property, products, and customer lists to Biolase in a $5.5 million, cash-and-stock deal. The company's financial position also was aided by another product, LaserSmile, which originally was developed as a tooth-whitening system, but later gained clearance from the FDA for periodontal procedures. By 2003, LaserSmile accounted for nearly 20 percent of Biolase's revenue total.

Biolase entered 2004 controlling 80 percent of the U.S. dental laser market. The company's market share represented a commanding lead but only a sliver of the overall market, falling considerably short of the expectations of Jones and his management team. "Dentists inflict pain," Jones said in a January 6, 2004, interview with *Investor's Business Daily*. "We're providing them with a revolutionary product that can change how the dentist is perceived."

Some within the dental community embraced the new technology with enthusiasm, a zeal reflected in an American Dental Association survey that reported the number of dentists incorporating laser technology into their practices more than doubled from 5.3 percent in 1998 to 11.4 percent in 2002. Further, there were reports nationwide that some dentists were coming out of retirement just to use laser technology, but Biolase primarily was attracting early adopters to the technology, not a massive wave of dentists that would indicate a genuine revolution within the industry. The arrival of the laser age to dentistry, it appeared, would take time, with the cost of the new technology and, to a lesser extent, familiarity with the technology proving to be the barriers to its widespread adoption. In the interim, Biolase led the charge of promoting dental lasers, but time was taking its toll on the company's financial condition. After posting its first profit in 2002, Biolase registered $19 million in net income in 2003 before recording a net loss in each of the ensuing three years, incurring $45 million in losses during the period.

DEBUT OF WATERLASE MD: 2004

Biolase made progress on several fronts midway through the decade. Its most notable achievement was the launch of a new Waterlase system, Waterlase MD. Introduced in October 2004, Waterlase MD upped the ante required to practice laser dentistry, selling for $70,000. The next-generation laser, touted as easier to use and more effective than its predecessor, sold well despite its increased price, securing its 1,000th customer just a year-and-a-half after its debut. The launch of Waterlase MD coincided with the first change in leadership in six years, as Jones took the title of vice-chairman and handed the duties of president and chief executive officer to Biolase's chief operating officer, Robert Grant. The new alignment of executives, organized "to spread awareness of the advantages of laser dentistry and broaden the use of its enamel-cutting technology in specialties such as orthopedics," according to the November 29, 2004, issue of *Business Week,* remained intact for less than two years. Jones took back the titles of president and chief executive officer in May 2006, reprising his role as Biolase's dominant personality during a busy period for the company.

As Biolase prepared for the future, much of its success depended on its efforts as a proselytizer of laser technology. Dentists, in droves, need to incorporate laser technology into their practices to fuel the company's financial growth. Toward this end, the company created Biolase University, a certification training and education program for dentists, in May 2006, the same month it moved its corporate headquarters from San Clemente to Irvine. In July 2006, further awareness of the company's Waterlase systems was ensured when the University of Florida College of Dentistry decided to integrate Waterlase dentistry into its course curriculum. The company also was applying its laser expertise to fields beyond dentistry. In mid-2006, the company received clearance to market Oculase MD, a laser system for general ophthalmic soft tissue surgical indications. In the years ahead, as the company preached the advantages of harnessing laser power and water in dentistry and other disciplines, its financial health hinged on its ability to develop effective devices and to communicate the worth of such devices to its target customers.

Jeffrey L. Covell

PRINCIPAL SUBSIDIARIES

BL Acquisition II, Inc.; BL Acquisition Corp.; Biolase Australia, Pty. Ltd.; Biolase Europe, GmbH (Germany); Biolase (NZ) Limited (New Zealand); Biolase Spain, S. L.; Societe Endo Technic, Inc. (France).

PRINCIPAL COMPETITORS

Lumenis Ltd.; Hoya Photonics Inc.; BSML, Inc.; Synergetics USA, Inc.

FURTHER READING

Benesh, Peter, "Biolase Technology Inc.," *Investor's Business Daily,* January 6, 2004, p. A8.

"Biolase Announces Agreement with the University of Florida College of Dentistry," *Internet Wire,* July 24, 2006.

"Biolase Launches Operations in Australia and New Zealand," *Internet Wire,* March 9, 2006.

"Biolase Moves into New Corporate Headquarters in Irvine, CA.," *Internet Wire,* May 1, 2006.

"Biolase Technology Launches Biolase University," *Dental Products Report,* May 2006, p. 37.

"Biolase to Enter into Strategic Relationship with Procter & Gamble," *Internet Wire,* June 29, 2006.

Herper, Matthew, "A Painless Root Canal?" *Forbes,* March 31, 2003, p. 119.

Kincade, Kathy, "Biolase Hits Paydirt in Dentistry," *Optoelectronics Report,* December 1, 2003, p. 4.

Luna, Nancy, "San Clemente, Calif.–Based Biolase Technology Goes Dental Without Drills," *Orange County Register,* July 13, 2003.

Marcial, Gene G., "More Dentists Are Drilling with Biolase," *Business Week,* December 8, 2003, p. 118.

———, "Painless Root Canals, Thanks to Biolase," *Business Week,* February 3, 2003, p. 114.

Milbourn, Mary Ann, "California Technology Firm to Restate Revenue, Launch Public Offering," *Orange County Register,* August 30, 2003.

Much, Marilyn, "Biolase Technology Inc.," *Investor's Business Daily,* May 15, 2003, p. A8.

Boardwalk Pipeline Partners, LP

——————— ■ ———————

3800 Frederica Street
Owensboro, Kentucky 42301
U.S.A.
Telephone: (270) 926-8686
Toll Free: (877) 686-3620
Fax: (270) 688-5872
Web site: http://www.boardwalkpipelines.com

Public Company
Incorporated: 2003
Employees: 1,100
Sales: $607.6 million (2006)
Stock Exchanges: New York
Ticker Symbol: BWP
NAIC: 486210 Pipeline Transportation of Natural Gas

■ ■ ■

Boardwalk Pipeline Partners, LP transports and stores natural gas in 11 states through 13,400 miles of pipeline and 11 underground storage fields. Boardwalk serves customers directly and indirectly throughout the northeastern and southeastern United States, counting natural gas producers, distributors, industrial companies, and marketing companies among its clientele. Boardwalk operates through three subsidiaries, Texas Gas Transmission, LLC, Gulf South Pipeline Company, LP, and Gulf Crossing Pipeline Company, LLC. Texas Gas operates 5,900 miles of pipeline stretching from eastern Texas to the Midwest, serving markets such as Memphis, Tennessee; Louisville, Kentucky; Cincinnati, Ohio; and Indianapolis, Indiana. The subsidiary also delivers natural gas to the Northeast through interconnects with other systems. Gulf South operates roughly 7,500 miles of pipeline in the Gulf Coast states of Texas, Louisiana, Mississippi, Alabama, and Florida. Gulf Crossing, expected to commence operations in 2008, will deliver natural gas through 355 miles of pipeline stretching from northern Texas to Louisiana. Boardwalk is owned indirectly by Loews Corporation, a diversified company with interests primarily in insurance (CNA Financial Corp.) and tobacco (Lorillard, Inc.).

ORIGINS

When Boardwalk was formed in 2003, it had no assets and no operations, existing in name only. The company was formed for the sole purpose of acquiring its first asset, a pipeline system with a more than 50-year history. Texas Gas Transmission Corp., formed in 1947, was regarded as a predecessor company to Boardwalk, giving the newly established master limited partnership a legacy in the field of transporting, gathering, and storing natural gas.

Texas Gas, whose headquarters in Owensboro, Kentucky, would become Boardwalk's headquarters, fell under the control of several different owners during its history. By the 1990s, the pipeline system that originated in eastern Texas and the Louisiana Gulf Coast area was owned by Transcontinental Gas Pipe Line Corp. (Transco), consisting of part of the assets that drew the interest of The Williams Companies, Inc., and set in motion the events that would lead to the formation of Boardwalk.

COMPANY PERSPECTIVES

Boardwalk has a unique combination of complementary pipelines. Our Gulf South pipeline gathers gas from the prolific basins between Texas and Alabama and delivers that gas to on-system markets and to off-system markets in the Northeast and Southeast. Our Texas Gas Transmission pipeline provides long-haul transportation from Gulf Coast supply areas to on-system markets in the Midwest and off-system markets in the Northeast. Together, our existing assets and our newly announced pipeline projects create a strategically interconnected grid of natural gas pipeline and storage assets that provide customers flexibility to access diverse supplies of gas in the Mid-Continent and Gulf Coast and to connect to other pipelines reaching the consuming regions of the Northeast, Midwest, and Southeast.

Based in Tulsa, Oklahoma, Williams began paving sidewalks in Fort Smith, Arkansas, in 1908 before establishing steel pipeline construction as its focus. The company's first major move to diversify occurred in 1966, when it purchased Great Lakes Pipe Line Company, the country's largest petroleum products pipeline, part of an ambitious expansion program that would later see the energy and construction company diversify into telecommunications. Williams began cobbling together a nationwide system of interstate natural gas pipelines in 1982 by acquiring Northwest Energy Company, establishing a presence in an industry that would be fleshed out with the purchase of Transco Energy in 1995. The acquisition of Transco spread Williams's operations to the East Coast, making it one of the largest transporters of natural gas by volume in the United States. Texas Gas, which played a large role in giving Williams its new stature, was a 48-year-old pipeline system by the time of the acquisition, having developed into a network that served customers in eight states to the north and east of its origination point in eastern Texas and the Louisiana Gulf Coast.

As part of the portfolio of properties owned by Williams, Texas Gas shared the fate of its parent company. The relationship made for a turbulent ride for the natural gas assets that Boardwalk would acquire. Williams, from the 1960s forward, developed into a conglomerate with wide-ranging interests, including a variety of energy-related businesses, telecommunications holdings, and agrichemicals interests, among others.

Expansion and diversification created a flourishing enterprise, but by the end of the 1990s the company's vibrancy began to diminish. Its stock reached $53 per share in 1999 and then began to spiral downward, plunging to less than $1 per share three years later. Reeling, Williams initiated a comprehensive restructuring program that saw it shed billions of dollars worth of assets in an effort to raise cash and regain a steady footing.

For Texas Gas, Williams's difficulties cast a cloud of uncertainty over the company's headquarters. In 1999, before its profound problems surfaced, Williams consolidated two of its natural gas pipeline units, merging the main offices of Williams Gas Pipeline-Central in Tulsa into the main office of Texas Gas in Owensboro, forming Williams Gas Pipeline-SouthCentral. As Williams's financial troubles flared, the situation at the Owensboro offices became tenuous. In April 2002, Williams Gas Pipeline-SouthCentral's general manager was promoted and transferred to Houston, creating a vacancy in Owensboro that Williams's senior executives chose not to fill. H. Dean Jones III, vice-president of customer service for the eastern region, found himself to be the highest-ranking executive in Owensboro and the de facto leader of the two pipeline systems. Any sense of unease felt by Jones and his colleagues about their future was confirmed in July 2002, when Williams's management put the Owensboro-based assets up for sale. In September 2002, AIG Higher Capital, a New York-based investment group that operated as a unit of American International Group, swooped in, paying $550 million for 6,000 miles of pipeline that constituted the non–Texas Gas assets merged into Owensboro in 1999. Before the end of 2002, Williams sold another pipeline system to another conglomerate, the Kern Rivet pipeline system, which was purchased by Warren Buffett's Berkshire Hathaway holding company for nearly $1 billion.

ACQUISITION OF TEXAS GAS: 2003

The assets shed in 2002 marked just the beginning of Williams's efforts to pare down its operations. The company sold more than $2 billion worth of assets in 2003, assets that would include Texas Gas. While Williams stripped away businesses, another company, Loews Corporation, was looking to move in the opposite direction. The New York-based, diversified holding company, right on the heels of Berkshire Hathaway and American International Group, was set to become the third conglomerate to enter the pipeline business within a year, attracted by the billions of dollars of assets for sale in the distressed energy merchant sector, a sector rocked by the spectacular collapse of Enron

KEY DATES

1947: Texas Gas Transmission Corp. is founded.
1995: The Williams Companies, Inc., acquires Texas Gas.
2003: Loews Corporation forms Boardwalk and acquires Texas Gas from Williams.
2004: Boardwalk acquires Gulf South Pipeline from Entergy-Koch, LP.
2005: Boardwalk completes an initial public offering of stock.

Corporation. For Williams, selling to cash-rich companies that were not previously active in the pipeline business meant the transactions closed quickly, eliminating the rigors of regulatory reviews, such as those mandated by Hart-Scott-Rodine antitrust legislation, and delays related to obtaining financing.

Loews, founded in 1946, was a company best known for its investments in insurance and tobacco, but, as shown with its acquisition of Texas Gas, it was always ready to delve into new businesses when presented with the right opportunity. The company owned an 89 percent stake in insurance firm CNA Financial Corporation and 100 percent of tobacco company Lorillard, Inc., as well as hotel chains and watch distributors. Its involvement in the energy business consisted of a 51 percent interest in Diamond Offshore Drilling, which owned 44 offshore drilling rigs, and a 49 percent stake in Hellespont Shipping, which owned a fleet of six, "ultra-large" crude tankers. The company's diversification, orchestrated by its founders, brothers Robert Tisch and Laurence Tisch, created a more than $17 billion-in-sales enterprise by 2002, when Loews began studying the pipeline market. The company surveyed the market for roughly a year before setting its sights on Texas Gas in 2003, the year Laurence Tisch's son, James Tisch, took over as Loews's chief executive officer. "We sensed there would be good values," Tisch remarked in an April 28, 2003, interview with *Gas Processors Report.*

Loews formed Boardwalk in April 2003 to facilitate the purchase of Texas Gas. The deal, which closed in May 2003, comprised a $795 million cash payment and the assumption of $250 million in Texas Gas debt, a $1.04 billion acquisition that marked Loews's entry into the pipeline business and the beginning of Boardwalk's life as a commercially active concern. By the time ownership of Texas Gas changed hands, the system comprised roughly 5,900 miles of pipeline running through Texas, Louisiana, Arkansas, Mississippi, Tennessee, Kentucky, Indiana, Illinois, and Ohio, with deliveries to the Northeast through interconnects with other systems. Texas Gas also owned 31 compressor stations and nine underground storage fields in Indiana and Kentucky. Revenues for the system totaled $267 million in 2002, from which the company derived $56 million in net income.

The acquisition of Texas Gas represented Loews's first step toward developing a pipeline arm to its holdings. The company, through Boardwalk, was on the prowl for more assets, seeking the steady cash flow typically generated by natural gas pipeline systems. A second system was acquired in December 2004, when Boardwalk purchased Gulf South Pipeline, a system also known within the industry as United Gas Pipe Line. Boardwalk paid $1.13 billion to New Orleans, Louisiana-based Entergy-Koch, LP for Gulf South, which operated 7,570 miles of pipeline in Texas, Louisiana, Mississippi, Alabama, and Florida, 29 compressor stations, and two natural gas storage fields in Louisiana and Mississippi. Together, Boardwalk's two systems comprised more than 13,000 miles of pipeline in 11 states and 11 underground storage fields in four states that were capable of 124 billion cubic feet of storage and four billion cubic feet per day of gas throughput. The two systems provided Boardwalk with a formidable profile in the industry and they also provided the company with its leadership. Dean Jones headed Texas Gas, serving as copresident of Boardwalk, while his counterpart at Gulf South, Rolf Gafvert, who joined Gulf South in 1992, held the identical title of copresident.

2008 OPENING OF THIRD PIPELINE SYSTEM

Gafvert and Jones relished the opportunities available to Boardwalk with deep-pocketed Loews ready and willing to assist in the company's expansion. For Jones in particular, who had no doubt felt Williams's waning interest in Texas Gas, the new arrangement sparked a palpable sense of excitement. Loews role as the majority stockholder in Boardwalk meant the company had instant access to funding to promote its development. "We want to be a much bigger company now that we have an opportunity to grow," Jones explained in a fall 2006 interview with *Exploration + Processing.* "We're fortunate to have the financial backing of Loews Corp. to assist us to accomplish anything that we set our minds to," he added. Gafvert echoed the sentiment, telling *Exploration + Processing,* "We have speed and execution. Because of our ownership with Loews, one of the things we do bring to the market is our projects are worked on and executed in a quick turnaround, which is important today."

As Boardwalk set out, the expansion-minded mood at the Owensboro main office was on display. Loews took Boardwalk public in November 2005, raising more than $300 million in an initial public offering of stock. Next, Boardwalk, with Loews's blessing, turned to expanding its operations. There were numerous expansion projects underway in 2005 and 2006, but none figured more prominently than the construction of a new pipeline that gave birth to a third operating subsidiary. Gulf Crossing Pipeline Company, LLC, was established to construct a 355-mile pipeline originating near Sherman, Texas, and ending near Tallulah, Louisiana. The $1.3 billion project, which also included the construction of four new compressor stations, was expected to commence operation in October 2008, adding a third dimension to Boardwalk's holdings. In the years ahead, further expansion projects were expected, and potentially additional acquisitions, as Boardwalk sought to spread its influence in the pipeline business. With the financial backing of Loews giving the company an advantage over many of its competitors, Boardwalk could justifiably look to the future with confidence.

Jeffrey L. Covell

PRINCIPAL SUBSIDIARIES

Texas Gas Transmission, LLC; Gulf South Pipeline Company, LP; Gulf Crossing Pipeline Company, LLC.

PRINCIPAL COMPETITORS

El Paso Corporation; Southwest Gas Corporation; TXU Corp.

FURTHER READING

"Boardwalk Pipeline Partners to Build Interstate Gas Pipeline and Expansion," *Pipeline & Gas Journal,* December 2006, p. 12.

"Boardwalk Pipeline Partners to Extend Two Pipelines," *Pipeline & Gas Journal,* February 2007, p. 10.

"Fayetteville Extensions Planned," *Oil Daily,* December 18, 2006.

"Holding Company Loews Enters Pipeline Business," *Oil Daily,* April 15, 2003.

Lawrence, Keith, "Williams Cos. Employment in Owensboro, Ky., Dwindles," *Messenger-Inquirer,* September 30, 2002.

Salgado, Brian, "Pipelines to Success," *Exploration + Processing,* Fall 2006, p. 24.

Shook, Barbara, "Loews to Raise $345 Million in IPO for Boardwalk Pipeline Partners," *Natural Gas Week,* August 22, 2005, p. 5.

"Williams Agrees to $1.045 Billion Sale of Texas Gas Transmission," *Pipeline & Gas Journal,* May 2003, p. 4.

"Williams Agrees to Sell Texas Gas Transmission to Loews for $1.045 Billion," *Gas Processors Report,* April 28, 2003.

"Williams Merging Central and Texas Gas," *Pipeline & Gas Journal,* January 2000, p. 4.

BOMBARDIER

Bombardier Inc.

———■———

800 Rene-Levesque Boulevard West
Montreal, Quebec H3B 1Y8
Canada
Telephone: (514) 861-9481
Fax: (514) 861-7053
Web site: http://www.bombardier.com

Public Company
Incorporated: 1942 as L'Auto-Neige Bombardier Limitee
Employees: 56,100
Sales: $14.78 billion (2006)
Stock Exchanges: Toronto
Ticker Symbol: BBD
NAIC: 336411 Aircraft Manufacturing; 336510
    Railroad Rolling Stock Manufacturing

■ ■ ■

Bombardier Inc. boasts a rich legacy of innovation in the motorized transportation industry and is among the most successful manufacturing companies in Canada. A leading maker of regional aircraft and business jets and passenger rail equipment, the company was also known for its recreational vehicles, including snowmobiles (the Ski-Doo and Lynx brands), personal watercraft (Sea-Doo), and all-terrain vehicles. After stumbling in the 1970s, Bombardier (pronounced bohn-BAR-dee-ay) reemerged as a force, particularly in the aircraft and rail equipment industries, in the final decades of the 20th century, enjoying healthy sales and profit gains. However, the staggering downturn in the airline industry early in the new millennium resulted in a reorganization which included divestment of the recreational vehicle business.

EARLY HISTORY: FOCUS ON SNOWMOBILES

Bombardier Inc. is the progeny of inventor and entrepreneur Joseph-Armand Bombardier, who was born near the eastern Quebec village of Valcourt in 1902. An inveterate tinkerer, Bombardier took it upon himself early in life to devise a solution to the difficulty of traveling during the winter when snow-covered roads in his native Quebec kept people isolated. At the age of 19, Bombardier started his own garage and worked as a mechanic, while he labored diligently in his spare time to create a vehicle that would allow easy winter travel, eventually building several prototypes that could travel on snow. Over a ten-year period, in fact, he crafted motorized test vehicles ranging from one-seat units to multipassenger carriers.

Bombardier finally came up with what he believed was a suitable solution to winter travel. In 1936 he submitted his patent application for the B7, a seven-passenger snowmobile that sported a revolutionary rear-wheel drive and suspension system (patent approval came in 1937). Bombardier soon found himself besieged with 20 orders for the innovative vehicle, and he quickly assembled a work crew, comprised largely of relatives and friends, in order to begin manufacturing B7s for country doctors, veterinarians, telephone companies, foresters, and others who benefited from easy winter travel. In 1940 he built a modern factory with an annual production capacity of 200 vehicles, and in 1941 he introduced a bigger version of the B7 named the B12. The B12, used for cargo and mail transport as well as ambulance and rescue services, resembled a small blue school bus with round passenger windows, tanklike treads on the rear, and skis on the front.

Despite strong demand, wartime material and fuel restrictions reduced Bombardier's output during the early 1940s. Nevertheless, the optimistic Joseph-Armand incorporated the company in 1942 as L'Auto-Neige Bombardier Limitée, or Bombardier Snowmobile Limited. The war turned out to be a boon for the company. That same year, the government ordered 130 B1s, which were a specially tailored version of the original B12. Moreover, in 1943 Bombardier was asked to design and produce a special armored all-track snowmobile, the Khaki, which led to the development of the armored Mark I. Between 1942 and 1946 Bombardier produced more than 1,900 tracked vehicles for the armed forces. Unfortunately, the company reaped few profits from the sales, and Joseph-Armand was even forced to give up the royalties for the use of his patents in all military vehicles.

The massive production boom did help Bombardier to hone his manufacturing and design skills, experience that proved useful after the war, when civilian orders for the company's snow vehicles ballooned. Between 1945 and 1952 the company shipped 1,600 B12s. It also began producing the C18, which was a larger version of the B12 that could carry 25 school children. By 1947 the company was generating annual sales of CAD 2.3 million and realizing profits of more than CAD 300,000. Unfortunately, sales plummeted to less than CAD 1 million in 1949 after the Quebec government implemented a snow-removal program for rural roads. Joseph-Armand scrambled to compensate for the setback, relying on his inventiveness to come up with new products that could utilize his patented technologies.

Among several new products the company tested during the late 1940s was the Tractor Tracking Attachment, a patented tread mechanism that could be attached to a tractor, thus improving performance in muddy terrain. Between 1949 and 1954 Bombardier sold thousands of the devices throughout North America, and cash from that successful product was dumped into research and development of a variety of all-terrain vehicles for the mining, oil, agriculture, and forest industries. Two of the most successful innovations introduced during that period were the Muskeg and the J5. The Muskeg was a breakthrough tractor-type machine that could perform multiple functions in difficult terrain. Joseph-Armand considered it one of his greatest inventions, and modern versions of the vehicle were still being produced in the early 1990s. The J5 was the first tracked vehicle designed specifically for logging.

By the end of the 1950s Bombardier's sales were approaching CAD 4 million annually as profits soared toward the CAD 1 million mark. It was during that time that Joseph-Armand, who was still managing the business, renewed his childhood dream of building a small snowmobile that could whisk a person over snow-covered terrain. With the advent of lighter engines, high-performance synthetic rubbers, and an improved tracking technology patented by his son Germain, Joseph-Armand believed that he could accomplish his goal. By 1959 the Bombardier team had developed a working prototype that lived up to Joseph-Armand's dream, and that year the company began mass production of the acclaimed Ski-Doo snowmobile. The first model sported five-foot wooden skis, a coil-spring suspension system, and could travel at speeds of 25 miles per hour.

The vehicles, which originally sold at a price of CAD 900 each, launched an entirely new industry that would explode during the next two decades. Although demand for the new snowmobile was slow in the first two years after its introduction—production rose from just 225 in 1959 to about 250 in 1960—in 1961 unit sales lurched to 1,200 before rocketing to more than 2,500 in 1962. Besides capturing the interest of trappers, foresters, prospectors, and other workers, the Ski-Doo became popular as a sport vehicle.

Bombardier continued to improve the vehicle and began introducing new lines. By 1964 the company was shipping more than 8,000 Ski-Doos annually, and Joseph-Armand died knowing he had realized his original dream of providing safe, practical, and economical transportation in isolated, snow-covered regions. During his career, Bombardier secured more than 40 patents, and he left his sons in charge of a financially sound company with more than CAD 10 million in an-

KEY DATES

■

1937: Joseph-Armand Bombardier receives approval of his patent for the B7, a seven-passenger snowmobile.

1942: Bombardier incorporates his company as L'Auto-Neige Bombardier Limitée, or Bombardier Snowmobile Limited.

1959: The Ski-Doo snowmobile makes its debut.

1967: Company is renamed Bombardier Limited.

1969: Company goes public.

1974: Contract with Montreal to supply 423 subway cars marks first major move into rail equipment.

1976: Bombardier enters the aviation industry through purchase of controlling interest in Herous Limited.

1986: Air carrier Canadair is purchased from the Canadian government.

1988: The Sea-Doo personal watercraft is introduced.

1989: Company buys Short Brother PLC, a Northern Ireland aircraft producer.

1990: Learjet Corporation, famed builder of business jets, is acquired.

1992: Company assumes a controlling stake in de Havilland, a maker of turboprop aircraft (five years later the remaining interest is acquired); the first Canadair Regional Jet (CRJ) is delivered.

1998: Deutsche Waggonbau AG, a Berlin-based maker of train and subway cars, is acquired.

1999: The first Global Express business jet is delivered.

2001: Adtranz is acquired for $725 million, making Bombardier the world's largest producer of passenger-rail equipment; company begins delivery of the CRJ 700.

2003: Recreational products segment is sold.

2004: Aerospace and transportation job cuts are announced.

2006: Despite challenges Bombardier Aerospace unit maintains strong market presence.

nual sales and profits of more than CAD 2 million annually. Germain, Joseph-Armand's eldest son, assumed the presidency, but passed the torch to his brother-in-law, Laurent Beaudoin, in 1966.

Beaudoin (pronounced bow-DWAN) was only 27 years old when he assumed the presidency at Bombardier Limited, as it was named in 1967. Also, he was joined by an aggressive young group of top managers that averaged 30 years in age. That group of executives successfully guided the company through its headiest growth stage; North American snowmobile shipments vaulted from 60,000 units in 1966 to a peak of 495,000 units annually in 1972, and Bombardier produced more than one-third of that number. During that period the company's sales and profits surged from CAD 20 million and CAD 3 million, respectively, to CAD 183 million and CAD 12 million, impressive growth that was achieved by attacking the giant U.S. market, unveiling a broad line of new snowmobiles, and pursuing an aggressive marketing initiative.

SNOWMOBILE DOWNTURN, DIVERSIFICATION

In 1969 Beaudoin took Bombardier public, planning to use the resulting cash to vertically integrate the company and profit from related economies of scale. In fact, during the 1960s and early 1970s Bombardier acquired several new companies, the largest of which was the Austrian firm Lohnerwerke GmbH. The two companies were merged to form Bombardier-Rotax in 1970. Lohnerwerke's subsidiary, Rotax, had previously supplied engines for Bombardier's Ski-Doos. Lohnerwerke, a tramway manufacturer founded in 1823, gave Bombardier an entry into the tram and rail transit industry. A year later, Bombardier also purchased its largest competitor, Bouchard Inc., which produced the third best-selling snowmobile on the market. As it turned out, Bouchard exited the snowmobile industry at an opportune time, as demand for the vehicles began tumbling shortly after the buyout.

Indeed, the energy crises of the early 1970s left the snowmobile industry gasping. Of 100 North American manufacturers, only six survived the ugly industry shakeout of the mid-1970s. The ever resilient Bombardier was one of those left standing. Confident that the industry would one day recover, Bombardier management remained committed to sustaining its leadership position and capturing as much market share as possible. Still, Bombardier suffered serious sales and earnings declines. Just as it had done following the creation of the Quebec snow-clearing program of 1949, Bombardier scrambled during the early and mid-1970s to develop new products to bolster sagging snowmobile sales. The Can-Am off-road motorcycle, which used parts supplied by manufacturers of Ski-Doo components, was introduced in 1972, and two years later the company began manufacturing a fiberglass sailboat. Bombardier also landed a big contract to produce stadium seats for the 1976 Montreal Olympic Games. In addition, the company entered the aviation industry in 1976 when it purchased a controlling interest in Herous Limited, a manufacturer of aircraft maintenance and landing gear.

In 1974 Bombardier had won a CAD 118 million contract with the city of Montreal to supply 423 subway cars by 1978. At the time, snowmobiles still accounted for about 90 percent of the struggling company's sales, so the subway car contract represented a major new push for Bombardier. Some analysts, however, frowned upon the move because most of North America's rail equipment manufacturers had already exited the business in the 1960s in light of foreign competition and stagnant demand. In contrast, Bombardier worked to acquire and master related technologies during the 1970s as part of an effort to position itself as a major player in the global rolling stock industry. In addition to the Montreal contract, Bombardier supplied 36 self-propelled commuter cars to Chicago in 1977, 21 locomotives and 50 rail cars to VIA Rail Canada in 1978, and 117 commuter cars to the New Jersey Transit Corporation in 1980. In 1981, moreover, Bombardier received an order for 180 subway cars to be used in Mexico City.

ACQUISITIVE DECADE

After slogging through the snowmobile industry downturn of the 1970s, Bombardier was beginning to reshape itself into a successful manufacturer of transit equipment by the early 1980s. Importantly, Bombardier landed a huge contract in 1982 to supply New York City with 825 subway cars. Also during the early 1980s, Bombardier diversified into military equipment, believing that it could implement the same strategy it was using to dominate the North American rail transit market. In 1977 the company had purchased the marketing rights, at a discount, to a truck developed by Am General Corporation of the United States, a deal that turned out to be a boon for the company. In 1981 the Canadian government awarded Bombardier a contract to supply 2,767 trucks. Bombardier delivered the last truck ahead of schedule in 1983, leading to a second order for 1,900 of the vehicles. The company also received a contract in 1985 to supply 2,500 trucks to the Belgian Army.

By the mid-1980s Bombardier was again generating hefty profits, despite turbulence in the North American transit market and ongoing sluggishness in snowmobile sales. Beaudoin, who was known as a savvy deal maker, capitalized on the downturn in the transit industry to increase market share and bolster its competitive

position. In 1987, for example, Bombardier acquired Pullman Technology, a division of Pullman-Peabody, followed the next year by the purchase of the Transit America division of The Budd Company. The company also acquired major interests in transit companies in Belgium and France. In the early 1990s Bombardier acquired UTDC, a major Canadian competitor, and Concarril, Mexico's top manufacturer of railway rolling stock. Those purchases cemented Bombardier's role as a leading global supplier of transit cars. That status was confirmed when Bombardier was awarded the contract to build specialized rail cars for the massive Eurotunnel, a transit system linking England and France beneath the English Channel.

At the same time Bombardier was expanding in the transit industry, the company was also launching an aggressive diversification drive into the aerospace market. That drive began with the 1986 purchase of the troubled air carrier Canadair from the Canadian government. The government had dumped $2 billion into the development of the Challenger corporate jet, a nine-seat craft that was to be the foundation of Canadair. Bombardier paid just $121 million for the company and was quickly able to turn the operation around through cost-cutting and aggressive marketing of the project's sophisticated technology. The acquisition effectively doubled Bombardier's size and represented its intent to become a player in the aerospace industry. To that end, in 1989 Bombardier purchased Short Brother PLC, a Northern Ireland aircraft producer, and the following year bought Learjet Corporation, builder of the well-known business jets.

BECOMING A GLOBAL LEADER IN AIRCRAFT AND RAIL

Meanwhile, Bombardier continued to firm up its position in the sporadic snowmobile market. Although the business represented less than 10 percent of sales by the early 1990s, Beaudoin refused to exit the market, citing Bombardier's historic expertise in the industry. Throughout the mid-1980s, in fact, Bombardier continued to beef up its snowmobile division with new technology and products. By the early 1990s Bombardier was still controlling about 50 percent of the Canadian snowmobile market and more than 25 percent of the entire North American market. In addition, Bombardier introduced the Sea-Doo watercraft in 1988 to compete in the growing market for individual sit-down jet-boats. The design was actually the offspring of a 1968 effort by Bombardier's research staff, and it was chosen as the number one watercraft of its type by *Popular Mechanics* in 1988. By the early 1990s Bombardier was serving about 40 percent of that emerging North American segment. Bombardier was also branching out globally with its motorized consumer products division, as evidenced by its 1993 buyout of the leading Finnish snowmobile maker.

Throughout the 1980s and early 1990s Bombardier grew and prospered by purchasing undervalued operations and turning them around with sound management, but not all of its efforts proved profitable. For example, several of its transit deals, including the giant Eurotunnel contract, actually lost money for the company. In general, though, Beaudoin's deals were successful and most of the company's operations thrived. As a result, Bombardier's sales mushroomed from CAD 1.4 billion in 1987 to an impressive CAD 4.4 billion in 1992. Profits rose at a rate of 15 percent annually during the period to CAD 133 million in 1992. Bombardier had become one of Canada's largest and most successful manufacturing companies, and it was steadily expanding throughout Europe and North America.

Further expansion of Bombardier's aerospace operations came in 1992 when the company gained a controlling 51 percent stake in Ontario-based de Havilland, a manufacturer of turboprop aircraft, such as the Dash 8 regional airplane. The Province of Ontario took the remaining 49 percent interest in de Havilland, which had been a division of Boeing, retaining the stake until January 1997, when Bombardier gained full control. Another key development in aircraft also occurred in 1992: the delivery of the first Canadair Regional Jet (CRJ), an aircraft that helped revolutionize the airline industry in the 1990s. The CRJ 100 was a redesigned version of Canadair's Challenger business jet, having been fitted with 50 seats and designed to fly routes of 650 to 1,500 kilometers (400 to 950 miles) in length. For consumers, it had the advantage over traditional turboprop regional planes, such as the Dash 8, of being a jet, and a particularly quiet one at that, while for airliners the plane's flight range made it ideal for routes longer than those that had been served by regional turboprops and shorter than those covered by conventional jets. Orders poured in for the CRJ during the mid-1990s as regional airliners proliferated and conventional airliners began setting up "spoke-to-spoke" routes in the "hub-and-spoke" system that had overtaken the industry. After delivery of the first CRJ 100 to Germany's Lufthansa CityLine in November 1992, Bombardier went on to deliver another 168 planes to 16 airlines in 11 countries by mid-1997. At that time the company had firm orders for another 86 CRJs and options from customers to purchase 198 more.

Bombardier continued to expand its operations and acquire new companies in the mid-1990s. In April 1995, for example, it purchased German transportation equipment manufacturer Waggonfabrik Talbot, which employed a workforce of about 1,200. Importantly, the wisdom of Bombardier's decision to retain its motorized consumer craft business became evident when that market rebounded in 1994. Buoyed by new product introductions, sales by that division surged 39 percent in 1994 to account for roughly 17 percent of company revenues. More importantly, profits from Ski-Doo and Sea-Doo products represented 37 percent of total company profits, making that division central to Bombardier's gains in that year. As a result of new acquisitions and improving markets, Bombardier's revenues sailed from CAD 4.77 billion in 1993 to CAD 5.94 billion in 1994, as net income climbed from CAD 177.3 million to CAD 247.3 million. Revenues increased still further in 1995, to CAD 7.12 billion, but net income dropped to CAD 158 million because of a CAD 155 million write-down of the company's 3 percent stake in Eurotunnel.

In April 1996 Bombardier was reorganized into five groups: Bombardier Aerospace, Bombardier Transportation (the rail operations), Bombardier Recreational Products, Bombardier Services (later Bombardier International), and Bombardier Capital. It was the first of these groups, Bombardier Aerospace, that led the company to new heights of prosperity in the final years of the 20th century. In addition to the continued success of the CRJ 100 regional jet, Bombardier successfully rolled out more aircraft models, including two new business jets. In 1998 came the first delivery of the Learjet 45 business jet, which had been jointly developed by Learjet, de Havilland, and Shorts. This super-light jet had a maximum range of 2,120 nautical miles and a cruising speed of 534 miles per hour. Within two years, Bombardier had delivered more than 100 of the new jets. During 1999, Bombardier completed another key introduction, the Global Express business jet, an ultra-long-range, high-speed corporate jet capable of circling the globe with just two stopovers. Bombardier invested CAD 400 million in the project, which began in the early 1990s and was codeveloped by Canadair, Learjet, de Havilland, and Shorts, with the assistance of 11 outside partners, who ponied up another CAD 400 million. The addition of Global Express gave Bombardier a full range of business jets, ranging from the lower-end Learjet through the middle-market Challenger to the high-end Global Express, which sold for $34 million.

With sales of regional jets booming and the red-hot U.S. economy driving sales of corporate jets to record levels (the U.S. market accounted for more than half of

Bombardier's overall revenues), Bombardier Aerospace's revenues skyrocketed, jumping from CAD 4.28 billion in 1996 to CAD 6.44 billion in 1998 to CAD 10.56 billion in 2000. By the latter year, aerospace operations accounted for two-thirds of overall revenues and more than 85 percent of the company's profits. The head of Bombardier Aerospace, Robert E. Brown, was rewarded for this stellar performance in February 1999 with a promotion to president and CEO of Bombardier Inc., with Beaudoin remaining chairman of the board.

It should be noted that a number of observers were critical of what they perceived as too-close ties between Bombardier and the government of Canada and pointed out that Bombardier's rapid ascension in the aerospace industry was aided by government subsidies, particularly in regard to the development of the CRJ. In fact, Bombardier's chief competitor in the area of regional aircraft, Empresa Brasileira de Aeron utica S.A. (Embraer) of Brazil, took its case of unfair trade practices to the World Trade Organization (WTO). Bombardier did likewise, accusing Embraer of gaining market advantages from its ties to the Brazilian government. At times the competitive battle between the world's two main regional jet makers threatened to escalate into an all-out trade war between their respective home nations. The conflict continued unresolved into the early 21st century, although a number of WTO rulings in the matter supported the Canadian position.

In the late 1990s and early years of the 21st century, Bombardier Transportation began playing a more prominent role within the company. In February 1998 Bombardier acquired Deutsche Waggonbau AG, a Berlin-based maker of train and subway cars, thereby doubling the size of its European rail equipment operations. In December of that same year, Bombardier signed its biggest rail contract ever, a $1.8 billion deal with Virgin Rail Group of Britain to build 78 high-speed diesel-electric locomotives and train coaches. The company entered the burgeoning Chinese market in November 1999 by establishing a joint venture that would construct a manufacturing facility in China to build 300 intercity mass transit railcars for the Ministry of Railways. In August 2000 Bombardier agreed to acquire Berlin-based DaimlerChrysler Rail Systems GmbH (known as Adtranz) from DaimlerChrysler AG for $725 million. Adtranz was a major maker of rail equipment with 1999 revenues of $3.4 billion and 22,000 employees. In addition to production of electric locomotives, Adtranz specialized in propulsion and train controls, services, and signaling, providing Bombardier Transportation with a broader range of activities and making Bombardier the world's largest producer of passenger-rail equipment. The acquisition of Adtranz, which was completed in May 2001 and was the largest

in company history, meant that 40 percent of Bombardier's revenues would be generated by the rail transportation unit.

In addition to creating a more powerful rail unit, Bombardier also worked hard to remain at the forefront of the regional aircraft and business jet sectors. Having concluded that there was still room in the market for regional turboprops, Bombardier in late 1999 made its first deliveries of the Dash 8-Q400, a 70-passenger twin-turboprop designed for regional airliners' high-density, short-haul routes. By early 2001, Bombardier had delivered 29 of the new models and had firm orders for an additional 33 and options on 32. In January 2001 deliveries started for the CRJ 700 model regional jet, a stretched, 70-seat version of the CRJ 100/200. Bombardier already had firm orders for 173 additional CRJ 700s and options had been taken on 313 more. Moreover, the company was already developing the next-generation CRJ, the 900, an 86-passenger model scheduled to enter airline service in early 2003. For all of its models of regional aircraft, Bombardier entered 2001 with firm orders for 574 units and 1,047 options, a backlog that represented potential sales of tens of billions of dollars. Also under development was the Bombardier Continental business jet, an all-new super midsize corporate jet designed for transcontinental flights. The company hoped to receive certification of the Continental by early 2003.

Meanwhile, in March 2001, Bombardier bolstered its recreational vehicles operations with the purchase of the engine assets of Outboard Marine Corporation, including the Evinrude and Johnson outboard marine engine brands. Despite this acquisition, recreational products, the founding business of Bombardier, had been left in the exhaust of the rapidly expanding aircraft and rail units. Only 11 percent of the revenues and 6 percent of the profits for the fiscal year ending in January 2001 came from recreational products.

The one cloud on the horizon was the impact that a prolonged economic slowdown might have on the company's operations, with business jet sales being particularly vulnerable during economic downturns. Furthermore, the regional jet industry that Bombardier had pioneered had never been through an economic downturn, providing an air of uncertainty surrounding the company.

IN THE WAKE OF THE 2001 TERRORIST ATTACKS

Following the September 11, 2001, terrorist attacks on the United States, pressure on the airline industry increased exponentially. Air passenger traffic in and out of Toronto, for example, fell by 37 percent in the wake of the attacks on the East Coast of the United States executed by commercial aircraft. Bombardier responded with employee layoffs and reduction of its fiscal 2002 profit growth target. The key airline industry had been under the pressure of falling fares prior to the attacks.

To worsen matters, *Canadian Business Online* explained, leadership turmoil erupted with the abrupt departure of the president and CEO of the aerospace operation. Pierre Beaudoin was named president and COO of Bombardier Aerospace in October. The grandson of the founder and son of the chairman joined the family controlled business by way of the recreational products in 1985. He moved to the aerospace division in February 2001, as president of the business jets unit.

Fiscal 2002 (year-end January) produced $21.6 billion in total revenue: 56 percent from the regional and business passenger aircraft aerospace operation; 32 percent from rail; and most of the remaining 12 percent from the recreational division. Net income was off 60 percent from the prior year to $390 million.

In June, CEO and President Robert Brown maintained Bombardier would achieve its predicted earnings growth per share of 10 percent, but by August, the company reduced fiscal year estimates by 21 percent. Its stock price took a beating. Bombardier attributed the downturn to the battered U.S. economy and its beleaguered airline industry. However, losses related to a three-week employee strike in April 2002 also had been accrued.

Troubles were not confined to aerospace. A $663-million Bombardier Capital Financing write-down, in 2001, well exceeded the segment's ten-year total profits, according to *Canadian Business*. Robert Fay, an analyst with Toronto-based Canaccord Capital Corp., told Rasha Mourtada: "'Looking at the current situation of Bombardier, that's probably the worst decision the management has made,' Fay says of the company's move into the manufactured housing and mortgage market by providing consumer lending." Analysts applauded when Bombardier abandoned the troublesome manufactured housing and customer finance areas.

However, the Canadian company's problems did not end there. The shaky performance of Adtranz and equipment failure on rail cars produced for Amtrak created other headaches. What was more, the WTO, in January 2002, determined Canada had illegally assisted Bombardier in its effort to gain an aircraft contract.

In December 2002, Brown left the company. Paul Tellier, a board member since 1997, was appointed president and CEO, taking command beginning in January 2003. The company reported fiscal year (ended January 31, 2003) revenue of $17.3 billion. With profits off, stock price and credit ratings came under pressure. Tellier, known for his role in the turnaround of Canadian National Railway, set a plan in motion to do the same for Bombardier. The finance unit, which was responsible for nearly 70 percent of debt, would be pared down. The company's dividend was cut by half. According to *Business Week*. Bombardier would concentrate on the aerospace and transportation units, which were of roughly equal size.

In August, Bombardier agreed to sell the recreational unit for CAD 1.23 billion in cash: 50 percent to Bain Capital of Boston; 35 percent to four of the founder's children; and 15 percent to Caisse de depot et placement du Quebec. The sale assisted in Tellier's drive to reduce debt, improve cash flow, and raise equity, according to the *New York Times*. The recreational vehicle unit, struggling with losses, had re-branded some of its products under the John Deere name during the year.

The sale of Military Aviation Services and Belfast City Airport added more to the Bombardier coffer. A deal to sell the bulk of Bombardier's Capital's business aircraft portfolio to GE Commercial Equipment Financing, for CAD 475 million, also was struck during 2003. In March 2004, Tellier proposed a transportation sector restructuring to reduce excess capacity, improve performance, and restore earnings capability, the Bombardier web site history recounted.

Losses continued in fiscal 2004. During the last three months of the calendar year the company announced a series of significant job cuts. In addition, another top management shakeup occurred in December 2004 with the resignation of Tellier, followed by the departure of two independent directors and two senior executives.

A new office of the president was created. Laurent Beaudoin served as chairman of the board and CEO of Bombardier Inc. and shared leadership responsibilities with presidents of transportation and aerospace, Andre Navarri and Pierre Beaudoin, respectively. Tellier's departure short-circuited a change in corporate governance in which the CEO and chairman roles were separated out. "In a further sign that the family is reasserting itself, son Pierre has also been appointed to the board. An unwinding of Bombardiers' multiple-voting shares, long sought by investors, seems as distant as ever," wrote Matthew McClearn for *Canadian Business*. During 2005, Bombardier Capital continued to wrap up business, making further divestitures including inventory finance operations and the manufactured housing portfolio.

For fiscal 2006, the company reported the transportation unit's 2004 turnaround initiative had started "to generate sustainable results." The segment recorded seven consecutive quarters of profits. Markets in China, southeast Asia, Russia, and Eastern Europe were being cultivated as a complement to the transportation unit's North American and European stronghold.

As for aerospace, despite the challenges of the times, Bombardier had maintained a strong regional aircraft market position: 55 percent of 22- to 99-seat aircraft and 37 percent of 100-seat. The company, furthermore, was seizing 60 percent of all new aircraft orders in the 20- to 99-seat category, according to a September 2006 *Airfinance Journal* article. The regional jet market was also expected to move toward the 100- to 149-seat level, bringing Bombardier into direct competition with Airbus and Boeing.

Dave Mote
Updated, David E. Salamie; Kathleen Peippo

PRINCIPAL OPERATING UNITS

Bombardier Aerospace; Bombardier Transportation. AEROSPACE: Headquarters (Canada); Toronto Site; Learjet Inc. (U.S.A.); Short Brothers plc (Northern Ireland); Flexjet (U.S.A.); Flexjet Asia-Pacific; Amphibious Aircraft (Canada); Skyjet (U.S.A.); Skyjet International Ltd. (U.K.). TRANSPORTATION: Headquarters (Germany); Locomotives (Switzerland); Rail Control Solutions (Sweden); North America (Canada); Total Transit Systems (U.S.A.); Bogies (Germany); Light Rail Vehicles (Austria); Propulsion and Controls (Switzerland); London Underground Projects (U.K.), Mainline & Metros (Germany); Services (Belgium).

PRINCIPAL COMPETITORS

Embraer - Empresa Brasileira de Aeronáutica S.A.; Siemens AG; Gulfstream Aerospace Corporation; Boeing Commercial Airplanes; Delta AirElite Business Jets, Inc.; Flight Options LLC; NetJets Inc.; CitationShares Holdings, LLC.

FURTHER READING

Barker, Robert, "Bombardier May Be Going Places," *Business Week,* June 16, 2003, p.96.
Bertin, Oliver, "Bombardier Targets New Niche," *Globe and Mail,* November 24, 1997, p. B8.
———, "A Global Gamble: Bombardier, the Montreal Maker of Snowmobiles, Jet Skis and Regional Airliners, Is Betting

$400-Million That Its New Executive Jet Will Solidify a World-Class Reputation and Give It More Respect at Home," *Globe and Mail,* August 24, 1996, p. B1.
Bombardier: A Dream with an International Reach, Montreal: Bombardier Inc., 1992.
Bombeau, Bernard, "Regional Manufacturers Carve Up the Market," *Interavia,* May 1997, pp. 33, 36–38.
Bourette, Susan, "Bombardier Rewards Brown by Promoting Him to Top Job," *Globe and Mail,* December 9, 1998, p. B1.
Came, Barry, "Sky King: Bombardier's New Regional Jet Is Revolutionizing the Way People Fly," *Maclean's,* August 11, 1997, pp. 30–36.
Chipello, Christopher J., "Bombardier, Going Outside Family, Names Brown CEO," *Wall Street Journal,* December 9, 1998, p. B13.
———, "Jet Maker Looks to the Old Economy: Bombardier of Canada Seeks a Smoother Ride with Railroad Deal," *Wall Street Journal,* September 12, 2000, p. A21.
Crowe, Nancy, "Bombardier Gears Up," *Vermont Business,* December 1986, p. 89.
DePalma, Anthony, "The Transportation Giant up North: Bombardier Rises, with Some Help from Friends in Ottawa," *New York Times,* December 25, 1998, p. C1.
"Family Affair: the Regional Jet Market Has Arguably Been a Victim of Its Own Success," *Airfinance Journal,* September 2006, pp. 34+.
Ferrabee, James, "Bombardier Stock on a Magic Carpet Ride," *Gazette,* December 19, 1994, p. C2.
———, "Confident Chunnel Man," *Gazette,* February 1995, p. D7.
Ford, Royal, "Red Line Cars Are Born in Vermont," *Boston Globe,* November 7, 1993, p. 69.
Gibbens, Robert, "Bombardier Buys German Railcar Firm," *Financial Post,* February 25, 1995, p. 19.
———, "Bombardier Is Aiming High," *Financial Post,* April 11, 1991, p. 21.
Goldsmith, Charles, "Gulfstream and Bombardier Stage Business-Jet Dogfight," *Wall Street Journal,* June 20, 1997, p. B4.
Hadekel, Peter, "Bombardier's Ski-Doo Division Is Profiting from Borrowed Techniques," *Gazette,* April 16, 1993, p. F1.
Koselka, Rita, "Let's Make a Deal," *Forbes,* April 27, 1992, p. 62.
Lang, Amanda, "Dynasties," *Globe and Mail,* Report on Business Magazine, June 1, 1995, p. 60.
Leger, Kathryn, "Tough Guy on the Tarmac: Laurent Beaudoin Keeps Bombardier on Top of Global Markets with a Combination of High Technology and Hardball," *Financial Post,* August 1, 1998, p. 8.
Livesay, Bruce, "Ceiling Unlimited: Bombardier's Global Ambition and Constant Innovation Have Propelled It to No. 1 in Our CEO Survey," *Globe and Mail,* March 28, 1997, p. 36.
Louiseize, Kelly, "Bombardier Wants Province's Help," *Northern Ontario Business,* October 2005, pp. 19+.

McArthur, Keith, "Bombardier Endures Jet Controversy," *Globe and Mail,* June 25, 2001, p. B3.

McClearn, Matthew, "Pilot to Bombardier: Bye," *Canadian Business Online,* December 2004.

McGovern, Sheila, "On the Move: The Snowmobiles Bombardier Built for Rural Quebec Are the Still-Thriving Roots of a World Transportation Empire That Includes Planes, Trains, and Sea-Doos," *Gazette,* November 1, 1993, p. C8.

Moorman, Robert W., "Bigger and Better," *Air Transport World,* May 1999, pp. 32–34+.

———, "Booming with Bombardier," *Air Transport World,* August 1998, pp. 102+.

———, "The Deal Maker: From Selling Snowmobiles to Saving Aircraft Companies, Laurent Beaudoin Has Made Bombardier a World-Class Player," *Air Transport World,* July 1992, p. 44.

Mourtada, Rasha, "Buckle Your Seat Belts," *Canadian Business Online,* September 2002.

Newman, Peter C., "A Lesson in How to Choose the Right Stuff," *Maclean's,* December 21, 1998, p. 50.

Pasztor, Andy, and Daniel Michaels, "Regional-Jet Makers, Flying High, See Clouds Looming: Economic Slowdown, Labor Disputes and Large-Plane Rivals Could Stall Demand," *Wall Street Journal,* July 12, 2001, p. B4.

Shalom, Francois, "Firefighting: Canadair Says Bomber's Problems Are Merely Glitches, and Promises to Fix Them for Unhappy French," *Gazette,* March 18, 1995, p. C3.

Sheppard, Robert, "The Nimble and the Bulky: Small Regional Jets and Giant Airliners Appear to Be the Way of the Future for the International Aviation Industry," *Maclean's,* August 7, 2000, pp. 24–25.

Shifrin, Carole A., "Bombardier Bets on New Regional Turboprop," *Aviation Week and Space Technology,* December 15, 1997, pp. 38–42.

Simon, Bernard, "Bombardier to Sell Unit to Cut Debt," *New York Times,* August 28, 2003, p. 1W.

Taylor, Peter Shawn, "A Sweet Deal," *Canadian Business Online,* November 2004.

Tremblay, Miville, *Le sang jaune de Bombardier: La gestion de Laurent Beaudoin,* Sainte-Foy, Quebec: Presses de l'Universit du Quebec, 1994, 131 p.

Velocci, Anthony L., Jr., "Claims, Counterclaims Intensify Gulfstream, Bombardier Rivalry," *Aviation Week and Space Technology,* June 28, 1999, p. 66.

Walmsley, Ann, "Meet the New Boss Same As the Old Boss?: Bombardier's Robert Brown Has a Tough Act to Follow As He Steps into Laurent Beaudoin's Shoes," *Globe and Mail,* March 26, 1999, p. 85.

Wells, Jennifer, "Bombardier's Big Gamble," *Maclean's,* September 2, 1996, pp. 36–38.

Yakabuski, Konrad, "Bob Brown in Command: Who Would Have Guessed That Plain Robert Brown—Spit-and-Polish Soldier, Career Civil Servant—Could Match Laurent Beaudoin's Fabled Record As CEO of Bombardier," *Globe and Mail,* Report on Business Magazine, October 27, 2000, p. 74.

———, "Bombardier Sets Out on a European Odyssey: Canadian Firm Establishes New Trade Beachhead on Old Continent," *Toronto Star,* December 19, 1993, p. D1.

Brasfield & Gorrie LLC

729 South 30th Street
Birmingham, Alabama 35233-2939
U.S.A.
Telephone: (205) 328-4000
Toll Free: (800) 239-8017
Fax: (205) 251-1304
Web site: http://www.brasfieldgorrie.com

Private Company
Incorporated: 1967
Employees: 2,740
Sales: $2 billion (2006 est.)
NAIC: 236210 Industrial Building Construction;
561110 Office Administrative Services

■ ■ ■

Brasfield & Gorrie LLC is one of the 30 largest construction companies in the United States, operating as a full-service general contracting, construction management, and design/build service provider in the Southeast. The company serves a variety of markets, including religious, office, parking, retail, education, and sports and leisure, but relies on healthcare construction for roughly one-third of its business. Brasfield & Gorrie ranks as the largest healthcare general contractor in the United States, as determined by *Modern Healthcare.* The company's second largest market is water and wastewater construction. Brasfield & Gorrie operates through 25 divisions that focus on specific, specialized construction markets. The divisions take direction from

five full-service offices in Atlanta, Georgia; Orlando, Florida; Nashville, Tennessee; Raleigh, North Carolina; and Jacksonville, Florida.

ORIGINS

Brasfield & Gorrie's evolution from an anonymous construction firm into a nationally recognized, regional powerhouse reflected the ambition and success of Magnus Miller Gorrie, the Alabama Engineering Hall of Fame inductee who orchestrated the company's spirited growth. Born in 1935, Gorrie grew up in Birmingham, Alabama, where his life's work would leave an indelible mark on the city's skyline. As a teenager, he began accumulating the savings that would fund his start as a construction entrepreneur, first delivering newspapers and later spending his summers working various construction jobs. The money earned from a paper route and part-time employment proved to be significant because Gorrie, whose father worked for International Business Machines Corporation (IBM), invested everything he earned, converting it into IBM stock. As the years passed and IBM's market value soared, a sizable nest egg developed, giving Gorrie the funds to start out on his own.

While Gorrie's holdings in IBM grew in value, he gained the experience he would use as an independent contractor. He attended Auburn University, graduating in 1957 with a degree in civil engineering. Next, he joined the U.S. Navy's Civil Engineering Corp., serving a three-year term before returning to Birmingham in 1960. He found employment with a firm name J.F. Holley, working in various areas of the building industry until the desire to strike out on his own induced him to tap into his IBM savings, which had been maturing for at least a decade. In 1964, the 28-year-old Gorrie found the vehicle to begin his entrepreneurial career, a general contracting firm named Thomas C. Brasfield Company. Owned by Thomas Brasfield, who had conducted business as a sole proprietor since 1921, the firm operated only locally, performing small commercial and remodeling work in Birmingham. At the time, Gorrie's savings amounted to $80,000, a considerable sum considering the average annual salary in the United States in 1964 was $4,743. Gorrie sold some of his IBM shares and paid Brasfield $45,000, which gave him control over the business, as much as $10,000 worth of equipment, an office, a secretary, and two supervisors. Gorrie quickly set to work to turn the 23-year-old business into a bustling, growing enterprise.

Gorrie inherited a business that was well known and respected within the Birmingham community. Because the firm had cultivated ties to the city, Gorrie chose to retain the name of the business and continued to operate it as the Thomas C. Bradfield Company at first while he concentrated on more important matters than signage. He bid low on projects, taking on the construction of small office buildings, schools, churches, and, most significantly, medical facilities, the company's largest single market in the 21st century. Revenues during his first year of operation reached $800,000. In 1967, he decided to add his name to the business's title, renaming the company Brasfield & Gorrie, and moved it to Birmingham's Southside, where it would remain for the next 40 years.

Brasfield & Gorrie had a permanent name and a permanent location by the end of the 1960s, but nearly everything else about the company was in flux. Change occurred in the form of market diversification, as the company developed the strengths that would define its success and shifted its strategic focus to take advantage of fluctuating market conditions. One of the first defining events in the company's development occurred in 1968, when it completed its first multistory, concrete project. The success of the project convinced Gorrie to specialize in concrete structures, leading to what would be hundreds of high-rise construction projects completed under the Brasfield & Gorrie banner.

EXPANSION

Gorrie wasted little time before making his company a recognized entity in the construction industry. In 1975, a decade after he purchased Thomas Bradfield's modest business, Gorrie leaped onto the national stage, drawing the attention of one of the country's most respected trade publications. *Engineering News-Record* listed Brasfield & Gorrie among the 400 largest contractors in the United States, an annual ranking that would include the Birmingham firm every year from 1975 into the 21st century. The firm's stature increased as its areas of expertise broadened. In 1977, a market of tremendous importance to Brasfield & Gorrie was entered when the firm took on its first water and sewage treatment contract, a project that soon led to a slew of requests to construct other plants. The rapid growth of Brasfield & Gorrie's water and wastewater business, which became a principal source of revenue, second only to healthcare construction, prompted Gorrie to form a separate operating division for such projects. The creation of the division represented the company's first step toward developing the decentralized organizational structure that took shape in the 1980s and 1990s.

Brasfield & Gorrie's ever increasing size demanded something other than a monolithic structure. The company needed an organizational framework that could make it more responsive to the needs of its clients, a necessity created by the firms' geographic expansion. During the early 1980s, the company took advantage of a major surge in condominium construction that spread across the Alabama Gulf Coast to the Florida Panhandle, demonstrating its increasing willingness to court business outside Birmingham. When the condominium construction market began to wane, Gorrie directed his work crews in Florida to move to the central part of the state, where another boom in construction was taking place. Brasfield & Gorrie, which was awarded a $25 million contract to construct the Orlando City Hall, anchored its presence in Florida by opening a full-service office in Orlando in 1985, the same year it opened an identical facility in Atlanta, Georgia. Branch offices (additional locations would be established in the years ahead) served as hubs for Brasfield & Gorrie's construction efforts throughout the Southeast, each equipped to serve the spectrum of the firm's markets: religious; multifamily; education; healthcare; industrial; parking; office; retail; sports and leisure;

KEY DATES

1921: Thomas C. Brasfield Co. is established in Birmingham, Alabama.
1964: M. Miller Gorrie acquires Thomas C. Brasfield Co.
1967: Gorrie changes the name of the company to Brasfield & Gorrie.
1968: Company completes its first multistory concrete project.
1977: The company begins building water and sewage treatment plants.
1985: Brasfield & Gorrie opens offices in Atlanta, Georgia, and Orlando, Florida.
1995: Gorrie's son, M. James Gorrie, is appointed president.
1998: Offices are opened in Raleigh, North Carolina, and Nashville, Tennessee.
2004: The company completes construction of the Georgia Aquarium.
2007: An office in Jacksonville, Florida, is opened.

mixed-use; and water and wastewater treatment. The branch offices, in turn, presided over the divisions comprising Brasfield & Gorrie's operations, the number of which reached six by the time the company entered the 1990s.

The 1990s saw Brasfield & Gorrie strengthen its already stalwart position within the construction industry. The company's Atlanta office was pressed to its limits early in the decade, given the herculean task of providing 50,000 yards of concrete for the construction of the Georgia Dome, the site of the 1996 Summer Olympics. The 1990s also witnessed the ascension of the second generation of Gorrie leadership. Gorrie's son, M. James Gorrie, rose through the ranks of the company before earning his promotion to the title of president in 1995. Miller Gorrie assumed the responsibilities of chairman and chief executive officer after his son became president. On the expansion front, two new, full-service offices opened in the late 1990s, doubling the size of the company's network. The offices, both established in 1998, were located in Raleigh, North Carolina, and Nashville, Tennessee.

BRASFIELD & GORRIE IN THE 21ST CENTURY

By the time Brasfield & Gorrie entered the 21st century, the company held considerable sway in the southeastern construction market. Four decades of expansion under the direction of Gorrie brought the Brasfield & Gorrie banner into 16 states, giving the company a large and geographically diverse customer base. The size of the company's customer base was significant because Brasfield & Gorrie generated roughly 85 percent of its business from repeat clients. Further, having customers located in 16 states mitigated the company's exposure to downturns in construction activity in particular regions, enabling it to respond to clients' requests in markets enjoying growth while it waited for anemic markets to regain their vitality. The result was a company spared the swings in the construction cycle that often hobbled firms wed to one or two markets. Between 2001 and 2006, years that included a nationwide economic recession, Brasfield & Gorrie completed an average of $1.02 billion in volume annually, enjoying steady business drawn from a broad geographic base.

Brasfield & Gorrie's organizational structure expanded as its customer base grew. The creation of divisions, which began in earnest during the 1980s, was the company's response to entering new markets and fleshing out its presence in existing markets. By 2004, when the company celebrated the 40th anniversary of Gorrie's purchase of the Thomas C. Brasfield Co., Brasfield & Gorrie comprised nearly 20 divisions, a number that would increase almost annually. There were 21 divisions by 2006 and 25 divisions in 2007, the year the company opened its first new full-service office in nearly a decade with the establishment of a facility in Jacksonville, Florida.

A look back at the accomplishments of Brasfield & Gorrie since the transfer of ownership from Brasfield to Gorrie revealed the depth and breadth of the company's activity during four decades of growth. The company had completed more than 35 million square feet of office construction, more than two million square feet of religious construction, more than nine million square feet of retail construction, and more than 12 million square feet of high-rise residential and hotel construction. Healthcare construction, the company's forte, amounted to more than 20 million square feet during Gorrie's era, accounting for one-third of Brasfield & Gorrie's business in the early 21st century.

As Brasfield & Gorrie charted its course for the future, the company figured to play a prominent role as a contractor of choice. The projects undertaken during the middle of the first decade of the 2000s revealed one of the nation's premier construction companies, a firm entrusted to manage complex and costly contracts. Brasfield & Gorrie was awarded arguably its most difficult project in 2002, when its Atlanta office was selected to build the more than $200 million Georgia Aquarium, the largest of its kind in the country and one of the largest in the world. The company was involved in the project from sketch to completion, officially breaking ground at the site, located on the Coca-Cola complex in downtown Atlanta, in May 2003. Funded by Home Depot cofounder Bernie Marcus, the aquarium measured 440,000 square feet, featuring a conference center large enough to accommodate 12,000 guests, a 1,600-car parking deck, a food court, facilities for school programs, and more than five million gallons of marine and fresh water. The facility, which was completed in late 2004, was a testament to Brasfield & Gorrie's capabilities, calling upon the company's skills honed in its water and wastewater business. One of the projects undertaken after the Georgia Aquarium project offered a more typical example of the company's work. In mid-2005, the company broke ground on the Bailey Medical Center Hospital, a 53-bed, acute-care facility located in Owasso, Oklahoma. A three-story, 138,000-square-foot, $55 million building, Bailey Medical was completed in late 2006, at which time Brasfield & Gorrie had $4.2 billion worth of work in progress or under contract.

Jeffrey L. Covell

PRINCIPAL COMPETITORS

Hardin Construction Company, LLC; Choate Construction Company; Alberici Corporation.

FURTHER READING

Barth, Cindy, "Brasfield & Gorrie Up for Project of the Year," *Orlando Business Journal,* October 6, 2000, p. 41.

"Brasfield & Gorrie Begins Construction on Bailey Medical Center," *Construction News,* August 15, 2005, p. 12.

Dorich, Alan, "Partners in Healthcare," *US Business Review,* July 2006, p. 25.

Miller, Joanna, "Underwater Dream Becomes a Reality," *Construction Today,* October 2005, p. 14.

Salgado, Brian, "Billion-Dollar Contractors," *Construction Today,* August 2005, p. 196.

Scalzitti, James, "Solid-Built Relationships," *Construction Today,* November–December 2005, p. 76.

Sloan, Barbara, "Building Success in Alabama," *Partners,* Summer 2004, p. 14.

Snyder, Jack, "After Helping Build City's Skyline, John Mills to Retire," *Orlando Sentinel,* April 12, 2006.

The Brickman Group, Ltd.

18227D Flower Hill Way
Gaithersburg, Maryland 20879
U.S.A.
Telephone: (301) 987-9200
Fax: (240) 683-2030
Web site: http://www.brickmangroup.com

Private Company
Founded: 1939 as Theodore Brickman Landscaping
   Company
Employees: 6,000
Sales: $550 million (2007 est.)
NAIC: 541320 Landscape Architectural Services;
   561730 Landscaping Services.

∎∎∎

In the green industry, few can top The Brickman Group, Ltd.'s beautiful landscape designs and their top-quality landscape maintenance services. Founded in 1939 in a suburb of Chicago, Brickman is one of the nation's largest and most respected horticultural firms. Brickman offers clients a wide range of services, including landscape architecture plans, enhancements to existing landscapes, sports field turf design and upkeep, tree care, irrigation, and lawn and landscape maintenance services. With annual revenues exceeding $500 million, Brickman Group continues to provide award-winning designs to clients large and small throughout the United States and Canada.

IN THE BEGINNING

The precursor to today's Brickman Group was founded by Theodore W. Brickman, Sr., as Theodore Brickman Landscaping Company. Brickman started the company in Glenview, Illinois, in 1939 to serve the horticultural needs of Chicago and its burgeoning suburbs. As an employee of the Chicago Park District, Brickman had gained valuable experience and knowledge of northern Illinois's plants, trees, and shrubs. Paramount to Brickman's early success was his belief in the "Golden Rule": do unto others as you would have them do unto you, applied equally to his personal and professional life.

The Golden Rule served Brickman well. By the 1940s he had a growing list of residential clients and commercial properties in and around Chicago. During the latter part of the decade and into the early 1950s, Ted's son Theodore, Jr., known as "Dick," completed his secondary education and headed for college. Dick earned a degree in landscape architecture and joined the family business.

Dick Brickman brought many ideas to the firm and one was the concept of "design/build" landscaping. The company had previously provided various landscape or horticultural services, but not landscape architecture. Dick helped the company segue into the design of landscaping plans, which encompassed "building" or installing the plants, bushes, trees, walkways, and retention walls needed to accomplish the design plan.

Dick began running the company in 1957 as Brickman expanded throughout the Chicagoland area. In 1959 Theodore Brickman & Company was incorporated in Long Grove, a suburb of Chicago.

Residential jobs in the suburbs of Chicago were no longer the company's biggest accomplishment, however, as it had earned a reputation for transforming the "concrete jungle" of the city itself in the 1960s. Dick's landscape designs took the often harsh and ugly reality of city living and created oases of lush greenery complete with atriums, walkways, trees and flowers, fountains, and precisely cut hedges and shrubs. In addition to gaining notice, the company began winning landscaping awards from various groups and organizations in the Midwest.

A NEW ERA

The 1970s proved a turning point for Brickman as the firm not only made its first acquisition, a tree-trimming service, and expanded outside the Midwest to the East Coast. It was also a time of growing environmental awareness, and Brickman was on the forefront of environmentally friendly landscaping practices. Yet the biggest development of the decade revolved around Ray Kroc, the owner of McDonald's Corporation.

Brickman & Company earned a rare distinction in 1971 when Ray Kroc signed the company to provide landscaping designs and services for McDonald's Corporation's new headquarters in Oak Brook, Illinois. While the design/build contract was prestigious, it was Kroc's second demand that changed the future of Brickman: Kroc wanted Brickman & Company to design, install, *and* maintain McDonald's landscaping. Brickman was well versed in landscaping designs and installations but had not provided maintenance services for its clients. Kroc's insistence forced Brickman into the lucrative though lesser known segment of the green industry.

The McDonald's contract proved a major success, impressing Kroc and Brickman's landscaping peers. Not only did the company win several awards for the property, including the Grand Award for landscape maintenance from the Professional Grounds Management Society and *Grounds Maintenance* magazine, but the Environmental Improvement Grand Award from the Professional Landcare Network. Additionally, Kroc signed Brickman to provide all landscaping services, including maintenance, for the life of the property.

MAINTAINING A GIANT

Brickman had become the largest landscaping services company in the United States by the early 1980s. The firm had expanded into states throughout the Midwest, East Coast, and Southwest, and had even provided design/build services for clients in Hawaii, on the West Coast, and Canada. Reincorporated in Delaware in 1986, The Brickman Group, Ltd., became the parent company of several operating units including Brickman Industries, Theodore Brickman Company, and Maple Leaf Nurseries.

The company hit another milestone in 1986 with the arrival of Scott Brickman, the third generation to join the family business. Like his father Dick, Scott had earned a degree in landscape architecture; he began his Brickman tenure as a project director. Revenues for 1986 reportedly reached $100 million, with ambitious plans underway for the future. Over the next several years as Scott Brickman worked his way up the corporate ladder, the company decentralized its corporate structure to allow regional managers to "bridge the gap" between local branches and corporate executives.

In 1989 Brickman celebrated its 50th anniversary yet also suffered the loss of its founder, Ted Brickman. At the time of his death, Brickman continued to dominate the landscape and horticultural services industry and had offices in Connecticut, Delaware, Georgia, Florida, Maryland, New Jersey, Pennsylvania, Virginia, and several locations in and around Chicago.

Throughout the early and mid-1990s Brickman continued to expand through acquisitions and new branch openings in the Midwest (Indiana, Ohio, and Wisconsin); ventured south to Florida and North Carolina; and increased its presence in Texas. The Brickman name had become synonymous with ingenious landscape designs featuring bright, vibrant colors, elaborate fountains, and beautifully crafted paths and walkways. For its efforts, the company earned accolades from a myriad of green industry magazines and associations.

There were two significant occurrences in 1998: the appointment of 35-year-old Scott Brickman as chief

KEY DATES

1939: Theodore Brickman Landscaping Company is founded in Glenview, Illinois.

1957: Ted Brickman's son Dick joins the family business as a landscape architect.

1959: Theodore Brickman & Company is incorporated.

1971: Ray Kroc signs Brickman as the landscaper for McDonald's Corporation.

1986: Scott Brickman, representing the family's third generation, joins the company; company is reincorporated in Delaware.

1989: Company celebrates its 50th anniversary; Ted Brickman passes away.

1990: Founder's Day is unveiled as a memorial to Ted Brickman.

1998: Scott Brickman is named chief executive of the company.

2005: Brickman helps victims of Hurricane Katrina.

2006: Scott Brickman is named Ernst & Young's Entrepreneur of the Year.

executive (his father Dick remained chairman) and the family's decision to sell a stake in the company to outside investors. The increased funding was key to Brickman's growth as the green industry became fiercely competitive.

In 1999 Brickman celebrated its 60th anniversary with revenues of about $180 million. The business had succeeded well beyond its mainstay operations of build/design and landscape maintenance to include tree care, irrigation, and even snow/ice removal services for the winter months. Brickman had locations throughout the country, and had finally expanded to the West Coast with offices in San Diego, California.

THE NEW CENTURY

In the new millennium, Brickman continued to acquire landscape firms and open satellite offices in underserved areas. Revenues for 2000 reached over $220 million and climbed to $272 million in 2001, helped by the purchase of Duke Realty Corporation's landscaping division and Brickman's segue into the athletic field market. Brickman's new SportsTurf Services unit was formed to provide both design and maintenance services for athletic fields throughout the country.

By 2002 Brickman was contending with aggressive competition from the TruGreen Companies, Davey Tree

Expert Company, and ValleyCrest Companies. According to *Landscape Management* magazine's annual top 100 landscape services firms for 2002, TruGreen brought in $1.5 billion to ValleyCrest's $620 million, while Davey Tree's $325 million was slightly ahead of Brickman's $323 million. TruGreen had the most branches/franchises at 300, with Brickman next at 96, trailed by ValleyCrest's 92 and Davey Tree's 65 branches.

In 2003 and 2004 Brickman continued to earn its reputation as one of the nation's preeminent horticultural firms with a professional staff able to handle virtually any landscape-related need. Available at any time were horticulturists (with experience in both regional and local plant life), licensed landscape architects, "seasonal color" designers (with degrees in horticulture and/or design to guarantee the most vibrantly colored flowers and trees), sports turf specialists (covering football fields, ballparks, and more), and irrigation specialists (to provide expert watering for all climates). Additionally, there were production specialists, educators, national account managers (for nationwide clients to insure consistency), regional managers, and branch managers, all serving the needs of Brickman's clients. Brickman's ongoing growth and profitability was reflected in revenues of $349.4 million in 2003 and $383.6 million in 2004, and earnings rising during the same period from $1.2 million to $9.2 million.

In the middle and following years of the first decade of the 2000s Brickman gave back to the community by donating funds for victims of Hurricane Katrina, as well as donations of time and money to Habitat for Humanity, the Red Cross, Ronald McDonald House, Lambs Farm (Illinois), Girls Hope/Boys Hope (Ohio), Camp Horizons (in Connecticut), and many more. In addition, Brickman continued to buy landscape firms, strengthening already established markets in the Midwest and East Coast, and gaining a foothold in areas dominated by competitors. To continue financing its expansion (there were 135 branches in 23 states by early 2007), a majority stake in the company was sold to Leonard Green & Partners LP, a Los Angeles-based private equity firm. The Brickman family and other small investors held the remaining interest in the company.

As Brickman approached its 70th anniversary in 2009, the company was still going strong and practicing founder Ted Brickman's sage words: "We are in business to serve and satisfy our customers by listening to them and responding with services that meet and exceed their expectations."

Nelson Rhodes

PRINCIPAL COMPETITORS

Davey Tree Expert Company, Inc.; Griffin Land & Nurseries, Inc.; TrueGreen Landcare LLC; ValleyCrest Companies.

FURTHER READING

Berberich, Steve, "Building a Landscape Firm Brickman by Brickman," *Gazette.Net,* December 2, 2005.

"Brickman Group Has Fourth Office in the Chicago Area," *Chicago Tribune,* June 2, 1991, p. 1C.

Gibson, Sue, "Acquisition Expands and Strengthens Brickman's Reach in Midwestern Markets," *Landscape Management,* September 2001, p. 16.

Heard, Jacqueline, "Landscape Architect Theodore Brickman, 82," *Chicago Tribune,* August 4, 1989, p. 10.

Hopp-Peters, Elizabeth, "Brickman Reaps Growing Profits of Landscaping," *Chicago Tribune,* October 5, 1986, p. 1.

"LM 100: Big 50 Companies," *Landscape Management,* July 2003, p. 24.

"McDonald's HQ Site for Sore Eyes," *Chicago Tribune,* May 1, 1988, p.1G.

Patta, Gig, "Landscapers Unaffected by Slowing Economy," *San Diego Business Journal,* August 20, 2001, p. 17.

Stahl, Jason, "Winner: Landscape Contracting—Bruce Hunt," *Landscape Management,* November 2000, p. 20.

BTG Plc

10 Fleet Place
Limeburner Lane
London, EC4M 7SB
United Kingdom
Telephone: (+44 020) 7575 0000
Fax: (+44 020) 7575 0010
Web site: http://www.btgplc.com

Public Company
Incorporated: 1981 as British Technology Group
Employees: 95
Sales: £50.2 million ($94.3 million) (2006)
Stock Exchanges: London
Ticker Symbol: BGC
NAIC: 523999 Miscellaneous Financial Investment Activities; 541690 Other Scientific and Technical Consulting Services

■ ■ ■

BTG Plc is a leading "technology transfer" company based in the United Kingdom. BTG acquires, invests in, patents, and licenses technologies developed in university-based and other research facilities, and also provides capital investment and related support services to companies developing BTG-held technologies under license. Since 2005, BTG has refocused its technology interests to the life sciences sector, targeting medical and pharmaceutical innovations and technology. The company's portfolio targets especially such areas of medical development as Aging, Drug Repositioning, Oncology, and Neuroscience. BTG holds the patent, for

example, for the hemophilia treatment BeneFix. The company also licenses the chronic lymphocytic leukemia drug Campath, which is also used as a treatment for multiple sclerosis. A promising compound in the group's pipeline is the varicose vein treatment Varisolve, which entered Phase III trials in Europe at the start of 2007. Other drugs under development include the cervix "ripener" Cervidil, pain treatment Combunox, iron reducer Ferriprox, and colorectal cancer drug Tomudex. For these and other compounds, BTG provides resource management services, sourcing (including locating partner companies to develop its technologies), and patent development and protection. BTG stemmed from the early 1980s merger of the National Research Development Corporation and The National Enterprise Board, and was privatized in 1992. The company is listed on the London Stock Exchange, and posted revenues of over £50 million ($94 million) in 2006. The company is led by Managing Director Louise Makin.

MARKETING BRITISH TECHNOLOGY IN 1948

BTG stemmed from the early 1980s merger of two British government bodies. The oldest of these was the National Research Development Corporation (NRDC), founded after the passage of the Development of Inventions Act of 1948. That legislation, and the NRDC itself, was designed to prevent the reoccurrence of what had occurred following the invention of penicillin. Although Alexander Fleming, a British scientist, was credited with discovering penicillin in 1928, he had not patented the molecule, in part because he had not yet

COMPANY PERSPECTIVES

There exists a paradox—the potential for medical breakthroughs has never been better, but the operating environment to do so has never been so difficult. The challenges presented by the relationship between innovators and the pharmaceutical industry are both profound and numerous. The industry finds itself at the centre of perhaps an unprecedented scrutiny from the public, from governments, from regulatory authorities, from health care providers, and from shareholders.

Over the last decade, these challenges have resulted in a phenomenon in the industry that has become known as The Innovation Gap: R&D spending going up, whilst the number of drugs reaching the market continue to decline. Addressing these challenges requires companies to think differently about how to make the difficult but rewarding transition from an idea to a potentially life changing product.

Success becomes a matter of finding innovation and managing the complex path to market.

At BTG, we have the ability to harness innovation and realise commercial value in the changing pharmaceutical environment. We are experts in sourcing, protecting and developing new products, and have the scale and experience to help transform the commercial potential of medical research programmes from around the globe. We are also independent, have a significant capacity for investment, and a deep pipeline of development projects which we believe make us a unique and attractive partner to researchers and the healthcare industry.

worked out a method for producing the antibiotic on a large scale. At the end of World War II, however, the British government was surprised to discover that an American corporation had since patented the production process for penicillin, not only depriving the United Kingdom of much needed royalties, but also obliging the country to purchase its supplies of penicillin from the United States.

In response, the Inventions Act vested the NRDC with the authority to "[secure], where the public interest so requires, the development or exploitation of inventions resulting from public research, and of any other

invention as to which it appears to the corporation that it is not being developed or exploited or sufficiently developed or exploited." The NRDC was established as part of the Board of Trade, and began reviewing patents and inventions being developed in the United Kingdom in the hope of discovering commercially marketable products.

At first, the NRDC's role consisted largely of identifying prospective candidates and then passing these ideas along to Britain's industry for development. The NRDC also helped export the United Kingdom's technology, arranging licensing agreements around the world. However, through the 1950s and especially into the 1960s, the NRDC took on a more and more active role in the development of the country's scientific breakthroughs, especially those made at public institutions. By the mid-1960s, the NRDC often took a direct role in setting up and managing industrial operations, as part of joint venture corporations. An example of the company's operations could be seen in the role it played in guiding the process of transforming hecogenin, a product of the waste juice of the sisal plant, into cortisone. For that effort, the NRDC went as far as establishing a factory in Africa, then funding the pilot plant that led to the successful production of cortisone in the space of less than three years.

During the 1950s and 1960s, the NRDC backed the development of a number of significant products. In 1957, for example, the corporation played a major role in the discovery and production of the important antiviral agent interferon. Just one year later, the company began its relationship with the famous Hovercraft technology. That investment also marked the corporation's departure from publicly funded research, and represented the NRDC's most significant private sector investment. Into the mid-1960s, NRDC spent more than £4 million assisting the development of Hovercraft's technology and commercial operations.

Toward the end of the 1960s, NRDC's total investments had topped £19 million, and included such projects as the development of large-screen cathode-ray tubes; microelectronics component production; and the extension of Hovercraft technology. By then, the corporation had become involved in some 60 joint ventures. Other significant discoveries backed by the NRDC into the 1970s included the creation of the cephalosporin class of antibiotics, in 1964; the invention of pyrethrin insecticides, in 1966; the development of cholesterol assay tests in 1971, and the development of magnetic resonance imaging (MRI) in 1975, all of which became significant revenue generators into the end of the century for the later BTG. In another extension, NRDC acquired a 45 percent stake in Data

Recording Instruments, a maker of computer peripheral equipment, in partnership with Grundy, of Teddington, in 1994.

PRIVATIZATION IN 1992

The mid-1970s was marked by the arrival of a new component to the British government's efforts to stimulate its domestic industry. In 1974, the government created a new state-controlled body, the National Enterprise Board (NEB), as part of the then-Labour dominated government to establish greater government control over the country's flagging industries. The hotly controversial NEB then took over the task of analyzing, and acquiring, many of Great Britain's leading corporations. In 1976, for example, the NEB became responsible for the British government's ownership of the Rolls-Royce corporations. The link between the NEB and the NRDC also began at this time. In 1975, for example, the NEB acquired a controlling share of Data Recording Instruments, buying out Grundy and acquiring part of the NRDC's stake as well.

The arrival of the Thatcher government in the late 1970s spelled the end of the era of direct government involvement in British industry, however. By 1981, the long-held Conservative Party's disapproval of the NEB led to it being merged into the NRDC. The merger cre-

ated a new government controlled corporation, British Technology Group (BTG). BTG's initial role was to oversee the divestment of corporations held by the NRDC and the NEB, both of which remained in existence for the first years of BTG. By 1983, BTG's new role was properly defined, calling for the body to become focused strictly on technology transfer. As such the government ordered BTG to hasten disposal of its investment portfolio. While BTG was given the right to retain revenues generated by its technology licenses, those created by its assets disposal were turned over to the British Treasury. BTG itself was meant to be privatized soon after its formation.

The process of winding down the former holdings and activities of the NRDC and the NEB was largely completed by 1984, at which time BTG's status as a technology transfer group was formally ratified by the British government. This gave the company the signal to launch a new investment campaign, during which BTG spent some £75 million in order to build its technologies portfolio. One of the company's most significant investments during this time was its acquisition of the patents for MRI, a major diagnostic breakthrough that had been developed by a British scientist. BTG began actively licensing MRI on a worldwide level starting from 1984.

While MRI technology swept the global medical community, other BTG investments proved more difficult to develop into profits. In 1987, for example, the company acquired the traction control and transmission research division of British auto maker Rover. The purchase gave the company control of the patents behind a new continuously variable automotive transmission, which promised far greater fuel efficiency. When BTG was unable to attract licensees from the automotive industry, the company decided to begin manufacturing its own transmissions, setting up subsidiary Torotrak. Production proved costly, however, dragging the company into losses by the late 1990s, and in 1998 Torotrak was spun off as a public company.

By then, BTG too had changed its corporate status. By the late 1980s, BTG and its management had increasingly begun to chafe under government ownership. Yet, despite the initial objective of privatizing the company at its creation, it was only in the early 1990s that the British government agreed to allow BTG to go private. In 1992, the company's management had lined up backing from the Cinven investment group, and BTG went private as part of a management buyout. By 1995, BTG had gone public, listing its shares on the London Stock Exchange.

BIOTECHNOLOGY FOCUS FOR THE NEW CENTURY

The public offering helped the company rapidly expand its portfolio of patents and technologies, so that by the middle of the decade the company boasted control of more than 9,000 patents supporting more than 1,300 inventions. Among the group's successes in the 1990s were the disposable contact lens, licensed to Bausch & Lomb, and Factor IX, later commercialized as Benefix, a treatment for hemophilia B. In 1999, the company acquired the patents to the highly promising varicose vein treatment Varisolve.

Through the 1990s, BTG's management earned itself an international reputation for the ferocity with which it protected its ever growing patent portfolio. As an example the company successfully defended its control of the technology behind the two-part hip cup, forcing a settlement with the Johnson & Johnson group. At the beginning of the next decade, the company was able to force both Microsoft and Apple to license their web-based software updating technology after it acquired Teleshuttle Corp., the company that held the patents to that technology, in 1998. In 2001, the company scored new success when it received approval from both the European Union and the United States to market the chronic lymphocytic leukemia drug Campath.

Despite these successes, BTG struggled through years of losses. Part of the group's difficulties came from the diversified nature of its portfolio, which spanned a wide range of technologies and industries. In 2004, the company brought in a new management team, led by Managing Director Louise Makin, former president of Baxter Healthcare's Biopharmaceuticals Europe division. Makin, seconded by CFO Christine Soden, set out to restructure the company, refocusing BTG around a new core of biopharmaceuticals. The company began divesting its noncore holdings, maintaining only revenue-generating assets outside of its core range. The restructuring effort, which left the group with a loss of £35 million on total revenues of just £38 million, soon paid off. By the end of 2006, with total revenues climbing past £50 million, the company posted profits of £1.4 million. With a growing number of highly promising drugs in its pipeline, BTG appeared to have discovered the formula for success in the new century.

M. L. Cohen

PRINCIPAL SUBSIDIARIES

British Technology Group; BTG Employee Share Schemes Ltd. (Guernsey); BTG International (Holdings) Ltd.; BTG International Inc. (U.S.A.); BTG International Ltd.; BTG Investment (Holdings) Ltd.; BTG Licensing Ltd.; Iclectus Ltd. (80.5%); Inter-Corporate Licensing Ltd.; Provensis Ltd.

PRINCIPAL COMPETITORS

Candover Investments plc; CVC Capital Partners Limited; Investcorp S.A.; Electra Investment Trust; 3i Group PLC; IP2IPO Group plc.

FURTHER READING

"BTG Acquires AD Therapies from Sankyo," *Pharma Marketletter*, November 17, 2003.

"BTG Boosts Delivery Portfolio," *Med Ad News*, June 2002, p. 18.

"BTG Launches Streaming Video Delivery Company," *New Media Age*, November 7, 2002, p. 10.

"BTG Says Licensee Cougar Presents Positive Data on Prostate Cancer Compound," *AFX UK (Focus)*, February 27, 2007.

"BTG Wins Battle Against US Giant," *Marketing Week*, August 18, 2005, p. 19.

Fortson, Danny, "Trading Ideas in Britain," *IP Law & Business*, July 2005.

Garrett, Alexander, "Technological Properties: The Value Is All in the Minds," *Observer*, July 20, 1997, p. 9.

Kenward, Michael, and Sarita Kendall, "When the Finest Minds Are up for Sale," *Financial Times*, July 4, 2001, p. 12.

"Microsoft and Apple Sued over Online Updates," *Information Week*, July 21, 2004.

Page, Nigel, "Taking IP to Market the BTG Way," *Pharma Marketletter*, November 17, 2003.

Perry, Joseph, "The BEI Company Study: BTG," *BioExecutive International*, January 2007.

CalAmp Corp.

1401 North Rice Avenue
Oxnard, California 93030
U.S.A.
Telephone: (805) 987-9000
Fax: (805) 987-8359
Web site: http://www.calamp.com

Public Company
Incorporated: 1981 as California Amplifier, Inc.
Employees: 350
Sales: $217.4 million (2006)
Stock Exchanges: NASDAQ
Ticker Symbol: CAMP
NAIC: 334220 Radio and Television Broadcasting and Wireless Communications Equipment Manufacturing

■ ■ ■

CalAmp Corp. is a provider of microwave amplification and conversion components integral in satellite television, wireless cable, and wireless broadband access systems. The company ranks as the leading supplier of direct broadcast satellite equipment in the United States, supplying satellite television operators such as EchoStar Communications Corporation, owner of the DISH Network, and The DirecTV Group, Inc. The company controls approximately 50 percent of the direct broadcast satellite market. CalAmp also provides wireless connectivity products for the telemetry and asset track-

ing markets, public safety communications, the health-care industry, and digital multimedia delivery applications.

ORIGINS

CalAmp was incorporated in 1981 as California Amplifier, Inc., the name it would operate under for nearly 25 years. The name change signified the adoption of a new business strategy for the Oxnard, California-based company, one of several major shifts in market focus the company would make during its history. Starting out under the California Amplifier banner, the company developed and manufactured microwave components and systems for commercial and consumer applications, but it primarily supplied the U.S. Department of Defense with its products. Prime market conditions greeted California Amplifier during its first decade of business, as military spending swelled during the two-term Reagan presidency, stoked by the decades-long rivalry between the United States and the Soviet Union. California Amplifier gained its financial footing as a defense contractor, but it was forced to abandon its primary source of revenue when the Cold War ended at the decade's conclusion. In 1989, the company severed its ties with the Department of Defense and focused all its research and development and marketing efforts on commercial and consumer applications. The transition—not the last the company would initiate because of changing market conditions—pointed California Amplifier in two directions: serving the wireless cable and satellite television markets.

At the beginning of the 1990s, California Amplifier organized itself along its two product lines, establishing a wireless cable television segment and a satellite television segment. For both segments, the company developed products that converted and processed signals that delivered programming to consumers' homes. Wireless cable used technologies similar to coaxial cable, multichannel television transmission, but eliminated the need for a cable connecting the headend/transmission site to each home. Instead, a wireless system comprised a headend/transmission site, a transmission tower, and at each subscriber's home, a reception antenna, a downconverter, and a decoder or set-top converter. In the satellite television segment, the company's product sales were generated primarily from downconverters, amplifiers, and integrated feedhorns and amplifiers used in home satellite dish applications.

California Amplifier enjoyed steady, encouraging financial growth from both its operating segments during the 1990s, aided by technological advancements and the passage of federal legislation. On the wireless cable side the company's customers, wireless cable operators, gained strength early in the decade thanks to rulings made by the Federal Communications Commission (FCC), the U.S. agency charged with regulating interstate and international communications by radio, television, wire, satellite, and cable. Between 1990 and 1991, the FCC made a series of rulings that enabled wireless cable operators to consolidate channel frequency licenses, which allowed operators to increase channel capacity on their systems. Of singular importance was the Cable Television Consumer Protection and Competition Act of 1992, regarded by industry experts as the most influential piece of legislation affecting wireless cable operators. The legislation forced programmers to make their service available to all operators at a fair and reasonable price, further stipulating that cable operators could not price their services differently in various areas, thereby preventing higher prices in regional areas where wireless cable operators focused their marketing efforts.

Like its wireless cable business, California Amplifier's satellite business benefited from the growth of service operators. The evolution of home satellite systems in the United States between the 1980s and 1990s turned "backyard" dishes into "pizza-box" dishes, securing a lasting place for satellite television in the consumer marketplace. During the early 1980s, home satellite systems utilizing C-Band dishes were capable of receiving a wide variety of television broadcast signals, including programming delivered by pay television operators, but in 1986 premium broadcasters began to scramble their transmission signals. Satellite installations, already limited by the five- to 12-foot diameter of the dishes, declined in the wake of the scrambling efforts. The industry, and California Amplifier's satellite business, received a revitalizing boost with the introduction of the Direct Broadcast System (DBS) in 1994. Using high-powered satellites and the digital Ku-Band, the DBS received a significant number of channels because the DBS satellite transmitted digital signals at high power levels, requiring dishes only 18 inches in diameter. Consumers, overwhelmingly, chose pizza-box-sized dishes over apparatus that filled most backyards.

California Amplifier made the transition from operating as a military supplier to operating as a commercial supplier without much trouble. The technology developed by the company was easily adapted to private sector applications, making for a seamless change in its market orientation. In 1992, sales eclipsed $20 million, jumped to $40 million two years later, and reached $61.5 million in 1996. The steady, substantial increases were recorded while the company experienced major changes in the relative importance of its two business segments. In 1994, California Amplifier relied on satellite television for two-thirds of its business, but within two years the company's wireless cable business became its primary revenue-generating engine, accounting for 70 percent of sales in 1996. California Amplifier's wireless cable sales shot upward thanks to strong international demand for its reception products and to the introduction of its broadband scrambling system, MultiCipher, while its satellite sales dipped as it made the switch from making C-Band dishes to the Ku-DBS alternative.

REORGANIZATION IN 1998

After a strong first half of the decade, California Amplifier demonstrated less financial vitality during the second half of the 1990s. The sales total recorded in 1996 became the decade's high, as the company suffered downturns affecting both its business segments. Sales dipped to $46.9 million in 1998 and to $37.1 million in 1999. More distressing, the company's record of consistent profits came to an end, halted by a $2.6 million net loss in 1998 and a $1.4 million net loss in 1999. In response, California Amplifier reorganized its structure, establishing three business units—satellite products, wireless cable products, and voice and data products—in January 1998. Further alterations were made in September 1999, when the company combined its wireless cable and voice and data units into a single entity, wireless access products.

The start of a new decade brought a welcomed change in the company's financial performance. After registering three consecutive years of declining revenue, California Amplifier generated $86.4 million in revenue in 2000, a 130 percent increase from the previous year that was drawn from an enormous increase in satellite-related sales. The company had purchased Gardiner Communications in April 1999, a $9 million transac-

tion that greatly bolstered California Amplifier's DBS product line. Satellite sales leaped 377 percent between 1999 and 2000, reaching $60 million, as the company fed the demand for dishes by operators such as DirecTV Inc. and EchoStar Communications Corp., owner of the DISH Network.

Acquisitions would figure more prominently in California Amplifier's expansion plans as the company moved forward. Its 20th anniversary in 2001 saw another major increase in revenue driven by a 40 percent increase in satellite sales and a 60 percent increase in wireless access sales. The company generated $125 million in revenue in 2001 and, for the first time in three years, it turned a profit, posting $5.2 million in net income. The financial gains were encouraging, but the company's management began to worry about the lack of balance between its two primary business segments. Satellite products accounted for 68 percent of California Amplifier's revenue in 2001, far more than the 25 percent generated by wireless access products. In the years ahead, Fred Sturm, who served as chief executive officer and president, and Ira Coron, who served as chairman, turned their attention to balancing California Amplifier's business, an objective they would achieve by completing a series of acquisitions.

BEGINNING AN ACQUISITION CAMPAIGN: 2003

Management's concerns about an over-reliance on satellite sales piqued in 2002 as the company felt the repercussions of its lopsided stance. Satellite sales began to falter during the year because one of its largest customers, the notoriously beleaguered WorldCom, canceled its orders. California Amplifier reduced its staff and sold a manufacturing plant during the year in response to the setback, which led to a decline in revenue to $100 million. A more positive response followed in December 2003, when the company announced it had agreed to acquire Vytek Corp. in a $77 million, all-stock deal. Based in San Diego, where it had relocated from White Plains, New York, in 2002, Vytek was a $38.4 million-in-sales company that derived 40 percent of its business from wireless products and 60 percent from software development and consulting. "As a result of this acquisition," Sturm remarked in a December 25, 2003, interview with the *Daily Deal,* "our customer base will grow and diversify beyond satellite television and telecommunications providers to include large- and medium-sized enterprise customers, thereby expanding our market reach and distribution channels." The acquisition was completed in April 2004, prompting California Amplifier to change its name to CalAmp Corp. and to reorganize its operations into a divisional structure. The satellite and wireless access units were combined with Vytek's products manufacturing business to form the products division. Vytek's service-oriented business, its principal area of focus, became CalAmp's solutions division.

In the wake of the third major restructuring effort in its history, the company launched an acquisition campaign aimed at entering new markets with higher growth and profit margin potential. In April 2005, CalAmp acquired Carlsbad, California-based Skybility, a developer and supplier of embedded cellular transceivers. The devices were used in telemetry and asset tracking applications. In May 2006, the company struck again, signing an agreement to acquire Dataradio, Inc., for $54 million. Based in Montreal, Canada, Dataradio set up networks that enabled emergency responders to use laptop computers to share information with dispatchers over private data networks. CalAmp followed up its acquisition of Dataradio by purchasing SmartLink Radio Networks Inc. for $8.1 million in March 2007, one of two acquisitions announced during the month. SmartLink, based in Connecticut, made a product that enabled public safety agencies operating on different radio systems to speak with each other in real time, possessing technology that complemented Dataradio's expertise. The other acquisition in March 2007 was the purchase of the vehicle finance division of AirIQ Inc., a $19 million deal.

CalAmp was preparing for the future by diversifying its market presence. The company's spending spree touched off by the acquisition of Vytek totaled nearly $90 million by mid-2007, pushing it into new markets, the data communications market in particular. Further acquisitions were anticipated in the years ahead as the company sought to diversify beyond its core competency in satellite product sales. CalAmp claimed to control roughly 50 percent of the DBS market in the United States, maintaining a commanding lead that, despite its efforts to diversify, it did not intend to relinquish. The company was in the final stages of developing products capable of receiving transmission signals from up to five different satellites, a necessity to meet the rigors of high definition television service. Accordingly, as CalAmp pressed ahead with its plans, the company looked to its nearly three-decade-long involvement in the satellite sector and to emerging markets for its future success.

Jeffrey L. Covell

PRINCIPAL SUBSIDIARIES

California Amplifier SARL (France); CalAmp Solutions Holdings, Inc.; CalAmp Solutions, Inc.

PRINCIPAL DIVISIONS

Products Division; Solutions Division.

PRINCIPAL COMPETITORS

Powerwave Technologies, Inc.; Motorola, Inc.; Andrew Corporation.

FURTHER READING

"CalAmp Will Buy Dataradio," *America's Intelligence Wire,* May 10, 2006.

"Camarillo, Calif.-based Amplifier Company Shows a Fiscal Year Profit," *Ventura County Star,* June 5, 2001.

Garcia, Shelly, "California Amplifier Meets Rapid Increase in Demand," *San Fernando Valley Business Journal,* December 8, 2003, p. 7.

Hiestand, Jesse, "California-Based Amplifier Manufacturer's Stock Resumes Trading on Nasdaq," *Daily News,* June 8, 2001.

Hopkins, Brent, "Lawsuit Sinks Shares of Satellite Products Firm California Amplifier Inc.," *Daily News,* April 27, 2004.

Martinez, Carlos, "Tech Transformation: Only Flexible Firms Have Survived Change," *San Fernando Valley Business Journal,* September 15, 2003, p. 1.

McLain, Jim, "CalAmp to Make Another Acquisition," *Ventura County Star,* March 28, 2007.

Monga, Vipal, "California Amp Gets Vytek in $77M Stock Deal," *Daily Deal,* December 5, 2003.

Pondel, Evan, "Camarillo, Calif-based Electronics Maker Gets New Chief Financial Officer," *Daily News,* July 25, 2001.

Woodard, Chris, "California Amplifier Inc.," *Investor's Business Daily,* August 7, 2000, p. A12.

Carlson Companies, Inc.

701 Carlson Parkway
Minnetonka, Minnesota 55305
U.S.A.
Telephone: (763) 212-1000
Fax: (763) 212-2219
Web site: http://www.carlson.com

Private Company
Incorporated: 1938 as the Gold Bond Stamp Company
Employees: 171,000
Sales: $4.93 billion (2005 est.)
NAIC: 721110 Hotels (Except Casino Hotels) and Motels; 483112 Deep Sea Passenger Transportation; 541611 Administrative Management and General Management Consulting Services; 561510 Travel Agencies; 561520 Tour Operators; 722110 Full-Service Restaurants

■ ■ ■

Carlson Companies, Inc., transformed from a trading stamp business to a highly diversified operation before honing in on the hospitality and travel industries. Carlson Hotels Worldwide, a leading hotel franchiser, includes the Radisson, Regent, Park Plaza, Park Inn, and Country Inn & Suite brands. Jointly owned Carlson Wagonlit Travel is the second largest travel management network in the world, after American Express. Among its other operations are T.G.I. Friday's restaurants, Regent Seven Seas Cruises, and Carlson Marketing, which ranks among the largest marketing agencies in the United States.

STARTING WITH TRADING STAMPS

The story of Carlson Companies begins with founder Curtis L. Carlson. Carlson was born in Minneapolis, Minnesota, in 1914, the son of a Swedish immigrant and a first-generation American. Early on he showed entrepreneurial talent when he farmed out paper routes to his younger brothers, realizing a small profit on their labor. Upon graduation from the University of Minnesota, Carlson went to work for Procter & Gamble Company selling soap, but, after a year, he decided to go into business for himself.

With $55 of borrowed capital, the 23-year-old Carlson registered the Gold Bond Stamp Company with the Clerk of District Court in Minneapolis on June 8, 1938, in the midst of the Great Depression. Carlson had noticed that the Leader, a downtown Minneapolis department store, gave away coupons to its customers with each purchase that could be saved up and redeemed for cash or prizes. The point of the coupons was to encourage customer loyalty and spur sales. Carlson reasoned that what worked well for department stores would also work well for grocery stores. He was familiar with both forms of retailing from his work at Procter & Gamble and from his childhood, when his father had worked in the food business.

Carlson set up a mail drop, rented desk space in a downtown Minneapolis building, and paid a secretary in a nearby office $5 a month to answer the phone. Hanging onto his regular job for four additional months, he spent his evenings and weekends selling reluctant small grocers on his new trading stamp idea. Five months after he quit his steady job, Carlson made his first sale, in March 1939, to a small grocer in south Minneapolis. The store owner purchased $14.50 worth of Gold Bond stamps to dispense, which customers would then present to Carlson for redemption. Carlson guaranteed that his client would have the exclusive right within a 25-block area to give out Gold Bond trading stamps. To call attention to the sales incentive, Carlson plastered the store with posters and banners and distributed balloons and refreshments. The idea was a success and, by the end of the year, Carlson had added 39 more grocery stores to his list of clients.

With this progress, Carlson moved his growing firm to an office in south Minneapolis, in between a Chinese restaurant and a pinball machine repair shop, and took on an additional employee to handle the administrative side of things while he sold the Gold Bond program to grocers. In addition, he roped his wife into the business, dressing her up in a golden majorette's costume with a feathered hat and positioning her at a card table inside stores during their gala inaugurations of the Gold Bond program. Mrs. Carlson's job was to explain to homemakers how to save the stamps and redeem them for cash.

In 1940, strapped for cash, Carlson sold six $100 shares in his enterprise to friends but planned to buy them back when he became more solvent, since he was intent on retaining control of the company himself. By 1941 his client list had grown to include 200 merchants in the Minnesota area. With the entry of the United States into World War II at the end of that year, however, the fortunes of the Gold Bond Stamp Company went into a dive: wartime shortages eliminated the need for merchants to provide incentives to their customers. When ration books replaced trading stamp books in shoppers' hands, Carlson's company lost two-thirds of its business within three months. Carlson reduced the company to a skeleton operation when his two employees entered the military, and he began moonlighting as a manager in his father-in-law's children's clothing store in downtown Minneapolis to make ends meet for the duration of the war.

RAPID EXPANSION FOLLOWING WORLD WAR II

In 1944, when Carlson was called up to join the war effort, he sold a half interest in the company to Truman Johnson, who had also been employed by Procter & Gamble, and left the business in his hands. At the war's end, the small firm was in dire need of rejuvenation. In 1946 Carlson vowed to expand the company into seven states within the next five years. Toward this end, he hired salesmen to work new territories, including next-door Wisconsin, and, farther afield, Texas, Indiana, and Oregon. In addition, the trading stamp concept was extended to outlets other than grocery stores. Accordingly, the Gold Bond stamp program was sold to gas stations, dry cleaners, and movie theaters. In a more imaginative vein, feed and grain millers, a turkey hatchery, and even undertakers signed on, as the men from Gold Bond urged merchants to invest 2 percent of their gross receipts in the incentive program, promising a 20 percent rise in sales.

By the early 1950s, Gold Bond stamps were offered in 11 midwestern states. In 1953 Carlson scored a major coup, leaving behind forever the days of individual sales to "mom and pop"-type stores, when the largest grocery chain in the nation, Super Valu Stores, Inc., based in Minneapolis, began offering Gold Bond trading stamps. In a switch to accommodate the wishes of the chain store, the stamps were redeemed for prizes, rather than cash, a much more complicated undertaking. Gold Bond was forced to open warehouses, maintain inventory, set up redemption centers, and hire people to staff them, a process by no means free of errors. Since Carlson had purchased stock in Super Valu when it implemented his program, he reaped a reward from the soaring value of the grocery store's stock, as well as from his own business, which notched $2.4 million in sales that year.

Through the connection with Super Valu, Gold Bond stamps gained a higher national public profile. When Kroger Company, a competing Midwest grocery store chain, approached the company about implementing a stamp program, Carlson inaugurated a second trading stamp, called Top Value Stamp Co., to avoid competition with the Super Valu line. Doubling the size of his company's workforce, Carlson expanded the Top Value line to grocery chains in other areas of the country, including the Northeast, Oklahoma, and Nebraska.

In 1957 Kroger, the company's original Top Value client, bought the Top Value portion of Carlson's business for $1 million. With this money, Carlson was able to buy out his more cautious partner, Truman Johnson, who had held a half-interest in Gold Bond since the war

KEY DATES

1938: Curtis L. Carlson launches Gold Bond Stamp Company.
1941: U.S. entry into World War II drives down business.
1946: Carlson embarks on expansion plan.
1953: Nation's largest grocery chain begins offering Gold Bond stamps.
1959: Diversification begins.
1962: Company purchases a Radisson Hotel.
1973: Name is changed to Carlson Companies.
1975: T.G.I. Friday's restaurants is purchased.
1979: Ask Mr. Foster Travel is acquired.
1989: Edwin C. "Skip" Gage begins short-lived term as CEO of Carlson Companies.
1998: Marilyn Carlson Nelson succeeds father as president and CEO.
1999: Founder dies; Carlson Nelson becomes chair.
2003: Curtis Nelson, son of Marilyn Carlson Nelson, rises to positions of president and COO of Carlson Companies.
2004: Carlson Companies produces record sales.
2006: Top management is reorganized.

years. Carlson regained full control of the company in 1958.

Rapid expansion of the company continued throughout the late 1950s. Safeway Stores Incorporated, another large chain of grocery stores in the West and Southwest, was added to the fold, and the company also entered the international arena, inaugurating trading stamp operations in Canada, the Caribbean, Japan, and other countries. By the 1960s, the trading stamp business had become ubiquitous, and Gold Bond was one of the largest companies in the field. All but one of the top 20 American grocery store chains offered the trading stamps, and half of all gas stations provided them as well.

BEGINNING TO DIVERSIFY

Nevertheless, the tide of consumer sentiment had begun to turn against the trading stamp industry. Trading stamps were blamed for inflated prices in stores: shoppers began to demand lower prices, not vouchers toward free prizes. Gold Bond lost Safeway's business, and it became clear that Gold Bond would have to diversify to other fields if it hoped to maintain its steady growth.

Carlson began diversification by purchasing real estate, buying large parcels of land in Minnetonka, a western suburb of Minneapolis, for future development. In addition, he purchased the Radisson Hotel, a high-profile property in downtown Minneapolis, in 1962, marking his company's entry into the hospitality industry. Both the hotel and the real estate transactions were intended to act as tax shelters for Gold Bond's earnings, enabling the company to retain as much of its profits as possible, so that it could use them to fuel further growth.

This growth took the company in a number of different directions. Throughout the 1960s, as the popularity of the trading stamp business continued to decline, Carlson's diversification and acquisition strategy took on more importance. As sole owner of Gold Bond, Carlson was able to manage his assets with virtually no outside surveillance or interference. Willing to take risks and amass debt, he sought to acquire businesses that were already in solid financial shape but had the potential to benefit from his company's proven sales savvy. The key elements of Carlson's philosophy of acquisition, then, were the capacity for growth and the possibility of replication. By 1973 the name of the Gold Bond Stamp Company had been changed to Carlson Companies, Inc., to better reflect the firm's expansion into new markets and businesses.

Companies purchased by Carlson included the Ardan Catalogue showrooms, a business related to the premium showrooms earlier opened by Gold Bond, and a number of properties that tied into the hotel business in some way, such as a wholesale food distributor called the May Company and the creation of a chain of restaurants and pubs known as the Haberdashery. In addition, the company had extended its Radisson Hotel franchise, opening additional facilities, first in Minnesota, and then in other areas of the United States.

Farther afield, Carlson invested in a $7 million hardboard plant in northwestern Wisconsin. Failed projects included a chain of grocery stores called Piggly Wiggly, an investment in Caribbean shrimp boats, and a money-losing meatpacking plant. All were eventually shed by the growing company.

Although the Carlson Companies underwent a slight recession in 1975, one acquisition made during that year proved to be a consistent money-earner. T.G.I. Friday's (from the expression "Thank God It's Friday"), a chain of 11 restaurant-bars based in Dallas and featuring eclectic decor and an airy, multiple-floor arrangement, grew to encompass 73 branches within eight years. T.G.I. Friday's was soon joined by another restaurant chain, Country Kitchen International, which catered to the family market, with down-home decor and low-priced meals.

In 1978 Carlson began the acquisition of WaSko Gold Products, a New York City-based jewelry manufacturer, for about $18.2 million. This company fit in well with Carlson's Ardan company, which specialized in jewelry sales. By this time, Carlson had added several other retail businesses, including Naum Brothers, a catalog showroom based in Rochester, New York; the Indian Wells Oil Company, E. Weisman, dealing in tobacco and candy sales; Jason Empire, Inc., an importer of binoculars and telescopes; and the Premium Corporation, which provided sales incentive programs similar to those offered by the Gold Bond Stamp business.

After gaining experience in the hotel industry through the ownership of the Radisson Hotel chain, Carlson Companies ventured into the travel agency business in 1979. The addition of the well-known Ask Mr. Foster Agency (later known as Carlson Travel Network and still later as Carlson Leisure Group), founded in 1888 in St. Augustine, Florida, opened the door to the travel services industry, which Carlson would eventually grow to dominate.

In 1980 Carlson Companies announced plans for the real estate development west of Minneapolis that its founder had acquired in the late 1950s and 1960s as a tax shelter. The company proposed a 307-acre development, to be anchored by a new corporate headquarters building. The project would include businesses, restaurants, and a hotel, and was slated to cost $300 million and be called Carlson Center. Carlson Companies continued to manage its acquisitions, purchasing shares in a company called Modern Merchandising and selling its groceries wholesaler, May Company, to another food company. The following year, Carlson added another company to its collection of marketing concerns, purchasing the E. F. MacDonald Company, a sales incentive and motivation business in Dayton, Ohio, and merging the company with its other holdings in this area.

By 1982 Carlson's holdings had grown to encompass 75 different companies with combined sales of $2.1 billion. Despite its move into a much broader arena of business, the conglomerate had managed to maintain a 33 percent compounded annual rate of growth for the 44th consecutive year. One of its holdings, Curtis Homes, offered a new approach to success in the housing construction market. Curtis Homes provided the basic outer shell of a house with the wiring and roof, leaving all inside finishing—floors, paneling, and so forth—to the buyer of the house. The end result

was a low-priced home for the buyer and big business for the company. As a result, Curtis Homes was able to turn a profit even when housing sales overall were in a slump. Carlson later sold this operation to a competitor in this field in order to concentrate on businesses with which he was more familiar.

Along with the acquisition of new companies, Carlson grew by fostering development within the properties it already owned. In the restaurant business, that meant a proliferation of outlets within each franchise. The Country Kitchen restaurant chain, for instance, included 285 restaurants by the early 1980s, most of which were in small towns across North America. T.G.I. Friday's, with the highest sales per unit ($3.45 million average per store) of any American restaurant chain (and a favorite of founder Curt Carlson), opened 17 new locations in one year alone. By 1992 Friday's had over 200 restaurants throughout the world, many of which were franchised. The Radisson Hotel chain had increased to two dozen sites, including one near the pyramids in Egypt. Radisson Hotels International, as it became known (it was later called Radisson Hotels Worldwide), together with other Carlson Hospitality hotels, inns, and resorts, by the mid-1990s numbered over 345 properties throughout the world.

Despite this progress, Carlson found its empire suffering from a recession in the early 1980s. In June 1983, *Business Week* reported several problems for Carlson. Although Country Kitchens had opened a large number of restaurants, the chain was plagued by poor management and bad relations with its franchise owners; it failed to meet a four-year sales goal by a large margin, fulfilling just over one-quarter of its targeted growth. Ardan, the catalog showroom, suffered from overexpansion, and its sales had not improved in several years. Radisson, the flagship hotel chain, seemed stalled in the doldrums of a highly competitive industry, apparently blocked from major advances. Business incentive programs and travel agency operations, too, had suffered in the recession.

Carlson Companies owed its historically steady and successful expansion over the course of decades to the tight control of its autocratic founder and sole owner, Curt Carlson. As Carlson neared the age of 80, however, it became clear that he would have to transfer some of his power to a capable successor. On January 1, 1983, Carlson appointed his son-in-law, Edwin C. (Skip) Gage III, to be executive vice-president. Gage had previously been the president of the Carlson Marketing Group, which ran the company's businesses associated with incentives and promotions; he had been groomed for many years to follow carefully in Carlson's footsteps.

Gage told *Business Week* that he planned to "concentrate on doing very well the things we already do."

FOCUSING ON HOSPITALITY, TRAVEL, AND MARKETING

In the mid-1980s, Carlson Companies began to evolve from a conglomerate with somewhat disparate holdings to a more tightly organized company, focused on the hospitality, travel, and marketing businesses and the strengthening of the synergistic ties between the three groups. In addition, the company began to shift its emphasis from owning hotels and travel agencies to franchising them. This enabled Carlson to expand rapidly without large outlays of capital in a time when cash was scarce. It also enabled the company to realize millions in fees and royalties from its franchisees.

In 1986 Carlson moved to cash in on its relationship with nearly 500 different travel agencies and raise the number of bookings for its 22 hotels. Also in that year, the company announced the formation of a new chain of hotels, called Country Inns by Carlson, to serve a more middle-class segment of the market than the full-service, upscale Radisson line. Country Inns by Carlson were decorated with homey touches, including fireplaces in the lobbies and down-filled quilts on the beds.

By the following year, under the leadership of Juergen Bartels, a German-born former president of the Ramada Inn chain, Carlson's hotel holdings ranked near the top ten in the nation in number of rooms. Through the careful selection of franchise holders and thorough staff training, the company sought to upgrade its properties and began to tailor its operations to fit the needs of the growing population of women business travelers. Building on these moves, Carlson set a new goal of becoming the preeminent travel company in the world. Towards this end, the company announced in the following year that it would nearly triple the number of hotels it owned, from 200 to 550, within the next few years.

In 1988 Carlson Companies underwent a corporate reorganization that resulted in the formation of Carlson Holdings, Inc., a parent company governance for all the properties of the Carlson family. This company consisted of three divisions: one to manage the family's investments, one to handle commercial real estate scattered throughout North America, and the third made up of Carlson Companies. The Companies moved into a new corporate headquarters in 1989, two gleaming towers of glass on the Carlson land west of Minneapolis in the suburb of Minnetonka. Shortly thereafter, as if to symbolize that a new era had begun with the company's move into new quarters, Curt Carlson staged a ceremony in the rotunda of the new building, turning over the reins of the company to his son-in-law Skip Gage, who took over as chief executive officer. Although a thousand employees turned out to applaud their new leader, his tenure was brief.

Under Gage's command, the company announced more ambitious plans for expansion and proceeded to extend its international holdings, purchasing A. T. Mays, a British travel agency, and changing the name of Ask Mr. Foster to Carlson Travel Network to reflect a more global outlook. Amid talk of operations in eight new countries and a goal of 3,000 worldwide travel agencies, economic reality began to intrude. In late 1990, the Carlson Travel Network was forced to put some home office employees on a shortened work week to avoid layoffs, as its business was damaged by tension over the impending Persian Gulf War, which battered the travel industry.

In 1991 the recession continued, and profits for Carlson Companies dipped. Despite the fact that he had undergone quadruple bypass heart surgery early in the year, Curt Carlson dismissed Gage, still new in his job, in November 1991 and reassumed control of the company. At the same time, Carlson promoted his eldest daughter Marilyn to vice-chairman, apparently grooming her to follow him (Gage was married to Carlson's younger daughter Barbara). Despite the decline in profits, Carlson returned to oversee a company with a small debt load, growing in its targeted industries at a furious rate. By 1992 Carlson was adding a travel agency a day to the more than 2,000 it owned, and a new hotel every ten days. It planned to double the number of T.G.I. Friday's restaurants it ran to 400 within four years. The company had operations in 38 countries, and it took to the high seas as well in May 1992, when it inaugurated service on a futuristic-looking cruise ship, the *Radisson Diamond,* through its newly formed Radisson Seven Seas Cruises luxury cruise line.

EXPANSION OF HOSPITALITY AND TRAVEL GROUPS

By the mid-1990s, Carlson Marketing Group was struggling. At that time, the group specialized in direct marketing; performance improvement programs such as incentive programs that reward top salespeople; loyalty marketing such as frequent-flyer programs; and event and sports management. This successor to the original trading stamp business generated only 5 percent of the revenue for Carlson Companies. The travel business generated 65 percent, while the hospitality operations contributed 30 percent. *Forbes* reported in October

1993 that the success of the travel and hospitality groups was at least partly attributable to Curtis Carlson allowing the heads of these groups considerable autonomy.

As head of the newly renamed Carlson Hospitality Worldwide, Bartels continued to achieve impressive, profitable growth with his consistent reliance on franchising; this trend continued under John A. Norlander, a 21-year veteran of Radisson and Carlson who took over for the departing Bartels in 1995. Friday's Hospitality Worldwide Inc., for example, had grown to more than 460 restaurants in 350 cities and 40 countries by mid-1997 and included not only the T.G.I. Friday's chain but also such spinoffs as Friday's Front Row Sports Grill and Friday's American Bar and such new concepts as Italianni's. By January 1998, Radisson Seven Seas Cruises boasted of six luxury liners with a total capacity of 1,202 berths, making it the fourth largest luxury cruise line in the world. In late 1996, Carlson formed a partnership with Four Seasons Hotels Inc. to expand the Four Seasons' Regent luxury-hotel chain. Regent had nine hotels located primarily in Asian cities; through the partnership, Carlson would concentrate on building new Regent hotels in North America and Europe.

Carlson Travel Group, meanwhile, was headed by longtime Carlson executive Travis Tanner. The 1990s were difficult ones for travel agencies and mergers became commonplace as competition heated up. Tanner engineered a merger for Carlson as well, with Carlson Travel Network linking with Paris-based Wagonlit Travel to form Carlson Wagonlit Travel (CWT) in 1994. CWT was 50-50 owned by Carlson Companies and Accor Group, a France-based company with additional interests in hotels and car rental. CWT immediately became the second largest travel agency in the world, trailing only American Express, with some 4,000 offices in more than 141 countries and annual sales in excess of $9.5 billion. After essentially operating as one agency for a couple of years, Carlson Travel and Wagonlit were formerly merged in early 1997, with headquarters in Miami, Tanner acting as chairman, and Herve Gourio, who had headed Wagonlit, as cochairman. Carlson Companies, meanwhile, created Carlson Leisure Group (CLG) to act as the U.S. licensee of the Carlson Wagonlit Travel brand name for leisure travel, as well as to oversee non-Carlson Wagonlit travel operations—for example, the 1997-launched Carlson Vacations, a leisure travel agency based in Russia. Also in 1997, CLG acquired Travel Agents International, a prominent U.S. leisure travel agency which made CLG the largest franchise travel agency company in North America, with more than 1,300 locations. In mid-1997 CLG expanded in the United Kingdom with the purchase of Inspira-

tions PLC and its 97-unit, Glasgow, Scotland–headquartered A.T. Mays travel agency, the fourth largest such agency in the United Kingdom.

ANSWERING QUESTIONS OF SUCCESSION

Systemwide revenue, which included all sales under the Carlson Companies brands whether owned or franchised operations, reached $20 billion in 1997. Previous year sales were reported as $13.4 billion. Carlson Hospitality Worldwide's hotel, restaurant, and cruise ship segment recorded its most successful year in history, according to a March 1998 *PR Newswire* release. Sales climbed 23 percent and cash flow from operations more than 50 percent. With one new location being added about every three days, the total number of locations climbed to 951 locations, in 60 countries, by year end. New among its brands were Regent International Hotels.

Carlson Companies celebrated its 60th anniversary in March 1998. During the festivities Curt Carlson named Marilyn Carlson Nelson his successor as president and CEO. Her father continued as chairman. When Curt Carlson died the following year, Carlson Nelson also took on the responsibility as chair.

In 2000 Carlson Companies' activities ranged from the acquisition of Park Plaza and Park Inn Hotel brands to the activation of customer loyalty program Gold Points' 24k.com web site. The Internet was a bustling market of shopping portals and loyalty programs by this time. The data gathering potential of the Internet lured businesses with the promise of customized marketing for individual consumers.

Carlson Companies' competition also had the potential to cross-market its customers. Cendant Corp. engaged in travel and real estate, Hyatt Hotels Corp. developed mixed-use retail, and Marriott International operated senior living facilities. Carlson itself was poised to open its first "lifestyle living complex" in 2001, according to a September 17, 2001, article in *Hotel & Motel Management*.

The terrorist attacks on New York City and Washington, D.C., on September 11, 2001 (9/11), in addition to killing thousands, levied a direct hit on the industries in which Carlson Companies operated. Consequently, systemwide sales remained flat in 2002 at $19.8 billion, according to *Travel Weekly*. While company owned and operated division sales had dropped slightly, improvements in productivity helped return operating income nearly to the level achieved in 2000.

Curtis Nelson succeeded his mother as president and COO of Carlson Companies, in early 2003. Marilyn Carlson Nelson continued as chair and CEO. Curtis Nelson's first job in the family-owned business had been as a County Kitchen restaurant dishwasher. During and after college, he held management positions with rival hotel operations before rejoining the family business. Marilyn Carlson Nelson's road to the top, by contrast, had taken years longer. Among the moves under her leadership were the reevaluation of the organizational structure and the profitable sale of British Travel firm Thomas Cook, David Saltman reported for *Chief Executive* in 2003. Externally, Nelson worked to help jump-start the struggling post-9/11 travel industry. Business and leisure travel produced 65 percent of annual sales, followed by marketing at 50 percent, and hospitality at 35 percent.

Systemwide sales climbed 5.5 percent to $20.9 billion in 2003, according to *Lodging Hospitality*. The addition of 97 hotels boosted properties to 883 operating in 67 countries by year end. Among the year's activities, Carlson Marketing Group acquired Peppers & Rogers Group, known for its customer-based business strategy expertise.

Carlson Companies announced it produced record sales during 2004. The travel and hospitality industries were on an upswing. For the following year, the *Star Tribune* reported the company's revenue as $34.4 billion. That figure did not reveal the whole picture, as David Phelps explained: "It's hard to measure the strength of Carlson Companies and its various segments because the company is closely held." Moreover, all the operations bearing the Carlson brand name factored into the figure.

Another aspect of the company became clouded as well, in 2006, when Marilyn Carlson Nelson consolidated senior management. As part of the move, the position of president of operations, held by Curtis Carlson, was eliminated. Nelson was offered the title of vice-chair, which he refused. The action placed a veil of uncertainty on leadership succession once again.

Phelps wrote, "Known for her passion for various Twin Cities civic projects, Carlson Nelson was seen initially as someone who lacked hands-on business experience. But her tenure as CEO has been viewed favorably from within the company and in the industry. She is credited with strengthening the professional management and promoting more women to positions of authority. An effective public speaker and community volunteer, Carlson Nelson was named by *Forbes* magazine as one of the 'world's most powerful women' in each of the past three years."

Meanwhile, Carlson and One Equity Partners acquired Accor's share of Carlson Wagonlit Travel, which in turn acquired Navigant International. The ad-

dition of the leading business travel firm doubled the company's North American presence.

Elizabeth Rourke
Updated, David E. Salamie; Kathleen Peippo

PRINCIPAL OPERATING UNITS

Carlson Restaurants Worldwide, Inc.; Carlson Hotels Worldwide; Carlson Marketing International Inc.; Carlson Wagonlit Travel, Inc. (55%).

PRINCIPAL COMPETITORS

American Express Company; Darden Restaurants, Inc.; Marriott International, Inc.; Gage Marketing Group; BCD Travel; Brinker International, Inc.

FURTHER READING

Andorka, Frank H., Jr., "Carlson Moves on After Leader's Death," *Hotel & Motel Management*, April 5, 1999, p. 23.

———, "Carlson Takes Changes in Stride," *Hotel & Motel Management*, April 20, 1998, pp. 3+.

Bain, Laurie, "Carlson Plays to Win," *Restaurant Business*, June 10, 1987, p. 161.

Barnfather, Maurice, "Capital Formation," *Forbes*, March 29, 1982, p. 94.

Button, Graham, "Still Hungry at 75," *Forbes*, December 11, 1989, p. 302.

"Carlson Celebrates 60 Years of Operation in Grand Style," *National Real Estate Investor*, May 1998, p. 8.

"Carlson Companies: Company Profile," *Nation's Restaurant News*, March 29, 1993.

"Carlson Companies Tops $20 Billion," *Lodging Hospitality*, May 1, 2004, p. 12.

"Carlson Cos. Tap Nelson As President, COO," *Travel Weekly*, March 10, 2003, p. 9.

Carlson, Curtis L., *Good As Gold: The Story of the Carlson Companies*, Minneapolis: Carlson Companies, Inc., 1994, 238 p.

"Curt Carlson: Will a One-Man Conglomerate Make Room at the Top?" *Business Week*, June 13, 1983.

Ellis, James E., "Curt Carlson Keeps It All in the Family," *Business Week*, September 30, 1991.

Ferguson, Tim W., "In Land of Lakes, He Cares Not if Economic Waters Are Rising," *Wall Street Journal*, October 23, 1990.

Flynn, Laurie J., "Carlson Revives Stamp Redemption Online," *New York Times*, August 28, 2000, p. C4.

Fredericks, Alan, and Nadine Godwin, "Carlson Sets $4 Billion Sales Goal for Empire of Travel Companies," *Travel Weekly*, October 8, 1997, p. 1.

Kho, Nguyen, "Life with Father," *Town & Country,* August 1992.

"Looking at the World Through Gold Glasses," *Forbes,* March 15, 1975.

McDowell, Edwin, "Mellowed by Age, but Still a Tough Boss," *New York Times,* April 5, 1992.

"1997 Was Record-Breaking Year for Carlson Companies, Inc.," *PR Newswire,* March 18, 1998.

Papa, Mary Bader, "A Son Named Marilyn," *Corporate Report-Minnesota,* March 1990, p. 27.

Papiernik, Richard L., and Bill Carlino, "T.G.I. Friday's Group Poised for $145M IPO," *Nation's Restaurant News,* August 30, 1999, p. 1.

Phelps, David, "Succession Shake-Up Rattles Carlson Cos.," *Star Tribune: Newspaper of the Twin Cities,* September 6, 2006, p. 1A.

Pine, Carol, and Susan Mundale, *Self-Made: The Stories of 12 Minnesota Entrepreneurs,* Minneapolis: Dorn Books.

Quintanilla, Carl, "Carlson Pushes Growth Despite Woes in Travel Industry," *Wall Street Journal,* March 9, 1995, p. B4.

Rowe, Megan, "Carlson's Culture," *Lodging Hospitality,* October 1996, pp. 26–28.

Salomon, Alan, "Hoteliers Diversify to Thrive," *Hotel & Motel Management,* September 17, 2001, p. 74.

Saltman, David, "Global Heavyweight: Marilyn Carlson Nelson Waited Nearly a Lifetime to Become CEO of Carlson Cos.," *Chief Executive,* August–September 2003, pp. 40+.

Stern, William, "Hanging On," *Forbes,* October 25, 1993, pp. 194, 198.

Walker, Angela, "Global Goals Power Carlson Wagonlit," *Hotel & Motel Management,* April 25, 1994, p. 6.

Weissmann, Arnie, "In a Family Way," *Travel Weekly,* September 1, 2003, p. 67.

White, Willmon L., *The Ultra Entrepreneur: Carl Carlson,* Phoenix: Gullers Pictorial, [1988], 139 p.

Wieffering, Eric J., "Carlson Companies: Smaller Than You Thought, Revisited," *Corporate Report-Minnesota,* May 1993, p. 44.

Chaoda Modern Agriculture (Holdings) Ltd.

———————■———————

Rm. 2705 27th Fl., China Resources Bldg.
26 Harbour Road
Wanchai,
Hong Kong
Telephone: (+852 0591) 8783 5933
Fax: (+852 0591) 8783 3208
Web site: http://www.chaoda.com

Public Company
Incorporated: 1994
Employees: 14,384
Sales: RMB 2.8 billion ($349.2 million) (2006)
Stock Exchanges: Hong Kong
Ticker Symbol: 0682
NAIC: 445110 Supermarkets and Other Grocery (Except Convenience) Stores; 112990 All Other Animal Production; 311421 Fruit and Vegetable Canning; 551112 Offices of Other Holding Companies

■ ■ ■

Chaoda Modern Agriculture (Holdings) Ltd. is China's leading producer of organic fruits, vegetables, livestock, cereals, teas, and other items for both the mainland and international market. The Fujian Province-based company, which is registered in the Cayman Islands and listed on the Hong Kong Stock Exchange, has also played an important role in helping to modernize China's vast agricultural sector. Avoiding the more polluted industrial areas, Chaoda has acquired thousands of small-scale farms, combining them into a total of more than 18,500 hectares of cropland, spanning 14 provinces. The company produces more than 150 species of fruits and vegetables, delivering more than 1.1 million tons per year, processed through 29 production centers. Much of the group's production is destined for the export market, and especially to Japan and Hong Kong, where the company's organic and/or "green" labeled produce command premium prices. The company has also launched exports to the European Union, starting with tangerines to the Netherlands in 2004. Since the early 2000s, Chaoda has also been developing its livestock and dairy operations, importing high-yield dairy cows from Australia as part of a breeding program. A major brand in China, Chaoda also operates its own chain of fruit and vegetable shops in the mainland. Agricultural products remain the company's primary revenue generator, accounting for 90 percent of its turnover of RMB 2.8 billion ($349.2 million) in 2006. Founder Kwok Ho remains company chairman as well as its largest shareholder, with a 35.33 percent stake in the company.

LAUNCHING CHINA'S GREEN REVOLUTION IN 1994

The agricultural community was one of the earliest targeted for reform during the change in Chinese economic policies under Deng Xiaoping in the late 1970s. Under the new reform policies, the government fazed out the previous communal farming model and its notoriously low production yields. Instead, the new reforms put into place a new farming model based on individual responsibility. Farming families were then given their own plots of land, assigned to them by local

COMPANY PERSPECTIVES

In these few years, we have established a comprehensive quality control system for agricultural produce, realizing unpolluted control of agricultural produce along the entire process from cultivation to consumption and creating a "Green and Organic Ecological Industrial Chain."

village authorities. These plots were generally quite small, often no more than 1.5 hectares. Farmers were given the right to grow cash crop vegetables and fruit, which they could sell at market or to wholesalers at a profit. At the same time, however, farmers were also required to respect certain quota requirements, notably for the production of cereals, rices, and other grains vital to the government's self-sufficiency goals.

The new model did indeed result in often significant production gains. However, farmers remained hampered by government-imposed pricing controls, and especially by the small sizes of their farms. Nonetheless, China's agricultural activity took off through the 1980s and into the early 1990s, transforming the country into the world's single largest agricultural region, responsible for some 40 percent of total world crop production.

In the meantime, China's race to industrialize its economy and near total disregard for environmental concerns resulted in the massive contamination of much of the country's most populated regions. The pollution of the country's rivers, groundwater, air, and soil inevitably led to a series of disasters and food-related health scandals in the early 1990s. In response, the Chinese government began developing a new series of more environmentally favorable farming and food standards, ranging from the less restrictive "green" label to the organic food standards in line with those found in the West.

The potential of this new market attracted a number of China's growing ranks of would-be entrepreneurs. Among them was Kwok Ho, son of a high-level People's Liberation Army (PLA) officer. Ho's father had been among those who successfully routed the Nationalist Party from the southern province of Fujian, and Ho himself was originally destined to join the country's military elite. Ho left school after completing only the elementary level, and at the age of 14 went to work in a factory owned by the PLA. Ho later experienced the farming life first hand when he, like many of his contemporaries, was forced into the fields

during the Cultural Revolution. Ho's connections within the PLA, which, in addition to its military and defense role, grew into one of China's largest industrial conglomerates, enabled him to launch a business of his own, that of importing and distributing integrated circuits. The reform and liberalization of the Chinese economy during the 1980s gave a boost to Ho's business, and by the beginning of the 1990s, Ho ranked among the country's wealthiest.

The government's decision to devalue the yuan in the early 1990s, however, cut sharply into the country's import trade. Ho's business too suffered from the downturn, and forced him to look elsewhere for his investment interests. The growing concern over the country's food supply attracted Ho's attention, as well as the highly fragmented, inefficient farming system in place throughout the country. The promise of further reforms, which enabled the company to negotiate with villages, rather than directly with farmers, were to make it easier for the company to negotiate land acquisitions. Ho recognized that by acquiring leases on farms (in China, all land remained the property of the state), he could institute a new type of farming model, largely inspired by the mass farming techniques deployed in the United States over the previous fifty years. Yet, given the increasing health concerns over pollution in China, Ho's vision held a major difference. Rather than rely on the massive use of pesticides, chemical fertilizers, weed killers, and the like that had largely "poisoned" the U.S. food supply, Ho set out to comply with the government's "green" standards.

Ho established the Chaoda Modern Agriculture Company in 1994 and began buying up plots of land, targeting the country's most rural areas still relatively spared from the pollution of China's industrialized regions. Under Chaoda's model, farmers were allowed to work their own land or otherwise find jobs within the company; they could also choose to lease their land to Chaoda, in exchange for an annual rent. Ho also recognized the need to invest in the development of new seeds and organic fertilizers in order to produce higher yields using organic farming techniques, setting up an initial investment of $120,000.

By the end of the decade, Chaoda had established itself as the leading producer of organic and green fruits and vegetables in China. The company's steady land acquisitions had enabled the company to boost its total acreage to 224 hectares in 1999, and again to more than 1,300 hectares in 2000. This expansion was aided by the runup to China's entry into the World Trade Organization, slated for the early years of the 2000s, when the country's agricultural sector would be opened to foreign

```
┌─────────────────────────────────────────┐
│                                         │
│           KEY DATES                     │
│              ■                          │
│  ─────────────────────────────────────  │
│  1994:  Kwok Ho founds Chaoda Modern    │
│         Agriculture Company in order to │
│         produce fruits and vegetables   │
│         for China's "green" and         │
│         organic sectors.                │
│  2000:  Chaoda goes public with listing │
│         on Hong Kong Stock Exchange;    │
│         total acreage tops              │
│         1,300 hectares.                 │
│  2006:  Chaoda's total acreage tops     │
│         18,500, as company announces    │
│         plans to double its acre-       │
│         age in near future.             │
│                                         │
└─────────────────────────────────────────┘
```

competition for the first time. This prospect in turn stimulated a widespread consolidation among the country's farms.

PUBLIC OFFERING IN 2000

Chaoda was not alone in vying for the country's organic foods market. By the beginning of the 2000s, the country counted nearly 750 companies working within the organic and/or green market, including an increasing number of food processing groups. Chaoda nonetheless remained the segment's leader, and also became the first of the country's agricultural groups to go public. In 2000, the company, registered in the Cayman Islands, listed its stock on the Hong Kong Stock Exchange. The success of the listing was underscored by the presence of Hong Kong tycoon Li Ka-shing among the initial investors, with a holding of more than 6 percent of Chaoda's stock. Kwok Ho retained majority control of the company, with more than 50 percent of shares (reduced to just over 35 percent by the midpoint of the first decade of the 2000s).

Despite Chaoda's strong growth, its overall market share in China remained tiny, just 0.02 percent in 2001, attesting to the enormity of the domestic market. Yet the quality of Chaoda's produce, as well as its commitment to the country's green and organic standards, had earned it a growing international clientele. Hong Kong became an early and prominent market for the company, where it could sell its crops at significantly higher prices than on the mainland. As a result, much of the company's best produce became destined for the foreign market. By the beginning of the 2000s, Chaoda fruits and vegetables were supplied directly to Hong Kong's ParknShop Supermarket (owned by Li Ka-shing) and Wellcome chains, as well as to a growing number of the island's wholesalers. Japan also became a major

export market for the company. By mid-2006, more than 30 percent of the group's production was destined for overseas markets.

In the mainland, the company sought continued expansion as well. In 2001, for example, the company finally broke into the important Beijing market, where an estimated 60 percent of all fruits and vegetables were contaminated, through a partnership with a local green distributor. By the end of that year, the company's revenues had grown to $72 million, and its payroll had swollen to 4,000. The company itself was described by *Businessweek* as "emblematic of where the government wants agriculture to go." Where much of the rest of the country's agriculture remained mired in the inefficient methods of the past, Chaoda had become highly profitable, and extremely competitive; indeed, in the mainland, the company boasted that it was able to maintain pricing of its organic produce at levels of the nonorganic market.

DIVERSIFICATION IN THE NEW CENTURY

In 2003, the Chinese completed a new round of reforms that provided for the further liberalization of the agricultural market. Major features of the new reforms included the dropping of requirements that all farms produce wheat, corn, and rice. The government also liberalized pricing, opened up new domestic markets, as well as stimulating the growth of the country's export market. Chaoda also took advantage of the government's backing of research and development efforts, and the company's own R&D budget grew to represent 5 percent of its total revenues.

Into the new century, Chaoda had increasingly sought to diversify its operations. The company launched its own chain of fruit and vegetable stores in 2000. By the end of 2001, the company owned 130 retail stores and ten wholesale markets, covering most of the country's major cities in the south and east. Chaoda also entered the production of organic fertilizers, and by the early 2000s operated 20 factories; the company also began working with the Fujian Academy of Agricultural Sciences to develop organic pesticides. Chaoda also began trading livestock, and entered dairy production at the beginning of the decade.

Chaoda hit a temporary snag in 2002, when its auditor, PricewaterhouseCoopers, refused to endorse its annual report. The company was also accused by some of misleading investors by claiming its production as organic. According to one source, however, some 90 percent of the company's production was more accurately described as conforming to the Chinese government's "green" standard, less stringent than the organic norms established in the West. Chaoda's troubles were compounded by its difficulties achieving promised growth rates of 30 to 60 percent. As a result, the investment community soured on the company and its share price plunged.

Into the middle of the first decade of the 2000s, Chaoda largely overcame investor hesitation, in part through its continued strong growth. By the end of 2003, the company had increased its total acreage to more than 11,000 hectares, and boosted its number of production facilities to 36 factories in 11 provinces. The company had successfully entered the market for high-end teas, while at the same further expanding its export market, including its first sales in the European market, of tangerines to the Netherlands, in 2004. In that year, the company moved to transform the Chinese dairy industry, importing more than 600 dairy cows from Australia as part of an effort to breed new high-yield cattle for the domestic market. In 2005, the company launched plans to develop a new cattle facility in Upper Mongolia with a planned capacity of up to 30,000 dairy cows.

In the meantime, the rapid consolidation of the Chinese agricultural market was further reflected in Chaoda's own growth. By the end of 2006, the company's total land area had soared past 18,500 hectares. In that year, the company announced plans to double that total before the end of the decade. By then, too, the company, considered one of the top brand names in its category in China, had raised its market share. Yet, with just 2 percent of the world's single largest agricultural market, Chaoda appeared ripe for continued growth into the future.

M. L. Cohen

PRINCIPAL SUBSIDIARIES

Chaoda Vegetable & Fruits Limited (Hong Kong); Desire Star (Fujian) Development Company Limited; Fujian Chaoda Green Agriculture Development Company Limited; Fujian Chaoda Liancheng Foodstuffs Company Limited; Fujian Chaoda Livestock Company Limited; Fuzhou Chaoda Modern Agriculture Development Company Limited; Huge Market Investments (British Virgin Islands); Inner Mongolia Chaoda Stock-breeding Co., Ltd; Insight Decision Limited (British Virgin Islands); Jiangxi Nanfeng Chaoda Fruits Company Limited; Timor Enterprise Limited (British Virgin Islands); Worthy Year Investments (British Virgin Islands).

FURTHER READING

"Chaoda for 200mn Yuan Livestock Venture," *Standard,* June 15, 2004.

Chung, Olivia, "Chaoda Plans to Diversify with High-End Teas," *Standard,* December 20, 2003.

Gu, Amy, "Chaoda Targets Dairy Market," *Standard,* October 22, 2005.

"Hong Kong Listed Chaoda Modern Agri Rating Upgraded to Ba2 from Ba3—Moody's," *AFX Asia (Focus),* March 1, 2007.

"Investors Forget Past Fears As Chaoda Reaps $1.3bn of Orders," *Euroweek,* February 4, 2005, p. 18.

Leemaster, Tim, "Chaoda Sells $1.3b Bonds to Fund Land Expansion," *Standard,* April 5, 2006.

Lo, Ken, "Chaoda Commits to Vegetable Processing Investment," *South China Morning Post,* November 26, 2005.

McConnell, Brook, "Ignore the Critics, Chaoda Is Good for the Long Run," *South China Morning Post,* September 24, 2006.

———, "Large-Scale Production Puts Chaoda in Front," *South China Morning Post,* April 11, 2004.

Oliver, Chris, "Chaoda Cream of the Crop on Mainland," *South China Morning Post,* July 31, 2005.

Roberts, Dexter, "Chaoda's Green Revolution," *Business Week,* September 10, 2001.

Stone, Andy, and Su-Ching Jean Chen, "The Industrialized Peasant," *Forbes,* January 8, 2007, p. 122.

China Automotive Systems Inc.

No. 1 Henglong Road
Yuqiao Development Zone
Shashi District
Jing Zhou City, Hubei Province 434000
China
Telephone: (+86 27) 5981 8527
Fax: (+86 71) 6832 9298
Web site: http://www.caasauto.com

Public Company
Incorporated: 1992 as Ji Long Enterprise Investment
  Limited
Employees: 1,965
Sales: $87.02 million (2006)
Stock Exchanges: NASDAQ
Ticker Symbol: CAAS
NAIC: 336399 All Other Motor Vehicle Parts
  Manufacturing

■ ■ ■

China Automotive Systems Inc. (CAAS) is one of that country's leading developers and manufacturers of power steering systems for the Chinese automotive market. The Jingzhou City-based group serves as a holding company controlling Great Genesis Holdings Ltd. That company owns 100 percent of Hong Kong-based Ji Long Enterprise Investment Limited, which in turn oversees the group's mainland holdings. These are composed entirely of a series of joint ventures, primarily established with foreign partners. The oldest joint venture is Shashi Jiulong Power Steering, founded in 1992, which produces power steering assemblies primarily for the light truck market. CAAS controls 81 percent of that company. Other holdings include Jingzhou Henglong Automotive Parts Co., Ltd., held at 44.5 percent, which produces rack and pinion power steering gears for cars and light duty vehicles; Shenyang Jinbei Henglong Automotive Steering System Co., Ltd., held at 70 percent, a producer of power steering parts; Zhejiang Henglong & Vie Pump-Manu Co., Ltd. (51 percent), which produces power steering pumps; and Universal Sensor Application Inc. (60 percent), which develops power steering sensor components in partnership with the United States' Sensor System Solution Inc. The company's most recent joint ventures include Wuhu Henglong Auto Steering Systems (77.3 percent), formed in partnership with a subsidiary of fast-growing automobile manufacturer Chery Automobile; and Wuhan Jielong Electric Power Steering Co. Ltd., held at 85 percent, which develops and produces electric power steering components.

CAAS focuses its production on the high-end components market, and supplies all of China's major automobile manufacturers, including the GM joint venture SAIC GM Wuling Automotive Co. Ltd. China Automotive Systems listed its stock on the NASDAQ via a reverse merger in 2003. The company is led by Chairman and CEO Hanlin Chen. Chen, a founding member of the company, claims to hold an M.B.A. from defunct Barrington University, described by the Government Accountability Office's Office of Special Investigations as a "diploma mill." In 2006, CAAS generated total sales of $87 million.

COMPANY PERSPECTIVES

CAAS' broad spectrum, high quality and reasonable price products, strong R & D capabilities and leading position will support it for continuous growth and to become an international power steering system supplier in the future.

1993: POWER STEERING PIONEER

China Automotive Systems Inc. (CAAS) originated as a holding company, Ji Long Enterprise Investment Limited, established in Hong Kong in 1992 in order to develop automotive components joint ventures on the Chinese mainland. Ji Long in turn was owned by the mainland-based Great Genesis Holding Company. Under Chinese ownership laws, the automobile market remained strictly limited, with foreign ownership restricted to less than 50 percent. Foreign ownership of automotive components producers, however, was not subject to the same restrictions, and therefore provided an attractive vehicle for foreign investors eager to gain a share of the soon-to-boom Chinese automotive market.

Nonetheless, for its first joint venture, Ji Long found a mainland partner, Hubei Military. The companies established Shashi Jiulong Power Steering Co. Ltd., held at 81 percent by Ji Long. By 1993, that company had launched production of power steering gears for the truck market. The joint venture's main customer at that time was China First Auto, in Changchun.

Hanlin Chen, who later served among other capacities as a board member of the Political Consulting Committee of Jingzhou City, and as vice-president of the Foreign Investors Association in Hubei Province, was named as the joint venture's general manager. Chen later claimed to have earned an M.B.A. from controversial distance-learning start-up Barrington University, nominally based in Alabama, in the United States. That university was later discredited, however, by the Government Accountability Office's Office of Special Investigations, which described that operation as a "diploma mill" selling diplomas "on a flat-fee basis."

The small scale of the Chinese automotive market during this period meant that the Jiulong joint venture grew only slowly in its first years. Into the mid-1990s, the company's production remained only at 200 sets per year. Starting from 1996, when the Chinese automotive industry entered its first growth phase, the Jiulong joint venture geared up its own gear production. By the end of the decade, the company's production had surged to more than 60,000 sets per year. This helped the group build its sales to $50 million by the beginning of the 2000s.

The rise of the automotive market, and Ji Long's growing manufacturing expertise, enabled the company to begin seeking to expand its production operations. In 1997, the Hong Kong-based holding vehicle established a new mainland joint venture, Jingzhou Henglong Automotive Parts Co. Ltd. The new company, held at 44.5 percent by Ji Long, targeted the car market, as well as light duty vehicles, with the production of rack and pinion power steering gears at the Jiulong factory. Following its creation, Hanlin Chen was named as chairman of Henglong as well.

The company quickly ramped up production capacity for both joint ventures, and by 2002 their combined output rate topped 230,000 sets per year. The company's extraordinary growth reflected the growth of the Chinese automotive market; by the end of 2003, production at the Jiulong and Henglong joint ventures topped 400,000 sets per year. While the company took advantage of the vast and inexpensive manual labor pool, it also launched a series of investments, spending more than $10 million to install improved and more automated production machinery. The completion of this investment program, launched in 2003, helped raise total production past 600,000 sets per year, with the potential to reach as much as one million sets per year.

2003: TAPPING THE U.S. INVESTMENT MARKET

The Great Genesis/Ji Long group had by then sought new production opportunities. In 2002, the company entered two more joint venture partnerships. The first of these was Shengyang Jinbei Henglong Auto-Steering System Co., in partnership with Shengyang Jinbei Automobile, with Ji Long controlling the majority stake of 70 percent. That company in turn was part of Brilliance Auto, one of China's leading automakers. The Shengyang joint venture specialized in the production of rack and pinion steering gears, and launched production on a 35,000-square-meter facility that same year. The second joint venture created that year was Zhejiang Henglong & Vie Pump Manufacturing Co., Ltd. Held at 51 percent by Ji Long, that company expanded the group's power steering components production range to include power steering pumps.

With the Chinese automotive industry growing by nearly 40 percent per year in the early years of the new century, Great Genesis/Ji Long sought to expand its

---

KEY DATES

1992: Hanlin Chen establishes Ji Long Enterprise Investment Limited; first joint venture, Shashi Jiulong Power Steering, launches production of power steering gears.

1997: Company creates power steering pump joint venture Jingzhou Henglong Automotive Parts Co. Ltd.

2003: Company goes public through reverse merger into U.S.-based Visions in Glass, and changes name to China Automotive Systems.

2006: China Automotive establishes two power steering components joint ventures, Wuhu Henglong Auto Steering Systems and Wuhan Jielong Electric Steering Systems Co.

2007: Company opens U.S. distribution and sales office in Detroit, Michigan.

---

capital base. In 2003, the company completed a reverse merger with a dormant U.S.-based company, Visions-in-Glass, Inc., which had been founded in 1999 as a web-based distributor of custom-designed stain glass and related items. After listing on the NASDAQ, however, Visions-in-Glass had largely ceased to exist. The reverse merger agreement, a controversial but not uncommon maneuver among companies seeking rapid access to investment capital, provided for Visions-in-Glass to acquire Great Genesis Holdings. Following the transaction, the company changed its name to China Automotive Systems Inc. Ji Long remained the company's holding vehicle for its joint ventures.

The public offering enabled Hanlin Chen and CAAS to envision growth beyond the Chinese market to include operations supplying the North American, European, and Korean automotive markets as well. For the time being, however, the company's expansion efforts focused on the Chinese market, which in less than ten years had risen to the ranks of the world's third largest automobile market.

In 2003, CAAS made a brief foray outside of the automotive market, forming the Jingzhou Henglong Fulida Textile Co., Ltd., environmental textiles joint venture. By the middle of the following year, however, the company decided to refocus itself around its steering and automotive components operations, and disposed of its holding in the textiles business to another vehicle owned by Hanlin Chane, Hubei Wanlong Investment Co.

In 2003, the company joined with Tsinghua University in order to found a research institute devoted toward developing electronic power steering and electronic hydraulic steering systems. Both technologies were expected to play an important role in providing greater fuel economy and environmental protection in the future. The following year, the company established a technology joint venture with Advanced Custom Sensors, of Irvine, California, to develop and produce sensors for automotive control systems. Production of the joint venture was slated to start in 2005. This joint venture was followed in 2005 by a second technology joint venture, with Sensor System Solutions, Inc., also based in Irvine.

CAAS's rise as a major producer of power steering components had in the meantime made it an important partner not only with nearly all of the major Chinese automakers, but also with the increasing number of foreign automakers establishing operations in the country. In 2004, for example, CAAS's international profile received a giant boost when it was named as the exclusive steering pump supplier to SAIC GM Wuling Co., established by the U.S. automaker to produce its Spark 1.0 vehicle for the Chinese market. Similarly, in 2005 the company entered an agreement to supply power steering components for the new Chinese-built Peugeot 206 launched in that country by the French automotive giant.

CAAS formed two new joint ventures in 2006. The first of these came with Chery Automobile Co., one of the fastest-growing non-state-owned automakers in China, to supply power steering components and systems. That joint venture was named Wuhu Henglong Auto Steering Systems, and began construction of a factory in Wuhu, Anhui, China. The second joint venture, Wuhan Jielong Electric Steering Systems Co., was set up with minority partner Hong Kong Tongda, in order to produce electric power steering systems and components. The company expected that operation to launch production by 2007, ramping up to full capacity of 300,000 sets per year by 2011.

As it entered the second half of the first decade of the 2000s, CAAS began seeking to make good on its international expansion objectives. The company began working with a venture capital firm in the United States seeking potential takeover targets, in part to acquire technology, but also to acquire customer contracts in that market. By 2006, the company had spotted a number of candidates, and had even signed a letter of intent for one purchase.

The company's first move into the United States, however, came at the beginning of 2007, with the opening of an office in Detroit, Michigan. As Hanlin Chen stated in a company press release: "We are very excited about the opening of our first office in the overseas market. We hope to leverage the resources available in the United States to upgrade our product quality, enhance new product R&D and extend our leadership in the Chinese domestic market." China Automotive Systems appeared ready to move into high gear as a major Chinese automotive components manufacturer.

M. L. Cohen

PRINCIPAL SUBSIDIARIES

Jingzhou Henglong Automotive Parts Co. Ltd. (44.5%); Shashi Jiulong Power Steering Co. Ltd. (81%); Shenyang Jinbei Auto Steering Systems Co. Ltd. (70%); Universal Sensors Inc. (60%); Wuhan Jielong Electric Power Steering Co. Ltd. (85%); Wuhu Henglong Auto Steering Systems (77.3%); Zhejiang Henglong & VIE Pump Co. Ltd. (51%).

PRINCIPAL COMPETITORS

Yuejin Motor Group; Shanghai Automotive Industry Corp.; Zonda Group; Xinxiang Yituo Ltd; Shanghai Huizhong Automobile Manufacture Company Ltd.; Jintan Changjiang Automobile Parts Factory; Dongfeng Auto Company Limited; Loudi Huada Automobile Gear Factory; Henan Jianghe Machinery Factory; Zhuhai National Motor Company Ltd; Dongfeng (Liuzhou) Automobile Company Ltd.; Shanghai Hezhong Automobile Parts Co.

FURTHER READING

"China Automotive Receives Steering System Development Contract from Dongfeng Peugeot Citroen China," *PrimeZone Media Network,* June 28, 2005.

"China Automotive Systems Inc. Planning an Office in Detroit," *Automotive News,* February 19, 2007, p. 32.

"China Automotive Systems, Inc. Signs Letter of Intent for Joint Venture with Advanced Custom Sensors, Seeks to Address Growing Demand for Sensor Technology in China," *PrimeZone Media Network,* August 3, 2004.

"China Automotive Systems Opens US Office," *just-auto.com,* February 6, 2007.

"China Automotive Systems Selected As Exclusive Supplier for Steering Pumps for General Motors Joint Venture in China, Also Selected by Dong Feng Liuzhou Motor Co. As Supplier," *PrimeZone Media Network,* November 29, 2004.

"Chinese Companies Look to Buy US Distribution Assets," *Mergers & Acquisitions Report,* June 5, 2006.

Joshi, Vijay, "China Automotive Soars on GM Venture Supply Deal," *CBS Marketwatch,* November 29, 2004.

Saint-Seine, Sylviane de, "China Made 206 to Get Local Steering System," *Automotive News Europe,* July 11, 2005, p. 1.

Citizens Financial Group, Inc.

One Citizens Plaza
Providence, Rhode Island 02903-1339
U.S.A.
Telephone: (401) 456-7000
Fax: (401) 455-5715
Web site: http://www.citizensbank.com

Wholly Owned Subsidiary of The Royal Bank of Scotland Group plc
Incorporated: 1871 as Citizens Savings Bank
Employees: 25,000
Total Assets: $160.83 billion (2006)
NAIC: 551111 Offices of Bank Holding Companies; 522110 Commercial Banking; 522120 Savings Institutions

∎ ∎ ∎

Citizens Financial Group, Inc., is a leading commercial bank holding company in the New England, Mid-Atlantic, and Midwest regions, and it ranked as the ninth largest commercial bank in the United States in terms of assets in late 2006. Wholly owned by The Royal Bank of Scotland Group plc, Citizens Financial owns retail banks in 13 states, operating more than 1,600 branches and approximately 3,100 ATMs. Citizens concentrates mainly on consumer, small-business, commercial, and corporate banking customers. It is ranked number two nationwide in both supermarket banking and U.S. Small Business Administration lending and number nine in commercial bank assets.

The group, which traces its origins back to the founding of Providence, Rhode Island-based High Street Bank in 1828, had assets of only about $1.5 billion when it went public in 1985. After being acquired by The Royal Bank of Scotland in 1988, Citizens began a period of spectacularly rapid growth through acquisition following the appointment of Lawrence K. Fish as chairman and CEO in 1992. Originally located in New England, Citizens made its big move into the Mid-Atlantic region through the 2001 acquisition of the regional banking business of Mellon Financial Corporation for $2.1 billion and into the Midwest via the 2004 purchase of Charter One Financial, Inc., for $10.5 billion. These and numerous smaller deals catapulted Citizens into the ranks of the top ten U.S. banks, with total assets of more than $160 billion.

19TH-CENTURY BEGINNINGS AS HIGH STREET BANK AND CITIZENS SAVINGS BANK

High Street Bank, which was chartered as a commercial bank, was founded in 1828 in Providence, Rhode Island's Hoyle Square, at the time one of the city's busiest intersections for travelers from the nearby manufacturing towns and from the countryside. Hoyle Square was named after the Hoyle Tavern, a very popular locale in the city, while the bank took its name from its offices, which were located in two rooms of a residence on High Street.

With Rhode Island serving as one of the main industrial areas of New England in the mid-19th century, competition was fierce in the commercial banking sector. Eventually, as the need for banks serving ordinary citizens increased, the directors of High Street Bank decided to branch out. In 1871 they obtained a second charter from the Rhode Island legislature that established Citizens Savings Bank, a mutual savings bank. Jessie Grant, the daughter of the bank's vice-president, made the first deposit into the bank on April 19 of that year, and by the end of the year the new bank had deposits of $52,000. The next 50 years consisted of a period of slow growth for both Citizens Savings and the Hoyle Square neighborhood as Providence's position as an industrial center and seaport deteriorated. By the early 1920s, the bank's future seemed more promising, so the bank built a new headquarters on the site of Hoyle Tavern, which had been torn down in 1890.

The Great Depression of the 1930s hit New England hard, with Rhode Island suffering particularly from the ongoing decline of its important textile industries. Citizens Savings saw its deposits decline and had to contend with increased numbers of defaulted mortgages, but because the bank's lending practices were fairly prudent, its travails were not as severe as those of many other financial institutions.

Recovery and change came during the 1940s. In 1943 Citizens Savings gained the ability to acquire stock in High Street Bank because of a change in Rhode Island investment law. Citizens quickly gained full control of its former parent, foiling an attempt by a High Street stockholder to take control of High Street Bank. In 1947 High Street Bank relocated its offices to those of Citizens Savings. One year later, High Street Bank was renamed Citizens Trust Company.

Citizens began developing a branch network in 1947, when it opened an office in Cranston, Rhode Island. Three years later the bank became a member of the Federal Deposit Insurance Corporation (FDIC). It was the first mutual savings bank to do so. Expansion continued in 1954 with the acquisition of Greenville

Trust Company. This added two more branches as well as assets of more than $8 million. Growth continued throughout the 1960s and 1970s. By 1971 Citizens Savings was the 80th largest mutual savings bank in the United States. Ten years later, the bank was operating 29 branches throughout Rhode Island, and assets totaled $971 million.

1981–92: EMERGENCE OF CITIZENS AS UNIT OF THE ROYAL BANK OF SCOTLAND

Also in 1981, George Graboys was named CEO of the bank. Graboys had practiced law before joining his family's asset-based lending company, U.S. Finance Corp., in the mid-1960s. After Citizens acquired U.S. Finance in 1969, Graboys began working within the commercial bank unit, then was elected president of Citizens Savings in 1975. It was during Graboys' tenure as CEO of Citizens that the bank would be transformed into a more modern financial institution as well as trade its independence for the security of a deep-pocketed parent.

Citizens avoided the fate of other savings and loan institutions during the disastrous and criminal savings and loan crisis of the 1980s by sticking to its conservative business and lending practices. Graboys did, however, respond surely to the key events of the decade for financial institutions: the deregulation of interest rates, the removal of interstate barriers, and increased competition. He sought to expand his bank's loan and retail banking businesses outside of Rhode Island and to engage in all aspects of retail banking and middle-market corporate lending. In 1983 the bank opened its first commercial loan office outside of Rhode Island, locating it in Boston. To prepare to convert from a mutual savings bank to a stock savings bank, Citizens Bank became a federal savings bank in October 1984. Then in mid-1985, Citizens Financial Group, Inc., was created as a bank holding company for both Citizens Bank and Citizens Trust. Citizens Financial then sold 4.3 million shares of common stock at $23 per share in an initial public offering. The new holding company began its existence with assets of $1.6 billion. The holding company structure enabled the group to move into other financial services businesses and into other geographic markets.

Graboys began using the proceeds from the stock offering to fund acquisitions. In 1986 the group acquired Gulf States Mortgage Company, an Atlanta-based residential mortgage origination and service firm with a loan portfolio of just over $1 billion. The new subsidiary was later renamed Citizens Mortgage

KEY DATES

1828: High Street Bank is chartered as a commercial bank based in Providence, Rhode Island.

1871: Directors of High Street Bank obtain a second charter for Citizens Savings Bank, a mutual savings bank.

1943: Citizens Savings gains control of High Street Bank, its former parent.

1947: Citizens begins developing a branch network.

1948: High Street Bank is renamed Citizens Trust Company.

1950: Citizens joins the Federal Deposit Insurance Corporation (FDIC), becoming the first mutual savings bank to do so.

1981: Citizens is operating 29 branches throughout Rhode Island and has assets of $971 million; George Graboys takes over as CEO.

1985: Citizens Financial Group, Inc., is created as a bank holding company for both Citizens Bank and Citizens Trust; Citizens Financial is then taken public.

1988: Fairhaven Savings Bank is acquired and becomes base for Citizens Bank of Massachusetts; The Royal Bank of Scotland Group plc acquires Citizens Financial, which begins operating as a wholly owned subsidiary.

1990: Citizens acquires Old Colony, the Rhode Island subsidiary of Bank of New England.

1992: Lawrence K. Fish is named chairman and CEO.

1993: Citizens enters the Connecticut market with the purchase of New England Savings, which becomes the base for Citizens Bank of Connecticut; Boston Five Bancorp, operating in the Boston area, is acquired.

1994: Neworld Bancorp and Old Stone Federal Savings Bank are acquired.

1996: Citizens Financial merges with First NH Bank (owned by Bank of Ireland), which is renamed Citizens Bank New Hampshire; Bank of Ireland now holds 23.5 percent stake in Citizens Financial, Royal Bank holds 76.5 percent stake.

1998: Royal Bank of Scotland pays Bank of Ireland $750 million to regain full control of Citizens Financial.

1999: Citizens acquires the retail banking unit of Boston-based State Street Corporation.

2000: Boston-based UST Corporation is acquired.

2001: Citizens acquires the regional banking business of Mellon Financial Corporation, including 345 branches in Pennsylvania, Delaware, and New Jersey, for $2.1 billion.

2004: Citizens moves into the Midwest via a $10.5 billion takeover of Charter One Financial, Inc.

2007: Stephen D. Steinour is named CEO of Citizens Financial, succeeding Fish, who remains chairman.

Corporation. In July 1988 Citizens Financial completed its first acquisition of a retail bank located outside Rhode Island by spending $39 million for Fairhaven Savings Bank, which was based in Fairhaven, Massachusetts, and had five branches in the southeastern portion of that state and $288 million in assets. Fairhaven Savings became the initial building block for Citizens Bank of Massachusetts, which would eventually become the group's largest retail banking unit.

By 1988 Citizens Financial was the fifth largest bank in New England but was far smaller than the top four at the time: Bank of Boston, Fleet Financial Group, Bank of New England, and Shawmut National. Graboys believed that Citizens needed to ally itself with a larger company if it were to have any chance of competing against its much larger rivals. At the same time, however, Graboys wished to keep his bank at least semi-independent. The solution to this dilemma was for Citizens to be acquired by a foreign bank that would allow it to operate as a separate U.S. bank. That bank turned out to be the Edinburgh-based Royal Bank of Scotland Group plc, which at the time was the sixth largest U.K. bank with assets of more than $36 billion. The Royal Bank paid about $440 million for Citizens in a transaction that was completed in December 1988. Citizens would be able to tap into the deep pockets of its new parent to fund further growth, while The Royal Bank gained a platform for U.S. expansion.

The well-run Royal Bank also helped Citizens survive a turbulent period for New England banking in the late 1980s and early 1990s, following the collapse of the New England real estate market and the resulting wave of loan defaults. Both Bank of New England and Bank of Boston fell into serious financial difficulties in the early 1990s; the former failed and was taken over by Fleet in 1991.

Citizens Financial began the 1990s by moving into a new 13-story headquarters called One Citizens Plaza. The building was located in downtown Providence at the confluence of the Moshassuck and Woonasquatucket rivers. Citizens' desire for growth through acquisition was initially stymied by the crisis in New England banking. A number of acquisition targets were dropped from consideration because of the level of nonperforming loans in their portfolios. In fact, Citizens reached an agreement to acquire BankWorcester Corporation of Worcester, Massachusetts, for $149 million in early 1990, only to pull out of the deal later in the year because of the growing size of BankWorcester's nonperforming assets. Graboys nevertheless completed one acquisition in late 1990, that of Old Colony, the Rhode Island subsidiary of the troubled Bank of New England. Citizens thereby added 22 branches to its Rhode Island network of 30 branches, giving it the largest branch network in the state. Adding Old Colony's $1.2 billion in assets moved Citizens from fourth to second place in size among the state's banks. Old Colony was founded in 1803 as Newport Bank, which was the 12th bank founded in the United States.

DOUBLING IN SIZE UNDER LAWRENCE K. FISH: 1992–95

By 1992 Graboys had accomplished a quadrupling of the bank's assets during little more than a decade of leadership, to $4 billion. That year, Lawrence K. Fish succeeded Graboys as chairman and CEO. A banking veteran, Fish was a former executive at Bank of Boston who received accolades for his efforts to revive the failing Bank of New England during his brief tenure from 1990 to 1991 as chairman and CEO of the Boston-based bank. The Royal Bank of Scotland handed Fish the mission of taking a more aggressive approach to expanding its U.S. subsidiary.

Fish quickly delivered for his new bosses, completing seven acquisitions from September 1992 through January 1995, in the process increasing Citizen's assets to more than $10 billion. A number of the deals were for failed banks and savings and loans that were being liquidated by the FDIC or the Resolution Trust Corporation (RTC), a U.S. government agency set up to sell insolvent financial institutions. This was the case

with the bank acquired in September 1992, Plymouth Five Cents Savings Bank, which was acquired from the FDIC and whose eight branches doubled the size of Citizens Bank of Massachusetts. Also bought from the FDIC was New England Savings Bank, acquired in May 1993. Citizens gained its first presence in Connecticut through the purchase of New London, Connecticut-based New England Savings, which became the base for Citizens Bank of Connecticut. New England Savings had 21 branches and $695 million in assets. Later in 1993, Citizens Financial completed its largest acquisition to date, the purchase of The Boston Five Bancorp and its 22 metropolitan Boston branches for $95 million. Boston Five, which boasted assets of $1.65 billion, also had an extensive New England mortgage operation, which was added to Citizens Mortgage, doubling that subsidiary's mortgage portfolio to more than $8 billion.

During 1994 Citizens Financial completed three more acquisitions: Neworld Bancorp, Coastal Federal Savings Bank, and Old Stone Federal Savings Bank. Boston-based Neworld had 14 branches in Boston and another eight on Cape Cod, bringing Citizens Bank of Massachusetts' branch total to 55. Purchased for $144.3 million, Neworld had assets of $1.1 billion. Coastal was another failed thrift and was purchased from the RTC for $10.7 million. This added nine branches and $100 million in assets to Citizens Bank of Connecticut. Also acquired from the RTC for $133.6 million was Old Stone, which was the fourth largest bank in Rhode Island with 28 branches and assets totaling $501 million. Citizens held 29 percent of the bank deposits in its home state, second only to Fleet's 34 percent. Also in 1994, Citizens Financial became one of the last large banks to begin selling mutual funds through its branches. It formed alliances with two major Boston-based fund managers, Fidelity Investments and Putnam Cos., to sell 30 of their stock and bond funds.

In early 1995 Citizens further entrenched itself in the Massachusetts market by acquiring Quincy Savings Bank for $141 million. Quincy operated 14 branches in Boston's suburban South Shore and had assets of $813 million. This latest acquisition increased the assets of Citizens Financial to $10.3 billion, more than double the figure when Fish took over. During the same period earnings tripled to $52.7 million as Fish found success with a strategy of positioning Citizens as a service-oriented, "supercommunity" banking franchise catering to the needs of working-class customers. This approach involved more of the old-fashioned human contact than the high-tech electronic services, such as ATMs and on-line banking, that rivals were rapidly adopting as the wave of the future. This focus on community banking also led Citizens to open its first supermarket banking branches in 1995 through a deal with Shaw's Supermarkets. Later deals placed Citizens branches within such supermarkets as Stop & Shop, Star, Victory, Shop'n'Save, and Wal-Mart.

1996–2000: ACCELERATING THE PACE OF GROWTH

In April 1996 Citizens Financial merged with First NH Bank. Based in Manchester, New Hampshire, First NH was the largest financial services firm in the state, and was owned by Bank of Ireland. The Royal Bank of Scotland paid $245 million in cash and notes to Bank of Ireland, which also gained a 23.5 percent stake in Citizens. The Royal Bank retained 76.5 percent ownership of Citizens. First NH was recast as Citizens Bank New Hampshire, bringing to Citizens Financial 73 bank branches, 12 supermarket banks, and 153 ATMs. The addition of $4 billion in assets made Citizens the third largest bank in New England, trailing Fleet (which had acquired Shawmut in 1995) and Bank of Boston. Citizens also leaped into the top 50 among U.S. banks.

The newly enlarged bank completed two more significant acquisitions within the next 12 months. In November 1996 Farmers & Mechanics Bank, based in Middletown, Connecticut, was acquired for $53.2 million in cash. The purchase expanded Citizens Bank of Connecticut by 12 branches and $569 million in assets. Citizens Bank of Massachusetts grew through the March 1997 buyout of Grove Bank, which was headquartered in Chestnut Hill, Massachusetts, and had ten branches in the lucrative suburban markets west of Boston. Purchased for $87 million, Grove Bank had assets of $747 million. Also in late 1996 and early 1997, Citizens Financial exited from the mortgage servicing market, believing that its Atlanta-based mortgage servicing unit was too small to compete with large national mortgage servicers. Citizens Mortgage continued to originate and process mortgages from the bank's New England branches. In late 1996 Citizens Capital, Inc., was formed as a Boston-based subsidiary specializing in investment financing for middle-market businesses needing capital for management buyouts, expansions, and mergers. In yet another development around this same time, Citizens in January 1997 launched a four-state marketing campaign featuring the slogan "Not Your Typical Bank." The campaign was designed to emphasize the bank's strategy of being a supercommunity bank offering the personal service of a smaller, neighborhood bank in contrast to the impersonal reputations of its much larger rivals.

Continuing to fill in geographic gaps in its New England base, Citizens spent $57.2 million for Bank of New Haven in August 1997. The $350 million in assets

bank operated 11 branches in Connecticut, bringing Citizens' network in that state to 41. In August 1998 Citizens Bank of Massachusetts expanded into Boston's northern suburbs with the purchase of Woburn National Bank and its five branches and $165 million in assets. One month later, The Royal Bank of Scotland regained full control of Citizens Financial by paying Bank of Ireland $750 million for its 23.5 percent stake. In October 1998 Citizens Bank of Connecticut added four branches of Branford Savings Bank, expanding its presence in the greater New Haven area. Later that same year, Citizens sold its Visa credit-card portfolio to Bankcard Services of MBNA, one of the giants of the credit card industry. Citizens continued to offer credit cards to its customers, but the cards would be serviced by MBNA instead of the bank.

While continuing to emphasize personal, branch-based banking, Citizens in 1999 also launched Citizens Bank Online, a full-service electronic banking and bill payment service. The year was also significant because of the merger of Fleet and BankBoston that created Fleet-Boston Financial Corporation, a $190 billion financial giant that ranked as the eighth largest bank in the United States. Citizens Financial thereby gained the number two spot among New England banks but with just $18 billion in assets was dwarfed by its much larger rival. This increased the pressure on Citizens to complete more acquisitions, and it did just that. In October 1999 the bank paid $350 million to acquire State Street Corp.'s retail bank, which included four branches in Boston and Quincy, Massachusetts, and a commercial loan portfolio totaling $2.2 billion. The deal was particularly significant for its bulking up of Citizens' commercial portfolio by nearly 50 percent, to $7 billion, or one-third of its total assets of $21 billion. Citizens was well-positioned to be a major player in New England in middle-market loans to corporations, small businesses, and nonprofits.

In January 2000 Citizens Financial completed its largest acquisition to date, the $1.4 billion purchase of Boston-based UST Corporation. This deal doubled the size of Citizens Bank of Massachusetts to $14 billion in assets, adding 87 more branches to that unit. It also increased Citizens Financial's commercial loan portfolio by another $4.4 billion. Citizens also gained United States Trust Company of Boston, UST's asset management unit, which had more than $3.5 billion under management for individual and institutional investors; and Brewer & Lord, a full-service insurance agency. Overall, the State Street and UST deals helped increase Citizens Financial's assets to nearly $31 billion by the end of 2000, making the bank one of the 30 largest banks in the nation. Meanwhile, Citizens' parent had also bulked itself up during 2000, acquiring National

Westminster Bank Plc for $33 billion and becoming one of the top three banks in the United Kingdom, with total assets of nearly $500 billion. For Citizens, having a larger Royal Bank of Scotland as a parent appeared likely to open up even more avenues for growth because the U.S. unit would generate a much smaller proportion of The Royal Bank's operating earnings.

2001–03: EXPANDING INTO THE MID-ATLANTIC REGION VIA MELLON DEAL

This soon proved to be the case as Citizens Financial announced in July 2001 that it would purchase the retail banking operations of Pittsburgh-based Mellon Financial Corporation for about $2.1 billion. The deal, completed that December, was Citizens' largest yet and also its first foray outside its New England base. Included in the purchase were 345 branches in Pennsylvania, Delaware, and southern New Jersey and $13.4 billion in consumer and commercial deposits, as well as $6.1 billion in loans, mainly to small and middle-market banking customers. In addition, Citizens gained another insurance agency, Norristown, Pennsylvania-based Clair Odell Group (later renamed Citizens Clair Insurance Group). Citizens instantly became the third largest bank in Pennsylvania and with more than $53 billion in total assets was one of the 20 largest commercial banks in the United States.

The integration of the Mellon operations went remarkably smoothly. Part of the reason for this was that Citizens retained nearly the entire workforce it inherited and did not embark on the round of branch closings that had become so typical of bank mergers. Citizens worked diligently to establish the Citizens name in the new territories it was entering, and it prevented large-scale defections by Mellon customers through such bold moves as lowering fees and deposit thresholds. As a result, Citizens made a strong entrance into the Mid-Atlantic region, despite the presence of entrenched competitors, including Pittsburgh-based PNC Bank and Philadelphia-based Sovereign Bancorp, Inc.

In the 24 months following the consummation of the Mellon deal, Citizens completed a series of smaller acquisitions that served to fill in gaps in its existing territories, particularly in Massachusetts and Pennsylvania. In the fall of 2002 the group spent $273 million for Medford Bancorp Inc., which operated 19 branches and had $1.4 billion in assets. Based in Medford, Massachusetts, the acquired bank had more than 100,000 accounts centering on the high-income area of Middlesex County, just northwest of Boston.

In January 2003 Citizens strengthened its presence in the greater Philadelphia market and gained its first foothold in the Reading, Pennsylvania, region by acquiring Commonwealth Bancorp of Norristown, Pennsylvania, for $450 million. Commonwealth operated 60 branches and 61 ATMs in southeastern Pennsylvania and had $1.8 billion in assets and deposits of $1.5 billion. Next, Citizens bought its third insurance agency, the Feitelberg Company, which was headquartered in Fall River, Massachusetts, and ranked as one of the largest insurance agencies in southeastern New England. In its next two deals, Citizens further strengthened its position in Massachusetts. In July 2003 the group laid out $285 million for Port Financial Corp., parent of CambridgePort Bank, which operated 11 branches and 15 ATMs and had $1.5 billion in assets. Late in the year, Citizens acquired another Middlesex County bank, Community Bancorp, in a $116 million deal. Based in Hudson, Massachusetts, Community operated ten branches and had assets of $457 million. Citizens Financial finished 2003 with total assets of nearly $77 billion.

2004: INTO THE MIDWEST THROUGH TAKEOVER OF CHARTER ONE

The group remained on the prowl for acquisitions in 2004. Citizens began the year by completing a $136 million acquisition of Thistle Group Holdings Co., parent of Roxborough Manayunk Bank, which ran 15 branches in the Philadelphia area (including one in Delaware) and had assets of $914 million. In March Citizens acquired the Bridgeport, Connecticut-based credit card business of People's Bank for $2.7 billion. About a year later, this unit, which had a loan portfolio of more than $2 billion, began operating as RBS National Bank, a subsidiary of Citizens Financial. In September 2004, meanwhile, Citizens expanded its credit card products operations by acquiring Atlanta-based Lynk Systems, Inc., an electronic payment processing firm, for $515 million. Lynk was later renamed RBS Lynk, Incorporated. In April 2004 the Philadelphia Phillies moved into their new ballpark, which was named Citizens Bank Park as a result of a $95 million naming rights deal between Citizens and the major league baseball team.

In August 2004, in the midst of a year in which its main rival, FleetBoston, was swallowed by Bank of America Corporation in a $48 billion deal, Citizens made a major move into the Midwest—and strengthened its position in New England and the Mid-Atlantic region—via its biggest acquisition yet, a $10.5 billion takeover of Charter One Financial, Inc. Cleveland-based Charter One had been founded in 1934 as First Federal Savings and Loan Association, which was one of the nation's first S&Ls to open following passage of the Home Owners Loan Act of 1933. Over the next 50 years the thrift expanded into the suburbs of Cleveland, then in 1982 was converted from a mutual to a public company and adopted the Charter One name. In the 1990s Charter One completed a string of acquisitions of other Midwestern thrift franchises, with the most significant being the 1995 merger with FirstFed Michigan Corp. and the 1999 buyout of St. Paul Bancorp Inc., the latter of which provided the thrift entrée into the lucrative Chicago market. In May 2002 Charter One converted itself from a thrift into a nationally chartered bank.

By the time of its takeover by Citizens Financial, Charter had assets of $41.3 billion and a workforce of 8,400 and was operating 616 branches in Ohio, Michigan, Illinois, Indiana, New York, Massachusetts, Vermont, Connecticut, and Pennsylvania. In the Midwestern states of Ohio, Michigan, Illinois, and Indiana, the acquired branches continued to operate under the Charter One name; they were managed out of a midwestern headquarters in Cleveland. The branches in the other states were converted to the Citizens Bank banner. The Charter One acquisition boosted Citizens Financial's asset base to $131 billion, making it the 12th largest commercial bank holding company in the United States, and increased its retail network to more than 1,530 branches and approximately 2,700 ATMs. It ranked as the ninth largest bank based on its deposits of more than $88 billion.

During 2005, when integration of Charter One took center stage, Citizens trimmed its workforce by about 1,100 as part of a cost-cutting initiative aiming to eventually generate $185 million in annual savings. That year, Citizens paid a $3 million civil fine to the State of Massachusetts after regulators uncovered what they called "unethical and dishonest conduct" in the sale of variable annuities to elderly investors. Securities regulators claimed that members of the bank's brokerage arm, CCO Investment Services Corp., had engaged in a pattern of targeting elderly bank depositors with sales pitches that misled them about the risks of buying variable annuities. The following year, regulators in Rhode Island fined Citizens $800,000 for engaging in the same practices in that state. Later in 2006, the National Association of Securities Dealers imposed $850,000 in fines on CCO for various violations of regulatory requirements following an investigation not related to the Massachusetts and Rhode Island cases. Citizens implemented a number of changes designed to correct the problems that had cropped up at CCO.

Also in 2006, The Royal Bank of Scotland combined its U.S.-based RBS Lombard business with the asset finance businesses of Citizens Bank and Charter One Bank, creating RBS Asset Finance, Inc., which began operating as a subsidiary of Citizens Financial. RBS Asset Finance focused mainly on equipment financing. Citizens Financial also sold its insurance brokerage business in the spring of 2006. Brewer & Lord, Citizens Clair, and the Feitelberg Co. were sold to Chicago-based Hub International Limited for around $83 million. At the same time, Citizens entered into an alliance with Hub, whereby Citizens began offering Hub insurance products to its customers at all of the branches in its 13-state network. Overall growth at Citizens Financial slowed considerably in 2006, with its earnings of $2.92 billion representing just a 2 percent increase over the previous year. Like many other U.S. banks, Citizens had been hurt by a narrowing spread between long- and short-term interest rates because this flattening yield curve cut into the money banks were able to make by lending at long-term rates while paying interest on short-term rate deposit accounts.

Having finally finished absorbing its monster purchase of Charter One, Citizens Financial began seeking bolt-on acquisitions once again. In February 2007 the group spent $180 million for GreatBanc, Inc., a Chicago-area bank with ten branches and $1.2 billion in assets. Citizens intended to seek additional acquisitions of this nature throughout the 13-state area in which it operated. The GreatBanc deal, however, turned out to be the last of Fish's tenure as CEO. In March 2007 The Royal Bank reorganized its North American operations, creating a new unit called RBS America to oversee both Citizens Financial and The Royal Bank's U.S. capital-markets business. Fish was named chairman of RBS America, and he also remained chairman of Citizens Financial. Ellen Alemany, a former executive at Citigroup Inc., was named CEO of RBS America, while the president of Citizens Financial, Stephen D. Steinour, was promoted to CEO. Largely through acquisitions, Fish had dramatically transformed Citizens Financial from the fifth largest bank in Rhode Island to the ninth largest in the country during his 15 years at the group, while maintaining a winning formula coupling customer service with a local, conservative approach to lending. Steinour, who in his previous roles at Citizens had been deeply involved in bank acquisitions and integrations, had the unenviable task of following up on this legendary performance.

David E. Salamie

PRINCIPAL SUBSIDIARIES

Citizens Bank of Rhode Island; Citizens Bank of Massachusetts; Citizens Bank New Hampshire; Citizens

Bank of Connecticut; Citizens Bank of Pennsylvania; Citizens Bank (Delaware); Citizens Bank, N.A.; Charter One Bank, N.A.; Citizens Automobile Finance, Inc.; Citizens Capital, Inc.; CCO Investment Services Corp.; CCO Mortgage Corp.; RBS Business Capital; RBS National Bank; RBS Lynk, Incorporated; RBS Asset Finance, Inc.

PRINCIPAL COMPETITORS

Bank of America Corporation; Sovereign Bancorp, Inc.; The PNC Financial Services Group, Inc.; JPMorgan Chase & Co.; KeyCorp; Fifth Third Bancorp; Huntington Bancshares Incorporated; Commerce Bancorp, Inc.; National City Corporation; Citigroup Inc.; HSBC USA Inc.; TD Banknorth Inc.; LaSalle Bank Corporation.

FURTHER READING

Arditi, Lynn, "Citizens Completes $350-Million Deal for State Street," *Providence Journal,* May 7, 1999, p. F1.

———, "Citizens to Buy Grove," *Providence Journal-Bulletin,* November 5, 1996, p. E1.

Bailey, Douglas M., "Scot Bank to Buy Citizens Financial," *Boston Globe,* April 29, 1988, p. 25.

Barry, David G., "Citizens Bank Buys into the Bay State," *Boston Business Journal,* March 10, 1995, pp. 26+.

Beckett, Paul, "Mellon Financial Sells Retail Bank for $2.1 Billion," *Wall Street Journal,* July 18, 2001, p. C11.

Blanton, Kimberly, "A Bigger Pond Still: Larry Fish Buys Another Boston Bank," *Boston Globe,* October 26, 1993, p. 37.

Browning, Lynnley, "Citizens Struggles to Keep That 'Local Bank' Image," *Boston Globe,* June 27, 1999, p. G1.

———, "Citizens to Buy State Street's Retail Bank," *Boston Globe,* May 7, 1999, p. C1.

———, "$1.4b Citizens-UST Deal Recasts Financial Scene," *Boston Globe,* June 22, 1999, p. A1.

Christie, Claudia M., "Businessperson of the Year," *New England Business,* December 1, 1988, p. 36.

"Citizens Plans to Buy Another Connecticut Bank," *Providence Journal-Bulletin,* June 14, 1996, p. G1.

Collins, William E., "Graboys of Citizens: Our Businessperson of the Year for 1989," *Ocean State Business,* January 15, 1990, p. 10.

Davis, Paul, "Citizens Acquires Bank in Mass.," *Providence Journal-Bulletin,* September 19, 1992.

———, "Citizens Acquires Connecticut Bank Chain," *Providence Journal-Bulletin,* May 22, 1993.

———, "Citizens Has Ill. Deal and Discusses Doing More," *American Banker,* October 31, 2006, p. 1.

———, "Citizens to Buy Boston Five," *Providence Journal-Bulletin,* April 14, 1993.

Engen, John, "Hitting for the Cycle," *USBanker,* August 2003, pp. 40–42, 44.

Fasig, Lisa Biank, "Bank on a Roll," *Providence Journal,* June 2, 2002, p. F1.

———, "Citizens Makes Deal for Massachusetts Bank," *Providence Journal,* June 14, 2002, p. G1.

———, "The Greening of Pa.: Citizens Completes Takeover of 345 Mellon Branches," *Providence Journal,* December 4, 2001, p. E1.

———, "With Mellon Deal, Citizens Financial's Business Model Branches Out," *Providence Journal,* July 18, 2001.

Forrest, Wayne, "Citizens Hooks Fish: Ex-BNE Chief to Lead Era of Expansion," *Providence Business News,* February 10, 1992, p. 1.

Gedan, Benjamin N., "Royal Bank Reorganizes Top Officers at Citizens," *Providence Journal,* March 24, 2007, p. F1.

Graham, George, and Victoria Griffith, "Bank Shuffles Cards in Boston's High Stakes Poker Game," *Financial Times,* June 22, 1999, p. 29.

Grimaldi, Paul, "Citizens to Buy Midwest Bank for $10.5 Billion," *Providence Journal,* May 5, 2004, p. A1.

Healy, Beth, "Larry Fish Prepares Citizens to Swim with the Big Banks," *Boston Business Journal,* December 3, 1993.

Hiday, Jeffrey L., "Citizens Financial Agrees to Acquire UST of Boston in a $1.4 Billion Deal," *Wall Street Journal,* June 22, 1999, p. A6.

———, "Citizens' NH Bank Purchase Puts It Among the Top 50 in Size," *Providence Journal-Bulletin,* December 19, 1995, p. E1.

Hirsch, Michelle, "Lawrence K. Fish: Citizen's New President Looks Forward to Next, 'Exciting,' Five Years," *Providence Business News,* April 26, 1993, p. 2.

Holtzman, Robert, "Thanks to Royal, Citizens Is Tops in New England," *Ocean State Business,* January 30, 1989, p. 1.

Hooper, Molly, "Rhode Island Thrift Plans to Go Public with Stock Offer," *American Banker,* May 8, 1985, p. 3.

Kapiloff, Howard, "Larry Fish Has Finally Made It Big—with Little R.I.'s Citizens Financial," *American Banker,* October 6, 1994, p. 4.

Kostrzewa, John, "Citizens Confirms Plans to Acquire BNE-Old Colony for $75 Million," *Providence Journal-Bulletin,* September 5, 1990, p. 5.

———, "Interest in Bank Expected to Soar," *Providence Journal-Bulletin,* March 22, 1988, p. 1.

———, "Royal Bank Agrees to Buy Citizens for $440 Million," *Providence Journal-Bulletin,* April 29, 1988, p. 1.

Kraus, James R., "Bank of Ireland Selling Its Stake in R.I. Regional," *American Banker,* August 20, 1998.

———, "Citizens Races Clock, New England Rivals for Size," *American Banker,* January 7, 1997, pp. 1+.

———, "Scottish, Irish Banks Merging Their Units in New England," *American Banker,* December 19, 1995.

Kutler, Jeffrey, and Mark Basch, "Which Is No. 1 Thrift?: Here's a Vote for Citizens Savings," *American Banker,* September 26, 1985, p. 3.

McPherson, David, "Citizens' Acquisitions Team: 24 Deals and Counting," *Providence Journal,* November 26, 2003, p. E1.

————, "Citizens to Buy Another Pa. Bank," *Providence Journal,* September 23, 2003, p. F1.

————, "Citizens to Buy Community National Bank," *Providence Journal,* July 31, 2003, p. E1.

————, "Citizens to Buy Mass. Bank," *Providence Journal,* April 18, 2003, p. G1.

————, "Citizens to Buy Pa. Bank," *Providence Journal,* October 1, 2002, p. E1.

————, "Citizens to Sell Off Brokerages," *Providence Journal,* March 2, 2006, p. E1.

————, "Industry Group Fines Citizens Brokerage Unit," *Providence Journal,* October 17, 2006, p. E1.

Milligan, Jack, "Savings Institution Turns National Bank: Phase Two for Charter One," *Community Banker,* June 2002, pp. 22–27.

Mollenkamp, Carrick, "Royal Bank of Scotland's To-Do List: Keep Stock Rising, Fix U.S. Business," *Wall Street Journal,* February 28, 2007, p. C3.

Moyer, Liz, "Bulking Up in Its Region, R.I.'s Citizens to Buy UST," *American Banker,* June 22, 1999, pp. 1+.

————, "Citizens Looks to Wider Horizons," *American Banker,* July 18, 2001, p. 1.

"Now There Are Two: Citizens Buys in As Fleet's Top Rival in R.I.," *Providence Journal-Bulletin,* July 10, 1994.

Plasencia, William, "Citizens Bank of R.I. Taking the Plunge in Funds," *American Banker,* May 5, 1994, p. 12.

Raghavan, Anita, Dennis K. Berman, and Joseph Hallinan, "Citizens Financial to Buy Charter One," *Wall Street Journal,* May 5, 2004, p. A3.

Rebello, Joseph, "Radical Ways of Its CEO Are a Boon to Bank," *Wall Street Journal,* March 20, 1995, p. B1.

Reed, Keith, "Fish Moves Up the RBS Ladder," *Boston Globe,* March 24, 2007.

Sabatini, Patricia, "Mellon Financial to Exit Retail Banking," *Pittsburgh Post-Gazette,* July 18, 2001.

Stape, Andrea L., "Citizens Pays R.I. Annuity Penalty," *Providence Journal,* April 15, 2006, p. D1.

————, "Citizens' Unit Pays Mass. Fine," *Providence Journal,* July 23, 2005, p. B1.

Stein, Charles, "Citizens Financial Group: Backed by Scottish Parent, Institution No Longer Content to Sit on the Sidelines," *Boston Globe,* November 9, 1997, p. E1.

Sundaramoorthy, Geeta, "RBS Recipe: Autonomy for U.S. Arm," *American Banker,* December 9, 2004, p. 1.

Syre, Steven, and Charles Stein, "Banks Driven to Get Deal Done: Citizens and UST Chiefs Pushed into Action by Fleet-BankBoston Merger," *Boston Globe,* June 22, 1999, p. D1.

Vogelstein, Fred, "Larry Fish on New England Acquisition Trail," *American Banker,* June 7, 1993.

Wyss, Bob, "Citizens to Purchase USTrust for $1.4 Billion," *Providence Journal,* June 22, 1999, p. A1.

CLAYTON WILLIAMS ENERGY, INC.

Clayton Williams Energy, Inc.

---

6 Desta Drive, Suite 3000
Midland, Texas 79705
U.S.A.
Telephone: (432) 682-6324
Fax: (432) 682-1452
Web site: http://www.claytonwilliams.com

Public Company
Incorporated: 1991
Employees: 180
Sales: $265.9 million (2006)
Stock Exchanges: NASDAQ
Ticker Symbol: CWEI
NAIC: 211111 Crude Petroleum and Natural Gas Extraction; 213112 Support Activities for Oil and Gas Field Exploration

■ ■ ■

Clayton Williams Energy, Inc., is an independent exploration and production company involved in oil and natural gas, specializing in drilling horizontal wells (wells drilled at angles greater than 70 degrees from vertical). The company operates primarily in Texas, Louisiana, and New Mexico, and to a lesser extent in Mississippi, Montana, Utah, and Colorado. Clayton Williams Energy holds interests in 891.9 net producing oil and gas wells with proved reserves of 271.5 billion cubic feet of gas equivalents. Its interests are located primarily in the Permian Basin in Louisiana and the Austin Chalk and Cotton Valley Reef formations in Texas. The company's portfolio is comprised of 44

percent of natural gas proved reserves and 56 percent oil and natural gas liquids. Nearly all of its revenues are generated from oil and gas sales, with a small percentage derived from natural gas services and drilling rig services.

ORIGINS

Clayton Williams Energy owes its existence to its eponymous founder, Clayton Wheat Williams, Jr., a fourth-generation Texan steeped in the traditions of oil and gas exploration. The "West Texas wildcatter," as industry publications often referred to Williams, delved into numerous ventures during a remarkably prolific career, displaying an ecumenical drive in the business world reminiscent of his father, Clayton Wheat Williams, Sr. Clayton, Sr., born in an officers' building within the abandoned Fort Stockton in Fort Stockton, Texas, laid multidirectional footsteps for his son to follow, traveling down a variety of paths during his business career. He left Texas A&M University in 1915 with a degree in electrical engineering and proceeded to distinguish himself as an engineer, military officer, geologist, oilman, rancher, civic leader, historian, and philanthropist, pursuing business interests with tireless, boundless enthusiasm. After his son was born in 1935, Clayton, Sr., divided his time between drilling for oil and running his cattle ranch in Fort Stockton, where Clayton, Jr., grew up as the son of Fort Stockton's most prominent citizen.

Clayton, Jr., like his father, threw himself into a variety of business ventures, becoming the west Texas wildcatter who presided over a formidable business empire that included 26 different companies founded by the Fort Stockton native. Clayton, Jr., known as "Claytie" to his friends, attended his father's alma mater, Texas A&M, leaving in 1954 with a degree in animal husbandry. After college, he spent two years in the U.S. Army before returning to Texas and following in the footsteps of his father, gaining employment in the oil fields of west Texas. Williams worked as lease broker with petroleum companies that held interests in the exploration and production of natural gas, as well as the transportation and extraction of natural gas and natural gas liquids. Once he began making a name for himself out of the shadow of his father, Williams delved into the discovery and development of oil and gas properties in numerous fields in Texas, New Mexico, and parts of the southeastern United States. He also displayed the same desire to jump into a variety of businesses that his father had. Williams diversified his business interests, investing his time and money into farming, ranching, real estate, and banking. At one point, he entered the telecommunications fray, forming long-distance company Clay-Desta, which drew its name from a combination of his given name and his wife's given name, Modesta.

Williams devoted himself to a bevy of business pursuits while presiding at his 43-square-mile "Happy Cove Ranch" in Texas, but he primarily figured as an oil and gas executive. In the course of his career, with the numbers growing with each passing month, Williams drilled more than 1,000 wells and took part in the effort to drill an additional 2,400 wells. His interests in the oil and gas market comprised a slew of oil and gas and gas gathering properties owned and operated in a decentralized manner, which, in aggregate, vaulted Williams into *Forbes* magazine's list of the 400 wealthiest Americans by the early 1980s. Clayton Williams Energy was created to give Williams's oil and gas assets cohesion, a company formed to consolidate nearly 40 years of Williams's activity in the sector into a single entity.

Before Williams gathered his assets into the company that would carry his name, he tried his hand at politics, launching a campaign that became notorious for one blunder in particular. The gubernatorial race in Texas in 1990 pitted Williams as the Republican contender against Democratic State Treasurer Ann Richards. Williams spent upward of $8 million of his own money in a race remembered for the personal attacks lodged by each candidate and for offensive remarks made by Williams. At a Dallas lunch event, Williams refused to shake Richards' hand, a slight greeted with disdain in a state that prided itself on chivalry. In another incident, Williams told a reporter that before he was married he used to cross the border into Mexico to frequent brothels, describing his behavior as part of the fun of growing up in Texas. Williams made other gaffes that drew attention to his campaign for the wrong reasons, but nothing compared to his remarks in March 1990 when reporters gathered at his ranch for a cattle-roping exhibition. Rain delayed the event, and in effort to entertain reporters, Williams, with television cameras recording the moment, said, "Well, bad weather is like rape; if it's inevitable, you might as well just relax and enjoy it," as reported in the November 4, 1990, edition of the *Sunday Times*. The comment unleashed a storm of outrage whose intensity only increased when an Austin, Texas, woman testified one week before the election that her attacker had quoted Williams while raping her. Williams lost the race to Richards and returned to his business endeavors, making the formation of Clayton Williams Energy the first item on his agenda.

ASSET CONSOLIDATION: 1991

Williams was 60 years old when he consolidated his assets into Clayton Williams Energy. He assumed the duties of president, chief executive officer, and chairman of the new company in September 1991, presiding over assets that had generated $47 million in revenue in 1990. The assets, which constituted Clayton Williams Energy's predecessor companies, were the product of Williams's acquisitions and investments over the span of decades, beginning with his first successful oil well in 1959. Williams began concentrating his exploration and drilling activity in the Cretaceous Trend in 1988, where the majority of Clayton Williams Energy's activity was centered in the 1990s. The Trend extended from south Texas through east Texas, Louisiana, and other southern states, a region that contained the Austin Chalk, Buda, and Georgetown formations. Clayton Williams Energy, upon its formation, touted itself as one of the leaders in horizontal drilling in the Trend, concentrating the bulk of its activity in the Giddings Fields, part of the Austin Chalk formation.

The other focus of operations in the years immediately preceding the formation of Clayton Williams Energy was in the Jalamat Field, an oil and gas field located in Lea County, New Mexico, that was discovered in 1935. Williams acquired the Jalamat Field in 1988 and immediately launched a major recompletion and workover program, investing in the refurbishment of existing and temporarily abandoned wells. Between 1988 and 1991, Williams drilled 95 wells in the Trend and Jalamat Field and discovered producing properties in 91 of the wells. Williams's success ratio led *Forbes,* in its November 11, 1991, issue, to refer to the oilman-rancher as "one of the most active and luckiest horizontal drillers in the country," and it gave his new company momentum to begin its corporate life.

Williams's success in finding producing properties, whether based on luck or skill, fueled Clayton Williams Energy's financial growth during the 1990s. He took the company public in May 1993, when investors were given an opportunity to share in the success of the Midland-based firm, which had generated $60 million in sales and posted $1.9 million in net income the previous year. Investors were betting on Williams's ability to avoid dry holes and find productive wells. Financial growth and profitability depended on continually assessing Clayton Williams Energy's strategy and changing course whenever market conditions or other factors dictated finding new exploratory prospects. Accordingly, the company's drilling profile was in flux, changing as Williams moved from field to field in search of oil- and gas-rich areas to sustain his company's financial growth.

Williams demonstrated the nimbleness required of a successful wildcatter as the 1990s progressed. In 1997 Clayton Williams Energy started several exploratory projects aimed at reducing its dependence on drilling in the Trend, directing its resources to formations in east central Texas, southern Texas, Louisiana, and Mississippi. The major shift in emphasis become more profound in 1998, when low oil prices forced the company to suspend drilling activities in the Trend. In 1999 another dramatic change to the company's drilling profile occurred when it sold its interests in the Jalamat Field.

CLAYTON WILLIAMS ENERGY IN THE 21ST CENTURY

Clayton Williams Energy entered the 21st century poised for growth. Historically low oil prices during the late 1990s held the company's financial growth in check, limiting revenues in 1998 to $51 million and forcing a decline in 1999 to $43 million. Escalating oil prices during the first years of the 21st century created a far more fertile economic climate for the company, producing the most substantial financial leaps in its history. Revenues eclipsed $100 million in 2000, more

than doubling in a year that saw Clayton Williams Energy establish a new core area of operation in southern Louisiana. The company focused its exploration efforts on the swamps in Plaquemines Parish situated between dry land and the Gulf of Mexico. In 2002 the company deepened its involvement in the area by purchasing all of the working interest in the Romere Pass Unit in Plaquemines Parish for $21.7 million.

As Clayton Williams Energy completed its first decade as a publicly traded company and prepared for its second, the company exhibited a more aggressive stance toward expansion. The biggest acquisition of the period occurred in mid-2004, when Williams orchestrated the acquisition of Southwest Royalties Inc. for $187.8 million, and a related limited partnership, Southwest Partners L.P., for $7 million. The two transactions added 187 billion cubic feet equivalent of proved reserves, nearly all of which were located in the Permian Basin. The deal doubled Clayton Williams Energy's reserve life and provided substantial exploitation opportunities, contributing to an increase in revenues to $193 million in 2004. "We are very excited about this acquisition," Williams noted in a May 24, 2004, company press release. "It increases our reserves by 150 percent, doubles our reserve life, and provides significant exploitation drilling opportunities."

In the years ahead, Clayton Williams Energy's drilling profile was guaranteed to change, but the company hoped its financial growth remained constant. The greatest uncertainty in regard to its future was the question of who would succeed Williams as the company's leader. Williams turned 77 years old in 2007, wielding considerable influence over the company as its chairman, chief executive officer, and president. The end of his tenure promised to mark a major transition for the company, one that represented a potential stumbling block as the company looked to the future.

Jeffrey L. Covell

PRINCIPAL SUBSIDIARIES

Warrior Gas Co.; Clayton Williams Trading Company; Clayton Williams Venezuela, Inc.; CWEI Acquisitions, Inc.; Clayton Williams Pipeline, Inc.; CWEI Romere Pass Acquisition Corp.; Warrior Mississippi Corporation; Southwest Royalties, Inc.; CWEI Longfellow Ranch I, L.P.; CWEI South Louisiana II, L.P.; Rocky Arroyo, L.P.; CWEI West Pyle/McGonagill, L.P.; CWEI South Louisiana III, L.P.; CWEI North Louisiana, L.P.; Floyd Prospect, L.P.; Southwest Royalties, Inc. Income Fund V; Southwest Royalties, Inc. Income Fund VI; Southwest Oil and Gas Income Fund VII-A, L.P.;

Southwest Royalties, Inc. Income/Drilling Program 1987-I, L.P.; Southwest Oil and Gas Income Fund VIII-A, L.P.; Southwest Royalties Institutional Income Fund VIII-B, L.P.; Southwest Combination Income/ Drilling Program 1988, L.P.; Southwest Oil and Gas Income Fund IX-A, L.P.; Southwest Royalties Institutional Income Fund IX-B, L.P.; Southwest Oil & Gas Income Fund X-A, L.P.; Southwest Royalties Institutional Income Fund X-A, L.P.; Southwest Oil & Gas Income Fund X-B, L.P.; Southwest Royalties Institutional Income Fund X-B, L.P.; Southwest Oil & Gas Income Fund X-C, L.P.; Southwest Royalties Institutional Income Fund X-C, L.P.; Southwest Oil & Gas Income Fund XI-A, L.P.; Southwest Institutional Income Fund XI-A, L.P.; Southwest Developmental Drilling Fund 1990, L.P.; Southwest Developmental Drilling Fund 91-A, L.P.; Southwest Developmental Drilling Fund 92-A, L.P.; Southwest Developmental Drilling Fund 1993, L.P.; Southwest Royalties Institutional Income Fund XI-B, L.P.; Southwest Developmental Drilling Fund 1994, L.P.; Floyd Prospect II, L.P.; West Coast Energy Properties GP, LLC; West Coast Energy Properties, L.P.

PRINCIPAL COMPETITORS

Chevron Corporation; EOG Resources, Inc.; XTO Energy Inc.

FURTHER READING

Breaux, Julie, "Midland, Texas–Based Clayton Williams Buys Oil, Gas Firm Southwest Royalties," *Odessa American,* May 25, 2004.

Cassidy, John, "Texan Cowboy Trips over His Election Spurs," *Sunday Times,* November 4, 1990.

"Clayton Williams Buys Assets," *Oil Daily,* May 4, 2004.

"Clayton Williams, GE in Energy Acquisition," *UPI NewsTrack,* August 15, 2006.

"Clayton Williams to See Red," *Oil Daily,* March 17, 1999.

Coghlan, Keely, "Clayton Williams Keeps on Drilling As Timely Price Hedging Pays Off," *Oil Daily,* May 12, 2000.

Fletcher, Sam, "Clayton Williams Swims Against the Tide to Find Success in Cotton Valley Gas Play," *Oil Daily,* December 8, 1999.

Gosmano, Jeff, "Clayton Williams Tops Energy Share Winners on Strong Reserves," *Oil Daily,* March 1, 2005.

Poole, Claire, "Claytie's Comeback," *Forbes,* November 11, 1991, p. 16.

CONMED Corporation

525 French Road
Utica, New York 13502
U.S.A.
Telephone: (315) 797-8375
Fax: (315) 797-0321
Web site: http://www.conmed.com

Public Company
Incorporated: 1970 as Concor Enterprises, Inc.
Employees: 3,100
Sales: $646.8 million (2006)
Stock Exchanges: NASDAQ
Ticker Symbol: CNMD
NAIC: 334510 Navigational, Measuring, Electromedical, and Control Instruments Manufacturing

■ ■ ■

CONMED Corporation (Conmed) is a NASDAQ-listed company based in Utica, New York, specializing in surgical and medical procedure instruments, especially single-use products. Markets served include arthroscopy, electrosurgery, endoscopy, endosurgery, gastroenterology, integrated systems, patient care, powered surgical instruments, and pulmonology. Conmed offers eight major types of products, including arthroscopy tools and implants; electrosurgery tools and accessories; powered instruments such as saws and drills; patient care systems to monitor vital signs as well as operating room products; IV/wound care systems; minimally invasive, endosurgery devices; and diagnostic and therapeutic products used in gastroenterologic and pulmonary

procedures. Conmed maintains 11 manufacturing plants and a sales network in the United States. The company also sells its products in more than 100 countries around the world, in nine countries through direct marketing and the rest through specialty distributors.

FORMATION AS CONCOR ENTERPRISES

Conmed was founded by Eugene R. Corasanti, a 1952 accounting graduate of Niagara University. An aspiring entrepreneur, he started a few businesses before assembling a group of investors to acquire Mohawk Hospital Supply, a Utica medical equipment supplier, in 1970. In that same year he formed Concor Enterprises, Inc., to house the asset. Soon Corasanti was looking to branch into manufacturing to expand the business, and after conferring with engineers he decided to produce a disposable EKG electrode. In April 1972 he changed the name of Concor Enterprises to Consolidated Medical Equipment Inc. Manufacturing of the product began in 1973, which Conmed considers the year that it was founded.

Disposable EKG electrodes proved to be a good choice of product. At the time disposable medical products were just beginning to become acceptable and the disposable electrode market was in its infancy. Consolidated Medical did so well with the electrodes that in the 1980s it added products used in electrosurgery, a method of using high frequency current to cut tissue and stem bleeding. Because it was used in about 80 percent of all operations, electrosurgery products offered a great deal of commercial promise. At first the company introduced disposable handheld pencils and

---

grounding pads, but in time added other electrosurgery products.

In July 1985 Consolidated Medical became Conmed Corporation. Two years later the company went public, issuing four million shares. In that same year the company completed its first acquisition, paying $126,000 in cash for Medac, Inc., but little more than two years after that the business was discontinued. Conmed's first significant acquisition came in August 1989 with the $5 million purchase of Aspen Laboratories, Inc., a unit of a Bristol-Myers Co.'s subsidiary, Zimmer Inc., which manufactured electrosurgical generators. Aspen, founded in Denver in 1975, made its mark by introducing the first disposable, hand-held electronic scalpel, capable of cutting and cauterizing. It then produced the first solid-state electrosurgical generator.

At the start of the 1990s Conmed posted annual revenues of more than $30 million. It made further acquisitions to bolster its position in the electrosurgery market. In 1991 it paid nearly $3.2 million to acquire the Concept electrosurgical disposables business of Linvatec Corp., another Bristol-Myers subsidiary. Sales increased to $38.5 million in 1991 and net earnings to $8.5 million. A year later sales improved to $42.6 million and earnings to $9.7 million. In July 1993 Conmed acquired Medtronic Andover Medical, Inc., for $21.8 million in cash from Medtronic, Inc. The Massachusetts-based company manufactured cardiac monitoring disposable products. Its addition helped to increase Conmed's sales to $53.6 million in 1993. That year was also noteworthy because Corasanti's son, Joseph J. Corasanti, joined the company as its general counsel. A graduate of Whittier College School of Law, he spent three years working as an associate attorney with the Los Angeles law firm of Morgan, Wenzel & McNicholas. Moreover, in 1993 Conmed unveiled a new electronic trocar system. Called TroGard, it allowed surgeons to make small punctures in a patient's abdominal wall using radio frequency energy transmitted through a pencil-tip-size handheld instrument. Once the body cavity was penetrated, the system instantly shut off energy. The punctures were then used to insert

instruments and camera systems. The product was rolled out in 1993 but did not make much of an impact until 1994 when it was featured on The Discovery Channel's "Cutting Edge Medical Report." Shortly after the program aired at 6:30 A.M., Conmed received telephone calls from more than 100 surgeons interested in trying out the system. Prior to the show the company had fewer than 30 customers for the product.

Conmed acquired a specialty ECG monitoring line from Becton Dickinson Vascular Access Company in November 1994. Later in the year it agreed to another deal, which was not completed until 1995: the $21.2 million stock swap of Irvine, California-based Birtcher Medical Systems. A competitor in the electrosurgery field, Birtcher also produced other hospital operating-room equipment. Also in 1995 Conmed acquired The Master Medical Corporation for $9.5 million and the assumption of another $500,000 in debt, adding a line of single-use IV fluid drop rate gravity controllers. As a result of acquired products and internally developed products, Conmed's sales approached $100 million in 1995 and net income increased to $10.9 million.

PURCHASE OF NEW DIMENSIONS IN MEDICINE: 1996

In a deal agreed to in 1995 but not completed until February 1996, Conmed acquired a competitor, Melville, New York-based New Dimensions in Medicine, Inc., for $31.6 million in cash and the assumption of $3.3 million in debt. As a result, Conmed added ECG electrode products, disposable electrosurgical products, and a number of wound care products. Revenues improved to $125.6 million in 1996 and net income grew to $16.3 million. A year later revenues reached $138.3 million, helped in part by the acquisition of the surgical suction-tubing product line of a C.R. Bard Inc. subsidiary. However, Conmed also recorded a $7 million loss in 1997, due in part to a disappointing performance by New Dimensions but mostly to a $34 million write-off of some research and development projects it inherited in the acquisition of Linvatec Corporation, which closed on the final day of 1997.

Although the write-down may have been a bitter pill to swallow, the $370 million Linvatec acquisition was the more important transaction in Conmed's history. Linvatec, yet another Bristol-Myers unit, manufactured and distributed arthroscopy products and powered surgical instruments. With $215 million in sales in 1996, Linvatec essentially tripled Conmed's business overnight, making Conmed the second largest producer of arthroscopy products and orthopedic

KEY DATES

1970: Eugene Corasanti forms Concor Enterprises, Inc.

1973: Company is renamed Consolidated Medical Equipment Inc., company begins manufacturing EKG electrodes.

1985: Name is shortened to CONMED Corporation.

1987: Company goes public.

1997: Linvatec Corporation is acquired.

2003: Conmed sues Johnson & Johnson Co.

2007: Joseph Corasanti become chief executive officer.

powered surgical instruments in the world. In 1998 Conmed posted revenues of $336.4 million and net income of $17.8 million. Also making a contribution to the balance sheet was the addition of the arthroscopy product line of Minnesota Mining & Manufacturing Co. (3M). The assets were folded into the Linvatec unit, as was the 1999 acquisition of 3M's line of powered surgical instruments, used to operate on soft tissue and bone. The 3M assets played a significant role in Conmed's 1999 performance. Sales increased 10.8 percent to $372.6 million. Arthroscopy sales grew by nearly 20 percent and about half of that improvement was due to the 3M acquisition. The powered surgical instrument segment also benefited from the addition of 3M assets, which accounted for 13.2 percent of increased sales, compared to the 7.3 percent contribution from internal growth.

Conmed entered the 21st century with a new president and chief operating officer. The posts were assumed by Joseph J. Corasanti who was being groomed to one day succeed his father. The company's momentum was blunted somewhat in 2000. Arthroscopy sales showed only slight improvement, but because the orthopedic and powered surgical instrument businesses continued to grow, Conmed was able to increase 2000 revenues by 5.2 percent to $395.9 million. Net income, in the meantime, fell from $27.2 million in 1999 to $19.3 million. The company enjoyed a better year in 2001, when sales increased 8.3 percent to $428.7 million and earnings rebounded to $24.4 million. The powered surgical instruments business was essentially flat but early in 2002 the company looked to improve that performance by launching a new line of battery-powered systems to replace an outdated line. Also boding well for the future were a pair of acquisitions from Imagyn Medical Technologies, Inc., in November 2000 and July 2001, which greatly enhanced Conmed's presence in the endoscopy segment.

Conmed completed several significant acquisitions at the end of 2002 and in 2003. In December 2002 it bought a pair of privately held companies: Portland, Oregon-based ValMed Corporation and Quebec, Canada-based NorTrex Medical Ltd. ValMed produced ceiling mounted service manager and lighting systems and centralized touch-screen consoles to control operating room lights and equipment. NorTrex offered similar products to Canadian intensive care units and other critical care areas in hospitals. The two companies formed the foundation for a new business unit: CONMED Integrated Systems, the mission of which was to provide a turnkey solution for hospital and surgery centers.

Early in 2003 Conmed paid about $48 million for Blue Bell, Pennsylvania-based Bionx Implants Inc., maker of self-reinforced polymer bioabsorbable suture anchors, screws, pins, stents, and other soft-tissue devices used in orthopedic surgery and sports medicine. Not only did the deal add to Conmed's slate of sports medicine products and nearly $19 million in annual revenues, it increased Conmed's research and development capability. Also in 2003 Conmed acquired Jacksonville, Florida-based Core Dynamics for $9 million in cash, a move that further built up the company's Endoscopy assets by adding Core's minimally invasive laparoscopic surgical devices, including trocars, cannulas, and laparoscopic suction/irrigation devices. The company also brought with it a reputation as an innovator, having developed the audible trocar, which signaled when the trocar tip had penetrated the peritoneal cavity. Conmed's revenues increased to $453 million in 2002 and approached the $500 million mark in 2003, topping $497 million. The company recorded earnings of $34.1 million in 2002 and $32 million in 2003.

LAWSUIT AGAINST JOHNSON & JOHNSON: 2003

Also of note, in November 2003 Conmed filed a federal lawsuit against Johnson & Johnson Inc. claiming that it used its position in the suture market to coerce hospitals to also purchase its endoscopy devices, which were more expensive than those offered by Conmed. In order to receive discounts and rebates on sutures, Conmed alleged, hospitals were often required to purchase 80 percent of their endoscopy products from Johnson & Johnson. Conmed estimated that were it not for Johnson & Johnson's practices it would be able to do more than $100 million in additional business each year, increasing its market share from less then 5 percent to more than 20 percent. Johnson & Johnson was already under investigation by the Federal Trade Commission as well as the attorneys general of Connecticut and New York concerning the way it marketed suture and endoscopy instruments. Conmed was not alone in challenging Johnson & Johnson. Earlier in the year California-based Applied Medical Resources Corp., a manufacturer of endoscopy instruments, filed a similar suit against Johnson & Johnson.

Conmed completed another important acquisition in 2004 that resulted in another new division. At the cost of $80 million Conmed acquired the endoscopic product line of C.R. Bard Inc., maker of single-use medical devices used in the gastroenterological and pulmonary markets to detect diseases of the digestive tract and lungs. They formed the basis of CONMED Endoscopic Technologies. Based in Billerica, Massachusetts, the unit generated about $54 million in sales in 2003. Added to Conmed's balance sheet for part of 2004 it helped boost Conmed over the $500 million mark to $558.4 million. The company enjoyed strong growth on every front, and hoped to build on that momentum in 2005. Although revenues increased to $617 million, Conmed fell short on its sales and earnings' goals.

At the end of 2006 Eugene Corasanti announced that effective with the start of 2007 he was turning over day-to-day control of the company he founded to his son, Joseph, although he planned to stay on as chairman. In his final year at the helm, Corasanti was able to correct some of the problems that cropped up in 2005, as revenues increased 4.8 percent to $646.8 million in 2006.

Ed Dinger

PRINCIPAL SUBSIDIARIES

Aspen Laboratories; CONMED Andover Medical, Inc.; CONMED Endoscopic Technologies, Inc.; CONMED Integrated Systems, Inc.; Linvatec Corporation.

PRINCIPAL COMPETITORS

Smith & Nephew plc; Stryker Corporation; United States Surgical Corporation.

FURTHER READING

"Cable Series Features Trocar System, Boosts Conmed's Visibility in Laparoscopic Market," *Health Industry Today,* September 1994, p. 5.

"Conmed Corp. to Purchase Bionx Implants Inc. for 2.54 Times Revenues," *Weekly Corporate Growth Report,* January 20, 2003, p. 3.

Mulder, James T., "Conmed Adds to Product Offerings," *Post-Standard* (Syracuse, N.Y.), August 19, 2004, p. C1.

———, "Conmed Sues Johnson & Johnson," *Post-Standard* (Syracuse, N.Y.), November 9, 2003, p. A1.

———, "No Pain, No Gain; Conmed's Surgical Tools Business Profits from Injuries to Aging Weekend Warriors," *Post-Standard* (Syracuse, N.Y.), August 29, 2005, p. 7.

———, "A Surgical Stock; Conmed Corp.'s Price Slides in 2002 amid Reports of Lower-Than-Expected Earnings," *Post-Standard* (Syracuse, N.Y.), January 27, 2003, p. 11.

———, "Utica's Conmed Sewed Up No. 2 Spot As Electrosurgical Supplier," *Syracuse Herald American,* December 18, 1994, p. F1.

Crawford & Company

5620 Glenridge Drive, NE
Atlanta, Georgia 30342
U.S.A.
Telephone: (404) 256-0830
Toll Free: (800) 241-2541
Fax: (404) 847-4025
Web site: http://www.crawfordandcompany.com

Public Company
Founded: 1941
Employees: 7,525
Sales: $900.4 million (2006)
Stock Exchanges: New York
Ticker Symbols: CRDA; CRDB
NAIC: 524210 Insurance Agencies and Brokerages;
524291 Claims Adjusting

■ ■ ■

Crawford & Company is the largest independent claims management firm worldwide, with more than 700 offices in 63 countries, including 400 branches throughout the United States. Primary service areas involve claims adjustment and risk management services to insurance companies and self-insured companies. These services include workers compensation claims management; property and casualty claims adjusting; medical services auditing and administration; risk assessment, prevention, and management; and catastrophe and environmental damage assessment. Internationally, Crawford & Company handles claims loss adjusting for many industries, including oil, energy, and engineering; construction; marine; aviation; livestock; entertainment; specie and fine art; and banking, financing, and political risk. The founder's family retains a 60 to 65 percent interest in the firm.

FOUNDING AND EARLY SUCCESS

Jim Crawford, an insurance claims manager, founded Crawford & Company on the idea that an independent claims adjuster service could offer insurance companies a more cost effective and efficient means for handling claims than in-house adjusters. This concept originated from Crawford's observation that milk from different companies would be more efficiently distributed, at less cost, if an independent company delivered milk for several dairies. Although the dairy companies eschewed the concept, Crawford realized he could apply it to the insurance industry's claims adjusting process. Thus, on May 27, 1941, Crawford opened Crawford & Company in Columbus, Georgia.

Values and vision were significant factors in the success of the company. Initially, Crawford set forth three principles: (1) "Honesty and integrity above all"; (2) "Hard work pays"; and (3) "Knowledge and creativity are power." Furthermore, Jim Crawford issued what became known as "General Memorandum No. 1," from which the company adopted the long-running slogan "Top Quality, Promptly." The slogan reflected his intention that all claims handled by Crawford & Company would be correct and thorough. Following this idea, Crawford placed great importance on providing continuous training and development for his associates, and he began an internal training program in 1946.

Quality training and service established Crawford & Company as the leading independent claims administration company in the United States. Crawford University (as it was named eventually) determined the standard of quality by which claims adjusters would be judged throughout the insurance industry.

The company attained success rapidly and expanded nationwide by handling casualty and workers' compensation claims for the largest insurance companies. Crawford operated offices in all 50 states. Such success allowed the company to initiate international expansion in 1957. Its first overseas office opened in London that year, followed by an office in Puerto Rico to serve Latin America. International development continued over the next decade, and, to celebrate the 25th anniversary of the company, in 1966, Crawford & Company opened new offices in Canada, Puerto Rico, and England, as well as in the United States. Jim Crawford did not live to oversee further development of the company, however; he died in 1963. Crawford & Company became a public company in 1968, when certain stockholders sold shares on the NASDAQ.

DIVERSIFICATION IN CLAIMS-RELATED SERVICES

During the early 1970s, Crawford & Company began to offer new services to the insurance industry, both within the field of claims adjusting and in supplementary services. In 1971, the company introduced MAYDAY, a claims referral service open 24 hours per day, seven days per week, the first such call center in the industry. Crawford's diversification beyond casualty claims adjusting included property claims adjusting, such as automobile and heavy equipment damage appraisals, as well as catastrophe-related property loss claims. The company began to offer health and rehabilitation claims administration and operated 70 offices by the end of the 1970s. Also, Crawford offered a comprehensive package of claims administration services for self-insured companies.

The company confronted many changes in the insurance industry during the early 1980s. For instance, price competition among property and casualty insurance companies resulted in an impetus to reduce costs by handling claims adjustments in-house rather than through independent claims adjusters. To accommodate this change, claims adjusters began to handle claims over the telephone, instead of through face-to-face interactions. Also, the movement toward self-insurance reduced reliance on independent adjusters as traditional insurance companies began to offer self-insurance services, effectively increasing Crawford's competition in this area. Crawford responded by adapting leading information systems. The acquisition of Risk Sciences Group, Inc., expanded Crawford's ability to provide clients with then cutting-edge online, interactive software. Risk Sciences integrated its Sigma+System with Crawford's existing software. For the first time, the new system allowed clients access to databases and other information from Crawford's existing information system.

New services within the Health and Rehabilitation department involved medical coordination, whereby a staff of nurses handled hospital charges, audits, disability cost analysis, and medical interpretation and research. The company met a critical need for oversight in worker's compensation cases, for evaluation of healthcare delivery. Increasing demand for this department's service prompted Crawford to expand its geographic reach with the opening of 19 locations in 1983, and 20 locations in 1984, to a total of 121 locations. In 1984, the company acquired IMARC, a job placement company, thereby enhancing Crawford's ability to provide complete rehabilitation services, from insurance claims administration, through healthcare delivery oversight, to the return to work after healing from an injury. By 1985, Health and Rehabilitation Services accounted for 14 percent of all services; medical coordination accounted for nearly 4 percent.

Risk Management Services became an important area of business, as companies sought to prevent accident and injury. Crawford introduced Risk Control Services in 1981 in order to provide programs designed to analyze "pure risk" in the areas of occupational health and safety, personal and family safety and health, as well as liability responsibilities for safety and health, and property and net income protection. Specific services included risk control management, measurement, maintenance, and education and training. Over time, Crawford added related services, such as the Value Appraisals and Risk Survey for identifying factors that contribute to loss.

KEY DATES

1941: Company is founded.

1946: Crawford initiates training program.

1957: International expansion begins with new office in London.

1968: Crawford & Company goes public with a listing on the NASDAQ.

1972: Crawford adds health and rehabilitation services.

1981: The Risk Control Group launches Crawford into risk management services.

1989: Public listing changes to New York Stock Exchange.

1994: International expansion includes acquisitions in England and Canada.

1996–98: Acquisition of the Thomas Howell Group boosts Crawford's global presence.

2004: Record year of hurricanes prompts company to upgrade its catastrophe preparation standards.

Growth at Crawford prompted a corporate restructuring of staff at the seven regional offices and at main headquarters. Crawford sought to improve service to clients through communication that would attune the company to client needs. With more than 4,000 claims specialists at 700 risk management service locations in the United States, Puerto Rico, and Canada, Crawford hoped to create a comprehensive approach to providing diverse services. Consolidation of claims and health and rehabilitation offices generated more effective communication between claims and rehabilitation specialists, as well as between employees and clients. The Total Risk Perspective, introduced in 1985, provided employees with the opportunity to exchange information to enhance the perspective brought to a client's needs through greater understanding of the entire enterprise. Also, the new structure heightened emphasis on marketing, including product development, and involved adding a director of marketing at each of the regional offices.

Crawford continued to develop programs for niche service markets within the insurance industry. In 1985 Crawford introduced a Lease End Inspection Service to provide administration of lease end settlements which were potentially costly and contentious. The new department served a growing market for third-party evaluations, particularly the fleet management and leasing agent markets, to which Crawford offered material damage appraisal services.

Acquisitions furthered Crawford's expansion in healthcare services. Crawford acquired the utilization review operations of Compass Health Management in early 1988, a move that opened the company to the employee group medical benefits market, a growing field with greater potential than workers compensation services. The 1989 acquisition of Efficient Health Systems, Inc., of Chicago, provided geographic expansion for Crawford's employee medical benefits services. The acquisition added maternity review to Crawford's service offerings. In expectation of future growth in long-term care insurance policies, Crawford introduced an assessment service in this field. Also, the company's hospital audit services department opened four new offices, in Michigan, Florida, Texas, and California, with the intention of expanding the service on a regional basis.

The company's catastrophe management and environmental pollution claims services grew unexpectedly during the 1980s. Hurricane Alicia's devastation in the Houston, Texas, area in the fall of 1983 significantly increased property claims and appraisal assignments. In 1985, the catastrophe services unit provided more than 300 property claims specialists as six hurricanes struck land, the first time this had occurred since 1916 and the first time Crawford experienced such demand for its services. After the devastation of Hurricanes Hugo and Jerry and the San Francisco earthquake, all in 1989, Crawford began to provide supervisory personnel as well as claims adjusters. Growth of Crawford's environmental pollution claims services accelerated with the *Exxon Valdez* Alaskan oil spill in 1990.

Throughout this period of diversification, Crawford experienced a steady increase in revenues, from $39.8 million in 1972 to $374 million in 1989. That year's revenues merited the company a listing on the New York Stock Exchange.

ACQUISITIONS CULTIVATE INTERNATIONAL EXPANSION

Expansion into the international marketplace began via a domestic link, when Crawford opened an office in Dallas in 1989 to provide claims adjusters and supervisors for London- and other foreign-based clients involved in underwriting insurance policies in the United States. The business grew rapidly, and the office required expansion within the first year.

Early international development focused on companies in England with extensive operations abroad.

In December 1990, Crawford acquired London-based Graham Miller Group Ltd., which provided loss adjusting services to international insurance underwriters through offices in 40 countries, including affiliate offices. Clients included the prominent Lloyd's of London. The fall 1994 acquisitions of Arnold & Green Ltd. (A & G) and the Brocklehurst Group expanded Crawford's presence in the United Kingdom. A & G handled employer's liability and public liability claims, product guarantees, indemnity errors and omissions, and contractors' all risk loss exposures. Brocklehurst handled property, aviation, marine, agriculture, and oil and energy risk loss exposures. Crawford integrated Brocklehurst and Graham Miller, but A & G remained a separate operating entity. Also, Crawford opened an office in London to provide healthcare management services, such as employer liability and return-to-work services.

The purchase of independent claims loss adjusting firms in Canada melded with Crawford's existing and recently acquired operations. In 1994, Crawford acquired Finnamore & Partners Ltd. of Halifax, Canada, which provided specialty claims adjusting services in the areas of marine, heavy construction, energy, environment, entertainment, commercial property, and professional liability. The acquisition of ACI Adjusters Canada, initiated in the spring of 1998, made Crawford Canada the largest independent in that country, with 80 offices providing claims administration and disability management.

In June 1996, Crawford increased its global claims management capabilities significantly when a subsidiary acquired a 60 percent interest in Swiss Reinsurance Group (Swiss Re) by acquiring the London-based operation, Thomas Howell Group. As one of the largest reinsurance companies worldwide, Swiss Re operated more than 70 offices in 30 countries. The new organization operated as Crawford-THG. Two years later, Crawford acquired the other 40 percent interest in a stock exchange with Swiss Re, making Crawford-THG a wholly owned subsidiary. Also, Crawford purchased 100 percent of Swiss Re's THG-Americas operation. International acquisitions connected Crawford with prominent insurance companies worldwide, which provided a base for further growth.

Asia became the focus of international business development in 2005. That year Crawford merged with Godfrey & Company of New Zealand. Operating for Crawford in New Zealand and the south Pacific islands, Godfrey & Company planned to initiate new claims loss-related services in the region. Crawford acquired a 26 percent interest in Puri Anuj & Associates Pvt. Ltd., in India, which handled full service insurance loss adjusting and claims settlement through three offices. The newly merged company operated as Puri Crawford & Associates. Crawford increased its activity in China with the purchase of a 25 percent stake in Tino Insurance Surveyors & Adjusters Co. Ltd. in China. Under the shareholding agreement, Crawford managed the organization, which operated as Crawford Tino Insurance and carried a staff of 35 at offices in Beijing, Shanghai, Shenzen, and Wu Han.

EXPANSION OF DOMESTIC INSURANCE-RELATED SERVICES

During the late 1990s, Crawford's focus returned to domestic operations. The January 1999 acquisition of The Garden City Group (GCG), specialists in administration of class action settlements and other large-scale litigation, provided Crawford with an entrance into this lucrative area of claims administration, including bankruptcies and mass torts. Synergy between GCG's operations and Crawford's large-volume property inspections capability enabled Crawford to offer "one-vendor service" in several kinds of large scale litigation cases. GCG served the northeastern United States primarily, with offices in Garden City and New York, New York; Washington, D.C., and Sarasota, Florida. Crawford expanded Garden City Group by opening offices in Reston, Virginia; Columbus, Ohio; and Seattle, Washington. The company intended to use these offices as outlets for obtaining new clients in each region. New contracts for the new subsidiary included administration of the medical screening component of a diet drug class action settlement.

Crawford entered new fields of operation in 2002 and 2003. The company launched its Dedicated Recovery Unit, based in Tulsa, Oklahoma, to handle specialized debt collection. In 2003, the company's Investigation Services unit launched an Accident Reconstruction Service. Service innovations included the independent Content Service, which provided price evaluation through a national database.

Other domestic growth occurred through new contracts with prominent national insurance companies. Cypress Property and Casualty Insurance Company of Florida named Crawford & Company as its primary vendor. Claims administration included property and casualty claims, cause and origin, catastrophe, contents valuation, subrogation, and investigation. The Hartford, a national investment and insurance company, expanded Crawford's preferred vendor relations from property claims adjustment to include cause and origin and surveillance claims services. International business relations with Lloyd's of London facilitated the appointment of Crawford as Lloyd's marine services agent in Norfolk, Virginia.

Crawford streamlined its service methods by using advanced technologies to facilitate administration as well as to integrate related claims services for reduced claims processing costs. Through a joint venture with Standard Insurance Company, Crawford initiated an "integrated disability management" (IDM) service. IDM consolidated information in order to provide a more conceptual view of disability and workers compensations claims, such as by factoring in related absenteeism and productivity issues. Also, through integration of disability insurance coverage and claims administration and management, the service would reduce costs by providing employees with a single point of contact.

A new unit, Crawford Integrated Services, offered a comprehensive workers' compensation claims process by combining the resources of the Risk Management and Healthcare Management Services divisions. Crawford Claims Advantage provided the foundation of the new service model. The proprietary software used interview material and evidence-based research to analyze risk factors for recovery, then to customize medical treatment for the injured employee. Among its other attributes, Crawford Claims Advantage identified issues that required additional attention, such as medical or vocational case management, which could prolong or delay claims resolution.

2004–05: RECORD-SETTING HURRICANE SEASON PROMPTS SERVICE UPGRADES

Increased activity in the company's Catastrophic Services Management division prompted Crawford to improve its preparation strategies. Toward this end, Crawford's risk control services formed an alliance with TropicalStormRisk in 2001. The consortium provided long-range forecasting for tropical cyclone strike numbers in the United States, the Caribbean, Japan, and Australia. The British government developed the technology, and the consortium included leading scientists and statisticians, as well as experts in the insurance industry. Crawford believed that correct prediction facilitated lead-time preparation and reduced risk.

Crawford handled a record number of claims due to unprecedented storm activity during 2004 and predictions for a similar level of activity in 2005 motivated the company to invest in its catastrophe services unit. First, Crawford increased its staffing capabilities through direct hire. By identifying and contacting freelance claims adjusters and reestablishing relationships with retirees, the company added more than 1,000 adjusters to its on-call list. To certify adjusters quickly, Crawford expedited the training process.

In order to improve claims loss administration, the company purchased a fleet of satellite communications trucks, 24,000-pound vehicles which provided 10 to 15 wireless telephone lines plus wireless Internet connections for about 250 users. The equipment allowed adjusters to upload claims and download information as needed to facilitate claims processing regardless of local communications infrastructure problems. Also, the technology enabled broadcasts to the company's Atlanta headquarters.

The predictions by the TropicalStormRisk consortium proved correct, as the 2005 Atlantic storm season produced some of the most devastating hurricanes on record. With a mobile unit stationed in Orlando, Florida, the company's satellite communications trucks received their first in-action test with Hurricane Dennis, which struck the Florida Panhandle as a category three storm in July. Before Hurricane Katrina, Crawford placed mobile crews in Baton Rouge, Louisiana, and in Mobile, Alabama. Hurricane Katrina, a category five hurricane and one of the most devastating storms on record, struck New Orleans and the Gulf Coast in August; then Hurricane Rita hit the southwest Louisiana coast and part of Texas as a category three hurricane. Hurricane Wilma, another category five storm, hit Florida and the Yucatan in Mexico in November 2005. Moreover, the long-term effects of Hurricane Katrina required the company to hire and train additional claims adjusters.

In providing claims adjusting and administration services during the 2004 and 2005 hurricane seasons, revenues at Crawford increased significantly. The increase compensated for a six-year shortfall in revenues due to a decrease in property and casualty claims administration business, the company's primary service areas.

Mary Tradii

PRINCIPAL SUBSIDIARIES

Crawford-THG Ltd.; Garden City Group, Inc; Risk Sciences Group, Inc.

PRINCIPAL DIVISIONS

Casualty Claims Services; Catastrophe Management Services; Class Action Services; Crawford Integrated Service; Workers' Compensation Claims Administration.

PRINCIPAL COMPETITORS

ChoicePoint Inc.; Claimsnet.com Inc.; Medco Health Solutions, Inc.

FURTHER READING

"Atlanta-Based Crawford & Company to Help with Hurricane Dennis," *PR Newswire,* July 11, 2005.

"Crawford & Company Catastrophe Service Revved-Up for 2005 Hurricane Season," *PR Newswire,* July 6, 2005.

"Crawford and Company Obtain Shareholding in Chinese Firm," *Europe Intelligence Wire,* November 24, 2005.

"Crawford & Company Strengthens Its Global Property & Casualty Unit," *PR Newswire,* January 16, 2006.

H O M E X

Seguro vives aquí

Desarrolladora Homex, S.A. de C.V.

Andador Javier Mina 891-B
Culiacán, Sinaloa 80200
Mexico
Telephone: (52 667) 7758-5800
Toll Free: (800) 224-6639 (in Mexico)
Fax: (52 667) 7758-5838
Web site: http://www.homex.com.mx

Public Company
Incorporated: 1989 as Proyectos Inmobiliarios de Culi-
      acán, S.A. de C.V.
Employees: 7,337
Sales: MXN 12.54 billion ($1.16 billion) (2006)
Stock Exchanges: Mexico City; New York (ADRs)
Ticker Symbols: HOMEX; HXM
NAIC: 236115 New Single Family Housing Construc-
      tion (Except Operative Builders)

∎ ∎ ∎

Desarrolladora Homex, S.A. de C.V. (Homex), is a
vertically organized home development company
focused on government-subsidized entry-level housing in
Mexico. Benefiting from efforts by the federal government to reduce the large housing deficit in a country
where demographics indicate a sharply rising formation
of new families, Homex builds many thousands of units
each year and has expanded its activities to include
developments in every part of Mexico. It is the fastest
growing of the nation's major publicly held home
developers.

THE FIRST DECADE: 1989–98

Homex got its start in 1989 when four sons of
Eustaquio de Nicolás Vera established, in Culiacán, Sinaloa, Proyectos Inmobiliarios de Culiacán, S.A. de C.V.
(Picsa), a real estate development firm. Its first jobs
involved the construction of commercial areas, but it
gradually focused on designing, building, and selling
houses. Picsa began producing government-subsidized
housing in 1991. By this time Mexico had a housing
deficit of at least six million units, and demand was
growing rapidly since more than half the population was
under 25 and certain to need new housing in the near
future. Homex started building low-cost housing for
government employees, financed by a fund known by its
Spanish-language acronym, Fovi.

The main need, however, was to construct housing
for the much larger number of poor Mexicans employed
in the private sector. An institute known by its Spanish-
language acronym of Infonavit was established in 1972
and was chiefly funded by a 5 percent payroll tax collected by employers. Infonavit purchased land, issued
mortgages, and hired contractors to build housing,
providing them with financing, but the process was
marked by inefficiency and corruption. A law passed in
1992 retained the institute's source of funding but
credited the money to individual workers' accounts. Infonavit continued to extend mortgages but no longer
was involved in buying land and hiring contractors.
Instead, it was authorized to make loans to construction
companies for this purpose and loans to commercial
banks extending the same types of mortgages and

COMPANY PERSPECTIVES

To improve the quality of life of our community through superior quality real estate developments.

credits. Picsa began building Infonavit-financed homes in 1993, and the institute's program quickly became its chief source of business.

Government deficit spending led to capital flight in 1994, resulting in the devaluation of the peso and an economic recession that persisted into the middle of the decade. Mortgage financing ground to a halt. Picsa, like many other Mexican firms, had debts to meet and little liquidity. "That was a mortal sin at the time," Eustaquio de Nicolás Gutiérrez, chief executive of the firm, later told Miriam Pineda of the Mexico City daily *Reforma*. "But we completely paid our debts by selling land earmarked for development. We learned a lot from the experience."

Primarily through Infonavit and Fovi, in 1997 the federal government was providing financing for about 80 percent of low-income housing in Mexico (excluding the large amount of informal construction done by and for poor people, most of them self employed). In that year Infonavit began to provide mortgages to workers earning more than the prior maximum of seven times the minimum wage of about $100 a month. Infonavit and Fovi were handling two-thirds of all mortgage originations in Mexico. A new government program, known by the acronym Prosavi, provided direct cash subsidies of at least 20 percent of the value of the house instead of simply offering below market interest rates. It was available to workers, whether or not formally employed, earning no more than three times the minimum wage.

Vying for this enhanced business were more than 2,000 construction firms, none of them holding more than 7 percent of the low-income housing market. Picsa was not one of the majors, but it was competing with them, especially along the U.S.-Mexican frontier, where whole subdivisions of 200 to 300 units were being constructed to accommodate a rapidly growing population. By mid-1998 Picsa was operating in 14 cities in seven states, most of them in western Mexico but also including Yucatán and Chiapas in the east. Half of these houses were for Fovi, Infonavit, and another federal agency, Fovissste. The other half were for Prosavi.

Since the average price of sale was very economical, only about MXN 90,000 (a little under $10,000), Picsa

needed simplified administration to make a profit at this level. All back office duties involving customers were directed from headquarters in Culiacán. The branch offices in the cities where the company was operating were staffed with only six people each, including sales personnel. Headquarters also maintained a close watch on materials, and any losses were deducted from the salaries of workers who were paid on the basis of how fast the homes were built rather than on a regular hourly wage. Picsa established its own software system to manage construction. In addition, to save money, the company avoided operating in big cities where the cost of land acquisition and labor was high.

RAISING BUILDINGS AND CAPITAL: 1999–2003

Picsa was renamed Desarrolladora Homex in 1999, when the company had become the fifth largest home-builder in Mexico and the largest one in the Prosavi program. By this time the company had constructed 14,000 subsidized homes and was expected to build 8,000 more before the year ended. It was, by that time, engaged in more than 50 subsidized housing developments in 18 cities and planned to enter two more cities by 2000.

In August 1999 Homex sold a 20 percent stake in the business to ZN México Capital Management LLC, a U.S.-based investment fund, for $12.5 million. ZN México, whose principals included José Juan Alvarez, Luis Alberto Harvey, and Arturo Saval, had as partners the investment bank Nexxus Capital and another U.S. investment firm, Zephyr Management, directed by Tom Barry. It administered two private capital funds and one publicly owned enterprise engaged in several emerging markets. Nexxus had aided a competitor of Homex, Consorcio Ara, S.A. de C.V., to convert to public ownership, and its investment in Homex was expected to have the same purpose.

In April 2001 Infonavit announced a new program that made nearly two million workers paying into its fund newly eligible for home mortgages. However, the economic slowdown in the United States that began in 2000 had spread to Mexico, resulting in fewer jobs and thus less money available for mortgage lending. Homex lost money in 2001 and had to postpone an initial public offering (IPO) of company shares until market conditions improved.

Homex moved into Guadalajara, Mexico's second largest city, in 2002, opening an office and planning to build 2,650 subsidized homes in a development named Hacienda Santa Fe. By this time the company had constructed more than 20,000 of these homes and

KEY DATES

1989: Company, known by the acronym Picsa, is founded.

1991: Picsa begins building government-subsidized low-income housing.

1998: Picsa is operating in 14 cities in seven Mexican states.

1999: The company is renamed Desarrolladora Homex.

2002: Homex gains a powerful backer in Chicago-based real estate tycoon Samuel Zell.

2004: Homex makes an initial public offering of stock in Mexico City and New York.

2005: The company acquires Casas Beta, Mexico's seventh largest homebuilder.

2006: Homex has built more homes this year than any of its competitors.

hoped to complete 10,000 in 2002 alone. That year the de Nicolás brothers found a powerful investor in billionaire real estate tycoon Samuel Zell. His international investment arm, Chicago-based Equity International Properties Ltd., purchased 22.3 percent of Homex for $32 million in 2002. Zell successfully lobbied Homex to adopt U.S. accounting standards. He also urged top managers to improve their English skills.

Homex enjoyed an excellent 2003, selling 13,396 homes, earning a return of about 11 percent on its revenues, and reducing its debt margin in relation to its assets. It had 32 housing developments in 20 cities in 14 states. The largest were in Culiacáan, Guadalajara, and Nuevo Laredo, but the company had, in mid-2004, also entered Acapulco, Metepec, Monterrey, Tapachula, and Tijuana. The future of housing continued to look bright because of high demand, with 5.3 million new homes forecast between 2004 and 2010.

PUBLIC COMPANY: 2004–06

Homex was ready to go public. Zell directed the IPO of stock, speaking to potential investors at meetings in Boston and New York and even deciding how many shares to allot different funds. The IPO, in Mexico City and New York, for some 20 percent of the company's shares in June 2004, was oversubscribed sixfold. About $160 million was raised, almost three-quarters in New York, where Homex became the first Mexican housing construction company to sell American Depositary Receipts (the equivalent of shares) on the New York

Stock Exchange. More than half the money was earmarked for investments such as buying more land for future development, and another one-fourth was designated to pay down debt.

Homex was the fastest-growing homebuilder in Mexico in 2004, advancing to fourth place. Unit sales had grown 64 percent since 2001, compared to average growth of 15 to 18 percent for the industry as a whole. It was the industry leader in Guadalajara and had operations in at least 20 Mexican cities. An article by David Isaac in *Investor's Business Daily* credited the company's business model for much of this growth. "The business model runs on a strong information technology system which we control out of our corporate office," Homex Chief Financial Officer Cleofas Hinojosa told Isaac. "We basically control every stage and every step of our construction with this information system. [It] allows us to very quickly and very effectively open branches in the cities we choose to go."

By 2004 the building sector had proved a success story for the administration of President Vicente Fox Quesada, who took office in late 2000 with the goal of nearly doubling the construction of new homes by 2006. Established in 2001, Sociedad Hipotecaria Federal, a government development bank covering housing, was directing funds to commercial banks and Sofoles, the acronym for single-purpose financial corporations engaged in activities such as mortgage lending. Sofoles made over two million loans in 2004, compared to less than one million in 2000. SHF's sales of packages of virtually default-free securities were intended to increase the pool of funds available to private home lenders, and thus to create more middle-income housing.

Homex significantly expanded its scope in April 2005, when it acquired Controladora Casas Beta, S.A. de C.V., for $194 million in cash and stock. Mexico's seventh largest homebuilder, Casas Beta had sold 11,055 homes in 2004 in three states, including México, and the Federal District (Mexico City), where Homex did not have a presence. The acquisition made Homex the second largest homebuilder in Mexico. By this time the value of the company's shares had more than doubled since its IPO of stock less than a year before. Zell's investment had, on paper, increased fourfold in value. Some financial analysts felt the stock was ripe for a correction, however, noting that only 10 percent of Homex's houses were in the growing middle-income market, which offered a higher profit margin than low-income housing. They were also concerned by the company's high level of uncollected invoices and its low land reserves compared to competitors, only enough for two years of construction.

In September 2005 Homex sold $250 million worth of ten-year senior guaranteed notes in order to lower its borrowing costs and extend debt maturity. This transaction, earmarked to repay $215 million in existing debt, about 80 percent of the total outstanding, was preparatory to a secondary stock offering in January 2006 that raised about the same amount and was applied to paying the shareholders of Casas Beta for the Homex stock they had received in selling the company, as well as Zell's Equity International Properties, which retained 13 percent of the shares at the end of the month. The de Nicolás family held 41 percent and public investors 46 percent; ZN México was no longer a shareholder.

Homex entered the cities of Puebla and Mexicali in 2006, raising its development activities to 28 cities in 18 states. It enjoyed another banner year, building 43,044 homes, more than any of its competitors, and raising its net profit to MXN 1.24 billion ($114.81 million) on revenue of MXN 12.54 billion ($1.16 billion), a 41 percent increase over the previous year. It was in a virtual dead heat with Corporación Geo in terms of annual revenue. The mainstay of the company's business continued to be construction of modest homes of between 42 and 76 square meters, with one to three bedrooms, bath, kitchen, living room–dining room, and one parking place. These houses averaged MXN 238,000 (about $22,000) in price in 2006. They constituted 90 percent of the homes that the company built in 2006, and about 75 percent of them were financed by Infonavit. Eustaquio de Nicolás remained chairman of the board, while Gerardo de Nicolás was chief executive.

Homex, like many Mexican enterprises, was eager to stress corporate social responsibility as part of its activities. Developers were obligated, by law, to set aside 10 percent of their land holdings for municipal use. Homex offered to develop schools, day care centers, parks, and other services on these tracts. The company conceded that such offers were also useful as marketing tools, since working parents would benefit from ease in placing and picking up their children. Homex also said that its workforce was fully employed and that it was cooperating with the federal government's institute for adult education by allowing the institute's teachers to offer classes on its construction sites, even ending the workday a little early for this purpose.

Robert Halasz

PRINCIPAL SUBSIDIARIES

Acro Homex, S.A. de C.V.; Administración Picsa, S.A. de C.V.; Altos Mandos de Negocios, S.A. de C.V.; Casas Beta del Centro, S.A. de C.V.; Casas Beta del Noreste, S.A. de C.V.; Casas Beta del Norte, S.A. de C.V.; Desarrolladora de Casas del Noreste, S.A. de C.V.; Homex Atizapán, S.A. de C.V.; Proyectos Inmobiliarios de Culiacán, S.A. de C.V.

PRINCIPAL COMPETITORS

Consorcio Ara, S.A. de C.V.; Corporación Geo, S.A. de C.V.; Urbi Desarrollos Urbanos, S.A. de C.V.

FURTHER READING

Abelson, Alan, "Big Repair Job," *Barron's*, September 19, 2005, pp. 5, 7.

Aguilar, Alberto, "Adquiere ZN México casi 20 por ciento de Homex antes Picsa," *Reforma*, September 22, 1999, p. 3.

———, "Nombres, nombres y … nombres," *Reforma*, April 25, 2005, p. 4.

Armendáriz, Alberto, "Arranco cotización de Homex con alza," *Mural*, June 30, 2004, p. 1.

Carstens, Catherine Mansell, "The Retirement Saving System," *Business Mexico*, April 1992, pp. 20–25.

"Da a conocer Homex su trayectoria inmobiliaria," *Mural*, December 4, 2005, p. 10.

Gallun, Alby, "Zell Does Well with Mexican Homebuilding," *Crain's Chicago Business*, June 28, 2004, p. 4.

Isaac, David, "Mexican Builder Hammers Out Growth Plan," *Investor's Business Daily*, March 22, 2005, p. A6.

León, Irina, "Qué es Picsa?" *Reforma*, June 15, 1998, p. 15.

Libaw, Oliver, "Affordable Housing: Bridging the Gap," *Business Mexico*, May 1997, pp. 26–28, 30.

Lyons, John, "Watching Zell's Neighborhood," *Wall Street Journal*, February 14, 2005, p. C4.

Millman, Joel, "In Cash-Short Mexico, Housing Is Sacred," *Wall Street Journal*, December 1, 1998, p. A18.

"Nombres, nombres y … nombres," *Reforma*, June 17, 2004, p. 5, and January 10, 2006, p. 3.

Pineda, Miriam, "Invertirán en empresas mexicanas," *Reforma*, October 25, 1999, p. 15.

———, "Semana Empresarial/Construyen el éxito," *Reforma*, November 1, 1999, p. 4.

Platt, Gordon, "Mexican Homebuilder Cuts Borrowing Costs," *Global Finance*, November 2005, p. 64.

Ruiz, Ramon, "Mortgaging for Growth," *Business Mexico*, March 2005, pp. 18–21, 49.

Rymer, Jerry, "Brick by Brick," *Business Mexico*, August 2001, pp. 27–29.

Velazco, Jorge, "Crece la competencia en mercado inmobiliario," *Mural*, June 3, 2002, p. 3.

Watson, Andrew, "Building Blocked," *Business Mexico*, November 2001, pp. 35–38.

driven to excel

Directed Electronics, Inc.

One Viper Way
Vista, California 92081
U.S.A.
Telephone: (760) 598-6200
Toll Free: (800) 876-0800
Fax: (760) 598-6400
Web site: http://www.directed.com

Public Company
Incorporated: 1982
Employees: 435
Sales: $437.79 million (2006)
Stock Exchanges: NASDAQ
Ticker Symbol: DEIX
NAIC: 334310 Audio and Video Equipment Manufacturing; 334290 Other Communications Equipment Manufacturing

■ ■ ■

Directed Electronics, Inc., is the number one American producer of aftermarket vehicle security and remote-start equipment, home loudspeakers, and aftermarket satellite radio receivers. The firm makes security products under the Viper, Python, Hornet, and Clifford brand names, while its speakers include Polk Audio, Definitive Technology, a/d/s, Orion, and Xtreme. Nearly half of revenues come from a line of satellite radio receivers produced for broadcaster Sirius. Directed Electronics products are sold by more than 3,400 retailers in the United States and in 70 countries abroad, including mega-chains Circuit City and Best Buy. To ensure proper installation, the firm offers training at its corporate headquarters in Vista, California, in a facility called "The Snake Pit."

EARLY YEARS

Directed Electronics dates its beginnings to 1982, when a bankrupt electronics firm was acquired by Darrell and Kathy Issa. Darrell Issa was a third-generation Lebanese-American who had dropped out of high school at the age of 17 to join the U.S. Army, receiving electronics training to be a bomb disposal technician and later earning a master's degree in business while on the Army payroll. After being discharged in 1980 and getting married, he drew on his training to cofound a small electronics-manufacturing firm, A.C. Custom, with his former scoutmaster. In 1982 Issa and his wife took control of the business and also bought one of its bankrupt customers, Directed Electronics, Inc. (DEI).

During his decade in the service Issa and an older brother had allegedly been involved with automobile theft (Issa denied the allegations; his brother was later convicted), and such experiences ironically inspired a new business direction. Through DEI Issa soon began to produce antitheft devices, digital keypads, and motion sensors as original equipment for carmakers including BMW, Mazda, General Motors, and Ford of Australia.

With the car alarm business taking off, in 1984 Issa sold A.C. Custom and two years later he moved with DEI to the San Diego area. He had intended to merge with a home security products manufacturer there, but the deal fell through when the firms' business models turned out to be incompatible.

In 1986 DEI changed direction from making alarms as original equipment to producing its own line of aftermarket models. Over the next several years such brands as Viper, Steal Stopper, and Hornet, with patented features including a shock sensor, would make DEI the largest U.S. manufacturer of aftermarket alarms. In 1990 the company also introduced a remote start system, which allowed users to turn on their vehicle from inside the house. DEI had annual sales of approximately $15 million.

The firm's products were largely sold through car audio stores, where employees had the skills needed to install them. Unlike some of its competitors, the company paid close attention to customer care, and its sales team was instructed to make sure that dealers provided good follow-up service. The price of a DEI security system ranged from $200 to $600.

MOVING TO LARGER QUARTERS: 1992

In early 1992 DEI more than tripled its available workspace by moving into a 66,000-square-foot facility. The company also filed suit against Chrysler Corporation, which had introduced a new limited-edition car called the Dodge Viper. DEI had been using its Viper trademark on clothing, watches, and coffee mugs, and took action when it discovered that the automaker was planning a similar promotional campaign.

In December a new car alarm option called Back Talk was introduced that played a recorded warning (voiced by Issa himself) which was intended to startle potential thieves. The company also settled its suit against Chrysler, agreeing to license the use of the Viper name to the automaker for an undisclosed amount of money. For 1992 DEI had record sales of $47 million and shipped 400,000 systems, 35 percent more than the

year before. In addition to its Vista, California, headquarters, the firm also had operations in Ohio and Connecticut.

In 1993 the company introduced several new products, including four Python midpriced car security systems; Failsafe, which was intended to shut down a car after a theft had taken place; Soft Chirp, a quieter overnight alarm; and Sound-Off, a sound-deadening material that could be installed under vehicles to dampen road noise. DEI had cornered 42 percent of the vehicle security market, and in 1994 Issa was honored by *Inc.* magazine as its "Entrepreneur of the Year."

In 1996 the company diversified yet again by introducing the Directed Audio line of automotive speakers, amplifiers, and installation products. When combined with the various offerings in the Viper, Python, Sidewinder, Hornet, and Wasp car security lines, the firm would offer a total of 700 different products. DEI's share of the competitive auto-security products market was slipping, however, having fallen to 27 percent.

In the fall of 1997 DEI was granted $177,000 by the California Employment Training Panel to cover the costs of a two-year program to train the majority of its 133 workers in team-building, customer service, automation, and technical skills. However, DEI President and CEO Issa had begun campaigning for the Republican nomination for U.S. senator by lambasting "big government," and after being stung by critics for seeking the handout, he announced the company would not accept it.

The firm was embroiled in a lengthy legal battle with Code-Alarm Inc. over claims of patent infringement by each. In June 1995 the latter had been ordered to pay DEI $5.9 million for violating a patent on a shock-sensor device, while a second suit alleging a similar violation was later settled in DEI's favor for $2 million. In the spring of 1998 Code-Alarm's claim that DEI had infringed its starter shut-off patent was dismissed and the patent itself declared invalid, and soon afterward Code-Alarm was ordered to pay DEI $10 million to settle yet another suit over shock-sensor technology, ending the battle between the companies.

TRIVEST BUYING CONTROL OF FIRM IN 1999

Though Issa had lost his bid for the Republican Senate nomination in 1998, a year later he ran for the U.S. House of Representatives, and that December he sold 80 percent of DEI to private equity firm Trivest, Inc., for approximately $160 million. The sale had been made in part to reduce the appearance of conflict of

KEY DATES

1982: Darrell Issa acquires control of Directed Electronics in Cleveland.
1986: Company moves to San Diego, California.
1990: Remote start product is introduced; firm becomes top maker of aftermarket car alarms.
1996: Car audio products debut.
1998: Firm is awarded $10 million to end long-running patent suit with Code-Alarm.
1999: Issa sells 80 percent of company to Trivest.
2000: Firm buys bankrupt car alarm maker Clifford Electronics.
2001: Car audio manufacturer ADS Technologies is acquired.
2002: Mobile video and GPS security products are added.
2004: Company buys speaker maker Definitive Technology; sales of Sirius radios begin.
2005: Company goes public on the NASDAQ.
2006: Acquisition of Polk Audio makes firm number one U.S. home speaker maker.

audio brands a/d/s, Precision Power, and Orion. ADS head Kurien Jacob was assigned by DEI to run its new car audio unit, based like ADS in Phoenix. The firm was also preparing to offer in-car video screens and DVD players under the Directed Video brand.

In early 2002 the company allied with Ford Motor Co. affiliate Wingcast and auto parts giant Delphi (which would supply components) to develop another new digital GPS-based antitheft tracking device, which was operated via the Internet and offered two-way wireless remote control of vehicle functions. Wingcast would supply live operators to facilitate use of the service. In 2003 an additional web-linked GPS car security system, Directrack, was introduced. It was an option in DEI's Viper, Python, Clifford, and Automate car security lines.

In August 2003 the company settled lawsuits against six competitors who agreed to license the disputed technology. At year's end a partnership was formed with Clarion Corp. of America, which would launch the DEI-manufactured Ungo Pro Security product line the following year. Another partnership was formed in the spring of 2004 with famed auto customization firm West Coast Customs (featured on MTV's hit "Pimp My Ride"), whose line of branded car audio and video products would be produced by DEI.

RECAPITALIZATION, SIRIUS DEAL IN 2004

In May 2004 a $185 million recapitalization of the firm was completed via Wachovia, CIBC World Markets, and Capital Strategies Ltd., with a special $109.4 million dividend paid to investors and the remainder used to pay down debt. In August the company signed a deal with satellite radio broadcaster Sirius to produce and distribute portable radio receivers including the Sirius Sportster that could be used in vehicles and elsewhere.

In September 2004 DEI acquired Definitive Technology LLP, a 14-year-old maker of high-quality home audio speakers, for close to $50 million. Its key management personnel were retained, and Definitive would form the basis of DEI's new Home Audio Division. For 2004 the company had sales of $206 million, with electronics superstore chain Best Buy accounting for one-fifth of the total.

In early 2005 DEI signed an agreement to become the exclusive supplier of vehicle security equipment to 600-store retail chain Circuit City, which some months earlier had dropped it after a long stretch selling its products. It also opened a new $500,000 educational facility called "The Snake Pit" which offered training for installers.

DEI's Vista, California, facility was now 180,000 square feet in size. Three-quarters of the firm's staff of

interest, as well as to give DEI funds to make acquisitions. Issa would remain president and CEO of the firm, which had annual sales of about $90 million.

In July 2000 DEI bought the assets of bankrupt Southern California firm Clifford Electronic, Inc., which made the Clifford and Avital brand car alarms, positioned at the high end of the market. Its $42 million in sales boosted DEI's share of the aftermarket car alarm sector back up to 40 percent. Only 20 of Clifford's 150 employees would be retained, with their work moving to DEI's 102,000-square-foot facility in Vista. In addition to aftermarket products, the firm was also producing items for car manufacturers' own brands.

In November 2000 Darrell Issa was elected to the U.S. Congress to represent California's 48th District, and he immediately stepped down as head of DEI. His replacement would be Jim Minarik, the president and CEO of vehicle entertainment systems maker Clarion Corp. of America. Minarik received an equity stake in DEI as part of his compensation package.

In the spring of 2001 DEI partnered with Seaguard Electronics to introduce the Valet Car-Com 2, a two-way Global Positioning System (GPS) vehicle location service, which could track stolen vehicles. It required payment of a subscription fee. November saw the firm acquire ADS Technologies, Inc., manufacturer of car

240 worked there, designing, testing, and shipping products that were manufactured overseas, primarily in Asia. The company also maintained smaller facilities in Louisville, Kentucky, and the United Kingdom, and operated a 24-hour call center to assist installers, which handled 17,000 to 33,000 calls per month. A database of 5,000 vehicle electronics system blueprints had been created to assist them with installation.

Acquisitions continued in July 2005 with the purchase of DesignTech International's line of vehicle security products for an undisclosed sum. New products announced during the year included a portable audio/video media player in the Directed Mobile Media line, priced at $449, and iPod and Sirius Sportster docking stations.

INITIAL PUBLIC OFFERING IN LATE 2005

In December 2005 the firm made an initial public offering (IPO) of stock on the NASDAQ, selling 9.38 million shares at $16 to net $84.4 million. The money was primarily used to pay down debt. Trivest and other selling shareholders including Issa kept about half the proceeds.

The company's sales grew by 60 percent during 2005 to top $304 million, with net earnings reaching nearly $14 million. Sirius satellite radio products accounted for $121 million, or 39 percent of the total. During the year the company had also begun selling do-it-yourself remote start products through retailers including AutoZone, Advance Auto, and NAPA.

In early 2006 a new portable navigation system using GPS technology was introduced, priced at $699, which appeared with some 150 other new products at the annual Consumer Electronics Show. In May the company bought the nonmanufacturing assets of Astroflex, Inc., a 17-year-old Canadian remote vehicle starter company with sales of approximately $5.5 million, and in July the Federal Communications Commission notified the firm that two of its Sirius receivers were out of compliance with regulations. They were quickly redesigned to correct the problem.

In August DEI won a bidding war to buy the third largest home and vehicle audio equipment maker in the United States, Polk Audio, agreeing to pay $136 million. When Polk's $86 million in sales were combined with those of Definitive Technology, DEI would be the top home audio speaker maker in the country. Polk, founded in 1972, would continue to be based in Baltimore, Maryland. The sale was funded by a new $141 million loan from Canadian Imperial Bank of Commerce and JPMorgan Chase. In the latter half of the year DEI also purchased its longtime Canadian distributor and top Canadian remote starter maker Autostart, while introducing HD Digital Radio receivers for car and home use, priced at between $250 and $300.

For 2006 revenues leaped to nearly $438 million, with a net profit of $21 million. Though Sirius equipment accounted for half the total, such sales were leveling off as regulators sorted out a proposed merger between Sirius and arch-rival XM, and DEI announced it expected them to decline as much as 22 percent over the next year.

In early 2007 the firm introduced a number of new products including an enhanced portable entertainment system and new overhead video monitors for cars, which featured built-in DVD players. In March a new brand, Polk Audio Designs, was introduced, which would be used for lower-priced products such as iPod accessories and radios. In the summer the firm's Snake Pit training center added Home Theater Residential Integration courses.

After 25 years Directed Electronics, Inc., had grown to become the leading maker of aftermarket car security systems in the United States, as well as the top producer of satellite radio receivers and home speakers. It also made a variety of other security and home and vehicle entertainment products, and with its management still seeking acquisitions, continued growth looked certain.

Frank Uhle

PRINCIPAL SUBSIDIARIES

DEI Sales, Inc.; DEI Headquarters, Inc.; DEI International, Inc.; Polk Holding Corp.; Polk Audio, Inc.; Britannia Investment Corp.; Directed Electronics Hong Kong Ltd.; Directed Electronics Canada, Ltd.; 436678 Canada, Inc.; 4366859 Canada Inc.

PRINCIPAL COMPETITORS

Audiovox Corp.; Clarion Corp. of America; Rockford Corp.; Klipsch LLC; Bose Corp.; Harman International Industries, Inc.; Alpine Electronics of America, Inc.; Mitek Corp.; JL Audio, Inc.; Audiobahn, Inc.; Crimestopper Security Products, Inc.; Paradigm Electronics, Inc.; B&W Group Ltd.; Sanyo Electric Co., Ltd.; Rosen Entertainment Systems; Stillwater Designs; Delphi Corp.

FURTHER READING

"Alarm Company, Chrysler Settle Viper Dispute," *Associated Press,* December 28, 1992.

Benson, Mitchel, "Senate Hopeful Got Grant for Company," *Wall Street Journal,* October 8, 1997, p. CA2.

"CFA IPO Spotlight: Directed Electronics Prospectus Info," *Dow Jones Corporate Filings Alert,* September 2, 2005.

"Code-Alarm Settles Dispute with Directed Electronics for $10 Million," *Dow Jones Online News,* June 19, 1998.

"Darrell Issa Sells 80 Percent Interest in Company He Founded," *Associated Press Newswires,* January 23, 2000.

"Delphi in Aftermarket Telematics Venture with Directed Electronics," *Autoparts Report,* May 3, 2002.

"Directed Electronics Sales Soar 69.2%," *TWICE,* March 31, 2006.

"Directed Forecasts Satellite Radio Sales Downturn," *Satellite Week,* March 26, 2007.

"Directed Shares Fall After FCC Notice," *Associated Press Newswires,* July 5, 2006.

Ferguson, Tim W., "Does Good Business Make Good Politics?" *Forbes,* June 1, 1998, p. 138.

Freeman, Mike, "The Audience Is Listening … and So Are Analysts to the Splash Directed Is Making in Home Audio," *San Diego Union-Tribune,* September 8, 2006, p. C1.

———, "Directed Electronics Comes Up Short," *San Diego Union-Tribune,* December 17, 2005.

———, "Vista-Based Directed Electronics Buys Assets of Bankrupt Rival," *San Diego Union-Tribune,* July 11, 2000, p. C3.

———, "Weak Sales for Holiday Season Hit Directed Electronics," *San Diego Union-Tribune,* December 7, 2006.

Gilroy, Amy, "Directed Launches Lower Cost WCC, Enters Nav," *TWICE,* January 16, 2006, p. 44.

———, "Directed to Offer Sirius Tuner," *TWICE,* August 12, 2004.

Kaye, Nick, "Have You Called Your Car Lately?" *New York Times,* November 5, 2004, p. 9.

King, Mike, "Directed Is Pushing All the Right Buttons," *Montreal Gazette,* February 8, 2007, p. B4.

Kinsman, Michael, "Directed Success," *San Diego Union-Tribune,* March 6, 2005, p. N4.

Lockwood, Herbert, "DEI Has Alarmingly Good Year; Expanding Internationally," *San Diego Transcript,* January 6, 1993, p. 1.

McCracken, Jeffrey, "Car-Alarm Dispute Gets Personal, Political," *Crain's Detroit Business,* November 10, 1997, p. 3.

Palenchar, Joseph, "Directed Buys Definitive Technology," *TWICE,* September 22, 2004.

———, "Directed Cuts Deal to Buy Polk Audio," *TWICE,* August 22, 2006.

Spaulding, Richard, "One Man's Tale Disarming and Alarming Too," *San Diego Evening Tribune,* September 25, 1990.

Williams, Lance, and Carla Marinucci, "Issa Was Charged in San Jose Car Theft," *San Francisco Chronicle,* June 25, 2003.

Wright, Patrick, "Vista Company Makes Noise with Polk Audio Purchase," *North Country Times,* August 24, 2006.

Domino Printing Sciences PLC

Trafalgar Way
Bar Hill
Cambridge, CB3 8TU
United Kingdom
Telephone: (+44 01954) 782551
Fax: (+44 01954) 782874
Web site: http://www.domino-printing.com

Public Company
Incorporated: 1978
Employees: 1,836
Sales: £208.35 million ($391.2 million) (2006)
Stock Exchanges: London
Ticker Symbol: DNO
NAIC: 333293 Printing Machinery and Equipment
   Manufacturing

■ ■ ■

Domino Printing Sciences PLC is one of the world's top two manufacturers of specialty printing equipment for packaging, product coding, and commercial printing applications. The company has traditionally focused on the continuous ink-jet (CIJ) printing market, a technology that enables printing and coding to irregular surfaces, such as cans, plastic bottles, cartons, and other primary packaging systems and surfaces. Domino's CIJ equipment is used, for example, in order to date stamp eggs. The company's equipment is also used for secondary packaging applications, including adding product identification systems to boxes, trays, and the like. The CIJ market remains the company's single largest revenue generator. In 2006, CIJ equipment alone accounted for 28 percent of the company's total turnover of £208 million ($391 million). In addition, some 34 percent of the company's revenues are generated through the sale of the proprietary, specialty inks required by its systems. The maintenance, including spare parts sales, and service of its equipment is also a major revenue area for the company, accounting for 24 percent of sales.

Despite its expertise in the CIJ market, and that market's continued position as the leading packaging printing technology, Domino has taken steps to position itself in two other emerging printing and coding technologies, those of laser printing, and, further down the road, drop-on-demand (DOD) printing. While the former offers the advantage of solvent-free inks, higher resolution and reliability, and lower ink usage, maintenance, and downtime, the latter provides a high degree of flexibility, enabling packagers to produce variable labels on demand, rather than be required to produce or purchase and stock large quantities of preprinted or prelabeled packaging. Based in Cambridge, England, Domino has operated on an international level almost since it was founded in 1978. England continues to account for 11 percent of group sales, while the rest of Europe, led by the French and German markets, supports 35 percent of the company's revenues. The United States, where the company operates a manufacturing and sales subsidiary, remains Domino's largest single market, at 21 percent of sales. Yet the fast-growing Chinese market, at 11 percent of group sales, is expected to be Domino's primary growth market. Domino is listed on the London Stock Exchange and is led by Chairman Peter J. Byrom and Managing Director Nigel Bond.

TECHNOLOGY PIONEER IN 1978

Domino Printing Sciences grew out of Cambridge Consultants Ltd., a research center that played a significant role in the developing U.K. high-technology sector. Cambridge Consultants had been founded in the early 1960s, as part of Cambridge University, in an effort to use that institution's expertise in order to support the growth of British enterprise. Sinclair Radionics was an example of an early outgrowth of Cambridge Consultants. In 1972, U.S. management consultants group Arthur D. Little acquired 80 percent control of Cambridge Consultants, which nonetheless remained at its Cambridge base.

During the 1970s, an engineer at Cambridge Consultants, Graham Minto, had begun working with continuous ink-jet printing (CIJ) technologies in an effort to overcome a number of the technologies advantages. CIJ was not new. It had originally been proposed in the late 19th century as a means for telegraph printing, and the first commercial applications of the printing technology dated back to the early 1950s. Through the 1960s and into the 1970s, CIJ printing had become a dominant printing technology, at least in the commercial sector, despite its many disadvantages. Indeed, the machinery was very expensive, required a great deal of energy and, because of a large number of moving parts, was often highly unreliable. CIJ printers were also known to be messy to operate, while incapable of achieving high-quality printing standards.

Improvements to the technology began to appear in the 1970s, however, and by the middle of the decade, had come to focus on the use of electrostatic charges to propel and deflect the ink. Minto himself had played a leading role in adapting new technology brought over from the United States, simplifying the technology in order to create a new generation of CIJ printers. By 1978, Minto had led the development of an innovative new CIJ printer, called the Unijet, which featured a single printing head. In order to commercialize his invention, Minto founded a new company, called Domino Printing Sciences, which licensed the technology from Cambridge Consultants.

Domino got off to a strong start: in the same year of its founding, the company's Unijet printer had captured the attention of both the printing and packaging industries. Even before its official launch, the Unijet had received its first industry award, winning the £10,000 TDC Innovator Award, sponsored by Technical Development Capital, a wing of the Industrial and Commercial Finance Corporation. The company had also lined up its first sales agents, marketing separately to the printing and packaging industries.

The Unijet proved highly reliable, while also less expensive than its largely U.S. counterparts, and these features enabled the company quickly to develop sales beyond the United Kingdom. Orders for the company's printing equipment rapidly spread to the European continent, and by the middle of the decade, Domino claimed the leadership in the CIJ market in the United Kingdom and in Western Europe. The company had also extended its reach into other high-growth markets, including Japan, where it launched sales through a distributor in 1981. By 1983, the company had entered the U.S. market, signing a manufacturing and sales agreement with American Technologies, part of American Can. American Technologies also handled distribution of Domino' systems and ink for the Australian and New Zealand markets. Exports rapidly became the driving force of the company's revenues, and by the end of the decade, Domino's equipment, inks, and services were available in 60 countries. Fully 80 percent of the company's revenues were generated outside of the United Kingdom.

REBUILDING

By then, Domino had grown from a four-person company into one of the world's leading printing equipment suppliers. The company had also prepared itself for future growth in 1985, listing its stock on the London Stock Exchange in an offering oversubscribed some 43 times. The public offering enabled the company to make a new series of investments, and especially in building up its specialty inks business. Indeed, while printer sales remained an important source of revenues, the company's margins remained relatively low, and the finite nature of the purchase

KEY DATES

1978: Graham Minto founds Domino Printing Sciences as part of Cambridge Consultants and launches first CIJ printing system.
1985: Already the European leader, Domino goes public on the London Stock Exchange.
1994: Company adds laser printing technology with acquisition of the Direct Digital Coder system from the United States' Directed Energy Inc.
2001: Canadian Inkjet Systems is acquired.
2006: Company acquires Mectec Elektronik and Enterprise Information Systems.

precluded future earnings potential. In contrast, the use of specialty inks developed by the company and delivered via proprietary cartridge systems provided the company with an important source of locked-in, ongoing, and high-margin revenues. In order to expand its ink capacity, the company created a dedicated research and development team, which worked on developing a variety of colored inks, edible inks, and other specialty inks, such as those capable of being read with ultraviolet lights.

In 1985, the company moved to form a true ink subsidiary, called Domino Amjet. That subsidiary began its operations in Liverpool. By the end of the year, Domino Amjet had been supplemented through the purchase of Chemelectron, at a cost of £596,000.

Yet Domino's growth hit a major hurdle in the second half of the 1980s. Flush with success, the company acquired its U.S. distributor in 1987, raising the purchase price through a new rights issue that year, and taking on some £23 million in debt to finance the purchase. The American Technologies acquisition, however, nearly broke the young British company. Soon after the purchase, the company realized that its new American subsidiary was rife with problems. For one, American Technologies had been producing Domino's printing systems under license for the United States and other markets. Yet the company had made a number of changes to Domino's manufacturing specifications; as a result, the equipment became prone to frequent breakdowns, and caused serious damage to Domino's reputation in the world's single largest CIJ printer market.

The investment community, already skittish due to a number of other soured acquisitions made by British

firms in the United States, reacted swiftly, and Domino's share price all but collapsed. Domino's future appeared clouded. In 1989, Minto resigned from his position in the company and was replaced by Managing Director Howard Whitesmith.

Whitesmith's own background was in manufacturing engineering, and by the late 1980s the Wraysbury native had extended his own experience from engineering to purchasing and materials management. Whitesmith was particularly interested in the Japanese kanban system of manufacturing, and especially its insistence on placing a great deal of individual responsibility on employees. As a result, the company rapidly gained greater manufacturing efficiency, while simultaneously raising its quality levels.

Whitesmith also set out to restructure the company's ailing American operations. The company took over direct managerial control of the subsidiary, restructured its manufacturing processes, and raised production to the same quality standards as its British plant. The company also worked hard to restore its reputation in the U.S. market, changing the subsidiary's name to Domino Amjet, and by the early 1990s was able to offer an industry leading five-year guarantee on its systems.

These efforts played a major role in helping the company gain a number of high-profile customers in the early 1990s. In 1992, for example, the company received an order for 500 printers from the British Post Office, the largest ever CIJ printer order placed in the United Kingdom at the time. By then, the company's sales topped £60 million.

Domino's position as the leading European producer of industrial ink-jet systems played a role in its strong recovery throughout the 1990s. A major boost for the company came when the European Commission instituted a new directive requiring that all food and beverage items sold in the European Union be labeled with "sell by" or "use by" dates. The new directive created a suddenly vast new market for the company. As a result, Domino's expansion was dramatic; in France, for example, the company's sales jumped by 80 percent in just one year. The company responded to the increase in business by expanding its production capacity on the European continent, establishing a new ink production headquarters near Frankfurt, Germany, in 1992.

NEW TECHNOLOGY
INVESTMENTS FOR THE FUTURE

Part of Domino's success lay in its customer service-driven model, as opposed to its competitors' technology driven operations. As a result the company succeeded in developing strong relationships with its customers, as well as a reputation for its service commitment. In the early 1990s, Domino extended its concept of customer service by adopting a new strategy of diversifying its variable printing technologies. This diversification was also seen as an important hedge against the eventuality that the market would abandon CIJ technology in favor of a rival technology, such as laser or the newly emerging DOD technology.

Acquisitions played an important role in Domino's diversification strategy. An early purchase was that of British company Packtrack, for £500,000 in 1992. That company specialized in a relatively low-tech, mimeographic technology that was nonetheless highly prized by certain customers, and served as a precursor of sorts for the DOD market.

Domino added laser technology in 1994, buying the Direct Digital Coder system that had been developed by Directed Energy Inc. That acquisition enabled the company to roll out its own laser systems, which, because they featured nonsolvent-based inks, were prized by the bakery and cereals sectors. The company launched its first laser system in 1994; by 1996, the company's active investment and development program enabled it to launch a second laser printer system. The extension into lasers played a role in the company's expansion into the fast-growing mainland Chinese market, where it established a joint-venture distribution subsidiary. The company then began marketing its laser printing systems to that country's tobacco industry, among others.

Domino also strengthened its international network, adding operations in India and Mexico. In 2001, the company acquired Canadian Inkjet Systems, which was renamed as Domino Printing Solutions. That year, also, the company acquired Alpha Dot, based in the United Kingdom, paying £3 million to acquire that company's expertise in coding and marking products. The company then unveiled its own DOD printing system, called Domino On Demand, in 2003.

New acquisitions toward the middle of the decade helped the company expand both its range of market and technologies. In 2004, the company boosted its presence in Germany, buying CIJ printer systems developer Wiedenbach Group. That purchase in particular provided Domino with enhanced capacity for printing on wires and cables. The following year, the company added new operations in the United States with the acquisition of Texas-based Citronix, which had developed its own CIJ printing systems.

Domino expanded again in 2006, buying Enterprise Information Systems, based in Dallas, Texas, and Sweden's Mectec Elektronik. That purchase marked Domino's entry into a new market, the print and apply labeling equipment sector. As it entered 2007, Domino had grown into a world leader in its industry. The company's diversified technological capacity provided the base for its future growth in the new century.

M. L. Cohen

PRINCIPAL SUBSIDIARIES

Domino (Australia) Pty. Ltd.; Domino Amjet BV (Netherlands); Domino Amjet GmbH (Germany); Domino Amjet Ibérica S.A. (Spain); Domino Amjet. Inc. (U.S.A.); Domino Coding Ltd. (China); Domino Deutschland GmbH; Domino Korea Pte Ltd.; Domino Printech India; Domino Printing Mexico; Domino Printing Solutions Inc. (Canada); Domino SAS (France); Domino UK Ltd.; Domino UK Ltd. (Dubai).

PRINCIPAL COMPETITORS

Videojet Inc.; RWE AG; Heidelberg USA Inc.; MAN AG; Xerox UK Ltd.; Metso Corp.; Heidelberger Druckmaschinen AG; Stork N.V.

FURTHER READING

"Domino Denies Takeover Rumours," *Printing World,* January 6, 2005, p. 10.

"The Domino Effect," *Food Trade Review,* January 2007, p. 66.

"Domino Moves into Print and Apply," *Packaging Today International,* November 2006, p. 6.

"Domino on Demand Brings New Focus," *Print Week,* July 17, 2003, p. 20.

"Domino's Milestone," *Food Trade Review,* January 2007, p. 9.

"EIS Deal Strengthens Domino's Technology," *Label & Narrow Web,* July–August 2006, p. 42.

Ferry, Jeff, "Domino Jets Ahead," *Management Today,* June 1992, p. 62.

Gimbel, Florian, "Domino Acquires Alpha Dot," *Financial Times,* July 12, 2001, p. 19.

Ducks Unlimited, Inc.

One Waterfowl Way
Memphis, Tennessee 38120-2351
U.S.A.
Telephone: (901) 758-3825
Fax: (901) 758-3850
Web site: http://www.ducks.org

Nonprofit Company
Incorporated: 1937 as Ducks Unlimited, Inc.
Employees: 650
Operating Revenues: $196.1 million (2005)
NAIC: 813312 Environment, Conservation, and
Wildlife Organizations

■ ■ ■

Ducks Unlimited, Inc., (DU) is an outdoor sports enthusiast's group dedicated to restoring and protecting waterfowl habitats. Its efforts extend beyond the United States to breeding grounds in Canada and wintering sites in Latin America and the Caribbean. DU is responsible for conserving about 12 million acres and has been a vocal proponent of preserving wetlands, to the benefit of many species besides ducks. The organization has roughly 750,000 members and about 60,000 volunteers.

SPORTING ORIGINS

North America was troubled by more than the Great Depression in the early part of the 1930s; a continental drought was depleting waterfowl populations at the same time. In the preceding decades, the U.S. government had begun to pass laws to protect migratory birds through such measures as hunting limits and establishment of refuges.

In October 1930 a group led by Joseph P. Knapp established More Game Birds in America, Inc., a foundation to promote scientific conservation of these species. Borrowing from the then radical gamekeeping ideas of St. Louis attorney and gamekeeper advocate Dwight C. Huntington, More Game Birds aimed to go beyond protecting naturally occurring animals from excessive hunting, to encourage propagation of these species in the wild.

Knapp, considered the driving force behind the creation of DU, had inherited a fortune and become successful in New York's printing and publishing industry, eventually gaining control of *Collier's Weekly* and putting together the Crowell-Collier Publishing Company. He was an avid duck hunter who lived part of the year in North Carolina, and had already set up another conservation agency, the Knapp Foundation Inc.

Other founders of More Game Birds included Arthur Bartley, an associate of Huntington's son; Pulitzer Prize–winning editorial cartoonist J. N. "Ding" Darling (who later became a vocal critic of Knapp); and John A. Hartwell, president of the New York Academy of Medicine.

The pioneering International Wild Duck Census of 1935 found that most waterfowl in North America were spawned on the vast prairies of Canada, so it was there that the first conservation efforts were centered. The wa-

COMPANY PERSPECTIVES

The vision of Ducks Unlimited is wetlands sufficient to fill the skies with waterfowl today, tomorrow and forever.

terfowl population was then estimated to number just 42 million (an earlier federal count put the number even lower). The federal Duck Stamp program provided funds for establishing refuges in the United States only.

INCORPORATED IN 1937

More Game Birds formed a successor organization to restore the Canadian breeding grounds. Ducks Unlimited, Inc., (DU) was established in Washington, D.C., in January 1937; More Game Birds transferred its assets to the new group three years later. (The organization's name is said to be a play on the "Limited" designation that usually follows corporate names in Canada.) Hartwell was DU's first president, though he was in poor health and served but a short time. By the time of DU's first meeting in March 1938, the organization claimed 6,270 members. Revenues were about $90,500, less than one-sixth of the original yearly goal.

Ducks Unlimited (Canada), the organization that would take the funds raised in the United States to work north of the 49th parallel, was formed in 1938. Its first general manager was Tom Main, while Judge W. G. Ross served as its first president. Work on the first restoration project soon commenced. This involved setting up a couple of dams to regulate water at Winnipeg's Big Grass Marsh. DU finished more than 100 projects affecting more than a million acres by 1943; the estimated waterfowl population had grown to about 140 million birds. Wartime shortages slowed the organization somewhat, and there was some disruption of personnel. Arthur Bartley, then general manager, was called to duty in 1943, and the next year DU's New York headquarters was requisitioned by the U.S. Navy. Nevertheless, the group saw its revenues increase from $185,000 in 1942 to $400,000 in 1945.

Wetter weather helped lift the waterfowl population to pre–Dust Bowl levels in the 1950s. DU's fund-raising reached new heights, exceeding $600,000 in 1956, when the group had about 25,000 members. DU had begun its first marine project, on Prince Edward Island, in 1951. By the end of the decade, it had nearly 500 projects in Canada.

INCREASING FUND-RAISING AND MEMBERSHIP

The group's headquarters moved from New York City to Chicago in 1965 in a project funded by the organization's president, Henry Schmidt. The next year, annual fund-raising exceeded $1 million.

DU's ranks swelled in the 1970s as the group mobilized a massive army of volunteers. Membership grew from 50,000 to five times that by the end of the decade. Fund-raising passed the $10 million mark in the middle of the decade. DU Canada, for so many years the spender of funds from the United States, started raising money itself in 1974.

The group expanded its geographic influence at the same time. In the early 1970s it began wetlands projects south of the border, establishing Ducks Unlimited de Mexico, A.C. The country was important to many waterfowl as a wintering site.

There was a blossoming of DU's relationship with Hollywood, as Bing Crosby and John Wayne participated in films celebrating the organization. Another screen legend, Clark Gable, had been an early member.

The 1980s saw a return of drought conditions and a subsequent reduction in game bird populations. A number of groups, including DU, came together to create the North American Waterfowl Management Plan in 1986. This aimed to restore populations to benchmarks set in the previous decade. In the same year, pioneering legislation was passed providing incentives for farmers to set aside marginally productive land for ten years or more. DU stepped up its policy efforts with the addition of regional offices in Bismarck, North Dakota, in 1984 and Sacramento, California, three years later.

A lobbying office was established in Washington, D.C., in 1989. In the same year, the North American Wetlands Conservation Act was passed, providing federal matching funds for a variety of environmental projects. This landmark legislation was renewed in 2002.

DU relocated its headquarters from Chicago to Memphis in 1992, two years after setting up a regional office in Jackson, Mississippi. Its membership numbered about 510,000 in the United States and 140,000 in Canada.

The organization had begun arranging easements for property owners who wanted to dedicate their land to conservation while maintaining ownership. Nevertheless, duck numbers fell to their lowest number yet recorded, about 30 million. Wet weather helped populations recover in the mid-1990s. A migration of 80 mil-

KEY DATES

1930: More Game Birds in America Foundation is established as major drought dries up waterfowl nesting grounds.

1937: Ducks Unlimited, Inc., is established to fund conservation projects in Canadian breeding grounds.

1951: Group begins first marine project on Prince Edward Island.

1965: Chicago becomes new headquarters for the organization.

1966: Annual fund-raising exceeds $1 million.

1974: DU begins wetlands projects in Mexico.

1992: Headquarters shifts from Chicago to Memphis.

1996: Annual migration of 80 million ducks is largest since the 1970s.

2006: Wetlands for Tomorrow campaign is launched, aiming to raise $1.7 billion within seven years.

lion ducks in 1996 was the largest since the 1970s; in 1999, an estimated 105 million were counted. DU added a regional office in Ann Arbor, Michigan, toward the latter part of the decade.

HABITAT FOR 2000 AND BEYOND

The group's Habitat 2000 program, begun in the mid-1990s, raised nearly $1 billion by 2001, and saw the number of members increase to 757,000. DU was on its way to protecting its ten millionth acre. The ducks continued to face challenges. Another drought reduced breeding populations on Canadian prairies. Lack of rainfall also caused some to remain in the north.

Like other nonprofit groups, DU lent its name to a variety of goods in order to raise royalties. In 2004, the organization took over licensing of images from the federal government's Duck Stamp program for consumer products.

DU budgeted millions to repair damage to Gulf Coast habitats caused by the Hurricanes Katrina and Rita in 2005. However, in the spring following the storm, its biologists reported that the storms had improved the ecosystem by opening up the marshes and providing an ample food supply.

DU had $196.1 million in revenue and support in the fiscal year ended June 30, 2005. The group claimed

750,000 members. More than three-quarters of them were in the United States. There were 3,665 local chapters in the United States and Canada. About 150 of the group's 650 or so professional employees worked at the Memphis headquarters. (DU claimed to have more waterfowl biologists on staff than any other public or private institution.)

DU kicked off another ambitious campaign, called Wetlands for Tomorrow, in 2006. This program aimed to raise $1.7 billion over the next several years in what was billed as the largest conservation campaign ever.

In 2007, its 70th anniversary year, DU was urging Congress to maintain protection of native grasslands in the Great Plains. A longstanding program that compensated farmers for allowing marginal areas to return to wetland was under threat from increasing land values and pressure to raise crops for biofuels.

Frederick C. Ingram

PRINCIPAL COMPETITORS

Audubon Society; National Wildlife Federation; The Nature Conservancy; Pheasants Forever Inc.; Sierra Club; U.S. Fish and Wildlife Service.

FURTHER READING

Bailey, Ken, "Flying High: DU Is Doing Better Than Ever at the Age of 60," *Outdoor Canada,* October 1998, p. 20.

Barrow, Mary Reid, "History Tells Us That Philanthropist Was North Landing River's Savior," *Virginian-Pilot and Ledger-Star* (Norfolk), Beach Journal, February 7, 1993, p. 7.

Behrens, Tom, "Beyond 'Gee Whiz'; Scientific Data Helping to Monitor, Protect Waterfowl Species," *Houston Chronicle,* Hunting & Fishing Sec., July 19, 2001, p. 12.

Bennett, David, "For 67 Years, Huge Membership, Science and Emotion," *Delta Farm Press,* May 7, 2004, p. 6.

Buchanan, Dave, "DU Turns 70 with Its Mission Intact," *Cox News Service,* January 31, 2007.

Causer, Craig, "Health and Conservation Groups Grow Program Services," *Non-Profit Times,* November 1, 2002, p. 35–36.

"Ducks Decline to 30 Million, Lowest in Recorded History," *Omaha World-Herald,* June 7, 1992, p. 18D.

Farrington, S. Kip, Jr., *The Ducks Came Back: The Story of Ducks Unlimited,* New York: Coward-McCann, Inc., 1945.

Hampton, Jeffrey S., "Sights Set on History; Philanthropist Joseph P. Knapp Was Leading Force Behind Preserving Wildfowl, Hunting," *Virginian-Pilot and Ledger-Star* (Norfolk), September 27, 1998, p. Y1.

McHugh, Paul, "Ducks Unlimited Comes to Aid of Wildlife," *San Francisco Chronicle,* December 21, 2000, p. D9.

Nichol, Bill, "Ducks Unlimited Turns 70," *Ducks Unlimited Magazine,* January/February 2007, http://www.ducks.org/DU_Magazine/DUMagazineJanFeb 2007/2973/DUTurns70.html.

Return to Big Grass: Ducks Unlimited, Leader in Wetlands Conservation, Long Grove, Ill.: Ducks Unlimited, Inc., 1986.

Saita, Anne, "Foundation's Largesse Felt Widely Across N. Carolina," *Virginian-Pilot and Ledger-Star* (Norfolk), November 6, 1995, p. B1.

Stevens, William K., "With Habitat Restored, Ducks in the Millions Create Fall Spectacle," *New York Times,* November 14, 1995, p. C4.

Tennyson, Jon R., *A Singleness of Vision: The Story of Ducks Unlimited,* Chicago: Ducks Unlimited, Inc., 1977.

Verrengia, Joseph B., "Duck Hunters Win One for Isolated Wetlands—Or Do They? Development Abounds in Bottomlands," *Associated Press Newswires,* South Wire, March 6, 2004.

Dynatec Corporation

—■—

9555 Yonge Street, Suite 200
Richmond Hill, Ontario L4C 9M5
Canada
Telephone: (905) 780-1980
Fax: (905) 780-1990
Web site: http://www.dynatec.ca

Public Company
Founded: 1980 as Dynatec Mining Limited
Employees: 1,100
Sales: $211.4 million (2006)
Stock Exchanges: Toronto
Ticker Symbol: DY
NAIC: 212393 Other Chemical and Fertilizer Mineral
  Mining; 213114 Support Activities for Metal Min-
  ing; 541380 Testing Laboratories

■ ■ ■

Ontario-based Dynatec Corporation took the leap from
contract mining into mine ownership in the early
2000s. Mining Services and Metallurgical Technologies,
the company's two primary divisions, have supported
the growth of the new ventures. Small in comparison to
other mine owners in the increasingly consolidated
industry, Dynatec has succeeded in overcoming obstacles
toward the construction of a large nickel mining project
on Madagascar.

BREAKING GROUND

Three engineers, Bob Dengler, Bill Shaver, and Fred Edwards, founded Dynatec Mining Limited in 1980,

concentrating on underground development work and
shaft sinking. "Initial growth was slow," the *Canadian
Mining Journal* recalled. The 1988 acquisition of a drilling operation prompted a name change and broadening
of business. The company began operating as Dynatec
International Limited, consisting of two key divisions:
Dynatec Mining Limited and Tonto Drilling Services.

In the early 1990s, the privately held Canadian
company led by Dengler engaged in business in the
United States, Mexico, South America, and the Pacific
Rim. The company's activities included mine contracting, construction, engineering consulting, diamond and
rotary drilling, and mine equipment manufacturing and
distribution, according to the *Globe & Mail.*

A big change came about in 1997. Dynatec merged
with Sherritt International Consultants, Inc. (SICI), a
metallurgical business. Sherritt's Toronto-based parent
company, the gas and oil drilling concern Sherritt
International Corp., immediately spun off the combined
businesses. Dynatec's Dengler headed the new entity,
with projected annual sales of CAD 150 million to
CAD 200 million. The Fort Saskatchewan, Alberta-
based SICI, armed with a half-century of metallurgy
experience, opened new doors for Dynatec Corporation.

"During years of mining we have operated in virtually every commodity minable. As we expanded we
began running small mining operations, gradually building up to larger, more comprehensive projects such as
Inco's Shebandowan nickel mine, the Ken Snyder gold
mine in Nevada and Goldcorp's Red Lake gold mine.
From geology and mine development through to mine
management, we can take on a project and bring it

COMPANY PERSPECTIVES

Dynatec Corporation is a growing mining company and a leading provider of mining and metallurgical services. Dynatec's strategy is to create shareholder value by applying its mining and metallurgical expertise to ownership positions in attractive mineral projects.

through to a producing mine. When we added our Metallurgical Technology division in the late 1990s we realized we could leverage our expertise to add greater value for our shareholders though mine ownership," Dengler recounted in the *Canadian Mining Journal.*

SEEKING NEW VENTURES

Dynatec and FNX Mining Co. Ltd. formed a joint venture in 2002 to buy mining rights to five dormant Sudbury basin mineral properties from Inco Ltd. FNX embarked on a multimillion-dollar exploration project during 2002 and 2003. Formed as a result of the impact of an asteroid, the northern Ontario site had produced CAD 330 billion worth of minerals, primarily nickel, over its lengthy history, the *National Post* explained. Interest in the area was renewed when geologists discovered deeper deposits of copper. Because the site had already been heavily mined, infrastructure such as ventilation shafts, tunnels, and electric wiring was largely in place in many locations.

"We're controlling our own destiny a lot more than in the past, and we're able to take advantage of our expertise for ourselves and for the joint venture, as opposed to just for our clients," Tony Makuch, operations manager for Dynatec, told the *National Post* in March 2003.

Yet while Dynatec held a 25 percent and FNX 75 percent interest in the Sudbury area properties, Inco continued to play a role. The mammoth mining concern not only held the right to process the ore FNX and Dynatec produced but could buy back the properties if it chose to do so.

The November 2003 commencement of commercial production at McCreedy West propelled Dynatec and FNX into the ranks of base and precious metal producers, the *Canadian Mining Journal* reported. The venture continued to prepare other Sudbury basin sites for production.

Meanwhile, Dynatec was expanding outside Canada. Under an August 2003 agreement with a

subsidiary of U.S.-based Phelps Dodge Corp., Dynatec would evaluate, develop, and operate the Ambatovy nickel project in Madagascar. Another move in 2003 banked on the successful transfer of Dynatec's drilling knowhow to the energy sector. Dynatec leased coal-bed methane rights in West Virginia, on its way to becoming a natural gas producer.

Dynatec recorded 2003 revenue of CAD 151.9 million. Upon a subsequent decision to sell the Drilling Services and Mineral Products Divisions, the amount was restated to CAD 106.7 million. Restated earnings were a loss of CAD 1.1 million. In 1999, Dynatec had bought an interest in Canadian industrial mineral producer Highwood Resources. Full ownership followed in 2002, leading to the creation of a Mineral Products division.

In April 2004, the estimated size of Madagascar's Ambatovy nickel project was increased by 20 percent, to 60,000 tonnes. The new projection boosted Dynatec's stock price. The Ambatovy development was expected to rank among the world's largest nickel mines when it began production.

Concurrently, several other big nickel projects were gearing up. Inco Ltd., the world's second largest nickel miner, planned to begin commercial production at a Labrador deposit in 2006. BHP Billiton PLC was positioning itself for a run at third place with Australian nickel projects slated for 2007.

In the process of shifting from engineering firm to active investor, the company continued to derive the bulk of its revenue from contract mining and consulting work such as Goldcorp's "blockbuster" Red Lake property, Drew Hasselback reported for the *National Post* article.

Yet by building a mining asset portfolio through joint ventures, Dynatec's revenue split was evolving. Company mines were expected to produce one-quarter and contract mining and engineering three-quarters of revenue by the end of 2004. Dynatec's 2003 revenue was almost entirely from mining, drilling, and metallurgical services. Contract revenue supported development projects such as Ambatovy as well as mines in the Sudbury basin and a coal-bed methane venture in West Virginia.

In 2004, about a third of the $128.4 million in Mining Services revenue was from the Sudbury Basin Joint Venture (SBJV). Another $16.1 million in revenue was related to its SBJV ownership position. Metallurgical Technologies brought in $4.4 million, bringing total revenue to $148.9 million.

KEY DATES

1980: Dynatec Mining Limited is founded by three engineers.
1988: Acquisition leads to name change and creation of two operating divisions.
1997: Company merges with metallurgical firm Sherritt International Consultants; goes public as Dynatec Corporation.
2002: Joint venture propels move toward mine ownership.
2003: Dynatec begins expanding internationally.
2005: Company sells drilling services business.
2006: Construction plans for Ambatovy nickel venture are back on course.

BEATING THE ODDS

Bruce V. Walter succeeded Dengler as president and CEO on January 1, 2005. Walter, former Sherritt Inc. president, ascended to leadership during a mining boom driven by high metal demand, strong prices, and willing investors. Dynatec, now both contract miner and mine owner and operator, also celebrated a quarter century in business during 2005.

Dynatec sold its Drilling Services to a subsidiary of Major Drill Group International for $17 million in February 2005. Following the sale, Dynatec employed 1,100, a majority working on the SBJV and Red Lake projects.

Capital cost of the Ambatovy nickel project, Dynatec's largest property, was projected to come in at CAD 2.25 billion. The agreement with Phelps Dodge, who needed a partner with nickel metallurgy expertise, initially allowed Dynatec a 53 percent interest for a $20 million expenditure on the project and the contribution of its commercial licenses for hydro-metallurgical technology. In January 2005, Dynatec's ownership climbed to 100 percent. Phelps Dodge received 20.9 million shares, or nearly 10 percent equity in Dynatec, and 100 preferred shares of a subsidiary, according to the *Canadian Mining Journal.*

A feasibility study projected a project life of 27 years. Expected to operate at below average cost, Ambatovy, a laterite ore project, was likely to earn money even when nickel prices dropped off. Although more than 50 percent of nickel production came from sulfide deposits, three-quarters of the world's known nickel resources were in laterite ore. Dynatec's work on Ambatovy positioned the company for the future. Still, as a

company with market capitalization of about CAD 240 million, Dynatec needed additional equity partners to get the big project off the ground.

Stable partnerships looked anything but certain for a time and many forecast doom for the project situated off the east coast of southern Africa. Dynatec shares fell 17 percent upon the late 2004 news that Impala Platinum had pulled out of its short-lived agreement to buy 37.5 percent of Ambatovy. However, in August 2005 Sumitomo Corporation joined the Ambatovy Nickel project as a 25 percent partner.

On another front, in February 2005, the SBJV announced news of a significant mineralization discovery. In the summer, Dynatec acquired indirect interest of Aurora Platinum Corporation, enhancing its Sudbury position. In October, Dynatec exchanged the Aurora holding and its 25 percent interest in the Sudbury Basin Joint Venture for 20.5 million common shares of FNX. With a 24.6 percent stake in FNX, Dynatec was the mining company's largest shareholder. Nevertheless, it was the mining and metallurgical technologies services that drove Dynatec's record operating earnings in 2005.

Meanwhile, work progressed on the U.S.-based coal-bed methane project. Site evaluation, completed in March 2004, led to pilot well gas production on the leased 42,053 acres in West Virginia during 2005. Testing continued into 2006.

Dynatec hit another speed bump in September 2006, when U.S. hedge fund Amaranth Capital Advisors LLC, Dynatec's largest shareholder, was forced to liquidate most of its holdings after a bad bet on natural gas prices.

However, the news brightened considerably the next month, when a group of Korean investors joined the Ambatovy project. Bringing in $852 million in financial support, according to the *National Post,* the Korean Resources Corp. consortium consisted of Daewoo International Corp., Keanganam Enterprises Ltd., and STX Corporation. Under the new partnership configuration Dynatec maintained a 40 percent share as mine operator. Sumitomo Corporation and the Korean group each held a 27.5 percent share. The Canadian-based designer and builder of the mine, SNC Lavalin Inc., agreed to buy 5 percent at the closing of the project debt financing.

Mining was expected to begin in 2010, producing 60,000 tonnes of nickel and 5,600 tonnes of cobalt annually. At a late October 2006 price of $14.34 on the London Metal Exchange, nickel was trading at three times the average price from 1990 to 2005. The Korean investors had committed to buying at least half the mine's output for the first 15 years of production.

Nickel, used in production of stainless steel and batteries, for example, was increasingly demanded by rapid growth economies, including China and India.

Yet Dynatec was competing in an industry controlled by companies valued in the tens of billions. Consolidation continued in 2006. Brazil-based CVDR, which was developing two nickel projects of its own in its home country, bought Inco for $17.5 billion. Inco, in turn, had a New Caledonia nickel project in development. Switzerland-based Xstrata PLC paid more than $20 billion for Falconridge Ltd., which was also developing a New Caledonia project. The giants had mines scheduled to go into production ahead of the Ambatovy.

Dynatec reported record revenue of $211.4 million for 2006. Anticipating the year ahead, the company said construction was on track to begin at Ambatovy around midyear. Also slated for 2007 was a decision on the future of the coal-bed methane initiative. As for the third ownership interest, Sudbury, contract mine production, development, and construction work continued.

Kathleen Peippo

PRINCIPAL SUBSIDIARIES

FNX Mining (24.5%); Ambatovy Nickel Project (40%).

PRINCIPAL DIVISIONS

Mining Services; Metallurgical Technologies.

PRINCIPAL COMPETITORS

Baker Hughes Incorporated; Layne Christensen Company; Major Drilling Group International Inc.

FURTHER READING

"Arizona, Utah Firms Hit with Record Fines," *Salt Lake Tribune,* August 5, 1994, p. A13.

Damsell, Keith, "Barrick Has 'the Most to Lose,'" *National Post,* June 14, 2000, p. C12.

"Dynatec Corporation," *Globe and Mail,* January 11, 2005, p. B9.

"Dynatec International Limited," *Globe and Mail,* April 10, 1991, p. B6.

Fisher, Howard, "Victims' Survivors Sue Mine Shaft's Builder," *Arizona Daily Star,* July 29, 1994, p. 4B.

Foster, Kevin, "Dynatec Lifts Projection for Madagascar Project," *American Metal Market,* April 7, 2004, p. 4.

Hasselback, Drew, "Cleaning Up After the Giants: Junior Firms Hope to Strike It Rich in Abandoned Ontario Mines," *National Post,* March 8, 2003, p. FP7.

———, "Dynatec Step Closer to Being Mining Player," *National Post,* April 6, 2004.

———, "Koreans Sink US$852M into Dynatec Plan: $2.5B Nickel Mine Proposed for Madagascar," *National Post,* October 31, 2006, p. FP4.

Kelly, Bruce, "Revival Plan Set for Yukon Mine," *American Metal Market,* June 9, 1998, p. 7.

Partridge, John, "Dynatec Partner Brightens Prospects," *Globe and Mail,* November 9, 2006, p. B19.

Ross, Ian, "Joint Venture Targets Former Inco Mines in Massive Exploration Program," *Northern Ontario Business,* September 2004, p. 12.

"Sherritt Buys Private Mining Services Company," *Globe and Mail,* August 20, 1997, p. B16.

"Sherritt Files Prospectus for Dynatec Interest," *Globe and Mail,* October 2, 1997, p. B2.

"$30M Exploration Program Targets Sudbury Basin," *Northern Ontario Business,* June 2004, p. 17.

Werniuk, Jane, "Look Who's All Grown Up," *Canadian Mining Journal,* April 2005, pp. 9+.

ECLIPSE
AVIATION

Eclipse Aviation Corporation

■

2503 Clark Carr Loop SE
Albuquerque, New Mexico 87106
U.S.A.
Telephone: (505) 245-7555
Toll Free: (877) 375-7978
Fax: (505) 241-8800
Web site: http://www.eclipseaviation.com

Private Company
Incorporated: 1998
Employees: 1,000
Sales: $186 million (2004 est.)
NAIC: 336411 Aircraft Manufacturing; 336413 Other
   Aircraft Part and Auxiliary Equipment Manufactur-
   ing; 541710 Research and Development in the
   Physical, Engineering, and Life Sciences

■ ■ ■

Eclipse Aviation Corporation is a pioneer in the very light jet (VLJ) industry. Since the beginning the company's stated aim has been to revolutionize aviation the way the personal computer did the computer industry: making it more affordable, accessible, and efficient on the wings of the "personal airplane." Eclipse's founder and many of its early backers came from the tech industry. They brought new concepts to the design, manufacture, and customer service of the company's first plane, the Eclipse 500. The company is based at Albuquerque's Sunport International Airport and has 190,000 square feet of facilities. It is also building a network of service centers across the country.

TECH BACKGROUND

Eclipse Aviation Corporation was formed in 1998 by Vern Raburn. Raburn had a degree in industrial engineering and more than two dozen years of experience in the information technology industry; he had led Microsoft Corporation's first consumer products efforts, and later was CEO of the Symantec virus protection software company and the pen-based computing business Slate.

Raburn also knew flying; he had accumulated more than 5,000 hours in his pilot's logbook, some of them while flying a business jet as head of the investment company of Microsoft cofounder Paul Allen. It was during this time that he conceived an idea for an economical business jet powered by a new class of small engines under development at Williams International.

Such a craft would be able to spare owners the frustration of traveling on major airlines through congested hubs. Instead, the personal jets could be piloted among thousands of secondary airports. If he could keep the costs down, he could reach a vast, untapped market of middle managers dissatisfied with commercial aviation but unwilling or unable to spend the $4 million or so to buy a traditional business jet.

Other savvy businesspeople agreed with the concept. One of the company's angel investors was Bill Gates, Raburn's best man at his wedding to another early Microsoft employee, Dottie Hall (she also went to work at Eclipse). Other influential backers included company Chairman Harold A. Poling, former CEO of the Ford Motor Company.

COMPANY PERSPECTIVES

We knew it was a tall order. When we set out to create the Eclipse 500 jet aircraft, we weren't taking advantage of an existing opportunity, but creating our own. But together with some of the best thinkers, doers, and design engineers in the jet aviation industry, and quite a few of the smartest people we know outside the industry, that's exactly what we did. Throughout the creation and refinement of the Eclipse 500, we've approached every goal with the determination to always take things to the next, higher level. Exactly where the world's first very light jet should be.

Eclipse Aviation was incorporated in Delaware on December 2, 1998. It set up a temporary base in Scottsdale, Arizona, but after an extensive search settled on a new home at Albuquerque's Double Eagle II Airport. New Mexico, a sparsely populated, rural state with few large companies, invested $15 million in the enterprise.

Within a couple of years, Eclipse had lined up 160 customers, each paying $155,000 deposits. This required a large leap of faith; the Eclipse was not only yet to achieve certification, but the engine was unproven. This turned out to be a classic risk/reward scenario: some of the original buyers were able to sell their deposits, and positions in the order book, for up to three times their original investment several years later, before the plane even entered production.

In 2000 the planned price was $837,500, or about one-quarter that of the most inexpensive existing business jets. Eclipse raised its asking price to $1.5 million by 2006. Deposits were not Eclipse's only source of funds. It raised more than $600 million from private investors in its first several years.

A parallel industry was evolving alongside the new VLJs in development, even before they had taken to the air. This was air taxis; a number of operators were planning to use VLJs to shuttle corporate travelers point-to-point for a price comparable with full-fare airline flights. Some of these ventures were quite speculative. In September 2001 Florida's Nimbus Group Inc., once an Internet auction firm, ordered 1,000 of Eclipse's planes for use in a massive air taxi service. However, this deal collapsed within months as Nimbus's share price fell.

The company originally aimed to deliver its first aircraft in 2004, but this date would be pushed back due to difficulties encountered in the daunting process of aircraft design. Since World War II, only a couple of new manufacturers (Lear and Robinson Helicopter) had successfully entered the U.S. market for factory-built aircraft (as opposed to experimental or kit planes).

FLYING IN THE FACE OF CONVENTION

By starting with the proverbial blank sheet, Eclipse was able to incorporate the latest technologies into its aircraft, such as just-in-time manufacturing and electronic instruments. Digital flight and engine controls reduced the complexity associated with flying jets. In addition, the Eclipse 500 would be much less expensive to operate than even its turboprop-driven rivals.

The manufacturing was as revolutionary as the aircraft itself. According to *Industrial Engineer,* the company looked for inspiration to Lexus automobiles, Dell computers, even Carrier air conditioners rather than the staid, reactionary assembly lines of the OEM aircraft industry. In the process, the company introduced new techniques to aviation, such as friction stir welding, which replaced the rivets that had been holding metal planes together since before World War II.

Eclipse aimed to outdo the traditional manufacturers in customer service as well. In 2005 it announced a program called JetComplete, which offered aircraft access at a fixed rate per flight hour, including maintenance (fuel and insurance were extra). Other customer amenities included Iridium satellite communications as a standard feature and Avio flight planning software. The company had begun to establish service centers within an hour's flight of nearly all its customers in the mainland United States. It signed up ETIRC Aviation Europe to handle sales and service in Turkey and the former Soviet Union.

FIRST FLIGHT IN 2002

Creating from scratch was a risky business, however, as illustrated in the company's experience with the 500's engine. The Eclipse 500 made its first test flight on August 26, 2002. However, problems soon emerged with the engine originally chosen for the design, leaving the company with what Raburn called "a million-dollar glider." Eclipse found Williams International's lightweight EJ-22 jet to be inadequate in power and reliability.

This was a huge setback; in fact, the Williams engine was what had originally inspired the Eclipse concept. The plane's design had relied on getting 770

KEY DATES

1998: Vern Raburn forms company to produce a very light jet, the Eclipse 500.

2000: Headquarters are established in Albuquerque, New Mexico; preliminary jet design is completed.

2002: The Eclipse 500 begins test flights.

2003: Pratt & Whitney agrees to develop customized engine for the Eclipse 500.

2006: Eclipse 500 receives FAA type certification.

2007: First aircraft is delivered to a customer.

pounds of thrust out of the 85-pound EJ-22, which had originally been developed for cruise missiles.

In early 2003, Pratt & Whitney Canada agreed to produce a replacement engine. Though based on its PW600 series, this required an investment of at least $10 million on Pratt & Whitney's part. Lining up such an established name as the venerable engine maker gave a huge boost of credibility to a company that had yet to certify a plane, Raburn told a local business journal. However, the change of plans delayed not just the plane's entry into full scale production; the building of a $75 million manufacturing plant at Double Eagle II was put on hold at the same time.

CERTIFICATION IN 2006

The Federal Aviation Administration (FAA) issued type certification for the Eclipse 500 in September 2006. This was a major achievement, signifying the agency found it to be a safe aircraft. Certification of the company's production line, allowing Eclipse to manufacture and deliver planes without having each one individually inspected, was the next step.

A couple of minor mechanical issues were discovered in what Raburn called "the most extensive testing process in the history of general aviation," but these were soon resolved. Eclipse officially delivered its first aircraft on January 4, 2007. The company had big plans, and by early 2007 had ramped up its employment to 1,000 workers. It was aiming to eventually have up to 2,000 employees producing 1,000 planes per year.

By early 2007, Eclipse had orders for 2,600 aircraft. It had started adding buildings to its Double Eagle II campus, with plans to start on a new assembly line after three years. Eclipse's economic impact was not limited to New Mexico, however. In 2006 the company made

an initial $10 million order with wiring harness manufacturer LaBarge Inc., which had plants in Arkansas and Missouri. Other vendors included Fuji Heavy Industries, which made the wings, and Mecaer Group, supplier of landing gear.

As Eclipse's first jet cleared more of the obstacles leading to full-scale production, it became the focus of much economic activity. A small hub of aviation-related industries began to gather in New Mexico, prompting talk of a regional cluster to perhaps one day rival those in Kansas (Cessna's home base) and Florida.

A consulting firm hired by Eclipse predicted the total market for VLJs to be worth $6.5 billion a year by 2017. The FAA expected roughly 5,000 VLJs to be flying by 2016, most of them as air taxis.

Frederick C. Ingram

PRINCIPAL COMPETITORS

Adam Aircraft, Inc.; Cessna Aircraft Company; Piper Aircraft Inc.

FURTHER READING

Averett, Steven, "Eclipsing the Past: Eclipse Aviation Wants to Change the Way You Fly," *Industrial Engineer,* September 2004, pp. 34–42.

Cohn, Meredith, "New Tiny Jets Aim to Revolutionize Air Travel," *Baltimore Sun,* August 13, 2006.

Domrzalski, Dennis, "ABQ Aviation Cluster Plans Build Momentum," *New Mexico Business Weekly,* February 2, 2004, http://albuquerque.bizjournals.com/albuquerque/stories/2004/02/02/story4.html.

———, "Eclipse Early-Purchasers Pocket Large-Dollar Position Premiums," *New Mexico Business Weekly,* August 12, 2005, http://albuquerque.bizjournals.com/albuquerque/stories/2005/08/15/story4.html.

———, "New Mexico Cities to Fight for Aviation Companies," *New Mexico Business Weekly,* October 11, 2002, http://albuquerque.bizjournals.com/albuquerque/stories/2002/ 10/14/story1.html.

———, "Raburn: Eclipse 500 or Die Trying," *New Mexico Business Weekly,* March 10, 2003, http://albuquerque.biz journals.com/albuquerque/stories/2003/ 03/10/focus1.html.

———, "Startup Eclipse Already an Economic Force," *New Mexico Business Weekly,* October 18, 2004, http://albuquer que.bizjournals.com/albuquerque/stories/2004/10/18/story 6.html.

"Eclipse Nears FAA Certification," *New Mexico Business Weekly,* May 2, 2006, http://albuquerque.bizjournals.com/albu querque/stories/2006/ 05/01/daily9.html.

"FAA Certification Leads to New Financing, Partnerships for Eclipse," *New Mexico Business Weekly*, July 28, 2006, http://albuquerque.bizjournals.com/albuquerque/stories/2006/07/24/daily27.html.

"First Eclipse Handover," *Flight International*, January 9, 2007.

Isen, Cheryl, "The Sky's the Limit for this Jet-Plane Entrepreneur," *Puget Sound Business Journal*, January 20, 2006, http://seattle.bizjournals.com/seattle/stories/2006/01/23/small b3.html.

Karlgaard, Rich, "Flying Eclipse's Pocket Jet," *Forbes*, August 15, 2005, p. 27.

Kestin, Hesh, "The Plane Truth," *Inc.*, June 1, 2002.

"LaBarge Inks $10M Eclipse Order Deal," *St. Louis Business Journal*, April 19, 2006, http://stlouis.bizjournals.com/stlouis/stories/2006/04/17/daily21.html.

Norris, Guy, "Eclipse Begins Work on New Facility," *Flight International*, February 27, 2007.

Raburn, Vern, "Why Eclipse Landed in Albuquerque," *New Mexico Business Journal*, February/March 2001, pp. 37–41.

Robinson-Avila, Kevin, "Design Tweaks Bring Eclipse 500 Up to Speed and Distance," *New Mexico Business Weekly*, February 12, 2007, http://albuquerque.bizjournals.com/albuquerque/stories/2007/02/12/story5.html.

———, "Eclipse Breaks New Ground for Attention to Customer Service," *New Mexico Business Weekly*, January 29, 2007, http://albuquerque.bizjournals.com/albuquerque/stories/2007/01/29/story2.html.

———, "Eclipse Glides Through Turbulence," *New Mexico Business Weekly*, December 25, 2006, http://albuquerque.bizjournals.com/albuquerque/stories/2006/12/25/story1.html.

Schonfeld, Erick, "The Little (Jet) Engine That Could: With a Revolutionary 85-Pound Engine and $60 Million in Backing, Vern Raburn Wants to Turn the World of Private Air Travel Upside Down," *Fortune*, July 24, 2000, pp. 132+.

Siebenmark, Jerry, "Flying Low: Eclipse Aviation's Business Jet Cheaper Than Ones Made in Wichita," *Wichita Business Journal*, February 25, 2002, http://wichita.bizjournals.com/wichita/stories/2002/02/25/ story1.html.

———, "Wichita Officials Keeping an Eye on Eclipse Aviation's Slow Progress," *Wichita Business Journal*, March 24, 2003, http://wichita.bizjournals.com/wichita/stories/2003/03/24/story4.html.

Siebenmark, Jerry, and Dennis Domrzalski, "A Call to Arms? Officials Keeping an Eye on N.M. Aviation Cluster," *Wichita Business Journal*, October 21, 2002, http://wichita.bizjournals.com/wichita/stories/2002/10/21/story3.html.

Wastnage, Justin, "Cancellation: Eclipse 500 Order Termination Signals End to Nimbus Taxi Plans; Deal Flounders When Manufacturer Returns Former Internet Auctioneer's Stock Deposit After Low Value Hinders Sale," *Flight International*, July 16, 2002, p. 39.

Eddie Bauer Holdings, Inc.

15010 NE 36th Street
Redmond, Washington 98052-5317
U.S.A.
Telephone: (425) 755-6100
Fax: (425) 755-7696
Web site: http://www.eddiebauer.com

Public Company
Founded: 1920
Incorporated: 1968 as Eddie Bauer, Inc.
Employees: 10,000
Sales: $1.01 billion (2006)
Stock Exchanges: NASDAQ
Ticker Symbol: EBHI
NAIC: 448140 Family Clothing Stores; 454110 Electronic Shopping and Mail-Order Houses

■ ■ ■

Eddie Bauer Holdings, Inc., together with its principal operating subsidiary, Eddie Bauer, Inc., is a catalog, storefront, and e-commerce retailer specializing in casual outdoor apparel and accessories. The company mails out approximately 80 million catalogs per year, with about a quarter of revenues stemming from catalog and web site orders. On the storefront side, there are around 280 Eddie Bauer retail stores located throughout the United States and Canada, with an additional 115 Eddie Bauer outlet stores; the latter offer lower-priced merchandise consisting of both excess merchandise from the retail stores and products designed specifically for the outlets. Through joint ventures, Eddie Bauer operates retail outlets and distributes catalogs in Japan and Germany. The company also licenses the Eddie Bauer brand to several other companies, including Ford Motor Company, which has made Eddie Bauer edition sport-utility vehicles since 1984; American Recreation Products, Inc., for camping gear and accessories; the Lane Company, for a line of Eddie Bauer furniture; Dorel Industries, Inc., which sells Eddie Bauer car seats; and Skyway Luggage Company, for luggage and travel accessories.

EARLY HISTORY

Created by the son of Russian immigrants, Eddie Bauer, Inc., began as a tennis racquet stringing business in Seattle, Washington. While his parents would eventually play a significant role in the development of Eddie Bauer, Inc., Eddie Bauer initially drew upon his childhood years on Orcas Island, a sparsely populated island near Seattle, as the inspiration for what eventually would become a billion-dollar retail business.

Those early years were spent fishing, hunting, and trapping on the wooded island, imbuing Bauer with a love of the outdoors. When his family moved to Seattle in 1912, Bauer was 13 years old and looking for work. He immediately gravitated toward the only full-line sporting goods store in the city, Piper & Taft, and landed a job as a stock boy. Over the years, Bauer watched and learned, eventually becoming adept at making guns, fly rods, and golf clubs. In addition to these talents, Bauer also developed considerable skill in stringing tennis racquets, winning the world speed championship while in a display window at Piper &

Taft, by stringing 12 racquets in slightly more than three-and-a-half hours. Still in his teens, Bauer already had gained the attention of Seattle's sporting community. He often was referred to in local newspapers for killing the biggest elk, or catching the most fish, or for winning rifle- and pistol-shooting competitions. This local recognition would serve Bauer well when, in 1919, with $25 in his pocket and $500 borrowed on a 120-day loan, he rented 15 feet of wall space in a gun shop for $15 a month and began stringing racquets on his own. In this venture, Bauer enjoyed immediate success, stringing enough racquets to accumulate $10,000 within his first year. In 1920, encouraged by his initial success, Bauer arranged for credit from a bank and opened his own shop, Eddie Bauer's Sport Shop, the predecessor of Eddie Bauer, Inc.

In addition to his renowned racquet-stringing abilities, Bauer also offered golf equipment and trout fishing flies during his first year of business, and the 20-foot storefront quickly became a haven for sporting enthusiasts throughout the Pacific Northwest. Bauer's success during these nascent years was in large part due to his reputation as an experienced outdoorsman and his active participation in the sporting community. He worked at his store from February through August each year, then hunted and fished throughout the winter. During these sojourns in the wild, he field-tested all of the equipment he sold in his stores, which, after the first year, included an array of outdoor equipment and clothing. Two years after he opened for business, this firsthand knowledge of his stock enabled him to offer an unconditional guarantee of satisfaction on all of the products sold in his store, a rarity for retail businesses during the 1920s; he also established a company creed. Bauer promoted sporting activities in his spare time, increasing the public's awareness of such sports as skiing by importing Norwegian hickory skis and persuading Norwegian skiers to come to the Pacific Northwest to help foster growth in the sport.

By 1924, Bauer had added a complete selection of fishing tackle, firearms, and skeet and trap equipment to his store and renamed it Eddie Bauer's Sporting Goods. Customers continued to flock to Bauer's store, lured by his unconditional guarantee and his knowledge of the outdoors. Eddie Bauer's Sporting Goods had quickly become a favorite place for outdoorsmen to outfit themselves for a wide variety of sporting endeavors. With a large and loyal clientele, Bauer's future success appeared as guaranteed as the products he sold, but, in the coming years, Bauer's position as a successful operator of a local sporting goods store would be elevated to a height not imagined even during the optimistic 1920s.

FROM SHUTTLECOCKS TO GOOSE DOWN JACKETS

Bauer's success had been predicated on his experience and interest in sporting equipment, so it was fitting that the innovation that would eventually launch his company into the upper echelon of the outdoor apparel industry came as a result, at least in part, of his desire to improve sporting equipment. In the late 1920s, Bauer attempted to improve the consistency of flight in badminton shuttlecocks. He imported premium feathers from Europe and developed a method using buckshot that achieved the desired results. In 1934 his design was patented and eventually adopted for use in the badminton world championships.

While investigating which type of feather would improve the flight of shuttlecocks, Bauer came across goose down, reminding him of an uncle who had once extolled the virtues of goose down's insulating quality. Years earlier, Bauer's uncle, a Cossack fighting in Manchuria during the Russo-Japanese War, had worn a coat lined with goose down to stave off the 50 degrees below zero winter weather. Bauer, who had suffered through many cold winters fishing and hunting in the mountains near Seattle, decided to use goose down to make a coat for himself. After designing and sewing a quilted goose down jacket for himself, Bauer discovered the truth of his uncle's story and soon was making down jackets for a few of his friends. The popularity of these jackets led Bauer to patent his design and begin production of America's first quilted goose down insulated jacket in 1936. Called the "Skyliner" and selling for $34.50, the jacket was an immediate success, particularly with Alaskan bush pilots, and led to the production of a wide assortment of garments with different quilting styles. Starting with ten seamstresses in 1936, Bauer needed 125 by 1940 to meet the voracious demand for his quilted jackets. By this time, Bauer had secured a virtual monopoly on the insulated jacket market, employing as many seamstresses as his rapidly expanding business required and purchasing all the European and North American goose down he wanted.

KEY DATES

1920: Eddie Bauer opens Eddie Bauer's Sport Shop in Seattle.

1922: Bauer begins offering his customers an unconditional guarantee of satisfaction.

1924: Store is renamed Eddie Bauer's Sporting Goods.

1936: Bauer patents and introduces the first goose down insulated jacket, marking the company's entrance into outdoor apparel.

1942: Bauer begins providing goose down products to the U.S. Army Air Corps.

1945: Company sends out its first mail-order catalogs.

1953: Company is reorganized as a 50-50 partnership between Eddie Bauer and William F. Niemi, Sr., under the name William F. Niemi Co., doing business as Eddie Bauer Expedition Outfitters.

1968: Bauer retires, selling his interest in the company to Niemi; the company is incorporated as Eddie Bauer, Inc.

1971: General Mills, Inc., acquires Eddie Bauer for $10 million.

1984: Through a licensing deal with Ford, the first Eddie Bauer edition SUV makes its debut.

1988: Spiegel, Inc., acquires the company for $260 million.

1991: Eddie Bauer Home makes its debut.

1993: Company enters into joint venture to open stores and start catalog operations in Japan.

1995: Joint venture is created to form retailing and cataloging operations in Germany.

1996: Company moves into e-commerce with the launch of www.eddiebauer.com.

2002: An enduring pattern of poor sales prompts the first of several rounds of store closings.

2003: Spiegel is forced to file for Chapter 11 bankruptcy protection.

2005: Out of the reorganization of Spiegel, Eddie Bauer Holdings, Inc., emerges as a new holding company for Eddie Bauer, Inc.; Eddie Bauer appoints its first board of directors and shuts down all of its Eddie Bauer Home stores.

2006: Eddie Bauer agrees to sell itself to two private equity firms for $286 million.

2007: Shareholders vote down the proposed sale.

WORLD WAR II CONTRIBUTIONS

This supply of goose down, however, ended just as Bauer's quilted down garments began to attract orders through the mail. When the United States entered World War II in 1941, the war production board requisitioned all of the goose down supply on the market and froze Bauer's existing supply. No longer able to purchase or use goose down, he was relegated to using eiderdown (down from an eider duck) as a replacement, a substitute that negatively affected his sales. It appeared as if his flourishing retail trade had been swept away from him, but whatever losses Bauer incurred as a result of the government's seizure, he more than made up for by providing goose down products to the U.S. Army Air Corps beginning in 1942. At first, Bauer provided the military with sleeping bags and snowshoes and binders, which he sold at retail prices, and eventually his business with the government increased considerably. Using the war production board's goose down, Bauer manufactured 25,000 flight suits and

nearly 250,000 sleeping bags for Air Corps flight crews and those fighting in the frigid Aleutian campaign. To satisfy the military's needs, Bauer constructed a production factory, invested roughly $200,000 in specially built machinery, and hired 400 power sewing machine operators to work in three shifts, seven days a week. This prodigious wartime production salvaged what otherwise could have been a recessive period for Bauer's company and, more importantly, it also carried the Eddie Bauer name across the nation. All of the garments Bauer manufactured for the military had the Eddie Bauer label stitched on them, the only garments during the war that carried the manufacturer's private label.

Although Bauer's civilian business slackened during the war, he continued to advertise to create a demand for his products when the war ended. Once it did, he steeled himself for an immediate return to the prosperous days of the late 1930s. Expectations ran higher, however, considering the tremendous strides in name recognition the company had made as a result of the war, so Bauer introduced a new way to bring his products to the public. In 1945, just as many of those who had worn Eddie Bauer products during the war were returning home, Bauer issued the company's first mail-order catalogs, through a division that had been formed in 1942 to sell the goose down products, Eddie Bauer Expedition Outfitters. Although the introduction of the catalogs represented a significant landmark in the company's history, a more pressing concern during these immediate postwar years overshadowed their import. Bauer's company seemed in danger of failing.

CONCENTRATING ON MAIL-ORDER CATALOGS

To fill the demands of his contract with the Air Corps, Bauer had invested in equipment that could serve his production needs only during the war. Both the profits and the machinery were temporary, so, once the war ended, Bauer was left with the machinery and nowhere to sell it, leaving him in a precarious situation. As he would later recall, "We were stuck with the machinery and I lost practically everything I owned, down to where I had to start all over again." To assist with this rebuilding process, Bauer entered into a partnership in 1953 with William F. Niemi, Sr., a friend with whom Bauer hunted and fished, and together they strengthened the company by placing an emphasis on the mail-order side of the business and concentrating on producing a larger selection of products (the company was officially called William F. Niemi Co. but was doing business as Eddie Bauer Expedition Outfitters). From this point forward until the 1970s, Bauer's company would be primarily a mail-order business. Before the end of the decade, Bauer would close his stores in Seattle and rely almost exclusively on purchases made through the mail, with the only retail sales being generated by a factory store in Seattle. In the late 1950s Bauer and Niemi also brought their sons into the partnership.

The changes made by Bauer and Niemi worked. By mailing catalogs to potential customers and outfitting those outdoorsmen who came to the factory in Seattle, the company generated $1 million in sales in 1960. Although Bauer's financial position had seemed bleak 15 years earlier, the widespread recognition of the Eddie Bauer name had always remained secure. A new generation of potential customers were being introduced to the Eddie Bauer line of products through the catalogs arriving in the mail. By this time, Bauer's company used nearly half of the world's supply of northern goose down and had outfitted every American expedition to the Himalayas over the previous ten years. When mountain climbers needed to train for assaults on the towering peaks in the Himalayan range, they often

selected the mountains in proximity to Seattle as suitable sites. By the 1960s, a visit to Bauer's factory store became a natural stop for climbers needing clothing and equipment, which further bolstered the nation's recognition of the Eddie Bauer name. When James W. Whittaker became the first American to reach the top of Mount Everest in 1963, he wore an Eddie Bauer parka, slept in an Eddie Bauer sleeping bag, and used Eddie Bauer gear, as did the entire expedition. Three years later, Bauer's company outfitted the American Antarctic Mountaineering Expedition, and it continued to produce the preferred gear for expeditions to follow in later years.

1968–71: BRIEF STAB AT INDEPENDENT EXPANSION

By 1968, annual sales at the company were approaching $5 million and professional management and financial planning was clearly needed at the rapidly growing firm. Eddie Bauer and his son decided to sell their half of the company to Niemi and his son, Bill Niemi, Jr., for $1.5 million; a group of investors who had helped finance the buyout gained stock in the company, which was incorporated as Eddie Bauer, Inc. The completion of the sale in June 1968 marked Eddie Bauer's retirement from the firm he had launched nearly 50 years earlier.

The new management team, headed by Niemi as chairman and Niemi, Jr., as president, made some initial moves back into retailing, opening the first store outside Seattle, in San Francisco, in 1968, and a new store in downtown Seattle, the company's first large store, in early 1970. The company also consolidated its scattered Seattle operations in a building on Airport Way in South Seattle that included administration, customer service, manufacturing, warehousing, and distribution at one location. By 1970 sales had surged to $9.1 million, with earnings exceeding $500,000. Needing capital to fund a more ambitious expansion, Eddie Bauer, Inc., made plans for an initial public offering (IPO) in the spring of 1970, but the underwriter of the IPO recommended a postponement following a stock market dip. It was at this point that the management concluded that the best course of action would be a sale of the undercapitalized company.

1971–88: THE GENERAL MILLS ERA

In March 1971 food conglomerate General Mills, Inc., purchased Eddie Bauer for about 311,000 shares of General Mills common stock, or about $10 million. The acquisition of Eddie Bauer was part of General Mills' aggressive move into specialty retailing. What General

Mills received was still essentially a mail-order business, with a small retail side. It was the latter segment of Eddie Bauer that General Mills wanted to fortify.

Several years passed, however, before the disparate merchandising philosophies of the two companies would effectively join together and even longer until Eddie Bauer obtained consistent leadership. From 1975 to 1978 the company went through four presidents, until finally settling on James J. Casey, who had joined Eddie Bauer three years earlier. At this time, the state of Eddie Bauer's product line was still in flux, as General Mills attempted to reshape its subsidiary's market appeal. Six months after Casey assumed leadership of the company, he maneuvered it away from a merchandising failure that had added golf and tennis apparel to the company's product line. For customers inured to a product line whose reputation had been built on manufacturing down parkas and outfitting expeditions to the Antarctic, the shift was a difficult one to make, and potential customers went elsewhere when purchasing items for warmer climes. Although General Mills continued to struggle with the specialty outdoor market niche, it had increased the number of Eddie Bauer retail locations. By the end of the decade, there were 16 retail stores and plans in place to double that figure. In General Mills' first year of ownership, Eddie Bauer posted $11 million in sales, and, with the boost in sales provided by the additional stores, sales climbed to $80 million, ranking the company second only to L.L. Bean, Inc., in the specialty outdoor market. The disparity between retail and catalog sales disappeared, with half of the total revenues generated by the stores, and 14 million catalog customers accounting for the remainder. In the meantime, the company moved its headquarters once again in 1973, settling into a 14-acre campus in Redmond, Washington.

By 1984, the changes initiated by General Mills had substantially altered the image Eddie Bauer projected to its customers. Apparel generated approximately 70 percent of the retail store revenues, and much of it did not resemble the clothing worn by members of a Mount Everest expedition, or even the clothing worn by weekend adventurers camping in the woods. Tents, backpacks, and fishing rods had slowly begun to disappear from the shelves of the company's stores and were replaced with oxford cloth shirts, lamb's wool sweaters, and other items uncharacteristic of the rugged, expedition outfitter. With 41 stores located in Canada and the United States, the company broadened its appeal, enough for Ford Motor Company to begin production of the Eddie Bauer Bronco II in 1984, and attracted a more diverse clientele. The expansion of the retail side of the business represented a move toward greater growth for the mail-order segment as well. In 1983 Eddie Bauer mailed 14 million catalogs, and, by the following year, 30 million catalogs were sent to potential customers, two million of which were printed in French to accommodate the company's burgeoning clientele in Canada. Plans called for further expansion of the company's retail business, some 60 stores over the next five years. To lead the company toward this goal, a switch in leadership was made. In 1984 Michael Rayden replaced Casey and began separating retail, mail order, and manufacturing into three distinct divisions.

By 1988, Eddie Bauer had 57 retail stores located in the United States and Canada. Yet just as General Mills was announcing further plans to augment Eddie Bauer's retail holdings, the corporation put Eddie Bauer up for sale along with another specialty clothing chain it owned, Talbots, in a bid to divest itself of all nonfood-related businesses.

1988–2005: THE SPIEGEL ERA

In 1988 Spiegel, Inc., a catalog marketer of apparel, home furnishings, and other merchandise, bought Eddie Bauer for $260 million, roughly equal to the sales the company generated at the time of its purchase. Wayne Badovinus was selected to lead Eddie Bauer and, over the next two years, 100 stores were added to the retail chain, bringing total sales up to $448 million. In 1991 Eddie Bauer's first "Premier" store was opened in Chicago, which housed all of the company's recently introduced specialty product lines. "All Week Long," Eddie Bauer's collection of women's sportswear and casual attire, first introduced as a catalog business in 1987, had evolved into a retail business by 1991 with the opening of its first store in Portland, Oregon, and was part of the Premier store concept. Also included in the Premier stores were "The Sport Shop at Eddie Bauer," featuring custom-built fishing rods, reels, and fishing flies, and "The Eddie Bauer Home Collection," which sold a wide assortment of indoor and outdoor furnishings. The addition of these specialty retail concepts, each first introduced in 1991, marked another dramatic leap in revenues. In the three years since Spiegel had purchased Eddie Bauer, the parent company had witnessed an increase in revenues from roughly $260 million, to nearly $750 million, occasioned primarily by the dramatic increase in Eddie Bauer's retail business. This expansion continued after 1991, giving the company 265 retail stores by the end of 1992. Eddie Bauer Home became the longest lasting of the new concepts, and by 1994 there were 15 such outlets in 11 states, and the company was mailing out separate Home catalogs six times per year. Revenues surpassed the $1 billion mark for the first time in 1993.

The mid-1990s were marked by continued expansion in North America as well as the company's first forays into overseas territory. The international expansion was pursued through joint ventures with units of Otto Versand (GmbH & Co.), a German mail-order giant controlled by the Otto family, which also controlled Spiegel. In 1993 Eddie Bauer entered into a venture with Otto-Sumisho, Inc., to open retail stores and sell through catalogs in Japan. Two years later the company joined with Otto Versand units Heinrich Heine GmbH and Sport-Scheck GmbH in another venture created to launch retail and catalog sales in Germany. By the end of the decade there were 35 Eddie Bauer stores in Japan and nine in Germany. A similar venture for the U.K. market was created in 1996 but was discontinued three years later, with catalog sales continuing through Eddie Bauer's German joint venture.

During 1995, when the company celebrated its 75th anniversary, Eddie Bauer launched a new retail and catalog concept, called AKA Eddie Bauer, selling upscale dress clothing for men and women and aiming at the burgeoning market for more casual work clothes. The company's All Week Long concept was discontinued, with those stores converted into AKA Eddie Bauer units. Even amidst a slump in the entire retailing industry, Eddie Bauer continued to expand in other ways as well. In 1996 came the debut of the EBTEK line of high performance outerwear and casual activewear featuring such fabrics as Goretex and Polartec 200. That same year, the company established a third distribution channel with the launching of its Internet web site. Bucking the early trend in e-commerce, eddiebauer.com was generating a profit within two years of its debut. During 1997 Eddie Bauer opened its 500th U.S. store.

With its Ford partnership continuing, Eddie Bauer entered into several more licensing deals in the late 1990s to further leverage its increasingly well-known name. In 1997 the company inked a deal with the Lane Company for the development of a line of Eddie Bauer furniture. The following year Eddie Bauer mountain bikes were launched with Giant Bicycle, Inc.; Eddie Bauer eyewear debuted through an agreement with Signature Eyewear, Inc.; and Eddie Bauer infant and juvenile car seats were introduced in conjunction with Cosco, Inc.

After adding a net 39 stores in 1998, and suffering from declining sales because of increased competition and a slow reaction to hot new fashion trends such as cargo pants, Eddie Bauer reined in its North American expansion the following year, when the chain's net gain was just nine stores. The company also made some alterations to its store concepts that year. Eddie Bauer

Home was revamped to include less in the way of upholstered furniture and tabletop items and more of the domestic items for bed and bath, such as bedding and towels. The 40 home stores also began featuring the Eddie Bauer Juvenile line of bedding and beds and increased its "baby by Eddie Bauer" line of infant bedding and furniture. The AKA Eddie Bauer concept was discontinued in the form of separate stores, and the AKA merchandise was integrated into adjacent Eddie Bauer sportswear stores.

With a revamp of its sportswear lines, Eddie Bauer managed to post a 6 percent increase in comparable store sales in 1999, compared with a 9 percent decrease the previous year. Overall revenues increased slightly that year, reaching $1.79 billion. During 2000, when Eddie Bauer planned to increase its North American retail units to 565 and to expand or remodel 40 existing stores, a milestone was reached when the first Eddie Bauer store opened in Hawaii, completing the chain's entrance into all 50 states.

The turnaround performance of 1999 did not last. In the summer of 2000, same-store sales began dropping precipitously, amounting to a 15 percent decline for the third quarter of that year. The consensus from analysts was that Eddie Bauer had veered too far to informal clothing styles and too young as well. The hot trend at the time was business casual clothing, and Eddie Bauer's styles had grown too informal for business attire. For the full year of 2000, the company suffered from a 9 percent drop in same-store sales and a 3 percent fall in catalog sales. The one bright spot was its web-based business, which remained profitable and enjoyed a surge in sales of 130 percent, to roughly $135 million.

In the fall of 2001 Eddie Bauer introduced an overhauled merchandise mix featuring a "classic casual" look aimed at men and women between the ages of 35 and 55. The timing of this launch proved unfortunate as it coincided with an economic downturn and retail slowdown following the September 11, 2001, terrorist attacks on the United States. Same-store sales plummeted 21 percent in September and 19 percent the following month. In January 2002 Richard T. Fersch, who had served as the CEO of Eddie Bauer since 1997, unexpectedly announced his retirement, prompted in part by the company's continued poor financial performance.

As the search began for a new leader at Eddie Bauer, the retailer's parent was itself experiencing serious financial difficulties stemming primarily from its money-losing credit-card division. In February 2002 Spiegel announced its intention to sell the troubled unit and also revealed plans to close 45 underperforming Eddie Bauer stores out of the total of 575. In July 2002 Fabian

Månsson was brought onboard as the new Eddie Bauer president and CEO. The flamboyant Månsson, born in Stockholm, had previously helped turn the Swedish firm Hennes & Mauritz AB into one of Europe's most successful retailers. Månsson immediately returned Eddie Bauer to its roots, launching new clothing lines and a marketing campaign that emphasized the outdoor heritage of the brand in the fall of 2002. Sales for the year amounted to only $1.42 billion, down more than 20 percent from the 1999 total.

In March 2003 Spiegel was forced to file for Chapter 11 bankruptcy protection as its financial situation deteriorated. One month later, Eddie Bauer retrenched once again, announcing that another 60 underperforming stores were to be closed. By the end of the year, plans were in place for a further 30 store closures. Despite a 7 percent jump in same-store sales in September—the first monthly gain of that sort in more than three years—Eddie Bauer's results for the full year were less encouraging: a 6 percent drop in same-store sales and a further decline in overall sales, to $1.3 billion.

2005: BEGINNING OF NEW ERA OF INDEPENDENCE

Still operating under bankruptcy protection, Spiegel placed Eddie Bauer up for sale in April 2004. That year, Eddie Bauer netted a profit of $108 million on revenues of $1.24 billion. Spiegel, in the meantime, sold its Newport News and Spiegel catalog businesses in 2004 but pulled Eddie Bauer off the block when no party came forward with an offer that matched what executives thought the retailer was worth. Then, in February 2005, Spiegel revealed plans to reorganize around Eddie Bauer, a plan that came to fruition on June 21 of that year. Out of the restructuring and bankruptcy emerged Eddie Bauer Holdings, Inc., a new holding company, initially wholly owned by Spiegel creditors, serving as the parent company for Eddie Bauer, Inc., and its subsidiaries. Eddie Bauer appointed the first board of directors in its 85-year history, and Månsson continued to lead the company as president and CEO. A stand-alone company for the first time in 34 years, Eddie Bauer began its new era focused on its 417-unit clothing store operation and its companion catalog and Internet channels. The 30 Eddie Bauer Home stores were closed during the second half of 2005. The company remained involved in home furnishings via arrangements in which it licensed the Eddie Bauer brand to other parties.

This new era began rather roughly. Same-store sales for the fourth quarter of 2005 fell more than 7 percent mainly because of another merchandising misstep. The fall and holiday apparel lines, which had been redesigned to be more fashionable with tighter styles and brighter colors, met with a cold reception from the brand's core customers. During the second half of the year, Eddie Bauer lost $22.8 million on sales of $593.7 million. In 2006 the retailer went back to a focus on clothing for the "modern outdoor lifestyle," began standardizing its stores around a 5,500-square-foot format, and launched its first full-scale customer loyalty program, called Eddie Bauer Friends. In October, stock in Eddie Bauer Holdings began trading on the NASDAQ.

At the same time, Eddie Bauer began exploring a possible sale of the company. In November 2006 the company reached an agreement to sell itself to Sun Capital Partners, Inc., and Golden Gate Capital, two private equity firms, for $286 million. Månsson contended that the deal would provide the company the additional time and resources necessary for his turnaround strategy to come to fruition. Many shareholders, however, were unhappy with the $9.25 per share price that had been negotiated, and in February 2007, at a special meeting, they voted down the sale. The next day, Månsson resigned and was replaced on an interim basis by Howard Gross, a board member with 35 years of retailing experience, including stints heading The Limited and Victoria's Secret chains. Ironically, one month later Eddie Bauer released its results for the fourth quarter of 2006, which showed the firm posting its first quarterly profit since its emergence out of Spiegel: $63.2 million on sales of $381.9 million. Same-store sales were up 4.6 percent for the quarter, a trend that appeared to be accelerating in 2007, when the increase was 9.5 percent for the first ten weeks of the year. These amounted to early, though far from certain, signs of a sustained turnaround for the legendary Eddie Bauer brand.

Jeffrey L. Covell
Updated, David E. Salamie

PRINCIPAL SUBSIDIARIES

Eddie Bauer, Inc.; Eddie Bauer of Canada, Inc.; Eddie Bauer Fulfillment Services, Inc.; Eddie Bauer Customer Services Inc. (Canada); Eddie Bauer Diversified Sales, LLC; Eddie Bauer Services, LLC; Eddie Bauer International Development, LLC; Eddie Bauer Information Technology LLC.

PRINCIPAL COMPETITORS

L.L. Bean, Inc.; Lands' End Inc.; The Gap Inc.; Target Corporation; Columbia Sportswear Company; The

North Face, Inc.; Patagonia; Recreational Equipment, Inc.; AnnTaylor Stores Corporation; Banana Republic Inc.; The Talbots, Inc.; Chico's FAS, Inc.; Coldwater Creek Inc.; J. Crew Group, Inc.; The J. Jill Group Inc.; J.C. Penney Corporation, Inc.; Federated Department Stores, Inc.; Nordstrom, Inc.

FURTHER READING

Allison, Melissa, "Eddie Bauer CEO out Day After Deal Dies," *Seattle Times,* February 10, 2007, p. E1.

Batsell, Jake, "Bankrupt Spiegel Puts Eddie Bauer Up for Sale," *Seattle Times,* April 7, 2004.

———, "Eddie Bauer Goes Indoors," *Seattle Times,* November 14, 2001, p. C1.

———, "Eddie Bauer Taps CEO with Roots in European Retail," *Seattle Times,* July 12, 2002, p. C1.

Chandler, Susan, "New Fashion Focus Helps Eddie Bauer Rebound," *Seattle Times,* August 29, 1999, p. F1.

Copple, Brandon, "Fashionably Late," *Forbes,* August 12, 2002, p. 46.

"Eddie Bauer: A Name You Can Trust," *Catalog Age,* September 1993, pp. 135–36.

"Eddie Bauer Catalog Sidesteps Recession Doldrums," *Direct Marketing,* November 1983, p. 72.

"Eddie Bauer: The Man Behind the Name," *Pacific Northwest Magazine,* May 1983, pp. 61–64.

Enbysk, Monte, "Snug Fit: Eddie Bauer Inc. Has Profited Handsomely from Acquisition by Spiegel," *Tacoma News Tribune,* February 27, 1994, p. F4.

"Evolution of a Down-Wear Retailer," *New York Times,* March 12, 1981, p. D4.

Fung, Shirley, "Troubled Bauer Shifts Gears," *Women's Wear Daily,* November 1, 2000, p. 8.

George, Melissa, "Why Eddie Bauer Is Lost in the Woods," *Crain's Chicago Business,* August 10, 1998, p. 1.

Green, Jeff, "Bauer Power," *Brandweek,* July 5, 1999, pp. 16–17.

Hanover, Dan, "EddieBauer.com Gets It Done," *Chain Store Age,* October 1998, pp. 197–98.

Harris, Craig, "Eddie Bauer Has First Profit Since Bankruptcy," *Seattle Post-Intelligencer,* March 15, 2007, p. D6.

Lim, Paul J., "Eddie Bauer Plans Aggressive Expansion," *Seattle Times,* January 18, 1996, p. C1.

Merrick, Amy, "Eddie Bauer CEO Says He Is Retiring Amid Sales Slump," *Wall Street Journal,* January 7, 2002, p. A18.

———, "Spiegel Files for Chapter 11," *Wall Street Journal,* March 18, 2003, p. B4.

———, "Spiegel Plans to Exit Bankruptcy As Operator of Eddie Bauer Chain," *Wall Street Journal,* February 22, 2005, p. B7.

Moin, David, "Spiegel to Shut 60 Eddie Bauer Units," *Women's Wear Daily,* April 29, 2003, p. 4.

Moriwaki, Lee, "It Takes More Than Flannel," *Seattle Times,* October 19, 1997, p. E1.

Nogaki, Sylvia Wieland, "Out of the Woods: Eddie Bauer Hikes Trail Leading to Higher Profits," *Seattle Times,* July 26, 1993, p. E1.

Ouchi, Monica Soto, "Eddie Bauer Deal Doesn't Sell," *Seattle Times,* February 9, 2007, p. E1.

———, "Judge OKs Spiegel Plan," *Seattle Times,* May 26, 2005.

———, "New Life for Eddie Bauer: Spiegel Reorganizes Around Its Outdoorwear Division," *Seattle Times,* February 19, 2005, p. E1.

Palmeri, Christopher, "Indoor Sportsman," *Forbes,* March 29, 1993, p. 43.

Palmieri, Jean E., "Eddie Bauer Looks Homeward," *Daily News Record,* October 7, 2002, p. 9.

Pasternack, Edward D., "Eddie Bauer Expanding in Japan and Germany," *Direct Marketing,* March 1996, pp. 36, 38–39.

"REI, Eddie Bauer Expand," *Chain Store Age Executive,* August 1987, pp. 46–47.

"Retreat, Hell: Four Contrarians Who Hear Opportunity Knocking," *Business Week,* January 14, 1991, p. 64.

Ricketts, Chip, "Eddie Bauer's Southern Expansion Push Includes Metroplex," *Dallas Business Journal,* February 26, 1990, p. 3.

Schwadel, Francine, "Waters Resigns from General Mills, Pursues Purchase of Units He Managed," *Wall Street Journal,* January 11, 1988, p. 32.

Schwadel, Francine, and Richard Gibson, "General Mills Is Putting Up for Sale Talbots, Eddie Bauer Clothing Chain," *Wall Street Journal,* January 8, 1988, p. 4.

———, "General Mills to Sell Last Retail Units, Talbots and Bauer, for $585 Million," *Wall Street Journal,* May 19, 1988, p. 4.

Spector, Robert, "Eddie Bauer's New Look," *Weekly,* January 2, 1985, pp. 20–22.

———, *The Legend of Eddie Bauer,* Lyme, Conn.: Greenwich Publishing, 1994.

Tice, Carol, "Shrink-to-Fit Bauer," *Puget Sound Business Journal* (Seattle), March 28, 2003, p. 1.

Tita, Bob, "Spiegel's Future Stands to Turn on Eddie Bauer," *Crain's Chicago Business,* March 10, 2003, p. 4.

Warren, James R., "Eddie Bauer's Guarantee Was Key to Firm's Success," *Seattle Business Journal,* June 13, 1983, pp. 6–7.

Young, Vicki M., "Eddie Bauer Acquired in $614M Equity Deal," *Women's Wear Daily,* November 14, 2006, p. 3.

———, "Eddie Bauer on the Block," *Women's Wear Daily,* April 24, 2006, p. 2.

ESCO Technologies Inc.

9900A Clayton Road, Suite 200
St. Louis, Missouri 63124-1186
U.S.A.
Telephone: (314) 213-7200
Toll Free: (888) 622-3726
Fax: (314) 213-7250
Web site: http://www.escostl.com

Public Company
Incorporated: 1990 as Esco Electronics Corp.
Employees: 2,365
Sales: $458.9 million (2006)
Stock Exchanges: New York
Ticker Symbol: ESE
NAIC: 334511 Search, Detections, Navigation, Guidance, Aeronautical, and Nautical System and Instrument Manufacturing

■ ■ ■

Formed out of the defense contracting business of Emerson Electric Co., St. Louis-based ESCO Technologies Inc. (Esco) has transformed itself into a manufacturer of engineered products and systems operating in three business segments to serve commercial and industrial customers. The company's Filtration/Fluid Flow unit is responsible for approximately 40 percent of revenues. With facilities located in North America, South America, and Europe, the subsidiaries operating in this segment provide filtration products used in the transportation, aerospace, healthcare, and industrial markets. Esco's Test segment accounts for about 28

percent of revenues. Subsidiaries design and manufacture products to help customers identify, measure, and contain magnetic, electromagnetic, and acoustic energy. Contributing about one-third of all revenues, Esco's Communications segment serves electric, gas, and water utility customers, providing meter-reading technology as well as video surveillance systems for security applications. Esco is a public company listed on the New York Stock Exchange.

19TH-CENTURY LINEAGE

Esco was spun off from Emerson Electric Co., which was established in St. Louis in 1890 to make electric motors and fans designed by a pair of Scotland-born brothers, Alexander W. Meston and Charles R. Meston. The company took the name of their financial backer, John Wesley Emerson, a Missouri judge and Union army officer. In the beginning Emerson focused on the sale of electric fans, a product that the company pioneered, but soon it applied its technology to any number of household, office, farm, and industrial products, including sewing machines, power tools, dental drills, and even player pianos. During World War II Emerson began its defense work. Just one day after the attack on Pearl Harbor, December 7, 1941, which led to the United States' entry into the war, Emerson received a contract to manufacture aircraft gun turrets. By the end of the war, the company had completed $100 million worth of defense contracts.

During the postwar years, Emerson struggled to reestablish itself. Defense work dwindled to just $1.5 million in 1947, while the company also had to contend

COMPANY PERSPECTIVES

Esco Technologies is a proven supplier of special purpose communications systems for electric, gas and water utilities, including hardware and software to support advanced metering applications. In addition, the Company provides engineered filtration products to the transportation, healthcare and process markets worldwide, and is the industry leader in RF shielding and EMC test products.

with giants General Electric and Westinghouse providing stiff competition in the commercial sector. Emerson launched a diversification effort in the 1950s, focusing on high-growth markets, a plan accomplished in large part through strategic acquisitions. The company also managed to build up its defense contracting, which contributed 30 percent of revenues in 1956. However, Emerson suffered a pair of setbacks in the 1960s that soured management on military work. In 1962 an aircraft fire-control systems contract was canceled, followed by the 1969 cancellation of the Cheyenne helicopter program, which in one stroke halved Emerson's defense-related sales. Management decided that it wanted no more than 15 percent of its annual revenues tied to military work.

Emerson benefited from the military buildup during the Reagan administration of the 1980s. The company owned six subsidiaries involved in the manufacture of such equipment as radar systems, electronic test equipment for jet fighters, heavy trailers used to transport M-1 tanks, mobile bridges, launching systems for the TOW antitank missile, antisubmarine systems, and valves and filters to keep submarines quiet and less susceptible to detection. These units included St. Louis-based Electronics & Space Corp.; Southwest Mobile Systems Corp., and Distribution Control Systems Inc.; Greenlawn, New York-based Hazeltine Corp.; Calabasas, California-based Rantec Microwave and Electronics Inc.; and South El Monte, California-based Vacco Industries. By the end of the 1980s these companies combined for nearly $600 million in sales, or about 8 percent of the parent company's $7.1 billion in total sales.

The prospects for Emerson's military business appeared dim, however. The surprisingly sudden end to the Cold War led to a contraction in the U.S. defense budget. Further complicating matters, the company had been embroiled in controversy with the government. In

January 1989 a pair of Hazeltine executives pled guilty to making false statements and defrauding the government, and the company paid $1.9 million in criminal and civil fines. The company was also having problems making progress on a new tail-end radar system for B-52 bombers that was adversely impacting relations with the U.S. Air Force. Meanwhile, Electronics & Space Corp. was accused of making false statements connected to four contracts between 1984 and 1986. This matter would be settled in May 1990 when Emerson entered a guilty plea and agreed to a $14 million settlement payment. The company's ability to bid on Pentagon contracts was placed under review. Emerson was also having trouble with the Federal Aviation Administration over delays in building a microwave landing system for airports.

Even as Emerson's defense operations were being reviewed by the government, the Emerson board of directors, according to the *St. Louis Business Journal*, "considered three alternatives: continuing the defense operations as part of Emerson, pursuing a joint venture or spinning off the business. After failing to find a joint venture partner, Emerson opted for the spinoff." In August 1990 Emerson formed a new company that took the name Esco Electronics Corp. after the October spinoff was completed. Emerson shareholders received one Esco share for every 20 Emerson shares they owned.

Heading Esco as chairman and chief executive officer was J. Joe Adorjan, who for the previous three years had overseen Emerson's defense subsidiaries. The company was listed on the New York Stock Exchange, where it was met with a tepid welcome. After opening at $5.25 a share, the price of Esco stock quickly tumbled. Investors concluded that Emerson was "discarding something that they can't sell," according to defense analyst Howard Rubell, quoted by Reuters. He added, "If Emerson thought this was such a good business, it would keep it."

Despite the Persian Gulf War, military budgets continued to decline, leading to steady layoffs at Esco in 1991. When the fiscal year came to a close in September 1991, the company posted a net loss of $67.4 million, much of it related to charges taken for contract cancellations and cost overruns. Essentially the only nondefense assets the company had to offer were a pair of communications products: a meter reading communications system and video surveillance technology that had monitored automated teller machines and stores. Esco was interested in diversifying further into commercial businesses, but was cautious. "It is our view," Adorjan told the *St. Louis Post-Dispatch*, "that if you do an autopsy of dead corporations in the defense industry in the next few years, one of the primary causes of death will be their rush into commercial business."

NEW CHIEF EXECUTIVE: 1992

In October 1992 Adorjan resigned to return to Emerson, where he took over as president. He was replaced as chairman and CEO at Esco by Dennis J. Moore, the company's president and chief operating officer. A 1961 graduate of the U.S. Naval Academy, Moore served as a U.S. Navy pilot in the Vietnam War. After his discharge in 1967 he went to work in the aerospace industry. Twenty years later he moved to St. Louis to become president of Electronics & Space Corp., and in 1989 became a group vice-president of Emerson's defense subsidiaries. Under Moore's guidance, Esco began to execute a diversification plan. While remaining a defense contractor, the company looked to pursue areas that fit in with its capabilities. Five areas were targeted: valves and filters; utility communications; test instrumentation; communications and antennas; and motion control. The company looked to grow internally by adapting some of its defense-based technologies to commercial use and externally through strategic acquisitions.

The first step taken in the diversification plan through external means was the $28 million September 1992 acquisition of Textron Filtration Systems, a California company that manufactured commercial and industrial filtration systems and parts used by chemical-processing, fluid-power, and aviation customers. The operation, renamed PTI Technologies Inc., was meant to complement Esco's Vacco Industries unit, which made submarine filters and valves. Next, in March 1993, Esco bought Electro-Mechanics Company, Inc. (EMCO), in a $4.6 million deal that added to the Rantec test business. Esco then added more filter assets to PTI in December 1993 with the $7.6 million acquisition of Schumacher Filters, Ltd., a U.K. company that gave PTI a European presence. A year later Esco acquired Ray Proof North America, maker of RF shield-

ing, a material that prevented damage from electromagnetic radiation. Ray Proof was then joined with Rantec and EMCO to establish EMC Test Systems.

Esco enjoyed a strong year in fiscal 1993. Sales grew 13 percent to $459.7 million and net income increased 271 percent to $5.2 million. Nevertheless, a few months later the company was forced to make layoffs at Electronics & Space because of continuing defense cuts. While defense work remained important, Esco in the second half of the 1990s began divesting defense assets while adding to its commercial business. "[Defense] was a good business for an operating unit with a $10 billion corporation," Moore told *Investor's Business Daily* to explain why Esco was too small to compete against such giant defense contractors as Raytheon. "But the projects are just too large and unwieldy for us. If you experience some delays, you could end up taking a $10 million to $15 million hit."

Hazeltine was sold to GEC-Marconi Electronics Systems Corporation for $110 million in cash in July 1996. As a result, defense work fell to about 70 percent of total revenues in fiscal 1996. Esco then beefed up its filter business with the $92 million acquisition of Filter-Tek and the thermoform packaging business of Schawk, Inc., in February 1997. This move pushed Esco's commercial sales past the 50 percent mark on an annualized basis. In fiscal 1997 revenues totaled $378.5 million and the company recorded net earnings of $11.8 million. While the defense business returned to profitability, Esco continued to take steps to exit the field while adding commercial assets.

In July 1998 Esco acquired Advanced Membrane Technology, which was then incorporated into PTI. This addition helped to fuel further growth in commercial sales, which increased to 57 percent of Esco's total sales of $365.1 million in fiscal 1998. As the year came to a close the company hired J.P. Morgan to provide advice on whether to divest Systems & Electronics, Esco's largest remaining defense unit. Because business conditions were not favorable, Esco elected to hold onto the subsidiary until September 1999 when it was sold for $92 million in cash to Engineered Support Systems, Inc. By unloading Systems & Electronics, Esco completed its transformation from a company that derived 95 percent of revenues from defense contracts in 1990 to one that had defense sales in the 10 percent range. Esco could devote more attention to its new major businesses, filtration/fluid flow, test, and communications.

NEW CENTURY, NEW NAME

In keeping with its new focus, Esco changed its name to ESCO Technologies, Inc., in 2000. All three major business areas enjoyed double-digit sales growth, as overall sales improved 23 percent to $300.2 million, compared to $243.3 million the year before when adjusted for the sale of Systems & Electronics. The company enjoyed internal growth through the introduction of new products and completed a pair of acquisitions over the course of the year. In March 2000, Esco bought the $7 million-per-year space products business of Eaton Corp., a California unit that manufactured fluid control components for launchers and aircraft. A month later Esco spent $25 million to acquire the Curran Company and an affiliated company, Lindren, Inc., suppliers of radio frequency shielding products used in electronics, communications systems, and medical equipment. The assets were folded into Esco's Test segment.

Esco completed another acquisition in 2001, paying $13.5 million for BEA Filtri S.p.A., an Italian supplier of microfiltration products to pharmaceutical, food and beverage, healthcare, and petrochemical customers. Not only did Esco add filtration products, it increased its European presence. In fiscal 2001, sales improved 15 percent to $344.9 million and earnings grew to $30.1 million. A year later sales reached $367.5 million and the company recorded net earnings of $21.8 million.

At the start of fiscal 2003, in October 2002, Moore turned over the chief executive officer role to Victor L. Richey, Jr. A former military intelligence officer, Richey had joined Emerson in 1985 and was part of the Esco spinoff. As a senior executive he made a valuable contribution to Esco's successful transition from defense to commercial work. He assumed the chairmanship as well in April 2003 when Moore retired as planned.

With Richey at the helm, Esco continued to make acquisitions to grow the business. In January 2003, the company paid $4 million for Austin Acoustics System, Inc., a Texas company that produced noise control chambers for the test, medical, and broadcast and music industries. The assets were added to Esco's Test segment. Later in the year, Esco divested its Power Systems and Microfiltration businesses for a combined $29.5 million. In addition, in fiscal 2003, Esco closed a filtration plant in Puerto Rico, transferring the production to other plants in Mexico and Illinois. Wall Street approved of the moves, as the price of Esco stock improved about 80 percent over the course of fiscal 2004.

More acquisitions followed. In November 2005, Esco acquired Nexus Energy Software, Inc., for $28.5 million, adding energy data management software to the company's meter reading systems. In February 2006, Esco paid $67.5 million for Hexagram, Inc., a radio frequency fixed-network automatic meter-reading company. When fiscal 2006 came to a close, Esco recorded an increase in revenues to $458.9 million and net income to $31.3 million.

Ed Dinger

PRINCIPAL SUBSIDIARIES

ETS-Lindren, L.P.; Filtertek Inc.; Hexagram, Inc; PTI Technologies Inc.; VACCO Industries.

PRINCIPAL COMPETITORS

CLARCOR Inc.; Donaldson Company, Inc.; Pall Corporation.

FURTHER READING

Byrne, Harlan S., "Esco Electronics: Acquisitions Help Wean It from Defense Business," *Barron's,* December 7, 1992, p. 47.

———, "Esco Technologies: Power Surge," *Barron's,* June 4, 2001, p. 42.

Carey, Christopher, "Esco Buys Filter Firm," *St. Louis Post-Dispatch,* December 2, 1993, p. 8C.

Deslog, Rick, "Moore, Richey Grow Pared-Down Esco," *St. Louis Business Journal,* April 8, 2002.

"Esco Electronics Corp.," *Wall Street Transcript,* September 6, 1993.

Flannery, William, "Emerson's Board OKs Spinoff," *St. Louis Post-Dispatch,* September 25, 1990, p. 7C.

Goodman, Adam, "Clouds Begin to Lift For Esco," *St. Louis Post-Dispatch,* February 5, 1991, p. 9B.

———, "Esco ... On Its Own Spinoff Hit with Losses in 1st Year," *St. Louis Post-Dispatch,* November 10, 1991, p. 1E.

Lawder, David, "Emerson Spinoff Faces Tough Environment," *Reuters,* September 21, 1990.

Reeves, Amy, "Still Learning New Tricks After Years in Business," *Investor's Business Daily,* July 6, 2001, p. A07.

Thimangu, Patrick L., "Richey Catches the Wave," *St. Louis Business Journal,* November 15, 2004.

FARO
The Measure of Success

FARO Technologies, Inc.

125 Technology Park
Lake Mary, Florida 32746-6204
U.S.A.
Telephone: (407) 333-9911
Fax: (407) 333-4181
Web site: http://www.faro.com

Public Company
Incorporated: 1981 as Res-Tech
Employees: 681
Sales: $152.4 million (2006)
Stock Exchanges: NASDAQ
Ticker Symbol: FARO
NAIC: 334519 Other Measuring and Controlling Device Manufacturing

■ ■ ■

Based in Lake Mary, Florida, FARO Technologies, Inc., designs, develops, manufactures, markets, and supports sophisticated three-dimensional measuring systems. It has more than 6,100 customers worldwide. The devices are used in a wide range of industries, including aerospace, automotive, consumer goods, food, heavy equipment, machine tools, medical systems, metal fabrication, mining, motion pictures and gaming, petrochemical, and pharmaceutical. FARO products can be used for alignment purposes, calibration, inspection, installation, reverse engineering, and other applications. The devices are capable of up to 0.0002 inches accuracy and have a range as far as 76 meters. Products include the FaroArm, an articulated arm married to computer

software to make factory floor measurements; the Laser ScanArm, which uses a laser probe to measure products without touching them; the Laser Tracker, which allows quality control personnel and engineers to measure and inspect parts, machine tools, and other objects; the FARO Gauge, another articulate arm device that uses computer software in building machine tools; and FARO Laser Scanner LS, which measures and collects data points to create a precise rendering of an object or area, facilitating inspection and reverse engineering efforts as well as design and architectural work. A public company listed on the NASDAQ, Faro operates sales offices around the world.

CANADIAN ROOTS: 1981

FARO was founded in 1981 as Res-Tech by a pair of biomedical engineering doctoral students at McGill University in Montreal, Canada: Simon Raab and Greg Fraser. Raab also held a degree in physics from the University of Waterloo, Canada, and a master's of engineering physics from Cornell University. Prior to his doctorate Fraser earned an undergraduate degree in mechanical engineering and a master's of theoretical and applied mechanics from Northwestern University. In 1983 the company assumed the FARO Technologies Inc. name, with Raab serving as chief executive officer. The firm was initially a research and development company, interested in developing software-aided devices to assist physicians in diagnostics and surgery. FARO's first product was introduced in 1984, an articulated-arm device used to measure laxity in the knee. Subsequent models introduced in the 1980s offered greater capabilities. The Genucom Knee Analysis System gener-

With more than 13,000 installations and 6,100 customers globally, FARO Technologies, Inc. (NASDAQ: FARO) and its international subsidiaries design, develop, and market portable, computerized measurement devices and software. The Company's products allow manufacturers to perform 3-D inspections of parts and assemblies on the shop floor. This helps eliminate manufacturing errors, and thereby increases productivity and profitability for a variety of industries in FARO's worldwide customer base.

ated a three-dimensional image of the knee, providing surgeons with far more information about the severity of an injury than they could achieve with mere touch. As a result, surgeons could make better informed decisions on how to correct the damaged knee. The device held obvious appeal for sports medicine, which dealt with a large number of severe knee injuries. Because so many high-salaried athletes were involved, sports medicine centers were willing to invest in the latest technology.

The partners had one failing, however. "As engineering egghead entrepreneurs, we didn't understand marketing," Raab told *Investor's Business Daily.* "We got only 10% market penetration among 9,000 knee surgeons." Ultimately the Genucom was discontinued. However, in the early years of the company, Raab and Fraser spent a great deal of their time on the road, either attending trade shows or demonstrating their devices at hospitals. Thus, they were able to interact with the users of their equipment and others, then use that feedback to further designs and develop new devices. In 1986 the company introduced Metrecom, a skeletal analysis system that detected abnormalities in the spine that caused neck and back problems. It was used by doctors as well as physical therapists and chiropractors to develop treatments. Two years later, FARO introduced a device called Surgicom to map the human brain by joining measurements with MRI and CAT scan information, allowing surgeons to locate difficult-to-find tumors and remove them with a minimum loss of bone and tissue.

In order to be closer to the bulk of their customers, Raab and Fraser decided to relocate to the United States. Because Raab had relatives living in central Florida the pair moved their operation to Lake Mary, Florida, in 1990. Around the same time, Raab and Fraser met a Martin-Marietta engineer who convinced

them that there was a market for their technology in the field of industrial measurement, in particular the need for a portable device similar to the ones FARO had already produced, but to measure large parts and assemblies. While there were industrial measuring devices on the market, they were cumbersome and sensitive, and housed in metrology laboratories where they could provide only limited help. No three-dimensional measuring systems were available to provide information on the factory floor where they were needed. Moreover, the software component of the available systems was arcane and not easily used by the assemblers and machinists.

SWITCH TO NEW MARKETS: 1992

Raab and Fraser decided to fill this gap, and in 1992 FARO focused on the manufacturing and industrial markets, the same year that the company was reincorporated in Florida. The direct sale of medical products was phased out and FARO's technology was licensed to two major neurosurgical companies, including Medtronic, Inc., which would incorporate the Surgicom advances into standard equipment used in neurosurgery around the world. By 1994 FARO had essentially reinvented itself while pioneering a new field that combined metrology with the software used in computer-aided design and computer-aided manufacturing. FARO called this new market Computer-Aided Manufacturing Measurement, or CAM2 as it would become known.

FARO developed the FaroArm, which looked like a miniature space shuttle arm and was the cornerstone of a portable measuring system that was tough enough to withstand the production environment, highly accurate, yet easy to use. The companion software component took the name AnthroCAM. The new industrial measuring devices were quickly embraced by the aerospace industry, used to measure inside jet engines and refurbish airplanes. Very quickly, the number of different applications mushroomed. By 1995 the FaroArm was being used by a casket company to locate and drill handle holes, reducing an eight-hour process to just 15 minutes; prosthetic companies were using them to fashion artificial limbs; anthropologists brought the devices with them on digs; race-car builders were using them to transfer wind tunnel information to the shop to create aerodynamic cars; and race-car organizations began relying on the FaroArm to conduct prerace inspections that were quicker and more accurate. Automakers also embraced the FaroArm, used in a number of applications including the analysis of test crashes. Business was so strong that by 1995 FARO opened a Detroit office. In that year the company also introduced

KEY DATES

1981: Company is founded in Canada as Res-Tech by Simon Raab and Greg Fraser.
1983: FARO name is assumed.
1984: Knee measuring device is company's first product.
1990: Company relocates to Florida.
1992: FARO becomes involved in Computer-Aided Manufacturing Measurement, CAM2.
1997: Initial public offering is held.
1998: CATS (Computer Aided Technologies) GmbH is acquired.
2002: SpatialMetrix Corp. is acquired.
2005: iQvolution AG is acquired.

an even smaller measuring device, a $3,000 unit that was marketed to artists and animators.

Sales grew from $4.7 million in 1992 to $5.1 million in 1993, before dipping to $4.5 million a year later. The company lost nearly $1 million during this period. FARO turned profitable in 1995 after making a concerted effort to reach international customers. Revenues increased to $9.9 million in 1995, with international sales contributing $2.1 million, and the company posted earnings of $1.6 million. A year later FARO opened sales offices in France and Germany, followed by a United Kingdom office in 1997. Domestically, the company also opened sales offices in Chicago, Dallas, Los Angeles, and Seattle. As a result of growing sales home and abroad, FARO's revenues increased to $14.7 million in 1996 and $23.5 million in 1997. During this period, the company recorded net income of $1.4 million in 1996 and $3.2 million in 1997.

In 1997 FARO went public. In an initial public offering of stock completed in September, the company sold 1.7 million shares, and individuals sold another 600,000 shares, netting $31.7 million for the company. The money was earmarked to pay down debt and provide funds for capital improvement, such as doubling the size of the Lake Mary facility to 35,000 square feet at a cost of $1 million, and general corporate purposes, including possible acquisitions.

FARO's first acquisition was completed in May 1998 when the company bought CATS Computer Aided Technologies GmbH, a German manufacturer of portable, three-dimensional measuring systems used in manufacturing quality control, for approximately $16 million in cash and stock. Not only did FARO expand

its reach to all areas of the factory floor, it hoped to take advantage of its international marketing organization to better promote the CATS system. Moreover, CATS' strong software capabilities helped to refine FARO's AnthroCAM system, resulting in the CAM2 Measure software program.

While FARO improved sales to $27.5 million in 1998, net income slipped to $500,000, primarily due to the CATS acquisition. The business continued to expand in 1999, when FARO also made progress with a branding initiative, introducing new logos and product names, as well as positioning statements. Furthermore, in 1999 the company established the MQC (Manufacturing Quality Group) to provide large and small manufacturers with quality assurance measurement services. In connection with this new unit, FARO opened a Detroit-based technology center to serve the automotive industry. When the year came to a close, FARO recorded an increase in sales to $33.1 million. Fourth quarter write-downs, however, resulted in a net loss of $400,000.

NEW CENTURY EXPANSION

Soon after the start of the 2000s, FARO opened a new European headquarters, located in a 14,000-square-foot facility in Stuttgart, Germany. The company also opened an office in Japan in 2000 to improve its position in the Asian market. FARO essentially broke even in 2000, netting almost $40,000 on revenues of $40.5 million. The strongest growth came from Germany, France, and the United Kingdom, where sales improved 33 percent. Sales in the United States also improved 13 percent over 1999.

FARO expanded its European presence in 2001 by opening sales offices in Turin, Italy, and Barcelona, Spain. Both countries had strong automotive and aerospace industries, making them logical customers for FARO's CAM2 products and services. Nevertheless, 2001 was a difficult year for FARO because of a slumping economy that adversely impacted the manufacturing sector, which was dealt a further blow by the terrorist attacks in the United States on September 11 that served to worsen economic conditions. Sales declined to $36.1 million and the company posted a net loss of more than $2.8 million.

Early in 2002, FARO diversified its product lineup through the acquisition of Kennett Square, Pennsylvania-based SpatialMetrix Corporation (SMX), a manufacturer of laser trackers and metrology software, and a provider of inspection services. That gave birth to the FARO Laser Tracker, which used an extremely precise laser beam to measure objects in a radius as large as 115 feet. The company also fortified its existing product by introducing new generation FaroArms, dubbed the Platinum FaroArm, FARO Gage, and Gage-PLUS, which were lighter, more durable, and provided even greater precision. FARO rebuilt sales and returned to profitability in the second half of 2002, although for the year it lost $2 million on sales of $46.2 million.

FARO's international business showed strong growth, especially in China, which was just beginning to incorporate many aspects of modern technology. FARO also looked to expand its range of customers, targeting small manufacturers and machine shops, who wanted to perform advanced measurements, CAD-to-part comparisons, and reverse engineering, but do so within a tight budget without sacrificing quality. To tap into this market, FARO in 2003 introduced the Advantage Line of Measurement Products, ranging in price from $19,900 to $69,900. On the other end of the spectrum, FARO unveiled the first fully integrated 3-D Laser ScanArm in 2003, combining the capabilities of the Arm's hand probe with a laser scanner. All of these positive developments combined to produce a banner year. Sales increased to $71.8 million and the company netted $8.3 million. Business continued to improve in 2004, when sales jumped to more than $97 million and net income approached $15 million.

In March 2005, FARO added more markets it could sell to, including mining, geology, architecture, petrochemical, and forensics, through the acquisition of iQvolution AG, a small German company that made three-dimensional laser scanning products used for factory planning, facility life-cycle management, quality control, and forensic analysis. Record results continued in 2005, as sales pushed past the $125 million mark, while the company netted $8.2 million.

Early in 2006 FARO made changes at the top management ranks when President and Chief Operating Officer Jay Freeland was named co-CEO with Raab. Freeland essentially took over day-to-day control of the company while Raab, who was also chairman of the board, focused on overall strategy as well as product and business development. Freeland was taking the helm at a time when FARO was clearly hitting its stride. New product launches continued in 2006, including a new low-cost version of the Laser Scanner product line, the FARO PowerGAGE that added CAD-to-part analysis capability for its Gage line, and an updated version of the company's laser scanning software. As the year came to a close Freeland was named CEO, while Raab remained on the board of directors as nonexecutive chairman, all part of a succession plan. When the numbers were tallied, FARO posted sales of $152 million in 2006 and net income of $8.2 million.

Ed Dinger

PRINCIPAL SUBSIDIARIES

CAM2 SRL; FARO Europe KG; FARO Japan KK; FARO Shanghai Co. Ltd.; FARO Worldwide Inc.

PRINCIPAL COMPETITORS

Delcam plc; Hexagon AB; Leica Geosystems Holdings AG.

FURTHER READING

Barth, Cindy, "FARO Shifting Customer Service to European HQ," *Orlando Business Journal*, January 21, 2000, p. 13.

Benesh, Peter, "Measuring Devices Find a Better Market," *Investor's Business Daily*, November 14, 2003, p. A06.

Dillon, Paul, "FARO Expands in Lake Mary, Will Hire Up to 100," *Orlando Business Journal*, July 4, 1997, p. 1.

"FARO Technologies Acquires SpatialMetrix," *Manufacturing Automation*, January–February 2002.

Lennon, Kim, "Ahead of the Cutting Edge," *St. Petersburg Times*, June 26, 1989.

Pfister, Nancy, and Justin Sapp, "FARO Ventures Abroad, Takes EDC's Top Export Award," *Orlando Business Journal*, May 5, 2000, p. 9.

Taylor, Gary, "FARO Technologies Inc. Changes the Way the World Takes Measurements," *Orlando Sentinel*, February 5, 1995, p. A5.

⁜ FirstMarblehead

The First Marblehead Corporation

———————■———————

The Prudential Tower
800 Boylston Street, 34th Floor
Boston, Massachusetts 02199-8157
U.S.A.
Telephone: (617) 638-2000
Toll Free: (800) 895-4283
Fax: (617) 638-2100
Web site: http://www.firstmarblehead.com

Public Company
Incorporated: 1994
Employees: 932
Sales: $563.6 million (2006)
Stock Exchanges: New York
Ticker Symbol: FMD
NAIC: 522291 Consumer Lending

■ ■ ■

The First Marblehead Corporation is a Boston-based, New York Stock Exchange–listed company that provides outsourcing services connected to the private education lending field. It works with 14 of the 20 largest originators of federally guaranteed student loans, including JP-Morgan Chase, Bank of America, HSBC, Wachovia, and PNC. Although First Marblehead is involved in the primary and secondary school market, most of its loan programs are related to undergraduate, graduate, and professional education. The company works on a fee basis with major banks, providing marketing research and program design, customer call center management, loan application and disbursement services, and loan servicing. First Marblehead also bundles education loans and sells the aggregated debt. First Marblehead was one of the first companies to exploit the divide that developed between the rising cost of education and the meager increases made to federal college loan programs in the final decades of the 20th century. With an estimated one-quarter of college students resorting to high-interest credit cards to finance their education, private loans made possible by First Marblehead offered near 6 percent became extremely attractive. Because student loans are not protected by bankruptcy, the default rate is also quite low, making it a safe niche for lenders as well. Serving as a facilitator, First Marblehead has carved out a lucrative business, so tempting that the company faces an influx of well-heeled competition looking to peel away some of its market share.

COMPANY FOUNDED: 1991

While First Marblehead was cofounded in 1991 by Daniel Maxwell Meyers and Stephen E. Anbinder, credit for the idea goes to Meyers. He grew up in Marblehead, Massachusetts, where he developed a profound respect for the value of education. His father, Newton Meyers, earned a degree from Brown University at the age of 18, the result of high test scores and a Navy program that was implemented during World War II. After completing his military service, the elder Meyers used the GI Bill to finance a degree from Harvard Business School. He was so enamored with education that on vacations the Meyers family often visited college campuses. When Newton Meyers died, Daniel's mother pursued her own college education, this despite being the daughter of first-generation Russian immigrants who were opposed

COMPANY PERSPECTIVES

First Marblehead is an industry leader in providing services for private, non-governmental, education lending in the United States.

to higher education for women. Nevertheless, she graduated from Salem State College in 1952 and then supported her four children, all of whom became college graduates.

Daniel Meyers received a degree in economics from Brandeis University in 1984. He then went to work on Wall Street, starting out in the mail room at E.F. Hutton, where one of the firm's traders took him under his wing and taught Meyers the basics of arbitrage and derivatives. Meyers proved to be a quick learner and a talented trader, who moved on to work at Prudential Bache Securities, L.F. Rothschild Unterberg Towbin, and Commodities Corporation. Later in the 1980s he became involved in asset-backed securities. This experience led him to wonder if there was a way to provide private college loans at reasonable interest rates through the securities market.

To flesh out the idea, Meyers took on a partner, a fellow trader named Stephen E. Anbinder, about 20 years his senior. A Harvard Business School graduate, Anbinder had spent a decade heading the fixed income capital markets group at Dillon Read & Company, a securities brokerage firm. In 1990 Meyers and Anbinder conferred with economist David Breneman, a Harvard professor who was an expert on the economics of higher education. "When Dan described his vision to me, I realized that this was a serious and valuable idea," Breneman told *UVA TopNews Daily*. "What impressed me most was his drive to help young people enter and complete college."

With Breneman serving on the company's advisory board and providing access to key people, Meyers and Anbinder launched First Marblehead in 1991 as a limited partnership. In August 1994 it was incorporated in Delaware. For the first ten years the company served individual colleges, raising money on Wall Street to provide a supplemental pool of loan money. The company reached a major turning point in June 2001 when it forged a strategic alliance with The Education Resources Institute (TERI), a Boston-based nonprofit company founded in 1985 to provide education financing and information services. At the cost of $9.2 million First Marblehead acquired TERI's loan processing

operations, forming the basis of a new subsidiary, First Marblehead Education Resources, which retained about 160 TERI employees. As part of the alliance, the unit continued to provide the loan origination and processing services related to TERI Education Loans as part of a master servicing agreement. More importantly, First Marblehead possessed the capabilities to service other lenders, in particular banks.

With the TERI assets in hand, First Marblehead was able to accelerate its growth. After posting revenues of $6.7 million and net income of $2 million in fiscal 2001, the company saw revenues soar to more than $41.3 million in 2002, yielding earnings of more than $12.2 million. Processing fees for TERI alone accounted for $14.2 million, structural advisory fees all but tripled to $14.8 million, while residuals increased from $1.1 million to $11.8 million. The company's administrative and other fees also increased by about a third to $475,000. The sharp growth continued in 2003, when processing fees from TERI increased to $20.6 million, administrative and other fees enjoyed threefold growth to $1.4 million, as did residuals to $30 million, and structural advisory fees improved to $39.3 million. Total revenues for the year reached $91.4 million and net income was an impressive $31.5 million.

INITIAL PUBLIC OFFERING: 2003

A few months after the close of fiscal 2003, First Marblehead went public. With Goldman Sachs & Co., J.P. Morgan Securities Inc., and Bear, Stearns & Co. Inc. serving as managing underwriters, the initial public offering of stock was conducted on October 31, 2003, and netted approximately $115.1 million for the company. A follow-on public offering of shares held by stockholders was conducted eight months later, but none of these proceeds went to the company.

First Marblehead continued to enjoy rapid growth in fiscal 2004, as it helped lend $1.8 billion to 200,000 students. As a result, its balance sheet showed sizable increases in all areas, especially structural advisory fees, which grew from $39.3 million to $98.2 million. All told, first Marblehead more than doubled total revenues to $199.3 million while posting net income of $75.3 million. Important factors in the company's strong performance were an increase in the number of people entering the traditional college age group, and rising tuition costs that far outpaced the amount of public loan funds that were available, forcing people to turn to private funding sources. First Marblehead was well positioned to take advantage of this situation because it was one of the few companies that could offer a full range of outsourcing services to lenders for private student loans. There was some concern among investors,

```
┌─────────────────────────────────────────┐
│                                           │
│           KEY DATES                       │
│              ■                            │
│  1991: Company is formed as a limited partnership. │
│  1994: Company incorporates in Delaware.  │
│  2001: Loan processing services of The Education │
│        Resources Institute are acquired.  │
│  2003: Company goes public.               │
│  2005: Cofounder Daniel Meyers resigns.   │
│                                           │
└─────────────────────────────────────────┘
```

however, that a large bank might grow interested in offering the same profitable services. First Marblehead hoped that banks remained more interested in focusing on the extremely lucrative federally guaranteed loan business and in converting those college-age borrowers into long-term customers. Moreover, the cost and bother of duplicating First Marblehead's operation would, it was hoped, serve as a deterrent to those considering entering the field.

Investors took notice of First Marblehead's stellar performance, bidding up the price of its stock, which in a matter of six months doubled its initial $16 price. The company continued to ride high in 2005. It found a new partner in FindTuition.com, part of CareerBuilder Inc., which offered financial aid research information to three million students. The web site began to market loans of a First Marblehead partner, Charter One Bank, and First Marblehead provided back-office support. For fiscal 2005 revenues increased to $418 million and net income approached an impressive $160 million. The company's stock price also topped $73 during the year.

RESIGNATION OF MEYERS: 2006

Fiscal 2006 proved troublesome, however. A major client, CFSI, announced that it planned to take in-house the services it had outsourced to First Marblehead. There was also concern that student-loan giant SLM Corp., "Sallie Mae," was going to encroach on the company's business. Then, in September 2006, Meyers abruptly resigned when it became known that he had exchanged gifts worth $32,000 with an employee of an important client. Although Meyers maintained that the gifts were purchased with his own money, the board concluded that his conduct had violated the firm's ethics policy. Soon the *Wall Street Journal* reported that Meyers had exchanged gifts, which included an expensive watch, with Kathy Cannon, a senior executive in Bank of America Corp.'s student-lending division, First Marblehead's second largest client.

Selected to replace Meyers was First Marblehead's president and chief operating officer, Jack L. Kopnisky,

who had only recently joined the company. However, the loss of its longtime CEO was a major blow to the company. "Meyers was the heart and soul of this company," industry analyst Matt Snowling told the *Boston Herald*. "He was the one, out there for years knocking on doors at schools and banks, building the business ... he's well-known in the educational community." By early October 2005, the price of First Marblehead shares slipped to $21. The price rebounded only to take another fall a month later when Bank of America announced it would not renew its contract with First Marblehead under the current terms. The two sides finally came to an accommodation a few months later, news that helped to buoy the price of First Marblehead stock. The situation improved even further when GE Consumer Finance decided to use the company to help it market a full suite of private student loans services under the GE Money banner, including financing programs for K–12 and continuing education programs in addition to undergraduate and graduate school.

Despite the turbulence, First Marblehead again produced strong results when 2006 came to a close. Revenues increased to $563.6 million and net income continued to climb to nearly $236 million. Shortly after the year ended, First Marblehead announced that it was seeking regulatory approval to acquire the $40 million asset, one branch Union Federal Savings Bank of North Providence, Rhode Island, which provided deposit and loan services to retail customers in the state. The deal was completed in November 2006. First Marblehead indicated that it planned to have Union Federal fund loans originated under its Astrive brand, but it was uncertain what further purpose there might be in owning a bank. Union Federal might simply serve as nothing more than a research-and-development lab, but, according to *American Banker,* it held "the potential to build a portfolio of loans; to fund loans for new partners not able to do so themselves; or to provide such partners with lines of credit to make their own loans." While the move offered long-range flexibility, it also created short-term risk, as some of First Marblehead's clients might chaff at the possibility of the firm offering direct competition.

While First Marblehead was busy acquiring a bank, it also took steps to diversify its client base in fiscal 2007. It expanded its relationship with the College Board, and also signed deals with KeyCorp, Ensure Bank, Monster.com, E-Loan, and ConnectEdu, a web site for high school students. Through the first six months of fiscal 2007, First Marblehead turned in outstanding results, recording an increase in revenues from $268.4 million to $500.7 million over the comparable period in fiscal 2006, while net income grew from $105.9 million to $222.2 million. Nevertheless, investors who had renewed their faith in the company after Meyers' departure became faint of heart again, as First Marblehead shares lost a fifth of their value in the early weeks of calendar 2007. "The most obvious worry," according to the *Wall Street Journal,* was "new federal legislation that could boost government's student-loan program and take business away from the private-loan sector that First Marblehead services." There was also concern that the loans First Marblehead arranged were being paid off faster than expected, a situation that would ultimately hurt earnings. Kopnisky suggested, however, that investors were behaving "very myopically," and overreacting to short-term events. Because the private-loan market was continuing to grow at a fast clip, he said he did not foresee a drop in overall demand for private loans or the services First Marblehead had to offer.

Ed Dinger

PRINCIPAL SUBSIDIARIES

First Marblehead Data Services, Inc.; First Marblehead Education Resources, Inc.; TERI Marketing Services, Inc.; First Marblehead Securities Corporation; GATE Holdings, Inc.

PRINCIPAL COMPETITORS

Citigroup Inc.; SLM Corporation; Wells Fargo & Company.

FURTHER READING

Benesh, Peter, "Loan Processor Gets High Marks from Street," *Investor's Business Daily,* May 4, 2004, p. A08.

Hechinger, John, "First Marblehead Says CEO Resigns over Gift Exchange," *Wall Street Journal,* September 28, 2005, p. B2.

Hechinger, John, and Anne Marie Chaker, "First Marblehead Chief's Exit Tied to Bank of America Official," *Wall Street Journal,* September 29, 2005, p. A11.

Hechinger, John, and Karen Richardson, "A Shortened Payment Plan; First Marblehead Investors Begin to Retreat," *Wall Street Journal,* March 9, 2007, p. C2.

"Honoring the Memory of a Family Friend and Educator," *UVA TopNews Daily,* January 11, 2005.

Reidy, Chris, "Ethics Violation Tests First Marblehead," *Boston Globe,* May 16, 2006.

———, "First Marblehead Chief Abruptly Quits over Gifts Exchange," *Boston Globe,* September 28, 2005.

Shenn, Jody, "Marblehead Bank Deal: Lab? Or Play for Funding?" *American Banker,* July 19, 2006, p. 1.

General Employment Enterprises, Inc.

———————————■———————————

1 Tower Lane, Suite 2100
Oakbrook Terrace, Illinois 60181
U.S.A.
Telephone: (630) 954-0400
Fax: (630) 954-0447
Web site: http://www.generalemployment.com

Public Company
Incorporated: 1962
Employees: 320
Sales: $20.1 million (2006)
Stock Exchanges: American
Ticker Symbol: JOB
NAIC: 561310 Employment Placement Agencies

■ ■ ■

General Employment Enterprises, Inc., offers professional staffing services to corporate clientele, providing temporary and permanent engineering, accounting, and information technology professionals through a network of branch offices. General Employment divides its business into two segments, offering placement staffing services and contract staffing services. Its placement staffing segment puts candidates into regular, full-time positions with employers. Contract services entail placing professional employees on temporary assignments under contracts with client companies. The company derives 51 percent of its annual revenues from contract staffing services and 49 percent from placement staffing services. General Employment operates 11 branch of-

fices located in Arizona, California, Illinois, Indiana, Massachusetts, North Carolina, Ohio, and Texas.

ORIGINS

General Employment traces its beginnings to the entrepreneurial efforts of F. L. Winslow, who founded an engineering staffing firm known as the "Engineering Agency" in 1893. More than a century passed from the opening of Winslow's small office to the modern version of the company in the 21st century, but the period of the greatest significance for understanding the history of the company began following World War II. The latter part of the 20th century marked the Imhoff era of General Employment's history, a period dominated by the personality and actions of Herbert F. Imhoff, Sr., that extended into the 21st century under the direction of his first-born son, Herbert F. Imhoff, Jr.

Herbert F. Imhoff, Sr., was 31 years old in 1958 when he joined the engineering staffing firm founded by Winslow. He spent the ensuing 43 years at the company, working full time until his death. Imhoff rose through the company's management ranks, earning his last promotion in 1964, when he was named chief executive officer and took charge of a company that supplied secretaries, clerical workers, accountants, and engineers on a permanent basis to corporate clientele. Imhoff led the company through its initial public offering (IPO) of stock in 1967, when shares in General Employment began trading in the over-the-counter stock market. The following year the company moved to the more prestigious American Stock Exchange. Imhoff presided over modest financial growth and physical

COMPANY PERSPECTIVES

Ours is a service business which is highly dependent upon the relationships and trust we develop with our clients. Our branch office personnel are on the phones every day, working to establish new relationships and to maintain existing ones. Our goal is to provide our clients with more than just a business service. We provide the personal service they expect from us— listening, understanding and responding to their needs.

expansion during his first decades in control. In 1982, he was joined by his son, Herbert F. Imhoff, Jr., who was known by his nickname "Corky." The younger Imhoff earned a law degree from Drake University in 1975 and worked as a practicing attorney and partner at a Chicago-based corporate law firm before joining General Employment as the company's general counsel. Herbert, Jr., like his father, climbed his way up the company's executive ranks, working alongside his father when General Employment faced the first great crisis in its history.

By the beginning of the 1990s, Herbert, Sr., had been in charge of General Employment for nearly 30 years. The company, throughout the period, had operated its employment agencies as separate subsidiaries, maintaining the distinct identities of its various entities until 1985, when the subsidiaries were merged into the parent company. In 1988, the company made one exception to the cohesiveness achieved three years earlier by establishing Triad Personnel Services Inc. as an Illinois-based subsidiary, but there were vestiges of the decentralized structure of General Employment that existed into the 1990s. The company operated under the trade names "General Employment," "Craig Agency," "Omni One," "Business Management Personnel," and "Triad Personnel Services" when Imhoff made arguably the boldest move in General Employment's history. His actions, which represented his response to General Employment's singular crucible, left an indelible mark on the history of the Oakbrook Terrace company.

FACING A CRISIS

The early 1990s changed the face of General Employment. A recession between 1990 and 1991 prompted companies nationwide either to trim their workforces or to suspend hiring activities, creating harsh conditions for staffing services firms of all types and sizes. General Employment, which subsisted solely on placing accountants, engineers, and similarly skilled professionals on a permanent basis, felt the sting of the times as its clients stopped expanding their payrolls. Imhoff, who watched his company sink into the red at the start of the decade, took action in 1992, when he faced a nearly $2 million operating loss. He decided to shift General Employment's focus away from the accountants and engineers who had represented the company's lifeblood for 99 years, and to specialize instead in providing information technology professionals to companies. Imhoff also created a second facet to General Employment's profile, establishing a contract services division in October 1992. Through its contract services business, which became the primary focus of the Triad Personnel Services subsidiary, General Employment began providing temporary and part-time professionals to companies for medium- to long-term work assignments.

The profound changes to General Employment's business and structure produced encouraging results. Between 1993 and 1995, revenues increased from $10.8 million to $16.7 million, a period that saw revenues from its fledgling contract services business increase from $2.3 million to $5.1 million. Perhaps more heartening, the company demonstrated strong profit growth, registering an increase in net income from $61,000 in 1993 to just over $1 million in 1995. The early results marked the beginning of what proved to be a highly successful decade for General Employment. The company offered its two types of services through branch offices, which numbered 24 by 1995, focusing on the market for computer programmers, systems analysts, and other information technology professionals, while at the same time emphasizing the contract services side of its business. Revenues jumped nearly 40 percent in 1996, when contract services accounted for nearly a third of the company's business, as companies clamored for the type of high-technology employees offered by General Employment. In 1997, after averaging 27 percent revenue growth for the previous three years, the company's stock value tripled. *Business Week* magazine took note, ranking General Employment 15th on its list of the "100 Best Small Companies in the United States." Imhoff responded to the company's surging growth by expanding its network of branch offices, opening nine new locations in 1997 and announcing plans for opening 12 new offices in 1998 and 16 new offices in 1999. "We're in the right place at the right time," he explained in a March 13, 1997, interview with Arlington Heights, Illinois's *Daily Herald*. "We have

---

KEY DATES

1958: Herbert F. Imhoff, Sr., joins General Employment.

1962: The company is incorporated.

1964: Imhoff is named chief executive officer of the company.

1967: General Employment completes its initial public offering of stock.

1992: General Employment begins offering contract services and focuses its efforts on the information technology field.

2000: The collapse of the technology sector forces General Employment to pare down its operations.

2001: Imhoff's son, Herbert F. Imhoff, Jr., is appointed chief executive officer.

2005: The company posts its first quarterly profit in three-and-a-half years.

2006: The company records $1 million in net income for the year.

---

people with the know-how. We're good at what we do. And, all of sudden, there is a fantastic need for what we do."

General Employment enjoyed the greatest financial and physical growth in its history during the 1990s, responding to the crisis early in the decade with a plan that fueled its robust expansion and broadened its market presence. The company moved into rapidly growing markets such as Atlanta, Georgia; Las Vegas, Nevada; San Diego, California; and Charlotte, North Carolina, sharing in the explosive advancement of the technology sector by supplying technology professionals. "We've been through some boom times," Imhoff reflected in an April 13, 1998, interview with the *Daily Herald,* "but never anything better than this." Unfortunately for General Employment, Imhoff's next statement proved to be prophetic. "This may be as good as it gets," he said.

BACKPEDALING IN THE EARLY 21ST CENTURY

On the march through most of the 1990s, General Employment entered the 21st century in retreat, forced to give up ground as its luster quickly faded. What had been largely responsible for its rise in the 1990s—supplying information technology professionals—caused its downfall when the technology sector imploded, leaving

General Employment heavily reliant on a moribund market. The disaster meant the company would be forced to look back at the late 1990s as its years of peak performance: net income reached a record high of $3.09 million in 1998, the same year its stock traded for $19 per share. Both figures fell well beyond the company's reach in the first years of the new century. Revenues reached a high of $39.8 million in 2000, when the company operated 42 branch offices in 14 states. Those figures, too, slipped from the company's grasp as it reeled backward, facing the second great crucible in its history.

The timing of the crisis could not have been worse. Just as the company realized the severity of its predicament, it also had to contend with a leadership crisis. In June 2000, while the technology sector was beginning to fall apart, Imhoff was diagnosed with lymphoma. He took a three-month leave of absence the following month, but by the fall of 2000 he was back working full time, focusing his attention on finding a solution to his company's woes. "I decided not to sit at home and worry about myself," he said in a November 9, 2000, interview with the *Daily Herald.* "I'd rather go to work." His efforts during the last months of his life centered on returning General Employment to its roots, back to the types of services that had supported the company for a century. "We had become a staffing company that was almost 90 percent devoted to placement of people in the information technology arena," he explained in a March 12, 2001, interview with *Crain's Chicago Business.* "Now, we're going to get back into fields like engineering and accounting and become more diverse in the process." The task of orchestrating the company's recovery was a chore passed from father to son. Herbert F. Imhoff, Sr., died in June 2001. Herbert F. Imhoff, Jr., was named chief executive officer of General Employment two months later.

Corky Imhoff inherited a company suffering from significant problems. His first years in control were spent on the defensive, time devoted to getting General Employment on sound financial footing. Cost-cutting initiatives were implemented, including eliminating half of the company's headquarters staff and selling a subsidiary, Generation Technologies Inc., to its management in 2004. Imhoff took a 20 percent cut in salary and a half-dozen senior executives also accepted reductions in pay, but the most visible aspect of the cost-cutting efforts entailed greatly reducing the number of branch offices operated by the company. General Employment operated 42 offices in 14 states in 2000, a physical presence that shrank to 19 offices in a ten-state territory by 2005. The effect of the cost-cutting measures was profound. General Employment, which boasted a market capitalization of $47 million in 1997, saw its value on Wall Street diminish to $10 million by 2005. Its stock, which had traded for $19 per share in 1998, was trading for $1.60 per share by 2006.

As General Employment planned for the future midway through the decade, there were signs that its health was on the mend, but much remained to be achieved. In the first fiscal quarter of 2005, ending December 31, 2004, the company posted a small profit of $119,000, the first net profit since the collapse of the technology sector in 2000. "I hope this is a turning point," Imhoff said in a March 7, 2005, interview with *Crain's Chicago Business.* "Of course," he continued, "we'd like to see more earnings, but we're encouraged that we seem to now be going in the right direction. The actions we've taken over the past few years have made a significant impact on our results." Steady growth continued to elude the company, however. One year later, in a March 6, 2006, interview with *Crain's Chicago Business,* Imhoff conceded his cost-cutting efforts had diverted attention away from pursuing growth opportunities. "We gave up some contracts with clients because there were lower-profit deals, and we haven't filled the pipeline with replacements as quickly as we should have," he said. "That's our fault." In the years ahead, Imhoff hoped to adopt a more aggressive approach to expansion and lead General Employment toward prosperity. His hopes were buoyed at the end of 2006, when the company registered $1 million in net income, the highest total in more than five years.

Jeffrey L. Covell

PRINCIPAL SUBSIDIARIES

Triad Personnel Services Inc.

PRINCIPAL COMPETITORS

Kforce Inc.; MPS Group, Inc.; Robert Half International Inc.

FURTHER READING

Comerford, Mike, "Imhoff, 74, Dies," *Daily Herald,* June 8, 2001, p. 3.

Eaton, Dan, "Tech Staffing Agency to Double Dublin Employees, Move Offices," *Business First-Columbus,* July 28, 2000, p. 5.

"General Employment Rides High-Tech Boom," *Daily Herald,* March 16, 1997, p. 1.

"Imhoff Takes 3-Month Leave of Absence," *Daily Herald,* July 13, 2000, p. 1.

Mawhorr, Sarah, "Cancer Doesn't Keep CEO from Work," *Daily Herald,* November 9, 2000, p. 1.

Murphy, H. Lee, "Boom Times: Gen'l Employment Expands to Hot New Markets," *Crain's Chicago Business,* April 13, 1998, p. 6.

———, "Gen'l Employment Enterprises Still Looking for Work," *Crain's Chicago Business,* March 8, 2004, p. 31.

———, "Growth Leaves General Employment Behind," *Crain's Chicago Business,* March 6, 2006, p. 13.

———, "Staffing Firm Going Back to Its Roots," *Crain's Chicago Business,* March 12, 2001, p. 51.

———, "Staffing Firm on the Upswing," *Crain's Chicago Business,* March 7, 2005, p. 22.

Schmitt, Anne, "The Right Place at the Right Time," *Daily Herald,* March 13, 1997, p. 1.

Silvestri, Scott, "General Employment Plans Expansion," *Daily Herald,* December 30, 1999, p. 1.

Tascarella, Patty, "Midwest Staffing Company Acquires 3-Year-Old Generation Technologies," *Pittsburgh Business Times,* April 20, 2001, p. 15.

GMH Communities Trust

10 Campus Boulevard
Newtown Square, Pennsylvania 19073
U.S.A.
Telephone: (610) 355-8000
Fax: (610) 355-8001
Web site: http://www.gmhcommunities.com

Public Company
Incorporated: 1985 as GMH Associates
Employees: 2,150
Sales: $293.13 million (2006)
Stock Exchanges: New York
Ticker Symbol: GCT
NAIC: 525930 Real Estate Investment Trusts

■ ■ ■

GMH Communities Trust is a real estate investment trust that specializes in housing at colleges and military bases. Originally a renovator of student housing, GMH began competing for military housing privatization contracts in the late 1990s.

Although the company's founder, Gary M. Holloway, began his career at an accounting firm (Touche Ross), the firm that bears his initials spent much of 2006 getting its financial house in order. This included restating results and firing a CFO who had complained of trouble at the top.

ORIGINS

The story of GMH Communities Trust begins in 1985, when Philadelphia area developer Gary M. Holloway, Sr., formed GMH Associates. This was originally a fictitious business name used to describe Holloway's development activities; a new entity, GMH Associates, Inc., was incorporated in 1990.

Holloway formed a property management firm as well in the late 1980s and a construction company was launched a few years later. GMH Realty, Inc., was formed in 1993 to sell the properties. This was not Holloway's first experience in the industry. After working at accounting firm Touche Ross, he had become chief financial officer of his father's business, Holloway Corp., before launching GMH in 1985.

Holloway invested in a variety of residential and commercial properties through partnerships. These holdings were worth about $35 million by 1994, according to the *Philadelphia Business Journal*.

Based in Newton Square, Pennsylvania, GMH Associates soon developed a specialty in taking over distressed campus housing projects at colleges and universities. GE Capital joined GMH in many of these deals; a joint venture between the two called GMH Capital Partners LP was formed around 2000.

The market for student housing was extremely fragmented, controlled by the schools themselves and local landlords. There seemed to be opportunity for a consolidator, but critics wondered why the academic institutions were willing to give up such a lucrative sideline.

INTO MILITARY HOUSING IN 1999

In 1999, GMH began competing to develop and manage military housing projects. The U.S. armed forces had found their stock of on-base housing to be severely dilapidated, so Congress authorized the Department of Defense to work with private parties to develop or rehabilitate communities at military bases. This was intended to accelerate the pace of development while shifting most of the capital burden to the private sector and saving money on construction costs.

GMH Associates boasted a real estate portfolio worth more than $1 billion by 2000. In 2002, GMH had revenues of $13.7 million, resulting in a net profit of $428,000.

PUBLIC IN 2004

A new entity, GMH Communities Trust, was created in May 2004 to take over a handful of predecessor companies that had been known as GMH Associates (College Park Management, Inc.; GMH Military Housing, LLC; 353 Associates, L.P.; and Corporate Flight Services, LLC). Founder Gary M. Holloway, Sr., remained chairman and CEO, while his son, Gary Holloway, Jr., was given responsibility for properties not folded into the company.

When formed, GMH Communities owned 38 properties totaling 22,000 beds and managed another 25 properties with 16,640 beds. The company had revenues of $75.85 million in 2004 and 1,200 employees. GMH reckoned itself the nation's leader in the college housing market: though there were a few other firms with national reach (two of these also went public around the same time as GMH), 97 percent of the $159 billion student housing industry was not yet controlled by large corporations or REITs (according to company figures reported by Dow Jones). GMH also claimed to be the third largest provider of privatized housing to the U.S. military, though it had a couple of serious rivals there, too.

Although it had lost $3 million on revenues of $18.8 million the previous year, GMH Communities conducted an initial public offering (IPO) on the New York Stock Exchange. The IPO, completed in early November 2004, raised $343 million, which was less than desired. During the year, GMH opted for status as a REIT, or real estate investment trust, which conveyed certain tax advantages. It acquired the sole general partnership interest in the operating company, GMH Communities LP. GMH had a couple of taxable REIT subsidiaries, College Park Management TRS, Inc., and GMH Military Housing Investments, LLC, which were owned by the GMH Communities TRS, Inc., subsidiary of the operating partnership.

The elder Holloway continued to own a stake in GMH after the IPO. Other leading shareholders included retired Admiral James Eastwood, and the former CEO of GE Capital Corporation, Denis Nayden. Another REIT, Vornado Realty, began investing in GMH in July 2004.

In spite of having what CEO Gary Holloway, Sr., called a "captive audience" for its campus and military properties, GMH Communities posted another large loss, $37 million, in 2004, though revenues quadrupled to nearly $84 million.

The IPOs of GMH and two other student housing REITs provided more capital for acquisitions, and seemed to drive up the price of available properties. (GMH also had a secondary offering in October 2005.) Nonetheless, GMH managed to post a $6.1 million net profit in 2005, as total revenues rose to $224 million. By this time, rental revenues had come to represent more than half of GMH's total.

A PROBLEM WITH "TONE AT THE TOP"

GMH delayed the reporting of its 2005 figures and lowered forecasts due to an internal investigation into "material weaknesses" in its accounting. The company's share price fell 25 percent immediately following this news.

Perhaps mitigating the damage was the assertion that Chairman and CEO Gary Holloway, who owned 20 percent of shares, was considering the purchase of the remainder of the company, though he backed down from this a few months later. The board was said to be discussing other "strategic alternatives" as well. GMH's chief financial officer, Bradley Harris, was fired and replaced in the interim by board member and key shareholder Dennis O'Leary. (It was Harris's March letter complaining of "tone at the top" that had prompted the internal investigation.) Almost inevitably, a class-action suit alleging securities fraud followed.

KEY DATES

1985: GMH Associates is established in Philadelphia area.

1999: GMH enters market for military housing privatization projects.

2004: GMH Communities Trust REIT is formed; company goes public on the New York Stock Exchange.

2006: Accounting concerns delay annual report, punish share price.

The company's auditor, Ernst & Young L.L.P., dropped the account in June 2006 without announcing a reason. The next month, the company hired a permanent CFO, J. Patrick O'Grady, a former partner with KPMG L.L.P. and Arthur Andersen L.L.P. At the end of July, GMH finally released its 2005 annual report.

In December 2006, the company announced it was not up for sale any more. Instead, it trimmed its quarterly dividend and focused on streamlining operations and finding better financing. Revenues had continued to climb in 2006, reaching $293 million for the year. However, profits were another story. GMH lost $5 million, roughly the same amount it spent on committees investigating its accounting controls in the first half. GMH emerged from the challenging year placing less emphasis on acquisitions.

Frederick C. Ingram

PRINCIPAL SUBSIDIARIES

College Park Management TRS, Inc.; GMH Communities TRS, Inc.; GMH Military Housing Investments, LLC.

PRINCIPAL COMPETITORS

Actus Lend Lease; American Campus Communities Inc.; Clark Realty Capital LLC; Education Realty Trust Inc.; Hunt Building Corporation; Lincoln Properties.

FURTHER READING

Aubin, Dena, "Demand for Better Campus Digs Fuels Bond Issuance," *Capital Markets Report*, June 17, 1999.

Bergstrom, Bill, "State Firm Helps Revitalize Military Housing," *Patriot-News* (Pennsylvania), February 29, 2004,

p. I1.

Crudele, John, "Beware of Termites with This Real Estate Option," *New York Post*, October 1, 2006, p. 28.

"GMH Communities IPO Raises Less Than Expected," *Reuters News*, October 28, 2004.

"GMH Communities Trust Delays Earnings, Shares Drop," *Reuters News*, March 13, 2006.

"GMH Communities Trust Ends Strategic Review, Decides Against Sale of Company, Slashes Dividend," *Associated Press Newswires*, December 18, 2006.

"GMH Files to Increase IPO Size to $400 Mln," *Reuters News*, August 11, 2004.

"GMH Latest 10k Delay, More Restatements Raise Concerns," *Dow Jones Newswires*, April 3, 2006.

Gopal, Prashant, "Vornado Increases GMH Stake; Sees Potential in Housing Firm," *Record* (Bergen, N.J.), October 20, 2005, p. B3.

Halbfinger, David M., "GMH Realty Has Built Nucleus of a Formidable Brokerage Firm," *Philadelphia Business Journal*, August 12–18, 1994, pp. 22, 27.

Hamerman, Joshua, "GMH Is Unlikely to Land Outside Interest," *Mergers & Acquisitions Report*, May 8, 2006.

Holcomb, Henry J., "GMH Has No Comment on Sale Report," *Philadelphia Inquirer*, September 20, 2006.

———, "GMH Issues Its Delayed 2005 Report: The Newton Square Firm Said That There Were Problems in Its Accounting and That They Were Being Corrected," *Philadelphia Inquirer*, August 1, 2006.

———, "GMH Postpones Earnings Report, Cites Internal Probe," *Philadelphia Inquirer*, March 14, 2006.

———, "Newton Square, Pa.–Based Real Estate Investment Firm Goes Public," *Philadelphia Inquirer*, October 29, 2004.

Jia, Denise, "GMH Communities CEO: No Longer Intends to Acquire Company," *Dow Jones Corporate Filings Alert*, July 13, 2006.

Kostelni, Natalie, "GMH, GE Capital Team Up," *Philadelphia Business Journal*, July 21, 2000, p. 1.

Kowsmann, Patricia, "GMH Communities Trust Sets CFO Salary at $300,000," *Dow Jones Corporate Filings Alert*, July 7, 2006.

Lambert, Phineas, "GMH Communities Has Tepid Debut," *TheDeal.com*, October 29, 2004.

Lee, Karen M., "GMH Communities Targeted in Purported Class Action," *Dow Jones Newswires*, April 5, 2006.

Loyd, Linda, "GMH Communities Trust Won't Be Sold; Shares Fall," *Philadelphia Inquirer*, December 18, 2006.

Mayor, Marc, "Le coin des insiders," *L'Agéfi Suisse*, March 11, 2005.

Morrissey, Janet, "GMH Communities to Seek Alternatives, May Soften Bad News," *Dow Jones Newswires*, March 13, 2006.

———, "GMH Trust Disappoints Street with Another Filing Delay," *Dow Jones Newswires*, June 30, 2006.

———, "Some REITs See Student Housing Investments As a Smart Bet," *Dow Jones Newswires*, March 11, 2005.

Walsh, Thomas J., "Brokerage Wins $30 Million Judgment," *Philadelphia Business Journal*, September 25, 1998, pp. 1f.

Goetze's Candy Company, Inc.

3900 East Monument Street
Baltimore, Maryland 21205
U.S.A.
Telephone: (410) 342-2010
Toll Free: (800) 295-8058
Fax: (410) 522-7681
Web site: http://www.goetzecandy.com

Private Company
Incorporated: 1958
Employees: 85
Sales: $5.8 million (2006 est.)
NAIC: 311340 Nonchocolate Confectionery Manufacturing; 311330 Confectionery Manufacturing from Purchased Chocolate; 424450 Confectionery Merchant Wholesale; 311320 Confectionery Manufacturing from Cacao Beans

■ ■ ■

Goetze's Candy Company, Inc., originally The Baltimore Chewing Gum Company, is family-owned and operated by the Goetze family. The company's assortment of soft caramels includes Caramel Creams (known in some regions of the country as Bulls-eyes) and Cow Tales in a variety of flavors. All of Goetze's candies are produced to order in the original manufacturing plant designed and built by R. Melvin Goetze, Sr., in 1928. Goetze's ships its candies throughout the United States and to Europe, Asia, Japan, and Australia.

INVENTION OF A NEW KIND OF CARAMEL

In 1895, August L. Goetze left his work as a printer and an engraver in Baltimore, Maryland. Joined by his son, William A. Goetze, he began manufacturing a variety of confections, including peanut chews, taffy, and chewing gum, in a basement kitchen at McDonogh and Madison Streets in the heart of the city. The company, which Goetze and his son named The Baltimore Chewing Gum Company, was located around the corner from Johns Hopkins Hospital. In February 1897, the business relocated to Ashland Avenue and Bond Street where it remained until 1928.

R. Melvin Goetze, Sr., son of William A. Goetze, joined the company in 1909. In 1917, he invented "chu-ees," a soft, chewy caramel and the precursor of what was to become the company's core product. Goetze and his father began experimenting with adding wheat flour to their caramel base and the result was a confection with some pastry-like qualities. "It doesn't stick to your teeth and it's not super-sweet, which is why adults seem to like it more than children," explained the company's fifth generation vice-president Mitchell Goetze of this confection, in a 2004 *Style* magazine. The Caramel Cream, which in some regions of the country came to be sold as a Bulls-Eye, had a sugar cream center, to enhance its sweetness.

Throughout the 1920s, the company's business grew steadily. August Goetze died in 1924 and, by 1928, The Baltimore Chewing Gum Company had to move to a new, 24,000-square-foot facility on Monument Street in order to handle production. Goetze, Sr.,

COMPANY PERSPECTIVES

Goetze's Candy Company is a fifth-generation, family-owned company manufacturing confections since 1895 and specializing in the combination of caramel and cream candies made from the finest quality ingredients.

planned and designed the entire plant and its equipment. He even designed and built the new machinery, which allowed for three times the company's output prior to the move.

According to the company's web site, The Baltimore Chewing Gum Company survived the stock market crash of 1929 due to its private, family-based ownership. Throughout the 1930s and the 1940s, the Goetzes owned and operated the company, which continued to thrive and to produce its small line of candies, which then still included chewing gum. In 1935, the third generation of Goetzes joined the family business. The company, which initially had sold its goods regionally, began to ship its candies throughout the United States. Its gum traveled as far as Hawaii and Puerto Rico. Still, the company followed a strict practice of "cook today and package tomorrow," producing only to-fill orders; it never stockpiled its items, making only as much as it could sell.

Then in 1942, sugar rationing began, and the company cut back on its candy production. The chicle used to produce its chewing gum also became expensive. The Goetzes decided to stop buying chicle and to produce only one candy, the Caramel Cream, by then the candy company's best-selling item.

FOCUSING ON CARAMEL SALES

The 1950s were a decade of change and focus for the small company, which, in 1951, changed its name to Goetze's Candy Company and, in 1958, incorporated under that name. Beginning in the 1950s, under the influence of R. Melvin Goetze, Jr., a third-generation family member, Goetze's Candy invested in automation as its primary means of improving the business. The company had the distinction of being the first to receive a delivery of corn syrup by tank truck in Baltimore in October 1951. Also that year, Goetze's Candy Company switched from wax paper to cellophane for twist-wrapping its Caramel Creams. By the end of the decade, the fourth generation of the Goetze family was entering the business.

Throughout the next four decades, Goetze's Candies created and tried marketing new flavors of its original caramel cream formula. Some, such as banana, peanut butter, cherry, licorice, and butter rum, came and went quickly. The company remained strictly family-owned and operated, honoring a commitment that the Goetzes made to their business and to future generations.

In a 1996 issue of *Candy Industry*, Spaulding Goetze, a fourth-generation member of the Goetze family, former commodity broker, and then president of the 101-year-old Goetze's Candy Company, explained the family's methods for keeping ownership of the company in the family. Only family members who worked for Goetze could become stockholders. However, the company did not guarantee a job for all Goetzes; only those truly interested were welcomed aboard. In fact, management expressly encouraged family members to work outside of the company for a while in order to maintain a smoothly run business.

In addition, the Goetze family developed a unique practice for transferring ownership of Goetze's Candy from one generation to the next. The up and coming generation had the responsibility for writing their parents' will. Spaulding Goetze stressed that this practice "[brought] everything out in the open so people aren't worrying about what they're going to get" and left family members free to concentrate on the business of running the company. What this meant, additionally, was that at no point did those in management feel free to sell the company.

NEW FLAVORS, NEW PRODUCTS, NEW SIZES

Shortly before Goetze's celebrated its 100th anniversary and the fifth generation of Goetzes joined the company in 1995, it introduced another new product, the Cow Tale in 1992. The Cow Tale, a long, thin, soft candy with a cream filling and caramel-like exterior, was produced originally only in one flavor, the same as that of Goetze's original vanilla Caramel Cream. However, after the Cow Tale became popular among both adults and children and assumed the status of the number one 25-cent candy item in the United States, Goetze's Candy introduced a second flavor, chocolate, and in 2000, a third, StrawberriCream. The company also began shipping its products worldwide in 1995, sending its Caramel Creams and Cow Tales to Europe, Asia, Japan, and Australia.

By 1998, the candy manufacturer was cooking and processing more than 60 tons of candy per day in the plant it had occupied since 1928. It still manufactured

KEY DATES

1895: August L. Goetze and his son, William A. Goetze, found The Baltimore Chewing Gum Company.

1897: The company relocates to Ashland Avenue and Bond Street, Baltimore, Maryland.

1928: The company moves to a new production facility and its permanent home on Monument Street.

1951: The company changes its name to Goetze's Candy Company.

1958: The company incorporates under the name Goetze's Candy Company, Inc.

1995: Goetze's Candy Company, Inc., begins shipping worldwide.

its original Caramel Cream products, and it continued to explore other flavors, such as old-fashioned caramel apple sticks with an apple-flavored cream center.

The candy industry enjoyed sales of $3.9 billion in 1999. However, the late 1990s introduced sharp increases in sugar prices and sugar shortages. Additionally there were changes afoot in the way in which candy was being marketed. According to Mitchell Goetze in a 2000 *National Petroleum News* story, "C-stores [had] moved away from their core products and started stocking a lot of novelty candies." In addition, larger-sized portions were becoming more common. Goetze began to sell its Cow Tales in seasonal tumblers of 25 units and its Caramel Creams in 2.5 pound tubs with snap-on lids and decorative exteriors.

Also by the new millennium, consolidation within the candy retailer and broker communities was providing both challenges and opportunities for small candy companies such as Goetze's. Many candy manufacturers, Goetze's Candy among them, began to turn to nontraditional retail opportunities, such as selling their confections to auto-parts or fabric stores. In 2000, it joined with six other candy makers to form the Confectioners Alliance, a group dedicated to increasing the placement and distribution of confectionary products, and cooperative efforts in direct and broker sales management, advertising, and promotion. The company also began to invest more heavily in Internet sales and sales to private label and contract manufacturers.

Spaulding Goetze, a fourth-generation chief executive, focused his family's attention on research and development of new products, on packaging, and on automating production and sales systems. In 2000, as fruit flavors entered the candy market, Goetze's Candy Company introduced StrawberriCream Caramel Creams and Cow Tales. After candy sales slipped in 2003 and 2004, candy manufacturers as a group began to focus on niche targets—aging baby boomers, diabetics, empty nesters, young adults, Hispanics and other ethnic groups, and tweens—to drive up sales. In 2004, Goetze's added a square caramel made with real cream, Goetze's Gourmet Caramels. In 2006, it introduced its Old-Fashioned Caramel Apple Cow Tales and added larger-size bags and packs of some of its other standards.

According to candy sources, caramel-based candies, less sweet and with more nostalgic appeal than chocolate confections, provided an opportunity for immediate growth in the years leading up to 2010. Still, as the collectively run Goetze's looked to the future, it still chose to maintain a low profile. "It's somewhat of a hobby," professed Mitchell Goetze in a 2004 *Style* article. "When you run an entity because it's something you love—it sounds corny, but it's true—your philosophy on why you show up every day really is different than when you always are wearing the business first." Despite this laid-back approach to doing business, the company still managed to turn out upwards of ten million pieces of candy during a typical eight-hour shift. The demand for its products might be attributed to the fact that "[c]aramel items continue to be perceived by consumers as 'higher-end,' as well as healthy and nutritious," according to Mitchell Goetze in a January 2002 *Confectioner* article. "They're something that parents can offer to children and not feel as bad about ... as they would some electric blue sour ball." It seemed safe to say that Goetze's candies would continue to make children as well as adults feel good for years to come.

Carrie Rothburd

PRINCIPAL COMPETITORS

Brach's Confections, Inc.; The Hershey Company; Tootsie Roll Industries, Inc.; Atkinson Candy Company; Cadbury Adams USA; Cadbury Trebor Bassett; Classic Caramel Company; Mars, Incorporated; Spangler Candy Company.

FURTHER READING

Henderson, Stephen G., "Ghouls Rule; This Year's Halloween Candy Is a Real Scream," *Baltimore Sun*, October 27, 2004, p. 1F.

Henry, Jim, "Keeping It in the Family: An Industry Discussion," *Candy Industry*, January 1996, p. 34.

Kimmerle, Beth, *Candy: The Sweet History,* Portland: Collectors Press, 2003, p. 106.

"Plenty on the Candy Plate," *Candy Industry,* November 2003, p. 24.

"Rising to the Top," *Professional Candy Buyer,* January–February 2002, p. 14.

Saccogna, Laura, "Sweet Profits with Candy," *National Petroleum News,* December 1, 2000, p. 20.

"Suppliers Form Candy Alliance in Response to Consolidation," *MMR,* May 28, 2001, p. 15.

Yockel, Michael, "As Good As It Goetze," *Style,* November 2004, p. 200.

Zind, Tom, "Caramels Capitalize on Boomer Nostalgia, While Adding New Dimensions to Attract the Youth Market," *Confectioner,* January 2002, p. 30.

Goldcorp Inc.

———————■———————

Park Place
666 Burrard Street, Suite 3400
Vancouver, British Columbia V6C 2X8
Canada
Telephone: (604) 696-3000
Toll Free: (800) 567-6223
Fax: (604) 696-3001
Web site: http://www.goldcorp.com

Public Company
Incorporated: 1994
Employees: 4,657
Sales: $1.71 billion (2006)
Stock Exchanges: Toronto New York
Ticker Symbols: G (TSX); GG (NYSE)
NAIC: 212221 Gold Ore Mining

■ ■ ■

Goldcorp Inc., true to its name, engages in gold mining, including exploration, extraction, processing, and reclamation. As an upstart company, Goldcorp resurrected the Red Lake Gold Mine. Located in Ontario, Canada's largest gold mine also claims status as one of the world's richest and lowest cost producers. The Wheaton River Minerals acquisition in 2005 broadened Goldcorp geographically, into Mexico, South America, and Australia. The next year, dual purchases of Barrick's Placer Dome assets and Glamis Gold Ltd. propelled Goldcorp into the world's upper echelon of gold mining companies.

GOING FOR THE GOLD

Rob McEwen, founder of Goldcorp Inc., "caught the gold bug as a teenager in the 1960s, listening to his father talk at the dining room table about his travels around the world, a return to hard currency and his investments in gold," *Canadian Business* recounted. McEwen then followed in his father's footsteps, entering the investment industry and, for a short time, partnering with him in the securities firm McEwen Easson.

Upon his father's death in 1986, McEwen gained control of Goldcorp. The senior McEwen had established the closed-end investment fund three years earlier. Holding shares in gold mining companies and bullion, the fund value plummeted in 1987. Investors wanted to shut it down, but McEwen had other ideas.

McEwen envisioned transforming the entity into an operating company. The transition was not simple. He faced stiff competition, when he moved to gain control of Dickinson Mines in 1989. The company primarily consisted of the Red Lake Mine, in northeastern Ontario and situated next to a well-developed Placer Dome Mine. The battle, once the mine had been acquired, was far from over. The mine was a high-cost operation. Despite naysayers, McEwen set out on the road to upgrade the company, from boardroom to drill site.

In March 1995, the discovery of deposits holding greater gold concentration validated McEwen's decision to take on Red Lake. A subsequent United Steelworkers strike coupled with a drop-off in the price of gold afforded McEwen an opportunity to overhaul the mine. Yet idling the mine, however timely, created other concerns.

Neighboring Placer Dome Campbell Mine sat on the same deposit as Red Lake. Fearing a takeover, McEwen took another risk. In March 2000, The Goldcorp Challenge was implemented. Goldcorp "posted all its proprietary mining data on a web site and asked the world to help them find Red Lake's next six million ounces of gold," *Canadian Business*'s Andrew Wahl related. In the end, McEwen usurped any Placer Dome advantage in a bid for Goldcorp, was directed to new deposits, and inspired to pioneer a mining virtual-reality lab. With the protracted strike over, laborers returned to a state-of-the-art mine able to produce ten times the gold at one-sixth the cost.

PATHS MERGING: 2001–04

Goldcorp moved to acquire Vancouver-based Wheaton River Minerals Ltd. in late 2004. Goldcorp predicted the new entity would be one of the world's lowest cost producers, producing 1.1 million ounces at $60 per ounce during 2005. Combined, Goldcorp and Wheaton held 10.5 million ounces proven and probable reserves, at least $500 million in cash and gold bullion, no debt, and a $3 million credit line, according to *American Metal Market*. Rob McEwen was slated to continue as chairman with Wheaton River's Ian Telfer as CEO.

"The closer we got to it, the better it looked," Telfer told *American Metal Market*. "Goldcorp was looking for growth and a resolution to their management situation and Wheaton River was looking for growth and to reduce its copper value. We do both, and we're excited about the potential for stock to go up."

Earlier in the year, McEwen had announced his plans to step away from his leadership position with the company he built. Under new management, Goldcorp was expected to concentrate growth in the Americas, primarily, followed by Australia.

The grand plan quickly grew complicated when Glamis Gold Ltd. made a hostile takeover bid for Goldcorp. The Reno, Nevada-based mining company had its eyes on Goldcorp's Red Lake operation. The Glamis offer was contingent on Goldcorp dropping Wheaton: two previous bids for Wheaton by other suitors had already been scuttled during 2004.

The strongest gold rally in more than two decades had driven both friendly and hostile takeovers in the industry. Since 2001 gold was up from about $250 per ounce to more than $450 per ounce, and industry watchers expected the price of gold to continue to rise, according to a February 2005 *Canadian Business* article.

The Glamis all-stock offer for Goldcorp was worth $3.5 billion, while the Wheaton stock swap was valued at $2.4 billion, John Gray reported for *Canadian Business*. The larger deal deteriorated, however, becoming "more like a bitter U.S.-style political campaign, complete with mudslinging, personal attacks and even negative advertising," Gray observed.

Ultimately, Goldcorp shareholders shut out Glamis and approved the Wheaton deal. The merger transformed Goldcorp from a company with a single significant gold property in northwestern Ontario, to an international gold and copper producer with mines in Mexico, Argentina, Australia, and Brazil. Annual gold production doubled from 600,000 to more than 1.2 million ounces, placing Goldcorp in fifth place among North American gold producers behind Barrick Gold, Placer Dome, Newmont Mining, and Kinross Gold, respectively. Goldcorp's elevated status made the company "attractive to not just gold investors, but pension funds and mutual funds, both in Canada and the U.S.," Telfer told *Canadian Business*.

Nonetheless, the industry trend toward consolidation most likely would dampen future deals, limiting the number of available companies and, consequently, driving up the cost of those remaining on the market. Rising gold prices, moreover, further increased valuation of potential purchase targets. As for buying less expensive start-ups, Goldcorp operations lacked experience in the early mine development phases, according to *Canadian Business*. Both McEwen's and Telfer's backgrounds were in the financial end of business. Yet both had built successful companies, albeit in decidedly different styles.

Telfer's ventures prior to Wheaton had their ups and downs. Telfer had helped elevate TVX Gold from speculative stock-play to respected producer. In the wake of that success, he entered into an Internet venture linking investors with small Canadian gold miners. Yet as with a lot of other dot-coms of the day, it went bust. Seeking to reverse his fortunes, Telfer teamed up to find a promising gold property. A $5.5 million investment by Telfer, Frank Guistra, Neil Woodyer, Pierre Lassonde, and Gene McBurney bought control of Wheaton River, in May 2001. Telfer was named chairman and CEO.

KEY DATES

1983: Goldcorp is established as an investment fund.

1986: Rob McEwen sets out on road to transform fund into operating company.

1995: Red Lake Mine shows signs of promising returns.

2000: In a risky bet, company posts its proprietary mining information online, which leads to rewarding innovation.

2005: Goldcorp merges with Wheaton River Minerals Ltd.

2006: Company engages in second largest gold deal to date.

Wheaton's largest existing asset, Golden Bear mine in northern British Columbia, was nearly depleted, so Telfer spent two years buying various mining interests in Mexico, Argentina, and Australia. Nevertheless, a corresponding jump in gold prices was required for the endeavor to claim success.

Telfer got the price rally he needed: profits and market capitalization skyrocketed. Still, Telfer's name was linked to his earlier failure. To enhance Wheaton's image, Telfer moved to merge with Toronto-based Iamgold Corp. in the spring of 2004. Unfortunately, piggybacking hostile takeover bids and shareholder resistance scuttled the deal.

Meanwhile, in December 2003, Goldcorp was trading at record highs, aided by a gold price in excess of $400 per ounce. Later, when the company sold off gold reserves and its top officer dumped about 39 percent of his stake in Goldcorp, shareholders grew edgy.

McEwen said the reserve sell-off was in response to pending Canadian tax law change in regard to bullion. As far as parting with his own shares in the company, McEwen pointed to family obligations as the precipitating cause. *Canadian Business* reported that behind the scenes McEwen was pursuing sale of the company.

Prolonged negotiations with Glamis Gold failed to bring a deal to a close. Consequently, McEwen turned his attention elsewhere. He had been captivated by the Wheaton story, as told by Telfer, at a Canadian Institute of Mining, Metallurgy and Petroleum event in the fall of 2004. In December, Goldcorp announced its bid for Wheaton.

When Glamis responded with its hostile takeover bid for Goldcorp, Telfer and McEwen joined forces to convince shareholders, particularly institutional shareholders, to support the Goldcorp/Wheaton merger. In January 2005, McEwen launched a web-based war of words against Glamis. In February, the Goldcorp board rejected a "sweetened" deal, John Gray reported for *Canadian Business*. Goldcorp shareholders, the recipients of a special dividend, then approved the Wheaton deal.

MINING FOR GREATER RICHES: 2005–07

At the start of 2005, Goldcorp's Red Lake and Wharf mines were producing 600,000 ounces per year. The Wheaton River deal, completed in April, pushed gold production to more than one million ounces. The stellar year continued. In June Goldcorp acquired a Mexican gold project; combined with an existing Los Filos property, Goldcorp aimed to put the largest gold mine in Mexico into operation in 2007. In the second half of the year, Goldcorp announced agreements to buy Placer Dome properties from Barrick Gold Corporation as well as Virginia Gold Mines, with its Eleonore gold exploration project in Quebec. The rash of purchases would catapult Goldcorp into the ranks of the top five gold mining companies worldwide and the top three in North America. Revenues hit $896.4 million for 2005, up from $191 million the prior year. The company also posted record net earnings, $286 million versus $51 million in 2004.

As for 2006, Goldcorp was not planning to replicate the prior year, at least in terms of acquisitions. "We will be slowing things down. Our objective was to get to two million ounces and we're now there," Telfer told the *Globe and Mail.*

Telfer's resolve did not last long. In September 2006, Goldcorp made an $8.6 billion offer to buy its once hostile suitor, Glamis. Although this time the deal was friendly, controversy abounded. "Mr. McEwen was the most vocal critic, claiming the deal was overly dilutive for Goldcorp shareholders and would see too much of Goldcorp's cash directed toward risky development projects," Wendy Stueck reported for the *Globe and Mail.*

Glamis reported record gold production of 434,010 ounces during 2005 and doubled its revenue. The Glamis mine portfolio included sites in Mexico, Central America, and Nevada. However, Goldcorp's biggest noninstitutional shareholder wanted a voice in whether it was wise to buy a company so keen on exploration. According to the agreement, only Glamis shareholders got a vote on the deal. McEwen, who still held about 1.5 percent of the company he founded, took his fight to the courts and lobbied shareholders for support.

The proposed all-stock purchase would rank as the second largest gold deal ever, behind Barrick Gold Corp.'s $10.4 billion acquisition of Placer Dome Inc. Goldcorp shares dropped 27.7 percent in the wake of the announcement of the deal, *Canadian Business* reported in October 2006.

McEwen said he would sell his Goldcorp shares if the Glamis deal proceeded. The price of gold, of course, would factor into the timing. Very early in November, gold sold for about $629 per ounce, off 12 percent from the 2006 high of $721.50 on May 11, according to *America's Intelligence Wire.* McEwen, who vacated his management position and board seat at Goldcorp following the Wheaton purchase, was still an active participant in the industry, holding an ownership share of U.S. Gold Corp., an exploration company based in Colorado.

In October 2006, Glamis shareholders approved the deal. The Ontario Superior Court of Justice shot down McEwen's appeal of a lower court ruling in November, allowing Goldcorp to complete the acquisition. The court found Goldcorp in compliance with all applicable business laws in the construction of the deal. Telfer took the chairmanship of the combined companies, and Glamis's top officer, Kevin McArthur, succeeded him as president and CEO.

Goldcorp posted annual earnings of $408.3 million in 2006, up 43 percent. Revenue climbed 91 percent to $1.71 billion. The company planned to spend $120 million on exploration of its own properties during 2007, *Canadian Business* reported. Goldcorp predicted production of 2.6 million ounces of gold at an average cash cost of $150 per ounce for the year.

The expanded Goldcorp held 11 mining operations and seven development projects. The Barrick and Glamis deals served to boost the company's gold reserves and resources from five million to ten million ounces. Goldcorp had set its sights on a 50 percent increase in production over the next five years.

Kathleen Peippo

PRINCIPAL COMPETITORS

AngloGold; Ashanti; Barrick Gold; Newmont Mining.

FURTHER READING

Bresnick, Julie, "Glamis Bid May Foil Wheaton's Goldcorp Plan," *American Metal Market,* December 17, 2004, pp.1+.

———, "Goldcorp, Wheaton River Agree to Tango … ," *American Metal Market,* December 7, 2004, p. 5.

"Goldcorp Completes Acquisition of Glamis Gold," *America's Intelligence Wire,* November 4, 2006.

"Goldcorp 4Q Earnings Fall 35 Percent with Special Items and Higher Mining Costs," *Canadian Business Online,* March 8, 2007.

Gray, John, "McEwen Abandons His Campaign," *Canadian Business Online,* November 7, 2006.

———, "My Last Boom," *Canadian Business,* February 28–March 13, 2005, pp. 28+.

Hendawi, Hamza, and Qassim Abdul Zahra, "Goldcorp Inc. Founder Will Sell if He Loses Battle: Opposes Glamis Takeover," *America's Intelligence Wire,* November 4, 2006.

Stueck, Wendy, "Goldcorp CEO Shoots Down Critics of Deal," *Globe and Mail,* September 2, 2006, p. B5.

Wahl, Andrew, "Most Innovative CEO 2006: Rob McEwen, US Gold Corp.," *Canadian Business,* October 9, 2006.

Wong, Craig, "Goldcorp Looks to the Drillbit for Growth After Year of Acquisitions," *Canadian Business Online,* March 8, 2007.

———, "Goldcorp Says 'Rush Is Over,' Will Slow Down," *Globe and Mail,* March 7, 2006, p. B3.

GOME Electrical Appliances Holding Ltd.

Rm. 6101, 61/F, The Center
99 Queen's Road
Hong Kong
Telephone: (+852) 2122-9133
Fax: (+852) 2122-9233
Web site: http://www.gome.com.hk

Public Company
Founded: 1987 as China Eagle Group
Employees: 22,171
Sales: CNY 49.84 billion (2006)
Stock Exchanges: Hong Kong
Ticker Symbol: SEHK
NAIC: 443111 Household Appliance Stores; 443112 Radio, Television, and Other Electronic Stores

■ ■ ■

GOME Electrical Appliances Holding Ltd. is the largest retailer of household appliances in China and one of the largest retail chains in the country. The company sells a complete line of small and large appliances, including televisions, stereos, air conditioners, mobile telephones, refrigerators, washing machines, and computers. GOME owns and operates more than 550 retail stores in 21 regions in mainland China; the stores are located in more than 100 large- and medium-sized cities. The company also operates several digital equipment stores specializing in computer hardware, software, and accessories. Through a partnership with Walgreens, the company is expanding into retail pharmaceutical and cosmetics under GOME Pharmaceutical Company.

Company founder Huang Guangyu, also known by his Cantonese name, Wong Kwong-yu, is one of the richest individuals in China through the success of GOME.

BEGINNINGS OF A RAGS-TO-RICHES SUCCESS STORY

The story of GOME's success began in a poor farming village in the Guangon province of southern China, where GOME founder Huang Guangyu traded in used books and sold discarded plastic bottles in order to contribute to the family income. Huang, then 16 years old, and his older brother, Huang Jungin, left Shantou in 1986 with the ambition to enter the retail trade on a different scale. In their first venture together, the two brothers purchased $500 in radio equipment and watches at the low prices available in Shantou, then sold them in the northern provinces of Inner Mongolia, where such products garnered a higher price. They relocated to Beijing and reinvested sales income to purchase clothing for resale. They returned to the electronics trade on January 1, 1987, with the opening of an electrical appliances outlet in a rundown market stall on Zhushikou Street. Among China's first private entrepreneurs, they profited by selling small, household appliances at prices lower than the competition and by offering customer service before and after the sale. Simply, the store succeeded through the combined ideas of "small profits, good sales, service comes first." Furthermore, the business thrived as China's "open-door" reform began to transform the country into a consumer-driven economy.

The company, operating as China Eagle Group, achieved success through real estate investment, as well.

In 1992 the company completed the Eagle Towers and Eagle Plaza development in Beijing. Eagle Towers, a commercial center with 7,000 square feet of retail space, was the largest such development in China, even a decade later. About this time, the individual business preferences of the Huang brothers emerged. Huang Jungin preferred the real estate business, while Huang Guangyu preferred retail. In 1992, they separated the two businesses according to assets, with Huang Guangyu obtaining complete control of the retail appliance business, and his brother taking the real estate business. Huang Guangyu retained the China Eagle Group name, but he operated the retail company as GOME Household Electrical Appliances Company.

EXPANDING WITH THE CHINESE ECONOMY

Though Huang did not finish middle school, he proved to be a sharp-minded entrepreneurial leader for the retail company and for China. The company opened several appliance stores throughout Beijing, and Huang became a primary mover in the development of Chinese retail chains by applying the GOME name to all stores in the network. Also, the company continued its business philosophy of low prices. Huang eliminated the markup cost of wholesale prices by dealing directly with manufacturers, and multiple store outlets allowed the company to obtain a high-volume inventory purchased at special rates. In turn, GOME offered appliances to Chinese consumers at a lower retail price than the competition. The lower prices often led to price wars, especially after GOME opened stores outside Beijing in 1999, the first in nearby Tianjin. Operating on high volume and low prices generated comparisons between Huang and Wal-Mart founder Sam Walton. The success

of GOME prompted a management seminar attended by government officials and respected academics to deliberate business development strategies based on the GOME model.

Huang expanded the network of retail appliance stores, with new outlets in Shenzhen, Shanghai, Changzhou, and other major cities. GOME opened 32 stores in seven cities in 2001 and 47 stores in 11 cities the following year. The company began locating new stores in secondary cities, such as Guangzhou, where the company opened 11 stores in 2002.

GOME grew with China's economy, both following and leading according to profit margins and consumer demands. In July 2001, as the market for mobile telephones exploded in China, GOME began to offer complete customer service, from phone purchase to calling plans and payment processing, in 20 cities. The company sold more than one million handsets in 2002 alone and another 900,000 phones during the first six months of 2003. As competition in refrigerators and other large home appliances decreased profit margins for those products, GOME expanded its small home appliance department, taking advantage of higher profit margins generated from market entry of those products. Moreover, GOME pressed the competition by purchasing a large inventory of specific appliances, such as televisions and mobile phones, thus instigating price wars in order to benefit the consumer and attract customers to its stores. When oxygen enrichment air-conditioners became the newest must-have appliance in China, GOME participated in market expansion for the product in China. GOME placed large orders of the appliance from Haier Group, which gave GOME initial selling rights, a sales lead ahead of other retailers.

In order to accommodate the widening array of available consumer products, as well as the growing demand for specific products, GOME initiated two new store concepts. One involved the development of specialty stores selling digital products exclusively. GOME began selling computers in late 2001, and in early 2003 the company opened its first computer specialty store in Zhongguancun Village in Beijing. GOME offered computers, hardware, software, printers, scanners, digital cameras, cellular telephones, compact discs, CD players, and other accessories. GOME planned additional stores for Shanghai, Guangzhou, Shenzhen, Xi'an, and Shenyung. The other store concept involved the development of larger retail centers. In December 2003, GOME opened its flagship superstore in Beijing Capital Stadium Shopping Center Supermarket. The largest appliance store in the chain, with 10,000 square meters, the superstore carried 120,000 kinds of electrical appliances available from

KEY DATES

1987: Huang brothers begin selling small appliances in market stall in Beijing.

1993: GOME brand name is applied to network of appliance stores.

1999: GOME opens first store outside Beijing and begins national expansion.

2002: China Eagle Investments acquires another company to obtain a "backdoor" listing on the Hong Kong stock exchange for GOME.

2004: China Eagle Investments is renamed GOME Electrical Appliances Holding Ltd.; GOME becomes the largest appliance retailer in China.

2006: New strategic directions involve raising profit margins and entering new retail sectors.

over 600 brands. GOME opened a superstore in Dongguan, in Guangdong Province, in 2003, as well. At the superstores, GOME highlighted digital products and other high-end goods that provided higher profit margins. Overall, GOME opened a total of 79 stores in 19 cities in 2003, bringing the company's total to 103 stores. That year, GOME became the largest retailer of household electronic appliances in China.

DOING BUSINESS IN HONG KONG

As the company expanded, Huang turned his attention to Hong Kong. Huang wanted to establish a retail presence in Hong Kong in order to gain a foothold for international expansion and to attract foreign investment. Both of the motives entailed becoming a publicly owned company through entry to the Hong Kong stock exchange. In order to expedite this process, and avoid China's nine-month listing process, the company obtained a "backdoor" listing through the acquisition of Capital Automation Holdings, Ltd., and two other companies in 2002 by China Eagle Investment Group, another Huang entity. Huang planned to follow this listing with an initial public offering (IPO) of stock, but an unsatisfactory investor market stalled that process. In the meantime, GOME opened its first retail outlet in Mong Kok in November 2003. The store sold digital information technology and audiovisual products. An additional three home appliance stores opened in May 2004.

In February 2004 GOME announced a new plan for an initial public offering of stock on the Hong Kong exchange, but the IPO had to be postponed again, due to lack of confidence in the Hong Kong stock market during a crisis. By July GOME solidified its plans for the IPO. Because foreign investors cannot own more than 65 percent of a retail business in China, Huang divided GOME into two companies. China Eagle held a 65 percent stake in the retail chain, and Huang's "parent group" retained private ownership of 35 percent of GOME stores. The publicly listed company carried the more profitable mature assets which would likely attract investment; Huang owned the stores with lower overall financial performance. Finally, in September 2004, China Eagle placed 300 million shares on the market at HKD3.98 per share ($.50 per share); the company offered 240 million shares to institutional investors. Of the 50 investors, about half were from Asia, 35 percent from Europe, and 15 percent from the United States. GOME raised HKD 1.2 billion ($600 million), which it applied to reduce debt, continue expansion, and upgrade the company's computer information system. Upon completion of the offering, China Eagle took the name GOME Electrical Appliances Holding, Ltd.

The corporate structure after the stock offering assessed a 25.1 percent public ownership of GOME Holding, which owned 116 retail stores. Huang retained 35 percent of GOME Electrical through his 74.9 percent ownership in the holding company. Plus, he owned 100 percent of Beijing GOME, the low performing group of 56 stores. Through a subsequent sale of stock and convertible notes, Huang's ownership decreased to 66 percent. GOME Holding planned to consolidate ownership of the retail chain at a later date.

CONSOLIDATING ITS POSITION IN MAINLAND CHINA

By the end of 2004, GOME had become the largest retailer of home appliances in China, and the company sought to maintain that position, through geographic expansion and acquisition. GOME made its first-ever acquisition in August 2005, with the purchase of Shenzhen e-Home, a chain of ten appliance retail stores in Shenzhen and Guangzhou. Shenzhen e-Home operated at a loss, and GOME executives believed that it would take three to six months to create profitability by merging the stores into the GOME sourcing and pricing strategy. The locations of the stores complemented GOME's existing sites.

Geographic expansion involved an investment of CNY 250 million to open 130 retail outlets, nearly doubling the chain network of the listed company which had reached 144 stores at the end of 2004. While most new stores were to be located in China's largest cities, including Beijing, Tianjin, and Shenzhen, other outlets expanded GOME's reach to the coastal area cities with populations of approximately 500,000. The company opened 115 stores during 2005, expanding the company's reach to a total of 69 cities. About half of the shops opened in the second-tier cities. These markets required more time to develop due to less wealth and, therefore, lower consumer purchasing power. Hence, the company's profit margin suffered on a sales-per-square-inch basis. While revenues increased 42 percent in 2005, to CNY 17.96 billion, ($2.2 billion), net profit increased only 2.7 percent, to CNY 498.59 million. GOME viewed the gain in market share as essential for the immediate intention of expansion, expecting the profit to increase over the long term. GOME's retail sector carried 6 to 7 percent of the mainland market, but the company aimed to achieve 15 percent market share by 2009. Moreover, the separate "parent group" owned by Huang had opened 120 stores in 2005 and operated a total of 176 stores in 61 cities.

In early 2006, GOME completed the consolidation of the 65 percent stake listed on the Hong Kong stock exchange with the parent group owned by Huang. GOME Electrical acquired GOME Appliance Company from Huang, allowing the Hong Kong listed company to control all assets. In conjunction with the consolidation, GOME issued 650 million new shares at HKD 8.05 in order to help pay for the acquisition of Huang's shares. Huang's shares were acquired in a stock exchange, with GOME issuing new shares to Huang. Thus, Huang's share of the holding company increased, from 66.04 percent, to 75.67 percent.

GOME further consolidated its position in the appliance retail market through the August 2006 acquisition of China Paradise Electronics Retail, the third largest electronics retailer in mainland China, with 205 stores. GOME acquired 98.24 percent of the stock for $680 million. With the acquisition GOME intended to buttress profit margins as well as to reinforce its competitive position. GOME expected the acquisition to reduce operating expenses through streamlined supply chain management, thus continuing the company strategy of high-volume sales based on low prices. China's entry into the World Trade Organization increased the presence of foreign companies, such as Best Buy, Wal-Mart, and Carrefour, into Chinese markets. Hence, the acquisition would strengthen GOME's competitive advantage in China. GOME integrated most of the China Paradise stores under the GOME brand, but maintained the China Paradise brand in the Yangtze River Delta to capitalize on strong public recognition in that region. In addition to strengthening market share in retail appliances, the

acquisition pushed GOME to second place among all retail chains in China.

During 2006, GOME changed its growth strategy. Rather than continuing rapid new-store development, the company planned to open only 30 stores between 2007 and 2010. Instead, GOME concentrated on improving profit margins. One aspect of this strategy involved developing special merchandising displays that gave prominence to higher margin goods in retail stores. The company had tried this strategy successfully for telecommunications products, then expanded it to home appliances during 2006. Similarly, in late 2006, the company initiated a retail cobranding agreement with Motorola, the best-selling handset brand at GOME. Under the agreement, Motorola's presence would increase both quantitatively and qualitatively. Motorola's sales space increased with the store-within-a-store concept and a shop design that highlighted the company's brand identity. Also, Motorola would improve service with direct, in-store support through training GOME retail associates. Motorola shops were established at 30 of GOME's largest retail outlets around China. To launch Motorola's new image, GOME and Motorola offered special prices on the popular A780 handset during "Moto Month."

GOME initiated a number of other strategies to increase profit margins, such as eliminating weekend discounts and seeking preferential access to new products which tended to carry high margins. In 2006 the company launched digital TVs through exclusive contracts from three major Chinese companies, Hisense Electric Company, Konka Group, and Sichuan Changhong Electric. Conversely, GOME reduced its reliance on domestic brand appliances when suppliers sought to reduce prices, opting for imported brands with higher profit margins. Also, GOME attempted to improve profit margins by establishing high-end shops under the name Eagle Electric Appliance. These stores offered specialized services and a more appealing shopping atmosphere. GOME opened one store each in the central business districts of Shenyang and Beijing. The concept failed, due to insufficient resources, so GOME turned those stores into regular appliance stores.

As the retail appliance market matured, high profit margins in other business sectors prompted GOME to pursue new opportunities. In the summer of 2006, Huang began negotiations for entry into the retail pharmaceutical and cosmetic industries through a partnership with Walgreens. Huang established a new entity, GOME Pharmaceutical Company, Ltd., and he planned to open ten stores in late 2006. Also, in early 2007, GOME began construction on the Eagle International Fashion Exchange Center, in Guangzhou, a high-end clothing exhibition center. With 600,000 square meters, 328,000 were designated for retail space, 30,000 for office space, 50,000 for hotels, and 12,000 square meters for exhibition space.

Mary Tradii

PRINCIPAL SUBSIDIARIES

China Paradise Electronics; GOME Pharmaceutical Company, Ltd.

PRINCIPAL COMPETITORS

Best Buy Company, Inc.; Shandong Sanlian Group; Shanghai Yolo Household Electrical Appliance Company, Ltd.; Shanghai Yongle Electronics; Suning Appliance Chains Group Company, Ltd.; Wal-Mart Stores, Inc.

FURTHER READING

"Band Leader GOME Won't Be Caught out When Retail Music Stops," *South China Morning Post,* March 24, 2006.

Chan, Carol, "GOME Buys e-Home Chain for 180m Yuan," *Asia Africa Intelligence Wire,* August 2, 2005.

Cheng, Andy, "GOME Offers $5.2b for Paradise; Falling Margins and Intensifying Competition Trigger Urge to Merge in Electronics Retail Sector," *South China Morning Post,* July 26, 2006.

———, "GOME Shifts Focus to High-Margin Brands," *South China Morning Post,* March 27, 2006.

"China Paradise to Add over 80 Outlets in Shanghai," *Alestron,* December 8, 2006.

"China's No. 1 Home Appliance Retailer Makes Overall Listing," *Alestron,* March 31, 2006.

"Chinese Retail Giant Records Sharp Hike in Revenue," *Asia Pulse News,* March 23, 2006.

"GOME AV Starts Eagle Plan," *Asia Africa Intelligence Wire,* April 23, 2004.

"GOME Built Its Largest Branch in Beijing," *Alestron,* December 4, 2003.

"GOME Buys Publicity Right for a Film, Cellphone," *Alestron,* December 23, 2003.

"GOME Chairman Nets $1.37b in Share Disposal; Wong Sells 220m Shares, Reducing His Stake in the Appliances Firm to 65.9pc.," *Asia Africa Intelligence Wire,* December 15, 2004.

"GOME Entering IT Market," *Alestron,* February 13, 2002.

"GOME Eyes High-End Market," *SinoCast, LLC China IT Watch,* October 2, 2006.

"GOME Finishes Back-Door Listing in Hong Kong," *Alestron,* September 14, 2004.

"GOME Gained Initial Right to Launch New Standard Digital TV," *Alestron,* September 11, 2006.

"GOME Ignites High-End Color TV Price War," *Asia Africa Intelligence Wire,* December 10, 2002.

"GOME Opens New Stores in HK," *Asia Africa Intelligence Wire,* May 11, 2004.

"GOME Plans to Open Specialty Store for Digital Products in Beijing," *Alestron,* January 8, 2003.

"GOME's Ambition in Mobile Phone Market," *Asia Africa Intelligence Wire,* July 24, 2003.

"GOME Shuffles Managerial Team," *SinoCast, LLC China IT Watch,* October 20, 2006.

"GOME Throws Arm into Garment Field," *Alestron,* January 24, 2007.

"GOME to Benefit Customer by CNY20bn Goods on Promotion," *Alestron,* November 21, 2006.

"GOME to Boost Profit Margin," *Business Daily Update,* September 8, 2006.

"GOME to Enter Pharma and Cosmetic Retail Industry," *China Business News,* August 8, 2006.

"GOME to Move on Secondary Cities in Pearl River Delta," *Asia Africa Intelligence Wire,* December 19, 2003.

Guerrera, Francesco, "GOME Reshuffle Will Boost Huang's Fortune: China," *Financial Times,* March 30, 2006, p. 29.

"Haier Allies with GOME for Promoting Air-Conditioner," *Asia Africa Intelligence Wire,* December 8, 2003.

Hannity, Sean, and Alan Colmes, "Mong Kok to Get First GOME Store, Hong Kong Imail," *America's Intelligence Wire,* September 25, 2003.

Ho, Prudence, "GOME Plans Stores in Lower-Tier Cities," *Standard,* March 23, 2005.

"Home Appliance Vendor GOME Plans HK Debut in Mid-2004," *Asia Africa Intelligence Wire,* February 27, 2004.

Hoogewerf, Rupert, "Huang Guangyu: China's Sam Walton," *Hunan Report,* http://www.hurun.net/showmagazineen content11.aspx.

Li, Sandy, and Fiona Lau, "GOME Chairman to Raise US$150m from Share Sale," *South China Morning Post,* April 7, 2006.

Lifen, Zhang, "Getting Rich Is Glorious; Case Study: GOME Electrical Appliances," *Financial Times,* December 7, 2004, p. 3.

"Merger Completes," *SinoCast, LLC China IT Watch,* November 3, 2006.

Mitchell, Tom, "Local Hero's Taste of Paradise: An All-Chinese Deal Shows the Mainland Mastering the HK Capital Market," *Financial Times,* August 2, 2006, p. 6.

"Motorola Partners with GOME for Retail and Logistics," *China Business News,* November 17, 2006.

"Samsung Fights in Beijing Market with GOME," *Alestron,* February 23 2004.

Tang, Gladys, and Elliot Wilson, "Cut-Priced GOME Offer Snapped Up," *Asia Africa Intelligence Wire,* September 28, 2004.

"Three Forces to Consolidate Small Home Appliance Market," *Alestron,* May 6, 2003.

Yuk-min, Hui, "GOME Electrical in Takeover Attempt," *Asia Africa Intelligence Wire,* January 18, 2005.

Graham Packaging
Holdings Company

■

2401 Pleasant Valley Road
York, Pennsylvania 17402
U.S.A.
Telephone: (717) 849-8500
Fax: (717) 848-4836
Web site: http://www.grahampackaging.com

Private Company
Incorporated: 1998
Employees: 8,400
Sales: $2.52 billion (2006)
NAIC: 326160 Plastics Bottle Manufacturing

■ ■ ■

Graham Packaging Holdings Company designs and manufactures plastic packaging for branded consumer products, selling its products to manufacturers involved in the food and beverage, household, personal care, and automotive lubricants product categories. The company serves customers such as PepsiCo, Inc., Tropicana Products, Inc., Shell Oil Co., Exxon Mobil Corp., and The Procter & Gamble Co. Graham Packaging Holdings operates 86 manufacturing facilities in North America, Europe, and South America. The company specializes in technology-based, custom blow-molded containers, operating a substantial number of its plants near its customers' manufacturing facilities. Sales to the food and beverage industry account for more than half of the company's annual revenues. Graham Packaging Holdings is majority-owned by a private investment firm, The Blackstone Group L.P.

ORIGINS

Graham Packaging Holdings, which touted itself as "riding the crest of conversion," hitched its growth to the conversion from glass, paper, and metal containers to plastic packaging. As increasing numbers of manufacturers turned to plastic for their packaging needs, the company's opportunities for growth increased commensurately. Accordingly, the company's fortunes were wed to one of the most notable technological revolutions of the 20th century, but Graham Packaging Holdings did not sit and wait for the conversion to plastic packaging to take place. Instead, the company took an active role in advancing the vanguard of the revolution, assuming such a role from its inception, when Donald C. Graham formed a design and engineering firm in York, Pennsylvania, in 1960. Initially known as Graham Container Corp., the company operated as a regional plastic bottle developer and manufacturer, winning the business of automotive lubricant maker BP Lubricants, household products manufacturer Clorox, and household products and personal care products manufacturer Procter & Gamble during its first decade in business.

From its first decade forward, the company positioned itself as a specialist. Graham Packaging Holdings focused on serving manufacturers who required a high degree of customized packaging, thereby garnering high profit margins and realizing high growth rates. The company applied its technological expertise to the automotive, food and beverage, household cleaning, and personal care markets, designing bottles, jars, tubes, canisters, jugs, and carafes that appeared on retail shelves as dish detergent, motor oil, juices, and a slew of other

COMPANY PERSPECTIVES

We design and make custom blow-molded plastic containers—bottles, jars, tubes, canisters, jugs, and carafes—for some of the best-known branded products in the world. Our attention-getting packaging is an important part of their branding. Through superior design, engineering, and technology—plus unparalleled customer service and quick and reliable delivery—we occupy a leading position in plastic containers for four market categories: food and beverage, household products, automotive lubricants, and personal-care and specialty products.

products. During the 1970s, a number of new customers turned to the York-based company for their packaging needs, including Group Danone, Unilever, and Pennzoil-Quaker State, becoming the first to sample the company's seminal technological achievement. The Graham Rotational Wheel, utilizing electromechanical, blow-molding technology, debuted during the decade, greatly improving production speed and giving engineers the ability to use virgin resins, high barrier resins, and recycled resins simultaneously with ease.

INTERNATIONAL EXPANSION

With its proprietary Graham Rotational Wheel, the company established itself as a leading producer of customized, blow-molded rigid plastic packaging, specializing in using high-density polyethylene (HDPE) resin. As new customers were signed—Colgate-Palmolive, Tropicana, and Church & Dwight were among the new additions in the 1980s—the company built new plants to the demands of its growing business, often establishing production facilities at its customers' locations. The company also ventured overseas for the first time, evolving beyond a regional scope to become an international force in the conversion to plastic packaging. By the end of the 1980s, the company had begun to expand into Europe and South America, where many of its U.S.-based customers maintained operations. On a corporate level, the end of the 1980s also marked the creation of the organizational structure that described the company at the beginning of the 21st century. In 1989 Graham Packaging Holdings' immediate predecessor, Sonoco Graham Company, was formed. In 1991 Sonoco Graham Company changed its name to Graham Packaging Company, by which point there were nearly 30 plants in operation in North America, France,

The 1990s represented a decade of profound change for the business that operated under the Graham Packaging Holdings banner. The period included the company's first major leadership change, a change in ownership, and the greatest growth in its history. The conversion to plastic, which the company had promoted since its inception, took hold during the decade, accelerating greatly as consumers and manufacturers realized the superior functionality, safety, and economics of plastic when compared to metal, glass, and paper. The conversion to plastic occurred most rapidly in the food and beverage sector, where Graham Packaging Holdings concentrated its efforts. The company established itself as the world leader in the production of HDPE containers, supplying packaging for noncarbonated, chilled juice, juice drinks, and liquid foods that utilized HDPE resins.

It also invested heavily in a relatively new type of plastic packaging using polyethylene terephthalate (PET) resins. PET containers were used for the hot-fill packaging of nonrefrigerated shelf-stable juices and juice drinks, able to withstand a production process in which bottles were filled at between 180 degrees and 190 degrees Fahrenheit to kill bacteria and permit the shipment and display of beverages in a shelf-stable state. Between 1992 and 1998, Graham Packaging Holdings spent nearly $170 million to build a nationwide network of plants geared for PET production.

The company's commitment to developing PET production capabilities coupled with its entrenched position in the HDPE market enabled it to attract a wealth of food and beverage business during the 1990s. New food and beverage customers during the decade included Arizona Beverages Company, Clement Pappas & Co., Coca-Cola North America, H.J. Heinz Company, Welch Foods, Inc., and The Quaker Oats Company. The influx of new customers enabled the company to record a compound annual growth rate of 88 percent in its food and beverage business between 1993 and 1998. Food and beverage sales, which accounted for roughly 3 percent of the company's revenues at the start of the 1990s, represented nearly more than one-third of its business by the end of the decade.

BLACKSTONE GROUP TAKES A MAJORITY INTEREST: 1998

As the company embraced the food and beverage industry, significant changes were underway at its main offices. In 1998 The Blackstone Group L.P., a private investment and advisory firm based in New York, acquired 85 percent of Graham Packaging Holdings from Donald Graham, who retained a 15 percent interest in the company he had founded 38 years earlier. Blackstone paid $208.3 million for control of the company, making an investment it eventually intended to cash in on by ushering Graham Packaging Holdings through an initial public offering (IPO) of stock.

Concurrent with the change in ownership came a change in leadership, as Graham passed the duties of chief executive officer to Phillip R. Yates, who joined the company during the early 1970s. Yates, who held a variety of executive management positions in sales, marketing, technology, and manufacturing during his tenure, was promoted from the offices of president and chief operating officer when he took over Graham's responsibilities, assuming control over a company that had grown enormously during his stay. Graham Packaging Holdings held sway as the dominant competitor in the market for one-quart, motor-oil containers, producing more than 1.4 billion HDPE containers in 1998, a figure that represented 73 percent of the one-quart, motor-oil containers produced domestically. The company's food and beverage business, which had achieved great strides in the years leading up to Blackstone's investment, generated nearly 38 percent of its revenues in 1998, helping cement the company's position as the global leader in HDPE containers and account for its role as an emerging contender in the PET market. Graham Packaging Holdings' involvement in the household cleaning and personal care market provided a significant third dimension to its business, a market in which the company ranked as a leading supplier of HDPE custom bottles for hair care, liquid fabric

care, and dish care products in North America. In all, the company operated 51 plants located in North America, Brazil, France, Germany, Hungary, Italy, Poland, Turkey, and the United Kingdom that generated $717 million in sales in 1999.

Under the ownership of Blackstone, Graham Packaging Holdings continued with its tradition of working closely with its customers. Roughly one-third of its plants were located at its customers' manufacturing facilities, which enabled it to cultivate a collaborative relationship with its clients. The partnerships resulted in custom packaging solutions tailored to the specific needs of a client that often yielded innovative products. In 1998, for instance, the company developed a blow-molded plastic can for frozen juice concentrates marketed by Welch Foods, an HDPE container that took seven years to develop. "We developed a new molding system which produces containers at a higher speed than any of our several hundred production lines in North America," a Graham Packaging Holdings executive explained in a March 8, 1999, interview with *Plastics News.* "We also developed a patented closure sealing system to meet the challenge of maintaining seal integrity through freeze-thaw cycles, while also providing easy opening." The package, leakproof and able to withstand the rigors of a microwave, was hailed by Welch Foods' chief executive officer in the same *Plastics News* article. "It's the first packaging innovation for frozen juices since the invention of the peel strip in 1979," said Daniel Dillon.

Graham Packaging Holdings, once under Blackstone's control, demonstrated an eagerness to sell itself on Wall Street. The company filed with the Securities and Exchange Commission (SEC) for a $253 million IPO in mid-2000, but the offering was canceled within months. "The market was not ready for us yet," Yates said in an October 3, 2000, interview with the *York Daily News.* The company made another attempt two years later, filing for a proposed $276 million IPO in May 2002. The underwriters reduced the size of the offering to $247 million shortly thereafter before canceling the IPO in July 2002, citing poor market conditions.

ACQUISITION OF OWENS-ILLINOIS'S PLASTIC CONTAINER UNIT: 2004

Graham Packaging Holdings failed to convert to public ownership during the first years of the 21st century, but the period witnessed the boldest move in its history. In 2004, Toledo, Ohio-based Owens-Illinois Inc., the largest manufacturer of glass containers in North America, was in the process of shedding assets to narrow its focus on glass manufacturing. The $6 billion-in-sales company decided to put its blow-molded plastic container business up for sale, presenting Yates and his management team with an opportunity to expand Graham Packaging Holdings' stature in the plastic container business. Yates swooped in, agreeing in mid-2004 to pay $1.19 billion for Owens-Illinois's plastics unit. "For our customers," Yates noted in a July 24, 2004, interview with the *York Daily Record,* "this means more resources resulting in even better value in terms of products, service, and innovative technology." The acquisition provided a massive boost to Graham Packaging Holdings' operations, adding 31 manufacturing facilities to the company's existing network of 57 plants and 5,000 employees to the company's existing payroll of 4,000 workers. Revenues of the combined company were expected to total $1.8 billion in North America and $2.2 billion worldwide.

As the company focused on assimilating the Owens-Illinois acquisition into its operations, a process that was expected to be completed by late 2007, it did not shy away from additional opportunities for expansion. In March 2005, five months after completing the Owens-Illinois acquisition, the company purchased four plants from Swedish container maker Tetra Pak. The four plants manufactured plastic bottles for nutritional beverages and dairy beverages for customers in Belgium, Brazil, Turkey, and the United States. The acquisition pointed to Graham Packaging Holdings' commitment to expand even as it applied its energies to completing the nearly two-year-long process of digesting the Owens-Illinois acquisition. "Our strategic plan," a senior executive explained in a March 13, 2005, interview with the *York Daily Record,* "is to grow both organically and through acquisitions that make sense."

The responsibility of executing Graham Packaging Holdings' strategy passed to different hands as the company prepared for its future. In December 2006, Yates was appointed as chairman and relinquished his post as chief executive officer, paving the way for the appointment of Warren Knowlton. Knowlton spent two decades at Owens-Corning before joining Pilkington PLC, one of the world's largest glass makers. After leaving Pilkington, Knowlton served as chief executive officer of Morgan Crucible PLC, a market leader in specialty carbon and ceramic products, the position he held when he was recruited by Graham Packaging Holdings. Knowlton took charge of a company that had displayed vigorous growth in the years immediately preceding his appointment as chief executive officer. Graham Packaging Holdings' revenues leaped from $906 million in 2002 to $2.52 billion in 2006. Knowlton's task centered on executing the company's commit

ment to expansion and presiding over its likely conversion to public ownership.

Jeffrey L. Covell

PRINCIPAL SUBSIDIARIES

Graham Packaging Company, L.P.; GPC Capital Corp. I; GPC Capital Corp. II; GPC Opco GP LLC; GPC Sub GP LLC; Graham Recycling Company, L.P.; Financière Graham Emballages Plastiques SNC; Financière Graham Packaging France SNC; Graham Emballages Plastiques S.A.S. (France); Graham Packaging Acquisition Corp.; Graham Packaging Argentina S.A.; Graham Packaging Belgium S.A.; Graham Packaging Canada Limited; Graham Packaging Comerc USA LLC.; Graham Packaging Company BV (Netherlands); Graham Packaging Company de Ecuador SA; Graham Packaging Company OY (Finland); Graham Packaging Consultores en Controles S.A. de C.V. (Mexico); Graham Packaging Controllers USA LLC.; Graham Packaging de Mexico S. de R.L. de C.V.; Graham Packaging do Brasil Industria e Comercio S.A. (Brazil); Graham Packaging Especialidades Tecnologicas S.A. de C.V. (Mexico); Graham Packaging Europe SNC (France); Graham Packaging European Services, Ltd.; Graham Packaging France Partners; Graham Packaging France, S.A.S.; Graham Packaging Holdings BV (Netherlands); Graham Packaging Hungary Kft.; Graham Packaging Iberica S.L. (Spain); Graham Packaging International Plastic Products Inc.; Graham Packaging Latin America, LLC; Graham Packaging Leasing S.A. de C.V. (Mexico); Graham Packaging Leasing USA LLC.; Graham Packaging Lummen NV (Belgium); Graham Packaging Minster LLC; Graham Packaging Noeux SARL (France); Graham Packaging PET Holdings S. de R.L. de C.V. (Mexico); Graham Packaging PET Technologies de Mexico S.A. de C.V.; Graham Packaging PET Technologies Inc.; Graham Packaging Plastic Products de Mexico S. de R.L. de C.V.; Graham Packaging Plastics Limited; Graham Packaging Plasticos de Venezuela C.A.; Graham Packaging Poland, L.P.; Graham Packaging Regioplast STS Inc.; Graham Packaging Technological Specialties LLC.; Graham Packaging U.K. Ltd.; Graham Packaging Villecomtal SARL (France); Graham Packaging West Jordan, LLC; Graham Packaging Zoetermeer BV (Netherlands); Graham Plastpak Plastik Ambalaj A.S. (Turkey); Industrias Graham Packaging de Irapuato S. de R.L. de C.V. (Mexico); Industrias Graham Packaging S. de R.L. de C.V. (Mexico); Lido Plast San Luis S.A. (Argentina); Lido Plast-Graham S.r.L. (Argentina); Graham Packaging Poland Sp. Z.o.o.; Polo GR Industria e Comercio, Ltda. (Brazil); Resin Rio Comercio Ltda. (Brazil); Servicios Graham Packaging S. de R.L. de C.V. (Mexico); Societa Imballagi Plastici, S.r.L. (Italy).

PRINCIPAL COMPETITORS

Amcor Limited; Ball Corporation; Consolidated Container Company LLC.

FURTHER READING

Adkins, Sean, "Springettsbury, Pa.-based Packaging Company Withdraws IPO Application," *York Daily Record*, October 3, 2000.

"Blackstone Group to Buy Plastics Biz for $1.2B," *New York Post*, July 5, 2004, p. 21.

Bothum, Peter, "Springettsbury, Pa.-based Plastic Packaging Company Considers IPO," *York Daily Record*, July 14, 2000.

Cecil, Andrea Maria, "Acquisition Part of Graham's Plan," *York Daily Record*, March 13, 2005.

Doba, Jinida, "Graham Packaging's GPC Unit Files for IPO," *Plastics News*, July 17, 2000, p. 4.

Esposito, Frank, "Graham Shuttering Ontario Plant," *Plastics News*, November 12, 2001, p. 1.

"Graham Packaging Holdings Co.," *Beverage Industry*, January 2007, p. 46.

Lauzon, Michael, "Graham Packaging Nixes Plan to Go Public," *Plastics News*, October 9, 2000, p. 4.

McMorris, Frances A., "Graham Cuts Offer Size," *Daily Deal*, January 15, 2003.

Starr, Michelle, "Graham Packaging Co. Inks $1.2 Billion Deal to Buy Plastic-Container Unit," *York Daily Record*, July 29, 2004.

———, "Snapple Sports New Look Made by York County, Pa., Company," *York Daily Record*, May 17, 2002.

Guardian Industries Corp.

2300 Harmon Road
Auburn Hills, Michigan 48326-1714
U.S.A.
Telephone: (248) 340-1800
Fax: (248) 340-9988
Web site: http://www.guardian.com

Private Company
Founded: 1932 as Guardian Glass Company
Incorporated: 1968
Employees: 19,000
Sales: $5 billion (2006 est.)
NAIC: 327211 Flat Glass Manufacturing; 327993 Mineral Wool Manufacturing; 336399 All Other Motor Vehicle Parts Manufacturing; 421310 Lumber, Plywood, Millwork, and Wood Panel Wholesalers; 421330 Roofing, Siding, and Insulation Material Wholesalers

■■■

From its origins at the height of the Great Depression as a small Detroit-based maker of automotive windshields, Guardian Industries Corp. has developed into one of the world's largest glassmakers. The company operates around two dozen float glass plants around the world, producing glass principally for the automotive and building product markets. Still making windshields, Guardian through its Automotive Products Group makes all components of car exteriors—including windows, moldings, and grilles—the only exception being body panels. In addition to its core float glass and

fabricated glass product operations, Guardian also owns Guardian Fiberglass, Inc., one of North America's largest manufacturers of fiberglass, and Guardian Building Products Distribution, Inc., a leading North American distributor of building products, including insulation, roofing products, windows, doors, and vinyl siding. Since its first venture overseas in 1981, Guardian has aggressively expanded its glass operations around the world, eventually generating 40 percent of its revenues outside North America. William Davidson has led Guardian since 1957, and he took the firm private in 1985. Davidson, according to *Forbes* magazine the richest person residing in the state of Michigan, also owns the Detroit Pistons professional basketball team and professional hockey's Tampa Bay Lightning.

1932–57: BEGINNINGS OF GUARDIAN GLASS AS WINDSHIELD FABRICATOR

In the early 1920s David E. Hokin began supplying windshields to Ford Motor Company by importing Czechoslovakian glass through Canada into Detroit, a route designed to circumvent the heavy duty that the United States imposed on European sheet glass. When Ford started outfitting its Model A cars with laminated glass windshields in 1928, Hokin established a new company, Laminated Glass Manufacturing Company, to produce laminated glass using a process originating in Czechoslovakia. This endeavor enjoyed a good start, but demand for the firm's windshields plunged when the boom times ended with the stock market crash of 1929 and the subsequent Great Depression. Hokin was finally forced to liquidate Laminated Glass in early 1932 when

COMPANY PERSPECTIVES

At Guardian, our longevity isn't too surprising. On the contrary, it's a testament to our ability to adhere to a business style that works.

Make aggressive moves. Choose wisely. Remain flexible. At Guardian, these concepts have driven our success for more than 70 years. Today, 19,000 employees across 19 countries on five continents subscribe to our way of success because it works.

Blending individual responsibility with a results-oriented mindset simply creates a foundation for quick decision making—and nearly unlimited visibility. By decentralizing authority, we combine the collective foresight of our family, and focus it all on growth.

And ultimately, that's what you'll find at Guardian's family of companies. Companies defined by sales, plants, products and careers that have a unique tendency to grow like crazy.

It's no wonder.

Ford stopped buying the firm's windshields because new technology had made them obsolete.

The company was quickly reorganized in a process initiated by Hokin's business attorney, David I. Hubar. In February 1932 a Hubar-led group of investors acquired the assets of Laminated Glass, which reemerged as Guardian Glass Company. The name played off the security and protection that the firm's windshields offered to occupants of vehicles, and this theme was carried over into the company logo, a large *G* surrounding a knight on a horse. Other key investors at Guardian's founding included Barney Wetsman and Frank Handler. Previously, Wetsman had successfully owned a clothing store, a construction company, and a theater, while Handler, a cousin of Wetsman, was the owner of a brokerage house in Buffalo, New York. Its main asset a small plant on St. Jean Avenue on Detroit's lower east side, Guardian Glass had a workforce of about 20 at its founding and was producing fewer than 100 windshields per day; first-year revenues amounted to around $130,000.

By 1936, Hubar and Wetsman had bought out all the other partners except Handler. Eventually, Wetsman bought out Hubar to become Guardian's largest shareholder, with a 51 percent interest; Handler owned the remaining 49 percent. In the meantime Bert Root, a former executive at Toledo, Ohio, glassmaker Libbey-Owens-Ford Company, had been brought onboard in 1934 to serve as president. Under Root's guidance, Guardian in 1938 set up a modern plant on West Lafayette Boulevard in Detroit, at a former sign factory. The plant's new equipment, which included a high-pressure autoclave, raised the quality of Guardian's products. At this time, in addition to turning out original equipment and replacement windshields for cars, trucks, and buses, Guardian was also producing safety glass for other applications. Gradually, the financial health of the company improved.

Wetsman died in 1940 following a heart attack, which led his brother Frank to join the firm as treasurer. A successful owner of theaters through a partnership, Frank Wetsman initially and reluctantly left Handler in charge of Guardian. The Wetsman family had grown to distrust Handler because in the late 1930s he had been imprisoned for more than three years after being convicted of swindling his brokerage firm customers. Nevertheless, Guardian prospered during World War II producing laminated windshields for military jeeps and trucks as it contributed to the manufacturing efforts that earned Detroit the sobriquet of "Arsenal of Democracy." The company suffered a blow in 1944 when Root died, and business dropped off in the immediate aftermath of the war.

In the postwar boom, demand for windshields surged as sales of automobiles and school buses skyrocketed. Curved windshields were among the design changes introduced by automakers during this period. In response, Guardian Glass in 1956 purchased a radiator foundry and machine shop on Campbell Avenue in Detroit from U.S. Radiator. The company installed machinery at this new plant for the production of curved laminated windshields, and the site also served as Guardian's headquarters.

While the firm was thus meeting the needs of its customers and also enjoying high demand for its products, Guardian was simultaneously flirting with bankruptcy. As the Wetsmans had feared, and eventually uncovered, Handler had been engaging in financial improprieties that left the company vulnerable. Frank Wetsman, however, never confronted his cousin about the financial wrongdoings, and he died of a heart attack in the spring of 1956.

1957–68: REVITALIZATION UNDER BILL DAVIDSON

Fortunately for the company, Wetsman had begun grooming a successor. In 1955 he had brought his oldest nephew, William M. (Bill) Davidson, onboard as

KEY DATES

1932: Guardian Glass Company is established as a small windshield fabricator in Detroit.

1957: William M. (Bill) Davidson gains full control of Guardian and files to reorganize the company under Chapter 11 bankruptcy protection.

1960: Guardian emerges from bankruptcy; eventually all its creditors are paid in full.

1968: Davidson consolidates his various business interests, including Guardian Glass and ten automotive glass distribution centers, within the newly constituted Guardian Industries Corp., which is taken public.

1970: Guardian begins manufacturing glass with the opening of a float glass plant in Carleton, Michigan.

1981: Company moves into Europe with the opening of a float glass plant in Luxembourg.

1985: Davidson takes Guardian Industries private through a $302 million leveraged buyout.

1990: Sales pass the $1 billion mark.

1998: Guardian acquires significant stake in Builder Marts of America.

2000: Cameron Ashley Building Products, Inc., is acquired.

treasurer. Born in Detroit in 1922, Davidson was a World War II veteran and an avid athlete who had earned a bachelor's degree in business from the University of Michigan and a law degree from Wayne State University after the war. After briefly working at a private law firm, he moved into the business world where he quickly made a mark by turning around the fortunes of two failed businesses: Frank W. Kerr Company, a pharmaceutical wholesaler, which he purchased in 1951, and Rupp & Bowman, a surgical supply company, bought the following year. As an adjunct to the Kerr business, Davidson partnered with Warren Coville, a local photographer, to form a photo processing firm called ABC Photo, Inc., in 1955.

After his uncle's death, Davidson sparred with Handler over control of the company. Davidson stopped Handler's attempts to sell Guardian, and he eventually fired his relative. Davidson then tried to buy out Handler's interest in the company. A deal was finally reached in 1957 after months of wrangling, with Handler selling his stake for $175,000.

Soon thereafter, Davidson filed to reorganize Guardian under Chapter 11 bankruptcy protection. As the reorganization progressed, Davidson attempted to boost sales by setting up a separate distribution company in 1958. This firm opened a wholesale distribution center in Detroit specializing in replacement windshields. One year later, production began at Guardian Glass's second laminating plant in Fort Lauderdale, Florida.

At the same time, Davidson was seeking to gain a greater share of the original equipment windshield market. Fortune intervened in the form of a Glass Workers Union strike that stopped production at nine U.S. glass plants in late 1958. Using glass supplied by Ford Motor, Guardian stepped in to fabricate windshields for American Motors Corp. (AMC). When the strike finally ended after 18 weeks, Guardian retained the AMC account and continued to supply that automaker for many years to come.

When Guardian emerged from bankruptcy in 1960, Davidson took the unusual step of committing to pay off the company's creditors in full. In part by pledging personal assets as collateral, Davidson fulfilled this commitment over the next several years. During this period, Guardian Glass grew at a steady if unspectacular rate, eventually reaching sales of $19 million by 1967. Davidson at the same time rapidly expanded his automotive glass distribution business. He set up additional distribution centers in New York, Georgia, Massachusetts, Illinois, Texas, Washington, D.C., Kansas, New Jersey, and California. The two businesses were closely linked: About 70 percent of the windshields produced by Guardian Glass were sold through Davidson's distribution centers; the remainder went directly to automakers to fulfill original equipment supply contracts.

1968–79: GLASS MANUFACTURING AS PUBLIC COMPANY

By the mid-1960s, Davidson had grown unsatisfied with the profits his company could make fabricating windshields and with his dependence on the big glass manufacturers. The U.S. glassmaking industry at the time was dominated by an oligarchy consisting of Pittsburgh Plate Glass Company (which was renamed PPG Industries, Inc., in 1968), Libbey-Owens-Ford (L-O-F), and Ford Motor. No company had entered the field in the United States since 1920, when Ford started making glass. At the same time, the industry was in the midst of a revolutionary transition to the float method of manufacturing, which the U.K. firm Pilkington Brothers Limited had introduced in 1959. In this process, molten glass was poured onto one end of a shallow bath of molten tin at about 1,800°F and formed into a ribbon that floated, frictionless and in a controlled atmosphere, down the bath through a temperature gradient falling to about 1,000°F at the other end. At this temperature the ribbon, fire finished, was cool enough to be taken off on rollers without marking the surface. This revolutionary new method of glassmaking produced polished plate glass much more economically by removing the large fixed capital investment in grinding and polishing machinery and by cutting working costs. After it started using the float method, Pilkington began licensing the process to other glass manufacturers. PPG became the first such licensee, in 1962. L-O-F and Ford soon followed suit.

Davidson embarked on a risky strategy to break into this entrenched field. First, on November 7, 1968, he consolidated his various business interests within one new company called Guardian Industries Corp. Included under this corporate umbrella were Guardian Glass, Guardian Photo, Inc. (the renamed ABC Photo), and Davidson's ten automotive glass distribution centers. This consolidation created a more powerful business that could more easily raise the large amount of capital needed for an entry into glassmaking. Soon after its creation, Guardian Industries held an initial public offering (IPO) of shares on the over-the-counter market. (The stock began trading on the American Stock Exchange in 1969.) Following the IPO, Davidson controlled 45 percent of the company's stock, other shareholders of the original companies held 29 percent, and the remaining 26 percent was in the hands of public shareholders, including employees.

One of the main reasons for going public was to facilitate acquisitions. Davidson had concluded that a new float plant would produce more glass than Guardian needed for its windshield requirements. He also wanted to diversify outside laminated glass. Tempered glass, which was heat-treated to create a stronger and more break-resistant product than ordinary glass, seemed the best bet as it was used to make both the side and rear windows of vehicles, and Guardian could thus offer automakers a full array of glass products. The tempered glass market also offered entrée into the architectural market as most patio and storm doors were made from tempered glass. In December 1969, then, Guardian Industries via a stock swap acquired Permaglass, Inc., a tempered glass fabricator based in Millbury, Ohio, that held more than 50 patents in the glass fabricating field and had annual sales of around $11 million. In addition to several U.S. plants in Ohio, California, and Florida, Permaglass also operated a plant

in Ontario, Canada, and had majority control of a business in Australia. This marked Guardian's first foray outside the United States.

While pursuing this acquisition, Guardian was moving ahead with construction of its first float glass plant. Davidson swooped in to hire Edward R. Sczesny (pronounced Sezny) away from Ford and placed him in charge of building the new plant. Sczesny had directed the installation of the Pilkington float glass process at the Detroit automaker. Then, when Pilkington turned down Guardian's request for a float license, Davidson elected to move forward anyway. Although the U.K. firm threatened Guardian with legal action if it proceeded to build a float plant without a license, Davidson took a calculated gamble. He and his legal advisors concluded that Pilkington risked jeopardizing its entire worldwide licensing program if it sued Guardian and lost.

Construction of the plant began in April 1969. It was located in Carleton, Michigan, just south of Detroit. As construction proceeded, Davidson worked to secure funding for the plant. The eventual $17 million construction cost was a huge amount for a firm the size of Guardian, and it was only after months of discussions with various banks that sufficient funding was secured. In August 1970 production began at the 275,000-square-foot facility, which had an initial capacity of 350 tons of glass per day.

Industry observers expected Pilkington to sue Guardian for violation of its patents, but instead the U.K. company had already reversed course and entered into negotiations with Guardian about a float license. The two sides reached a deal in May 1971. Guardian entered into an ongoing royalty license agreement, but it successfully negotiated lower payments than those of other Pilkington licensees on the grounds that it had received no technical assistance from Pilkington in setting up the plant. This better deal infuriated the entrenched U.S. glassmakers, but they had little recourse. Guardian continued to make royalty payments to Pilkington until 1977, when a final lump-sum payment was negotiated and paid.

Davidson's huge gamble quickly paid off. The Carleton plant was profitable within seven months of startup, and by 1972 Guardian Industries' net income was more than three times the level of three years earlier. A major financial restructuring in 1972 vastly improved the company's balance sheet, and early the following year Guardian's stock began trading on the New York Stock Exchange. Also in 1973 the installation of a second float line at the Carleton plant more than doubled the plant's capacity at a cost of $20 million. Company revenues reached the $100 million mark in

1974. In the meantime, Guardian moved into new headquarters in the Detroit suburb of Novi in 1972.

During and in the wake of the severe recession of 1974–75, which hit the automotive industry particularly hard, Guardian shifted more of its attention and resources to architectural glass. In 1974 the company acquired Webster, Massachusetts-based Glass Guard Industries, which produced tempered and insulated glass for the architectural market, and Guardian later began producing window glass for residential construction as well as reflective glass. By the end of the 1970s, the architectural market was responsible for 75 percent of Guardian's glass sales.

As the heavy weight of glass made long-distance shipping economically unfeasible, Guardian began planning for additional float glass plants around the United States. Its second float plant opened in Kingsburg, California, in 1978 and its third in Corsicana, Texas, in 1980. From its three plants, Guardian was able to capture about 13 percent of the U.S. glassmaking market. Guardian Photo, in the meantime, transformed itself from a regional to a national player by acquiring the photofinishing business of GAF Corporation in 1978 for around $6 million. By purchasing GAF's 17 photofinishing plants in 13 states, Guardian Photo became one of the top four players in its industry in the United States, with annual revenues of more than $70 million, which represented about 30 percent of Guardian Industries' overall total.

1980–85: THE EUROPEAN INVASION

In 1979, when total revenues reached $280 million, Guardian was already in the planning stages for another large gamble: an invasion of the European glassmaking market. Before this plan reached fruition, however, the company diversified further in the United States when it began making fiberglass insulation at a plant in Albion, Michigan, in 1980. Prior to launching this venture, Guardian had hired a number of employees away from Johns-Manville Corporation, and the latter firm sued Guardian in 1981 accusing it of duplicating its patented technology for making fiberglass insulation out of glass. Manville won a judgment against Guardian, which after a lengthy battle in the courts was forced to pay Manville $40.6 million in early 1991.

Guardian made its move into Europe through a Luxembourg-based joint venture called Luxguard. The company owned 70 percent of the venture, while Ferdinand Kohn, a local businessman involved in the distribution and fabrication of glass products throughout Europe, held the remaining 30 percent. In

November 1981 production began at the new plant, which was situated in Bascharage, Luxembourg, and had a capacity of 500 tons of glass per day. Guardian's push into Europe shook up the entrenched players there— Pilkington in particular, which filed several lawsuits against Guardian, the first even before the plant was completed. The two companies eventually reached a worldwide out-of-court settlement in 1986, the terms of which were never disclosed.

Neither the lawsuits nor the settlement slowed Guardian's expansion. In 1984 the company acquired a 48 percent stake in the Spanish glassmaker Villosa, which operated a plant in Llodio, Spain. Guardian installed a 500-ton float line at this plant the following year and then acquired full control of the company in 1986. Back in North America, the company in the early 1980s acquired a number of fabricators of glass products as well as a float glass plant in Floreffe, Pennsylvania. In 1985 Guardian opened a new automotive glass fabrication plant in Auburn, Indiana, which specialized in producing original equipment windshields and side windows for General Motors Corporation.

1985 FORWARD: TREMENDOUS GROWTH AS A PRIVATE COMPANY

From its 1968 IPO to 1984, Guardian increased its revenues from $34.2 million to $543 million. During the same period, earnings had grown at a rate of 21 percent per year, peaking at $39 million. Davidson, however, grew to believe that the company's stock was undervalued and destined to remain so for some time. He concluded that the time was right to take the company private once again, a move that would also prevent Guardian from falling victim to a hostile takeover while also freeing management from some of the constraints under which public companies must operate. In July 1984, then, Davidson announced his intention to purchase the 57.3 percent of the company he did not already own at $24 per share, well above its level of $15.25 per share before the offer. After the company board approved the $302 million leveraged buyout in January 1985, Davidson completed the transaction one month later.

In the wake of the buyout, Guardian's debt ballooned from around $150 million to $450 million, and its debt rating was downgraded to "junk" status. Over the next couple of years, Davidson reorganized the firm into four semiautonomous groups—the Glass Group, the Automotive Group, Guardian Photo, and the Insulation Group—and focused mainly on reducing the debt load. In 1986 the insulation operations were expanded through the opening of a new fiberglass plant in Mineral Wells, Mississippi. In May of that year, Guardian's flagship Carleton plant was hit by an acrimonious strike of United Auto Workers (UAW) members. The company eventually hired strikebreakers to keep the plant operating, and in October, following a controversial ruling by the National Labor Relations Board, both the strikers and the so-called replacement workers were allowed to participate in a decertification vote. As a result of the dual vote of workers and strikers, the UAW was ousted from the plant, and the strike was broken. Guardian's employee relations reputation was sullied by the events at Carleton.

By mid-1987, the debt reduction program had succeeded in returning Guardian's debt rating to investment grade status. Not coincidentally, the company announced new growth initiatives at this same time, including the construction of two new float glass plants, each capable of producing 600 tons a day—one in North America, one in Europe. The former was located in Richburg, South Carolina, near Charlotte, and was designed to serve customers in the southeastern United States. Guardian's third European float plant was sited in Luxembourg at Dudelange, 12 miles from the Bascharage facility. These plants, both of which commenced operations in late 1988, increased Guardian's glass manufacturing capacity to beyond 5,000 tons per day. They also helped propel the company's sales past the $1 billion mark in 1990.

Guardian accelerated its growth in the early 1990s, vastly expanding its number of float glass plants and moving into various developing markets. New float plants commenced production in Maturin, Venezuela (1990); Orosháza, Hungary (1991); Nong Khae, Thailand (1992); and Gujarat, India, and Tudela, Spain (1993). Guardian also set up a distribution subsidiary in Japan as part of an attempt to break into that important market, which was protected by restrictive trade barriers. In the meantime, Guardian's glass operations cast an increasingly large shadow over Guardian Photo. The photofinishing unit had seen its revenues rise to more than $100 million by 1985, but sales then stagnated. The time seemed right to divest this noncore asset, and Guardian Industries sold it to Qualex Inc. in 1991.

Having outgrown its Novi offices, Guardian in 1995 moved into new headquarters in Auburn Hills, Michigan, north of Detroit. The 55-acre site was adjacent to the Palace of Auburn Hills, a sports arena that Davidson had partially financed. The Detroit Pistons, acquired by Davidson in 1974, played professional basketball at the Palace. Also in 1995, Guardian launched a $500 million expansion program through which it opened new float glass plants in Al-Jubail,

Saudi Arabia, and Thalheim, Germany, in 1996 and a second plant in Thailand at Rayong in 1997. Distribution centers were also established in Argentina and South Africa in 1997. Several acquisitions of fabricators of glass products, particularly mirrors, in the United States in the early 1990s increased the company's appetite for raw glass. Guardian therefore boosted its U.S. capacity by building new float plants in DeWitt, Iowa, in 1996, and in Geneva, New York, two years later.

By 1995 revenues from Guardian's Automotive Group had reached $500 million, or 30 percent of the company total. At this time, automakers were increasingly seeking to contract with suppliers who could deliver entire systems. Guardian therefore moved to transform its Automotive Group from a supplier of automotive glass to one capable of supplying a vehicle's entire exterior trim and molding system. It achieved this position by acquiring a 70 percent stake in Automotive Molding Company, based in Warren, Michigan, which produced molding, trim, and other exterior vehicle components at four plants in Michigan and Georgia. This $125 million deal was followed by the opening of a new automotive trim plant in Morehead, Kentucky, in 1998. That same year, Guardian took its new automotive strategy international by purchasing Lab. Radio, an automotive manufacturer in Valencia, Spain. This acquisition meshed with Guardian's 1993 entry into the European automotive glass business through the opening of a plant in Grevenmacher, Luxembourg.

Guardian Fiberglass, which had sales of about $75 million in 1990, expanded in the 1990s by opening new plants in Erin, Ontario, in 1994, and Inwood, West Virginia, two years later. Also in 1998, Guardian Industries took an even greater leap into building products when it acquired a large stake in Builder Marts of America (BMA), a privately held wholesaler of building materials to more than 1,000 lumber and building material retailers across the country. Based in Greenville, South Carolina, BMA had annual sales of $590 million. In 1999 BMA merged with Ace Hardware's lumber and building materials division to become the nation's largest wholesale buying and distribution group in the lumber, building materials, and millwork industry. Guardian Fiberglass and BMA were grouped within a newly formed Building Materials Group, which engineered yet another deal in 2000. The group acquired Dallas-based Cameron Ashley Building Products, Inc., for approximately $160 million in cash and the assumption of $177 million in debt. With annual revenues of around $1 billion, Cameron Ashley had a network of more than 160 branches in the United States and Canada from which it distributed roofing, millwork, pool and patio enclosure materials, insulation, siding, and other building products to independent building material dealers, professional builders, large contractors, and mass merchandisers. In 2003 Guardian acquired full control of BMA and then merged its operations with those of Cameron Ashley to form Guardian Building Products Distribution, Inc., a $2 billion distribution unit.

As its building products operations took a rapidly enlarged place with the company fold, Guardian Industries continued its steady expansion of its core glass manufacturing business. In addition to expanding and renovating existing facilities, new float glass plants were opened in Częstochowa, Poland, in 2002, and Goole, England, in 2003. Guardian also entered into a joint venture in 2003 to purchase the Egyptian Glass Company, which was operating a float plant outside of Cairo. In 2004 production began at Guardian's 24th float glass plant, which was located in El Marqués, Mexico. Guardian also took a more aggressive approach toward developing new glass products in the early 21st century, an initiative launched in 2000 with the opening of a 50,000-square-foot science and technology center across the street from the firm's first float plant in Carleton, Michigan. Among the new products the firm subsequently unveiled were SunGuard, a line of solar control coated glass products designed for commercial buildings; DiamondGuard, a scratch-resistant coating product; and ClimaGuard, touted as the first glass technology offering complete protection from ultraviolet radiation.

By 2006 Guardian Industries' revenues had reached $5 billion, a remarkable achievement for a company whose sales were a mere $22 million in 1968. Davidson's bold moves into glass manufacturing and into the markets of Europe and elsewhere overseas had paid off handsomely, and made him a billionaire. In addition, the broadening of the automotive unit and the diversification into building products meant that Guardian was much more than just a glassmaker. As the firm celebrated its 75th anniversary and Davidson's 50th year at the helm in 2007, the growth initiatives continued. Guardian was in the midst of investing an additional $537 million in major capital expenditures, including a new float plant under construction in Ryazan, Russia. The company had also entered into a joint venture to build another float plant in the United Arab Emirates. The 84-year-old Davidson was also making plans for succession, though he announced no intentions to retire. He planned to keep Guardian Industries family-owned, but he also indicated that employees would own and control a significant portion of the company.

David E. Salamie

PRINCIPAL SUBSIDIARIES

Guardian Automotive Corporation; Guardian Automotive Products, Inc.; Guardian Building Products, Inc.; Guardian Building Products Distribution, Inc.; Guardian Fiberglass, Inc.; Guardian Glass Company; Guardian Industries Canada Corp.; Guardian Building Products Distribution Canada, Inc.; Guardian Industries VP, S de RL de CV (Mexico); Guardian De Argentina S.R.L.; Guardian do Brasil Vidros Planos Ltda. (Brazil); Guardian de Colombia S.A.; Guardian de Venezuela S.A.; Guardian Industries France SAS; Guardian Flachglas GmbH (Germany); Guardian Oroshaza Co. Ltd. (Hungary); Guardian Europe S.A. (Luxembourg); Guardian Luxcoating S.A. (Luxembourg); Guardian Luxguard I S.A. (Luxembourg); Guardian Luxguard II S.A. (Luxembourg); Guardian Automotive E.S.A. (Luxembourg); Guardian Industries Poland Sp.z.o.o.; Guardian Glass España, C.V., S.L. (Spain); Lab. Radio, S.A. (Spain); Guardian Industries UK Ltd.; Saudi Guardian International Float Glass Co., Ltd. (Saudi Arabia); Egyptian Glass Company; Guardian Africa Corp. Ltd. (South Africa); Gujarat Guardian Limited (India); Guardian Japan, Ltd.; Guardian Industries Corp Ltd. (Thailand).

PRINCIPAL COMPETITORS

Nippon Sheet Glass Company, Limited; Compagnie de Saint-Gobain; Asahi Glass Company, Limited; Pilkington Group Limited; PPG Industries, Inc.; Apogee Enterprises, Inc.; Owens Corning Sales, LLC; Vitro, S.A. de C.V.; Johns Manville Corporation; Safelite Group, Inc.

FURTHER READING

Adler, Alan L., "The Glass Wall: Auburn Hills' Guardian Industries Chips Away at Barriers to the Japanese Glass Industry," *Detroit Free Press,* January 29, 1996, p. 6F.

Applebaum, Phillip, *The Wetsmans: Odyssey of an American Family,* [Mich.?]: William Morse Davidson, 1994, 315 p.

Barkholz, David, "Guardian Strikers Are Replaced Permanently," *Crain's Detroit Business,* July 28, 1986, p. 1.

Berss, Marcia, "Nice Guys Finish Last," *Forbes,* July 6, 1992, pp. 92+.

"Board of Guardian Industries Clears Buyout Proposal," *Wall Street Journal,* January 21, 1985.

Brenners-Stulberg, Linda, "Executive Wants to Buy Guardian," *Detroit Free Press,* July 10, 1984, p. 4C.

Campanella, Frank W., "Growth in Glass: Process Leading Guardian to Sixth Year of Earnings Gains," *Barron's,* August 10, 1981, p. 48.

Chipello, Christopher J., "Japan Glass Market Proves Hard to Crack," *Wall Street Journal,* August 7, 1991, p. A8.

Dawkins, William, "Raging Bull Charges European Glass," *Financial Times,* June 7, 1990.

Dietderich, Andrew, and Terry Kosdrosky, "Man of the Moment: Davidson Shines with Pistons, Lightning, and Business Interests," *Crain's Detroit Business,* June 21, 2004.

Gallagher, John, "Guardian Pays $40.6-Million Judgment," *Detroit Free Press,* February 9, 1991, p. 7B.

"Guardian Industries Celebrates 70th Anniversary by Focusing on the Future," *U.S. Glass,* February 2003, pp. 32+.

"Guardian Industries: Focusing on Volume Turns Losers Around," *Business Week,* March 12, 1979, pp. 120, 122–23, 125.

"Guardian Industries: The Profitable Side of Glass," *Financial World,* August 15, 1978, p. 34.

"Guardian Wins Bidding War for Cameron," *National Home Center News,* May 22, 2000, pp. 4, 18.

Kinkead, Gwen, "The Raging Bull of Glassmaking," *Fortune,* April 5, 1982, pp. 58–62, 64.

Lifton, Kimberly, "Guardian Floating Overseas," *Crain's Detroit Business,* August 28, 1995, p. 1.

"Little Glass Fortress," *Forbes,* October 16, 1978, pp. 182, 184.

Longo, Don, "BMA Stands Ready As Deals Are Sealed," *National Home Center News,* July 3, 2000, pp. 5, 32.

"Offer for Guardian Industries Planned by Its President," *Wall Street Journal,* July 10, 1984.

Pryweller, Joseph, "Guardian Unit Acquires Spanish Auto Trim Supplier," *Crain's Detroit Business,* February 16, 1998, p. 21.

Raphael, Steve, "Guardian Faces $100M Damages," *Crain's Detroit Business,* May 30, 1988, p. 1.

——, "Patently Tough," *Crain's Detroit Business,* June 20, 1988, p. 1.

Rodengen, Jeffrey L., *The Legend of Guardian Industries,* Fort Lauderdale, Fla.: Write Stuff Enterprises, 2004, 224 p.

Rohan, Barry, "Guardian Loses Patent Suit, Assessed $38 Million," *Detroit Free Press,* July 18, 1989, p. 5C.

Saunders, John, "Union Ousted at Guardian," *Detroit Free Press,* October 18, 1986, p. 8C.

Sherefkin, Robert, "Major Move for Guardian: Invests $80M in Warren Firm," *Crain's Detroit Business,* January 15, 1996, p. 1.

Snavely, Brent, "Guardian Grows As Davidson Plans for Future," *Crain's Detroit Business,* March 12, 2007, p. 1.

Szczesny, Joseph, "Guardian Stretches Out Overseas," *Oakland (Mich.) Press,* March 15, 2007.

Walsh, Tom, "Little-Known Guardian Makes the Right Moves," *Detroit Free Press,* March 4, 2007, p. 1E.

Hallmark Cards, Inc.

2501 McGee Street
Kansas City, Missouri 64108-2615
U.S.A.
Telephone: (816) 274-5111
Toll Free: (800) 425-5627
Fax: (816) 274-5061
Web site: http://www.hallmark.com

Private Company
Incorporated: 1923 as Hall Brothers, Inc.
Employees: 16,000
Sales: $4.1 billion (2006)
NAIC: 511191 Greeting Card Publishers; 322233 Stationery, Tablet, and Related Product Manufacturing; 322299 All Other Converted Paper Product Manufacturing; 323118 Blankbook, Looseleaf Binders, and Devices Manufacturing; 339942 Lead Pencil and Art Good Manufacturing; 453110 Florists; 453220 Gift, Novelty, and Souvenir Stores; 513210 Cable Networks; 533110 Lessors of Nonfinancial Intangible Assets (Except Copyrighted Works)

■ ■ ■

Hallmark Cards, Inc., is the world's largest greeting card company, creating 19,000 different designs and related products each year in more than 30 languages, and distributing them in more than 100 countries. In addition to the Hallmark flagship, the company also markets cards under the Ambassador and Expressions from Hallmark brand names. The company's products are sold in Hallmark retail outlets and other specialty stores, through mass merchandise stores (around 30,000 in the United States alone), and via the hallmark.com web site. Of the 3,700 Hallmark Gold Crown stores in the United States, the company's premier channel of distribution, about 450 are company-owned outlets, with the remainder independently owned and operated under licensing agreements.

Over the years, Hallmark has branched out into other products and services that use creativity and emotion to help people connect, including stationery, party goods, gift wrap, photo albums, cut flower arrangements, home decor, collectibles, books, and Christmas ornaments. In the late 1990s, the company acquired several specialized greeting card companies that operate as wholly owned subsidiaries, including DaySpring Cards, Inc., the leader in Christian personal expression products; Sunrise Greetings, producer and distributor of warm, sophisticated greeting cards including its flagship Sunrise Greetings line and the humor card line Weiner-Dog; William Arthur, which offers customized holiday cards, wedding invitations, fine stationery, and other high-end products; and Image Arts, which specializes in discount cards and boxed holiday cards for mass retailers and deep-discount stores. Hallmark's Crayola, LLC, subsidiary (formerly known as Binney & Smith Inc.) specializes in personal skill development products, including Crayola crayons, Magic Markers, Silly Putty art materials, creativity software, model kits, and art supplies for professionals and students. The firm launched *Hallmark Magazine*, a women's lifestyle magazine, in 2006. Hallmark also holds a 67 percent stake in Crown Media Holdings, Inc., a publicly traded company that owns and operates two cable television channels: the Hallmark Channel and the Hallmark Movie Channel. Even with the company's diversification, the greeting card remains Hallmark's mainstay, so much so that Hallmark has often been mistakenly credited with inventing it. The founding Hall family still owns about two-thirds of the private company's stock.

EARLY HISTORY

Hallmark was founded by Joyce C. Hall, a native of Norfolk, Nebraska, who as a teenager ran a postcard company with his older brothers. In 1910 Hall, still only 18, left the family business he had founded after a traveling salesman convinced him that Kansas City, Missouri, would serve him better as a wholesaling and distribution center. Almost immediately after arriving in Kansas City, Hall set up a mail-order postcard company in a small room at the Young Men's Christian Association, where he remained until his landlord complained about the volume of mail Hall was receiving. The new company was named Hall Brothers, a name justified the following year when Rollie Hall came to Kansas City to join his brother in the business.

At that time, picture postcards were all the rage in the United States, with the best ones imported from Europe. Very early on, however, Joyce Hall came to believe that the postcard's appeal was quite limited. They were novelty items rather than a means of communication; with the leisure time required to write long letters diminishing, and the long-distance telephone call still a rare phenomenon, people would need a shorthand way of reaching each other by mail. Greeting cards suggested themselves as a viable alternative, so in 1912 Hall Brothers added them to its product line.

The outbreak of World War I bore out Hall's contention. The supply of postcards from Europe dried up, but domestic products were of inferior quality and their popularity waned. Greeting cards stepped into the breach. In 1914 Hall Brothers bought a small press and

began publishing its own line of Christmas cards. In 1915 a fire destroyed the company's entire inventory, putting it $17,000 in debt, but Joyce and Rollie Hall rebuilt the business. In 1921 they were joined by their brother William Hall. By 1922 Hall Brothers had recovered to the point where it was employing 120 people, including salespeople in all 48 states. Also that year, it diversified for the first time and started selling decorative gift wrap.

In 1923 the company formally incorporated under the name Hall Brothers, Inc., and two years later the Hallmark brand name appeared on the company's products for the first time. Over the next two decades, the company would attack its market aggressively through advertising. In 1928 Hall Brothers became the first greeting card company to advertise nationally when it took out an ad in *Ladies' Home Journal.* In 1936, with the national economy emerging from the worst of the Great Depression, Hall Brothers went on the attack again, introducing an open display fixture for greeting cards that Joyce Hall had developed with the help of an architect. Previously, cards had always been kept under store counters, out of customers' sight and usually in a disorganized state. In 1938 Hall Brothers advertised in the broadcast medium for the first time when it began sponsoring "Tony Won's Radio Scrapbook" on WMAQ radio in Chicago. Meantime, the company's first licensing deal was concluded in 1932, when it gained the right to use Walt Disney characters on its products.

When the United States entered World War II, the company pitched an appeal to friends and loved ones of military personnel with the slogan "Keep 'em happy with mail." Hall Brothers would find its most famous and enduring slogan in 1944, however, when it started using the tagline "When you care enough to send the very best," which had been suggested a few years earlier by Sales and Advertising Manager Ed Goodman. After the war, a staff artist created the company's logo, consisting of a five-pointed crown and the Hallmark name in script letters. Hall Brothers trademarked the logo in 1950.

HALLMARK HALL OF FAME, RETAIL SHOPS, AMBASSADOR CARDS

The company established another landmark in advertising on Christmas Eve 1951, when it sponsored a television production of Gian Carlo Menotti's opera *Amahl and the Night Visitors.* This was the first of the famous Hallmark Hall of Fame series, which two years later presented a production of *Hamlet* starring the noted British Shakespearean actor Maurice Evans. That broadcast marked the first time the entire play had ever

KEY DATES

1910: Joyce C. Hall sets up a mail-order postcard company in Kansas City, Missouri.

1911: Hall's company begins operating under the name Hall Brothers.

1912: Greeting cards are added to the product line.

1923: Company is incorporated as Hall Brothers, Inc.

1925: The Hallmark brand name is used for the first time.

1928: Hall Brothers becomes first greeting card company to advertise nationally with an ad in *Ladies' Home Journal.*

1938: First radio advertising through sponsorship of "Tony Won's Radio Scrapbook" on Chicago's WMAQ.

1944: First use of the slogan "When you care enough to send the very best."

1950: Company trademarks its famous logo, consisting of a five-pointed crown and the Hallmark name in script letters.

1951: Hallmark Hall of Fame series is launched with the company's sponsorship of a television production of the opera *Amahl and the Night Visitors.*

Early 1950s: First retail shop specializing in Hallmark cards opens.

1954: Company changes its name to Hallmark Cards, Inc.

1959: The Ambassador Cards line is launched to serve shoppers at mass merchandisers.

1967: Springbok Editions, maker of jigsaw puzzles, is acquired.

1984: Binney & Smith, maker of Crayola crayons and other art products, is acquired.

1986: Irvine O. Hockaday, Jr., becomes the first person outside the Hall family to serve as CEO; Shoebox Greetings line of nontraditional cards is launched.

1994: RHI Entertainment, Inc., is acquired and is renamed Hallmark Entertainment, Inc.; the Hallmark Gold Crown Card, a frequent-buyer reward program for customers of selected Hallmark retail stores, is introduced.

1997: Expressions from Hallmark is launched, marking the debut of the Hallmark brand in the mass merchandising market; William Arthur, Inc., maker of customized and prepackaged stationery products, is acquired; company web site adds e-commerce features.

1998: Hallmark completes several acquisitions: U.K.-based Creative Publishing, Editions DALIX of France, and the U.S. firm InterArt Holding; a significant stake in the Odyssey channel is acquired.

1999: A line of 99-cent greeting cards is introduced under the Warm Wishes brand; DaySpring Cards is acquired.

2000: A partial offering of stock in Crown Media Holdings, Inc., is completed.

2001: The Odyssey channel is relaunched as the Hallmark Channel.

2002: Following Hockaday's retirement, Donald J. Hall, Jr., grandson of the founder, is named CEO.

2006: Hallmark's new "Say It with Music" greeting cards are an instant hit; *Hallmark Magazine* is launched.

2007: Binney & Smith is renamed Crayola, LLC.

been seen on U.S. television. As Joyce Hall himself often said, "Good taste is good business."

Also in the early 1950s, Hall Brothers began opening the first of thousands of retail shops specializing in Hallmark cards. In 1954 the company changed its name to Hallmark Cards, Inc., having already used Hallmark as a brand name for 31 years. In 1959 the company introduced its Ambassador Cards line to tap into the lucrative market presented by shoppers at mass merchandisers such as supermarkets, discount stores,

and drugstores. The next year Hallmark introduced its own line of party decorations and began featuring characters from Charles M. Schulz's "Peanuts" comic strip on its products.

In 1966 Joyce Hall retired as president and CEO of the company he had founded. Handing the reins to his son, Donald Hall, Joyce Hall nevertheless remained active in company affairs as chairman until his death in 1982. Joyce Hall was not only a wealthy and successful businessman when he died, but also a member of the

French Legion of Honor and a commander of the British Empire. He had been friends with British Prime Minister Winston Churchill and with U.S. Presidents Harry Truman and Dwight Eisenhower. For the latter Hall Brothers custom-designed an official presidential Christmas card in 1953.

Among Donald Hall's first important moves as CEO of Hallmark were the 1966 establishment of Hallmark International to further expand the company abroad and the 1967 acquisition of Springbok Editions, maker of jigsaw puzzles. The next year, the company broke ground on the Crown Center, a $500 million retail, commercial, and residential complex intended to revitalize an area near downtown Kansas City and financed entirely with company funds. Hallmark created a new subsidiary, Crown Center Redevelopment Corporation, to oversee it.

ACQUISITIONS: 1979–89

In 1979 Hallmark acquired Georgia-based lithographer Litho-Krome Corporation. In 1981 the company formed a division, Hallmark Properties, to create and administer licensing projects. This division went on to create Hallmark's Rainbow Brite, Purr-Tenders, and Timeless Tales character merchandise, and also oversaw the company's licenses for Peanuts and Garfield cartoon characters. Later this division would be renamed Hallmark Licensing (in 1992) and its licensed properties would include Harry Potter, Dr. Seuss, Barbie, Winnie the Pooh, Looney Tunes, Blue's Clues, and Batman.

The Crown Center development suffered a disaster in 1981 when two suspended walkways at the center's Hyatt Regency hotel collapsed, killing 114 people and injuring 225. After his father's death in 1982, Donald Hall added the chairmanship to his duties as CEO. In 1984 Hallmark acquired Binney & Smith, the Pennsylvania-based maker of Crayola crayons and Liquitex art materials. In 1986 Donald Hall retired as CEO and handed the post to the company president, Irvine O. Hockaday, Jr., who thus became the first person outside the Hall family to run the company.

In 1987 Hallmark, after being a prominent advertiser in the broadcast media for many years, became an owner as well when it acquired a group of Spanish-language television stations from Spanish International Communication. The next year, it added another station purchased from Bahia de San Francisco Television. Also in 1988, Hallmark acquired a Spanish-language network, Univision, and amalgamated all of its holdings in a subsidiary, Univision Holdings. Based in New York, the subsidiary ran the nine full-power stations under the name Univision Station Group.

During the mid-1980s small greeting card companies began competing for Hallmark's market position with a diverse array of cards that became favorites. In the mid-1980s Hallmark fought back with its Personal Touch and Shoebox Greetings series (the latter debuting in 1986). Many of these cards, however, bore a resemblance to rival designs that some found too striking. In 1986 Blue Mountain Arts, Inc., which produced nonoccasion cards featuring poetry and pastel illustrations to produce a concentrated emotional effect, sued Hallmark for copyright and trade infringement and unfair competition. The initial decision went against Hallmark, which appealed ultimately to the U.S. Supreme Court. When the Supreme Court refused to hear the case in 1988, Hallmark agreed to discontinue its Personal Touch line. Financial terms of the settlement were not disclosed.

DIVERSIFICATION IN THE FACE OF INCREASING COMPETITION

Hallmark's biggest challenge during the early 1990s was confronting its continuing loss of market share to the number two and three companies in the greeting card industry, American Greetings Corporation and Gibson Greetings, Inc., respectively. From 1990 to 1995, it was estimated that Hallmark's market share fell from 50 percent to 45 percent. The reason for Hallmark's decline rested in the very backbone of its empire: the specialty card and gift shops that sold the Hallmark brand, which by the early 1990s numbered more than 10,000. Over a long period, these shops had fallen victim to changing buying patterns in particular among women, who still bought 90 percent of all cards sold. Pressed for time, more and more consumers were opting to purchase cards at one-stop shopping outlets—supermarkets, drugstore chains, and large discounters—such as Wal-Mart Stores, Inc. In the early 1970s more than half of all cards were sold in specialty shops; by the early 1990s only about 30 percent were. American Greetings and Gibson, which did not have such extensive ties to the card shops, were able to recognize the trend and shift to accommodate it. Hallmark, however, was in a bind. Continuing to rely so heavily on specialty shops would do nothing to halt its market share decline, but it could not simply abandon the shops, for doing so would bankrupt many of them, not something a company as paternalistic as Hallmark could seriously consider.

One strategy was to diversify away from greeting cards even further. In 1990 Hallmark acquired Willitts Designs, a maker of collectibles, but sold the company only three years later. Likewise, Hallmark's venture into Spanish-language television was abandoned in 1992 at a loss of $10 million when Univision was sold to Grupo Televisa. Cable television was Hallmark's next foray with the 1991 formation of a Crown Media, Inc., subsidiary to which was added Cenom Cable in St. Louis, through the purchase of a controlling interest for $1 billion. In 1994 this venture too was cast aside when Hallmark sold Crown Media to Charter Communications Inc. for $900 million.

During this period Hallmark also updated its product line, offering a more high-tech approach to card purchasing. In 1991 the "Personalize it!" in-store kiosk was introduced (later called Touch-Screen Greetings), through which customers were able to create computer-generated personalized greeting cards. The following year Hallmark filed suit for infringement of its kiosk patent against American Greetings and its Creata-Card kiosk. The suit was settled in 1995 with each company receiving a worldwide, nonexclusive license to use the technology; no other details on the settlement were provided at that time.

Moreover, in 1994, Hallmark developed recordable greeting cards in partnership with Information Storage Devices. Initially retailing for $7.95 each, these cards allowed a sender to record a personal message, which would then play back each time the card was opened. Also in 1994 came the debut of the Hallmark Gold Crown Card, a frequent-buyer reward program for customers at selected Hallmark retail stores. Two years later, the Hallmark stores participating in the reward program were rebranded under the Hallmark Gold Crown name through a $100 million remodeling program in which the stores were also provided with a fresh look. In addition to the frequent-buyer program, the Gold Crown stores differed from regular Hallmark stores in several respects; they had their own lines of cards and exclusive merchandise, and they were all owned by individuals and were not franchises.

In the face of declining profits brought on by declining market share, Hallmark went through a series of reengineering and restructuring efforts in the early 1990s in an attempt to hold costs down. U.S. and Canadian operations were consolidated, and a 1995 restructuring brought together for each Hallmark card brand its administrative, marketing, and product development functions.

Additional diversification moves in the area of entertainment were made in the mid-1990s. In 1994 Hallmark acquired RHI Entertainment, Inc., for $365 million. RHI was the television production company responsible for Hallmark's Hall of Fame productions. Hallmark thus acquired the world's leading producer of family-oriented entertainment, which it promptly renamed Hallmark Entertainment, Inc., and set up as a subsidiary of Hallmark Cards. Then in 1995, Hallmark

purchased a 9.9 percent stake in European broadcaster Flextech for $80 million. Flextech and Hallmark created a family-oriented international cable television network, the Hallmark Entertainment Network, which commenced operations in Ireland and the United Kingdom in 1996. Next, Hallmark Entertainment, Inc., teamed up with the Jim Henson Company in 1998 to launch the Kermit Channel, a pay television channel featuring general family entertainment fare. Also in 1998, Hallmark purchased a significant stake in the Odyssey channel, a cable network that had been launched in 1988 as a religious channel and that was in the process of being transformed into a family-oriented entertainment channel.

Given the uneven success of Hallmark's other ventures, greeting cards remained the company's most important endeavor. New promotions of Hallmark cards in the mid-1990s included a "sneak-a-peek" advertising campaign, comprising a series of commercials in which people were caught looking at the backs of the cards they had received, just to make sure they were Hallmarks. Continuing to seek ways to reverse the decline in its share of the greeting card market, the Hallmark brand was introduced into the mass merchandiser market for the first time with the 1997 launch of Expressions from Hallmark. The cards featured the Hallmark logo on the back and were initially marketed though more than 5,000 discounters, supermarkets, and drugstores. This move angered many owners of Hallmark retail stores, who feared that their sales would suffer. In 1999 came the debut of yet another new line called Warm Wishes, which featured cards priced at 99 cents and aimed at increasingly value-conscious consumers. The Warm Wishes line debuted in more than 17,000 retail outlets across the United States. The new initiatives appeared to be working, as Hallmark reported that its share of greeting card sales in the U.S. retail market increased from 47 percent in 1997 to 51 percent in 1998 to 52 percent in 1999.

Although the company had been involved in the online world in various ways since the mid-1980s, Hallmark's first serious move into the Internet came in 1996 with the launch of its corporate web site, hallmark.com. Primarily offering corporate news and product information, the site did offer some early versions of free electronic greeting cards (or e-cards). In November 1997 an overhauled hallmark.com went live with a much more extensive selection of free e-cards, some e-cards that sold for $1.50, and new e-commerce features, such as the online retailing of gift products, including jewelry, flowers, and stuffed animals. In late 1999 Hallmark began offering all of its e-cards free of charge.

The pace of acquisitions quickened in the late 1990s as Hallmark continued to diversify. In 1997 the company purchased William Arthur, Inc., a West Kennebunk, Maine-based maker of customized and prepackaged stationery products. Overseas growth was pursued as well in response to U.S. greeting card sales being flat for several years. Hallmark in 1998 acquired Creative Publishing plc, a leading U.K. maker of boxed and seasonal cards, for about $310 million. Creative was merged into the company's existing U.K. business, which was renamed Hallmark Cards (Holdings) UK. The purchase of Creative increased Hallmark's share of the U.K. greeting card market to nearly 30 percent, making it the number one player there. Hallmark similarly expanded in France in 1998 through the purchase of Editions DALIX. Two more acquisitions were completed in the United States in 1998: Bloomington, Indiana-based InterArt Holding Corporation, maker of high-quality greeting cards and related products whose product line included items designed by artist Mary Engelbreit; and Tapper Candies, a maker of candy, toys, and party favors based in Cleveland. During 1999 Hallmark acquired DaySpring Cards, Inc., the leading creator of Christian personal expression products. Adding the Siloam Springs, Arkansas-based DaySpring provided Hallmark with increased access to the fast-growing Christian card market. A second acquisition in 1999 brought The Picture People into the Hallmark fold. Based in Foster City, California, The Picture People operated a national chain of mall-based portrait studios.

In mid-1999 Hallmark launched an ambitious ten-year strategic plan, aiming to triple revenues by 2010, to $12 billion. The company planned to remain centered around its core greeting card business, but would also pursue growth and expansion in five additional business platforms: "caring gift solutions, memories, life celebrations, personal development, and family entertainment." Subsequent developments in greeting cards included the launch of Hallmark en Español, a line of more than 1,000 Spanish-language greeting cards (relaunched in 2003 as Sinceramente Hallmark); the introduction of Hallmark Fresh Ink, a line of hipper, sometimes risque cards aimed at women between the ages of 18 and 39; and the signing of Maya Angelou to a licensing deal to develop cards and specialty gifts featuring newly written poetry and sentiments from the poet laureate. As the 21st century began, Hallmark had to contend with an enlarged competitor in the form of American Greetings, which purchased the number three card company, Gibson Greetings, in 2000. Following the deal, American controlled 40 percent of the U.S. card market, compared to Hallmark's market share of just over 50 percent. Also in 2000, Hallmark acquired Gift Certificate Center, an online provider of gift certificates for business and consumer use; this subsidiary was renamed Hallmark Insights in 2006.

In the area of family entertainment, meantime, Hallmark in May 2000 made a partial offering of stock in Crown Media Holdings, Inc., a subsidiary of Hallmark Entertainment that operated and distributed the Hallmark Entertainment Network, the Kermit Channel, and the Odyssey channel. Hallmark retained a 49.1 percent stake in Crown Media and 90 percent of its voting rights. In 2001 Odyssey's name was changed to the Hallmark Channel, and the network began stepping up its showings of Hallmark Hall of Fame productions. Crown Media also began rebranding its Hallmark Entertainment Network outlets located outside the United States under the Hallmark Channel name.

Later in 2001 Hallmark lost a major account when Kmart Corporation elected not to renew its contract with the greeting card giant and to instead make American Greetings its exclusive card supplier. The impact of this decision was less than severe given Kmart's shaky financial condition and its subsequent major round of store closings; Hallmark continued to supply both Wal-Mart and Walgreen Co., two retailers that were growing steadily. In September 2001 Crown Media acquired Hallmark Entertainment's library of more than 700 films for $815.3 million in stock and assumed debt. As a result of this transaction, Hallmark Cards' stake in Crown Media was boosted to approximately 67 percent.

2002 AND BEYOND: NEW ERA OF HALL LEADERSHIP

At the end of 2001, Hockaday retired having shepherded the company through a decade and a half during which revenues increased from less than $1.5 billion to more than $4 billion. As a result of Hallmark's aggressive diversification during his tenure, revenue from non-greeting card operations increased from half of the total to two-thirds. Taking over as CEO on January 1, 2002, was Donald J. Hall, Jr., grandson of the founder, whose father remained chairman. The 45-year-old Hall, Jr., had spent more than 30 years at Hallmark working in a variety of areas, most recently as executive vice-president of strategy and development. Since 1996 he had also served as vice-chairman of the company's board, a position he retained. The return of the founding family to day-to-day management was not surprising given that the Hall family continued to own more than three-quarters of the company's stock; the remainder was in the hands of Hallmark employees.

The new leader acted quickly to put his own mark on the company. He shelved Hockaday's much-ballyhooed goal of tripling sales by 2010 because he concluded that it had become a distraction. At this time, greeting card sales remained stagnant while Hallmark concurrently faced a plethora of new paper-based card competitors and also witnessed the ascendance of new technologies, including instant and text messaging, providing consumers with other options for personal expression. Under these market pressures, Hallmark began seeking opportunities to shave costs, and in mid-2002 it started shutting down the manufacturing plant at its downtown Kansas City headquarters, shifting the production to other factories. In 2004 the company outsourced a portion of its information-technology services. Such restructuring moves contributed to a reduction in the worldwide workforce from 20,000 in 2002 to 18,000 in 2005.

In the fall of 2004 the company launched a program to revitalize its network of Hallmark Gold Crown stores. Rolled out over a span of years, the program involved putting a fresh mix of Hallmark products in the stores and reorganizing their layouts into product departments based on consumer needs. The design changes were aimed at making it easier to navigate through the stores and more convenient to shop there.

At the same time, Hall, Jr., began pulling back from some of his predecessor's diversification initiatives. In late 2005 Hallmark sold Picture People in a typical divestment of a noncore asset. The company also significantly scaled back its entertainment operations. In early 2006 the Hallmark Entertainment production company was sold to the unit's president, Robert Halmi, Jr., and the private investment firm Kelso & Co. This move followed Crown Media's April 2005 sale of its international business to a British investor group, which reduced Crown's main assets to the Hallmark Channel and the film library Hallmark had sold it in 2001. In August 2005 Hallmark placed Crown Media itself on the block but failed to find a buyer. *Business Week* reported in January 2007 that Hallmark was once again seeking to sell Crown, which had lost nearly $1.7 billion since being taken public in 2000, while its stock had fallen 72 percent. Although the Hallmark Channel was one of the most-watched cable networks, it generated correspondingly small fees from cable distributors mainly because the viewers tended to be older and thus less appealing to advertisers.

In the meantime, Hallmark boosted sales at its Gold Crown stores with the introduction in 2006 of a new line of "Say It with Music" greeting cards, retailing at $4.99 apiece. Although sound cards were not new,

the new Hallmark line offered better sound quality via digital technology and featured songs from original artists, such as Earth, Wind and Fire's "Sing a Song" and George Thorogood's "Bad to the Bone." The sound cards, which lasted two years and could be played 200 times, were an instant hit, representing Hallmark's biggest greeting card introduction since the debut of Shoebox Greetings two decades earlier. Based on this success, Hallmark began expanding the line to include cards using dialogue and music from television shows and movies.

Another new initiative in 2006 was the launching of *Hallmark Magazine,* a women's lifestyle magazine focusing on family, friends, home, and community that began with an initial circulation of 400,000 copies. Three years in the making, the magazine was envisioned as an extension of the Hallmark brand, one that could help promote the brand and fill a gap in the market. A companion web site, located at hallmarkmagazine.com, debuted in 2006 as well. At year-end, Hallmark melded its sales, category management, and customer strategy and planning divisions into a new division called customer development. This realignment, which resulted in the elimination of 160 full-time positions, was part of the firm's ongoing efforts to improve its operations' efficiency and effectiveness.

In early 2007 Binney & Smith changed its name to Crayola, LLC. Successful new product introductions at Crayola, which had been going through a reengineering effort, helped drive sales up 9 percent in 2006 to $534 million. Hallmark reported that its overall 2006 sales of $4.1 billion represented a 5 percent increase, after eliminating divested operations from the 2005 total. The company continued to seek ways to bolster its core operations. In February 2007, for example, Hallmark introduced Journeys, a new line of encouragement cards available exclusively at Gold Crown outlets that offered personal messages of support for someone undergoing chemotherapy, quitting smoking, fighting depression, dealing with a loved one in the military, caring for an aged parent, or contending with other difficult times. Through such new product development efforts, Hallmark Cards showed its determination to remain at the top of the greeting card industry as its centenary neared.

Joan Harpham
Updated, Douglas Sun; David E. Salamie

PRINCIPAL SUBSIDIARIES

Crayola, LLC; Crown Center Redevelopment Corporation; Crown Media Holdings, Inc. (67%); DaySpring

Cards, Inc.; Hallmark Insights; Halls Merchandising, Inc.; Image Arts; Irresistible Ink, Inc.; Litho-Krome Company; Sunrise Greetings; William Arthur; Hallmark Cards Australia, Ltd.; Hallmark Belgium N.V.; Hallmark Canada Inc.; Nihon Hallmark K.K. (Japan); Hallmark Mexicana, S. de R.L. de C.V. (Mexico); Hallmark Cards Nederland, B.V. (Netherlands); Hallmark Cards New Zealand Ltd.; Hallmark Cards Iberica, S.A. (Spain); Hallmark Cards PLC (U.K.).

PRINCIPAL DIVISIONS

Hallmark International.

PRINCIPAL COMPETITORS

American Greetings Corporation; CSS Industries, Inc.; Taylor Corporation.

FURTHER READING

Beatty, Sally, "Hallmark, Media Firms Pool Interests to Build Network," *Wall Street Journal,* July 5, 2000, p. B4.

Chandler, Susan, "Can Hallmark Get Well Soon?" *Business Week,* June 19, 1995, pp. 62–63.

Coleman, Calmetta Y., "Hallmark to Buy U.K. Card Firm for $310 Million," *Wall Street Journal,* July 10, 1998, p. B4.

Ebeling, Ashlea, "Wild Card," *Forbes,* November 13, 2000, pp. 250–51.

Fitzgerald, Kate, "Hallmark Alters Focus As Lifestyles Change," *Advertising Age,* October 25, 1994, p. 4.

Flint, Joe, "Odyssey Cable Network to Change Its Name to Hallmark Channel," *Wall Street Journal,* March 29, 2001, p. B15.

Frazier, Mya, "Battle for Retail Real Estate: American Greetings, Hallmark Duke It Out in $7 Billion Industry," *Cleveland Plain Dealer,* November 8, 2000, p. 1C.

"From Someone Who Loves You," *Economist,* August 10, 1991, p. 63.

Fuller, Jennifer Mann, "Going for the Gold: Hallmark Cards Makes Strong Investment to Ensure Success of Its 4,800-Store Network," *Kansas City (Mo.) Star,* December 17, 1997, p. B1.

Grover, Ronald, "Far from Hallmark's Best Moment: The Hall Clan Wants to Sell Its Money-Losing TV Channel, but Buyers Aren't Exactly Lining Up," *Business Week,* January 29, 2007, p. 85.

Hall, Joyce C., with Curtiss Anderson, *When You Care Enough,* Kansas City, Mo.: Hallmark, 1979, 269 p.

Hamilton, Martha M., "Floral Retailers Bunch Up in a Crowded Field: Is There Room to Bloom for New Competitors?" *Washington Post,* February 12, 2000, p. E1.

Hayes, David, "Cyber Greetings: Sending Instant Holiday Cards Is Just a Click Away," *Kansas City (Mo.) Star,* December 21, 1996, p. B1.

Helliker, Kevin, "Hallmark Finds Another Market Niche: The Sorrowful," *Wall Street Journal,* December 24, 1998, p. B1.

Hirshey, Gerri, "Happy Day to You," *New York Times Magazine,* July 2, 1995, pp. 20+.

Howard, Elizabeth G., "Hallmark's $4 Billion Formula," *Kansas City Business Journal,* June 16, 1995, p. 17.

Kinni, Theodore B., "The Reengineering Rage," *Industry Week,* February 7, 1994, p. 11.

Mann, Jennifer, "Angelou, Hallmark Team Up," *Kansas City (Mo.) Star,* November 14, 2000, p. D4.

———, "At Hallmark, a Hall Again Takes Charge," *Kansas City (Mo.) Star,* October 5, 2001, p. A1.

———, "CEO Ruminates on Hallmark," *Kansas City (Mo.) Star,* October 9, 2001, p. D4.

———, "Greeting Card Firms in Patent Dispute: Suits Come and Go Between Hallmark, American Greetings," *Kansas City (Mo.) Star,* February 1, 2001, p. C1.

———, "Hallmark Attacking Competitor over Technology: Web Site for American Greetings Corp. Is Focus of Lawsuit," *Kansas City (Mo.) Star,* June 3, 2000, p. C1.

———, "Hallmark Cards Divests Production Company," *Kansas City (Mo.) Star,* December 9, 2005, p. C1.

———, "Hallmark Greets Fresh Challenges," *Kansas City (Mo.) Star,* February 13, 2005, p. A1.

———, "Hallmark Makes Changes in Profit Sharing," *Kansas City (Mo.) Star,* November 1, 2002, p. C1.

———, "Hallmark Plans Buyout in U.K.," *Kansas City (Mo.) Star,* July 10, 1998, p. A1.

———, "Hallmark to Start a Site for Retailers: Ebizmix.com Has Already Lined Up 70 Suppliers," *Kansas City (Mo.) Star,* June 7, 2000, p. C1.

———, "Progress Is Slow for Hallmark.com: Web Site Has Plenty of Visitors So Far, but Few Purchases," *Kansas City (Mo.) Star,* June 13, 2000, p. E9.

Nelson, Emily, "Dearest Mom, Greetings from My CD-ROM," *Wall Street Journal,* September 4, 1996, p. B1.

Orenstein, Susan, "Roses Are Red, Violets Are Blue, Hallmark's Online, but What Can It Do?" *Industry Standard,* November 20, 2000.

Schiller, Zachary, and Ron Grover, "And Now, a Show from Your Sponsor," *Business Week,* May 22, 1995, pp. 100–2.

Stern, William M., "Loyal to a Fault: Its Brand Name Is August, Its Profits a Wow! But Hallmark Cards Had Better Get with It—Now!" *Forbes,* March 14, 1994, pp. 58–59.

Story, Louise, "Brought to You by That Logo on the Hallmark Greeting Card," *New York Times,* December 27, 2006, p. C3.

Weiner, Steve, "Do They Speak Spanish in Kansas City?" *Forbes,* January 25, 1988, p. 46.

Young, Gordon, "Card Sharks," *Utne Reader,* May/June 1993, p. 132.

Heelys, Inc.

3200 Belmeade Drive, Suite 100
Carrollton, Texas 73006
U.S.A.
Telephone: (214) 390-1831
Toll Free: (866) 433-5464
Fax: (214) 390-1661
Web site: http://www.heelys.com

Public Company
Incorporated: 2000 as Heeling Sports Limited
Employees: 33
Sales: $188.2 million (2006)
Stock Exchanges: NASDAQ
Ticker Symbol: HLYS
NAIC: 316211 Rubber and Plastics Footwear
Manufacturing

■ ■ ■

Heelys, Inc., manufactures and distributes the unique, patented athletic footwear with wheels in the heels, invented by company founder Roger Adams. Heelys, as the sneaker-skates are called, allows those wearing the shoes to walk or glide without changing foot gear. The wheels are detachable, but the idea behind the sneaker-skate is to transition easily between walking and rolling. It can take someone minutes or days to learn how to ride on the wheels, to master the subtle shift of one's body weight without falling. The trick is to balance one's body by placing one foot forward and leaning backward on the heel of the back foot to engage the wheel, then to push forward with the front foot. Ten-sion in the hips, knees, and ankles supports the body in motion. There are two stop options. The "soft stop" involves shifting to the back of one heel, preferably in a manner that will not wear the sole down too quickly. The "hard stop" involves placing the entire foot down to the ground, but one should be prepared to run a few steps to account for momentum. In the case of a forward fall, a somersault is safer than falling on one's hands. Heelys provides written use and safety instructions on "heeling" with each pair of shoes and on the company's web site, and distributes instructional videos to retail stores. Heelys recommends the use of helmets and knee and wrist pads, and the company offers its own brand of these products.

Heelys footwear is available in a variety of styles and colors in children and adult sizes. The company markets masculine styles under such names as Atomic, Rebel, Torch, and Octane and feminine styles under Whirl, Bliss, Glitz, and Spree. Heelys offers a lightweight model, the Slicker 9016. Other products include wheel replacements, a wheel removal tool, and Sole Saver heel plugs that fit into the space left in soles when the wheels are detached.

CHILDHOOD MEMORIES LEADING TO INSPIRATION

Roger Adams' invention of wheeled athletic shoes stemmed from a lifelong love of skating which began in the family business. His parents owned and operated several roller skating rinks, including the largest in the Pacific Northwest, Adams-Tacoma Roller Bowl. Adams could skate at the age of nine months, before many

COMPANY PERSPECTIVES

What are Heelys? Shoes that roll!

children even walk, and he is listed in the *Guinness Book of World Records* as the youngest person to roller skate. Yet while other members of his family pursued skating-related business opportunities, Adams became a clinical psychologist. The invention of Heelys occurred during a midlife crisis. For higher income Adams had taken a position as a mental health supervisor, work he disliked, particularly as it required him to be on call 24 hours a day. The stress of a divorce exacerbated his unhappiness. The idea for Heelys occurred while Adams vacationed in Huntington Beach, California, in 1998, and reflected on the happier times of his life. Sitting outside, watching people go by—walking, rollerblading, bicycling—Adams thought there must be some new way to move. Then the idea for a gliding shoe came to him. As Adams described it, according to Michael E. Ross of *MSNBC*, "I had the idea of a shoe that could roll on command by just shifting your body weight. It was like a flash; the hair stood up on the back of my neck."

Adams had always loved to tinker with different technologies, such as light sensors, hydraulic jacks, and automatic door openers, so it did not take long for him to create a prototype of the wheeled shoe. Adams spent two days in his garage creating the first pair of Heelys out of a pair of Nike running shoes. He applied a hot butter knife to the heels to make room for the wheels. A rod through the heel and a skateboard wheel bearing allowed for the placement and movement of the metal wheels. He tinkered with the shoes, working with local teens and falling to the ground himself many times as he tested them, before a final prototype emerged.

Initially, Adams thought he would produce and market sneaker-skates by licensing the invention to a major footwear company. Sketchers rejected the idea. He then obtained $2.4 million in venture capital from Capital Southwest, an opportunity that gave Adams greater control over the product. Adams established Heeling Sports Limited (HSL) in May 2000. He hired his consultant, Mike Staffaroni, former vice-president of the global Rollerblade division at Benetton Group, as vice-president of marketing. In September, just in time for the Christmas shopping season, Adams introduced Heelys skate-shoes to retailers at a trade show. He offered limited distribution of 30,000 pairs to skate shops and specialty footwear stores, such as Gadzooks and Foot Locker. The first retailer to carry the product sold

its entire inventory in a matter of hours, and other retailers sold out within a few days. Sales tripled every month afterward and within nine months, the company sold 500,000 pairs nationwide as a full-scale, spring launch broadened distribution.

Staffaroni, who became chief executive officer of HSL in January 2001, chose to stimulate interest in Heelys through public exposure to the product as a unique footwear phenomenon. The company hired young enthusiasts to demonstrate "heeling" as sport. The group, called Team Heelys, traveled to shopping malls, skate parks, and other public places and performed a variety of tricks, such as backwards skating, spins, and aerial stunts. Moreover, the wheels allowed those wearing Heelys to travel up to 30 miles per hour. The novelty of Heelys stunned and fascinated people who had not seen the sneakers with hidden wheels. Moreover, HSL further stimulated excitement over the footwear by sending Team Heelys to places where distribution had not begun. In other words, HSL teased audiences in order to make Heelys even more desirable, especially among trend-setting teens. The sneaker-skates attracted the attention of sports and fashion magazines, which touted Heelys as the latest, must-have thing. Also, HSL touted practical usage of the wheeled shoes, as workers at Home Depot and Office Max wore them in order to negotiate the large sales floor very quickly. University students liked Heelys for crossing campus quickly between classes.

Adams continually improved his invention to create a faster, smoother ride. He experimented with soft urethane polymer, but the material did not hold up well. He resolved that problem by layering hard urethane around a soft urethane tire, then applying a coat of soft urethane for the outer layer. Also, by summer 2001, in time for back-to-school shopping, HSL offered Heelys in a variety of styles and colors, using names attractive to teens, such as Stealth, Rage, and Predator. In late 2001, the company introduced a lighter weight shoe, called Slick 9016, which included a wider wheel for more effective clearance over the rough texture and cracks in pavement that can hinder a smooth ride. Other features included a 45-degree heel for braking, and reinforced bearings and axle.

In late 2001, just before the holiday shopping season, HSL launched its first major advertising campaign, with the intention of broadening Heelys position from the skater market into the mainstream market. The campaign included a 30-second television spot to air on MTV, a three-minute video for in-store use, newspaper ads, and promotions at street fairs. The television commercials showed walking feet that convulse as they were digitally transformed into gliding

KEY DATES

1998: Adams invents sneakers with wheels hidden in the heels.

2000: Limited distribution of Heelys sneaker-skates begins.

2001: Full-scale national distribution and limited international distribution begins.

2002: Adams obtains patent on wheeled footwear design.

2006: Initial public offering raises $135 million in capital investment for future growth.

feet. Posters for in-store and other print advertising replicated the commercials by picturing swaths of blurred color and snippets of details. The Dallas agency in charge of the campaign, Pyro Brand Development, created the tagline "Freedom is a wheel in your sole."

Heelys gained media exposure from entertainers who danced in the lightweight Slick 9016s in music videos and public performances. Of particular influence, the R&B/hip-hop star Usher walked, rolled, and danced in a pair of Heelys in a video for his successful *8701* CD. In the video, Usher dances with friends in a crowded room when he unexpectedly glides in the direction of the camera, then makes a dance move whereby he drops to the floor to show the audience the wheel in the heel. Little X featured Heelys for dance in the video "U Don't Have to Call," another chart-topping song. Flo-ology, a California street dance company, discovered Heelys at a trade show for action sports retailers in Long Beach and incorporated the sneaker-skates into some of their dance performances. Flo-ology founder Odie liked Heelys because they provided forward movement but carried the body in a stable state. The advent of the Heelys dance movement surprised and delighted Adams.

The acquisition of other footwear companies in 2002 provided HSL with athletic shoe technology to further improve the Heelys product. Axis brand athletic shoes featured air-shock technology, and Soap "grinders," used in a manner similar to skateboards, held plates on the sole that allowed one to ride down a rail without a skateboard. Adams combined Soap and Heelys' apparatus to create the Grind-and-Roll shoe, capable of movement similar to and distinctive from skateboarding and inline skating. Other product developments included a pair of two-wheeled Heelys, to make the product easier for children to use. In 2003 the company launched a selection of Heelys in colors and styles at-

tractive to girls. The introduction of Sole Saver heel plugs provided customers with the option of a finished footwear look when the wheel is removed.

EXPERIENCING RAPID WORLDWIDE SUCCESS

From the beginning, Adams and Staffaroni intended to introduce Heelys into international markets. They contracted with distributors who had exclusive rights to defined areas. In February 2001 the company made its first international shipment to Japan, where Murasaki Sports, a 60-outlet chain of sporting goods stores, sold 30,000 pairs of Heelys within the first six months. During 2001, HSL initiated distribution in Canada and the United Kingdom and, by the end of the year, in Germany, France, Sweden, Iceland, and elsewhere in Europe. Because of the density of populations in Hong Kong and South Korea, Heelys quickly became a broadly popular item in those countries. Several large retailers carried the product in Korea and within about two years 37 Heelys stores operated in the country. By early 2004 HSL distributed Heelys in 50 countries, expanding worldwide by the end of 2005. Markets included Mexico, Australia, and countries in Central America, South America, the Caribbean, and Eastern Europe.

Abroad, as in the United States, entertainers became enthusiastic about the possibilities of Heelys, particularly in Korea. There, pop singer Seven danced in Heelys in a music video, while JTL and other well-known dance groups integrated Heelys into their dance routines.

Due to the popularity of Heelys in Asia, counterfeit copies produced in China emerged in stores in Japan and China. The counterfeit manufacturers gave the fake products similar names, such as Heatys and Neo Heel, and produced exact replicas of the original Heelys, including box and tags. The knock-offs were priced at 25 to 50 percent below the price of authentic Heelys; hence, sales of these items cut deeply into sales of Heelys. In 2005 HSL responded by hiring attorneys in Hong Kong to represent HSL to government agencies. However, slow, unsatisfactory results led the company to file a suit so the problem could be addressed through the court system. HSL held a patent and a trademark file in China, but given the difficulty of safeguarding intellectual property rights in China, the company did not expect good results. Moreover, the company was concerned that the poor quality of the knock-offs might damage Heelys' reputation if children hurt themselves falling down in the counterfeit shoes. To counter the competition, Heelys distributors emphasized the quality and safety of the authentic sneaker-skate.

PREPARING FOR FUTURE GROWTH

Though still a small company, HSL expected to generate a critical mass of customers in the United States during the 2006 holiday shopping season. Heelys experienced solid sales growth in 2005, with $44 million in revenues, a 106 percent increase over 2004. During the first six months of 2006, sales of $44.6 million matched those of the entire previous year. This represented a 177 percent increase over the first six months of 2005, at $16.1 million in sales. By mid-2006, Heelys were available in more than 7,400 stores nationwide. These included outlets of the major sporting goods chains, such as The Sports Authority, Dick's Sporting Goods, Modell's, Journeys, and Big 5 Sporting Goods, as well as certain department stores, such as Nordstrom and Mervyn's. Zappos.com sold the shoes via the Internet.

To promote the product to a mainstream audience as the holiday season approached, Heelys initiated a partnership with Subway restaurants in the United States and Canada in November 2006. With the purchase of a Kid's Pak meal, customers received a free toy, such as a Heelys dog tag, a backpack hanger, or a set of stickers. Once again the best advertising occurred through word-of-mouth buzz among teens. Fans of Heelys footwear made videos of themselves and their friends doing tricks with the sneaker-skates, then uploaded the videos onto Youtube.com, an enormously popular web site.

The expectation of continued high growth prompted HSL to seek capital investment through an initial public offering (IPO) of stock; HSL registered the offering in September. The company addressed a number of concerns before continuing the stock offering. First, Staffaroni hired executives capable of effectively managing growth, including a vice-president of marketing and a vice-president of design and development. Also, the company took the name of its product and reincorporated as Heelys, Inc., in Delaware. One problem involved the company's limited product line, an issue that made the company something of a risk to Wall Street analysts. Heelys wheeled footwear accounted for 95 percent of revenues, with the balance stemming from the sale of protective gear, replacement wheels, and heel plugs, as well as revenue from the two sport shoe companies that HSL acquired in 2002. To address this concern, the company introduced a limited line of apparel, screen-printed T-shirts and hats; shipments began in August 2006. Heelys intended to use the IPO capital to transform the company into an action-sports lifestyle company through the acquisition of similar companies and new product development.

Heelys' stock debuted on the NASDAQ in early December 2006, at the price of $21 per share. The stock rose quickly, opening at $30.30 per share and closing at $32.60 per share, a 55 percent increase in the course of one day of trading. With an offering of 6.425 million shares, the company raised $135 million. The offering ranked seventh among all IPOs during 2006 and second for the apparel or footwear industry.

Mary Tradii

FURTHER READING

Applegate, Jane, "Teens Are Trend Setters," *Los Angeles Business Journal*, August 27, 2001, p. 29.

Carfano, Jennifer, "Keep on Rolling; After Debuting Its Footwear Line Stateside, Heelys Is Now Picking up Momentum Overseas," *Footwear News*, September 3, 2001, p. 16.

Clack, Erin, "Heelys Preps for IPO; Six-Year-Old Firm Adding Execs, Expanding Global Presence and Pushing into New Categories," *Footwear News*, November 13, 2006, p. 2.

Griffin, Cara, "Heelys Cleans up with Purchase of Soap Brand," *Sporting Goods Business*, November 2002, p. 8.

"Heels on Wheels; The Next Big Thing?" *Business Week Online*, August 2, 2001.

"Heelys," *High Point Enterprise*, January 4, 2007.

"Heelys' Legal Footwear Feud: Heelys Is Accusing Miami-Based Levy Marketing of Selling a Knockoff of Its Trademark Wheeled Sneakers," *Miami Herald*, December 13, 2006.

"Heelys' Skate Shoes Roll Toward IPO," *Europe Intelligence Wire*, September 13, 2006.

Hill, J. Dee, "Pyro Pushes Heelys in Mainstream," *Adweek Southeast*, December 10, 2001, p. 6.

Lynn, Lee, "Heel Your Heelys," *Asia Africa Intelligence Wire*, May 14, 2003.

Ross, Michael E., "Heelys Are the Latest in Mobility," *MSNBC*, April 27, 2004.

"Shortsteps," *Sporting Goods Business*, November 10, 2000, p. 18.

"South Florida Teens Head over Heelys for Latest Foot Gear," *South Florida Sun-Sentinel*, July 17, 2001.

"These Shoes Are on a Roll: But More Schools and Stores Are Asking Kids to Cool Their Heelys," *Charlotte Observer*, January 2007.

"Update 9-Heelys Rolls into Top IPO List of 2006," *America's Intelligence Wire*, December 8, 2006.

"US CO Heelys Debuts Skate Shoes on Korean Market," *AsiaPulse News*, April 4, 2002, p. 0463.

Young, Katherine, "In Slow Pursuit of Counterfeiters: Heelys Maker Finds China Is Spinning Its Wheels," *Dallas Morning News*, July 18, 2006.

Hercules Technology Growth Capital, Inc.

400 Hamilton Avenue, Suite 310
Palo Alto, California 94301
U.S.A.
Telephone: (650) 289-3060
Fax: (650) 473-9194
Web site: http://www.herculestech.com

Public Company
Incorporated: 2003
Employees: 26
Sales: $29.5 million (2006)
Stock Exchanges: NASDAQ
Ticker Symbol: HTGC
NAIC: 523999 Miscellaneous Financial Investment Activities

∎ ∎ ∎

Hercules Technology Growth Capital, Inc., is a finance company that invests in technology-related companies. Hercules, specializing in debt financing, targets segments of the technology industry populated with companies whose products or services require advanced technologies, including computer hardware and software, networking systems, semiconductors, Internet consumer and business services, telecommunications, renewable or alternative energy, and life sciences. The company's investments related to life sciences include medical device and biopharmaceutical concerns. Hercules' investment portfolio includes more than 50 companies and represents $283 million in committed capital. The company's investments range from $250,000 to $18.5

million. Biopharmaceuticals ranks as the largest category in Hercules' portfolio, accounting for 40 percent of its investments. Software ranks as the second largest category, accounting for 14 percent of the company's investments. Hercules' main offices are located in Palo Alto, California, and are supported by branch locations in Boston, Chicago, and Boulder, Colorado.

ORIGINS

Instead of looking to Roman mythology for inspiration in naming their enterprise, the founders of Hercules might have looked to Egyptian mythology as a source, specifically the fable of the phoenix, a bird that consumed itself by fire and rose renewed from its ashes. Hercules arose from the ashes of Comdisco, Inc., whose spectacular fall at the end of the 20th century spawned a number of new commercial finance companies, each positioned in the same niche of the industry that Comdisco once occupied and each led by former Comdisco executives. TriplePoint Capital, Pinnacle Ventures, Redpoint Ventures, Lighthouse Capital Partners, and VantagePoint Venture Partners were some of the companies, along with Hercules, whose executive ranks were populated with Comdisco veterans. For each, and Hercules in particular, Comdisco's rise and fall offered a prologue to the development of a new generation of commercial finance entities.

Based just outside of Chicago in Rosemont, Illinois, Comdisco was incorporated as Computer Discount Corporation in 1969, two years before shortening its name to Comdisco. The company ranked as the largest dealer of used IBM computer equipment in the United

COMPANY PERSPECTIVES

We recognize that selecting the right capital provider to fund your company's growth is an important and complex decision. You want a seasoned investor with extensive financial resources, but you also want a committed long-term partner with whom you share common goals and values. At Hercules Technology Growth Capital, we support our entrepreneurs not only with customized financing solutions and capital, but also with perspective, experience, and insight. When we enter a partnership with you, we share a common goal—the continued growth and success of your company throughout its business lifecycle.

States by 1972, the same year it completed its initial public offering (IPO) of stock. Comdisco developed into a technology services and equipment leasing company of note during the ensuing years, enjoying sufficient success to finance forays into other business lines. The company diversified by forming divisions such as Comdisco Technical Services, Comdisco Disaster Recovery Services, and Comdisco Healthcare Group. Of significance to Hercules was the creation of Comdisco Ventures in 1987, the year Comdisco's annual sales eclipsed $1 billion for the first time. The division, an outgrowth of Comdisco's equipment leasing business, was started and led by Jim Labe, regarded as one of the pioneers of the venture leasing and lending segment of the commercial finance industry. The business built by Labe provided a blueprint for Hercules' development nearly two decades later, demonstrating the gains to be achieved in supplying what variously was referred to as "venture lending," "venture debt," and "debt financing." It was a type of financing Hercules would call "structured mezzanine financing," and it produced vigorous financial growth under the Comdisco Ventures banner.

Debt financing was a relatively new approach adopted by venture capitalists during Comdisco Ventures' era, and one widely used during Hercules' formative years. Debt financing usually came in two forms, venture lending and venture leasing. Venture lending provided companies with capital needed for operating expenses, while venture leasing supplied companies with capital for purchasing equipment or other tangible assets. A venture capital firm involved in debt financing, unlike a traditional lender such as a bank, was not bound to rigid state and federal regula-

tions, enabling it to offer more competitive rates and to enjoy greater freedom in structuring the loan, including as subordinated debt (usually involving warrants that allowed the holder to purchase stock at a set price at a certain time) and as convertible debt (a loan the lender may convert into equity at a liquidity event). For start-up ventures, debt financing offered an attractive way to obtain capital. "Debt," an executive of a venture debt company explained in the November 1, 1999, issue of *Venture Capital Journal,* "allows young companies to preserve their equity capital and to spend more time developing their technologies, so that when they go out for subsequent rounds of equity financing, they have demonstrated further progress and can command higher valuation, which is less dilutive to the company. The bottom line is that debt is less expensive than equity."

Comdisco Ventures, starting out by providing equipment-based financing, gradually expanded its services to include subordinated debt and convertible debt and became a prominent player in the commercial finance sector. The division committed more than $1.7 billion to roughly 675 venture capital-backed companies during its first dozen years in business, developing into a major contributor to Comdisco's financial stature by the end of the 1990s. Comdisco Ventures accounted for 27 percent of Comdisco's earnings before taxes in 1999 and it promised to play an even greater role in the coming years, as Jim Labe, serving as chief executive officer, ramped up the division's activities in providing lease and debt financing. The division committed $731 million to start-up ventures in 1999, roughly two-and-a-half times the volume recorded the previous year. Debt, by the end of the decade, was figuring more prominently in the capital structure of funding early-stage companies, particularly companies involved in the Internet, e-commerce, and telecommunications sectors. Comdisco Ventures satisfied the demand, supplying start-up ventures with much needed capital and tying itself to the rampant growth of the dot-com industry. Within two years, the division increased its outlay of venture debt, leasing, and equity financing to more $3.5 billion, setting itself up for a quick and numbing collapse when the technology sector was ripped apart. "They were trying to grab hold of the tech gold rush," an analyst remarked in the October 1, 2001, issue of *Business Week,* "and it bit them." Comdisco's chief executive officer conceded mistakes were made at the once-robust division, telling *Business Week* "some basic questions about each investment should have been asked but weren't."

COMDISCO VENTURES' FALL
LEADS TO HERCULES' RISE

In a matter of months, a thriving business was torn to shreds. The market value of Comdisco Ventures' public

2003: Hercules is established in December.

2004: The company launches investment operations in September.

2005: Hercules completes its initial public offering of stock in June.

2006: Revenues increase nearly threefold to $29.5 million.

holdings, valued at $683 million in September 2000, hurtled downward, plunging to $5 million eight months later. The division provided financing to a number of Internet failures, including furniture e-tailer Living.com, real estate web site IProperty.com, and the online hardware store Homewarehouse.com, which were three of the 50 companies in its portfolio that went out of business between 1999 and 2001. The division, which halted its investments in January 2001, quickly became mired in a financial morass that crippled its parent company, causing a $30 million loss for Comdisco in the first quarter of 2001 after contributing $110 million in profit the previous quarter. In July 2001, battered mightily by the one-time gem of its holdings, Comdisco threw up its hands and filed for protection under Chapter 11 of the U.S. Bankruptcy Code, forcing a number of executives to plot the next move in their career paths.

Despite Comdisco Ventures' failure, debt financing remained a popular tool for venture capital firms during the first years of the new century. In an investment climate characterized by risk aversive behavior and an anemic IPO market, venture debt continued to be an attractive form of financing for lenders and borrowers alike, evinced by the numerous Comdisco Ventures alumni who founded their own debt financing companies, the founders of Hercules included. Manuel A. Henriquez, Glen C. Howard, and H. Scott Harvey joined forces in December 2003 to establish Hercules, each bringing a wealth of experience to the new venture.

Henriquez took the titles of chairman and chief executive officer when Hercules opened its offices in Palo Alto, California. A graduate of Northeastern University, Henriquez worked for BancBoston Ventures, the Bank of Boston's early-stage venture capital fund, and Robertson Stephens & Co.'s late-stage equity venture fund, CrossLink Capital, before joining Comdisco Ventures in 1997. He joined the division as a managing director, a position he held until being named president and chief investment officer in late 1999.

Henriquez left Comdisco Ventures before its collapse, resigning in August 2000 to become a partner at VantagePoint Venture Partners, a $2.5 billion, multistage technology venture fund.

Glen Howard received his undergraduate degree from the University of Arizona and his graduate degree in business administration from Saint Mary's College. He worked for Comdisco, Inc., before he joined the company's venture lending division, rising to the post of vice-president before joining Comdisco Ventures in 1997. Howard began as a senior associate and was named a managing director in late 1999, a title he held until the division's demise. After leaving Comdisco Ventures in mid-2001, Howard spent two years as a partner in Pearl Street Group, a specialty finance company, leaving the firm in late 2003 to join his former colleague Henriquez and cofound Hercules.

The third member of the founding team, H. Scott Harvey, came from the senior ranks of Comdisco, Inc., as well, but unlike Howard, he never made the move to the venture lending division. The legal expert of the founding team, Harvey received his law degree from the John Marshall Law School, which earned him a post as Comdisco, Inc.'s corporate counsel in 1983. After eight years as corporate counsel, he became vice-president of marketing, administration, and alliances, serving in such capacity until 1997. Next, Harvey was named deputy general counsel of Comdisco, Inc., remaining a legal adviser until July 2002, weeks before the company emerged from Chapter 11 proceedings with a mandate to sell all its assets.

FIRST INVESTMENTS: 2004

The three founders established Hercules to invest in structured mezzanine debt (the company's term for venture debt) and equity in technology-related companies. The subsectors of the technology industry targeted by the company included computer software and hardware, networking systems, semiconductors, information technology infrastructure, online consumer and business services, telecommunications, renewable or alternative energy, medical devices, and biopharmaceuticals. The company did not make its first investment until nearly a year after its formation, officially commencing operations in September 2004.

Hercules' first two full years of investing activity gave industry observers a sense of the investment firm's strategy for the future. The company set the range of its investments between $1 million and $20 million, although it claimed to have the capability to underwrite transactions up to $30 million. In 2005, Hercules committed $177 million in capital, directing nearly one-quarter of its investments to biopharmaceutical companies. The company debuted on the NASDAQ Global Market during the year, completing an IPO in June, when shares in Hercules were offered for $13 per share. In 2006, Hercules more than doubled its commitment to biopharmaceuticals, investing $115 million in the life sciences segment. The company invested in structured mezzanine financing and, to a lesser extent, senior debt and equity in companies such as Acceleron Pharma, Merrimack Pharmaceuticals, and Omrix Biopharmaceuticals. Hercules, which committed $283 million in capital in 2006, also stepped up its involvement with software companies, investing $40 million in companies such as Atrenta, GameLogic, and Intelliden.

Hercules was beginning what its founders hoped to be a long and profitable stay in the commercial finance sector. The company's initial financial results suggested it was on the right track. In 2005, the company generated $10.6 million from interest and fees, realizing $1.2 million in net investment income. In 2006, exponential increases were recorded, as its revenues swelled to $29.5 million and net investment income shot upward to $10.4 million. In the years ahead, the company's investment team hoped to continue achieving robust financial growth, as Hercules matured into a prominent player in its industry.

Jeffrey L. Covell

PRINCIPAL SUBSIDIARIES

Hercules Technology II, L.P.; Hercules Technology SBIC Management, LLC; Hercules Funding I LLC; Hercules Funding Trust I; Hydra Management LLC; Hydra Management Co., Inc.

PRINCIPAL COMPETITORS

Lighthouse Capital Partners; Redpoint Ventures; Triple-Point Capital.

FURTHER READING

"Hercules Technology Growth Capital Inc. Provides $10M to Labopharm Inc. US Subsidiary," *Asia Africa Intelligence Wire,* July 11, 2005.

"Hercules Technology Growth Capital Provides $7.5M Financing to Luminous Networks," *Wireless News,* September 6, 2005.

Lau, Debra, "The Growing Attraction of Debt," *Venture Capital Journal,* November 1, 1999.

Rose, Barbara, "Comdisco Pumps Up Venture Cap Unit," *Crain's Chicago Business,* January 31, 2000, p. 6.

Tait, Nikki, "Comdisco Considers Sale of Venture Arm," *Financial Times,* March 14, 2001, p. 34.

"Windspeed Takes Over Comdisco," *Private Equity Week,* March 1, 2004, p. 13.

"The Wrong Move?" *Business Week,* October 1, 2001, p. EB22.

Holiday Retirement Corp.

2250 McGilchrist Street SE, Suite 200
Salem, Oregon 97203
U.S.A.
Telephone: (503) 370-7071
Fax: (503) 364-5716
Web site: http://www.holidaytouch.com

Private Company
Incorporated: 1971 as Holiday Management
Employees: 7,500
Sales: $1 billion (2006 est.)
NAIC: 623311 Continuing Care Retirement Communities; 623213 Homes for the Elderly; 623990 Other Residential Care Facilities; 624120 Services for the Elderly and Persons with Disabilities; 237210 Land Subdivision; 531110 Lessors of Residential Buildings and Dwellings; 531311 Residential Property Managers; 531390 Other Activities Related to Real Estate

∎∎∎

Holiday Retirement Corp. and its affiliates manage more than 300 facilities in the United States, Canada, and the United Kingdom. The company is the largest retirement community operator in the United States and Europe with fully integrated development, construction, ownership, and management arms. Holiday's management company primarily serves the middle class in small towns, relying on resident couples in their 50s to manage its facilities.

1963–83: BUILDING A CHAIN OF INDEPENDENT LIVING FACILITIES

In 1963, William (Bill) Colson and his father, Hugh, started a construction company called Colson & Colson. Hugh Colson had been a carpenter, and the Colson family had been poor throughout Bill's childhood and young adult years. In fact, Bill, who had the reputation of being a humble and private man, had worked as a dishwasher to pay for his schooling and "barely made it through two years at Bakersfield Junior College" in California, according to a 2004 *Oregonian* article.

In 1970, the Colsons entered into a joint venture with Carl Campbell of Wenatchee, Washington, to build one of the first senior housing facilities in San Diego, California. At the time, retirement communities represented a fledgling industry with unsure prospects, and Bill Colson "wasn't convinced" of the wisdom of the venture. "It wasn't a nursing home, and it wasn't an apartment.... I didn't know what to think," he told *Oregonian* in 2004. The trio formed Holiday Management in 1971.

Throughout the 1970s and 1980s, Holiday Management grew slowly but steadily. Then during the mid-1980s, with financing readily available, there was a surge in senior housing projects in the United States. The time was ripe; with 32 million people approaching age 65 and older during the early 1990s, the need for senior living communities was on the rise. However, lack of experience and undercapitalization led to failure for many new housing businesses. Many of these

COMPANY PERSPECTIVES

Our belief, and the one that Holiday Retirement is based on, is to treat people the way we would like to be treated ourselves. With this attitude, Holiday's managers and employees can provide a stable and caring environment that allows seniors to enjoy retirement to the fullest.

projects were too expensive, too large, built in isolated locations, or lacked needed healthcare services. In addition, the over-60 population was not yet sold on the concept of senior housing, and rooms stood empty.

Beginning in 1983, Holiday Management, which included Colson & Colson Construction, developed and constructed retirement facilities through partnerships or limited liability corporations. The Colsons formed Holiday Retirement Corp. in 1987 and hired Daniel Baty, former chief executive of Hillhaven, the nation's second largest nursing home chain, to become their chief executive officer.

EXPANSION INTO CANADA AND EUROPE

When Baty took charge of Holiday, the company consisted of 40 independent living facilities. By the early 1990s, after expanding into Canada, Holiday had 130 facilities with 13,000 units in North America. In 1994, the company added close to 3,000 units spread across 18 properties to bring this number to about 150. There were more than 17,000 units by 1995. Holiday also then managed 16,000 units in about 130 properties. By that time, it topped both the owner and manager lists for senior housing and was by far the nation's largest owner of senior housing. It continued to top the lists in 1995 and 1996.

The key ingredients of Holiday's success were its focus on simple systems, common purchasing, dietary planning, and consistent operating policies and procedures with divisional and regional management of facilities. Suites in a typical Holiday facility did not have kitchens because Holiday served three meals a day in a group dining room. Homes also provided housekeeping and linen services and transportation in a luxury minivan.

Holiday did not use radio or television ads to appeal to its target market, the 65-plus demographic group, because people in the senior generation did not watch a lot of television. Rather, its direct marketing efforts consisted of personalized two- or three-page letters. Holiday also kept in mind that it was marketing to two groups of people, the prospective residents and their children, the "influencers." While the influencers were more concerned with issues of safety and meals, the top priority for the actual potential residents was the availability of formal and informal social activities.

Holiday branched out into Europe in 1995 when it entered into a joint venture to acquire Peverel, the United Kingdom's largest retirement home manager. Peverel managed more than 21,000 retirement homes in about 500 developments in the United Kingdom. The company continued to grow, both in size and revenue, and in 1996, Holiday did nearly $600 million in revenue. It opened a home in Clevedon, North Somerset, England, in 1996.

By 1997, Holiday Retirement Corp. operated 177 retirement complexes with more than 21,500 units. That year was a period of dynamic growth for the senior housing industry. Colson was able to say in the October 1997 *National Real Estate Investor* that "[Holiday's] typical project is ... 110 to 120 units. When we open it, we're preleased about 48 percent, and we'll hope to be stabilized in eight to 12 months."

However, 1998 and 1999 were merely modest years for domestic senior housing, with the largest organizations expanding their capacity only slightly because of the constrained availability of capital. Holiday, however, continued its international expansion and added 23 domestic properties. In 1998, it purchased most of Medotels from French Accor SA. In 1999, it added the Seriance Group in France, which became the fifth largest assisted living management operation in that country. It also opened its second establishment in the United Kingdom, called The Hawthorns, which offered three-course meals for lunch.

It also stepped up its growth in Canada, whose senior housing industry, according to some sources, was about 15 years behind that of the United States. "The other competitors [in senior housing] are starting to move," said Colson in a 1998 *Ottawa Citizen,* "and [we] want to be on the leading edge." By 1999, there were more than 225 retirement facilities with 27,000 units in 39 states, Canada, and the United Kingdom. Also in the late 1990s, Holiday overhauled its information technology infrastructure.

2000–06: A PERIOD OF RAPID BUILDING

In 2000, Holiday began XL Management to take over its assisted living facilities. Until that time, the company

KEY DATES

1963: Bill Colson and his father start a construction company called Colson & Colson.
1971: Colson founds Holiday Management Company with two other shareholders.
1987: Holiday Retirement Corp. is formed.
1995: Holiday enters into a joint venture to acquire Peverel in the United Kingdom.
1998: Holiday purchases most of Medotels from French Accor SA.
1999: The company establishes the Seriance Group in France.
2000: The company starts XL Management.

predominantly a middle-class clientele. "We aren't after the rich and we aren't after the poor. We are after the middle American ... the person who has worked their whole life and has a little bit in savings and a little bit in social security," Colson announced.

As Colson looked to the future, he saw the possibility of stepping up the pace of building again by the year 2010. "We may just have to kick the management company in the pants and do 30 to 40 new buildings per year" to keep up with the growth of the over-60 population. Fortress Investment Corp., a real estate investment and finance company located in New York City, purchased the company in late 2006. However, day-to-day management of the company remained with Holiday.

Carrie Rothburd

had had assisted living wings in only a few properties, but from 2000 to 2004, XL Management grew slowly to reach a total of 16 facilities. According to Colson in a 2004 *Multifamily Executive* article, slow growth was necessary because "[w]hen you are dealing with seniors and health issues, you don't want to go too fast."

By 2001, there were about 2,100 continuing care communities throughout the United States, serving roughly 600,000 people, according to the American Senior Housing Association. The population in these communities exceeded the 500,000 seniors living in assisted living projects, which had blossomed as an alternative to more expensive nursing homes in the 1990s. Colson opened 27 new properties. "We opened a new building every 13 or 14 days," Colson recalled in *Multifamily Executive* in 2004. "That's hard for the management company. It's hard to hire new people and fire up a building that often."

By 2003, Holiday had a total of about 30,000 units in more than 250 retirement communities in the United States, Canada, and the United Kingdom. It sold Seriance in 2003, and, in 2004, it ranked seventh among the top 150 private Oregon-based corporations as ranked by *Oregon Business* magazine. It was the largest domestic owner of senior housing for the 11th consecutive year with close to 35,000 units in almost 300 properties and the second largest property manager.

In 2005, the company slowed its building pace. It raised average rents 3 percent. The company that liked having a "small frog in every pond," according to Colson in the 2004 *Multifamily Executive* article, continued to shy away from large metropolitan areas and to serve

PRINCIPAL COMPETITORS

Health Care Property Investors, Inc.; Life Care Centers of America; Nationwide Health Properties, Inc.; ACTS Retirement - Life Communities, Inc.; Emeritus Corporation; Atria Senior Living Group, Inc.; Health Care REIT, Inc.; Kindred Healthcare, Inc.; LTC Properties, Inc.; McCarthy & Stone plc; National Health Investors, Inc.; Senior Housing Properties Trust; Ventas, Inc.

FURTHER READING

Adolph, Carolyn, "Angry Seniors Fight to Keep Their Way of Life," *Gazette*, August 11, 1995, p. A1.

Crone, Teresa, "Spring Garden, Pa., Rejects Construction of Proposed Retirement Home," *York Daily Record*, September 20, 2000.

Foong, Keat, "Holiday Retirement Creates For-Seniors-Only Marketing," *Multi-Housing News*, December 2000, p. 1.

Garcia, Sandra, "Colson, Slavin Still Constructing Despite Seniors Sector Slowdown," *Commercial Property News*, September 16, 2001, p. 1.

Lucas, John, "Uncle Sam's Age-Old Recipe for Gracious Living," *Daily Telegraph*, February 17, 2001, p. 12.

McGraw, Carol, "It's in the Details," *Oregonian*, April 4, 2004, p. 1.

Oser, Alan S., "When Navigating the Nursing Home Maze, Slow Down," *New York Times*, March 21, 2001, p. 2.

Rose, Michael, "Holiday Retirement Corp. Is Among the World's Largest Operators in the Expanding Business," *Statesman Journal*, January 25, 2004.

Shaver, Les, "Senior Centric: Colson Focuses on Middle-Class Active Adults," *Multifamily Executive*, May 15, 2004.

Hopson Development Holdings Ltd.

———— ■ ————

Suites 3305–3309
33rd Fl. Jardine House
1 Connaught Place
Central Hong Kong,
Hong Kong
Telephone: (+852) 2537 3086
Fax: (+852) 2537 2834
Web site: http://www.hopson.com.cn

Public Company
Incorporated: 1992
Employees: 3,596
Sales: HKD 8.86 billion ($790.7 million) (2006)
Stock Exchanges: Hong Kong
Ticker Symbol: 00754
NAIC: 237210 Land Subdivision; 236116 New Multi-Family Housing Construction (Except Operative Builders); 236117 New Housing Operative Builders

■ ■ ■

Hopson Development Holdings Ltd. is one of the largest and fastest-growing property development groups in the mainland Chinese market. The Hong Kong-based company, founded only in 1992, is a leading developer in its original base in Guangzhou, in Guangdong Province, considered to be one of the primary industrial and economic centers of the mainland's economic boom at the dawn of the 21st century. Hopson's share of the Guangzhou market stands at more than 7 percent. Since the early 2000s, however, Hopson has systematically expanded its landholdings and development projects throughout China, and especially into the country's other major property markets, notably Beijing, Shanghai, Tianjin, and Huizhou. At the middle of the decade, Hopson's total landbank stood at more than 14 million square meters, much of which had been acquired at low prices during the property dip at the beginning of the decade. Hopson maintains a highly active property development portfolio, with more than 75 projects under construction at mid-decade, most of which are either wholly or majority owned by the company. Some 30 of the group's current projects were launched in 2006 alone. The company's own development operations focus on the residential market. Hopson also holds investments in existing properties, with an emphasis on retail developments and car parks. Hopson has been listed on the Hong Kong Stock Exchange since 1998. The company remains controlled by founder Chu Mang-Yee, whose 63 percent shareholding has placed him among the world's billionaires. Other major strategic investors include Temasek Holdings subsidiary Aranda and U.S.-based investment group Tiger Global LP. In 2006, Hopson posted revenues of HKD 8.86 billion ($790.7 million).

MAINLAND PROPERTY PIONEER IN 1992

Prior to the 1990s, the property development market in mainland China did not exist. Strict controls by the Chinese government over housing and other developments, as well as the government's policy of maintaining ownership of all land in the country, meant that, with the loosening of economic policy in the early 1990s, the stage was set for a real estate boom that transformed

China into one of the world's most vibrant property markets.

The explosive growth of the country's industrial sector in the late 1980s and especially into the 1990s not only drew an increasing proportion of the population into the country's urban areas, it also helped create a new and fast-growing middle class. The appearance and rapid development of this class, accompanied by the rise of a wealthy class, in turn inspired new demands for higher-end residential properties than those built under the authority of the Communist government. In response, the government began reforming its real estate policies to allow for private development. While the land itself remained the property of the Chinese government, prospective developers were now able to acquire the right to build on the properties, generally accompanied by long-term leases in the range of 70 years or more. These reforms created new opportunities for the country's would-be property developers.

Among them was Chu Mang-Yee, who had established his career within the Chinese government bureaucracy. While serving the government, Chu gained experience working within the construction and property development area. This experience enabled Chu to become one of the early entrants into the newly emerging private sector property development market, and in 1992 Chu became one of the founders of a new company, Hopson Development Holdings.

Hopson initially focused on the Guangzhou region. The main city of Guangdong Province, Guangzhou (once more commonly known as Canton) became one of the first areas in the country to enjoy free trade zone status, placing the city at the center of China's industrial boom in the late 1980s and 1990s. The city's proximity to Hong Kong also made it a highly prized location.

Led by Chu, Hopson began acquiring a significant landbank in Guangzhou, rapidly becoming one of the market's leaders.

Hopson's strategy was to focus on acquiring less centrally located properties. By adding holdings in less developed areas outside of the city's central areas, and along its outskirts, the company was able to build a strong landbank at a reduced cost. Nonetheless, Hopson chose its acquisitions carefully, picking up sites in highly strategic locations, particularly those with access to the city's highway and other transport infrastructure.

The company clearly targeted the rising middle- and upper-middle class markets with the construction of a number of large-scale residential complexes. Hopson focused especially on two of Guangzhou's fastest-growing sections, Tianhe and Haizhu. The Tianhe sector alone counted for more than 70 percent of the company's total landbank into the late 1990s.

The Gallopade Park complex provided an example of Hopson's project development work during this period. Launched in the early 1990s, the completed Tianhe District project encompassed a total of 68 mid-rise residential towers, accompanied by a two-tower research center, three office blocks, and a two-tower training center. The company's Huajing New City development, built during the same period near the Kowloon-Canton train terminal, and in proximity to the Huanan Expressway, initially consisted of four high-rise residential buildings, as well as 23 mid-rise buildings and office and retail complexes. In later phases, that site was expanded through the construction of an additional 22 high-rise residential towers, as well as a four-story retail and leisure center. Other projects launched and/or completed during the 1990s including Jinan Garden, Fairview Garden, Regal Court, Grandview Place, Riverside New City, and Parkview Villa. The company also launched a development in Yuexiu District, where it built the Zhujiang International Building, combining service apartments with retail and parking spaces.

The company's brisk expansion allowed it to claim some 7 percent of the Guangzhou residential development market by the late 1990s. The company had also seen strong revenue growth, with its turnover rising from just HKD 120 million in 1995 to more than HKD 1.3 billion by 1998.

In order to fuel its further expansion, and to continually replenish its landbank, Hopson Development listed its shares on the Hong Kong Stock Exchange, and moved its headquarters to that city in 1998. Following the listing, Hopson began acquiring new landholdings, a process which also included acquiring majority, if not full, control of most of its major development projects. At the same time, Hopson

KEY DATES

1992: Hopson Development Holdings is founded by Chu Mang-Yee and others to develop new residential and commercial properties for the Guangzhou region.

1998: Hopson goes public, listing shares on the Hong Kong Stock Exchange.

2002: Company launches drive to diversify geographic focus, adding first properties in Beijing and Tianjin markets, before expanding into Shanghai and Huizhou areas.

2006: Company raises HKD 1 billion through sale of 60 million shares in order to acquire new properties.

focused on expanding a number of its existing sites. As an example, the company acquired the neighboring properties to its Pleasant View Garden site, in order to more than triple the total surface area of that development.

EXPANDING BEYOND GUANGZHOU

As its properties reached completion and the first residents took possession of their homes and offices, Hopson responded by establishing its own property management subsidiary, Guangdong Esteem Property Services Limited, in 2000. The new subsidiary also helped boost the company's effort to attract new residents following the institution of new housing reforms by the Chinese government, which were enacted to encourage the market's transition from one based on large-scale institutional purchases of residential properties to an individual-based housing market. Hopson itself successfully made this transition, and into the early 2000s, more than 85 of its property sales came from the individual market.

By 2001, Hopson's landbank stood at more than 4.2 million square meters. The company's growth was aided by the strong growth in the Guangzhou market in general, among the most vibrant in China, and in the world. Indeed, by the early 2000s, China's GDP topped 7 percent, ranking the country among the world's top performers. Yet the Guangzhou market was responsible for a significant part of that growth, as its own GDP nearly doubled the national average, nearing 14 percent.

Concerns that China's construction market was overheating, which prompted a new series of reforms by

the Chinese government, caused a dip in market prices at the beginning of the 2000s. Hopson took advantage of the softened prices to make massive new additions to its landbank, placing the company in a strong position as the property development market—buoyed by China's entry into the World Trade Organization and its upcoming hosting of the 2008 Olympic Games—continued its steady expansion.

Hopson itself became determined to expand beyond its core Guangzhou market in the early 2000s, and a significant part of its new land acquisitions came as part of a strategy to increase its geographic scope. For that effort, the company became determined to build a presence in a number of other major mainland markets, including Beijing, Shanghai, Tianjin, and Huizhou.

Hopson quickly made good on its expansion plans. In 2002, the company invested nearly HKD 937 million in a joint venture with Guangdong Zhujiang Investment, already a partner with Hopson in a number of its Guangzhou developments. The joint venture quickly bought five properties, including three in Beijing's Chaoyang District totaling more than 1.3 million square meters for a total investment of nearly HKD 700 million. At the same the company added its first property development in Tianjin, a 2.5-million-square-meter tourist and resort development. The company also boosted its Guangzhou presence with the launch of a 74,000-square-meter development there.

Hopson soon added properties in other major Chinese urban markets, including its first entry into Shanghai toward the middle of the decade. In 2005, the company further enhanced its position in the Beijing market, acquiring two adjoining sites in the centrally located Chaoyang district. The company announced plans to build a combined residential and retail complex with a total area of nearly 170,000 square meters, at a cost of more than HKD 1 billion. By then, the company's total landbank was nearly 13 million square meters.

The move into Beijing, as well as further expansion into Shanghai and Tianjin, helped raise Hopson into the top ranks of the mainland's fast-growing property development groups. By the end of 2005, Hopson could already claim the number three position. In 1995 the company added a new chief executive officer, Wu Jiesi, formerly with Guangdong Investment and a former mayor of Shenzhen, who announced plans to take the market's lead by as early as 2007. As part of this effort, the company brought in two new strategic investors, Aranda, part of Singapore's Temasek Holdings, and the U.S.-based investment group Tiger Fund. The share sale enabled the company to raise nearly $1 billion in new funding.

Continued concerns for what many considered to be an overheated housing market led the Chinese government to enact new restrictions on property development. With its large landbank, Hopson was able to profit from the new measures, which by limiting future property developments, helped raise prices in the company's existing markets. The company also shifted its efforts to acquiring stakes in existing developments, such as the May 2006 purchase of a nearly 61 percent stake in Beijing Dongfangwehhue, then in the process of developing a 15,834-square-meter site in the Dongcheng District, one of the most active areas of Beijing. The remaining shares of that company were held in large part by Chu Mang-Yee's brother and brother-in-law.

Hopson also took steps to restructure its portfolio in order to take advantage of continuing gains by the real estate market. In July 2006, for example, the company sold off its 50 percent holding in a major commercial development in Shanghai, the Hopson International Tower, raising $150 million. Yet acquisitions of new properties remained a company priority, as the company continued a spending spree of more than HKD 2.5 billion through 2006. At the end of that year, the company took steps to boost its treasury for a new round of acquisitions. In November 2006, the company raised nearly HKD 1 billion through the placement of 60 million shares on the market. The company followed this offering with a convertible bond sale, adding an additional $235 million to its treasury. With a landbank topping 14 million square meters into the beginning of 2007, Hopson Development Holdings had developed into a leading player in the booming Chinese real estate market.

M. L. Cohen

PRINCIPAL SUBSIDIARIES

Guangdong Esteem Property Services Limited.

PRINCIPAL COMPETITORS

China Poly Group Corp.; Shanghai Alison Group Company Ltd.; China Vanke Company Ltd.; Baoye Group Company Ltd.; North China Pharmaceutical Company Ltd.; China Enterprise Company Ltd.; Nanjing Xingang High-Tech Company Ltd.; Shenzhen Changcheng Investment Holding Company Ltd.; Shanghai Industrial Development Company Ltd.; Shui On Land Ltd.; Beijing Vantone Pioneer Real Estate Company Ltd.

FURTHER READING

Chan, Doris, "Hopson Makes Move into Lucrative Beijing Market," *South China Morning Post,* January 11, 2002.

Cheung, Jackie, "Hopson in $996m Share Sale to Buy Land," *Standard,* November 4, 2006.

"HK Equities Red Hot with IPOs, Block Trades," *Euroweek,* January 19, 2007.

"Hopson's Renminbi Bonds to Debut in Hong Kong," *Alestron,* January 23, 2007.

"Hopson to Invest RMB 1.1bn on Properties," *Sing Tao Daily,* December 8, 1999, p. 15.

Li, Sandy, "Hopson Prepares $1bn Injection for Guangdong Sites," *South China Morning Post,* December 8, 1999.

"Stepping into the Limelight," *Asiamoney,* November 2006.

Wang, Raymond, "$500m Gain for Hopson in Shanghai Project Deal," *Standard,* July 26, 2006.

Yeung, Frederick, "Hopson New Profit Leaps 181% on Land Boom," *South China Morning Post,* April 14, 2006.

Huawei Technologies Company Ltd.

■—■

Bantian, Longgang District
Shenzhen, 518129
China
Telephone: (+86 0755) 2878 0808
Fax: (+86 0755) 2878 9251
Web site: http://www.huawei.com

Private Company
Incorporated: 1988
Employees: 61,000
Sales: $11 billion (2006 est.)
NAIC: 334220 Radio and Television Broadcasting and Wireless Communications Equipment Manufacturing; 334210 Telephone Apparatus Manufacturing

■ ■ ■

Huawei Technologies Company Ltd. is one of the world's fastest-growing telecommunications equipment producers, and is also one of China's largest technology-based companies. Located in Shenzhen, the free trade zone established opposite Hong Kong, Huawei has established a reputation for high-quality, cutting-edge technologies, and is the leading provider of a full range of telecommunications equipment, including switches, routers, ASIC chipsets, other fixed-line and wireless telecom infrastructure components, and mobile telephone handsets. The company's low-cost manufacturing base has allowed it to compete on an international level, particularly in the Asian region. Yet Huawei has also made strong inroads into Western markets. In 2006, for example, European telecommunications giant Vodafone

Plc picked Huawei to supply its 3G mobile telephone handsets. While its manufacturing base remains in China, Huawei has built an internationally operating research and development (R&D) network, with R&D subsidiaries, offices, and partnerships in Bangalore, Dallas, California's Silicon Valley, Stockholm, and Moscow, supplementing its six R&D facilities in China. Some 48 percent of the company's 61,000 employees are dedicated to R&D as part of the company's drive to establish itself as a technology leader in the global telecommunications industry. This effort has allowed the company to build a patent base of more than 2,500 approved patents, with another 17,000 patent applications in the pipeline.

Despite its success, Huawei remains somewhat controversial—it has been accused of patent infringement, corporate espionage, and technology theft in the past. Its private status, and the secretive nature of founder and Chairman Ren Zhengfei, has led to speculation that the company is in fact owned and run by the People's Liberation Army (the company denies this). The company claimed annual revenues of $11 billion, of which 65 percent were generated outside of China.

TELECOM UPSTART IN 1988

Huawei Technologies was founded in 1988 by Ren Zhengfei, an officer in the People's Liberation Army, later a member of the Chinese government. Ren's relationship with the Communist government, and with the PLA, later raised security questions in regards to the company's international expansion, and at least at the

VISION: To enrich life through communication.
MISSION: To focus on our customers' market challenges and needs by providing excellent communications network solutions and services in order to consistently create maximum value for customers.

Customer Focus Strategy: Serving our customers is the only reason Huawei exists; Customer demand is the fundamental driving force of our development. High quality, excellent service, low operating costs, and giving top priority to meeting customer requirements to enhance their competitiveness and profitability. Continuously performing management transformation to realize efficient process-based organization operation for ensuring high quality end-to-end delivery. Developing with our peers in the industry as both competitors and partners to jointly create a favorable environment and share the benefits of the value chain.

beginning, it appears that Huawei was directly owned and controlled by the PLA. The company later claimed to have restructured its ownership, with its employees, possibly through one or more unions, controlling the majority of the company's shares. The reclusive Ren, who refused interviews and otherwise reportedly patterned himself after Chairman Mao, was said to own 1 percent of the company.

Huawei (the word stands for "achievement" in Chinese) established its operations in the growing city of Shenzhen. That city, which was little more than a small fishing village in the late 1970s, had become one of China's fastest-growing cities following the establishment of a free trade zone there amid the debut of China's economic reforms in 1979. Shenzhen's proximity to Hong Kong, facing the then-British city on the opposite bank of the Shenzhen River, as well as its natural harbor facilities, made an important part of China's goal of establishing its own homegrown industrial and technological capacity.

Yet at first Huawei relied on foreign technology, and functioned as little more than an importer of PBX switches for China's antiquated telephone system. Telephone penetration had traditionally been extremely low in the country, with just 200,000 lines in a nation of more than one billion at the beginning of the 1990s. The country's ambitions of rejoining the global

industrial economy, however, guaranteed explosive demand for telecommunications infrastructure and end-user equipment in the coming years. While China eagerly imported existing technologies into the country, notably through a vast number of joint ventures and technology transfer agreements with foreign partners, the government also pressed the development of homegrown technologies.

The country, and Huawei, could build its ambitions on the vast pool of technology graduates produced each year by the country's universities. The relatively low wages and seemingly unlimited number of engineers provided a huge resource for the company as it launched its own research and development program within a year of its founding. By the beginning of the 1990s, the company had succeeded in producing its first PBX switch. Geared specifically to the Chinese market, that switch boasted a 10,000-circuit capacity. Backed by the government, Huawei gained contracts for its PBX switching equipment throughout China.

The company's continued development efforts led to the launch of its C&C08 digital switch in 1993. By 1995, the company had begun to apply for, and earn, its own patents, and in that year the company set up its own Intellectual Property Rights department. Huawei continued to extend its R&D capabilities, opening a second research facility in Beijing in 1995, followed by an R&D center in Shanghai in 1996. These efforts helped the company roll out its HONET range of integrated access network and SDH equipment that same year. Also in 1996, the company signed its first international contract, supplying fixed-line equipment to Hong Kong-based Hutchison Whampoa.

ESTABLISHING TECHNOLOGY PARTNERSHIPS IN 1997

Partnerships with a variety of international companies played a major role in helping the company ramp up its technologies. This was especially true as the developing GSM mobile telephone standard presented new opportunities for the company's expansion. Where previous fixed-line and PBX-based telecommunications equipment were already mature technologies when Huawei was founded, the new wireless communications and mobile telecommunications market helped level the playing field somewhat. Faced with a lowered barrier to entry into the global technology race, Huawei quickly established a network of partnerships with many of the industry's major players. This effort led the company to set up a series of shared research and development facilities with such partners as Texas Instruments, Cisco Systems, Motorola, Intel, Sun Microsystems, Altera,

KEY DATES

1988: Huawei is established in Shenzhen by Ren Zhengfei as an importer of PBX network equipment before launching its own research and development operations.

1996: Company signs first international supply contract, with Hutchison Whampoa in Hong Kong.

1999: Huawei sets up first international R&D center in Bangalore, India.

2001: Company establishes European sales subsidiary.

2006: Company wins contract to supply UMTS handsets to Vodafone.

Qualcomm, Microsoft, and Infineon, starting from 1997. While the company's aggressive pursuit of technology would later lead to new questions regarding the company's intentions—in 2002 Cisco Systems filed a lawsuit against Huawei, alleging patent infringement and corporate espionage, among other incidents—Huawei rapidly gained expertise in the new telecom market. By 1997, the company had debuted its own GSM-platform based equipment

Huawei extended its R&D network again in 1998, opening a center in Nanjing. The following year, the company set up its first wholly owned international R&D network, in Bangalore, India. That center became the company's largest overseas operation, with more than 1,000 employees. In 2000, the company added two new U.S. centers, targeting the high-tech corridors of Dallas and California's Silicon Valley. By then, the company had increasingly begun to extend its operations throughout the Asian Pacific, and by 2001 claimed to be the leading producer of optical line products for the region. The South American region proved to be another strong market for the company, which established its first sales office for that continent in Brazil in 1999, followed by the establishment of a technology training center in 2000. By then, the company claimed total sales of more than $2.65 billion, though just $100 million was generated outside of China.

Huawei's commitment to the GSM standard enabled it to target entry into the European market, which had begun building a continent-wide GSM network in the mid-1990s. Huawei moved to expand its presence in Europe and in 2000 formed a sales subsidiary in England. Over the next several years, the company expanded throughout the region, opening support offices in 26 countries. The company also entered the computer information systems market, launching a subsidiary in Moscow. Increasingly, Huawei had begun to compete head-to-head with the European market's telecom equipment giants, including Siemens, Nokia, and Ericsson. A major contract for the company came in 2001 when it received the contract to deploy a 10Gbps SDH system for the city of Berlin. Huawei's cost-competitiveness enabled its international sales to build rapidly; by the end of 2002, international sales had already topped $500 million. This growth was especially impressive given the global slump in telecommunications spending at the beginning of the decade.

Back at home, Huawei remained the dominant telecommunications equipment supplier, a position reinforced by its selection by China Mobile to roll out what became the world's first and largest wireless LAN network in 2001. While China remained by far the company's main market, Huawei continued to build both its reputation and global presence into the middle of the first decade of the 2000s. The company gained a major position in the Middle East, launching a next-generation UMTS network for Emirates Telecommunications Corporation in 2003. In 2004, the company added to its international clientele with the launch of a UMTS network for the Netherlands' Telfort.

Huawei's reputation remained shrouded in controversy, however. In 2000, the company had been accused of bypassing the Iraqi embargo, with an equipment supply contract. The company later claimed not to have fulfilled the contract; the incident, however, was said to have influenced the U.S. government's continued suspicions of the company. As a result, if Huawei had achieved success in most of the world's market, its presence in the United States remained highly limited.

The lawsuit filed against it by Cisco Systems in 2002—alleging that the company had stolen Cisco's technology and software in an effort to woo Cisco's customers away—had the paradoxical effect of boosting Huawei's stature. The lawsuit's implicit recognition of Huawei as a rival for Cisco placed Huawei among the global industry's major players, and in the end served to enhance Huawei's reputation. The two companies ultimately reached an amicable settlement, and Cisco dropped the lawsuit in 2003. Nonetheless, questions over Huawei's ownership, and intentions, continued to pose problems for the company. In India, for example, its attempt to expand its operations there was blocked by the Indian government in 2005. Similarly, the company's interest in British electronics and technology flagship Marconi in the early 2000s raised an alarm among members of the British Parliament. That company was ultimately acquired by Sweden's Ericsson. A new incident, when a member of Huawei's staff was caught taking photographs of Fujitsu networking equipment after hours at a trade show, in 2004, raised further doubts about the company's commitment to developing its own technology.

Nevertheless, the company continued to attract new and high profile contracts. By the end of 2006, the company appeared to have joined the global big league. After being awarded a contract to supply European telecom giant Vodafone's UMTS infrastructure equipment, including its full Spanish rollout, Vodafone tapped Huawei again in 2006 to supply its first series of UMTS handsets. Part of the company's success was attributed to its flexibility; not only was it able to agree to Vodafone's request for a midpriced multimedia-equipped telephone, it also agreed to brand the telephones under the Vodafone name. By the end of 2006, the company's sales had risen past $11 billion. International sales by then represented the majority of the company's operations, at 65 percent of sales. With an ever growing homegrown technological foundation, Huawei was prepared to make a bid for the industry leadership in the new century.

M. L. Cohen

PRINCIPAL SUBSIDIARIES

Huawei Technologies operates subsidiaries in Brazil, China, India, Malaysia, Moscow, South Africa, the United Kingdom, and the United States.

PRINCIPAL COMPETITORS

Siemens AG; Sony Ericsson Mobile Communications; Hitachi Ltd.; Fujitsu General Ltd.; Motorola Inc.; Nokia Corp.; NTT DoCoMo Inc.; LG Electronics; Sharp Corp.; Reliance Industries Ltd.; Sanyo Electric Company Ltd.; Alcatel-Lucent S.A.

FURTHER READING

Einhorn, Bruce, "China's Huawei Gives It Up for Vodafone," *Business Week,* October 2, 2006.

Fitchard, Kevin, "Made in China," *Telephony,* February 5, 2007.

Flannery, Russell, "Mystery Man," *Forbes,* December 27, 2004, p. 148.

Forney, Matthew, "Ren Zhengfei: Modeled After Mao," *Time,* April 18, 2005, p. 85.

Kripalani, Manjeet, Jack Ewing, and Bruce Einhorn, "Huawei: More Than a Local Hero," *Business Week,* October 11, 2004, p. 180.

Meyer, Chris, "Keep the R&D Flag Flying," *MEED Middle East Economic Digest,* December 16, 2005, p. 16.

"See Huawei Run," *Economist,* March 5, 2005, p. 61.

Simons, Craig, "The Huawei Way," *Newsweek International,* January 16, 2006.

Huntington Bancshares Incorporated

Huntington Center
41 South High Street
Columbus, Ohio 43287-0001
U.S.A.
Telephone: (614) 480-8300
Toll Free: (800) 480-2265
Fax: (614) 480-5284
Web site: http://www.huntington.com

Public Company
Founded: 1866 as P. W. Huntington & Company
Incorporated: 1905 as The Huntington National Bank of
    Columbus
Employees: 8,081
Total Assets: $35.33 billion (2006)
Stock Exchanges: NASDAQ
Ticker Symbol: HBAN
NAIC: 551111 Offices of Bank Holding Companies;
    522110 Commercial Banking; 522120 Savings
    Institutions

■ ■ ■

Huntington Bancshares Incorporated is a regional bank holding company in the Midwest, operating principally through The Huntington National Bank. Based in Columbus, Ohio, with around $36 billion in assets in early 2007, Huntington operates more than 380 branches and nearly 1,000 ATMs in Ohio, Michigan, West Virginia, Indiana, and Kentucky. Huntington offers commercial and consumer banking services, mortgage banking products, automobile financing,

equipment leasing, investment management, and brokerage, trust, and insurance products and services. Huntington's rich history spans more than 140 years.

MID-19TH-CENTURY FOUNDING BY P. W. HUNTINGTON

P. W. Huntington formed the Huntington National Bank in 1866. He had to do something big. After all, P. W. was one of the most recent additions to a long line of Huntingtons who had helped shape the United States. In 1633 Simon and Margaret Huntington left Norwich, England, with their daughter and four sons to settle in the tiny town of Roxbury, Massachusetts. Simon died of smallpox during the voyage, but the family prospered, married, and multiplied. Benjamin Huntington, P. W.'s great-grandfather and the descendant of one of Margaret's sons, helped to start the Revolutionary War by calling the first revolutionary meeting in Norwich, Connecticut, in 1774. Another Huntington, Samuel, was president of the Continental Congress from 1779 to 1781, signed the Declaration of Independence, and helped construct the Constitution; some historians have even referred to Samuel as the nation's true first president. The Huntington after which P. W. was named, Pelatiah Webster, was a well-known political economist, author, and teacher during the late 1700s.

P. W. himself was born in 1836, went to work at the age of 14 on a whaling vessel that sailed to Russia, and began a job as a messenger in a Columbus, Ohio, bank when he was 17. After working for 13 years in the rapidly growing Columbus banking industry, P. W.

COMPANY PERSPECTIVES

We are a bank whose size makes people feel right at home, yet is more than large enough to provide them with access to all the resources they need. We like to think of Huntington as a local bank with national resources, and it's just one of the things that makes us great.

started his own banking enterprise, P. W. Huntington & Company. The bank grew quickly. P. W. built a five-story building in 1878, Columbus's first "skyscraper," and began to get his sons involved with the bank's operations. Four of P. W.'s five sons became partners during the 1890s and early 1900s, eventually assuming executive management positions. The bank was incorporated in 1905 as The Huntington National Bank of Columbus.

Huntington moved to a new, larger building in 1916 to house its burgeoning operations. P. W. died in 1918 shortly after turning the bank over to his sons. By the time of his death, however, he had built the bank into a leading financial institution in Columbus. Francis, or "F. R.," became president and provided active leadership for 14 years. One of F. R.'s most important contributions during his short term as president was the initiation of an acquisition program; in 1923, Huntington purchased the State Savings Bank & Trust Company and the Hayden-Clinton National Bank of Columbus, thus swelling its capital base considerably.

As a result of its acquisitions, Huntington became active in the trust business. In fact, by 1930 the bank's trust assets totaled more than all its other banking assets combined. F. R. died in 1928 at the age of 52, but not before constructing a large addition onto the bank's existing building. The grand complex received worldwide attention when it was unveiled in 1926. Shortly thereafter, F. R.'s brother, Theodore, or "T. S.," assumed the presidency. One year later, the Great Depression began.

Fortunately for the bank's investors, T. S. maintained the strict, low-risk banking strategy during 1928 and 1929 that had been initiated by his father and followed by F. R. as well. P. W. believed in high liquidity, large cash reserves, and cautious investments. P. W. had once turned away a giant $500,000 deposit from a railroad, saying to one of his sons, "We should not owe that much money to anyone." P. W. was also known for collecting sticks on his walk to work in the morning. He

burned them in the company's fireplaces to save money on heating fuel. Like his father, F. R. carefully avoided the urge to invest in the plethora of speculative opportunities that arose during the Roaring Twenties.

POSTWAR END OF HUNTINGTON FAMILY LEADERSHIP

As a result of its discipline, Huntington survived the Depression while many of its industry peers shrank into oblivion. T. S. guided the company for only four years before stepping aside for health reasons. He handed the company off in 1933 to the youngest Huntington brother, B. Gwynne, or B. G. Known for his almost limitless energy, B. G. successfully guided the bank through the perilous Depression and World War II years before ceding his duties as president and becoming chairman of the board in 1949. B. G. served as chairman during Huntington's rapid postwar expansion. His death in 1958 marked the end of 92 years of guidance for Huntington National by the men of the P. W. Huntington family. Exemplifying their leadership during that period was the motto carved into the stone in the bank's main lobby, "In Prosperity Be Prudent; In Adversity Be Patient."

B. G. Huntington was succeeded as president by John E. Stevenson. Stevenson, who had worked in the Columbus banking industry since 1907 and had come to Huntington by way of the 1923 mergers, was a strong and decisive leader. One of his most notable achievements as chief executive of Huntington was extending the bank's reach through the addition of branches. During the early 1960s, Huntington built several branches and acquired a number of banks that it turned into Huntington branches. Stevenson also oversaw Huntington's entry into new services, namely installment and mortgage loans and retail lending. Noted for his emphasis on loyalty, Stevenson is recorded in company annals as having told a colleague, "Run the place as though you owned it, but never fool yourself into thinking that you do." Clair E. Fultz assumed Stevenson's duties as president in 1963.

Although the Huntington National Bank benefited from an astute, dedicated management team during its 1950s and 1960s growth years, much of its success was attributable to the healthy expansion of the local economy. Indeed, Columbus's population soared from 70,000 in 1940 to 376,000 by 1950 and to 471,000 by 1960, making it the second largest city in Ohio. The boom in housing, industry, and retail sectors created huge opportunities for Huntington to increase its lending activities and attract a steady supply of deposits. Huntington flourished. Between 1958 and 1966, in fact, its assets doubled. By the mid-1960s, the bank was

KEY DATES

1866: P. W. Huntington starts his own banking enterprise, P. W. Huntington & Company, in Columbus, Ohio.

1905: Bank is incorporated as The Huntington National Bank of Columbus.

1923: Bank completes its first acquisitions: the State Savings Bank & Trust Company and the Hayden-Clinton National Bank of Columbus.

1958: Era of Huntington family leadership ends; John E. Stevenson becomes first nonfamily member to serve as bank president.

1966: Huntington Bancshares Incorporated is formed as a holding company for The Huntington National Bank.

1972: Huntington National becomes the first U.S. bank to open a 24-hour, fully automated banking office.

1982: Bank doubles in size via acquisition of Union Commerce Corporation of Cleveland.

1986: Allowed to bank outside of Ohio for the first time following Congressional approval of interstate branch banking, Huntington acquires banks in Indiana, Kentucky, and Michigan.

1997: Huntington acquires First Michigan Bank Corporation in a $1.2 billion deal.

2002: Company divests its Florida banking operations.

2006: Huntington acquires Unizan Financial Corp. of Dayton, Ohio, and reaches an agreement to acquire Sky Financial Group, Inc., of Bowling Green, Ohio, for $3.6 billion.

separated into eight major divisions, was operating 15 offices in the Columbus area, was lending money for all types of consumer and business needs, and had implemented computer systems to reduce its escalating load of paperwork.

EXPANSION UNDER HUNTINGTON BANCSHARES UMBRELLA

The year 1966 marked Huntington's 100th anniversary. It also signaled the start of a new era of expansion for the bank that occurred during the late 1960s and 1970s. By 1965, Huntington's trust division had grown so large

that a separate building, connected to the main bank by an underground tunnel, was created to separately house that operation. In 1966 Huntington created an international banking division that would eventually provide important financial services for foreign banks and companies. Among other accomplishments, in 1972 Huntington National became the first bank in the United States to open a 24-hour, fully automated banking office. Called the "Handy Bank," the concept was soon copied around the world.

Importantly, Huntington National formed Huntington Bancshares Incorporated in 1966 as a means of extending its reach into other parts of Ohio that were previously off limits under federal banking laws. Huntington Bancshares became the parent of Huntington National Bank and subsequently conducted a string of acquisitions during the late 1960s and 1970s. Under the direction of a new president, Arthur D. Herrmann, who took office in 1975, Bancshares created new financial services divisions to place under its corporate umbrella. In 1976, for instance, the Huntington Mortgage Company was founded; by 1979 it was the largest construction lender in central Ohio. The Huntington Leasing Company was started in 1977, and doubled its assets by 1979. By 1979, in fact, Huntington Bancshares Inc. had assets of nearly $2.5 billion (up from just $400 million in 1966) and was operating 97 offices through 15 affiliated banks.

State deregulation of the banking industry in 1979 provided new opportunities for Huntington to enlarge its already ballooning organization. Under the direction of Frank A. Wobst, who became president of Huntington in 1981, Huntington National opened new branches in Kayton, Akron, and Cincinnati. Those gains were augmented by several new acquisitions by Bancshares, including two pivotal purchases in 1982: Reeves Banking and Trust Company of Dover and, more importantly, Union Commerce Corporation of Cleveland. As a result of expansion and acquisition, Huntington Bancshares became Ohio's fourth largest bank holding company in 1982, with $5 billion in assets, 176 branch offices, and operations in 94 Ohio cities.

COMMENCEMENT OF MULTISTATE BANKING OPERATIONS

Huntington was again aided by deregulatory efforts in 1985, but this time at the federal level. Congress approved interstate banking regulations in that year that allowed Huntington Bancshares and other multibank holding companies to become active in other states. Huntington's management determined that its national expansion objectives could best be achieved by establishing separate holding companies in different states. It formed Huntington Bancshares Indiana, Inc., for example, and set up similar holding companies in Kentucky and Michigan. In 1986 Huntington completed four major acquisitions of banks in those three states, and also extended operations of some of its subsidiaries into Florida, Delaware, New Jersey, Pennsylvania, and several other states. All the while, Huntington continued to strengthen its presence in its core Ohio markets.

Although Huntington's rampant growth during the 1970s and 1980s may appear to reflect a divergence from the cautious growth strategies employed by the Huntington family, it was really more symbolic of industry trends dominant during that period. Indeed, as smaller U.S. banks found themselves under increasing pressure to compete against nonbank financial institutions that were encroaching on their traditional turf, the number of banking entities in the United States plunged from about 13,000 in 1983 to less than 10,000 by 1990. Meanwhile, the number of multibank holding companies, such as Huntington Bancshares, grew from about 300 to around 1,000. Huntington did increase its exposure to risk, but it pursued a generally safe strategy during the 1980s.

Huntington's shakiest move was its $2 billion 1982 Union Commerce acquisition. Although it doubled Huntington's size, the purchase left the company loaded with debt that took six years to pare. Wobst and his colleagues learned from the troubled 1982 acquisition, and pursued a less aggressive growth plan throughout the remainder of the 1980s. Nevertheless, a steady stream of purchases combined with Huntington's expansion into a range of new financial services generated strong asset, revenue, and profit growth for the holding company during most of the decade. By 1989, Huntington boasted $10.9 billion in assets and 248 offices in 11 states. Furthermore, the bank was gearing up for faster growth in the 1990s.

Although industry trends favored Huntington's rapid rise during the latter half of the 20th century, the primary source of its success was sound management. After all, many of Huntington's competitors had suffered irreversible defeats during the late 1970s and early 1980s, and many others had engaged in risky investment strategies that were about to damage them severely in the early 1990s. In contrast, Huntington remained comparatively healthy. It refused to be drawn into imprudent growth tactics to compete with its faster growing peers, such as industry leader Banc One. "In the 1960s and 1970s they (Banc One) made a lot more money than we did," Wobst acknowledged in the

September 13, 1993, issue of *Forbes*. "If we had tried to grow as fast as they did, we wouldn't be around anymore."

The chief executives that had provided Huntington's sound management during the 1980s represented an eclectic mix of skills and backgrounds. Wobst was born in Germany, studied law, and immigrated to the United States in 1934 when he was 24. Unable to speak English, Wobst learned the language and worked his way up to the presidency of the company after being in the United States for only 23 years. Wobst became chairman and chief executive in 1984, ceding his presidential duties to 40-year-old Zuheir Sofia. Sofia, a native of Lebanon, came to the United States as a teenager and joined Huntington's start-up international division in 1971. By 1984 he was practically running the company.

ACCELERATING THE RATE OF EXPANSION

During the early 1990s Wobst and Sofia sustained, and even accelerated, the expansion rate they had achieved in the 1980s. They also succeeded in strengthening the holding company's balance sheet and improving its productivity and profitability. Huntington celebrated its 125th anniversary by offering a range of new financial and banking services. It began sponsoring low-income community development loan programs, for example, and started offering cut-rate, at-home banking for low- and moderate-income customers. Huntington also hopped into the surging mutual fund and insurance markets, offering its own proprietary products. Importantly, the bank continued to expand through cautious acquisitions, including gaining a toehold in retail banking in Florida. The move to Florida provided Huntington with the ability to maintain banking relationships with its midwestern customers who retire and move to the Sunshine State.

Perhaps Huntington's greatest accomplishment during the late 1980s and early 1990s was its development and implementation of cutting-edge information systems that were slashing its labor costs and improving service. It poured millions of dollars into, for example, a system that allowed customers to pay bills through a touch-tone telephone. It also created a service that let customers talk to staff to make investments, loan inquiries, or account transactions by phone, 24 hours per day. It worked to developed a telephone with a screen that would let its customers pay bills, book airline tickets, and access other Huntington services. In 1994 Huntington opened a $4 million operations center in West Virginia, where it planned to consolidate its account management operations. "We have used technology very smartly," Sofia said in an August 1993 issue of *Columbus Dispatch,* "and all of the sudden it is beginning to pay off for us."

Other aspects of Huntington's operations were also paying off in the early 1990s. In 1992 Huntington Bancshares' earnings surpassed $50 million before rocketing almost 50 percent in 1993 to $103 million. Furthermore, the holding company's total base of assets ballooned to $16 billion. By early 1994, its assets had risen to $18 billion, an increase of more than 60 percent since 1989. Huntington had become the 40th largest bank in the United States (by assets) by 1994, and was operating more than 450 banking and financial services offices in 17 states. Befitting the legacy of fiscal propriety initiated by P. W. Huntington in the 1860s, the company's financial health was among the best in the industry going into the mid-1990s. In addition, its stock price surged more than 25 percent during 1993, reflecting Huntington's potential for future expansion.

In the mid-1990s Huntington substantially bolstered its presence in the Florida market. In 1995 the bank acquired three, smaller-size privately owned banks in Florida, more than doubling its asset base in that state to some $600 million. Huntington then pushed its Florida assets past the $1 billion mark in January 1996 when it acquired Peoples Bank of Lakeland, a commercial bank with ten offices in the Lakeland area and assets of approximately $550 million. Later that year, Huntington began offering its customers online banking through Huntington Web Bank. Through this service, Huntington became the first bank in the nation to offer online bill paying.

Further deregulation of the financial services sector enabled Huntington to enter the insurance sector in the mid-1990s. After moving into the insurance market in Michigan in 1995, Huntington the following year acquired Columbus-based life insurance agency Tice & Associates, Inc. Its insurance offerings widened in 1997 through the establishment of Huntington Property and Casualty Insurance Agency, Inc., and then in January 1998 the company acquired another Ohio insurance agency, Cleveland-based Pollock & Pollock, Inc.

Huntington also remained active on the bank acquisition front during this period. In Florida, the bank continued to concentrate on the central part of that state, acquiring Citi-Bancshares, Inc., of Leesburg, Florida, in February 1997 and The Bank of Winter Park that October. The former operated ten branches and had assets of $548 million, while the latter had assets of $90 million. Then in June 1998 Huntington doubled its Florida operations by purchasing 60 former Barnett Bank branches from NationsBank Corporation for $523 million. The deal strengthened Huntington's presence in

central Florida, with the addition of branches stretching from Tampa to Daytona Beach. In the meantime, Huntington completed its largest acquisition yet, the September 1997 purchase of First Michigan Bank Corporation for approximately $1.2 billion in stock. Based in Holland, First Michigan had $3.6 billion in assets and 90 banking offices concentrated in the western part of the state, particularly in Grand Rapids, Holland, Kalamazoo, and Muskegon.

By the end of 1998, Huntington ranked as the 31st largest bank in the United States with assets of $28.3 billion and 529 branches in six states, including 187 in Ohio, 135 in Michigan, and 126 in Florida. That year, takeover activity in the banking industry subsided because of slumping stock prices, and banks began cutting costs as an alternative way of increasing profits. Late in 1998, then, Huntington launched a realignment effort aimed at yielding annual pretax savings of $125 million. The restructuring included layoffs for 1,000 employees, or about 10 percent of the workforce, the closure or sale of 39 branches, and the consolidation of loan-processing offices. Furthermore, as part of an effort to free up resources to invest in operations with higher growth potential, Huntington in October 1999 sold its credit card portfolio to Chase Manhattan Bank, resulting in a net gain of $108.5 million.

EARLY 21ST CENTURY: RESTRUCTURING UNDER NEW LEADERSHIP

Huntington Bancshares began the 21st century in growth mode, adding to its western Michigan operations the ten branches of Traverse City-based Empire Banc Corporation, which had assets of just over $500 million. This June 2000 acquisition, however, came in the midst of a very difficult year. First, the integration of First Michigan had been far from smooth. Huntington fired a number of that bank's executives, upsetting many customers, who took their business elsewhere, including to bank start-ups led by some of the executives who had been terminated. Following these problems in Michigan, Huntington's Florida operations began struggling because of a drop-off in loan originations. Then in the third quarter of 2000, the company was forced to take a $33 million charge to write down the value of its auto-leasing portfolio. All told, net income for 2000 fell 22 percent to $328 million, while the firm's stock price fell sharply and by early 2001 was barely up from its level six years earlier.

Pressure from angry shareholders played at least a partial role in the appointment of a new chief executive in February 2001. Thomas E. Hoaglin, a former executive at Bank One Corporation, succeeded Wobst as

CEO that month and took over the chairmanship six months later. In July 2001 Hoaglin launched a major restructuring, which involved decentralizing operations, cutting the bank's dividend by 20 percent, and closing 38 branches in the Midwest. The most visible part of the plan, however, was Hoaglin's refocusing on the Midwest and his reversal of his predecessor's move into Florida. In September 2001 Huntington reached an agreement to sell its Florida banking business to Sun-Trust Banks, Inc., for $705 million in cash. The deal closed the following February. Later in 2002 Huntington acquired Haberer Investment Advisor, Inc., a Cincinnati-based investment advisory firm with approximately $500 million in assets under management, and LeaseNet Group, Inc., a $90 million leasing company headquartered in Dublin, Ohio. As part of the decentralization effort and also aiming to forge closer relationships with bank customers, Huntington repositioned itself as the "local bank with national resources." Hoaglin's initiatives paid off in 2002 when earnings were up sharply from the previous year.

Huntington's auto-leasing business was a source of further headaches as the bank in 2003 was forced to restate its earnings for prior years three times because of faulty accounting practices that had been adopted in the late 1990s in connection with auto leases. As the Securities and Exchange Commission (SEC) launched an investigation into the matter, Huntington moved to reduce its exposure to the automobile lending and leasing business by selling off more than $1.1 billion in car loans. In January 2004 Huntington reached an agreement to acquire Unizan Financial Corp., a bank based in Canton, Ohio, for $587 million in stock. Late in the year, however, Huntington was forced to put this deal on hold after the Federal Reserve and the Office of the Comptroller of the Currency launched their own probes of the company, focusing on the wider issues of financial reporting and accounting procedures and corporate-governance practices. In the spring of 2005 Huntington reached separate deals with the banking regulators and the SEC. In the case of the SEC, Huntington and three current and former officers, including Hoaglin, agreed to pay more than $8.6 million in civil penalties as part of the settlement. The bank also worked for months with the banking regulators to address their concerns, a process that stretched into late 2005.

With these regulatory issues resolved, Huntington resubmitted its takeover of Unizan to the Federal Reserve Board, which approved the deal in January 2006. The deal was consummated two months later, at a final price of $610 million in stock. Huntington thus added 42 more branches to its Ohio operations, entered the Canton market for the first time, and gained market share in both Dayton and Columbus. At the time of the

acquisition, Unizan had assets totaling $2.5 billion. Also in early 2006, Huntington agreed to purchase the naming rights for a new stadium in Columbus. Scheduled to open in 2008, Huntington Park was to be the new home for the Columbus Clippers, the top minor league baseball team for the New York Yankees.

With low interest rates putting pressure on earnings and the bank's core midwestern market in a prolonged state of economic stagnation, Huntington faced the choice of either aggressively pursuing further acquisitions or becoming increasingly at risk of being swallowed up itself. Hoaglin signaled his preference for the former by reaching an agreement in December 2006 to acquire Sky Financial Group, Inc., for $3.6 billion in stock and cash, a deal that would rank by far as the largest in company history. Sky, which was founded in Bowling Green, Ohio, in 1952 as Bowling Green Banking Co., had been an active consolidator since 1998, growing during that period from $2.2 billion in assets to $17.6 billion. Still based in Bowling Green, Sky was operating more than 330 branches and 400 ATMs in Ohio, central Indiana, northern West Virginia, southern Michigan, and western Pennsylvania. About 70 of the combined banks' 710 branches were earmarked for closure as part of the integration process. In addition to gaining its first presence in Pennsylvania, Huntington by buying Sky stood to gain the number one positions in the Ohio cities of Canton, Toledo, and Youngstown and also to become the number three bank in Indianapolis. Furthermore, it would become the nation's 24th largest bank, with total assets topping $54 billion. The deal was also slated to set up a succession plan at Huntington as Marty Adams, the head of Sky Financial, would become president and COO of Huntington, and he would succeed Hoaglin as CEO at the end of 2009 and as chairman in early 2011. Even before the Sky acquisition was complete, Hoaglin made it clear this would not be the company's last deal in the Midwest, telling *American Banker*, "We have a lot of growth that we'd like to see in other midwestern states."

Dave Mote
Updated, David E. Salamie

PRINCIPAL SUBSIDIARIES

The Huntington National Bank.

PRINCIPAL COMPETITORS

JPMorgan Chase & Co.; National City Corporation; Fifth Third Bancorp; Citizens Financial Group, Inc.; KeyCorp; U.S. Bancorp; Comerica Incorporated.

FURTHER READING

Amatos, Christopher A., "Banker Sees Technology As Source of Profits," *Columbus (Ohio) Dispatch,* December 29, 1992.

Brenowitz, Stephanie, "Huntington Names Chief Executive," *Columbus (Ohio) Dispatch,* January 19, 2001, p. 1C.

————, "Huntington's Wobst Will Leave Top Job," *Columbus (Ohio) Dispatch,* April 20, 2001, p. 1E.

Burns, Adrian, "Sky's Chief Expected to Bring Values, Ability to Huntington," *Business First-Columbus,* March 2, 2007, p. A1.

De Lisser, Eleena, "Huntington to Buy Florida Branches from NationsBank," *Wall Street Journal,* December 10, 1997, p. B12.

Engen, John, "Hunter or Hunted?" *U.S. Banker,* June 2006, pp. 27–28, 30.

Foster, Pamela E., "Bad Loans Prompt Huntington to Trim Jobs," *Business First-Columbus,* June 22, 1992, sec. 1, p. 3.

Fultz, Clair E., *Huntington: A Family and a Bank,* Columbus, Ohio: Huntington Bancshares Inc., 1985, 92 p.

————, *The Huntington: A Story of the Huntington National Bank of Columbus,* New York: Newcomen Society in North America, 1966, 32 p.

Hohmann, George, "Huntington Banks Building $4 Million Fairmont Facility," *State Journal,* May 1994, Sec. 1, p. 22.

Hoke, Kathy, "Shaking Up Huntington," *Business First-Columbus,* July 13, 2001, pp. A3, A36.

"Huntington Bank Gets High Marks for Customer Service, Technology," *Business First-Columbus,* December 14, 1992, sec. 1, p. 6.

"Huntington Celebrates 125th Anniversary with Lasting Contributions," *Columbus (Ohio) Dispatch,* February 16, 1992.

"Huntington COO Sees Long-Range Plans Paying Off," *Columbus (Ohio) Dispatch,* August 9, 1993.

Matthews, Tom, "Huntington, Officers, SEC Settle Case," *Columbus (Ohio) Dispatch,* June 3, 2005, p. 1H.

Miller, James P., "Huntington Bancshares Plans to Slash 10% of Its Work Force to Boost Earnings," *Wall Street Journal,* October 15, 1998, p. A6.

Murray, Matt, "Huntington Bancshares Agrees to Buy First Michigan for $897 Million in Stock," *Wall Street Journal,* May 6, 1997, p. A6.

Novack, Janet, "A Nice, Boring Bank," *Forbes,* September 13, 1993, pp. 56–57.

Pramik, Mike, "First Year Good One for CEO," *Columbus (Ohio) Dispatch,* April 30, 2002, p. 1E.

————, "Huntington Agrees to Buy Unizan," *Columbus (Ohio) Dispatch,* January 28, 2004, p. 1D.

————, "Huntington Bank Continues on Path Blazed by Wobst," *Columbus (Ohio) Dispatch,* December 23, 2001, p. 1E.

————, "Huntington Says Midwest Key to Bank's Turnaround," *Columbus (Ohio) Dispatch,* July 12, 2001, p. 1A.

————, "Huntington to Sell Florida Offices," *Columbus (Ohio) Dispatch,* September 27, 2001, p. 1B.

————, "Making Change," *Columbus (Ohio) Dispatch,* December 23, 2001, p. 1E.

Shingler, Dan, "Huntington Does Growing with Caution," *Crain's Cleveland Business,* February 17, 1992, p. 13.

Stammen, Ken, "Two More Agencies Examining Huntington: Bank's Application to Acquire Unizan Put on Back Burner," *Columbus (Ohio) Dispatch,* November 2004, p. 1E.

Sundaramoorthy, Geeta, "Huntington's Turnaround: At This Midtier, Shades of the Old Bank One," *American Banker,* June 1, 2004, p. 1.

Tatge, Mark, "Piggy Bank," *Forbes,* April 30, 2001, pp. 56, 58.

"Thomas Hoaglin: Huntington's Mr. Fix-It," *U.S. Banker,* August 2001, p. 10.

Trowbridge, Denise, "Huntington Will Buy Sky Bank," *Columbus (Ohio) Dispatch,* December 21, 2006, p. 1G.

Wahl, Melissa, "Huntington Prefers Quiet Growth," *Business First-Columbus,* May 1, 1995, pp. 1, 59.

Wilson, Paul, "Unizan Purchase Is Given Go-Ahead," *Columbus (Ohio) Dispatch,* January 27, 2006, p. 1G.

Wolf, Barnet D., "Huntington Bank Ready to Make Move into Florida," *Columbus (Ohio) Dispatch,* April 12, 1998, p. 1H.

————, "Huntington Offers Settlement: Bank Willing to Pay $7.5 Million to SEC," *Columbus (Ohio) Dispatch,* April 26, 2005, p. 1E.

Huron Consulting Group Inc.

---

550 West Van Buren Street
Chicago, Illinois 60607
U.S.A.
Telephone: (312) 583-8700
Fax: (312) 583-8701
Web site: http://www.huronconsultinggroup.com

Public Company
Incorporated: 2002
Employees: 1,035
Sales: $321.9 million (2006)
Stock Exchanges: NASDAQ
Ticker Symbol: HURN
NAIC: 541611 Administrative Management and General Management Consulting Services; 541618 Other Management Consulting Services

■ ■ ■

Huron Consulting Group Inc. offers financial and operational consulting services to corporate clientele. Huron's financial consulting services are targeted for companies in distress, enabling them to contend with challenges related to bankruptcy, litigation, and regulatory investigations and compliance. The firm's operational consulting services are designed to help financially sound companies enhance revenues and operational efficiency. Based in Chicago, Huron maintains branch offices in Boston; Charlotte, North Carolina; Houston; Los Angeles; New York City; San Francisco; and Washington, D.C. The firm also operates document review centers in Miramar, Florida; Raleigh, North Carolina; and Rock Hill, South Carolina.

ORIGINS

The spectacular, highly publicized collapse of Enron Corporation between 2001 and 2002 had a profound effect on the formation of Huron and the business environment in which the consultancy firm operated. The scandal, a maelstrom of corruption, fraud, and unscrupulous accounting practices, turned an energy-trading company with claimed revenues of $111 billion into a corporate junkyard within a matter of months, making for one of the most notorious cases of managerial malfeasance in modern business history. Investors, employees, and California consumers and businesses, saddled with inflated electricity prices, were among the many victims of Enron's torrid plummet, as was the credibility of U.S. business culture, which was undermined by the "squirrelly behavior of six- and seven-figure accountants, lawyers, CEOs, bankers, and financial analysts who failed at their duty with Enron," as *Business Week* noted in its January 28, 2002, issue. The failure of those with influence cast a pall over the corporate landscape, begging for stricter controls and stricter enforcement by federal authorities. In terms of litigation avoidance and compliance, everything changed in the corporate world after the fall of Enron—creating a fertile environment for enterprising lawyers and consultants—for the type of company Huron would become.

To ensure that the sweeping devastation caused by the Enron scandal would not be repeated, the U.S.

COMPANY PERSPECTIVES

In today's competitive environment, consulting companies must never lose sight of the fact that consulting is a relationship business and must resist the temptation to market their services as products. The work itself becomes routine and unrewarding, and ultimately less valuable for the client. Clients will begin to view the consultant as simply one vendor among many, and base their purchasing decisions solely on price. When this happens, profit margins will decrease and attrition rates will climb. The answer is to focus on value, which is demonstrated by results that meet the client's overall objectives. These results can only be achieved through the implementation of specialized services delivered by teams of talented consultants who understand the needs and wants of their clients.

Congress intervened. Chief among the pieces of legislation enacted in the wake of Enron's collapse (and the other spectacular corporate disaster of the time, WorldCom) was the Sarbanes-Oxley Act, a law created to protect shareholders and the public from accounting errors and fraudulent practices in the corporate setting by stipulating the type and duration of record storage. Federal officials also imposed other corporate regulations, the Securities and Exchange Commission stepped up enforcement actions, and laws were passed restricting auditors from performing consulting work, all of which created market opportunities for Huron. The firm's indebtedness to the collapse of Enron ran deeper, however. The scandal put a group of financial and operational consultants out of work and forced them to start over, a reiteration of professional lives that was manifested as Huron. The first courtroom casualty of the investigation into Enron was Arthur Andersen LLP, one of the "Big Five" accounting firms that performed auditing, tax, and consulting services for the world's largest corporations. In June 2002, Arthur Andersen LLP was found guilty of obstruction of justice, but before a Houston, Texas, jury delivered its verdict, the company had begun to unravel. Its staff of professionals had begun to flee, including a group of financial and operational consultants led by Gary Holdren, a partner and Midwest director of global client services of Arthur Andersen LLP.

The Holdren-led group founded Huron in March 2002, establishing the firm in Chicago, the same headquarters of its former employer, Arthur Andersen LLP. For start-up capital, the fledgling firm relied on Lake Capital Management LLC, a company armed with a $500 million investment fund that picked Huron as its first investment recipient. Lake Capital provided a $100 million investment to the 213 financial and operational consultants composing Huron when the firm commenced operations in May 2002. Holdren, who took the titles of chairman, chief executive officer, and president, set up Huron as a consulting business unaffiliated with a public accounting firm, giving the firm greater flexibility in the post-Enron marketplace. Because Huron was established as an independent consulting firm, the company was not subject to the legal restrictions placed on public accounting firms, namely, restrictions that prohibited public accounting firms from providing certain nonaudit services to their audit clients. Holdren, instead, marshaled his forces to focus on two areas of business, financial consulting and operational consulting, the two segments that composed Huron.

Huron's two business segments provided a wide range of services, services tailored to serve both financially sound and financially distressed corporate clientele. On the financial side, the firm offered analyses and advice to resolve challenges stemming from litigation, disputes, investigations, regulation, and financial distress. Within the financial consulting segment, the disputes and investigations subcategory offered financial analyses to aid law firms and corporations ensnarled in disputes, lawsuits, and regulatory or internal investigations, including forensic accounting expertise to reconstruct complex corporate transactions and events.

Economic consulting, another subcategory of the financial segment, included economic and statistical analyses to support litigation, regulatory hearings, and public policy issues. A third subcategory, corporate advisory services, provided assistance to financially floundering companies, partnering Huron consultants with the management of the distressed client to assess the viability of the business and to develop and to implement a turnaround plan. Within the valuation services subcategory, Huron's financial consulting segment also offered valuation services that determined the value of assets in connection with acquisitions and bankruptcies. The final subcategory, the firm's interim management/focused consulting practice, specialized in distressed healthcare companies, providing onsite senior management, suggesting revenue-cycle improvements, and developing cost-reduction initiatives.

While Huron's financial consultants ministered to the stricken, its operational consultants engaged in more cheerful meetings with their clients. The segment

KEY DATES

2002: Huron is founded in March and commences operations in May.
2003: Huron launches its healthcare practice.
2004: The firm completes its initial public offering of stock.
2005: An acquisition spree begins with the purchase of Speltz & Weiss LLC.
2006: MSGalt & Company, Aaxis Technologies Inc., and Document Review Consulting Services LLC are acquired.
2007: Huron completes the acquisition of Wellspring Partners LTD and Glass & Associates, Inc., in January.

provided services to help clients improve the efficiency of their business by increasing revenue, reducing costs, and managing regulatory compliance issues. Like the financial segment, the operational segment comprised several subcategories, beginning with the firm's higher education practice, which served colleges, universities, hospitals, and academic medical centers by helping such organizations tackle issues related to research administration, regulatory compliance, clinical research, technology planning, and financial management and strategy.

The legal business consulting practice worked in concert with clients' in-house legal departments to improve their organizational design and business processes and with management to assist in the use of outside counsel. Within the legal business consulting practice, a wide range of digital evidence, discovery, and records management services were offered, including computer forensics, data management, document processing, and numerous other services.

A third subcategory focused exclusively on healthcare businesses, providing services to both providers and payers. For providers, the healthcare practice helped hospitals, physicians, and other healthcare organizations improve their operations by performing assessments and implementing solutions addressing cost reduction and efficiency. For payers, the firm focused on compliance and government contracting issues related to federal healthcare programs such as Medicare.

Another subcategory dealt with strategic sourcing, a practice devoted to helping clients navigate through all areas of the procurement process. Strategic sourcing consultants addressed the needs of clients' chief financial officers and chief procurement officers, offering services related to accounts payable and invoice audits, outsourcing advice, contract compliance, and spend analysis, among other services. The final subcategory in the operational segment, performance improvement, comprised consultants who helped clients align their business models, improve efficiency, and realize optimal value from strategic transactions such as mergers and spinoffs.

HURON'S FIRST MONTHS IN BUSINESS

With its own business strategically aligned, Huron set out to win the confidence and the business of the corporate community. The firm generated $1.5 million in its first month of operation, drawing its business from the relationships its billable professionals had cultivated with individuals working in corporations, academic institutions, and leading law firms. Personal contacts, from the start and during the ensuing years, served as Huron's principal means of developing new business, making the addition of new consultants akin to developing new products: as more consultants joined the firm, revenues, theoretically, would increase. Consequently, increases in the firm's payroll, particularly in the number of billable professionals, provided a meaningful yardstick of Huron's expansion, with each new consultant hired bringing his or her own network of business relationships that increased the firm's financial stature. By the end of 2003, Huron's first full year of operation, considerable growth had been achieved in this area. The firm's workforce doubled, lifting revenues above the $100 million mark, helping make Holdren one of the most influential consultants of 2003, as selected by *Consulting Magazine*.

During Huron's first months in operation, the firm relied heavily on the financial side of its business. Turnaround work, such as navigating United Airlines' parent, UAL Corp., through bankruptcy proceedings, fueled the firm's growth. The business derived from turnaround contracts put Huron on its feet, but the need for such consulting work began to diminish by the end of 2003. The firm responded by emphasizing its operational consulting services, namely advising healthcare companies on how to be more efficient and expand into new markets. Huron's efforts in accentuating its healthcare business were bolstered significantly by the arrival of four senior consultants from Cap Gemini Ernst & Young's healthcare practice to the firm's Chicago headquarters in the fall of 2003. As a result, Huron's operational consulting revenues leaped 160 percent between 2003 and 2004, balancing the company's financial footing as it prepared to complete an initial public offering (IPO) of its stock. The firm completed its IPO in October 2004, becoming a publicly traded company two months before it announced revenues had eclipsed $150 million. With more than 600 employees, including billable professionals and administrative staff, Huron had achieved impressive growth during its first two years in business, but the pace of the firm's expansion was about to pick up after the IPO as the Chicago consulting firm turned to the quickest mode of expansion: completing acquisitions.

ACQUISITIONS: 2005–07

Huron added revenue-generating consultants in bunches following its IPO, fleshing out the financial and operational segments of its business by purchasing rivals. The firm's acquisition campaign touched off in May 2005 with the purchase of Speltz & Weis LLC, a consulting firm founded in 2001 by David Speltz and Timothy Weis, who created the firm to lead Syracuse, New York's Crouse Hospital out of bankruptcy. The $17 million transaction added 30 consultants to Huron's ranks, strengthening the firm's interim and crisis-management practice that served the healthcare industry. The deal gave Huron a full menu of service offerings to distressed hospitals and other healthcare facilities, a potentially lucrative market in Holdren's eyes. "I think most of us will agree the healthcare system in the United States has major challenges," he said in a May 16, 2005 interview with *Crain's Chicago Business,* shortly after the Speltz & Weis deal closed. "The consulting dollars spent in the country are in the billions. The changes over the next several years in the healthcare sector will create great opportunities for Huron."

Revenues slipped past $200 million in 2005, more than double the total generated two years earlier, as Huron's expansion efforts elevated its stature within the consulting industry. The firm's acquisitive activity resumed after nearly a yearlong hiatus, with the operational side of its business benefiting from the absorption of a rival. In April 2006, Huron purchased MSGalt & Company, an advisory firm that developed and implemented programs to improve shareholder returns. Next, Huron completed two acquisitions in one month, adding consultants from Document Review Consulting Services LLC and Aaxis Technologies Inc. in July 2006. Document Review, as its name indicated, provided comprehensive document-review services provided by experienced contract reviewers. Aaxis, which strengthened Huron's legal business consulting practice, offered electronic data discovery support to litigation teams and corporate counsel.

By the end of 2006, a look at the yardstick that measured Huron's expansion showed considerable progress. The number of revenue-generating professionals employed by the firm had nearly quadrupled, jumping from the 213 consultants employed at the firm's inception to 842 operational and financial advisers four years later. The expertise of the professionals added to the firm's payroll produced a balanced consulting practice, with the 344 billable professionals working in the financial consulting segment generating 48 percent of Huron's revenue in 2006 and the 498 billable professionals grouped in the operational side generating 52 percent of the firm's revenue. As Huron headed toward its fifth anniversary, plotting its course for the future, the firm was expected to continue expanding through acquisitions.

Activity in early 2007 suggested as much, marking the completion of the firm's largest transaction in its history. Huron acquired Glass & Associates, Inc., a turnaround and restructuring consulting firm, in January, but the deal was overshadowed by the $65 million acquisition of Wellspring Partners LTD during the month. The purchase of Wellspring, which added 65 consultants and $55 million in revenue, expanded Huron's healthcare practice fourfold, broadening its service offerings and extending its geographic reach. In the years ahead, further acquisitions on the scale of the Wellspring deal promised to make Huron a formidable force in the consulting industry, as the Holdren-led organization entrenched itself in the marketplace by helping clients overcome disaster and seize opportunities.

Jeffrey L. Covell

PRINCIPAL SUBSIDIARIES

Huron Consulting Group Holdings LLC; Huron (UK) Limited; Huron Consulting Services LLC; Wellspring Management Services LLC; Aaxis Technologies, Inc.; FAB Advisory Services, LLC.

PRINCIPAL COMPETITORS

FTI Consulting, Inc.; LECG Corporation; Navigant Consulting, Inc.

FURTHER READING

Becker, Cinda, "Consolidation Action," *Modern Healthcare,* May 16, 2005, p. 17.

Evans, Melanie, "Huron Consulting's Expansion," *Modern Healthcare,* January 8, 2007, p. 7.

"Ex-Arthur Andersen Execs File IPO As Deals Emerge," *America's Intelligence Wire,* May 14, 2004.

Murphy, H. Lee, "Huron Takes Plunge As IPO Market

Opens," *Crain's Chicago Business,* May 16, 2005, p. 50.

Nussbaum, Bruce, "Can You Trust Anybody Anymore?" *Business Week,* January 28, 2002.

Reynolds, Adam, "Huron Consulting Is IPO of the Week," *America's Intelligence Wire,* October 13, 2004.

Sachdev, Ameet, "Chicago Private Equity Firm Takes Plunge with Second Consulting Firm Stake," *Chicago Tribune,* October 3, 2003.

Singh, Shruti Date, "Growing Economy to Test Huron," *Crain's Chicago Business,* August 9, 2004, p. 4.

Integra LifeSciences Holdings Corporation

311 Enterprise Drive
Plainsboro, New Jersey 08536
U.S.A.
Telephone: (609) 275-0500
Fax: (609) 275-5363
Web site: http://www.integra-ls.com

Public Company
Incorporated: 1989 as Integra LifeSciences Corp.
Employees: 1,180
Sales: $419.3 million (2006)
Stock Exchanges: NASDAQ
Ticker Symbol: IART
NAIC: 334516 Analytical Laboratory Instrument Manufacturing

■ ■ ■

Integra LifeSciences Holdings Corporation is a Plainsboro, New Jersey-based medical device company that focuses on neurosurgical/orthopedic implants and medical/surgical equipment. It started out involved in the development of biomaterials used to help regenerate skin, used on burn victims to establish a base for skin grafts and on patients undergoing brain surgery who relied on the absorbable material to help in the replacement of large sections of scalp. Integra continues to offer dermal regeneration and engineered wound dressings but has since added implants used in bone regeneration, the repair of peripheral nerves, and in small bone and joint fixation. Products in the company's equipment group complement the implant business and include

ultrasonic surgery systems for tissue removal, brain measuring devices, cranial stabilization and brain retraction systems, devices used to cut and enter the cranial cavity, and equipment to drain cerebrospinal fluid from the brain. Integra also offers instruments used in general, neurosurgical, dental, spinal, and plastic and reconstructive surgery. Integra's products are sold around the world through a direct sales force as well as independent distributors. Integra is a public company listed on the NASDAQ.

FOUNDING IN 1989

Integra was founded in the Philadelphia, Pennsylvania, area by Richard Ernest Caruso in 1989. He was born in Atlantic City in 1943 and used his ability to play football to earn a scholarship to Susquehanna University, where he graduated with an accounting degree in 1965. The following year he earned an advanced business degree from Bucknell University and began his business career as an auditor at Price Waterhouse and Co. in Philadelphia. In 1969 he went to work at LFC Financial Corp., a project financing company located in Radnor, Pennsylvania, that was in effect the restructured and relocated Lytton Financial Corp., a Los Angeles savings and loan firm that had been built by former theatrical press agent and screenwriter Bart Lytton but had been ruined by the crash of the California housing market in the 1960s. Caruso became an executive vice-president and principal at LFC and over the course of more than 20 years at the firm originated some $3 billion of creative lease and project finance transactions.

Although considered a successful man, Caruso was not satisfied with his life. In an interview with *eVentur-*

ing, Caruso admitted, "I did not personally feel successful because, in my mind, I could not point to any substantive real accomplishment other than my financial success." Thus, in 1987 he took a partial sabbatical to earn a Ph.D. from the London School of Economics, establish the Uncommon Individual Foundation to help entrepreneurs to develop and pursue dreams, and find a new business challenge for himself, one that would involve new technology and benefit mankind. He became interested in the idea of developing technology to replace body parts. In 1989, despite an utter lack of medical training, he formed a company focused on regenerative medicine, setting up shop in the Radnor Corporate Center. He soon came across an artificial skin technology that caught his attention, developed by Harvard's Dr. John Burke and Dr. Ioannis Yannas of the Massachusetts Institute of Technology (MIT).

Burke was the director of the Burn Center at Massachusetts General Hospital and Shriners Burns Institute in the early 1970s when he developed a major advance in the treatment of serious burns. By completely removing severely burned skin he hoped to reduce the potential of wound infection, but it also meant an immediate skin graft. At first he relied on skin donors who shared similar genetic markers with the patient. The drawback of this method was the need for immunosuppressant drugs to fend off the body's impulse to reject the graft, resulting in a highly compromised immune system and the possibility of other lethal threats. Burke also tried using the patient's own skin, but with severely burned patients there was limited amounts of skin to be harvested. Burke began searching for another way to rebuild a patient's skin, using a synthetic material. He recruited a partner to help pursue this idea, teaming up with an MIT professor of polymer science and engineering named Dr. Ioannis Yannas. Together they developed a scaffold made from the protein collagen that could be laid down over a wounded area after burned skin was removed and provide a medium in which a patient could regenerate tissue. While this scaffold would be eventually absorbed by the patient's body, a second top layer, a flexible silicon sheet that mimicked the protective function of the top layer of skin, was ultimately removed.

Burke and Yannas's "artificial skin" was patented in 1980 and subsequently licensed by Kansas City, Missouri-based Marion Laboratories, founded by Ewing Marion Kauffman, better known to the public as the owner of the Kansas City Royals Major League Baseball franchise. He invested between $35 million and $50 million in developing the wound care product and along the way acquired a Plainsboro, New Jersey, company called Colla-Tec, Inc., to produce the necessary raw collagen. Clinical trials began in 1986, but three years later Kauffman merged Marion with Merrell Dow Pharmaceuticals to form Marion Merrell Dow, Inc. Burke and Yannas's product still needed further development before it could be presented to the Food and Drug Administration (FDA) for regulatory approval, but because there was not a large enough market for the product, Merrell Dow shelved the project and Colla-Tec was put up for sale. MIT then arranged to take back the product license by promising to pay half of the royalties it might receive by reselling the license.

CARUSO JOINS COMPANY FULL TIME: 1992

Learning that the artificial skin project was on the market, Caruso persuaded Drs. Burke and Yannas as well as MIT to relicense their technology to his company. In 1991 Integra acquired Colla-Tec and two months later acquired some of the technology of Marion Merrell's Wound Care Division. All of these assets were then packaged into a new subsidiary, Integra (Artificial Skin) Corp. Caruso continued his role at LFC, which also invested in Integra. Then, in 1992, he left LFC, bought back all the stock the firm held in Integra, and went to work for the start-up on a full-time basis.

The company began the process to receive FDA clearance for the Integra Artificial Skin Dermal Regeneration Template, while beefing up its capabilities through further acquisitions and adding absorbable medical products used to help with wound care, surgical bleeding, and drug delivery. These products also brought in revenues while the artificial skin product gained regulatory approval. Integra was able to post sales of $8.7 million in 1994 and $10.2 million a year later, but it also lost more than $27 million during this period, much of it due to development work on regenerative technologies for cartilage and peripheral nerves.

In 1995 Integra went public through a reverse merger with a bankrupt listed company, San Diego-based Telios Pharmaceuticals. Early in 1996 Integra made a public offering of stock raising $35 million in much needed cash. More than just providing a convenient way to take Integra public, the Telios acquisition also provided a wealth of intellectual capital,

```
┌─────────────────────────────────────────┐
│                                         │
│            KEY DATES                    │
│                ■                        │
│  ─────────────────────────────────────  │
│  1989:  Company is formed.              │
│  1991:  Wound Care Division of Marion   │
│         Merrell Dow is acquired.        │
│  1995:  Company goes public through     │
│         Telios Pharmaceuticals          │
│         acquisition.                    │
│  1997:  Stuart Essig is named CEO.      │
│  2001:  NeuroSupplies, Inc., is         │
│         acquired.                       │
│  2005:  Newdeal group of companies is   │
│         acquired.                       │
│                                         │
└─────────────────────────────────────────┘
```

including technologies that could be applied to such areas as tissue engineering, cancer treatment, inflammation, immune system regulation, and thrombosis.

A month after the stock offering, in March 1996, the FDA cleared Integra Artificial Skin, which became the first tissue regeneration product to reach the market. Moreover, the company soon received approval from a number of other countries as well. However, the product had a limited market, essentially severe burn patients, and sales did not accelerate sharply. Revenues reached $13.1 million in 1996 and $14.7 million in 1997, while the company lost another $17 million. Clearly a change of direction was needed and to help achieve it Caruso recruited a new chief executive. In late 1997 he hired 36-year-old Stuart M. Essig, a managing director at Goldman, Sachs & Co. where he supervised the medical technology practice.

Essig lacked operational experience, but Integra already had a solid management team in place. Instead, his role was to improve the company's visibility on Wall Street and to find a way to better commercialize the artificial skin product. According to *Investor's Business Daily,* Essig "could have chosen any range of therapeutic targets. But he settled on neurosurgery, or surgery of the brain, spine, neck and central nervous system." Not only was it a fragmented field with no dominant player, the number of neurosurgeons were small enough that a limited sales force could market to them.

REVERSE STOCK SPLIT: 1998

In order to make Integra's stock more attractive to institutional investors, in May 1998 Essig engineered a 1-for-2 reverse stock split. By reducing the number of outstanding shares he was able to inflate the share price, making it more noticeable. Essig also looked to use his experience in mergers and acquisitions to build up a slate of products to create a neurosurgery brand by purchasing established companies. In September 1998

Integra acquired Rystan Company, Inc., the maker of Panafil, an agent used to remove ("debride") burned skin and other wounds. The company then sold the product line to Healthpoint, Ltd., and entered into a comarketing agreement to sell Panafil to burn centers. Integra's telemarketing unit also agreed to sell the product along with Accuzyme, Healthpoint's debriding agent. In addition, in 1998 Integra entered into several business alliances. Sulzer Calcitek, which marketed some of the company's dental products, agreed to fund research to develop the next generation of BioMend, an absorbable tissue product used to restore gum tissue after oral surgery, which had received FDA clearance in 1995. A Johnson & Johnson company, DePuy, agreed to work with Integra on a cartilage regeneration product. Furthermore, Bionx Implants, Inc., and Linvatec Corporation reached deals to develop orthopedic implants.

More repositioning was in store for 1999. In March Integra spent $25 million to acquire the Wisconsin-based NeuroCare Group, a major provider of neurosurgery products, including instruments, monitors, and implants. Integra's research and development efforts were also beginning to pay off, as a pair of internally developed products were launched in 1999: DuraGen Dural Draft Matrix for use in conjunction with cranium and spine surgery, and the Biomend Extend Absorbable Collagen Membrane, used to repair tissue after periodontal surgery. With a wealth of new products to sell, Integra began to experience a significant increase in sales. Revenues improved from $17.5 million in 1998 to $42.9 million in 1999, due almost entirely to the NeuroCare acquisition.

Expansion through acquisitions continued in the new century for Integra as it grew into a one-stop shop for neurosurgeons. In 2000 it bought Clinical Neuro-Care Systems, Inc., for $6.8 million to pick up external ventricular drainage systems and cranial access kits, and it spent another $11.6 million in cash for the cryosurgery product line and handheld neurosurgical instruments of NMT Medical, Inc. The following year Integra acquired a German company, GMSmbH, to add the LICOX Brain Tissue Oxygen Monitoring System at the cost of $2.3 million. A French company, Satelec Medical, maker of an ultrasonic surgical aspirator console and associated handpieces, was also bought for $3.7 million. Finally, in December 2001 Integra paid $4.3 million for NeuroSupplies, Inc., a major specialty distributor to neurologists, hospitals, and others. These new products helped to boost revenues to $71.7 million in 2000 and $93.4 million in 2001, and the company was finally able to turn a profit, recording net earnings of $26.2 million. The company's performance caught the attention of investors, who bid up the price of Integra's stock by 93 percent in 2001. The company was also able to raise $113 million in a secondary offering of stock in August 2001.

Integra continued to expand its sales and distribution channels and bolster its product lines through acquisitions in 2002. They included Signature Technologies, Inc., a contract manufacturer of titanium and stainless steel implants; the neurosciences division of NMT Medical Inc., which added hydrocephalus valves; the NeuroSensor Monitoring system from Novus Monitoring Limited of the United Kingdom; and Padgett Instruments, Inc., a well-established marketer of instruments and other products used in reconstructive, plastic, and burn surgery. Integra also raised another $120 million in a placement of convertible notes to provide it with plenty of ready cash to fuel even further growth.

Revenues increased to $117.8 million in 2002 and net income approached $35.3 million. Momentum carried into the following year for Integra, which improved sales 58 percent to $185.6 million in 2003. The company launched several new products, including a next-generation dural graft product called DuraGen Plus. Acquisitions kept pace as well. JARIT Surgical Instruments, a marketer of surgical instruments used in virtually every surgical discipline, was added at the cost of $42.7 million. In August Integra purchased Tissue Technologies, Inc., the maker of the UltraSoft line of facial implants. Also acquired were Spinal Specialties, Inc., maker of chronic pain management kits, and Reconstructive Technologies, Inc., which offered a tissue expansion device.

Integra introduced close to 20 new products in 2004 and completed four more acquisitions, including the Sparta Surgical line of surgical instruments and critical care devices; R&B Instruments line of spinal and neurosurgical instruments; the Schaerer Mayfield USA, Inc., line of cranial stabilizing and positioning systems as well as skull pins, clamps, headrests, and other associated products; and Berchtold Medizin-Elektronik GmbH, a German manufacturer of electrosurgery generators and an ultrasonic surgical aspirator and related products. The addition of these products helped Integra to increase sales to $229.8 million in 2004.

Revenues increased to $277.9 million in 2005 and earnings totaled $37.2 million. All told, the company introduced 15 new products. The year also saw Integra become involved in an entirely new business that focused on the pathologies of the foot and ankle, supported by the acquisitions of the Newdeal group of companies, a French maker of foot and ankle surgery products. The combination of internally developed products and acquired products proved to be a successful formula in 2006. Integra increased sales to $419.3 million while recording net income of $29.4 million.

Ed Dinger

PRINCIPAL SUBSIDIARIES

Integra Healthcare Products LLC; Integra LifeSciences Corporation; Integra NeuroSciences (International), Inc.; Integra NeuroSciences (IP), Inc.; J. Jamner Surgical Instruments, Inc.; Jarit Instruments, Inc.; Newdeal, Inc.; Spinal Specialties, Inc.

PRINCIPAL COMPETITORS

B. Braun Medical Ltd.; Codman & Shurtleff, Inc.; Medtronic, Inc.

FURTHER READING

Davis, Alison, "Fact Sheet: NIGMS-Supported Basic Research on Skin Replacement Following Burn or Trauma Injury," *National Institute of General Medical Sciences,* June 18, 1999.

Goldblatt, Dan, "Integra LifeSciences Hires a Heavy Hitter," *Business News New Jersey,* January 19, 1998, p. 1.

———, "Integra's Big Score," *Business News New Jersey,* March 20, 1996, p. 14.

Grugal, Robin M., "Integra LifeSciences Holdings Corp. Plainsboro, New Jersey Shift to Neurosurgery Is a Brainy Move After All," *Investor's Business Daily,* February 20, 2002, p. A09.

Reeves, Amy, "Integra LifeSciences Holdings Corp. Plainsboro, New Jersey Overhaul Helps Med Firm Skin the Competition," *Investor's Business Daily,* July 30, 2001, p. A09.

"Shared 'Uncommon' Vision Leads to Birth of Regenerative Medicine," http://www.eventuring.org, November 21, 2006.

Smith, Carol, "Artificial Skin Offers Genuine Hope," *Seattle Post-Intelligencer Reporter,* February 23, 2001.

International Profit
Associates, Inc.

—■—

1250 Barclay Boulevard
Buffalo Grove, Illinois 60089
U.S.A.
Telephone: (847) 808-5590
Fax: (847) 808-5599
Web site: http://www.ipa-iba.com

Private Company
Incorporated: 1991
Employees: 1,800
Sales: $250 million (2006 est.)
NAIC: 561110 Office Administrative Services

■ ■ ■

International Profit Associates, Inc. (IPA), is a controversial small business management consulting firm based in Buffalo Grove, Illinois. The company claims to have helped more than 175,000 small and medium-size businesses by offering corporate strategy, tax advice, mergers and acquisitions help, and executive coaching services. Sister company Integrated Business Analysis provides similar services in Canada. IPA associates itself with prominent politicians, including former Presidents Gerald Ford, George H. W. Bush, and Bill Clinton, all of whom have spoken at the company's annual Christmas "Celebration of Success" dinner, and then touts these appearances in its promotional materials. IPA also makes contributions to politicians, but some have returned the company's money in light of persistent complaints from clients and employees and the criminal record of its chief executive, John R. Burgess. Clients are

usually contacted first by a telemarketer who sets up an appointment with a field salesperson whose task is to persuade the business owner to contract for a survey analysis.

The company's main selling ploy is to promise that the client will see a three dollar return on every dollar spent on consulting fees. The survey analyst spends two or three days studying the business, then provides an oral analysis, the purpose of which is to convince the client to bring in a team of IPA consultants to address the problems the analyst has uncovered. IPA has received an unsatisfactory rating from the Better Business Bureau of Chicago and Northern Illinois because of a steady stream of complaints about its high-pressure sales tactics, the dubious suggestions it provides clients, and the aggressive way it pursues debts. The company's practices have also prompted an investigation by the Illinois attorney general, and the Chicago office of the Equal Employment Opportunity Commission filed a federal lawsuit in the early 2000s on behalf of more than 100 women, former employees who have alleged sexual harassment by Burgess and other executives.

COMPANY FOUNDED: 1991

IPA was founded in 1991 by Burgess and two colleagues, Charles W. Morton and Bruce Tulio, who worked for the consulting firm of George S. May International Co. Born in Cranston, Rhode Island, in 1949, Burgess grew up in less than privileged circumstances, according to a 2000 profile in *Inc.* magazine. At the age of 12 he launched his business career by selling eggs door to door, then held a number of jobs to work his way through school at Roger Williams College and later the New England School of Law. Instead of practicing law he spent three years working for Pillsbury Co. as a soybean-meal trader. When he left, Pillsbury sued to recover more than $70,000 in commissions that it claimed were based on inaccurate trading profits. In the end the two sides reached a settlement and Burgess paid Pillsbury $10,000.

While wrangling with Pillsbury, Burgess began practicing law in the Buffalo, New York area in the late 1970s. He developed a thriving practice that gained a reputation for representing women involved in divorce cases. After about five years his license was suspended when he pleaded guilty in Erie County Supreme Court, related to an incident with a 16-year-old prostitute in his law-office building, and he paid a $500 fine. He continued to practice law but complaints from clients began piling up at the Grievance Committee of the Eighth Judicial District of New York. According to *Inc.,* the most serious charge was "$40,000 inexplicably missing from an escrow account of a deceased 38-year-old nurse's estate that Burgess had represented." As a result of that case, court records indicate he was disbarred in July 1987. Then, in March 1988 he pleaded guilty to attempted grand larceny, for which he was fined $1,000 and sentenced to three years of probation. Burgess reached bottom in May 1989 when he and his wife filed for Chapter 7 personal bankruptcy.

Undaunted, Burgess reinvented himself as a small business consultant, finding work with George S. May as an executive survey analyst. He was apparently well suited to the work, rising quickly through the ranks so that in a mere two years he was the head of the survey department. Just as quickly, Burgess left the firm, the circumstances of his departure proving somewhat murky. Burgess told *Inc.* that he was disenchanted with

May's "perpetual turnover, and they expected me to yell and scream all day long. I was too young to have a heart attack and die." In subsequent court fights with May, however, a different story emerged in court testimony and sworn depositions. May's president, Donald Fletcher, testified that Burgess brought a prostitute into the company's boardroom in August 1991 and when Fletcher confronted him, Burgess admitted the incident. Fletcher then said he gave Burgess the choice of resigning or being fired. In a sworn deposition Burgess acknowledged that he had a prostitute in the May boardroom, but maintained that it "had very little to do with my resigning."

Regardless of the circumstances, Burgess left May in the late summer of 1991. Having signed a noncompete clause at May, which prohibited him for going to work with a May competitor, Burgess decided to start a rival firm. More than 20 former coworkers attended an organizational meeting at his apartment, and ten signed on, including his two cofounders and eight others. Cofounders Morton and Tulio were not strangers to legal problems either. Morton was convicted of a misdemeanor in 1988 for stealing Hummell figurines from three Pittsburgh, Pennsylvania, stores, while a year later across the state in Philadelphia Tulio pleaded guilty to involvement in the manufacture of a major ingredient of methamphetamine. Tulio would soon have a falling out with Burgess and leave IPA, and Morton sold out several years later and retired.

Burgess and his partners incorporated IPA in Illinois and set up shop in Wheeling, Illinois, the three of them sharing two desks. The company led a hand-to-mouth existence in the early days, relying on the credit cards of employees to make ends meet while it drummed up business and fought off the legal challenge of May, which took little time to take the new firm to court, alleging that IPA appropriated trade secrets and used May's forms and programs. It was just the first of more than a dozen lawsuits the two companies traded over the next decade. In 1996 Burgess provided *Crain's Chicago Business* with his explanation for the animosity between the two firms: "They don't like us because of the 585 people who work here, 200 came from there." He added that May "just wants to control the marketplace. They want to deny us our right to compete."

IPA would be taken to court by a wide variety of other litigants as well. According to *Inc.,* employee Karen Marchesseault "sued IPA and Burgess, Tulio, and Morton to recover $40,000 in travel expenses charged to her American Express cards. An employee temp agency, a snowplowing service, a bank, and even IPA's former law firm were among creditors who sued to collect on

KEY DATES

1991: Company is founded.
1993: Company moves to Buffalo Grove, Illinois.
1995: Canadian operations are launched.
1997: IPA Advisory & Intermediary Services is established.
2000: Second Buffalo Grove facility is acquired.
2003: Accountancy Associates, LLC, and ITA Implementation Services are formed.

IPA's allegedly unpaid bills." Many other lawsuits would be filed by former employees over unpaid commissions and by clients dissatisfied with the work the company performed.

HEADQUARTERS MOVE TO BUFFALO GROVE: 1993

Although in the early months IPA spent more on legal bills than it received in revenues, it began to grow steadily. It claimed revenues of $5 million in 1992. A year later the company moved to Buffalo Grove, Illinois, where it built a new headquarters. In 1994 revenues reached $24 million, according to the company. IPA expanded into Canada with the launch of Integrated Business Analysis. With sales of more than $33 million in 1996, IPA laid claim to being the fastest growing management consulting company in the industry.

The company achieved this growth by churning through hundreds of employees who, according to *Crain's Chicago Business,* had "abruptly quit or been fired." Every two weeks a dozen to two-dozen business analysts were recruited, lured in part by classified ads that read, "Self-motivated individuals with strong communications skills and a burning desire to succeed can realistically earn a six-figure income while enjoying extensive travel throughout the U.S." The accepted applicants then paid their own travel expenses in order to attend a one-week training class at the Buffalo Grove site. Here they learned how to "condition" prospective clients into contracting IPA consulting services by creating a sense of urgency. According to training materials quoted by *Crain's,* "Through the practice of dropping bombs on the client during the course of the survey, and leaving the client with a crisis at the end of the day, the client's temperature is risen and urgency is instilled." As a result, the client often sought IPA services and did not have to be sold directly. The next day IPA consultants arrived to begin work, giving clients little time to have a change of heart. At the other end of the transaction were telemarketers who worked in two six-hour shifts, cold calling small businesses and setting up appointments for the sales reps, who paved the way for the analysts by making a two-hour pitch that culminated in a flat-fee agreement for a survey. The analyst, in effect, was just another salesperson involved in the process of landing a client. Overseeing it all was Burgess monitoring whiteboards that kept track of hourly quotas and demanding that the different units keep up the expected pace.

Burgess spent some of IPA's profits on its annual "Celebration of Success" dinner and began inviting, and paying, politicians to be keynote speakers. In 1997 former President Gerald Ford spoke. A year later it was Bob Dole, former senator and unsuccessful presidential candidate. In 1999 former President George H. W. Bush spoke, receiving a reported $82,000. In 2001 the man who beat him, Bill Clinton, would be the Christmas speaker, his fee: $125,000. His wife, Hillary Clinton, spoke at the gala in 2004. Burgess was photographed with the speakers and the pictures were often included in sales materials, providing IPA with reflected credibility. Along the way, IPA executives contributed generously to a wide assortment of state and national officeholders, although a number of them began to return the money as IPA received increasingly unfavorable notice in the press.

In the second half of the 1990s, IPA expanded its service offerings by creating what it called strategic alliances but were in effect subsidiaries. It formed IPA Advisory & Intermediary Services in 1997 to help small companies in such areas as mergers and acquisitions, debt financing, and equity investments. To keep up with the company's growth, IPA began construction on a 50,000-square-foot headquarters in 1998. A year later the company said it topped the $100 million mark, and boasted that it had reached this distinction faster than any other management consulting company. Also in 1999 IPA formed a second strategic alliance, International Tax Advisors, Inc. This unit provided strategic tax planning services and also handled problems that clients might have with tax collection agencies. Moreover, at the end of the decade IPA began offering to business owners professional development coaching.

With business continuing to grow, IPA expanded its headquarters to 93,000 square feet by acquiring a second facility in Buffalo Grove. A year later the company reported $150 million in annual sales, and in 2002 claimed that between its U.S. and Canadian operations it employed more than 1,500 people. Two more strategic alliances were formed in 2003: Accountancy Associates, LLC, and ITA Implementation Services to provide such services as tax planning, estate structuring and succession planning, and accounting compliance.

REVENUES REACH $250 MILLION: 2006

In 2006 the IPA family of companies claimed to reach $250 million in annual revenues. However, IPA also continued to court controversy in the new century. Complaints continued to pile up at the Better Business Bureau, and although IPA maintained that it resolved all of them, it was classified as having an unsatisfactory record because the root causes had not been addressed. In February 2005 the company reached an agreement with the Wisconsin attorney general's office to cease deceptive business practices.

In May 2006 the *New York Times* reported that the Illinois state attorney general's office had received more than 200 complaints against IPA since 2001 and was investigating the company. Moreover, since the early 2000s IPA had been contesting a lawsuit filed by the Equal Employment Opportunity Commission on behalf of more than 100 women. The suit, the *Times* reported, asserted that IPA "executives routinely harassed female subordinates with crude comments, groping and demands for sex. Mr. Burgess himself was accused by a former employee of making comments about her body and 'telling her that her future with the company depended on having sex with him,' the lawsuit said." "'This is probably the most egregious case of sex harassment that the Chicago district office has seen,' the commission's lead attorney, Diane Smason, observed. 'The owner of the company engaged in harassment, and that set the tone for the company, on down.'"

In addition to legal fees and political donations, IPA spent considerable amounts of time and money on charitable activities. It organized an annual company blood drive for the American Red Cross, and made contributions to such causes as the Chicago public schools, the Columbine Memorial, the Susan G. Komen Breast Cancer Foundation, the U.S. Holocaust Memorial Museum, and the Special Olympics Windy City Rubber Ducky Derby.

Ed Dinger

PRINCIPAL SUBSIDIARIES

Integrated Business Analysis; Advisory & Intermediary Services; International Tax Advisors; ITA Implementation Services.

PRINCIPAL COMPETITORS

The Corporate Executive Board Company; George S. May International Company; GP Strategies Corporation.

FURTHER READING

Fuller, James, "Company's Founder Has a Past of Highs and Lows," *Daily Herald* (Arlington Heights, Ill.), January 10, 2004, p. 7.

Hall, Dee J., "Businessman Settles Suit Against IPA," *Wisconsin State Journal,* April 15, 2006, p. B5.

Johnson, Julie, "Complaints Follow Small Biz Consultant," *Crain's Chicago Business,* February 16, 2004, p. 1.

McIntire, Mike, "Rubbing Shoulders with Trouble, and Presidents," *New York Times,* May 7, 2006, p. 1.

Oloroso, Arsenio, Jr., "This Consultancy's on Fast Track," *Crain's Chicago Business,* July 29, 1996, p. 1.

Rosenbloom, Joseph, "'I'm John Burgess. I'm Here to Help You,'" *Inc.,* June 2000, p. 68.

The Supply Chain Company™

i2 Technologies, Inc.

1 i2 Place, 11701 Luna Road
Dallas, Texas 75234-6026
U.S.A.
Telephone: (469) 357-1000
Toll Free: (877) 926-9286
Fax: (469) 357-1798
Web site: http://www.i2.com

Public Company
Founded: 1989 as Intellection
Employees: 2,044
Sales: $279.7 million (2006)
Stock Exchanges: NASDAQ
Ticker Symbol: ITWO
NAIC: 511210 Software Publishers; 541511 Custom
Computer Programming Services

■ ■ ■

i2 Technologies, Inc., develops and implements software designed to simplify supply and demand chain management processes for maximal efficiency and cost savings to manufacturers and retailers. Software components provide support for different aspects of the supply chain process: forecasting demand; determining materials/parts procurement and delivery; inventory control; production planning and scheduling; order fulfillment; and distribution logistics. i2 products ease analysis of multiple streams of information and events that may affect management decisions. The uniqueness of i2's software lies in the ability to account for unexpected events and to provide a feedback loop that allows for rapid

rescheduling without slowing the movement of numerous production or distribution orders. i2 is the innovation leader in supply and demand chain management solutions; however, due to management missteps, i2's market share does not reflect this technological advantage. Nevertheless, i2 utilizes its technological advantage to specialize in custom design of sophisticated supply and demand chain management systems. With more than 900 customers, i2's primary base is involved in the manufacture of high-tech, automotive, aerospace, defense, industrial, metals, and consumer products; the company also serves the retail and distribution sectors. FreightMatrix.com provides online logistical support for the transportation component of supply chain planning. i2 offers its products through alliances with IBM, Accenture, Infosys, and other software service providers, as well as through its own sales team.

SEEDS OF A SOFTWARE
TECHNOLOGY INNOVATION

Before developing an interest in computer technology and founding i2, Sanjiv Sidhu followed in the footsteps of his father, a chemist who directed India's system of government laboratories. Sidhu attended the elite Hyderabad Public School in southern India, and at Osmania University he obtained a degree in chemical engineering. He moved to the United States in 1980 and entered Oklahoma State University, where he received a master's degree in chemical engineering. Sidhu started a Ph.D. program in systems and control engineering at Case Western University in Cleveland, but quit in his eagerness to enter the world of work. In 1984 he obtained a technical staff position at the

COMPANY PERSPECTIVES

What makes i2 *the* supply chain company? We focus all our efforts on delivering solutions and services that bring bottom-line benefits to our customers. We're passionate about leading the charge and setting the standards—for the new generation of supply chain management technology. It's only through our customers' successes that we can become truly successful as a company.

industrial systems division at Texas Instruments (TI) in Tennessee, but as computer technology accelerated, Sidhu developed a passion for the potential of computer applications to solve business problems. In order to pursue this passion, Sidhu requested a transfer to TI's artificial intelligence laboratory in Dallas. There he saw the potential of applying new artificial intelligence techniques to create effective supply chain management processes. In 1988 Sidhu left TI to experiment with supply chain management software applications. Supported by his then-pregnant wife, Lekha, Sidhu spent two years programming software in the couple's two-bedroom apartment.

Sidhu's innovations involved changing the way systems worked with data to supply materials to the factory floor in a timely and cost effective manner. The standard manufacturing resource planning (MRP) software started from the delivery due date and worked backward to determine the sequence of supply and production schedules. The limitations of this method included an inability to respond quickly to unexpected occurrences, such as a machinery breakdown, a material supply problem, or a customer order change. While the use of relational database programs had increased flexibility of MRP and enterprise resource planning (ERP) software, it retained limitations of data and methods based on rigid assumptions about production and supplier lead times. Sidhu was not concerned with replacing such platforms, but to develop complementary software that would improve flexibility and functionality by implementing a concurrent supply chain planning strategy.

To achieve this, Sidhu applied concepts of constraint propagation, a subdiscipline of artificial intelligence which focused on the limitations involved in completing a specific task in order to determine how to perform that task. Sidhu accounted for multiple, global supply streams and complex contingencies, and he considered the interdependence of the whole system of materials availability, the production process, and delivery logistics, as well as fixed constraints, such as maximum production capacity and delivery date. Through mathematical modeling, Sidhu replicated real-life production runs in a virtual environment. An algorithm search evaluated various manufacturing plans by processing thousands of these virtual production runs; then it offered a selection of the best options. Thus, the software eliminated the guesswork usually involved in production planning. Sidhu's innovation potentially saved manufacturing companies the cost of holding excess materials inventory or the loss of business due to production delays. Other software capabilities, such as forecasting, auditing production capacity, recording due dates, and monitoring inventory, provided additional information for production run modeling. In effect, Sidhu's supply chain philosophy facilitated the industrial shift from mass production to "order-driven" production.

DEVELOPING A BUSINESS STRATEGY FOR PRAGMATIC UTILIZATION

Sidhu formed Intellection in 1989 and began to offer software design services in supply chain management. Initially, he developed custom software based on a customer's existing, proprietary mainframe or minicomputer system. Over time he developed a pre-configured template adaptable to enterprise resource applications. At this point Sidhu created a partnership with Ken Sharma, another TI alumnus. In marketing the software, Sharma contributed expertise as a manufacturing management consultant.

To start the marketing process, Sidhu and Sharma attended a trade show in New Orleans, but they found it difficult to convince potential customers of the validity of their method. Then, in 1991, Intellection found its first major customer in Timken, Co., a multimillion-dollar steel manufacturer. Very quickly after software implementation, Timken observed a 30 percent reduction in inventory, a 50 percent reduction in "cycle time" for steel bar products, and a 25 percent improvement for on-time delivery of finished products. Intellection found another customer in Solectron, a computer circuit board maker in Silicon Valley. Solectron purchased a $500,000 software package and recouped the investment within nine months through a 30 percent increase in inventory turnover and a 25 percent reduction in carrying costs. By focusing on the money-saving potential of their software, rather than the technical specifications, Intellection began to attract more customers. In the years that followed the company obtained business from a number of *Fortune* 500 companies.

KEY DATES

1988: Sanjiv Sidhu quits his full-time job to develop innovative supply chain software.

1989: Company is founded as Intellection.

1991: The company achieves its first successful implementation of supply chain software with a major customer.

1996: Company, now known as i2 Technologies, Inc., initiates public stock offering; revenues reach $76 million.

2000: i2 launches online trading and distribution products; revenues reach $1 billion.

2001: The high-tech investment bust and product integration issues trouble i2.

2003: SEC probe, NASDAQ delisting, and loss of market share exacerbate problems.

2004: i2 introduces closed-loop supply chain concept into marketing strategy.

2005: New CEO Michael McGrath restructures organization; NASDAQ relists i2.

Intellection expanded by opening several offices nationwide which provided onsite consulting and customer training. The company formed marketing partnerships with other software sales and implementation companies, such as Baan, IBM, SAP, System Software Associates (SSA), and Marcam. These companies sold i2 software, given the brand-name Rhythm in 1992, in conjunction with other MRP and ERP products, including Oracle and PeopleSoft; in return, Intellection paid royalties on sales. With software packages priced from $100,000 to $12 million, depending on specific components, revenues doubled every year between 1991 and 1995, from $1.6 million in 1991 to $26 million in 1995.

The rapid pace of growth continued in 1996, particularly as the company, by this time operating under the name i2, pursued international expansion. In late 1995, i2 had its software and program manuals translated into Spanish, Japanese, German, and French. Over the next year, i2 opened sales, service, and/or support offices in Australia, Canada, Belgium, Denmark, Germany, the United Kingdom, Japan, Singapore, and Mexico. In 1996 overseas revenues accounted for 26 percent of revenues of $76 million. In 1997, i2 opened offices in Korea, India, Hong Kong, and Taiwan.

After an initial public offering of stock in 1996 raised funds to continue research and development and

operations expansion, the pattern of success continued in 1997. That year i2 introduced an upgraded version of its software. Though new competitors in supply chain management software had emerged, including SAP, Oracle, and J.D. Edwards, i2's upgrades were considered to be at least a year ahead of software offered by these companies. Sales to high technology companies, such as Dell Computer and Compaq Computer, supported i2 sales as well as its technology lead, as no one wanted their competition to have an advantage through the efficiency of the most advanced supply chain management technology available. As such, revenues more than doubled again, to $200.07 million in 1997.

APPLYING EXPERTISE TO CREATE INTERNET TECHNOLOGY

When the Internet evolved as an avenue for the conduct of business during the late 1990s, Sidhu saw the potential value that i2's supply chain management capabilities might bring to web-based business transactions. In order to apply Rhythm technology to the needs of Internet operations, i2 acquired companies involved in Internet development. Notably, the acquisition of Smart Technologies provided i2 with external, customer-facing e-commerce technology to complement its back-of-the-house supply chain systems. Under the name "Intelligent eBusiness," i2 launched Internet-based supply chain products which simplified customer order fulfillment through links to one or more suppliers. i2 intended the products to provide a single hub for online trading within an industry community.

The notion of facilitating online trading manifested in the development of TradeMatrix.com, introduced by i2 in October 1999. From the web-based platform buyers could search for the best price of a product based on volume of purchase, and sellers could provide accurate information as to order fulfillment. Working with major software and hardware companies, i2 developed a similar virtual trading hub for the semiconductor procurement in the electronics industry, HightechMatrix.com, introduced in January 2000. To support the transportation logistics element of supply chain management, i2 launched the online service FreightMatrix.com.

To strengthen its position in the field of business-to-business supply chain transactions, i2 acquired Aspect Development, a major competitor, for $9.3 billion through a stock exchange. i2 gained a database management system covering 17 million parts from 7,000 manufacturers. Another acquisition, of Supplybase, Inc., gave i2 the capability, via the Internet, to match buyers with suppliers of custom parts and assemblies in the high-technology, automotive, medical, and consumer electronics industries. By providing much needed content for supply chain transactions, the acquisition of the two companies would shift i2's role in e-commerce, from that of portal server and software provider to that of lead contractor for complete business-to-business vendor management projects.

Toward that end, in August 2000, i2 launched the TradeMatrix Network, Internet-based tools for publishing, searching, and managing content. The Discovery Content Management Solution Suite provided a 10,000-product template for the publication of product information on the web. Other capabilities included buyer search and match, customized pricing and contract terms, and collaboration with suppliers. The Supplier Network would provide users access to many of the largest maintenance, repair, and operations suppliers (MRO), accounting for approximately five million products, ranging from janitorial and office supplies to industrial and electrical raw materials.

TURMOIL FOLLOWING HIGH-TECH EXPLOSION

i2 experienced some success with its online marketplace tools, implementing a number of public and private systems; however, progress stalled along with confidence in Internet stocks and high technology in 2000. Disenchantment with the financial performance of high technology companies thwarted investment in the stock market, while disappointment with human limitations to effectively and quickly activate new technologies thwarted investment in large software systems. While i2 attained an achievement highpoint, reporting $1 billion in revenues for 2000, this event occurred along with these market changes and as major problems came to light at i2.

For i2, as for other companies, software implementations often stalled in large-scale, complex customization projects. At i2, such problems reached a climax in February 2001, when Nike missed its sales targets due to an inventory forecasting mishap. Though the software implementation by Cisco Systems involved products from other companies, Nike publicly attributed the problem to i2's software. As a result of faulty data, Nike shouldered $2.25 billion in excess inventory. The situation caused loss of customer and investor confidence in i2 and the financial problems that followed.

i2's attempt to address these new difficulties began with Sidhu's resignation as CEO, though he retained the position of chairman of the board; company President Greg Brady became CEO. Brady attempted a 120-day turnaround plan that included layoff of 10 percent of employees in May 2001 and improvements to

sales and service. Yet the damage had been done. After a continual, spectacular rise in revenues during the 1990s, i2 sales declined 12 percent in 2001, to $986 million. Moreover, the company reported an operating loss of $149 million, not including a $7.75 billion write-down in goodwill and termination of certain research and development projects. By April 2002 Brady resigned, and Sidhu resumed the CEO position.

Financial problems persisted as i2 lost significant market share. Potential customers purchased supply chain software from financially secure companies, even though those products did not provide the same quality of capability as i2 software. The company experienced a devastating second quarter in 2002, with a 52 percent decline in revenues, compared to the previous year, and a net loss of $757.4 million. In July, i2 announced another round of measures to reduce costs by at least 30 percent. These included layoffs of as many as 1,400 of 4,800 employees. i2's focus on the Internet had impeded satisfactory customer service, so the move generated fear that concurrent product implementations might be hindered by staff turnover. i2 pruned nonessential products, closed offices, scaled back system support, and began to relocate some technology development to India.

Two events compounded the turmoil. First, i2 announced a Securities and Exchange Commission (SEC) probe into the company's accounting practices, requiring a reaudit to begin from 1998. During the reaudit process i2 failed to file its 2002 annual report to the SEC, causing the NASDAQ to stop trading the stock on March 31, 2003, and to delist the stock on May 9. The following July, the reaudit revealed a total revenue reduction of $359.7 million in sales reported as earnings before payments were received. As much as $232 million represented potential future sales, however. Cumulative net losses increased to $297.1 million.

During its financial problems, i2 persevered in restructuring its product line to ease implementation and in restoring customer confidence. In March 2003, the company launched i2 Six, the newest version of its supply chain management software. Master Data Management, the key component to the success of the software, used existing ERP applications to derive critical data for supply chain planning. New features included faster information processing, industry specific templates, and a virtual modeling process that accounted for transportation and other supplier information in real time. i2's Six software provided a tool kit to ease data integration and workflow development. Customer service improvements involved simplifying communications by assigning account managers to specific customers. Business optimization entailed follow-up to product implementation and flexible software license pricing. Also, i2 developed a plan to analyze persistent problem areas and institute change within 90 days.

With the release of Six Two software, Sidhu began to use new language to more accurately describe i2's software capabilities, from simply "supply chain management" to "supply and demand chain management." He emphasized the "closed-loop" approach to supply chain management, a next-generation technology that extended from the planning component to tracking and executing the plan through continuous feedback. With the closed-loop method, i2 sought to compete with broad-based ERP vendors, who had gained market share during i2's retrenchment. i2 worked with Payless and Bed Bath & Beyond to develop these tools for retail companies, an area of significant sales growth and growth potential. While i2's confidence increased with a new vision for supply and demand chain technology, customer and investor confidence remained uncertain, as revenue declined, from $494.9 million in 2003, to $389.3 million in 2004.

An infusion of capital in April 2004 supported i2's goal to resolve the past and turn the company toward stability and profitability. Sidhu invested $20 million to cover a $10 million penalty to the SEC for i2's accounting irregularities, and Q Investments, a major shareholder and convertible debt holder, invested $100 million. Along with investment came two new board members, one of whom, Michael McGrath, became CEO of i2 in February 2005. McGrath brought several years experience in software consulting, as a principle in a major consulting firm. Having followed i2 for many years, McGrath believed that the company had solid product viability, but the financial organization continued to trouble the company. Along with other cost-cutting measures, McGrath executed a 15 percent reduction in the workforce, from 2,000 people to 1,700. He sold nonessential data and content businesses, garnering $43 million. McGrath applied the funds toward total debt reduction of $210 million.

To generate revenue, i2 focused on its core competency, supply chain management, but with the intention of selling next-generation solutions rather than software licenses. i2 succeeded in selling small, manageable systems that could be broadened incrementally through implementation of complementary software until a complete custom system was in place. Even though i2 continued to lead in supply chain innovations, in order to compete the company needed to provide a more efficient means of delivering services and to provide extraordinary cost savings through complex customization. This meant offering clients a streamlined approach to integration with existing enterprise systems.

Toward this end, in June 2005 i2 introduced the Agile Business Process Platform, software architecture for vertical market integration. The flexibility of service oriented architecture (SOA) carried potential to transform the field of supply chain management, so an early lead in this area gave i2 a competitive advantage. Other new i2 products and enhancements, such as its order cycle management process, order hub infrastructure, and transportation logistics capabilities, further solidified the company's technological lead in handling complex supply and demand chain processes.

The combination of cutting costs and continuing supply chain innovations effected positive change at i2. The NASDAQ relisted the company on July 21, 2005, and i2 became profitable on the strength of new business. For 2005, i2 reported $43 million in net operating profit from $337 million in revenues. Profitability gave i2 maneuverability to position itself for growth. In February 2006, i2 acquired RiverOne, a supply chain software vendor with customers in electronics manufacturing services not served by i2. Also, RiverOne contributed collaboration capabilities to i2's existing tools. Though the divestment of certain businesses at i2 caused revenues to decline to $280 million in 2006, positive evaluations of its products buttressed investor confidence, and the company's stock value rebounded to around $30 per share in early 2007.

Mary Tradii

PRINCIPAL SUBSIDIARIES

i2 Ltd. (U.K.); i2 Technologies BV (Netherlands); i2 Technologies Gmbh (Germany); i2 Technologies Pty Ltd. (Australia); i2 Technologies Nv (Belgium); i2 Technologies Pte Ltd. (Singapore); i2 Technologies Sarl (France).

PRINCIPAL DIVISIONS

Automotive; Aerospace and Defense, Industrial, and Metals (AAIM) Industry Group; Consumer Products Industry Group; High Tech Industry Group; Retail and Distribution Industry Group.

PRINCIPAL COMPETITORS

Adexa, Inc.; Agile Software Corporation; Ariba, Inc.; JDA Software Group; Oracle Corporation; SAP Aktiengesellschaft.

FURTHER READING

Ahles, Andrea, "Deal Will Give Software Firm Infusion of Cash," *Fort Worth Star-Telegram*, April 29, 2004.

Aston, Adam, "A Supply-Chain Whiz Comes Back Wiser; Says Returning i2 CEO Sidhu: Smaller Projects Are Smarter," *Business Week,* June 3, 2002, p. 78B.

Bartholomew, Doug, "Supply Chain Moves Online," *Industry Week,* March 20, 2000, p. 52.

Beller, Peter C., "Death-Defying Acts," *Forbes,* January 8, 2007, p. 44.

Blanchard, Dave, "Closing the Loop: i2 Technologies' Sanjiv Sidhu on the Current State of the Supply Chain Market," *Logistics Today,* November 2003, p. 44.

"B2B Software: i2's New Products Let Businesses Share More Info.," *Investor's Business Daily,* May 10, 2001, p. A04.

Callahan, Sean, "Partners' Campaign a Study in Quickness; IBM, i2, Ariba e-Marketplace Coalition," *B to B,* September 11, 2000, p. 14.

Deck, Stewart, "IBM, i2 Plan Integration of Tools, Services; Kicker Goes in Here," *Computerworld,* August 9, 1999, p. 8.

"EXE, i2 Collaborate on Supply Chain Software," *Logistics Management & Distribution Report,* June 30, 1999, p. 77.

Goldstein, Alan, "Founder Returns As CEO of Texas-Based i2 Technologies," *Dallas Morning News,* April 16, 2002.

Grygo, Eugene, "i2 Adds Sourcing Info to Supply-Chain Apps," *InfoWorld,* March 20, 2000, p. 14.

Harreld, Heather, "i2 in Order Management—Supply-Chain Software Leader Moves to Help Users with Complex Procurement," *InfoWorld,* October 29, 2001, p. 24.

"i2 and IBM Join Forces to Deliver Transportation Management Solution Through a Software As a Service Model," http://www.i2.com/news/releases/view.cfm?id= 0BDF66F3-65B1-A0F9-2096BCDDA75ED93A.

"i2 CEO Aims for Profitability; Michael McGrath, the New Leader of the Supply-Chain Software Vendor, Says Customers Expect Faster Benefits from Major Initiatives," *Information Week,* March 25, 2005.

"i2 Introduces Breakthrough Content Management Solution to Manage and Access E-Marketplace Product Information," *Canadian Corporate News,* August 11, 2000, p. 1008221c8311.

"i2 Looks to Stage a Comeback; The Supply-Chain Vendor Will Start Trading on Nasdaq Again Starting July 21, Following Several Years of Financial and SEC Troubles," *Information Week,* July 18, 2005.

"i2 Outlines Strategic Direction and Unveils TradeMatrixNetwork at EDay 2000," *Canadian Corporate News,* August 11, 2000.

"i2 Rolls out HightechMatrix.com," *Electronic Buyers' News,* January 3, 2000, p. 52.

"i2 Springs Back Against ERP Giants," *eWeek,* November 16, 2004.

"i2 Technologies to Beef up Asian Presence," *New Straits Times,* October 12, 2000.

"i2: The Early Bird Gets the Market," *Business Week,* October 25, 1999, p. 158.

Karpinski, Richard, "Web Links Supply Chain to Storefront," *Internet Week,* June 21, 1999, p. 8.

McHugh, Josh, "Bowling Ball, Marble and Garden Hose: How an Indian Immigrant Chemical Engineer Helped U.S. Industry Improve Its Work Flow," *Forbes,* October 21, 1996, p. 84.

Michel, Roberto, "Inside i2's Lean Planning," *Manufacturing Systems,* July 2000, p. 20.

Rampey, Jennifer, "i2 Leaders Sparked Company's Growth, Passion from Employees," *Dallas Business Journal,* June 28, 1996, p. C7.

"Restructuring for i2," *Journal of Commerce,* July 15, 2005.

Songini, Marc L., "i2 Completes Reaudit, but Obstacles Remain; Software Vendor Faces SEC Probe, Purchase Delays," *Computerworld,* July 28, 2003, p. 10.

———, "i2 Looks to Simplify Supply Chain Software with Upgrade: New Release Includes Vertical Industry Templates, Support for Web Services," *Computerworld,* March 24, 2003, p. 16.

———, "i2's Closed Loop Vision Garners User Support: Bundling of Technologies and Processes Promises a Dynamic Supply Chain," *Computerworld,* November 15, 2004, p. 10.

———, "i2 Users Concerned About Vendor's Finances, Future; Problems Continue to Raise Doubts Despite Improved Relations," *Computerworld,* May 19, 2003, p. 1.

———, "New i2 CEO to Resize, Refocus Troubled Firm; McGrath Will Refocus Offerings, Cut up to 400 Jobs," *Computerworld,* March 7, 2005, p. 20.

———, "Users Keep Faith As i2 Plans Layoffs, Other Cuts; Supply Chain Vendor Seeks Turnaround After Ninth Straight Loss," *Computerworld,* July 22, 2002, p. 14.

Taschek, John, "Big Payouts Get Results with i2," *PC Week,* October 6, 1997, p. 94.

Teresko, John, "Supply-Chain Solutions," *Industry Week,* July 5, 1999, p. 18.

"The 'Velvet Hammer' of E-Commerce," *Business Week,* August 28, 2000, p. 70N.

"Will i2 Revolutionize B2B Sourcing?" *Automotive Manufacturing & Production,* December 1999, p. 46.

Wilson, Tim, "Customers Stay Put As i2 Struggles—Though Feeling Impact, Many Aren't Making Major Changes in Their Deployment Plans," *Internet Week,* August 13, 2001, p. 11.

"WRAP: i2 Technologies to Buy Aspect Development for $9.3 Billion," *Futures World News,* March 14, 2000.

The J. M. Smucker Company

One Strawberry Lane
Orrville, Ohio 44667-0280
U.S.A.
Telephone: (330) 682-3000
Toll Free: (888) 550-9555
Fax: (330) 684-3370
Web site: http://www.smuckers.com

Public Company
Founded: 1897
Incorporated: 1921
Employees: 3,500
Sales: $2.15 billion (2006)
Stock Exchanges: New York
Ticker Symbol: SJM
NAIC: 311211 Flour Milling; 311225 Fats and Oils Refining and Blending; 311230 Breakfast Cereal Manufacturing; 311412 Frozen Specialty Food Manufacturing; 311421 Fruit and Vegetable Canning; 311423 Dried and Dehydrated Food Manufacturing; 311514 Dry, Condensed, and Evaporated Dairy Product Manufacturing; 311822 Flour Mixes and Dough Manufacturing from Purchased Flour; 311911 Roasted Nuts and Peanut Butter Manufacturing; 311999 All Other Miscellaneous Food Manufacturing; 312111 Soft Drink Manufacturing

∎ ∎ ∎

The J. M. Smucker Company (generally called Smucker's) has been the top producer and marketer of jams, jellies, and preserves in the United States, mainly under the flagship Smucker's brand, for nearly three decades, but the firm has developed—principally through two major acquisitions in 2002 and 2004—a wide-ranging portfolio of branded foods. In addition to two other leading U.S. brands, Jif peanut butter and Crisco cooking oils and shortening, Smucker's also produces Pillsbury flour, baking mixes, and ready-to-spread frostings; Hungry Jack pancake mixes, syrup, and potato side dishes; Martha White baking mixes and ingredients; Pet canned milk products; and Smucker's Uncrustables frozen sandwiches. The company operates about 20 manufacturing and processing facilities in the United States and Canada. Smucker's distributes its products in more than 45 countries worldwide, with foreign sales accounting for 19 percent of the total, but 90 percent of the non-U.S. revenues are generated in Canada. The familiar corporate slogan, "With a name like Smucker's, it has to be good," alludes both to the company's founding family and its reputation for high-quality products. The firm is also known for its insistence on independence: Members of the Smucker family continue to head the company, and they control about 9 percent of the firm's common shares.

FOUNDING ERA WITH JEROME MONROE SMUCKER AT THE HELM

The company was founded in 1897 by Jerome Monroe Smucker, a Mennonite from the small agricultural community of Orrville, Ohio, about 45 minutes south of Cleveland. The Mennonites' traditional disdain for modernization did not keep Smucker from rational and efficient business practices. He applied his education from a two-year business course at a nearby academy to the management of four farms and a creamery that shipped butter as far as New York City. The success of his businesses allowed him to expand operations around the close of the century, when Smucker bought a cider mill and began pressing apples from an orchard planted in the early 19th century by Johnny Appleseed. To even out the seasonality of apple cider sales, Smucker began to make apple butter from his Pennsylvania Dutch grandfather's recipe. Smucker's steam-powered press and secret method for capturing the vapors usually lost in cooking gave the spread a unique flavor that soon drew more customers than the cider mill and creamery. Smucker staked his name and reputation on each crock of apple butter, hand-signing the paper lid on every package.

The family-owned business prospered. J. M. Smucker's eldest son, Willard, began delivering the 25 cent, half-gallon tubs in a wagon at the age of ten. By 1915, the first year for which records are available, the business was bringing in nearly $60,000 and netting almost $3,000 annually. Sales had topped $147,000 by 1921, the year The J. M. Smucker Company was incorporated and capitalized at $100,000.

Smucker's offered a full line of preserves (generally made from whole fruit or large pieces of fruit) and jellies (made from strained, pure fruit juice). J. M. Smucker owned 94 percent of the private company's stock; his sons and daughters split the remainder. The company had grown to such a scale that in 1928 the Pennsylvania Railroad built a special siding to the Smucker plant, as the company's products were distributed in ever increasing volume throughout Ohio, Pennsylvania, and Indiana.

Sales continued to grow in spite of the October 1929 stock market crash, nearing $319,000 in 1931. Still, the company did not emerge from the crisis unscathed: It recorded two consecutive years of losses in 1932 and 1933. Throughout this period, J. M. Smucker began to delegate authority to Willard, who directed the establishment of Smucker's first facility outside Ohio in 1935. The plant was located in the state of Washington, chosen for its high-quality, low-priced apples, which were preprocessed, then shipped to Orrville for cooking. The move set Smucker's up for national distribution and marked the first step toward the vertical integration that would become a company hallmark.

Packaging and marketing were taken for granted at Smucker's until 1938, when Willard decided that the traditional crockery was too heavy and awkward to ship. He wanted to shift to a more modern glass package without losing the Smucker reputation for "old-fashioned" quality. The glass jar he designed and later trademarked reflected the old crock, and its label, showing a pioneer woman boiling up a batch of apple butter over an open fire, reinforced Smucker's quaint image. The new package was a success; after its introduction, sales surpassed the $1 million mark in 1939. The new jar and label also garnered the company an award from the National Packaging Show for best packaging design success. National distribution of Smucker's products began in 1942.

The war years at Smucker's were characterized by labor, glass, and fruit shortages, but the company withstood such hardships to celebrate its 50th anniversary in 1947. Founder J. M. Smucker, too, endured just long enough to see his business through five decades: he passed away at the age of 90 the following year.

GROWTH AND DIVERSIFICATION UNDER SECOND- AND THIRD-GENERATION LEADERSHIP

The second generational transfer of power at Smucker's began in the late 1950s, when son Paul joined Willard in drawing up a plan for future growth and diversification. Like his father, Paul had started working in the family business at a young age. From the age of 13, according to the *Wall Street Journal*, "after school and during the summer months, he did everything from janitorial work to assisting the cook." Paul earned a business degree from Miami (Ohio) University in 1939,

KEY DATES

1897: Jerome Monroe Smucker opens a cider mill in Orville, Ohio, and later begins making apple butter.

1921: Smucker incorporates his company as The J. M. Smucker Company.

1923: Company expands its product offerings to include a full line of preserves and jellies.

1935: Firm moves toward national distribution with establishment of fruit processing plant in the state of Washington.

1959: Company goes public.

1962: The enduring "With a name like Smucker's, it has to be good" slogan is used for the first time.

1979: Smucker's attains the number one spot among U.S. jelly and jam manufacturers.

1988: International expansion begins via two acquisitions in Canada.

2000: Smucker's Uncrustables frozen sandwiches make their debut.

2002: In a $781.5 million stock transaction, Smucker's acquires the Jif peanut butter and Crisco shortening brands from the Procter & Gamble Company.

2004: Company acquires International Multifoods Corporation in an $871 million deal that brings Pillsbury baking mixes, Hungry Jack pancake mixes and syrup, and other brands into the fold.

then returned to Orrville to work full time as a cost accountant at a salary of $100 per month. After marrying and serving in the Navy for three years during World War II, Paul was put in charge of a recently acquired applesauce factory. Despite the venture's failure, Paul's responsibilities increased: he was promoted to corporate secretary in 1946, treasurer in 1949, executive vice-president in 1954, and president in 1961.

In spite of merger offers from such respected giants of the food industry as Quaker Oats, Ralston Purina, Beatrice Foods, and Borden, the family opted to remain independent. In 1959 they offered one-third of the company to the public, raising $2.3 million for capital investments. At the time, Smucker's had annual sales of $11.4 million and earnings of $812,000. The family business legacy under Paul Smucker included an aver-

sion to long-term debt and "an almost obsessive concern for avoiding any move that might adulterate his company's products or blemish the corporate image," according to the *Wall Street Journal.*

Paul Smucker led a two-decade period of dramatic growth through increasing vertical integration, product diversification, acquisition, and national advertising and market penetration that culminated in the company's 1980 dominance of the fruit spread market. From early in its history, the company sought control of all aspects of production. Contracting directly with farmers for fruit crops precluded buying produce on the open market and empowered Smucker's to control production from seed to jam. Along with this vertical integration came vertical quality control. Beginning in 1946, Smucker's paid U.S. Department of Agriculture inspectors to oversee every aspect of its production, earning the company the designation "U.S. Grade A Fancy." This evidence of quality assurance allowed Smucker's a higher markup and better shelf placement.

Smucker's maintained its quality control as it expanded. The company opened a manufacturing plant in Salinas, California, that increased production capacity by 40 percent in 1960. Acquisitions, including $4 million (annual sales) West Coast jam and jelly maker Mary Ellen's, Inc. (1963) and Pennsylvania peanut butter manufacturer H.B. DeViney Company, Inc. (1965), helped extend Smucker's geographical reach, augmented its annual sales volume, and increased product variety. Smucker's most successful and innovative internally developed product was a candy-cane-striped mixture of peanut butter and jelly dubbed "Goober Jelly." The company expanded its product line to over 100 varieties, including ice cream toppings, which accounted for 20 percent of sales by 1960. By the late 1960s, jellies, jams, and preserves comprised less than two-thirds of sales. Product acquisitions and internal developments helped diversify the company's offerings, but not all new product launches and acquisitions were successful. The 1965 purchase of Wooster Preserving Company and the 1966 purchase of H.W. Madison Co., both pickle concerns, became oft-noted examples of failure.

In spite of Willard Smucker's general disdain for advertising, the company hired Wyse Advertising of Cleveland to produce radio spots in 1961. The agency thought up the enduring "With a name like Smucker's, it has to be good" slogan the following year. Family members did not relish the thought of making fun of their own name at first, but the tagline's phenomenal success on the West Coast persuaded them to use it for the brand's New York launch in the later years of the decade.

Sales doubled from $14.6 million in 1961 to $30 million in fiscal 1965. Smucker's stock more than tripled from its $20 issue price to $67.50 in 1965, when it was split 3-for-1 and listed on the New York Stock Exchange. Despite its growth, the company ranked second to grocery chain A&P's Ann Page store brand at the end of the decade. Smucker's increased its advertising budget to $1.3 million to accommodate network television, and continued to push for first place.

Profits more than tripled to $3 million between 1959 and 1969, then dropped almost 13 percent in the 1970 fiscal year in spite of a sales increase. The company continued to have troubles throughout the decade. Not able to increase prices as fast as inflation boosted overhead, the Smuckers' steadfastly refused to compromise quality to pad earnings. As a result, profit margins shrunk from 16 percent in 1964 to 11 percent in 1970. Smucker's instituted cost-cutting measures, including the consolidation of three packing operations into two and corresponding workforce reductions that reduced the payroll by 15 percent between 1973 and 1984. The 1969 and 1971 acquisitions of manufacturing operations in Oregon, Tennessee, and California enhanced economies and enabled Smucker's to sell its excess fruit to competitors.

Still the number two jelly manufacturer (now trailing Welch's) in 1974, Smucker's launched a concerted effort to dominate the industry. The company broadened its institutional markets and rounded out consumer jelly lines with the introduction of "Smucker's for Kids," a lower-priced line, as well as low-calorie and all-natural products. The combination of increased advertising, more thorough market penetration (especially in the South), and the 1979 acquisition of the Dickinson's line of gourmet preserves and jellies, catapulted Smucker's to the number one spot among jelly and jam manufacturers, with over one-fourth of the market, in 1979. Over the course of the decade, sales increased almost three times to $145.8 million, and profits nearly doubled to $5.9 million.

The 1970s also saw the ascent of Smucker's fourth generation of family leadership, when Timothy Smucker was appointed vice-president of planning. The assignment marked a new, more modern approach to strategic, tactical, and operational planning, as the company began to rival some of the world's largest food companies in its specialized niche. Timothy refined the "Basic Beliefs" first outlined by his father in 1967, including commitments to quality, personal and business ethics, growth, and independence. He incorporated them into a detailed blueprint for the company's future. Timothy was promoted to president and chief operating officer and brother Richard earned the title chief administrative officer in addition to executive vice-president in 1981.

STEADILY EXPANDING

As the leader of the highly competitive, but slow growing, jam and jelly market, Smucker's found itself ever more dependent on heavy advertising expenditures, acquisitions, and product launches to increase sales and earnings in the 1980s. A four-year plant expansion program was announced in 1982 on the heels of a 39 percent year-to-year earnings gain. Magic Shell brand ice cream toppings were purchased from Foremost-McKesson in 1980 and Knudsen & Sons, Inc., a manufacturer of pure fruit juices, joined the family of companies in 1984. The 1987 purchase of R-Line Foods complemented Smucker's institutional operations. Also in 1987 Timothy Smucker was named chairman and Richard Smucker assumed the presidency, while Paul Smucker remained involved in the business as chairman of the executive committee.

Smucker's began international efforts in the late 1980s. In 1988 it acquired Canada's Good Morning brand marmalade (citrus jelly made of small pieces of fruit) and Shirriff ice cream toppings, as well as Elsenham Quality Foods, Ltd., a British manufacturer of specialty preserves, marmalades, and fruit chutneys. Henry Jones Foods, producer of "one of Australia's oldest and best-known labels," IXL preserves and jams, was purchased the following year. Sales more than doubled from $151 million in 1980 to $367 million in 1989, and earnings quadrupled during the same period from $6.7 million to $27.6 million. By 1993, international sales comprised almost 8 percent of Smucker's annual total.

Smucker's entered the 1990s with 38 percent of the domestic jam and jelly market. The fourth generation leaders set an even loftier goal for their namesake brand and company: a 70 percent share. However, with tenacious, experienced rivals such as Kraft and Welch's as well as locally strong store brands, the company had its work cut out for it. In 1994 Smucker's ended its 35-year relationship with Wyse Advertising in favor of Leo Burnett Company, Inc., an agency company executives believed could support the brand's aspirations.

In the early 1990s, members of the Smucker family continued to control over half of the company's stock, and evinced no intentions of relinquishing that majority rule. As consolidation within the food industry gained momentum, the family shored up its takeover defenses by creating a new class of nonvoting stock. This allowed older members (Paul Smucker, for example) to plan their estates without relinquishing influence. From 1990 to 1993, sales increased over 16 percent to $491.3 million, as Smucker's sought to increase per capita consumption of its products, as well as increase its market share in each category.

Smucker's in the mid-1990s continued to pursue acquisitions, some of the international variety and some aimed at broadening the product portfolio. In July 1993 the firm significantly expanded its presence in the Canadian market by acquiring the jam, preserve, and pie filling business of Montreal-based Culinar, Inc., for $16.1 million. In March of the following year, Smucker's completed its largest purchase yet, acquiring the Mrs. Smith's frozen pie business from the Kellogg Co. for $84.1 million and thereby expanding into the frozen food section of the supermarket and gaining a foothold in the dessert category. Later in 1994 Smucker's acquired After The Fall Products, Inc., a maker of natural fruit juices and sodas based in Brattleboro, Vermont, and the Laura Scudder's brand of natural peanut butter. After The Fall fit in well alongside Smucker's Knudsen natural-beverage brand.

Whereas the After The Fall and Laura Scudder's brands enjoyed steady growth following their arrival at Smucker's, the Mrs. Smith's deal quickly turned sour. Part of the problem was poor timing. The Mrs. Smith's acquisition had occurred at a time when sales of frozen pies were shrinking, in part because of the growth of in-store bakeries. Mrs. Smith's was also in the process of an expensive national rollout of a new line of lower-calorie desserts. The new product flopped, however, and it was pulled from the market in 1995. By the fall Smucker's had decided to return to its core product areas and divest the Mrs. Smith's line. Two separate deals to sell the line, a November 1995 agreement with SBI Brands Inc. and a March 1996 agreement with ConAgra Foods, Inc., fell apart soon after they were announced when the parties were unable to come to final terms. Ultimately, Smucker's succeeded on its third try, offloading Mrs. Smith's at a loss to Flowers Industries Inc. in May 1996. In the meantime, disappointing results at Elsenham Quality Foods led Smucker's to sell this U.K. business in December 1995, incurring a loss there as well.

In 1997, when Smucker's celebrated its 100th year, the company continued the fight to maintain its dominance of the jelly and jam sector in the face of the increasing encroachment of private-label products. Smucker's acquired Kraft Foods, Inc.'s U.S. fruit spread business, which held around 2 percent of the market, and also introduced the reduced-calorie Smucker's Light line. Another noteworthy product introduced in 1997 was Smucker's Snackers, a prepackaged peanut butter, jelly, and crackers snack kit. Shelf stable, meaning that

refrigeration was not required, the product was designed for children to take to school and proved to be a hit. The firm also began pursuing cobranding and licensing deals that year. Smucker's teamed up with Brach & Brock Confections, Inc. (later known as Brach's Confections, Inc.) to produce Brach's Smucker's jelly beans and fruit chews. Via a licensing deal with Mars, Incorporated, Smucker's introduced Dove ice cream toppings.

Acquisitions remained on the agenda in the late 1990s, as Smucker's also developed new sales channels. In 1998 Henry Jones Foods, Smucker's Australian subsidiary, acquired the Allowrie jam brand, the number four jam brand in Australia. The following January, Smucker's acquired the Adams brand of natural peanut butter from Agrilink Foods, Inc. Adams products were available exclusively in the northwestern United States and western Canada. In late 1998 Smucker's entered the mail-order business, sending out hundreds of thousands of catalogs in its first mailing. The company soon launched online sales as well, and in May 1999 the firm opened its first retail store. Located in Orrville about three miles south of the company headquarters and called Simply Smucker's, the 3,100-square-foot store offered more than 350 Smucker's products and gifts and served as a brand showcase. With food manufacturers fighting for retailers' shelf space, these new sales channels provided Smucker's with the ability to directly connect with its customers and offer products to them that might not be available at the local supermarket. In the meantime, the involvement of the third generation of Smuckers in the business ended with the death of Paul Smucker in December 1998 at age 81. Smucker's concluded the 1990s by posting net income of $37.8 million for fiscal 1999 on sales of $602.5 million.

EARLY 21ST CENTURY: CREATING A MULTIBRAND FOOD EMPIRE VIA ACQUISITIONS

Smucker's entered the 21st century still an independent company but a conservatively run one perhaps in danger of being swallowed up by one of the food industry's ever larger giants. Just a half a decade later, the company had tripled its sales thanks primarily to two major acquisitions that belied Smucker's sleepy image. The company began the decade, however, continuing to pursue smaller deals. In early 2000 Smucker's purchased a plant in Brazil to process fruit-based ingredients for the Dannon Company, Inc., a move that supported Smucker's position as a major supplier of fruit ingredients for Dannon yogurt. Later in the year Henry Jones Foods made another acquisition in Australia, adding the Taylor Foods line of prepared sauces and marinades. Smucker's also simplified its share structure in 2000, creating a single class of common stock. Perhaps the most significant outcome here was that the Smucker family's voting interest in the company was reduced from 75 percent to around 34 percent. Smucker's also scored big in 2000 on the new product development front when it introduced Uncrustables, a package of frozen peanut-butter-and-jelly sandwiches on crustless white bread. Like the Snackers product, Uncrustables was primarily aimed at children and was designed to be particularly convenient for school lunches or for snacking at anytime of the day, needing only to be thawed for about 20 minutes before being ready to eat. Even before launching Uncrustables into the consumer market, Smucker's had successfully introduced the product into school lunch programs around the country as part of the firm's growing food-service business.

In early 2001 Timothy and Richard Smucker began serving as co-CEOs of Smucker's, adding this title to their previous duties as chairman and president, respectively. Smucker's enhanced its industrial business in October of that year by acquiring International Flavors & Fragrances Inc.'s fruit and vegetable preparation businesses, which had operations in the United States and Brazil. The much larger news that month, however, involved Smucker's reaching an agreement to acquire the Jif peanut butter and Crisco cooking oil and shortening brands from the Procter & Gamble Company (P&G). This deal, completed in June 2002, thoroughly transformed Smucker's. Beforehand, the company generated about half of its revenues from fruit spreads. Afterward, Smucker's had a balanced portfolio of three brands, each of which was responsible for around one-quarter of sales with all three holding the number one position in their respective categories in the United States. Acquiring Jif was particularly significant given the synergies between this top peanut butter brand and Smucker's core jellies and jams; in fact, Smucker's had coveted Jif for decades as Paul Smucker had approached P&G officials about buying it as far back as the 1970s.

On the revenue front, the purchase nearly doubled Smucker's sales, which totaled $1.31 billion for the fiscal year ending in April 2003. That the deal was structured as a tax-free transaction using Smucker's stock was also significant. P&G first spun Jif and Crisco off to P&G shareholders and then Smucker's immediately acquired the brands. P&G shareholders received one Smucker's share for every 50 P&G shares they owned, which translated into an acquisition price of $781.5 million in stock. Because of the payment in

stock, the Smucker family's stake in the company was further reduced by more than half, down to around 16 percent.

During fiscal 2003, in addition to increasing marketing support for Jif and Crisco by 50 percent, Smucker's also made a series of restructuring moves aimed at cutting costs. Three plants were shut down in the United States, the workforce was cut by 335 jobs, and the company stopped making about 1,000 products that collectively were generating less than 2 percent of sales. In May 2004 production began at a new $70 million facility in Scottsville, Kentucky, dedicated solely to production of the expanding Uncrustables line. Electing to concentrate more keenly on its North American branded, retail foods operations, Smucker's in 1994 sold Henry Jones Foods to SPC Ardmona Ltd. for $35.7 million and also offloaded its industrial ingredient businesses in the United States and Brazil. In January 2004 Smucker's, with a longstanding reputation as a good employer, was named as the best place to work in the nation by *Fortune* magazine, becoming the first manufacturing company to receive this distinction.

In June 2004 Smucker's completed its second transformative acquisition of the new century. Having gained a foothold in the baking aisle via the addition of Crisco, the company took a major leap into that section by acquiring International Multifoods Corporation (IMC) of Minnetonka, Minnesota. Purchasing IMC brought into the Smucker's fold the Pillsbury line of baking mixes and ready-to-spread frostings; Hungry Jack pancake mixes, syrup, and potato side dishes; Pet evaporated milk; and Martha White baking mixes. Smucker's also gained several Canadian brands: Robin Hood flour, Bick's pickles and condiments, and Golden Temple flour and rice. The purchase price was approximately $871 million in cash, stock, and assumed debt; the stock included in the deal further reduced the Smucker family's stake in the company to around 12 percent. The deal pushed revenues over the $2 billion mark for fiscal 2005, while the net income figure of $129.1 million was more than three times the figure for 2000. Fruit spreads accounted for only around 14 percent of overall revenues. Thanks to the addition of the Canadian brands, revenue generated north of the border jumped from just $64.3 million in 2004 to $338.8 million in 2005, representing more than 16 percent of the total.

During 2005, while working to integrate the IMC brands into its existing operations, Smucker's sold some peripheral businesses it had inherited, including IMC's foodservice and bakery products units in the United States and a Canadian foodservice business operating under the Gourmet Baker name. Net sales were up 5 percent in fiscal 2006 to $2.15 billion, driven largely by a 29 percent increase in sales of Uncrustables products. Annual revenue from this line, which had been expanded to include such sandwiches as peanut butter and honey on wheat bread and grilled cheese, had grown to more than $85 million. In the fall of 2006 Smucker's unloaded another noncore asset, its Canadian grain-based foodservice and industrial businesses, and it acquired the White Lily brand from C.H. Guenther & Son, Inc. The White Lily line, which generated annual sales of $33 million, encompassed flours, cornmeal, muffin mixes, grits, and frozen biscuits, making a neat fit with Smucker's other baking brands.

As part of an industry trend, Smucker's in January 2007 announced that it had reformulated its entire line of Crisco shortening products to nearly eliminate artery-clogging trans fats from their formulas. Looking ahead, Smucker's had set an overall long-term sales growth target of 8 percent per year, with half of this increase slated to come from its core business and new products and half from acquisitions. In April 2007 the company announced a significant acquisition aimed at helping it stay on track with these targets. Smucker's agreed to purchase Eagle Family Foods Holdings, Inc., a private company based in Columbus, Ohio, for $133 million in cash and the assumption of $115 million in debt. Eagle was the largest producer of sweetened condensed and evaporated milk in the United States and Canada, marketing under the Eagle and Magnolia brands, and it also owned a grab bag of other brands, including None Such mincemeat, Kava acid-neutralized coffee, and Borden eggnog. Eagle's revenues for fiscal 2006 totaled $206 million.

April Dougal Gasbarre
Updated, David E. Salamie

PRINCIPAL SUBSIDIARIES

J.M. Smucker LLC; Smucker Fruit Processing Company; The Dickinson Family, Inc.; J.M. Smucker (Pennsylvania), Inc.; Mary Ellen's, Incorporated; Smucker Quality Beverages, Inc.; Juice Creations Co.; Knudsen & Sons, Inc.; Santa Cruz Natural Incorporated; Rocket Juice Company; Smucker Holdings, Inc.; Simply Smucker's, Inc.; Smucker Direct, Inc.; Smucker Latin America, Inc.; J.M. Smucker de Mexico, S.A. de C.V.; Smucker Hong Kong Limited; JM Smucker (Scotland) Limited; Smucker-IMC, Inc.; Fantasia Confections, Inc.; IMC North America, Inc.; IMC U.S., Inc.; Inversiones 91060, C.A. (Venezuela); Martha White Foods, Inc.; IMC Bakery International, Inc.; Smucker Brands, Inc.; Smucker Bakery Manufacturing, Inc.; RHM Corporation (Canada);

RHM Management Inc. (Canada); RHM Canada LP; Smucker Foods of Canada Co.

PRINCIPAL COMPETITORS

Unilever; National Grape Cooperative Association, Inc.; ConAgra Foods, Inc.; B&G Foods, Inc.; Kraft Foods Inc.; Ralcorp Holdings, Inc.; Tropicana Products, Inc.; The Coca-Cola Company; General Mills, Inc.; Pinnacle Food Group, Inc.; Dean Foods Company.

FURTHER READING

Adamy, Janet, "Smucker Agrees to Acquire Maker of Pillsbury Mixes," *Wall Street Journal,* March 9, 2004, p. A3.

Barker, Robert, "No Suckers, Those Smuckers," *Business Week,* March 4, 2002, p. 112.

Brown, Paul B., "A Bread-and-Butter Business," *Forbes,* January 30, 1984, p. 77.

Byrne, Harlan S., "J. M. Smucker Co.: 'Why Can't We Be Like a Gerber?' Asks Jam Company," *Barron's,* April 9, 1990, p. 60.

Clark, Sandra, "Living Up to Its Name: Smucker Delivers on Its Promise," *Cleveland Plain Dealer,* November 1, 1992.

DeFotis, Dimitra, "Time to Jam," *Barron's,* February 28, 2005, p. T5.

Ellis, William Donohue, *"With a Name Like ... ,"* Orrville, Ohio: J. M. Smucker Company, 1987, 161 p.

Ethridge, Mary, "Smucker Jelly Goes Well with Jif Peanut Butter, Crisco Oil," *Akron (Ohio) Beacon Journal,* October 11, 2001, p. A1.

——, "Smucker's Leaves Advertiser," *Akron (Ohio) Beacon Journal,* March 29, 1994, p. D6.

"False Teeth and Jelly," *Forbes,* November 1, 1968, pp. 21–22.

Goforth, Candace, "Smucker Named Top Place to Work," *Akron (Ohio) Beacon Journal,* December 30, 2003, p. A1.

Groseclose, Everett, "The Scions: Paul H. Smucker Takes Great Pains to Preserve His Products' Quality," *Wall Street Journal,* February 3, 1975, pp. 1, 21.

"Increased Ad Spending, New Executives Boost Smucker Market Share," *Wall Street Journal,* December 26, 1979, p. 2.

Kirk, Jim, "Smucker Jells for Burnett," *Adweek* (Midwest Edition), March 28, 1994, pp. 1, 5.

Malcolm, Andrew H., "Of Jams and a Family," *New York Times Magazine,* November 15, 1987, pp. 82+.

McEnaney, Maura, "Smucker Has Eyes on Frozen Pies," *Akron (Ohio) Beacon Journal,* March 1, 1994, p. D7.

Murray, Matt, "A Maker of Sugary Jellies Spreads Out into Natural and Organic Fruit Juices," *Wall Street Journal,* July 8, 1994, p. B1.

——, "Smucker's Deal for Mrs. Smith's Is Proving to Be a Pie in Face," *Wall Street Journal,* November 22, 1995, p. B1.

Nelson, Emily, and Devon Spurgeon, "It's a Natural: P&G Sells Jif to J. M. Smucker," *Wall Street Journal,* October 11, 2001, p. B1.

Phalon, Richard, "Closely Guarded Honey Pot," *Forbes,* November 25, 1991, pp. 48–50.

Pledger, Marcia, "J. M. Smucker Simply Opens Its 1st Retail Store in Orrville," *Cleveland Plain Dealer,* May 6, 1999, p. 1C.

———, "Work Force Helped Mold New Smucker," *Cleveland Plain Dealer,* May 23, 1999, p. 1H.

"Quality Image Gains Sales for Top Jam Maker," *New York Times,* September 13, 1980, pp. L27, L30.

"Recipe for Success at J. M. Smucker Accents Quality As Key Ingredient," *Barron's,* May 1, 1967, p. 22.

Russell, John, "Down-Home Empire: Orrville's J. M. Smucker Co. Enjoys Small-Town Image While Dominating Industry and Preparing to Spread," *Akron (Ohio) Beacon Journal,* April 11, 2004, p. D1.

———, "Smucker Pinches Doughboy," *Akron (Ohio) Beacon Journal,* March 9, 2004, p. A1.

"The Savvy Saleslady of Strawberry Lane," *Sales Management,* September 1, 1971, p. 21.

Smucker, Donovan E., *Jerome M. Smucker: Pioneer Ohio Mennonite Entrepreneur,* Lima, Ohio: Fairway Press, 1995, 60 p.

"Smucker Spreads Out Beyond Jam and Jelly," *Business Week,* November 13, 1965, pp. 194–95.

Spethmann, Betsy, "So Long, Smucker!" *Brandweek,* July 10, 1995, p. 24.

Thomas, Emory, Jr., and Matt Murray, "Flowers to Buy Mrs. Smith's Unit from J. M. Smucker," *Wall Street Journal,* May 2, 1996, p. B8.

Weber, Joseph, "Keeping Out of a Jam," *Business Week,* October 4, 2004, pp. 104, 106.

Wells, Melanie, "The Perfect Combo: The Quiet Family-Run Smucker Is Taking on New Brands—and the Big Time," *Forbes,* April 15, 2002, p. 226.

Wilson, Paul, "$248 Million Buy: Smucker Acquires Eagle Brands," *Columbus (Ohio) Dispatch,* April 3, 2007, p. 1C.

Zawacki, Michael, "Family Values," *Inside Business,* October 2004, pp. 98–100.

Jacmar Companies

2200 West Valley Boulevard
Alhambra, California 91803-1928
U.S.A.
Telephone: (626) 576-0737
Toll Free: (800) 540-0737
Fax: (626) 458-9224
Web site: http://www.jacmar.com; http://www.
shakeys.com

Private Company
Founded: 1960
Employees: 700
Sales: $100 million (2007 est.)
NAIC: 424490 Other Grocery and Related Products
Wholesalers; 422420 Packaged Frozen Food
Wholesalers; 722211 Limited-Service Restaurants

■■■

While few have heard of the Alhambra, California-based Jacmar Companies, many have heard of at least one of its major subsidiaries, Shakey's Pizza. Jacmar bought its first Shakey's Pizza franchise in 1964 and continued to open the family-style pizza parlors along the West Coast. Jacmar's other major subsidiary, Jacmar Foodservice Distribution, supplies restaurants and fast-food outlets throughout Southern California with fresh and frozen food products and service items. In addition to Shakey's and its distribution service, Jacmar Companies also owns a partial interest in the BJ's Restaurants chain located primarily along the West Coast.

IN THE BEGINNING

The Jacmar Companies' primary claim to fame is its Shakey's Pizza chain, with several dozen restaurants sprinkled throughout the United States. The original Shakey's Pizza concept was created by Sherwood "Shakey" Johnson and "Big Ed" Plummer in 1954. Sherwood Johnson earned the nickname "Shakey" after contracting malaria during World War II. Like everything else in life, Johnson treated his "shakes" with humor and did not let the infirmity keep him down. Partnering with Plummer, the two opened a small hole in the wall at 57th and J Streets in Sacramento, California, serving beer and providing live entertainment. The entertainment was mostly Johnson, who loved to play Dixieland jazz on his piano.

With the profits from the first few nights, Johnson bought pizza makings for his patrons. The beer, pizza, and jazz went over big and word of "Shakey's" spread beyond the Sacramento area. As more money rolled in, Johnson expanded the menu and Plummer furnished the parlor with an eclectic mix of items from old-fashioned checkered tablecloths to goofy, irreverent signs on the walls.

As the popularity of Shakey's grew, Johnson and Plummer opened a second pizza parlor in Portland, Oregon, in 1956, then decided franchising was the way to go. The partners began selling franchising rights in 1957. A few years later, as Shakey's Pizza locations began opening in cities up and down the West Coast, a young entrepreneur named William "Bill" Tilley, was looking for an opportunity to get into the burgeoning foodservice industry. He had created a company called

Jacmar in 1960 to oversee his interests and was looking for opportunities. Tilley set his sights on opening his own Shakey's franchise and signed on with Johnson and Plummer, opening his first Shakey's Pizza in 1964.

As Tilley got his Shakey's off the ground, so did hundreds of others. In 1967, by the time Johnson decided to retire, there were more than 250 Shakey's locations in the western United States. Johnson sold his half interest in Shakey's for $3 million to Colorado Milling and Elevator Company, and Plummer reportedly sold his interest a year later for triple the price. As the founding fathers of Shakey's rode off into the sunset, Tilley's fortunes were rising and Shakey's seemed unstoppable. The first Shakey's outside the United States opened in 1968, in Manitoba, Canada.

MAJOR COMPETITION

By the 1970s Shakey's "old-tyme" appeal had attracted the interest of the oil-rich Hunt family. The Dallas-based Hunt Resources International bought Shakey's Pizza, Inc., in 1974. The chain had more than 300 locations throughout North America and had spread from the California coast all the way into the Midwest. The following year Shakey's went global with new restaurants opening in Asia. The concept proved wildly popular as new Shakey's pizza parlors popped up along the Pacific Rim.

Stateside, the foodservice industry, and the pizza segment in particular, had become hugely profitable. Shakey's enjoyed major success and was, for a time, the nation's largest pizza franchise with over 400 units. It was also the first pizza restaurant of its kind, offering fun, food, and music, and appealed to kids and parents alike. Yet the very aggressive Pizza Hut, owned by soft-drink giant PepsiCo, became a powerhouse, rolling out locations nationwide. Smaller, regional chains began popping up, and some started cutting into Shakey's bottom line: Round Table Pizza, a fellow West Coast chain, and two Texas-based franchises, Mr. Gatti's and Pizza Inn, gathered momentum and planned to open new locations in and around California.

With its corporate parent concerned about little more than the cash Shakey's was generating, the chain soon found itself in the midst of a serious pizza war. Mr. Gatti's and Pizza Inn were gaining popularity, as was newcomer Godfather's Pizza out of Omaha, Nebraska. Pizza Hut, too, continued to build new restaurants across the country. By the time Pizza Hut tested a new product called "pan pizza" at the end of the decade, Shakey's was still holding its own, but its foundation had begun to crumble. The Hunt brothers, much more interested in minerals than pizzas according to some, had seemingly neglected the restaurant chain and provided little if any corporate guidance.

The 1980s brought a new double-edged threat: the advent of delivery and two direct competitors for Shakey's family-friendly fare. Delivery was less dangerous to Shakey's than ShowBiz Pizza Time and Chuck E. Cheese. While most pizza parlors offered carryout and some provided neighborhood delivery, Domino's turned the industry on its ear by delivering its pizzas anywhere and fast. Shakey's had always been about relaxing and enjoying a meal in a comfortable, eclectic atmosphere. Sales were not severely impacted by the wildly popular Domino's Pizza, but ShowBiz and Chuck E. Cheese were attracting kids in droves.

To ward off competition, Shakey's updated its restaurants, added more menu items and buffets, and increased the "fun" quotient for kids with more games and amusements. Unfortunately, ShowBiz and Chuck E. Cheese were newer and bigger, and became the rage. Shakey's did, however, offer something ShowBiz and Chuck E. Cheese did not have, parent-friendly perks such as alcohol and jazzy music. Shakey's was also fortunate in another way: ShowBiz and Chuck E. Cheese were busy competing against each other, giving the older pizza chain a little breathing room.

In 1984 the Hunt brothers agreed to sell Shakey's Inc. after the company had failed to bring in a profit on sales of $162 million for the fiscal year, which ended in September. Two of Shakey's largest franchisees, Gary Brown and Jay Halverson, bought the ailing pizza chain of about 300 restaurants for $17 million. The new owners closed underperforming stores as Shakey's struggled to keep even a tiny slice of the pizza market. Pizza Hut completely dominated the industry, while ShowBiz, Chuck E. Cheese, and Mr. Gatti's all capitalized on the kid-friendly "eatertainment" segment.

Within five years, after many Shakey's locations had succumbed to their rivals, the franchise company's American holdings, which numbered about 215 restaurants and reportedly had sales of $130 million, was sold to Singapore's Inno-Pacific Holdings, Inc. Inno-Pacific owned numerous Shakey's restaurants in

KEY DATES

1954: Sherwood "Shakey" Johnson and "Big Ed" Plummer open the first Shakey's pizza parlor.

1956: A second Shakey's Pizza opens in Portland, Oregon.

1957: Johnson and Plummer begin franchising Shakey's.

1960: William H. "Bill" Tilley forms Jacmar in California.

1964: Tilley opens his first Shakey's Pizza franchise.

1967: Johnson retires and sells his half interest in Shakey's to Colorado Milling and Elevator Company for $3 million.

1968: Plummer sells his stake for $9 million as the first Shakey's opens in Canada.

1974: Hunt Resources International buys Shakey's Pizza, Inc.

1975: The first Shakey's Pizza locations open in Asia.

1989: Shakey's domestic operations are bought by Inno-Pacific Holdings, Inc.

2000: Jacmar acquires a majority stake in Chicago Pizza & Brewery Company.

2002: Jacmar unsuccessfully floats a buyout offer for Shakey's Pizza, Inc.

2004: Jacmar buys Shakey's U.S. operations from Inno-Pacific Holdings.

2007: Redesigned Shakey's Pizza restaurants open in California and other states.

Asia, where the chain continued to thrive, and had bought a majority stake in Shakey's International, the international franchising rights segment of the chain, the previous year.

TRANSITIONS

Jacmar's pizza holdings, which consisted of more than a dozen Shakey's locations clustered in Southern California, had survived the multiple ownership changes of its franchiser and continued to do well. Part of its success came from Jacmar's other business unit, its Food Distribution Service (FDS). The distribution service was making a name for itself along the West Coast. Jacmar FDS provided a wide range of foodservice items to its clients which included four- and five-star restaurants, fast-food outlets, and delicatessens. Jacmar provided table linens, flatware, paper products, janitorial needs, as well as a variety of prepared foods (frozen, chilled, or dry), fruits, vegetables, and dairy products.

Jacmar also had its own delivery fleet and professionally trained staff available six days per week. Business had grown so much FDS had announced plans to build a new distribution center. The 82,000-square-foot state-of-the-art facility would be built in Irwindale and service a region stretching from Santa Barbara to San Diego and everywhere in between. Construction was completed on the distribution center in 1999.

For Shakey's owners, history began repeating itself as new corporate parent Inno-Pacific Holdings was far more interested in its Asian assets than the franchisees in the United States. Former owners Brown and Halverson had closed numerous unprofitable stores and pushed new initiatives to strengthen the remaining pizza parlors. While same-store sales had stabilized, everything began sliding downward after Inno-Pacific's acquisition. Shakey's lagged far, far behind Pizza Hut and Domino's, as both had thousands of locations and revenues in the billions. Other pizza chains grew by mergers or acquisitions; ShowBiz and Chuck E. Cheese became CEC Entertainment, while Mr. Gatti's and upstart Little Caesar Enterprises bought smaller chains.

Even though Shakey's had managed to hold on in California and a few other western states, a national identity crisis had robbed the brand of its charm. There was little cohesion among franchisees, and no one, including Inno-Pacific Holdings, seemed to know what to do. Was Shakey's a family-friendly sit-down restaurant or an "eatertainment" unit that served pizza? As the new century approached, customers and franchisees needed answers.

NEW MILLENNIUM, NEW IDENTITY, 2000–04

The dawn of the 2000s brought Shakey's to a critical juncture: sink or swim. Many franchises were closing or bought by rivals, but Jacmar's restaurants, the largest franchisee with 19 locations, remained profitable. Jacmar also bought into another West Coast chain, Chicago Pizza & Brewery Inc. The Huntington Beach-based casual dining chain boasted Chicago-style pizza, sandwiches, appetizers, and a wide selection of beer.

In December 2000 Jacmar increased its stake in Chicago Pizza & Brewery and became the publicly traded company's largest shareholder. Chicago Pizza & Brewery, like its Shakey's holdings, were already serviced by its food distribution unit. In 2002 Jacmar approached Shakey's corporate parent, Inno-Pacific Holdings, about buying back the pizza chain's domestic operations. The offer was reportedly ignored and Jacmar's chairman, Bill Tilley, vowed to let its Shakey's franchise license expire rather than keep working with Inno-Pacific.

Two years later, in 2004, when Jacmar again broached the subject of buying Shakey's U.S. operations, Inno-Pacific was much more receptive, since numerous franchisees had filed suit for breach of contract. Jacmar bought Inno-Pacific's U.S. holdings, 63 Shakey's locations, for $4.5 million. Inno-Pacific held on to its own Shakey's restaurants, which numbered about 200 in Japan, the Philippines, and Singapore.

After the acquisition Shakey's USA became a wholly owned subsidiary of Jacmar Companies. Jacmar President James A. Dal Pozzo announced plans to revitalize the Shakey's brand, to straighten out the legal issues of its current franchisees, and to either lure back previous owners or attract new ones. "Generations of Californians remember Shakey's as a place their parents brought them for food, fun, and entertainment," Dal Pozzo told *Nation's Restaurant News* (September 12, 2004). "We plan to reinvigorate the brand, refresh our menu, and update our stores so generations to come can make their own memories at Shakey's." While most Shakey's locations were in California, a few survived in Arizona, Georgia, Idaho, and Washington.

FORGING AHEAD WITH A NOD TO THE PAST, 2005 AND BEYOND

Whether the once mighty Shakey's empire could be reconstructed remained to be seen. Jacmar's other interests continued to be successful; both its Food Distribution Service and the Chicago Pizza & Brewery (renamed BJ's Restaurants Inc.) were profitable. Shakey's, however, had the toughest competition since kid-friendly, entertaining pizza parlors had become very popular. The Texas-based chains Mr. Gatti's and Chuck E. Cheese were direct competitors, building large complexes filled with games and amusements.

While Shakey's had no plans for huge playground-like units, the chain was remodeling both the inside and outside of its eateries. A new 6,000-square-foot prototype, according to *Nation's Restaurant News* (July 18, 2005), was on the drawing board. The new building provided seating for 220 patrons and would cost about $850,000 to construct. Inside, Shakey's wanted to return to its roots, playing on the nostalgic style of the original Shakey's restaurants with checkered tablecloths, silly signs, and staff dressed in striped shirts, black bowties, and straw hats.

Shakey's rebirth was spearheaded by Arthur Gunther, former president of Pizza Hut, who came on board as a consultant and interim CEO in February 2005 until the chain's new chief executive, Tim Pulido, was hired by Dal Pozzo and Tilley in March 2006. Pulido, a former executive with both Pizza Hut and McDonald's Corporation, believed Shakey's prospects for the future were excellent, especially with Jacmar's solid foodservice industry experience behind it.

Nelson Rhodes

PRINCIPAL SUBSIDIARIES

Jacmar Food Distribution Services; Jacmar Pacific Pizza; Shakey's USA, Inc.; BJ Chicago LLC.

PRINCIPAL COMPETITORS

DPI West, Inc.; CEC Entertainment Company; Pizza Hut Shamrock Foods, Inc.

FURTHER READING

Bluth, Andrew, "Huntington Beach, Calif.-based Pizza Firm Sold to Food-Service Distributor," *Orange County Register,* December 22, 2000.

Coomes, Steve, "Jacmar to Spend $4.5 Million on Shakey's Pizza Chain," July 16, 2004, http://www.pizzamarketplace.com/article.php?id=3306.

———, "Poised for a Comeback," http://www.pizzamarketplace.com/article.php?id=3673, December 1, 2004.

———, "Talking Points: Tim Pulido, New CEO at Shakey's Pizza," http://www.pizzamarketplace.com/article.php?id=3306, March 20, 2006.

Gorman, John, "Pizza with the Works Means Buffet at Resurgent Shakey's," *Chicago Tribune,* January 4, 1988, p. 1.

"Jacmar Arm Acquires Chicago Pizza & Brewery," *Nation's Restaurant News,* January 8, 2001, p. 47.

Jennings, Lisa, "Ex-Pizza Hut Leader Shaking Things Up at Shakey's with Expansion Plan," *Nation's Restaurant News,* July 18, 2005, p. 4.

Liddle, Alan J., "Shakey's Seeks Steadier Ground After Buyout by Jacmar," *Nation's Restaurant News,* September 13, 2004, p. 8.

Maese, Kathryn, "A Slice of the Pie," *Los Angeles Business Journal,* September 13, 2004, p. 27.

"Shakey's Parent: Buyout by Franchisee Underway," *Nation's Restaurant News,* May 24, 2004, p. 206.

"Singapore Group Buys Shakey's Inc.," *New York Times,* February 10, 1989, p. D4.

PURDEY

James Purdey & Sons Limited

Audley House
57–58 South Audley Street
London, W1K 2ED
United Kingdom
Telephone: (+44 20) 7499 1801
Fax: (+44 20) 7355 3297
Web site: http://www.purdey.com

Wholly Owned Subsidiary of Compagnie Financière Richemont SA
Founded: 1816
Incorporated: 1925
Employees: 59
Sales: £5.75 million ($10 million) (2006 est.)
NAIC: 332994 Small Arms Manufacturing

■ ■ ■

James Purdey & Sons Limited is considered one of the top makers, if not the top maker, of fine sporting guns and rifles in the world. Its reputation for excellence was set soon after James Purdey established the business in London in 1816, and it quickly became the gunmaker of choice for gentry and royalty. From 1868 on, the company has been granted Royal Warrants of Appointment from members of the British monarchy, a prestigious honor allowing a manufacturer to advertise royal patronage.

Purdey guns are bespoke, meaning they are crafted to fit the shooter. The firm makes only about 75 guns per year, most of them shotguns used in hunting or target shooting, though some buyers are collectors and

therefore never shoot them. It can take as many as 750 man-hours to handcraft a Purdey gun (and from 18 to 24 months of actual time on the calendar), which serves to justify the hefty prices, from $89,000 to well over $100,000 for a single gun, depending on whether a customer wants any elaborate engraving on the metalwork or other features that can add tens of thousands of dollars to the price. At the company's factory, about 35 workers, all of them men, ply their trade largely using hand tools, each craftsman handling one section of the gun—the barrel, the action, or the stock. Purdey also draws on a pool of highly skilled, independent engravers.

In its entire history of nearly 200 years, James Purdey & Sons has made only a little more than 30,000 guns, each one individually numbered. The company was owned by the Purdey family until 1946, when the Seely family acquired it. In 1994 it was acquired by Compagnie Financière Richemont SA, a global luxury goods company based in Switzerland that owns many other famed brands, including Cartier jewelry, Piaget watches, Montblanc writing instruments, and Alfred Dunhill leather goods, menswear, and accessories.

EARLY 19TH-CENTURY BEGINNINGS

The James Purdey who founded the company was born in the Whitechapel district of London in 1784. His parents had eight children, but as was typical of the day only he and his sister Martha survived early childhood. Purdey was exposed to gunmaking from an early age as his father was a blacksmith, and blacksmiths in those

COMPANY PERSPECTIVES

In the world of gunmaking the name Purdey is synonymous with the highest standards of quality, the company striving not just to maintain, but to constantly improve upon, its own high standards of engineering precision in gunmaking. Purdey numbers among its clients some of the world"s most demanding and discerning people, and has held Royal Warrants of Appointment to all British monarchs since the reign of Queen Victoria.

days were often involved in gunmaking. Furthermore, his sister, ten years his senior, married Thomas Keck Hutchinson, a gunmaker, in 1793. Five years later, Purdey began an apprenticeship under his brother-in-law, which he completed in 1805. He next spent three years working for the top London gunmaker of the time, Joseph Manton. During his stint honing his craft as a journeyman under Manton and developing relationships with the master gunmaker's customers, Purdey worked alongside Thomas Boss, who was an apprentice at Manton's firm. Boss went on to found his own company in 1816, and, like the company that Purdey formed that same year, Boss & Co. endured into the 21st century as a renowned maker of high-end guns.

Purdey left Manton's firm in 1808 to join the enterprise of another important gunmaker of the time, Alexander John Forsyth. Forsyth is credited with the invention of the percussion lock, a key component of the percussion system of ignition that began replacing the flintlock system in the 1820s. In the percussion system, still in use in the early 21st century, a hammer hits a detonating compound, which explodes and ignites the main charge in the gun. At Forsyth's firm, Purdey began work as a lock filer and stocker (the latter task involved carving gun stocks from wood and fitting them to the guns' metal parts), but he was soon promoted to company foreman. At the end of 1812, Purdey was admitted to the Freedom of the Gunmakers' Company, an essential step for a journeyman hoping to set up his own business and take on an apprentice.

In the spring of 1816, at the beginning of the turbulent post–Napoleonic Wars period, Purdey opened his own shop in London at 4 Princes Street, off Leicester Square. (It should be noted that the company itself has always claimed 1814 as its founding year, but Donald Dallas, author of the firm's definitive history, has concluded that James Purdey "most probably" set up his business in the spring of 1816.) Having already established a reputation as an excellent craftsman during his employment with Manton and Forsyth, and determined to make guns of only the highest quality, Purdey was soon flourishing in his new endeavor. Initially focusing on flintlock guns, Purdey produced about 12 guns per year during his firm's first years with production rising steadily to around 165 by 1825. In the early 1820s he began transitioning to percussion guns as the new technology became established among gun owners. In addition to making new guns—including sporting guns (or shotguns), rifles, and dueling and other types of pistols—Purdey also fitted percussion locks to old flintlock guns, offered his customers repair and maintenance services, and sold shooting accessories, such as gun cases, powder flasks, shot belts, and cartridges.

Having outgrown his small shop, Purdey in late 1826 moved into the former premises of Manton's company on Oxford Street. Manton had run into financial difficulties and was forced into bankruptcy earlier in the year. In his new, larger quarters, which were also located in a more commercially viable area, Purdey was able to expand his trade, with production averaging around 265 guns per year in the late 1820s. Trade with India began in 1826, and Purdey also began manufacturing and selling guns of a lower quality, which merchants purchased for resale. The core of the company's business, however, was with the more well-to-do: British nobility, clergymen, and royalty. Queen Victoria purchased a pair of Purdey pistols in 1838, one year after her accession to the throne.

Production at Purdey's firm dropped to around 150 guns per year in the later 1930s and then further to around 120 per year in the 1940s. This falloff, however, did not necessarily reflect any problem with the business, because the higher figures for the immediately prior period stemmed from the high demand that arose with the advent of the new percussion system. In a more distressing development, Purdey's company fell into financial difficulties by 1847 and was nearly forced out of business. Cash flow problems were the apparent cause of this crisis and likely stemmed from the reluctance or slowness of customers to pay what they owed the company, although the turbulent political and social climate that led up to the revolutionary year of 1848 in Europe may have contributed as well. Purdey was saved through the intervention of Lord Henry Bentinck, who in some discreet manner restored the company's finances and kept its order book full. By the 1850s, however, Purdey had built up substantial debts either through profligate spending or an inability to manage his business properly anymore because of advancing age. These

KEY DATES

1816: James Purdey sets up shop as a gunmaker at 4 Princes Street, off Leicester Square, in London.

1826: Purdey moves his business to larger quarters on Oxford Street.

1858: Purdey turns over control of the business to his son, also named James Purdey.

1863: James Purdey the Younger patents the Purdey bolt.

1877: Company name is changed to James Purdey and Sons.

1878: Queen Victoria grants the firm a Royal Warrant of Appointment.

1882: Headquarters are moved to Audley House, 57–58 South Audley Street.

1900: Athol Purdey succeeds his father, James the Younger, as head of the company.

1925: Firm is converted into a limited liability company, James Purdey & Sons Limited.

c. 1929: Athol Purdey retires; his sons, Jim and Tom, are given the company helm.

1946: The Seely family acquires a controlling interest in the company.

1949: Purdey & Sons acquires James Woodward & Sons and the rights to its over-and-under gun.

1994: Purdey & Sons is acquired by Vendôme, majority owned by Compagnie Financière Richemont SA; Richemont later gains full control of Vendôme and Purdey.

circumstances led Purdey to transfer control of the business to his son, also called James Purdey.

SECOND HALF OF THE 19TH CENTURY: JAMES PURDEY THE YOUNGER AT THE HELM

James Purdey the Younger was born in 1828 at the building on Oxford Street that served as both the company headquarters and the family home. He served an apprenticeship under his father from 1843 to 1850. The elder James was 73 years of age when he turned the business over to his son at the beginning of 1858; he died five years later. James the Younger assumed control of the company at age 29. In 1860 he was admitted to the Freedom of the Gunmakers' Company. In his early years of leadership he worked assiduously to reduce the debt his father had accumulated and put the company on a firmer financial footing.

Purdey took charge at a time of another key transition in gun design, the change from muzzle-loading weapons, which were loaded at the open end at the front of the barrel, to breech-loading guns, which were loaded at the rear of the barrel (the breech). Purdey has been credited, however, with the development of the well-known Express rifle, a muzzle-loader that originated in the early 1850s. Its name had derived from its likeness to an express train; its shot was fast, powerful, and straight. By 1870, however, breech-loaders had largely supplanted muzzle-loaders at the Purdey company. In 1868, meanwhile, the firm was granted a Royal Warrant of Appointment from the Prince of Wales. This was followed ten years later by the granting of a Royal Warrant by Queen Victoria. Each reigning British monarch thereafter did likewise.

During his period of helmsmanship, Purdey was at the forefront of advances in gun design, taking out several important patents in the process. None, however, was more important than his 1863 patent for the Purdey bolt, which in conjunction with the top lever patented in 1865 by gunmaker William Middleditch Scott created a bolt action mechanism for opening and closing breech-loading guns that remained the standard right into the 21st century. This invention enabled a sportsman to easily open his gun using his thumb on the top lever without having to change his grip on the gun's stock. It also enabled the gun to be easily snapped shut. After entering into a licensing arrangement with Scott's firm, Purdey was able to license what was often called either the Purdey lever or Purdey action to a large number of rival gunmakers, thereby garnering substantial revenue for his firm.

In the late 1870s the Purdey company departed from its normal standards of gunmaking by offering for sale different grades of guns, from best grade A to the cheapest grade E, with prices ranging from £58 down to £20. Only the grade A guns were entirely built by the company and conformed to the usual high standards. Other grades were either entirely or partially produced by other gunmakers. This practice pushed the company's sales up to around 350 guns a year by the mid-1880s, and the extra sales translated into healthy profits. Sales of the lower grades began tailing off in the 1890s, however, and the firm eventually concluded that the practice of using multiple grades was tarnishing its well-earned reputation for excellence. Following World War I, the company returned to making only top-grade guns and rifles.

In the meantime, the hammerless gun, in which the mechanism for firing was contained entirely within the gun's stock, began its ascendancy in the early 1870s. James Purdey made another shrewd maneuver in this area, purchasing the rights to a spring-cocked hammerless action invented in 1880 by Frederick Beesley, who had left Purdey's company two years earlier. As was the case with the Purdey lever, Purdey was able to license Beesley's hammerless action to other gunmakers, and thereby generate further revenue, because of the superiority of its design. Sales of hammerless guns gradually surpassed that of hammer guns over the course of the 1880s, particularly in the later years of the decade with the advent of the hammerless ejector gun, which included a mechanism that automatically threw each empty cartridge case out of the gun when the breech was opened. Since the addition of the ejector mechanism, no major changes were subsequently made to the basic design of the Purdey shooting gun, although a continual process of refinement occurred.

James Purdey cemented his company's position at the top of the London gunmakers with the construction of Audley House at the corner of South Audley Street and Mount Street in the prestigious area of Mayfair. In 1882 the company moved its headquarters to the grand new, five-story building at 57–58 South Audley Street, where it remained based into the early 21st century. The building included some workshop space below ground, but Purdey did not want the main factory and its attendant noise at the location because of the lavish showroom that was installed on the first floor. Therefore the Purdey factory was located nearby at 37 North Row, where it remained until 1900 when it was moved to 2 Irongate Wharf, off Praed Street.

James Purdey's plan of succession was to pass the business on to his two eldest sons, James III, born in 1854, and Athol Stuart, born in 1858. By 1877 the two brothers, then aged 24 and 19, respectively, had established themselves at the firm, and as a first step in the succession process, James the Younger changed the name of the company to James Purdey and Sons, though he did not confer any partnership rights. The rationale for the change was to familiarize customers with the existence of the sons within the firm. James III, however, never a well man, succumbed to tuberculosis in 1890 at age 36. In 1900 James the Younger retired, and control of the company passed to Athol Purdey. He was assisted by his brother Cecil Purdey, who was born in 1865 and had been brought into the firm in the late 1880s. James the Younger died in 1909 just short of his 81st birthday, leaving an estate valued at more than £200,000—a more than considerable sum at the time. He left the gunmaking business to Athol and Cecil, with shares of two-thirds and one-third, respectively.

SURVIVING THE PERIOD OF WORLD WARS AND DEPRESSION

When World War I broke out in 1914, James Purdey and Sons had around 108 employees. One-third of the workforce eventually joined the armed forces during the war. Orders for the company's high-end guns fell off substantially with Europe embroiled in war, so much so that profits fell from around £8,000 in 1912 to just £725 in 1915 when the firm was in danger of bankruptcy. To save the company, Athol Purdey turned the attention of what remained of his highly skilled workforce to military contracting. Among the gun-related parts the company produced during the war were muzzle protectors designed to prevent mud from getting into the barrel of rifles in trench warfare conditions, telescopic sights for snipers' rifles, and the Norman sight, a self-adjusting sight for aircraft machine guns that had been invented by a Cambridge University professor. Though Purdey and Sons had produced a few sporting guns in the early years of the war, by 1917 the company had turned its full attention to war production, and in 1918 not one gun left the factory.

In the immediate aftermath of World War I, Purdey and Sons recovered somewhat, producing about 200 sporting guns per year, well below the prewar average of around 300 guns. With the European markets far from returning to normal, the company began making inroads into the American market, which enjoyed a postwar boom in the 1920s and had hitherto been largely untapped. Athol Purdey embarked on a sales trip to the United States in 1922, during which he took several orders, and many more followed in the ensuing years.

Despite this burgeoning new market, a distinct drop in gun production, from around 230 in 1923 to around 165 in 1925, left the company in need of an injection of capital. Thus, in October 1925 the firm was converted into a limited liability company, James Purdey & Sons Limited, and preferred shares in the company were sold to the Oliver family for £24,400. The connection here was Bee Oliver, who had become the second wife of James Alexander (Jim) Purdey, son of Athol, in 1923. Athol was named chairman, while Cecil, Jim, and Jim's brother, Thomas Donald Stuart (Tom) Purdey, served as directors. With these developments, the Purdey family for the first time in the history of the company was not fully in charge.

Thanks to the infusion of capital and the booming U.S. market, Purdey & Sons prospered over the next several years with gun production surging back up to 300 guns by 1928 and net profits totaling almost £10,000 in 1927. The company used some of its funds to buy 36 acres of property to establish a shooting ground at Eastcote, South Harrow, near London. In addition to being used as a testing ground, customers could use the grounds for shooting practice and receive instruction from experts. Around 1929, Athol Purdey retired, leaving his two sons, Jim and Tom, in charge of the firm, the fourth generation of Purdeys at the helm.

The worldwide Great Depression of the 1930s hit Purdey & Sons hard. Sales to American customers dried up almost completely, while overall gun production fell to only around 100 per year during the early 1930s. The firm suffered a net loss of £500 in 1931, making it necessary to impose austerity measures, including laying off 26 gunmakers, or one-quarter of the workforce. A good portion of these workers were rehired in the late 1930s when business began picking up again and annual gun output had returned to the 200 level. In the meantime, in another economizing move, Purdey & Sons sold its Eastcote shooting grounds in 1936. In its stead, the company entered into an agreement to rent the West London Shooting Grounds at Northolt for testing and instruction, an arrangement that continued into the early 21st century. In 1935 the Oliver family decided to sell their stake in the company, and their shares were purchased by Sir Wyndham Portal of Laverstock (later Lord Portal) and Major Godfrey Miller-Mundy of Redrice, Hampshire.

In April 1939, on the eve of another world war, Athol Purdey died at age 81. During World War II, as was the case with the previous world war, Purdey & Sons produced very few of its trademark sporting guns and instead concentrated on filling war contracts. Among the items produced were rifle gauges, molds for aircraft electrical equipment, rifle chamber caps, and pop-rivet tools used in the construction of aircraft fuselages. In April 1941 Audley House was damaged in a German bombing raid. Two years later, Cecil Purdey died at age 78, thus ending the involvement in the firm of the third Purdey generation.

Late in 1943 Lord Portal and Major Miller-Mundy sold their preferred shares to Ivan Cobbold, a longtime customer and friend of the company. In June of the following year, however, Cobbold was killed by a German V1 bomb. His shares were eventually sold, in March 1946, to Sir Hugh Seely (later Lord Sherwood), who had served as under-secretary of state for air during the war, and who was the majority owner of Purdey & Sons.

POSTWAR CHALLENGES

The prospects for selling luxury goods such as high-end sporting rifles seemed bleak in the austere environment of postwar Europe. Labor costs had increased markedly during the war, pushing up the price that Purdey & Sons would need to charge for its guns to make a profit. At the same time, the new Labour government enacted a highly progressive income tax that diminished the disposable income of Purdey customers; dozens of customers in the United Kingdom abruptly canceled their gun orders. Jim and Tom Purdey went so far as to suggest that the company concentrate its efforts on tool and mold manufacturing, which seemed to have better prospects, and drop gunmaking altogether. Lord Sherwood, however, felt that guns were Purdey's business and that was where the company should stake its future. His view won out, although Purdey & Sons continued to operate a toolmaking business as a sort of backup option until 1961.

For Purdey & Sons to prosper in the postwar era, it needed to place a greater emphasis on attracting customers in the United States, which was experiencing a postwar boom. In that market, however, there was a greater demand for over-and-under guns, that is, guns with two barrels, one atop the other, in contrast to the side-by-side gun, in which the barrels are opposed horizontally. Purdey & Sons had occasionally made over-and-under guns, but its twin-barrel guns were more typically the side-by-side variety. In 1949 the company made a key acquisition, purchasing James Woodward & Sons, a London gunmaker with roots dating back to the mid-1840s that was on the brink of insolvency. Woodward had earned a reputation for making very elegant and finely finished guns, and most importantly held the rights to a highly successful over-and-under gun. Though the purchase price of a little more than £444 included the rights to the James Woodward & Sons name, Purdey elected to begin making the Woodward over-and-under gun under the Purdey brand. The first such gun was delivered in 1950.

When Tom Purdey retired in 1955, a period began in which no member of the Purdey family was involved in the day-to-day management of the company. Purdey died two years later. Lord Sherwood became chairman of Purdey & Sons upon Tom Purdey's retirement, a position he held until his death in 1970. His brother, Sir Victor Seely, briefly took over the chairmanship before passing it on to Richard Beaumont in July 1971. Beaumont, a nephew of Lord Sherwood, had joined Purdey & Sons in 1947 and was made a director in 1953.

The next serious challenge for Purdey was the sustained inflationary economy of the late 1960s and early 1970s. The company was forced to substantially increase the wages it paid its gunmakers, which in turn meant that the prices of new guns had to be raised. Between 1968 and 1976, for example, the cost of a side-by-side gun jumped from £1,100 to £4,500. Compounding the situation was that most orders for new guns were on a fixed-price basis, but it took as long as four years to deliver a gun. Thus, a gun ordered at a fixed price of £1,500 in 1969 might actually cost £2,500 to build over the next few years because of the high rate of inflation. To escape this recipe for bankruptcy, Purdey began introducing surcharges on delivery and eventually included in order contracts an open-ended escalation clause. These measures, coupled with an easing in inflation, returned the company to more secure footing by the late 1970s.

Toward the end of the 1970s, the company introduced a line of Purdey clothing and accessories. During the 1980s, the company was producing between 60 and 70 guns per year, with prices starting at £23,000. The acquisition of James Woodward & Sons had proved critical as approximately 65 percent of Purdey's customers in the 1980s were Americans. The firm's overall export figure for new guns was approximately 85 percent.

1994 FORWARD: THE RICHEMONT ERA

Wishing to retire, Beaumont engineered the sale of Purdey & Sons to Vendôme, a luxury goods consortium controlled by Compagnie Financière Richemont SA, a Swiss holding company for the Rupert family's international interests. Among the luxury brands owned by Vendôme/Richemont were Cartier jewelry, Baume & Mercier and Piaget watches, and Montblanc pens. The deal was concluded in October 1994 for an undisclosed sum. Three years later, Richemont acquired full control of Vendôme, making Purdey a wholly owned subsidiary of Richemont. Shortly after the takeover of Purdey, Richard Purdey, six generations down the direct line of descent from the company founder and grandson of Jim Purdey, took charge of the company as chairman.

In the years following the Richemont takeover, James Purdey & Sons was reinvigorated in various ways. While the traditional techniques used to make guns at Purdey remained largely intact, the new owners did install some computer numerical controlled machinery to ease some of the gunmakers' burden, to further improve the technical precision of the guns, and to improve productivity. According to a December 29, 2004, article in the *Financial Times,* cost-saving measures and an increasing emphasis on generating revenues from nongun products, particularly clothing and accessories, enabled Purdey to move from a £265,000 loss (on revenues of £4.5 million) in 2001 to nearly breaking even in 2004 (not counting one

extraordinary expense, a £296,000 infusion into the firm's pension fund). In 1997, in the meantime, Purdey reintroduced to the market the Woodward name, offering both over-and-under and side-by-side models under that brand.

The biggest change, however, was the adoption of a more assertive marketing orientation. The firm adopted a new logo that featured the single word *Purdey,* and in 1999 it opened its first shop outside Audley House, on New York's Upper East Side at 844 Madison Avenue, where it began selling guns, clothes, and accessories. In the spring of 2006 the company hired the public relations firm Brian MacLaurin Associates to increase general awareness of the brand, such as by promoting Purdey's efforts in conservation. Later that year, Purdey launched online shopping for its clothing, accessories, and gift lines. At the same time, Purdey brand products were being increasingly distributed through prestigious specialty stores in Europe and the United States. In 2000, meanwhile, 184 years after its founding, James Purdey & Sons produced its 30,000th gun, a unique gun it called the Millennium Gun.

David E. Salamie

PRINCIPAL COMPETITORS

Holland & Holland Limited; Boss & Co.

FURTHER READING

Beaumont, Richard, *Purdey's: The Guns and the Family,* Newton Abbot, Devon, U.K.: David & Charles, 1984, 248 p.

"Corporate Profile: Gunmakers James Purdey and Sons," *Observer* (London), April 15, 1990, p. 33.

Dallas, Donald, *Purdey: Gun and Rifle Makers; The Definitive History,* London: Quiller Press, 2000, 245 p.

Fallon, James, "Vendôme Acquires U.K. Gun Makers," *Women's Wear Daily,* October 11, 1994, p. 28.

Mason, John, "Purdey Welcomes Russia's Gun Buyers," *Financial Times,* December 29, 2004, p. 14.

Middleton, Drew, "A Home of Guns for a King," *New York Times,* June 9, 1985, p. XX6.

Reed, Stanley, "Almost Too Pretty to Shoot," *Business Week,* July 17, 2006, p. 76.

Rigby, Rhymer, "Simply the Best," *Management Today,* December 1995, pp. 70+.

Unsworth, L. Patrick, *The Early Purdeys,* London: Christie's, 1996, 278 p.

Wighton, David, "Purdey Goes Out with a Bang," *Financial Times,* October 6, 1994, p. 23.

Wright, Rupert, "A Shot of Luxury for the Glorious Twelfth," *Times* (London), August 12, 2000, p. 22.

Kendle International Inc.

1200 Carew Tower
441 Vine Street
Cincinnati, Ohio 45202
U.S.A.
Telephone: (513) 381-5550
Toll Free: (800) 733-1572
Fax: (513) 381-5870
Web site: http://www.kendle.com

Public Company
Incorporated: 1989 as Kendle Research Associates, Inc.
Employees: 3,050
Sales: $373.9 million (2006)
Stock Exchanges: NASDAQ
Ticker Symbol: KNDL
NAIC: 541710 Research and Development in the Physical, Engineering, and Life Sciences

∎ ∎ ∎

Kendle International Inc. is a global clinical research organization (CRO) serving the biopharmaceutical industry on a contract basis. The company shepherds new drugs and treatments through the clinical trials required to win regulatory approval, providing patient recruitment, clinical monitoring, data management and analysis, late phase help with scientific events, education, and publications, and consulting services connected to the regulatory approval process. In addition, Kendle International offers its proprietary suite of software solutions, TrialWare, which helps clients to manage the database of information generated in clinical trials and share it with others. The company has worked with 46 of the top 50 pharmaceutical companies and has been involved in the regulatory process in 80 countries. A public company listed on the NASDAQ, Kendle International maintains its headquarters in Cincinnati, Ohio.

COMPANY FOUNDED: 1981

Kendle International was founded in 1981 by its chairman and chief executive officer, Candace Kendle, and president and chief operating officer, Christopher C. Bergen—friends at the time but now married. Neither of Kendle's parents had the opportunity to attend college. They were fortunate, in fact, to escape the coal mines. "My grandparents," Kendle told *PharmaVOICE* in a 2005 profile, "walked out of the coal mines of Kentucky, traveling 360 miles with nine children, because they were determined to get out. This type of commitment is sewn throughout the fabric of my family tree." She grew up in Cincinnati and graduated from high school in 1964. Interested in pursuing science and math, she initially enrolled in nursing school, where she was quickly disenchanted. She then enrolled at the University of Cincinnati in 1965, becoming only one of six women in the College of Pharmacy. After graduating with a bachelor of science in pharmacy in 1970 she stayed at the school to complete her Ph.D. two years later. She served her residency at Cincinnati Children's Hospital Medical Center, then relocated to the University of North Carolina School of Public Health where she received an Epidemiology Fellowship and served as an instructor at the university's School of Pharmacy. Kendle then became a professor at North

Kendle is a global clinical research organization that provides the biopharmaceutical industry with outstanding strategy as well as a full complement of quality clinical development and regulatory services to accelerate the drug development process. We live our "Real people. Real results." statement every day as we work in partnership with companies to help speed their drugs to market, making a real difference to the quality of life of people around the world.

Carolina, attaining the rank of associate professor by the time she left in 1979. She took over as director of the Children's Hospital of Philadelphia, Department of Pharmacy, and also served as a professor of Pediatrics at the University of Pennsylvania, School of Medicine. By this time she was married with two young sons, and although she enjoyed the academic life she was forced to make changes after she and her husband were divorced.

"There was only one reason we started Kendle," she explained to *PharmaVOICE*. "I needed some personal flexibility with regard to caring for my family." She decided to return home to Cincinnati to start a small consulting firm, a city where she had well over 100 family members. Her parents were not able to help her finance the business, but they provided board for Kendle and the boys and helped with the childcare. A bedroom in the house became the company's first headquarters. Kendle also had a partner in Bergen, a colleague at The Children's Hospital where he served as an administrator. A Princeton University graduate, he also held an M.B.A. from the University of Pennsylvania's prestigious Wharton School.

Over the next decade Kendle and Bergen grew the business together and nurtured their relationship, ultimately getting married. Kendle's basic vision for the company, Kendle Research Associates, Inc., was to take advantage of a developing trend among drug developers to contract out research to small laboratories. What she offered was to oversee clinical drug development and the testing of new drugs on humans. The data required by the U.S. Food and Drug Administration to gain regulatory approval had to be precise, and Kendle quickly built a reputation for reliability.

Because many of the pharmaceutical firms were located on the East Coast, operating out of Cincinnati was a disadvantage, but as long as Kendle and Bergen were able to string one contract to the next they were

content with their lot. All that changed in the early 1990s when the large pharmaceutical firms began outsourcing even more of their operations in an effort to cut costs. While theoretically this should have presented more opportunities for Kendle Research, it also created competition, and the new companies that were becoming involved in the CRO field were much larger and took away a major slice of the company's business. In 1991 the company lost $1 million worth of contracts, or about half of its revenues. Kendle held off on trimming payroll for as long as possible, exhausting the company's $1 million line of credit before starting to lay off people.

In order to remain in business, Kendle and Bergen had no choice but to sell out or grow larger. They elected to grow larger but they lacked the marketing skills necessary to do so. To gain more knowledge Kendle took a crash course at Harvard Business School and Bergen soon joined her as well. They reorganized Kendle Research with an emphasis on marketing and began to regrow the business. Sales totaled in the $2.5 million range in 1992 and 1993, and the company returned to profitability in 1993, but it was in 1994 that Kendle Research finally turned the corner. Revenues increased to $4.4 million and net income increased to $458,000 from $252,000. In addition, the company introduced TrialWare. A year later Kendle Research opened a sales office in Los Angeles and sales grew to $6.1 million. Offices were then established in Chicago, and Princeton, New Jersey, and revenues doubled to $13 million, with net income of $1.1 million.

IPO FUNDS 1997 ACQUISITIONS

By 1997 Kendle Research was poised to transform itself from a niche contractor into a full-service company with global scope. To become involved in Europe, it acquired U-Gene Research B.V. for $15.9 million in June 1997. Based in Utrecht, Netherlands, U-Gene conducted clinical drug trials in the Netherlands, the United Kingdom, and Italy. It owned and operated a state-of-the-art 38-bed testing facility. Kendle Research also reached an agreement to acquire another independent research firm, Munich, Germany-based GMI Gesellschaft fur Angewandte Mathematik und Informatik. To pay for these transactions, Kendle Research changed its name to Kendle International Inc. and conducted an initial public offering (IPO) of stock underwritten by Lehman Brothers Inc. and J.C. Bradford & Co. Completed in August 1997 the IPO netted $49.6 million for the company. A week later the GMI acquisition was completed, using $10 million of that cash and another $2 million worth of common stock. With these new

KEY DATES

1981: Company is founded.
1991: Loss of contracts leads to expansion.
1997: Company goes public as Kendle International.
2001: AAC Consulting Group, Inc., is acquired.
2003: Company enters Latin American market.

operations in the fold, Kendle International enjoyed a surge in revenues to $44.2 million, while net income improved to $1.9 million.

In February 1998 Kendle International completed its first domestic acquisition, paying $14.4 million in cash and stock for ACER/EXCEL Inc., a New Jersey-based full-service CRO. The company also brought with it a presence in the Pacific Rim through a drug development services joint venture located in Beijing, China. Kendle International also completed a secondary offering of stock in 1998, raising another $100 million. For the year, revenues increased to $89.5 million and net income totaled almost $7.2 million.

The company continued to grow in the final year of the 1990s, and built up its global operations in anticipation of winning even more contracts. It completed five acquisitions in 1999. A minority interest was taken in Digineer, Inc., a healthcare consulting and software development company. U.K.-based Research Consultants (International) Holdings Ltd., a regulatory affairs company, was added at the cost of $4.4 million in cash plus stock. In June 1999 Kendle International paid $2.7 million in cash for ESCLI S.A., a French contract research firm. The following month the company acquired Health Care Communications Inc. and its affiliate Health Care Communications Ltd. at the cost of $5.7 million in cash and stock, establishing the foundation for Kendle International's medical communication/meeting and medical society management division. The extra workload did not materialize as expected because the pharmaceutical industry underwent a period of consolidation and volatility, which began in late 1999 and carried through 2000, resulting in a temporary shift in focus from drug development to mergers and acquisitions, and a reduction in spending on CROs. When 1999 came to an end, Kendle International recorded revenues of $117.1 million and net income of $7.7 million, but the following year the company posted a net loss of $2.1 million on revenues of $120.5 million. The meager increase in sales was especially disappointing in light of the March 2000 introduction of a suite of

Internet-based products: TrialBase, TriaLine, and TrialFax.

During the difficulties of 2000, Kendle international took a hard look at its operations and polished its drug development process to better position the company when the pharmaceutical industry had completed its shakeout. The company also bolstered its presence in the Asia-Pacific region through the $2.2 million cash and stock acquisition of SYNERmedica Pty Ltd., an Australian CRO.

Business picked up in 2001 and Kendle International returned to profitability in the first quarter. By the end of the year revenues had improved to $154.3 million and net income totaled $4.2 million. The company also continued to grow externally, acquiring Rockville, Maryland-based AAC Consulting Group, a regulatory and validation services company for $10.9 million in cash plus stock. In addition, in 2001 Kendle International forged an alliance with Pharmacia Corp., becoming only one of two primary providers of clinical research services to the London-based firm, which two years later was bought by Pfizer, Inc.

GENERIC DRUG CAPABILITIES: 2002

Kendle International continued its global expansion in 2002, establishing alliances with CROs in Mexico and Bulgaria. The company also expanded its customer base to include smaller pharmaceutical and biotech firms, which lacked the resources of industry giants and could make good use of Kendle International's expertise. Moreover, the company continued to add what it had to offer clients. In 2002, for example, Kendle International became involved in generic drug development with the acquisition of Clinical and Pharmacologic Research, Inc., a Morgantown, West Virginia-based company that laid the foundation for the Kendle Bioequivalence and Pharmacokinetics unit.

In 2003 Kendle International took a step back to reorganize its business into five specialized operating units. It also took some write-downs that resulted in a $54.8 million net loss on revenues of $165.2 million for the year. Nevertheless, the company was still able to expand into Latin America through the acquisition of a Mexican CRO, Estadisticos y Clinicos Asociados, SA.

The reorganization effort was completed in 2004 and the company expanded its worldwide reach during the course of the year and into early 2005 by opening new offices in Romania and Bulgaria to gain a foothold in Eastern Europe. The company made further inroads in Latin America with a new office in Peru. It also took steps to open offices in New Delhi, India, and Johannesburg, South Africa. In 2004 Kendle International outpaced the marketplace by growing revenues 10 percent to $172.9 million. After two years of posting net losses, the company earned $3.6 million.

Kendle International enjoyed an even better year in 2005 as the company's refined business model continued to bear fruit. Revenues improved 17 percent to more than $202 million, while net income almost tripled to $10.7 million. Strong growth continued in 2006, when the company posted revenues of $373.9 million. The company also bolstered its Latin America business with the acquisition of International Clinical Research and expanded its customer base with the addition of the Phase II–IV Clinical Services business of Charles River Laboratories, Inc.

Ed Dinger

PRINCIPAL SUBSIDIARIES

Kendle U.K. Inc,; Kendle GmbH (Germany); Kendle International B.V. (Netherlands); Kendle International Holdings Pty Limited (Australia); ACER/EXCEL Inc.; Kendle Canada; Kendle International, S.A. de C.V. (Mexico).

PRINCIPAL COMPETITORS

Covance Inc.; PAREXEL International Corporation; Quintiles Transnational Corp.

FURTHER READING

"A Candid Visionary," *PharmaVOICE*, November 2005.

Curtis, Richard, "Kendle Top Local Public Co. Exec," *Cincinnati Business Courier,* February 17, 2004.

Daumeyer, Rob, "Kendle Overcomes Scare to Flourish," *Cincinnati Business Courier,* July 1, 1996, p. S10.

Galuskza, Peter, "Kendle International: The $44 Million Mom-and-Pop," *Business Week,* June 1, 1998, p. 74.

Tortora, Andrea, "TEST PILOT (Kendle International Inc. Is Doing Well)," *Business Courier Serving Cincinnati–Northern Kentucky,* October 19, 2001, p. 1.

Warrick, Camilla, "Kendle Molding Jobs to Fit the Person," *Cincinnati Post,* January 18, 1999.

Yeager, Chris, "Steady Growth," *Business Courier Serving Cincinnati–Northern Kentucky,* November 10, 2000, p. 22B.

Kenexa Corporation

650 East Swedesford Road, 2nd Floor
Wayne, Pennsylvania 19087
U.S.A.
Telephone: (610) 971-9171
Fax: (610) 971-9181
Web site: http://www.kenexa.com

Public Company
Founded: 1987 as Raymond Karsan Associates
Employees: 693
Sales: $65.6 million (2005)
Stock Exchanges: NASDAQ
Ticker Symbol: KNXA
NAIC: 511210 Software Publishers; 518210 Data Processing, Hosting, and Related Services; 541611 Administrative Management and General Management Consulting Services

■ ■ ■

Kenexa Corporation provides a comprehensive set of products and services designed to assist clients in the human resources management processes of recruiting and retaining quality employees. Through computer software or web-based subscriptions, Kenexa provides customers with tools they need to effectively handle talent acquisition and employee performance management. Talent acquisition products include applicant tracking systems that store and organize data on potential hires. These include Kenexa Recruiter, for the medium to large organization with a centralized human resources department; Kenexa Recruiter BrassRing, for decentral-

ized or multinational organizations; and Kenexa Store-Front, for retail or hourly positions. Applicant screening products include Kenexa Selector behavior and personality tests, PeopleQuest prerecorded telephone interviews, and Prove It! skills testing. For designing in-person interviews, the company offers Kenexa Insight and Kenexa Interview Builder. With Kenexa offers an "onboarding" process for proper paperwork completion and company orientation on an employee's first day at work.

Employee performance management products include CareerTracker, designed to be used by employees and managers to determine career pathways based on personal and company goals as they influence measures of performance and suggest areas of self-development. For managers, the product facilitates succession planning. Kenexa bStrategic deepens management's ability to analyze employee data in connection with performance goals. Other products are designed to gain employee feedback, including Employee Engagement Surveys and Exit Interviews. Kenexa provides professional consulting services to assist clients in the customization and implementation of the company's proprietary systems.

IMPROMPTU PARTNERSHIP LEADS TO COMPANY FOUNDING

Kenexa originated as Raymond Karsan Associates (RKA), an executive recruitment firm specializing in the insurance industry. The company name extended from the last names of founders Barry Raymond and Nooruddin "Rudy" Karsan. The two men met when Raymond, then an executive recruiter, interviewed Karsan, then an actuary for Mercantile & General Reinsurance Company of Toronto, for Raymond's client in the insurance industry. Raymond and Karsan established a rapport immediately and found they had complementary business skills. Raymond suggested that he and Karsan form a partnership in the field of executive recruitment, and Karsan's interest in entrepreneurship prompted him to accept the invitation.

At first, Raymond and Karsan simply pursued business opportunities in a fun, casual manner, without formal strategy or market research. Then, in 1991, as revenues neared the $1 million mark, they began to take a more conceptual approach to business growth. Their strategy involved providing a complete range of services complementary to the executive search and hiring process. By offering a variety of services, RKA sought to stun its clients with its ability to address any need. Moreover, Raymond and Karsan never said no to a customer, believing they could find a solution to any human resources management problem. Frequently, RKA acquired a company that already offered a service in order to assist a client. Karsan, who became chief executive officer in 1991, attributed the growth of the company to a willingness to say yes to any idea, as long as it involved a well-defined goal. Over time, RKA's management consulting services came to include organizational change and planning, compensation structure, standards of competency and performance, and employee development, the latter involving methods of promoting employee satisfaction and directing career pathways.

During the early 1990s, demand for computer-based technologies led RKA to the development of information management systems which simplified human resource processes. Because the company had little capital to invest in technological development, Karsan proposed a merger with the firm that already handled RKA's information technology. Then, in 1993, RKA introduced its first computerized talent management system, which transformed proprietary knowledge into software which assisted customers in recruiting, training, and retaining employees. In 1995, the company began to offer software for performance management and employee research. The introduction of software applications for outsourced employment processing began in 1996.

Thus, between the mergers and acquisitions and a general rise in new customers, RKA grew rapidly. By 1996, the company had grown from one full-time employee to 144 employees and from one office to 22 offices nationwide. With revenue nearly doubling every year, from $3.7 million in 1993 to $27.9 million in 1996, RKA attained a place on the Philadelphia 100, a list of the fastest-growing companies. *Inc.* magazine listed RKA on its list of the 500 fastest-growing companies nationwide for four years in a row, from 1995 through 1998.

TECHNOLOGY: CENTRAL CORPORATE STRATEGY

During the late 1990s, much of the company's growth occurred through several mergers and acquisitions that broadened the company's technology products and service capabilities. Prominent merger partners included Advanced Consulting Inc., an award-winning multimedia company specializing in custom, computer-based training and intranet training. The 1997 merger with Human Resources Technologies contributed a variety of customized services in executive search, recruitment, and development. Enhanced Communications Inc. provided RKA with unique training programs in a variety of management areas and in several media formats. Enhanced Communications offered unique training programs in the fields of financial services, information technology, and other professional services industries.

The greatest impact on growth occurred when RKA began to offer consulting and maintenance services for Oracle databases and applications. Toward that end, in 1998 RKA merged with Technology Partners Corporation, which offered Oracle products for several business management and information management applications, including online publishing. The January 1999 merger with Software Support Services further contributed to RKA's capabilities in applying Oracle applications and technology to human resources management processes. Working exclusively in Oracle software, S3 brought substantial expertise to RKA. The focus on Oracle product implementation substantially expanded RKA's client list of several *Fortune* 500 companies. By the end of 2000 Oracle services accounted for 85 percent of the company's $60 million in revenues.

```
┌─────────────────────────────────────────┐
│                                          │
│             KEY DATES                    │
│                ■                         │
│  1991: Rudy Karsan becomes CEO of Raymond│
│        Karsan Associates (RKA), as company turns
│        toward comprehensive service.     │
│  1993: The company's first human resource manage-
│        ment computer software is launched.│
│  1998: For the fourth consecutive year, RKA ranks
│        on the Inc. 500 list of fastest-growing
│        companies.                        │
│  1999: Company realigns its growth strategy toward
│        the development of Internet products.│
│  2000: Company is renamed Kenexa Corporation.│
│  2004: Subscription-based Internet products account
│        for 79 percent of revenues.       │
│  2005: Kenexa initiates public offering of stock.│
│  2006: Kenexa Research Institute is established.│
│                                          │
└─────────────────────────────────────────┘
```

While revenues continued to increase, further growth required an infusion of outside capital to cover the cost of developing Internet products and services, as well as day-to-day operations. In December 1999, RKA obtained $22 million in venture capital funds, primarily from Parthenon Capital of Boston and secondarily from Shad Run Investments LP and TSG Co-Investors LLC. A credit facility through Fleet National provided an additional $10 million. The company sought to obtain further resources through an initial public offering of stock, as announced in June 2000, but delayed the offering after the investor interest in Internet companies waned significantly. In the meantime, Kenexa obtained $58 million venture capital funds from Wafra Partners, a group owned by the Public Institute for Social Security of Kuwait, and Parthenon Capital. An additional $6 million was received from Westbury Partners in April 2001.

RKA used $7 million to purchase Barry Raymond's ownership. To reflect the change in ownership, the company changed its name to TalentPoint in May 2000. However, the use of the word "talent" made the name similar to other companies, including TalentPlus, which filed a lawsuit to stop the company from using TalentPoint. The company changed its name to Kenexa the following November.

The majority of investment capital was intended to develop proprietary Internet products, to be available on-demand through a paid subscription. Kenexa concentrated on the development of talent acquisition and performance management products branded and trademarked with the Kenexa name. In 2000, Kenexa introduced a web-based career development tool, called Kenexa CareerTracker. The system parlayed the company's knowledge in this area into a user-friendly tool whereby employees set goals in conjunction with their employers' framework of goals and performance standards. Performance, skill, aptitude, and personality measurements provided employees with a tool for realistic self-development on the career path. Managers used CareerTracker to organize information on people who hold potential for promotion. Moreover, the system allowed managers to interface with employee input in order to match individual ambitions and abilities with organizational goals and succession planning. Kenexa introduced upgraded versions of existing products, such as Enterprise Staffing Solutions and a specialized version, Healthcare Staffing Solutions. The latter facilitated the large scale recruiting for nursing and other healthcare professionals staffing through a unique process. An improved version of Prove It! offered a skills assessment for Microsoft Office software, such as Word, Excel, and Powerpoint.

As the company's focus on Internet tools progressed, Kenexa streamlined its product offering to eliminate training and to emphasize talent acquisition and maximization as a holistic process. In 2004, Kenexa launched Kenexa CARE, a software application designed to manage employee recruitment for hospital staffing by capturing candidate data in a format that facilitated candidate tracking during the entire recruitment process. Recruiter Express provided applicant tracking for small businesses with less than 1,000 employees and fewer than three active recruiters. Kenexa's StoreFront, introduced in November, offered applicant tracking designed for the needs of retail businesses in recruiting and hiring hourly employees. Through application online at remote sites or at an in-store kiosk, StoreFront streamlined the screening process and allowed for immediate or quick interview arrangements. With Interview Builder, Kenexa offered access to interview questions and links to interview resources on the web. Through job analysis, the system provided questions based on tasks and skills required of a position. The program scored candidate responses to interview questions for further analysis. By the end of 2004, subscription-based products accounted for 79 percent of revenues.

A partnership with Swiftknowledge, Inc., in 2005 led to the development of Kenexa bStrategic, an in-depth and complex analysis tool. The system used data on recruitment, applicant tracking, and employee and performance information, as well as finance and accounting information, to align human resource functions with organizational goals.

By June 2005 the company was prepared to seek funds for additional acquisitions and further product development, as well as to initiate international expansion, through an initial public offering (IPO) of five million shares of stock, priced at $12 per share. The initial offering, plus a secondary offering of 750,000 shares, raised $61.7 million net, though reacquiring stock of private investors left the company with $21 million in capital for the planned acquisition of Webhire, Inc.

KENEXA DEVELOPS GLOBAL MARKET STRATEGY

Kenexa continued its acquisition and expansion efforts by entering the global arena for employment process outsourcing services, particularly in Asia. Industry observers expected revenues in human capital management to reach $2 billion in Asia by 2008. The company planned to invest approximately $6 million to establish a presence in India. In April 2004, the company acquired Oramasters, a human resource solutions company based in Hyderabad, India, which specialized in Oracle products. Kenexa planned to expand operations at the center to accommodate customer support as well as augment continuing product development. In October 2006, Kenexa opened a new facility in Visakhapatnam, India, intended to serve India and Asia-Pacific operations. Kenexa opened offices in Hong Kong, Taiwan, and Malaysia as well. To serve these markets, the company launched its Enterprise Human Capital Management technology, a product designed for global employee performance management.

In August 2005 Kenexa augmented previously established offices in Canada when the company acquired the assets of Scottworks, a human resources consulting firm in Toronto. Scottworks specialized in employee and organizational feedback, sales and service improvement, team-building, and management development. In particular, Scottworks' multirater feedback system provided Kenexa with a significant new tool in obtaining employee opinions throughout an organization.

In Europe Kenexa established offices in the Netherlands and Germany, and in November 2006, acquired Psychometric Services Limited (PSL), a candidate assessment solutions provider in London, England. PSL specialized in personality and ability tests used for screening and selections of prospective employees. Kenexa acquired the company for $7.6 million. In addition to its expertise in psychological assessment, PSL would contribute an impressive client list, in both business and government.

CONTINUING PRODUCT DEVELOPMENT

Kenexa continued to improve its product offerings in 2006. In January Kenexa completed its acquisition of recruitment and new hire software company Webhire for $34 million. Webhire provided Kenexa with a new product, onboarding software designed to facilitate a new employee's first day on the job. This product provided Kenexa with an important link between the recruitment and employee retention process.

In order to provide broader and deeper knowledge about best practices in employee satisfaction, the company formed Kenexa Research Institute in October 2006. Toward that end, Kenexa acquired Gantz Wiley Research (GWR), whose assets included the WorkTrends database of employee survey results. Hence, the institute would include a library of more than 30 years of employee surveys on such topics as leadership, customer service, and employee engagement with organizational goals. Moreover, GWR principal Jack Wiley attained international prestige for his High Performance Model, which revealed the connections between employee opinions, customer loyalty, and business achievement. Wiley became executive director of the Kenexa Research Institute.

Kenexa improved its recruitment technology with the $115 million acquisition of BrassRing, a competitor in talent management technology. Based in Waltham, Massachusetts, BrassRing offered consulting, recruitment, and recruitment software. Observers noted that BrassRing carried better enterprise software which would benefit Kenexa. Indeed, Kenexa acquired the company in October and launched a new product in December. Kenexa Recruiter BrassRing Release 9, an applicant tracking system with more than 70 upgrades in functionality, derived its improvements from BrassRing's technological capabilities. The new system served organizations of more than 10,000 employees and addressed the needs of global organizations with multiple language and customization options for application of the technology to local needs. Kenexa planned to repay debt related to the acquisition of BrassRing through an offering of stock in early 2007.

While Kenexa was already recognized as a leader in human capital management, by 2007 industry observers placed Kenexa among the top companies in its field. In 2005 *HRO Today* ranked Kenexa as number one among 13 full-service recruitment process providers, in terms of range and quality of services. In 2006 *Workforce Management* placed Kenexa as the third ranking provider of applicant tracking system software providers, with more than 400 active clients.

Mary Tradii

PRINCIPAL SUBSIDIARIES

BrassRing, LLC; Kenexa Technology, Inc.; Knowledge Workers, Inc.

PRINCIPAL COMPETITORS

Authoria, Inc.; Lawson Software, Inc.; Peopleclick, Inc.; Taleo Corporation; Vurv Technology, Inc.; Workstream, Inc.

FURTHER READING

Frauenheim, Ed, "Kenexa-BrassRing Deal Could Trigger More Consolidation," *Workforce Management*, October 23, 2006, p. 4.

———, "Sector Tightens Again As Kenexa Acquires Webhire," *Workforce Management*, January 16, 2006, p. 6.

"India's Kenexa Acquires UK's PSL," *AsiaPulse News*, November 23, 2006.

Kasrel, Deni, "HR Company Capitalizes on Outsourcing," *Philadelphia Business Journal*, October 21, 1996.

"Kenexa Buys Oramasters," *Asia Africa Intelligence Wire*, April 3, 2004.

"Kenexa in Talks to Take over HR Solution Firm," *Economic Times*, April 13, 2005.

"Kenexa Introduces Interview Builders, Web-Based Solution Streamlines Hiring Process," *Customer Interaction Solutions*, January 2005, p. 28.

"Kenexa Introduces Recruitment Management Solution for Corporations with Fewer Than 1,000 Employees, University Physicians, Inc. Implements Kenexa Recruiter Express As Its Web-Based Applicant Tracking System," *Internet Wire*, February 10, 2004.

"Kenexa on Expansion Path, Lines Up New Product," *India Business Insight*, October 11, 2006.

"Kenexa Plans $6m for India Centre," *Asia Africa Intelligence Wire*, October 2, 2004.

Key, Peter, "Kenexa Has Been Reeling in the Funds," *Philadelphia Business Journal*, March 9, 2001, p. 3.

———, "Kenexa Logs Positive News amid Job Cuts," *Philadelphia Business Journal*, December 14, 2001, p. 4.

———, "What's in a Name? Ask the Kenexa Folks," *Philadelphia Business Journal*, December 8, 2000, p. 8.

"Meet Rudy Karsan," March 2000, http://www.inc.com/articles/2000/03/17619_Printer_Friendly.html.

Meyer, Gary, "Succession Plans Made Easier," *HRMagazine*, February 2001, p. 129.

"New Institute Aims to Advance the Science of Employee Research," *Training Journal*, October 2006, p. 6.

"Strategic HR," *HRMagazine*, July 2005, p. 128.

Kerry Group plc

Prince's Street
Tralee, County Kerry
Ireland
Telephone: (+353 66) 718 2000
Fax: (+353 66) 718 2961
Web site: http://www.kerrygroup.com

Public Company
Founded: 1972 as North Kerry Milk Products Limited
Incorporated: 1986
Employees: 23,289
Sales: EUR 4.65 billion ($6.13 billion) (2006)
Stock Exchanges: Dublin London
Ticker Symbol: KYGA
NAIC: 311222 Soybean Processing; 311411 Frozen Fruit, Juice, and Vegetable Manufacturing; 311412 Frozen Specialty Food Manufacturing; 311421 Fruit and Vegetable Canning; 311423 Dried and Dehydrated Food Manufacturing; 311511 Fluid Milk Manufacturing; 311512 Creamery Butter Manufacturing; 311513 Cheese Manufacturing; 311612 Meat Processed from Carcasses; 311615 Poultry Processing; 311813 Frozen Cakes, Pies, and Other Pastries Manufacturing; 311822 Flour Mixes and Dough Manufacturing from Purchased Flour; 311920 Coffee and Tea Manufacturing; 311930 Flavoring Syrup and Concentrate Manufacturing; 311942 Spice and Extract Manufacturing; 311991 Perishable Prepared Food Manufacturing; 311999 All Other Miscellaneous Food Manufacturing; 312112 Bottled Water Manufacturing

Kerry Group plc is one of the main global suppliers of food ingredients and flavors as well as a leading processor and marketer of branded consumer foods mainly in Ireland and the United Kingdom. The Irish firm operates manufacturing plants in 19 countries, with sales of its 10,000-plus products reaching more than 140 countries. Kerry's ingredients operations, which generate around two-thirds of its overall revenues, supply multinational and other food processors with seasonings, coating systems, sweet ingredients, nutritional systems, fruit preparations, bakery ingredients, specialty proteins, and other ingredients and flavors. The balance of revenues is derived from the company's own branded food processing operations, which include processed meats and specialty poultry products (Ballyfree, Mattessons, Richmond, and Wall's), dairy products and juices (Dawn), dairy spreads (Low Low, Kerrymaid, and Move Over Butter), cheese and cheese snacks (Cheestrings and Golden Vale), chilled and frozen ready meals (Denny and Rye Valley), sandwiches (Freshways), chilled desserts (Dawn), and mineral water (Kerry Spring). Kerry also operates an agribusiness division, which represents the company's founding focus and is responsible for coordinating the company's 5,700-strong contingent of raw milk and other dairy suppliers. Geographically, Kerry derives about 65 percent of its revenues in Europe, 27 percent in the Americas, and 8 percent in the Asia-Pacific region. Kerry Co-operative Creameries Limited holds a 28 percent stake in Kerry Group.

COMPANY PERSPECTIVES

Kerry Group will be a major international specialist food ingredients corporation; a leading international flavour technology company; a leading supplier of added value brands and customer branded foods to the Irish and UK markets.

BEGINNINGS AS DAIRY PROCESSOR, THEN DAIRY CO-OP

Kerry Group traces its origins to the founding in 1972 of North Kerry Milk Products Limited (NKMP) to operate a newly built dairy ingredients processing plant in Listowel, County Kerry, Ireland. NKMP had three shareholders: Dairy Disposal Company, Ireland's state-owned dairy processing company, which owned a 42.5 percent stake; a federation of eight small farmer cooperatives in Kerry, which also owned 42.5 percent; and the U.S. firm Erie Casein Company, Inc., which held the remaining 15 percent. The company was set up to manufacture milk protein (casein), a dairy ingredient used in food processing, plastics, and glue. The plan was to export the casein to the United States, hence the involvement of Erie Casein. During its first year, NKMP produced 2,000 tons of casein from 16 million gallons of skim milk, earning profits of EUR 127,000 on sales of EUR 1.3 million. Heading the company from its formation was 27-year-old Denis Brosnan, the second son of a local dairy farmer, who had earned bachelor's and master's degrees in food science from University College Cork.

When Ireland joined the European Economic Community (EEC) in 1973, small dairies in the nation began merging in order to compete with the larger milk companies operating within the EEC. After securing an injection of capital from milk suppliers in County Kerry, NKMP joined this wave of consolidation by acquiring Dairy Disposal Company and its creameries for EUR 1.5 million. NKMP also purchased six of the eight independent farmer cooperatives that had joined in at the founding. As a result of these maneuvers, NKMP was made a subsidiary of the newly formed Kerry Co-operative Creameries Limited, which began trading in January 1974. Kerry Co-op started out as the smallest of Ireland's six major agricultural cooperatives. Revenues in its first year were EUR 29 million. From these beginnings, Kerry grew over the next two decades into one of the world's leading specialist food ingredients producers and distributors. The introduction

of the company on the Dublin and London stock exchanges in the mid-1980s made millionaires out of many of the co-op's founding members.

A primary component in Kerry's growth was its steady expansion through acquisition, as well as a willingness to invest in new production and other facilities. Through the 1970s, Kerry Co-op grew to include a large number of dairy farms and processing plants in the counties of Cork, Killarney, Galway, and Limerick, supplying to the company's Dairy Disposal Company. By the mid-1980s, Kerry Co-op counted several thousand members.

In the early 1980s, Kerry began branching out from its dairy core into other food product categories. An early addition was the pork products category, which the company entered with the acquisitions of two prominent Irish pork products producers, Duffy Meats and Henry Denny & Sons, both acquired in 1982. The move into food processing raised Kerry to a prominent position in Ireland's food industry. By the middle of the decade, Kerry Co-op's annual sales topped IR£200 million. In 1983, in the meantime, Kerry bought out Erie Casein's 15 percent interest in it and also began laying the foundation for international growth by establishing U.S. and U.K. headquarters, in Chicago and London, respectively.

1986: FORMATION OF KERRY GROUP PLC

By the mid-1980s the little dairy co-op had expanded to include a number of manufacturing and other food processing facilities, located throughout Ireland and Northern Ireland. Needing capital to fund further growth, Kerry Co-op made a novel move: It restructured in 1986 as a full-fledged corporation. Kerry Group plc was incorporated and then acquired the property and assets of Kerry Co-op in exchange for 90 million common shares in Kerry Group. Then in October 1986 an initial public offering (IPO) of shares in Kerry Group was made via a listing on the Irish stock exchange. Following the IPO, Kerry Co-op retained a large stake in Kerry Group. Brosnan continued to manage the company as chief executive of Kerry Group. The newly public company reported strong growth after its first full year of operations, with revenues nearing IR£300 million, and net profits of nearly IR£6.3 million.

Brosnan led Kerry on an accelerated drive to build the business into a vertically integrated food production conglomerate, doubling the company's revenues before the end of the decade. The company continued its expansion in Ireland with the 1986 acquisition of

KEY DATES

1972: North Kerry Milk Products Limited (NKMP) is created to operate a dairy ingredients processing plant in Listowel, County Kerry, Ireland; Denis Brosnan is the managing director.

1974: NKMP is made a subsidiary of the newly formed Kerry Co-operative Creameries Limited.

1982: Kerry Co-op begins branching out with the acquisition of two Irish producers of pork products.

1986: Kerry Group plc is incorporated, acquires the property and assets of Kerry Co-op, and is then taken public; Kerry Co-op ends up with a large stake in Kerry Group.

1988: Kerry Group acquires the U.S.-based Beatreme Food Ingredients.

1994: Company completes an important food ingredients acquisition, that of DCA.

1998: Kerry acquires the food ingredients division of Dalgety PLC.

2001: Golden Vale plc, an Irish producer of dairy products, prepared meals, and snacks, is acquired; Brosnan steps down as chief executive at year-end, with Hugh Friel succeeding him.

2004: Kerry acquires the food ingredients business of Quest.

Snowcream Dairies Moate, and the formation of a Convenience Foods division, bringing the company into this increasingly prominent market, particularly with the steady adoption of this food trend among European consumers. Parallel to this move was the stepping up of Kerry's specialty ingredients business. At the same time, Kerry also established a presence in the United States, opening a dairy processing facility in Jackson, Wisconsin, in 1987. Kerry continued to build its U.S. presence, adding additional facilities in Wisconsin and Illinois especially. Part of the company's U.S. growth came from the acquisition of existing businesses, including the important 1988 acquisition of Beatreme Food Ingredients from Beatrice Corporation for $130 million. The purchase of Beatreme proved to be a watershed move and a quite risky one as the price paid was equivalent to Kerry's market capitalization at the time.

Rounding out the 1980s, Kerry's acquisitions included Grove and Ballytree, adding turkey products to the company's food production division. These companies were added in 1988, as was S.W.M. Chard, which gave Kerry a presence in the English market. At the end of 1989, Kerry, which had reached revenues of IR£584 million, began looking to expand onto the European continent. This was achieved the following year when the company purchased Milac, of Germany.

At the end of 1991, Kerry's annual sales surged to IR£755 million. The company had continued to invest in its British expansion, acquiring Eastleigh Flavors for its ingredients business in 1990, as well as food processors A.E. Button and Sons and Miller-Robirch. The company added several more U.K.-based businesses in the early 1990s, including the foods division acquisition of Buxted Duckling and the food ingredients producer Tingles Ltd. The Irish poultry processing company Kantoher Food Products was also acquired in 1992. At the same time, Kerry increased its market focus with the formation of Kerry Spring Water in Ireland in 1993. Between 1990 and 1993, Kerry also added Dairyland Products and Northlands to its ingredients division, both in the United States. These were joined by the company's move into Canada, with the 1993 acquisitions of Malcolm Foods and Research Foods, in Ontario and Vancouver. In 1994 Kerry widened its presence in the Americas through the commissioning of a state-of-the-art dairy processing facility in Irapuato, Mexico; this plant was set up to supply both the Mexican and Central American markets. Back in Ireland, the company began construction on one of the pork processing industry's most advanced plants, in Shillelagh.

MAJOR ACQUISITIONS: DCA AND DALGETY FOOD INGREDIENTS

Kerry's acquisition drive continued into the late 1990s, bringing the company into France and Italy, with the purchases of Ciprial S.A. and its Aptunion, Ravifruit, Gasparini, and Gial subsidiaries in 1996; into Poland, with the acquisition of U.K.-based Margetts in 1994; to Malaysia, in 1997, with the purchase of SDF Foods; and Brazil, with the acquisition of Star & Arty in 1998. In the United Kingdom, Kerry added both Mattessons and Wall's to its list of brands.

Two important acquisitions highlighted Kerry's expansion. The first came in 1994, when the company acquired the food processing business of DCA, elevating the company to a major position among North America's specialty ingredients producers, especially among the coatings and bakery market segments. DCA was acquired from Allied Domecq plc for $402 million.

In addition to bolstering the group's North American position, the DCA purchase also introduced it to the Australian and New Zealand markets. After digesting this purchase, including restructuring its U.S. holdings into the new subsidiary, Kerry Inc., Kerry Group once again began eyeing a new large-scale acquisition.

The opportunity for renewed expansion came in February 1998, when Kerry Group announced its agreement to purchase the food ingredients businesses of the U.K.-based Dalgety PLC. For a price of IR£384 million, Kerry acquired Dalgety Food Ingredients' plants in the United Kingdom and in Hungary and the Netherlands—new markets for Kerry—as well as plants in France, Italy, and Germany. The Dalgety acquisition firmly established Kerry as the top specialty ingredients producer in Europe, and one of the world's leaders in its specific categories. It also marked the firm's entrance into a new market sector through Dalgety's flavors operations. Moreover, it helped boost Kerry's revenues beyond EUR 2 billion for its 1998 fiscal year.

Among other 1998 acquisitions, Kerry purchased the ingredients businesses of Burns, Philp & Company Ltd., which had manufacturing bases in Australia and New Zealand, and this deal led to a major expansion of Kerry's seasonings, flavors, coatings, marinades, and bakery ingredients business in the Asia-Pacific region. On the consumer foods side, the company completed a new manufacturing plant in Burton-on-Trent to position itself for further growth in the burgeoning market in the United Kingdom for chilled ready meals. In 1999 Kerry strengthened its position in snack seasoning by acquiring the German firm Tukania Proca GmbH.

At the same time, Kerry was turning its attention to two new markets: the Far East and South America. Both of these markets represented a huge pool of potential customers, both for the company's own food products and brands, and for its ingredients products. The company's initial forays into these markets included plant acquisitions in Malaysia and Brazil.

Important changes in Kerry Group's ownership structure also occurred in the late 1990s. The company adopted a rule change in 1996 that allowed Kerry Co-op's interest in Kerry Group to drop below 51 percent to as low as 20 percent without an additional rule change. After this change was adopted, the co-op distributed one-quarter of its shares in Kerry Group to the individual cooperative members, thereby reducing the co-op's stake from 52 percent to 39 percent. By 1999 the co-op's stake had been further reduced to 37 percent.

EARLY 21ST CENTURY: MORE DEALS, SMALL AND LARGE

The dealmaking continued in the new century as Kerry Group acquired the U.S.-based Shade Foods and Specialty Food Ingredients, the European arm of Shade Foods, from the Swiss agricultural commodities group Andre in 2000 for approximately $80 million. The acquired units manufactured flavored particulates and specialty chocolate coatings for producers of ready-to-eat cereals, ice cream, and dairy, confectionery, and bakery products. In a similar vein, Kerry purchased York Dragee, a U.K.-based company providing chocolate inclusions and coated particulates to the cereal, confectionery, bakery, and ice cream sectors across Europe. Strengthening its U.S. operations, Kerry completed a third 2000 acquisition, paying ConAgra, Inc., $35 million for Armour Food Ingredients, a leading producer of savory flavorings, cheese and dairy flavorings, and specialty lipid powders. Also in 2000 Kerry sold the North American bakery business it had acquired as part of the purchase of DCA to the Pillsbury Company for a little over $100 million. For the year pretax profits were up 16 percent to EUR 173.2 million, while revenues were up nearly 7 percent to EUR 2.62 billion.

The year 2001 proved momentous for Kerry on the leadership front as Brosnan stepped aside from day-to-day operations at year-end, becoming nonexecutive chairman, while Hugh Friel took over as chief executive. Friel had been Kerry's deputy all the way back to the group's founding in 1972. During his final year as chief executive, Brosnan spearheaded several more acquisitions, which in the aggregate cost Kerry EUR 617 million. The largest and most significant of these by far was the September purchase of Golden Vale plc for a total cost, including assumed debt, of EUR 391 million. Operating 13 manufacturing facilities in Ireland and the United Kingdom, Golden Vale was a major food processor, specializing in cheeses, dairy spreads, prepared meals, snack products, milk, butter, and dairy ingredients.

Kerry Group remained on course following the change in chief executives, as Friel maintained the firm's steady expansion, primarily through acquisition. Though considerable sums were spent on acquisitions in 2002 and 2003—EUR 273.4 million and EUR 207.7 million, respectively—the focus in these years was on smaller, bolt-on acquisitions that built on the existing operations rather than pushing the company into new sectors. In consumer foods, for example, convenience foods remained a high priority, and Kerry picked up two Irish companies in 2002. These were Deli Products Ltd., producer of chilled convenience "food-to-go," and sandwich maker Freshways. A year later the company acquired the ready meals and chilled dessert business of Hibernia Foods plc. Another important development in 2002 was the creation of a new flavor division called Mastertaste, which served to provide a higher profile for this portion of Kerry's ingredients business. Mastertaste aimed to offer a wide range of innovative, high-quality, authentic flavors for food and beverage applications. In August 2003 Brosnan retired from the company board, and Denis Buckley, a Kerry Group director since its creation in 1986, was named the new chairman.

Friel accelerated the pace of acquisition in 2004, spending EUR 711.7 million on deals that year, more than half of which was used for just one purchase. In April, Kerry acquired the food ingredients business of Quest from Imperial Chemical Industries PLC for EUR 366.9 million. The acquired unit, which produced yeasts, proteins, emulsifiers, and cultures used in snack, bakery, dairy, and pharmaceutical products, had operations in the Netherlands, the United States, Canada, Malaysia, the Philippines, Ireland, and the United Kingdom. It became the basis for a new Kerry Bio-Science division, which was focused on so-called bio-ingredients and pharma-ingredients. Among the other acquisitions completed in 2004, several were smaller purchases of ingredients and flavors companies, including Ernsts Food Ingredients, Manheimer, Flavurence, Laboratorios Krauss, Fructamine, Oregon Chai, and Extreme Foods.

The Quest deal helped push Kerry Group's revenues over the EUR 4 billion mark in 2004. This blockbuster acquisition was followed by a return to more modest dealmaking. In March 2005 Kerry significantly expanded its operations in China by acquiring Hangzhou Lanli Food Industry Company Limited and also endeavoring to build a new factory in Hangzhou to supply ingredients and flavorings to both Chinese food companies and multinationals with operations in China, such as Groupe Danone, Unilever, and Nestlé S.A. Later in 2005 Kerry acquired Noon Group Limited for around £124 million (EUR 179 million) to augment its position in the fast-growing chilled ready-meals market. London-based Noon produced Indian, Thai, Oriental, and other Asian precooked meals mainly for major U.K. supermarket chains.

During 2006 Kerry completed only two acquisitions of any note, the spring purchases of two U.S. food ingredients businesses, Custom Industries, supplier of powders to the bakery and ready-to-eat cereal sectors, and Nuvex Ingredients, producer of high-protein and fiber nutritional lines for makers of breakfast cereals, functional foods, and nutritional snacks. The two companies were purchased for a combined $83 million (EUR 68 million). One of the main reasons for the slowdown in acquisition activity was that private-equity firms, flush with cash, were in the midst of a major acquisition spree that was driving prices higher than Kerry was willing to pay. In illustration, in August 2006 the company pursued an acquisition of the European frozen foods business of Unilever, which included the Birds Eye brand, but was outbid by the U.K. private-equity group Permira Advisers LLP.

Overall, 2006 proved to be difficult for Kerry Group. Results in the first half of the year were hampered by an unprecedented surge in energy and energy-related costs plus a falling dollar, forcing the company to issue its first profit warning since becoming a publicly traded company. In September the firm launched a restructuring program through which it intended to sell or close 11 manufacturing sites by the end of 2007. Pretax profits fell sharply in 2006, down 25 percent to EUR 221.1 million, and after-tax profits were down as well after Kerry took a EUR 73 million write-off in connection with several divestments completed during the year. The company nevertheless managed to achieve a sales increase of nearly 5 percent to EUR 4.65 billion. Early results from 2007 were more positive than the previous year, which signaled brighter prospects for Kerry Group and perhaps a return to more robust acquisition activity.

M. L. Cohen
Updated, David E. Salamie

PRINCIPAL SUBSIDIARIES

Ballysimon Warehousing Limited; Castleisland Cattle Breeding Society Limited; Charleville Research Limited Services; Dawn Dairies Limited; Duffy Meats Limited; Freshways Limited; Glenealy Farms (Turkeys) Limited; Golden Vale Dairies Limited; Golden Vale Farms Limited; Golden Vale Food Products Limited; Golden Vale Foods Limited; Henry Denny & Sons (Ireland) Limited; Irish Cold Stores Limited; Kerry Agribusiness Holdings Limited; Kerry Creameries Limited; Kerry Farm Supplies Limited; Kerry Ingredients (Ireland) Limited; Kerrykreem Limited; Platters Food Company Limited; Rye Valley Foods Limited; Snowcream (Midlands) Limited; National Food Ingredients Limited; National Rusks Limited; William Blake Limited; Henry Denny & Sons (NI) Limited (U.K.); Dairy Produce Packers Limited (U.K.); Golden Cow Dairies Limited (U.K.); Leckpatrick Dairies Limited (U.K.); Diversity Foods Limited (U.K.); Kerry Foods Limited (U.K.); Kerry Savoury Foods Limited (U.K.); Noon Group Limited (U.K.); Dairyborn Foods Limited (U.K.); Cereal Innovations Limited (U.K.); Dale Country Foods Limited (U.K.); EBI Foods Limited (U.K.); Kerry

Ingredients (UK) Limited; Gordon Jopling (Foods) Limited (U.K.); Kerry Group B.V. (Netherlands); Kerry Bio-Science B.V. (Netherlands); Kerry Ingredients B.V. (Netherlands); Kerry Foods France Sarl; Kerry Ingredients France S.A.S.; Kerry Ingredients GmbH (Germany); Kerry Ingredients (Denmark) A/S; Kerry Ingredients Italia S.p.A. (Italy); Mastertaste S.p.A. (Italy); Kerry Polska Sp. z.o.o. (Poland); Kerry Hungaria KFT (Hungary); Kerry Ingredients Australia Pty. Limited; Kerry Ingredients (NZ) Limited (New Zealand); Flavurence Corporation (U.S.A.); Geneva Flavors Inc. (U.S.A.); Guernsey Bel, Inc. (U.S.A.); GB Seasonings Inc. (U.S.A.); Kerry Biofunctional Ingredients Inc. (U.S.A.); Kerry Holding Co. (U.S.A.); Kerry Inc. (U.S.A.); Mastertaste Holding Co. (U.S.A.); Nuvex Ingredients Inc. (U.S.A.); Hickory Specialties, Inc. (U.S.A.); Jana's Classics, Inc. (U.S.A.); Oregon Chai, Inc. (U.S.A.); Stearns & Lehman, Inc. (U.S.A.); Kerry (Canada) Inc.; Rector Foods Limited (Canada); Nutrisens Inc. (Canada); Kerry Ingredients (de Mexico) S.A. de C.V.; Kerry do Brasil Ltda. (Brazil); Kerry Bio-Science Egypt Misr L.L.; Kerry Ingredients South Africa (Pty) Limited; Kerry Ingredients (Thailand) Limited; Kerry Food Ingredients (Philippines), Inc.; Kerry Ingredients (S) Pte Limited (Singapore); Kerry Ingredients (M) Sdn. Bhd. (Malaysia); Kerry Japan Kabushiki Kaisha; Kerry Food Ingredients (Hangzhou) Company Limited (China); Kerry Ingredients Trading (Shanghai) Limited (China); Kerry Limited Liability Company (Russia).

PRINCIPAL DIVISIONS

Kerry Bio-Science; Kerry Foods; Kerry Ingredients; Mastertaste.

PRINCIPAL COMPETITORS

Givaudan SA; International Flavors & Fragrances Inc.; Symrise GmbH & Co. KG; McCormick & Company, Incorporated; Glanbia plc; Firmenich SA; Northern Foods plc; Uniq plc; Greencore Group plc; Bakkavör Group hf.; Perkins Foods Holdings Ltd.; Premier Foods plc; Cargill, Incorporated; Danisco A/S; Associated British Foods plc.

FURTHER READING

Boyle, Pat, "Kerry Group Reveals Ingredients of $440m U.S. Quest Takeover," *Irish Independent* (Dublin), March 3, 2004.

Canniffe, Mary, "Kerry Group Annual Profit Surges 18.6% to £51.2m," *Irish Times* (Dublin), March 5, 1997.

——, "Kerry Group Pays $35m for Food Firm Armour to Expand Its Capacity in U.S.," *Irish Times* (Dublin), October 18, 2000, p. 19.

——, "Kerry Group Well Positioned to Raise Profits," *Irish Times* (Dublin), March 5, 1997.

Coyle, Dominic, "Kerry Group Pays $62m for Two U.S. Flavour and Ingredient Companies," *Irish Times* (Dublin), October 11, 2003, p. 16.

Firn, David, and Astrid Wendlandt, "ICI Sells Food Unit to Kerry for $440m," *Financial Times*, March 3, 2004, p. 22.

Harding, Ted, "Kerry Group Set to Exceed the Revised Profit Forecasts," *Sunday Business Post* (Dublin), March 9, 1998.

Kennelly, James J., *The Kerry Way: The History of Kerry Group, 1972–2000*, Dublin: Oak Tree Press, 2001, 457 p.

"Kerry Buys Malaysian Food Company," *European Report*, May 1, 1996.

"Kerry: Picking the Right Strategy," *Dairy Industries International*, July 1994, p. 31.

"Kerry Weathering Storm but Doubts Remain," *Irish Examiner* (Cork), February 28, 2007.

McGrath, Brendan, "Co-op to Cut Stake in Kerry Group to 39%," *Irish Times* (Dublin), May 16, 1996, p. 17.

——, "Kerry Group Looks to Far East Market," *Irish Times* (Dublin), May 27, 1997.

——, "Kerry in $80m Buy from Swiss," *Irish Times* (Dublin), October 1, 1999, p. 51.

——, "Kerry Targets South American Market," *Irish Times* (Dublin), August 16, 1999, p. 16.

——, "Mega Deals Create £600m Debt," *Irish Times* (Dublin), January 27, 1998, p. 18.

Micheau, Ed, "Kerry's Global Kingdom," *Business and Finance*, March 16, 2000.

Mudd, Tom, "Global Movers and Shakers: Kerry Group and Nestlé Expand Existing Markets while Nurturing New Opportunities," *Industry Week*, August 21, 2000, pp. 71, 73, 75.

——, "Milk Money: Denis Brosnan Turns a Tiny, Irish Dairy Co-op into a Lucrative, Worldwide Food Conglomerate," *Industry Week*, January 15, 2001, pp. 65, 67–69.

O'Kane, Paul, "Co-op Transformed by Commonsense Approach," *Irish Times* (Dublin), November 8, 1994, p. 14.

——, "Kerry Eyes Up a Kingdom," *Sunday Tribune* (Dublin), March 2, 2003, p. 3.

——, "Kerry Goes into Orbit with U.S. Fruit Juice Buy," *Sunday Tribune* (Dublin), September 14, 2003, p. 1.

O'Mahony, Brian, "Kerry to Remain Cautious on Acquisitions," *Irish Examiner* (Cork), August 31, 2005.

O'Sullivan, Jane, "Kerry Buys Four Companies for EUR 170m," *Irish Times* (Dublin), May 11, 2004, p. 19.

——, "Kerry Buys Two U.S. Firms for $83m," *Irish Times* (Dublin), April 12, 2006, p. 17.

——, "Kerry Group Chief Is in No Rush to Change Winning Recipe," *Irish Times* (Dublin), February 28, 2003, p. 61.

————, "Kerry Group Pays £394m for Food Ingredients Businesses of Dalgety," *Irish Times* (Dublin), January 27, 1998, p. 18.

————, "Kerry's Spend Hits $135m As It Buys Two U.S. Food Firms," *Irish Times* (Dublin), April 3, 2003, p. 16.

Shanahan, Ella, "Charm Offensive Yields Brosnan's Finest Hour," *Irish Times* (Dublin), August 20, 2001, p. 16.

Slattery, Laura, "Kerry Group Profits Fall 26% Despite Rise in Sales," *Irish Times* (Dublin), February 28, 2007, p. 19.

Smith, Peter, "Noon Products Sold to Kerry Group for £125m," *Financial Times*, August 6, 2005, p. 3.

Smyth, Jamie, "Kerry Group Buys Chinese Firm," *Irish Times* (Dublin), January 21, 2005, p. 11.

Taaffe, Claire, "Kerry Group: Big Cheeses of Marketing," *Business and Finance*, July 1, 2004.

Toops, Diane, "Taking the High Road with Kerry Group's Denis Brosnan," *Food Processing*, September 1995, pp. 19–21.

Wagner, Jeffrey, Yane Chandera, and W. D. Dobson, "The Evolution of Ireland's Kerry Group/PLC: Implications for the U.S. and Global Dairy-Food Industries" (Babcock Institute Discussion Paper), Madison: Babcock Institute for International Dairy Research and Development, University of Wisconsin, 2000, 22 p.

Wall, Vincent, "Sensing the Future," *Business and Finance*, January 11, 2001, p. 8.

Walsh, Kerri, "Kerry Buys Two Food Ingredients Makers," *Chemical Week*, April 26, 2006, p. 54.

Webb, Nick, "Kerry Made by Sealing a Friel Deal," *Sunday Independent* (Dublin), March 14, 2004.

Kyphon Inc.

1221 Crossman Avenue
Sunnyvale, California 94089
U.S.A.
Telephone: (408) 548-6500
Fax: (408) 548-6501
Web site: http://www.kyphon.com

Public Company
Incorporated: 1994
Employees: 885
Sales: $407.8 million (2006)
Stock Exchanges: NASDAQ
Ticker Symbol: KYPH
NAIC: 339112 Surgical and Medical Instrument Manufacturing

■ ■ ■

Kyphon Inc. is a medical device company focused on a minimally invasive treatment of spinal fractures it calls balloon kyphoplasty, the name drawn from the Greek word *kyphos,* or "bent." It is essentially an improved form of vertebroplasty, a procedure in which cement is injected into the fissures of collapsed vertebra to provide reinforcement and pain relief, although the vertebra remain collapsed. Carried out under local or general anesthetic, kyphoplasty relies on small balloons, about the size of a thumb, introduced into collapsed vertebra of a patient through small incisions on both sides of the spine. The balloons, or tamps, are gradually inflated to lift crushed or collapsed vertebra—the result of osteoporosis, cancer, or other causes—to near their normal

height. The cavity created by the balloons is then filled with Kyphon's proprietary cement or some other bone filler. It hardens in about 15 minutes. All that remains are the incisions, which can be closed by simple Band-Aids.

The procedure lasts about 45 minutes, and when it is completed patients are able to walk immediately, most of them experiencing a tremendous relief from pain as well as some correction in height. Kyphoplasty also provides better control over cement than does vertebroplasty, which carries a greater risk of cement leaking into a patient's lungs or organs and creating severe complications. More than 10,400 physicians in the United States, Europe, and some countries in Asia are trained in the balloon kyphoplasty procedure. The company also offers the X-STOP Interspinous Process Decompression system to treat lumbar spinal stenosis, another minimally invasive spine therapy, added through the acquisition of St. Francis Medical Technologies. Based in Sunnyvale, California, Kyphon is a public company listed on the NASDAQ.

FOUNDER'S BACKGROUND

The man who conceived of balloon kyphoplasty was Dr. Mark A. Reiley. After receiving an undergraduate degree from Claremont College in California, he earned his medical degree from George Washington University School of Medicine in Washington, D.C., in 1979. He then received five years of orthopedic training at the University of California, San Francisco, where he was a fellow in the Musculoskeletal Tumor Clinic at the school's medical center. It was here that Reiley attended a patient who suffered from multiple compression fractures of the spine. His efforts to provide help were frustrated by the instability of the bones and pain caused by the fractures. He began thinking of a way to stabilize such injuries.

As an orthopedic surgeon in Berkeley, California, Reiley toyed in 1984 with the idea of restoring the lost shape of a vertebra by creating a gap that could be filled with bone cement. According to *Forbes,* "He dove into spines of cadavers with tiny jacks, scrapers, expandable rotors, lasers and ultrasound when he happened upon a stock of balloons used to clear small kidney stones." Reiley tried out the balloons on the cadavers, and then began working with surgical product developer Arie Scholten, to establish the basic elements of balloon kyphoplasty.

Reiley and Scholten looked for a way to develop the procedure commercially and bring it to patients. They turned to the obvious places, the top orthopedic and spine companies, but the procedure they proposed seemed too radical and no one was interested. It was at this point, through a chance encounter, that Reiley met a former biotech executive named Karen Talmadge, who held a doctorate in biochemistry from Harvard University and had dealt with the orthopedics sector while serving as a chief executive. She was intrigued enough by the elegance of the procedure to study clinical literature, and soon realized that it had a great deal of commercial potential due to the large number of patients suffering from the kind of spinal fractures the procedure could address.

INCORPORATION OF KYPHON: 1994

In early 1994 Reiley, Scholten, and Talmadge incorporated Kyphon in Delaware. Talmadge engaged in the task of attracting venture capital to make the company operational. It proved to be a tough sell, however. Talmadge spent nearly three years attempting to gain support from venture capitalists but with no success. They expressed concerns about the procedure winning U.S. Food and Drug Administration (FDA) clearance and the willingness of insurers to reimburse for

it. "But what these reasons told me," Talmadge said in an interview with *Medical Device Link,* "was that investors were most concerned about the risk associated with backing an idea that would change the practice of medicine."

In 1996 Talmadge finally found someone she thought would be open to backing a revolutionary medical approach: Jack W. Lasersohn, a general partner at the Vertical Group, a Summit, New Jersey-based venture capital firm that specialized in medical technology and biotechnology. Talmadge had attended a lecture Lasersohn delivered about the medical devices that investors had failed to back because of a reluctance to challenge accepted medical practices. In particular he referred to the promise of balloon angioplasty, a procedure being developed to open constricted arteries. Afterward Talmadge met with Lasersohn, who was indeed receptive to Kyphon's use of balloons to repair spinal fractures. "I have to admit, this was one of the best ideas I had ever heard," Lasersohn told *San Jose Business Journal.* "I love balloons, and the spine, well that's an enormous market."

Lasersohn then sold the New York-based private equity fund Warburg Pincus & Co. on the idea, and together the two firms provided $1 million in seed money. Kyphon sought input from the leaders in the spine field, targeting the most skeptical, in the belief that when the procedure gained regulatory approval their endorsement would carry the most weight in the marketplace. In July 1998 the FDA approved the use of inflatable bone tamps, and in that same year the first balloon kyphoplasty procedure was performed. The company continued to raise venture capital money, which ultimately totaled $40 million. Talmadge, who had served as the company's chief executive since its founding, stepped down in November 1998, replaced by Richard D. Murdock, the former CEO of CellPro, a provider of blood cancer treatments.

Early in 1999 Kyphon began to assemble a direct sales and marketing operation and by the end of the year posted sales of $261,000. In May 2000 the company initiated a full commercial rollout of what it called the KyphX System in the United States and sales began to grow at an exponential rate, as positive results from clinical studies and the company's educational efforts made steady progress in convincing doctors to consider the new procedure and then received training to perform it. Sales increased to more than $6 million in 2000 and topped $36 million in 2001.

IPO: 2002

In July 2001 Gary L. Grenter was named president and CEO. He was the former chief executive at Biolectron,

KEY DATES

1994: Company is founded.
1996: Funding is secured.
1998: Inflatable bone tamps are approved by Food and Drug Administration (FDA).
2004: FDA approves bone cement.
2007: St. Francis Medical Technologies Inc. is acquired.

Inc., a company involved in the spinal fusion, fracture healing, and arthroscopy market. Under Grenter, Kyphon took steps to go public. After the company failed at one attempt, it succeeded in May 2002 with US Bancorp Piper Jaffray managing an initial public offering (IPO) of stock that raised $103 million for the company. Grenter's tenure did not last much longer, however. He resigned to "pursue other interests," and the reins were turned over to Richard W. Mott, named president and CEO in September 2002. Mott had been a top executive at Wilson Greatbatch Technologies, Inc., a maker of implantable medical device components. He took over a company that had a great deal of potential but lacked administrative structure and a clearly defined strategy. It fell on Mott to build a foundation that would allow the company to retain talent and attract new employees. Because Kyphon did not even have a human resources officer, one of Mott's first tasks was to fill that position. He recruited Steve Ham, a former Hewlett-Packard executive, who played a key role in fleshing out Kyphon's corporate culture. At the heart of it lay education. Just as the company grew by educating physicians about balloon kyphoplasty, so too did it invest in the continued education and personal development of its employees, as well as their families. Ham also played an important part as Kyphon expanded its organizational infrastructure, adding more senior leadership to support a rapidly growing workforce.

Sales increased to $76.3 million in 2002. The following year the company expanded its sales team, which helped grow revenues to more than $131 million in 2003 and led to the first profitable year in Kyphon's history. When the company netted $27.3 million. To support its growth, Kyphon moved into a new corporate headquarters in Sunnyvale with more than twice the space of the previous facility. The number of spine specialists trained worldwide in the procedure numbered 3,900, up from 2,700 in 2002 and 1,500 in 2001. Kyphon also set itself up for continued growth through the launch of a dozen new products in 2003. In addition,

the company completed the acquisition of a German biomaterials company, Sanatis GmbH for $4.5 million, picking up the right to a calcium-containing bone filler.

At this stage Kyphon was not able to offer a complete system, and surgeons relied on bone cement produced by other companies. Neither could Kyphon make claims about the clinical benefits of balloon kyphoplasty. These drawbacks ended in 2004 when Kyphon made further filings with the FDA and received clearance to sell a bone cement specifically for use in the spine. The FDA also agreed that the clinical data the company provided about the effects of the procedure was sufficient to allow Kyphon to promote claims about the effectiveness of the treatment. Sales increased to $213 million in 2004, and helping to fuel further growth the company also received good news on other fronts. The Centers for Medicare & Medicaid Services established reimbursement codes for balloon kyphoplasty, a move supported by the American Medical Association, setting the stage for physician and hospital reimbursement for the procedure across the country.

About 50,000 patients worldwide underwent balloon kyphoplasty in 2004, a number that increased to 73,000 in 2005, leading to a 43 percent increase in sales to $306 million and net income of $29.8 million. The company enjoyed continued growth in 2005, when sales improved to $407.8 million and net income approached $40 million. Success did not come without some measure of controversy, however. Early in 2006 Kyphon and Dr. Harvinder Sandhu, who had licensed an expandable, mechanical bone tamp to the company, sued Medtronic Sofamor Danek, accusing it of trade secret theft, fraud, breach of contract, and other charges. In the late 1990s Medtronic had elected not to license Sandhu's invention and a year later patented a device to treat vertebral compression fractures using a similar bone tamp. Medtronic maintained that because Kyphon was the only domestic player in this niche market it was simply trying to keep Medtronic and others from entering it. Four months later Medtronic filed its own lawsuit against Kyphon, alleging that four of its patents related to balloon-dilation catheters and spinal treatment had been violated.

Also in 2006 Kyphon was joined in a different kind of controversy, stemming from the days it had reached out to prominent spine researchers. One of the most prominent in the field was Cleveland Clinic orthopedic surgeon Dr. Isador Lieberman, who had been a major supporter of balloon kyphoplasty. However, in late 2006 he was regaled in the press for also having a financial interest in Kyphon, receiving valuable stock options in a company whose procedure he was touting. Lieberman was well aware of the clinic's conflict-of-interest policy because he sat on the panel that dealt with the issue. He was required to tell patients of his financial interests if they asked, but did not have to volunteer the information. While Lieberman argued that his support of balloon kyphoplasty was based on the efficacy of the procedure, he was also connected to seven other orthopedic device manufacturers, from whom he might receive stock, royalties, and consulting fees.

To help sustain its strong growth and achieve some diversity, Kyphon reached agreement on three acquisitions in 2006. Early in the year it acquired InnoSpine, Inc., which held FDA-cleared technology for the diagnosis and possible treatment of axial low back pain caused by disc degeneration. Late in the year, Kyphon announced two agreements with an Israeli company, Disc-O-Tech Medical Technologies, Ltd., to acquire its spine-related assets, which included a vertebroplasty system and the B-Twin Expandable Spinal System, which uses an expandable interbody device to treat degenerative disc disease in the lumbar and cervical spine. Kyphon also agreed to acquire St. Francis Medical Technologies Inc., an acquisition that was completed in January 2007. The Alameda, California-based company brought with it the X-STOP System to treat lumbar spinal stenosis.

Ed Dinger

PRINCIPAL SUBSIDIARIES

InnoSpine, Inc.; St. Francis Medical Technologies, Inc.

PRINCIPAL COMPETITORS

Biomet, Inc.; Stryker Corporation; United States Surgical Corporation.

FURTHER READING

Benesh, Peter, "Its Surgeries Will Really Get Your Back Up," *Investor's Business Daily,* November 30, 2005, p. A05.

Cutland, Laura, "Medical Startup Success Was a Test of Founder's Backbone," *San Jose Business Journal,* July 25, 2005.

Dobson, Roger, "'Balloon' to Cure a Crumbling Back," *Daily Mail,* July 15, 2003, p. 38.

Elliott, Alan R., "Medical Supplier Puts Its Back into Pain Relief," *Investor's Business Daily,* August 13, 2003, p. A08.

Grossman, Robert J., "Developing Talent," *HRMagazine,* January 2006, p. 40.

Halasey, Steve, "Growing Up, Globally," *Medical Device Link,* November/December 2006, http://www.devicelink.com.

Herper, Matthew, "The Inflatable Spine," *Forbes,* June 7, 2004, p. 227.

"Kyphon: A Trial Balloon Succeeds in Spine," *In Vivo,* July 2002.

Much, Marilyn, "Thanks to the FDA, It Gets a Selling Boost, Kyphon Inc.," *Investor's Business Daily,* July 14, 2004, p. A06.

Rutchick, Joel, "Surgeon Kept Quiet About Stake in Company," *Cleveland Plain Dealer,* December 10, 2006, p. A1.

MacNeil/Lehrer
Productions

‣

2700 South Quincy Street
Arlington, Virginia 22206
U.S.A.
Telephone: (703) 998-2111
Fax: (703) 820-6266
Web site: http://www.pbs.org/newshour

Private Company
Incorporated: 1981 as MacNeil Lehrer Gannett Productions
Employees: 100
Sales: $32.5 million (2005 est.)
NAIC: 512110 Motion Picture and Video Production

■ ■ ■

MacNeil/Lehrer Productions (MLP) is a private media production company owned by James Lehrer and Robert MacNeil, in partnership with Liberty Media Co. Lehrer and MacNeil are veteran public television newsmen, whose show the *MacNeil/Lehrer NewsHour* ran from 1983 to 1995, and continues as the *NewsHour with Jim Lehrer.* The production company puts out the awarding-winning daily *NewsHour,* as well as other documentary television programming. While the *NewsHour* runs on public television (PBS), the company produces television specials for regular broadcast and cable television networks as well. MLP also offers a host of client services, such as video production and interactive multimedia, web site design, museum exhibits, teleconferencing, and other educational and community outreach programs. The company produces interactive

web DVDs used for education and training. Its clients for its multimedia services include the National Endowment for the Humanities and the National Institutes of Health. The company also finds and distributes archival news footage for clients, and produces videography and distance learning packages. MLP has facilities in Washington, D.C., San Francisco, and Denver.

TWO NEWSMEN COMING TOGETHER

MacNeil/Lehrer Productions was founded in 1981, but its roots go back years before that, through the intertwined careers of its two principals. Robert MacNeil was born in Canada in 1931, and began his career as an actor in radio dramas. He eventually stopped pursuing acting and found work at a television news company in London. He next spent five years working for the Reuters wire service, until he became London correspondent for NBC. In the mid-1960s, NBC had him coanchor a weekend news program, the *Scherer-MacNeil Report.* MacNeil did not at the time enjoy being a news anchor, and in 1967 he went back to London to work for the British Broadcasting Company (BBC). In 1971, he returned to the United States and worked for the National Public Affairs Center for Television (NPACT), based in Washington, D.C. NPACT produced news for public television, and because of its critical views, the company outraged the Nixon administration. MacNeil's then broadcast partner, Sander Vanocur, resigned over conflict with the administration, and James Lehrer was hired as his replacement. MacNeil and Lehrer first worked together providing PBS's extensive coverage of the Watergate hearings.

James Lehrer had studied journalism at the University of Missouri and then worked as a reporter for the *Dallas Morning News* beginning in 1959. He resigned from that paper after only a few years, when its editorial board quashed a potentially unsettling series of articles he had written about the political leanings of a local civil defense group. The city's rival paper, the *Dallas Times-Herald*, then picked Lehrer up. He eventually became the *Times-Herald*'s city editor. However, a part-time consulting position at Dallas's PBS television station KERA soon consumed all of Lehrer's interest. He left print journalism to produce KERA's news show, and then in 1972 he moved to Washington to work as the public affairs coordinator for PBS. In 1973 PBS teamed Lehrer with MacNeil, and they produced a documentary series called *America '73*. Then they joined forces again for PBS's Watergate hearings coverage.

MacNeil went back to work for the BBC after the Watergate hearings ended, but in 1975 he was back in New York hosting an evening news program for the PBS affiliate WNET, the *Robert MacNeil Report*. Within a few months, MacNeil's New York news show went into nationwide broadcast with Lehrer joining from Washington. This show was called the *MacNeil/Lehrer Report*.

The *MacNeil/Lehrer Report* was different from other network news shows both in its sober tone and its unusual format. The original *Report* viewed five days a week for a half-hour, and it focused on a single issue. No other news show had such in-depth coverage. However, the show seemed more for connoisseurs than for a broad market, and it struggled at first to define itself and its audience. Its staidness was a throwback to the television news shows of the 1950s and 1960s, while commercial television news in the 1970s was shifting to shorter and more sensational or entertaining stories. The *MacNeil/Lehrer Report* provided the kind of news that was becoming increasingly rare on television.

Eventually the show won a small but loyal following. Its future, though, did not seem assured in its early days, and the anchors took the unprecedented step of forming their own production company. In 1981, MacNeil and Lehrer went into partnership with the media company Gannett Co. and formed MacNeil Lehrer Gannett Productions. Gannett owned 50 percent, and the two anchors 25 percent each. At that time, the new company's only product was the *MacNeil/Lehrer Report*, and this was the only news show in the country owned by its anchors. This unique arrangement gave the two newsmen an unusual amount of editorial control. It also potentially buffered them from the low pay of PBS. Public television stars typically made only about a third of what their colleagues on regular network television were paid. MacNeil Lehrer Gannett gave the newscasters an entrepreneurial vehicle that made up for the lower salaries on public television.

EXPANDED FORMAT

In 1983, the *MacNeil/Lehrer Report* doubled its airtime, becoming the *MacNeil/Lehrer NewsHour*. The expanded format required much time and energy from its hosts. Yet MacNeil and Lehrer used their production company to make documentaries, often using weekends and vacations to work on these projects. In 1984, the company produced a documentary called *My Heart, Your Heart*, which was an autobiographical account of Lehrer's experience with a heart attack a few months earlier. The company also distributed a 12-hour documentary about China, called *The Heart of the Dragon*.

In 1986, Gannett's five-year commitment to the production company expired, and Gannett sold its portion of the company to MacNeil and Lehrer, who were now sole owners. The company was then renamed MacNeil/Lehrer Productions. Because its work was shown on public television, MLP was able to attract corporate donors. Robert MacNeil was consumed for three years with a project he coauthored, an extensive documentary called *The Story of English*. He used vacation time to travel to far-flung parts of the English-speaking world to film, though he had no monetary backing. Yet by the time the series was ready to air in 1986, General Foods had contributed half the production costs plus $350,000 for marketing, and the Andrew W. Mellon Foundation granted MLP an additional $500,000.

By the mid-1980s, MLP was financially viable. According to a *New York Times* profile of the company (November 9, 1986), the two principals were able to pay themselves upward of $300,000 a year each, a substantial sum though still well below what news anchors of similar prominence made at commercial

KEY DATES

1973: MacNeil and Lehrer first work together.
1981: Company is founded.
1983: *MacNeil/Lehrer Report* becomes *MacNeil/ Lehrer NewsHour*.
1986: *Story of English* airs; Gannett's partnership expires and company is renamed MacNeil/ Lehrer Productions (MLP).
1995: MacNeil retires from *NewsHour;* Liberty Media buys two-thirds of MLP.
1996: *Online NewsHour* debuts.
2001: MLP puts out first interactive web DVD.

networks. Profit on the company's documentary projects was said to be next to nothing at that point. By 1990, though, MLP was making a documentary about health-care for network television, moving it to the broader audience that network television attracted.

CHANGING COMPETITIVE LANDSCAPE

By the early 1990s, the *MacNeil/Lehrer Report* was an established and respected fixture in the television news universe. Its viewership was quite small compared to network news. Viewership statistics can be compiled in different ways, for example, by how many people watch the entire show every night, how many people see a minimum number of minutes of it, how many people see any of the show during a fixed period of weeks or months. Because these statistics are gathered different ways, direct comparisons can be misleading. Yet by any measure, the *MacNeil/Lehrer NewsHour* was a niche vehicle, with less than half the viewership of the least popular mainstream network news show. Network news had never been the real competition for *MacNeil/Lehrer,* as the show prided itself on its civility and seriousness, while network television news shows were looking for entertainment value. *MacNeil/Lehrer* was able to add highly respected journalists to its roster, for example, national news correspondent Charlayne Hunter-Gault and congressional correspondent Roger Mudd. The show garnered top journalism awards year after year, including the widely recognized Emmy and Peabody awards.

Nevertheless, the early 1990s were financially difficult times for the *MacNeil/Lehrer NewsHour,* and for public television in general. The Cable News Network (CNN) debuted in 1980, and by the 1990s had

changed television news drastically with its round-the-clock broadcasting and many serious news and talk shows. Whereas the *MacNeil/Lehrer NewsHour* had once been a lonely alternative to commercial network news, with the prevalence of cable in the 1990s, viewers had many more news options. The *NewsHour,* still the principal product of MLP, found itself trimming its budget in the mid-1990s as public television membership fell and corporate underwriting was harder to get. The show operated with an annual budget of around $26 million, which it ratcheted down as it lost underwriter support.

In the early 1990s, the *NewsHour* received $6 million each from two corporate underwriters, PepsiCo and AT&T. AT&T and then PepsiCo stopped underwriting, and they were replaced by the agricultural firm Archer Daniels Midland and the insurer New York Life. By 1995, the show was making do with several million dollars less than a few years earlier, and the situation did not seem as if it would turn around by itself. Financial troubles also plagued the New York public television station WNET where MacNeil's portion of the show was shot (Lehrer was in Washington, D.C.). WNET discussed closing down, and MLP President Al Vecchione suggested that the *NewsHour* needed to streamline in order to cut costs.

In the midst of these difficulties, Robert MacNeil announced that he would retire after the 20th anniversary of the show, in 1995. He continued as a partner in MLP, and planned to devote more time to writing and to producing other shows besides the *NewsHour.* The *NewsHour* went on without him, produced in Washington as the *NewsHour with Jim Lehrer,* and using a variety of hosts for different story segments. The production company got a financial boost in 1995 when Liberty Media, a media conglomerate, bought a two-thirds share.

NEW PRODUCTS AND PROGRAMMING

While the *NewsHour* proceeded without him, Robert MacNeil devoted his time to producing other programming, both for television and for new media. MLP put out an innovative program in 1996 titled *The National Issues Convention,* which allowed people across the country to participate in opinion polling relating to that year's presidential election. The production company also partnered with NBC News to cover both the Democratic and Republican national conventions. The year 1996 also saw the debut of a web-based version of the *NewsHour,* called simply enough the *Online NewsHour.* This site attracted more traffic than any other of PBS's many web sites. The company expanded its web offerings in 1998 with *NewsHour Extra,* a version of the *Online NewsHour* targeted for middle school and high school students. During the next presidential cycle in 2000, MLP was again active in political documentary programming and coverage of the national party nominating conventions.

In 2001, the company began its experiments with interactive web-DVDs. With a grant from the Corporation for Public Broadcasting, it produced the *NewsHour Digital Prototype,* a multimedia mixture of audio, video, and text in which audiences could participate. MLP then made similar interactive web-DVD products for the National Endowment for the Humanities and for the National Institutes of Health.

The *NewsHour,* MLP' main product, continued to hold its small but devoted audience through the early 2000s. A segment called "Jobless Recovery: Non-Working Numbers" won journalism's prestigious Peabody Award in 2004. This story seemed typical of the *NewsHour*'s style, a seemingly dry topic, unemployment statistics, which other television news would not have bothered with, explored with depth and clarity. Industry magazine *Broadcasting and Cable* (May 17, 2004) described the award-winning piece as "underscoring the importance of economic issues while cutting through their inherent complexities in a lucid manner." Despite the changes brought by cable networks and the opportunities MLP itself took in exploring new media, the *NewsHour* still did very much what it had always done, delivering steady, studied programming on issues that were elsewhere neglected or scorned.

By the middle of the first decade of the 2000s, MacNeil/Lehrer Productions was quite a different company than the one it had originated as. While it still had a nightly news show as its main product, it also had a slew of other products. The company made educational videos, produced web sites, put out its interactive DVDs, and sponsored complex media projects that fostered civic engagement and debate. It was in many ways a 21st-century media company, experimenting with new forms and blurring the boundaries between web and television. At the same time, its television news show remained much as it always had, something of a throwback to the news shows of the mid-20th century. The company was thus an interesting mix of modern and traditional, and perhaps it was this mixture that allowed it to survive and prosper despite the transformation of news, media, and television during its lifetime.

A. Woodward

PRINCIPAL COMPETITORS

Cable News Network LP, LLLP; Harpo Inc.

FURTHER READING

Blau, Eleanor, "MacNeil/Lehrer Gets an Impressive Financial Commitment," *New York Times,* August 4, 1988, p. C23.

Burka, Paul, "The News About Jim Lehrer," *Texas Monthly,* October 1995, p. 58.

Carter, Bill, "MacNeil to Retire from 'Newshour' in '95 After 20 Years," *New York Times,* October 11, 1994, pp. C15, C18.

Fabrikant, Geraldine, "A Supporting Actor Takes Center Stage," *New York Times,* May 15, 1996, p. D1.

Gerard, Jeremy, "On Public Television, No Fireworks Is Just Fine," *New York Times,* November 29, 1990, p. C22.

"Jobless Recovery: Non-Working Numbers," *Broadcasting & Cable,* May 17, 2004, p. S20.

"MacNeil and Lehrer Form Venture with Gannett Co.," *Wall Street Journal,* September 14, 1981, p. 36.

"MacNeil and Lehrer PBS's Winning Team," *Broadcasting,* August 3, 1987, p. 95.

"MacNeil/Lehrer/Vecchione," *Broadcasting,* June 4, 1990, p. 95.

"NewsHour Lures Viewers Wanting More Than Shouting Matches," *PR Week,* February 24, 2003, p. 13.

Rathbun, Elizabeth, "PBS's Late-Night News Challenge," *Broadcasting & Cable,* June 7, 1999, p. 8.

Reibstein, Larry, "Good Night, Robin," *Newsweek,* October 30, 1995, p. 88.

Sterngold, James, "There's More to MacNeil/Lehrer Than Covering the News," *New York Times,* November 9, 1986, p. H27.

MannKind Corporation

28903 North Avenue Paine
Valencia, California 91355
U.S.A.
Telephone: (661) 775-5300
Fax: (661) 775-2081
Web site: http://www.mannkindcorp.com

Public Company
Incorporated: 1991 as Pharmaceutical Discovery Corp.
Employees: 428
Stock Exchanges: NASDAQ
Ticker Symbol: MNKD
NAIC: 325412 Pharmaceutical Preparation Manufacturing; 325414 Biological Product (Except Diagnostic) Manufacturing

■ ■ ■

MannKind Corporation is a biopharmaceutical company committed to developing therapeutic products to treat diabetes, cancer, inflammatory, and autoimmune diseases. The first product expected to reach the market is the company's Technosphere Insulin System, which consists of a proprietary dry-powder formulation of insulin that is inhaled deep into the lungs using an inhaler dubbed MedTone. MannKind began clinical trials with diabetes patients in 2006. The Technosphere Insulin System, if approved by the U.S. Food and Drug Administration (FDA), was expected to make its commercial debut in 2010. Longer range plans called for the development of a cancer vaccine for patients with solid tumors. The company received approval from the FDA to begin Phase 1 clinical trials of its cancer vaccine at the end of 2006.

FOUNDER'S BACKGROUND

When Alfred E. Mann turned 79 in 2004, there was little time in his schedule to celebrate his birthday. The tireless billionaire, a prolific entrepreneur and munificent philanthropist, was spending 45 hours per week running the riskiest venture in his career, Mann-Kind, which was slated for its public debut midway through the year. Mann also was devoting another 45 hours per week to guiding another of his companies, Advanced Bionics Corp., a maker of cochlear implants for the deaf. When Mann fulfilled his duties at Mann-Kind and Advanced Bionics, his 90-hour workweek stretched into triple digits. He sat on the board of six other companies he had either founded or purchased, which filled another ten hours of his weekly schedule, leaving him hard-pressed to find the time for any extracurricular activities, birthday celebrations included.

Mann was born in 1925 in Portland, Oregon, the son of a Polish mother and English father who had immigrated to the Pacific Northwest. Mann, whose older brother became a founding member of the Juilliard String Quartet and whose younger sister became a concert pianist, lived above a small neighborhood grocery store his father owned, growing up during the Great Depression. Perhaps motivated by the devastating economic conditions surrounding him, Mann began working at an early age, selling magazine subscriptions and operating a lemonade stand, the first entrepreneurial

COMPANY PERSPECTIVES

At MannKind, our focus is the discovery, development and, ultimately, the commercialization of therapeutic products for diseases for which there is a significant unmet medical need, such as diabetes and cancer.

venture in the career of a serial entrepreneur. Selling lemonade on a street corner was a childhood standard, however, offering nothing that distinguished Mann from any other ten-year-old. The first sign that Mann was an exception from the norm appeared in his academic performance. "I was a very avid student in school," he reflected in a February 24, 2003, interview with the *Los Angeles Business Journal.* "I studied like hell." He was selected as class valedictorian when he finished high school, earning the distinction and completing his course work at the age of 15. After high school, Mann worked in a shipyard until the Japanese attack on Pearl Harbor in December 1941 motivated him to join the U.S. Army Air Corps. Mann's academic career resumed after his service during World War II. He enrolled at the University of California, Los Angeles (UCLA) and earned an undergraduate and graduate degree in physics, completing his studies in 1951.

After leaving UCLA, Mann accepted a job offer from Technicolor, which soon touched off what would be an exceptionally active career as a high-technology entrepreneur, one that met perhaps its greatest challenge with MannKind. Mann's focus on the intricacies of the light spectrum while at UCLA led to his work on light filters and other related projects at Technicolor, which drew the attention of the U.S. Army, intent on developing the first heads-up fighter-aircraft display. Technicolor and the U.S. Army began working on the project, but Technicolor soon decided against continuing the collaborative effort. Mann, who had worked on the project, was approached by the U.S. Army soon afterward for his expertise in developing a light filter for a guidance system for an antitank missile. The two parties signed a contract for $11,200 that gave birth to Mann's first company, Spectrolab, in 1956, which distinguished itself as a developer of filters that improved the performance of solar cells used to power U.S. spacecraft. The United States' efforts to best the Soviet Union in the exploration of outer space provided fertile ground for Mann's second entrepreneurial venture, Heliotek, which became the leading supplier of solar power systems to the U.S. space program before the end of the 1950s. In 1960, Mann's first demonstration of founding one company

after another was followed by another signature trait of his dealings in the business world: a buyout of his creations that delivered handsome payoffs. Textron, an aggressive conglomerate of the era, bought both of Mann's companies, paying $11 million for Spectrolab and Heliotek and hiring Mann to lead the companies under the Textron corporate umbrella.

As his career played out, Mann often stayed with his ventures after they were purchased by another company, but his entrepreneurial inclinations always drove him to walk a more solitary path. Such was the case with his next company, Pacesetter, Inc., which manufactured pacemakers. Both Spectrolab and Heliotek made rechargeable batteries while under Mann's management, which led Mann, encouraged by scientists at Johns Hopkins University, to launch Pacemaker as a producer of a pacemaker that could be recharged through a vest worn by a patient. The business began as a research side venture in 1969, but by 1972 Mann was ready to leave Textron and invest his own money and time into the company. After switching to long-lasting lithium batteries in 1976, Mann had produced another coveted commercial entity, one that was purchased by Siemens AG in 1985 for $150 million, half of which went into Mann's pockets. As he had with Spectrolab and Heliotek, Mann remained in charge of Pacesetter after it was purchased by its German suitor, staying within the organization for the next seven years. Eventually, Mann was propelled by the drive that later would spur him as an octogenarian to work 100 hours per week. A new idea, his greatest financial success in the years before MannKind's founding, pulled him away from the Siemens fold, making him one of the wealthiest individuals in the United States.

Mann launched MiniMed Inc. as a side venture in 1979, paralleling the way Pacesetter began a decade earlier. The commonality between the two companies ran deeper: MiniMed was established to develop an implantable insulin pump using the same type of rechargeable technology used by Pacesetter. In terms of its perceived market value, however, MiniMed stood in sharp contrast to Pacesetter. MiniMed became the world's leading manufacturer of insulin pumps, controlling 80 percent of the insulin pump market.

Mann's success with MiniMed laid the foundation for MannKind, proving to be instrumental to the company's formation and ability to operate in the costly field of biopharmaceutical development. Mann registered the biggest payday of his career when he sold MiniMed, giving him a massive personal fortune to finance the development of MannKind. In 2001, Medtronic Inc., a Minneapolis, Minnesota-based biomedical device maker, agreed to pay $4.2 billion for

```
┌─────────────────────────────────────────────┐
│                                             │
│              KEY DATES                       │
│                 ■                           │
│  ─────────────────────────────────────────  │
│  1991:  Pharmaceutical Discovery Corp. is   │
│         founded.                            │
│  1999:  Alfred Mann acquires majority       │
│         control of CTL ImmunoTherapies      │
│         Corp.                               │
│  2001:  Mann merges AlleCure Corp. and CTL  │
│         into Pharmaceutical Discovery,      │
│         giving the new entity the name      │
│         MannKind Corporation.               │
│  2004:  MannKind completes its initial      │
│         public offering of stock.           │
│  2006:  The company begins Phase 3 clinical │
│         trials on the Technosphere Insulin  │
│         System and begins early-stage       │
│         trials on a cancer vaccine.         │
│                                             │
└─────────────────────────────────────────────┘
```

MiniMed and a research affiliate, Medical Research Group Inc., a deal that netted Mann more than $1 billion. MiniMed also played a role in the first steps toward forming MannKind. In early 1998, while Mann was presiding over MiniMed's insulin pump business, a Toronto entrepreneur named John Simard called Mann, looking for help in obtaining pumps for cancer vaccine trials he wanted to begin in Europe. A year earlier, Simard had founded CTL ImmunoTherapies Corp., a one-man operation that had taken on the daunting task of curing cancer. Mann was intrigued by CTL's prospects and agreed to provide pumps and to invest $500,000 in the company's development. A little more than a year after his first contact with Simard, Mann increased his commitment, investing several million dollars to take an ownership share in CTL, which relocated to Chatsworth, California, to be closer to its new owner. "I really intended it to be more of a philanthropic effort, although it was a business," Mann said of his investment in CTL in a March 29, 2004, interview with the *Daily Deal.* "I wasn't as concerned with making money as curing cancer."

MANNKIND TAKING SHAPE IN 2001

Mann's altruistic motivations would serve him well as he began to redirect his energies from MiniMed toward MannKind. The company was formed by combining CTL with two other companies, Valencia, California-based AlleCure Corp. and Danbury, Connecticut-based Pharmaceutical Discovery Corp. (PDC). AlleCure, an early-stage company like CTL, was developing immunology products to help prevent and treat allergies, basing its efforts on the work of Swiss scientist Rolf Zinkernagel, recipient of the 1996 Nobel Prize for

Medicine. PDC, founded in 1991, developed drug delivery technologies, specializing in pulmonary delivery systems. Mann merged CTL and AlleCure into PDC in December 2001, a transaction that coincided with PDC changing its name to MannKind Corporation. "There is a lot of interest and synergy between them," Mann said in a May 14, 2001, interview with the *Los Angeles Business Journal,* referring to the three entities composing his new company. "It lets us create a very powerful and diverse pharma company. We will take it public—market willing—some time in the late third or early fourth quarter."

Mann entered a new realm once he switched from guiding MiniMed to spearheading MannKind's development. Medical device makers such as MiniMed and Mann's other ventures faced a far less rigorous, time-consuming, and capital-intensive regulatory approval process than the arduous struggle pharmaceutical concerns faced. Gaining FDA approval meant passing through three phases of trials that took years and hundreds of millions of dollars to complete, a process during which MannKind would generate no revenues and rack up heavy annual losses. The pressures imposed by the approval process had a defining influence on MannKind, forcing Mann to alter his priorities. He had intended to focus on developing cancer vaccines, early trials of which proved promising, but mounting losses convinced him to make cancer treatments a secondary objective. MannKind, instead, would focus on a project closer to receiving FDA approval, pinning its efforts on treating diabetes with an inhaled form of insulin. Plans to develop cancer vaccines and treatments for inflammatory and autoimmune diseases remained in place, work that was conducted at the company's Valencia-based research operations, but most of the company's attention was focused on operations at PDC's former headquarters in Danbury, Connecticut, where research, development, and manufacturing of the Technosphere Insulin System took center stage.

Technosphere promised to offer diabetics a way of maintaining proper glucose levels that eliminated the need to inject insulin subcutaneously. The system used a proprietary dry-powder formulation that was inhaled deep into the lungs using a special inhaler developed by MannKind, the MedTone. Aside from eliminating the use of a needle, Technosphere was shown to absorb rapidly into the bloodstream following inhalation, performing most of the glucose-lowering activity of insulin within three hours of administration, roughly the same time glucose became available after ingesting food and much quicker than injected insulin.

As MannKind sought to gain FDA approval for Technosphere, the company chewed through hundreds of million of dollars, substantial chunks of which were supplied by Mann. Against the backdrop of the company's efforts to enter the market, anticipation of its debut on Wall Street occupied the interest of industry onlookers. Initially, Mann had declared he intended to complete an initial public offering (IPO) of stock in late 2001, but market conditions were not favorable for a conversion to public ownership. Another attempt was scheduled for mid-2002, but Mann canceled plans for an IPO. "We met with bankers and they told me that, because of my track record with companies and my reputation, that we could go public now," Mann said in an April 8, 2002, interview with the *Los Angeles Business Journal*. "But I don't believe the market is ready," he added. After again canceling plans for an IPO in early 2003, the company finally completed its public offering in July 2004, when it raised net proceeds of $83.2 million.

MANNKIND BANKING ON THE FUTURE

The money raised from the IPO provided some financial relief, but not nearly enough to end the company's worries. MannKind was a developmental-stage company, and it would remain so well into Mann's 80s. The company began the third and most expensive phase of the FDA approval process in late 2006, by which point more than $650 million had been spent trying to bring Technosphere to market. Analysts predicted Technosphere would not reach doctors' offices until at least 2010. The company also began early-stage clinical trials on its experimental cancer drug, MKC1106-PP, in late 2006, opening up another costly yet potentially lucrative avenue for Mann and his successors to pursue. MannKind's fate entirely rested on future developments, but as the company progressed toward its goal of becoming a commercially active concern, it stood to benefit from the persistence and enormous wealth of its creator.

Jeffrey L. Covell

PRINCIPAL DIVISIONS

MannKind Endocrinology; MannKind Immunology.

PRINCIPAL COMPETITORS

Pfizer Inc.; Novo Nordisk A/S; Eli Lilly and Company.

FURTHER READING

Coates, Chris, "Burning Cash, MannKind Is Raising More Money," *San Fernando Valley Business Journal*, December 4, 2006, p. 11.

————, "MannKind Stock Soars on Prospects for New Drug," *San Fernando Valley Business Journal*, July 17, 2006, p. 10.

Darmiento, Laurence, "Biotech Mogul Mann Delays One IPO and Gets Set for Another," *Los Angeles Business Journal*, January 13, 2003, p. 12.

————, "Mann Still Tireless in Research Quest," *Los Angeles Business Journal*, February 24, 2003, p. 1.

Garcia, Shelly, "MannKind Making Another Attempt to Launch IPO," *San Fernando Valley Business Journal*, May 10, 2004, p. 1.

Ibold, Hans, "Mann Slates Biotech IPO by Year End," *Los Angeles Business Journal*, May 14, 2001, p. 3.

Jaffe, Joshua, "Reaching for the Impossible?" *Daily Deal*, March 29, 2004.

Martinez, Carlos, "Biotech Billionaire Says Market Not Ready for IPO," *Los Angeles Business Journal*, April 8, 2002, p. 11.

Netherby, Jennifer, "Alfred Mann's Magic Boosts Company's Cancer Vaccine," *Los Angeles Business Journal*, March 27, 2000, p. 10.

Pondel, Evan, "Valencia, Calif.-based AlleCure Developing Vaccine Against Bee Venom," *Daily News*, April 2, 2002.

Marble Slab Creamery, Inc.

3100 South Gessner Road, Suite 305
Houston, Texas 77063-3743
U.S.A.
Telephone: (713) 780-3601
Fax: (713) 780-0264
Web site: http://www.marbleslab.com

Wholly Owned Subsidiary of NexCen Brands, Inc.
Incorporated: 1983
Employees: 37
Sales: $90 million (2006 est.)
NAIC: 722213 Snack and Nonalcoholic Beverage Bars;
533110 Lessors of Nonfinancial Intangible Assets
(Except Copyrighted Works)

■ ■ ■

Marble Slab Creamery, Inc., is one of the three largest players in the emerging category of ice cream shop chains specializing in hand-mixed, superpremium ice cream. Founded in 1983, making it the original in the category, but far smaller than the category leader, Cold Stone Creamery, Marble Slab Creamery runs a franchise-based chain of more than 350 units in the United States, which are scattered across 35 states, primarily in the South, Midwest, and Southwest. A much smaller number of stores also operate in Canada and the United Arab Emirates. Each store offers its customers three dozen or more flavors of ice cream, which is superpremium quality, meaning it contains 14 percent or more butterfat and a lower amount of air than regular ice cream. The ice cream is made fresh

daily in the stores, as are the waffle cones the ice cream is served in. Like those of the chief competitors, Marble Slab outlets turn their business into a show. After selecting an ice cream flavor, a customer chooses from an assortment of what the company calls "mixins"—various fruits, nuts, candies, and cookies. The server scoops the ice cream onto a frozen slab of marble (or granite) and then blends the toppings into the ice cream and scoops the concoction into a waffle cone. The stores also offer specialty desserts, frozen yogurt, smoothies, and blended coffee drinks. In early 2007 Marble Slab Creamery was acquired by NexCen Brands, Inc., which simultaneously acquired the number three player in this same category, MaggieMoo's International, LLC.

BIRTH OF THE CONCEPT IN HOUSTON

Marble Slab Creamery was founded in Houston in 1983 by Sigmund Penn and Tom LePage. Penn had experience in the food industry having helped expand his family's New York bakery business into a 55-store operation before moving to Houston where he started a variety of fast-food restaurant chains. LePage, a Minnesota native, had a long career in marketing and sales and was Penn's neighbor and tennis partner. The two friends eventually agreed to open an ice cream store and, as part of their research efforts, visited several upscale shops, including an outlet of Boston-based Steve's, considered the first to offer "mixins," and White Mountain Creamery in Washington, D.C.

In August 1983 Hurricane Alicia slammed into Houston, knocking out power to Penn's home. The

COMPANY PERSPECTIVES

Since 1983, Marble Slab Creamery has set its standards of quality unusually high. Every batch of our superpremium ice cream is homemade, and we hand-roll our freshly baked waffle cones in each store. As for mixins, we offer only the freshest fruits, the finest nuts, the sweetest candies, and the yummiest cookies around. So whatever your order, you can be sure it's fresh and filled with fabulous flavor.

Penns temporarily moved in with the LePages, which gave Penn and LePage an opportunity to test recipes using Penn's new cone-making machine. Two months later, the partners opened their store, called Cones 'n Cream, at the Carillon Shopping Center in Houston. The store offered rich, all-natural superpremium ice cream, made daily right on the premises, with "mixins" to order folded into the ice cream on a frozen marble slab in front of the customer. The customized ice cream mixture was then scooped into a freshly baked waffle cone. Using a cold slab kept the ice cream hard as the extras were blended in. Sales at the new store grew steadily from $1,100 the first week to $3,000 a week by January 1984 and $5,000 a week by March 1984.

Among the early developments for the nascent operation was a name change. After their application for a trademark on Cones 'n Cream was rejected on the grounds that the name was "too generic," the cofounders scrambled to come up with a new name. They soon settled on Marble Slab Creamery, though the name later proved misleading. Penn discovered that marble slabs eventually begin to break when they are exposed to a repeated process of being chilled and then warming up, prompting a switch to granite slabs (but not another name change). Less than a year after the first store opened, Penn and LePage began franchising the concept.

1986: BEGINNING OF THE HANKAMER ERA OF LEADERSHIP

One of the first franchisees, Ronald J. Hankamer, played the lead role in the next phase of the company's history. Hankamer was a partner in a family-owned hotel business, Southwest Inns Ltd., a major developer and operator of Holiday Inns in Texas. From his involvement in this business, he had gained experience with both franchising and the food industry as he was in charge of operations and managed the motels' restaurants and cof-

fee shops. He became acquainted with Marble Slab in 1983 when it was still known as Cones 'n Cream. His middle-school-age sons had been pestering him to check out the increasingly popular ice cream shop offering premium ice cream and a show to go with it. After taking his whole family to the shop, he was so impressed with the concept that he immediately set out to become a franchisee. He opened his franchised shop, under the Marble Slab Creamery name, in southwest Houston in late 1984. The store enjoyed strong sales from the very beginning and was immediately profitable.

By April 1986 there were 14 Marble Slab Creamery outlets, about half in Houston with the remainder in other Texas cities such as San Antonio and Galveston, as well as Tulsa, Oklahoma; and Ames, Iowa. By this time, some of the franchisees were becoming concerned about food costs, and Hankamer had concluded that a greater emphasis on store operations was needed for the franchises to thrive. He therefore approached the company founders about buying them out. Penn and LePage agreed to sell the business to Hankamer and his family for around $250,000.

Among the key early changes that Hankamer imposed was to alter the franchisee training program to unify and standardize the stores. After consulting with an interior design firm, he began allowing franchisees to choose from just three standard color schemes. He also conferred with restaurant consultants to develop plans that helped franchisees schedule their employees so as to lower their labor costs. By stepping up the chain's expansion, Hankamer created a larger overall system that provided franchisees with more clout to negotiate lower food costs from suppliers. Growing exclusively through franchising, Hankamer concentrated initially on the Sun Belt, where people eat more ice cream, closing locations that had been opened in farther-flung locales, such as Iowa. By 1995 the chain had reached the 50-unit mark, with locations in Texas, Louisiana, New Mexico, Arizona, and California. Around ten more stores debuted in 1996, including the first in Florida. Most of the Marble Slab Creamery outlets at this time were located in strip shopping centers, with about a quarter found in enclosed malls. In 1997 systemwide sales jumped 30 percent, reaching $13 million.

LAUNCH OF PERIOD OF ACCELERATING GROWTH

In the late 1990s and into the early 21st century, Marble Slab accelerated its growth, spreading into additional states in the Southeast, Midwest, and Southwest. By the end of 2000 there were 179 Marble Slab Creamery outlets in 21 states. Systemwide sales had surged to $30 million, while the company itself was

```
┌─────────────────────────────────────────────┐
│                                               │
│              KEY DATES                        │
│                   ◆                           │
│  1983:  Sigmund Penn and Tom LePage open an   │
│         ice cream shop in Houston called      │
│         Cones 'n Cream; the name is later     │
│         changed to Marble Slab Creamery.      │
│  1984:  Franchising begins.                   │
│  1986:  The cofounders sell the company to    │
│         franchisee Ronald J. Hankamer and     │
│         his family for $250,000.              │
│  2001:  Store count reaches 200.              │
│  2007:  Marble Slab Creamery is sold to       │
│         NexCen Brands, Inc., for $21 million. │
│                                               │
└─────────────────────────────────────────────┘
```

generating revenues of $2.1 million. All of the stores were franchised except for the original location in the Carillon Shopping Center, which remained company owned. This locale, situated just three city blocks away from the corporate headquarters, served as a research and development test center as well as a franchisee training facility. Hankamer continued to place great emphasis on the quality of the ice cream. The ice cream was made at seven independent dairies, which distributed an ice cream base to the stores, where flavorings were added and the ice cream was refrozen. Hankamer also instituted a rigorous inspection program through which field supervisors were charged with carrying out unannounced store visits to evaluate cleanliness, quality, and service. On the marketing side, the company supplemented word-of-mouth advertising with billboard and radio advertisements, and because many of its stores were in shopping centers with movie theaters, it increasingly used movie-theater onscreen ads.

By mid-2001 the Marble Slab system had reached 200 units. Over the next several years, the company opened around 30 additional franchised outlets each year, including the first stores in Canada and the United Arab Emirates. The company took a conservative approach to international development as Hankamer believed that a too-rapid expansion could prove to be a recipe for failure. In 2003 Marble Slab sold a master franchise for all of Canada to a Calgary-based company in a deal calling for the development of at least 70 units north of the border over a 30-year period. Two years later a firm based in Dubai was selected to open a minimum of 50 stores across the Middle East.

Also in the early 2000s, Marble Slab began marketing more toward children, introducing a kids club and a cartoonish mascot named Slabby who personified an ice cream cone. Competition in the hand-mixed, superpremium ice cream category was heating up at this time. Stone Cold Creamery, a chain founded in Scottsdale, Arizona, in 1988, surged past Marble Slab into the top position, with more than 500 units and systemwide sales of $155 million in 2003. Since its founding in Kansas City, Missouri, in 1989, MaggieMoo's International, LLC, had opened more than 100 stores, achieving 2003 systemwide sales of nearly $30 million. By comparison, the 300-unit Marble Slab generated systemwide sales of $60 million in 2003, an increase of nearly 43 percent over the previous year. Also that year, Marble Slab introduced an overhauled store design for its new units featuring an upscale interior that was chosen to better match the quality of the company's product. The 1,200-square-foot design incorporated softer colors, graphic imagery, and enhanced lighting, and it created a "slab theater" at the front of the store to entice shoppers inside. One other noteworthy addition was an open shelf, located about 5 feet above the counter, filled with the chain's signature mixins ingredients.

In 2004, as the company made a major push into California and began moving into the Northeast as well, Marble Slab launched its first major television advertising campaign. The spots emphasized the quality and freshness of the chain's ice cream as well as the showy way in which its ice cream concoctions were created. The freshness angle was promoted by noting that the milk in its ice cream had no additives and the product went from cow to counter in ten days.

2007: ACQUISITION BY NEXCEN BRANDS

The steady growth at Marble Slab Creamery continued as systemwide revenues surged to approximately $90 million by 2006, when the store count exceeded 350 units and the chain's reach extended to 35 states, Canada, and the United Arab Emirates. In February 2007 Hankamer sold the company to NexCen Brands, Inc., for $16 million plus an additional payment of $5 million in either cash or stock due one year later. NexCen simultaneously purchased MaggieMoo's for $16.1 million in cash and stock. Based in New York City, NexCen evolved out of Aether Systems, Inc., one of the once-high-flying casualties of the dot-com bust. In 2006 NexCen began focusing on brand management, seeking to acquire and manage consumer brands in industries in which intellectual property played a central role. The company purchased franchise-based footwear retailer Athlete's Foot Brands, LLC, that year and clothing designer Bill Blass Holding Co., Inc., early in 2007. Its acquisitions of Marble Slab and MaggieMoo's were its first within the quick-service restaurant sector.

NexCen's executives had no immediate plans to change either chain, although they saw some synergies between the two brands in operational areas, such as back-office functions. They envisioned Marble Slab and MaggieMoo's both continuing their plans of expansion as the two concepts had established their own niches within the hand-mixed, superpremium category: Marble Slab was positioned as more "adult and sophisticated," while MaggieMoo's was "more for kids." For Marble Slab, which at the time of the acquisition had about 165 stores under development, its new ownership was likely to mean a bigger marketing push and an increased emphasis on overseas expansion. NexCen planned to leverage the international franchise network of Athlete's Foot, which extended to 40 countries, to the benefit of its newly acquired ice cream chains.

David E. Salamie

PRINCIPAL COMPETITORS

Cold Stone Creamery; International Dairy Queen, Inc.; Baskin-Robbins; Friendly Ice Cream Corporation; Ben & Jerry's Homemade Inc.; Carvel Corporation; Bruster's Real Ice Cream, Inc.; Dippin' Dots, Incorporated; W. H. Braum, Inc.

FURTHER READING

Aronovich, Hanna, "Mixing It Up," *Food and Drink,* August 2006, pp. 76, 78.

Barbaro, Michael, "Buyout Firm Said to Be in Deal to Unite No. 2 and No. 3 Chains in Premium Ice Cream," *New York Times,* February 25, 2007, p. C3.

Benedict, Daniel, "Expanding Marble Slab Wants to Be Ice Cream of Crop," *Houston Chronicle,* September 14, 1987, Business sec., p. 1.

Crecca, Donna Hood, "How Sweet It Is," *Chain Leader,* March 2004, pp. 72, 74+.

Crown, Judith, "Marble Slab Creamery Chain Sold," *Houston Chronicle,* June 12, 1986, Business sec., p. 6.

———, "Superpremium Ice Creams Heat Competition," *Houston Chronicle,* January 5, 1986, Business sec., p. 1.

Elder, Laura Elizabeth, "Big Dipper," *Houston Business Journal,* February 2, 1996, pp. 27A–28A.

Hassell, Greg, "Scoop du Jour: Marble Slab Finds the Right Mix," *Houston Chronicle,* May 21, 1998, Business sec., p. 1.

Littman, Margaret, "Summer Job: Marble Slab Creamery Launches a New Summer Ad Campaign As Ice Cream's High Season Heats Up," *Chain Leader,* August 2004, pp. 32–33.

Lohmeyer, Lori, "New Decor, 'Slab Theater' Treat Ice-Cream Chain to Image Revamp," *Nation's Restaurant News,* October 6, 2003, p. 42.

"Marble Slab Creamery Boasts New Stores," *Shopping Center World,* November 1996, p. 17.

Mayk, Lauren, "Ice Cream Rivals Go at It," *Sarasota (Fla.) Herald-Tribune,* June 25, 2003, p. D1.

Mui, Ylan Q., "They'll Scoop to Conquer: Eclectic NexCen Tries Buying MaggieMoo's," *Washington Post,* February 26, 2007, p. D1.

Murphy, Kate, "Slabs Are Joining Scoops in Ice Cream Retailing," *New York Times,* October 26, 2006, p. C6.

Rickey, Gail, "Hurricane Alicia Spawns Marble Slab Creamery," *Houston Business Journal,* January 27, 1986, p. 14.

Ruggless, Ron, "NexCen to Acquire Marble Slab, MaggieMoo's Ice Cream Brands," *Nation's Restaurant News,* February 26, 2007, pp. 4, 49.

Sicard, Allyson, "The Scoop," *Shopping Center World,* May 2001, p. 48.

Waters, C. Dickinson, "Cold War Looms As Ice-Cream Operators Heat Up Expansion Plans," *Nation's Restaurant News,* July 23, 2001, pp. 8, 152.

Wollam, Allison, "Sweet Dreams: Marble Slab Among Cream of the Franchise Crop in Growth," *Houston Business Journal,* January 19, 2001, p. 23.

Zuniga, Jo Ann, "Rocky Road: Marble Slab Franchise Holders and Corporate Headquarters Are in an Icy Dispute over Financial Expectations," *Houston Chronicle,* October 27, 2002, Business sec., p. 1.

Match.com, LP

8300 Douglas Avenue, Suite 800
Dallas, Texas 75225
U.S.A.
Telephone: (214) 576-9352
Fax: (214) 576-9350
Web site: http://www.match.com

Wholly Owned Subsidiary of IAC/InterActiveCorp
Incorporated: 1993 as Electric Classifieds, Inc.
Employees: 275
Sales: $249.5 million (2005)
NAIC: 541690 Other Scientific and Technical Consulting Services

■ ■ ■

A subsidiary of Internet conglomerate IAC/InterActiveCorp, Dallas-based Match.com, LP is one of the world's largest online dating portals. In addition to its flagship www.match.com web site, the company operates more than 30 other dating sites in 18 local languages, serving more than 15 million registered users in over 240 countries. It claims to be responsible for at least 250,000 marriages a year. In brief, the web sites allow adults (presumably single) to post personal profiles and pictures, telling perspective dating partners their preferences in terms of age, body type, ethnicity, religion, location, and so on. While anyone is able to register to review likely matches, only paid subscribers are able to contact other singles or reply to e-mail messages, with the web site serving as an anonymous conduit. In addition, Match.com offers a variety of value-added services. Subscribers receive access to a weekly online magazine, *Happen,* focusing on dating advice. The MatchFolio premium service is essentially a personal shopper assigned to assist subscribers in their quest to find the best matches among the hundreds that are posted on the site. Match.com Mobile allows subscribers to search and communicate through their cell phones. Chemistry.com is another premium service, one that allows a subscriber's profile to be shared only with candidates who pass muster with a personality test. The company has also teamed up with "Dr. Phil" McGraw, the popular relationship and self-help counselor, to create MindFindBind With Dr. Phil, a three-part online program to help singles achieve the right state of Mind in order to Find a potential partner and Bind together in a lasting relationship.

FOUNDER ENROLLED AT NORTHWESTERN UNIVERSITY: 1981

Match.com was founded by Gary Kremen. A child of teachers, he was raised in Skokie, Illinois, where during his high school years in the late 1970s he taught himself how to program computers and became involved in computer hacking and other petty acts of vandalism. At the behest of his parents, Kremen was one day kept an extended period at the local police station after being picked up for some infraction and received a glimpse of life behind bars. The experience was frightening enough to motivate him to focus more attention on his studies. Despite less than stellar grades he was able to gain admission to Northwestern University through a well-crafted admission's essay that argued he could provide

COMPANY PERSPECTIVES

Match.com has one simple mission: to take the lottery out of love. It's been the idea that's inspired us since 1995, when we first had the idea of using this new-fangled technology called the Internet as a better way for people to find each other.

some diversity to the student mix. In 1981 he enrolled at Northwestern, majoring in both electrical engineering and computer science.

After college Kremen went to work doing computer security programming for The Aerospace Corporation, a government aerospace contractor in Silicon Valley, and was introduced to the precursor on the Internet, ARPA-NET, established by the U.S. Department of Defense. Recognizing the potential of the technology, Kremen decided he wanted to become an entrepreneur to take advantage of it, because as he told the *San Jose Mercury,* "while engineering is cool, money is where the power is." In 1987 he enrolled at Stanford Business School to gain more skills. Two years later he graduated and became partners with a friend, Ben Dubin, to establish Los Altos Technologies, a security software company. Yet even as he was developing this business, which he and Dubin would sell in 1996, Kremen in the early 1990s began pursuing new business ideas based on the Internet.

Kremen was quick to realize the importance of the .com and .net domain names that were being offered free of charge in the early 1990s. "I saw the future," he told *DN Journal,* "I could see the next 15–20 years laid out in front of me. I knew there would be a real estate grab and that generic domains would be big." He also became convinced that the Internet offered a perfect medium for online classified advertising, and so he registered for domain names that might serve as classified ad headings, such as Jobs.com, Autos.com, Housing.com, and even Sex.com.

CREATION OF ELECTRIC CLASSIFIEDS: 1993

In 1993 Kremen teamed up with Peng Tsin Ong, a Singapore-born veteran of high-tech start-ups, to found Electric Classifieds, Inc., in San Francisco. In order to launch the business and prove that online classifieds were viable, Kremen decided to concentrate on personal ads. Someone was already operating a small e-mail-based

dating service using the domain name Match.com. Kremen acquired it for $2,500 in 1994. Ong developed the database system. Other Stanford graduates were also brought in, Simon Glinksy to develop the business plan to attract investors, and Fran Maier, who was not only instrumental in tailoring the site to make it more inviting to women but promoted the idea of a membership business model. The developing business began to attract the attention of venture capitalists. Kleiner Perkins Caufield & Byers offered to invest, but Kremen declined the offer because the venture capital firm wanted to merge Electric Classifieds with Architext, a company that would ultimately become Excite.com, and Kremen would not be retained as chief executive. Instead, Electric Classifieds drummed up $1.7 million in seed money elsewhere, mostly Silicon Valley's Canann Partners.

Match.com went live in April 1995. After two months it boasted about 3,000 listings, according to a July 1995 article in *Forbes. DN Journal* claimed that the site had 7,000 members at this stage and that the business was growing at a 10 percent clip each week. Money was made by charging responders $5 to $8 to send e-mail messages to that person. Given that this was a new technology, it was not surprising that most of the users were located in San Francisco and that the ratio of men to women was four to one.

Match.com received a good deal of media attention, and Kremen was not shy about telling the press that he decided to start the company because he was not able to get a date. One of the resulting stories used a picture of him holding flowers and looking forlorn, the headline reading, "Why the Founder of Match.com Can't Get a Date." The publicity helped Electric Classifieds to raise an additional $7.5 million in another round of venture capital funds. Kremen had planned to expand Electric Classifieds the following year to offer used cars and real estate ads, but according to *DN Journal,* "his investors were satisfied with the horse they were on and he wound up being outvoted." *Wired* offered a different take on what happened next, maintaining "The board wanted him to start developing other classifieds and stop messing around with lonely-heart ads. 'They were embarrassed by it,' Kremen remembers." What is not in dispute is that Kremen and his board of directors had a contentious relationship. Although regarded as smart, Kremen was also perceived as difficult to work with.

In 1997 the investors engineered an $8 million sale of Match.com to Cendant, a Connecticut consumer services company. Kremen opposed the deal but was unable to block it. He received $50,000 and a lifetime Match.com account under the username "The Founder." Kremen went on to become involved in a

KEY DATES

1993: Electric Classifieds, Inc., is established.
1995: Match.com site goes live.
1997: Cendant acquires Match.com.
1999: Cendant sells Match.com to Ticketmaster Online-CitySearch Inc.
2004: Jim Safka is named CEO.
2006: Dr. Phil McGraw is signed to endorsement deal.

wide variety of Internet ventures, but became best known for a long-term battle he waged against a twice-convicted felon named Steve Cohen, who forged a letter to the company that controlled registered domain names, Network Solutions, claiming that Kremen had given him the rights to Sex.com. Cohen then made about $500,000 a month selling banner ads to other adult sites. Kremen spent years in court before gaining back the domain name, and then found himself a very much conflicted participant in the adult entertainment industry. He also won a $65 million judgment against Cohen, who then fled the country and remained on the loose until 2007, all the while claiming he was broke. About all that Kremen received from Cohen was a poorly kept mansion in Rancho Santa Fe, California, and a ramshackle house on the border with Mexico.

SALE OF MATCH.COM: 1999

With the money received from the sale to Cendant, Electric Classifieds attempted to build up nondating businesses, but it was unable to compete against Craigslist, which offered a free classified listing service that proved highly popular. Cendant held on to Match.com for less than two years, selling it for $50 million in May 1999 to Ticketmaster Online-CitySearch Inc., a unit of USA Networks, Inc., which later became IAC/InterActiveCorp. Ticketmaster Online-CitySearch offered such local online services as city entertainment guides, live-event ticketing, and local auctions. At the time of the sale, Match.com had built up its number of registered users to 1.8 million.

Match.com sought to achieve growth through partnerships with leading Internet portals, and through a network of affiliates in other countries. In 2000 revenues improved to $29.1 million. By 2001 Match.com had grown its number of daily page views to five million. By signing marketing agreements with America Online and Microsoft Network in April of that year the

site doubled its number of page views overnight. To promote the brand and stimulate revenues, Match.com launched its first national television campaign in the fall of 2001. At this point it was the second largest company in its category, trailing Yahoo! Personals.

Early in 2002 a new CEO, Tim Sullivan, was installed. The vice-president of e-commerce for Ticketmaster Online/Citysearch, Sullivan was familiar with Match.com because his sister had used the site to find a boyfriend, who eventually became her husband. He quickly took steps to expand the company, establishing MatchTravel, a service to host singles' vacations around the world, and by the end of 2002 the company added to its office in London and Sydney by launching some two-dozen local-language dating sites around the world. Match.com surpassed Yahoo! and in 2003 grew revenues to $185.3 million.

While all appeared to be going well for Match.com, beneath the surface there was cause for concern. In 2003 Match.com experienced an erosion in its subscriber base, and the only reason the company continued to show growth was because of the acquisition of UDate.com. In fact, growth in the category was tailing off at a rapid pace, as many users seemed to grow disenchanted with online matchmaking.

In 2004 a new chief executive, Jim Safka, was hired to take Match.com to the next level. He was well qualified for the job, having served as brand manager for Intuit and heading online marketing for AT&T Wireless. Safka set out to increase the number of daters in all age groups in order to attract more daters and increase subscribers. After spending about three months studying the data, he concluded that older daters were more likely than younger daters to subscribe. It was hardly a revelation to the company's founders. Fran Maier on her blog (http://franmaier.typepad.com) opined: "Back when Match.com was started we knew that women over 29 and men over 32 were much more likely to pay (and this was more than 10 years ago when the net was dominated by more men and younger people overall)." Nevertheless, Match.com and the other dating sites had spent the past decade chasing a younger market.

Safka directed his staff to make the site more user friendly to older daters. After just four months under Safka, Match.com increased paid subscribers by 10 percent. Business continued to grow in 2005 and early in the year the number of paid subscribers topped the one million mark for the first time. The company also added premium services, such as Chemistry.com, a site that relied on a personality test developed by anthropologist Helen Fisher of Rutgers University to screen candidates. By the end of the year revenues approached $250 million.

To make a further appeal to an older demographic and bring more legitimacy to online matchmaking, in January 2006 Match.com hired Dr. Phil McGraw, an arrangement that the company said was a partnership rather than a celebrity endorsement deal. His value to Match.com's new strategy was clear: By being associated with Dr. Phil, the company hoped to reach his core audience, which skewed toward older women, and if they came to the site, the men would follow. Moreover, Match.com planned to charge an additional $9 per month for Dr. Phil's MindFindBind program. To help these new users make sense of online dating, Match.com introduced a revamped Starter Kit in late 2006. Match.com also began to apply its new model overseas, where its chief rival, Meetic, continued to target young daters. However, it was not alone in marketing to an older demographic. A more recent entry in online dating, eHarmony.com, was enjoying strong growth among older Americans and was heavily promoted on television. In light of this competition and what appeared to be a slowing market, it was an open question whether Match.com would be able to maintain growth in the years to come.

Ed Dinger

PRINCIPAL SUBSIDIARIES

Chemistry.Com; Match.com International; Match.com Mobile.

PRINCIPAL COMPETITORS

eHarmony.com, Inc.; Friendster, Inc.; Tickle Inc.; Meetic

FURTHER READING

Bosman, Julie, "Online Dating Service Teams Up with Dr. Phil," *New York Times,* January 13, 2006, p. C5.

Churbuck, David C., "Help Wanted: On-Line Publisher," *Forbes,* July 3, 1995, p. 80.

Doscher, Megan, "The Best Way to ... Find Love: If There's One Person Out There for You, Can the Internet Really Be the Matchmaker?" *Wall Street Journal,* December 6, 1999, p. R34.

Jackson, Ron, "Be Careful What You Wish For: The Continuing Saga of Gary Kremen and Sex.com," *DN Journal,* March 2006.

Krieger, Todd, "Love and Money," *Wired,* September 1995.

O'Brien, Chris, "Internet Maverick," *San Jose Mercury News,* September 17, 2006.

———, "The Prisoner of Sex.com," *Wired,* August 2003.

Silver, Sara, "Internet Romance: How Match.com Found Love Among Boomers," *Wall Street Journal,* January 27, 2007, p. A1.

Tedeschi, Bob, "Online Matchmakers Are Helping to Bolster the Finances of the Corporate Parents As They Raise the Romantic Hopes of Clients," *New York Times,* February 4, 2002, p. C6.

Meyer International Holdings, Ltd.

382 Kwon Tong Road
Kwon Tong
Kowloon,
Hong Kong
Telephone: (+852) 2797-1228
Fax: (+852) 2763-5598
Web site: http://www.meyer.com

Private Company
Incorporated: 1951 as Meyer Manufacturing Co. Ltd.
Employees: 5,000
Sales: $287 million (2005 est.)
NAIC: 335211 Electric Houseware and Fan Manufacturing

■ ■ ■

Meyer International Holdings, Ltd., is the Hong Kong-based holding company for a family-owned business involved in manufacturing and distributing more than a dozen cookware brands. The Cheng family, headed by Stanley K. Cheng, controls Meyer Manufacturing Co. Ltd., the Hong Kong-based manufacturing arm of its business that is supported by production facilities in Thailand, China, and Italy. Distribution and marketing affiliates are located in the United States, the United Kingdom, Italy, Thailand, China, Australia, Singapore, Malaysia, Canada, and Japan. The U.S. affiliate, Meyer Corporation, U.S., ranks as the largest cookware distributor in the United States and the second largest distributor in the world. Meyer's cookware is made from stainless steel, hard-anodized aluminum, and nonstick aluminum. The two most important brands sold by the company are its Circulon and Anolon brands, which were developed by the company. Other brands either acquired by Meyer or licensed for distribution are Prestige, Raco, Silverstone, KitchenAid, Farberware, Essteele, Fujimaru, NapaStyle, Select, and Meyer Commercialware. Meyer produces more than 30 million pans annually, touting itself as the global leader in the production of hard-anodized, nonstick cookware.

ORIGINS

Meyer's prominence in the cookware industry was the work of Stanley K. Cheng, who changed the orientation of his family's business to create something more profound than a so-called category killer. Cheng created a category, carving out a new niche in the cookware market, and then, after defining it, went on to dominate it. He was born in Hong Kong in 1948, one of six children in a family that drew its income from manufacturing metal products and a host of other business ventures. The family business sprang from the Chiap Hua Group, a network of individual entities involved mainly in the production of metal products that was established in China in 1922. Cheng's father, Cheng Chik Chi, joined the Chiap Hua Group in 1937, when he and three of his brothers set up the firm's operations in Hong Kong. With the Hong Kong operations as a starting point, Cheng's father and uncles built a bustling business empire that included a rolling mill, real estate and mortgage financing interests, iron and steel works, a ship salvaging operation, and numerous other ventures. Of particular importance to the future of

COMPANY PERSPECTIVES

We specialize in the distribution of metal cookware and other kitchen products. Our cookware is made by our own affiliate factories throughout the world, including Italy, Thailand, and China. We focus on developing high quality, top performing cookware, utilizing cutting edge technology and designs. We offer cookware made from stainless steel, hard-anodized aluminum, and nonstick aluminum. Offering different brands enables us to distribute different levels of cookware to tailor to specific cooking and lifestyle needs.

the cookware industry was the family's aluminum manufacturing plant, which produced flashlights, hinges, camping lanterns, and tennis rackets. The Anglicized name of the family business, a transliteration of the Chinese characters for "beautiful" and "Asia" ("mai" and "yah"), was Meyer Manufacturing Co. Ltd.

Cheng would take the Meyer name to new heights, but before he did so he moved overseas to finish his education. He attended the University of Oregon and Oregon State University during the mid-1960s, earning degrees in business administration and mechanical engineering. He returned to Hong Kong in 1971, ready to make wholesale changes in his family's aluminum manufacturing business. He quickly changed the strategic direction of Meyer Manufacturing, directing company officials to make the switch to producing a line of cookware. The company's first line of products, a private label line of inexpensive, 12-gauge aluminum cookware, made its market debut in London in 1972, but Cheng's entry into the business did not bring immediate success. He ultimately wanted to market products under his own brand, and, more than anywhere else, he wanted to market his products in the United States. When he signed a five-year alliance with Ekco Products in 1977, he gained entry into the U.S. market for the first time, but marketing an aluminum-ware line under the Ekco name failed to meet his expectations. "That arrangement," Cheng recalled in a May 28, 1984, interview with *HFD-The Weekly Home Furnishings Newspaper,* "never really worked out very well and we were happy to see the deal run out in 1981." Cheng wanted to enter the U.S. market with his own product, one that embodied innovation and

elevated the stature of the Meyer name. Within a few years of ending his company's relationship with Ekco, Cheng's dream came true.

Cheng established Meyer's U.S. base of operations in Milwaukee, Wisconsin, in the early 1980s, the starting point of his assault on the U.S. market. Initially, Cheng misfired. He introduced a line of high-end aluminum cookware, positioning Meyer for the first time in the more upscale segment of the market, but he encountered a host of competitors battling it out with price promotions that obscured Meyer's product line. "We didn't really have a focus," a company executive, Jon C. Rieden, conceded in a December 17, 1990, interview with *HFD-The Weekly Home Furnishings Newspaper.* "We had kind of a shotgun approach." Several new executives with experience in the U.S. market were recruited to help distinguish the company in the saturated market, but unquestionably the greatest contributor to Meyer's success in the United States, and elsewhere, was the inventiveness of Cheng. Tapping into his skills as an engineer, Cheng developed what became Meyer's seminal product, the Circulon line of cookware.

DEBUT OF CIRCULON: 1984

Introduced in 1984, Circulon represented a new category in the cookware market, the first line of nonstick, hard-anodized pans. The breakthrough product featured an aluminum core sandwiched between a hard-anodized exterior and a hard-anodized nonstick surface, enabling the use of Teflon at high temperatures. The pan's interior, a titanium composite, featured a series of tiny peaks and valleys that Cheng patented as Meyer's "Hi-Low" process. The small grooves reduced abrasion of the Teflon surface, which became the basis of the line's marketing slogan, "Food Won't Stick for 10 Years." After more than a decade of applying its energies to the cookware segment, Meyer confirmed its position as preeminent manufacturer with the release of the Circulon line. The brand became an immediate commercial success, developing within a few short years into the most popular single line of cookware in the world. "Circulon gave us a unique product," Rieden said in his December 17, 1990, interview with *HFD-The Weekly Home Furnishings Newspaper.* "We went from the shotgun to the rifle."

The Circulon line gave Meyer a cookware line to rally around, a brand that distinguished the company and attracted the attention of retailers. Gourmet specialty stores and department stores, in particular, inundated Meyer with orders for Circulon, excited that, for the first time, they could offer customers a nonstick, hard-anodized product. As sales mounted, Cheng quickly followed his success with Circulon by introduc-

```
┌─────────────────────────────────────────┐
│                                          │
│            KEY DATES                     │
│                ■                         │
│  ─────────────────────────────────────   │
│  1951:  Meyer Manufacturing Co., Ltd.,   │
│         is founded in Hong Kong.         │
│  1971:  Stanley K. Cheng steers Meyer    │
│         into the cookware business.      │
│  1984:  Meyer unveils its Circulon       │
│         brand, the first line of hard-   │
│         anodized, nonstick cookware.     │
│  1986:  Meyer introduces the Anolon      │
│         brand of cookware.               │
│  1992:  Meyer moves its U.S.-based       │
│         operations to California.        │
│  1996:  Marketing and distribution       │
│         operations are established in    │
│         Australia.                       │
│  2006:  Meyer forms an alliance with     │
│         celebrity chef Rachel Ray.       │
│                                          │
└─────────────────────────────────────────┘
```

ing the Anolon line in 1986, a dishwasher-safe, nonstick line of cookware made with a thicker gauge of aluminum than Circulon pans. Together, the two cookware lines formed the foundation of Meyer's business, giving Cheng a base to build upon in the coming years.

Cheng, presiding as president and chief executive officer, expanded aggressively as he redefined the cookware market. Although success in the U.S. market had occupied his attention, he by no means limited his expansion efforts to courting American retailers. Cheng intended to make Meyer a global force. A network of Meyer subsidiaries were established to serve as marketing and distribution arms of Cheng's expanding empire, each fed by manufacturing facilities in Hong Kong, Thailand, Italy, and China. In the early 1980s, Cheng established Meyer Group Limited in the northwest of England at roughly the same time he established U.S. headquarters in Milwaukee and formed a Canadian subsidiary, Meyer Canada Inc. Further expansion in the 1990s fleshed out Meyer's geographic presence.

While his company spread its presence across the world map, Cheng was on the move as well. In 1992, he relocated his U.S. subsidiary, Meyer Corporation U.S., to Vallejo, California, and moved his family to the San Francisco Bay Area city. Cheng directed Meyer's worldwide operations from his offices in Vallejo and began to express his entrepreneurial bent in endeavors aside from cookware. In 1996, he purchased a 127-acre ranch in Napa Valley and established a vineyard, Hestan Vineyards, that began producing wines bearing the Meyer name, among other labels. Despite making the

foray into running a winery, Cheng did not let his attention stray from expanding his cookware business. In 1996, the same year he purchased his Napa Valley ranch, Cheng acquired the Raco cookware brand in Australia and used the acquisition to establish Meyer Cookware Australia Pty. Ltd., the Australian marketing arm of his operations. The following year he bolstered his U.K. operations by purchasing the Prestige brand of cookware, which had enjoyed nearly a half-century of recognition in the United Kingdom and nearby export markets.

With his own brands and those acquired from other manufacturers, Cheng maintained a formidable presence in the cookware segment. His position was strengthened further by adding a third mode of expansion. He began licensing brands from other companies, notably KitchenAid and Farberware, which enabled his U.S. subsidiary to become the largest distributor in the country and the second largest in the world. As Meyer pushed past its 30th anniversary in the cookware market, Cheng continued to seek new avenues of growth, ensuring that his company maintained its aggressive edge.

MEYER IN THE 21ST CENTURY

By the beginning of the 21st century, three decades of expansion put the Meyer corporate banner in nearly every corner of the world. At the heart of the sprawling empire was the company's manufacturing facility in Thailand, which dwarfed its other production plants in Italy and China. Over the years, capital improvement programs at the Thailand facility increased its manufacturing space to more than one million square feet, a figure that did not include a 300,000-square-feet rolling mill, which enabled the company to manufacture more than 90 percent of the materials used to make its products. The Thailand facility produced an average of 100,000 pans per day, 300 days a year, providing sufficient volume to serve Meyer affiliates in North America, Europe, Asia, and Australia.

The demand for the more than 100 cookware lines either made by or represented by Meyer promised to grow as Cheng kept the Meyer name at the forefront of the cookware market. During the first years of the 21st century, Cheng struck two deals that strengthened the already stalwart position of his company. In 2004, he joined Copia, a Napa Valley-based culinary organization, and Purcell Murray, the largest U.S. distributor of high-end kitchen appliances, in becoming part of Gaspergoo, a family entertainment property. The Gaspergoo franchise, launched by a filmed entertainment and lifestyle brand company named Zoup-ah!, was expected to include a television and home video series, licensed consumer products, cooking schools, and a chain of themed restaurants. Meyer signed on to provide housewares to the Gaspergoo franchise. In a September 2004 press release issued by Zoup-ah!, Cheng commented on the deal. "We are very excited to be working with Gaspergoo on the development of a comprehensive new line of quality houseware products for families," he said. "We believe that the Gaspergoo brand of housewares will be a big success due to the rapidly rising family focus on nutrition and cooking, and based on several of Meyer's groundbreaking design innovations."

Cheng's other notable partnership formed during the first half of the decade allied Meyer with a popular personality in U.S. culinary circles. In 2006, he reached an agreement with Rachel Ray, a celebrity chef, daytime talk-show host, and star of cable television's Food Network. Under the terms of the agreement, Meyer was selected to be the exclusive distributor of Ray's cookware collection, which included hard-anodized, nonstick pans, stockpots, sauté pans, and griddles.

Cheng's accomplishments in the years leading up to Meyer's 35th anniversary in the cookware market were indicative of a leader who eschewed complacency. In the years ahead, Cheng's attention to opening up new business channels for Meyer promised to fuel the company's steady rise, ensuring that the Meyer name would stand for excellence in cookware well into the future.

Jeffrey L. Covell

PRINCIPAL SUBSIDIARIES

Meyer Manufacturing Co. Ltd.; Meyer Corporation, U.S.; Meyer Guangzhou (China); Meyer Beijing (China); Meyer Zhaoqing Products Co. Ltd. (China); Nippon Meyer Co. Limited (Japan); Meyer Group Ltd. (U.K.); Meyer Prestige Limited (U.K.); Meyer Cookware Australia Pty. Ltd.; Meyer Canada Inc.; Meyer Europe SRL (Italy); Meyer Housewares Pte. Ltd.; Meyer (Thailand) Limited; Meyer Housewares (Malaysia) Sdn. Bhd.; Myrex International Ltd.

PRINCIPAL COMPETITORS

Corning Incorporated; Mirro Operating Company, LLC; Noritake Co., Limited.

FURTHER READING

Blackwood, Francy, "Cooking at Last," *HFD-The Weekly Home Furnishings Newspaper,* December 17, 1990, p. 62.

"Meyer Corporation," *Gourmet Retailer,* December 2000, p. 135.

"Meyer Corporation," *Gourmet Retailer,* December 2001, p. 134.

Quail, Jennifer, "The All-American Way," *HFN-The Weekly Newspaper for the Home Furnishing Network,* March 1, 2004, p. 10.

Zapfel, Dolph, "Hong Kong Produces a Heavyweight," *HFD-The Weekly Home Furnishing Newspaper,* May 28, 1984, p. 102.

MicroStrategy Incorporated

1861 International Drive
McLean, Virginia 22102
U.S.A.
Telephone: (703) 848-8600
Fax: (703) 848-8610
Web site: http://www.microstrategy.com

Public Company
Incorporated: 1989
Employees: 1,005
Sales: $313.8 million (2006)
Stock Exchanges: NASDAQ
Ticker Symbol: MSTR
NAIC: 511210 Software Publishers

■ ■ ■

A public company listed on the NASDAQ, MicroStrategy Incorporated is a McLean, Virginia-based developer of business intelligence software, serving a wide variety of financial services companies, pharmaceutical firms, retailers, telecommunications companies, consumer products companies, healthcare companies, insurance firms, media organizations, transportation companies, and government entities. The company's business platform, MicroStrategy 8, allows users to mine databases for information, such as customer behavior and sales trends, that can be used to make business decisions or serve other functions, including fraud detection. The system also enables users to build reports and disseminate them to others by e-mail, through wireless devices, or over the Internet. The company also offers support, education, and consulting services. Offices are maintained at about a dozen locations in North America; two cities in Latin America; nearly 20 sites in Europe, Africa, and the Middle East; and five cities in the Asia Pacific region. MicroStrategy's software products are sold through distributors and are also available through the company's online store.

COMPANY FOUNDED: 1989

Of MicroStrategy's three cofounders—Michael Saylor, Sanju K. Bansal, and Thomas Spahr—Saylor was the guiding spirit and dominant personality. The son of an Air Force sergeant, he used an ROTC scholarship to earn degrees in both engineering and the humanities at the Massachusetts Institute of Technology (MIT). His plans of becoming an Air Force fighter pilot and possibly an astronaut were dashed when a physical revealed a heart murmur, disqualifying him. Instead, he took a job with a New York consulting firm to write a financial computer simulation model for du Pont's global titanium business. When asked to sign a noncompete agreement, he refused and approached du Pont about working directly for them. In 1989, after completing the titanium project in 18 months, the 24-year-old Saylor told du Pont that he wanted to start his own consultancy to handle the company's work. He quit before he even had an answer, but a month later du Pont agreed to his proposal and gave him a $100,000 cash advance on a $250,000 contract, as well as office space and computer equipment. Thus, MicroStrategy was born as a Wilmington, Delaware-based company.

To help him launch his start-up, Saylor recruited

COMPANY PERSPECTIVES

Our mission is to empower every business user to make more informed decisions by providing timely, relevant, and accurate answers to their business questions. To achieve this mission, we endeavor to build the best business intelligence software in the world—a single, integrated platform supporting all styles of business intelligence through the easiest-to-use interface and delivery channel possible. We provide superior analytical performance to every business user in the format that suits them best—from high-level dashboards, to custom reports, to advanced analysis. We meticulously engineer our software to guarantee its reliability, scalability, security, and ease of administration for organizations of all sizes.

Indian-born Bansal, an MIT fraternity brother, who left the consulting firm of Booz Allen to become MicroStrategy's chief operating officer. Their first hire was a chief information officer, Spahr, another MIT graduate who had known Saylor since their junior high days in Dayton, Ohio. Du Pont served as MicroStrategy's incubator. "In essence," Saylor told *Washington Techway* in a 2000 profile, "we had no marketing costs, no sales cost, no facilities cost, a decent contract and a chance to get going." The relationship with du Pont also meant that MicroStrategy would not need outside investors and was free to pursue its own interests.

MicroStrategy started out focusing on high-level computer simulations, but Saylor quickly concluded that the demand for such work was limited and he began searching for another way to use the technology to help a broad spectrum of companies solve business problems. Using a spreadsheet program called Wingz as a platform, in order to save money, MicroStrategy began developing executive information systems (EIS) to consolidate and present summary-level analysis of database information to executives for decision making. Du Pont's fluorochemicals division, for example, used an EIS developed by MicroStrategy to break down its global business by region, industry, segment, and product.

INTRODUCTION OF EIS TOOL KIT: 1992

The company was not alone in pursuing the EIS niche, but what separated it from the pack was the 1992

introduction of the "EIS Tool Kit," a Wingz-based software product that permitted the creation of an EIS without programming. Hence, a smaller company that could not afford to build an EIS was able to create an EIS using the tool kit in a matter of days. Saylor admitted to *Washington Techway* that the product was really little more than a "sales gimmick," something to impress potential customers: "Just add 10 man-years of work, and you get an application." Nevertheless, the product led to a sale to McDonald's in 1993, providing MicroStrategy with an opportunity to gain experience in practical data mining. With billions of records pulled from thousands of franchises in its database, McDonald's wanted to use that information to do optimal marketing, to determine the sales impact of changes in price, advertising, menu, and any number of other factors. MicroStrategy graduated from summary-level analysis to doing detailed analysis. In the course of developing the McDonald's system, Saylor came to understand the potential of data mining. "I realized it was going to be big," Saylor told *Washington Tech,* "because with people collecting tons of data, you could make amazing conclusions from it. It was a fun business. It was intellectual. It was hard work."

MicroStrategy switched from being a consulting company to a software company, and began developing proprietary data-warehouse analysis tools. The company posted revenues of $4.2 million in 1993. It employed about 50 people, but Saylor and Bansal were so optimistic about the company's future that in early 1994 they decided to double employment. They also decided that they needed to relocate to a better technology hub than Wilmington, Delaware. Moreover, most of their employees were not yet married or homeowners, making a move something that needed to be done sooner rather than later. After considering Boston and San Francisco, they settled on the Washington, D.C., area, and in late 1994 moved the business to northern Virginia.

After completing the move, MicroStrategy introduced its first major product, DSS Agent (Decision Support System Agent), a sophisticated data-mining tool that allowed users to query the contents of enterprise data warehouses. It essentially laid the groundwork for a new segment of the business intelligence market that would become known as relational online analytical processing (ROLAP). The company began to grow at a rapid pace. After recording sales of less than $5 million in 1994, MicroStrategy grew revenues to $9.8 million in 1995 and $22.6 million in 1996.

The company by this time had developed its own unique culture, which was very much a reflection of Saylor. He told *Forbes,* "Our culture is part intellectual,

KEY DATES

1989: Company is founded in Wilmington, Delaware.
1994: Headquarters moves to northern Virginia.
1996: First web-based interface is introduced.
1998: MicroStrategy goes public.
2000: Company is forced to restate earnings.
2005: MicroStrategy 8 is launched.

part military, part fraternity, part religion." New employees, for example, were put through a six-week, six days-a-week, 16 hours-a-day "boot camp." At the same time, employees were free to question authority, and everyone took a cruise together each winter. The company's religion was the power of database mining, and its chief evangelist was Saylor, who began to gain press attention for his views on the future of technology. He was called a visionary and boy wonder. A *Newsweek* profile on him ran with the headline "Caesar and Edison ... and Saylor?" He spoke of purging the world of ignorance, of "database resonance," making database information available to a wider group of people, and "query tone," essentially a database dial tone, meaning that users could make use of stored information as easily as they used a telephone. Someone visiting a city, for example, could mine a database to find the best place to have a shoe repaired in a particular neighborhood. What was radical about Saylor's vision, according to Stewart Alsop writing in *Forbes*, "is that to answer some questions, a computer program would have to use data traditionally considered proprietary or otherwise off-limits. To find the best hotel, for instance, the software in Saylor's vision might have to examine transactions on corporate credit cards. To find the best doctors, the software would need to access and analyze patients' records."

Saylor, of course, embraced the Internet. MicroStrategy began adopting its flagship product for the Web in 1996, providing an interface to allow clients to use the Internet or an intranet to query a database without having to install any specialized software. It would take several more years, however, to refine the interface and allow the system to browse through hundreds of thousands of items.

TAKEN PUBLIC: 1998

MicroStrategy began signing up new clients at an accelerated clip, so that sales more than doubled to $53.6

million in 1997. Saylor was ready to take MicroStrategy public. In preparation, he read about 500 prospectuses to find the structure he liked, one in which insiders received ten votes a share. "The more I studied, the more I realized that there were two types of IPOs," Saylor told *Fortune*. "There's the IPOs that the entrepreneurs do when they want to get rich really quick, and then there's the IPOs done by the billionaires, the moguls, like Murdoch, Malone, Redstone, Craig McCaw, Ralph Lauren." MicroStrategy's original underwriter, Goldman Sachs, did not support Saylor's scheme, which he attributed to the firm's reluctance to set up a precedent for other entrepreneurs and cede leverage over MicroStrategy, "including not having the ability to merge us out of existence." Instead, Saylor took his offering to Merrill Lynch, which in June 1998 conducted the stock offering, raising $48.1 million for the company. Insiders did not sell any of their shares, although before the offering they split a $10 million dividend. The stock opened at $12 a share on the NAS-DAQ and in a matter of hours doubled. A month later MicroStrategy stock reached $44.50, making Saylor a paper billionaire. Over the next two years the stock continued to soar.

Saylor also continued to pursue his revolutionary dreams. Not content with just serving business clients, he wanted to make his technology part of people's daily existence, so that in time they could not envision life without it. In 1998 he made a tour to pitch his idea of a personal information network to companies. He envisioned an information network that could supply personalized investment, news, weather, sports, and other information to subscribers through e-mail, fax, or cell phones. When no one expressed an interest, Saylor decided to go it alone, creating an Internet business he called Strategy.com. Then in January 1999 a pager company, Metrocall, agreed to license the technology and by the end of the year 40 more companies followed suit, including NCR, Earthlink, and Ameritrade. Perhaps even more ambitious was Angel.com, a service akin to having a guardian angel on your shoulder whispering advice. Using voice recognition software, the angel, essentially a smart telephone with an earpiece, communicated with a user through a series of prompts, providing information, including marketing messages for which Saylor hoped to receive a transaction fee.

In early 2000 Saylor prepared to take Strategy.com public and made headlines by pledging $100 million of his own money to start a free online university and by renting Washington's FedEx Field to host a Super Bowl party for more than 5,500 people. However, other events intervened that caused the cancellation of the offering and the shutdown of the nascent business. Instead the URL directed traffic to MicroStrategy's home page.

Angel.com, on the other hand, evolved into a provider of on-demand IVR (interactive voice response) and call center solutions to corporate customers. The bursting of the dot-com bubble certainly had an adverse impact on the development of these businesses, but even before the demise of the technology sector early in the new century MicroStrategy was staggered by its own problems.

The price of MicroStrategy's stock spiked to $333 a share in March 2000, increasing Saylor's personal worth to $14.5 billion, but it all came crashing down when the company was forced to restate its financial results for 1998 and 1999 due to improper accounting practices that booked revenues before they were actually received. The price of MicroStrategy stock collapsed and soon the company was being investigated by the Securities and Exchange Commission (SEC) and facing a lawsuit from shareholders. Instead of a $1 billion stock offering that had been in the works, the company had to settle for a much needed $125 million private placement of convertible preferred stock. Staff cuts of about 10 percent and other cost-saving measures were instituted, including the elimination of the annual cruise.

In December 2000 MicroStrategy reached a settlement with the SEC in which Saylor, Bansal, and Chief Financial Officer Mark Lynch each agreed to pay fines of $350,000 without admitting wrongdoing. The company also agreed to implementing a number of accounting changes and the appointment of an independent director to keep tabs for the SEC. Chastened by the experience, Saylor made other changes as well. He relinquished the presidency, bringing in Eric Brown to take over the post. Saylor also scaled back his ambitions, playing down the revolutionary talk in favor of focusing MicroStrategy on what was its core business: developing software that companies could use to analyze the databases to identify trends, producing actionable information that could result in reduced costs or enhanced revenues. The company also looked to broaden its customer base beyond major corporations, and to target smaller businesses it opened an online store and allowed customers a month to evaluate the software free of charge. It was also in 2001 that one of the cofounders, Thomas Spahr, left the company, reportedly under benign circumstances. He expressed satisfaction with the job he had performed in developing the company's internal information systems and technology, but said he was ready to take some time off and perhaps later start his own company.

Spahr's more visible cofounders, meanwhile, continued to rebuild MicroStrategy. It fared far better than the vast majority of high-tech companies during the early 2000s. For one, it had a client list that included a large number of global companies and had solid revenues to point to, unlike so many high-flying tech companies that had soared in the late 1990s only to crash and burn in the new century. As 2002 came to a close, MicroStrategy returned to profitability and its stock price began to regain lost value. Although revenues dropped to $147.9 million, the company netted $38.1 million in 2002. The sales force was expanded, leading to an increase in sales to $175.6 million in 2003 and $231.2 million in 2004, when the company introduced MicroStrategy Office, allowing nontechnical employees to take advantage of business intelligence tools. In 2005 MicroStrategy 8 was introduced, adding more capabilities, including the ability to easily tap into separate systems, such as finance and human resources, and enhanced web-based reporting functions. Sales increased to $268.6 million in 2005 and $313.9 million in 2006, and net earnings during this period improved from $64.7 million to $70.9 million. MicroStrategy had clearly found its niche. While Saylor, now over 40 years of age, was no longer the boy wonder, and his musings no longer drew comparisons to Thomas Edison, only time would tell if his visions for the future were prescient or merely precocious.

Ed Dinger

PRINCIPAL SUBSIDIARIES

Alarm.com, Incorporated; MicroStrategy Administration Corporation; MicroStrategy Management Corporation; MicroStrategy Services Corporation.

PRINCIPAL COMPETITORS

Business Objects S.A.; Cognos Incorporated; Hyperion Solutions Corporation.

FURTHER READING

Alsop, Stewart, "Now I Know How a Real Visionary Sounds," *Fortune*, September 8, 1997, p. 161.

Borrell, Jerry, "Fighting Back," *Upside*, November 2001, p. 38.

Fisher, Eric, "MicroStrategy Sees 'Hypergrowth' in On-Line Databases," *Washington Times*, May 25, 1998, p. 9.

Glanz, William, "Humbled by Downfall, Saylor Changes His Image," *Washington Times*, February 19, 2001, p. 4.

Harbert, Tam, "Stars of the New Millennium," *Electronic Business*, January 1999, p. 34.

Ignatius, David, "The Brash Boy Wonder," *Washington Techway*, January 17, 2000, p. 31.

McCartney, Laton, "Battling Back," *Upside*, July 2000, p. 68.

Novack, Janet, "Database Evangelist," *Forbes*, September 7, 1998, p. 66.

Roth, Daniel, "The Value of Vision," *Fortune*, May 24, 1999, p. 285.

Saylor, Michael, "'If I Had Had More Experience, if I Was More Careful, if I Was More Competent, Maybe This Couldn't Have Happened,'" *Fast Company,* June 2001, p. 161.

Thomas, Evan, "Caesar and Edison and ... Saylor?" *Newsweek,* January 1, 2000, p. 48.

Usher, Anne, "Will MicroStrategy Survive?" *Washington Techway,* October 9, 2000, p. 42.

Mr. Gatti's, LP

5912 Balcones Drive, Suite 200
Austin, Texas 78731
U.S.A.
Telephone: (512) 459-4796
Fax: (512) 454-4990
Web site: http://www.mrgattis.com

Wholly Owned Subsidiary of Blue Sage Capital, LP
Founded: 1964
Employees: 400
Sales: $150 million (2006 est.)
NAIC: 722211 Limited-Service Restaurants

■ ■ ■

Mr. Gatti's, LP is a venerable competitor among small to midsize U.S. pizza restaurant chains. Since at least the 1980s, when Mr. Gatti's (or Gatti's) was beginning to make a name for itself, pizza has been a staple of the American diet. With the introduction of "deep dish" pizza and the ease of delivery, pizza went from Italian specialty to national fame, with Pizza Hut and Domino's dominating the industry. Small regional chains such as Gatti's (over half of its 150 locations are found in Texas) have built a loyal following with unique pies, buffets, and a family atmosphere. The large-format game-filled GattiTown and GattiLand locations compete against CEC Entertainment's Chuck E. Cheese chain, while Gatti's To Go carryout or delivery-only units, operating near colleges and in heavily populated suburban areas, keep Domino's on its toes.

THE BEGINNINGS, 1964–79

James R. Eure, a retired Air Force lieutenant colonel who served during World War II, loved pizza. His penchant was not for ordinary pizza, but lovingly crafted pies with tangy tomato sauce, provolone cheese, and the finest sausage and pepperoni. Colonel Eure, as he was called, wanted to introduce the community of Stephenville, Texas, to his particular style of pizza. In 1964 he borrowed money and opened a small pizzeria to serve his neighbors and friends, who praised his astoundingly good pies.

The Colonel decided to take his pizza expertise to a bigger area, so he and his wife Patti moved about 250 miles south to Austin, in 1968. The next year, 1969, the Colonel opened the "Pizza Place" with high hopes. He already had the real estate mantra "location, location, location," going for him, since Austin was home to the University of Texas. It proved an excellent venue for the Colonel's tasty, one-of-a-kind pies. Word spread quickly and demand grew, so much so that the Colonel opened several other locations in the Austin area.

Within five years there were 13 Pizza Places, but the Colonel was not satisfied. He wanted to take his pies beyond Austin to the rest of Texas and into neighboring states. He also wanted a more distinctive name, so he took his wife Patti's maiden name, Gatti, and added "Mr." Mr. Gatti's soon became synonymous with the tagline "The Best Pizza in Town," and the Colonel meant it, from his specially formulated tomato sauce to his real smoked provolone (not mozzarella) cheese.

COMPANY PERSPECTIVES

At Gatti's, we know there's no shortcut to quality. Since 1969, every ingredient has been selected to fit our high standards and exceed other's. We are one of the few pizza restaurants that use 100% real smoked provolone cheese. Here, cheese is more than a topping used to cover and hold ingredients, it's our key ingredient. Our dough is made fresh each and every day by hand in our own kitchens. Our signature pizza sauce recipe has been entrusted to the tomato experts at Heinz and is adhered to with exacting standards. Our delicious pepperoni is made especially for us by the meat experts at Hormel and can't be found anywhere else. Quality ingredients is what makes Gatti's the best pizza in town. Our founders Colonel Eure and his wife Patti "Gatti" Eure wouldn't have had it any other way.

In 1974 the Colonel was approached by investors who wanted to expand Mr. Gatti's through franchising. Colonel Eure accepted their offer and sold the company. Under the new ownership, Mr. Gatti's was transformed: locations were updated with a stylish new decor, and the first franchised unit opened in Cedar Park, north of Austin.

Mr. Gatti's continued to grow, opening new locations in central Texas, then past its border. During this time, two factors shaped the future of pizza and the foodservice industry: the advent of "fast" delivery and the arrival of "deep dish" or pan pizza. Delivery had long been available at small pizza parlors, but the arrival of Domino's significantly changed the market. The Ann Arbor, Michigan-based chain spread like wildfire, setting up shops near colleges and military bases. While aware of Domino's growth, Mr. Gatti's did not consider the delivery chain much of a threat, since Gatti's patrons sought not only delicious pies but a comfortable dining experience as well.

In 1978 Mr. Gatti's was bought by Texas entrepreneur L. D. "Brink" Brinkman of the Kerrville-based LDB Corporation, one of the nation's largest carpet and flooring manufacturers. At the time of the acquisition, Mr. Gatti's was Brinkman's first foray into the foodservice industry and had a few analysts scratching their heads. Nevertheless, Brinkman was a fan of the Lone Star chain and had the funds for its expansion.

PIZZA TAKES OFF: 1980–86

By the early 1980s more and more Americans were eating out, both in fast-food establishments and at sit-down restaurants. Deep dish pizza, launched nationwide by Pizza Hut (though it had long been a favorite in Chicago), was the rage. Mr. Gatti's, like most pizzerias, had some version of the thick crusted pie on its menu. Domino's Pizza, meanwhile, had continued to grow at an unprecedented rate and pizza purveyors large and small began delivery services to compete.

By 1981 Mr. Gatti's franchises had popped up throughout Texas and into Louisiana, Kentucky, and Tennessee with the total number of locations reaching 260. Other developments in the pizza market were spurred by health concerns, as customers sought alternatives to pizza, considered too heavy or filling, for lunch. Mr. Gatti's acknowledged the trend by offering weekday lunch buffets in 1982, while Pizza Hut responded with its "Personal Pan" pizzas. Other chains followed suit offering buffets, smaller pies, pizza by the slice, or adding salads to their lunchtime fare.

Pizza Hut continued to dominate the market with more than $1 billion in sales for 1982 and over 4,000 eateries. As the Hut hit its billion-dollar milestone, Domino's was second in the number of units with over 1,000 and revenues of $400 million. Regional chains had continued to extend their territories, with Mr. Gatti's testing the waters to the north and east while the California-based Round Table Pizza worked its way east and southward. Round Table garnered steady growth from 350 locations in 1984 to 460 in 1985, with revenues of $134 million and $162 million, respectively. Mr. Gatti's had reached 350 locations nationwide, yet had sales of only $130 million for 1985.

Mr. Gatti's planned to open from 50 to 75 new units annually in two dozen states. In addition to tweaking the menu with pasta dishes and sandwiches, several Mr. Gatti's had also begun delivery service and saw a healthy jump in sales. In both the Austin and Louisville, Kentucky, areas, Mr. Gatti's offered "one-number" dialing, advertising one phone number for the entire metro area to be routed to the closest unit for delivery. Within months, the ease of one-number dialing led to a dramatic sales increase, so much so that delivery king Domino's followed suit for its major metropolitan areas.

Despite the popularity of the pizza market, which had surpassed burger chains in unit growth (31,000 pizzerias versus 26,500 burger outlets for 1985), according to *Restaurant Business* magazine, several chains began to lose their footing. Godfather's Pizza, once ranked third in the nation, behind Pizza Hut and Domino's, was bought by the Pillsbury Company and imploded due to mismanagement and slumping same-store sales. Mr.

KEY DATES

1964: Colonel James R. Eure begins making pizzas in Stephenville, Texas.

1969: Colonel Eure opens "The Pizza Place" in Austin, Texas.

1974: A group of investors acquires Mr. Gatti's from the Colonel.

1981: Mr. Gatti's is acquired by L.D. Brinkman Corporation.

1982: Mr. Gatti's begins serving a weekday lunch buffet.

1984: One-number delivery dialing is introduced in Austin and Louisville, Kentucky.

1986: Mr. Gatti's buys several regional pizza chains.

1989: The company celebrates its 25th anniversary.

2004: Blue Sage Capital, LP buys Mr. Gatti's from LDB Corporation.

2005: New CEO Mike Mrlik takes the helm.

Gatti's, too, experienced problems with market saturation and lower same-store sales in some areas. To counteract slipping sales, Gatti's began renovating its older pizzerias and explored new venues including trendy Ventura County, California.

PIZZA WARS: 1987–99

Near the end of the decade the top two pizza chains were still Pizza Hut and Domino's, the latter breaking records for both unit growth and revenues. Other pizza chains were caught up as mergers and acquisitions ruled the industry. The ShowBiz Pizza Time and Chuck E. Cheese Pizza entertainment chains merged, while Mr. Gatti's and Little Caesar Enterprises bought smaller chains. Michigan-based Little Caesar quietly bought 11 outlets, and Mr. Gatti's acquired 44 units.

Mr. Gatti's buying spree consisted of three purchases: 14 of its franchised units in and around Nashville; the 19-unit "Musselman's" chain; and an 11-unit pizza chain called Red Geranium, bringing Mr. Gatti's total outlets to 337 for 1987. Mr. Gatti's also continued its popular "Call 1" program, expanding the delivery system into all of its markets and offering some a 30-minute delivery time, Domino's claim to fame.

Mr. Gatti's remodeling of older stores continued, bringing in a new three-room design. The main dining area was considered the "entertainment" room with a large-screen television, while there was a smaller

"Garden" room for patrons seeking more quiet, and the third was a party room for local events. Salad bars, which had remained a big draw during lunch, were being installed at all outlets, and the "No-Wait" lunch buffet had been expanded to three or four days in most chains. Some Mr. Gatti's offered a dinner buffet as well, on selected evenings.

By 1988 revenues for Mr. Gatti's reached $143 million, with 325 locations nationwide. The company's management, however, had been in flux, with several chief executives in as many years. Brinkman himself finally took the helm, planning to open up to a dozen company-owned locations and two dozen franchises in Mr. Gatti's 17-state region.

The 1990s, however, proved difficult for Mr. Gatti's as sales fell and competition from Pizza Hut, Domino's, Little Caesar's, and such regional chains as Donato's, Shakey's, CiCi's, and Pizza Inn took their toll. The company filed for Chapter 11 bankruptcy protection in 1991 and began reorganizing. Within two years, Mr. Gatti's had shed underperforming units and was climbing out of debt.

The new and improved Mr. Gatti's of the middle and late 1990s was streamlined and focused on its core business: making delicious pizzas and providing a pleasant dining experience for its customers. The chain had succeeded in raising same-store sales and had decided to try something new: an entertainment concept similar to Chuck E. Cheese called "GattiTown." The $3 million 27,000-square-foot prototype opened in its home base of Austin, with plenty of seating for dining, large-screen TVs, and a huge video and gaming arcade for kids.

THE NEW MILLENNIUM

At the beginning of the 21st century, Mr. Gatti's seemed to be on solid ground. The company's GattiTown entertainment complex had been a success and several more were built in Texas. Within a few years, however, the pizza chain was facing an uncertain future. Parent company LDB Corporation was in financial trouble and by 2003 was forced into bankruptcy.

In November 2004 Brinkman, which had owned Mr. Gatti's for 26 years, sold the pizza chain to the Austin-based Blue Sage Capital, LP, a private equity firm, for a reported $24 million. Blue Sage partner Jim McBride told the *Austin Business Journal* (December 9, 2004) Mr. Gatti's was more than worthy of saving: "It's Texas-based, family-owned and in need of a transition. And the company is mature, profitable and has solid growth prospects." Blue Sage was also involved with another foodservice chain, the Illinois-based Cosi, Inc., and was helping fund a national rollout of the sandwich and coffee chain.

In May 2005 Mr. Gatti's named a new chief executive and president, Michael Mrlik II, formerly of New World Restaurant Group, Inc. (owner of Einstein's Bagels, Noah's Bagels, and New World Coffee). Mrlik replaced Don Brinkman, son of L. D., who had stayed with Mr. Gatti's after the chain was sold. All was not, however, smooth sailing. Blue Sage filed suit against LDB Corporation in April 2006, alleging the former owner had not been truthful about the pizza chain's financial status and a myriad of issues facing the franchise.

Perhaps to leave behind the past and concentrate on the future, Mr. Gatti's became simply "Gatti's" as Blue Sage looked to expand the chain. The huge, game-filled GattiTown and GattiLand "eatertainment" complexes continued to perform well and Blue Sage had financed the opening of two dozen locations ranging from 19,000 to 30,000 square feet. In 2007 there were 150 Gatti's locations in Texas, Louisiana, Kentucky, North Carolina, South Carolina, Tennessee, Indiana, and Virginia. Texas, its home base, still had the highest concentration of outlets, with over 80 locations.

Nelson Rhodes

PRINCIPAL OPERATING UNITS

GattiLand; GattiTown; Gatti's To Go; Mr. Gatti's Pizza.

PRINCIPAL COMPETITORS

CEC Entertainment Inc.; CiCi Enterprises, Inc.; Domino's Pizza, Inc.; Little Caesar Enterprises, Inc.; Papa John's International, Inc.; Pizza Hut, Inc.

FURTHER READING

Byrne, John, "Making Money with Music," *Forbes,* March 12, 1984, p. 130.

Greenwood, Giselle, "Gatti's Expanding 'Eatertainment' Concept," *Austin Business Journal,* May 6, 2005.

Higginbotham, Stacey, "Blue Sage Buys Mr. Gatti's," *Austin Business Journal,* December 9, 2004.

"Investment Firm Sues Mr. Gatti's Over Sale," *Austin Business Journal,* March 27, 2006.

Kochak, Jacque, "Franchising's New Mobility," *Restaurant Business,* March 20, 1986, p. 137.

———, "New Products Deliver Quality and Freshness," *Restaurant Business,* September 20, 1985, p. 101.

———, "Pizza Market Is on the Move," *Restaurant Business,* May 20, 1986, p. 99.

Mehlman, William, "LD Brinkman on Flying Carpet Ride to New Profit Heights," *Insiders' Chronicle,* June 27, 1983, p. 1.

Nathanson, Ari, "Blue Sage Invests in Family, Food, Fun," *Buyouts,* January 3, 2005.

Raffio, Ralph, "Franchising: The Growth Leaders," *Restaurant News,* March 1, 1983, p. 103.

Robinson-Jacobs, Karen, "Pizza Maker Is Reinventing Itself with GattiTown," *Dallas Morning News,* July 21, 2006.

Romeo, Peter, "Pizza Delivery Boom Lures New Players," *Nation's Restaurant News,* April 6, 1987, p. F2.

———, "Pizza 'Swap-Out' Hits Small Chains," *Nation's Restaurant News,* February 2, 1987, p. 1.

Sadler, Don, "Emphasis on Fun," *American Executive,* July 2006, p. 92.

Strenk, Tom, "Gatti's Gets the Call," *Restaurant Business,* June 10, 1987, p. 148.

Morrow Equipment Co. L.L.C.

3218 Pringle Road SE
Salem, Oregon 97302
U.S.A.
Telephone: (503) 585-5721
Toll Free: (800) 505-7766
Fax: (503) 363-1172
Web site: http://www.morrowequipment.com

Private Company
Incorporated: 1968 as Morrow Crane Co.
Employees: 70
Sales: $50 million (2006 est.)
NAIC: 532412 Construction, Mining, and Forestry
    Machinery and Equipment Rental and Leasing

■ ■ ■

Morrow Equipment Co. L.L.C. owns and operates the largest fleet of tower cranes in North America. It is an exclusive distributor for Liebherr cranes, which are manufactured in Germany. Morrow provides construction and materials for a wide range of services at its 23 locations in the United States, Canada, Mexico, Australia, and New Zealand.

1968–72: BUILDING THE FIRST DOMESTIC FLEET OF TOWER CRANES

John and Richard Morrow acquired their first tower crane in 1968. After their father, Bob Morrow, who owned Morrow Construction, used their crane in his construction business, their brother, Bobby, suggested that they buy and rent cranes to building contractors. Seizing upon what proved to be a profitable idea, John and Richard established Morrow Crane Co. Richard worked as crane operator and John as company salesman. The two set out to persuade the construction industry to switch from the then current standard mobile cranes, with ground-level cabs and angled booms, to European-made tower cranes.

In the late 1960s, tower cranes were not commonly in use in the United States. The advantage of tower cranes is that they do not take up a large amount of space on the ground, and they stretch up to 100 stories high, making use of a horizontal boom. The simplest cranes were extended by adding sections of the vertical shaft, which the operator climbed at the start of his shift. Other cranes had the capability of being attached to the side of the building under construction. The crane helped construction workers move equipment and materials around the job site and enabled them to raise whatever they needed, such as buckets of wet cement or steel beams.

Crane operators are, by all accounts, a "special breed," according to a 2001 article in the *St. Louis Post-Dispatch,* since their job requires that they possess extraordinary depth perception and provide extraordinary care and attention to detail. Otherwise the cargo they move using the crane could swing into a building or fellow workers. They also need to be extremely coordinated to perform their job. Their left hand operates a joystick that raises and lowers loads. A second joystick, which they operate with their right hand, sends and retrieves the trolley along the crane's "jib" or arm and rotates the crane jib and cab 360 degrees. Their right foot operates a brake that secures the crane in position. A series of ladders with landings every 20 feet leads to the crane cab, and operators are paid for 30 minutes of climbing to work each day. Because they spend all day alone in a small space high above the ground, some operators equip their crane cabin with air conditioners, microwaves, hotplates, radios, and televisions. With overtime, many crane operators earn more than $100,000 a year.

The Morrow brothers claimed that the tower cranes they provided were faster and more stable than some other cranes and that the operator, who worked in a cab at the top of the tower, had a better view of the job site. Others, too, saw advantages to using tower cranes, and Morrow Crane Co. grew throughout the first half of the 1970s. In 1974, Morrow made a bid to American Pecco Corp., a manufacturer of cranes, to become Pecco's Northwest dealer. When Pecco rejected that bid, the Morrows raised the stakes by buying the distribution rights to German competitor Hans Liebherr's tower cranes for Washington and Oregon. Liebherr was the world's largest maker of tower cranes. This arrangement contributed greatly to developing the business for the next five years.

Then, in 1979, Liebherr decided to get out of the cyclical United States crane business, and Morrow Crane agreed to buy Liebherr's fleet of nine cranes on the condition that Liebherr grant the company the sole right to distribute Liebherr's cranes in the United States and Canada.

Following this deal, business for Morrow really took off in the 1980s. The company introduced the first self-erecting tower crane, the Liebherr FasTower, already popular in Europe, to the North American construction industry, in 1981. The self-erecting design of this crane eliminated the main disadvantage of a static tower crane, which was the need for a costly foundation structure and for a second crane to install the tower. The new cranes caught on rapidly, and, by 1982, the Morrow

Crane Company could boast that it was "far ahead of where we thought we'd be in sales in one year," according to an *Engineering News-Record* article.

In 1982, Morrow built its corporate headquarters on a ten-acre site in southeast Salem. The company developed a fleet of cranes and made a name for itself in the international construction industry. Christian Chalupny, a Liebherr employee, joined Morrow as president and chief executive officer of the company. Offices in Australia and New Zealand followed.

1993–2002: BECOMING THE LARGEST SUPPLIER OF TOWER CRANES IN THE WORLD

A little more than a decade later, in 1993, with close to 15 offices in the United States, Australia, and New Zealand, and employment at 35, Morrow Crane merged with American Pecco Corp. of Millwood, New York, and became Morrow Equipment Co. of Salem, Oregon. Before the merger, each of the two companies had annual sales of about $25 million. Christian Chalupny remained president and chief executive officer of the merged company, whose fleet included about 400 tower cranes and 100 hoists. Hoists are the elevators outside of buildings that lift people and materials. The merger helped the company weather a nationwide slowdown in commercial real estate construction by eliminating significant tower crane competition.

Throughout the mid-1990s, with increased construction, cranes became a constant part of the building landscape. Then, in 1995, Morrow helped put the first tower crane into the natural world as well. The University of Washington and the Wind River Ranger District purchased a tower crane from Morrow for use in observing the forest canopy in the Gifford Pinchot National Forest. In 1998, the company helped place a second crane in a lowland tropical rainforest in far north Queensland for use by James Cook University's Cooperative Research Centre for Tropical Rainforest Ecology & Management. Liebherr took four months to build the specially designed crane to Morrow's specifications. Parts of this crane had to be brought into the forest and lowered to the ground by helicopter.

Between 1998 and 2002, Morrow bought about 200 cranes, bringing its inventory close to 500. By 2001, Morrow was believed to be the world's largest supplier of tower cranes, with monthly rentals of its equipment ranging from $8,000 to $30,000, depending upon the size of the crane. A typical contract required that the contractor pay liability insurance. By 2004, the company was the 105th largest private company in the state of Oregon.

KEY DATES

1968: The Morrow brothers found Morrow Crane Co.
1974: Morrow buys Oregon and Washington distribution rights to Hans Liebherr cranes.
1979: Liebherr grants Morrow distributorship rights to all of the United States and Canada.
1982: Morrow builds its corporate headquarters in Salem, Oregon.
1993: Morrow merges with American Pecco Corp. and changes its name to Morrow Equipment Co. L.L.C.

By 2005, an unforeseen problem had arisen throughout the construction industry. The country was experiencing a building boom, and there were too few cranes to meet demand. In fact, demand was so high that companies had to reserve cranes for use six months or more ahead of time. The situation spelled good news for Morrow, which by then had about 500 cranes, each of which cost upward of $1 million. In response to demand, it moved its cranes frequently around the country and sometimes even across international borders. If business was slow, for example, in the Midwest or California, it would move its cranes to where the work was. On average, eight 40- to 48-foot flatbeds were required to move one crane. These cranes typically rented for $40,000 to $80,000 per month.

"[I]t's busy everywhere," Andrew Morrow, Salem regional sales rep for Morrow, told the *Seattle Times* in 2006. "It's a struggle right now trying to get people to plan far enough in advance to be sure that we have the tower crane they need."

Between 2005 and 2006, the company bought more than 100 new cranes, yet it still did not "have enough of them," according to Chalupny in a 2006 *Daily Journal of Commerce* article, to satisfy the demands of domestic contractors. "Based on the backlog we have and what we hear from contractors, there's so much work in the pipeline we don't see any signs of this cooling any time soon. We see this going on maybe two or three years more." The company would certainly grow along with the nation's skylines.

Carrie Rothburd

PRINCIPAL SUBSIDIARIES

Morrow Equipment Co. LLC Australia; Morrow Equipment Co. LLC New Zealand; Morrow Equipment Co. LLC Canada; Morrow Equipment Co. LLC Mexico.

PRINCIPAL COMPETITORS

Potain Tower Cranes, Inc.; Electric Tower Cranes, Inc.; Lorain Division of Koehring Co.; Mobile Crane.

FURTHER READING

"Builders Face Towering Problems: Too Few Cranes," *Seattle Times,* December 12, 2005.

Hudson, Repps, "Morrow Equipment of St. Louis Supplies the World Construction Ladders to the Sky," *St. Louis Post-Dispatch,* July 5, 2001, p. C8.

Martinis, Cheryl, "Building a Better Crane Company," *Oregonian,* December 17, 1993, p. D1.

Prince, Seth, "Skyline Streaked with Towering Cranes, Portland Rising," *Oregonian,* April 17, 2006, p. 20.

Reiner, Vivienne, "Tree Rex Evolves," *Weekend Australian,* July 4, 1998, p. 50.

"Tower Crane Shortage Means Project Delays for Portland Contractors," *Daily Journal of Commerce,* February 7, 2006.

THE MYRIAD RESTAURANT GROUP

Myriad Restaurant Group, Inc.

180 Franklin Street
New York, New York 10013
U.S.A.
Telephone: (212) 219-9500
Fax: (212) 219-2380
Web site: http://www.myriadrestaurantgroup.com

Private Company
Incorporated: 1993
NAIC: 722110 Full-Service Restaurants

■ ■ ■

Myriad Restaurant Group, Inc., is a private New York City-based company headed by celebrity restaurateur Drew Nieporent, operating 11 upscale restaurants as well as Crush Wine & Spirits, a Manhattan wine shop. New York operations include Montrachet, a three-star restaurant that was Nieporent's first eatery; Tribeca Grill, launched with actor Robert De Niro; Japanese restaurant Nobu and its cousins, Nobu Next Door and uptown's Nobu Fifty Seven; Mai House, a Vietnamese restaurant; and Centrico, a Mexican restaurant. Myriad restaurants outside of the city include Rubicon in San Francisco; Nobu London; the Coach House on Martha's Vineyard; and Proof on Main in Louisville, Kentucky. In addition, Myriad manages about ten restaurants for Interstate Hotels, Starwood Resorts & Hotels Worldwide, Inc.; Sports Club/LA; and the Boca Raton Resort & Club. The company also offers consulting services covering all aspects of a restaurant's operation, including the conception, design, and development of new restaurants. Clients include Interstate Hotels, Host Marriott, Marriott International, and the Neiman-Marcus department store chain.

FOUNDER: 1977 CORNELL GRADUATE

Born in New York City in 1955, Drew Nieporent and his brother Tracy grew up in Manhattan with their father, a French-born attorney for the State Liquor Authority, and their mother, a noted radio actress turned casting agent. Because their father did legal work for restaurants he was able to take the family to a wide variety of restaurants, from the exclusive to the more mundane. The boys were also able to meet some of the best restaurateurs in the city. Early on, as a result, Nieporent became fascinated with the restaurant trade and decided to pursue a career in it. At first he wanted to become a chef, and at the age of ten got his start when he began helping his mother to prepare dinner for guests. During his high school days he worked the grill at a McDonald's and at an Upper East Side restaurant called the Duck Joint. His interests shifted to the front of the house after he was admitted to the acclaimed Cornell University School of Hotel Management and during the summer months gained further experience working on the cruise ships *Sagafjord* and *Vistafjord*. After receiving his degree in 1977, Nieporent began his career working as a back waiter, bringing the food from the kitchen but not to the table, at Maxwell Plum's, a large Upper East Side restaurant that appealed to a broad range of customers through a large menu, moderate prices, and sense of excitement. It was a combination that Nieporent would file away for future reference.

In little more than a year Nieporent was running the dining room at Maxwell Plum's. He then went on to work at such popular Manhattan restaurants as Tavern on the Green, La Reserve, Le Perigord, Le Regence, La Plaza Anthenee, and one of the best French restaurants, La Grenouilie, where he was honored to become the first American captain. Within a half-dozen years of graduating from Cornell, Nieporent was eager to strike out on his own. One day while jogging he took a closer look at Manhattan's Tribeca area, the so-called Triangle Below Canal Street. At the time it remained a light industrial area with no restaurants, theaters, or clubs of any significant repute. Nieporent, however, sensed that the neighborhood held potential and, also of importance, the rents were reasonable. He then asked his brother Tracy if he wanted to join him in the venture.

By this time Tracy Nieporent had become an advertising executive at Young and Rubicon but was losing interest in the advertising field. He readily agreed to become involved in starting a restaurant, and the two brothers scouted Tribeca, finally leasing space in a former industrial building located on West Broadway, the site featuring exposed pipes and original plaster ceilings. They scraped together their savings and borrowed money from their parents to raise about $100,000. For a chef Drew Nieporent hired French-trained American David Bouley, a virtual unknown at the time, but Nieporent was familiar with him because he had sampled his cooking when Bouley was working at a San Francisco restaurant. Nieporent's vision was to create an accessible French restaurant, one that offered menus written in English and affordable upscale cuisine, but avoided the arrogance of a wait staff that was unwilling to answer the questions of diners who did not speak French or lacked an extensive knowledge of wine. The brothers struggled for a name for their restaurant, finally settling on Montrachet, the name on a bottle of burgundy that caught Drew Nieporent's eye.

OPENING OF MONTRACHET: 1985

Montrachet opened to the public in April 1985 and two months later received a three-star rating from *New York Times Magazine.* Cab drivers soon learned to navigate the obscure streets of Tribeca to bring diners to the new hot spot in town. Bouley also became a well-known chef, but soon he and Drew Nieporent fell out. The food bills were too high, and Bouley obsessed over each plate, causing backups in the dining room, which limited turnover and the restaurant's ability to turn a profit. Their relationship finally dissolved when, according to *New York Times Magazine,* "Bouley left the kitchen to discuss business opportunities with some diners.... 'He was cuckolding me right in front of my nose,' Nieporent says." Bouley was fired, given $37,000 in severance, and went on to establish a four-star eponymous restaurant nearby.

Despite the loss of Bouley, Montrachet was able to keep its rating and maintain its popularity. In the late 1980s actor Robert De Niro, a Tribeca resident, became a regular customer. At the time he was planning a film center in the neighborhood and wanted to have a restaurant on the ground floor, essentially a meeting place where directors, producers, and the like could gather to discuss projects. The public would be welcome as well. De Niro and Nieporent agreed to become partners in a new restaurant, which would take the name Tribeca Grill. Some 20 investors were also involved, including such celebrities as Bill Murray, Mikhail Baryshnikov, Sean Penn, Ed Harris, and Christopher Walken. Tribeca Grill opened in 1990 and was immediately popular with celebrities and the people who liked to be in their company. It established the Nieporent "custom blend," in the words of *New York Times Magazine:* "professional service, dependable food, sharp-focused restaurant identity and high-octane glitz."

The success of Tribeca Grill also solidified Nieporent's reputation as a restaurateur and opened up many new opportunities. His brother quit his job in advertising and joined him full time in 1991. Nieporent turned his attention to Long Island and the trendy Hamptons area. In 1992 he became partners with advertising executive Jerry Della Femina and some other investors to open a pair of restaurants. In early 1994, however, the partnership split up over a money dispute.

In 1993 Nieporent formed Myriad Restaurant Group to launch new restaurants and provide consulting and management services. In that same year the company began offering operational advice to the Charles Hotel in Cambridge, Massachusetts. A year later Myriad opened a pair of restaurants. In Tribeca, Nieporent and De Niro again joined forces to open

KEY DATES

1985: Drew Nieporent opens first restaurant, Montrachet.
1990: Nieporent teams up with Robert De Niro to open Tribeca Grill.
1993: Myriad Restaurant Group is incorporated.
1994: Nobu opens.
1997: Nobu London opens.
2005: Centrico opens.

Nobu, offering the Japanese-Peruvian fusion cuisine of Chef Nobu Matsuhisa. It quickly became one of the most sought after reservations in town. Across the country, in San Francisco, Nieporent and De Niro struck again. De Niro brought in other investors, including Francis Ford Coppola and Robin Williams, to open a restaurant in a former Wells Fargo bank in San Francisco's financial district. It took the name Rubicon from one of Coppola's Napa Valley wines, and featured a menu focused on wine and cheese.

The consulting and management business also thrived. By the mid-1990s, Myriad's roster of clients grew to include the Queen Elizabeth II, Harley-Davidson Café, the Hotel Macklowe, Interstate Hotels, Joseph Phelps Vineyards, Jordan Vineyard and Winery, and Pine Island Grill on Long Island Sound. Nieporent also continued to expand his stable of Tribeca eateries. In 1995 he established TriBakery, a venture that not only sold breads and pastries at retail and featured a small café but also served as a central bakery for Myriad's other restaurants in the neighborhood. Later in the year he opened Layla ("night" in Arabic), a Middle Eastern restaurant. Myriad collaborated with Interstate Hotels in 1996, opening the Steelhead Grill in Pittsburgh's Marriott City Center. After that operation was on its feet, Myriad turned its attention to a wine and cigar venture in Manhattan, The City Wine and Cigar Co. In 1997 Nieporent decided to make better use of the space in TriBakery by adding a neighborhood Italian restaurant concept called Zeppole, which operated at night. This represented one of the rare times Nieporent miscalculated, however. Zeppole was soon closed, although the central bakery remained. Layla was also experiencing some difficulties and was forced to curtail its hours, eliminating lunch.

LONDON OPENING: 1997

In the second half of the 1990s, Myriad made a foray beyond the United States. The company transferred the Nobu concept to London, England, where in 1997 it opened Nobu London in the Metropolitan Hotel on Old Park Lane near Hyde Park. It became the first Asian restaurant to receive a Michelin star, one of the most coveted ratings. The original Nobu, in the meantime, remained highly popular. To accommodate demand Myriad opened Nobu Next Door, which as the name suggests, was located next door. It featured the same menu as the original restaurant, but distinguished itself by not accepting reservations (except for large parties), making it especially appealing to a late-night crowd. In the spring of 1999 Myriad opened Nobu Las Vegas. Around the same time the company also opened the Berkeley Bar & Grill in Manhattan, the first venture to be entirely financed by Myriad, and closed City Wine and Cigar Co. Also of note during the late 1990s, the company worked with Interstate Hotels to open The Coach House in Martha's Vineyard, and with Starwood Hotels and Resorts Worldwide to open a restaurant called HeartBeat inside the new W Hotel located at 49th Street and Lexington Avenue, the first Manhattan restaurant for Nieporent outside of the Tribeca area. Myriad also worked with Starwood to open Icon in the W Court Hotel in Manhattan's Murray Hill section, and Earth & Ocean in a Seattle W Hotel in late 1999.

By 2000, Myriad owned or operated nearly 20 restaurants in New York, San Francisco, Las Vegas, Pittsburgh, Boston, Denver, Seattle, and London. The slate was soon whittled down by the closing of Berkeley Bar & Grill, but the company also became involved in South Florida for the first time with the opening of Rocca Mare ("Castle by the Sea" in Italian) in the tony Boca Raton Resort & Club.

With a large portion of its operations located in Tribeca in the shadow of the World Trade Center, the terrorist attacks of September 11, 2001, forced the closure of the restaurants for two weeks, costing the company more than $1 million in sales. Moreover, it took some time for people to visit Tribeca in the same numbers as before the attacks. Making matters worse, the economy stumbled, forcing a period of retrenchment for Myriad, which included Layla closing its doors.

Myriad was expanding again by 2005 when it opened a midtown Manhattan wine store called Crush Wine & Spirits. In that same year the company took the Nobu concept uptown, opening Nobu Fifty Seven on 57th Street two blocks south of Central Park, and it opened its first Mexican restaurant, Centrico, located on West Broadway. In 2006 Myriad scored a pair of successes when it opened Mai House, a Vietnamese restaurant, in Tribeca, and Proof on Main in Louisville, Kentucky, located in the 21C Historic Hotel and

Museum and featuring modern American cuisine with Tuscan influences. Also in the works was a partnership with Virgin Atlantic founder Richard Branson to develop a pair of restaurants at the Virgin Spa at Natirar in New Jersey, scheduled to open in 2008.

Ed Dinger

PRINCIPAL OPERATING UNITS

Centrico; The Coach House; Mai House; Montrachet; Nobu; Nobu Next Door; Nobu London Nobu Fifth Seven; Proof on Main; Tribeca Grill; Rubicon.

PRINCIPAL COMPETITORS

B.R. Guest Inc.; Palm Management Corp.; Patina Restaurant Group LLC.

FURTHER READING

Cannon, Leann, "Myriad Restaurant Group," *Nation's Restaurant News,* January 30, 2006, p. 142.

Gupte, Pranay, "Montrachet Founder Eyed Manhattan Early One," *New York Sun,* March 31, 2005.

Lubow, Arthur, "Who Is the Best Restaurateur in America?" *New York Times Magazine,* March 1996.

"Master of a 'Myriad' of Concepts," *Nation's Restaurant News,* September 1999, p. 16.

Parseghian, Pamela, "Drew Nieporent: Restaurateur with a Theatrical Legacy Always Casts About for the Next Big Opening," *Nation's Restaurant News,* January 2000, p. 142.

Rothstein, Mervyn, "Drew Nieporent, Empire Builder," *Wine Spectator,* November 15, 1994.

Zuber, Amy, "Drew Nieporent," *Nation's Restaurant News,* January 1997, p. 166.

National Research Corporation

1245 Q Street
Lincoln, Nebraska 68508
U.S.A.
Telephone: (402) 475-2525
Toll Free: (800) 388-4264
Fax: (402) 475-9061
Web site: http://www.nationalresearch.com

Public Company
Incorporated: 1981
Employees: 773
Sales: $43.7 million (2006)
Stock Exchanges: NASDAQ
Ticker Symbol: NRCI
NAIC: 541710 Research and Development in the Physical, Engineering, and Life Sciences

■ ■ ■

National Research Corporation (NRC) provides the healthcare industry in the United States and Canada with survey-based performance measurement, analysis, and tracking services, used to provide better patient care, meet regulatory requirements, and provide a point of comparison between competitors. The company's wide range of clients includes managed care organizations, medical groups, hospitals, health systems, medical groups, federal and state agencies, and employers. The *Healthcare Market Guide* is NRC's oldest product, which is now delivered online. Drawing data from 200,000 households, it compiles a consumer-reported assessment of hospitals, health systems, and health plans in the United States, used by clients to assess and improve their place in the healthcare marketplace. The *Guide* also delivers information about consumers' healthcare Internet usage, and the Product Line Preference Report offers a detailed profile of consumers who prefer a client's facility. In addition, NRC's annual "Consumer Choice" awards are presented to the most highly regarded hospitals in nearly 200 U.S. markets. The NRC+Picker unit uses survey information to uncover the patient experience at hospitals, and then offers solutions to help clients implement changes to achieve patient-centered care.

NRC also provides health plans, physician organizations, and healthcare purchases with several other profile and survey products. Senior Health Profiles, for example, identifies high-risk Medicare enrollees. Acting for the client, the company sends a Senior Health Questionnaire to a clients' enrollees. Using the responses, NRC then determines Pra (Probability of Repeated Admission), Frailty, and Depression Scale scores, and produces a High-Risk Report for each high-risk enrollee. The information can then be used to plan effective interventions and other purposes. The unit also provides Good Health Profiles to help health organizations with care and disease management interventions for the under-65 population. NRC is based in Lincoln, Nebraska. Although a public company listed on the NASDAQ, NRC is 70 percent owned by founder and CEO Michael D. Hays.

COMPANY FOUNDED: 1981

NRC was founded in Lincoln, Nebraska, by Michael Hays in 1981. Little is known about Hays, who is reluctant to grant interviews and provides only a minimum amount of personal information in the company's filings with the Securities and Exchange Commission. According to those filings, he was born in the mid-1950s and served seven years as vice-president of SRI Research Center, Inc, a Lincoln polling company that was founded in 1975 by Jim Clifton, the son of the cofounder of Selection Research Inc. The two companies were operated separately until Selection Research acquired the famous Gallup Organization in 1988 and SRI was ultimately brought into the fold. From the start Hays looked to carve out a niche serving the information needs of the healthcare industry.

In September 1988 Hays was joined by Jona S. Raasch, a veteran of the A.C. Nielsen Corporation. He took over as NRC's vice-president and chief operations officer. In that same year NRC began publishing the *Healthcare Market* on a biannual basis, gathering an ever increasing storehouse of hospital consumer data. The company sold the market information and competitive intelligence product to hospitals at a discounted prepublication price. It then provided a steady source of income as a renewable, stand-alone syndicated product. NRC also received income from custom research projects and a renewable performance tracking service that took the name The NRC Listening System.

By 2002 NRC revenues reached $2.6 million. The company began exhibiting strong growth in 1994 when revenues surged to $6.8 million, a more than twofold increase over the previous year. The company's renewable performance tracking services led the way, due to the healthcare industry's increasing emphasis on patient satisfaction. In 1991 the National Committee for Quality Assurance began accrediting managed care organizations and required that an independent third party conduct an annual standardized member satisfaction survey. This requirement resulted in more tracking projects from current clients as well as an increase in new clients. Revenues from tracking services, as a result, grew from $4.4 million in 1994 to $9.6 million in 1996, when total revenues reached $12.6 million. Operating income also increased from $1.7 million in 1994 to $3.7 million in 1996.

The need for tracking services increased even further when a leading healthcare organization accrediting body, The Joint Commission on Accreditation of Healthcare Organizations, broadened its performance measurement requirements, and the government administrator of Medicare benefits, the Health Care Financing Administration, required health maintenance organizations to determine the senior population's satisfaction with their services. Moreover, a number of states passed managed care bills that included consumer-rights provisions, spurring further business for NRC, which saw the number of clients increase from 155 in 1994 to 210 in 1996.

IPO: 1997

NRC went public in 1997. In a preliminary step, the company was reincorporated in Wisconsin in September of that year, and then with William Blair & Company and Robert W. Baird & Co. Incorporated acting as underwriters, the company netted $16.8 million in an initial public offering (IPO) of stock, priced at $15 per share. In addition, Hays benefited from the sale of a reported 850,000 shares, which fetched $17.5 million before expenses. NRC's proceeds were earmarked for general corporate purposes as well as to pay special cash bonuses to members of Hays's executive team. The company held out the possibility of using some of the cash to make acquisitions of complementary businesses, and having publicly traded stock at its disposal was expected to help in the financing of these deals. The common stock was also used to retain and attract key employees.

The downside of being a public company soon became apparent, however. In early December NRC's largest client, Kaiser Permanente-Northern California Region, opted to hire a different company to handle its performance measurement studies in 1998. Kaiser had accounted for 31 percent of NRC's total revenues in 1996 and 40 percent in 1997. The next largest client, the U.S. Department of Defense, accounted for just 15 percent. Kaiser's loss was a clear blow to the company, despite assertions that this was an isolated event and not part of a trend. Nevertheless, investors abandoned the stock, which had been approaching $20 a share but tumbled to less than $2.

NEW COMPUTER SYSTEM HELPING 2000 RESULTS

The addition of new clients resulted in an increase in revenues to $18.2 million in 1999, and NRC realized $1.7 million in operating income. With QualPro in operation for an entire year, NRC began to reap the benefits of its new computer system in 2000. Although revenues improved only slightly to $18.3 million, operating income doubled to $3.3 million, as did net income to $2.7 million. Because of lower margin contracts in 2001, sales dipped to $17.7 million in 2001; nonetheless, the company was still able to net $1.7 million. NRC also completed another significant acquisition in May 2001, paying $4.1 million for the healthcare survey business of The Picker Institute, which included patient and employee surveys. Founded by Harry and Jean Picker, the institute was at the forefront of the patient-centered care movement, using surveys to determine what patients wanted, what was important to them, and what helped or hurt them in managing their own health problems. NRC was allied with this highly respected organization and Hays became an adviser to Picker.

NRC benefited from the new Picker products and the addition of the U.S. Department of Veteran Affairs in early 2002, as well as other new clients, which led to a 26.7 percent jump in revenues to $22.4 million and net income of $3.8 million. Sales increased further in 2003, when revenues improved to $26.9 million and net income to $4.4 million, spurred in part by an acquisition that expanded the company's operations to Canada, which required similar public reporting. In May 2003 NRC had paid approximately $1.4 million for Toronto-based Smaller World Communications Inc., a provider of survey-based performance measurement services to the Canadian healthcare industry.

NRC launched a three-year plan in 2004 to build its sales force from six associates to 36, and saw an immediate return on its investment. For the year the company experienced a 10.3 percent increase in revenues to $29.7 million and an improvement in net income to $4.5 million. Nevertheless, Hays in his annual shareholders' letter maintained that the "2004 performance was not up to our expectations. While top line growth in our core business was satisfactory, this growth was offset by volatility in federal government sector revenues." While no major change of course was planned, Hays did promote Joseph W. Carmichael to president in 2004.

Problems with federal sector contracts continued in early 2005, leading to a slow start, but conditions improved significantly in the second half of the year, resulting in an increase in sales to $32.4 million and net

With Kaiser still in the fold, NRC posted record revenues of $16.3 million in 1997 and operating income of $3.2 million. A year later the company improved sales 8.5 percent to $17.7 million. While the company was able to add some new clients, it mostly made up the loss of the Kaiser contract through the June 1998 acquisition of Healthcare Research Systems for $5.5 million plus the assumption of debt and other liabilities. As a result of charges incurred in the transaction, NRC reported a $67,000 loss in operating income in 1998. Based in Ohio, Healthcare Research System offered comparable survey-based performance measurement, analysis, and tracking services to healthcare clients. In addition to adding new clients, the acquisition provided NRC with some new services and products to offer existing clients. The company also looked to expand its opportunities by opening sales offices in Boston and Ann Arbor, Michigan. The Michigan office focused solely on securing state and federal government contracts.

To improve the productivity and efficiency of the enlarged operation, NRC invested in its information technology to create a fully automated production system (QualPro). The company attempted to put the new system online in early 1999 but encountered numerous problems, which were ironed out over the next few months and finally implemented. The investment positioned NRC to take advantage of approaching opportunities, as consumers began demanding an increased amount of information about the healthcare system. Baby boomers were dealing with elderly parents and becoming concerned about their own future healthcare requirements. Never shy about making their needs known, the boomers were driving a demand for more and better information about healthcare plans. NRC sought to be ahead of the curve as it headed into the new century.

income to $5.2 million. NRC also took steps during the year to prepare the ground for future growth by completing another acquisition. In September 2005 it paid $3.5 million in cash for Geriatric Health Systems, LLC, a California-based company that performed surveys on insurance risk, patient outcomes, and member satisfaction for health plans in 40 states, including half of the largest payers.

NRC grew even larger and created some diversity in May 2006 when it acquired San Diego-based The Governance Institute (TGI) for $19.8 million. After 20 years in business TGI was a well established company that hosted conferences to provide strategic advice to key executives at hospitals and health systems. As a result of these acquisitions, NRC's revenues increased to $43.7 million in 2006 and net income totaled $5.9 million. With industry trends favoring it and a well-rounded slate of products and services, NRC appeared to be poised to enjoy steady growth in the years to come.

Ed Dinger

PRINCIPAL SUBSIDIARIES

Smaller World Communications, Inc.; The Governance Institute.

PRINCIPAL COMPETITORS

The Gallup Organization; Press Ganey Associates, Inc.; Verispan, L.L.C.

FURTHER READING

Cayton, Rodd, "Investors Like National Research," *Lincoln Journal Star,* July 23, 2006.

Crum, Rachelle, "Natl. Research Buys Conference Producer," *Tradeshow Week,* June 19, 2006, p. 3.

Jordan, Steve, "Lincoln, Neb.-based Firm Credits Computer System for Fivefold Earnings Gain," *Omaha World-Herald,* August 2, 2000.

Larson, Virgil, "Lincoln, Neb.-based National Research Says Profits Grew 53 Percent," *Omaha World-Herald,* November 6, 2002.

Olberding, Matt, "National Research Buys California Company," *Lincoln Journal Star,* September 20, 2005.

Piersoli, Richard, "National Research of Lincoln Buys San Diego Company," *Lincoln Journal Star,* May 31, 2006.

Nature's Path Foods, Inc.

9100 Van Horne Way
Richmond, British Columbia V6X 1W3
Canada
Telephone: (604) 248-8777
Fax: (604) 248-8760
Web site: http://www.naturespath.com

Private Company
Incorporated: 1985
Employees: 310
Sales: CAD 130 million ($111 million) (2006 est.)
NAIC: 311230 Breakfast Cereal Manufacturing; 311340 Nonchocolate Confectionery Manufacturing; 311412 Frozen Specialty Food Manufacturing; 311812 Commercial Bakeries; 311821 Cookie and Cracker Manufacturing; 311822 Flour Mixes and Dough Manufacturing from Purchased Flour; 311823 Dry Pasta Manufacturing; 311919 Other Snack Food Manufacturing; 311942 Spice and Extract Manufacturing

∎ ∎ ∎

Headquartered in Richmond, British Columbia, near Vancouver, Nature's Path Foods, Inc., is the largest maker of organic cereals in North America. The firm's two main manufacturing plants—located in Delta, British Columbia, and just across the U.S. border in Blaine, Washington—produce 70 tons of organic cereal each day. In addition to its flagship hot and cold cereal lines, Nature's Path also produces organic energy and cereal bars, granola bars, breads, pastas, toaster waffles and pastries, baking mixes, cookies, and crackers. The products are marketed under four main brands: Nature's Path, EnviroKidz, Optimum, and LifeStream. Enjoying growth of 25 percent per year, the company generates 70 percent of its revenues in the United States, 27 percent in Canada, and the remaining 3 percent overseas. Family owned and operated, Nature's Path since its founding in 1985 has been headed by the husband-and-wife team of Arran and Ratana Stephens.

THE PATH TO NATURE'S PATH

Arran Stephens was born in 1944 on British Columbia's Victoria Island, the third and youngest son of Rupert and Gwen Stephens. His earliest roots were in the organic field as his father owned an organic berry farm on the island, using kelp as fertilizer and sawdust as a mulch. In 1957 Rupert Stephens sold the farm and moved the family to Hollywood, where he pursued a successful songwriting career, penning tunes for Ricky Nelson, Lou Rawls, and others. As a teenager in California, Arran Stephens, who had been named after an island off the southwestern coast of Scotland, discovered the counterculture and dropped out of school in the tenth grade. A brief stint as a painter led to shows in San Francisco and New York. (Artistic talent ran in the family: One of his brothers is the well-known painter and sculptor Godfrey Stephens.)

Stephens returned to Canada in 1967 after a spiritual quest led him to spend seven months in India. Though he had only seven dollars in his pocket, he was able to open the Golden Lotus, one of the first vegetarian restaurants on the West Coast of Canada, after borrowing CAD 1,500 from friends. After a slow begin-

COMPANY PERSPECTIVES

It has been said, "you are what you eat." What we eat is directly transformed into blood, bones, skin, muscle and consciousness. So, where does the food we're eating come from?

We believe food, organically grown, is better for you and better for the environment. Organic foods contain no preservatives or additives, and are grown without synthetic pesticides, herbicides or fungicides which agribusiness typically sprays onto our food. These chemicals can then find their way into the soil, water, air and eventually our bodies.

Just as eating wholesome organic food helps to make healthy bodies, organic farming helps make healthy soil and a healthy planet. Our farmland is a thin layer of living earth blanketing the planet and needs to be nurtured and renewed continually. Organic farming practices enrich the soil and improve a farm's biodiversity, resulting in less soil erosion and more drought resistant farmland.

It was Hippocrates who suggested that we let food be our medicine and medicine be our food. Nothing can replace the richness and complexity of nutrients found in a varied diet of fresh, organic whole foods, and Nature's Path organic breakfast cereals are a great way to get started, every day.

ning, the Golden Lotus eventually earned steady business in part thanks to the influx of draft dodgers coming into Vancouver across the U.S. border and in part because of a very positive review published in the *Georgia Straight,* an influential Vancouver alternative newspaper.

During a second trip to India in 1969, Stephens had an arranged marriage to Ratana Mala Bagga, a college lecturer with a master's degree who hailed from a family once in the confectionery business. Upon their arrival back in Vancouver, the couple found that several Golden Lotus employees were clamoring to turn the restaurant into a cooperative. Not wishing to participate in such a venture, the couple sold the restaurant to the newly formed co-op for CAD 2,500. (It eventually folded in the early 1970s.)

Continuing his entrepreneurial ways, Stephens and a partner opened up LifeStream, the first large natural foods store in Vancouver, at the beginning of 1971. The store eventually moved into wholesaling and also developed a wide range of natural products that were marketed under the LifeStream brand, including breads, granola, energy bars, and soy-based vegetarian entrees. Sales grew rapidly, exceeding CAD 12 million by 1981, when LifeStream employed 100 people. Along the way, a third partner was brought into the operation. Difficulties with the partnership, however, led to the sale of LifeStream in 1981 to Nabob Foods Limited of Burnaby, British Columbia. Two years later, Nabob Foods and the LifeStream brand were acquired by Kraft, Inc.

1985: FOUNDING OF NATURE'S PATH FOODS

In the meantime, a noncompete agreement barred Stephens from starting another natural foods manufacturing company. Thus, he and Ratana opened up a new natural foods restaurant in Vancouver called Woodlands. In 1985, once the noncompete period had ended, the couple began making and selling bread out of the back of the restaurant under the Manna brand. The first product was an organic, sprouted, whole-grain bread. This marked the beginnings of Nature's Path Foods, Inc.

Slow at first, sales of Manna began accelerating after the Vancouver-based Woodward's department store chain agreed to stock the product on its shelves. Because bread had limited distribution possibilities, Stephens began investigating other lines with longer shelf lives, eventually settling on cereal as a good prospect for wider growth. In 1988 Nature's Path entered what was destined to become its signature field with the introduction of its first cereals—Organic Multigrain, Multigrain and Raisin, and Millet Rice Flakes. The cereals were sugarless, sweetened only with fruit juice, and used only grains grown without pesticides, herbicides, or fungicides.

As sales of the cereals began to take off, Stephens took a large gamble. Needing to meet the surging demand, and wanting to be freed from importing his cereal from the United States, he began building a CAD 6 million organic cereal production plant in Delta, British Columbia. The huge project, which was launched in 1989, nearly bankrupted the company. When the 54,000-square-foot plant was completed the following year, it was the first organic cereal plant in the world to be certified such by a third party. The risky investment quickly paid off. Nature's Path was soon turning its first profit, and in 1991 it introduced its biggest-selling product yet, Heritage Flakes. This cereal remained the firm's top seller for nearly a decade.

KEY DATES

1985: Arran and Ratana Stephens launch Nature's Path Foods, Inc., in Vancouver, selling organic bread under the Manna brand.

1988: Nature's Path introduces its first cereals.

1990: Construction is completed on the firm's organic cereal plant in Delta, British Columbia.

1991: Heritage Flakes cereal is introduced.

1999: Production begins at the company's second plant, located in Blaine, Washington.

2000: Company introduces the Optimum and EnviroKidz cereal brands.

2004: An expansion that doubles the size of the Blaine plant is completed.

Between 1988 and 1994 Nature's Path was one of the fastest-growing British Columbia-based businesses, enjoying twelvefold sales growth. During these early years, the company was unable to afford the high slotting fees that the major supermarket chains were charging manufacturers to stock their products. Nature's Path therefore concentrated on getting its cereals onto the shelves of smaller stores. Eventually, consumer demand grew to the point where the larger supermarkets were in essence forced to carry the Nature's Path line and also offered the company more reasonable fees for doing so.

By 1995 the company was doing so well that Arran and Ratana Stephens sold their restaurant to concentrate full time on Nature's Path. That same year, the Stephens family bought LifeStream back from Kraft. Most of the LifeStream products were eventually discontinued, though the two top LifeStream cereals were converted from "natural" to 100 percent organic and relaunched under the Nature's Path brand. In 1997 the company introduced a line of frozen breakfast waffles under the LifeStream brand. The LifeStream line eventually became one of the top-selling brands of natural waffles in North America.

By the late 1990s the Delta plant was no longer able to keep up with demand, which was increasing at a steady rate of 20 percent per year. Nature's Path therefore endeavored to build a second cereal plant and elected to site it in the United States, which had evolved into the firm's largest market. By having a facility in the United States, the company would avoid the hassles of trucking both raw materials and finished products across the border. Production at the new $9 million plant, which encompassed 70,000 square feet, began in August 1999. It was located in Blaine, Washington, just south of the Canadian border and only about 20 miles from Delta, British Columbia.

EARLY 21ST CENTURY: NEW BRANDS, EXPANDING LINE OF PRODUCTS

In 2000 Nature's Path added two new important brands to its growing lineup, one aimed at adults and one at children. On the adult side, the company introduced the Optimum brand, which featured cereals that doubled as both organic products and so-called functional foods, that is, products with health-promoting and/or disease-preventing properties. The first product in the line, Optimum Power, was a blend of organic flax/bran flakes, soy threads, Kamut puffs, and organic, freeze-dried blueberries. In addition to the blueberries, much touted for their health benefits, a serving of Optimum Power also offered 40 percent of the recommended daily intake of calcium and 100 percent of vitamin B12 and folic acid. Optimum Power, after only 14 months on store shelves, became the top-selling organic cereal in North America. Additional varieties of Optimum cereal were introduced over the next few years. Optimum frozen waffles debuted in 2001.

For children, Nature's Path introduced EnviroKidz cereals, the first line of certified organic cereals for kids. Sporting kid-friendly packages depicting endangered species, the line consisted of traditional breakfast favorites, such as Amazon Frosted Flakes, Orangutan-O's, and a puffed corn cereal called Gorilla Munch. In addition to being organic, the cereals contained no genetically modified ingredients. Also, Nature's Path committed to donating 1 percent of the line's sales to charities specializing in habitat conservation, the protection of endangered species, and the environmental education of children. By 2006, the annual disbursement from this commitment had reached CAD 500,000.

While the overall cereal market remained flat in North America, as consumers increasingly turned to such breakfast alternatives as bagels, croissants, and breakfast pastries, organic cereals were enjoying stellar growth, with Nature's Path leading the way as the number one brand. The Blaine plant eventually was doubled in size at a cost of $3 million, and the company in 2004 also inaugurated its own 105,000-square-foot distribution center in Richmond, British Columbia. In addition to increasing its cereal-making capacity, the expansion of the Blaine plant also involved the installation in 2003 of a major food bar production line. That year, Nature's Path successfully introduced EnviroKidz organic crispy rice bars. These were followed by the debut of Nature's Path granola bars in 2004 and Optimum energy bars one year later.

In the meantime, the company in 2003 hired its first organic program manager, Dag Falck, an agronomist from Norway who had experience in western Canada both as an organic farmer and as an independent organic inspector. One of his duties was ensuring that there was sufficient organic production to keep up with Nature's Path Foods' ever expanding needs. Falck was active in encouraging conventional farmers to convert to organic farming and provided assistance to them in making the transition.

In 2004 Nature's Path showed its firm commitment to the environment when it began packaging its products in a lighter-weight box called the EnviroBox. Representing a 10 percent reduction in packaging, the new box was estimated to reduce the company's annual consumption of paperboard by 75 tons. That same year, Nature's Path continued to expand its array of product offerings, introducing its Signature Series line of organic cookies and crackers as well as three varieties of EnviroKidz cookies. Next, the firm ventured into the baking mix category, introducing cookie, brownie, and pancake mixes in 2005. Then, one year later, Nature's Path unveiled a line of organic, whole-grain, and flax pastas under the LifeStream brand. By this time the company, through a partnership based in St. Charles, Illinois, was also distributing individual serving-sized portions of its cereals to educational institutions, including school districts in Illinois and California and such postsecondary schools as Harvard University and the University of British Columbia.

By 2006 Nature's Path Foods was the clear leader in organic hot and cold cereals in North America. With a line of products steadily expanding beyond cereals, the company's sales had reached approximately CAD 130 million and were increasing at a 20 percent clip each year. Stephens had been approached numerous times by venture capital firms and major food companies about selling the company, but he and his wife were not interested. With two of their four children already working at the company, they hoped to keep Nature's Path a family firm. Going forward, one of the firm's pressing needs was to add more manufacturing capacity to keep up with the rapid growth. Unable to expand the Blaine plant, Nature's Path began exploring the possibility of building a new plant in the U.S. Midwest. Doing so made financial sense because of the potential savings in transportation costs given that the company was shipping increasing amounts of its products from the West Coast to both the Midwest and the East Coast. For the

same reason, it also made a lot of environmental sense, an important consideration for Stephens and his firm. In addition to continuing to develop new products and doing so quickly enough to stay ahead of the burgeoning array of competitors in the organic food industry, Nature's Path Foods also planned to be more aggressive in marketing both itself and its products. In particular, the company sought to highlight its 30-plus-year history, its family ownership, and its independence and to emphasize its status as a pioneer, one that had been producing organic products long before doing so had become fashionable.

David E. Salamie

PRINCIPAL COMPETITORS

Small Planet Foods, Inc.; Kellogg Company; The Hain Celestial Group, Inc.; Barbara's Bakery Inc.; Golden Temple; Van's International Foods, Inc.; Dr. August Oetker KG.

FURTHER READING

Carstairs, Catherine, "Interview with Arran Stephens," June 30, 2003, http://www.naturespath.com/newsroom/for_the_media.

Cooper, Carolyn, "Going with the Grain," *Food in Canada*, January/February 2007, pp. 42+.

"Creating a Successful Trend, Naturally: Nature's Path Turns Organic Culture into Big Business," *Richmond (B.C.) Review*, December 10, 2005, Business sec., p. 18.

Ennen, Steve, "The Fastest Grain in the West: New Plant Handles Demand for North America's Top Maker of Organic Cereals," *Food Processing*, December 2000, pp. 53–56.

Evans, Mark, "The Meatless Route to Success," *Financial Post* (Toronto), May 29, 1991, sec. 1, p. 39.

Gallagher, Dave, "Nature's Path Begins Work to Double Plant's Size," *Bellingham Business Journal*, September 2002, p. A8.

Gorlick, Arthur C., "Cereal Plant Mixes Grains, Jobs in Blaine," *Seattle Post-Intelligencer*, August 14, 1999, p. B3.

"Greening Up the New Bottom Line," *Richmond (B.C.) Review*, October 2, 2004, Business sec., p. 12.

Hunter, Jennifer, "Setting Up Stateside," *Maclean's*, March 8, 1999, pp. 38+.

Janoff, Barry, "All-Natural Kids," *Progressive Grocer*, May 2000, pp. 141–42.

Roskelly, Nick, "Organic Trailblazers: Tracing the Footsteps of Nature's Path," *Stagnito's New Products Magazine*, March 2004, pp. 36, 38.

Stephens, Arran, *Journey to the Luminous*, Vancouver, B.C.: Eton-Wolf Publishing, 1999, 370 p.

———, *Moth and the Flame,* http://www.mothandthe flame.com/moth.html.

Wilhelm, Steve, "Nature's Path Foods Is Preparing for a Boom in Organic Food Sales," *Puget Sound Business Journal* (Seattle), August 30, 2002, p. 3.

———, "Nature's Path to Expand Cereal Factor in Blaine," *Puget Sound Business Journal* (Seattle), August 31, 2001, p. 24.

Won, Shirley, "It Doesn't Have to Be Lonely at the Top," *Globe and Mail,* June 3, 2006, p. B12.

Northern and Shell
Network plc

Northern and Shell Building
Number 10 Lower Thames Street
London, EC3R 6EN
United Kingdom
Telephone: (+44 0871) 434 1010
Fax: (+44 020) 7308 5077
Web site: http://www.northernandshell.com

Private Company
Incorporated: 1974
Employees: 1,239
Sales: £475 million ($960 million) (2006 est.)
NAIC: 511120 Periodical Publishers; 511110 Newspaper Publishers; 513120 Television Broadcasting

■ ■ ■

Northern and Shell Network plc (Northern & Shell) is the holding company behind one of England's major publishing and media groups. The controversial company, formerly one of the United Kingdom's leading publishers of "top-shelf" pornographic magazines, has transformed itself into a major newspaper publisher, through its acquisition of the Express Newspapers group, including the *Daily* and *Sunday Express* and *Daily* and *Sunday Star*. Following the sale of most of its pornographic magazine titles, Northern & Shell's magazine operations have been refocused largely around a core group of celebrity titles, including flagship *OK!* That weekly magazine, which claims the top spot in the highly competitive U.K. celebrity magazine market, also serves as Northern & Shell's international flagship. Since 2004, the company has launched an Australian version of the title, backed by the creation of an Australian subsidiary. In 2006, Northern & Shell launched a North American edition of *OK!* In other markets, the company has signed a number of partnerships, allowing for licensed versions in China, the Philippines, Thailand, Singapore, India, Turkey, Mexico, Greece, the Middle East, and Malaysia. In 2007, the company also expected licensed local editions of the title to launch in Spain, Russia, and South Africa. Since the mid-1990s, Northern & Shell has also been active in the satellite television market, producing its own range of programming, as well as its own channels, including Television X and its spinoffs, and the pay-per-night Red Hot, both offering varying degrees of pornographic fare. Northern & Shell operates its own printing plant in Preston, in Lancashire; the company also owns a 50 percent stake in a plant in West Ferry, in London's Docklands. Northern & Shell Network remains 100 percent owned by founder Richard Desmond. The company reported sales of approximately £475 million ($960 million) in 2006.

FOUNDING A PUBLISHING EMPIRE IN 1974

Richard Desmond's first contact with the world of business came at the age of five—Desmond's father, a salesman, had lost his hearing and would bring his son along to interpret for him. Desmond quit school at the age of 14, and took up playing drums at the start of the British pop revolution. As he told *Forbes:* "I wanted money and self-esteem, and I needed something to get me there quick." In order to buy his first drum set, Desmond

COMPANY PERSPECTIVES

The Core Values: Northern & Shell was founded in December 1974 with the vision of becoming a significant force in British and worldwide media. That ambition was developed through a broad portfolio of magazines and broadcast interests and came of age with the acquisition of Express Newspapers in November 2000.

Today, Northern & Shell owns four national newspapers and is a 50 percent joint venture partner in two more in Eire. It also dominates important parts of the consumer magazine market in the UK and worldwide with 12 foreign editions, operates in all major areas of publishing and has diverse interests in television, print, distribution, investment and property.

The strengths of the network lie in its skill in identifying key areas of commercial growth and its decisiveness and creative drive in developing brands that excel in these markets. Essential to the operation is the building of dedicated teams with pride in what they produce and a willingness to respond to customer needs.

Northern & Shell is determined to maintain all its products and activities as benchmarks of excellence to its readers, customers, advertisers and business partners.

worked for a time at a nightclub in London, where he came into contact with many stars of the day. While drumming was to remain a lifelong hobby, Desmond's interests lay more in business, particularly sales. After a first job selling classified ads for newspapers, Desmond began selling ads for pop magazines. This led him to open his own music store. At first Desmond sold records, but soon added sales of musical equipment. By the early 1970s, Desmond had added a second store.

Desmond's popularity among the bustling London music scene, by then the center of the global recording industry, brought him into contact with Ray Hammond, who had developed the idea for a monthly magazine titled *International Musician and Recording World.* Unlike existing music magazines, which were fan-oriented magazines focused on the players, Hammond's magazine was geared toward the musicians themselves, and featured a high proportion of equip-

ment reviews, often written by the musicians themselves. Hammond recruited Desmond to the project, and together they found financing with Malcolm Green. With Hammond serving as editorial director, Desmond's connections in the music industry, and Green's backing, *International Musician* launched in 1974.

The magazine was an instant success, and formed the basis of the Northern & Shell publishing group. *International Musician* quickly imposed itself as a leader in its category in the United Kingdom, remaining in publication through the 1980s. Success in the United Kingdom also led Northern & Shell to develop U.S. and German versions as well. The magazine proved especially popular with musical equipment manufacturers, providing a focused market for their products. The magazine's strong advertising sales led Desmond to recreate the *International Musician* concept for other markets, and by the end of the decade Northern & Shell had launched some 20 different titles, each catering to a specific market, such as stamp collecting or bicycling.

Hammond and Desmond remained partners through the 1970s, founding a second business together, The Advertising Practice. That company, which focused on the consumer products sector, served as a complement to Northern & Shell's growing range of specialist and hobbyist magazines. Hammond left the company in 1980, however, in order to pursue a career in writing and public speaking, becoming one of the United Kingdom's most well-known "futurologists." Desmond then became 100 percent owner of Northern & Shell.

Northern & Shell might have remained a modest magazine publishing company if not for Bob Guccione, the notorious publisher of *Penthouse.* New Jersey–born Guccione had in fact gotten his start in publishing in London in the mid-1960s, when he worked as a journalist and photographer for *London American* magazine. In 1965, Guccione decided to launch his own magazine, patterned after the successful *Playboy* magazine. By 1969, Guccione had transferred the magazine to the United States, where *Penthouse* quickly became the major rival to the *Playboy* empire. Into the early 1980s, as Guccione sought to establish a media empire, he decided to launch a new U.K. edition of his flagship magazine. For that, he contacted Richard Desmond.

Desmond agreed, taking over the U.K. license for *Penthouse* in 1982. Under Northern & Shell, *Penthouse UK* soon established itself as a leading men's magazine. It also provided the springboard for the company's first real fortune. As he had done with his hobbyist titles, Desmond quickly moved to replicate his success with

KEY DATES

1974: Richard Desmond establishes Northern and Shell Network plc (Northern & Shell) in partnership with Ray Hammond in order to launch *International Musician* magazine; company then launches series of 20 similar hobbyist-oriented titles.

1982: Desmond receives U.K. license to produce local edition of *Penthouse* magazine, beginning Northern & Shell's emergence as a leading publisher of pornographic magazines.

1993: Northern & Shell enters mainstream magazine market with launch of *OK!* celebrity title.

1995: Company enters satellite television market with launch of The Fantasy Channel (later Television X).

2000: Northern & Shell acquires Express Newspapers for £125 million.

2004: Company sells pornographic magazine titles and launches Australian edition of *OK!*

2006: U.S. edition of *OK!* is launched, as well as franchised editions in China, Malaysia, Thailand, Greece, Singapore, and elsewhere.

2007: Company shuts down *Happy!* magazine, launched in 2005.

GOING LEGIT IN THE NEW CENTURY

Desmond's advertising interest allowed him to expand into other media categories in the 1980s. The company became one of the first to move its headquarters to the London Docklands area. There, Northern & Shell set up its own production studios, where it began producing advertisements for the British television market. In the mid-1990s, the company moved to leverage this experience for its entry into the emerging satellite television market. This led the company to launch its own satellite programming, including a soft porn channel, The Fantasy Channel (later Television X), which debuted in 1995. Through the end of the decade, Northern & Shell developed Television X into four channels. By the 2000s, the company had added pay-per-view and pay-per-night programming as well, notably through its Red Hot channel.

In the meantime, Northern & Shell had been pursuing other directions. A dispute with its printer and distributor in 1991 had nearly forced Northern & Shell's collapse, when the larger company refused to distribute the company's magazines. Desmond fought back, threatened to sue, and eventually forced the distributor to agree to the settlement. Under that agreement, Northern & Shell transferred its hobbyist titles to the distributor in exchange for the right to keep its pornographic titles and a cash payment of more than £60 million.

The cash package allowed Desmond to develop new ambitions for his company. In 1993, Desmond approached United Newspapers, later known as United Business Media, with an offer to buy out its ailing national daily, the *Daily Express*. The deal never came to fruition.

Instead, Desmond turned to a new project, that of entering the U.K. mass market magazine sector. Desmond identified the potential for the underdeveloped celebrity market, which, in the early 1990s was occupied primarily by *Hello!* magazine. That title, however, focused especially on gossip and photos involving European royalty. Desmond's idea was to develop a title that focused on the British celebrity circuit. Backed by an investment of some £30 million ($50 million), *OK!* debuted in 1993. Desmond's longstanding connections with the U.K. music scene, including his friendships with such noted personalities as Robert Plant, Roger Daltrey, Phil Collins, and Paul McCartney, as well as his willingness to pay celebrities for exclusive photos and news, ensured that *OK!* became a quick success.

OK!'s growing circulation encouraged Desmond's new goal of joining the upper echelons of the U.K. publishing industry. When news came that United

Penthouse, and by the late 1980s had launched the first in a stream of "specialist" pornographic magazines. Despite the specific and, for many, repugnant nature of their titles, Northern & Shell's "top shelf" (so-called because they were kept on the top shelves of newsstands) magazines were generally considered to remain within the soft porn category. Northern & Shell also took over the U.K. license for *Penthouse*-spinoff *Forum.*

Following criticism from a member of Parliament, who complained of the sexist nature of Desmond's men's titles, the company struck back, launching *For Women.* That title became a new success for the company, selling more than 600,000 copies. Into the early 1990s, Desmond also made a move into the United States, operating a telephone sex line in New York City. That operation allegedly brought Desmond into conflict with the Mafia, under circumstances that were to remain a mystery (and denied by Desmond). By the end of that decade, Northern & Shell had given up its *Penthouse* license.

Newspapers was seeking a buyer for its Express Newspapers division, including the *Daily* and *Sunday Express,* as well as the tabloid format the *Daily Star,* Desmond moved swiftly, beating out competitors with an offer of £125 million. United accepted, and Northern & Shell became the owner of one of the United Kingdom's oldest and largest national daily newspapers. The move proved highly controversial, sparking a furor in the press, and earning Desmond the nickname of "Dirty Des."

Desmond moved to cut costs at the *Daily Express,* which for years had been struggling with declining circulation and mounting losses, slashing some 25 percent of its staff. The revitalized newspaper returned to profitability, while its circulation stabilized. Meanwhile, the *Daily Star* proved the more robust of the two, growing strongly into mid-decade.

Desmond attempted to entrench himself deeper into the U.K. newspaper market, announcing his plan to bid for the *Telegraph* group of newspapers. Once again surrounded by controversy, Desmond decided that his stable of pornographic titles had become a burden, and sold most of those titles in 2004. Ultimately, Desmond's bid for the *Telegraph* group failed, however.

In 2004, Desmond was approached by a U.S. publisher with an offer to buy the *OK!* franchise in order to develop it internationally. Instead, Desmond adopted the idea as his own. By the end of that year, the company had started up a subsidiary in Australia, which launched an Australian edition of *OK!* Elsewhere, Northern & Shell developed a network of partners, which acquired the license to produce local editions of *OK!* In this way, Northern & Shell expanded its range of operations to China, the Philippines, Thailand, Singapore, India, Turkey, Mexico, Greece, the Middle East, and Malaysia. In 2007, the company also expected licensed local editions of the title to launch in Spain, Russia, and South Africa. In 2006, meanwhile, Northern & Shell itself oversaw the launch of a U.S. edition of *OK!*

Desmond continued to target the mainstream magazine market into the middle of the first decade of the 2000s. The company launched a youth-oriented celebrity magazine titled *New!* in 2003. In 2005, the company believed it had spotted a new gap in the market, and launched the shopping-oriented title *Happy!* That magazine failed to build sufficient circulation, especially after rivals including Emap launched similar titles. By March 2007, Northern & Shell decided to throw in the towel, shutting down *Happy!* Despite this setback, the company's *OK!* franchise continued to grow strongly, while its control of the *Daily Express* and *Daily Star* maintained Northern & Shell's position at the center of the U.K. media market.

M. L. Cohen

PRINCIPAL SUBSIDIARIES

Broughton Printers Limited; Express Newspapers; Northern & Shell Distribution Limited; Northern & Shell Finance Limited; Northern & Shell Group Limited; Northern & Shell Magazines Limited; Northern & Shell North America Limited (U.S.A.); Northern & Shell Pacific Limited (Australia); Northern & Shell plc; Portland Enterprises Limited; Portland Television Limited; RHF Productions Limited.

PRINCIPAL COMPETITORS

VNU Business Media Europe Ltd; Pearson PLC; Reed Elsevier PLC; Daily Mail and General Trust PLC; The Thomson Corporation PLC; Emap PLC; Associated Newspapers Ltd.; Informa PLC; Guardian Media Group PLC; BBC Worldwide Ltd.

FURTHER READING

Griffiths, Ian, and Dan Milmo, "Desmond Takes His Pound of Flesh from Porn Empire Sale," *Guardian,* June 21, 2005, p. 17.

Jackson, Sally, "*OK!* Boss to Dish Up More Glossy Goss," *Australasian Business Intelligence,* October 11, 2006.

Johnson, Branwell, "Will Desmond Get More Than Just a Happy Hour?" *Marketing Week,* February 24, 2005, p. 19.

Madslien, Jorn, "Profile: Richard Desmond," *BBC News Online,* February 12, 2004.

"Northern & Shell Downplays London Ambitions," *Guardian Unlimited,* July 13, 2006.

O'Connor, Ashling, "Evolution of a Media Magnate," *Financial Times,* July 20, 2001, p. 12.

"OK! Tops the Celebrity Magazines," *Guardian Unlimited,* February 15, 2007.

"Shopping Magazine *Happy!* Closes," *Guardian Unlimited,* March 23, 2007.

Terazono, Emiko, "Express to Cut a Tenth of Workforce," *Financial Times,* October 31, 2006, p. 22.

Nufarm Ltd.

———■———

103–105 Pipe Road
Laverton North, VIC 3026
Australia
Telephone: (+61 03) 9282 1000
Fax: (+61 03) 9282 1007
Web site: http://www.nufarm.com

Public Company
Incorporated: 1956
Employees: 2,315
Sales: AUD $1.67 billion ($1.26 billion) (2006)
Stock Exchanges: Australian
Ticker Symbol: NUF
NAIC: 325320 Pesticide and Other Agricultural Chemical Manufacturing; 325311 Nitrogenous Fertilizer Manufacturing

■ ■ ■

Nufarm Ltd. is Australia and New Zealand's leading crop protection specialist. Herbicides form by far the largest part of Nufarm's operations, representing 86 percent of its total revenues of AUD 1.67 billion ($1.26 billion) in 2006. The company's herbicide production focuses on its range of phenoxy-based products, used for controlling and eliminating broadleaf weeds. Nufarm is one of the world's leading producers of phenoxy-based herbicides, which have been in use since the 1950s. The company is also one of the agrochemical industry's leading producers of generic and branded glyphosate herbicides, the largest-selling type of herbicide in the world. Nufarm's glyphosate operations include its

exclusive license to produce and market the Roundup herbicide brand in Australia and New Zealand. While herbicides remain Nufarm's core product category, the company has been developing a more diversified crop protection portfolio since the middle of the first decade of the 2000s. The company's fungicide production accounts for 10 percent of sales, while its youngest product line, insecticides, represented 4 percent of sales in 2006. In addition to its crop protection operations, Nufarm produces and distributes seeds, including the license to develop and market Roundup Ready canola for the Australian market, acquired in September 2006; the company has been divesting its other noncore operations, including its animal health operations and its chlor-alkyl chemicals production.

Australia remains Nufarm's largest market, accounting for 38 percent of sales. New Zealand adds just 3 percent to sales. Since the early 1990s, the company's geographic diversification strategy has enabled it to develop strong operations in North, Central, and South America, which combine to represent 32 percent of sales, and in Europe, which accounts for 23 percent of sales. The company's European presence was boosted in 2006 with the purchase of Italy's Agrosol SRL, based in Ravenna. Nufarm is listed on the Australian Stock Exchange and is led by Managing Director and CEO Doug Rathbone.

AUSTRALIAN CROP PROTECTOR IN 1956

Nufarm was originally established by Max Fremder as a distributor of phenoxy-based herbicides to the agricultural market of Victoria, Australia. Fremder's

COMPANY PERSPECTIVES

Nufarm Limited manufactures and markets a wide range of quality crop protection products. Our mission is to meet the interests of all stakeholders in a manner that shows we care about: the growth and success of the business; the wellbeing of our employees; the environment and the communities in which we operate; our customers and suppliers; and the reputation and performance of our products and service.

company grew strongly, backed by the boom in Australia's agricultural sector during the 1960s and 1970s. By 1972, the company had a new large-scale manufacturing plant in Laverton. That site also became the company's headquarters.

The global agricultural market was then at the beginning of a massive transformation. While much of the world's agricultural markets remained tied to a model based largely on smaller-scale, low-yield farms, the United States had inaugurated the new agro-industrial era. This new model focused on a smaller number of extremely large-scale farms, which, through the unbridled use of herbicides, pesticides, and other so-called crop protection products, raised per-acre production levels far beyond what had previously been obtainable. The development of more and more effective, and selective, crop protection products, such as the phenoxy-based herbicides, the first of which, 2.4D and known as Weedone, occurred during the 1940s. The shift of Australia's agricultural market to the newer large-scale, chemical-intensive methods provided new opportunities for Nufarm into the early 1980s.

By then, Nufarm had come under the leadership of Doug Rathbone, who held degrees both in chemical engineering and commerce. Rathbone, who became managing director of Nufarm in the late 1970s, recognized that the still small company, with sales of just AUD 100 million at the start of the 1980s, needed a larger partner in order to gain a leadership in the Australian market. By 1982, Nufarm had found its partner, in the form of chemicals producer and distributor Fernz Corporation, based in New Zealand. Fernz, originally known as Fertilizers of New Zealand, initially acquired an equity investment in Nufarm, before taking full control of the company and moving its headquarters to New Zealand in 1987. Rathbone then became managing director of the larger company, and obtained a seat on the board.

Before long, the Nufarm operations, and agrochemicals in general came to represent the fastest-growing part of Fernz, as Nufarm rapidly became the leading producer of herbicides in Australia and New Zealand. Yet the company's success, and its history producing such notorious chemicals as DDT, also made it a target of the Australian section of environmental activist group Greenpeace. In 1990, the company was accused of having caused massive pollution at its Melbourne plant. The scandal forced a government investigation that shut down the plant for some three months. While Nufarm was cleared of wrongdoing in the end, the episode proved a public relations disaster for the company.

INTERNATIONAL EXPANSION STARTING IN 1991

This led the company instead to make a move into international markets in the early 1990s. The company founded its first foreign distribution subsidiary in 1991, in Malaysia. The company then opened an office in Singapore the following year, and launched its first manufacturing operations in the region at this time as well. Before long, Nufarm's Asian operations had reached Indonesia, Thailand, Japan, the Philippines, and China.

Nufarm's Asian business was destined to remain just a small part of the company, however. Instead, Nufarm increasingly turned its attention toward the West. The company, which had launched exports of phenoxy herbicides to the United States in 1988, entered that market directly in 1992, setting up its first office there. The United States provided the base for the company's further expansion throughout the region, with new subsidiaries added in Canada by the middle of the decade. Into the 2000s, the company had entered the South American market as well.

Europe, however, provided the group's primary expansion grounds during the 1990s, in part because the consolidation and restructuring of the European Union's agricultural chemicals sector had placed a large number of businesses up for sale. Fernz Nufarm, as the company became known into the middle of the decade, first targeted the United Kingdom. While its expansion into the American and Asian markets had been especially through the development of a distribution market, Nufarm targeted the manufacturing sector for its European expansion. In 1994, the company made its first European purchase, buying Rhone Poulenc's phenoxy herbicides production facility in Belvedere, England.

Austria became the company's next new market, when it bought Agrolinz, based in Linz, Austria. That

KEY DATES

1956: Max Fremder founds Nufarm in order to manufacture and distribute phenoxy herbicides in Victoria, Australia.

1982: Under Managing Director Doug Rathbone, Nufarm is acquired by New Zealand's Fernz Corporation.

1991: Nufarm begins international expansion, establishing subsidiary in Malaysia.

1994: Company completes its first European acquisition, in the United Kingdom.

2000: Fernz Nufarm refocuses around core crop protection operations, moving its headquarters and stock listing to Australia and renaming itself as Nufarm Ltd.

2001: Nufarm acquires Agtrol International in United States.

2006: Nufarm acquires Agrosol crop protection business in Italy.

acquisition not only gave the company a strong position in the Austrian market, it also gave it control of Agrolinz's strong exports operations. Following the completion of the acquisition in 1995, the Austrian unit was renamed as Nufarm GmbH & Co. Kg.

The company's new U.K. and Austrian operations helped shift its geographic focus, so that more than two-thirds of its revenues were generated outside of Australia and New Zealand. The company's internationalization continued into 1996, with the acquisition of Akzo Nobel's Crop Protection Chemical division. Based at a facility in Rotterdam, in the Netherlands, the Akzo Nobel operation focused on the production of MCPA, related to Nufarm's core 2-4D products, adding annual production capacity of 11,000 tons per year. The acquisition, which cost Nufarm AUD 20 million, further increased the share of international revenues to 78 percent. Nonetheless, the company had not neglected its home market. In 1996, also, the company paid AUD 51 million to buy specialty chemicals group Laporte Plc, adding its range of construction and timber protection chemicals.

Yet the crop protection market remained the company's fastest-growing segment. The company added a new major market when it bought France's CFPI (Compagnie Française de Produits Industriels), which had been founded in 1928. CFPI had been producing Weedone under license since the 1940s, and had also

developed a strong business developing crop protection products specifically for the wine industry. The company completed the CFPI purchase by 1998. The addition of CFPI also gave the company an entry into Spain, while boosting its U.S. operations as well. That same year, the company boosted its North American presence, buying Rhone Poulenc's phenoxy herbicide manufacturing operations in the United States and Canada, which gave it control of the Weedone brand. The company also bought a stake in (and later full control of) Westrade USA Inc., in partnership with du Pont, for the production of the trifluralin herbicide. Meanwhile, the group's relationship with Rhone Poulenc expanded with the spinoff of CFPI's ethephon growth regulator business into a joint venture majority controlled by the chemicals giant.

That spinoff came as part of Nufarm's decision to focus its business on its herbicides and pesticides operations. In 1999, the company sold its fertilizer operations, which had remained primarily based in New Zealand, while the company's crop protection operations in the region were concentrated in Australia. As a result, Nufarm decided to move its headquarters to its main Laverton North facility in Victoria, delisting its shares from the New Zealand stock exchange. The company then formally adopted the new name of Nufarm Ltd., and shifted its listing to the Australian Stock Exchange.

CROP PROTECTION STRATEGY FOR THE NEW CENTURY

Nufarm continued to build up its diversified geographic base at the beginning of the 2000s. The company returned to the United States in 2001, buying Agtrol International, which also had strong operations in France. The Agtrol purchase was also part of the company's newly emerging product diversification strategy, adding Agtrol's production of fungicides, including vine protection products. By the end of 2001, Nufarm had not only entered a new geographic market, it had added a third component to its crop protection package. This came through the acquisition of a 14 percent stake in India's Excel Industries Limited, a producer of insecticides.

Back at home, Nufarm boosted its domestic presence with the purchase of Artfern's pesticides and specialty chemicals manufacturing operations, including its sulfonyl urea herbicides, in 2001. The following year, the company acquired another Australian herbicide producer, Crop Care Australasia, which had been set up as a joint venture between two other companies, Orica and Incitec.

Nufarm boosted its product portfolio again in 2002, when it acquired the production and marketing license for Australia and New Zealand for Monsanto's Roundup brand. The company later increased its share of the Roundup brand in these markets when it bought the license for Roundup Ready canola seeds and traits in September 2006.

By then, Nufarm had further strengthened its position in the global crop protection market, becoming one of the leading crop protection specialists. In 2004, The company reached an agreement with BASF of Germany to acquire the distribution license for that company's cereal fungicides, including the Sportak and other brands. This deal followed the company's acquisition of all of BASF's internationally based phenoxy herbicides operations.

Nufarm also made its entry into the Latin American market in 2004, buying 49.9 percent of Brazil's Agripec Quimica e Farmacêutica SA. The purchase, at a cost of $120 million, placed Nufarm in the top ranks of that country's crop protection market. It also provided the springboard for the company's further penetration in the South American region. By 2006, Nufarm had added operations in Colombia as well, buying Agroquimicos Genéricos SA, based in Cali. That company specialized in the production of generic herbicides and other agricultural chemicals, and helped boost Nufarm's profile not only in Colombia, but in Venezuela, Peru, and the other Andean region markets.

Nufarm continued to seek additions to its product portfolio as well. In August 2006, for example, the company reached a multiyear supply and distribution agreement for Bayer CropScience's diflufenican (DFF), a cereal-specific weed killer, and DFF-based products for the European market. At the same time, Nufarm entered a new market, through its September 2006 acquisition of the crop protection distribution business of Agrosol SRL, based in Italy. With sales nearing AUD 1.7 billion ($1.3 billion), Nufarm had established itself as one of the world's leading pure-play global crop protection companies.

M. L. Cohen

PRINCIPAL SUBSIDIARIES

Agripec Quimica e Farmaceutica SA (Brazil); Agrogen Nufarm de Colombia; Ag-Seed Research Pty Ltd.; Crop Care Australasia Pty Ltd.; Croplands Equipment Pty Ltd.; Croplands Equipment Pty Ltd. (New Zealand); Framchem S.A. (Egypt); Kwinana; Nufarm Agriculture Inc. (Canada); Nufarm Americas; Nufarm b.v. (Netherlands); Nufarm Chemical (Shanghai) Co., Ltd. (China); Nufarm Chile Ltda.; Nufarm Coogee Pty Ltd.; Nufarm Deutschland GmbH; Nufarm do Brasil Ltda.; Nufarm España S.A. (Spain); Nufarm GmbH & Co. KG (Austria); Nufarm Italia srl; Nufarm K.K. (Japan); Nufarm Malaysia Sdn Bhd; Nufarm NZ (New Zealand); Nufarm Portugal Ltda.; Nufarm S.A. (Argentina); Nufarm S.A. (France); Nufarm SRL (Romania); Nufarm Turf and Specialty (U.S.A.); Nufarm UK Ltd.; Nugrain Pty Ltd.; Nuseed; Pt Nufarm Indonesia.

PRINCIPAL COMPETITORS

BASF AG; Pfizer Inc.; Novartis Inc.; Bayer AG; AstraZeneca PLC; Idemitsu Kosan Company Ltd.; OMV AG; ConAgra Foods Inc.; Syngenta International AG.

FURTHER READING

"Aceto, Nufarm to Form US Herbicide JV," *Chemical Week,* October 15, 2003, p. 4.

Alperowicz, Natasha, "Bayer and Nufarm Sign Herbicide Deal," *Chemical Week,* August 9, 2006, p. 14.

Forster, Christine, "Nufarm to Sell Canadian Fertilizer Business, Warns on Profits," *Chemical Week,* July 25, 2001, p. 14.

————, "Strong Demand, Acquisitions Lift Nufarm's Profits," *Chemical Week,* April 21, 2004, p. 20.

"Nufarm Buys Stake in South American Agchems Maker," *Chemical Week,* September 29, 2004, p. 6.

"Nufarm Receives EPA Registration for Imidacloprid Insecticide," *Grounds Maintenance,* May 26, 2006.

Young, Ian, "Nufarm to Buy Herbicide Business from BASF," *Chemical Week,* January 21, 2004, p. 20.

Orascom Construction
Industries S.A.E.

∎

PO Box 1191
Corniche El Nil
Abu El Ela
Cairo,
Egypt
Telephone: (+20 02) 4611111
Fax: (+20 02) 4619400
Web site: http://www.orascomci.com

Public Company
Incorporated: 1950
Employees: 40,000
Sales: EGP 16.48 billion ($2.87 billion) (2006)
Stock Exchanges: Cairo
Ticker Symbol: OCIC
NAIC: 236210 Industrial Building Construction;
237110 Water and Sewer Line and Related
Structures Construction; 327310 Cement
Manufacturing

∎ ∎ ∎

Orascom Construction Industries S.A.E. (OCI) has emerged as a globally competitive construction and construction materials group. One of Egypt's largest companies, OCI serves as a holding company for more than 20 subsidiaries active in 30 countries. More than 72 percent of the group's total revenues, which neared EGP 16.5 billion ($2.9 billion) in 2006, come from outside of Egypt. OCI originated as a construction company in 1977 and construction remains the group's main business, accounting for 75 percent of its revenues

and nearly half of its profits. OCI's construction operations focus primarily on the North African, Middle East, and Central Asian regions. The company's operations encompass many of the region's largest construction projects, including the world's tallest building under construction in the mid-2000s in Dubai. In addition to its own construction business, OCI has established a number of international partnerships, including 50 percent of Besix, Belgium's largest construction company, and 48 percent of Contrack Construction of the United States.

Since the mid-1990s, OCI has invested heavily in developing its building materials operations, and especially cement production. In Egypt the company operates Egyptian Cement Company, which accounts for 50 percent of total cement sales. Since the 2000s began, OCI has invested heavily in developing an extensive international cement production network. Algeria is the group's primary foreign market, adding 31 percent of cement sales; the company also has cement, concrete, and aggregate plants in Turkey, Pakistan, Iraq, and Spain. OCI's total cement production topped 21 million tons in 2006 and is expected to top 36 million tons per year by the end of the decade. Other building materials operations in OCI's portfolio include the joint ventures National Steel Fabrication Company and Alico Egypt, while OCI also holds a 50 percent stake in Egyptian Container Handling Company (ECHCO), a terminal handling and port management services company, and 20 percent of Nile Valley Gas Company, which provides natural gas distribution and transportation services in partnership with British Gas and Edison International. One of the top five companies on the

Cairo Stock Exchange, OCI is part of the larger Orascom group of companies, which include Orascom Telecom and Orascom Hotels and Development. OCI is led by CEO Nassef Sawiris, son of founder and Chairman Onsi Sawiris.

FOUNDING A DYNASTY IN 1977

Onsi Sawiris was born into a well-to-do Coptic Christian family based in Sohag, in northern Egypt. Sawiris's father had been a lawyer and landowner, and Onsi, as youngest son, was expected to oversee the family's land. As such, Sawiris went to university where he earned an agricultural engineering degree. Yet Sawiris had little interest for farming, and was discouraged from taking over the family's farms by the local peasants, who viewed him as an outsider. Instead, in 1950, Sawiris decided to found his own business, a construction contracting firm. That business quickly grew beyond the Sahag region, and before long had begun to receive larger contracts in the Delta region. The company moved its headquarters to Cairo, and by the end of the 1950s had begun to receive large scale public works contracts, including contracts to construct a network of canals and basins for the Ministry of Irrigation.

Sawiris's company became large enough to be caught up in the nationalization policies put into place by Gamal Abdel Nasser, as the Egyptian leader moved to shore up his waning government in the early 1960s. The Sawiris firm became known as Nasr Civil Works Company (and remained a leading Egyptian construction group into the next century). Sawiris, who sought to flee the country, instead lost his passport and was forced to work as an employee for the company he had founded. It was not until 1966 that Sawiris was given back his passport and allowed to leave Egypt. Sawiris' wife and children, including sons Naguib, Samih, and Nassef, remained in Egypt, while Sawiris went to Libya.

There Sawiris set up a new construction business, and through the 1970s had become successful enough to send his sons to Cairo's German School, and then overseas to complete their university studies. Naguib attended Zürich's prestigious Polytechnic School, Samih studied engineering in Berlin, and youngest son Nassef attended the University of Chicago.

The Camp David Peace Accords signed between Egypt and Israel under the guidance of President Jimmy Carter in 1976 formed a turning point in Sawiris's career. As a result of the peace treaty, the Libyan government turned against Egypt, and the Egyptians then living in the country. Sawiris was forced to return to Egypt, and once again start his career from scratch.

Onsi Sawiris returned to the industry he knew so well, forming Orascom Construction in 1977. The company started from almost nothing, with just five employees, as Sawiris struggled to pay for his sons' education. Soon, however, Sawiris benefited from the booming post–treaty Egyptian economy, and Orascom Construction grew strongly into the 1980s. With their education completed, the Sawiris sons joined their father in the family business.

The Sawiris' business interests rapidly evolved beyond construction, although that industry remained central to the family's growing fortune. Hired to remodel a number of movie theaters, the company later moved into the operation of the cinemas themselves. Similarly, the company entered the restaurant and hotel industries as well. In the early 1990s, the family also made the decision to enter the telecommunications market, becoming the first company to be awarded a mobile telephone license.

Onsi Sawiris transferred control of his companies to his sons in the 1990s. Naguib took over as head of Orascom Telecom, while Samih became head of the Orascom hotel branch. Youngest son Nassef was placed in charge of developing Orascom Construction Industries (OCI), serving as CEO, while his father remained chairman.

VERTICAL INTEGRATION FROM 1995

OCI quickly grew into what *Business Today Egypt* called "the quiet star of the Orascom empire." Taking the helm of the company, Nassef Sawiris led OCI on a drive toward vertical integration. One of the company's first extensions was the creation of the National Steel Fabrication Company joint venture with Consolidated Contractors, in 1995. The company operated a factory producing steel components for the construction and petroleum markets.

KEY DATES

1950: Onsi Sawiris establishes first construction business in Egypt, which is nationalized in 1961.

1977: Sawiris sets up new business in Egypt, Orascom Construction, which rapidly grows into one of Egypt's largest companies.

1995: Son Nassef Sawiris takes over as CEO of Orascom Construction and leads it on diversification strategy into cement production and other construction materials production.

1999: Orascom Construction Industries (OCI) goes public and becomes a top five company on the Cairo Stock Exchange.

2003: OCI acquires 50 percent stake in Besix, in Belgium; begins construction of first foreign cement plant in Algeria.

2007: Company announces plans to build cement factories in Turkey, Saudi Arabia, and Indonesia, boosting total production to 36 million tons per year.

From steel, OCI turned its attention to a more crucial material for its construction operations. The deregulation of the Egyptian cement market, which had previously been under government control, provided a new opportunity for OCI. In 1996 the company founded Egyptian Cement Company (ECC) as majority partner in a joint venture with global cement giant Holcim. ECC then launched construction of its first cement production facility. That plant was operational by 1998, and became the first private cement producer to enter the booming Egyptian construction market. Steady expansion of the ECC transformed it not only into the largest single cement production facility in the Middle East, but placed it among the largest cement factories in the world.

OCI's vertical integration effort led it in several new directions in the late 1990s. The company joined with Alico, an architectural products producer based in the United Arab Emirates, to form the Alico Egypt joint venture in 1999. That company built its own factory in Ain Sokhna, in Egypt, which focused on the production of aluminum and glass-based architectural products, such as facades, windows, doors, and curtain walls. Alico Egypt quickly became a leading fixture in Egypt, serving as supplier for such high-profile projects as Nile City,

Heliopolis City, and the Cairo airport. The joint venture also became a major exporter, shipping some 25 percent of its production throughout the North African and Middle Eastern regions.

With its growing cement and building materials operations, OCI put into place a new facet of its vertical integration strategy, creating a new logistics and transport wing. In 1998, the company set up a new joint venture, Egyptian Container Handling Company, or ECHCO, which provided materials handling and port management services, including majority ownership and management of a new facility at Sokhna Port. That same year, OCI became majority partner in the launch of Suez Industrial Development Company, which acquired the concession to more than nine million square meters of land in the northwest Gulf of Suez, including more than four million square meters of prime industrial property. In another, more diversified joint venture, OCI partnered with British Gas and Edison International to found the Nile Valley Gas Company, which began construction of a natural gas transportation and distribution network serving southern Egypt.

GLOBAL CEMENT PRODUCER IN THE NEW CENTURY

By 1999, OCI had already topped revenues of EGP 2 billion ($574 million). The company went public that year, listing its stock on the Cairo Stock Exchange in an offer that valued the company at EGP 2.66 billion ($764 million). OCI quickly joined the Cairo exchange's top five companies, along with sister companies Orascom Telecom and Orascom Hotel Development.

The economic crisis that struck Egypt at the end of the 1990s prompted OCI to begin developing itself into an international construction and construction materials group for the new century. For its new strategy, OCI sought out strategic holdings in already established companies. OCI's first venture overseas brought it to the United States, where it purchased a 45 percent stake in Contrack Construction in 1998. That company, founded in Washington, D.C., in 1985, had from its start maintained a presence in Egypt, opening an office in Cairo that same year. Focused on providing subcontracting services to U.S. government projects in Egypt and the Middle East, Contrack emerged as a prime contractor by 1990. Through the 1990s, Contrack continued to expand its presence in the Middle East and in Egypt, setting up Contrack Engineering in Cairo, then opening offices in Qatar and Bahrain. In the next decade, Contrack expanded into Afghanistan, Uzbekistan, and Iraq as well. OCI benefited directly from the Iraqi reconstruction effort following the U.S. invasion of that country, winning a $325 million contract there.

OCI entered the European construction market in 2003, backing a management buyout of Besix, one of the largest construction groups in Belgium. Founded in 1909 as Société Belge des Bétons (SBB), that company had launched operations in the Middle East in the mid-1960s. By the end of the 1980s, the company had expanded into the Eastern European market, while into the early 1990s, the Middle East and Egypt provided one of its fastest-growing markets. OCI's share of Besix, which produced revenues of more than $1 billion in the middle of the first decade of the 2000s, stood at 50 percent.

In the meantime, OCI's cement production operation had become one of its fastest-growing operations. The company expanded its Egyptian production, adding a second plant in the late 1990s, then launching construction of a third plant in 2001. The company's dual expertise in construction and cement production also made it a natural choice for large-scale cement plant construction projects, such as a $30 million contract to supply steel structures and other equipment for a plant in Libya.

Yet increasingly OCI's cement production interests turned toward expanding its own network overseas. The company became the first private company to be awarded permission to build a cement plant in Algeria. That country quickly became OCI's second largest cement market, accounting for more than 30 percent of its production.

Into the middle of the first decade of the 2000s, OCI stepped up its international expansion. The company entered Pakistan in 2004, buying a 51 percent stake in the Pakistani Cement Company, based in Chakwal, with a production capacity of 2.2 million tons. In Algeria, the company launched construction of a new white cement factory, with a capacity of 550,000 tons. The company also launched construction of new plants in Nigeria, Iraq, and the United Arab Emirates, with most of those factories expected to come online by the end of 2007. By the beginning of that year, OCI had expanded its European presence, through Besix, with a move into the Spanish aggregates market. The company also announced its intentions to build cement production facilities in Turkey, Saudi Arabia, and Indonesia. The completion of these projects was expected to boost OCI's total cement production past 36 million tons,

compared to 21 million tons in 2006. With world-class status in both the construction and construction materials market, OCI emerged as the true star in the Sawiris family empire.

M. L. Cohen

PRINCIPAL SUBSIDIARIES

A-Build Egypt (50.1%); Alico Egypt (50%); BESIX Group (50%); Cementech Limited; Contrack Group; Egyptian Basic Industries Corporation (30%); Egyptian Container Handling Company (50%); Egyptian Gypsum Company (45%); Egyptian Maritime Services (90%); MBT Egypt (50%); National Pipe Company (40%); National Steel Fabrication (50%); Nile Valley Gas Company (20%); Orascom Road Construction (90%); SCIB Chemical (15%); Sokhna Port Development Company (70%); Suez Industrial Development Company (60.5%); United Paints & Chemicals (50%).

PRINCIPAL COMPETITORS

Tata Sons Ltd.; Holcim Ltd.; General Organization for Cement and Building Materials; Al Ghurair Group of Cos.; ERCE GIC; Alghanaem Industries; ETA ASCON.

FURTHER READING

"Egypt's Orascom to Build Cement Factory in Indonesia," *AsiaPulse News,* December 5, 2006.

Hassan, Fayza, "A Capital Idea," *Al Ahram Weekly,* July 22, 1999.

Mostafa, Hadia, "Business Secrets of the Sawiris Family," *Business Times Egypt,* February 2005.

"The New Pharaohs," *Economist,* March 12, 2005, p. 63.

Nield, Richard, "Great Leaps Forward," *MEED Middle East Economic Digest,* October 21, 2005, p. 39.

"OCI Buys in Spain," *MEED Middle East Economic Digest,* October 27, 2006, p. 24.

"OCI Pushes into Europe," *MEED Middle East Economic Digest,* November 3, 2006, p. 33.

"Orascom Builds up Construction Empire," *MEED Middle East Economic Digest,* May 28, 2004, p. 17.

"Orascom Cons. Inds- Cement JV in Saudi Arabia," *AFX CNF,* February 28, 2007.

"Orascom Construction Industries Acquires Cement Bags Manufacturer," *Internet Wire,* January 4, 2006.

"Orascom Looks East for Cement," *MEED Middle East Economic Digest,* March 2, 2007, p. 21.

Ormat Technologies, Inc.

6225 Neil Road, Suite 300
Reno, Nevada 89511-1136
U.S.A.
Telephone: (775) 356-9029
Fax: (775) 356-9039
Web site: http://www.ormat.com

Public Subsidiary
Incorporated: 1994
Employees: 733
Sales: $268.94 million (2006)
Stock Exchanges: New York
Ticker Symbol: ORA
NAIC: 221119 Other Electric Power Generation (Primary); 237990 Other Heavy and Civil Engineering Construction; 333611 Turbine and Turbine Generator Set Units Manufacturing; 221122 Electric Power Distribution

∎ ∎ ∎

Ormat Technologies, Inc. (OTI), is the third largest geothermal power producer in the United States and one of the world's leading renewable energy companies. The Reno, Nevada-based independent power producer, a subsidiary of the Yavne, Israel-based Ormat Industries Ltd., develops, builds, owns, and operates geothermal power plants in the western United States, Guatemala, Kenya, Nicaragua, and the Philippines. Ormat's entire product line, in use in 71 countries on six continents, includes recovered energy systems and remote power equipment. The company's technology is centered around high-efficiency turbines that are uniquely designed to generate electricity from low-heat sources. OTI's reputation as an alternative energy business is built upon its expertise at turning hot water and steam from local sources into electricity in a process that reinjects 100 percent of all geothermal fluid produced and consumes no water or chemicals.

PIONEERS LOOKING FOR A MARKET IN 1965

Ormat Technologies, Inc., was officially founded as a U.S. corporation on September 15, 1994, but the Ormat story really began in 1965 when Lucien and Yehudit Bronicki, a husband-and-wife team, established Ormat Turbines Ltd. in Yavne, Israel. After learning the Israeli science agency he worked for was abandoning his experimental work on a solar-powered turbo-generator, the 31-year-old Lucien sold his most valuable possession, his apartment, and used the proceeds to start a company and continue his research.

The persistent engineer quickly devised the Organic Rankine Cycle (ORC), which according to company literature "is a thermodynamic process where heat is added to a fluid at a constant pressure, the fluid is vaporized and then expanded in a vapor turbine, which drives a generator, producing electricity." The company's Organic Rankine Cycle modular power plants, known as Ormat Energy Converters (OECs), were capable of generating electricity from locally available heat sources, including steam and hot water, industrial waste heat, solar energy, and biomass, or low-grade fuels.

Ormat Technologies, Inc.

Over the past four decades, Ormat has pioneered a number of significant advances in the geothermal and recovered energy industries, laying the foundation for the rapid and profitable growth that Ormat Technologies, Inc., is experiencing today. Ormat's engineers have developed highly original designs for turbines and other generation equipment components, which have been optimized through the rigorous application of advanced thermodynamics and fluid dynamics. Ormat's unique position of being both an independent power producer, as well as a manufacturer of geothermal and recovered energy equipment, provides the company with a thorough firsthand understanding of customer needs and the ability to develop creative solutions based on field-tested experience.

Ormat initially found a market for its OEC technology in remote power generators called Closed Cycle Vapor Turbogenerators (CCVTs). Ormat's CCVTs generated 200 to 4,500 watts and operated on natural gas, propane, diesel fuel, or kerosene in extreme heat or cold. The small but powerful units were virtually maintenance-free and found worldwide use in telecommunications, lighting and security systems, battery-charging, and other remote power applications. The Russian company Gazprom, one of the world's largest natural gas production and transmission firms, began using Ormat CCVTs in 1973. In 1976, Ormat began supplying offshore gas platforms with CCVTs and 122 of the remote power units were installed along the Trans-Alaska Pipeline. In 1979, the Siberian railway began powering their communications system with Ormat CCVTs.

In the late 1970s, the company built a small salinity gradient solar-pond power plant near the Dead Sea, but Mr. Bronicki was unable to convince the Israeli government to fund a more ambitious solar energy project. It was then that the company began to develop geothermal systems to harness steam, heat, or hot water from geysers or hot springs on the earth's surface. The company's patented turbines were uniquely suited to the task. Conventional steam turbines required water temperatures of at least 160 degrees Celsius to produce grid-level power. Ormat's OECs permitted grid-level power generation with water or steam at temperatures as low as 80 degrees Celsius.

SETTING UP SHOP IN THE UNITED STATES: 1983

In late 1983, Ormat formed a partnership with Pennsylvania-based LFC Financial Corp. and established Ormat Energy Systems, Inc. In 1984, the subsidiary opened an office in Sparks, Nevada, and acquired the development rights to California's East Mesa Geothermal Field. The 24 megawatt (MW; one MW equals the amount of electricity it takes to power 1,000 homes) Ormesa I Project delivered power to the grid in December 1986 as planned and paid back a $50 million U.S. Department of Energy loan a year ahead of schedule. Its success at the time demonstrated the technical and economic feasibility of larger-scale geothermal power plants.

In 1986, Ormat once again partnered with LFC Financial in the formation of the Sparks, Nevada-based OESI Power Corporation. In April 1988, Ormat Energy Systems acquired a 25 percent interest in Puna Geothermal Ventures on the island of Hawaii. In June, the company bought the other 75 percent and became the sole owner of the site-specific subsidiary. The proposed $100 million plant was the first privately owned and operated commercial geothermal project licensed in the state and was scheduled to begin delivering up to 12.5 MW to Hawaiian Electric Industries Inc. by 1990. In February 1990, 11 months after a contract was signed, electricity began flowing from two OEC modular units, part of New Zealand's first geothermal power plant.

In April 1991, OESI reported net income for 1990 of $2.7 million on revenue of $66.1 million, and in May, the company raised $31.5 million in an initial public offering (IPO) on the American Stock Exchange. Ormat Turbines' stake in OESI fell from 32.9 percent to 22.9 percent after the company's sale of 2.25 million shares at $14 per share. At the time, OESI operated and maintained five geothermal projects in the United States totaling 49.9 MW. In addition, three units representing 29.5 MW were under construction and another five projects totaling 102 MW were under active development. On November 22, OESI halted stock sales after the share price dropped from $9.50 to $6.50, the result of investor concerns over delays and significant cost overruns in the Puna project caused by an explosion at a well drilling site in June. In December, OESI acquired 20 percent of Portland, Oregon-based LFC Power Systems Corp., operator of nine power plants in four states, including the Ormesa I geothermal facilities in California's Imperial Valley.

On the parent company's home front, in May 1991, Yavne-based Ormat Industries, Ormat Turbines' newly created parent company, staged a very successful

National Oil Company (PNOC), a government-owned corporation, to be the turnkey contractor for a 125 MW geothermal plant in the Upper Mahiao geothermal field. The $180 million build-operate-transfer project called for Ormat to manufacture and build the power plant, and California Energy Inc. of Omaha, Nebraska, to manage the financing and operate the facility, which was expected to produce electricity by mid-1996. Two smaller Ormat plants in the Philippines, each under 20 MW, were scheduled to become operational in 1994.

In April 1994, the effects of the Puna delays and the Rye Patch write-off became apparent for OESI. The company reported a net loss for 1993 of $32.1 million on revenues of $38.2 million. On March 29, 1995, OESI saw its stock "bounce back" from a low of 1.6 cents to close at 12.5 cents. August brought the final blow to the company when OESI announced its loss of $51.4 million for 1994. In December, Ormat Inc., which held 86.4 percent of OESI stock, paid remaining shareholders 12 cents per share and took the company private.

In June 1995, Ormat Inc. was awarded another PNOC contract for a $40 million, 49 MW geothermal power plant on the island of Leyte in the central Philippines. Ormat Industries landed a contract in late October to build a 25 MW geothermal power plant in Guatemala. The $65 million Zunil I project also included a 30-year power purchase agreement between Nevada-based Ormat International, Inc., and Guatemala's state-owned electric utility.

In February 1996, Ormat Industries announced another geothermal project for New Zealand, a turnkey contract to build a $32 million, 20 MW power plant on an active geothermal site in the Rotokawa region. In May, the company said it would build a fourth project in the Philippines, a $65 million, 50 MW geothermal power plant. In August, Ormat finally won a power plant contract in Israel, a $43 million, 30 MW, 50 percent shale-oil powered demonstration plant located in Nahal Zin, in southern Israel. Ormat also announced in August a contract for a $16 million, 7 MW plant for Ethiopia, where the company had been active in the 1970s. In December, Ormat International reached an agreement with state-owned Vietnam Electricity Corp. to build that nation's first geothermal plant.

In May 1997, Ormat received an order for its fourth New Zealand geothermal facility, a $24 million, 10 MW plant for the Ngawha geothermal field in Northland. Signaling its strategy to invest directly in power plants instead of just building and supplying them with equipment, Ormat Turbines in July acquired

IPO on the Tel Aviv Stock Exchange (TASE). The Bronicki family retained 67.9 percent ownership of the company. May 1991 also brought a partnership with Enin, the Soviet energy institute, to establish geothermal power stations in the Soviet Union and to import Russian technology used in power stations fueled by shale oil. Total revenues for Ormat Industries for the whole of 1991 were $71 million.

OESI moved its headquarters to Portland, Oregon, in the second quarter of 1992 and in September resumed operations at its Puna project in Hawaii. However, the company received bad news in May 1993 when General Electric Capital Corp., the construction lender and minority partner in the company's $40 million, 12.5 MW Rye Patch geothermal project in Pershing County, Nevada, withdrew its financing for the plant.

EXPANDING WORLDWIDE IN 1993

In September 1993, Ormat landed its biggest deal to date. Another U.S. subsidiary, Ormat Inc. of Sparks, Nevada, signed an agreement with the Philippine

30 percent of two state-owned 470 MW coal-fired plants in Karaganda, Kazakhstan. Ormat took over operations of the plants with an option to buy up to 70 percent of the facility.

Ormat advanced its Kazakhstan project in June 1998, when it formed Karaganda Power, a partnership with London-based International Power. In September, the partners completed the purchase of 70 percent of the electricity production and transmission company from the Kazakhstan government and committed $110 million to a three-year plan to refurbish the facilities. On another continent, Ormat International signed a deal in November to build the first phase of a $172 million geothermal plant in Kenya.

Ormat Industries landed its first deal in Nicaragua in March 1999, a 15-year contract to operate the 27 MW Momotombo geothermal power plant. The plan called for Ormat to invest $15 million in upgrades, drill additional geothermic wells, and boost the plant's operating capacity and profitability. In June, Ormat Industries established OPTI Canada, Inc., and partnered with Calgary-based Suncor Energy Inc. to test the commercial viability of Ormat's technology for producing synthetic crude oil at a pilot plant at one of Suncor's northern Alberta oil sand leases.

In July 2000, OPTI announced plans to build a $450 million, 30,000 barrel-a-day, heavy-oil-recovery facility not far from its Burnt Lake pilot plant. The Long Lake Project was based on OrCrude technology, an Ormat-developed steam-assisted gravity drainage process to heat bitumen to its melting point so that it could then be brought to the surface and converted on-site into synthetic crude. The plant was scheduled to start producing 20,000 barrels per day in 2002, which the company planned to sell in the U.S. refinery market.

REINVESTING IN THE UNITED STATES: 2001

In 2001, Ormat Industries continued its transition from a technology vendor to an independent power producer. In July, the company acquired two geothermal power plants in the United States that it had helped build a decade earlier. In separate deals, Ormat bought the 20 MW Brady Power Partners station for $20.5 million from the Florida Power & Light Energy Company, and the 10 MW Desert Peak plant for $10.5 million from the Mid American Group. Located in Churchill County, Nevada, both plants had long-term power purchase agreements with Sierra Pacific Resources. In November, Calgary-based Nexen Inc. joined OPTI, replacing Suncor, in its heavy oil project in Alberta's Athabasca oil sands region.

In February 2002, Ormat Industries announced it would build an $18.7 million, 18 MW power plant at the Miravalles geothermal field in Costa Rica. In March, International Power sold Ormat its share in Karaganda Power. In April, Ormat Nevada Inc., yet another Sparks-based subsidiary, bought the 74-megawatt Ormesa complex of geothermal power plants in Imperial County, California, for $41 million. The deal with FPL Energy and Caithness Energy gave Ormat control of six individual power generators and included the 40 MW Ormesa Project and the 20 MW combined Geo East Mesa Units 2 and 3. The Ormesa and GEM plants came with long-term contracts to sell power to Southern California Edison and generated about $30 million in annual revenue. In September, Ormat unloaded its 50 percent stake in a coal-fired power plant in Kazakhstan.

In 2003, Ormat Industries continued its U.S. expansion with the July acquisition of the Ormat-built Steamboat geothermal complex in Steamboat Hills, Nevada, about ten miles from the company's U.S. headquarters in Sparks. In two separate deals, the company bought four Steamboat power plants with 47 megawatts in total generating capacity and some adjacent land suitable for geothermal development. In October, Ormat Industries signed a contract for its fifth geothermal power plant in New Zealand, a $22 million, 16.5 MW facility. On December 18, 2003, Ormat made its biggest deal to date when it completed a $214 million acquisition of three California geothermal power plants from the bankrupt Covanta Energy Corp. In that one transaction, the company doubled the size of its U.S. operations and became the third largest player in the geothermal sector in North America. The deal included a 52 MW plant in Heber, leasing rights to a 48 MW Second Imperial Geothermal Co. plant, and 50 percent of the Mammoth Pacific Power Plants in the Sierra Nevada Mountains. Sales from the power facilities were expected to generate about $80 million annually.

In February 2004, the company began operating a 4.5 MW Ormat Recovered Energy Generation system at a natural gas processing plant in Louisiana. The heat recovery system, the first of its kind in the United States, used otherwise wasted heat from hot exhaust of two gas turbines. In April, OPTI Canada raised $301.4 million in an IPO under the symbol OPC on the Toronto Stock Exchange to finance part of its 50 percent share of a $3.4 billion oil sands project in northern Alberta. In May, Ormat Nevada paid $20 million to acquire the 12.5 MW Steamboat Yankee geothermal project in Washoe County, Nevada. In June, Ormat Nevada paid $71 million to become the sole owner of the 30 MW Puna geothermal plant in Hawaii, a project Ormat helped build a decade earlier.

GAINING STEAM IN 2004

Ormat Technologies, Inc.'s November 2004 IPO on the New York Stock Exchange capped a two-year restructuring for Ormat Industries and its worldwide holdings and subsidiaries. OTI emerged in the new order as the owner and operator of Ormat Industries' entire portfolio, which at the time included 12 geothermal power stations in the United States, Israel, Guatemala, Kenya, Nicaragua, and the Philippines, and another three projects under construction. Opening at $15.20 per share and trading under the ticker symbol ORA, the sale of 7.18 million shares of common stock, about 26 percent of the company, netted Ormat Technologies $100.2 million. TASE-traded, Yavne-based Ormat Industries, where the majority of Ormat's senior management and all of its production and manufacturing facilities remained, essentially became a holding company with shares in OTI and a 30 percent stake in OPTI Canada. At the time, the Bronicki family collectively owned 34.9 percent of Ormat Industries; Lucien Bronicki remained company chairman and chief technology officer, and Yehudit Bronicki continued to serve as CEO and president.

In February 2005, OTI won a contract to build a $25 million, 14 MW geothermal power plant on São Miguel Island in the Azores, its third island project. In March, OTI subsidiary Ormat Nevada, Inc., broke ground on the 20 MW Galena Geothermal Project No. 1, the first geothermal plant built at the Steamboat, Nevada, location since 1991. OTI reported in March that total revenues of $219.2 million for 2004 were up 83.5 percent from 2003. Net income rose year to year from $15.5 million to $17.8 million. May brought another groundbreaking for a geothermal plant at the Heber Geothermal Facilities Complex. The 10 MW plant was part of an 18 MW enhancement of Ormat's Heber facility. In June, OTI signed a 25-year agreement to sell Basin Electric Power Corp. 22 MW of Recovered Energy Generation systems for its gas compressor stations along the Northern Border Pipeline in North and South Dakota.

From December 2004 to January 2006, OTI's share price rose 143 percent. In March 2006, OTI reported record total revenues for 2005 at $238 million but said net income fell from $17.8 million to $15.2 million. In April, OTI netted $117.2 million from the sale of 3.5 million shares at $35.50 per share in a follow-on public offering, and in the same month moved its headquarters from Sparks to Reno, Nevada. Ormat returned to its solar roots in May when a 1 MW OEC became

operational as part of the first solar trough power plant in Arizona. OTI's Recovered Energy Generation (REG) business continued to grow in June with a $29 million supply and construction contract for three REG power plants from an independent power producer in Western Canada. In June, OTI became the sole owner of the 24 MW Ormat-built Zunil Geothermal Project in Guatemala.

In July 2006, OTI subsidiary Ormat International, Inc., became a one-third partner in the largest single-contract project to date in the geothermal industry worldwide, a $600 million, 340 MW power plant for Sarulla, Indonesia. In September, Ormat Industries announced that it would invest $63.5 million over the next five years to build a demonstration biodiesel plant, and in December, the company sold four million shares in OPTI Canada Inc. for $69 million to fund its experiment. Ormat's stake in OPTI fell to 5.3 percent after the sale. In late December, OTI secured significant geothermal leases in North Brawley, California, where it planned to build a 50 MW plant by 2008.

January 2007 brought Ormat its tenth New Zealand supply contract, a deal to build a $20 million, 12 MW geothermal power plant in Ngawha. In February, OTI began a $32 million, 35 MW expansion of its Olkaria III geothermal power plant in Kenya. On February 28, OTI reported that annual revenues for 2006 were up 13 percent to $268.9 million and net income jumped 127 percent to $34.4 million. Revenues from electricity generation totaled $195.5 million. In March, parent company Ormat Industries reported $290.9 million in total revenue for 2006. The company said net profits of $198.1 million were up 478.4 percent due to capital gains from the dilution in the company's stake in OTI and the sale of investments in OPTI Canada, Inc.

As 2007 began, geothermal energy was being used as a source of direct heat and electrical power generation in over 30 countries, but it represented less than 2 percent of worldwide electricity production. The International Energy Agency had predicted that geothermal power could triple in market share by 2030, to 167 terawatt hours each year, equal to nearly half of the electricity produced in an average-sized European country. With more than 40 years of alternative energy experience and a consistent revenue stream as an established independent power producer of geothermal energy, OTI and its subsidiaries appeared well positioned to take advantage of the worldwide trend away from fossil fuels and toward more environmentally friendly energy production and consumption.

Ted Sylvester

PRINCIPAL SUBSIDIARIES

Ormat Inc.; Ormat International, Inc.; Ormat Nevada, Inc.

PRINCIPAL COMPETITORS

CalEnergy Generation; Calpine Corporation; Fuji Electric Corp. of America; Mitsubishi Heavy Industries America, Inc.; Siemens AG (Germany); Caithness Energy, L.L.C.

FURTHER READING

Ankori, Merav, "Calpine's Pain Ormat's Gain?" *Israel Business Arena,* December 21, 2005.

———, "Ormat Sees 78% Energy Production Growth by 2008," *Israel Business Arena,* June 26, 2006.

Cohen, Neil, "Alternative Energy," *Jerusalem Post,* 12 April 1995.

"Exclusivity in a Growing Market," *Israel Business Today,* April 14, 1993.

Gerstenfeld, Dan, "Ormat Subsidiary to Invest $500 Million in Canadian Heavy Oil Venture," *Jerusalem Post,* November 1, 2001.

"Good Experience with 5-MW Solar Pond Power Plant," *Innovation A.G. Publications Ltd.,* December 1, 1991.

Hamburg, Ken, "OESI Power Sees Shares Bounce Back," *Portland Oregonian,* March 29, 1995.

"Hawaii Geothermal Project Must Stop Until Officials Probe Well Blowout," *Independent Power Report,* August 2, 1991.

Kanon, Sharon, "One Day, One House," *Jerusalem Post,* July 12, 1991.

Muscal, Tal, "Ormat Buys Three California Power Plants for $214 Million," *Jerusalem Post,* November 24, 2003.

"OrCal: California Steaming," *Project Finance,* December 1, 2005.

"Ormat Digs in Its Own Backyard," *Power,* May 1, 2005.

"Ormat Energy Completes 100% Buyout of Planned 30-MW Hawaiian Project," *Independent Power Report,* June 3, 1988.

"Ormat Industries Expands Development with Plan to Buy Up to 90 MW in Nevada," *Global Power Report,* June 8, 2001.

"Ormat, Mission, Magma Awarded 200 MW of Philippine Geothermal Contracts," *Independent Power Report,* April 23, 1993.

"Ormat Nevada Goes Geothermal, Buys 60 MW for $41-Million," *Megawatt Daily,* April 16, 2002.

"Ormat Secures Ngawha Contract," *Power in Asia,* January 18, 2007.

Paz, Zvika, "Power to Ormat," *Israel Business Arena,* June 5, 2002.

"Smart Solutions for Global Warming; From Geothermal to Biomass, Israeli Energy Pioneer Ormat Industries Is Advancing Alternative and Renewable Energies Around the World," *BusinessWeek Online,* November 1, 2006.

Solomon, Shoshanna, and Amy Teibel, "Focus: Ormat Tech IPO Seen Hot amid High Oil Prices," *Dow Jones International News,* November 9, 2004.

Trifonovitch, Kelli Abe, "Steaming Ahead," *Hawaii Business,* October 1, 2002.

"Unused Heat from Industrial Plants Utilized for Power by Israeli Firm," *International Solar Energy Intelligence Report,* November 14, 1994.

Oxfam

Oxfam GB

---

274 Banbury Road
Oxford, OX2 7DZ
United Kingdom
Telephone: (+44 0) 1865 312610
Web site: http://www.oxfam.org.uk

Nonprofit Company
Incorporated: 1943
Employees: 4,500
Operating Revenues: £310.5 million ($528 million)
   (2006)
NAIC: 624190 Other Individual and Family Services;
   813319 Other Social Advocacy Organizations

■ ■ ■

Oxfam GB is the founding member of Oxfam International, one of the world's leading and most well-known charitable organizations, providing aid and development services to victims of war, poverty, and natural and manmade disasters. Oxfam provides both direct and infield aid and assistance, develops public awareness campaigns, coordinates assistance and relief efforts, and solicits charitable contributions. The company operates a national chain of charitable, volunteer-based thrift shops, as well as a growing number of used bookstores, and the fair-trade chain of Progresso coffee shops. Oxfam GB also oversees its own publishing unit, producing a series of internationally recognized country guides. Much of the organization's financial funding comes through such bodies as the European Commission, the Department for Inter-

national Development, the United Nations, the Big Lottery Fund, Comic Relief, Vodafone Group Foundation, the Bill and Melinda Gates Foundation, the Disasters Emergency Committee, and many others. Donations and legacies accounted for nearly 38 percent of the group's operating revenues of £310.5 million ($528 million), while government bodies and public authorities provided more than 15 percent of the organization's funding. The group's retail operations generated 20 percent of its total income during that year.

Oxfam GB, based in Oxford, also provides the coordinating secretariat for Oxford International. Other members in the worldwide organization include Oxfam units in the United States, France, Germany, Belgium, Canada, Australia, New Zealand, Spain, the Netherlands, Ireland, and Hong Kong. Oxfam GB's operations are led by Director Barbara Stocking.

RESPONDING TO THE GREEK FAMINE IN WORLD WAR II

The origins of Oxfam can be traced back to the Allied blockade of Nazi-occupied Greece and the resulting famine there. British war policy of the time was conducted along the lines of "total war," which made little distinction between civilian and military, and placed the burden of caring for an occupied population on the occupying force. As a result of this policy, the British government insisted on maintaining a hermetically sealed blockade of Greece, allowing no civilian aid or relief from Britain to enter the country.

The first signs of famine in Greece had appeared by 1941 and by the end of the war, the country had

COMPANY PERSPECTIVES

Oxfam's Purpose: Oxfam works with others to overcome poverty and suffering.

witnessed death rates as high as 1,500 people per day. In Great Britain, a growing number of people had become alarmed at the situation in Greece, and had begun to demand that the British government alter its total war policy in order to allow relief to get through to the population. By 1942, a growing number of Famine Relief committees, created in large part through the efforts of Quaker activist Edith Pye, had begun to appear throughout the United Kingdom. In Oxford, a group of local scholars, clergymen, and pacifists joined together to form the Oxford Committee for Famine Relief toward the end of 1942. Leading that effort was Gilbert Murray, a professor of Greek at Oxford University, and Canon T. R. Milford, of the University Church. Another founding member, Cecil Jackson-Cole, provided the committee with needed business experience in his role as honorary secretary. The committee formally registered as a charitable organization in 1943. In that year, the committee organized its first "Greek Week" campaign to raise awareness and funding. That effort enabled the group to generate donations of nearly £13,000, a significant amount given the penury of the times, toward the relief effort in Greece. Because of the British government's continued refusal to allow British aid to penetrate the blockade of Greece, that sum was turned over to the Greek Red Cross.

The Oxford Committee, which increasingly began to refer to itself in the shortened form of "Oxfam," continued to solicit donations and to appeal for a relaxation of the Greek blockade throughout the war. With the Nazi defeat in World War II and the end of the blockade, the committee wound down its Greek Relief Fund. During the immediate postwar years the Oxford committee, together with the many other local relief committees established during the war, continued to collect donations in order to provide funding for relief operations being set up across war-torn Europe. In 1948, the Oxford committee established its first office, on Broad Street in Oxford, to serve as a collection center for donations. At that time, the committee borrowed an idea pioneered by the Salvation Army in the United States, and opened its own retail charity gift shop in the storefront below the office. This became the United Kingdom's first such permanent charity shop, and inspired the creation of a national chain of stores.

With its donations increasing, the committee then turned to supporting the relief efforts underway in the Middle East.

The creation of the Marshall Plan, which oversaw the European-wide relief and reconstruction effort starting in 1949, led a large number of the British relief committees to wind up their operations that year. The Oxford committee, however, chose to pursue operations, and adopted a new mission, directly opposed to the principles of total war and establishing the goal of providing "the relief of suffering arising as a result of wars or other causes in any part of the world." The committee's campaign helped play a role in defining the newly redeveloped Geneva Convention, passed in 1949 and providing explicit protection for civilians during wartime.

DIRECT ACTION

Into the early 1950s, Oxfam's operations focused especially on the European region, and in particular in providing funding for the continent's refugee relief efforts—the last of the European refugee camps was to close only in 1959 after campaigning from Oxfam and other relief organizations. By then, Oxfam had expanded its geographic focus to a global level. Already in 1951 the committee provided funding for the famine relief effort in Bihar, India, following a natural disaster there. Two years later, the committee launched a collection effort that ultimately provided £60,000 for relief efforts in war-stricken Korea. The group also began developing its international network during this time, starting with a partnership with the future Oxfam Australia, established in 1953.

Oxfam had also developed a keen sense of marketing and promotion, helping to raise its profile not only among the British public, but throughout the world. By the end of the 1950s, Oxfam was already pulling in more than £1 million in donations per year. The committee played a major role in the development of a new vision of charitable organizations in general and of international relief operations in particular, targeting the endemic poverty in regions that became known as the "developing" world. In 1960, for example, Oxfam joined with a number of other international bodies, and most notably the United Nations Food and Agriculture Organization, to launch the "Freedom from Hunger." This effort broke away from traditional charitable activities to instead focus on providing training and tools for people to grow their own food. Over a five-year period, Oxfam's efforts helped that campaign raise more than £7 million in the United Kingdom.

The Oxfam name was formally adopted in 1965. By then, the group had already evolved from an organization accepting charitable donations to an active relief organization. The start of this change stemmed from the group's decision in 1961 to send its first field director to southern Africa in order to coordinate its relief and development spending with local relief operations. Increasingly, however, Oxfam sought to become involved directly in the relief effort. This led to the group's first direct relief action when famine struck Bihar, India, again in 1966. In response, Oxfam sent a team of volunteers in order to operate a food distribution program. By the early 1970s, the organization had become involved in more than 800 projects in 19 countries, and included 11 dedicated expatriate staff members.

Oxfam's operation model had also begun to catch on internationally in the 1960s, leading to the creation of the first international Oxfam International affiliates, in Belgium and Canada, both in 1963. An affiliate was created in the United States in 1970, followed by the creation of Oxfam Ireland in 1971, and Oxfam Quebec in 1973.

At home, in its gift shops, Oxfam promoted sales of handicrafts made by small-scale producers in developing areas, providing training and funding, and guaranteeing fair pricing. This effort, originally launched as the Bridge Programme in 1964, later evolved into the Oxfam Fair Trade Company. By the early 1970s, the gift shops had become Oxfam's primary source of funding, selling both donated goods and handicrafts from around the world. A steady string of new Oxfam stores opened throughout the United Kingdom. The organization also launched a successful mail-order operation in the 1970s, which grew into a £1 million-per-year operation by the 1980s.

GLOBAL RELIEF LEADER IN THE NEW CENTURY

Fund-raising for the organization took off in the 1980s as well, in particular through such highly publicized global events as Band Aid and Comic Relief. In 1984 alone these efforts helped boost Oxfam's total income past £50 million. At the same time, Oxfam began taking steps to build its retail wing. In 1985, the group created a central clearance center in Ipswich, which took on remaindered items from the organization's retail network. In this way, the group slowly transformed the image of its chain of charity shops from a somewhat dusty, often shabby collection of odds and ends to a more modern retail format. As a result, the retail division's sales grew strongly into the 1990s, allowing the organization to step up development of the network. By the middle of the first decade of the 2000s, the operation boasted more than 750 stores.

Oxfam also began testing out new retail areas. In 1988, the group opened its first used bookstore; it was not until nearly a decade later, however, that this format became truly successful. By the 1990s, Oxfam had begun to roll out a chain of used bookstores, becoming a major challenger in the British retail book market. By then, too, Oxfam had opened its first furniture stores, in 1989. During the 1990s, the group branched out into retail fashions, launching the Nologo and Original fashion stores in London. By the end of that decade, the group's used bookstore format had begun to catch on with British consumers, and by 2005, the group rolled out plans to open as many as 20 bookstores per year. At that point, Oxfam was already the second largest seller of used books in all of Europe.

At the beginning of the 1990s, Oxfam took a role in the establishment of the fair-trade movement. The company helped establish the Cafédirect fair-trade coffee branch, launched in partnership with Traidcraft, Equal Exchange, and Twin Trading in 1991. The following year, Oxfam joined in the formation of the Fairtrade Foundation, in partnership with CAFOD, Christian Aid, Traidcraft, the World Development Movement, and New Consumer. These efforts ultimately led Oxfam to rebrand its Bridge Programme shops under the Oxfam Fair Trade Company in 1996.

By then, Oxfam International, which based its secretariat in Oxford, had expanded to include a number of new affiliates, including branches in Hong Kong in 1984, the Netherlands in 1994, Germany in 1995, and Spain in 1997. In 1998, after completing a strategic review of its operations, Oxfam GB decided to restructure, splitting off its operations in Ireland into a separate organization. Oxfam GB continued to maintain oversight over the group's operations in Scotland and Wales.

Donations and government grants and subsidiaries had come to form the majority of Oxfam's total income into the mid-first decade of the 2000s, roughly 53 percent of the group's £310.5 million income in 2006. Yet the group's retail operations remained important both for their revenues, accounting for some 20 percent of total income, and especially for their role in raising and maintaining public awareness for Oxfam and its various campaigns. Into the middle of the first decade of the 2000s, Oxfam expanded its retail presence in two different directions. In the first, it formed a partnership with abebooks.co.uk, the world's leading online rare books retailer, to sell its own books online. This effort was followed in 2004 with the opening of the group's first Progresso coffee shop, featuring fair-trade coffee in a bid to rival coffee retailers such as Starbucks. By 2007, the company had established plans to open as many as 20 Progresso coffee shops throughout the United Kingdom. By then, Oxfam had established itself as one of the world's largest and most respected relief organizations.

M. L. Cohen

PRINCIPAL COMPETITORS

Unicef; International Red Cross; CARE; Greenpeace International; International Medical Corps; Inter-national Rescue Committee; Médecins Sans Frontières/Doctors Without Borders.

FURTHER READING

Algie, Matthew, "Oxfam to Launch Fair Trade Coffee Shops," *just-food.com,* May 13, 2004.

Black, Maggie, *A Cause for Our Times: Oxfam the First 50 Years,* Oxford: Oxfam GB, 1992.

————, "The End of Total War," *New Internationalist,* February 1992.

Coulter, Paddy, "Jim Howard: Oxfam's Mr Fixit in the World's Troublespots," *Guardian,* May 29, 2003, p. 25.

Danby, Sandra, "From All Good Bookshops," *Bookseller,* July 2, 2005, p. 22.

"Oxfam Anal Main Text," *Estates Gazette,* May 21, 2005.

"Oxfam GB Executing 30 Mln Pound Dev't Works," *Africa News Service,* November 1, 2006.

"Oxfam Invites Users to Build a Campaign," *Revolution,* December 31, 2006, p. 9.

"Oxfam Marketing Team Falls out over Charity's Fundraising Strategy," *Marketing Week,* October 20, 2005, p. 3.

"Oxfam Overhauls Image of Stores," *PR Week,* July 9, 2004, p. 8.

"Oxfam UK Holds Pitch for Youth Initiatives Brief," *Marketing,* February 21, 2007, p. 6.

Pacific Internet Limited

———————————■———————————

89B Science Park Drive
The Rutherford 118261
Singapore
Telephone: (+65) 6872 0322
Fax: (+65) 6872 6334
Web site: http://www.pacific.net.sg

Public Company
Incorporated: 1991 as TechnologyNet
Employees: 1,066
Sales: SGD 188.8 million ($123.1 million) (2006)
Stock Exchanges: NASDAQ
Ticker Symbol: PCNTF
NAIC: 518111 Internet Service Providers

■ ■ ■

Pacific Internet Limited (PacNet) is one of the Asian region's leading independent Internet service providers (ISPs). The Singapore-based company offers wireless, fixed line, and broadband Internet access to both corporate and consumer markets, as well as a range of Internet-based services, such as e-mail and e-mail security, web site hosting, backup, and international roaming. Pacific Internet is also a leading provider of content, offering online travel services through its Safe2Travel subsidiary; VoIP telephony services, including PacNet Vocal, through a partnership with Skype; online financial services through partner banks; as well as its PacFusion site, one of the most popular sites in Singapore. While Pacific Internet got its start in Singapore, the company has long been one of the most

international of the region's ISPs, extending its Internet access services to Hong Kong, Thailand, Australia, the Philippines, Malaysia, and, since 2006, the mainland Chinese market as well. Founded as a private university network in 1991, PacNet was the first Asian ISP to list its shares on the NASDAQ. Temasek Holdings, a Singapore government investment vehicle, indirectly controls one-third of PacNet's stock. In 2006, the company posted revenues of SGD 188.8 million ($123.1 million). The company is led by President and CEO Teck Moh Phey.

UNIVERSITY NETWORK ORIGINS IN 1991

Although Pacific Internet grew into one of the most international of the Asian-Pacific region's independent Internet service providers, its origins lay in the creation of a small in-house network for the National University of Singapore's research and development activities. Created in 1991, TechnologyNet, also known as TechNet, operated as a closed network for the university's academic community, under the guidance of the National Science and Technology Board of Singapore. TechNet was also granted one of only a few Internet access licenses awarded by the Singapore government during this time.

By the mid-1990s, the rise of the Internet, spurred on the by the creation of the World Wide Web graphical interface, clearly pointed the way of the future for the telecommunications market. A number of new players in Singapore became determined to enter this market, including the city state's telephone monopoly,

Singapore Telecommunications, and its cable television operator, StarHub, among others. The market for Internet services also attracted a number of the state's major corporations. Among them was conglomerate Sembawang Group, which, through its venture capital SembVentures (later SembCorp Ventures), established Sembawang Media to develop a number of Internet-based interests. SembVentures also targeted the ISP market directly, and in 1995 bought TechNet and its Internet access license. By September of that year, Sembawang Media had readied the launch of the state's first "telco-neutral" ISP, Pacific Internet Corporation Pte. Ltd. (PacNet).

PacNet quickly expanded its ambitions beyond Singapore, in part because of the market's limited consumer population and the presence of state-controlled incumbent Singapore Telecommunications, as well as the low initial Internet penetration rate in the country. The company also recognized an opportunity to establish itself as an early player in what promised to become a highly international market, especially in the Asian-Pacific region. In 1996, therefore, PacNet targeted the Hong Kong market, buying a 50.1 percent stake in Pacific Supernet Ltd., also held by Sembawang. PacNet later increased its holding in Pacific Supernet to 100 percent, at which time the Hong Kong operation was rebranded under Pacific Internet. Back at home, PacNet launched the country's first cybercafé, providing wireless Internet access at a site on Boat Quay in 1996.

PacNet next targeted the Philippines market, forming a joint venture with that country's Prime World Digital Systems, which had pioneered the Internet market in that country, in 1997. The following year, PacNet acquired a 40 percent stake in Prime World, which then changed its name to Pacific Internet Philippines. By the middle of the first decade of the 2000s, the Philippines unit had readopted the Prime World name, while PacNet had increased its equity stake to more than 53 percent.

In the meantime, interest in the Internet was building rapidly among Singapore's consumer and corporate markets. PacNet became a major beneficiary of this interest, and through 1998 the company's subscriber base grew by more than 75 percent. At the end of the year, PacNet boasted nearly 187,000 dial-up subscribers, representing nearly 40 percent of the total subscriber market. At the same time, success in both the Hong Kong and Philippines markets encouraged the company to target further international growth. PacNet's sights fell on the vast Indian market, launching negotiations with a local partner to enter the newly deregulated market there.

BUILDING AN INTERNATIONAL NETWORK IN 1999

Seeking funding for its expansion goals—which included plans to expand into Australia, China, South Korea, Indonesia, Taiwan, and elsewhere in the region—PacNet became the first Singapore ISP to list its shares on the NASDAQ in 1999. The move was meant to tap the international investment community's growing interest in the Asian telecommunications market in general, and the Internet sector in particular. As growth in the relatively mature U.S. market slowed, the Asian markets, expected to grow by more than 500 percent into the early 2000s, represented an extremely attractive market for investors.

The successful public offering, and a secondary offering just five months later, enabled PacNet to expand rapidly into the year 2000. The company launched its operations in India, forming a partnership with Thakral Brothers (Pte) Ltd. to extend its global roaming services to that market in May 1999, before launching full commercial Internet services there in 2000. By then, PacNet had also expanded into Australia, buying that country's Mira Networking in May 1999. That purchase was followed by the acquisition of another Australian Internet provider, Zip World, in June 1999. At the beginning of 2000, PacNet boosted its Australian presence again, purchasing Kralizec Pty Ltd. and its Zeta Internet ISP unit there. That company, originally formed in Sydney in 1985, had been one of the first in the country to launch commercial Internet services in 1994.

PacNet continued to build its Australian operations through 2000, notably through the acquisition of Hub Communications Pty. Ltd. in February 2000. That company, founded in 1995, provided Internet access services for the Brisbane area, and also operated a chain of Internet cafés in Brisbane. Following the launch of ADSL-based broadband services in Australia, PacNet added again to its holdings there, buying Newcastle-based Hunterlink Pty, the leading ISP in the Hunter Valley region.

At home, the Singapore company faced rising competition, notably with the entry of StarHub into the ISP market. Nonetheless, the company continued to

KEY DATES

1991: TechnologyNet (TechNet) is created as closed academic network for the National University of Singapore.

1995: Sembawang Group acquires TechNet and its Internet service license and relaunches it as commercial Internet service provider Pacific Internet (PacNet).

1996: Company completes its first international expansion, into Hong Kong.

1999: PacNet lists its shares on the NASDAQ.

2005: Company forms joint venture with Zhong Ren Telecom to launch integrated IP communications services in southern China.

2006: PacNet announces plan to establish data center to serve mainland Chinese market.

build strongly, and consistently won the *Computer World* award for "Best ISP in Singapore" and even the award for "Best Asian ISP." The company began rolling out its broadband services in Singapore and Hong Kong. In 2000, also, PacNet launched its own web portal, PacFusion, which developed into the most frequently visited site in Singapore by the end of the decade. The company had also been building up its range of content and services. In 2000, the company paid $5 million for an 85 percent stake in Internet travel services provider Safe and Mansfield. That business was redeveloped into the company's Safe2Travel web site. At the same time, PacNet formed a partnership with Standard Chartered Bank to provide online banking services. Other partnerships included deals with financial services group GohDirect, web-based e-mail services through Webmail.com, and online wine sales through WineSong.

LEADING ASIAN INDEPENDENT ISP FOR THE NEW CENTURY

PacNet extended its international reach again in 2000. The company formed a subsidiary in Thailand, Pacific Digiway Ltd., which in turn acquired a 49 percent stake in Bangkok-based ISP World Net & Services Co., which then adopted the Pacific Internet brand. PacNet's stake in that operation was later raised to 74 percent. Also in 2000, PacNet made preparations to enter the Malaysian market; the company commenced full-scale services there in 2002.

By the middle of 2000, PacNet counted more than 312,000 dial-up subscribers, and a steadily growing

number of broadband customers as well. The latter market became the hottest Internet growth market leading into the new century; at the beginning of 2001, PacNet had become the first in Singapore to launch unlimited Internet access via broadband. By the end of the year, the company had introduced wireless broadband services as well, and had created a partnership with Hutchison Max Telecom to provide Internet access to its Orange mobile telephone customers. The company also increasingly developed a range of services for the corporate market, such as the creation of a data center in Singapore in 2001, at a cost of SGD 5 million. The company also launched Smart-Lan services that year.

Pacific Internet's expansion drive nonetheless came at a cost. By 2001 the company's losses for the year neared $7 million on revenues of $76.4 million. Yet the company's losses proved temporary as the growth of the broadband market in particular helped it return to profitability by the end of 2002. In Singapore, PacNet extended its broadband reach into the cable television market. The company also began testing its Powerline service, in order to supply Internet access through the electrical utility network, primarily to remote regions with no telephone access. In 2005, the company teamed up with Internet-based telephone company Skype to provide VoIP services for its Singapore customers. Similarly, the company made a new acquisition in Australia, acquiring T3 Communications in 2005, in a move to strengthen its provision of bundled telephony and broadband services to the Australian small- and midsized business markets.

PacNet increasingly began targeting interests in the fast-growing mainland China market. The company had already begun to supply corporate Internet services to that market through its Hong Kong operations. In 2002, for example, the company launched BizVoice, providing IP-based communications services between Hong Kong-based companies and their mainland offices. The company also developed Chinese-language versions of its online gaming platforms.

By 2005, the company was ready to enter the mainland market directly, forming a 50-50 joint venture with Zhong Ren Telecom to develop and market an integrated IP-based communications service for the southern China market. By December 2006, the company had announced plans to expand its mainland presence with the launch of data center services there. Targeted at the corporate market, the company expected the new data center to serve as a bridge between its northern Chinese and Hong Kong operations, and the southern Chinese market.

By the beginning of 2007, PacNet had established itself as a leading telco-independent Internet group for the Asian-Pacific region. The company's early move into broadband access played an important part in its growth, and by the end of 2006 already accounted for more than 47 percent of total revenues. With an average penetration rate of just 10 percent throughout the Asian-Pacific region, and as low as just 4.5 percent in such major markets as India, Pacific Internet's international network strategy could look forward to strong growth in the years to come.

M. L. Cohen

PRINCIPAL SUBSIDIARIES

Hunterlink Pty Limited (Australia); Pacfusion Limited; Pacific Internet (Australia) Investment Pty. Limited; Pacific Internet (Australia) Pty. Limited; Pacific Internet (Hong Kong) Limited; Pacific Internet (Malaysia) Sdn. Bhd.; Pacific Internet Corporation (Hong Kong) Limited; Pacific Internet Corporation Pte Ltd.; Primeworld Digital Systems, Inc. (Philippines); T3 Communications Investment Partners Pty Ltd. (Australia); Zip World Pty Ltd. (Australia).

PRINCIPAL COMPETITORS

Singapore Telecommunications Ltd.; StarHub Ltd.

FURTHER READING

"Pacific Internet Bringing It Together," *Telecom Asia,* July 2000, p. 46.

"Pacific Internet Plots Regional Expansion," *TelecomWeb News Digest,* May 9, 2006.

"Pacific Internet Targets China," *TelecomWeb News Digest,* January 3, 2006.

"PacNet NetworkGuard Introduced by Pacific Internet," *Corporate IT Update,* November 13, 2006.

"PacNet to Become First Asian ISP on NASDAQ," *Network Briefing,* December 11, 1998.

"Reach and Expertise," *Telecom Asia,* July 2002, p. 31.

"Singapore: After Two Years of Losses, Pacific Internet Returns to the Black with a New Profit of $1.7 Million for 2002," *Telecom Asia,* March 2003, p. 14.

Zane, Ruth Suarez, "Asian ISP Continues Expansion, Despite Faltering Stock Prices," *ISP Business News,* February 19, 2001.

Paramount Resources Ltd.

———————— ■ ————————

4700 Bankers Hall West
888 3rd Street SW
Calgary, Alberta T2P 5C5
Canada
Telephone: (403) 290-3600
Fax: (403) 262-7994
Web site: http://www.paramountres.com

Public Company
Incorporated: 1978
Employees: 232
Sales: $312.6 million (2006)
Stock Exchanges: Toronto
Ticker Symbol: POU
NAIC: 211111 Crude Petroleum and Natural Gas
    Extraction; 213112 Support Activities for Oil and
    Gas Field Exploration

■ ■ ■

Calgary-based Paramount Resources Ltd. engages in exploration, development, processing, transportation, and marketing of natural gas and petroleum. Its core interests lie largely in western Canada. Over the course of more than 30 years, founder Clay Riddell has grown the company from a speculative enterprise to a competitive mid-sized energy producer.

MAPPING THE FUTURE

Clay Riddell started out in modest circumstances, as the son of a Winnipeg mail carrier. Summers during high school and college were spent mapping rock outcrop-

pings in northern Canada. Riddell graduated in 1959 from the University of Manitoba. His first job was with California Standard Co., now Chevron Corp., as a junior geologist. During much of the 1960s he searched for oil in Alberta and the Northwest Territories. At the end of the decade he struck out on his own.

In 1974, Riddell established Paramount Oil & Gas Ltd. By 1978 he was ready to take his aspirations public, as Paramount Resources Ltd. Selling 40 percent of the company, he raised $5 million. Shareholders, then, had to cultivate the skill of patience. "I once got a letter from a shareholder, well, sort of a letter—it was written on a brown paper bag. He told me I had the perfect formula for going broke," Riddell told *Canadian Business.* The company finally began production early in the 1980s. The first successful well was drilled in the Northwest Territories.

Economic conditions of the early 1980s presented challenges for small energy producers such as Paramount Resources. In 1982, the company's asset value was an estimated $80 million. As the company continued to develop natural gas interests in northeastern Alberta, the important U.S. market was headed toward a decline. Delays in bringing gas to market had already been detrimental to the company's cash flow. Riddell was not to be deterred. Despite internal and external pressures he stuck to his guns, concentrating on natural gas exploration through the 1980s and 1990s.

SHIFTING SANDS: 2000–02

The first half of 1999 oil prices shot upward, taking the stock of oil and gas companies along for the ride.

Grown to the rank of a midsized producer, Paramount Resources had already made Clay Riddell a fortune. "Considered a textbook company in terms of its operations," according to *Canadian Business,* Paramount was turning heads with a Northwest Territory gas find and a project in California. Still, all was not rosy. Barriers to growth had also cropped up.

Oil sands joint venture Gulf Canada Resources Ltd. succeeded, in early 2002, in shutting down natural gas production in an area of northern Alberta it hoped to develop. Paramount Resources was among the gas producers opposing the order geared toward maintaining the natural gas pressure level required to pump heavy oil known as bitumen. According to the *Globe and Mail,* the Alberta energy regulator found bitumen to be a "significant energy resource for the province" which warranted "consideration for future development." The Alberta Energy and Utilities Board hearing lasted 47 days and resulted in a total of 146 natural gas wells ceasing production.

Better news came as 2000 wound down. Cold weather drove North American natural gas prices to record highs, breaking the $6 per million British thermal unit mark. By comparison, natural gas had sold for less than $3 in late 1999 and for $2 in late 1998. "We're sure excited about the prices we're seeing," COO Jim Riddell told the *Globe and Mail* in November 2000. Analysts expected prices to settle back into the $4 range as temperatures moderated and producers cranked up production in response to demand. Crude oil prices topped $35.70 per barrel on October 12, spiking, for a time, energy stocks. Yet likewise, oil prices were expected to drop back, to the $25 per barrel range.

Big U.S. and Canadian energy producers snapped up midsized Canadian independents to fuel their own growth beginning about midway through 2000 and into early 2001. Energy trusts also got into the act, one made more attractive by reduced premiums on the sector's stocks, the *Globe and Mail* reported. Canadian intermediates ranged from a market value of $300 million to roughly $1 billion. Producers with equity value exceeding $1.5 billion filled out the top echelon. The smaller junior producers, also trading at a reduced multiple, found themselves under the gun as well. Paramount, valued at $940 million, was sheltered by Riddell's controlling interest.

Riddell had blended four elements into a formula for success, according to the *National Post.* "He built his billion-dollar company from scratch in 23 years through a combination of drilling in remote regions, cash flow, bank debt, and when things got tough, asset sales to avoid dilution through share offerings." Riddell's emphasis on natural gas set him and Paramount Resources apart from other energy producers, and the strategy produced its own set of risks and opportunities. Natural gas, generating relatively fewer harmful emissions than other fuels, was predicted by some as a potential beneficiary of stricter environmental laws, driving up demand in the future. Paramount, meanwhile, had to hedge against price volatility. Its natural gas fields in Alberta and the Northwest Territories made up about 94 percent of its assets.

As far as the industry's consolidation trend was concerned, Riddell predicted that as companies grew larger, they would abandon their smallest, riskiest projects, providing opportunities for start-ups.

By the end of 2001, Riddell had built a fortune valued around $500 million, according to *Canadian Business.* Outside the energy business, Riddell's other interests included thoroughbred horses and an upscale Calgary restaurant.

Riddell owned 48.5 percent of Paramount Resources, which generated $391.5 million in revenue during 2000. More than 90 percent was from natural gas sales. Even though Paramount ranked among Canada's top gas exploration companies and was one of the first to concentrate its efforts in that energy sector, it remained dependent on high gas prices and strong demand to stay ahead of the curve.

In 2002, a Paramount Resources-led group of Canadian producers finally received compensation for a mandated shut down of gas wells adjacent to the northern Alberta oil sands deposits. Initially denied claims of an estimated $200 million in annual revenue losses, the group was granted CAD 85 million from the Alberta government. In 2001, Conoco had bought Gulf Canada, developer of the $1.3 billion oil sands project, and played a role in the deal, according to the *Oil Daily.* Paramount Resources, meanwhile, had used the detailed bitumen maps it developed to support its stance in the conflict to guide acquisition of oil sands leases of its own.

KEY DATES

1969: Geologist Clay Riddell acts on his entrepreneurial instincts.
1978: Riddell sells 40 percent of his company in a public offering.
2003: Company spins off Paramount Energy Trust.
2005: Company creates Trilogy Energy Trust:
2007: MGM Energy Corp. is created to explore Arctic.

NEW TACTICS: 2003–07

In February 2003, Paramount Resources spun off northeast Alberta natural gas properties into Paramount Energy Trust. Shareholders of the trust would receive the bulk of its cash flow. The shift of assets into such investment vehicles was a trend among Canadian oil and gas concerns, according to the *Daily Oil*. While independent oil firms funneled their profits into exploration, a trust looked toward low-risk drilling and acquisitions to keep wells flowing.

As a side note, Riddell expanded his interests into another arena, gaining part ownership of the Calgary Flames during the year. Corporate makeover plans continued into 2004, and the market approved. Paramount Resources' stock price jumped in September when the board authorized examination of restructuring options to increase shareholder value, according to the *National Post*. Announcement of public and private equity financings followed in October. The pair of placements would bring in CAD 116.5 million.

In February 2005, the company set a date for a shareholder vote on another spinoff. The *Globe and Mail* reported that the action would essentially divide the company in half, about 25,000 barrels of oil equivalent a day going to the trust and about 20,000 remaining in Paramount.

The strong oil sector increased Clay Riddell's net worth by more than 88 percent in 2005. At CAD 2.35 billion Riddell climbed to 11th place, up from the 23rd spot, on the *Canadian Business* list of the country's wealthiest citizens.

Trilogy Energy Trust, holding assets in central Alberta, had been spun out in 2005 and headed by Clay Riddell's son Jim. Paramount Resources' remaining conventional asset production climbed an average of 18 percent during the year, according to the annual report. Other highlights included new oil and gas discoveries and promising coal methane production development.

Additionally, Paramount Resources received a positive oil sands interest evaluation regarding potential recoverable bitumen.

As for the energy industry, crude oil prices recorded all-time highs. The numbers were driven in part by hurricane damage on the U.S. Gulf Coast. In contrast, North America's unprecedented warm weather in early 2006 had a dampening effect on gas prices.

With oil price predictions ranging from $55 to $75 a barrel and natural gas prices in a slump, the oil sands took on increasing significance for the Canadian economy, the *National Post* observed in March 2006. The country's biggest oil sands player was Canadian Natural Resources Ltd. Globally, OPEC members and Russia ranked as the top oil exporters. In either case, governments controlled output or owned the oil companies. On the buy side of the market, China, the United States, and Europe drove demand.

In January 2007 Paramount created MGM Energy Corp., spinning out far northern exploratory properties. Henry Sykes, former Conoco Phillips in Canada president, was tapped to lead the company, and Bob Peterson, former Imperial Oil Ltd. CEO, joined the board. Imperial spearheaded a drive to build the Mackenzie natural gas pipeline reaching into the Arctic. MGM would focus its attention on exploring and developing production in the region.

Riddell was betting on a repeat of earlier success with drilling in locations eschewed by other producers. Large companies had dropped out of the race to develop the region in response to pipeline problems, leaving room for smaller players. MGM planned to add as many interests as possible to its existing assets in the central Mackenzie Valley.

Kathleen Peippo

PRINCIPAL COMPETITORS

Canadian Natural Resources Limited; EnCana Corporation; Penn West Energy Trust.

FURTHER READING

Bell, Andrew, "Natural Gas Prices Hit Record Highs," *Globe and Mail*, November 15, 2000, p. B19.

Cattaneo, Claudia, "A 75th Birthday Gift for Pioneer?" *National Post*, January 16, 2007, p. FP2.

Critchley, Barry, "If It Worked the First Time ... : Paramount Says It's Going to Convert to a Trust—Again," *National Post*, February 7, 2005, p. FP4.

Ebner, Dave, "Paramount Resources Spins Off Energy Trust," *Globe and Mail*, December 14, 2004, p. B10.

Francis, Diane, "Canada Attractive for Oil Investors: Calgary Is As Important As Houston in Oilpatch," *National Post,* March 21, 2006, p. FP2.

————, "Happiness Is Never Giving Up Control: Oilpatch Takeovers Don't Worry Paramount's Riddell," *National Post,* June 21, 2001, p. C3.

Jang, Brent, "Canadian Oil Barons Hear a Familiar Tune: Another One Bites the Dust," *Globe and Mail,* February 10, 2001, p. B9.

————, "Gulf Canada Oil Sands Project Approved," *Globe and Mail,* April 4, 2000, p. B6.

Kelly, Patrick, "Canada's Rich Get Richer, Especially in the Oil Patch," *National Post,* December 6, 2005, p. A3.

Magnan, Michelle, "Clay Riddell," *Canadian Business,* February 12, 2007, p. 86.

McCallum, Anthony, "Market Perspective: Small Petroleum Firms See Strong Performance," *Globe and Mail,* December 9, 1982, p. B17.

"Paramount Considers Options," *Oil Daily,* September 29, 2004.

"Paramount Resources Ltd.," *Canadian Corporate News,* March 19, 2007.

"Producers Paid to End Dispute," *Oil Daily,* March 1, 2002.

Verburg, Peter, "Mr. Modesty," *Canadian Business,* December 2001.

————, "Party On!" *Canadian Business,* August 27, 1999, pp. 21+.

Perkins Foods Holdings Ltd.

Regus House, Victory Way
Admirals Park, Crossways
Dartford, Kent DA2 6AG
United Kingdom
Telephone: (+44 0) 1322 303068
Fax: (+44 0) 1322 303086
Web site: http://www.perkinsfoods.co.uk

Private Company
Incorporated: 1948 as John Perkins (Meat Packers) Ltd.
Employees: 2,978
Sales: £400 million ($680 million) (2006 est.)
NAIC: 311612 Meat Processed from Carcasses; 311412
Frozen Specialty Food Manufacturing

■ ■ ■

Perkins Foods Holdings Ltd. is one of the United Kingdom's leading holding companies focused on the fresh, chilled, and convenience foods segments. The Dartford, Kent-based company operates through two main divisions: UK Fresh Division and European Convenience Division. The UK Fresh Division, based primarily on Fresh-Pak Chilled Foods Ltd., is the company's largest division. Fresh-Pak, founded in the 1980s and acquired by Perkins in the mid-1990s, is one of the United Kingdom's largest suppliers of chilled prepared foods, with a range including sandwich fillers, mayonnaise, snack salads, dips, and hard-boiled eggs. The European Convenience Division, largely focused on the Luxembourg and French markets, includes Fraisnor SA in France, and Tavola in Luxembourg, among others.

A third Perkins division, the Dutch Convenience Division, includes Bakker Lekkerkerk, Brink Pluimveeprodukten, and VDM, in the Netherlands. Formerly a public company, Perkins was taken private in a management buyout backed by ABN-AMRO; in the middle of the first decade of the 2000s, Perkins has begun to sell a number of its holdings, including its U.K.-based Chilled Foods Division and its Netherlands-based meats and meat products subsidiary Enkco BV, both sold to Cranswick Plc in 2005, and Le Magicien Vert, in France, sold to Delpeyrat in 2006. These sales were made in order to test the waters for a possible breakup of the group in the second half of the decade. Perkins Foods Holdings is led by Chairman Allan Price.

BUTCHER BEGINNINGS IN 1948

Before emerging as one of a number of rapidly growing food-based holdings companies in the late 1980s, Perkins originated as a small butcher company, founded by John Perkins in 1948. That company, John Perkins (Meat Packers) Ltd., remained focused on the butcher meats market for the next several decades, evolving into a prominent supermarket supplier by the mid-1980s. In 1985, John Perkins Meats went public, listing its stock on the London Stock Exchange's Unlisted Securities Market (USM). That listing, however, was described as a near flop, and only the last-minute decision of Atlanta Securities Investment, the investment division of the Grovebell group run by British-Asian entrepreneur Vasant Advani to subscribe to the entire share offering, saved the listing.

The share purchase initially appeared to be part of

KEY DATES

1948: John Perkins (Meat Packers) Ltd. is established.

1985: Perkins goes public on the London Stock Exchange's Unlisted Securities Market.

1987: Perkins is acquired through management buy-out led by former Ross Foods executives Michael Davies and Howard Phillips, who launch company on acquisition drive.

1989: Sell-off of original John Perkins meat business occurs as company focuses on frozen and chilled prepared foods and fresh produce.

1998: Company sells fresh produce and expands frozen and chilled foods operations.

2000: Company goes private in management buyout backed by ABN-AMRO.

2006: Perkins completes sale of various divisions as part of possible larger breakup.

Advani's diversification plans for Brookbell, which at the time had been making a drive to enter the medical equipment manufacturing sector. By 1987, however, Perkins, and especially its USM listing, became a target of interest for two former Ross Foods executives, Michael Davies and Howard Phillips, who took over the company by buying out the shares still held by the Perkins family. Davies became chairman of the company, while Phillips took on the managing director position.

Davies and Phillips immediately set Perkins on a new course, essentially using the company, and especially its public listing, to embark on a stream of acquisitions. As such, Perkins became part of an ongoing trend in the British and European food sector at the end of the 1980s and into the early 1990s. The run-up to the lowering of trade barriers among European Union members in 1992 had sparked a widespread consolidation effort among European food companies. At the same time, dramatic changes were occurring within the food industry. The prepared foods segment had begun to grow strongly in the late 1970s and through the 1980s, in part because of the large-scale arrival of women into the workforce. With less time to cook, consumers turned to the growing list of prepared foods on offer. Manufacturers encouraged this trend, spending massively on advertising, which played an important role in convincing consumers that, indeed, they did not have enough time to cook a proper meal for themselves. The higher value-added nature of prepared foods, and

the potential for further reducing costs and driving up profit margins through the inclusion of a growing list of additives and food substitutes, represented billions of future profits for the food industry.

Perkins embarked on a large-scale acquisition drive into the 1990s. Along the way, the company shed the original John Perkins (Meat Packers) operation, which was spun off into a management buyout in 1989. Between 1987 and 1991, Perkins completed an impressive list of 25 acquisitions, spending more than £154 million, compared to the company's sales of less than £22 million in 1987.

Perkins targeted two primary areas for its initial growth phase. On the one hand, the company entered the booming market for "out of season" fruits and vegetables, largely through its acquisition of a Dutch specialist in this area, Hage BV, in 1989. That company dealt directly with the Netherlands' army of greenhouse growers, but also negotiated for exclusive supply contracts for fruits and vegetables from around the world. Far larger than Perkins itself, the Hage acquisition helped transform Perkins into one of the fastest-growing of the new food products consolidators in the United Kingdom at the beginning of the 1990s.

The entry into the Netherlands formed part of the group's larger objectives of extending its operations outside of the United Kingdom and establishing itself as a North European foods group. Perkins continued to seek further acquisitions in the Netherlands, and into the early 1990s targeted a new area, mushrooms, through the purchases of Champifri, Champex, and Holland Champignons, which operated in the freezing and chilling; distribution; and canning segments, respectively.

Perkins other major target market was for value-added convenience food products. For this, the company centered on both the chilled and frozen foods categories. Again, Perkins' interest led it to a series of international acquisitions, including Bakker Lekkerberk, a frozen fish fillet specialist, and Van der Made, a specialist in prepared frozen potato meals, both in 1989, and Enkco BV, in 1991, in the Netherlands. Other acquisitions of the period included Peppino's Pizza and G&K Potato in Germany, Luxembourg's Cogel, a pasta dish producer and distributor primarily active in France, and the United Kingdom's Anchor Seafoods, Studleigh-Royd, and sausages specialist Fellside Foods, among many others.

The company's acquisition drive helped boost the company's total sales past £133 million by 1989 and again to nearly £200 million by the end of 1990. If fresh foods, led by the Hage division, had been the company's largest operation at the end of the 1980s, in the early 1990s frozen foods emerged as the company's primary growth driver. By the end of 1991, growth at this division especially helped push the group's total revenues past £260 million.

Through the first half of the decade, however, Perkins suffered from a general backlash against the United Kingdom's large number of "growth-by-acquisition" companies. Like Perkins, these companies had begun as small operations using acquisitions to fuel larger ambitions. Into the early 1990s, as the British and European economies slid into an extended recession, a large number of these companies had collapsed. Among the surviving companies, many found their profits hammered. In the case of Perkins, which was considered to have more successfully structured its acquisition plan than its rivals, profit growth largely stagnated into the middle of the decade. As a result, the investment community turned against the company. Throughout much of the rest of the decade, the company's share price remained consistently undervalued.

BREAKING UP IN PRIVATE

Perkins' acquisition effort slowed considerably through the mid-1990s, as the company instead focused on consolidating its operations. Through this period, Perkins narrowed its range of operations around a core of Frozen Foods, Chilled Foods, and Fresh Fruits and Vegetables. The company's attempt to enter the mushroom market had been less than successful, and these operations were reorganized as noncore business. By 1996, the company had also shed its shellfish businesses as well.

As part of its emergence as a matured food products group, Perkins began seeking synergies among its various operations. The company's Bakker and Enkco divisions, both in Holland and focused on similar product categories but differentiated end markets, began to coordinate their operations during the second half of the 1990s. The company's Cogel distribution operation, based in Luxembourg, which already oversaw its Tavola branded pasta production operations, took over distribution of the popular German Peppino brand. As a result, Peppino was able to make rapid inroads into the French market as well. At the same time, the Tavola brand also served as a distribution vehicle for the production of another Perkins holding, VDM in the Netherlands, which specialized in the production of stir-fry ready meals. Similarly, Perkins' G&K operations in Germany launched other products in the VDM into the German market. By 1998, the company's sales topped £388 million.

Into the late 1990s, as the European economy once again entered a growth phase, Perkins began to seek new expansion opportunities. The growth of the company's frozen and chilled foods operations, and the relatively poor growth at its fresh produce operation, encouraged the company to exit that business. In 1998, the company agreed to sell that division to Greenery International for £123 million. Instead, Perkins invested an initial £9.7 million in the acquisition of Fresh-Pak Chilled Foods, based in Leicestershire, in England. That company, originally founded as Fresh-Pak Eggs in the early 1980s, had evolved into a major producer of sandwich fills, snack salads, and dips.

That acquisition signaled the launch of a new acquisition drive by the company. Between 1999 and 2000, the company acquired several more companies, including France's Traditions d'Asie and Le Magicien Vert, both ethnic foods specialists; Fraisnor, a producer of chilled pasta meals, also based in France; a stake in British ethnic food group Mrs Lam's; the Dutch poultry products group Brink Pluimveeprodukten Holking BV; and Britain's Lenders Foods Ltd., which produced stir-fry ready meals and sauces. These acquisitions helped rebuild the company's revenues after the sell-off of its product division, with sales nearing £375 million.

Despite its strongly focused growth strategy, Perkins not only remained hampered by the investment community's mistrust of midsized food stocks, its shares remained undervalued, placing it at the bottom of the list, despite a stronger performance than many of its rivals. The company's low share price soon positioned Perkins as a potential takeover target. By 2000, the company had been approached by Irish foods group, Greencore. The two sides were unable to agree on a selling price, however.

In frustration, then Perkins Chief Executive Ian Blackburn declared to the *Financial Times:* "The stock market is there to provide capital to enable businesses to grow. Our business has grown substantially over the past three years, but our market value has come down." In the end, Blackburn and other Perkins executives led a new management buyout, valued at £230 million, backed by Dutch banking giant ABN-AMRO, in December 2000.

Through the first half of the decade, Perkins continued to invest in its ongoing operations. In 2003, for example, the company spent £7.5 million on the construction of a new factory for its U.K.-based fresh foods operations, under the Fresh-Pak Chilled Foods subsidiary. Yet, as it approached mid-decade, the company, and especially ABN-AMRO, appeared to be seeking to cash in on the buyout investment. In 2004, the company announced its decision to put up for sale its U.K.-based Chilled Foods division, in part to test the water for a further breakup of the group's holdings.

The Chilled Foods division was sold to rival U.K. foods group Cranswick in 2005. The company continued to streamline its holdings, and in March 2006 announced the sale of the Le Magicien Vert ethnic foods operation to French foie gras group Delpeyrat. By the end of that year, the company had completed the sale of its Enkco BV operations in the Netherlands, as well, again to Cranswick. While the company regrouped around a new core featuring its Fresh-Pak business, the future existence of a Perkins Foods Holdings had increasingly become doubtful.

M. L. Cohen

PRINCIPAL SUBSIDIARIES

Bakker Lekkerkerk BV (Netherlands); Brindélices (France); Brink Pluimveeprodukten BV (Netherlands); Deli-Fresh Chilled Foods Limited; Fraisnor SA (France); Fresh-Pak Chilled Foods Limited; Le Gourmet Beaujolais (France); Perkins Foods France; Perkins Foods Luxembourg sa; Perkins Frozen Foods International bv (Netherlands); Tavola (Luxembourg); VDM (Netherlands).

PRINCIPAL COMPETITORS

Unilever; Grampian Country Food Group Ltd.; Brake Brothers Ltd.; Northern Foods PLC; Uniq PLC; Bernard Matthews Ltd.; Cranswick PLC; Farmfoods Ltd.; Kerry Foods Ltd.; Tulip Ltd.; Warburtons Ltd.; Roach Foods Ltd.; Prize Foods Group Ltd.

FURTHER READING

"ABN Eats Up Perkins," *European Venture Capital Journal,* February 2001, p. 77.

Bawden, Tom, "Amro Puts Perkins Division on Sale to Test the Water," *Times,* October 20, 2004, p. 44.

"Cranswick Acquired Perkins Chilled Foods," *Grocer,* August 5, 2006, p. 31.

"Making an Ethnic Meal of It," *F&CF Europe,* September 2002, p. 10.

Murray-West, Rosie, "Managers to Take Perkins Private," *Daily Telegraph,* December 19, 2000.

"Perkins Foods Invests £7.5m in New Barnsley Site," *Food Trade Review,* October 2003, p. 607.

"Perkins' £184.5m Deal," *Birmingham Post,* December 19, 2000, p. 26.

"Perkins Strong on Acquisitions," *Eurofood,* March 16, 2000.

"Perkins Takes Axe to Its Cost Base," *Grocer,* July 21, 2001, p. 4.

Todd, Stuart, "Delpeyrat Acquires Perkins Foods Subsidiary," *just-food.com,* March 1, 2006.

"Tough Trading Condition in the Market for Burgers and Ribs Are Blamed by Processor Perkins Frozen Foods' Management As the Company Prepares to Close Its Factory at Penrith in Cumbria," *Grocer,* November 24, 2001, p. 21.

PILKINGTON
Pilkington Group Limited

Prescot Road
St. Helens, Merseyside WA10 3TT
United Kingdom
Telephone: (+44 1744) 28882
Fax: (+44 1744) 692660
Web site: http://www.pilkington.com

Wholly Owned Subsidiary of Nippon Sheet Glass
Company, Limited
Founded: 1826 as The St. Helens Crown Glass
Company
Incorporated: 1894 as Pilkington Brothers Limited
Employees: 23,600
Sales: £2.58 billion ($4.49 billion) (2006)
NAIC: 327211 Flat Glass Manufacturing

■■■

Pilkington Group Limited is one of the largest glass-makers in the world, specializing in flat glass principally for the automotive and building products industries with sales about equally divided between the two. Approximately 64 percent of Pilkington's sales originate in Europe, 22 percent in North America, and around 7 percent each in South America and the Asia-Pacific region. The company operates 26 float glass plants in 13 countries—Finland, France, Italy, Germany, Poland, Russia, Sweden, the United Kingdom, the United States, Argentina, Brazil, Chile, and Australia—and has interests in 12 more located in Italy, Spain, Brazil, Mexico, and China. Pilkington invented the float glass process, which is the standard method for producing

high-quality flat glass. Pilkington's rise to international preeminence occurred during the mid- to late 20th century. The firm's long history of independence ended in June 2006 when it was acquired by Nippon Sheet Glass Company, Limited, and it has since operated as a wholly owned subsidiary of the Japanese firm.

19TH-CENTURY ROOTS: BECOMING THE U.K. GLASS LEADER

The St. Helens Crown Glass Company, Pilkington's original name, was formed in 1826 at St. Helens, then a small town in northwestern England (near Liverpool) at the heart of a coal-mining area of about 10,000 people. Cheap coal had already attracted a number of furnace industries, including glass. Of the six local men who became partners in the new crown, or window, glass business, two already owned a glassworks in the district. One of the others, the son of a leading coal owner in the area, became the new company's bookkeeper and was joined by the local solicitor. The other two, originally brought in only for their capital, were William Pilkington, son of a local doctor who had done well in distilling, and his brother-in-law Peter Greenall, who was in charge of the local brewery. When the two technical men had to withdraw from the glass-making venture because of an attempt to evade paying excise duty on their flint glass, William Pilkington—who had been apprenticed to a Liverpool distiller, ran the family distillery, and was already considered an astute business-man—was called in to take charge. William's elder brother, Richard Pilkington, was brought in when it was discovered that the bookkeeping partner was not keeping the books properly. The local solicitor chose this critical moment to withdraw from the venture. Thus, almost by accident, the Pilkington brothers found themselves landed with a tiny, struggling glassworks, much less profitable than the family distillery.

Skilled glassblowers, drawn mainly from Dumbarton, Scotland, where a glass manufacturer had gone bankrupt, provided the necessary technical expertise, and Peter Greenall, a partner in Parr's Bank at Warrington, saw to it that the struggling young business (which was renamed Greenall & Pilkington in 1929) received an overdraft far larger than its size warranted. William Pilkington, as salesman, traveled through Great Britain and Ireland seeking orders while his brother stayed at home and looked after the works and office. Business grew with the increasing demand for glass for the many new houses being built. A second furnace was built in 1834 and a third in 1835. Peter Greenall, who became a member of Parliament in 1841, remained an important, but silent, partner in the business, until his death in 1845, when the firm became Pilkington Brothers (PB).

Once the company was in operation, progress was determined partly by a willingness to accept technical change and partly by the initiative and drive of the new generations. The founders each had six sons, and two from each side became partners.

The taxation system for glass manufacturers favored crown glass against its more efficiently produced rival, sheet glass. PB's willingness to venture into sheet glass in the early 1840s stood it in good stead a few years later when the duties on glass were removed. Cheaper sheet glass from continental Europe, and especially from Belgium, drove out of business those U.K. manufacturers who had clung to crown glass. By the 1850s there were only three U.K. survivors: Chance Brothers of Smethwick near Birmingham; James Hartley & Son of Sunderland in the northeast, which had previously been the center of the industry in the United Kingdom; and PB, which thrived in this more competitive climate. Between 1849 and 1854 PB's labor force rose sharply from 450 to 1,350.

The second generation, whose influence began to make itself felt from the later 1860s as the founders retired, embarked upon a vigorous export drive. In the early 1870s, PB surpassed its two remaining U.K. rivals by replacing pot furnaces, which necessitated 24-hour intervals between weeklong glass-making campaigns while the pots were recharged and reheated, with Siemens's glass-making tanks, which allowed continuous round-the-clock production and much more cost-effective eight-hour shifts. PB also chose the very profitable years of the early 1870s to build a new factory for the manufacture of polished plate glass, used in larger windows and mirrors. Intensive foreign competition soon drove the other longer-established U.K. plate glass manufacturers out of business, but PB survived, because it alone had another profitable product to sustain it. In 1903 it emerged as the sole U.K. producer of plate glass. By then Hartley & Son had gone out of business and Chance Brothers, which had failed in its attempt to enter plate glass manufacturing and had delayed in introducing tank furnaces for sheet, was very much a runner-up. PB had emerged as the undisputed leader in flat glass manufacture in the United Kingdom, though it was still subject to continued fierce competition from European producers. Between 1874 and 1894 the firm's capital had grown more than ninefold, from £150,000 to £1.4 million. In 1894 the business was then made a private limited company, Pilkington Brothers Limited, with £800,000 in ordinary shares and £600,000 in 5 percent debentures. There were then ten family shareholders, three of the four senior partners having each brought in two of their sons.

Even during the hard years between 1874 and 1896, PB managed to flourish. Despite reinvestment of £1.25 million, £725,000 was distributed among the family. Between 1894 and 1914, the company did even better: nearly £3 million was reinvested and approximately £2.3 million distributed. The four Pilkingtons of the second generation reaped the financial rewards of their success on a scale far greater than did their fathers.

EARLY 20TH CENTURY: SAVING ITSELF FROM NEAR DISASTER

The third generation, which took over in the Edwardian period, did not match its predecessors' impressive performance. This may have been due to unexpected family losses. One son was killed in the Boer War (1899–1902). Another died of tuberculosis, and his twin brother, Austin Pilkington, who was himself an able manager, fell ill with tuberculosis in 1907 and, in a last attempt to save his life, was sent from the smoke and chemical fumes of St. Helens to live in the dry, thin air

KEY DATES

1826: The St. Helens Crown Glass Company is formed at St. Helens, England, to make window glass.

1829: Company is renamed Greenall & Pilkington.

1849: Company is renamed Pilkington Brothers.

1894: Company is incorporated as Pilkington Brothers Limited.

1903: Pilkington emerges as the sole U.K. producer of plate glass.

1936: An agreement is reached with Chance Brothers whereby Pilkington will buy its old rival over a number of years.

1952: Pilkington completes its acquisition of Chance; Alastair Pilkington invents the revolutionary float glass process.

1967: Pilkington stops making polished plate glass.

1970: Company goes public.

1980: Majority stake in Flachglas AG, the leading German flat glass maker, is acquired.

1985: Company changes its name to Pilkington Brothers plc.

1986: The glass-making interests of Libbey-Owens-Ford are acquired; company fends off a hostile takeover attempt by U.K. conglomerate BTR.

1987: Revlon's Barnes-Hind and Coburn Vision Care companies are acquired; company is renamed Pilkington plc.

1992: Roger Leverton becomes the first outsider named Pilkington chief executive; company expands into Eastern Europe for the first time with two investments in Polish ventures.

1993: The glass processing and distribution business of Heywood Williams is acquired; company acquires 50 percent of Societa Italiana Vetro SpA (SIV), the Italian state-owned glass-maker; heightened competition, economic recession, and an ill-conceived diversification lead the company to post a bottom-line loss.

1995: Pilkington gains full control of SIV; the company begins restructuring its operations into three business lines: automotive products, building products, and technical glass products.

1996: The divestment of Pilkington Visioncare is completed.

1997: Leverton is ousted by a board frustrated by the slow pace of restructuring; Paolo Scaroni is appointed as the new chief executive and begins a massive restructuring.

2006: Nippon Sheet Glass Company, Limited (NSG) acquires Pilkington for £2.2 billion ($4.1 billion), making the renamed Pilkington Group Limited a wholly owned subsidiary of NSG.

of Colorado, where he recovered. Another son, who became company chairman in 1914, died in 1921 at the age of 50, and at about the same time another decided to retire, mainly on grounds of ill health, at the age of 42. In the 1920s the main responsibility for running the company and earning profits upon which the growing number of nonexecutive family members depended, fell to the fully recovered Austin Pilkington, together with his younger brother Cecil, a natural sciences graduate from Oxford who became the firm's technical director. They were joined by Edward Cozens-Hardy (Lord Cozens-Hardy after his elder brother's death in 1924), formerly a partner in the London electrical engineering consultancy of O'Gorman and Cozens-Hardy, whose sister, Hope, had married Austin Pilkington. Cozens-Hardy had moved north and taken Austin Pilkington's place at PB in 1908, but had stayed on after his brother-in-law's return.

Just before World War I, this weakened third generation made two decisions that were to lead to much subsequent trouble. Having moved into the continuous melting of sheet glass in the 1870s, it made the mistake of opting for drawn cylinder machinery. This machinery replaced glassblowers but not the flatteners who had to reheat the cylinders and slit them open in order to produce the panes of glass. The large cylinders blown by machine could be made only one at a time. Instead the company should have opted for either the Libbey-Owens-Ford (LOF) or the Fourcault process, which drew the sheet of glass directly from the tank. Although these flat drawn processes were still being developed, preference for the compromise deprived PB of what was soon to prove the better alternative and nearly caused it to abandon sheet glass manufacture altogether during the 1920s. The decision also involved PB in a disastrous sheet glass venture in Canada in order to protect its drawn cylinder process rights. Second, having sensibly acquired, as a defense against European competitors, an interest in a small plate glassworks at Maubeuge in northern France in the 1890s, it unwisely decided to put down a second plate glassworks in the United Kingdom near the east coast, fearing that European competitors might establish their own factories on British soil if it did not do so. This factory, decided upon just before World War I, was built near Doncaster at great cost during the postwar boom. It swallowed up not only many of the vast reserves accumulated before and during that war but also £1 million of new capital, which had to be raised from the family in 1920.

PB saved itself by taking a world lead in plate glass manufacture at St. Helens. In the early 1920s, in collaboration with the Ford Motor Company of Detroit, it developed a new process that enabled a roughly cast ribbon to be cast continuously by pouring the molten glass out of the tank, instead of having to be ladled from pots to form a single plate of glass at a time, each side of which had to be ground and polished separately. Associated with the continuous flowing of the glass ribbon was a long series of grinding and polishing heads under which the ribbon was passed to produce the high-quality glass with more perfect parallel surfaces than had previously been possible. It was this extraordinarily costly process that float glass was to replace, but, being to a large degree continuous—a twin grinder was developed that ground both sides of the ribbon simultaneously, but not a twin polisher—it was less costly than the intermittent processes it replaced. Such high-quality polished plate glass, being thicker than the sheet glass then made, and more lustrous, commanded high prices that would not only cover the costs but also bring in good rates of profit. Sheet had saved plate at Pilkington in the later 19th century. Now the situation was reversed.

Having managed to save its sheet glass production during the 1920s, thanks to plate glass profits, PB then had a stroke of good fortune. The U.S. plate glass manufacturer Pittsburgh Plate Glass Company (PPG) developed its own method of drawing sheet glass directly from a tank that was superior to that of LOF or Fourcault. PB secured a license for this process in 1929. PPG machines, installed at St. Helens in the early 1930s and subsequently improved there, enabled the company to regain some of its market. The flat glass industry fared better in the United Kingdom because it supplied two markets, the building and motor trades, which survived the depressed years of the 1930s better than most others. There was also money to be made out of raw glass, particularly plate glass, when it was processed into safety glass. PB acquired a majority share in a fac-

tory built just outside St. Helens by Triplex (Northern) Limited, which came into production in 1930. Soon afterward it also became involved in safety glass processing plants in Canada, South Africa, and Australia. In 1936, an agreement was reached with Chance Brothers whereby PB would buy its old rival over a number of years. By 1939 it had already acquired nearly half of Chance's shares. It completed the takeover in 1952.

Austin and Cecil Pilkington retired from day-to-day management of the company at a critical moment in 1931, when PB recorded its first loss. Control passed to an executive committee that Cozens-Hardy set up with himself as chairman. His right-hand man was Ronald Weeks, who had been recruited from Cambridge in 1912 and had played a notable part in the management of the plate glass factory, subsequently marrying into the Pilkington family. Weeks was to gain a national reputation during World War II as General Weeks, deputy chief of the Imperial General Staff and afterward as chairman of Vickers and director of other companies. He became Lord Weeks in 1956. It was under this regime during the early 1930s that the fourth generation of the family began to play a greater part.

Geoffrey Langton Pilkington, who was much older than his cousins, had been a director since 1919 and served as company chairman from 1932 to 1949. The others, some of whom had entered the business from university in 1927, served a rigorous probation; one of them did not make the grade. Harry Pilkington and Douglas Phelps, the son of a Pilkington daughter, reached the executive committee in 1934; Roger Percival, the son of another Pilkington daughter, followed in 1936, and Peter Cozens-Hardy in 1937. By then Lawrence Pilkington, Harry Pilkington's brother, and Arthur Pilkington, after five years as a regular officer in the Coldstream Guards, had entered the company and joined the executive committee in the 1940s, followed by a much younger member, David Pilkington, born in 1925. This team was to succeed more spectacularly than any of its predecessors.

When PB closed its Maubeuge factory in 1935, as part of the general rationalization of the European plate glass industry that followed an agreement between the European and U.S. manufacturers reached the previous year, it ceased to manufacture any glass outside the United Kingdom. It was soon, however, the major participant in the establishment of a window glass factory built at Llavallol outside Buenos Aires, a joint European venture to safeguard the Europeans' Argentine market. This factory had hardly come into production when World War II broke out and the Pilkington management there had to struggle hard to maintain and extend it during the war years, when communication between Llavallol and St. Helens was difficult and technical assistance from the parent company was unobtainable.

POSTWAR ERA: THE FLOAT GLASS PROCESS AND DIVERSIFICATION

Lord Cozens-Hardy retired in 1939, and Sir Ronald Weeks did not return to the company after the war. With Douglas Phelps as chairman of the executive committee from 1947, succeeded by Arthur Pilkington in 1965, and Harry Pilkington, the future Lord Pilkington, as company chairman from 1949, the fourth Pilkington generation saw the company's assets grow from £12.5 million in 1949 to £206 million in 1973, when Lord Pilkington retired from the chairmanship. This growth was due to the outstanding success of the float glass process and also to diversification into what were, for PB, new branches of the glass industry.

In some respects, change was forced on the company rather than welcomed by it. Manufacture of sheet glass in South Africa in 1951, for instance, came about because the South African government, determined to develop a manufacturing industry in that country, proposed to allow a rival to build a sheet glass factory if PB did not do so. PB's interests would have been best served by exporting as much U.K. glass as possible and thus keeping its machines at home working at full capacity. For similar reasons, PB sheet glass manufacture had to be started in Canada in the same year and in India, with local as well as Pilkington capital, in 1954. In Australia, where Australian Window Glass (AWG) had a financial stake in Pilkington's safety glass processing plants, PB took a share in AWG when PB helped to modernize AWG's obsolete sheet glass factory in 1960. A few years later, PB and AWG took over an aspiring local manufacturer in New Zealand who had attempted to make sheet glass but soon had failed. PB's window glass operations in Argentina, started just before World War II, were developed and led in due course to the acquisition of a sheet glass works in Brazil. Although PB sacrificed sheet glass exports to these factories, it never lost those of plate glass: Maintaining a plate glass factory in these countries would have been far too costly. Manufacture of higher quality glass overseas had to await the development of the less costly float glass process, which tipped the scales further in the direction of manufacture abroad rather than at home.

The float glass process was invented by Alastair Pilkington in 1952. In this process, molten glass was poured onto one end of a bath of molten tin at about 1,000 degrees Celsius and formed into a ribbon that floated, frictionless and in a controlled atmosphere,

down the bath through a temperature gradient falling to about 600 degrees Celsius at the other end. At this temperature the ribbon, fire finished, was cool enough to be taken off on rollers without marking the surface. This revolutionary new method of glassmaking produced polished plate glass much more economically by removing the large fixed capital investment in grinding and polishing machinery and by cutting working costs.

To obtain perfectly parallel distortion-free surfaces, the polished plate glass process required 20 percent of the original rough-cast glass to be ground off by many grinding and polishing machines, with vast expenditure of electrical energy. Having experimented with the new process and developed a full-scale production plant during the 1950s, PB began to sell its own float glass before the decade was out and licensed the process to other glass manufacturers from 1962, with PPG being the first licensee. Plate glass could no longer compete at the quality end of the market nor, from the early 1970s, when float technology had progressed further, could the cheaper sheet glass.

Pilkington built more float lines at St. Helens, and manufacturers elsewhere in the world sought Pilkington licenses and expertise. Its growing industrial muscle and rising license income led to Pilkington building its own float plant in Sweden in the mid-1970s. Others came onstream in overseas markets it already dominated: Australia in 1973, and a second in 1988; South Africa in 1977; and Argentina in 1989. Its factories in Brazil were operated jointly with Saint-Gobain and in China with the People's Republic. It also acquired a majority, in Flachglas AG, the leading German producer, in 1980, followed by the 1986 purchase of the glass-making interests of Libbey-Owens-Ford Company, second in this field in the United States.

Alastair Pilkington, who invented the float glass process, was unrelated to the St. Helens glass-making family and was a mechanical sciences graduate from Cambridge University. Although not a member of the Pilkington family, he came to St. Helens as a family trainee in 1947. By the time the float process was being developed, he was already on the board pleading its case. He became a fellow of the Royal Society in 1969 and was knighted the following year. Between 1973 and 1980 he was chairman of the company.

PB was brought into glass fibers and optical glass as a result of its acquisition of Chance Brothers in the years after 1936. The latter had acquired the U.K. and British Empire rights to glass fiber manufacture from 1930 and had long specialized in optical glass. Glass Fibres Ltd. was formed jointly by PB and Chance Brothers in 1938. A glass fiber factory was built at St.

Helens after the war, and others followed at home and abroad to make glass silk for weaving and fibers for insulation and reinforcement. In the late 1980s Pilkington Reinforcements Limited stood as the world's leading supplier of special reinforced belting for engines and machinery for power transmission.

Chance Brothers' interest in optical glass went back to the 19th century and its world-renowned lighthouse department. During World War II Chance Brothers and Pilkington operated a shadow plant, a duplicate located away from the original factory as a precaution against bombing, at St. Helens and continued to undertake defense contracts afterward. Beginning in 1957, on the initiative of Lawrence Pilkington, optical and ophthalmic glass began production at a specially built works at St. Asaph in north Wales, which soon became the largest producer of unpolished spectacle discs in Europe. In 1966 PB and Perkin-Elmer, a subsidiary of the U.S. multinational Perkin-Elmer Corporation, joined forces at St. Asaph to make optical and electro-optical systems. The joint venture became Pilkington P.E. in 1973, when Pilkington acquired the U.S. company's stake in the business. This side of the business was strengthened greatly by later acquisitions, notably the purchase of Barr and Stroud, the Scottish optical and precision engineers, in 1977; Sola Holdings of Australia in 1979; Syntax Ophthalmic Inc. in 1985; and Revlon's Barnes-Hind and Coburn Vision Care companies in 1987. At the end of the 1980s, the business was divided into Pilkington Visioncare, its ophthalmic side, which was growing throughout the world, including China and Japan, and Pilkington Optronics, the electro-optical side, which supplied the U.K. defense industry, primarily through Barr & Stroud and Pilkington P.E.

The fourth Pilkington generation oversaw this vast expansion overseas and diversification at home as well as the development of float glass and many other activities. They were served loyally by senior managers who acted like proconsuls on their behalf abroad and by others at home who accepted greater responsibility as the business grew and its committee system was expanded. From the mid-1960s, when Arthur Pilkington became chairman of the executive committee, much of the company's business devolved to the five divisional boards. One or two outstanding managers had joined the executive committee from the 1930s. A few more followed Alastair Pilkington to the top. Harry Pilkington, the company's chairman, was a businessman with a remarkable head for figures, a clear, analytical brain, limitless energy, and a great devotion to work. In addition to his demanding corporate responsibilities, he managed to fit in the presidency of the Federation of British Industries in London and the chairmanship of a royal commission.

The Pilkington family influence persisted for some years after the company went public in 1970. Lord Pilkington, created honorary life president when he retired in 1973, used to come into the office regularly until shortly before his death in 1983, and the fourth generation was represented on the board until 1985 when the youngest, David Pilkington, retired. In 1985 Pilkington Brothers Limited became Pilkington Brothers plc, and in 1987 the company dropped "Brothers" entirely from its official name. Pilkington became a holding company for a number of major subsidiaries, of which there were 45 in 1990. Economy and efficiency became the watchwords, especially in the difficult years of the early 1980s, when nearly £100 million was spent in redundancy payments in the United Kingdom alone. While this changed the atmosphere at St. Helens, it revived the company's fortunes and enabled it to ward off a takeover bid from the London-based conglomerate BTR in 1986. As the company entered the 1990s, only one Pilkington remained on the board, Chairman Sir Antony Pilkington, son of Arthur Pilkington, knighted for his service to U.K. business in 1990.

REFOCUSING ON GLASS AND RESTRUCTURING

Pilkington entered a traumatic period in the early 1990s. Competition in the glass sector had intensified in the 1980s following the entrance of U.S. and Japanese glassmakers into the European market and the expansionary moves of French archrival Compagnie de Saint-Gobain. Pilkington was also buffeted by the effects of the deep recession that began in the late 1980s and continued into the early 1990s, with two of the company's main markets, the automotive and building sectors, being particularly hard hit. Compounding the situation was Pilkington's ill-timed, if not ill-conceived, diversification into eyecare products. In hindsight, the purchase of Barnes-Hind was particularly troublesome. Barnes-Hind specialized in hard contact lenses and solutions, a part of the eyecare market that, soon after Pilkington bought into it, was eclipsed by the rapid growth of soft and disposable lenses. The combination of all of these negatives led revenues to decline from £3 billion in 1989 to £2.6 billion in 1993, and pretax profits to slump from £300 million to £41 million over the same period. The bottom line for 1993 was an actual loss.

According to Andrew Lorenz, writing in *Management Today,* Pilkington's difficulties in this period also stemmed from its corporate culture, which had not yet fully transitioned from that of a family firm to that of a public company. It was more than symbolic, then, that in 1992 Roger Leverton become the first outsider named Pilkington chief executive. Antony Pilkington remained chairman but retired in 1995 and was succeeded by Nigel Rudd, the first non-Pilkington chairman; Rudd took the position as a nonexecutive chairman, leaving Leverton the distinct head of operations. During this leadership transition, Pilkington made the clear decision to refocus on its core flat and safety glass operations, to bolster these operations through new investment and acquisitions, and to begin disposing of noncore activities. Among the first operations jettisoned were the cement and rubber reinforcement businesses, insulation contracting, and the company's holdings in South Africa. A 50 percent interest in Pilkington Optronics was also quickly sold off, but the troubled eyecare business, Pilkington Visioncare, proved harder to divest. In 1993 Coburn Optical was divested, then Sola was sold that same year for £200 million. Two more Visioncare businesses were sold in 1995—the lens care operations of Pilkington Barnes-Hind and Paragon Optical—and the exit from ophthalmics was completed the following year with the sale of the Pilkington Barnes Hind contact lens business to Wesley Jessen Corporation.

On the acquisitions front, Pilkington moved into the Eastern European market for the first time in 1992 with the purchase of a 45 percent stake in International Glass Poland, a processor and distributor of glass building products, as well as the establishment of a joint venture, 40 percent owned by Pilkington, for the purpose of constructing that country's first float glass plant. Back home, the company moved toward vertically integrating its U.K. operations through the 1993 acquisition of the glass processing and distribution business of Heywood Williams for £95 million.

Also in 1993 Pilkington formed a joint venture with an Italian firm, Techint Finanziaria, to acquire Societa Italiana Vetro SpA (SIV), the state-owned glassmaker, which the Italian government had decided to privatize. Pilkington paid about £43 million for its share. Two years later the company bought out its partner for £128 million to take full control of SIV, which was a market leader in vehicle glass for such manufacturers as Fiat S.p.A., Volkswagen AG, Renault S.A., and PSA Citroën S.A. Through its acquisition of SIV, Pilkington increased its share of the European automotive glass market from 16 percent to 34 percent. Growth in 1994 came through expansion in the emerging markets of China, Brazil, and Chile, and by the purchase of full control of the company's Finnish float glass subsidiary, Lahden Lasitehdas OY. In 1995 Pilkington acquired the Interpane Group's glass processing and distribution businesses in Switzerland, Denmark, and Norway for £58 million.

By early 1996 Leverton's efficiency drive led to annual cost savings of £230 million. The workforce was reduced by 15 percent, to 36,000, and productivity was increased by 32 percent. Also, Pilkington's management structure in Europe was overhauled, beginning in 1995. Previously the European operations were organized geographically on a country-by-country basis. Leverton reorganized Pilkington Europe into three business lines: automotive products, building products, and technical glass products, which included specialized mirrors, solar energy panels, and glass for the electronics industry. Leverton then followed up with a series of major restructuring programs to further improve efficiencies in various operations.

Yet in May 1997, in the wake of dismal results for the 1997 fiscal year, the board of directors concluded that the pace of the restructuring was proceeding too slowly and ousted Leverton. Paolo Scaroni was promoted to chief executive from his position as head of the company's worldwide automotive products operations. Scaroni had previously led a rapid restructuring of SIV, and had once served as global head of the glass-making operations of Saint-Gobain.

Aiming to make Pilkington the world's most efficient glassmaker, Scaroni immediately quickened the restructuring pace, launching a two-year overhaul that cut a further 7,500 jobs from the workforce and shuttered 70 distribution and fabrication operations in Europe. The restructuring led Pilkington to take £225 million ($376 million) in writeoffs for the 1998 fiscal year, leading to a net loss of £186 million ($303 million) for the year. In late 1998 Pilkington announced another 1,500 job cuts spread across its worldwide operations, then in mid-1999 announced plans for an additional 2,500 job cuts, this time with an emphasis on Germany and North America. By this time Pilkington had improved its competitiveness in Europe, and began turning its attention to improving the profitability of its U.S. operations.

At the same time Scaroni began seeking opportunities for growth through acquisition and the establishment of joint ventures, following the company's return to profitability in the 1999 fiscal year. In early 2000, then, Pilkington doubled its holding in a Chinese affiliate, Shanghai Yaohua Pilkington, to 16.7 percent; increased its stake in Pilkington Sandoglass Sp. z o.o., a Polish float glass subsidiary, to 75 percent; and formed a joint venture with German glass processor Interpane International Glas to build the world's first integrated float glass manufacturing, laminating, and coating plant. Later in the year Pilkington completed a deal with Nippon Sheet Glass Company, Limited, whereby the former bought out the latter's minority holdings in several Pilkington automotive glass subsidiaries, including Libbey-Owens-Ford, which was subsequently renamed Pilkington North America Inc., and Pilkington Automotive UK Limited. In return, the Japanese firm took a 10 percent stake in Pilkington. With full control of these operations, Pilkington gained greater freedom to implement additional restructuring initiatives.

Several other deals were completed in the fiscal year ending in March 2001. The company acquired full control of Pilkington Sandoglass, later renamed Pilkington Polska Sp. z o.o., and then in December 2000 announced plans to build a second float glass plant in Poland, this one through a joint venture with Saint-Gobain. Pilkington also consolidated its position as the leading automotive glass supplier in China by acquiring a 51 percent stake in Shanghai FuHua Glass Company in a transaction completed jointly with the affiliated firm Shanghai Yaohua Pilkington. In 2001 Pilkington's building products side began selling a self-cleaning glass. Called Activ, this glass incorporated a permanent coating of titanium oxide that attracted water and made it run down the glass in a continuous sheet, taking dirt particles with it. Also that year, Nippon Sheet Glass increased its stake in Pilkington to just over 20 percent.

For fiscal 2002, Pilkington reported a net profit of £74 million ($105 million) on £2.81 billion ($4 billion), a good result given the beginnings of a downturn in the global glass market. It was at this inauspicious moment that Scaroni, having transformed Pilkington from a struggling U.K. manufacturer to one of the most efficient glassmakers in the world, abruptly quit to head Enel S.p.A., the Italian electricity giant. Taking over as chief executive in May 2002 was Stuart Chambers, who had been in charge of the building products division and had a background in marketing. Chambers brought the restructuring program that Scaroni had started to a successful conclusion by 2004 and also worked to pay down the company's debt load in order to free up capital to fund growth initiatives. Between March 2003 and March 2005 net debt was reduced from £861 million ($1.36 billion) to £572 million ($1.08 billion). Plans were in place to increase investment in emerging countries, particularly Russia and China. During fiscal 2005 Pilkington increased its ownership interest in and took over management control of three automotive glass plants in China and also entered into a joint venture to build a float line in Russia.

2006: THE NIPPON SHEET GLASS TAKEOVER

At this stage in its long history, Pilkington ranked as the world's second largest glassmaker (with a global market share of 19 percent), trailing only Japan's Asahi Glass Company, Limited (23 percent), and as one of the four global players in the industry, the other two being Saint-Gobain of France and the privately held U.S. firm Guardian Industries Corp. Among the second-tier manufacturers was Nippon Sheet Glass (NSG), still holding its 20 percent stake in Pilkington. With ample access to financing and motivated to become a serious rival to Asahi, NSG in November 2005 made a friendly offer to take over Pilkington for 150 pence per share, or approximately £2 billion ($3.5 billion). The Pilkington board rejected this bid and two additional sweetened offerings before accepting NSG's 165 pence per share offer in February 2006. The deal, completed that June, valued Pilkington at £2.2 billion ($4.1 billion). Thus ended a 180-year span of independence as the newly named Pilkington Group Limited became a wholly owned subsidiary of NSG.

Chambers carried on as chief executive of Pilkington. Initially at least, there was only a minor amount of integration stemming from the takeover as the deal was largely aimed at turning NSG into one of the global glass-making leaders. Pilkington continued to pursue growth opportunities in emerging markets. In November 2006 the firm entered into a joint venture to build and operate a float glass manufacturing line in Abu Dhabi. Yet another of Pilkington's joint ventures launched construction of a float glass production line in Kazakhstan in March 2007. Meanwhile, in a potentially troubling development, the European Commission that same month filed antitrust charges against Pilkington and Asahi Glass's Belgian unit, Glaverbel S.A., following a two-year investigation into allegations of price-fixing in the flat glass sector.

T. C. Barker
Updated, David E. Salamie

PRINCIPAL SUBSIDIARIES

EUROPE: Pilkington United Kingdom Limited; Pilkington Automotive Limited; Pilkington Technology Management Limited; Pilkington Deutschland AG (Germany; 95%); Pilkington Automotive Deutschland GmbH (Germany; 95%); Pilkington Austria GmbH; Pilkington Norge AS (Norway); Pilkington Schweiz AG (Switzerland); Pilkington Floatglas AB (Sweden); Pilkington Automotive Sweden AB; Pilkington Automotive Finland OY; Pilkington Lahden Lasitehdas OY (Finland); Pilkington France SA; Pilkington Danmark A/S (Denmark); Pilkington International Glass Poland Sp. z o.o.; Pilkington Polska Sp. z o.o. (Poland); Pilkington Italia SpA (Italy). NORTH AMERICA: Pilkington North America Inc. (U.S.A.); L-N Safety Glass SA de CV (Mexico). REST OF THE WORLD: Pilkington

(Australia) Limited; Vidrieria Argentina S.A. (51%); Pilkington Automotive Argentina S.A.; Pilkington Brasil Limitada (Brazil); Pilkington (New Zealand) Limited; Guilin Pilkington Safety Glass Co. Limited (China); Changchun Pilkington Safety Glass Co. Limited (China; 73%). HOLDING AND FINANCE COMPANIES: Pilkington Brothers Limited; Pilkington Italy Limited (U.K.); Pilkington Finance Limited; Pilkington Nederland Holdings BV (Netherlands); Pilkington Germany Holdings BV (Netherlands); Pilkington International Holdings BV (Netherlands); Pilkington Holding GmbH (Germany); Dahlbusch AG (Germany; 99%).

PRINCIPAL COMPETITORS

Compagnie de Saint-Gobain; Asahi Glass Company, Limited; Guardian Industries Corp.

FURTHER READING

Arbose, Jules, et al., "Why Once-Dingy Pilkington Has That Certain Sparkle," *International Management,* August 1986, pp. 44+.

Barker, T. C., *An Age of Glass: The Illustrated History,* London: Boxtree, 1994, 144 p.

———, *The Glassmakers,* London: Weidenfeld and Nicolson, 1977, 557 p.

———, *Pilkington Brothers and the Glass Industry,* London: Allen and Unwin, 1960, 296 p.

Batchelor, Charles, "Pilkington Hopes to Look Through Glass More Brightly," *Financial Times,* March 14, 2000, p. 26.

Betts, Paul, "Unleashing the Power of Experience," *Financial Times,* October 3, 2002, p. 14.

Blitz, Roger, "Japanese Break Through a Glass Barrier," *Financial Times,* June 26, 2006, p. 23.

Caulkin, Simon, "Pilkington After BTR," *Management Today,* June 1987, pp. 42+.

Dawkins, William, and Charles Leadbeater, "People in Glass Houses Start to Throw Stones," *Financial Times,* May 8, 1990, p. 21.

Graham, George, and Andrew Taylor, "Pilkington Drops Licensing Policy: Glassmaker Bows to Pressure As US Steps Up Anti-Trust Battle," *Financial Times,* May 27, 1994, p. 18.

Gresser, Charis, "Make or Break Time for Pilkington," *Financial Times,* October 30, 1997, p. 18.

———, "A Real Test of Endurance: Is Pilkington Fit Enough to Stay the Course," *Financial Times,* November 1, 1997, p. 5.

Gresser, Charis, and Sheila Jones, "Pilkington to Shed 6,000 Jobs in Restructuring," *Financial Times,* October 30, 1997, p. 17.

Guthrie, Jonathan, "Pilkington Sheds Flab but Makeover Is Incomplete," *Financial Times,* October 30, 1998, p. 22.

———, "Pilkington's Purge Fails to Cut Much Ice," *Financial Times,* June 5, 1998, p. 26.

Harney, Alexandra, "Stones Rain In on Pilkington's Glass House," *Financial Times,* May 15, 2002, p. 20.

Leadbeater, Charles, and Ian Hamilton Fazey, "Pilkington Integrates European Operations," *Financial Times,* October 9, 1991, p. 17.

Lorenz, Andrew, "Pilkington Picks Up the Pieces," *Management Today,* March 1996, pp. 37–40.

Lorenz, Christopher, "Transparent Move to European Unity," *Financial Times,* July 24, 1992, p. 15.

McDonough, Tony, and Mike Chapple, "Pilkington Takeover: End of an Era for Glass Giant," *Daily Post* (Liverpool, England), February 28, 2006.

Morais, Richard C., "Glassmaker to the World," *Forbes,* January 22, 1996, p. 48.

Novak, Viveca, "U.S. Wins Accord with British Firm on Glass Factories," *Wall Street Journal,* May 27, 1994, p. A12.

Parkin, R. A., *The Window Glass Makers of St. Helens,* Sheffield, U.K.: Society of Glass Technology, 2000, 122 p.

"Pilkington: Facing Up to a Cruel World," *Economist,* October 12, 1991, p. 78.

Pretzlik, Charles, "Pilkington to Cut More Jobs," *Financial Times,* June 4, 1999, p. 23.

Saigol, Lina, Kaori Suzuki, and David Turner, "Pilkington Agrees to £2.2bn Takeover by NSG," *Financial Times,* February 28, 2006, p. 19.

Salmans, Sandra, "The Pilkingtons of Britain: 5th in Line Takes Over Glassmakers," *New York Times,* July 27, 1980, p. F1.

———, "Pilkington's Progressive Shift," *Management Today,* September 1980, p. 66.

Spiegelberg, Richard, "Floating Glass," *Times* (London), June 26, 1970, p. 23.

———, "Floating the Float People," *Times* (London), November 20, 1970, p. 29.

Teitelbaum, Henry E., "Pilkington's Fragile Fortunes: Glassmaker Seeks to Stoke Turnaround amid Industry Downturn," *Wall Street Journal Europe,* January 28, 2003, p. M3.

Tieman, Ross, "Cracking Start by Scaroni," *Financial Times,* May 23, 1997, p. 25.

———, "Singing Sweet Music to Analysts and Shareholders," *Financial Times,* June 6, 1997, p. 29.

Urry, Maggie, "Pilkington Hopes for a Clear Recovery," *Financial Times,* June 18, 1993, p. 17.

———, "Pilkington Hopes to Put a Shine on Its Prospects," *Financial Times,* December 10, 1992, p. 21.

———, "Pilkington's Future Is As Clear As Glass," *Financial Times,* November 7, 2003, p. 25.

———, "Thriving on the Glass Revolution," *Financial Times,* February 28, 2006, p. 22.

Wagstyl, Stefan, "Pilkington Cuts 1,900 Jobs in Restructuring," *Financial Times,* March 28, 1996, p. 21.

Wighton, David, "Recovery Reflects Cost Cutting at Pilkington," *Financial Times,* November 23, 1994, p. 32.

Wilsher, Peter, "A Right Moving Story," *Management Today,* December 1991, p. 27.

PolyOne

PolyOne Corporation

▬

33587 Walker Road
Avon Lake, Ohio 44012-1145
U.S.A.
Telephone: (440) 930-1000
Toll Free: (866) 765-9663
Fax: (440) 930-1750
Web site: http://www.polyone.com

Public Company
Incorporated: 2000
Employees: 4,600
Sales: $2.62 billion (2006)
Stock Exchanges: New York
Ticker Symbol: POL
NAIC: 325211 Plastics Material and Resin Manufacturing; 325991 Custom Compounding of Purchased Resins; 325132 Synthetic Organic Dye and Pigment Manufacturing; 325998 All Other Miscellaneous Chemical Product and Preparation Manufacturing

■ ■ ■

PolyOne Corporation is one of North America's leading producers and distributors of polymer compounds. Major business segments focus on thermoplastic compounds and color and additive concentrates for the plastics industry, and the company also distributes to the North American market a vast array of resins produced by more than 20 major suppliers (including itself). Two joint ventures comprise the firm's resin and intermediates segment: OxyVinyls, a venture with Occidental Chemical Corporation, produces polyvinyl chloride (PVC) resins, vinyl chloride monomer, and chloride and caustic soda, and is 24 percent owned by PolyOne; while SunBelt, a venture with Olin Corporation, produces chlorine and caustic soda, and is 50 percent owned by PolyOne. Around two-thirds of the company's sales are generated domestically, with 17 percent originating in Europe, 11 percent in Canada, and 5 percent in Asia.

PolyOne was formed in August 2000 from the merger of two Cleveland-area firms, M. A. Hanna Company and The Geon Company. Founded in the late 19th century, M. A. Hanna was a major mining company before making a dramatic shift into polymers in the mid-1980s. Geon, which had been spun off from The BFGoodrich Company in March 1993, traced its roots back to Goodrich's founding of the vinyl plastics industry in 1926.

M. A. HANNA'S EARLY YEARS

Marcus Alonzo Hanna, the namesake of M. A. Hanna Company, was born in 1837 on his parents' Lisbon, Ohio, farm. His father, Dr. Leonard Hanna, moved to Cleveland in 1852 after competition from railroads undermined the family investment in a canal project. After trying a grocery business, Dr. Hanna joined with his brother Robert and another investor in a copper and iron trading venture in the late 1850s. The partners soon expanded operations to include coal mining.

When young "Mark" was expelled from Western Reserve College for distributing a risque flyer at a

COMPANY PERSPECTIVES

We provide value to our customers through our ability to link our knowledge of polymers and formulation technology with our manufacturing and supply chain processes to provide an essential link between large chemical producers (our raw material suppliers) and designers, assemblers and processors of plastics (our customers). We believe that large chemical producers are increasingly outsourcing less-than-railcar business; polymer and additive producers need multiple channels to market; processors continue to outsource compounding; and international companies need suppliers with global reach. Our goal is to provide our customers with specialized material and service solutions through our global reach and product platforms, low-cost manufacturing operations, a fully integrated information technology network, broad market knowledge and raw material procurement leverage. Our end markets are primarily in the building materials, wire and cable, automotive, durable goods, packaging, electrical and electronics, medical and telecommunications markets, as well as many industrial applications.

student event, he went to work for his father as a warehouse clerk. Mark worked as a deckhand and purser on his father's Great Lakes ships, then joined the Union Army in the Civil War. Dr. Hanna died in 1862 after a long illness, and his minerals trading firm dissolved. At war's end, Hanna began a courtship with Charlotte Rhodes that launched the company that would keep his name long after it passed from his family's hands.

Hanna's future father-in-law, Daniel P. Rhodes, was a rigid Democrat who initially opposed his daughter's involvement with Hanna, an active Republican. However, when Rhodes's son left Rhodes & Co. and Hanna made some ill-fated investments, Hanna joined his father-in-law's pig iron and iron ore business. Hanna aggressively acquired more mines and diversified Rhodes & Co. into lake steamers, docks, warehouses, and shipbuilding. His entry into Rhodes & Co. coincided with a dramatic expansion of the Midwest's commercial and industrial influence. The company stimulated this growth at its very source: It brought coal from Ohio and Pennsylvania to the shores of Lake Erie to fuel midwestern industries, and shipped iron ore and pig iron to regional steel factories.

Daniel P. Rhodes died in the 1880s, and Hanna inherited the conglomerate that by that time included mining, shipping, street and freight railways, hotels, and a bank. Hanna's brothers, Howard Melville and Leonard Colton, and a partner, Arnold C. Saunders, renamed the business M. A. Hanna & Company in 1885.

The new company purchased interests in iron ore, coal mines, and blast furnaces. Mark Hanna was soon known for his compelling personality, sharp business sense, and energetic bearing. He became a prominent industrial executive, builder of a shipping line, and owner of Cleveland's opera house. As his business influence grew, he aspired to political power as well. Hanna purchased the *Cleveland Herald* newspaper to boost Republican support, and financed the gubernatorial and presidential campaigns of William McKinley. His massive $3.5 million campaign contributions earned him the nickname "Red Boss" ("red" for iron dust and "boss" for his political activities), a U.S. Senate seat, and the rancor of some of the nation's largest newspapers. Hanna turned the company over to his brothers in 1896 so that he could chair the National Republican Committee full time. He was elected a U.S. senator in 1897, and served until his death in 1904.

Howard M. and Leonard C. Hanna continued on with the family business. Howard would become known as the businessman of the family, and his son would lead the company in the early 20th century. Leonard was remembered more for his civic and philanthropic contributions to the city of Cleveland. Marcus Hanna's corporate legacy would end with son Daniel R., whose involvement precipitated a leadership crisis at Hanna.

Howard Melville Hanna, Jr., Daniel's cousin, was groomed for leadership of the family company. When, in 1915, he grew disgusted with Daniel's playboy lifestyle and apparent lack of commitment to the business, Howard bought out Daniel's share of the Hanna company. Within the next six years, Leonard C., Howard, Sr., and cousin Daniel all died, leaving Howard, Jr., to steer the Hanna ship virtually alone. The abrupt change in leadership had coincided with lagging earnings, tax hikes, a decline in the coal industry, and lessened demand for iron ore.

INCORPORATING AND GOING PUBLIC

George M. Humphrey became Hanna Company's last partner when he invested in the firm in 1922. He had joined the company in 1917 as a legal advisor, and quickly built a promising business and personal relationship with Howard Hanna, Jr. A. C. Saunders continued as a partner until 1922, when the M. A. Hanna Company was incorporated with Matthew Andrews as

KEY DATES

1885: After inheriting his father-in-law's conglomerate, Marcus Alonzo Hanna renames it M. A. Hanna & Company.

1896: Moving into the political arena, Hanna turns over the company to his brothers.

1922: M. A. Hanna Company is incorporated and taken public.

1926: The BFGoodrich Company founds the vinyl plastic industry when a company scientist develops polyvinyl chloride (PVC); the company later markets PVC resin under the trade name Geon.

1943: The Goodrich Chemical Company is established and builds the first commercialized PVC plants.

1958: Hanna Mining Company, an affiliate of M. A. Hanna, is taken public.

1965: M. A. Hanna is liquidated, leaving Hanna Mining as an autonomous corporation.

Early 1980s: After fending off a takeover attempt, Hanna Mining begins selling off its mining assets.

1985: Hanna Mining reassumes the M. A. Hanna Company name.

1986: New CEO Martin Walker leads M. A. Hanna's switch from mining to plastics.

1993: The Geon Company is spun off from Goodrich as an independent, publicly traded firm.

1997: Geon acquires Synergistics Industries Limited.

1998: Geon combines its PVC business with that of Occidental Chemical Corporation to form the joint venture OxyVinyls.

2000: M. A. Hanna and Geon merge to form PolyOne Corporation.

2004: PolyOne divests its rubber compounding business.

chairman of the board and Howard M. Hanna, Jr., as president. Humphrey and Hanna used the influx of capital from that first stock offer to encourage growth at the company's profitable divisions, and sold Hanna's losing divisions. Their work to promote efficiency during the 1920s helped carry M. A. Hanna through the Great Depression profitably.

When Chairman Matthew Andrews died in 1929, Howard M. Hanna, Jr., was elected chairman and

George M. Humphrey was made president. Humphrey was instrumental in the creation of National Steel Co. that year. In conjunction with the national trend toward vertical integration, National Steel combined the Great Lakes Steel Co., a sheet steel business in Detroit, with Pittsburgh's Weirton Steel and Hanna's Lake Superior iron ore properties, ships, and lakefront blast furnaces.

The consolidation enabled National Steel to integrate all aspects of the steel business, from raw materials to finished product, in one company. Ernest Weir, of Weirton, served as chairman of the new company, George Fink of Great Lakes Steel was president, and George Humphrey chaired the executive committee. In exchange for its iron ore operations, Hanna received more than one-fourth of National Steel's capital stock, making Hanna the conglomerate's biggest shareholder. Having the most modern plants in the United States on the eve of the Great Depression made National Steel one of the country's most efficient and profitable steel works.

Although the company's primary activities were still concentrated in coal, iron ore, blast furnaces, and lake shipping, they were set off into separate companies with Hanna exchanging its assets for common stock of large affiliates such as National Steel Corp., Consolidation Coal Co., and eventually, Hanna Mining Co.

VARIOUS OPERATIONS AND INVESTMENTS

The Hanna company had three primary spheres of operation in the 1930s. The oldest was the ore and lake coal group, which incorporated Hanna's 20 Lake Superior ore mines, a mine in Missouri, and one in New York. National Steel became a "cash cow" for this division of Hanna—it could count on the associated company as a customer in bad times, such as the Depression, yet continue to sell to National's competitors as well. The ore and lake division also included the Franklin Steamship Corp., a subsidiary that provided shipping on commission for other companies. In 1945 Franklin Steamship was consolidated with the rest of Hanna's iron ore businesses as Hanna Coal & Ore Corp. Later named Hanna Mining Company, Franklin Steamship would evolve into Hanna's primary business in the 1960s.

Hanna's Susquehanna Collieries division, the company's second sphere of operation, handled the company's anthracite coal assets, which included three Pennsylvania mines with combined capacity of 12,000 tons daily by 1946. The company's third division concentrated on investments in a wide variety of industries, including rayon, oil, plastics, copper, tobacco, and banking. The division grew increasingly important in the 1930s and 1940s. Hanna purchased significant interests in: Standard Oil (0.3 percent); Seaboard Oil of Delaware (0.8 percent); Cleveland's National City Bank (5.1 percent) in 1933; Industrial Rayon Co. (17.2 percent) in 1935; Union Bank of Commerce (8.4 percent) in 1941; Consolidated Natural Gas (0.3 percent) in 1943; Durez Plastics & Chemicals (11.6 percent) in 1945; and Pittsburgh Consolidation Coal (37.8 percent), which was formed in 1945.

In 1946 Hanna transferred its stock holdings in Northwestern-Hanna Fuel Co., which operated six coal docks in upper lake ports, and all of its coal mine operations in Ohio, to the Pittsburgh Consolidation Coal Co. for $2.43 million and 325,000 common shares. Hanna retained management of the shipping and mining interests as part of its lake coal business.

The company's sizable investments entitled it to a voice in the management of many of the companies it financed, and, by the end of World War II, Hanna decided "to concentrate our holdings in a few companies in which we have confidence and then help in every way we can to build those companies into the strongest possible position in their respective fields." M. A. Hanna closed 1946 with $77 million in assets and holdings in some of North America's most important companies. Its own operations were conducting research to make lower grades of Lake Superior ore available, and exploring manganese deposits in Arizona and minerals deposits in South America.

EVOLVING INTO HANNA MINING

During the 1950s M. A. Hanna evolved through exchanges of stock and property into an investment company, while the Hanna Mining subsidiary concentrated on production and shipping. In 1951 M. A. Hanna acquired Canada's Empire Hanna Coal Co., Ltd., and made it into a division. Hanna Mining Company went public in 1958 and purchased 84,300 class B shares in M. A. Hanna. M. A. Hanna, in turn, owned 46 percent of Hanna Mining. The two companies also shared several board members.

The 1950s also saw Hanna Mining in a controversy over government nickel contracts. As the only nickel miner in the country, Hanna Mining produced emergency military stockpiles of the metal between 1953 and 1960. The U.S. Senate accused Hanna Mining of excessive profit-taking during hearings in the early 1960s, charging that the company made $10 million profit after taxes on an investment of $3.6 million.

In 1961, after Gilbert W. Humphrey (son of George M. Humphrey) had advanced to president and

CEO of M. A. Hanna, the company announced plans to dispose of direct business activities. By doing so, M. A. Hanna became the United States' largest closed-end investment company, with assets of about $500 million. As part of the plan, mining, shipping, and dock operations of companies affiliated with M. A. Hanna and the company's substantial investment in Iron Ore Co. of Canada were sold to Hanna Mining. M. A. Hanna's anthracite coal properties were sold to a new independent group, Empire Hanna Coal was purchased by outside interests, and Hanna's Great Lakes coal and vessel fueling business was sold to Consolidation Coal Co.

Within just three years, the market value of M. A. Hanna's three principal holdings—National Steel Corp., Consolidation Coal Co., and Hanna Mining Co.—had grown to $422.9 million. In 1964 Hanna Mining's directors were so confident in the new organization of their company that they proposed a three-for-one stock split and a dividend increase. In less than a year, though, the company's fortunes changed, and M. A. Hanna proposed that it be liquidated, leaving Hanna Mining as an autonomous corporation. Hanna Mining purchased one million shares of National Steel from M. A. Hanna and became the operating agent for National Steel iron ore mines and ships. M. A. Hanna sold its bituminous coal properties to Consolidation Coal Co. for $5.5 million.

After the liquidation, Hanna Mining became the focus of the management's worldwide operations. Hanna Mining reported six consecutive years of record high profits. The increases came from flourishing investments in Iron Ore Co. of Canada and National Steel. Overseas mining activities in Australia, Guatemala, and Brazil also contributed to Hanna's prosperity. Hanna enjoyed steadily increasing earnings in the 1970s, when the company entered into joint mining ventures in Liberia, Colombia, Australia, and Brazil, and established a copper mining project in Arizona. Within just one year at the end of the decade, earnings tripled.

SHIFTING TO POLYMERS AND PLASTICS AND READOPTING THE M. A. HANNA NAME

The company reached record sales in 1981 of $400 million with $44 million in net income. Yet Hanna plummeted from that summit in the 1980s when foreign competitors initiated their devastating assault on the U.S. steel industry. The situation was exacerbated when, in 1981, Canadian financier Conrad Black of Norcen Energy Resources, Ltd., initiated a yearlong takeover battle. Black's purchase of a large block of Hanna stock in October 1981 quickly captured the attention of

Hanna Chairman Robert F. Anderson and other members of the board. After a relatively brief, but heated federal hearing, Black and Hanna forged a standstill agreement that gave Black 20 percent of Hanna in exchange for $90 million. Black became a director, and the last descendant of an M. A. Hanna & Company partner, George M. Humphrey II, resigned from his position as senior vice-president by 1984.

In 1982 Hanna lost $80 million on $300 million in sales, and was forced to shut down all of its operations (except one Brazilian iron ore mine) for three weeks in December of that year. During that break, the company essentially abandoned its long-held position in mining and began a massive restructuring. Between 1982 and 1986 Hanna racked up more than $320 million in losses, and its roster of employees plunged from 8,000 to 3,500. Between 1980 and 1985 Hanna Mining sold 60 percent of its coal and iron businesses and a batch of preferred stock to finance an acquisition binge that concentrated on distribution and compounding in two fields: construction aggregates and polymers. Soon after, Hanna closed its last U.S. iron mine. In May 1985 the exit from mining was confirmed when the company reassumed the M. A. Hanna Company name.

When Martin D. Walker was brought onboard from Rockwell International as CEO and chairman in 1986, he led the switch from mining to plastics. (The planned move into aggregates never materialized because Hanna was outbid by an English firm for an aggregates company.) Within less than a year, the company spent half a billion dollars to convert itself from a major mining company to an influential polymer compounder, plastics distributor, and colorants producer. In 1986 the company purchased Burton Rubber Processing; colorants processors Allied Color Industries, Inc., and Avecor; and Day International, Inc., a major processor, distributor, and manufacturer of polymer printing blankets. Hanna also purchased PMS Consolidated, the world's leading plastic colorants processor; Colonial Rubber Works, a big compounder; and Cadillac Plastic, the number one distributor of plastic shapes, in 1987. The purchases revived Hanna's sales from $130 million in 1986, with a $104 million loss, to $460 million in 1987, and a $37 million net. Hanna surpassed $1 billion in worldwide sales before the decade was out.

FURTHER EVOLUTION THROUGH ACQUISITIONS, RESTRUCTURINGS, AND JOINT VENTURES

In 1990 Hanna acquired leading French plastics colorant producer Synthecolor S.A., a company with an estimated $25 million in annual sales. In 1991 Hanna

purchased Seattle plastics distributor FibreChem for $70 million, and enlarged its formulated colorants capacity with the opening of a new PMS Consolidated plant. The addition of DH Compounding Company, a joint venture with Dow Chemical Co., that same year gave Hanna a total of four compounding units. Another Canadian takeover threat was thwarted that year, when Brascan Limited, a Canadian natural resources conglomerate, gobbled up 30 percent of Hanna, which repurchased the stock at a premium to avoid the takeover.

CEO Walker told *Chemical Week* in 1991 that Hanna hoped to become "less a subcontractor and more a proprietary company" in the last decade of the 20th century. The decision to refocus came on the heels of an early 1990s recession that highlighted Hanna's dependence on contract work that distanced the company from the end users of its products and services. In 1992 the company sold a portion of its interest in Iron Ore Company of Canada to Mitsubishi Corporation and also divested the oil interests of Midland SouthWest Corporation.

M. A. Hanna completed several more acquisitions in the mid-1990s to both strengthen its U.S. operations and make further inroads into overseas markets. In June 1993, for example, the firm acquired Cookson America Inc.'s engineered materials division, which included Monmouth Plastics Company, a leading producer of flame retardant polyolefins, and Texapol Corporation, a major producer of engineered thermoplastic compounds, including nylon, acetal, and polycarbonate. The following July, Hanna purchased Theodor Bergmann GmbH & Co. Kunststoffwerk KG, one of Germany's largest producers of specialty and reinforced thermoplastic compounds. Also venturing into Asia, Hanna established a plastics-compounding joint venture with a state-owned manufacturer in China in January 1996, the same month it completed an acquisition of CIMCO, Inc., a producer of thermoplastic compounds and plastic components based in Costa Mesa, California, that generated about half of its sales in Asia and operated one plant in Singapore in addition to its two U.S. plants and one under construction in France. In March 1996 Hanna acquired Manchester, England-based Victor International Plastics, Ltd., from Rexam PLC. Victor, which generated annual sales of more than $50 million, produced color concentrates used to dye plastic. Hanna in early 1997 began building a manufacturing plant near Shanghai, China, for the production of color and additive concentrates.

During this same period, M. A. Hanna restructured a number of the businesses it had acquired during its spending spree, amalgamating them into larger business units. Thus, several regional resin distribution subsidiaries were merged to form the M. A. Hanna Resin Distribution business unit, and M. A. Hanna Engineered Materials was formed by consolidating Colonial Plastics, Monmouth Plastics, and Texapol Corp. Similar mergers in 1995 created M. A. Hanna Color and M. A. Hanna Rubber Compounding. That same year, Hanna divested Day International in order to focus on its polymer businesses with higher growth potential, and it also sold the last of its mining assets, offloading its remaining 8.14 percent in Iron Ore Company of Canada. By 1996 M. A. Hanna had doubled its revenues since the beginning of the decade, generating net sales of $2.07 billion, with 20 percent coming from outside the United States; the net income figure of $53.8 million for the year was almost half that of the previous year, but the difference was mainly attributable to the 1995 divestments.

At the beginning of 1997 Walker was succeeded as CEO by Douglas J. McGregor, who Walker had hired away from Rockwell International in 1988 and made president of Hanna in 1989. McGregor became chairman as well in June 1997, upon Walker's retirement. Under McGregor, Hanna continued to complete acquisitions and enter into joint ventures, but the company began losing customers as a result of an overfocus on integrating acquisitions and the distraction of the implementation of a new information technology system. The lost customers drove down earnings and the firm's stock price. In August 1998 the company launched a restructuring of its custom-formulated color business unit, eventually shutting down five plants and eliminating around 300 jobs from the workforce. Despite this and other moves, Hanna continued to falter, and McGregor abruptly stepped down in October 1998.

Walker returned as interim chairman and CEO, focusing on winning back lost customers. In June 1999 Phillip D. Ashkettle was hired as the new CEO, having spent the previous six years engineering a turnaround at Reichhold, Inc., a producer of specialty polymers, adhesives, and polymer systems based in North Carolina. At the beginning of 2000, Walker retired once again as Ashkettle added the chairmanship to his duties. In May of that year, M. A. Hanna agreed to merge with The Geon Company.

GEON ROOTS: PIONEERING PVC EFFORTS OF GOODRICH

The BFGoodrich Company was founded in 1870 by Dr. Benjamin Franklin Goodrich in Akron, Ohio. The original Goodrich product was a cotton-covered fire hose. Research and development was always given a high priority at Goodrich, and within its first 20 years, the company became known as the rubber industry problem-solver. The first rubber research laboratory in the United States was set up by Charles Cross Goodrich, son of the founder, in 1895. The Goodrich inventors improved on all types of products, including golf balls. In addition, they developed an efficient rubber reclamation process that would be used by the industry for decades.

Polyvinyls were the fortuitous result of the Goodrich policy of research and development. A company scientist working on developing a rubber product that adhered to metal discovered a chemical product that did just the opposite. In addition, the new product did not deteriorate when exposed to rubber-damaging processes. By pioneering polyvinyl chloride in 1926, Goodrich founded the vinyl plastic industry. Early PVC applications included waterproof raincoats and umbrellas. The company's polyvinyls became known as Geon and Koroseal and the versatile materials, which could be used in soft or hard form, eventually found their way into a variety of commonly used products, including electrical insulation, floor tiling, garden hoses, draperies, and luggage.

In the 1930s Goodrich scientific developments included the first airplane deicer, the endless band vehicle track used for farm and military vehicles, and the first commercial production of synthetic rubber. Of these developments, company President John Lyon Collyer saw great potential in and put great emphasis on the production of synthetic rubber. There was an enormous market for U.S.-made rubber because, prior to World War II, the nation was importing 90 percent of its rubber supply from the Far East. During the war Goodrich became heavily involved in rubber production for the military.

Though Goodrich focused on rubber, it also saw potential in its chemical business. The Goodrich Chemical Company was established in 1943 and built the first commercialized PVC plants. Its main products were vinyl materials (Geon), plasticizers, special-purpose rubbers, rubber manufacturing chemicals, and general chemicals. In 1948 a new research center was opened to further pure science, as well as applications, in the fields of rubber, chemicals, plastics, chemurgy, and the new field of nuclear energy.

By the early 1950s the company's largest division was tires, but the company could not seem to capitalize on its research and creativity. After inventing the first radial tires in the 1960s, Goodrich could not sell them to car manufacturers or American consumers. Five years later, French tire manufacturer Michelin successfully introduced radial tires. Goodrich's marketing ineptness, which wasted its pioneering research, was recognized throughout the industry. "Long the tire industry research leader," *Forbes* contributor Robert J. Flaherty wrote, "Goodrich has been the butt of a joke repeated in Akron for four decades: Goodrich invents it, Firestone copies it and Goodyear sells it."

A bitter takeover attempt in 1969 forced the Goodrich board to make some changes. In 1972, O. Pendleton Thomas, an oil company executive, took over command of Goodrich and restructured, closing money-losing plants and modernizing others. Thomas also implemented cutbacks on the types of tires produced and moved toward greater emphasis on chemicals and plastics. Thomas timed the company's shift away from tires well, for the 1970s marked the downfall of the American tire industry.

In 1979, when John D. Ong took over as chair and CEO, Goodrich was fourth among tire manufacturers, behind Goodyear, Firestone, and Michelin. The recession years of the early 1980s were some of the worst in history for the tire industry. In 1981 Goodrich dropped out of the original-equipment tire market, no longer selling directly to the automobile manufacturers, and instead concentrated on the higher-margin replacement tire market. In spite of the recession, the company was able to break even.

INCREASED FOCUS ON CHEMICALS AT GOODRICH

In the wake of the tire industry downfall, Ong expanded Goodrich's PVC business. By the end of 1981, 51 percent of total assets and one-third of the company's $3 billion in sales were attributable to Goodrich's chemical group. The 100-year-old tire manufacturer was on its way to becoming a chemical company. Goodrich focused on one product group, polyvinyl chloride resins and compounds, an area in which it had already become a dominant supplier. Uniroyal, another American tire manufacturer, was also moving in the direction of chemicals, creating a broad product mix of chemicals and elastomers (a plastic and rubber combination). Other tire manufacturers, pressed by foreign competition and the longer lasting radial tire, were also increasing their chemical production, but not in the sweeping way in which Goodrich and Uniroyal were proceeding.

Unfortunately, excess capacity and poor pricing plagued the PVC business in the early 1980s, when the industry was in its deepest decline since the Great Depression. Total PVC production in the United States fell by 6.6 percent from 1981 to 1982, dropping plant capacity to 55 percent. In 1982 general-purpose PVC was selling at 25 cents a pound, two cents below the

industry recognized break-even point for PVC manufacturers. That year Goodrich lost more than $30 million.

By the spring of 1983 the PVC market was in an upswing and Goodrich increased its PVC prices eight cents per pound in April. Goodrich had about 23 percent of the market at the time and was the only fully integrated PVC supplier in the world, with seven plant sites in production. The company was not only twice the size of second-ranked Tenneco but was also the low-cost producer. Even though Goodrich was increasing its debt load to expand its PVC business, buyers on Wall Street seemed to approve, with the stock reaching a 14-year high. The company recorded profits of $35 million on revenues of $3.2 billion. From 1979 to 1983 Ong had cut the workforce by 30 percent to 30,000 and put $1.3 billion into operations. He was also touting PVC as the basis of the company's growth. Capacity utilization was up to 80 percent in the plants.

The 1983 upswing in the PVC industry was short-lived, leaving a glut of the product from industry-wide plant expansions. In 1984, 200 jobs, or 25 percent of salaried employees, were cut from Goodrich's Chemical Group. The industry had adequately adjusted to the cyclical nature of its business. Low-margin commodity resins (providing the seasonal construction industry with pipes, siding, flooring coverings, and other building uses) were the mainstay of the industry, using almost 50 percent of all PVC. To establish steadiness for Goodrich's PVC business, Ong pursued production of finished PVC products such as bottles, a potentially huge market.

Goodrich's strategy in the mid-1980s was to expand specialty chemical activities and increase investment in aerospace activities. The company made four chemical manufacturer purchases and four aerospace acquisitions in three years. Goodrich also increased its research and development expenditures and created separate sales forces for the three specialty chemical units. In the second quarter of 1984, specialty resins, which were enhanced with heat stabilizers and other additives, accounted for 55 percent of Goodrich's PVC sales, significantly more than the industry-wide average of 40 percent.

In 1984, however, *Business Week* claimed that Goodrich was experiencing a high turnover of management and that the Geon division, with two operating chiefs in three years, was experiencing low employee morale. Market miscalculations and management mistakes had plagued Geon for some time. The $700 million sunk into the PVC division from 1979 to 1984 had yielded an operating income of only $131 million. With its staff of applications researchers and marketers,

Goodrich found itself competing with bare-bones operations such as Formosa Plastics and Shintech.

In the mid-1980s Goodrich tried to streamline its PVC production. Goodrich closed an outmoded, high-cost PVC resin facility, eliminating 170 million pounds per year of capacity. Nevertheless, Goodrich remained the largest PVC producer in the United States, with more than one billion pounds per year. The company also sold its unprofitable Convent, Louisiana, plant. The $250 million ethylene dichloride plant, completed in 1981, was part of the company's move toward backward integration into chemicals that were used to produce PVC. The Convent project was begun when it was cheaper to produce intermediate products because of scarcity of raw materials and high inflation. A predicted long-term chemical shortage failed to materialize and elevated gas prices boosted the energy cost to run the plant. In addition, PVC growth was overestimated and the price of low-grade resin, which made up a large segment of the market, was unstable. A total of $500 million in assets were divested in the restructuring. Those pieces of the business consisted of 25 percent of 1984 revenues generated, but operated at a loss of $22 million. After restructuring, Goodrich was down more than a billion in sales from its sales peak of $3.3 billion in 1984. However, PVC was still the world's second largest-selling plastic and the Geon Vinyl Division remained the largest producer of PVC in North America, grossing $865.8 million in 1985.

Specialty chemicals and aerospace were the clear focus of the company in the late 1980s because of their fast growth potential. Ann Slakter wrote in 1986, "Goodrich is heavily committed to the PVC business; its product line includes general- and special-purpose resins, special-purpose vinyl chloride monomer and caustic soda." In 1987 Geon Vinyl Division had sales of $1.06 billion and an operating income of $143.5 million. PVCs consisted of 49 percent of the company's total sales of $2.17 billion, with specialty chemicals bringing in 32 percent of sales, aerospace 15 percent, and industrial products 4 percent. While over 50 percent of the company's revenues had been from tires in the early 1980s, Goodrich moved further from its tire roots in 1986 by entering into a 50-50 joint venture with Uniroyal that combined their tire operations. When U.S. demand for PVC was high and export demand strong because of a weak dollar in 1988, Goodrich sold its 50 percent stake in Uniroyal-Goodrich Tire, leaving Goodrich with core businesses of polyvinyl chloride, special chemicals, and aerospace.

In 1989 William Patient, a chemical industry vice-president forced into early retirement, was hired to run the Geon division. In 1991 Goodrich entered the PVC recycling business by becoming one of three partners in the first large commercial PVC recycling facility, located in Hamilton, Ontario. Goodrich was responsible for purchasing and recompounding the PVC that was reclaimed. In another recycling partnership, the company introduced the first blow-molded bottles using recycled PVC. Still, in 1991 the Geon division lost $135 million on $1.2 billion in revenues. Patient saw that Goodrich was pushing itself as a specialty chemical maker but really was a high-cost producer of a commodity product. Goodrich was spending a lot on research and development instead of cutting costs.

1993: SPINOFF OF GEON FROM GOODRICH

In March 1993 Geon was spun off from Goodrich, with Patient staying on as president, CEO, and chairman. Patient told *Forbes,* "We took a clean sheet of paper and started over." During the week following the announcement of the initial public offering, Goodrich stock plummeted some 18 percent. Goodrich had been selling itself as a PVC and chemical company and the impending sale came as a surprise to shareholders and analysts who had foreseen a strong resurgence in the PVC industry and had bought Goodrich shares as a value play. While the Geon Division had produced 35 percent of sales and consisted of 50 percent of the company's assets, it also had experienced six quarters of losses since 1991. Geon sold at $18 per share in April in the first of two offerings. The second public offering in November sold at $20 per share. Goodrich raised $700 million in the sale and planned to increase its investments in aerospace and specialty chemicals.

Newly independent, The Geon Company was the third largest PVC resin supplier in North America, with 1.94 billion pounds of capacity. Shintech had 2.3 billion pounds of capacity per year, followed by Occidental Chemical Corporation with 2.1 billion. At the time of the sale the PVC maker had 2,500 employees; 14 businesses with resin-making compounding sites in the United States, Canada, and Australia; and a 50 percent share in a PVC compounding plant in England. Shintech was a low-cost resin and compounding company.

In a strategy designed to make Geon the recognized low-cost provider in the industry, product offerings in both resins and compounds were reduced and consolidated. The number of raw materials needed for manufacturing processes was also reduced. While this was being accomplished, Geon began targeting high-performance custom-molded compounds for future growth, thereby shifting the company away from some of the volatility in the PVC resins business.

In 1993 the U.S. PVC industry sold a record 10.5 billion pounds on the heels of eight consecutive years of 6 percent average growth. The upswing was led by an improved housing market and construction demand for residential siding, windows, and flooring. The industry was again at a high rate of capacity and the year ended unusually, with price increases and no typical year-end slowdown.

Because of the economic recession in Europe and Japan, though, world growth in PVC was weak in 1993, at 5 percent, and U.S. exports were flat. The majority of Geon PVC sales, 87 percent, were in North America. The Far East PVC growth was twice that of North America but Geon had only a small part of that market. The company's fiscal 1993 debt-to-capital ratio was 32 percent. Revenues broke down with 52 percent coming from vinyl resins, 39 percent from vinyl compounds, 9 percent from vinyl chloride monomer (VCM), licensing, and other income. The number of employees had fallen by 35 percent since 1991 and was at 1,930 by year-end. Three high-cost resin plants had been closed, eliminating 500 million pounds or 25 percent of 1991 total resin production capability. In contrast to its position in 1991, when it was losing money and was a high-cost commodity producer, Geon by the end of 1993 was trimmer, more focused, and in the black, with its stock reflecting a healthy 32 percent total return since the initial public offering.

In 1994 Geon announced plans to increase VCM capacity in one of its plants at least 50 percent by 1996. The move made the company less dependent on competition for raw materials while providing the raw material for PVC production at a lower cost than could be obtained by purchasing it from an outside supplier. Because of environmental concerns, chlorine use was declining in the paper industry, which lowered demand for one of the raw materials that Geon continued to purchase.

By 1996, as a result of the company's efficiency efforts, Geon was producing 20 percent more PVC resin than it had been four years earlier even though it had closed three resin plants that accounted for 25 percent of its capacity. That year, however, Geon sputtered to a full-year profit of only $12.2 million, compared to the $71.3 million figure for 1995, thanks to a brutal combination of a drop in PVC prices and increases in raw material costs. Results for 1997 were only marginally better as overcapacity in the PVC industry grew worse following the outbreak of the Asian financial crisis. That year, Geon promoted Thomas Waltermire from CFO to chief operating officer, placing him in charge of day-to-day operations and positioning him to succeed Patient. The firm also shifted into growth mode

by completing its first acquisition since gaining independence from Goodrich. In October, Geon acquired Synergistics Industries Limited of Mississauga, Ontario, a maker of plastic compounds and liquid plasticizers used in consumer products, such as medical bottles, and construction materials, such as electrical wire and cable insulation and jacketing. Purchased for $86.5 million, Synergistics had six manufacturing sites in the United States and Canada and generated $293 million in revenues in 1996.

Attempting to escape from the cyclicality of the highly competitive commodity PVC resin business, Geon in December 1998 combined its PVC business with that of Occidental Chemical (OxyChem) to form the joint venture OxyVinyls. Geon held a 24 percent stake in the venture, while OxyChem held the other 76 percent. Following this move, Geon was able to concentrate more of its resources on value-added, higher-priced products such as vinyl compounds, specialty resins, and performance polymers. These areas were built up through a series of acquisitions in 1998 and 1999, including the purchases of five formulators of plastisols, highly plasticized PVC compounds. In July 1999 Geon also acquired Virginia-based O'Sullivan Corporation for approximately $191 million, gaining a manufacturer of polymer films used in automobile interiors, book binders, medical bags, and other products. O'Sullivan became the core of Geon's engineered films operations. Also in 1999 the company consolidated its plastic compounding operations by shutting down two plants, one in Ontario and one in Texas, resulting in a workforce reduction of about 250. Midyear, Waltermire succeeded Patient as CEO of Geon, and it was under Waltermire's watch that Geon agreed to merge with M. A. Hanna.

2000: HANNA + GEON = POLYONE

In a stock-swap deal announced in May 2000 and completed that September, M. A. Hanna and Geon merged to form PolyOne Corporation. The combination created the world's largest polymer company, with a range of operations consisting of polymer compounds, color and additive systems, specialty resins, rubber compounds, engineered films, and polymer distribution. PolyOne began with a workforce of around 9,000 and 80 manufacturing sites around the world. On a pro forma basis, combined revenues exceeded $3 billion. The firm was initially headquartered in Cleveland, but it later moved to the nearby city of Avon Lake, where Geon had been based. On the management front, Ashkettle, who had headed Hanna, had been slated to serve as chairman and CEO of PolyOne, but he abruptly resigned from Hanna just before the merger was consummated. As a result, Waltermire took control as PolyOne's first chairman, president, and CEO.

PolyOne got off to a very rough start in part because of the double whammy of an economic downturn and high oil prices, the latter of which drove up raw material costs. Operationally, the company was also hampered because the dozens of acquisitions that Hanna had made in the years leading up to the merger had not been adequately integrated. Thus, the management team at PolyOne launched a string of streamlining initiatives that by mid-2003 had reduced the number of plants to around 65 and the workforce to around 7,200. As this restructuring unfolded in the midst of the economic downturn, the company suffered net losses for both 2001 and 2002: $46.1 million and $58.9 million, respectively. Revenues for both years were around $2.5 billion.

Seeking to cut its high debt load of nearly $800 million and to focus its attention on a few core businesses, PolyOne in October 2003 announced plans to divest three businesses—rubber compounding, engineered films, and specialty resins—that accounted for one-fourth of its 2002 sales. The company intended to concentrate on plastics compounding, colors and additives for the plastics industry, and the distribution of resins. In August 2004 PolyOne sold its rubber compounding business to an investment group for about $120 million. The following October the company reached an agreement to sell its engineered films unit to an investor group consisting of members of the unit's management team and the private equity firm Matrix Capital Markets for gross proceeds of $26.7 million. As part of the deal, which closed in February 2006, PolyOne retained an 18 percent stake in the divested business.

Later in October 2005, Waltermire unexpectedly stepped down from his leadership position. Taking over as CEO on an interim basis was Patient, the former head of Geon, who had served as nonexecutive chairman of PolyOne since November 2003. In December 2005, during Patient's interim term as CEO, the company announced that it had been unable to find a buyer willing to pay "acceptable terms" for the specialty resins business and that unit would therefore be retained. PolyOne brought onboard a new leader in February 2006, naming Stephen Newlin chairman, president, and CEO. Newlin had previously spent three years as an executive at Ecolab Inc. and 23 years at Nalco Chemical Company, two specialty chemical concerns.

Among Newlin's initial efforts at PolyOne was an attempt to bring more balance into the mix of industries to which the firm supplied compounds and other products. The company, which had been heavily dependent on the recession-prone building and construction and automobile industries, began making a more concerted effort to capture business in higher-growth areas, such as electronics. PolyOne continued to earmark much of the cash it generated to pay down long-term debt, which was reduced to $567.7 million by the end of 2006. Another of Newlin's goals was to increase overseas sales, which accounted for about one-third of overall 2006 revenues. Toward that end, PolyOne in 2006 began building a plant in Kutno, Poland, to serve the markets of Eastern Europe and also set up a business development office in India to establish a beachhead in that rapidly developing market. Already running three plants in China and generating about $65 million in annual sales there, PolyOne in late 2006 announced an agreement to acquire Ngai Hing PlastChem Company Ltd., operator of a vinyl compounding plant in the southern Chinese city of Dongguan. In February 2007 PolyOne revealed plans to establish a research and service center in northeastern China. Through such initiatives, it seemed possible that the high expectations that had accompanied the creation of PolyOne might finally be realized.

Jay P. Pederson, April S. Dougal
Updated, David E. Salamie

PRINCIPAL SUBSIDIARIES

Auseon Limited (Australia); Compounding Technology, Euro S.A. (France); Conexus, Inc.; DH Compounding Company; Geon Development, Inc.; Hanna France SARL; Hanna PAR Corporation; Hollinger Development Company; L. E. Carpenter & Company; LP Holdings (Canada); M.A. Hanna Asia Holding Company; M.A. Hanna Export Services Company (Barbados); M.A. Hanna Plastic Group, Inc.; M.A. Hanna de Mexico, S.A. de C.V.; MAH Plastics Company; O'Sullivan Plastics Corporation; O'Sullivan Films Holding Corporation; POL Plastics Company; Polymer Diagnostics, Inc.; PolyOne, LLC; PolyOne Belgium SA; PolyOne Canada, Inc.; PolyOne Color and Additives Germany, GmbH; PolyOne Corporation UK Limited; PolyOne Czech Republic; PolyOne Deutschland, GmbH (Germany); PolyOne Distribution de Mexico S.A. de C.V.; PolyOne Engineered Films, Inc.; PolyOne Funding Corporation; PolyOne International Financial Services Company (Ireland); PolyOne International Trading (Shanghai) Co., Ltd. (China); PolyOne Italy, Srl; PolyOne Management International Holding, S.A. (Spain); PolyOne Spain, S.A.; PolyOne France S.A.S.; PolyOne Hungary, Ltd.; PolyOne Polska

(Poland); PolyOne Poland Manufacturing; PolyOne-Shenzhen Co. Ltd. (China); PolyOne Shanghai, China; PolyOne Singapore, Ltd.; PolyOne-Suzhou, China; PolyOne Sweden, AB; PolyOne Th. Bergmann, GmbH (Germany); PolyOne Termoplasticos do Brasil Ltda. (Brazil); PVC Powder Blends LP (90%); Regalite Plastics Corporation; Shawnee Holdings, Inc.; Star Color Co. Ltd. (Thailand); Tekno Polimer Group (Turkey); PolyOne Wilflex Australasia Pty. Ltd. (Australia).

PRINCIPAL COMPETITORS

Ferro Corporation; A. Schulman, Inc.; Spartech Corporation; Shintech, Inc.; Georgia Gulf Corporation; Formosa Plastics Corporation; BASF Aktiengesellschaft.

FURTHER READING

Adams, Jarret, "Geon Reformulates for the Future," *Chemical Week*, September 30, 1998, p. 49.

"Behind the Revolving Door at B.F. Goodrich," *Business Week*, October 15, 1984, pp. 150–53.

Berman, Phyllis, "Here We Go Again," *Forbes*, July 15, 1985, pp. 32–33.

Blackford, Mansel G., and K. Austin Kerr, *BFGoodrich: Tradition and Transformation, 1870–1995*, Columbus: Ohio State University Press, 1996, 507 p.

Brockinton, Langdon, and W. David Gibson, "From the Tire Industry: Growth in Chemicals," *Chemical Week*, August 31, 1988, pp. 26–29.

Byrne, Harlan S., "M. A. Hanna: The Right Chemistry," *Barron's*, September 30, 1996, p. 23.

Byrne, John A., "A New Act in Akron," *Forbes*, November 21, 1983, pp. 78–79.

Cimperman, Jennifer Scott, "Geon Profits Jump Despite Dip in Sales," *Cleveland Plain Dealer*, June 23, 2000, p. 31S.

——, "Hanna, Geon Plan to Merge," *Cleveland Plain Dealer*, May 9, 2000, p. 1C.

——, "PolyOne to Close Up to 12 Factories," *Cleveland Plain Dealer*, April 3, 2001, p. 1C.

Coeyman, Marjorie, "Geon Learns to Stand on Its Own," *Chemical Week*, December 15, 1993, pp. 45–46.

Coeyman, Marjorie, Maurice Martorella, and Emily Plishner, "Geon VMC Expansion Will End Its Merchant Buying," *Chemical Week*, March 30, 1994, p. 9.

Collyer, John Lyon, *The B.F. Goodrich Story of Creative Enterprise: 1870–1952*, New York: Newcomen Society, 1952, 32 p.

Croly, Herbert, *Marcus Alonzo Hanna: His Life and Work*, Hamden, Conn.: Archon Books, 1965, 495 p.

Esposito, Frank, "Newlin Takes Customer-Focused Approach," *Plastics News*, June 21, 2006, p. 19.

Flaherty, Robert J., "Harvey Firestone Must Be Spinning in His Grave," *Forbes*, September 15, 1980, pp. 158–64.

Flint, Troy, "Geon Forms Venture with Occidental," *Cleveland Plain Dealer*, June 26, 1998, p. 1C.

——, "Geon Plans to Close Plants in U.S., Canada, Cut 250 Jobs," *Cleveland Plain Dealer*, November 19, 1998, p. 2C.

——, "Hanna to Trim 260 Workers, Shut Plants," *Cleveland Plain Dealer*, August 7, 1998, p. 1C.

Gardner, Greg, "One Startling Transformation: Hanna Co. Changes into Major Player in Polymers Market," *Akron (Ohio) Beacon Journal*, August 15, 1988, p. B1.

Gerdel, Thomas W., "Avon Lake Polymer Firm Names New Top Executive," *Cleveland Plain Dealer*, February 15, 2006, p. C1.

——, "Geon's Chief Executive Stepping Down," *Cleveland Plain Dealer*, April 28, 1999, p. 1C.

——, "Getting Back on Track," *Cleveland Plain Dealer*, November 29, 1998, p. 1H.

——, "Hanna Names New President," *Cleveland Plain Dealer*, May 26, 1999, p. 1C.

——, "Hanna's Last Iron Mine in U.S. to Shut," *Cleveland Plain Dealer*, May 14, 1985, p. 1E.

——, "M. A. Hanna Replaces Top Exec," *Cleveland Plain Dealer*, October 9, 1998, p. 1C.

——, "PolyOne Chief Unexpectedly Quits," *Cleveland Plain Dealer*, October 8, 2005, p. C1.

Gleisser, Marcus, "Hanna Family in High and Low Society," *Cleveland Plain Dealer*, October 9, 1984, p. 14E.

——, "Hanna Has Come Long Way, Marcus," *Cleveland Plain Dealer*, October 8, 1984, p. 14E.

——, "Hanna Mining Seeks Revival of Old Name," *Cleveland Plain Dealer*, March 21, 1985, pp. 1C, 2C.

——, "Hanna Promoting President to CEO," *Cleveland Plain Dealer*, September 6, 1996, p. 1C.

——, "Last Humphrey Leaves Hanna," *Cleveland Plain Dealer*, September 22, 1984, p. 3B.

——, "'60s Caught Hanna in Debate About U.S. Nickel Contracts," *Cleveland Plain Dealer*, October 8, 1984, p. 14E.

——, "Takeover Attempt Tangled Affair," *Cleveland Plain Dealer*, October 10, 1984, p. 5B.

Grant, Alison, "PolyOne Selling Units to Pay Debt, Change Focus," *Cleveland Plain Dealer*, October 22, 2003, p. C1.

Hairston, Deborah W., "A Retreading for Goodrich," *Chemical Week*, June 26, 1985, pp. 8, 10.

Kimelman, John, "Ohio Nocturne," *Financial World*, June 7, 1994, pp. 40–41.

Kindel, Stephen, "Goodrich and Geon: Who Needs This Deal?" *Financial World*, May 11, 1993, p. 18.

Krouse, Peter, "CEO Seizes Chance to Make PolyOne Reach Full Potential," *Cleveland Plain Dealer*, January 4, 2007, p. C1.

——, "Growing Pains Plague PolyOne," *Cleveland Plain Dealer*, January 20, 2003, p. E1.

——, "Hanna CEO's Firing Still Raises Questions," *Cleveland Plain Dealer*, March 26, 2003, p. C1.

————, "Smaller but Stronger After Concentrating on the Core," *Cleveland Plain Dealer,* November 7, 2004, p. G1.

Leaversuch, Robert D., "BFGoodrich Is Exiting PVC Supply; Vinyl Div. to Become Independent," *Modern Plastics,* March 1993, pp. 20–21.

Lerner, Ivan, "M. A. Hanna and Geon Unite As a Specialty Polymers Powerhouse," *Chemical Market Reporter,* May 15, 2000, pp. 3, 34.

————, "PolyOne Continues Reconfiguring and Restructuring Process," *Chemical Market Reporter,* August 13, 2001, p. 19.

Lubove, Seth H., "M. A. Hanna to Buy Day International for $348.9 Million," *Wall Street Journal,* July 13, 1987.

Machan, Dyan, "Starting Over," *Forbes,* July 4, 1994, pp. 53–56.

McConville, Daniel J., "M. A. Hanna Prepares for Better Days," *Chemical Week,* June 19, 1991, pp. 25–26.

McGough, Robert, "High Iron," *Financial World,* April 11, 1992, pp. 26–27.

McGregor, Douglas J., *M. A. Hanna Company: A Case Study in Corporate Transformation,* New York: Newcomen Society of the United States, 1998, 20 p.

Mullin, Rick, "Hanna's Ambitious Five-Year Plan," *Chemical Week,* April 9, 1997, pp. 36–37.

Phillips, Stephen, "Goodrich to Spin Off Geon Unit," *Cleveland Plain Dealer,* February 18, 1993, p. 1D.

Plishner, Emily S., "M. A. Hanna Looks to Compound Bottom Line Growth," *Chemical Week,* April 28, 1998, p. 79.

"PolyOne Shines Financially, Grows Globally," *Plastics News,* February 26, 2007, p. 22.

Prizinsky, David, "Hanna Looking to Exit Iron Ore, Coal Businesses," *Crain's Cleveland Business,* November 5, 1990, p. 3.

————, "A Master Makeover: Former Hanna Boss Guided Century-Old Company's Reinvention As a Polymer Force," *Crain's Cleveland Business,* April 3, 2000, p. 62.

————, "Spinoff of Resin Biz Pays Off for Geon," *Crain's Cleveland Business,* March 20, 2000, p. 2.

Rose, William Ganson, *Cleveland: The Making of a City,* Kent, Ohio: Kent State University Press, 1990.

Sabath, Donald, "Hanna Chairman Has High Expectations," *Cleveland Plain Dealer,* May 23, 1989.

Schiller, Zachary, "Goodrich: From Tires to PVC to Chemicals to Aerospace ... ," *Business Week,* July 18, 1994, pp. 86–87.

————, "Goodrich: 'Something Very Drastic ... Had to Be Done,'" *Business Week,* July 1, 1985, p. 27.

————, "The Iron Age Is Waning for M. A. Hanna," *Business Week,* August 10, 1987, p. 70H.

Slakter, Ann, "BFGoodrich Tires of Tires," *Chemical Week,* January 6–13, 1988, pp. 13–14.

————, "A New President for a 'New' Goodrich," *Chemical Week,* October 8, 1986, pp. 30–34.

Stringer, Kortney, "Geon to Acquire Vinyl-Products Firm," *Cleveland Plain Dealer,* June 3, 1999, p. 1C.

"Tire Companies Beef up Chemicals," *Chemical Week,* May 4, 1983, pp. 30–34.

Tullo, Alex, "OxyChem and Geon Form Joint Venture for Polyvinyl Chloride Resin Business," *Chemical Market Reporter,* June 29, 1998, pp. 1, 32.

Verespej, Michael A., "Stability Before Growth," *Industry Week,* April 15, 1996, pp. 12, 14, 16.

Walsh, Kerri, "Ashkettle Departs Hanna," *Chemical Week,* August 23–30, 2000, p. 7.

————, "Hanna Gets Back on Its Feet," *Chemical Week,* February 16, 2000, p. 56.

————, "Walker Works to Rebuild Hanna," *Chemical Week,* December 9, 1998, p. 76.

Westervelt, Robert, "PolyOne Starts Up Under the Gun," *Chemical Week,* January 31, 2001, pp. 42–43.

Williams, Monci Jo, "Hanna the Transformed," *Fortune,* August 28, 1989, p. 83.

Winter, Ralph E., "Geon, Growing Fast, Expects Jump in Earnings," *Wall Street Journal,* May 10, 1999, p. B5A.

————, "Hanna Focuses on Regaining Sales, Improving Customer Service, CEO Says," *Wall Street Journal,* December 16, 1998, p. B5A.

————, "Hanna Is Hurt in Short Term by Revamping," *Wall Street Journal,* December 13, 1991.

Yerak, Rebecca, "Geon's Chances Pay Off," *Cleveland Plain Dealer,* February 1, 1994, p. 1F.

Zawacki, Michael, "Plastics, Pressure, and Profits," *Inside Business,* September 2004, pp. 38–40.

Potlatch Corporation

601 West Riverside Avenue, Suite 1100
Spokane, Washington 99201-0603
U.S.A.
Telephone: (509) 835-1500
Fax: (509) 835-1559
Web site: http://www.potlatchcorp.com

Public Company
Incorporated: 1903 as Potlatch Lumber Company
Employees: 3,900
Sales: $1.61 billion (2006)
Stock Exchanges: New York Chicago
Ticker Symbol: PCH
NAIC: 525930 Real Estate Investment Trusts; 113110 Timber Tract Operations; 113310 Logging; 321113 Sawmills; 321212 Softwood Veneer and Plywood Manufacturing; 321219 Reconstituted Wood Product Manufacturing; 322110 Pulp Mills; 322130 Paperboard Mills; 322291 Sanitary Paper Product Manufacturing

■ ■ ■

Potlatch Corporation is a real estate investment trust (REIT) that owns and manages around 1.5 million acres of timberland in Arkansas, Idaho, Minnesota, Wisconsin, and Oregon. Through Potlatch Forest Products Corporation, the firm's taxable REIT subsidiary, Potlatch operates 13 manufacturing facilities in Arkansas, Idaho, Illinois, Michigan, Minnesota, and Nevada that produce lumber, plywood, particleboard, bleached paperboard, and private-label consumer tissue

products, including bathroom tissue, facial tissue, paper towels, and napkins. Potlatch sells its products mainly in the United States, but is a major international supplier of bleached paperboard. The company, which was established in the mountainous, evergreen forests of northern Idaho in 1903, reorganized itself as a REIT at the beginning of 2006 in order to take advantage of the special tax treatment for REITs.

EARLY HISTORY

The early history of Potlatch is closely tied to the more general history of the U.S. logging industry. In the United States logging began in New England, where forests were cleared, often carelessly, to make room for the country's first towns and farms and to provide lumber for buildings, fuel, and furniture. Once thought to be a virtually inexhaustible resource, these forests were nearly depleted by the mid-1800s, and logging companies thus began to spring up in the Midwest, especially in the "North Woods" of Wisconsin, Michigan, and Minnesota. By the 1890s much of these vast midwestern pine forests also were cleared, forcing lumbermen to look to the South and to the far Northwest for new regions of forested land.

Also in the 19th century the railroads were spreading their tracks to the outer edges of the nation. The Utah Northern extended its line in 1874 just across the southern Idaho border and several years later began to lay additional tracks to reach the mining communities farther north. By 1883 Northern Pacific had built a line from St. Paul, Minnesota, to Tacoma, Washington, which wound its way through such towns in northern Idaho as Bonner's Ferry and Sandpoint. Without the railroads to carry logs and lumber products, dreams of harvesting Idaho's evergreen forests would never have been realized.

As the railroads brought settlers to the Western frontier, stories of the land's riches were carried back east. Northern Idaho, cut off from the southern part of the state by the deep gorge of the Salmon River, was uncharted for the most part, but many midwestern timbermen began to hear of the area's towering stands of white pine and other valuable trees. Frederick Weyerhaeuser of St. Paul, Minnesota, a powerful lumber capitalist and one of the founders of Potlatch, saw an exhibit of Idaho timberland at Chicago's 1893 World's Fair, and it was he who led the charge of Midwest lumber companies to the Northwest. He did this with the help of the "Weyerhaeuser syndicate," a group of midwestern businessmen who had long worked together to secure timber for their individual mills. In 1900 his syndicate bought an astonishing 900,000 acres of timberland in the Pacific Northwest, thus forming Weyerhaeuser Timber Company, and that year Weyerhaeuser himself toured on horseback northern Idaho's stands of white pine. Soon the syndicate was buying additional Northwest timberland from railroads, state auctions, and homesteaders; other midwestern companies, trusting Weyerhaeuser's judgment, quickly followed.

In northern Idaho's Palouse, Potlatch, and Elk River basins, thousands of acres of timberland were being purchased by midwestern companies, but most went to just two men: William Deary of Northland Pine Company, a firm established by the Weyerhaeuser syndicate, and Henry Turrish of Wisconsin Log & Lumber Company. Although competitors, Deary and Turrish were by 1902 buying land together, in part for convenience but also to keep land prices lower. The owners of Northland and Wisconsin Log & Lumber soon recognized the value of this collaboration, and the following year they decided to merge their Idaho timberland under a new firm, which they called Potlatch Lumber Company. When the company was formed it owned more than 100,000 acres, but it quickly gained additional land, as well as two mills, when it bought nearby Palouse River Lumber Company and Codd Lumber Company in 1903 and 1904, respectively.

Backed with an initial $3 million in capital, Potlatch Lumber Company was established with great hopes but with little recognition of the difficulties posed by the area's rugged environment. Its name, derived from the northwest Indian word *patshatl,* which referred to an elaborate ceremony of gift-giving, was selected because the Potlatch River cut through the company's land. The first president of Potlatch was Weyerhaeuser's son, Charles, and the vice-president was Turrish, but the dominant personality of the company was Deary, who was appointed general manager. One of the first goals of Potlatch was to plan and build a magnificent new sawmill, which Deary decided to place along the Palouse River about 15 miles north of Moscow, Idaho. Opened on September 11, 1906, the structure was some 300 feet long, 100 feet wide, and 70 feet tall, and its giant Corliss engine gave the mill an annual capacity of 135 million board feet. Production began with 125 employees.

To house these employees, the company decided to build a town on two hills overlooking the sawmill. By the mill's opening day there were 128 completed homes, and soon there was also a hotel, two churches, a large general store, and an elementary and high school. Called Potlatch, this attractive, well-designed town was a great source of pride for the company but also a considerable drain on funds. The company continued to own and maintain the town until the 1950s.

Another major investment by the early company was its 45-mile railroad line, which, when completed in 1907, ran from Palouse, Washington, east through Potlatch and other towns, ending in Bovill, Idaho. It was used to carry logs from the company's timberland to the new mill, as well as to transport finished lumber to connecting railroads at Palouse and Bovill.

Despite Potlatch Lumber Company's high-quality timber, modern sawmill, and new railway, its early years were disappointing and often marked by losses. The first

KEY DATES

1903: William Deary and Henry Turrish merge their Idaho timberland in a new company called Potlatch Lumber Company.

1906: Potlatch opens a sawmill near Moscow, Idaho.

1931: Potlatch merges with Clearwater Timber Company and Edward Rutledge Timber Company to form Potlatch Forests, Inc.

1950: Company pioneers in the production of bleached paperboard from wood waste.

1956: Company merges with Arkansas-based Southern Lumber Company.

1964: Company expands into Minnesota with the acquisition of Northwest Paper Company.

1965: Headquarters shifts to San Francisco.

1971: Richard B. Madden becomes CEO and begins trimming the company to concentrate on four core areas and initiates a capital expenditure program.

1973: Company changes its name to Potlatch Corporation.

1981: Company builds the first U.S. plant to make oriented strand board.

1994: John M. Richards is named chairman and CEO.

1997: Corporate headquarters relocates to Spokane, Washington.

1999: A deal with Anderson-Tully Company to form Timberland Growth Corporation, a timber-based REIT, falls apart; L. Pendleton Siegel is named chairman and CEO.

2002: Potlatch divests its printing paper operations.

2004: Company sells its oriented strand board plants in Minnesota.

2006: Potlatch is converted to a real estate investment trust; Michael J. Covey is brought on-board as CEO.

dividend was not paid until 1911, and even that was just 3 percent, a low figure in the high-risk lumber business. A few years later the company was paying 10 percent, but the average dividend from 1903 to 1923, when the company's holdings had reached some 170,000 acres, was just 3.6 percent. Before his death in 1914, Frederick Weyerhaeuser reportedly said the company was appropriately called Potlatch because he

had given it so much money with little return. Other Idaho timber companies had similarly poor records.

The company's tree-cutting policy contributed to this shaky financial picture. Instead of selectively cutting the area's white pine, ponderosa pine, and Douglas fir—the species most in demand—the company cut all trees in its path, even those, such as tamarack, that often cost more to harvest than was economical. Other problems included the company's high capital costs (for the railway, mill, and town), rugged terrain and inaccessible timber areas, deep winter snow, the relatively few trees per acre, and heavy state taxes. The 1914 opening of the Panama Canal had an especially harsh impact on Potlatch and other Idaho timber companies. Before the canal's opening, Potlatch benefited from rail costs cheaper than those paid by its Pacific Coast rivals, who were hundreds of miles farther from the major Eastern markets. After 1914 companies located on the Pacific Coast were able to send their timber to these markets by boat, at a cost one-third cheaper than rail, thus undercutting the price of lumber sold by Potlatch and other Idaho timber firms.

GREAT DEPRESSION: CRISIS AND MERGER

As early as 1926 the entire Northwest lumber industry was suffering from overproduction and declining prices. When the Great Depression hit the country in 1929, causing a precipitous drop in new building construction, Potlatch found itself facing potential bankruptcy, as did northern Idaho's other major timber companies, Clearwater Timber Company and Edward Rutledge Timber Company, which had been established in 1900 and 1902, respectively, by the Weyerhaeuser syndicate. The Clearwater mill was located just south of Potlatch in the town of Lewiston, and the mill of Edward Rutledge was found farther north in Coeur d'Alene.

After considerable debate among stockholders, the financial crisis was resolved by merging the three companies into an organization called Potlatch Forests, Inc. The new corporation, headquartered in Lewiston, was headed initially by John Philip Weyerhaeuser, Jr., a grandson of Frederick Weyerhaeuser, and later, in 1935, by the older Rudolph M. Weyerhaeuser, one of the founder's sons. Effective April 29, 1931, the merger did not remove the companies' common problem of a weak market but did provide for better efficiency. Some timber in the Clearwater land, for example, could be taken more economically to the Potlatch mill. Expensive machinery could be shared between the three concerns. The merger also allowed for a more ambitious attempt at selective cutting, which Clearwater had begun in 1929. The goal of selective cutting was to fell only mature or diseased trees, allowing the younger, healthy ones to stand for future generations of logging. Reforestation, however, did not begin until 1954.

Despite these gains, the Depression remained a difficult period for Potlatch, which was forced to cut its prices and the wages of its workers. The Coeur d'Alene mill was closed for some time beginning in 1932, and that year its operations in the town of Potlatch were open only to ship lumber held in storage. Losses were reported in all but two years of the 1930s, resulting in a total deficit of $8.7 million for the decade. During this period, however, the company did develop an important new product, Pres-to-logs, a slow-burning, virtually smokeless fuel made of compressed sawdust, wood chips, and splinters. The logs were ideal for fireplaces located in homes or on railcars, where smoke had to be kept to a minimum. A first in the industry, Pres-to-logs were made by a process involving extreme heat, high pressure, and moisture.

POSTWAR ERA: NEW PRODUCTS AND GEOGRAPHIC EXPANSION

World War II brought increased demand for lumber to build houses, military camps, and other facilities for soldiers, and Potlatch, benefiting from booming lumber orders, gained badly needed profits. From 1940 to 1945 the company's after-tax profits surpassed $5 million, of which $1.2 million was placed in a reserve fund for future upgrading of its mills and machinery and for introducing new products. By the war's end, the company was poised for strong, sustained growth, which would be overseen by George F. Jewett, a grandson of the founder, who became president of Potlatch in 1946. Three years later Jewett was elected the company's first chairman of the board, a position that was filled later by Edwin Weyerhaeuser Davis, another grandson, in 1957 and then by Benton R. Cancell in 1962.

The company's profitable postwar era was distinguished by its large number of new products. The first to be introduced was veneer, or thin sheets, of white pine, which Potlatch hoped would be popular for home paneling. To make this product, giant logs of white pine had to be peeled and then made into rolls. In 1949, after three years of developing the process, the company began making white pine veneer, but the project quickly came to be too expensive and problematic. By 1952 the operations were successfully converted to make a different product, plywood, which was made from layers of Douglas fir, white pine, Ponderosa pine, or larch.

An especially important new product for Potlatch was paperboard, a thick paper with a variety of uses,

such as making milk cartons and other containers. To manufacture the product, the company in 1950 built a new bleach kraft pulp and paper mill, located in Lewiston, which was the first in the United States to produce bleached paperboard from sawmill wood waste, namely chips. Within the next few years Potlatch introduced "Lock-Deck" laminated decking, "Pure-Pak" cartons for milk, and additional paperboard items, such as paper plates and meat trays. By the early 1960s the company had also purchased a mill for folding paperboard and entered a new line of products by acquiring Clearwater Tissue Mills, Inc.

To obtain the raw materials for these new products, Potlatch began to expand its timber reserves. In 1956 it merged with Southern Lumber Company, an Arkansas firm founded by the Weyerhaeuser syndicate in 1882. With the subsequent purchase of Bradley Lumber Company, also located in Arkansas, Potlatch controlled more than 100,000 acres of Arkansas timberland, mostly of southern yellow pine, oak, and other hardwoods. Directing its sights to Minnesota, Potlatch merged in 1964 with another Weyerhaeuser creation, Northwest Paper Company, a producer of printing and writing paper. Established in 1898, Northwest owned about 220,000 acres of forested land in Minnesota, where jack pine, aspen, red pine, and balsam fir were the most common species. With these mergers, Potlatch had become a national company, and the small town of Lewiston subsequently proved to be a difficult place from which to manage its new holdings. As a result, the company's headquarters were moved to San Francisco in 1965, and a few years later, in 1973, the company changed its name from Potlatch Forests, Inc., to Potlatch Corporation.

THE MADDEN ERA, 1971–94: REFOCUSING AND CAPITAL EXPENDITURES

By 1971, when Richard B. Madden became CEO, the company had diversified into some 20 separate product lines, including modular housing and corrugated boxes, and its sales had reached $356 million. Potlatch also was investing millions of dollars to reduce its air and water pollution. Not simply taking over the reins, Madden spent much of his first year developing what became the company's guiding business philosophy: "Potlatch will be a company characterized by a growing profit and reasonable rate of return that is achieved by talented, well-trained, and highly motivated people. It will be a company that is properly supported by a sound financial structure and will feature a keen sense of social responsibility."

Using this simple statement, Madden then initiated an intensive review of the company's many components. The result was a decision to sell its less profitable activities and to concentrate on just four product lines: wood products (lumber, plywood, and particleboard), printed papers, pulp and paperboard, and tissue products. Moreover, the company decided to focus on "higher-value-added" products, or those that had a relatively high value compared with the cost of the raw materials. Such products tended to be less affected by recurring business cycles. In printed papers, for example, Potlatch concentrated on high grades of coated paper, the type commonly used for annual reports and advertising brochures.

Beginning in the mid-1970s and extending into the 1980s and 1990s, the company combined these shifting priorities with a new program of capital expenditures. In 1981, for example, Potlatch built in Minnesota the first U.S. plant to make oriented strand board (OSB). An alternative to plywood, OSB was a multilayered board made from strands of aspen "oriented" in various directions; the strands were held together by a mixture of wax and resin and compressed under intense heat. By 1991 the company was making more than a billion square feet of OSB in two varieties: Oxboard, with five layers, and Potlatch Select, with three. Although capital projects were curtailed during the recession of the early 1980s, by the late 1980s Potlatch was again spending large sums of money to retool its plants and machinery. Projects completed by the early 1990s included a $40 million upgrade of the Lewiston sawmill and log processing center; a $400 million modernization of the Lewiston pulp and paperboard mill; a new $27 million lumber mill in Warren, Arkansas; and, as part of a $107 million upgrade of its tissue operations, a new "twin wire" tissue machine in Lewiston. In 1993 Potlatch completed construction of a new $25 million tissue complex in North Las Vegas, Nevada, to service the southwestern market; that year, the company also began a multiyear, $525 million expansion of its pulp and printing paper mill in Cloquet, Minnesota.

This program of capital expenditures was reflected in the company's skyrocketing sales and healthy profit margins. Total sales jumped from $356 million in 1971, the year Madden became chairman of the board, to $504 million in 1975, $820 million in 1980, $950 million in 1985, and $1.37 billion in 1993, Madden's last full year as chairman. Even during the down years of the cyclical forest products industry, Potlatch managed to stay in the black. In the early 1990s earnings were highest in its wood products, such as lumber and oriented strand board, and, owing to difficult market conditions, considerably lower in printing paper and pulp and paperboard.

NEW LEADERSHIP

In May 1994 John M. Richards, president and COO, was named to replace Madden as chairman and CEO. L. Pendleton Siegel was promoted to Richards's former position. Capital expenditures continued in 1994, as Potlatch opened a new $27 million sawmill in Warren, Arkansas. Also in 1994, Potlatch expanded into northeastern Oregon when it began developing a 22,000-acre plantation for the growing of hybrid poplar trees, which could be harvested in six years, rather than the usual 50 to 70 years. The trees were slated to supply the bleached pulp mill in Lewiston beginning in the early 21st century and were viewed as a method to reduce the company's dependence on outside fiber sources. In December 1995 the company filed suit against Beloit Corporation alleging that Beloit had installed a defective pulp washer system at the Lewiston pulp mill. In June 1997 a jury awarded Potlatch damages of $95 million, but the judgment was thrown out in 1999 by the Idaho Supreme Court, which returned the suit to a lower court. Potlatch's continued pursuit of the case was halted when Beloit filed for bankruptcy protection.

In a cost-saving move, Potlatch in 1997 relocated its corporate headquarters to Spokane, Washington, the closest city to Lewiston with a major airport. The following year Potlatch began planning a complex merger of its Arkansas timberland with that of Anderson-Tully Company located in Mississippi and Arkansas into a newly formed real estate investment trust (REIT) called Timberland Growth Corporation. This deal fell apart during 1999, however, following the weakening of markets in Asia and the United States. In the middle of that year, Richards retired as chairman and CEO, with Siegel taking over those positions. Late in the year Potlatch completed the costly expansion of its Cloquet mill. The firm posted profits of $40.9 million for 1999 on net sales of $1.68 billion.

EARLY 21ST CENTURY: RESTRUCTURING AND A NARROWING FOCUS

Potlatch optimistically entered the 21st century under new leadership and with a 15-year $2 billion capital improvement program behind it, only to face a sharp market downturn that sent it into the red. For the first time in 30 years, prices for both wood and paper products were depressed at the same time, a situation compounded by rising energy costs. Burdened by a heavy debt load of more than $800 million that had been swollen in part to fund the large capital expenditures of the 1990s, Potlatch was forced to restructure. By early 2001, the company had trimmed about 9 percent of its workforce, or around 600 workers, and shut down its Jaype plywood plant near Pierce, Idaho. Restructuring charges of $28.3 million contributed to a net loss for 2000 of $33.2 million, the firm's first money-losing year since 1993.

Potlatch fared little better in 2001 when the economic downturn and competition from overseas hurt sales. As a result of continued low prices, the firm's printing paper business operated at a loss for the year, contributing to an overall loss of $79.4 million. By early 2002, when its debt load had ballooned to more than $1 billion, Potlatch announced its plan to divest the printing paper unit, an admission that its upgrade of the Cloquet mill had been a costly mistake. In May of that year, the company sold the Cloquet mill to the South African firm Sappi Limited for $485.5 million in cash and at the same time shut down its printing paper mill in Brainerd, Minnesota. The Brainerd mill was subsequently sold in early 2003 for $4.4 million. Potlatch also closed down its Bradley hardwood mill in Warren, Arkansas, in 2002, as it exited from the hardwood lumber business. In disposing of these properties, the company incurred pretax charges of $276.2 million, which largely contributed to a net loss for the year of $234.4 million. The divestments cut revenues to $1.29 billion, down from the previous year's total of $1.81 billion, while also enabling the debt load to be substantially reduced to $638.3 million. One bright spot during the year was the strength of the firm's consumer products division. In the fall, Potlatch launched a $66 million expansion of its tissue-conversion plant in Las Vegas.

In 2003, while celebrating its 100-year anniversary, Potlatch returned to the black, posting profits of $50.7 million on surging revenues of $1.51 billion. Among the factors helping the company were higher prices for its consumer products, an easing of oversupplied markets, and a softening of the U.S. dollar against foreign currencies, which favored U.S. producers rather than overseas importers. Facing few opportunities to grow its consumer products division in the West, where Potlatch produced 90 percent of the private-label tissue products sold in grocery stores, the company in 2003 laid plans to expand the division into the Midwest. In the middle of the following year, production commenced at a new tissue-converting plant in Elwood, Illinois, near Chicago. Also during this period, Potlatch was working to burnish its image as a responsible environmental steward of its large timber holdings. For example, in the spring of 2004 the nonprofit Forest Stewardship Council (FSC) gave its seal of approval to Potlatch's Idaho forestland following a rigorous environmental audit. Later, Potlatch became the first public company whose lands were 100 percent certified by the FSC.

Seeking to pay down its debt still further, Potlatch in September 2004 sold its three oriented strand board plants in Minnesota to Ainsworth Lumber Co. Ltd. of Vancouver, British Columbia, for approximately $452 million in cash. By the end of 2004, the firm was able to cut its debt load to $336.5 million. Proceeds from the sale also went toward a special dividend of $2.50 per share distributed to company stockholders. A $163.1 million after-tax gain on the sale pushed 2004 profits up to $271.2 million. Within its narrower product lines—which encompassed lumber, plywood, particleboard, bleached paperboard, and tissue products—Potlatch was pushing to develop new products. For instance, in 2005 the firm introduced fire-resistant cedar decking, a product created in response to the increasing number of wildfires that had been blazing across the West. Also debuting in 2005 was an RV-friendly toilet paper called SepticSure, which was able to break down within 30 seconds after a flush. Potlatch also expanded its lumber operations in May 2005 via the acquisition of a sawmill in Gwinn, Michigan, from Louisiana-Pacific Corporation.

2006: CONVERSION TO REIT

At the beginning of 2006 Potlatch joined an industry trend by converting to a real estate investment trust, mainly for tax reasons. Prior to the conversion, the company transferred all of its manufacturing operations into Potlatch Forest Products Corporation, a taxable REIT subsidiary. Whereas the operations of this subsidiary remained subject to federal corporate income taxes, earnings from the 1.5 million acres of timberland owned by the parent, principally the sale of standing timber, were no longer subject to these taxes. Soon after the conversion, Potlatch nearly tripled the regular quarterly dividends it paid to shareholders and also completed a special one-time distribution to shareholders amounting to $165 million in cash and $356 million in stock. The conversion to a REIT also coincided with a shift in leadership. In February 2006 Siegel stepped down as company president and CEO while remaining chairman. Brought onboard as Siegel's successor was Michael J. Covey, who had been an executive vice-president at Plum Creek Timber Company, Inc., where he had a played a key role in that firm becoming the nation's first timber REIT in 1999. At the end of 2006 Covey took over the Potlatch chairmanship as well.

In its first year as a REIT, Potlatch posted earnings of $139.1 million on revenues of $1.61 billion. Going forward, the company planned to be much more active in buying and selling property, as the REIT structure made such maneuvers more tax efficient. Following an acre-by-acre review of its holdings, Potlatch found that as much as 20 percent of its timber holdings, or about 300,000 acres of land, were more valuable for recreation cabins, trophy homes, and hunting grounds than for growing trees; this land was therefore earmarked for sale over a ten-year period. In the meantime, the company began scouting for timberland to add to its portfolio. In January 2007 Potlatch completed its first land acquisition as a REIT, and its first significant such purchase in 13 years, buying 76,000 acres of hardwood forest located in north-central Wisconsin. Seeking to derive additional value out of its landholdings, Potlatch in April 2007 began charging for recreational access to most of its 665,000 acres of forestland in Idaho.

Thomas Riggs
Updated, David E. Salamie

PRINCIPAL SUBSIDIARIES

Potlatch Forest Holdings, Inc.; Potlatch Forest Products Corporation; The Prescott and Northwestern Railroad Company; St. Maries River Railroad Co.; Warren & Saline River Railroad Company; NaturNorth Technologies, LLC.

PRINCIPAL OPERATING UNITS

Resource; Land Sales and Development; Pulp and Paperboard; Consumer Products; Wood Products.

PRINCIPAL COMPETITORS

Weyerhaeuser Company; Georgia-Pacific Corporation; Kimberly-Clark Corporation; The Procter & Gamble Company; Cascades Inc.; Longview Fibre Company; Plum Creek Timber Company, Inc.

FURTHER READING

"At Potlatch, Caution Is the Key," *Business Week,* January 11, 1988, p. 72.

Blackman, Ted, "Team Concept Involves Crews in All Aspects of Mills," *Forest Industries,* November 1991, p. 14.

Caldwell, Bert, "The REIT Stuff: Complex Potlatch Deal Represents 'New Approach to Doing Business,'" *Spokane (Wash.) Spokesman Review,* March 1, 1998, p. A12.

Hansen, Dan, "Groups Threaten Suit Over Pollution Permit: Activists Say Potlatch's Discharge Endangers Fish," *Spokane (Wash.) Spokesman Review,* August 13, 1998, p. B2.

Harrison, Andy, "Potlatch Expands in Major Market Sectors," *Pulp and Paper,* February 1995, pp. 34–35.

Hidy, Ralph W., Frank Ernest Hill, and Allan Nevins, *Timber and Men: The Weyerhaeuser Story,* New York: Macmillan, 1963.

Jones, Grayden, "Potlatch Picks Spokane for Corporate HQ," *Spokane (Wash.) Spokesman Review,* May 20, 1997, p. A1.

Keenan, William, Jr., "Potlatch's Strategy for '80s Centers on Production, Energy, Raw Materials," *Paper Trade Journal,* February 28, 1981, pp. 26+.

Koncel, Jerome A., "Potlatch Keeps It Simple to Achieve Solid Successes," *American Papermaker,* June 1990, pp. 26–29.

Kramer, Becky, "Knocking on Wood: Potlatch Corp. Opens Its Books to Forest Certification Systems," *Spokane (Wash.) Spokesman Review,* December 14, 2003, p. D1.

———, "Potlatch Chief Siegel to Resign," *Spokane (Wash.) Spokesman Review,* December 6, 2005, p. A12.

———, "Potlatch Earns Seal of Approval," *Spokane (Wash.) Spokesman Review,* April 21, 2004, p. A1.

———, "Potlatch Hails Sale of Plants," *Spokane (Wash.) Spokesman Review,* August 27, 2004, p. A12.

———, "Potlatch Move Seen As Boon to Shareholders," *Spokane (Wash.) Spokesman Review,* September 21, 2005, p. A8.

———, "Potlatch on a Major Roll," *Spokane (Wash.) Spokesman Review,* August 3, 2003, p. D1.

———, "Potlatch Sells Minnesota Paper Plant," *Spokane (Wash.) Spokesman Review,* March 19, 2002, p. A8.

———, "Potlatch to Charge Recreation Fee," *Spokane (Wash.) Spokesman Review,* February 24, 2007, p. A8.

———, "Potlatch to Sell Timberland," *Spokane (Wash.) Spokesman Review,* December 12, 2006, p. A1.

Louis, Arthur M., "Potlatch Moving Out of S.F.: New Headquarters Will Be in Spokane," *San Francisco Chronicle,* May 20, 1997, p. C1.

Madden, Richard B., *"Tree Farmers and Wood Converters": The Story of Potlatch Corporation,* New York: Newcomen Society in North America, 1975, 24 p.

McCoy, Charles, "Potlatch Corporation Expects Earnings Recovery to Take Root: Concern's Timber Holdings Are Largely Immune to Spotted-Owl Controversy," *Wall Street Journal,* April 13, 1992, p. B4.

Mehlman, William, "Leverage, Spotted Owl Seen Pulling Hard for Potlatch," *Insiders' Chronicle,* August 19, 1991, pp. 1, 14–15.

Nelson, Warren, and Marc Lerch, "Potlatch Mill Saves Energy Costs by Using Wide-Gap Heat Exchanger," *Pulp and Paper,* March 1990, pp. 212–13.

Petersen, Keith C., *Company Town: Potlatch, Idaho, and the Potlatch Lumber Company,* Pullman, Wash.: Washington State University Press, 1987, 284 p.

Read, Paul, "Industry Is Tough on Potlatch," *Journal of Business–Spokane,* April 5, 2001, p. A1.

———, "A Look Inside Potlatch Corp.," *Journal of Business–Spokane,* December 4, 1997, p. A1.

———, "Potlatch Positioned for Payoff," *Journal of Business–Spokane,* May 20, 1999, p. A1.

Ripley, Richard, "Factors Break Right As Potlatch Regains Footing," *Journal of Business–Spokane,* November 26, 2003, p. A5.

———, "Potlatch Charts New Direction," *Journal of Business–Spokane,* June 13, 2002, p. A1.

Stepankowsky, Paula L., "Potlatch Could Become REIT, but Its Investors Are Skeptical," *Wall Street Journal,* December 21, 2005.

Strenge, Rob, "Potlatch Works to Certify Lands," *Journal of Business–Spokane,* December 6, 2001, p. A1.

Wiegner, Kathleen K., "Down from the Clouds," *Forbes,* March 1, 1982, pp. 43+

————, "To Make Your Company Raider-Proof, Run It Right," *Forbes,* November 3, 1986, pp. 106+.

Qatar Airways Company Q.C.S.C.

Qatar Airways Tower
P.O. Box 22550
Doha,
Qatar
Telephone: (+974) 449 6000
Fax: (+974) 462 1533
Web site: http://www.qatarairways.com

Private Company
Incorporated: 1993
Employees: 6,550
Sales: $1.5 billion (2006 est.)
NAIC: 452990 All Other General Merchandise Stores; 481111 Scheduled Passenger Air Transportation; 481112 Scheduled Freight Air Transportation; 481211 Nonscheduled Chartered Passenger Air Transportation; 481212 Nonscheduled Chartered Freight Air Transportation; 488119 Other Airport Operations; 722320 Caterers

■ ■ ■

Qatar Airways Company Q.C.S.C. is the official airline of the country on its namesake peninsula. It combines high levels of service with competitive pricing in an attempt to stand out in a region known for luxurious air travel. After a troubled start as a budget carrier, the airline upgraded its product to attract more business and first-class flyers. It invested in lavish in-flight entertainment systems and ordered billions of dollars worth of new aircraft. Its own international route network has expanded to connect continents; Qatar Airways also has codeshare agreements with several world airlines.

Qatar Airways is half-owned by the government of Qatar, the rest by private investors. One of the fastest-growing airlines in the world, it carries more than six million passengers a year. In addition to the airline, Qatar Airways Company operates Doha International Airport and duty-free shops and catering operations there.

ORIGINS

In 1993, a group of investors and corporate interests in Qatar came together to organize an airline to provide direct connections between the capital of Doha and other regional centers. At the time, connections to Europe or Asia were usually routed through Bahrain, an island to the north of the Qatar peninsula. In addition to convenience, there was the hope that better connections would help diversify the oil-dependent economy.

The airline's start-up capital was a relatively paltry $7 million (QAR 25 million), all supplied by local, private interests. The largest shareholders were Qatar Insurance and Al Muftah, owning 10 percent each. Chosen to lead the new airline was Sheikh Hamad Bin Ali Bin Jabor Al Thani, a pilot credited with a number of intrepid aviation achievements.

Qatar Airways began flying on January 20, 1994, with an initial flight from Doha to Sharjah and Dubai. Within a few months, the route network included Abu Dhabi, Amman, Kuwait, and Cairo and even stretched

Qatar Airways is the national carrier of the State of Qatar. Currently undergoing rapid expansion, Qatar Airways is one of the fastest growing airlines operating one of the youngest fleets in the world.

outside the Middle East to London, England; Bombay, India; and Colombo, Sri Lanka. It was soon preparing to extend this reach even further through routes operated jointly with other carriers.

Entry into the Doha-Dubai route brought the company into direct competition with Emirates Airlines, which had become a global powerhouse since its launch in the mid-1980s. With its high standards of passenger service and low cost operations, Emirates was taking business from more established European and U.S. airlines on long-haul routes, helping to make Dubai a global hub in the process. It would eventually be a model, as well as rival, to the upstart from Qatar. However, Qatar Airways' original aim was to provide convenient point-to-point routes rather than lavish amenities.

There was also the matter of Gulf Air, an airline formed in the early 1970s by a handful of regional governments, including Qatar, which held a 25 percent stake (it had not yet invested in Qatar Airways). The Qatari government withdrew from Gulf Air in 2002. This freed up traffic rights to a number of countries that had blocked additional carriers from Qatar on the basis of bilateral agreements.

Initial equipment was comprised of a couple of Airbus A310s; a Boeing 737 arrived in the summer. All were leased and previously owned. These planes carried 124,000 people during the carrier's first full year in business. Robust long-haul traffic growth prompted the airline to acquire a couple of used Boeing 747 jumbo jets in 1995, while two Lockheed Tristars were purchased to charter and lease out. Hamad told *Airline Business* that secondhand aircraft were preferred for the start-up in order to greatly lower capital requirements and to reduce the risk of costly technical problems.

Qatar Airways broke even in its first year, when it carried 124,000 passengers. It also had a small but vital cargo business. By 1996, the airline was flying 448,000 passengers a year. However, lucrative business and first-class traffic was lacking.

RECAPITALIZATION AND RELAUNCH: 1997

After a couple of years as a budget carrier, in 1997 Qatar Airways was recapitalized and relaunched as a premium airline in order to attract lucrative business and first-class passengers. A new CEO, Akbar Al Baker, arrived from the country's Civil Aviation Department. He promptly cut the number of routes by a third while upgrading levels of service to rival the opulent offerings of other airlines in the region. The carrier invested in lavish in-flight entertainment systems and lulled business class travelers with such amenities as lie-flat seating.

Qatar Airways began flying Airbus aircraft exclusively after its relaunch, though its four Boeing 727 continued to be used for a while after being refurbished. The big Boeing 747s were leased out and replaced with smaller A300s, allowing for more frequent flights to London. The upgraded interiors offered more room and better in-flight entertainment systems. Also improved was the quality of food onboard.

By 2001, Qatar Airways was carrying about 1.5 million passengers a year. Though still tiny by world standards, it billed itself as the world's fastest-growing airline. The fleet numbered a dozen aircraft by the end of 2001, but with traffic increasing 35 percent a year, more capacity was needed for Qatar Airways to continue to grow.

Qatar Airways was affected by the downturn in the aviation industry that plagued airlines around the world following the September 11, 2001, terrorist attacks on the United States. However, it remained committed to expansion. Passenger count rose by one-half in 2002 to 2.5 million. Its route network included 38 destinations, including 11 in the Indian subcontinent. There were 21 Airbuses in the fleet. Qatar Airways ordered $5 billion of aircraft from Airbus in June 2003, an ambitious commitment to its long-term future.

In spite of difficulties such as the war in Iraq, the Persian Gulf continued to emerge as a hub for global crossings between Europe and Australasia. New entrants were tempted into the market, such as Abu Dhabi's Etihad Airways.

Revenues were up to $1.5 billion by the year ended March 31, 2006. The company was operating at a loss, though its subsidiaries such as the duty-free stores were profitable. The carrier prepared to operate its own flights to North America after adding service to a handful of U.S. cities via a codeshare arrangement with Lufthansa in May 2006. Qatar Airways had four dozen planes by the end of 2006, plying the skies between 70 cities.

The airline had a year earlier announced its intentions to acquire 20 Boeing 777s for its long-haul fleet at

---

KEY DATES

■

1994: Qatar Airways begins operations as a budget carrier.
1997: Airline is relaunched with four aircraft.
2002: Government of Qatar withdraws from Gulf Air; fast-growing Qatar Air has 21 planes.
2005: Fast-growing airline orders billions of dollars worth of new aircraft.

---

a cost of $4.6 billion, but this was delayed, as was an even larger order for five dozen Airbus A350s worth $10 billion. Qatar Airways was an extremely important client for Airbus, being the launch customer for a version of the A350 as well as for the 550-seat A380 super jumbo, due for delivery in 2009. It planned to use a pair of the giant planes on the crowded Doha-London route. The airline also ordered 30 Boeing 787 Dreamliners in 2007, reported the *Seattle Post-Intelligencer.*

FACILITIES AND FUEL FOR THE FUTURE

Qatar was building a new airport as it vied with its neighbors for a leading share of transcontinental traffic. A $120 million, highly automated catering facility at the new airport was opening in 2007. The first phase was expected to open two years later at a cost of $2.5 billion; the rest would be completed by 2015.

Qatar Airways was planning to become the world's first airline to use diesel fuel produced from natural gas. Qatar's liquefied natural gas industry was booming, giving its residents some of the highest per-capita incomes in the world, and stimulating the economy. It was also helping propel the state's own airline to new heights. The airline expected its fleet to number 110 aircraft by 2015.

Frederick C. Ingram

PRINCIPAL SUBSIDIARIES

Doha International Airport; Qatar Aircraft Catering Company; Qatar Airways Holidays; Qatar Aviation Services; Qatar Distribution Company; Qatar Duty Free; United Media International.

PRINCIPAL COMPETITORS

Emirates Group; Etihad Airways P.J.S.C.; Gulf Air Company GSC.

FURTHER READING

Bates, Joe, "Committed to Excellence: Middle Eastern Airlines Pride Themselves on the Quality and Variety of Their Onboard Catering Offer," *Travel Retailer International,* November/December 2006, pp. 21+.

Curley, Bob, "Next Up: Middle Eastern Airlines Are Reshaping International Travel," *Business Traveler USA,* October 2006, pp. 40–44.

Guild, Sara, "Solo Act in Doha," *Airline Business,* January 1996, pp. 44+.

Hindley, Angus, "New National Carrier Heads for the Sky," *MEED Middle East Economic Digest,* September 2, 1994, pp. 14+.

———, "A Passing Cloud," *MEED Middle East Economic Digest,* November 9, 2001, pp. 36+.

———, "Qatar Airways: Flying in the Face of Detractors," *MEED Middle East Economic Digest,* November 10, 1995, p. 11.

"In for the Long Haul: The Fortunes of Qatar Airways Reflect Its Home Country's Economy—It Is Expanding Rapidly," *MEED Middle East Economic Digest,* October 17, 2003, pp. 46+.

Kj, Max, "Qatar Airways: Focus on Expansion," *Flight International,* April 1, 2003, p. 36.

Lennane, Alex, "Guessing Game: No One Is Entirely Sure What Is Happening at Qatar Airways," *Airfinance Journal,* September 2006, pp. 14–15.

Lutaud, Léna, "Qatar Airways, les ailes du désert," *Le Figaro,* February 28, 2005, p. 14.

Nelms, Douglas W., "Quick Turnaround: New Management and a New Philosophy Are Leading to New Success for Qatar Airways," *Air Transport World,* March 2000.

Okong'o, Peter, "Crunch Time for Qatar Airways," *Nation* (Kenya), November 1, 2005.

Pilling, Mark, "Total Control: It Is with an Iron Grip on All Aspects of Its Business Affairs That Akbar Al Baker, Chief Executive of Qatar Airways, Has Thrust the Flag Carrier of This Gulf State into the Mainstream," *Airline Business,* March 2006, pp. 30–34.

"Qatar Airways' Global Vision," *Duty Free News International,* ARI-ME 10th Anniversary Report, October 13, 2003, pp. 30–37.

"Qatar Airways to Use GTL As Jet Fuel," *Gasification News,* March 15, 2007.

"Qatar Airways Unveils New Terminal," *Gulf News,* November 24, 2006.

"Qatar's Ambitious Vision: Boosted by Last Year's $5.1bn Order for New Aircraft, Qatar Airways Is Positioning Itself for the Future As One of the World's Leading Carriers. And Inflight Sales Are Taking Off," *Duty Free News International,* pp. 85, 87.

Rimmer, John, "Reaping the Whirlwind: Fuelled by the Aggressive Expansion of Its Owner Qatar Airways, Qatar Duty Free Claims to Be Among the Fastest-Growing Travel-Retail Operations in the World," *Duty Free News International,* December 1, 2005, pp. 44–46.

————, "Rising Star: Dubai, Bahrain and Abu Dhabi Beware. A New Retail Force Is Emerging in Qatar, Where Airport Investment Is Fuelling Rapid Sales Growth. But Will Qatar Duty Free Match the Achievements of Its Illustrious Neighbours?" *Travel Retailer International,* August/September 2004, pp. 17–18.

Trevidic, Bruno, "Qatar Airways deviant le premier gros client de l'Airbus A350," *Les Echos,* June 14, 2005, p. 25.

Turney, Roger, "Converting Qatar; Little Qatar Airways Is Pushing onto the World Stage and Cargo Service Is Part of the Strategy," *Air Cargo World,* July 2003, pp. 16–17.

Vandyk, Anthony, "Airlines Exploding Quietly; Little-Known Qatar Airways Is Growing, Though Virtually a One-Man Operation," *Air Transport World,* Vol. 33, No. 5, p. 83.

Velocci, Anthony L., Jr., "Qatar Takes on Rivals with Low Fares, New Routes," *Aviation Week & Space Technology,* August 22, 1994, pp. 34+.

Wallace, James, "Qatar Airways Is Mystery Customer; Dreamliner Order Made by Key Airbus Client," *Seattle Post-Intelligencer,* April 26, 2007, p. E1.

Whitaker, Richard, "Second to None? Qatar Airways Ahead of Forecasts After Second Launch," *Airline Business,* November 1997, pp. 44+.

Whyte, Al, "Finding Five Billion," *Trade Finance,* October 2003, pp. SS23.

Qatar National Bank SAQ

PO Box 1000
Cornish Street
Doha,
Qatar
Telephone: (+974) 4407407
Fax: (+974) 4413753
Web site: http://www.qnb.com.qa

Public Company
Incorporated: 1964
Employees: 600
Total Assets: QAR 50.06 billion ($13.76 billion) (2005)
Stock Exchanges: Doha
Ticker Symbol: QNBK
NAIC: 522110 Commercial Banking; 522293 International Trade Financing

■ ■ ■

Qatar National Bank SAQ (QNB) is Qatar's largest commercial bank. The company's total assets of QAR 50 billion (($13.7 billion) give it control of some 45 percent of the country's total banking assets. QNB provides a full-range of commercial banking and investment services and products to both the retail consumer and corporate sectors. The company also serves the government treasury; the Qatari government has held a 50 percent stake in the bank since its inception in 1964. QNB operates throughout Qatar, with 39 branches and offices, including branches in the Grand Hamad, Ritz Carlton Doha, Sheraton Doha, and Doha Marriott hotels. QNB also operates a network of 100 automated

teller machines (ATMs), and, since 2006, offers online banking services. Overseas, QNB operates international branch offices in London, Paris, Singapore, and Yemen, along with a representative office in Libya. Into the middle of the first decade of the 2000s, QNB has begun to expand its range of services. In 2005, for example, the company opened a dedicated Islamic bank, QNB Al Islam, becoming the first commercial bank in Qatar to provide banking services in accordance with *sharia* law. The company has also launched an effort to develop its international presence. For this, the company has targeted the wealth management and private banking sector, acquiring London's Ansbacher Group in 2004. Ansbacher, which operates offices in London, Switzerland, the Channel Islands, and in the Dubai International Finance Center, then became the first financial company to receive permission to open an office in the Qatar Financial Center in Doha. QNB is listed on the Doha Securities Market. Yousef Hussain Kamal is company chairman, with Ali Shareef Al-Emadi serving as acting chief executive officer. Sheikh Hamad Bin Faisal Al-Thani, a member of the ruling Al-Thani family, is QNB's vice chairman.

FIRST QATARI BANK IN 1964

For much of the first half of the 20th century, Qatar remained an economic backwater under the British Empire. The tiny emirate's main industry, and primary source of capital, had been pearl fishing. Yet, the dual blows of the global depression in the early 1930s and the invention of the cultured pearl by Japan toward the end of the decade, had left Qatar's economy largely in ruins. New hope came, however, with the discovery of

COMPANY PERSPECTIVES

QNB's cornerstone values: Prosperity, Community, Growth, and Focus are the essence of our motto, "Together Forward." This embodies the spirit of QNB and we intend to make a positive difference by giving back to the community and embedding the country's wealth within every facet of the society. "Together Forward" emphasizes on our commitment to go beyond just extending a helping hand.

large oil deposits in the Persian Gulf. By the end of the 1940s, Qatar was already on its way to becoming one of the world's richest per-capita countries.

The first bank to enter this new Qatari market was Britain's Eastern Bank, which merged with Chartered Bank, setting up offices in Qatar in 1948. That bank was soon followed by rival British Bank of the Middle East, and then by the Ottoman Bank. Toward the end of the 1950s and into the 1960s, several new banks appeared in Doha, including Jordan's Arab Bank, and Lebanon's Intra Bank.

By then, the ruling Al-Thani family had already begun its drive toward full independence from the United Kingdom. Despite its tiny size—Qatar's total population, including expatriates and other foreigners, numbered just 80,000 at the beginning of the 1970s—Qatar's existing and potential wealth was enormous. The ruling family recognized the need to retain a greater share of the fast-flowing oil profits within its borders. In 1964, therefore, the Qatari government established the country's first Qatari-owned bank. Called the Qatar National Bank (QNB), the new bank was in fact established as a commercial bank. The Qatari government held 50 percent of the new bank's stock, with Sheikh Khalifi Al-Thani serving as chairman. The remaining 50 percent was held by Qatari investors. Although not a fully fledged national bank, QNB nonetheless served as the depositary for government funds, and was given the mission to "encourage economic development and to support the national economy." Two years later, the Qatari government set up the Qatar and Dubai Currency Board, to govern the rial shared between the two emirates. That body provided the country's currency functions in the absence of a true central bank.

QNB remained a small player in its own market through the end of the decade. Founded with assets equivalent to £1.2 billion, QNB built up assets of more than £9.5 billion by 1970. Yet QNB's growth continued to be overshadowed by its foreign-owned competitors, which boasted total assets of nearly QAR 415 billion (£36 billion) at the end of the decade. While QNB had been steadily profitable, with profits rising to £467 million at the end of the decade, its true growth came only in the wake of Qatar's independence in 1970. The bank also had to contend with the entry of a number of new foreign rivals, including Tehran-based Bank Saderat Iran, the United Bank of Karachi, the Bank of Oman, and New York's First National City Bank.

Qatar's declaration of independence, and the subsequent economic and political reforms carried out by the government into 1972, set the stage for QNB to emerge as Qatar's single most dominant bank. The new government quickly moved to take control of the country's banking sector, issuing Decree Law No. 4 in 1970. The legislation severely limited the operations of foreign banks in Qatar, restricting new foreign banks seeking to enter the country to just a single branch and putting a cap on further expansion, including mergers, by existing foreign banks. The foreign banks were also required to maintain minimum interest-free deposits with QNB, and to invest 50 percent of each branch's total deposit directly into the Qatari economy.

The new legislation stimulated the appearance of a local banking industry, with the first new domestic bank, Commercial Bank of Qatar, appearing in 1975. By the early 1980, a third bank, Doha Bank, had also been created. Nonetheless, QNB remained far and away the dominant fixture in the Qatari banking sector, representing 60 percent of all deposits in the country. QNB had also become the country's largest lender, holding 36 percent of the credit market. QNB's stature, and the rising importance of Qatar in the regional and international economy, had led QNB to become the first Qatari bank to establish offices outside of Qatar, with the opening of its first branch in London in 1976. By 1981, the company had entered France as well, opening an office in Paris.

NEW PRODUCTS AND MARKETS IN THE NEW CENTURY

As Qatar's main bank, QNB played the role of pioneer, introducing a wide range of modern banking services. These included the introduction of credit cards and ATMs for the retail sector. The bank also began expanding its network throughout the country, in order to serve its fast-growing population; from just 70,000 in the early 1970s, Qatar's total population swelled to more than 700,000 by the year 2000. By the middle of the first decade of the 2000s, QNB had built up a

KEY DATES

1964: Qatar National Bank is established as first Qatari-owned commercial bank in Qatar.

1976: First international branch is opened in London.

2004: Company acquires Ansbacher Group Holding Limited in London, adding private asset and wealth management services.

2006: Qatar National launches regional expansion strategy, acquiring licenses to open offices and branches in Yemen, Libya, Singapore, Dubai, and Kuwait.

2007: Company receives license to operate in Oman.

network of 39 branches and offices. The bank catered to its increasingly international clientele by adding a number of locations in the country's leading hotels, the Grand Hamad, Ritz Carlton Doha, Sheraton Doha, and Doha Marriott.

QNB's dominance of the Qatari banking sector meant that, however vibrant Qatar's economy might be, the bank's future growth prospects there remained limited. As a result, in the early 2000s, QNB began developing a new strategy based on the creation of new banking products and services on the one hand, and expanding into new markets on the other. In 2002, the bank began its first move into the regional market, expanding its business activities into Saudi Arabia and Iran. In that latter market, for example, QNB became a major investor in the Iran Eurobond launched in July of that year. At home, QNB launched a new electronic banking system, providing for Internet-based credit cards. The new system later enabled the bank to launch Qatar's first real-time online banking system, introduced in 2006.

QNB also laid plans to expand its physical presence in the Middle East and North African regions. In 2004, the bank joined with the Bank of Beirut and Emirates Bank International in order to apply for a banking license in Syria. The bank also eyed the Yemen and Libyan markets, especially as the latter emerged from the long-held economic sanctions levied against it by the international community. The bank applied for and received licenses to operate in both countries.

QNB also sought to expand its range of services, and in 2005 the bank launched its own Islamic banking affiliate, QNB Al Islami. The *sharia*-compliant bank

then opened its first branch in Doha that year. While a number of other Islamic banks already operated in Qatar, the creation of QNB Al Islami was the first by one of the country's commercial banks, underscoring the rising importance of that banking market.

At the same time, QNB made a major move into the booming private wealth and asset management sector, buying London-based Ansbacher Group Holdings Ltd. in 2004. Founded in 1894 as Henry Ansbacher & Co., that firm had become a leading trader in U.S. securities in London by the 1930s, and a leading U.K. stockbroker. Ansbacher later expanded into the offshore banking market, establishing offices in Switzerland, and acquiring operations in the Cayman Islands and the Bahamas. The acquisition of Ansbacher, at a cost of $250 million, provided a major entry for QNB into the wealth management field. In particular, the Ansbacher acquisition was seen as a key element in QNB's regional expansion strategy, allowing the bank to target the high-end sector in its new markets. Following its acquisition, Ansbacher established new branches in Dubai's International Finance Center. In 2006, Ansbacher was also the first financial body authorized to open an office in the new Qatar Finance Center in Doha.

With the Ansbacher acquisition under its belt, QNB began rolling out its regional expansion strategy. By the end of 2006, QNB had opened a representative office in Libya, and added branches in Singapore and Kuwait as well. The company also announced plans to open a full branch in Yemen, which was expected to be operational by June 2007. By then, the bank had already expanded in the Dubai market, and, in March 2007, announced that it had been granted a license to operate in Oman as well. Through its continued international expansion effort, QNB hoped to become one of the top five banks in the region by the end of the decade.

M. L. Cohen

PRINCIPAL SUBSIDIARIES

Ansbacher Group Holdings Limited (U.K.); QNB International Holdings Limited (Luxembourg).

PRINCIPAL COMPETITORS

HSBC Bank Middle East Limited; Bank Saderat Iran B Qatar; Commercial Bank of Qatar; Arab Bank PLC; Doha Bank; BNP Paribas Doha; Qatar International Islamic Bank; Ahli Bank QSC; United Bank Ltd.; Standard Chartered Bank B Qatar; MashreqBank Psc B Qatar; Qatar Industrial Development Bank.

FURTHER READING

"Ansbacher Takes Expansion Step in Dubai," *Banker,* January 1, 2005.

Avery, Helen, "Ansbacher Opens New Opportunities in Qatar," *Euromoney,* December 2004, p. 20.

"Local Clout," *MEED Middle East Economic Digest,* October 14, 2005, p. 44.

"Making Hay," *MEED Middle East Economic Digest,* June 9, 2006, p. 50.

Melly, Paul, and Eleanor Gillespie, "Qatar: Competition Hots up for Local Custom," *Banker,* June 1, 2006.

"Qataris Get Oman Licence," *MEED Middle East Economic Digest,* January 19, 2007, p. 26.

"Qatar National Bank Flies East, West and South," *MEED Middle East Economic Digest,* September 8, 2006, p. 41.

"Qatar National Bank Wins Full Service Kuwaiti Licence," *MEED Middle East Economic Digest,* December 8, 2006, p. 36.

"QNB Aims to Join Gulf Top Five," *MEED Middle East Economic Digest,* July 19, 2002, p. 6.

"QNB First in Libya," *Middle East,* October 2006, p. 53.

"QNB the First Qatari Bank to Open a Full Services Branch in Kuwait," *Middle East,* December 10, 2006.

"QNB to Manage Al Rayyan IPO," *MEED Middle East Economic Digest,* January 13, 2006, p. 25.

Qatar Telecom QSA

PO Box 217
Corniche Street, W Bay
Doha,
Qatar
Telephone: (+974) 4400766
Fax: (+974) 4830011
Web site: http://www.qtel.com.qa

Public Company
Incorporated: 1972 as Qatar National Telephone Service
Employees: 1,832
Sales: QAR 4.42 billion ($820 million) (2006)
Stock Exchanges: Doha London Bahrain
Ticker Symbol: QTEL
NAIC: 517212 Cellular and Other Wireless Telecommunications; 517110 Wired Telecommunications Carriers

■ ■ ■

Qatar Telecom (Qtel) Q.S.C. is the former telecommunications monopoly of that country, offering fixed line, wireless mobile, and broadband and Internet access services. The company enjoys one of the highest mobile telephone penetration rates in the world, with a 102 percent coverage; Qtel's fixed line rates represent 25 percent of the country's potential subscriber base, while Internet access lags at just 8 percent. Qtel offers a range of modern telecommunications services, including 3G mobile telephony offerings such as mobile television, as a "triple play" package of television, Internet access, and VoIP telephony services. With revenues of more than QAR 4.4 billion ($820 million) in 2006, Qtel is also Qatar's largest and most profitable public company. The former state-controlled telephone monopoly has been pushing into the international market ahead of the loss of its monopoly, which was ended by royal decree in November 2006. The company is lead partner, with TDC International of Denmark, in Nawras, which successfully won its bid for the second GSM-based mobile telephone license in Oman. The company signed a strategic agreement with Singapore Technologies Telemedia, acquiring a 25 percent stake in Indonesia's Asia Mobile Holdings in 2007. The company also owns a stake in Singapore's Starhub. In March 2007, Qtel announced the purchase of majority control of Kuwait-based Wataniya. That agreement extended Qtel's regional footprint to include Qatar, Kuwait, Tunisia, Algeria, Iraq, Saudi Arabia, the Maldives, and Palestine. The $3.7 billion purchase was part of Qtel's objectives of breaking into the global telecom market's top 20 by 2020.

Qtel is listed on the Doha, London, and Bahrain stock exchanges, although the Qatar government retains a 55 percent stake in the company. Sheikh Abdullah Bin Mohammed Bin Saud Al-Thani, a member of the ruling Al-Thani family, is company chairman, while Dr. Nasser Marafih serves as chief executive officer.

CREATING QTEL IN 1987

Telecommunications came rather late to the tiny country of Qatar, when the first private telephone exchange, with a capacity of 50 lines, was installed in Doha in 1949. At the time, Qatar remained an

COMPANY PERSPECTIVES

Our Vision: To be among the top 20 Telecommunications Companies in the world by 2020.

impoverished backwater under British protection; the emirate's primary industry, pearling, had been devastated in the 1930s by the twin blows of the global recession, and especially by the introduction of cultured pearls, introduced by Japan during that decade. Yet the discovery of oil represented new hope for Qatar. The new source of income brought further investments in the telecommunications sector, and led to the creation of a public telephone network in 1953. Initial capacity of the network was just 150 telephone lines. Qatar's oil deposits later allowed it to emerge as one of the world's richest countries per capita.

Independence in 1971 and the economic boom following the Arab oil embargo in the early 1970s created new momentum for the country. In the early 1970s, the decision was made to develop a modern telecommunications infrastructure. The Qatari government turned to the United Kingdom's Cable & Wireless Ltd., forming Qatar National Telephone Service (QNTS), which was set up to provide domestic telephone services. Cable & Wireless was granted the concession for international telephone services. Work on installation of the network was carried out under the auspices of the newly created Telecommunications Department, established in 1973 under the Ministry of Communications and Transport. The full rollout of the new telephone network was completed by 1975. The following year, the company commissioned the Doha Earth Station, positioning the country as a major hub in the region's international satellite-based telecommunications grid. A second earth station was added in 1985. By then, QNTS had become one of the first in the region to add mobile telephone services, using the analogue-based Mobile Automated Telephone Service (MATS) standard. The country later acted as a founding partner behind the launch of the Arabsat satellite in 1986, establishing a third earth station that year. Also that year, the company inaugurated its first fiber-optic link, between Doha and Khalifa City.

Despite these achievements, telephone penetration in Qatar remained low, with poor service levels. The Qatari government took full control of QNTS in 1987, which was merged with two other existing telecommunications operations to form Qatar Public Telecommunications Corporation (QPTC). Under terms of its founding agreement, QPTC was granted the monopoly over the country's telecommunications sector through to the year 2013.

QPTC then began to institute a new program of modernizing the country's telecommunications sector. In 1991, the company introduced the first public payphone. In that year, also, QPTC launched its own paging service, boasting national coverage. One year later, QPTC fully digitized the country's telephone network, making it one of the region's most advanced. QPTC was also given control of the country's cable television monopoly, launching Qatar Cablevision in 1993. Like the vast majority of its telecommunications operations, the company's cable television operations were transmitted via satellite through its existing earth station network. By then, QPTC's expansion of its operations allowed it to top 110,000 telephone lines, enabling it to claim penetration rates of more than one-fifth of the total population.

QPTC was also the first in the region to launch new generation mobile telephone services. This came with the 1994 launch of Qatarnet, which introduced cellular telephone services based on the GSM standard. The company was somewhat slow to complete its base station grid, however, and continued to receive complaints about the lack of coverage, even in certain parts of the capital city, Doha, into the 2000s.

Nonetheless, QPTC remained committed to developing its range of services through the end of the decade. The company rolled out its new high-speed paging service, called Flex, in 1996. In that year, also, the company brought the Internet to Qatar, launching its first Internet access packages. Like other telecommunications offerings, however, Internet access remained tightly controlled by the Qatari government.

PRIVATIZATION IN 1998

The introduction of new services allowed QPTC to grow strongly through the decade, and by the late 1990s the company was already one of the largest and most profitable in the country. The company's growth had received a major boost from the government's massive investment in developing its liquefied natural gas industry, which not only stimulated the economy, but also brought in a surge in demand for the company's telecommunications services. The country's rising population, as Qatar became a magnet for a growing number of foreign nationals, helped push the company's total subscriber base past 150,000. QPTC's own investments, which boosted its total capacity to 350,000 lines, positioned the company for future growth.

The Qatar government had begun moving toward a policy of privatization of its state-controlled assets, as

KEY DATES

1949: First private telephone exchange is installed in Qatar.

1953: First public telephone exchange is commissioned.

1972: Qatari government forms Qatar National Telephone Service in partnership with Cable & Wireless Ltd.

1987: Qatar Public Telecommunications Corporation (QPTC) absorbs existing telecom companies in Qatar and becomes state-owned monopoly.

1994: QPTC launches GSM-based Qatarnet mobile telephone service.

1998: Privatization of QPTC creates Qatar Telecom (Qtel), which lists on Doha Securities Market, then later adds stock to London and Bahrain stock exchanges.

2002: "Q-Turn" restructuring program is launched.

2004: Qtel wins bid for second GSM license in Oman, and forms Nawras, which begins service in 2005.

2006: Qtel loses monopoly in Qatar.

2007: Company pays $3.7 billion for Kuwait-based Wataniya, with mobile telephone operations in seven countries in Middle East and North Africa.

part of a larger effort by the ruling Al-Thani family to transition toward a democratically elected government in the 2000s. As one of the country's largest and most profitable companies, QPTC became a flagship of sorts for the government's privatization policies. In 1998, the company listed its stock on the Doha Securities Market, and changed its name to Qatar Telecom (Qtel) Q.S.C. The following year, Qtel added its listing to the London Stock Exchange as well, followed by a listing on the Bahrain Stock Exchange in 2001, and on the Abu Dhabi Securities Market in 2002. Nonetheless, the Qatari government retained 55 percent of the company.

The first decade of the 2000s saw a boom in the company's mobile telephone services, especially following the launch of its prepaid service, Hala. By the middle of the decade, the company's mobile telephone operations were its largest, bypassing its fixed line operations, which grew only slowly to achieve a market penetration of 26 percent at mid-decade, to achieve a market penetration of 102 percent. At the same time,

Qtel continued to roll out new services, such as high-speed ADSL based Internet access in 2002, called BarQ Platinum. The company also opened its first retail store, featuring a one-stop shopping concept, at the City Center Mall in Doha.

Qtel's enhanced service offering came in part due to the unusual restructuring exercise launched by the company in 2002. Dubbed "Q-Turn" and devised by the McKinsey consulting firm, the restructuring exercise was unusual in that it involved transforming an already highly profitable company. As part of its restructuring, the company reorganized its operation, boosted its customer services division, while also stepping up the pace of its new services and product offerings.

The Q-Turn program, which took two years to complete, was designed to prepare the company for the next phase in its expansion. At home, the company's monopoly was slated to come to an early end, amid the government moves to institute new democratic reforms. At the same time, Qtel's domestic growth prospects had increasingly reached their limit, while former bestsellers, such as its paging service, had gone into decline. The company's improved customer service offering was designed to help maintain customer loyalty in a postmonopoly marketplace, while also developing new markets for products and services.

INTERNATIONAL EXPANSION FOR THE NEW CENTURY

Nonetheless, Qtel recognized that its true survival as a public telecommunications company depended on its ability to expand beyond Qatar's borders. Despite its relative lack of experience, Qtel became determined to break into new markets. This effort was quickly rewarded, when the company won its bid to acquire the second GSM license in Oman in 2004. For this, the company formed the joint venture Nawras with minority partner TDC International. By 2005, Nawras was operational, and quickly gained a 20 percent share of the Omani market.

Partnerships remained an important component in the company's international ambitions. The company teamed up with Singapore Technologies Telemedia and investment bank Naeema Holding to bid for one of the GSM licenses on offer in Egypt in 2005, placing the company in head to head competition with Vodafone. By June 2006, the company had passed the first round of the selection process.

In the meantime, Qtel sought new international prospects and in November 2006 the company raised $2 billion in loans in order to fund its war chest. That fund-raising effort coincided with the Qatari government's announcement in November 2006 that it was ending Qtel's monopoly, opening the domestic market to competition. The first rival to Qtel's home base was expected to appear as early as the end of 2007.

Qtel braced itself for the competition, in part by rolling out new services, including 3G mobile telecommunications services, which included an innovative mobile television service. The company also launched its own "triple play" package of Internet access, telephone, and television.

Yet the company's future hopes were pinned on the international market and the ambitious goal of breaking into the global top 20 by 2020. In November 2006, the company bought 38.2 percent of Navlink, a data services company majority owned by AT&T and focused on the Middle East market. In January 2007, Qtel teamed up with Singapore Technologies Telemedia again, this time paying $635 million to buy a 25 percent share of Asia Mobile Holdings. That purchase gave Qtel a share of Telemedia's Starhub, in Singapore, and PT Indosat, in Indonesia. The latter was already the second largest mobile provider in its market, with more than 14 million subscribers.

Elsewhere in the region, Qtel, in partnership with Atco Clearwire Telecom, became one of ten bidders for a fixed-line license in Saudi Arabia. The decision for that bid was expected to come late in 2007. In the meantime, Qtel made a leap into the regional big leagues at the beginning of March 2007, when it agreed to pay $3.7 billion for 51 percent of Wataniya, a Kuwait-based group focused on mobile telephone operations in the Middle East and North Africa. The Wataniya purchase expanded Qtel's presence to Kuwait, Tunisia, Algeria, Iraq, Saudi Arabia, the Maldives, and, by the end of 2007, Palestine. With plans for more acquisitions, Qtel appeared determined to become a telecommunications major in the years to come.

M. L. Cohen

PRINCIPAL SUBSIDIARIES

Omani Qatari Telecommunications Company S.A.O.C. (55%); Qtel Investment Holdings B.S.C.; TDC–Qtel MENA Investcom B.S.C. (79%).

PRINCIPAL COMPETITORS

Vodafone Egypt; Oman Telecommunications Company; Emirates Telecommunications Corporation; MobiNil; Khaled Ahmed Al-Jafaly Co.

FURTHER READING

Dunkley, Clare, "Preparing for Round One," *Meed Middle East Economic Digest*, September 24, 2004, p. 32.

"An Exception to the Rule," *Meed Middle East Economic Digest*, October 18, 2002, p. 39.

Hindley, Angus, "Qtel Keeps the Customer Satisfied," *Meed Middle East Economic Digest*, April 4, 1997, p. 11.

Irish, John, "Doha Calling: As the Spectre of Competition Looms at Home, Qatar Telecom Is Brushing Up Its Act and Exploring Overseas," *Meed Middle East Economic Digest*, June 9, 2006, p. 63.

"Qatar Establishing New Connections," *Middle East*, August–September 2003, p. 37.

"Qtel Enters Asia," *Meed Middle East Economic Digest*, January 19, 2007, p. 21.

"Qtel Eyes Top Three Spot," *Meed Middle East Economic Digest*, June 2, 2006, p. 34.

"Qtel Loses Monopoly Status After Banks Bid $2bn Facility," *Euroweek*, November 10, 2006.

"Qtel Plans War Chest," *Meed Middle East Economic Digest*, September 15, 2006, p. 40.

"Sector Open for Business," *Meed Middle East Economic Digest*, November 10, 2006, p. 27.

"A Turn for the Better," *Meed Middle East Economic Digest*, October 17, 2003, p. 48.

Regent Communications, Inc.

2000 Fifth Third Center
511 Walnut Street
Cincinnati, Ohio 45202
U.S.A.
Telephone: (513) 651-1190
Fax: (513) 651-1195
Web site: http://www.regentcomm.com

Public Company
Incorporated: 1996 as JS Communications
Employees: 890
Sales: $85.03 million (2006)
Stock Exchanges: NASDAQ
Ticker Symbol: RGCI
NAIC: 513112 Radio Stations

∎ ∎ ∎

Regent Communications, Inc., owns nearly 70 radio stations in 13 small and midsize markets around the United States. The Ohio-based firm operates in a total of nine states, with its largest presence in New York. Regent's strategy is to establish clusters of stations so that it can reduce operating costs by combining core functions, while working to increase listenership at each to maximize ad revenues. The publicly held Regent is run by cofounder and 50-year radio veteran William Stakelin.

ROOTS

Regent Communications officially dates its beginnings to 1996, but the firm's origins go back much further. It was founded by a pair of radio veterans, William "Bill" Stakelin and Terry Jacobs, the latter of whom had been an insurance industry executive before founding a company called Jacor Communications, Inc., in 1979 to assemble a string of radio stations. Jacor grew rapidly during the 1980s before heavy debt put it in financial peril, and in 1992 investor Samuel Zell took it over. A year later Jacobs left to found a new company called Regent Communications, which began buying stations to take advantage of Federal Communications Commission (FCC) rule changes that allowed ownership of up to two AM and two FM stations in a single market, double the previous amount.

Over the next two years Regent acquired stations in Ohio, Kentucky, Indiana, and Nevada, and in the summer of 1995 the firm nearly doubled in size with the purchase of Apollo Radio Holding Co. for $50 million. Founded in 1988, Apollo operated three stations in Salt Lake City, two in Kansas City, and two in Charleston, South Carolina. Apollo President Bill Stakelin, who had gotten his start in radio as a teenager in the late 1950s, would become executive vice-president and chief operating officer of Regent.

In early 1996 the FCC increased radio station ownership limits again, and soon afterward Regent bought several stations and sold a handful of others to boost its holdings to 20. In October 1996 the company was acquired by the revitalized Jacor in a stock swap worth $120 million, plus $5 million in cash and the assumption of $64 million in debt. Jacor, which had closed a $770 million purchase of Citicasters, Inc., briefly became the third largest radio station group in the United States before itself being swallowed by industry giant Clear Channel Communications.

Just a month after Regent's sale to Jacor was announced, Terry Jacobs and Bill Stakelin formed a new radio station acquisitions firm called JS Communications, which soon afterward took the name Regent Communications, Inc. Jacobs would serve as the reconstituted Regent's CEO and chairman, with Stakelin its president and chief operating officer.

WAVE OF ACQUISITIONS BEGINNING IN 1997

A spring 1997 deal to buy four stations from Jacor fell through, but in the fall an agreement was reached to pay approximately $23 million to buy the six AM and ten FM stations of the Park Lane Group, located in California and Arizona, as well as a firm called Alta California Broadcasting, which owned four stations near Redding, California. A short time later publicly traded Faircom, Inc., merged with Regent, which brought the company six stations in Ohio and Michigan. Other acquisitions in Arizona and California boosted the firm's holdings to 32 by the spring of 1998. Funding for the buying spree was derived in part from a private equity sale to a group led by Waller-Sutton Media Partners LP.

In June 1998 Regent's stock began trading on the OTC Bulletin Board. In July another station in Lancaster, California, was purchased, KAVC-FM (later known as KOSS), which boosted the firm's holdings in the area to three.

Acquisitions continued in early 1999 with the purchase of three St. Cloud, Minnesota, stations and three in Erie, Pennsylvania. In the summer an agreement was reached to buy a total of nine country and adult contemporary stations in Utica/Rome and Watertown, New York, from Forever Broadcasting for $44

million plus 100,000 shares of preferred stock. This was followed a month later with a deal to acquire three stations in El Paso, Texas, for $23.5 million from New Wave Broadcasting, L.P. For fiscal 1999 the firm's revenues reached $23.9 million, up from $14.8 million a year earlier, while its net loss widened from $4.5 million to $6.8 million.

In January 2000 Regent completed a new stock offering on the NASDAQ, selling 16 million shares for $8.50 each to net $136 million. The money would be used to pay down debt and make further acquisitions.

CLEAR CHANNEL DEAL BRINGS NEW YORK, MICHIGAN STATIONS

In March the company reached an agreement to swap 11 of its Ohio and California stations and $67 million in cash for nine Clear Channel Communications stations in Grand Rapids, Michigan, and Albany, New York. The deal was precipitated by Clear Channel's purchase of rival AMFM Inc., which required the sale of 110 stations in 37 markets to comply with FCC rules. The agreement was subsequently restructured to include an additional Grand Rapids station, while three of the California stations were retained by Regent and the cash amount was upped by $13.5 million. Albany and Grand Rapids would subsequently become two of the firm's largest markets.

In April Regent was granted a $125 million credit line from FleetBoston Financial, and in June a deal was cut to buy three stations in St. Cloud, Minnesota, for $5 million from StarCom, Inc., while a $10 million stock buyback program was initiated. In the fall the firm sold three of its California stations to Concord Media Group for $13.5 million. For fiscal 2000 Regent's earnings topped $44.1 million, with a net profit of nearly $13.9 million.

In January 2001 the company reached an agreement with NextMedia Group, Inc., to buy WJET-FM in Erie, Pennsylvania, for $5 million, and in May a deal was cut with The Cromwell Group, Inc., to buy six stations serving Peoria, Illinois, for $20 million. Summer saw the firm purchase two stations in Grand Rapids and Flint, Michigan, for a total of $7 million, and announce plans to buy seven others in Lafayette, Louisiana, for $38.6 million from Comcorp.

In November 2001 Regent sold 900,000 shares of stock for $5.75 each in a private placement that raised $5 million, and a few weeks later it bought two more Flint, Michigan, stations for $1.3 million from Covenant Communications, giving it a total of six in the market. The company now owned 58 radio stations.

In April 2002 Regent sold 10.5 million additional shares of common stock for $7.50 each to net $74 mil-

near Lancaster, Pennsylvania, plus $3.7 million, for five in Bloomington, Illinois. The firm had 75 stations in 15 markets.

KEY DATES

1996: Terry Jacobs and Bill Stakelin found JS Communications and rename it Regent.
1997: Company prepares to buy more than two dozen radio stations in small and midsize markets.
1998: Regent stock begins trading on the OTC bulletin board.
2000: Stock moves to the NASDAQ as firm nets $136 million in new offering; Regent gets ten New York and Michigan stations in swap with Clear Channel.
2002: New stock offering raises $74 million; 12 stations are purchased from Brill Media.
2005: Jacobs retires as CEO; Stakelin assumes top post.
2006: Company acquires five stations in Buffalo, New York, for $125 million.

TERRY JACOBS STEPS DOWN IN 2005

In July 2005 Regent cofounder Terry Jacobs retired as chairman and CEO and took the job of vice-chairman. President and Chief Operating Officer Stakelin would add the title of CEO, while board member William Sutter was elevated to the job of chairman. Jacobs, 62, would focus his energies on a real estate firm he had started with his sons. During the summer the company also announced its second $20 million stock buyback program in two years, as part of an ongoing effort to boost shareholder value.

During the year the firm moved its five Albany stations into a newly purchased building, as it also began upgrading some outlets to offer high-definition digital broadcasts, a format that had been created several years earlier but seen little interest as yet from the public. Digitally equipped stations could simultaneously broadcast their regular AM or FM signal along with a new digital frequency that gave crisper sound. Online audio streaming of all of the company's FM radio stations had recently been accomplished, as well.

Revenues for 2005 topped $85.6 million, while a net loss of $6.6 million was recorded due to a $20.8 million impairment charge from such intangible assets as broadcast licenses. The large write-down was the result of new federally mandated accounting requirements for public firms, and other radio companies had taken similar charges, which were based on comparing a station's assessed market value to its book value. Stations that had increased in value did not get factored into the equation, so the net result was always negative.

The firm was also seeing its ad revenues falling due to competition from satellite radio broadcasters XM and Sirius, the rising popularity of personal music players including iPods (most of which did not include a radio tuner), and the gradual shift of ad dollars to the Internet. Because of these and other factors, the average time Americans spent listening to radio was down 14 percent compared to a decade earlier, according to research firm Arbitron.

Responding to such challenges, Regent worked to build value within its existing properties. At Grand Rapids rock station WGRD, which had fallen to the low end of the local Arbitron top ten, Regent engineered a dramatic turnaround by launching a new morning show called "Free Beer and Hot Wings," which soon stood at number one in the ratings in the coveted

lion in new capital, and in August a 12-station acquisition from Brill Media Co. was announced. The $62 million bankruptcy auction deal would bring stations serving markets in Pennsylvania, Indiana, Kentucky, Colorado, and Minnesota. The firm had also made upgrades to several stations and launched a handful of others, including the popular KKQZ-FM in Colorado.

In February 2003 Regent swapped four of the Brill stations in Duluth, Minnesota, plus $2.7 million in cash for five stations in Evansville, Indiana, owned by Clear Channel Communications. Revenues for the year jumped to $80.6 million while a profit of $5.7 million was reported.

Nearly 85 percent of Regent stations' advertising revenues came from local businesses, significantly more than the industry average of under 80 percent. With such major consolidators as Clear Channel and Infinity Broadcasting cutting costs by using generic-sounding DJ's or syndicated programs, Regent President Bill Stakelin defended the firm's local emphasis to *Billboard*, stating "Radio is not a national medium ... radio's strength is localism." Regent stations invested in community outreach, with on-air personalities frequently attending public events and sales representatives working with local businesses to create ads, many of which were recorded at the stations themselves.

In early 2004 the company engineered a station swap with Citadel Broadcasting Corp., in which Regent would give up four Erie, Pennsylvania, stations and two

18- to 34-year-old male demographic. The show garnered nearly four times the listeners of its closest rival, and was later syndicated to several other Regent stations.

In May 2006 the firm bought two FM stations in Peoria, Illinois, for $12.5 million from AAA Entertainment, while selling three others there for $2.8 million. The new stations, WZPW and WXMP, were more powerful Class B stations, while those sold were all of the weaker Class A type.

In the summer Regent sold its ten Chico and Redding, California, stations for $17.5 million and jettisoned WYNG-FM in Evansville, Indiana, for $1.5 million, while cutting a deal to buy WNYQ-FM in Albany, New York, for $4.9 million. The latter would boost its presence in that market to one AM and five FM stations. The company had been working to improve its position there after WGNA-FM had lost the popular syndicated Howard Stern show when the "shock jock" was hired by satellite company Sirius. The station was subsequently reformatted to play rock music, while the adult contemporary WNYQ was given the nickname "The Buzz" and its listenership boosted with the addition of a top-rated morning show poached from a competitor. Another Albany FM station was also reformatted to sports talk, while the company's AM outlet there was relaunched with female-oriented talk.

$125 MILLION, FIVE-STATION CBS DEAL: FALL 2006

In September Regent made its largest acquisition to date with the purchase of five stations in Buffalo, New York, from CBS Radio Assets for $125 million. Buffalo was ranked the 41st largest radio market in the United States, and it would become the largest that the firm had a toehold in. The new stations included three of the area's top four rated ones as well as the most popular, country formatted WYRK-FM. Combined with its other upstate New York clusters in Albany, Watertown, and Utica/Rome, Regent ad sales representatives could sell coverage of a broad swath of the state to advertisers. Financing for the CBS deal was derived from $240 million in credit obtained from Banc of America Securities. When the dust had settled the firm would own 68 radio stations in 13 markets, including two of the four most popular in ten of them. For 2006 revenues dropped slightly to $85 million, while a huge $26.6 million loss was reported due to a $48.8 million write-down of impairment to intangible assets.

In early 2007 the company revised its stations' web sites to make them more content-rich, which encouraged users to stay there longer and, it was hoped, look at more of the advertisements they were running. With the Buffalo deal completed, Regent management told stock analysts that the firm was planning to fine-tune its holdings in the near term rather than seek further acquisitions.

A decade after Terry Jacobs and Bill Stakelin founded the second incarnation of Regent Communications, Inc., the company was working to strengthen its portfolio of radio station clusters while facing the industry trends of declining listenership and reduced advertising dollars. Despite these challenges, the firm's seasoned management team remained committed to its goal of offering radio with a significant amount of local content to stations in small and midsize markets.

Frank Uhle

PRINCIPAL SUBSIDIARIES

Regent Broadcasting Management, LLC; Regent Broadcasting LLC.

PRINCIPAL COMPETITORS

Clear Channel Communications, Inc.; Cumulus Media Inc.; CBS Radio, Inc.; Citadel Broadcasting Corp.; Entercom Communications Corp.; Saga Communications, Inc.

FURTHER READING

Bachman, Katy, "Regent's Terry Jacobs to Retire," *Mediaweek*, July 28, 2005.

Heine, Paul, "Is Smaller Better?" *Billboard Radio Monitor*, December 10, 2004.

Hennessey, Raymond, "Radio-Station Operator Regent Communications Makes Strong Debut on Nasdaq," *Dow Jones Business Wire*, January 25, 2000.

Lerner, Richard, "Starting Over," *Greater Cincinnati Business Record*, October 31, 1994, p. 16.

Miller, Nick, "Jacor Adds to Its Empire with Regent," *Cincinnati Post*, October 10, 1996, p. 6B.

———, "Regent Is Acquiring 9 N.Y. Radio Stations," *Cincinnati Post*, August 4, 1999, p. 10C.

———, "Regent Radio Group Goes Public, Grows," *Cincinnati Post*, June 18, 1998, p. 10C.

Peale, Cliff, "Local Radio Mogul Spurs Investors," *Cincinnati Post*, January 21, 1999, p. 8B.

"Regent Commun., Clear Channel in Station Exchange Pact," *Dow Jones News Service*, March 13, 2000.

"Regent Commun. to Buy 7 La. Radio Stations for $39.6M," *Dow Jones News Service*, August 29, 2001.

"Regent Commun. to Buy 12 Radio Stations from Brill Media," *Dow Jones News Service*, August 23, 2002.

"Regent to Exchange Duluth, Minnesota Stations," *Dow Jones News Service,* February 27, 2003.

Rhodes, Gary, "Radio Market Heats Up—Jacor Expatriate Heads New Firm," *Cincinnati Post,* October 29, 1993, p. 6B.

Stammen, Ken, "Regent Tunes in to Growth," *Cincinnati Post,* September 18, 2000, p. 7B.

Zier, Julie A., "Regent Communications Absorbs Apollo," *Broadcasting & Cable,* July 3, 1995, p. 28.

SonicWALL, Inc.

———■———

1143 Borregas Avenue
Sunnyvale, California 94089
U.S.A.
Telephone: (408) 745-9600
Fax: (408) 745-9300
Web site: http://www.sonicwall.com

Public Company
Incorporated: 1991 as Sonic Systems
Employees: 404
Sales: $135.3 million (2005)
Stock Exchanges: NASDAQ
Ticker Symbol: SNWL
NAIC: 511210 Software Publishers; 334119 Other
    Computer Peripheral Equipment Manufacturing

■■■

SonicWALL, Inc., develops Internet security infrastructure products designed to provide secure access to wired and wireless broadband customers operating small- to medium-sized networks. The company's product lines offer firewall security and virtual private networking functionalities, e-mail security, backup and recovery, content security management, centralized management and reporting, and secure remote access capabilities. SonicWALL also offers services such as content filtering, antivirus protection, and intrusion prevention on a subscription basis. Its products are sold to distributors such as Tech Data Corporation and Ingram Micro Inc., who, in turn, sell the SonicWALL line to value-added resellers. SonicWALL sells its products on a global basis, generating 30 percent of its annual revenue from overseas business. The company's headquarters in Sunnyvale, California, occupy 86,000 square feet of office space. Sales and support offices are located in the United Kingdom, France, Sweden, Norway, Switzerland, the Netherlands, Germany, Australia, Brazil, Mexico, Japan, Singapore, Hong Kong, and China.

ORIGINS

SonicWALL's founders spent most of their first decade in business designing and selling a different type of product than the network security products that defined the company in the 21st century. The change in strategic direction made by brothers Sreekanth Ravi and Sudhakar Ravi stemmed not from failure, but from a perceived chance for greater opportunity, one that seduced the two young entrepreneurs to abandon a profitable and growing business and pursue a different course. The brothers, separated in age by one year, both attended the Champaign-Urbana campus of the University of Illinois before different interests pulled them in different directions. Sreekanth Ravi, the younger of the pair, jumped into the business world, founding a manufacturer of high-performance video products named Generation Systems. His brother continued his education, earning his master of science degree in computer science from Stanford University. When Sreekanth Ravi sold Generation Systems to a publicly traded computer products company in 1990, he was ready to try his luck as an entrepreneur again. For his second venture, he enlisted the help of his brother, who was involved in semiconductor research at

Stanford. When the brothers came together in February 1991 to found SonicWALL's first incarnation, Sreekanth Ravi was 25 years old and Sudhakar was 26 years old.

The Ravis named their Santa Clara, California-based start-up Sonic Systems. Sreekanth Ravi took the titles of chairman, chief executive officer, and president. Sudhakar Ravi served as Sonic Systems' vice-president of engineering. The pair focused their efforts on developing networking products for Apple Macintosh computers, a market far smaller than the one targeted by the Ravis at the end of the decade. Sonic Systems' devices enabled Macintosh computers to connect to networks using Ethernet communications standards, which had been developed by Xerox during the 1970s. By the time the Ravis started their business, Ethernet standards had become the most widely used technology to facilitate communication among computers on a local area network, providing fertile market conditions for Sonic Systems to gain its footing. By 1995, the Ravis had turned their first profit, posting $251,000 in net income on $10.4 million in revenue.

A CHANGE IN STRATEGY IN 1997

The financial figures recorded in 1995 represented record-high totals for Sonic Systems as an Ethernet-based company. The Ravis soon began to turn their attention to the business opportunities created by the growth of the Internet, specifically the security concerns of small- to medium-sized businesses that increasingly were accessing the Internet for a variety of purposes, including communications, information gathering, and commerce. The brothers remained committed to their original business plan through 1996, when Ethernet-related sales totaled $9.3 million, but in 1997 they began to test the waters of the Internet security market. The turning point in their business occurred in October 1997, when Sonic Systems introduced the SonicWALL DMZ, an Internet security appliance with a list price of roughly $1,800. The debut of their first Internet security hardware gave the Ravis their first stream of

revenue, $250,000 by the end of the year, from the market that soon would provide the sole means of support for their business.

The release of the SonicWALL DMZ marked the beginning of the company's transformation into an Internet security appliance maker, a process that would take 26 months to complete and turn Sonic Systems into SonicWALL. The Ravis decided to concentrate their effort on the Internet security market in 1998, when volume shipments of SonicWALL appliances commenced. They also began offering content filtering subscriptions to customers in 1998, giving them the option of receiving lists of objectionable web sites on a weekly basis. As the company's security business ramped up, its Ethernet-related business began to fade. In 1998, the company generated $2.3 million in revenue from the sale of security appliances and $5.1 million from Ethernet sales. In 1999, the company's Ethernet sales dipped to $1.6 million, while Internet security sales mushroomed to $19.4 million. The final stages of the transformation occurred during the last months of 1999, beginning with a change in the company's name to SonicWALL, Inc., in August. In November, boasting a young and growing product line of security hardware, the company sold its promise on Wall Street, completing an initial public offering (IPO) of stock. In December, it stopped shipping Ethernet-related products, ending its involvement in its original line of business.

Entering a new century with a new name and a relatively new line of business, the Ravi brothers essentially were starting anew with SonicWALL. The switch to selling Internet security products, according to the company's filing with the Securities and Exchange Commission on February 23, 2000, was a seamless transition, free from requiring "any significant restructuring of personnel, facilities, manufacturing, or operations." There were, however, a number of new senior executives who arrived during the critical stage of the company's transformation into a security appliance producer. Between April 1998 and September 1999, the company's main offices, which had been relocated to Sunnyvale, California, underwent a changing of the guard, taking in a new vice-president of business development, a new chief financial officer, a new vice-president of sales, a new vice-president of operations, and a new vice-president of engineering. Sudhakar Ravi, who had served as the company's vice-president of engineering since 1991, became the company's chief technical officer in September 1999. With a new cadre of senior executives at his side, Sreekanth Ravi, who continued to hold the three most powerful posts at the company, began fleshing out SonicWALL's presence in the security appliance market.

KEY DATES

1991: SonicWALL is founded as Sonic Systems, a developer of Ethernet devices for Apple Macintosh computers.

1997: Sonic Systems introduces its first Internet security appliance, the SonicWALL DMZ.

1998: The company decides to focus its efforts on the Internet security market.

1999: Sonic Systems changes its name to SonicWALL, completes its initial public offering of stock, and ships its last Ethernet devices.

2000: SonicWALL acquires Phobos Corp.

2003: Matt Medeiros is appointed president and chief executive officer.

2005: SonicWALL acquires Lasso Logic and enKoo.

2006: An e-mail security vendor, MailFrontier, is acquired.

Sreekanth Ravi began to make bold moves before SonicWALL completed its first year as a publicly traded company. In October 2000, he reached an agreement to acquire a Murray, Utah-based company name Phobos Corp. whose history mirrored SonicWALL's evolution. Founded in 1995, Phobos initially made Ethernet cards for high-speed networks, but after butting up against stiff competition and realizing that Ethernet cards faced a future of dwindling profit margins, the company's management switched course. In 1998, Phobos began applying its expertise in networking to developing products for coordinating traffic on servers and providing encryption capabilities. Sreekanth Ravi agreed to pay nearly $280 million in cash and stock for Phobos, a purchase price exponentially greater than the less than $3 million in sales the Utah company generated from its new business line in 1999, but financial stature mattered little in the reasoning behind the acquisition. Instead, Ravi was focused on technology, specifically a circuit board for servers that offloaded the encryption needed for secure online transactions. By adding Phobos' Secure Sockets (SSL) and load-balancing technologies to SonicWALL's security appliances, Ravi hoped to expand his reach beyond small-sized and midsized business customers and attract larger customers.

As SonicWALL began its pursuit of customers who operated large networks, leadership changes occurred for the first time in the company's history. Ravi, who had held the three most powerful positions at the company since its inception, began to cede some of his power. In October 2001, Cosmo Santullo was hired to serve as SonicWALL's president and chief executive officer. Santullo spent two decades working in various capacities for IBM Corporation, his lengthy stay there ending in 1998. For seven months he served as senior vice-president of global marketing for EMC e-Business Solutions before being promoted to president. He vacated his post after five months, leaving EMC to join Mirror Image Internet, Inc., a provider of Internet content delivery systems based in Woburn, Massachusetts. Santullo served as the company president and chief executive officer for nearly two years, leaving the firm to join SonicWALL. After joining SonicWALL, Santullo remained in Massachusetts, commuting across the country to the company's main offices in Sunnyvale for ten months before resigning in August 2002, unwilling to make a permanent move to California.

Instead of reclaiming his titles as chief executive officer and president, Ravi turned to SonicWALL's vice-president of partners, alliances, and strategic accounts, Mike Roach, to serve in such capacities on an interim basis. A permanent replacement was hired in March 2003, when Matt Medeiros joined the company. A graduate of the University of San Francisco, Medeiros held executive positions at NeXT Computer, Apple Computer, Optical Polymers Group, and Allied Signal before serving as the president and chief executive officer of the components division at Phillips Electronics, the position he held prior to joining SonicWALL. The appointment of Medeiros as the day-to-day leader of the company coincided with the selection of a new chairman. Ravi passed the duties to a board member, Chuck Kissner, but continued to serve as director of the company.

ACQUISITIONS AND A PROFIT IN THE EARLY 21ST CENTURY

Medeiros took charge of a company whose financial record in the Internet security market offered room for improvement. Sales grew robustly at first, jumping to $112 million in 2001, before sliding downwards to $103 million in 2002. SonicWALL's sales decreased to $94 million during Medeiros's first year at the helm, but of greater concern was the company's problem with profitability. Years of annual losses pocked the company's foray into the Internet security market, representing a glaring blemish that Medeiros intended to remove. SonicWALL lost $20 million in 2001, $93 million in 2002, and $17 million during Medeiros's first year in charge.

SonicWALL's development during this period was highlighted by several acquisitions. In November 2005, the company paid nearly $16 million for Lasso Logic, Inc., a California-based provider of backup and recovery solutions for data protection. At the same time, the company acquired assets related to remote access technology owned by enKoo, Inc., paying $2.4 million for technology it intended to incorporate into Sonic-WALL products that featured virtual private networking and SSL. Shortly after completing the acquisitions, Medeiros could point to success on the financial front, giving cause for celebration as SonicWALL celebrated its 15th anniversary. After sales increased to $125 million in 2004 and jumped again to $135 million in 2005, the pattern of declining revenue appeared to have stopped. More important, the company reversed the pattern of annual losses as well. After posting a loss of $313,000 in 2004, SonicWALL generated a profit in 2005, registering $6.2 million in net income.

Buoyed by the company's improved financial performance, Medeiros began preparing for the future, intent on making growth and profitability bywords in the years ahead. Early in 2006, during SonicWALL's 15th anniversary, Medeiros completed an acquisition that he hoped would contribute to the company's financial stature. He paid $31 million for e-mail security vendor MailFrontier, a company whose products monitored e-mail traffic for viruses, spam content, phishing attacks, and other threats. Medeiros intended to add MailFrontier's messaging security software and hardware to SonicWALL's range of products, a product line that was expected to become more comprehensive in the years ahead.

Jeffrey L. Covell

PRINCIPAL SUBSIDIARIES

SonicWALL B.V. (Netherlands); Phobos Corporation; Lasso Logic, Inc.; SonicWALL Switzerland; SonicWALL Norway.

PRINCIPAL COMPETITORS

Check Point Software Technologies Ltd.; Cisco Systems, Inc.; NetWolves Corporation.

FURTHER READING

Boulton, Guy, "Sunnyvale, Calif.-based Tech Firm Buys Murray, Utah, Counterpart," *Salt Lake Tribune,* October 18, 2000.

Howell, Donna, "Security Firms Looking High and Low to Find Additional Customers," *Investor's Business Daily,* March 18, 2002, p. A4.

——, "SonicWall Appoints New CEO," *Asia Africa Intelligence Wire,* March 20, 2003.

Savage, Marcia, "Breaking the Sonic Barrier," *Computer Reseller News,* December 18, 2000, p. 59.

"SonicWall CEO Cosmo Santullo Resigns," *eWeek,* August 2, 2002.

"SonicWall Strengthens E-Mail Security," *eWeek,* February 8, 2006.

ThyssenKrupp AG

August-Thyssen-Strasse 1
Düsseldorf, 40211
Germany
Telephone: (+49 211) 824-0
Fax: (+49 211) 824-36000
Web site: http://www.thyssenkrupp.com

Public Company
Incorporated: 1999
Employees: 187,586
Sales: EUR 47.13 billion ($59.79 billion) (2006)
Stock Exchanges: Frankfurt Düsseldorf London
Ticker Symbols: TKA (Frankfurt, Düsseldorf); THK (London)
NAIC: 233310 Manufacturing and Industrial Building Construction; 331111 Iron and Steel Mills; 331221 Rolled Steel Shape Manufacturing; 331513 Steel Foundries (Except Investment); 333921 Elevator and Moving Stairway Manufacturing; 336312 Gasoline Engine and Engine Parts Manufacturing; 336330 Motor Vehicle Steering and Suspension Components (Except Spring) Manufacturing; 336611 Ship Building and Repairing; 541330 Engineering Services; 561210 Facilities Support Services

■ ■ ■

The engineering and steel powerhouse ThyssenKrupp AG was created in March 1999 from the merger of two of Germany's oldest industrial giants, Thyssen AG and Fried. Krupp AG Hoesch-Krupp. One of the largest companies in Germany, ThyssenKrupp has five main divisions. ThyssenKrupp Steel specializes in flat steel products and holds the number two spot in that sector in Europe, behind Arcelor Mittal. ThyssenKrupp Stainless is the world's leading producer of flat stainless steel and nickel alloys. ThyssenKrupp Technologies plans and constructs chemical, cement, and other plants; creates surface mining systems; builds frigates, submarines, and other marine vessels; produces components for mechanical engineering and the automotive industry; and is one of the world's top 20 auto suppliers, producing components, assemblies, and systems for chassis, body, and powertrain applications. ThyssenKrupp Elevator is the world's third largest maker of elevators and escalators. ThyssenKrupp Services is involved in the material and process services for the production and manufacturing industries.

THYSSEN'S EARLY HISTORY

Thyssen (pronounced TISS-in) traces its origins to a steel plant in Bruckhausen near Hamborn on the Rhine, which started operations in December 1891 and later formed the core of the Thyssen empire. The plant was built by August Thyssen, a 50-year-old entrepreneur who had already built up a steel and engineering business called Thyssen & Co. August had worked in his father's banking business in Eschweiler and later as a manager-partner of a steel mill, called Thyssen, Fossoul & Co. In 1871, the year of Germany's first unification, he set up his own business at Mulheim in the Ruhr area with 35,000 talers and a paternal grant of the same sum. August Thyssen's business expansion in the 1880s included the purchase of large coal mines. He gradually

COMPANY PERSPECTIVES

Present in the markets of the future: ThyssenKrupp is already an international company today, with strong positions on the European and North American markets. The Group is represented in more than 70 countries with 66% of sales coming from customers abroad. But a further leap lies ahead as we invest in the growth markets of tomorrow—Southeast Asia, Latin America, Central and Eastern Europe. These are regions offering huge growth potential which we will be able to tap systematically with our capabilities and strong customer relationships.

Our Group is becoming increasingly global in all areas. Rising orders from our international customers together with joint ventures and acquisitions have significantly strengthened our worldwide business. More than one in two ThyssenKrupp employees work outside Germany in one of our roughly 600 foreign subsidiaries and associated shareholdings.

bought into the Gewerkschaft Deutscher Kaiser coal pits and took the mining company over entirely in 1891. Thyssen & Co.'s Mulheim factories soon became unsuitable for August's expansion plans as the site was too small and lay too far away from a river, which he needed for transport. In 1889 he decided to build the steel plant at Bruckhausen, installing six furnaces using the modern Siemens-Martin technique, and a rolling mill with five trains for the first step. August also wanted to control his own crude steel supplies, building a plant in 1895 in Bruckhausen, which started operations two years later.

August's companies expanded quickly in the years leading up to World War I, securing their own coal and iron ore supplies. His drive for self-sufficiency made him buy into raw materials suppliers in France, North Africa, and Russia. By 1904, August's rolled steel production had hit 700,000 tons a year, putting him ahead of other producers in Germany. The demands made by Germany's military authorities during World War I buoyed Thyssen's business in the same way as other German industries, but Germany's defeat had catastrophic consequences for the company. Its foreign property was confiscated, its plants in the Ruhr Valley were put temporarily under French control, and earnings were battered by the postwar hyperinflation.

August's shrunken business empire became profitable again only in late 1924. The octogenarian August concentrated on mechanizing production to cut costs, and initially resisted overtures from other German steel producers to form a cartel. However, Thyssen gave up its independence soon after August's death in 1926, joining four other coal and steel enterprises to form Vereinigten Stahlwerke AG (Vst). Thyssen made up more than a quarter of Vst's paid-up capital of 800 million reichsmarks, and Fritz Thyssen became chairman of the supervisory board. Vst was decentralized in 1934; five steel mills in the western part of the Ruhr district were grouped into August Thyssen-Hütte AG based in Duisburg.

Fritz Thyssen, the elder son of August, is remembered more for his association with Adolf Hitler than for his business skills. Frustrated by his father's long tenure at the head of the company, Fritz channeled his energies into right-wing politics aiming to subvert the Weimar Republic. He became an early supporter of the Nazi Party. Fritz later fell out with the Nazis and recanted in a ghostwritten autobiography titled *I Paid Hitler*. He fled Germany in 1939, was captured in Vichy, France, and incarcerated from 1941 to November 1943 in a mental asylum and then in concentration camps until the end of the war. After World War II, Fritz's break with the Nazis was largely accepted by a denazification court, which fined him 15 percent of his German properties. At the end of 1948 he immigrated to Latin America.

Vst and Thyssen's main works, renamed ATH AG, fared just as badly under the Nazis. The Four Year plan of 1936, devised by Hitler to prepare Germany for war, restricted raw material supplies and made cost-effective production almost impossible. During the war years, ATH, like other German companies, became a supplier to war production, although in 1942 Nazi hard-liners accused the company of defeatism. In the autumn of 1944, Allied bombing raids destroyed many of ATH's factories, with production in its huge plants ceasing altogether.

POSTWAR EMERGENCE AS AUGUST THYSSEN-HÜTTE

Worse was to follow. The victorious Allies allowed limited repairs at ATH's factories, and the first steel mills at Thyssen-Hütte, the main works of ATH, began operating again in October 1945 but only temporarily. In April 1946 the Allies agreed to stop reconstruction while they decided what to do with German industry, which they blamed for arming Hitler. In February 1948 the Allies decided to dismantle Thyssen-Hütte as part of

KEY DATES

1811: Friedrich Krupp establishes a cast-steel factory in Essen.

1850s: The Krupp company expands into the production of railroad equipment and cannon-making.

1891: August Thyssen gains full control of the Gewerkschaft Deutscher Kaiser coal mine in Hamborn, and operations begin at a new steel plant that Thyssen builds on that site—events that are considered to comprise the origin of the Thyssen group.

1903: The Krupp company is converted into a stock corporation called Fried. Krupp AG.

1919: Under the Treaty of Versailles, Krupp is barred from most armament production.

1926: Following the death of the founder, the bulk of the Thyssen group is merged into Vereinigten Stahlwerke AG (Vst).

1933: Period begins when Krupp's operations are closely tied to the policies of the Nazis.

1934: Vst is decentralized, with August Thyssen-Hütte AG established as one of its operating companies.

1943: Krupp is converted into a sole proprietorship and transferred into the control of Alfried Krupp von Bohlen und Halbach.

1945: Krupp is placed under Allied control.

1953: Following a postwar period of dismantling and liquidation, August Thyssen-Hütte AG is reestablished as a public company; Alfried Krupp von Bohlen und Halbach resumes management of Krupp.

1968: Krupp is converted into a limited liability company, Fried. Krupp GmbH.

1973: August Thyssen-Hütte acquires Rheinstahl AG, which becomes the core of its engineering group.

1977: August Thyssen-Hütte simplifies its name to Thyssen AG.

1978: Thyssen diversifies further, acquiring the Budd Company, a U.S. auto components maker.

1982: Thyssen spins off its steel operations into the semi-independent Thyssen Stahl AG.

1992: Krupp merges with steelmaker Hoesch AG to form Fried. Krupp AG Hoesch-Krupp.

1993: The new Krupp becomes a publicly traded company for the first time in its long history.

1997: Following a failed hostile takeover of Thyssen by Krupp, the two companies merge their flat steel operations into a joint venture called Thyssen Krupp Stahl AG.

1999: Thyssen and Krupp complete a full merger of their operations, creating ThyssenKrupp AG.

2006: Twice thwarted in its attempt to acquire Canadian steelmaker Dofasco Inc., ThyssenKrupp announces plans to build a new steel plant in the United States.

---

their war reparations from Germany. Factories were exploded or stripped of machinery. The destruction of the Thyssen-Hütte and other works of Vst was halted only in November 1949 with the Petersberg Treaty, an agreement signed between the Allies and the new government of the Federal Republic of Germany. At the same time the Allies broke up the Vst group into 16 successor companies. They also separated the steel companies from their mining firms. All that remained of August Thyssen-Hütte AG was the core business of the former Thyssen-Hütte at Hamborn. Nevertheless, it restarted its first blast furnace in 1951. Business improved once the Allies lifted steel production limits one year later.

In May 1953 August Thyssen-Hütte AG was relaunched as a public company with the successors of Fritz Thyssen as minority shareholders. Eventually, a consortium company belonging to the Fritz Thyssen family and the Commerzbank AG and Allianz AG insurance group was created and held a stake in Thyssen of more than 25 percent.

Thyssen's postwar history was dominated by two management board chairmen, Hans-Günther Sohl, who ran the company from 1953 to 1973, and his successor, Dieter Spethmann, who retired in 1991. Sohl rebuilt ATH as Germany's biggest steelmaker, and Spethmann presided over its often difficult diversification into new product areas.

ATH flourished in the 1950s on booming steel demand, building new facilities to make flat rolled steel. The company invested some DM 700 million up to 1958 and spent DM 800 million alone on a new Beeckerwerth plant. Thyssen also expanded by buying companies, taking over four major producers by 1968: Niederrheinische Hütte AG, Deutsche Edelstahlwerke AG, Phoenix-Rheinrohr AG, and Hüttenwerk Oberhausen AG. It also expanded into trading and services by buying into Handelsunion AG from 1960 onward. The future core of the Thyssen Handelsunion AG subsidiary, Handelsunion traded in steel, scrap metal, and raw materials, and also offered transport services. Thyssen also forged alliances with other large German steel producers to make production more cost-effective, signing an agreement with Mannesmann in 1970 on steel pipe and rolled steel manufacturing.

Expanding steel output was still the ATH strategy at the beginning of the 1970s, when less expensive imports from newly emerging steel producing companies began to undercut European producers. Thyssen's steel production peaked at 17 million tons in 1974, the same year that the first major steel crisis hit world manufacturers. Like other German producers, Thyssen suffered from 1969 and 1973 revaluations of the deutsche mark, high wage costs, and the imposition of environmental controls. The oil price rise of 1973 delivered another blow to the industry as costs soared and demand shrank.

THYSSEN DIVERSIFYS

ATH decided to scrap all plans to expand steelmaking capacity and to withdraw from sectors where competitors were undercutting the company's prices. Instead, Thyssen invested in streamlining production and in diversifying away from steel. In 1974, Thyssen took over Rheinstahl AG, the group's high technology engineering group which in 1976 was renamed Thyssen Industrie AG. The parent company itself changed its name to simply Thyssen AG in 1977. The following year Thyssen bought a U.S. car components maker, The Budd Company.

These acquisitions, however, initially caused problems. Rheinstahl had a number of steel mills, which increased Thyssen's capacity to 21 million tons a year. The company was forced to close nearly 30 plants in the Thyssen group between 1974 and 1980. The number working in Thyssen's West German steel plants decreased to fewer than 75,000 in 1979 from 85,000 five years earlier. Budd made money for Thyssen in the first two years after the takeover. The second oil crisis in 1979 pitched the U.S. economy into recession and caused heavy losses at Budd; the company only saw a

turnaround in 1982. One of the biggest loss makers was Budd's railway equipment division; it had signed four large contracts in 1981 at fixed prices that never covered production costs. The division's workforce was cut to 700 from 2,500. Budd then concentrated on its core auto-components market, cutting its workforce from 21,500 in 1978 to fewer than 12,000 in 1986.

Thyssen's diversifications were continually dogged by the decline of the steel industry. Spethmann was determined to restructure Thyssen using the company's own financial resources. He opposed acceptance of subsidies such as those propping up rival state-owned steelmakers in Belgium, the United Kingdom, and France, but the near collapse of steel prices forced Thyssen to accept European Community production quotas and subsidies in 1980. The steel crisis continued, however, forcing the creation of Thyssen Stahl AG in 1982 as an independent steel group, in a bid to find partners to help reduce costs. Spethmann made the first of many overtures to archrival Fried. Krupp GmbH for merging production but was rebuffed. Thyssen therefore imposed a tough program of cuts, with a reduction to the 1991 level of 11 million tons capacity from 16 million tons. Losses at Budd and at Thyssen Stahl forced the group to suspend dividend payments for two years in 1982. An improvement in the world economy prompted Thyssen to restart dividend payments at five marks a share, though losses at Thyssen Stahl continued until 1987.

In the 1980s, Thyssen linked its name to high technology projects in the transport sector. It lead-managed a consortium developing the Transrapid train, capable of speeds of up to 500 kilometers an hour. The Transrapid was sold as a revolutionary form of transport running on a magnetic field rather than on wheels. The train had no engine on board and relied on electromagnetic motors in the track. Thyssen wanted to lay a Transrapid track from the northern port city of Hamburg to Munich in the south, but received government backing only for a smaller pilot track in North Rhine Westfalia state. The government was not entirely convinced that all of Transrapid's technical problems had been solved, and was worried about funding a white elephant project. A bitter row broke out before the government gave approval. Thyssen accused Bonn officials of trying to sabotage the project, which the company wanted to sell abroad.

Thyssen's image suffered in the 1980s when a book was published accusing Thyssen Stahl of malpractices in its treatment of Turkish guest workers. Thyssen successfully contested the book in court, however, and author Günter Wallraff had to delete passages from his best-seller, titled *At the Very Bottom*.

DECLINING FORTUNES LEAD TO RESTRUCTURING

Taking over Spethmann's chief executive post in 1991 was Heinz Kriwet, who presided over some of the company's darkest days. In the aftermath of the reunification of Germany, Thyssen reacted cautiously, shying away from buying into East Germany's decrepit steel industry. Instead, it concentrated on setting up 27 smaller ventures in the engineering and services sector, involving investments of some DM 500 million. It also signed another 40 cooperation deals with state-owned companies in the former communist country. The early years of the 1990s also saw Thyssen diversify again, through an entrance into the telecommunications industry, including the formation of an alliance with U.S. telecom firm BellSouth, with the partners hoping to grab a piece of an industry that was in the process of being deregulated in Germany.

Declining steel demand in the early 1990s had a major impact on Thyssen, leading to several years of declining profits before the company posted a net loss of DM 994 million for the 1992–93 fiscal year. During that year the company shed more than 7,000 jobs from its workforce as part of a rationalization program. Thyssen also began aggressively pursuing alliances with other companies in a near desperate attempt to cut costs and reduce losses. The most important of these was a linkup with Fried. Krupp AG Hoesch-Krupp, the new name for Fried. Krupp GmbH after it acquired ailing Rhineland steelmaker Hoesch AG through a hostile takeover. In 1995 Thyssen and Krupp merged their stainless steel operations in a joint venture called Krupp-Thyssen Nirosta, which was 60 percent owned by Krupp and 40 percent owned by Thyssen. Nirosta instantly became the largest stainless-steelmaker in the world, with annual capacity of 1.2 million metric tons and annual revenues of DM 4.5 billion ($3.2 billion). In September 1995, meanwhile, two great-grandsons of Thyssen's founder, August Thyssen, sold their remaining stakes in the company, thereby severing the final ties between the Thyssen family and the company.

In March 1996 Kriwet took over as chairman of Thyssen, while Dieter Vogel, who had headed the group's trading and services division, stepped into the chief executive slot. In August 1996 Vogel and nine other Thyssen executives were arrested as part of an investigation into whether Thyssen executives had mishandled DM 73 million ($49 million) in funds connected to the privatization of a former East German metals trading company. In late 1997 he was formally charged in connection with this investigation. For the year ending in September 1996, Thyssen reported a 36 percent decline in pretax profits. In response to these

struggles, the company announced a major restructuring in late 1996 aiming for the withdrawal from or scaling back of activities in noncore areas, including long steel products, defense equipment, and coal and oil trading. Further, after failing in the summer of 1996 to forge a link in the telecommunications sector with Deutsche Bahn, the German national railway, Thyssen scaled back its involvement in that sector. In late 1997 Thyssen sold its stake in a German cellular-phone operator to Veba AG and RWE AG for DM 2.26 billion ($1.26 billion). Also in 1997 Thyssen merged its shipbuilding operations with those of Preussag AG to form the largest shipbuilding concern in Germany, with annual sales of DM 3.5 billion ($1.83 billion).

In March 1997 Krupp initiated a hostile takeover of Thyssen, which failed, but led to the late 1997 creation of Thyssen Krupp Stahl AG, a flat steel joint venture; additional negotiations then resulted in the March 1999 merger of the two companies to form ThyssenKrupp (these events are described in more detail below). Meantime, Thyssen finally appeared to have turned around its financial difficulties: sales were on the rise and net income was a very strong DM 2.19 billion by the 1997–98 fiscal year. The company's renewed focus was evident in its pursuit and completion of several significant acquisitions. In 1997 Thyssen acquired U.S.-based Copper and Brass Sales Inc., a leading trading and service center for nonferrous metals in North America. That same year, Thyssen paid $675 million to acquire another U.S. firm, Giddings & Lewis, Inc., the largest machine-tool maker in the United States. Giddings fit in well with Thyssen's already considerable auto-related operations, since the Fond du Lac, Wisconsin-based firm derived about 40 percent of its revenue from that industrial sector. In early January 1999 Thyssen, through its Thyssen Industries unit, purchased the North American elevator operations of Dover Corporation, including the Dover Elevator brand, for $1.1 billion. Thyssen was already one of the top elevator firms worldwide, and with the addition of Dover Elevator became one of the top three or four companies in that area.

KRUPP'S NAPOLEONIC ERA ROOTS

The company that would eventually be known as Fried. Krupp GmbH, and then Fried. Krupp AG Hoesch-Krupp, was established on November 20, 1811, by Friedrich Krupp, member of a family of merchants whose roots in Essen can be traced back to 1587, and his two partners, brothers Georg Carl Gottfried von Kechel and Wilhelm Georg Ludwig von Kechel. They set up a factory for making English cast steel and products manufactured from it. There was a ready market for these products because of Napoleon's Continental Blockade, which prevented imports of cast steel from England. The two partners contributed the metallurgical knowledge, while Friedrich Krupp handled the commercial side and provided the necessary capital. When the steelmaking experiments of the two partners—and later of a third, Friedrich Nicolai— proved unsuccessful, Friedrich Krupp ran the factory on his own from 1816 onward and developed a process for making high-quality cast steel on a factory scale. His products included cast-steel bars, tanner's tools, coining dies, and unfinished rolls. In the years that followed, however, Friedrich Krupp failed to operate the factory at a profit. Competition was severe, particularly from Britain, and while Krupp's prices were too low, his production costs were too high. In addition, product quality varied because, owing to a lack of funds, Krupp occasionally had to use inferior raw materials. Only the family's considerable assets, which in the end were totally consumed, prevented the firm from going bankrupt. When Friedrich Krupp died in 1826, production had almost come to a standstill.

Therese Krupp, his widow, kept the firm going, supported by her relatives and her 14-year-old eldest son, Alfred. With only a few workers at first, the manufacture of cast steel continued. When in 1830 Alfred Krupp started to manufacture finished products, he was able to endorse these with his personal guarantee of quality. Output, however, remained at a low level.

Only after 1834 did the firm experience vigorous expansion. The lifting of customs barriers by the German Customs Union (an agreement between the German states, before their unification, to remove trade barriers between them and create a single economic entity) in 1834 boosted sales, and the purchase of a steam engine, financed by a new partner, helped to make production more cost efficient. Alfred Krupp endeavored above all to perfect the manufacture of high-precision rolls, which he later supplied additionally in rolling machines and rolling mills. With his two brothers, he developed a mill in the early 1840s for stamping, rolling, and embossing spoons and forks in one operation. Krupp took numerous journeys to find customers abroad, particularly in France, Austria, and Russia. A long sojourn in England enabled him to widen his knowledge of steelmaking and factory organization.

The firm's expansion did not follow a steady course, mainly because the market for rolls and rolling mills was limited. Further, there was no replacement market, because Krupp's rolls were virtually indestructible. The attempt to establish cutlery factories succeeded only in Austria, where in 1843 Krupp, together with Alexander Schoeller, founded the works at Berndorf near Vienna, which from 1849 onward was managed by his brother Hermann. The search for new applications for his high-quality but expensive cast steel was unsuccessful at first. The general economic malaise that set in around 1846–47 hit the cast-steel works badly. In April 1848 Alfred Krupp, sole owner, could save it from ruin only by selling off personal assets and then by winning a major order from Russia for cutlery machinery.

KRUPP EXPANDS INTO RAILWAY EQUIPMENT AND CANNON-MAKING

Around 1850 business started to pick up again. The burgeoning of the railways opened up a virtually unlimited market for Krupp's hard-wearing cast steel. Along with axles and springs, the firm's most important product in this field was the forged and rolled seamless railway tire. Invented by Alfred Krupp in 1852–53, this proved able to withstand the increasing track speeds without fracturing. In 1859 the breakthrough into cannon-making was achieved with an order from Prussia for 300 cast-steel cannon-barrel ingots.

To secure sales, Alfred Krupp sought new markets on other continents. He journeyed abroad, established agencies, and participated in international exhibitions. At the Crystal Palace Exhibition held in London in 1851, Krupp displayed a cast-steel cannon barrel that attracted great interest; for a cast-steel ingot weighing approximately 40 hundredweight he received the highest accolade, the Council Medal.

At an early stage Krupp introduced new, economic steelmaking processes, for instance the Bessemer process in 1862 as well as the open-hearth process in 1869. For products that had to be particularly tough, crucible steel remained his most important starting material. It was around this time that Krupp adopted a policy of acquiring ore deposits, coal mines, and iron works to secure the company's rapidly growing requirement of raw materials. With the swift expansion of the company—in 1865 the workforce totaled 8,248 and sales 15.7 million marks—it became necessary to delegate managerial tasks. In 1862 Alfred Krupp established a corporate body of management bearing joint responsibility for the affairs of the firm. His general directive of 1872 laid down the principles to be applied in running his enterprise as well as the social welfare policy to be pursued.

From the outset Alfred Krupp strove to create and maintain a loyal set of highly skilled employees. Only thus could he guarantee the high quality of his products. To alleviate the social problems caused by industrialization he introduced employee welfare schemes, at the same time enjoining his workers not to become involved in trade-union or social-democratic activity. As early as 1836 he set up a voluntary sickness and burial fund, which became a compulsory sickness and death benefit insurance scheme in 1853. In 1855 Alfred Krupp established a pension scheme and in 1858 a company-owned bakery that evolved into the employees' retail store. In 1856 the first hostels were built offering board and lodging to bachelor workers. The year 1861 saw the construction of the first company dwellings for foremen. Worker's housing estates, incorporating schools and branches of a retail store, followed in 1863, and from the early 1870s grew apace. In 1870 a company hospital was established.

In the years up to 1873 the firm continued to expand strongly. However, in the economic slump of 1874 it almost suffered financial collapse because Krupp had raised large bank loans without arranging adequate security. Thereafter the company entered a phase of steady development. The gunnery division was engaged in efforts to develop better field, siege, and naval guns. The divisions producing machinery components, shipbuilding material, and railway equipment were expanded. When Alfred Krupp died in 1887, the firm's employees numbered 20,200 and sales for 1887–88 amounted to 47.5 million marks.

Even during his lifetime Alfred Krupp was known as the Cannon King, mainly because during the Franco-Prussian War of 1870–71 Krupp's cast-steel guns had proved superior to the French bronze cannon. The way the firm presented itself to the public reflected the spirit of the times and for decades the manufacture of guns was given a prominence beyond its actual share of production. In fact, until 1905 armaments generally accounted for less, and in some cases considerably less, than 50 percent of output; in the years leading up to World War I the proportion was between 50 and 60 percent.

ACQUISITION OF GRUSON WORKS AND GERMANIA SHIPYARD

Alfred's only son and heir, Friedrich Alfred Krupp, continued the expansion of the enterprise into a horizontally and vertically integrated concern. Entry into the production of armor plate at the behest of the Imperial Navy led in 1892–93 to the acquisition of the strongest competitor in this field, the Gruson works in Magdeburg. Production of armor plate was then concentrated in Essen, while work in Magdeburg

focused on the design and construction of plant and machinery.

At the urgings of his directors, as well as of Emperor Wilhelm II and the Imperial Navy, Krupp decided in 1896 to take over the Germania shipyard in Kiel. The plant was leased that year, and acquired in 1902. At this time Admiral Tirpitz, secretary of state for the Imperial Navy, introduced the program for the expansion of the German fleet under the Fleet Acts. The resultant boost to the German shipbuilding industry also benefited the Germania yard where, in addition to merchant vessels, warships clad in Krupp armor plating were built. The year 1902 saw the building of the experimental submarine *Forelle,* forerunner of the U-boat. At the same time the company began producing diesel engines at the Germania yard, following the development of the first working diesel engine in 1897 by Rudolf Diesel in collaboration with Krupp and Maschinenfabrik Augsburg.

The construction in 1897 of a large integrated iron and steel works at Rheinhausen strengthened the company's solid footing in iron and steel. A few years later the Thomas process was adopted there for the mass production of steel. Further ore and coal mines were acquired to cover the increasing raw materials requirements. Friedrich Alfred Krupp was particularly interested in the technology of steelmaking. He introduced scientific research into steel at Krupp and thus created the springboard for the successful development of special-steel production.

Friedrich Alfred Krupp expanded the employee welfare and benefit schemes, not only at Essen but also at the outlying works. He widened the scope of the health funds, built new housing estates, and created the Altenhof estate for retired and disabled workmen. He established educational and leisure amenities for his employees, in particular a lending library with numerous branches and an educational society.

During his lifetime Friedrich Alfred Krupp was caught in the crossfire of public debate. While to many he was a successful industrialist with a sense of national responsibility, his critics saw him as a capitalist entrepreneur who, through his links with the Imperial House and his support of the German Navy League, a nongovernment association formed to promote the strengthening of the German fleet, exerted influence on the country's naval policy in order to gain lucrative contracts for his company. The spectacular acquisitions of the Gruson works and the Germania yard readily lent themselves to such an interpretation.

In later literature too, Friedrich Alfred Krupp has been presented in controversial terms. Research has proven, however, that it was not he who initiated the program of naval expansion started in 1897–98. The main impetus came from Admiral Tirpitz and the circle of people close to Emperor Wilhelm II. Friedrich Alfred Krupp only acted in response to this policy.

When Friedrich Alfred Krupp died suddenly at the age of 48 in 1902, Bertha Krupp, the elder of his two daughters, inherited the company, which, as recommended in the will of the later owner, was converted into a stock corporation in 1903, when it became known as Fried. Krupp AG. Almost all the shares remained in the ownership of Bertha Krupp. When in 1906 she married Gustav von Bohlen und Halbach, counselor to the Royal Prussian Legation at the Vatican, Wilhelm II as king of Prussia accorded Gustav the right to bear the name Krupp von Bohlen und Halbach and to pass on this name to his successors as owners of the company. After the wedding Gustav Krupp von Bohlen und Halbach was appointed to the supervisory board of Fried. Krupp AG, which he chaired from 1909 until the end of 1943.

In the years leading up to World War I, order books were healthy and the company continued to expand. By 1903 the workforce had increased to 42,000 and by 1913 to 77,000, with sales rising from 91.4 million marks in 1902–03 to 430.7 million marks in 1912–13. The increase in productivity mainly reflected the expansion of the Rheinhausen iron and steel works and the resultant fundamental reorganization of production in Essen.

In 1908 electric steelmaking was introduced at the Essen works. After a few years the company was making electric steels of such quality that they were able to partly replace high-grade crucible steel. Intensive research into alloying came to fruition in 1912 with the development of stainless chromium-nickel steels which, besides being resistant to corrosion, were also able to withstand the effects of acid and heat and were thus suitable for a wide range of applications.

The continuation and expansion of employee benefits and welfare remained key elements of corporate policy. Margarethe Krupp, the widow of Friedrich Alfred Krupp, established a domestic nursing service and provided the financial base for the Margarethenhöhe garden suburb. The company continued to build housing estates for its workers, these efforts being increasingly supplemented by independent housing associations closely linked to Krupp. Convalescent homes and a dental clinic were built, and the Arnoldhaus lying-in hospital was founded.

KRUPP INCREASING MUNITIONS PRODUCTION DURING WORLD WAR I

World War I brought an increase in armaments production and a further expansion of the company. In order to fulfill government contracts, munitions output was doubled in the first year of the war and by the third year it had reached more than five times its pre-1914 level. This output was achieved, particularly after 1916, by building huge new factories and increasing the workforce substantially. In November 1918 Krupp's employees totaled 168,000. Well-known products in these years were the 16.5-inch Big Bertha gun (named after Bertha Krupp), 27 of which went into action in 1914; the merchant submarines *Deutschland* and *Bremen,* built at the Germania yard in 1915–16; and the long-barreled "Paris gun" with a range of 85 miles, of which seven were built.

Both at the time and in some of the subsequent literature the firm and the Krupp family were accused of having been the main beneficiaries of the war. More recent researchers have demonstrated how inaccurate a picture this was. Compared with other companies only a relatively small portion of the profits initially earned were distributed to the shareholders, whereas the main part was invested in the new factory buildings which later were of little use. High personnel and welfare costs during but especially immediately after the war and the cost of converting to peacetime manufacture exhausted the company's substantial reserves. With the end of hostilities the demand for armaments ceased. Under the Treaty of Versailles (1919) the company was prohibited from making ammunition, and cannon manufacture was allowed only to a limited extent. Krupp changed its production and embarked on the manufacture of locomotives, motor trucks, agricultural machinery, and excavators. The cost of reorganization, the wages for workers actually no longer needed, and the losses incurred through dismantling, inflation, and the dispute over the Ruhr River, when the government implemented a strategy of passive resistance to the occupation of the region by French and Belgian troops, plunged the company into a crisis in the mid-1920s that threatened its very existence. Gustav Krupp von Bohlen und Halbach had no choice but to implement drastic cutbacks. Having initially refused for social reasons, he reduced the workforce within two years from 71,000 to 46,000. Unviable operations were closed down, production was streamlined, and newly launched but unprofitable mechanical engineering activities were discontinued. Even then the company would not have overcome the crisis had it not been for the financial support it received from a combination of government agencies and banks.

Gustav Krupp von Bohlen und Halbach rejected the proposal of his directors that the Krupp works be closed down or incorporated in Vereinigte Stahlwerke, a combination of German steel companies, which was about to be established. He did, however, finally accept the suggestion made by Krupp Director Otto Wiedfeld, who from 1922 until early 1925 was the German ambassador to the United States, that the company be rehabilitated by selling a 50 percent shareholding to the British government. This plan had to be quickly abandoned, however, because the German government felt its policy of rapprochement with France might be jeopardized.

In the years that followed, the company gained a more stable footing, mainly by streamlining the fabricating operations and expanding the production of special steels. Between 1927 and 1929 a blast-furnace plant was added to the melting shops and rolling mills in the Borbeck district of Essen to form an integrated iron and steel works. One of the most modern in Europe, it enabled the production of special steel to be increased further. In 1926 Krupp introduced Widia sintered carbide, a product that, by virtue of exceptional hardness and wear resistance, brought a major breakthrough in tool engineering.

CLOSE ALLIANCE WITH NAZIS

The Great Depression, which first hit the world economy in 1929, brought this revival to an abrupt halt. The workforce, which by 1928 had risen to 92,300, fell back to 46,100 by 1932. Sales dropped from 577.5 million reichsmarks in 1929 to 240 million in 1932. After 1933 Germany experienced an economic upturn during which corporate policy at Krupp became closely entwined with the economic policy of the National Socialists. Governmental efforts to achieve self-sufficiency included the development of the country's iron ore deposits. The Renn process introduced by Krupp in 1929 permitted these inferior ores to be reduced economically. A coal conversion plant was built for producing petrol from coal. Increasing demand for rolled-steel products, especially for building the new autobahns, spawned the expansion of Krupp's structural engineering shops in Rheinhausen. Under the Four-Year Plan the state took increasing control of industry and at Krupp the production of locomotives, motor trucks, and ships was stepped up against the will of the company's directors. They wanted to give priority to the successful production of special steels and their fabrication for use in chemical process plant and other applications. In 1938, following the death of proprietor Arthur Krupp, son of Hermann Krupp, the Berndorf works near Vienna was incorporated in the concern. Krupp also

expanded its shipbuilding activities by acquiring a majority shareholding in Deutsche Schiff-und Maschinenbau Aktiengesellschaft "Deschimag" in 1940–41. Sales rose from 809.6 million reichsmarks in 1937–38 to 1.1 billion in 1942–43; in the same period the number of employees rose from 123,400 to 235,000.

In the 1920s Krupp had, at the behest and later with the financial support of the German Reichswehr Office, undertaken design work of a military nature going beyond the tight restrictions imposed by the Treaty of Versailles. The resulting vehicles and equipment were manufactured in collaboration with other firms. In the 1930s work on the design and manufacture of armaments was stepped up, and during the war these activities were greatly intensified, controlled as they were by the state's grip on the economy. Weapons made up a much smaller proportion of total output than during World War I, however, because the manufacture of motor trucks, locomotives, bridges, ships, and especially submarines, continued at a high level.

Research has shown that in spite of claims to the contrary, Gustav Krupp von Bohlen und Halbach, president of the federation of German industry from 1931 to 1934, did not support Hitler or the Nazi Party before they came to power. In keeping with his sense of national loyalty, however, he expressed his support for the state after Hitler's appointment as Reichskanzler.

At the end of 1943 the firm was reconverted into a sole proprietorship and transferred to Gustav's eldest son Alfried. The armaments authorities and semiofficial control committees were intervening more and more in industrial activity. Out of loyalty to his war-torn country Alfried endeavored to meet the demands imposed, though the lack of skilled workers, air raids, and the relocation of operations made this increasingly difficult. Like most of the armament factories in Germany during the war, Krupp used forced labor, as most of its workers had been called up for military service.

At the end of the war large areas of the works lay in ruins and much of what remained, like the iron and steel works in Essen-Borbeck, was compulsorily dismantled. The Gruson works and Berndorfer Metallwarenfabrik were expropriated by order of the Allies, and the Germania shipyard, also severely damaged by bombing, was dismantled and liquidated.

Gustav Krupp von Bohlen und Halbach was indicted for war crimes by the International Military Tribunal in Nuremberg but was found to be physically and mentally unable to stand trial. The suggestion made by the American, Russian, and French prosecuting counsels that his son Alfried be indicted in his place was rejected by the British prosecutor on the grounds that they were not conducting a game in which one player could be replaced by another. Nevertheless, Alfried Krupp von Bohlen und Halbach was put under arrest by the American occupation troops in Essen on April 11, 1945. His property was confiscated, and he was kept in prison until he was accused before a U.S. military court in 1947 together with members of the firm's senior staff. This was one of three trials against industrialists. Alfried Krupp von Bohlen und Halbach and his leading staff were accused of having planned and participated in a war of aggression, but were declared not guilty of these charges. Of the other charges of the indictment, criminal spoliation in occupied countries and promotion of slave labor, they were found guilty on July 31, 1948. In 1951 their prison terms were cut short and they were released. Two years later Alfried Krupp von Bohlen und Halbach resumed the management of his firm, which since 1945 had been under the control of the British military government.

POSTWAR REBUILDING OF KRUPP

The company's situation was perilous. On top of the losses already mentioned came the Allied divestment order under which Krupp was compelled to sever and sell its mining and steelmaking operations. The firm thus faced the loss of its raw materials base, in particular its vital steel interests. In 1951 Alfried Krupp von Bohlen und Halbach had declared that he would never again produce weapons. The object, therefore, was to shape a newly structured concern from the remaining manufacturing and engineering activities, comprising the locomotive and motor truck works, the Widia hard-metal plant, the forging and foundry shops, and the structural engineering operation in Rheinhausen. This restructuring was achieved in the years that followed. New markets were opened in the developing countries for the engineering and construction of industrial plants. Together with Berthold Beitz, whom he had appointed as his chief executive at the end of 1953, Krupp contributed personally to this effort by making numerous order-winning trips abroad. The range of manufacturing and engineering activities was made as varied as possible in order to assure continuity of employment in the face of changing markets. In 1958 sales, including the coal and steel operations still subject to the divestment order, amounted to DM 3.3 billion, generated by a workforce of 105,200. Krupp had become the highest-revenue German company.

The Allied divestment order could only be complied with to a minor extent for lack of purchase offers. In 1960 Krupp therefore combined its remaining coal and steel operations and strengthened this base in

1965 through a merger with Bochumer Verein für Gusstahlfabrikation, a steel company in Bochum in which a majority shareholding had been acquired at the end of the 1950s. Krupp thus regained a position in the production of special steels, which it had lost with the dismantling of the Borbeck steel plant. In 1961 the company opened a plant in Brazil to make drop forgings for internal combustion engines and vehicles. In 1964 Krupp acquired a majority shareholding in Atlas-Werke AG, Bremen, including MaK Maschinenbau GmbH, Kiel.

In line with the general economic situation, the company followed a positive course into the mid-1960s, apart from a brief downturn in 1963. Nevertheless, until withdrawn in 1968, the divestment order prevented the company from developing a comprehensive long-term policy of corporate restructuring and investment. The financial crisis into which the company plunged in 1967 was largely triggered by the high level of supplier credits that had to be granted in the strongly expanding export business. As security for the banks, the federal and state governments provided guarantees, which, however, did not need to be taken up. The guarantees were subject to the condition that the sole proprietorship Fried. Krupp be converted into a stock corporation. This requirement dovetailed with the decision already taken by the owner to adapt the enterprise to the requirements of modern business and secure its future by changing its legal structure. In the terms of his will, Alfried Krupp von Bohlen und Halbach provided for the establishment of a nonprofit foundation. Since his son Arndt had renounced his inheritance before his father's death, leaving the way clear for the firm to be converted into a corporation, ownership of the late owner's private assets and the corporate property combined in the firm of Fried. Krupp was vested in the foundation. Alfried Krupp thus continued in modern form the idea formulated by his great-grandfather that ownership incurs social responsibility: The company would be run as a private-sector enterprise but its earnings used to serve the community at large.

FRIED. KRUPP GMBH IN 1968

Alfried Krupp von Bohlen und Halbach died in July 1967. In 1968 the firm was entered in the Commercial Register as a limited liability company, Fried. Krupp GmbH, with capital stock of DM 500 million. Managerial responsibility was assigned to an executive board having the same powers as the management board of a stock corporation under German law. All shares in Fried. Krupp GmbH were placed in the ownership of the Alfried Krupp von Bohlen und Halbach Foundation, whose object was to preserve the company's coherence and to serve the public benefit. Berthold Beitz was chairman of the foundation's board of trustees. From 1970 to 1989 he was chairman of the supervisory board of Fried. Krupp GmbH. The foundation funded projects in Germany and abroad in the fields of science and research, education and training, public health, sports, literature, and the fine arts. Between 1968 and 1990 the foundation awarded grants totaling around DM 360 million.

In 1969 the coal mining assets were severed from the group and transferred to Ruhrkohle AG. Over the subsequent years activities in the engineering and construction of industrial plant were expanded, especially with the acquisition of Polysius AG and Heinrich Koppers GmbH. The steelmaking arm further strengthened its special-steel operations by acquiring Stahlwerke Südwestfalen AG.

In 1974 the state of Iran acquired a 25.04 percent interest in the stock capital of the steel subsidiary Fried. Krupp Hüttenwerke AG, strengthening the equity base. In 1976 Iran also acquired a 25.01 percent stake in Fried. Krupp GmbH, whose capital stock was increased to DM 700 million by the summer of 1978. Following the Iranian Revolution of 1979, these ownership interests were held by the Islamic Republic of Iran.

The 1980s saw the implementation of various restructuring schemes. Krupp sold its interests in shipbuilding, an area of heavy losses. The steelmaking sector reduced its output of tonnage steel and in 1988 the plan to close the iron and steel works in Rheinhausen was met by a campaign of protest from the workforce. The works were kept in operation to a limited extent. At the same time Krupp further strengthened its activities in special steel—for example, by acquiring VDM Nickel-Technologie AG in 1989—as well as in mechanical engineering and electronics. In 1989 Gerhard Cromme became chairman and chief executive of Krupp. By 1990 the company, having successfully completed the restructuring, was back in the black and paid its first dividend in 16 years.

HOSTILE TAKEOVER OF HOESCH IN 1992

In 1991 Krupp secretly paid DM 500 million ($294 million) to take a 24.9 percent stake in Hoesch AG, a neighboring and struggling steelmaker headquartered in Dortmund with a history dating back to the 1820s. Hoesch was having difficulty competing with its much larger rivals as the early 1990s were marked by overcapacity in steel throughout Europe. German steelmakers were particularly vulnerable because steel prices in that country were the highest in Europe. Krupp saw a

takeover of Hoesch as a great opportunity to rationalize the two companies' operations and cut costs. In December 1991 Krupp increased its stake in Hoesch to nearly 51 percent. Hoesch continued to resist being taken over, but by mid-1992 Krupp had won the battle and a merger of the two firms was backdated to January 1 of that year, creating Germany's second largest steel producer (trailing Thyssen).

The newly and cumbersomely named Fried. Krupp AG Hoesch Krupp, still headed by Cromme, had steelmaking capacity of around eight million metric tons and sales of about DM 28 billion ($18.9 billion). The new Krupp had six divisions: steel, engineering, plant construction, automotive supplies, trade, and services. In January 1993 Krupp became a publicly traded company for the first time in its long history, though as late as the 1997–98 fiscal year the Alfried Krupp von Bohlen und Halbach Foundation still held a 50.47 percent stake while the Iranian government held 22.92 percent. The restructuring that followed the takeover of Hoesch included the elimination of more than 20,000 jobs and the closure of one of the combined company's two main integrated steel plants. Two years of heavy losses followed before Krupp posted a modest net profit of DM 40 million ($29.2 million) for 1994.

THE LONG ROAD TO THE THYSSEN-KRUPP MERGER

Following Krupp's 1994 takeover of Accial Speciali Terni, an Italian stainless steelmaker, the company in 1995 merged its enlarged stainless steel operations with those of Thyssen in the Krupp-Thyssen Nirosta joint venture, 60 percent owned by Krupp and 40 percent owned by Thyssen. In March 1997 Krupp launched a DM 13.6 billion ($8 billion) hostile takeover bid of the larger Thyssen. This move led to fierce protests from workers fearful of another round of massive industrial layoffs, as had occurred after the Krupp takeover of Hoesch. When Cromme, dubbed the "job killer" because of those same layoffs, met with protesting workers he was pelted with eggs and tomatoes. With Thyssen's leadership resisting the attempted takeover, Krupp soon abandoned its hostile bid.

Nevertheless, Thyssen agreed to discuss with Krupp a merger of the two firm's flat steel operations, with the negotiations leading to the establishment in September 1997 of Thyssen Krupp Stahl AG, which was 60 percent owned by Thyssen and 40 percent owned by Krupp. Ekkehard Schulz, who had headed Thyssen Stahl, was named chief executive of the joint venture. The companies immediately announced that 25 percent of their flat steel workforce, or about 6,300 people, would lose their jobs as part of a restructuring.

Krupp and Thyssen were not finished with their dealmaking, however, and surprised many analysts in November 1997 with an announcement of a full merger of their entire companies. A key factor driving the merger was the increasing globalization of the world economy. The two industrial giants needed to be even larger in order to effectively compete on a global scale. After overcoming numerous hurdles, the companies consummated their union in March 1999 with the formation of ThyssenKrupp AG. Vogel, Thyssen's chief executive, still had the criminal charges hanging over him, and lost a battle to run the new company. Cromme and Schulz were named co-chief executives of the new company, which organized itself into six main divisions: Thyssen Krupp Steel, Thyssen Krupp Automotive, Thyssen Krupp Industries, Thyssen Krupp Engineering, and Thyssen Krupp Materials & Services. The company expected to slash annual costs by DM 1 billion ($557 million) through the merger and intended to cut 2,000 of its 173,000 jobs. Revenues were estimated at DM 70 billion ($39 billion). One other consequence of the merger was that the large stakes held by the main shareholders of Krupp were significantly diluted; the Alfried Krupp von Bohlen und Halbach Foundation held an initial 16.82 percent interest in ThyssenKrupp while the Iranian government held 7.64 percent. When combined—and these two parties sometimes had joined to block certain board initiatives at Krupp—they held about 24.5 percent of Thyssen-Krupp, which was just less than the 25 percent needed for a formal "blocking minority" per German law.

CHASINGING DEALS IN THE EARLY 21ST CENTURY

Just six months after the historic merger, ThyssenKrupp announced plans to shift its focus to higher-margin engineering businesses by spinning off its steel division through an initial public offering (IPO). Then in April 2000 the company, seeking to bolster its engineering operations, made an offer of EUR 8.7 billion for Mannesmann AG's Atecs Mannesmann unit, which included a variety of machinery and automotive-electronics businesses. Mannesmann opted instead for a higher joint offer from Siemens AG and Robert Bosch GmbH, and in August 2000 ThyssenKrupp had to abandon its steel IPO because of a downturn in the steel market. Forced to scrap its shift in focus, and facing much criticism about the slowness of its decision-making process, the company shook up its top management structure in 2001. Jettisoning the dual-management scheme, ThyssenKrupp named Schulz sole chief executive, while Cromme was moved into the chairmanship of the firm's supervisory board.

Firmly in control, Schulz set as one of his primary initial goals the trimming of the company's hefty debt burden as net debt stood at EUR 7.7 billion at the end of the 2000–2001 fiscal year. Numerous noncore operations were divested to raise funds to pay down the debt. These efforts, however, which cut net debt to EUR 4.9 billion by early 2003, were not enough to keep Standard & Poor's (S&P), the rating agency, from downgrading ThyssenKrupp's debt to junk status. Around this same time, the company spent EUR 406 million to buy back part of the Iranian government's stake, cutting it to less than 5 percent. This move was necessary to keep ThyssenKrupp from being blacklisted by the U.S. government following passage of a new law. Companies faced the possible loss of government contracts if a foreign government providing "support for acts of international terrorism" owned a large stake in them. In 2004 further U.S. pressure forced ThyssenKrupp to end the presence of a representative from the Iranian government on its supervisory board.

In the spring of 2003 ThyssenKrupp launched a new initiative to shave debt, again focusing on the divestment of noncore businesses. Through the end of the 2004–2005 fiscal year, the company shed 29 companies with combined sales of EUR 4.36 billion ($5.15 billion). Among the most significant of these divestments were Novoferm GmbH, a maker of steel doors, door frames, garage doors, and industrial doors, sold to Sanwa Shutter Corporation in 2003 for EUR 174 million; Triaton GmbH, an information technology services provider, sold to Hewlett-Packard Company in 2004 for EUR 249 million; the company's residential real estate business, sold in early 2005 for EUR 1.94 billion to a consortium comprising the U.S. investment bank Morgan Stanley and the German real estate company Corpus-Immobiliengruppe; and Thyssen-Krupp's metal-cutting business, sold in the fall of 2005 to Maxcor, Inc. The disposal program succeeded in eliminating the company's net debt and also led the S&P to boost the firm's credit rating back to investment grade. The changes to the conglomerate's portfolio were also paying dividends on the bottom line. For the fiscal year ending in September 2005, ThyssenKrupp achieved its best results since the 1999 merger: net income of EUR 1.02 billion ($1.23 billion) on net sales of EUR 42.06 billion ($50.72 billion).

The postmerger consolidation phase complete, Schulz next shifted ThyssenKrupp's focus to growth, aiming to push the company's sales to EUR 50 billion. In November 2005 the company made a bold bid to become more of a global player in steel by launching a EUR 3.5 million ($4.1 billion) offer for Dofasco Inc., the largest Canadian maker of flat rolled steel. The following January, however, ThyssenKrupp conceded defeat on a takeover battle for Dofasco that broke out between itself and Luxembourg-based Arcelor S.A. In a neat twist, Arcelor itself almost immediately faced a hostile takeover at the hands of Mittal Steel Company N.V. of the Netherlands. As part of its offer, Mittal pledged to sell Dofasco to ThyssenKrupp upon completion of the deal to gain approval from U.S. regulators for the Arcelor takeover. Then, however, Arcelor transferred control of Dofasco to a Dutch foundation as it attempted to thwart Mittal's gambit. Mittal still prevailed, though, and completed its acquisition of Arcelor, forming Arcelor Mittal, by far the world's largest steelmaker. Despite the deal's completion, ThyssenKrupp saw its North American ambitions thwarted again as the foundation controlling Dofasco refused to sell it.

Even before the Dofasco saga had completely played itself out, ThyssenKrupp in August 2006 launched a strategy for North American growth by announcing plans to spend EUR 2.3 billion ($2.94 billion) to build a steel-processing plant in the United States. By February 2007 the company had narrowed its site options for the carbon and stainless facility to either outside Mobile, Alabama, or in St. James Parish on the Mississippi River in Louisiana. ThyssenKrupp hoped to open the plant by 2010.

At the same time, the company began overhauling its automotive operations, which had operated in the red during fiscal 2005–2006. In November 2006 ThyssenKrupp sold its North American body and chassis operations to Ontario-based Martinrea International Inc. for $275 million. The divested operations had annual sales of EUR 1 billion ($1.3 billion). Several other automotive operations were either sold or restructured, and ThyssenKrupp's slimmed-down automotive division was dissolved, with the remaining operations merged into the ThyssenKrupp Technologies division.

There were two other developments of this period worthy of note. In December 2006 the Alfried Krupp von Bohlen und Halbach Foundation increased its ThyssenKrupp shareholding to more than 25 percent, giving it a blocking minority. This move angered a number of shareholders, but Schulz viewed it positively as a potential defensive measure at a time rife with industry takeovers. In February 2007 the European Commission imposed large fines on ThyssenKrupp and four other elevator manufacturers for fixing prices and engaging in rigged bidding in Belgium, Germany, the Netherlands, and Luxembourg between 1995 and 2004. ThyssenKrupp was hit with the toughest penalty, EUR 479.7 million ($630 million). In the meantime, the company's results for fiscal 2005–2006 were even better than those of the previous year. Net sales jumped 10 percent to EUR 47.13 billion ($59.79 billion), while net income surged 67 percent, reaching EUR 1.7 billion ($2.16 billion).

Dieter Müller and Renate Köhne-Lindenlaub
Updated, David E. Salamie

PRINCIPAL SUBSIDIARIES

ThyssenKrupp Steel AG; ThyssenKrupp Stainless AG; ThyssenKrupp Technologies AG; ThyssenKrupp Elevator AG; ThyssenKrupp Services AG; Grupo ThyssenKrupp S.A. (Spain); ThyssenKrupp Austria GmbH & Co. KG; ThyssenKrupp Canada, Inc.; ThyssenKrupp (China) Ltd.; ThyssenKrupp France S.A.S.; ThyssenKrupp Italia S.p.A. (Italy); ThyssenKrupp Nederland B.V. (Netherlands); ThyssenKrupp Participaciones, S.L. (Spain); ThyssenKrupp UK Plc; ThyssenKrupp USA, Inc.

PRINCIPAL COMPETITORS

Arcelor Mittal; POSCO; Nippon Steel Corporation; JFE Holdings, Inc.; United States Steel Corporation; Shanghai Baosteel Group Corporation; Corus Group plc; Acerinox, S.A.; Otis Elevator Company; Schindler Holding Ltd.

FURTHER READING

Atkins, Ralph, "A Deal Forged from the Ashes of a Hostile Takeover," *Financial Times,* July 31, 1997, p. 28.

Atkins, Ralph, and Kirsten Bialdiga, "Thyssen Foundation Lifts Stake Above 25%," *Financial Times,* December 2, 2006, p. 21.

Betts, Paul, "Steel Major Braces Itself for New Round of Consolidation," *Financial Times,* January 16, 2002.

Bowley, Graham, "Thyssen, Krupp to Cut 6,300 Jobs," *Financial Times,* September 4, 1997, p. 36.

Brierley, David, "Battle for Thyssen Krupp," *European,* November 13, 1997, p. 26.

———, "Thyssen Steeled for the Fight," *European,* November 28, 1996, p. 24.

Buck, Tobias, "Brussels Imposes Euros 992m Fine on Life Cartel," *Financial Times,* February 22, 2007, p. 8.

Burchardt, Lothar, "Zwischen Kriegsgewinnen und Kriegskosten: Krupp im Ersten Weltkrieg," *Zeitschrift für Unternehmensgeschichte* 32 (1987), pp. 71–122.

Epkenhans, Michael, "Zwischen Patriotismus und Geschäftsinteresse: F. A. Krupp und die Anfänge des deutschen Schlachtflottenbaus, 1897–1902," *Geschichte und Gesellschaft* 15 (1989), pp. 196–226.

Esterl, Mike, "Thyssen Considers U.S. Expansion, Will Sell Parts Unit," *Wall Street Journal,* August 12, 2006, p. A10.

———, "A Trimmer ThyssenKrupp Seeks Fat Deal," *Wall Street Journal,* December 12, 2005, p. B2.

Fear, Jeffrey R., *Organizing Control: August Thyssen and the Construction of German Corporate Management,* Cambridge, Mass.: Harvard University Press, 2005, 956 p.

Fisher, Andrew, "German Steelworkers Turn Heat on Banks," *Financial Times*, March 25, 1997, p. 26.

Fuhrmans, Vanessa, "ThyssenKrupp Calls Off IPO of Steel Unit As Shares Fall," *Wall Street Journal*, August 17, 2000, p. A17.

Gall, Lothar, *Krupp: Der Aufstieg eines Industrieimperiums*, Berlin: Siedler, 2000, 398 p.

Gall, Lothar, ed., *Krupp im 20. Jahrhundert: Die Geschichte des Unternehmens vom Ersten Weltkrieg bis zur Gründung der Stiftung*, Berlin: Siedler, 2002, 719 p.

Gibson, Richard, Carl Quintanilla, and Brandon Mitchener, "Thyssen Agrees to Buy Giddings for $675 Million," *Wall Street Journal*, June 13, 1997, pp. A3, A12.

Guzzo, Maria, "ThyssenKrupp Mill a 'Go' Regardless of Dofasco," *American Metal Market*, December 4, 2006, p. 6.

Harnischfeger, Uta, "ThyssenKrupp Forges Ahead," *Financial Times*, February 14, 2003, p. 26.

———, "ThyssenKrupp Retakes Iran Stake," *Financial Times*, May 20, 2003, p. 17.

"Hunting Hoesch," *Economist*, October 19, 1991, pp. 86, 88.

James, Harold, *The German Slump: Politics and Economics, 1924–1936*, Oxford: Clarendon Press, 1986, 469 p.

"The King and Them," *Economist*, January 27, 1990, pp. 73+.

Klass, Gert von, *Krupps: The Story of an Industrial Empire*, translated by James Cleugh, London: Sidgwick and Jackson, 1954, 437 p.

Kohl, Christian, "A Global Vision for Steelmakers Thyssen, Krupp," *American Metal Market*, February 10, 1999, p. 8A.

Köhne-Lindenlaub, Renate, "Krupp," in *Neue Deutsche Biographie*, vol. 13, Berlin: Duncker Humblot, 1982.

Krupp: A Century's History of the Krupp Works, 1812–1912, Essen: Krupp Works, 1912.

Lindemann, Michael, "How Cromme Engineered the Rebirth of a German Titan," *Financial Times*, March 14, 1996, p. 31.

———, "Thyssen Poised for Disposals After Setback in All Activities," *Financial Times*, January 31, 1996, p. 34.

Lindemann, Michael, and Quentin Peel, "Married Without a Honeymoon," *Financial Times*, May 19, 1994, p. 30.

Lindenlaub, Jürgen, and Renate Köhne-Lindenlaub, "Unternehmensfinanzierung bei Krupp, 1811–1848: Ein Beitrag zur Kapital-und Vermögensentwicklung," *Beiträge zur Geschichte von Stadt und Stift Essen* 102 (1988), pp. 83–164.

Manchester, William, *The Arms of Krupp, 1587–1968*, Boston: Little, Brown, 1968, 976 p.

Marsh, Peter, "ThyssenKrupp Pursue Entry to U.S. Markets," *Financial Times*, October 29, 2002, p. 29.

Marsh, Peter, and Richard Milne, "ThyssenKrupp Puts Dofasco Behind It and Rethinks Its U.S. Options," *Financial Times*, January 25, 2006, p. 34.

Muhlen, Norbert, *The Incredible Krupps: The Rise, Fall, and Comeback of Germany's Industrial Family*, New York: Henry Holt, 1959, 308 p.

Nash, Nathaniel C., "Family Sells Last of Stake in Thyssen," *New York Times*, September 5, 1995, pp. D1, D7.

Norman, Peter, "Contrasting Response to Strategic Marriage," *Financial Times*, November 6, 1997, p. 34.

———, "Krupp-Thyssen Merger Mired in Rivalry," *Financial Times*, November 21, 1997, p. 26.

———, "Steel Groups Give in to Lure of Wedlock," *Financial Times*, November 5, 1997, p. 31.

———, "Thyssen and Krupp Outline Merger Gains," *Financial Times*, February 7, 1998, p. 17.

———, "Thyssen, Krupp Seek Breakthrough," *Financial Times*, January 5, 1998, p. 28.

———, "Thyssen Krupp Terms Agreed," *Financial Times*, September 12, 1998, p. 21.

———, "Troubles Just Starting for 'Krupp-Thyssen,'" *Financial Times*, March 26, 1997, p. 28.

Parkes, Christopher, "Hauled down the Merger Aisle," *Financial Times*, January 6, 1992, p. 13.

———, "Taking a Long-Term View of German Steel," *Financial Times*, April 21, 1992, p. 35.

Peel, Quentin, "Breaking Point for Nerves of Steel," *Financial Times*, February 25, 1993, p. 23.

Penson, Stuart, "Thyssen + Krupp = World's Largest Stainless Maker," *New Steel*, April 1995, pp. 58+.

Plumpe, Werner, and Jörg Lesczenski, "Die Thyssens," in *Deutsche Familien: Historische Portraits von Bismarck bis Weizsäcker*, edited by Volker Reinhardt, Munich: Beck, 2005.

Reier, Sharon, "Krupp's Blitzkrieg," *Financial World*, December 10, 1991, pp. 26–28.

Richter, Mathilde, "ThyssenKrupp to Buy Majority Stake in HDW," *Wall Street Journal Europe*, May 18, 2004, p. A5.

Robertson, Scott, "ThyssenKrupp Launching New Strategies for Growth," *American Metal Market*, August 14, 2006, pp. 1, 4.

Roth, Terence, "Krupp, Hoesch Map Out Merger Plans," *Wall Street Journal*, October 22, 1991, p. A9C.

Schröder, Ernst, *Krupp: Geschichte einer Unternehmerfamilie*, 3rd ed., Göttingen: Muster-Schmidt Verlag, 1984, 103 p.

Stenglein, Frank, *Krupp: Höhen und Tiefen eines Industrieunternehmens*, Munich: Econ Verlag, 1999.

"Die Thyssen-Gruppe," *Usines et Industries*, December 1986.

Tinnin, David B., "Reforging an Old Steelmaker," *Fortune*, June 16, 1980, pp. 112+.

Treue, Wilhelm, *Die Feuer Verlöschen nie. August Thyssen-Hütte, 1890–1926*, Düsseldorf: Econ-Verlag, 1966.

Treue, Wilhelm, and Helmut Uebbing, *Die Feuer Verlöschen nie. August Thyssen-Hütte, 1926–1966*, Düsseldorf: Econ-Verlag, 1969.

Turner, Henry Ashby, Jr., *German Big Business and the Rise of Hitler*, New York: Oxford University Press, 1985, 504 p.

Uebbing, Helmut, *Wege und Wegmarken: 100 Jahre Thyssen*, Berlin: Siedler, 1991, 348 p.

Wessel, Horst A., ed., *Thyssen & Co., Mulheim a.d. Ruhr: Die Geschichte einer Familie und Ihrer Unternehmung*, Stuttgart: F. Steiner, 1991, 227 p.

TODCO

2000 West Sam Houston Parkway South, Suite 800
Houston, Texas 77042-3615
U.S.A.
Telephone: (713) 278-6000
Fax: (713) 278-6101
Web site: http://www.theoffshoredrillingcompany.
com

Public Company
Incorporated: 1997 as R&B Falcon Corporation
Employees: 2,420
Sales: $912.1 million (2006)
Stock Exchanges: New York
Ticker Symbol: THE
NAIC: 213111 Drilling Oil and Gas Wells

■ ■ ■

TODCO (The Offshore Drilling Co.) is a New York Stock Exchange-listed company based in Houston that provides contract oil and gas drilling services, mostly to major international oil companies, state-owned oil companies, and independent oil and gas companies. TODCO's fleet is composed of 64 drilling rigs, including 24 shallow water jackups, 27 inland barge rigs, nine land rigs, three submersible drilling units, and one platform rig. They operate in the shallow waters and inland areas of the Gulf of Mexico as well as the Caribbean Basin off the shores of Mexico, Venezuela, and Trinidad. TODCO also holds a 25 percent interest in Delta Towing, which operates a fleet of more than 40 support vessels, including inland tugs, offshore tugs,

crewboats, deck barges, shale barges, spud barges, and a single offshore barge. In addition to the Houston home office, TODCO maintains operational offices in Houma, Louisiana; Maturin, Venezuela; La Romaine, Trinidad; Luanda, Angola; Rio de Janeiro, Brazil; and Ciudad del Carmen, Mexico. Warehouse and yard facilities are located in Houma, La Romaine, and Maturin.

FOUNDING OF PREDECESSOR COMPANY: 1935

TODCO's roots date back to the Great Depression of the 1930s when two true pioneers of the oil and gas industry, J. W. "Jack" Bates, Sr., and George M. Reading, became partners. Bates came west to California after receiving a degree from Dartmouth College, starting out in the oil industry at the lowest ranks, working as a mule skinner. Reading was a University of California-educated mining engineer. The two men met in Texas in 1930 when Bates was general superintendent for Roxanna Petroleum, which later took the name Shell Oil Company, and Reading was one of his drilling contractors. In 1935 they became partners, forming Tulsa, Oklahoma-based Reading & Bates Drilling Co. with three drilling rigs they acquired on credit. The company enjoyed steady growth drilling contract wells in Oklahoma, Texas, and Kansas. In 1949 Jack Bates, Jr., took over the presidency, then two years later took on a partner of his own, Charlie Thornton, a former Gulf Oil petroleum engineer who headed a Canadian subsidiary. In 1955 they incorporated Reading & Bates Offshore Drilling Co., a subsidiary that would one day become part of TODCO. Its rigs operated in the Gulf of Mexico as well as the Persian Gulf in the Middle East. The company became one of the first drilling contractors to work in the North Sea, and in the late 1960s began growing its fleet and adding capabilities, such as pollution control technology and ocean engineering.

Reading & Bates continued to operate land rigs in Iran, but in the late 1970s the Shah was overthrown in a revolution and the equipment was confiscated. Having lost most of its land rigs, Reading & Bates simply exited this part of the business. The company was involved in exploration and other areas, but following the collapse of the oil and gas industry after the price of oil fell to the $8–$10 per barrel range in 1986, Reading & Bates undertook a restructuring. In 1989 it moved its headquarters to Houston and by 1991 divested most of its assets in order to concentrate on offshore drilling contracting, especially deepwater and difficult environments. A new unit was also formed in 1990, Reading & Bates Development Co., to provide floating production platform services and other specialized drilling services as well as to invest in wells the company drilled.

The decision to focus on deepwater drilling was made in part because oil prices were rising in the early 1990s, making it economically viable for oil companies to drill in deepwater, which was a more costly endeavor. Moreover, many of the most promising energy plays left to exploit were located in the deepest parts of the ocean. At the time, offshore contract drilling was a highly fragmented field, so much so that the top three companies controlled little more than a quarter of the market. Oil producers, as a result, were in an enviable position, able to take advantage of any dip in oil or gas prices to demand a reduction in the day rate of drilling rigs. If the contractors tried to grow their business by building more rigs, they only added to the total number of rigs available, worsening the supply/demand imbalance. Hence, the wisest course of action was to acquire competitors' rigs, and in the mid-1990s there was a great deal of consolidation in the field. Sonat Offshore tried to acquire Reading & Bates but was

rebuffed. Reading & Bates tried to acquire Norway's Transocean ASA but lost out to Sonat. The two companies merged to become Transocean Offshore.

READING & BATES MERGING WITH FALCON DRILLING: 1997

In 1997 Reading & Bates found a willing partner in Falcon Drilling Company, whose chief executive, Steven A. Webster, was a longtime friend of Reading & Bates's CEO, Paul Loyd. They became acquainted at Harvard Business School, where they both graduated in 1975. They then worked together as consultants in Saudi Arabia and became partners in some small ventures. In 1988 Webster founded Falcon as an offshore drilling contractor. He grew the business rapidly, focusing on shallow water, and took it public in 1995. By the time it merged with Reading & Bates, Falcon operated the largest fleet of barge rigs in the world, and was worth $1.6 billion.

In July 1997 R&B Falcon Corporation was formed to accommodate the $2.5 billion stock swap, which in order to avoid taxes was structured as a pooling of interests. The two partners were considered a good fit because there was little overlap in their activities, with Reading & Bates focusing on deep water and Falcon on shallow water. The previous year, Falcon did about $319 million in business while Reading & Bates posted revenues in the neighborhood of $290 million. Combined they were large enough to finance the building of deepwater drilling ships, in high demand but which cost as much as $300 million to build. With Webster serving as CEO and Loyd assuming the chairmanship, the company looked to focus on drilling and to avoid taking equity in any of the wells it worked on. The Total Offshore Production Services (TOPS) unit of Reading & Bates Development had pursued an equity strategy, but the wells had not delivered, hurting profits of the parent company. In 1997 the unit spent $77.4 million on dry holes. Even before the merger was completed R&B Falcon began to talk about spinning off TOPS, but when oil and natural gas prices dropped the sale was put on hold.

Despite the fall in oil prices, the company completed a major acquisition in 1998, using about $415 million in stock to acquire Cliffs Drilling Co., a contract drilling company that operated 16 jackup drilling rigs, 11 land drilling rigs, and three platform rigs along the Gulf Coast of Texas and Louisiana, and in Venezuela. The company also offered engineering services and operated in the Middle East. By the end of

KEY DATES

1935: Reading & Bates Drilling Co. is formed.
1955: Reading & Bates Offshore Drilling Co. is formed.
1988: Falcon Drilling Company is founded.
1997: Reading & Bates and Falcon merge to form R&B Falcon Corporation.
2000: R&B Falcon is acquired by Transocean.
2002: R&B Falcon is renamed TODCO.
2004: Transocean spins off TODCO.

1998, low oil prices began to hurt R&B Falcon's main business as oil companies began terminating rig contracts.

With the entire industry enduring tough times, R&B Falcon surprised everyone when it was able to complete a $1 billion bond offering. The funds were much needed, in light of the company's $2.7 billion long-term debt load. More than half of the money raised was earmarked to refinance the debt. Webster had always been known as someone proficient in growing companies by taking on debt, but conditions were such that a more cautious approach was in order. Hence, in May he stepped down in what was described as an amicable parting and Loyd took over as chief executive while retaining the chairmanship. Webster stayed on as a member of the board and held the title of nonexecutive vice-chairman.

After the OPEC cartel cut production in 1999, commodity prices began to rise and in the summer of 2000 R&B Falcon was finally able to sell its exploration and production assets in the Gulf of Mexico, receiving more than $127 million from Enterprise Oil, a U.K.-based company. The company's other production properties were also put on the block, but just a month later the entire company was acquired by Transocean Sedco Forex Inc. in a stock transaction valued at more than $5.8 billion, plus the assumption of $3 billion in debt.

Transocean had been the major player in the consolidation that had taken place in the offshore contract drilling segment. The company's lineage dated back to 1953 when the pipeline company Southern Natural Gas Co. (SNG) acquired the DeLong-McDermott contract drilling joint venture and renamed it The Offshore Company. A year later the unit began operating its first jackup drilling rig in the Gulf of

Mexico and, like Reading & Bates, was one of the first to work the North Sea in the 1960s. The company drilled its first deepwater well in Asia in the 1970s. The parent company changed its name to Sonat in 1981 and The Offshore Drilling Company became Sonat Offshore Drilling Inc. In 1993 Sonat spun off Sonat Offshore and by 1995 had sold all of its stake in the former subsidiary.

During the wave of consolidation that swept the offshore drilling business in the mid-1990s Sonat Offshore merged with Transocean to form Transocean Offshore in 1996. Transocean had been formed in the mid-1970s by a Norwegian whaling company that decided to diversify and became involved in semisubmersibles, self-propelled, seagoing barges that served as living quarters and a base of operations for offshore drilling operations. It was an especially attractive acquisition target because of its considerable North Sea assets. In 1999 Sonat Offshore became even larger when it merged with Sedco Forex Limited, the offshore drilling subsidiary of Paris-based Schlumberger Ltd. The Sedco component had been founded in 1947 as the Southeastern Drilling Company in the United States to operate in shallow marsh water. It later expanded to deeper water and was acquired by Schlumberger in 1984, and a year later it was combined with Forex. Established in France in 1942, Forex initially provided land drilling services in France, North Africa, and the Middle East. It became involved in offshore work through a joint venture with Languedocienne called Neptune. Forex eventually acquired complete ownership of Neptune, and in 1972 Schlumberger acquired all of Forex.

The combination of Transocean and Sedco Forex took the name Transocean Sedco Forex Inc. It instantly became the world's fourth largest oilfield service company and was added to the Standard & Poor's 500 Index on the first day it began trading on the New York Stock Exchange in 2000. With the acquisition of R&B Falcon, completed in January 2001, it grew even larger, becoming a $14 billion company.

ADOPTION OF TODCO NAME: 2002

While Transocean achieved scale it took on considerable debt to do so. In the fall of 2002 Transocean announced that it planned to spin off the Gulf of Mexico shallow and inland water assets of R&B Falcon through an initial public offering (IPO) of stock, while keeping the deepwater assets, in order to pay down debt and hone its focus on the deepwater business. In preparation for this move R&B Falcon was renamed TODCO in December 2002.

The IPO was supposed to be held in early 2003, but because of a struggling economy it was postponed until February 2004. TODCO did not received any of the proceeds but gained its independence at a time when the market was undergoing a resurgence as oil and gas prices soared. Transocean steadily divested its interest in TODCO, selling the final shares by May 2005.

Serving as TODCO's president and chief executive officer was Jan Rask who had been heading it as a Transocean unit since July 2002. He brought to the job considerable experience as a top executive with a number of contract drilling companies, including Arethusa (Off Shore) Limited, Marine Drilling Companies, Inc.; and Pride International, Inc.

In 2004 TODCO posted revenues of $351.4 million, a significant increase over the $227.7 million the prior year due to improved market conditions in the Gulf of Mexico. In 2005 the company reactivated seven rigs, six of them located in the Gulf, as demand for shallow water drilling rigs continued to grow. For the year TODCO generated revenues of $534.2 million and net income of $59.4 million. The company's remaining deactivated rigs, six jackups and ten inland barges, were put into service in 2006 as revenues soared to $912.1 million and earnings more than tripled to $183.6 million. Because contract drilling was a cyclical business, such explosive growth was not likely to last for an extended period, but TODCO looked to exploit the fat times for as long as they lasted.

Ed Dinger

PRINCIPAL SUBSIDIARIES

The Offshore Drilling Company; TODCO Mexico Inc.; TODCO Management Services Inc. LLC; Cliffs Drilling Company.

PRINCIPAL COMPETITORS

GlobalSantaFe Corporation; Parker Drilling Company; Pride International, Inc.

FURTHER READING

Cummins, Chip, "Transocean to Buy Rival R&B Falcon in Stock Deal Valued at $5.35 Billion," *Wall Street Journal,* August 22, 2000, p. A2.

Davis, Michael, "President Resigns at R&B Falcon," *Houston Chronicle,* April 8, 1999, p. 1.

———, "Reading & Bates Continues to Take Risks, Adapt, Innovate," *Houston Chronicle,* May 4, 1997, p. 8.

———, "Reading & Bates, Falcon to Combine," *Houston Chronicle,* July 11, 1997, p. 1.

Greer, Jim, "Drilling Spin-Off Ends IPO Drought," *Houston Business Journal,* February 16, 2004.

Lipin, Steven, and Peter Fritsch, "Falcon Drilling Plans $2.5 Billion Merger," *Wall Street Journal,* July 11, 1997, p. A3.

Paganie, David, "TODCO Carries Momentum into 2006 with Reactivation of Seven Cold-Stacked Rigs," *Offshore,* January 2006, p. 42.

Snow, Nick, "Transocean Spin-Off Receives Mixed Reviews," *Oil & Gas Investor,* September 2002, p. 102.

Srinvasan, Kristen, "Tapping In: The Offshore Drilling Co. Has Found a New Momentum in Its Industry with the Help of Its Employees and Their Idea," *US Business Review,* December 2005, p. 119.

Umpqua Holdings Corporation

———— ■ ————

1 SW Columbia Street, Suite 1200
Portland, Oregon 97258
U.S.A.
Toll Free: (866) 486-7782
Fax: (936) 639-2337
Web site: http://www.umpquabank.com

Public Company
Incorporated: 1953 as South Umpqua State Bank
Employees: 1,396
Total Assets: $7.34 billion (2006)
Stock Exchanges: NASDAQ
Ticker Symbol: UMPQ
NAIC: 522110 Commercial Banking; 551111 Offices of
    Bank Holding Corporation

■ ■ ■

There are more than 130 Umpqua Bank "stores" in Oregon, Washington, and northern California, mostly in small towns. These stores often serve as the local hot spot, hosting free movie nights, yoga classes, and book clubs. Umpqua Bank is the wholly owned subsidiary of Umpqua Holdings Corporation, which also owns brokerage firm Strand, Atkinson, Williams and York.

SERVING BUSINESSES IN
DOUGLAS COUNTY, OREGON

In 1953, with one bank and six employees, South Umpqua State Bank opened in Canyonville, Oregon. For close to 30 years, the rural institution, named after a

river in Oregon, served mostly small- and medium-sized businesses of the Canyonville and Roseburg area timber industry, as well as some farmers, professionals, and other retail customers. The bank's mission was to help farmers and other "little guys" cash checks and take out loans when bigger banks denied them service. Under the direction of some of its founders, South Umpqua State Bank eventually grew to include six locations.

In the early 1980s, as the recession, coupled with competition from the South and Canada, virtually eliminated the market for local timber, banking fell upon hard times in the Pacific Northwest. As many Oregon mills shut down, a wave of bankruptcies and business closings followed. Thirteen Oregon banks failed, and state-chartered Oregon domestic banks experienced a negative return on assets in 1982 and 1983.

A few community banks survived, South Umpqua State Bank among them. By the mid-1980s, although it still had a higher than average loan loss, the bank returned to profitability. For South Umpqua, which served a community of about 25,000, the return on assets was 0.78 percent and return on equity 11.75 percent in 1984.

LEADING THE WAY IN RETAIL
STRATEGIES FOR FINANCIAL
SERVICES

Throughout the remainder of the 1980s and the first half of the 1990s, South Umpqua Bank had six branches serving Douglas County, Oregon. By November 1994, however, the bank's market share had

COMPANY PERSPECTIVES

One of the buzz words in our company is empowerment. It's empowerment at all levels of the organization from the newest associate to the most senior manager. Every store manager has decision-making ability to make the right decision for the customer.

stagnated as major competitors, such as Wells Fargo and Bank of America, began encroaching on its territory with supermarket and pharmacy outlets. New President and CEO Raymond Davis responded to these competitive pressures by initiating a dramatic makeover of the approximately $160 million-in-assets institution.

Davis, a former CPA, had started working in banks while attending his hometown college, the University of Nevada, Reno. He became an executive officer of a small bank in Reno before moving to Atlanta, Georgia, to become president of the U.S. Banking Alliance, a consulting firm that evaluated bank performance. In this capacity, he had the opportunity to learn and record the best ideas of other financial institutions.

South Umpqua State Bank's main concern, when Davis took charge, was to "differentiate ourselves from other banks. We realized that we could not do this with resources, i.e. cash, people, branches, computers—since the big banks ha[d] so much more than we do," he explained in a 1999 *Retail Banker International* article. Thus, working with Stern Marketing Group of Berkeley, California, Davis inaugurated an image overhaul to address banking's "bifurcation dilemma," the situation whereby the teller line and transactions were in front of the branch and the account representatives and managers sequestered in back.

After the overhaul, all South Umpqua State Bank staff shared in one "universal job." They were trained to provide customer service and to sell the bank's entire product line during a six-week course that included units on manners and public speaking. They worked on commission and roamed the floor, greeting and assisting customers.

Another innovation that Davis instituted at South Umpqua was the "investment opportunities center," with financial periodicals and a television set tuned to business programming, a self-service post office, a coffee bar, and interactive product displays. The prototype branch measured only 2,400 square feet, a 40 percent reduction in South Umpqua's typical branch size, and

had no walled teller windows or sales desks. It included a new logo, a fir tree, emphasizing the bank's roots in the local logging community.

Matching the increased emphasis on friendly banking, South Umpqua also instituted a measurable quality service program. A computer-based program measured the level of service every store and every department of the bank provided. Each sales associate's and store's performance was evaluated each month based on quantifiable factors; total deposits, loan growth, and the production of new accounts were all factored into internal measures to arrive at a monthly "return on quality" for each branch.

By early 1997, product sales had increased by 40 percent, and South Umpqua's account base was up by 21.5 percent, outstripping the business growth of its nearest competitor by 10 percent. Encouraged, the bank expanded from 6 to 11 branches and moved into nearby Lane County, Oregon, with three banks in Eugene and one in Springfield. In early 1998, with $253 million in assets, South Umpqua, which had sold stock directly to its customers for years, launched its initial public offering to fund its further expansion plans.

A year later, in 1998, the company reorganized itself as a bank holding company called Umpqua Holdings Corporation with the renamed South Umpqua Bank its wholly owned subsidiary. In April, the bank entered the Portland market with a loan origination office. By year's end, with more than two-thirds of its branches converted to retail centers, South Umpqua had outstripped rivals US Bancorp and Wells Fargo in regional market share. One of the fastest growing banks in the western states, by 1999, South Umpqua Bank had doubled its assets to about $340 million, having averaged growth in revenues of more than 20 percent for the past few years.

Capitalizing on this growth, South Umpqua acquired an old-line Portland brokerage firm, Strand, Atkinson, Williams and York, in 1999. This firm had incorporated in 1928, and, at the time of the purchase, had about 4,000 clients and 25 employees and offices in Portland and Medford, Oregon, and Kalama, Washington. Umpqua gave its new subsidiary the capital base it needed to expand its stock and bond underwriting and in return received brokerage expertise and contacts. In 1999 Umpqua Bank also installed ATMs in nine Price Chopper stores from Albany to Grants Pass, Oregon, continuing its expansion at the ground level.

Despite a positive reception overall by the public, the bank garnered questionable media attention in 1999 when nine environmental groups spearheaded a bank boycott to force board Chairman Allyn Ford to

KEY DATES

1953: South Umpqua State Bank opens in Canyonville, Oregon.
1994: Raymond Davis becomes company chief executive.
1996: The bank introduces its "store" concept.
1998: The company creates Umpqua Holdings Corporation with South Umpqua Bank as a wholly owned subsidiary.
1999: South Umpqua acquires Strand, Atkinson, Williams and York.
2000: South Umpqua State Bank merges with Valley of the Rogue Bank and forms Umpqua Holdings Corporation; William Haden becomes chief executive of South Umpqua Bank; the company acquires Adams, Hess, Moore & Co.
2001: South Umpqua Holdings moves to Portland.
2002: Umpqua Holdings purchases Centennial Bancorp.
2004: Umpqua Holdings merges with Humboldt Bancorp; the company opens Umpqua University & Support Center.
2006: Umpqua purchases Western Sierra Bancorp.

withdraw his own company's plans to log federal old growth forests near Eugene. Davis insisted that the boycott was misdirected because "South Umpqua Bank and Roseburg Forest Products do not have anything to do with one another." Although some people closed their accounts as a result of the boycott, and although a second and third boycott occurred in 2001, their actions did not have any appreciable effect on the bank.

South Umpqua renamed itself South Umpqua Bank in 2000 and stepped up its acquisition efforts. It merged with Valley of the Rogue Bank, creating the third largest Oregon-based commercial bank with more than $750 million in assets. Valley of the Rogue Bank had been founded in 1968 and had purchased five other banks before the merger, becoming southern Oregon's largest community bank. After the merger, Davis remained president and chief executive of Umpqua Holdings, while William Haden, president and chief executive of Valley of the Rogue Bank, became president and chief executive of the newly named Umpqua Bank. All told, the new financial institution had 27 banks along the I-5 corridor and in southern Oregon and 54 ATMs scat-

tered across the state. Also in 2000, South Umpqua Bank acquired a second Portland brokerage firm, Adams, Hess, Moore & Co.

Umpqua Holdings moved its headquarters to Portland in 2001, leaving Umpqua Bank behind in Roseburg. The downturn in the economy made it harder for many banks to stay independent, and Umpqua continued its string of acquisitions. It purchased Independent Financial Network, of Coos Bay, Oregon, a multibank holding company with 14 banks on or near the Oregon Coast with $389 million in assets and Linn-Benton community bank of Albany, Oregon, in 2001.

In 2002 Umpqua Holdings purchased Centennial Bancorp, whose subsidiary, Centennial Bank, had 15 branches in the Portland area, including two in Vancouver, Washington, and another eight in Eugene, Oregon, and along the coast. Founded in Eugene in the early 1970s, Centennial had been a leading lender to business, and the fourth largest Oregon-based bank. The move created the largest banking company based in Oregon and boosted Umpqua's assets to $2.5 billion. It also increased Umpqua Bank's Portland presence. Umpqua Holdings merged with Humboldt Bancorp in northern California in 2004, closing out the year with 92 stores and $4.5 billion in assets.

Umpqua took its store concept one step further with its new destination stores in 2003. These bank stores were reminiscent of an art gallery, Internet café, and luxury hotel lobby rolled into one with the teller row partitioned by lamps instead of walls, and money handed to the customer on a tray with a gold-wrapped chocolate coin. To prepare staff for its new customer service responsibilities, Umpqua negotiated with the Ritz-Carlton to provide staff training emphasizing hospitality. Umpqua University & Support Center, in Roseburg, which housed the bank's training facility, human resources, retail support, and the consumer and business lending departments, opened in 2004 to create a central location for staff trainings.

Paving the way for and underscoring the community aspect of its new destination concept, Umpqua focused on launching several community service programs. In 2001 it began its "Wish Upon a Star" program with Douglas, Jackson, and Josephine radio stations, a monthlong holiday program that granted wishes to individuals in financial need. In 2003 it introduced Green Accounts that allowed account holders the choice of donating the interest on their account to a local nonprofit, originally one of several environmental groups, but later other nonprofits as well.

In 2004 it developed its Connect Volunteer Network, a volunteer program that provided each full-time Umpqua Bank associate with 40 hours of paid volunteer time. Nearly 800 of Umpqua Bank's 900 eligible employees enrolled as soon as they were able. Connect extended to northern California shortly thereafter. The bank also offered the online Umpqua Read Club in partnership with Powell's Books.

Total market share for Portland's flagship next generation store increased sixfold between 2003 and 2004, prompting Umpqua to open other next generation stores elsewhere in its territory. It opened a second store in Bend and a first in Medford, Oregon, in 2004, both featuring this next generation design. After testing out a loan production office in Bellevue, Washington, it opened its first full-service, destination store in Seattle area in 2005.

It also began to open new "neighborhood stores," which were smaller and faster to build. In addition to bank products, these stores offered retail space for distinctive merchandise from local businesses, and an electronic daily specials menu advertising neighborhood information, resources, and events. They also featured a Discover Wall, an interactive multiscreen display providing information on such topics as area home prices. The Discover Wall included Discover Local Music, which allowed people to download recordings by area artists onto CDs.

In 2006 Umpqua grew from close to 100 to slightly more than 125 banks when it acquired Western Sierra Bancorp and subsidiaries, Western Sierra Bank, Central California Bank, Lake Community Bank, and Auburn Community Bank. This acquisition increased its presence in the greater Sacramento and San Joaquin Valley area. The next year, it purchased North Bay Bancorp and its principal operating subsidiary, The Vintage Bank along with its Solano Bank division, adding another ten northern California banks.

As impressive as Umpqua's growth appeared on its own, it was even more impressive viewed in light of the decline of the timber industry and then the tech bust of 2000 in the Pacific Northwest. Oregon and Washington had the highest unemployment rates in the nation. Yet Umpqua grew, from less than 1 percent of Oregon deposits in 1999, to 6.2 percent in early 2005 or 3 percent of deposits in both Oregon and Washington. By 2007 it had 134 branches with more than $7 billion in deposits, up from close to $5 billion in 2005.

Davis took into account some of the challenges that came with such substantial growth in a 2007 *Bank Marketing International* article: "As we have grown so rapidly—we have become the largest community bank in the Northwest—we face the challenge of remaining agile and nimble." At a time when U.S. banks were opening branches faster than ever (1,500 from 2004 to 2005 alone) and a time when younger customers wanted to do everything online, how well the bank would continue to grow, according to Davis, was "a scary question to think about."

Nonetheless, Umpqua called itself the "world's greatest bank" and had been judged the best place to work among the state's large employers by *Oregon Business Magazine* in 2004 as well as one of the "best ideas" of 2005 by *BusinessWeek*. In addition, *Fortune* ranked it 34th on its list of the "100 Best Companies to Work For" in 2007. Challenges aside, Umpqua clearly seemed to be doing many things right.

Carrie Rothburd

PRINCIPAL SUBSIDIARIES

Strand, Atkinson, Williams & York.

PRINCIPAL COMPETITORS

Bank of America Corporation; Washington Mutual, Inc.; Wells Fargo & Company; West Coast Bancorp; Bank of the West; KeyCorp; U.S. Bancorp; Washington Federal, Inc.

FURTHER READING

"Blazing the Oregon Trail," *Bank Marketing International,* March 1997, p. 9.

"Consumer Banking the Friendly Way," *Retail Banker International,* July 30, 1999, p. 12.

Gilstrap, Michelle, "Banking with a Smile," *Display & Design Ideas,* November 1, 2004.

Kalb, Loretta, "Oregon-Based Umpqua Banks Aims to Be Unique in Banking in Northern California," *Sacramento Bee,* July 25, 2004.

Kuehner-Hebert, Katie, "'Neighborhood Store' Latest Branch Model from Umpqua," *American Banker,* March 24, 2006, p. 3.

———, "Unorthodox Branch Style Gets More So at Umpqua," *American Banker,* June 20, 2003, p. 5.

Schmermund, Kathleen, "Umpqua Promotes Musicians, Loans," *American Banker,* June 29, 2005, p. 5.

Stiles, Greg, "Roseburg, Oregon–Based Umpqua Bank Named Best Place of the Year to Work in State," *Mail Tribune,* March 3, 2004.

"Umpqua Bank: Leading the Way in Customer Experience," *Bank Marketing International,* January 29, 2007, p. 6.

VeraSun Energy Corporation

—■—

100 22nd Avenue
Brookings, South Dakota 57006
U.S.A.
Telephone: (605) 696-7200
Fax: (605) 696-7250
Web site: http://www.verasun.com

Public Company
Incorporated: 2001
Employees: 195
Sales: $557.8 million (2006)
Stock Exchanges: New York
Ticker Symbol: VSE
NAIC: 325998 All Other Miscellaneous Chemical Product Manufacturing; 325193 Ethyl Alcohol Manufacturing

■ ■ ■

VeraSun Energy Corporation is the second largest ethanol producer in the United States (trailing Archer Daniels Midland Company), operating plants that convert corn into biofuel. VeraSun operates plants in Aurora, South Dakota; Fort Dodge, Iowa; and Charles City, Iowa. Each plant produces more than 100 million gallons of ethanol annually. The company also has three plants in various stages of construction in Welcome, Minnesota; Hartley, Iowa; and Reynolds, Indiana. VeraSun, using a process it developed to use oil extracted from distillers grains, plans to begin production of biodiesel in 2008, by which point it expects to be producing 560 million gallons of ethanol annually. The

company has signed partnership agreements with Ford and General Motors to build fuel stations capable of supplying E85 (85 percent ethanol, 15 percent gasoline) fuel to properly equipped cars and trucks. VeraSun brands its E85 product as "VE85," which is available at select locations in South Dakota, Minnesota, Illinois, Pennsylvania, Missouri, Indiana, and Iowa.

ORIGINS

Donald L. Endres brought both an understanding of agriculture and confirmed success as an entrepreneur to the founding of VeraSun, boasting ideal attributes for the challenges that lay ahead. He was raised in Watertown, South Dakota, the son of a corn farmer whose father was a corn farmer. Endres's brothers followed in the footsteps of their father and grandfather, adding a third generation of corn farmers to the family history. Endres shot off in an entirely different direction, becoming an entrepreneur in the technology sector after earning a bachelor of science degree in animal science from South Dakota State University. He displayed a Midas touch, leading a group of associates through several multimillion-dollar technology ventures that enriched all involved. In one such venture, Endres teamed with William L. Honnef to launch an Internet gift certificate company named ExpressGold.com. The pair sold the company to CyberSource Corporation in January 2000, cashing out for $75 million. Honnef, who had earned his undergraduate degree from Indiana University of Pennsylvania, was selected by his alma mater as "Entrepreneur of the Year" in 2000, a distinction South Dakota State University also bestowed on Endres in 2000.

One year after they collected their awards, Endres and Honnef were ready to launch their next venture. VeraSun began to take shape in 2001, and it took Endres back to his agricultural roots. "We knew there was an energy shortage," Endres explained in a February 11, 2005, interview with *Top Producer*, "so we looked at wind power, biodiesel, and ethanol. Ethanol had the unique potential to have more positive impact in the region. We had been successful in the past, but unlike previous ventures, this looked like a unique opportunity to involve the community."

Endres also was more than familiar with the intricacies of ethanol production. In 2000 he cofounded Glacial Lakes Energy, a farmer-owned, limited liability company (LLC) that operated an ethanol plant in his hometown. He also invested in Badger State Ethanol, a Monroe, Wisconsin, LLC. His plans for VeraSun differed from the two other ventures, however, distinguished by the scale of the operations he and Honnef were contemplating in 2001. Glacial Lakes operated a plant that annually produced 45 million gallons of ethanol. Badger State's facility had an annual capacity of 40 million gallons of ethanol. Endres, looking to optimize efficiencies and distribution, envisioned VeraSun as a producer of much greater magnitude, a company whose annual capacity would approach that of the nation's largest ethanol producer, agricultural giant Archer Daniels Midland Company. "First," Endres explained in his interview with *Top Producer*, "we saw 30-million-gallon, then 50-million-gallon, now 100-million-gallon plants. That's the life cycle of all businesses. As they mature, they become more efficient. In the ethanol industry, one means of capturing efficiencies is through scale. Buying inputs is just easier when you're bigger, and you can sell in bigger volumes to petroleum companies."

Endres set his sights on building not just one, but a series of ethanol plants capable of producing 100 million gallons per year (MGPY) or more. The objective was ambitious, calling for substantial financial resources to achieve. To make VeraSun more attractive to investors, Endres organized the company as a C-corporation, a move that also enabled VeraSun's board of directors to execute decisions far more quickly than allowed by the one-person, one-vote structure of a farmer-owned cooperative. Endres pitched his business plan to investors, drawing the interest of one venture-capital firm, Bluestem Capital Company, in particular. With the help of Bluestem, a Midwest-focused, Sioux Falls, South Dakota-based firm, Endres was able to raise more than $100 million to equip VeraSun with the capital to build its first ethanol plant.

As VeraSun's financing was being arranged, Endres and his team began scouting for the location of the company's first plant. Research efforts led the team to east-central South Dakota, specifically near the town of Aurora, a corn-rich area in proximity to the Dakota Minnesota & Eastern railroad that offered outlets to ethanol and grain byproduct markets. Plans for the 417-acre Aurora site called for the construction of a 100 MGPY plant that was expected to be completed in March 2004, when VeraSun was slated for its debut in the fast-growing ethanol market.

As a biofuel alternative to gasoline, ethanol represented a ray of hope for a country facing numerous challenges on the energy front. U.S. dependence on foreign oil, escalating gasoline prices, and excessive carbon dioxide emissions were issues that could be addressed, in part, by using alternative fuels, and ethanol was one of the leading alternative fuels causing a stir of interest as VeraSun began building its plant in Aurora. A high-octane, anhydrous (water free) alcohol, ethanol was most widely used as a blending ingredient in gasoline because it released less carbon dioxide than conventional gasoline and offered a replacement for phased-out methyl t-butyl ether (MTBE), which had been the gasoline additive of choice until it was discovered to be a soil and aquifer contaminant. Ethanol, produced by fermenting yeast with the starch or sugar in a wide variety of crops, presented none of the environmental problems posed by MTBE. Further, in cars and trucks designated as flex-fuel vehicles (FFVs), blends of 85 percent ethanol and 15 percent gasoline (E85) could be used, by far eclipsing MTBE's role as an oxygenate.

For his Aurora plant, and others to follow, Endres chose to use a dry-mill process of converting corn into ethanol, turning to the crop cultivated by his grandfather, father, and brothers. In the dry-mill process, each bushel of corn yielded roughly 2.8 gallons of ethanol and roughly 18 pounds of distillers grains, a high quality, nutritious livestock feed.

KEY DATES

2001: VeraSun Energy Corporation is founded.

2003: VeraSun completes the construction of its first ethanol plant, a facility in Aurora, South Dakota.

2004: Construction of a second ethanol production plant begins in Fort Dodge, Iowa.

2006: VeraSun completes its initial public offering of stock and announces its intention to produce biodiesel.

2007: The company's third ethanol plant, a facility in Charles City, Iowa, begins production in April, the same month construction of a sixth plant in Reynolds, Indiana, begins.

ETHANOL PRODUCTION BEGINS IN 2003

For a company waiting to receive its first stream of revenue, word of the construction activity in Aurora provided welcomed news. The plant was finished ahead of schedule, opening in November 2003 and commencing production the following month. The 100 MGPY capacity of the plant, which operated 24 hours per day, seven days per week, represented a boon to corn farmers, requiring more than 35 million bushels of corn annually, and to VeraSun's coffers, giving it ethanol to sell and annual production of 320,000 tons of distillers grains, enough to feed more than 600,000 dairy cattle per day. The debut of the Aurora plant was a celebratory event, but before VeraSun produced its first gallon of ethanol, Endres had already moved on to his next project. In December 2003, *Alternative Transportation Fuels Today* reported that city officials in Fort Dodge, Iowa, had been approached by VeraSun representatives. The inquiries led to the formalization of plans for a second VeraSun production facility, which commenced construction in September 2004. The 110 MGPY Fort Dodge facility started producing ethanol in October 2005, two months after expansion of the Aurora plant lifted capacity to 120 MGPY.

VeraSun ranked as the second largest ethanol producer in the country by the time the Fort Dodge facility went online, its rise through the ranks of a highly fragmented industry a testament to Endres's drive to expand. Additional plants would soon follow—the purchase of a 228-acre farm in Floyd County, Iowa, in late 2005 became the site of the company's Charles City plant—but Endres attended to other matters as well,

namely, promoting the use of ethanol and preparing for VeraSun's debut as a publicly traded company. One of the major concerns in the ethanol industry was the lack of an extensive infrastructure to deliver biofuel to consumers. Of the more than 180,000 fuel stations blanketing the country, only 500 were equipped to offer E85. VeraSun, which had branded its E85 product as "VE85" in May 2005, assumed an active role in establishing a network of ethanol fuel stations. In late 2005, the company signed a partnership agreement with Ford Motor to expand the fueling infrastructure for FFVs. In June 2006, one day after U.S. automakers announced they intended to double the production of FFVs by 2010, VeraSun and Ford said they intended to add more than 50 stations offering E85 in Missouri and Illinois in an effort to create an "ethanol corridor" in the Midwest. At roughly the same time, VeraSun allied itself with General Motors and Shell Oil Products U.S. in an effort to build 26 new E85 refueling stations in the greater Chicago area.

VERASUN'S PUBLIC DEBUT IN 2006

Against the backdrop of construction efforts, VeraSun began the process of converting to public ownership. Pacific Ethanol, with plans to dot the West Coast with production plants, became the first pure-play ethanol company to trade publicly in the United States, completing an initial public offering (IPO) in March 2005 that caused a stir of excitement in the investment community (the company's shares shot up 165 percent in value within a year). VeraSun and another ethanol producer, Aventine Renewable Energy, queued up next, filing with the Securities and Exchange Commission in early 2006 in preparation for their public debuts. Vera-Sun proposed a $150 million offering, hoping to use the proceeds to build two ethanol plants in the upper Midwest, but the size of the offering soon increased. After announcing an eightfold increase in profits for the first fiscal quarter of 2006, the company doubled the size of its IPO, seeking to draw more than $300 million from Wall Street. When the company's IPO was completed in June 2006, the perception of VeraSun's value among investors gave the offering another boost, resulting in a $419 million offering. VeraSun raised gross proceeds of $253 million, giving it the capital to pursue its goal of increasing production to 560 MGPY by the end of the first fiscal quarter in 2008.

In the wake of the stunning success of its IPO, VeraSun redoubled its expansion efforts and broadened its strategic scope. The company began construction of two plants in November 2006, a 110 MGPY facility in Hartley, Iowa, and a 110 MGPY facility in Welcome,

Minnesota, that set it on track to achieve its production goal for early 2008. November also marked the announcement of VeraSun's intent to make history in the alternative fuels industry. The company revealed it had discovered a way to produce biodiesel, a clean-burning, renewable fuel, from oil extracted from distillers grains. By removing the oil from distillers grains, the company both increased the value of the oil for fuel use and improved the quality of the resulting distillers grains as a livestock feed because the process concentrated protein and reduced fat content in the grains. VeraSun immediately began scouting for locations for a 30 MGPY biodiesel production facility, with construction expected to start in 2007 and production to commence in 2008. The completion of the facility was expected to make VeraSun the first company to develop a large-scale commercial facility for biodiesel from a coproduct of the ethanol production process, thereby enabling the company to produce two biofuels from the same feedstock.

The frenetic pace of expansion during VeraSun's first five years of business promised to continue as the company plotted its future course. The Charles City plant opened in April 2007, three months ahead of schedule, the same month the company announced the location of its sixth ethanol plant, a 110 MGPY facility in Reynolds, Indiana. Construction of the Reynolds facility was expected to be completed before the end of 2008, but it was not expected to be the last plant built under the VeraSun banner. With ethanol and biodiesel offering Endres two avenues of growth to pursue, the company figured to play a leading role in the biofuel market for years to co me.

Jeffrey L. Covell

PRINCIPAL SUBSIDIARIES

VeraSun Aurora Corporation; VeraSun Fort Dodge, LLC; VeraSun Charles City, LLC; VeraSun Marketing, LLC; VeraSun Hartley, LLC; VeraSun Granite City, LLC; VeraSun Reynolds, LLC; VeraSun Welcome, LLC.

PRINCIPAL COMPETITORS

Archer Daniels Midland Company; US BioEnergy Corporation; Hawkeye Renewables, LLC; Aventine Renewable Energy Holdings, Inc.

FURTHER READING

Barack, Lauren, "Farmable Fuel of the Future: Don Endres of VeraSun Energy," *On Wall Street,* January 1, 2007.

Barzak, Ibrahim, "Ethanol Maker VeraSun Doubles Size of IPO As Quarterly Profit Soars," *America's Intelligence Wire,* May 24, 2006.

"Ethanol Companies Line Up for IPOs," *Investment Dealers' Digest,* April 10, 2006.

"Floyd County, Iowa, to Sell Former Farm to VeraSun Energy," *Waterloo Courier,* November 25, 2005.

"Ford and VeraSun Announce Partnership to Drive Ethanol Infrastructure," *Asia Africa Intelligence Wire,* November 4, 2005.

"GE to Promote E-85 During NASCAR Races," *World Fuels Today,* February 9, 2006.

Gullickson, Gil, "VeraSun a Risin'," *Top Producer,* February 11, 2005.

Lammers, Dirk, "Shares of Ethanol Producer VeraSun Jump 24 Percent in IPO," *America's Intelligence Wire,* June 14, 2006.

"VeraSun Announces Innovative Process for Biodiesel Production," *Chemical Business Newsbase,* November 3, 2006.

"VeraSun Breaks Ground on Iowa Ethanol Plant," *Feedstuffs,* October 4, 2004, p. 24.

"VeraSun Building Minnesota Plant," *Europe Intelligence Wire,* November 30, 2006.

"VeraSun Completes Expansion at South Dakota Ethanol Plant," *Alternative Transportation Fuels Today,* August 10, 2005, p. 1.

"VeraSun Considers Local Ethanol Plant Development in IA," *Alternative Transportation Fuels Today,* December 12, 2003.

"VeraSun Energy Announces Ethanol Plant Construction," *Feedstuffs,* February 24, 2003, p. 27.

"VeraSun Ethanol Plant Commences Operations," *Alternative Fuels Today,* November 25, 2003, p. 1.

"VeraSun Looks to Acquire Land in Iowa for New Ethanol Plant," *Alternative Transportation Fuels Today,* August 30, 2005.

VistaPrint Limited

——■——

Canon's Court
22 Victoria Street
Hamilton, HM 12
Bermuda
Telephone: (441) 295-2244
Toll Free: (800) 721-6214
Web site: http://www.vistaprint.com

Public Company
Founded: 1995
Employees: 770
Sales: $152.1 million (2006)
Stock Exchanges: NASDAQ
Ticker Symbol: VPRT
NAIC: 323119 Other Commercial Printing

■■■

VistaPrint Limited helped modernize the traditional short-run printing industry by capitalizing on the growing acceptance of the Internet and developing new computer technologies. The company's self-service web site, vistaprint.com, groups similar orders together to end the long waits, exorbitant costs, and lengthy processes typically associated with individualized, high-quality printing services. The company's eight million worldwide customers are small businesses and individuals who request products such as business cards, brochures, invitations, and holiday cards. Before the emergence of affordable online printing services, these customers would have been priced out of conventional methods of printing. With the demand for self-service printing growing at an impressive rate, VistaPrint services 120 countries and processes nearly 20,000 orders per day.

MADE IN FRANCE; REMADE IN AMERICA, 1995 TO 2000

As a former consultant to Microsoft, Robert S. Keane knew his way around the Internet. He had a B.A. in economics from Harvard University, an M.B.A. from France's INSEAD international business school, and had worked as a graphic design consultant for small businesses in Europe. Based on his knowledge of the desktop publishing software market, Keane believed online printing would not only be a successful business enterprise but possibly the future of small-job printing needs.

Keane came up with a business plan and sought financial backers for an online printing company, VistaPrint.com S.A. One of his early investors was his father, Kevin Keane, chairman of the Buffalo, New York-based Mod-Pac Corporation, a printing company that specialized in conventional printing services. The younger Keane hoped his start-up would benefit both businesses: VistaPrint's online services would attract thousands of small orders and Mod-Pac was equipped to process them.

In addition to his father's support, Keane hoped to lure several larger investors from the venture capital market. Initially, few caught on to the idea. However, Sofinnova Partners, one of France's leading venture capital firms, believed the printing industry was ready for a change and agreed to provide funding for

COMPANY PERSPECTIVES

VistaPrint Limited (Nasdaq: VPRT) is the leading on-line supplier of high-quality graphic design services and customized printed products to small businesses and consumers. VistaPrint offers custom designed, full-color, low-cost printed products in small quantities. Over 8 million small businesses and consumers have already chosen VistaPrint for products ranging from business cards and brochures to invitations and thank you cards.

VistaPrint. Olivier Protard, managing partner at Sofinnova Partners, later told the *European Venture Capital Journal* (November 2005), "When we funded VistaPrint, the company consisted of one American guy with a French colleague in a small, cramped office." Over the next decade, VistaPrint raised a total of $65 million from investors including the London-based Saffron Hill Ventures and several East Coast firms including Highland Capital Partners, Windspeed Ventures, and Window to Wall Street.

While investors were optimistic, European customers were not buying. Because Sofinnova had a presence in the United States, Keane and his major investors decided in 2000 to move VistaPrint's operations to Massachusetts. The new company, VistaPrint Corporation, became part of the Boston start-up scene and concentrated its efforts on U.S. customers and tapping into American funding opportunities. Just five months after the company's relocation, VistaPrint had 40,000 customers who had accessed and paid for its online printing services. In turn, the company was able to raise additional funding to expand its services.

As the digital age gained momentum, e-printing services were relatively widespread. Web sites such as iPrint.com, mimeo.com, and Kinkos.com all offered on-line, self-service printing. VistaPrint set its business apart by offering 250 free business cards to its customers for trying its service. Customers who sampled these cards paid a $4.95 delivery fee, and accepted a VistaPrint advertisement on the backs of their cards. More than half the customers who tried the business cards returned as paying customers. Customers who reordered paid only about $40 for 500 or $50 for 1,000, remarkably lower prices than at traditional printing companies. While VistaPrint's pricing was similar to their online competitors, customers valued the opportunity to sample the product before placing a larger order.

FREE SAMPLES NET BIG RETURNS

VistaPrint's sampling program was one of the keys to its early success and the company was in the black by 2001, just one year after bringing its operations to the U.S. printing industry. As customers returned and placed orders for higher quantities, VistaPrint began offering additional products such as letterhead, envelopes, postcards, return address labels, and magnets.

Although sampling programs could be costly, VistaPrint was able to keep costs at a minimum through a proprietary software program, VistaStudio. The desktop publishing application, set up on a browser rather than a server, significantly reduced response time and allowed VistaPrint to provide a three-business-day turnaround on orders. The software allowed users to choose from thousands of professionally designed templates and 70,000 graphics in VistaStudio's image bank, or upload their own designs. According to *Inc.* magazine's "Best of the Web" September 2000 issue, a panel of CEOs who tested nine self-service online printers praised VistaPrint's "user-friendly approach" over that of its competitors.

While VistaStudio allowed the company to quickly process orders by the thousands, VistaPrint needed a printer who could keep up with their growing demands. In September 2002 Robert Keane worked out a ten-year exclusive with his father's printing company, Mod-Pac, to print all of VistaPrint's North American clients. As fate would have it, Keane's younger brother, Daniel Keane, had graduated from Dartmouth University and joined their father at Mod-Pac Corporation. The Keane trio prospered, for a while.

For over a year, Mod-Pac and VistaPrint enjoyed mutual success. VistaPrint's revenue increased substantially, leaping from 2002's $16.9 million to $35.4 million in 2003. In addition, the company raised $30 million in venture capital. Mod-Pac, too, benefited from its alliance with VistaPrint: the Buffalo printer's revenues climbed as did profits as well as its stock price, from $4 in March 2003 to $18 in August 2003.

PRIVATE TO PUBLIC

By July 2004 Robert Keane made a surprisingly bold decision to cut all apron strings. He decided having his own printing plants was more profitable than relying on Mod-Pac's services. With a $22 million cash payment, Robert Keane dissolved his printing agreement with father and brother and moved all printing operations to the Netherlands and Canada. VistaPrint opened a 54,000-square-foot printing plant in Venlo, Netherlands, and began shipping products to Europe in the spring of 2004.

KEY DATES

1995: Robert Keane launches VistaPrint.com S.A. in Paris, France.

2000: VistaPrint Corporation is incorporated in Waltham, Massachusetts.

2001: An offer of free business cards helps VistaPrint acquire 85,000 new paying customers.

2002: The company reincorporates as VistaPrint Limited with executive offices in Bermuda.

2004: A new 54,000-square-foot printing plant opens in the Netherlands.

2005: VistaPrint goes public on the NASDAQ.

2006: The company's stock price triples, reaching a high of $37.75.

2007: VistaPrint is awarded its 13th U.S. patent.

In 2005 VistaPrint had a workforce of 400, over five million small business clients, and had built a 68,000-square-foot printing plant in Windsor, Ontario, to serve North American markets. Its two printing plants cut costs and expedited service by combining orders into "gang runs." Though the plants received more than 10,000 orders per day, another proprietary software program called VistaBridge sorted similar orders into the same batches for printing on the company's 40-inch presses. Production labor took as little as 60 seconds per order, allowing VistaPrint to process thousands of small orders at the same time, rather than separately processing each individual order.

Rapid production turnaround, financial stability, low overhead, and a growing customer base set the stage for an attractive initial public offering (IPO). In September 2005 VistaPrint conducted an IPO of 10.02 million shares at $12 each. Within two months the stock had climbed to $19.74 per share. VistaPrint ended fiscal 2005 (June) with $90.9 million in revenue, a 55 percent increase from 2004's $58.8 million. Mod-Pac, the family business run by Daniel Keane, struggled to replace the business it had lost from VistaPrint. Its stock tumbled to $11 per share as VistaPrint's approached $34 in early 2006.

Although Daniel considered legal action against Robert and VistaPrint, alleging he was a coinventor of VistaPrint's technology, the younger Keane also thought about competing directly with VistaPrint by entering the online printing market. Ultimately, Daniel Keane went in another direction, telling the *Buffalo News* (February 9, 2007) his goal was to strengthen Mod-Pac's "commercial printing business by building ties to printed products distributors and industry groups."

OFF AND RUNNING

VistaPrint's success was due, in part, to the uniqueness of its printing technology. While printing was an age-old industry, Robert Keane had taken the basics of graphic design and printing and changed them to meet the needs of 21st-century businesses. Keane estimated the small business/home office market was valued at $19 billion, telling *Graphic Arts Monthly* (August 2006), there were "38 million self-employed individuals or clients at firms with fewer than 10 workers in the U.S. and Europe." Providing affordable printing services to these customers was a quick and easy process with VistaPrint's proprietary software programs, technology so valuable the company applied for patents to protect it.

VistaPrint added a full-time patent attorney to its staff and had acquired 12 U.S. patents by 2006 with more than 40 others pending worldwide. The company also continued to attract new customers through e-mail newsletters, advertising weekly and monthly specials, and tailored marketing campaigns to its established clients. As a result, by spending $13.3 million in advertising for fiscal 2006, VistaPrint ended the year with revenues of $152.1 million, an increase of 67 percent from 2005. Additionally, average daily orders increased 50 percent for the fiscal year from 15,000 orders in 2005 to 18,000 in 2006. The company also enjoyed continued success on the stock market with its share price rising to a high of $37.75.

Though many online businesses came and went in the dot-com era, VistaPrint succeeded in a volatile market by developing groundbreaking technology that offered customers a high-quality, low-cost alternative to traditional printing services. As more small and home businesses abandoned brick-and-mortar printers for the ease of the Internet, VistaPrint's services grew to meet clients' needs. The invention of self-service, online printing had forever changed the conventional printing industry.

Jodi Essey-Stapleton and Nelson Rhodes

PRINCIPAL OPERATING UNITS

VistaPrint B.V. (Netherlands); VistaPrint España S.L. (Spain); VistaPrint Jamaica Limited; VistaPrint North America Services Corp. (Canada); VistaPrint USA Incorporated.

PRINCIPAL COMPETITORS

AlphaGraphics, Inc.; FedEx Kinko's Office and Print Services, Inc.; Microsoft Corporation; Office Depot,

Inc.; OfficeMax, Inc.; PrintingForLess.com, Inc.; Staples, Inc.; Taylor Corporation.

FURTHER READING

Allchorne, Tom, "Made in Europe, Big in America," *European Venture Capital Journal,* November 2005, p. 24.

"Best of the Web," *Inc.,* September 2000, p. 119.

Cross, Lisa, "Selling Online," *Graphic Arts Monthly,* August 2006, p. 20.

Enright, Allison, "Samples Eliminate Fear Factor," *Marketing News,* October 15, 2005.

"Free Business Card Service Now Offered via Co-Branded Platform," *Direct Marketing,* March 2001, p. 65.

Holian, Janet, "Automating Short Runs," *Graphic Arts Monthly,* April 2006, p. 8.

Keri, Jonah, "VistaPrint Pulls Back After Successful IPO," *Investor's Business Daily,* December 2, 2005, p. B08.

Madrid, Allan, "Gang Run," *Graphic Arts Monthly,* August 2005, p. 52.

Robinson, David, "Competitive Brothers Staying Out of Court," *Buffalo News,* February 27, 2006.

———, "Mod-Pac Narrows Operating Losses," *Buffalo News,* February 9, 2007.

Sheahan, Matthew, "VistaPrint Raises $52M Series B," *Private Equity Week,* November 15, 2004.

Tam, Pui-Wing, "Office Technology; The New Paper Trail," *Wall Street Journal,* February 13, 2006, p. R8.

Taub, Eric, "It's Just Like Oz, with You Behind the Curtain," *New York Times,* February 22, 2005, p. G2.

Taulli, Tom, "The Patented Path to Profits," *Forbes,* April 28, 2006.

WD-40 Company

1061 Cudahy Place
San Diego, California 92110-3929
U.S.A.
Telephone: (619) 275-1400
Toll Free: (800) 448-9340
Fax: (619) 275-5823
Web site: http://www.wd40.com

Public Company
Incorporated: 1952 as Rocket Chemical Company
Employees: 244
Sales: $286.9 million (2006)
Stock Exchanges: NASDAQ
Ticker Symbol: WDFC
NAIC: 324191 Petroleum Lubricating Oil and Grease Manufacturing; 325611 Soap and Other Detergent Manufacturing; 325612 Polish and Other Sanitation Good Manufacturing; 325613 Surface Active Agent Manufacturing; 325998 All Other Miscellaneous Chemical Product and Preparation Manufacturing

■ ■ ■

Since the 1950s, the San Diego-based WD-40 Company has dominated the U.S. market for its namesake multipurpose lubricant. The WD-40 substance is a petroleum-based lubricant, moisture retardant, cleaner, and rust preventative. It is used in around 80 percent of American households and is one of the best-known brands in the country. One of the product's strengths is its versatility: it has been found to improve the performance of sewing machines, attract fish, loosen rusted nuts and bolts, and unfreeze door locks and handles. Sold through mass merchandisers, hardware stores, home improvement centers, warehouse club stores, automotive stores, and industrial distributors and suppliers, WD-40 is sold in more than 160 countries worldwide. A one-product company until 1995, WD-40 Company also produces 3-in-One Oil, a lower-priced general purpose lubricant; Lava and Solvol heavy-duty hand cleaners; and several household cleaning product brands—2000 Flushes, X-14, Carpet Fresh, Spot Shot, and 1001. An increasingly global firm, WD-40 generates around 44 percent of its revenues outside the United States, with Europe responsible for 28 percent and 7 percent originating in the Asia-Pacific region. The company's lubricants franchise accounts for about two-thirds of overall revenues, with household products bringing in 31 percent and hand cleaners the remaining 2 percent.

1953: THE BIRTH OF WD-40

Although WD-40 has been a household name for several decades, it did not begin as a household product. In 1953 Norm Larsen of Rocket Chemical Company developed WD-40 as a corrosion protector for missile covers for the San Diego-based Convair, an aerospace and defense contractor and a division of General Dynamics Corporation. Eventually, WD-40 was intended for use on the National Aeronautics and Space Administration's Atlas missile. The name WD-40 stands for "water displacement, formulation successful in 40th attempt," because it was on the 40th try that Larsen perfected the product. Employees at General Dynamics discovered that WD-40 was perfect for a variety of home uses, and they began sneaking the lubricant home from work. By 1955, Larsen began experimenting with putting WD-40 in aerosol cans, and in 1958, Rocket Chemical Company responded to the consumer market for a home lubricant by contracting with an aerosol packager and preparing WD-40 for commercial sales.

Rocket Chemical Company, which was founded in 1952 by Larsen and three investors, was a one-room operation with a three-person staff. (One of the three investors was Sam Crivello, who was on the company board for many years, and whose son Mario continues to hold a seat on the board and also maintains a stake in the company totaling more than 5 percent.) In addition to WD-40, the company produced rust resistors and removers for metal parts and tools for the aerospace industry. In 1960 the company grew to include seven employees with sales of about 45 cases per day. Rocket Chemical Company sales representatives sold the product out of their cars to San Diego sporting goods and hardware stores. A slight recipe change in 1961— adding a dose of mineral spirits to the original formula to cover the petroleum scent—was the only adjustment ever made to Larsen's original formula as of the early 21st century. Hurricane Carla, which ravaged the Florida coast in 1961, increased WD-40's business dramatically, as it was used by hurricane victims to recondition water-damaged vehicles and machinery.

ONE PRODUCT TRANSFORMS A COMPANY

By 1965, WD-40 sales were so successful that Rocket Chemical Company ceased production of all other products to focus solely on the lubricant. Sales surpassed $1 million in 1968, and when John Barry became president the next year, the firm officially changed its name to WD-40 Company. In 1969 sales reached $2 million.

With a mandate to accelerate both revenues and earnings, Barry piloted WD-40 to a position of prominence as an untouchable one-product company. The brother-in-law of one of the three original investors in Rocket Chemical Company, Barry garnered his marketing know-how working at companies including 3M, Avery Label, and Adams Rite. With a virtually unknown product and no working capital, Barry's marketing strategies were straightforward and simple, emphasizing free samples (including 10,000 WD-40 samples each month sent to soldiers in the Vietnam War to keep their weapons dry), trade shows, and magazine advertising. Product awareness was built through manufacturers' representatives, who worked on commission and sold the product to wholesalers only. No written contracts were held between WD-40 and the manufacturers' representatives, and the relationship could be terminated with 30-day notice. The underlying philosophy behind these strategies was to market the company's one product to its full potential, diversifying the uses of the product, not the product itself, while keeping costs down.

GOING PUBLIC, NEW GROWTH

In January 1973 WD-40 went public. Prior to this first offering, the company was a Subchapter-S corporation. Shareholders gave up this election by going public, receiving looser restrictions on their estates and tax benefits in exchange. Heavy demand escalated the initial price of a 40,000 share offering to $16.50 from the originally intended $15 a share, and later in the year shares surged to $34, before dropping again to $15 at the end of the year. The initial offering generated net proceeds of approximately $590,000, of which $350,000 was used for a new plant, with the remainder added to working capital. The company paid half its earnings in dividends, increasing dividends with earnings growth. The next year, the company moved its headquarters to its present location on Cudahy Place in San Diego. Prices in 1974 were raised by 10.6 percent.

In 1978, after 25 years of business, sales reached $25 million. The following year, sales increased to $34 million, with earnings of $5 million. Sales and earnings had increased at a ten-year compounded rate of approximately 35 percent. The company remained tightly held, with over half of the stock held by officers, directors, and relatives of the original three Rocket Chemical Company investors. The wholesale price of the company's product rose 43 percent between 1969 and 1981, while the U.S. wholesale price index increased

KEY DATES

1953: Norm Larsen of Rocket Chemical Company develops WD-40 as a corrosion protector for missile covers.

1958: Rocket Chemical begins packaging WD-40 for the consumer market in aerosol cans.

1969: Name of firm is changed to WD-40 Company.

1973: WD-40 goes public.

1993: Sales reach the $100 million mark.

1995: Era as one-product company ends with the acquisition of 3-in-One Oil.

1999: WD-40 acquires the Lava brand of heavy-duty hand cleaners.

2001: Global Household Brands is acquired, adding the X-14, Carpet Fresh, and 2000 Flushes brands to the company stable.

2002: Company acquires Spot Shot carpet stain remover.

2005: WD-40 Smart Straw and WD-40 No-Mess Pen make their debuts.

132 percent during this period. Costs at WD-40 had always been low, because the focus on one product meant there were no research and development costs. The company at this time had only 32 employees, with a sales force of 65 manufacturers' representatives selling the product to about 14,000 wholesalers. The entire manufacturing operation was staffed by one part-time employee, who created the WD-40 concentrate from a mixture of off-the-shelf chemicals. About 28 percent of sales were spent on sales, marketing, and administration. Also, because the company had no debt, minimal overhead, and rented its office space, WD-40 paid about 5 percent back to investors.

By 1979, 35 million cans of WD-40 were being sold, with 55 percent purchased by homeowners and sporting enthusiasts and the remainder purchased by commercial and industrial users. The first price increase since 1974 raised the cost of the cans by 15 to 16 percent. Half of the company's total assets were held in cash, with after-tax net earnings around 16 percent. In 1981 the company was selected by *Forbes* as one of the small, emerging growth companies on its "Up-and-Comers List." Continuing to experiment with innovative sampling as a marketing strategy, WD-40 entered into a partnership that year with Wagner Spray Tech, a spray gun manufacturer in Minneapolis. WD-40

samples were included in spray gun packages, along with instructional brochures. Both companies shared equally in the costs and profits of the sample program.

INTERNATIONAL EXPANSION

By 1985, sales had increased to $57.3 million, with a 21 percent increase the following year to $69.4 million. Earnings in 1986 were $11.6 million, and shares were sold at a new all-time high of $33.50, a 44 percent gain. Having already achieved great success with its one product in the United States in the 1980s, it was time for WD-40 Company to expand its presence in the world market. International sales at this time represented less than 5 percent of total sales (not including Canada). In 1986, rather than renewing its contract with its U.K. distributor, the company built its own plant in Milton Keyes (near London). The next year an official U.K. subsidiary, WD-40 Company Limited, was established to manufacture, produce, and oversee distribution of WD-40 in Europe, the Middle East, and Africa. Since that year, when sales for the United Kingdom and Europe were $10 million, earnings grew rapidly. By 1992, sales attributed to France, Spain, and the Middle East had reached $17.5 million. Continuing to emphasize overseas expansion, the company bolstered its sales force in Europe by adding new sales representatives in France, Spain, and Italy. Shortly thereafter, Barry began sales expansion to Australia and the Pacific Rim. By 1988, European, Australian, and Asian markets accounted for 21 percent of revenues.

Sales reached $71 million in 1987, and company stock hit a high of $46. However, the October 19, 1987, crash of the stock market, resulting in a 508-point drop in the Dow Jones Industrial Average, caused WD-40's stock to drop to the mid-$20s in November. With fewer than 100 employees, the company was still able to net $11 million in 1987. Every dollar of that $11 million was paid in dividends. At this time, the company had no debt and $18 million in cash, with a market value of $231 million.

In 1988 WD-40 changed its sales strategy, shifting from salesperson commissions to direct sales. This policy was implemented as a means to increase business with large retailers, who formed a significant portion of the company's sales, with 40 percent of sales originating in 50 of the company's 12,000 accounts. Large retailers preferred the elimination of intermediary distributors, as a cost-cutting factor. Responding to this desire, WD-40, using a contract clause allowing the termination of the hiring agreement on either side with 90 days notice, decided to eliminate 12 distributors and instead hire direct salespersons to cater to the large accounts. Good earnings prospects and an increased dividend brought

WD-40's stock to an October high of $33.25, and sales rose to $80 million, with net income increasing 40 percent to $25.4 million. The new sales strategy, however, proved dangerous to the company's earnings in the long run.

Eight of the 12 distributors sued WD-40, claiming that the company had promised them job security in exchange for company loyalty. In 1992 the distributors were granted a $10.3 million settlement. WD-40 appealed the decision. In the meantime, two additional distributors, who had not joined the original suit, filed a separate lawsuit in 1992, using the same lawyers. In 1993 this second suit was settled, granting the distributors $2.5 million. In 1994 the original case was again decided in favor of the distributors, costing the company $12.6 million. Perhaps, because sales had skyrocketed from $80 million in 1988 to $100 million in 1992, due in part to the new sales strategy, the settlement fee may not actually have presented a real loss to the company. The year 1994 was the first in a decade in which WD-40 had flat earnings, but profits still totaled $12.6 million on record sales of $112 million.

Competition had never presented a challenge to WD-40. Though the formula for the lubricant was a guarded secret, the company had chosen never to patent it. Although WD-40 was physically indistinguishable from other products—such as 3M's Q4, Borden's Ten*4, and Valvoline's 1-2-99—no contender had presented even a minor challenge, and WD-40 has buried over 200 competing products over the years. This included, as of 1988, 14 billion-dollar companies, whose economic clout was unable to unseat WD-40's blue-and-yellow can.

After over two decades of leadership, Barry retired to become chairman of the board in 1990, replaced by Gerald Schleif as president and CEO. Schleif was previously WD-40's executive vice-president and CFO and had served the company for 21 years. In 1990 WD-40 increased the price of its product for the first time in nine years, raising it by 9 percent. The company was named among "100 of America's Best Companies" by *Fortune* magazine in 1991. A new international subsidiary, WD-40 Ltd. (Australia), was established that year, to market the product in New Zealand, Southeast Asia, and the Far East, and a sales manager was employed to handle Hong Kong in 1992.

By that year, WD-40 had an 83 percent share of the multipurpose lubricant market, with sales of $99.9 million (an 11.3 percent increase over the previous year's sales of $89.8 million). Stock was trading at $52. Two-thirds of those sales were generated in the United States, and WD-40 Company targeted international expansion as the key to increased growth, setting a goal of a 50:50 ratio.

WD-40 celebrated its 40th anniversary in 1993, breaking the $100 million sales mark with revenues of $104.4 million. Plans for the anniversary bash included a commemorative anniversary can. The company was featured among the "top ten most profitable" companies on the NASDAQ in 1993. Statistics revealed that four out of every five American households used WD-40, and that 81 percent of industrial and trade consumers also chose the product. Weekly sales in the United States amounted to more than one million cans of the petroleum-based lubricant.

FROM ONE-PRODUCT FIRM TO "FORTRESS OF BRANDS"

A major new direction was implemented in December 1995. After more than 40 years as a successful single-product company, WD-40 acquired 3-in-One Oil from the U.K. firm Reckitt & Colman plc for $15.4 million. 3-in-One's history dated back to 1894 when George W. Cole of Asbury Park, New Jersey, invented it as a product with three uses in the care and maintenance of bicycles: lubrication, rust prevention, and cleaning. It eventually developed into a well-established, low-priced, general purpose lubricant. Its positioning as a multiuse product meshed well with that of WD-40, and the two products had carved out specific niches in their method of delivery: 3-in-One's precise applicator drip spout versus WD-40's aerosol spray. At the time of its acquisition by WD-40 Company, 3-in-One was generating annual sales of $14.4 million.

In 1996 WD-40 developed and launched a new product, T.A.L. 5, a premium, extra-strength lubricant (the initials standing for "triple additive lubricant"). A new corporate logo was designed to reflect the integration of the two new products. In that same year, WD-40 changed its propellant from hydrocarbon to CO_2, reducing its volatile organic compounds content to comply with new environmental regulations. WD-40 continued its growth that year, with sales of $131 million and income of $21.3 million. International sales grew to $51.4 million, a 28 percent increase over the previous year, with international business accounting for 44 percent of sales, and with WD-40 marketed in over 135 countries and 30 different languages.

Following Schleif's retirement in 1997, Garry O. Ridge was named president and CEO of WD-40. Hailing from Australia, Ridge had joined the firm ten years earlier to head its Australian subsidiary. Later, he was placed in charge of all international operations. Under

Ridge's leadership, WD-40 quickened both its new product development efforts and its pace of acquisition, concentrating in the latter case on brands already ranking either number one or two in their respective categories. He greatly expanded the firm's portfolio of brands, widening it outside of lubricants; Ridge eventually liked to tell people that WD-40 was in the "squeak, smell, and dirt" business. The leader also conveyed the firm's strategy during this period as expanding from a "brand fortress" focusing on one product to a "fortress of brands."

The "dirt" side entered the picture in April 1999 when WD-40 acquired the Lava brand of heavy-duty hand cleaners from Block Drug Company, Inc., for $23.3 million. Lava, another venerable brand dating back to 1893, was generating a little more than $9 million in annual sales; users of Lava soaps overlapped quite a bit with the users of WD-40 lubricants, making for a complementary fit. At the time Lava was principally available as a bar soap, although a liquid version had been developed but not fully marketed. WD-40 quickly unveiled larger versions of liquid Lava and successfully introduced them into hardware stores. Also in 1999, the company discontinued sales of T.A.L. 5 as the product fell far short of attaining annual sales of $20 million—Ridge's threshold for a product to be considered a success. In the meantime, sales of 3-in-One increased smartly in 1999 when the product was repackaged to include a telescoping applicator spout. With a resemblance to an old-fashioned oilcan, the new 3-in-One packaging featured an extendable spout designed for poking into hard-to-reach places. In 2000 WD-40 followed up its acquisition of Lava with the purchase of Solvol from Unilever. Solvol was the leading brand of heavy-duty soap in Australia, New Zealand, and the Pacific Islands. Revenues passed the $150 million mark in 2000.

In April 2001 WD-40 completed its largest acquisition yet, buying Global Household Brands for a total of $72.9 million, including $66.8 million in cash. WD-40 thereby moved into the household cleaning products sector (encompassing both the "smell" and the "dirt" of Ridge's formulation), picking up X-14 brand mildew stain removers and bathroom cleaners, Carpet Fresh rug deodorizer, and 2000 Flushes, a long-duration automatic toilet bowl cleaner. Collectively, these brands were generating $70.5 million in revenues at the time they were purchased. To fund the deal, WD-40 had to break with tradition. Known historically for paying out most of its earnings in dividends and for having a very low debt load, the company slashed its dividend by 20 percent while its long-term debt ballooned from $10.9 million to $76.6 million.

The debt load was increased further to $96.6 million and the dividend cut again to help fund the May 2002 acquisition of Heartland Corporation for $47.2 million. Via this deal, WD-40 gained Spot Shot carpet stain remover, a neat fit alongside Carpet Fresh. The addition of Spot Shot, a brand generating nearly $33 million in annual sales, helped company sales jump 32 percent in fiscal 2002, to well over $200 million. Despite the dividend cuts, WD-40 was still paying out about 50 percent of its earnings to shareholders in the form of dividends, a rate much higher than that of other consumer products companies.

During 2003, as it worked to integrate and expand the marketing reach of its newer brands and also celebrated its 50th birthday, WD-40 was also active in extending its two oldest brands. The firm introduced the WD-40 Big Blast can, which featured a wide-area spray nozzle for faster and more efficient deliveries of the product over larger areas. Also debuting in 2003 was the 3-in-One Professional line of specialty lubricating products, which included a silicone spray, a white lithium grease, and a high-performance penetrant. This line was expanded the following year with several new formulations, including an engine starter and conditioner. The entire Professional line was introduced in an aerosol format, while the high-performance penetrant was also available in 3-in-One's familiar drip form.

WD-40 also continued its acquisition spree in 2004, completing in April an $11.4 million purchase of the 1001 brand of carpet and household cleaning products from PZ Cussons Plc, and thereby expanding into the U.K. market. Later in the year the Lava brand was extended via the launch of the Lava Pro line of solvent-based heavy-duty hand cleaners. WD-40's most significant line extensions, however, involved the company flagship. Debuting in mid-2005 were the WD-40 Smart Straw and the WD-40 No-Mess Pen. The former addressed a longstanding issue—WD-40 users complaining about losing the thin plastic straw attached to the cans with tape. Market research had revealed that 80 percent of WD-40 users had lost one of the straws. The company responded with Smart Straw, which featured two spraying options: a stream through a newly designed, permanently attached straw or, with the straw folded down, a wide-area spray. The No-Mess Pen, meanwhile, stored a low-odor version of the WD-40 formula in a pen-shaped applicator that offered portability and the ability to precisely apply the product. While WD-40 was a product more typically used by men than women, the company hoped the No-Mess Pen might win over more female customers. In their first year on store shelves, the two new WD-40 products helped push the brand's sales up nearly 10 percent.

WD-40's unbroken record of growth continued in fiscal 2006, when sales increased 9 percent to $286.9 million. Net income, however, rose only 1 percent to $28.1 million in part because of the rising costs of components and raw materials. In addition to the acquisitions and new products, efforts to pursue growth overseas were also paying off, particularly in Europe, and Russia and China were being targeted as two markets with especially high growth potential. During fiscal 2007 WD-40 launched a new phase in its penetration of the Chinese market by opening up a direct sales office in Shanghai. As it continued to develop and expand its "fortress of brands" and pursue global growth, WD-40 Company set ambitious financial goals for itself, including reaching around $400 million in sales and more than $40 million in net income by fiscal 2010.

Heidi Feldman
Updated, David E. Salamie

PRINCIPAL SUBSIDIARIES

WD-40 Manufacturing Company; WD-40 Products (Canada) Ltd.; WD-40 Holdings Limited (U.K.); WD-40 Company Limited (U.K.); WD-40 Company (Australia) Pty. Limited; HPD Holdings Corp.; HPD Laboratories, Inc.; HPD Properties, LLC; Heartland Corporation; Shanghai Wu Di Trading Company Limited (China).

PRINCIPAL COMPETITORS

Radiator Specialty Company; CRC Industries, Inc.; The Clorox Company; Church & Dwight Co., Inc.

FURTHER READING

Barrett, William P., "Johnny One-Note," *Forbes,* March 8, 1999, pp. 76–77.

Bauder, Don, "WD-40 Eases Its Way into Wall Street's Heart," *San Diego Union-Tribune,* November 29, 1998, p. I2.

Bounds, Gwendolyn, "More Than Squeaking By: WD-40 CEO Garry Ridge Repackages a Core Product," *Wall Street Journal,* May 23, 2006, p. B1.

Carnes, Kathryn, "WD-40 Co.: Building on Demonstrable Value," *Lubricants World,* June 2001, pp. 16–17.

Cone, Edward, "WD-40: Small Companies, Big Returns," *Baseline,* October 1, 2003, p. 32.

Cowan, Alison Leigh, "Terminating Outside Sales Staff Proves Costly to WD-40," *New York Times,* July 23, 1993, p. C4.

Freeman, Adam L., "WD-40 Looks to Do Lots More Than Squeak By," *Wall Street Journal,* January 22, 2003, p. B4B.

Freeman, Mike, "WD-40 to Purchase Australian Soap Maker Solvol," *San Diego Union-Tribune,* September 9, 2000, p. C1.

Green, Frank, "Not Just Squeaking By: WD-40's Garry Ridge Promotes Teamwork over Traditional CEO Approach," *San Diego Union-Tribune,* October 4, 2005, p. C1.

——, "WD-40 Buys Household Products Firm," *San Diego Union-Tribune,* March 27, 2001, p. C1.

——, "WD-40: Going Smoothly," *San Diego Union-Tribune,* October 9, 1997, p. C1.

——, "WD-40 to Add 3 Products to Its Inventory," *San Diego Union-Tribune,* September 30, 1999, p. C1.

"How to Be Happy in One Act," *Fortune,* December 19, 1988, p. 179.

Ignelzi, R. J., "WD-40 @ 50," *San Diego Union-Tribune,* November 10, 2003, p. D1.

Kichen, Steve, and Jon Schriber, "Life in the Fast Lane," *Forbes,* November 9, 1981, pp. 188–89.

Kinsman, Michael, "WD-40 Acquires Carpet Spot Remover," *San Diego Union-Tribune,* May 10, 2002, p. C2.

Lazo, Shirley A., "WD-40 Does It Again," *Barron's,* July 3, 1995, p. 38.

Murray, Thomas, "The 5 Best-Managed Companies," *Business Month,* December 1989, pp. 27, 43–43.

"Now 35 Million Consumers Push WD-40's Profit Button," *Inc.,* October 1979, pp. 64–68.

Palmer, Jay, "The Cult of WD-40," *Barron's,* December 3, 2001, pp. 19–20.

Perry, Tony, "This Company Is No Squeaky Wheel When It Comes to Self-Promotion," *Los Angeles Times,* December 16, 1992, p. B1.

Repaci, Louis, "Sampling Program Meets Marketing Objectives of 2 Different Companies," *Marketing News,* April 16, 1982, p. 3.

Richman, Louis S., "What America Makes Best," *Fortune,* Spring/Summer 1991, pp. 78–87.

Riggs, Rod, "Success Builds England Plant for WD-40 Co.," *San Diego Union,* August 17, 1985, p. E1.

"Schleif Named to Two WD-40 Executive Posts," *Los Angeles Times,* September 26, 1990, p. D7.

Tivenan, William, "WD-40," in *Encyclopedia of Consumer Brands,* Vol. 2, edited by Janice Jorgensen, Detroit: St. James Press, 1994, pp. 572–74.

Vezina, Meredith, "Still Slick After 40 Years, WD-40 Keeps Sliding Along," *San Diego Business Journal,* September 13, 1993, p. 16.

Witness Systems, Inc.

---

300 Colonial Center Parkway, Suite 600
Roswell, Georgia 30076-4893
U.S.A.
Telephone: (770) 754-1900
Toll Free: (888) 394-8637
Fax: (770) 754-1873
Web site: http://www.witness.com

Public Company
Incorporated: 1988
Employees: 900
Sales: $221.8 million (2006)
Stock Exchanges: NASDAQ
Ticker Symbol: WITS
NAIC: 511210 Software Publishers

■ ■ ■

Witness Systems, Inc., is the technological leader in software and services designed to assist clients in monitoring and analyzing customer service interactions. Witness Systems products allow supervisors to capture and listen to conversations between employees and customers while simultaneously viewing the computer screens that employees access for information during the course of a call. Call monitoring provides call center managers with the information they need to evaluate and train agents so as to develop a quality service experience for customers. The platform for this technology is Witness's Impact 360 Workforce Optimization, a single architecture that supports the four aspects of call center management: call monitoring, workforce scheduling,

performance evaluation, and e-learning. In addition to its call center and Internet protocol telephony solutions, Witness offers similar monitoring technology with back office and retail financial services solutions under the Impact 360 brand. Witness serves more than 2,000 clients, including many *Fortune* 500 companies. The company provides software licensing and related services from offices in Australia, Brazil, Canada, Germany, Hong Kong, Japan, Mexico, the Netherlands, the United Kingdom, and Vietnam. Development operations are located in India and at the company's Atlanta, Georgia, headquarters. Witness's main international office is located in the United Kingdom.

TECHNOLOGY BREAKTHROUGH

Witness Systems evolved from Tesdata Systems Corporation, a publicly owned, computer testing and monitoring company, known for its Smart network monitoring equipment. The Witness brand developed with voice and data synchronization, an innovation that made the company a technological leader in customer service telephone call monitoring. Voice and data synchronization captured verbal activity from a call and synchronized it with views of the computer screens accessed by the service representative during the call. Thus, Witness gave customer service supervisors the ability to review each customer encounter as it had occurred, in order to identify the training needs of individual representatives. Witness Systems formed as a private company in 1988, focusing on market and product development for the Witness technology.

The next significant technological change occurred in 1991, when Witness Systems transferred its call monitoring application from the mainframe computers to desktop computers. Several improvements accompanied the change, such as preserving on hard disk a digital recording of telephone calls and data screens. Supplemental capabilities included information management for use in employee performance evaluations and information security measures.

Beginning in January 1995, Jim Judson provided strategic direction as president of Witness Systems. Under Judson, the path of product development followed from listening to customers about their specific needs, leading the company to add several enhancements and options. In 1997 the company introduced improvements to the software's security capabilities, file and search capabilities, and replay speed and efficiency. A new central control console facilitated administration. The new Witness Evaluation and Report module improved on existing performance summarization. Simultaneous review, evaluation, and scoring could be achieved using forms, charts, and graphs customized according to the needs of individual call centers. Another enhancement involved the ability to monitor calls based on specific events, such as a sales campaign or by caller, as determined by customer account number. System improvements, ease-of-use, and a focus on accountability garnered the company industry accolades. Four leading call center industry publications named the Witness call monitoring system "Product of the Year" for 1998. Also, *Call Center Magazine* named Judson a Call Center Pioneer, in recognition of his attention to customer needs and requests.

During his three-year tenure at Witness, Judson positioned Witness financially for continued, rapid growth. In 1997, he obtained capital investment from Battery Ventures and a credit facility from Silicon Valley Bank. That year, in July, Witness hired several engineering, finance, and marketing executives to support growth. Overall, staff at the company increased from 22 in early 1997 to 90 in mid-1998. Under Judson's leadership, revenue increased 300 percent, to $6 million in 1997; however, the company reported a loss of $2.3 million. The pace of growth accelerated after Judson left Witness in January 1998. Interim CEO Craig Richards

oversaw the company in 1998. That year Witness opened its first international office, in Leeds, England, a leading base for call centers in the United Kingdom. Overall, sales doubled to $13.2 million in 1998; however, net loss doubled as well, to $5.3 million.

Under new CEO David Gould, Witness moved forward in its pursuit of growth, and by February 2000 the company was prepared for an infusion of new capital investment through an initial public offering of stock. Witness offered 3.8 million shares at $20 per share. The price rose to around $40 per share within the first month of trading. Witness applied the proceeds to pay debt, to fund working capital and operating losses, to invest in sales and marketing and research and product development, and to further international expansion. In April, Witness opened an office in Stockholm, Sweden, to serve the Scandinavian countries and Iceland. The June opening of the Sydney, Australia, office addressed demand in Hong Kong, Singapore, Japan, and New Zealand. In August, Witness opened an office in Amsterdam, Netherlands, to take advantage of the high level of trilingual capabilities of many people.

INTERNET-BASED TECHNOLOGY SPURRING GROWTH

The development of Internet technology opened new areas of expansion for Witness. In February 2000, the company introduced eQuality Interactive, a suite of call monitoring technologies designed for Internet-based customer interactions. The products recorded web chats between agents and customers for performance evaluation and analysis. In March, Witness extended the eQuality Interactive product with eQuality Response, an e-mail interactions monitoring program. In contrast to telephone interactions, written communications required a different set of skills and, therefore, different evaluation techniques. In addition to sorting recordings by customer representative, the software sorted calls by customer, who might encounter more than one representative during different shifts. In November 2001, Witness began to offer monitoring for online self-service transactions, whereby supervisors reviewed customer interfaces with a web site.

A natural extension of the call recordings and performance evaluations provided by eQuality involved the new field of e-learning. In response to customer suggestions, Witness developed e-learning software which utilized information garnered from call monitoring to create online training. In addition to improving the general quality of customer interactions, the e-learning tool offered training for new product or service introductions, special sales, up-selling, and cross-selling. Witness benefited from this early entry into e-learning,

KEY DATES

1988: Innovation in voice-data synchronization provides basis for Witness call monitoring system.

1995: Jim Judson provides strategic leadership as president of Witness Systems.

1998: Customer-focused technology improvements lead to industry accolades for Witness products.

2000: Witness launches Internet-based technologies under the eQuality brand.

2005: Acquisition of Blue Pumpkin provides technology to unify call monitoring solutions on a single platform.

2007: Verint Systems acquires Witness for $950 million.

which proved to be a significant area of growth in 2002 when the economy and other call center service companies stagnated. To build on this strength, Witness launched a Business Consulting Services Group to assist customers in designing their online training program. Further development of e-learning occurred through a partnership with Phasient Learning Technologies, maker of training simulation products. In cooperation with Phasient, Witness developed eQuality Producers, with which call center managers could create training materials from agent calls by editing the calls to produce customer service training simulations.

Another avenue for growth through Internet technology pursued by Witness involved voice over Internet protocol (VoIP). In April 2003 Witness announced its intention to acquire Eyretel plc, a company that provided call monitoring technology to the financial services industry, specifically, in monitoring financial transactions. Eyretel's presence in Europe and Asia complemented Witness's strength in the United States. Through rapid integration with Eyretel, Witness exceeded its goal of achieving $18 million in annual savings through streamlined operations; the company attained that goal within four months. Significantly, the acquisition benefited Witness through Eyretel's lead in the development of VoIP, which would facilitate call monitoring from a remote site. Also, Eyretel had signed a contract with Cisco Systems' Call Manager product line; thus, Witness expanded on that partnership to bundle its software with Cisco's. Witness further strengthened its VoIP capabilities through an agreement

with Avaya, Inc., whose Communication Manager product, as well as its VoIP capabilities, complemented Witness's call monitoring systems. Witness's lead in VoIP supported a 60 percent increase in revenue in 2003, to $108 million. By September 2004, Witness introduced enhanced Internet protocol (IP) software for recording, categorizing, and storing IP telephony calls. In particular eQuality Contact Store enhanced user handling from a remote site and integrated calls from all locations for easier access and navigation through stored material.

Other new developments in call monitoring technology involved improvements to eQuality's analytical capabilities. In March 2004, Witness offered integrated information to ease navigation through recorded customer interactions and to facilitate identification of patterns. In April 2004, Witness formed an Alliance with CallMiner, Inc., in order to combine the eQuality customer interaction recording software with CallMiner's CoreEngine and TrendMiner programs. Speech recognition and related technologies would be applied to improve information retrieval. Potentially, a new product could chart topics that arose during customer calls through key words or phrases and then provide statistics for trend analysis. The alliance culminated in eQuality Call Miner, which analyzed speech patterns to identify specific words or phrases which could be utilized to choose calls for performance analysis by conversational context. Also, the voice recording could be converted to text for manager analysis.

ACQUISITIONS SUPPORT COMPREHENSIVE PRODUCT STRUCTURING

During 2005 and 2006, Witness purchased several companies of complementary technologies with the intention to unify eQuality products into a comprehensive system to be available on a single platform. Toward that end, in December 2004 Witness announced it would acquire Blue Pumpkin Software, Inc., a leader in performance optimization software for workforce management. Blue Pumpkin's forecasting, scheduling, adherence, and planning software would enhance similar applications offered by Witness. Located in Silicon Valley, Blue Pumpkin specialized in small- and medium-sized businesses and had offices in Petach Tikva, Israel. The $75 million transaction, completed in February, entailed a payment of $40 million from existing cash resources and $35 million in Witness stock, or 2.1 million shares. In order to retain the quality staff at Blue Pumpkin, Witness offered stock options to 120 employees.

Synthesis of Blue Pumpkin and Witness capabilities manifested in the October 2005 introduction of Witness Impact 360 software and services. With the new product Witness offered clients a unified architectural platform and user interface which integrated the four primary functions of call center management: call monitoring, workforce scheduling, performance evaluation, and e-learning. Hence, 360 Impact was intended to optimize and simplify call center management by connecting separate but interrelated functions under one enterprise software system. Furthermore, the system would provide significant cost savings to customers who would otherwise purchase separate programs for each function. Product upgrades in 2006 included improvements to schedule forecasting and implementation capabilities, particularly in collaboration with outsourced call centers. Also, enhancements would allow for more accurate identification of peak and low call times.

Three additional acquisitions furthered development of the 360 Impact product, particularly for the retail financial services industry. In November 2006, Witness acquired Demos Solutions Consulting Group, Ltd., and Exametric, Inc., both of whom catered to the financial services industry with enterprise productivity and resource planning solutions. Hence, with the acquisitions, Witness sought to expand its customer base to banking entities. Witness paid $29 million in cash for both companies, and would pay as much as $18 million over the next few years, depending on revenue growth. The two acquisitions led to the November 2006 introduction of its specialized workforce management software, called Impact 360 for Retail Financial Services. The program was designed to synchronize retail outlets, customer contact centers, and certain accounting functions under one enterprise solution. Impact 360 would facilitate analysis and action on information about employee performance and customer interface. Other capabilities included forecasting customer volume in order to determine staffing; tracking, capturing, and analysis of employee keystrokes and screen navigation; customization of forms, reports, and graphs to summarize and evaluate employee performance; and determining training requirements. With the third acquisition, of Amae Software in December 2006, Witness obtained a user-friendly customer survey software that would enhance Witness's Impact 360 Workforce Optimization suite with a customer feedback option.

Witness's technological lead with the comprehensive Impact 360 package garnered repeat customer business, as well as new clients. In the last quarter of 2005, Impact 360 accounted for 25 percent of sales, compared to only 10 percent of sales from bundling for complete package solutions during the previous quarter. During 2005, Witness added 357 new clients and 75 percent of license revenue originated from sales to existing clients. Growth continued apace in 2006, with revenues reaching $221 million.

OWNERSHIP AND EXECUTIVE CHANGES

In early 2007 a number of surprising events occurred at Witness Systems. First, a Securities and Exchange Commission investigation into backdating stock options, which began in the fall of 2006, led to the resignation of CEO Dave Gould. Then, rumors swirled around the possibility of NICE Systems, Inc., acquiring Witness. Unexpectedly, Verint Systems, Inc., won the competitive bidding process, with a $950 million cash offer; it was $150 million higher than NICE's bid. Finally, despite an options backdating probe at Verint, which led to the delisting of Verint from the NASDAQ, the acquisition process continued, awaiting only the approval of shareholders and boards of directors.

The merger between Verint and Witness would combine each company's unique area of superiority, Witness's in call monitoring and Verint's in performance analysis. Also, the two companies offered strengths in different markets, with Verint operating in defense and enterprise sectors and Witness operating in numerous civilian industries. Despite these different areas of expertise, the two companies shared similar corporate cultures, with an orientation to customer-focused product development.

Mary Tradii

PRINCIPAL COMPETITORS

ASC Telecom LP; Autonomy Corporation plc; Cacti, Inc.; Consensus Communications, Inc.; ECI Telecom, Ltd.; Envision Telephony, Inc.; NICE Systems, Ltd.

FURTHER READING

Bednarz, Ann, "Witness Watches Web Customers Help Themselves; New Tools Gauge the Effectiveness of Customer Self-Service Tools," *Network World,* November 12, 2001, p. 25.

Benesh, Peter, "Witness Systems, Inc., Roswell, Georgia; Remember, the Goal Is Customer 'Service,'" *Investor's Business Daily,* March 31, 2004, p. A08.

"Call Center Product Roundup," *Telecommuting Review: The Gordon Report,* September 1, 1991, p. 6.

Colkin Cuneo, Eileen, "Witness Buying Financial Transaction Recording Firm," *CommWeb,* April 23, 2003.

Dawson, Keith, "Witness Partners with Simulation Developer," *CommWeb,* January 3, 2003.

"Dynatech, Tesdata Call off Merger Talks," *Electronic News*, June 25, 1984, p. 71.

"FCG Soft Sets up Centre for Witness," *Asia Africa Intelligence Wire*, February 12, 2005.

Fraswer, Sarah, "Witness[ing] a Shift in the Call Center," *Customer Interface*, November–December 2002, p. 42.

Fuffardi, Michelle, "Witness' Impact 360 Workforce Optimization for the Retail Financial Services Industry," *CommWeb*, November 20, 2006.

Habib, Shiri, "'This Is a Good Deal for Verint,'" *Israel Business Arena*, February 13, 2007.

Loughin, Nancy, "Witness System a Good Tool for Remote Supervision of Online Workers—As Long As It's Used Properly," *Telecommuting Review: The Gordon Report*, November 1, 1987, p. 8.

O'Herron, Jennifer, "Using Speech Rec to Mine Recorded Calls," *CommWeb*, April 27, 2004.

Pender, Lee, "Suite Keeps Eye on Service Reps," *PC Week*, January 17, 2000, p. 17.

Peters, Andy, "Alpharetta Software-Maker Opens Office in England," *Atlanta Business Chronicle*, August 7, 1998, p. 10A.

Sangaran, Shyla, "Enhanced Call Centre Workforce Management," *Asia Africa Intelligence Wire*, November 7, 2005.

Schelmetic, Tracey E., "Witness Systems Announces Acquisitions," *Customer Interaction Solutions*, November 2006, p. 15.

———, "Witness Systems Announces Enhancements to Impact 360," *Customer Interaction Solutions*, August 2006, p. 19.

Seyfer, Jessie, "Backdating Shadows Don't Darken $950 Million Deal," *CommWeb*, March 15, 2007.

Sheff, Harry, "Witness Systems Updates Impact 360 Recording Engine; The Workforce Optimization Software Gets an Upgrade, One Month After Unveiling," *CommWeb*, November 15, 2005.

Walker, Tom, "Software Firm Will Face SEC Inquiry," *Atlanta Journal-Constitution*, October 31, 2006.

———, "Software Maker Witness Systems to Be Acquired by Verint in $950 Million Deal," *Atlanta Journal-Constitution*, February 13, 2007.

"Witness Australian Expansion," *Call Center Solutions*, June 2000, p. 41.

"Witness' e-Learning Helps Contact Centers to Train and Retain Agents," *Customer Interface*, August 2000, p. 81.

"Witness Establishes Nordic Presence," *Call Center Solutions*, April 2000, p. 38.

"Witness Improves Analysis Tools; An Integration Between Two Data Analysis Components of Their eQuality Suite Gives Users More Information About What's Really Going on in the Call Center," *CommWeb*, May 18, 2004.

"Witness India Centre to Be APAC Hub," *Business Line*, March 4, 2006.

"Witness' New Customer Feedback Software; Witness Systems Acquired Amae Software to Add Their Customer Survey Tools to the Impact 360 Workforce Optimization Suite," *CommWeb*, December 12, 2006.

"Witness Opens in Amsterdam," *Call Center Solutions*, August 2000, p. 44.

"Witness/Pumpkin Pitch End-to-End Workforce Optimization," *WebbCom*, March 9, 2005.

"Witness Releases Enhanced Workforce Management Solution," *Customer Interface Solutions*, June 2005, p. 36.

"Witness Systems Allies with CallMiner," *Customer Interaction Solutions*, April 2003, p. 30.

"Witness Systems Buys Blue Pumpkin for $75m," *Asia Africa Intelligence Wire*, December 21, 2004.

"Witness Systems Debuts New Training Tool," *Call Center*, December 1, 2003, p. 8.

"Witness Systems Enhances IP Recording Software," *Customer Interaction Solutions*, September 2004, p. 31.

"Witness Systems Expands Business Consulting Services," *Customer Interaction Solutions*, August 2002, p. 16.

"Witness Systems Introduces eQuality," *Call Center Solutions*, February 2000, p. 33.

"Witness Systems Presents E-mail Evaluation Application," *Call Center Solutions*, March 2000, p. 26.

Index to Companies

Listings in this index are arranged in alphabetical order under the company name. Company names beginning with a letter or proper name such as Eli Lilly & Co. will be found under the first letter of the company name. Definite articles (The, Le, La) are ignored for alphabetical purposes as are forms of incorporation that precede the company name (AB, NV). Company names printed in **bold** type have full, historical essays on the page numbers appearing in bold. Updates to entries that appeared in earlier volumes are signified by the notation **(upd.)**. Company names in light type are references within an essay to that company, not full historical essays. This index is cumulative with volume numbers printed in bold type.

A

A and A Limousine Renting, Inc., **26** 62
A & A Medical Supply, **61** 206
A&E Plastics, **12** 377
A&E Television Networks, 32 3–7
A&K Petroleum Company *see* Kerr-McGee Corp.
A&M Records, **23** 389
A&N Foods Co., *see* Nippon Suisan Kaisha, Ltd.
A&P *see* The Great Atlantic & Pacific Tea Company, Inc.
A & W Brands, Inc., 25 3–5 *see also* Cadbury Schweppes PLC.
A-dec, Inc., 53 3–5
á la Zing, **62** 259
A-Mark Financial Corporation, 71 3–6

A-1 Supply *see* International Game Technology.
A-R Technologies, **48** 275
A.A. Mathews *see* CRSS Inc.
A. Ahlström Oy *see* Ahlstrom Corp.
A.B. Chance Industries Co., Inc. *see* Hubbell Inc.
A.B.Dick Company, 28 6–8
A.B. Leasing Corp., *see* Bozzuto's, Inc.
A.B. Watley Group Inc., 45 3–5
A-BEC Mobility, **11** 487
A.C. Delco, **26** 347, 349
A.C. Moore Arts & Crafts, Inc., 30 3–5
A.C. Nielsen Company, 13 3–5 *see also* ACNielsen Corp.
A/E/C/ Systems International, *see* Penton Media, Inc.
A.E. Fitkin & Company, **6** 592–93; **50** 37
A.E. Lottes, **29** 86
A.G. Becker, **20** 260
A.G. Edwards, Inc., 8 3–5; **32** 17–21 **(upd.)**
A.G. Industries, Inc., *see* American Greetings Corp.
A.G. Stanley Ltd. *see* The Boots Company PLC.
A.H. Belo Corporation, 10 3–5; **30** 13–17 **(upd.)**
A.H. Robins Co., *see* Wyeth.
A. Hirsch & Son, **30** 408
A. Hölscher GmbH, **53** 195
A. Johnson & Co. *see* Axel Johnson Group.
A.L. Pharma Inc., 12 3–5 *see also* Alpharma Inc.
A.L. Van Houtte Inc. *see* Van Houtte Inc.
A. Leon Capel and Sons, Inc. *see* Capel Inc.

A.M. Castle & Co., **25** 6–8
A. Michel et Cie., **49** 84
A. Moksel AG, 59 3–6
A. Nelson & Co. Ltd., 75 3–6
A.O. Smith Corporation, 11 3–6; **40** 3–8 **(upd.)**
A.P. Møller - Maersk A/S, 57 3–6
A.P. Orleans, Inc., *see* Orleans Homebuilders, Inc.
A.S. Abell Co., **IV** 678
A.S. Watson & Company Ltd., 84 1–4
A.S. Yakovlev Design Bureau, 15 3–6
A. Schilling & Company *see* McCormick & Company, Inc.
A. Schulman, Inc., 8 6–8; **49** 3–7 **(upd.)**
A. Sulka & Co., **29** 457
A.T. Cross Company, 17 3–5; **49** 8–12 **(upd.)**
A.T. Massey Coal Company, Inc., **34** 164; **57** 236
A.T. Mays, **55** 90
A-T-O Inc. *see* Figgie International, Inc.
A.W. Baulderstone Holdings Pty. Ltd., **55** 62
A.W. Faber-Castell Unternehmensverwaltung GmbH & Co., 51 3–6
A. Wilhelmsen A/S, **74** 278
AA Energy Corp., *see* AMR Corp.
AADC Holding Company, Inc., **62** 347
AAF-McQuay Incorporated, 26 3–5
AAI Corporation, **37** 399
Aai.FosterGrant, Inc., **60** 131, 133
AAON, Inc., 22 3–6
AAPT, **54** 355–57
AAR Corp., 28 3–5
Aardman Animations Ltd., 61 3–5
Aareal Bank AG *see* DEPFA BANK PLC.
Aarhus United A/S, 68 3–5

Adage Systems International, Inc., *see*
Systems & Computer Technology
Corp.
Adam, Meldrum & Anderson Company
(AM&A), **16** 61–62; **50** 107
Adam Opel AG, **7** 6–8; **21** 3–7 (upd.);
61 6–11 (upd.)
Adams/Cates Company, **21** 257
Adams Childrenswear *see* Sears plc.
The Adams Express Company, **86** 1–5
Adams Golf, Inc., **37** 3–5
Adams Media Corporation *see* F&W
Publications, Inc.
Adaptec, Inc., **31** 3–6
Adar Associates, Inc. *see* Scientific-Atlanta,
Inc.
ADC of Greater Kansas City, Inc., **22** 443
ADC Telecommunications, Inc., **10**
18–21; **30** 6–9 (upd.)
Addison Communications Plc, **45** 272
Addison Corporation, **31** 399
Addison Structural Services, Inc., **26** 433
Addison Wesley, **IV** 659
Adecco S.A., **36** 7–11 (upd.)
Adeletom Aviation L.L.C., **61** 100
Adelphia Communications Corporation,
17 6–8; **52** 7–10 (upd.)
Ademco *see* Alarm Device Manufacturing
Co.
Adero Inc., **45** 202
ADESA, Inc., **71** 7–10
Adesso-Madden, Inc., **37** 372
ADI Group Limited *see* AHL Services,
Inc.
Adia S.A., **6** 9–11 *see also* Adecco S.A.
Adiainvest S.A. *see* Adecco S.A.
adidas Group AG, **14** 6–9; **33** 7–11
(upd.); **75** 12–17 (upd.)
Aditya Birla Group, **79** 1–5
Adler, **23** 219
Adler Line *see* Transatlantische
Dampfschiffahrts Gesellschaft.
ADM *see* Archer Daniels Midland Co.
ADME Bioanalyses SAS *see* Eurofins
Scientific S.A.
Administaff, Inc., **52** 11–13
Administracion Corporativa y Mercantil,
S.A. de C.V., **37** 178
Admiral Co. *see* Maytag Corp.
ADNOC *see* Abu Dhabi National Oil Co.
Adobe Systems Incorporated, **10** 22–24;
33 12–16 (upd.)
Adolf Würth GmbH & Co. KG, **49**
13–15
Adolfo Dominguez S.A., **72** 3–5
Adolph Coors Company, **I** 236–38; **13**
9–11 (upd.); **36** 12–16 (upd.) *see also*
Molson Coors Brewing Co.
Adolphe Lafont, *see* Vivarte SA.
ADP *see* Automatic Data Processing, Inc.
Adria Produtos Alimenticios, Ltd., **12** 411
Adrienne Vittadini, **15** 291
ADS *see* Aerospace Display Systems.
Adstaff Associates, Ltd., **26** 240
Adsteam, **60** 101
ADT Automotive, **71** 8–9
ADT Ltd., **26** 410; **28** 486; **63** 403

ADT Security Services, Inc., **12** 9–11;
44 6–9 (upd.)
Adtran Inc., **22** 17–20
Adtranz *see* Bombardier Inc.
Advacel, **18** 20; **43** 17
Advance Auto Parts, Inc., **57** 10–12
Advance Circuits Inc., **49** 234
Advance Gems & Jewelry Co., Ltd., **62**
371
Advance/Newhouse Communications, **42**
114
Advance Publications Inc., **IV** 581–84;
19 3–7 (upd.)
Advanced Aerodynamics & Structures Inc.
see Mooney Aerospace Group Ltd.
Advanced Broadband, L.P., **70** 325
Advanced Casino Systems Corporation,
21 277
Advanced Circuits Inc., **67** 3–5
Advanced Colortech Inc., **56** 238
Advanced Communications Engineering
see Scientific-Atlanta, Inc.
Advanced Communications Inc. *see*
Metrocall, Inc.
Advanced Data Management Group S.A.,
23 212
Advanced Fiberoptic Technologies, **30** 267
Advanced Fibre Communications, Inc.,
63 3–5
Advanced Gravis, **28** 244; **69** 243
Advanced Logic Research, Inc., *see*
Gateway, Inc.
Advanced Marine Enterprises, Inc., **18**
370
Advanced Marketing Services, Inc., **34**
3–6
Advanced Medical Optics, Inc., **79** 6–9
Advanced Metallurgy, Inc., **29** 460
Advanced Micro Devices, Inc., **6**
215–17; **30** 10–12 (upd.)
**Advanced Neuromodulation Systems,
Inc.**, **73** 14–17
Advanced Parking Systems Ltd., **58** 184
Advanced Plasma Systems, Inc., **48** 299
Advanced Pollution Instrumentation Inc.,
62 362
Advanced Semiconductor Engineering, **73**
301
Advanced Structures, Inc., *see* Essef Corp.
Advanced System Applications, **11** 395
Advanced Technology Laboratories, Inc.,
9 6–8
Advanced Telecommunications, Inc. *see*
Eschelon Telecom, Inc.
Advanced Tissue Sciences Inc., **41** 377
Advanced Web Technologies, *see* Miner
Group Int.
AdvanceMed LLC, **45** 146
AdvancePCS, Inc., **63** 336
Advanstar Communications, Inc., **57**
13–17
Advanta Corporation, **8** 9–11; **38** 10–14
(upd.)
Advanta Partners, LP, **42** 322
Advantage Company, *see* LDDS-Metro
Communications, Inc.
The Advantage Group, Inc., *see*
Habersham Bancorp.

Advantage Health Plans, Inc., **11** 379
Advantage Health Systems, Inc., **25** 383
Advantage Publishers Group, **34** 5
Advantest Corporation, **39** 350, 353
Advantica Restaurant Group, Inc., **27**
16–19 (upd.)
Advantra International NV *see* Punch
International N.V.
Adventist Health, **53** 6–8
The Advertising Council, Inc., **76** 3–6
Advertising Unlimited, Inc., *see* R.L. Polk
& Co.
The Advisory Board Company, **80** 1–4
Advo, Inc., **6** 12–14; **53** 9–13 (upd.)
Advocat Inc., **46** 3–5
AEA *see* United Kingdom Atomic Energy
Authority.
AEA Investors Inc., **22** 169, 171; **28** 380;
30 328
AECOM Technology Corporation, **79**
10–13
AEG A.G., **I** 409–11
AEG Hausgeräte, **53** 128
Aegek S.A., **64** 6–8
Aegis Group plc, **6** 15–16
AEGON N.V., **III** 177–79; **50** 8–12
(upd.) *see also* Transamerica–An
AEGON Company
AEI Music Network Inc., **35** 19–21
Aeneas Venture Corp., **26** 502
AEON Co., Ltd., **V** 96–99; **68** 6–10
(upd.)
AEP *see* American Electric Power Co.
AEP Industries, Inc., **36** 17–19
Aer Lingus Group plc, **34** 7–10
Aera Energy LLC, **41** 359
Aérazur, **36** 529
Aereos Del Mercosur, **68** 365
Aerial Communications Inc., **31** 452
Aeries Health Care Corporation, **68** 299
Aero Mayflower Transit Company *see*
Mayflower Group Inc.
Aero O/Y *see* Finnair Oy.
**Aeroflot—Russian International
Airlines**, **6** 57–59; **29** 7–10 (upd.)
Aerojet-General Corp., **63** 6–9
Aerolíneas Argentinas S.A., **33** 17–19;
69 9–12 (upd.)
Aeroméxico, **20** 168
Aeromotive Systems Co., **55** 31
Aeronautics Leasing, Inc., **39** 33
Aeronca Inc., **46** 6–8
Aeropar Participacoes S.A., **73** 166
Aeropharm Technology, Inc., **63** 233–34
Aéroports de Paris, **33** 20–22
Aeroquip Corporation, **16** 7–9 *see also*
Eaton Corp.
Aerosance Inc., **62** 362
Aerosonic Corporation, **69** 13–15
Aerospace Display Systems, **36** 158
Aerospace International Services, **41** 38
Aerospace Products International, Inc., **49**
141
The Aérospatiale Group, **7** 9–12; **21**
8–11 (upd.) *see also* European
Aeronautic Defence and Space
Company EADS N.V.
Aerostar, **33** 359–61

Aircraft Modular Products, **30** 73
Aircraft Turbine Center, Inc., **28** 3
AirFoyle Ltd., **53** 50
Airgas, Inc., 54 7–10
Airguard Industries, Inc., *see* CLARCOR Inc.
AirLib *see* Société d'Exploitation AOM.
Airline Interiors Inc., **41** 368–69
Airlines of Britain Holdings, **34** 398; **38** 105–06
Airlink Pty Ltd *see* Qantas Airways Ltd.
Airopak Corporation *see* PVC Container Corp.
Airport Leather Concessions LLC, **58** 369
Airrest S.A., **64** 359
Airshop Ltd., *see* Jalate Inc.
Airstream *see* Thor Industries, Inc.
AirTouch Communications, 11 10–12
see also Vodafone Group PLC.
Airtours Plc, 27 27–29, 90, 92
AirTran Holdings, Inc., 22 21–23
AirWair Ltd., **23** 399, 401–02
AirWays Corporation *see* AirTran Holdings, Inc.
Aisin Seiki Co., Ltd., III 415–16; **48** 3–5 (upd.)
AIT Worldwide, **47** 286–87
Aitchison & Colegrave *see* Bradford & Bingley PLC.
Aitken, Inc., **26** 433
AITS *see* American International Travel Service.
Aiuruoca, **25** 85
Aiwa Co., Ltd., 30 18–20
Ajax Repair & Supply, **58** 75
Ajinomoto Co., Inc., II 463–64; **28** 9–11 (upd.)
AJS Auto Parts Inc., **15** 246
AK Steel Holding Corporation, 19 8–9; **41** 3–6 (upd.)
Akamai Technologies, Inc., 71 18–21
Akane Securities Co. Ltd., *see* ORIX Corp.
AKAY Flavours & Aromatics Ltd., **70** 56
Akbank TAS, 79 18–21
Akemi, Inc. *see* FinishMaster, Inc.; Maxco Inc.
Aker RGI, **32** 99
AKG Acoustics GmbH, 62 3–6
AKH Co. Inc., **20** 63
Akin, Gump, Strauss, Hauer & Feld, L.L.P., 33 23–25
Akorn, Inc., 32 22–24
Akro-Mills Inc., *see* Myers Industries, Inc.
Akron Extruders Inc., **53** 230
Aktia Sparbank Abp, **69** 177, 179
Aktiebolaget SKF, III 622–25; **38** 28–33 (upd.)
Aktieselskabet Dampskibsselskabet Svendborg, **57** 3, 5
Akzo Nobel N.V., 13 21–23; **41** 7–10 (upd.)
Al-Amin Co. For Securities & Investment Funds *see* Dallah Albaraka Group.
Al Copeland Enterprises, Inc., **7** 26–28; **32** 13–15
Al Habtoor Group L.L.C., 87 9–12

Al-Tawfeek Co. For Investment Funds Ltd. *see* Dallah Albaraka Group.
ALA *see* Americal Library Association.
Alaadin Middle East-Ersan, **IV** 564
Alabama Farmers Cooperative, Inc., 63 20–22
Alabama Gas Corporation, **21** 207–08
Alabama National BanCorporation, 75 21–23
Alabama Power Company, **38** 445, 447–48
Alabama Shipyards Inc., **21** 39–40
Aladdin Mills Inc., **19** 276; **63** 300
Alagasco, **21** 207–08
Alagroup, **45** 337
Alain Afflelou SA, 53 30–32
Alain Manoukian *see* Groupe Alain Manoukian.
Alamac Knit Fabrics, Inc., *see* WestPoint Stevens Inc.
Alamito Company, **6** 590
Alamo Group Inc., 32 25–28
Alamo Rent A Car, 6 348–50; **24** 9–12 (upd.); **84** 5–11 (upd.)
Alamo Water Refiners, Inc. *see* The Marmon Group, Inc.
ALANTEC Corporation, *see* FORE Systems, Inc.
ALARIS Medical Systems, Inc., 65 17–20
Alarm Device Manufacturing Company, *see* Pittway Corp.
Alaron Inc., *see* The Marmon Group, Inc.
Alascom, Inc. *see* AT&T Corp.
Alaska Air Group, Inc., 6 65–67; **29** 11–14 (upd.)
Alaska Commercial Company, **12** 363
Alaska Native Wireless LLC, **60** 264
Alaska Railroad Corporation, 60 6–9
Alaska Steel Co., **19** 381
Alatas Mammoet, **26** 279
Alba Foods, **27** 197; **43** 218
Alba-Waldensian, Inc., 30 21–23 *see also* E.I. du Pont de Nemours and Co.
Albany Cheese, **23** 219
Albany International Corporation, 8 12–14; **51** 11–14 (upd.)
Albany Molecular Research, Inc., 77 9–12
Albaugh Inc., **62** 19
Albemarle Corporation, 59 23–25
Alberici Corporation, 76 12–14
Albert E. Reed & Co. Ltd. *see* Reed International PLC.
The Albert Fisher Group plc, 41 11–13
Albert Heijn NV, *see* Koninklijke Ahold N.V. (Royal Ahold).
Albert Nipon, Inc., *see* The Leslie Fay Company, Inc.
Albert's Organics, Inc. *see* United Natural Foods, Inc.
Alberta Energy Company Ltd., 16 10–12; **43** 3–6 (upd.)
Alberta Gas Trunk Line Company, Ltd. *see* Nova Corporation of Alberta.
Alberto-Culver Company, 8 15–17; **36** 23–27 (upd.)

Albertson's, Inc., II 601–03; **7** 19–22 (upd.); **30** 24–28 (upd.); **65** 21–26 (upd.)
Albion Industries, Inc., *see* The Marmon Group, Inc.
Albright & Wilson Ltd., **12** 351; **38** 378, 380; **50** 282; **59** 25
Albuquerque Gas & Electric Company *see* Public Service Company of New Mexico.
Albuquerque Gas, Electric Light and Power Company, **6** 561–62
Alcan Aluminium Limited, IV 9–13; **31** 7–12 (upd.)
Alcan Inc., **60** 338
Alcatel S.A., 9 9–11; **36** 28–31 (upd.)
Alchem Capital Corp., *see* Delta Woodside Industries, Inc.
Alchem Plastics *see* Spartech Corp.
Alco Health Services Corporation, III 9–10 *see also* AmeriSource Health Corp.
Alco Office Products Inc., **24** 362
Alco Standard Corporation, I 412–13
ALCO Trade Show Services, **26** 102
Alcoa Inc., 56 7–11 (upd.)
Alden Merrell Corporation, **23** 169
Alderwoods Group, Inc., 68 11–15 (upd.)
Aldi Einkauf GmbH & Co. OHG, **13** 24–26; **86** 10–14 (upd.)
Aldila Inc., **46** 12–14
Aldiscon, **37** 232
Aldus Corporation, 10 34–36 *see also* Adobe Systems Inc.
Alert Centre Inc., **32** 373
Alès Groupe, 81 10–13
Alestra, **19** 12
Alex & Ivy, *see* The Bombay Company, Inc.
Alex Lee Inc., 18 6–9; **44** 10–14 (upd.)
Alexander & Alexander Services Inc., 10 37–39 *see also* Aon Corp.
Alexander & Baldwin, Inc., 10 40–42; **40** 14–19 (upd.)
Alexander Hamilton Life Insurance Co., *see* Household International, Inc.
Alexander Howden Group, *see* Alexnder & Alexander Services Inc.
Alexander's, Inc., 45 14–16
Alexandria Petroleum Co., **51** 113
Alfa Corporation, 60 10–12
Alfa-Laval AB, III 417–21; **64** 13–18 (upd.)
Alfa Romeo, 13 27–29; **36** 32–35 (upd.)
Alfa, S.A. de C.V., 19 10–12
Alfa Trading Company, **23** 358
Alfalfa's Markets, *see* Wild Oats Markets, Inc.
Alfesca hf, 82 1–4
alfi Zitzmann, **60** 364
Alfred A. Knopf, Inc., *see* Random House, Inc.
Alfred Bullows & Sons, Ltd., **21** 64
Alfred Dunhill Limited, *see* Vendôme Luxury Group plc.
Alfred Marks Bureau, Ltd. *see* Adia S.A.
Alfred McAlpine plc, **51** 138

Atlantic Container Lines Ltd., **23** 161
Atlantic Energy, Inc., 6 449–50
Atlantic Envelope Company, **54** 251–52, 255
The Atlantic Group, 23 31–33
Atlantic Mutual, **41** 65
Atlantic Premium Brands, Ltd., 57 56–58
Atlantic Records Group, **26** 150; **64** 115
Atlantic Refining Co. *see* Atlantic Richfield Co.
Atlantic Research Corporation, *see* Sequa Corp.
Atlantic Richfield Company, IV 375–77; 31 31–34 (upd.)
The Atlantic Seaboard Dispatch *see* GATX.
Atlantic Southeast Airlines, Inc., 47 29–31
Atlantic Southern Properties, Inc. *see* Atlantic Energy, Inc.
Atlantic Wholesalers Ltd., *see* George Weston Ltd.
Atlantis Energy Inc., **44** 182
Atlantis Group, Inc., **17** 16; **19** 50, 390
Atlantis Plastics, Inc., 85 14–17
Atlantis Resort and Casino *see* Sun International Hotels Ltd.
Atlas Air, Inc., 39 33–35
Atlas Air Worldwide Holdings, Inc., **60** 238
Atlas America, Inc., **42** 311
Atlas Bolt & Screw Company *see* The Marmon Group, Inc.
Atlas Cement Company, **31** 252
Atlas Copco AB, III 425–27; 28 37–41 (upd.); 85 18–24 (upd.)
Atlas Eléctrica S.A., *see* Electrolux AB.
Atlas Hotels, Inc., **V** 164
Atlas Securities, **47** 160
Atlas Tag & Label, *see* BISSELL, Inc.
Atlas Van Lines, Inc., 14 37–39
Atlas Ventures, **25** 96
Atlatec SA de CV, **39** 192
Atmel Corporation, 17 32–34
Atmos Energy Corporation, 43 56–58
Atmospherix Ltd. *see* Blyth Industries, Inc.
Atochem S.A., I 303–04, 676 *see also* Total-Fina-Elf.
AtoHaas Americas, **26** 425
Atoll Soft Nederland BV, **72** 35
Atomic Austria GmbH, **41** 14–16
Atos Origin S.A., 69 45–47
Atossa HealthCare, Inc. *see* Nastech Pharmaceutical Company Inc.
ATR, **7** 9, 11
Atrix Laboratories, Inc. *see* QLT Inc.
ATS *see* Magasins Armand Thiéry et Sigrand.
ATT Microelectrica España, **V** 339
Attachmate Corporation, 56 19–21
ATTC Manufacturing Inc., **48** 5
Attic Futura *see* PMP Ltd.
Attica Enterprises S.A., 64 43–45
Atwater McMillian *see* St. Paul Companies, Inc.
Atwood Mobil Products, 53 52–55
ATX Technologies, Inc., **32** 374

ATx Telecom Systems Inc., **31** 124
Au Bon Marché, **26** 160
Au Bon Pain Co., Inc., 18 35–38
AU Optronics Corporation, 67 38–40
Au Printemps S.A., V 9–11 *see also* Pinault-Printemps-Redoute S.A.
Aubert & Duval Holding *see* Eramet.
Auchan, 37 22–24
The Auchter Company, 78 21–24
Auctentia Subastas S.L., **60** 146
Audible Inc., 79 42–45
Audifon U.K. Ltd., **56** 338
Audio Accessories, Inc., **37** 301
Audio International Inc., **36** 159
Audio King Corporation, 24 52–54
Audio/Video Affiliates, Inc., *see* REX Stores Corp.
Audiofina, **44** 377
Audiovox Corporation, 34 48–50
Audits & Surveys Worldwide Inc., **28** 501, 504
Auerhahn, **60** 364
Augat Inc., **54** 373
Aughton Group, *see* Associated British Foods plc.
August Max Woman *see* United States Shoe Corp.
August Schell Brewing Company Inc., 59 66–69
August Storck KG, 66 21–23
Ault Incorporated, 34 51–54
Auntie Anne's, Inc., 35 55–57
Aura Books plc, **34** 5
Aurea Concesiones de Infraestructuras SA *see* Abertis Infraestructuras, S.A.
Aurec Information and Directory Systems *see* Amdocs Ltd.
Aurigene Discovery Technologies Limited, **59** 168
AurionGold Limited, **61** 293
Aurora Casket Company, Inc., 56 22–24
Aurora Dairy Corporation, **37** 195, 198
Aurora Foods Inc., 32 67–69
Aurora Systems, Inc., **21** 135
Aurrera S.A., **35** 459
Aurum Corp., **38** 431
Ausimont S.p.A., *see* Solvay S.A.
Ausplay, *see* Little Tikes Co.
Aussedat-Rey, **23** 366, 368
Austal Limited, 75 36–39
The Austin Company, 8 41–44; 72 14–18 (upd.)
Austin Nichols, *see* Pernod Ricard S.A.
Austin Powder Company, 76 32–35
Austin Quality Foods, **36** 313
Austins Steaks & Saloon, Inc. *see* WesterN SizzliN Corp.
Australia and New Zealand Banking Group Limited, II 187–90; 52 35–40 (upd.)
Australian Airlines *see* Qantas Airways Ltd.
Australian and Overseas Telecommunications Corporation *see* Telecom Australia.
Australian Consolidated Press, **27** 42; **54** 299
Australian Mutual Provident Society, **IV** 61, 697

Australian Tankerships Pty. Ltd., **25** 471
Australian Telecommunications Corporation, **6** 342
Australian Wheat Board *see* AWB Ltd.
Austria Tabak, **55** 200
Austrian Airlines AG (Österreichische Luftverkehrs AG), 33 49–52
Austrian Star Gastronomie GmbH, **48** 63
Authentic Fitness Corp., 20 41–43; 51 30–33 (upd.)
Auto Helloes Co. Ltd., **76** 37
Auto Parts Wholesale, **26** 348
Auto Shack *see* AutoZone, Inc.
Auto Value Associates, Inc., 25 26–28
Autobacs Seven Company Ltd., 76 36–38
Autobytel Inc., 47 32–34
Autocam Corporation, 51 34–36
Autodesk, Inc., 10 118–20
Autogrill SpA, 49 31–33
Autoliv, Inc., 65 53–55
Autologic Information International, Inc., 20 44–46
Automated Loss Prevention Systems, **11** 445
Automated Sciences Group, Inc. *see* CACI International Inc.
Automated Security (Holdings) PLC, *see* Sensormatic Electronics Corp.
Automatic Coil Corp., **33** 359, 361
Automatic Data Processing, Inc., III 117–19; 9 48–51 (upd.); 47 35–39 (upd.)
Automatic Liquid Packaging, **50** 122
Automatic Payrolls, Inc. *see* Automatic Data Processing, Inc.
Automatic Retailers of America, Inc., *see* Aramark Corporation
Automatic Sprinkler Corp. of America *see* Figgie International, Inc.
Automatic Toll Systems, **19** 111
Automatic Voting Machine Corporation *see* American Locker Group Inc.
AutoMed Technologies, Inc., **64** 27
Automobiles Citroën, 7 35–38
Automobili Lamborghini Holding S.p.A., 13 60–62; 34 55–58 (upd.)
Automotive Diagnostics, *see* SPX Corp.
Automotive Group *see* Lear Corp.
Automotive Industries Holding Inc., **16** 323
AutoNation, Inc., 50 61–64
Autonet, **6** 435
Autonom Computer, **47** 36
Autoroutes du Sud de la France SA, 55 38–40
Autosite.com, **47** 34
Autotote Corporation, 20 47–49 *see also* Scientific Games Corp.
Autoweb.com, **47** 34
AutoZone, Inc., 9 52–54; 31 35–38 (upd.)
AVA AG (Allgemeine Handelsgesellschaft der Verbraucher AG), 33 53–56
Avado Brands, Inc., 31 39–42
Avalon Correctional Services, Inc., 75 40–43

Bank of New South Wales *see* Westpac Banking Corp.

Bank of New York Company, Inc., II 216–19; 46 59–63 (upd.)

The Bank of Nova Scotia, II 220–23; 59 70–76 (upd.)

The Bank of Scotland *see* The Governor and Company of the Bank of Scotland.

Bank of the Philippine Islands, 58 18–20

Bank of Tokyo-Mitsubishi Ltd., II 224–25; 15 41–43 (upd.)

Bank of Wales plc, *see* The Governor and Company of the Bank of Scotland.

Bank One Corporation, 36 68–75 (upd.) *see also* J.P. Morgan Chase.

BankAmerica Corporation, II 226–28 *see also* Bank of America.

BankAtlantic Bancorp., Inc., **66** 273

BankBoston *see* FleetBoston Financial Corp.

Bankers Life and Casualty Co., *see* Conseco Inc.

Bankers Life Association *see* Principal Mutual Life Insurance Co.

Bankers National Life Insurance Co., *see* Conseco Inc.

Bankers Trust Co., **38** 411

Bankers Trust New York Corporation, II 229–31

Bankhaus August Lenz AG, **65** 230, 232

Banknorth Group, Inc., 55 49–53

Bankrate, Inc., 83 38-41

Bankruptcy Services LLC, **56** 112

Banksia Wines Ltd., **54** 227, 229

BankWatch, **37** 143, 145

Banner Aerospace, Inc., 14 42–44; 37 29–32 (upd.)

Banner Life Insurance Company, *see* Legal & General Group plc

Banorte *see* Grupo Financiero Banorte, S.A. de C.V.

Banpais *see* Grupo Financiero Asemex-Banpais S.A.

BanPonce Corporation, **41** 312

Banque Bruxelles Lambert *see* Bank Brussels Lambert.

Banque de Bruxelles *see* Bank Brussels Lambert.

Banque de France, **14** 45–46

Banque de la Société Générale de Belgique *see* Generale Bank.

Banque de Paris et des Pays-Bas, **33** 179

Banque Indosuez, **52** 361–62

Banque Internationale de Luxembourg, **42** 111

Banque Lambert *see* Bank Brussels Lambert.

Banque Nationale de Paris S.A., II 232–34 *see also* BNP Paribas Group.

Banque Paribas *see* BNP Paribas Group.

Banque Sanpaolo of France, **50** 410

La Banque Suisse et Française *see* Crédit Commercial de France.

Banta Corporation, 12 24–26; 32 73–77 (upd.); 79 50–56 (upd.)

Bantam Doubleday Dell Publishing Group, *see* Random House Inc.

Banyan Systems Inc., 25 50–52

Baoshan Iron and Steel, **19** 220

Baosteel Group International Trade Corporation *see* Shanghai Baosteel Group Corp.

BAP of New York, Inc., **15** 246

Baptist Health Care Corporation, 82 37–40

Bar-S Foods Company, 76 39–41

Bar Technologies, Inc., **26** 408

Barastoc Stockfeeds Pty Ltd., **62** 307

Barat *see* Barclays PLC.

Barber Dental Supply Inc., **19** 291

Barberet & Blanc, **I** 677; **49** 350

Barcel, **19** 192

Barclay Furniture Co., *see* LADD Furniture, Inc.

Barclay White Inc., **38** 436

Barclays PLC, II 235–37; 20 57–60 (upd.); 64 46–50 (upd.)

BarclaysAmerican Mortgage Corporation, 11 29–30

Barco Manufacturing Co., **16** 8; **26** 541

Barco NV, 44 42–45

Barcolo Manufacturing, **15** 103; **26** 100

Barden Companies, Inc., 76 42–45

Bardon Group *see* Aggregate Industries plc.

Bareco Products, **15** 352

Barefoot Inc., **23** 428, 431

Barilla G. e R. Fratelli S.p.A., 17 35–37; 50 77–80 (upd.)

Baring Brothers & Co., Ltd., **39** 5

Barings PLC, 14 45–47

Barker & Dobson, **47** 367

Barlow Rand Ltd., I 422–24

Barlow Specialty Advertising, Inc., **26** 341

Barmag AG, 39 39–42

Barneda Carton SA, **41** 326

Barnes & Noble, Inc., 10 135–37; 30 67–71 (upd.); 75 50–55 (upd.)

Barnes Group, Inc., 13 72–74; 69 58–62 (upd.)

Barnett Banks, Inc., 9 58–60 *see also* Bank of America Corp.

Barnett Inc., 28 50–52

Barney's, Inc., 28 53–55

Barnstead Thermolyne Corporation, *see* Sybron International Corp.

Baroid, **19** 467–68

Baron de Ley S.A., 74 27–29

Baron Industries Corporation, **53** 298

Baron Philippe de Rothschild S.A., 39 43–46

Barr *see* AG Barr plc.

Barr & Stroud Ltd., *see* Pilkington plc.

Barr Pharmaceuticals, Inc., 26 29–31; 68 46–49 (upd.)

Barracuda Technologies, **47** 7, 9

Barratt Developments plc, I 556–57; 56 31–33 (upd.)

Barrett Business Services, Inc., 16 48–50

Barricini Foods Inc., **27** 197

Barrick Gold Corporation, 34 62–65

Barris Industries, Inc., **23** 225

Barry Callebaut AG, 29 46–48; 71 46–49 (upd.)

Barry Controls, *see* Applied Power, Inc.

Barry's Jewelers *see* Samuels Jewelers Inc.

Barsab Investment Trust *see* The South African Breweries Ltd.

Barsotti's, Inc. *see* Foster Wheeler Corp.

Bartlett & Co., **33** 261

Barton & Ludwig, Inc., **21** 96

Barton Beers, Ltd., **29** 219

Barton Incorporated, *see* Canandaigua Brands, Inc.

Barton Malow Company, 51 40–43

Barton Protective Services Inc., 53 56–58

Barwig Medizinische Systeme *see* OEC Medical Systems, Inc.

The Baseball Club of Seattle, LP, 50 81–85

Baseline, **58** 167

BASF Aktiengesellschaft, I 305–08; 18 47–51 (upd.); 50 86–92 (upd.)

Bashas' Inc., 33 62–64; 80 17–21 (upd.)

Basic Resources, Inc. *see* Texas Utilities Co.

BASIS Information Technologies, Inc., **11** 132

The Basketball Club of Seattle, LLC, 50 93–97

Basketball Properties Ltd, **53** 166

Baskin-Robbins Ice Cream Co., **29** 18

Bass Anglers Sportsman Society Inc., **52** 192

Bass Brewers Ltd., **15** 441; **29** 85

Bass Brothers Enterprises Inc., **28** 107; **36** 472

Bass Charington, **29** 84

Bass PLC, I 222–24; 15 44–47 (upd.); 38 74–78 (upd.)

Bass Pro Shops, Inc., 42 27–30

Bassett Boat Company, **30** 303

Bassett Furniture Industries, Inc., 18 52–55

Bassett Lowke Ltd., **60** 372

Bassett-Walker Inc. *see* VF Corp.

BAT Industries plc, I 425–27 *see also* British American Tobacco PLC.

Bata Ltd., 62 27–30

Batavia Wine Company, *see* Canandaigua Brands, Inc.

Bateaux Parisiens, **29** 442

Bates, *see* Wolverine World Wide, Inc.

Bates Manufacturing Company, **10** 314

Bates Worldwide, Inc., 14 48–51; 33 65–69 (upd.)

Batesville Casket Company *see* Hillenbrand Industries, Inc.

Bath & Body Works, **11** 41; *see also* Intimate Brands, Inc.

Bath Iron Works Corporation, 12 27–29; 36 76–79 (upd.)

Bath Plus Inc., **51** 196

Batkor Finances BV, **68** 64

Baton Rouge Gas Light Company *see* Gulf States Utilities Co.

Battelle Memorial Institute, Inc., 10 138–40

Batten Barton Durstine & Osborn *see* Omnicom Group Inc.

Braathens ASA, **47** 60–62

Brabants Dagblad BV, *see* N.V. AMEV.

Brach's Confections, Inc., 15 63–65; **74** 43–46 **(upd.)**

Braden Manufacturing, **23** 299–301

Bradford & Bingley PLC, 65 77–80

Bradford Exchange Ltd. Inc., **21** 269

Bradington-Young LLC *see* Hooker Furniture

Bradlees Discount Department Store Company, 12 48–50

Bradley Air Services Ltd., 56 38–40

Bradley Lumber Company, *see* Potlatch Corp.

Bradstreet Co. *see* The Dun & Bradstreet Corp.

Brady Corporation, 78 50–55 **(upd.)**

Bragussa, **IV** 71

Braine L'Alleud Bricolage BV, **68** 64

BRAINS *see* Belgian Rapid Access to Information Network Services.

Brake Bros plc, 45 57–59

BRAL Reststoff-Bearbeitungs-GmbH, **58** 28

Bramac Dachsysteme International GmbH, **70** 363

Bramalea Ltd., 9 83–85

Brambles Industries Limited, 42 47–50

Brammer PLC, 77 64–67

The Branch Group, Inc., 72 43–45

Brand Companies, Inc., *see* Chemical Waste Management, Inc.

Branded Restaurant Group, Inc., *see* Oscar Mayer Foods Corp.

Brandeis & Sons, **19** 511

BrandPartners Group, Inc., 58 36–38

Brandt Zwieback-Biskuits GmbH, **44** 40

Brandywine Asset Management, Inc., **33** 261

Brandywine Holdings Ltd., **45** 109

Brandywine Valley Railroad Co., *see* Lukens Inc.

Braniff Airlines, **36** 231

Brannock Device Company, 48 68–70

Brascan Corporation, 67 71–73

Brasfield & Gorrie LLC, 87 72–75

Brasil Telecom Participaçoes S.A., 57 67–70

Brass-Craft Manufacturing Co. *see* Masco Corp.

Brass Eagle Inc., 34 70–72

Braud & Faucheux *see* Manitou BF S.A.

Brauerei Beck & Co., 9 86–87; **33** 73–76 **(upd.)**

Braun GmbH, 51 55–58

Brauns Fashions Corporation *see* Christopher & Banks Corp.

Brazcot Limitada, **53** 344

Brazil Fast Food Corporation, 74 47–49

Brazos Gas Compressing, *see* Mitchell Energy and Development Corp.

Brazos Sportswear, Inc., 23 65–67

Bredel Exploitatie B.V., *see* United Dominion Industries Ltd.

Breed Corp., **63** 224

Breg, Inc. *see* Orthofix International NV.

Bremer Financial Corp., 45 60–63

Brenntag AG, 8 68–69; **23** 68–70 **(upd.)**

Brent Walker Ltd., **49** 450–51

Brentwood Acquisition, Inc., **68** 299

Brentwood Associates Buyout Fund II LP, **44** 54

Brentwood Corporation, **61** 398

Bresler's Industries, Inc., **35** 121

Bresser Optik, **41** 264

Brewster Lines, **6** 410

Breyers Ice Cream Co. *see* Good Humor-Breyers.

BRI International *see* Quintiles Transnational Corporation

Briazz, Inc., 53 76–79

The Brickman Group, Ltd., 87 76–79

Bricorama S.A., 68 62–64

Bricotruc, **37** 259

Bridel, **19** 49–50; **25** 85

Bridge Communications Inc., **34** 442–43

The Bridge Group, **55** 41

Bridgeport Machines, Inc., 17 52–54

Bridgestone Americas Holding Inc., **64** 133

Bridgestone Corporation, V 234–35; **21** 72–75 **(upd.); 59** 87–92 **(upd.)**

BridgeStreet Corporate Housing Worldwide Inc., **58** 194

Bridgewater Properties, Inc., **51** 229

Bridgeway Plan for Health, **6** 186

Bridgford Company, **13** 382

Bridgford Foods Corporation, 27 71–73

Brierly Investment Limited, **19** 156

Briggs & Stratton Corporation, 8 70–73; **27** 74–78 **(upd.)**

Brigham Exploration Company, 75 72–74

Brigham's Inc., 72 46–48

Bright Horizons Family Solutions, Inc., 31 71–73

Bright of America Inc., **12** 426

Bright Star Technologies, **13** 92; **15** 455; **41** 362

Brighter Vision Learning Adventures, **29** 470, 472

Brighton & Hove Bus and Coach Company, **28** 155–56

Brightpoint, Inc., 18 74–77

Brightwork Development Inc., **25** 348

Briker, **23** 231

Brillianty Alrosa, **62** 9

Brillion Iron Works Inc., **23** 306

Brillstein-Grey Entertainment, 80 41–45

Brin's Oxygen Company Limited *see* BOC Group plc.

The Brink's Company, 58 39–43 **(upd.)**

Brinker International, Inc., 10 176–78; **38** 100–03 **(upd.); 75** 75–79 **(upd.)**

Brinson Partners Inc., **41** 198

BRIO AB, 24 81–83

Brio Technology, **25** 97

Brioche Pasquier S.A., 58 44–46

Briones Alonso y Martin, **42** 19

Brioni Roman Style S.p.A., 67 74–76

BRISA Auto-estradas de Portugal S.A., 64 55–58

Brisco Engineering, **41** 412

Bristol Gaming Corporation, **21** 298

Bristol Hotel Company, 23 71–73

Bristol-Myers Squibb Company, III 17–19; **9** 88–91 **(upd.); 37** 41–45 **(upd.)**

Bristow Helicopters Ltd., 70 26–28

Britannia Soft Drinks Ltd. (Britvic), 71 69–71

Britannica Software, *see* Encyclopaedia Britannica, Inc.

Britannica.com, *see* Encyclopaedia Britannica, Inc.

Britches of Georgetowne, *see* CML Group, Inc.

BRITE *see* Granada Group PLC.

Brite Voice Systems, Inc., 20 75–78

BriteSmile, Inc., **35** 325

British Aerospace plc, I 50–53; **24** 84–90 **(upd.)**

British Airways plc, I 92–95; **14** 70–74 **(upd.); 43** 83–88 **(upd.)**

British American Cosmetics, **I** 427

British American Financial Services, **42** 450

British American Tobacco PLC, 50 116–19 **(upd.)**

British and Foreign Steam Navigation Company, **23** 160

British and North American Royal Mail Steam Packet Company *see* Cunard Line Ltd.

British-Borneo Oil & Gas PLC, 34 73–75

British Broadcasting Corporation Ltd., 7 52–55; **21** 76–79 **(upd.)**

British Bus Group Limited, **69** 43

British Coal Corporation, IV 38–40

British Columbia Packers, *see* George Weston Ltd.

British Columbia Telephone Company, 6 309–11

British Data Management, Ltd., **33** 212, 214

British Electric Traction Company *see* Rentokil Initial Plc.

British Energy Plc, 49 65–68 *see also* British Nuclear Fuels PLC.

British European Airways *see* Jersey European Airways (UK) Ltd.

The British Film Institute, 80 46–50

British Gas plc, V 559–63 *see also* Centrica plc.

British Home Stores PLC *see* Storehouse PLC.

British Independent Television Enterprises Ltd. *see* Granada Group PLC.

British Insulated Callender's Cables Limited *see* BICC PLC

British Interactive Broadcasting Ltd., **20** 79

British Land Plc, 54 38–41

British Leyland Motor Corporation, *see* Jaguar Cars Ltd.

British Linen Bank, *see* The Governor and Company of the Bank of Scotland.

British Midland plc, 38 104–06

The British Museum, 71 72–74

British Nuclear Fuels PLC, 6 451–54

British Oxygen Co *see* BOC Group.

Buffalo Paperboard, **19** 78

Buffalo Wild Wings, Inc., 56 41–43

Buffets, Inc., 10 186–87; **32** 102–04 (upd.)

Bugaboo Creek Steak House Inc., **19** 342

Bugle Boy Industries, Inc., 18 87–88

Buhrmann NV, 41 67–69

Buick Motor Co. *see* General Motors Corp.

Build-A-Bear Workshop Inc., 62 45–48

Builders Concrete *see* Vicat S.A.

Builders Square *see* Kmart Corp.

Building Materials Holding Corporation, 52 53–55

Building One Services Corporation *see* Encompass Services Corp.

Building Products of Canada Limited, **25** 232

Buitoni SpA, *see* Nestlé S.A.

Bulgari S.p.A., 20 94–97

Bull *see* Compagnie des Machines Bull S.A.

Bull S.A., 43 89–91 (upd.)

Bulletin Broadfaxing Network Inc., **67** 257

Bulley & Andrews, LLC, 55 74–76

Bullock's, **31** 191

Bulova Corporation, 13 120–22; **41** 70–73 (upd.)

Bumble Bee Seafoods L.L.C., 64 59–61

Bundall Computers Pty Limited, **56** 155

Bundy Corporation, 17 62–65

Bunge Ltd., 62 49–51

Bunzl plc, IV 260–62; **31** 77–80 (upd.)

Burbank Aircraft Supply, Inc., **14** 42–43; **37** 29, 31

Burberry Ltd., 17 66–68; **41** 74–76 (upd.)

Burda Holding GmbH. & Co., 23 85–89

Burdines, Inc., 60 70–73

Bureau de Recherches de Pétrole, **21** 203–04

The Bureau of National Affairs, Inc., 23 90–93

Bureau Veritas SA, 55 77–79

Burelle S.A., 23 94–96

Burger King Corporation, II 613–15; **17** 69–72 (upd.); **56** 44–48 (upd.)

Burgess, Anderson & Tate Inc., *see* U.S. Office Products Co.

Burgundy Ltd., **68** 53

Bürhle, **17** 36; **50** 78

Burhmann-Tetterode, **22** 154

Buriot International, Inc., **53** 236

The Burke Company, *see* Tridel Enterprises Inc.

Burke Mills, Inc., 66 41–43

BURLE Industries Inc., *see* Sensormatic Electronics Corp.

Burlington Coat Factory Warehouse Corporation, 10 188–89; **60** 74–76 (upd.)

Burlington Industries, Inc., V 354–55; **17** 73–76 (upd.)

Burlington Motor Holdings, **30** 114

Burlington Northern Santa Fe Corporation, V 425–28; **27** 82–89 (upd.)

Burlington Resources Inc., 10 190–92 *see also* ConocoPhillips.

Burmah Castrol PLC, IV 381–84; **30** 86–91 (upd.) *see also* BP p.l.c.

Burndy, **19** 166

Burney Mountain Power, **64** 95

Burns & Ricker, Inc., **40** 51, 53

Burns & Wilcox Ltd., **6** 290

Burns-Alton Corp., **21** 154–55

Burns International Security Services, 13 123–25 *see also* Securitas AB.

Burns International Services Corporation, 41 77–80 (upd.)

Burns Lumber Company, Inc., **61** 254, 256

Burns, Philp & Company Ltd., 63 83–86

Burnup & Sims, Inc., **26** 324

Burpee & Co. *see* W. Atlee Burpee & Co.

Burr-Brown Corporation, 19 66–68

Burris Industries, **14** 303; **50** 311

Burroughs & Chapin Company, Inc., 86 52–55

Burroughs Corp. *see* Unisys Corp.

Burt's Bees, Inc., 58 47–50

The Burton Group plc, V 20–22 *see also* Arcadia Group plc.

Burton Rubber Processing, *see* M. A. Hanna Co.

Burton Snowboards Inc., 22 118–20, 460

Burtons Gold Medal Biscuits Limited, *see* Associated British Foods plc.

Busch Entertainment Corporation, 73 73–75

Bush Boake Allen Inc., 30 92–94 *see also* International Flavors & Fragrances Inc.

Bush Brothers & Company, 45 71–73

Bush Hog, **21** 20–22

Bush Industries, Inc., 20 98–100

Bush Terminal Company, **15** 138

Business Communications Group, Inc. *see* Caribiner International, Inc.

The Business Depot, Ltd., **10** 498; **55** 353

Business Express Airlines, Inc., **28** 22

Business Information Technology, Inc., *see* Ciber, Inc.

Business Men's Assurance Company of America, 14 83–85

Business Objects S.A., 25 95–97

Business Post Group plc, 46 71–73

Business Resources Corp., **23** 489, 491

Business Software Association, **10** 35

Business Software Technology, *see* Legent Corp.

Business Wire, **25** 240

Businessland Inc., **6** 267

Buster Brown & Company *see* Brown Shoe Company, Inc.

BUT S.A., *see* Kingfisher plc.

Butler Bros., **21** 96

Butler Cox PLC, **6** 229

Butler Group, Inc., **30** 310–11

Butler Manufacturing Company, 12 51–53; **62** 52–56 (upd.)

Butterfield & Butterfield *see* eBay Inc.

Butterfield & Swire *see* Swire Pacific Ltd.

Butterick Co., Inc., 23 97–99

Buttrey Food & Drug Stores Co., 18 89–91

Butzbacher Weichenbau GmbH & Co. KG, **53** 352

Buxton, **23** 21

buy.com, Inc., 46 74–77

Buzztime Entertainment, Inc. *see* NTN Buzztime, Inc.

BWAY Corporation, 24 91–93

BWP Distributors, **29** 86, 88

Byerly's, Inc. *see* Lund Food Holdings, Inc.

Byron Weston Company, **26** 105

C

C&A, 40 74–77 (upd.)

C&A Brenninkmeyer KG, V 23–24

C&D *see* Church & Dwight Co., Inc.

C&G *see* Cheltenham & Gloucester PLC.

C & G Systems, *see* Thermadyne Holding Corp.

C & H Distributors, Inc., *see* GEHE AG.

C&J Clark International Ltd., 52 56–59

C&K Aluminio S.A., **74** 11

C&K Market, Inc., 81 59–61

C & O *see* Chesapeake and Ohio Railway.

C&S Co., Ltd., **49** 425, 427

C&S/Sovran Corporation, *see* Bank of America Corp.

C & S Wholesale Grocers, Inc., 55 80–83

C&W *see* Cable and Wireless plc.

C-COR.net Corp., 38 118–21

C-Cube Microsystems, Inc., 37 50–54

C-Mold *see* Moldflow Corp.

C.A. Delaney Capital Management Ltd., **32** 437

C.A. La Electricidad de Caracas, 53 18

C.A. Muer Corporation, **65** 205

C.A. Swanson & Sons *see* Vlasic Foods International Inc.

C Corp. Inc. *see* Alimentation Couche-Tard Inc.

C.D. Haupt, *see* Jefferson Smurfit Group plc.

C.E. Chappell & Sons, Inc., **16** 61–62; **50** 107

C.E.T. *see* Club Européen du Tourisme.

C.F. Burns and Son, Inc., **21** 154

C.F. Martin & Co., Inc., 42 55–58

C.F. Orvis Company *see* The Orvis Company, Inc.

C. Hoare & Co., 77 76–79

C.H. Boehringer Sohn, 39 70–73

C.H. Guenther & Son, Inc., 84 39–42

C.H. Heist Corporation, 24 111–13

C.H. Masland & Sons *see* Masland Corp.

C.H. Robinson Worldwide, Inc., 11 43–44; **40** 78–81 (upd.)

C.I. Traders Limited, 61 44–46

C. Itoh & Co., I 431–33 *see also* ITOCHU Corp.

Citizens Financial Group, Inc., 42
76–80; 87 104–112 (upd.)
Citizens Gas Co., **6** 529
Citizens Gas Fuel Company *see* MCN
Corp.
Citizens Gas Supply Corporation, **6** 527
Citizens Insurance Company of America,
63 29
Citizens National Gas Company, **6** 527
Citizens Savings and Loan Society *see*
Citizens Mutual Savings Bank.
Citizens State Bank, **41** 178, 180
Citizens Utilities Company, 7 87–89 *see*
also Citizens Communications
Company
Citrix Systems, Inc., 44 96–99
Citroën *see* Automobiles Citroën; PSA
Peugeot Citroen S.A.
City and Suburban Telegraph Association
see Cincinnati Bell Inc.
City Brewing Company LLC, 73 84–87
City Capital Associates, **31** 211
City Centre Properties Ltd. *see* Land
Securities PLC.
City Collection Company, Inc., **58** 184
City Developments Limited, **71** 231
City Light and Traction Company, **6** 593
City Light and Water Company, **6** 579
City Market Inc., *see* Dillon Companies
Inc.
City National Bank of Baton Rouge, **11**
107
City of Seattle Water Department, **12** 443
City of Westminster Assurance Company
Ltd., **59** 246
City Public Service, 6 473–75
Civic Parking LLC, *see* Central Parking
Corp.
Civil & Civic Contractors *see* Lend Lease
Corporation Ltd.
Civil Aviation Administration of China,
31 102; **33** 98
CJ Banks *see* Christopher & Banks Corp.
CJ Corporation, 62 68–70
CKE Restaurants, Inc., 19 89–93; **46**
94–99 (upd.)
CKS Group Inc. *see* marchFIRST, Inc.
CKS Inc., **23** 479
Clabir Corp., **12** 199
Claire's Stores, Inc., 17 101–03
Clairol, *see* Procter & Gamble Co.
CLAM Petroleum, *see* Louisiana Land and
Exploration Co.
Clancy-Paul Inc., *see* InaCom Corp.
Clapp-Eastham Company *see* GenRad,
Inc.
Clara Candy, **15** 65
CLARCOR Inc., 17 104–07; **61** 63–67
(upd.)
Clare Rose Inc., 68 83–85
Claremont Technology Group Inc., **31**
131
Clariden Bank, **21** 146–47; **59** 142, 144
Clarify Corp., **38** 431
Clarion Company Ltd., 64 77–79
Clark & McKenney Hardware Co. *see*
Clarcor Inc.
Clark Bar Candy Company, **53** 304

The Clark Construction Group, Inc., 8
112–13
Clark, Dietz & Associates-Engineers *see*
CRSS Inc.
Clark Equipment Company, 8 114–16
Clark Filter, Inc., *see* CLARCOR Inc.
Clark Retail Enterprises Inc., **37** 311
Clark-Schwebel, Inc., **28** 195
Clarkins, Inc., **16** 35–36
Clarksburg Casket Co., **56** 23
CLASSA *see* Compañia de Líneas Aéreas
Subvencionadas S.A.
Classic FM plc, **39** 198–200
Classic Vacation Group, Inc., 46 100–03
Clause/Tézier, **70** 346; **74** 139
Claxson Interactive Group, **54** 74
Clayco Construction Company, **41**
225–26
Clayton Brown Holding Company, **15**
232
Clayton Dubilier & Rice Inc., **25** 501; **29**
408; **40** 370; **49** 22
Clayton Homes Incorporated, 13
154–55; **54** 76–79 (upd.)
Clayton-Marcus Co., *see* LADD Furniture,
Inc.
Clayton/National Courier Systems, Inc.,
see Consolidated Delivery & Logistics,
Inc.
Clayton Williams Energy, Inc., 87
113–116
CLE *see* Compagnie Laitière Européenne.
Clean Harbors, Inc., 73 88–91
Cleancoal Terminal, *see* Westmoreland
Coal Co.
Clear Channel Communications, Inc.,
23 130–32 *see also* Live Nation, Inc.
Clear Shield National Inc., *see* Envirodyne
Industries, Inc.
Clearly Canadian Beverage Corporation,
48 94–97
Clearwire, Inc., 69 95–97
Cleary, Gottlieb, Steen & Hamilton, 35
106–09
Cleco Corporation, 37 88–91
Clemente Capital Inc., **25** 542
Cleo Inc., **35** 131 *see also* Gibson
Greetings, Inc.
Le Clerc, **21** 225–26
Clessidra SGR, **76** 326
Cleve-Co Jig Boring Co., **23** 82
Cleveland-Cliffs Inc., 13 156–58; **62**
71–75 (upd.)
Cleveland Cotton Products Co., **37** 393
Cleveland Electric Illuminating Company
see Centerior Energy Theodor.
Cleveland Fabric Centers, Inc. *see*
Fabri-Centers of America Inc.
Cleveland Grinding Machine Co., **23** 82
Cleveland Indians Baseball Company,
Inc., 37 92–94
Cleveland Iron Mining Company *see*
Cleveland-Cliffs Inc.
Cleveland Precision Instruments, Inc., **23**
82
Cleveland Range Ltd. *see* Enodis plc.
Cleveland Twist Drill Company *see*
Acme-Cleveland Corp.

Click Messenger Service, Inc., *see*
Consolidated Delivery & Logistics, Inc.
Click Trips, Inc., **74** 169
Click Wine Group, 68 86–88
ClickAgents.com, Inc., **49** 433
Clicks Stores *see* New Clicks Holdings
Ltd.
ClientLogic Corporation *see* Onex Corp.
Clif Bar Inc., 50 141–43
Clifford & Wills, *see* J. Crew Group Inc.
Clifford Chance LLP, 38 136–39
Cliffs Corporation, *see* Cleveland-Cliffs
Inc.
Climaveneta Deutschland GmbH *see*
De'Longhi S.p.A.
Clinical Partners, Inc., **26** 74
Clinical Pathology Facility, Inc., **26** 391
Clinique Laboratories, Inc., **30** 191
Clinton Cards plc, 39 86–88
Clipper Group, **12** 439
Clipper, Inc., **IV** 597
La Cloche d'Or, **25** 85
Cloetta Fazer AB, 70 58–60
Clopay Corp., **34** 195
The Clorox Company, III 20–22; **22**
145–48 (upd.); **81** 83–90 (upd.)
Close Brothers Group plc, 39 89–92
Clothesline Corporation, **60** 65
The Clothestime, Inc., 20 141–44
Clougherty Packing Company, 72
72–74
Clover Club, **44** 348
Clovis Water Co., **6** 580
Clow Water Systems Co., **55** 266
CLRP *see* City of London Real Property
Company Ltd.
CLSI Inc., **15** 372; **43** 182
Club Corporation of America, **26** 27
Club de Hockey Canadien Inc., **26** 305
Club Méditerranée S.A., 6 206–08; **21**
125–28 (upd.)
Club Monaco Inc., **62** 284
ClubCorp, Inc., 33 101–04
Cluett Corporation, *see* Celebrity, Inc.
Cluster Consulting, **51** 98
Clydesdale Group, **19** 390
CM&P *see* Cresap, McCormick and
Paget.
CMAC Investment Corporation *see*
Radian Group Inc.
CMC *see* Commercial Metals Co.
CME *see* Campbell-Mithun-Esty, Inc.;
Central European Media Enterprises
Ltd.; Chicago Mercantile Exchange Inc.
CMGI, Inc., 76 99–101
CMI International, Inc., *see* Hayes
Lemmerz International, Inc.
CMIH *see* China Merchants International
Holdings Co., Ltd.
CML Group, Inc., 10 215–18
CMO *see* Chi Mei Optoelectronics Corp.
CMP Media Inc., 26 76–80
CMP Properties Inc., **15** 122
CMS Energy Corporation, V 577–79;
14 114–16 (upd.)
CMS Healthcare, **29** 412
CN *see* Canadian National Railway Co.

Discovery Partners International, Inc., **58** 93–95

Discovery Toys, Inc., *see* Avon Products, Inc.

Discovery Zone, **31** 97

Discreet Logic Inc., 20 185–87

Disctronics, Ltd., **15** 380

Disney *see* The Walt Disney Co.

Disneyland Paris *see* Euro Disney S.C.A.

Disnorte, **51** 389

Distillers Co. plc, I 239–41 *see also* Diageo PLC.

Distribución y Servicio D&S S.A., 71 123–26

Distribuidora Bega, S.A. de C.V., **31** 92

Distribuidora de Produtos de Petróleo Ipiranga, **67** 216–17

Distribution Centers Incorporated *see* Exel Logistics Ltd.

Distribution Centre Sdn. Bhd., **62** 268

Distrigaz S.A., 82 91-94

DITAS *see* Türkiye Petrolleri Anonim Ortakliği.

Divani & Divani *see* Industrie Natuzzi S.p.A.

DIVE!, **26** 264

Diversey Corp., **I** 275, 333; **26** 305–06; **32** 476

Diversified Agency Services, *see* Omnicom Group Inc.

Diversion Entertainment, Inc., **58** 124

Diversity Consultants Inc., **32** 459

Divesco Inc., **58** 333

DiviCom, **43** 221–22

Dixie Carriers, Inc., *see* Kirby Corp.

Dixie Container Corporation, **12** 377

Dixie Crystals Brands, Inc., **32** 277

The Dixie Group, Inc., 20 188–90; **80** 88–92 (upd.)

Dixie-Narco Inc., *see* Maytag Corp.

Dixie Offshore Transportation Company *see* Kirby Corp.

Dixie Power & Light Company, **6** 514

Dixie Yarns, Inc., **19** 305

Dixieland Food Stores, *see* Fleming Companies, Inc.

Dixieline *see* Lanoga Corp.

Dixon Industries, Inc., 26 117–19

Dixon Ticonderoga Company, 12 114–16; **69** 129–33 (upd.)

Dixons Group plc, V 48–50; **19** 121–24 (upd.); **49** 110–13 (upd.)

DJ Moldings Corp., **18** 276

DJ Pharma, Inc., **47** 56

Djarum PT, 62 96–98

Djedi Holding SA, **23** 242

DKB *see* Dai-Ichi Kangyo Bank Ltd.

DKNY *see* Donna Karan International Inc.

Dl Radiators France S.A.R.L. *see* De'Longhi S.p.A.

DLC *see* Duquesne Light Co.

DLJ *see* Donaldson, Lufkin & Jenrette.

DLJ Merchant Banking Partners II, **21** 188; **36** 158–59

DLL *see* David Lloyd Leisure Ltd.

DM Associates Limited Partnership, **25** 127

DMAX-Ltd., **57** 190

DMB&B *see* D'Arcy Masius Benton & Bowles.

dmc2 Italia SrL, **56** 127

DMGT *see* Daily Mail and General Trust.

DMI Furniture, 46 147–50

DMP Mineralöl Petrochemie GmbH, **IV** 487

DMV Stainless, **54** 393

DNATA, **39** 137, 139

DNN Galvanizing Limited Partnership, *see* Dofasco Inc.

DNP DENMARK A/S, **IV** 600

Do It All, *see* Alliance Boots plc.

Do it Best Corporation, 30 166–70

Dobbs House, **21** 54

Dobbs Houses Inc., **15** 87

Dobrogea Grup S.A., 82 95-98

Dobrolet *see* Aeroflot.

Dobson Communications Corporation, 63 130–32

Dobson Park Industries, **38** 227

Doc Green's Gourmet Salads Inc., **64** 327, 329

Doc Holliday's Pawnbrokers and Jewelers, Inc., **61** 55

Docks de France, **37** 23; **39** 183–84

Doctor's Associates Inc., 67 142–45 (upd.)

The Doctors' Company, 55 125–28

Doctors Without Borders *see* Médecins Sans Frontières.

Documentum, Inc., 46 151–53

DOD Electronics Corp., **15** 215

Dodge & Day *see* Day & Zimmermann, Inc.

Dodge Motor Company, **20** 259

Doduco Corporation, **29** 460–61

Doeflex PLC, **33** 79

Dofasco Inc., IV 73–74; **24** 142–44 (upd.)

Dogan Sirketler Grubu Holding A.S., 83 107-110

Dogi International Fabrics S.A., 52 99–102

Doherty, Mann & Olshan *see* Wells Rich Greene BDDP.

Dolan Design, Inc., **44** 133

Dolby Laboratories Inc., 20 191–93

Dolce & Gabbana SpA, 62 99–101

Dole Corporation, **44** 152

Dole Food Company, Inc., 9 175–76; **31** 167–70 (upd.); **68** 115–19 (upd.)

Dollar Bills, Inc. *see* Dollar Tree Stores, Inc.

Dollar Express Inc., **62** 104

Dollar General, **26** 533

Dollar Thrifty Automotive Group, Inc., 25 142–45

Dollar Tree Stores, Inc., 23 176–78; **62** 102–05 (upd.)

Dollfus Mieg & Cie *see* Groupe DMC.

Dollond & Aitchison Group, **49** 151–52

Dollywood Corporation *see* Herschend Family Entertainment Corp.

Dolmar GmbH, **59** 272

Dolomite Franchi SpA, **53** 285

Dolphin Book Club, *see* Book-of-the-Month Club.

Dolphin Services, Inc., **44** 203

Dom Perignon, **25** 258

Domain.com, Inc. *see* StarTek, Inc.

Domain Home Fashions *see* Aga Foodservice Group PLC.

Domaine Carneros, **43** 401

Domaines Barons de Rothschild, **36** 113, 115

Doman Industries Limited, 59 160–62

Dome Petroleum, Ltd., **IV** 401, 494; **12** 364

Dominick International Corp., **12** 131

Dominick's Finer Foods, Inc., 56 87–89

Dominion Bond Rating Service Ltd., **65** 244

Dominion Bridge Company, Limited, *see* United Dominion Industries Ltd.

Dominion Homes, Inc., 19 125–27

Dominion Industries Ltd., **15** 229

Dominion Resources, Inc., V 596–99; **54** 83–87 (upd.)

Dominion Salt Ltd., **62** 307

Dominion Textile Inc., 12 117–19

Domino S.p.A., **51** 324

Domino Printing Sciences PLC, 87 136–139

Domino Sugar Corporation, 26 120–22

Domino's, Inc., 7 150–53; **21** 177–81 (upd.); **63** 133–39 (upd.)

Domtar Inc., IV 271–73

Don Canham Enterprises *see* School-Tech, Inc.

Don Massey Cadillac, Inc., 37 114–16

Don's Foods, Inc., **26** 164

Donaldson Company, Inc., 16 178–81; **49** 114–18 (upd.)

Donaldson, Lufkin & Jenrette, Inc., 22 188–91

Donaldson's Department Stores, **15** 274

Donatos Pizzeria Corporation, 58 96–98

Donegal Parian China Ltd. *see* Belleek Pottery Ltd.

Dong Guan Highsonic Electronic Products Company, **62** 150

Dong Yang Department Store Company, **62** 174

Dong-Myung Industrial Company Ltd., **64** 270

DongGuan Leeway Footwear Company Ltd., **68** 69

Dongguan Shilong Kyocera Optics Co., Ltd., **21** 331

Dongguan Xinda Giftware Co. Ltd., **60** 372

Dongil Frozen Foods Co., *see* Nippon Suisan Kaisha, Ltd.

Dönkasan, **55** 188

Donna Karan International Inc., 15 145–47; **56** 90–93 (upd.)

Donnellon McCarthy Inc., **12** 184

Donnelly Corporation, 12 120–22; **35** 147–50 (upd.)

Donning Company Publishers *see* Walsworth Publishing Company, Inc.

General Fire Extinguisher Co. *see* Grinnell Corp.

General Foods Corp., **I** 608, 712; **V** 407; **26** 251; **44** 341 *see also* Kraft Foods Inc.

General Frozen Foods S.A. *see* Vivartia S.A.

General Furniture Leasing *see* CORT Business Services Corp.

General Growth Properties, Inc., 57 155–57

General Host Corporation, 12 198–200

General Housewares Corporation, 16 234–36

General Injectables and Vaccines Inc., **54** 188

General Instrument Corporation, 10 319–21 *see also* Motorola, Inc.

General Insurance Co. of America *see* SAFECO Corp.

General Maritime Corporation, 59 197–99

General Merchandise Services, Inc., **15** 480

General Mills, Inc., II 501–03; **10** 322–24 (upd.); **36** 234–39 (upd.); **85** 141–49 (upd.)

General Motors Acceptance Corporation, **21** 146

General Motors Corporation, I 171–73; **10** 325–27 (upd.); **36** 240–44 (upd.); **64** 148–53 (upd.)

General Nutrition Companies, Inc., 11 155–57; **29** 210–14 (upd.)

General Office Products Co., *see* U.S. Office Products Co.

General Packing Service, Inc., **19** 78

General Parts Inc., **29** 86

General Petroleum Authority *see* Egyptian General Petroleum Corp.

General Physics Corporation, *see* National Patient Development Corp.

General Portland Inc., **28** 229

General Printing Ink Corp. *see* Sequa Corp.

General Public Utilities Corporation, V 629–31 *see also* GPU, Inc.

General Radio Company *see* GenRad, Inc.

General Railway Signal Company *see* General Signal Corp.

General Re Corporation, III 258–59; **24** 176–78 (upd.)

General Sekiyu K.K., IV 431–33 *see also* TonenGeneral Sekiyu K.K.

General Shale Building Materials Inc. *see* Wienerberger AG.

General Signal Corporation, 9 250–52 *see also* SPX Corp.

General Telephone and Electronics Corp. *see* GTE Corp.

General Telephone Corporation *see* GTE Corp.

General Tire, Inc., 8 212–14

General Turbine Systems, **58** 75

General Utilities Company, **6** 555

General Waterworks Corporation, **40** 449

Generale Bank, II 294–95 *see also* Fortis, Inc.

Generale Biscuit Glico France S.A. *see* Ezaki Glico Company Ltd.

Générale Biscuit S.A., **II** 475

Générale de Banque, **36** 458

Générale de Mécanique Aéronautique, *see* Avions Marcel Dassault-Breguet Aviation

Générale de Restauration, **49** 126

Générale des Eaux Group, V 632–34 *see* Vivendi Universal S.A.

Générale Occidentale, **II** 475; **IV** 614–16

Générale Restauration S.A., **34** 123

Generali *see* Assicurazioni Generali.

Génération Y2K, **35** 204, 207

Genesco Inc., 17 202–06; **84** 143–149 (upd.)

Genesee & Wyoming Inc., 27 179–81

Genesee Iron Works *see* Wickes Inc.

Genesis Health Ventures, Inc., 18 195–97 *see also* NeighborCare,Inc.

Genesis Microchip Inc., 82 133–37

Genesse Hispania, **60** 246

Genetic Anomalies, Inc., **39** 395

Genetics Institute, Inc., 8 215–18

Geneva Metal Wheel Company, **20** 261

Geneva Rubber Co., *see* Park-Ohio Industries Inc.

Geneva Steel, 7 193–95

Geneve Corporation, **62** 16

GENEX Services, Inc., **52** 379

Genix Group *see* MCN Corp.

Genmar Holdings, Inc., 45 172–75

Genoc Chartering Ltd, **60** 96

Genosys Biotechnologies, Inc., **36** 431

Genovese Drug Stores, Inc., 18 198–200

Genpack Corporation, **21** 58

GenRad, Inc., 24 179–83

Gensec Bank, **68** 333

GenSet, *see* Thermadyne Holding Corp.

Genstar, **22** 14; **23** 327

Genstar Rental Electronics, Inc., **58** 110

Genstar Stone Products Co., **15** 154; **40** 176

GenSys Power Ltd., **64** 404

GenTek Inc., **37** 157; **41** 236

Gentex Corporation, 26 153–57

Genting Bhd., 65 152–55

Gentiva Health Services, Inc., 79 189–92

GenTrac, **24** 257

Gentry Associates, Inc., **14** 378

Gentry International, **47** 234

Genty-Cathiard, **39** 183–84; **54** 306

Genuardi's Family Markets, Inc., 35 190–92

Genuin Golf & Dress of America, Inc., **32** 447

Genuine Parts Company, 9 253–55; **45** 176–79 (upd.)

Genzyme Corporation, 13 239–42; **38** 203–07 (upd.); **77** 164–70 (upd.)

Genzyme Transgenics Corp., **37** 44

Geo. H. McFadden & Bro., **54** 89

GEO SA, **58** 218

GEO Specialty Chemicals, Inc., **27** 117

geobra Brandstätter GmbH & Co. KG, 48 183–86

Geodis S.A., 67 187–90

Geofizikai Szolgáltató Kft., **70** 195

Geographics, Inc., **25** 183

GEOINFORM Mélyfúrási Információ Szolgáltató Kft., **70** 195

Geomarine Systems, **11** 202

The Geon Company, 11 158–61

Geon Industries, Inc. *see* Johnston Industries, Inc.

GeoQuest Systems Inc., **17** 419

Georesources, Inc., **19** 247

Georg Fischer AG Schaffhausen, 61 106–09

Georg Neumann GmbH, **66** 288

George A. Hormel and Company, II 504–06 *see also* Hormel Foods Corp.

George Buckton & Sons Limited, **40** 129

The George F. Cram Company, Inc., 55 158–60

The George Hyman Construction Company, *see* The Clark Construction Group, Inc.

George K. Baum & Company, **25** 433

George Kerasotes Corporation *see* Carmike Cinemas, Inc.

George P. Johnson Company, 60 142–44

George R. Rich Manufacturing Company *see* Clark Equipment Co.

George S. May International Company, 55 161–63

George Smith Financial Corporation, **21** 257

George Weston Limited, II 631–32; **36** 245–48 (upd.)

George Wimpey plc, 12 201–03; **51** 135–38 (upd.)

Georgetown Group, Inc., **26** 187

Georgia Carpet Outlets, *see* The Maxim Group.

Georgia Cotton Producers Association *see* Gold Kist Inc.

Georgia Federal Bank, **I** 447; **30** 196

Georgia Gas Corporation *see* Atlanta Gas Light Company

Georgia Gulf Corporation, 9 256–58; **61** 110–13 (upd.)

Georgia Hardwood Lumber Co., *see* Georgia-Pacific Corporation

Georgia-Pacific Corporation, IV 281–83; **9** 259–62 (upd.); **47** 145–51 (upd.)

Georgia Power & Light Co., **6** 447, 537; **23** 28

Georgia Power Company, **38** 446–48; **49** 145

Georgia Steel Supply Company, **70** 294

Georgie Pie, **V** 35

GeoScience Corporation, *see* Tech-Sym Corp.

Geosource Inc., **21** 14

Geotec Boyles Brothers, S.A., **19** 247

Geotecnia y Cimientos SA, **55** 182

Geotek Communications Inc., 21 238–40

GeoTel Communications Corp., **34** 114

GeoVideo Networks, **34** 259

Geoworks Corporation, **25** 509

Geraghty & Miller Inc., **26** 23

Hasbro, Inc., III 504–06; 16 264–68
    (upd.); 43 229–34 (upd.)
Haskel International, Inc., 59 218–20
Haslemere Estates, 26 420
Hassenfeld Brothers Inc. *see* Hasbro, Inc.
Hastings Entertainment, Inc., 29
    229–31
Hastings Manufacturing Company, 56
    156–58
Hatch Grinding, 29 86, 88
Hatfield Jewelers, 30 408
Hatteras Yachts Inc., 45 175
Hattori Seiko Co., Ltd. *see* Seiko Corp.
HAULOTTE, 51 295
Hauni Maschinenbau AG, 60 193
Hauser, Inc., 46 224–27
Hausted, Inc., 29 451
Havas, SA, 10 345–48; 33 178–82
    (upd.) *see also* Vivendi Universal
    Publishing
Haverty Furniture Companies, Inc., 31
    246–49
Havertys, 39 174
Haviland Candy Co., 15 325
Haw Par Corporation, 56 362
Hawaii World, 62 276
Hawaiian Airlines Inc., 22 251–53
    (upd.) *see also* HAL Inc.
Hawaiian Electric Industries, Inc., 9
    274–77
Hawaiian Trust Company *see* Bank of
    Hawaii Corp.
Hawaiian Tug & Barge, *see* Hawaiian
    Electric Industries, Inc.
Hawk Corporation, 59 221–23
Hawk Model Co., 51 368
Hawker Siddeley Group Public Limited
    Company, III 507–10
Hawkins Chemical, Inc., 16 269–72
Haworth Inc., 8 251–52; 39 205–08
    (upd.)
Haxton Foods Inc., 21 155
Hay Group, 42 329–30
Hayes Aircraft Corp., 54 283
Hayes Corporation, 24 210–14
Hayes Lemmerz International, Inc., 27
    202–04
Hayes Microcomputer Products, 9 515
Hayes Wheel Company, *see* Kelsey-Hayes
    Group of Companies
Haynes Publishing Group P.L.C., 71
    169–71
Hays plc, 27 205–07; 78 149–53 (upd.)
Hazel-Atlas Glass Co., 15 128
Hazelden Foundation, 28 176–79
Hazeltine, Inc., *see* Emerson.
Hazelnut Growers of Oregon, *see*
    Diamond of California.
Hazleton Laboratories Corp., 30 151
Hazlewood Foods plc, 32 251–53
Hazzard and Associates, 34 248
HBO *see* Home Box Office Inc.
HBOS, 71 324–26
HCA—The Healthcare Company, 35
    215–18 (upd.)
HCG *see* Harrell Construction Group,
    LLC.
HCI *see* Holland Chemical International.

HCI Construction, 61 125, 127
HCI Direct, Inc., 55 196–98
HCI Distribution Company, 61 125–26
HCR Manor Care, *see* Manor Care, Inc.
HCS Technology, 26 496–97
HDI (Haftpflichtverband der Deutschen
    Industrie Versicherung auf
    Gegenseitigkeit V.a.G.), 53 159–63
HDM Worldwide Direct, 16 168 *see also*
    Euro RSCG Worldwide S.A.
HDOS Enterprises, 72 167–69
HdP *see* Holding di Partecipazioni
    Industriali S.p.A.
HDR Inc., 48 203–05
HDS *see* Heartland Express, Inc.
Head N.V., 55 199–201
Head Sportswear International, 15 368;
    43 374
Heads and Threads, *see* Alleghany Corp.
Headwaters Incorporated, 56 159–62
Headway Corporate Resources, Inc., 40
    236–38
Headway Technologies, Inc., 49 392–93
Healing Arts Publishing, Inc., 41 177
Healix Health Services Inc., 48 310
Health and Diet Group, 29 212
Health Care & Retirement Corporation,
    22 254–56
Health Communications, Inc., 72
    170–73
Health Development Corp., 46 432
Health Maintenance Organization of
    Pennsylvania *see* U.S. Healthcare, Inc.
Health Management Associates, Inc., 56
    163–65
Health-Mor Inc. *see* HMI Industries.
Health O Meter Products Inc., 14
    229–31
Health Plan of America, 11 379
Health Risk Management, Inc., 24
    215–17
Health Services Capital Corporation, 64
    27
Health Systems International, Inc., 11
    174–76
Healthcare, L.L.C., 29 412
Healthcare Products Holdings, Inc., 70
    142
HealthCare USA, 59 139
HealthCo International, Inc., 19 290
Healthdyne, Inc., *see* Matria Healthcare,
    Inc.
HealthExtras, Inc., 75 185–87
Healthmagic, Inc., 29 412
HealthRider Corporation, 38 238
HealthRite, Inc., 45 209
Healthshares L.L.C., *see* Nichols Research
    Corp.
Healthsource Inc., *see* CIGNA Corp.
HealthSouth Corporation, 14 232–34;
    33 183–86 (upd.)
Healthtex, Inc., 17 223–25 *see also* VF
    Corp.
HealthTrust, III 80; 15 112; 35 215, 217
Hearing Aid Specialists Pty Limited, 56
    338
The Hearst Corporation, IV 625–27; 19
    201–04 (upd.); 46 228–32 (upd.)

Heartland Components, *see* Illinois Tool
    Works Inc.
Heartland Express, Inc., 18 225–27
Heartland Homes, Inc., 41 19
Heartland Industrial Partners L.P., 41 94
Heartland Securities Corp., 32 145
The Heat Group, 53 164–66
Heatcraft Inc., *see* Lennox International
    Inc.
Heatilator Inc., *see* HNI Corp.
Heating & Cooling Supply, Inc., 52
    398–99
Hebdo Mag International, Inc. *see* Trader
    Classified Media N.V.
Hebei Hualong F&N Industry Group, 75
    288
Hebei Longteng Paper Corporation, 63
    316
Hechinger Company, 12 233–36
Heckett Technology Services Inc., *see*
    Harsco Corp.
Heckler & Koch GmbH, *see* British
    Aerospace plc.
Hecla Mining Company, 20 293–96
Hede Nielsen A/S, 47 219
Heekin Can Inc., 13 254–56 *see also* Ball
    Corp.
Heelys, Inc., 87 213–216
Heery International, Inc., 58 156–59
Hees International Bancorp Inc. *see*
    Brascan Corp.
Hefei Rongshida Group Corporation, *see*
    Maytag Corp.
Hegenscheidt-MFD GmbH & Co. KG,
    53 352
HEI Diversified, Inc., *see* Hawaiian
    Electric Industries, Inc.
HEICO Corporation, 30 236–38
Heide Park, 55 378
Heidelberger Druckmaschinen AG, 40
    239–41
Heidelberger Zement AG, 31 250–53
Heidemij *see* Arcadis NV.
Heidi Bakery, *see* Giant Food LLC.
Heidrick & Struggles International,
    Inc., 28 180–82
Heijmans N.V., 66 176–78
Heil Company, 28 103
Heileman Brewing Co *see* G. Heileman
    Brewing Co.
Heilig-Meyers Company, 14 235–37; 40
    242–46 (upd.)
Heineken N.V., I 256–58; 13 257–59
    (upd.); 34 200–04 (upd.)
Heinrich Bauer North America, 7 42–43
Heinrich Bauer Verlag, 23 85–86
Heinrich Koppers GmbH, IV 89
Heinz Co *see* H.J. Heinz Co.
Heinz Deichert KG, 11 95
Heinz Italia S.p.A., 15 221
Heitman Properties, 60 184
HEL&P *see* Houston Electric Light &
    Power Co.
Helados La Menorquina S.A., 22 515
Helen of Troy Corporation, 18 228–30
Helena Rubenstein, Inc., *see* L'Oréal.

Hillenbrand Industries, Inc., 10
349–51; 75 188–92 (upd.)
Hillerich & Bradsby Company, Inc., 51
161–64
The Hillhaven Corporation, 14 241–43
see also Vencor, Inc.
Hillos GmbH, 53 169
Hills & Dales Railway Co. *see* Dayton
Power & Light Co.
Hills Brothers Inc. *see* Nestlé S.A.
Hills Pet Products, *see* Colgate-Palmolive
Co.
Hills Stores Company, 13 260–61
Hillsborough Holdings Corporation *see*
Walter Industries, Inc.
Hillsdale Machine & Tool Company, *see*
Tecumseh Products Co.
Hillsdown Holdings, PLC, II 513–14;
24 218–21 (upd.)
Hilti AG, 53 167–69
Hilton Active Apparel, *see* K2 Inc.
Hilton Group plc, III 91–93; 19
205–08 (upd.); 62 176–79 (upd.); 49
191–95 (upd.)
Hindalco Industries Limited *see* Aditya
Birla Group
Hindustan Lever Limited, 79 198–201
Hines Horticulture, Inc., 49 196–98
Hino Motors, Ltd., 7 219–21; 21
271–74 (upd.)
HIP Health Plan, 22 425
Hipercor, S.A., V 52; 26 129
Hiram Walker Resources Ltd., I 262–64
Hiram Walker-Consumers' Home Ltd. *see*
Consumers' Gas Company Ltd.
Hiram Walker-Gooderham & Worts Ltd.,
29 18
Hire-Purchase Company of Ireland, 16
13; 43 7
Hiroshima Yakult Co., 25 449
The Hirsh Company, *see* Knape & Vogt
Manufacturing Co.
Hirth-Krause Company *see* Wolverine
World Wide Inc.
Hirz, 25 85
Hispanic Broadcasting Corporation, 35
219–22
Hispanoil *see* Hispanica de Petroleos.
History Book Club, *see*
Book-of-the-Month Club.
Hit de Venezuela, 54 73
HIT Entertainment PLC, 40 250–52
Hit or Miss *see* The TJX Companies, Inc.
Hitachi, Ltd., I 454–55; 12 237–39
(upd.); 40 253–57 (upd.)
Hitachi Metals, Ltd., IV 101–02
Hitachi Zosen Corporation, III 513–14;
53 170–73 (upd.)
Hitchiner Manufacturing Co., Inc., 23
267–70
Hi3G, 63 208
HL&P *see* Houston Lighting and Power
Co.
HMI Industries, Inc., 17 233–35
HMO-PA *see* U.S. Healthcare, Inc.
HMSHost Corp., 49 31; 63 322
HMV Group plc, 59 228–30
HNI Corporation, 74 148–52 (upd.)

Ho-Chunk Inc., 61 125–28
Hoan Products Ltd. *see* Lifetime Hoan
Corp.
HOB Entertainment, Inc., 37 191–94
Hobart Corporation *see* KitchenAid, Inc;
Whirlpool Corp.
Hobby Lobby Stores Inc., 80 139–42
Hochtief AG, 33 194–97
The Hockey Company, 34 215–18; 70
124–26 (upd.)
Hocking Glass Company, *see* Anchor
Hocking Glassware.
Hockleys Professional Limited, 55 281
Hodes *see* Bernard Hodes Group Inc.
Hodgart Consulting *see* Hildebrandt
International.
Hoechst AG, I 346–48; 18 234–37
(upd.)
Hoechst Celanese Corporation, 13
262–65
Hoenig Group Inc., 41 207–09
Hoesch AG, IV 103–06
Hofbräuierzentrale GmbH Saarbrücken,
41 222
Hoffman Corporation, 78 158–12
Hoffman Enclosures Inc., 26 361, 363
Hoffmann-La Roche & Co *see* F.
Hoffmann-La Roche & Co.
Hoffritz, *see* Lifetime Brands, Inc.
Hofmann Herbold & Partner, 34 249
Hogan & Hartson L.L.P., 44 220–23
Hogatron, 60 364
Hogue Cellars, 50 520
Hohner *see* Matth. Hohner AG.
Hojgaard & Schultz, 38 436
HOK Group, Inc., 59 231–33
Hokkaido Electric Power Company Inc.
(HEPCO), V 635–37; 58 160–63
(upd.)
Hokuriku Electric Power Company, V
638–40
Holberg Industries, Inc., 36 266–69
Holcemca B.V., 51 29
Holcim, Ltd., 51 27, 29; 59 111, 115
Holco BV, 41 12
Hold Everything, *see* Williams-Sonoma,
Inc.
Holden Ltd., 62 180–83
Holden Meehan *see* Bradford & Bingley
PLC.
Holderbank Financière Glaris Ltd., III
701–02 *see also* Holnam Inc
Holding di Partecipazioni Industriali
S.p.A., 52 120, 122
N.V. Holdingmaatschappij De Telegraaf,
23 271–73
Holec Control Systems, 26 496
Holes-Webway Company, 40 44
Holga, Inc., *see* HNI Corp.
Holiday Corp., 16 263; 38 76; 43 226
Holiday Inns, Inc., III 94–95 *see also*
Promus Companies, Inc.
Holiday Rambler Corporation, *see*
Harley-Davidson, Inc.
Holiday Retirement Corp., 87 221–223
Holiday RV Superstores, Incorporated,
26 192–95
Holland & Holland, 49 84

Holland & Knight LLP, 60 171–74
Holland America Line *see* Carnival Corp.
Holland Burgerville USA, 44 224–26
Holland Casino, 23 229
Holland Chemical International, 59 391
Holland Graphic Occasions, 64 226
The Holland Group, Inc., 82 174–77
Holland Motor Express, *see* TNT
Freightways Corp.
Holland Studio Craft, 38 402
Holland Sweetener Company V.O.F. *see*
Tosoh Corp.
Hollander Home Fashions Corp., 67
207–09
Holley Performance Products Inc., 52
157–60
Hollinger Hardware Limited *see* Home
Hardware Stores Ltd.
Hollinger International Inc., 24 222–25;
62 184–88 (upd.)
Hollingsead International, Inc., 36
158–60
Hollister Company, 75 7
Holloway-Staubach Corporation *see* The
Staubach Co.
Holly Corporation, 12 240–42
Holly Sugar Company *see* Imperial Holly
Corp.
Hollywood Casino Corporation, 21
275–77
Hollywood Entertainment Corporation,
25 208–10
Hollywood Media Corporation, 58
164–68
Hollywood Park, Inc., 20 297–300
Hollywood Park Race Track, 29 118
Hollywood Pictures, *see* Walt Disney Co.
Holme Roberts & Owen LLP, 28
196–99
Holmen AB, 52 161–65 (upd.)
Holmes International *see* Miller Industries,
Inc.
Holnam Inc., 8 258–60; 39 217–20
(upd.)
Holophane Corporation, 19 209–12
Holson Burnes Group, Inc., 14 244–45
Holsten Brauerei AG, 35 256, 258
Holt and Bugbee Company, 66 189–91
Holt, Rinehart and Winston, Inc., *see*
Harcourt Brace and Co.
Holt's Cigar Holdings, Inc., 42 176–78
Holtzbrinck *see* Verlagsgruppe Georg von
Holtzbrinck.
Holvis AG, 15 229
Holyman Sally Ltd., 29 431
Homart Development Co., 57 156
Homasote Company, 72 178–81
Home and Community Care, Inc., 43 46
Home Box Office Inc., 7 222–24; 23
274–77 (upd.); 76 178–82 (upd.)
Home Builders Supply, Inc. *see* Scotty's,
Inc.
Home Choice Holdings, Inc., 33 366–67
The Home Depot, Inc., V 75–76; 18
238–40 (upd.)
Home Entertainment of Texas, Inc., 30
466
Home Hardware Stores Ltd., 62 189–91

Imetal S.A., IV 107–09
IMG, 78 177–80
Imhoff Industrie Holding GmbH, 53 315
IMI plc, 9 288–89; 29 364
IMIWeb Bank, 50 410
Imlo, 26 22
Immeon Networks LLC, 54 407
Immersion Corporation, 28 245
Immobilier Batibail, 42 152
Immucor, Inc., 81 192–96
Immunex Corporation, 14 254–56; 50 248–53 (upd.)
Imo Industries Inc., 7 235–37; 27 229–32 (upd.)
Imo Pump, 58 67
Impala Platinum Holdings Ltd., IV 91–93; 63 38–39
Impark Limited, 42 433
IMPATH Inc., 45 192–94
Imperial Airways see British Overseas Airways Corp.
Imperial Business Forms, 9 72
Imperial Chemical Industries plc, I 351–53; 50 254–58 (upd.)
Imperial Commodities Corporation see Deli Universal NV.
Imperial Feather Company, 19 304
Imperial Holly Corporation, 12 268–70 see also Imperial Sugar Co.
Imperial Industries, Inc., 81 197–200
Imperial Metal Industries Ltd. see IMI plc.
Imperial Oil Limited, IV 437–39; 25 229–33 (upd.);
Imperial Packing Co. see Beech-Nut Nutrition Corp.
Imperial Parking Corporation, 58 182–84
Imperial Products, Inc., 62 289
Imperial Sports, 19 230
Imperial Sugar Company, 32 274–78 (upd.)
Imperial Tobacco Company see B.A.T. Industries PLC.
Imperial Tobacco Group PLC, 50 259–63
Implantes Y Sistemas Medicos, Inc., 72 262
Implats see Impala Platinum Holdings Ltd.
IMPO Import Parfumerien, 48 116
Imported Auto Parts, Inc., 15 246
Impressions Software, 15 455
Impulse Airlines Pty Ltd. see Qantas Airways Ltd.
Impulse Designs, 31 435–36
IMRA America Inc., 48 5
IMRS see Hyperion Software Corp.
IMS Health, Inc., 57 174–78
IMX Pharmaceuticals, 59 285
In Focus Systems, Inc., 22 287–90
In-N-Out Burgers Inc., 19 213–15; 74 153–56 (upd.)
In-Sink-Erator, 66 195–98
INA Corporation see CIGNA Corp.
INA-Holding Schaeffler KG, 62 129
InaCom Corporation, 13 276–78
Inalca S.p.A. see Cremonini S.p.A.
Inamed Corporation, 79 213–16

Incentive Group, 27 269
Inchcape PLC, III 521–24; 16 276–80 (upd.); 50 264–68 (upd.)
INCO-Banco Indústria e Comércio de Santa Catarina, 13 70
Inco Limited, IV 110–12; 45 195–99 (upd.)
Incon Research Inc., 41 198
InControl Inc., 11 460
Incredible Universe, 12 470; 36 387
Incyte Genomics, Inc., 52 174–77
Indel, Inc., 78 181–84
Indemnity Insurance Company see CIGNA Corp.
Independent Delivery Services, Inc., 37 409
Independent Election Corp. of America, 47 37
Independent Exhibitions Ltd., see Penton Media, Inc.
Independent Grocers Alliance see IGA.
Independent News & Media PLC, 61 129–31
Independent Print Media Group, 74 283
Independent Stave Company, 28 223
India Exotics, Inc., see Celebrity, Inc.
Indian Airlines Corporation see Air-India.
Indian Airlines Ltd., 46 240–42
Indian Archery and Toy Corp., see Escalade, Inc.
Indian Iron & Steel Company Ltd. see Steel Authority of India Ltd.
Indian Oil Corporation Ltd., IV 440–41; 48 210–13 (upd.)
Indiana Bell Telephone Company, Incorporated, 14 257–61
Indiana Electric Corporation, 6 555
Indiana Energy, Inc., 27 233–36
Indiana Gaming Company, 21 40
Indiana Gas & Water Company, 6 556
Indiana Parts and Warehouse, 29 86, 88
Indiana Power Company, 6 555
Indiana Protein Technologies, 55 233
Indiana Tube Co., 23 250
Indianapolis Brush Electric Light & Power Company, 6 508
Indianapolis Cablevision, 6 508–09
Indianapolis Light and Power Company, 6 508
Indianapolis Motor Speedway Corporation, 46 243–46
Indianapolis Power & Light Company, 6 508–09
Indianapolis Pump and Tube Company, see Arvin Industries, Inc.
IndianOil Companies see Indian Oil Corporation Ltd.
Indigo Books & Music Inc., 58 185–87
Indigo NV, 26 212–14 see also Hewlett-Packard Co.
Indigo Systems Corp. see FLIR Systems, Inc.
The Inditex Group see Industria de Diseño Textil S.A.
Indo Mobil Ltd., 48 212
Indresco, Inc., 22 285; 52 215
Induba, S.A. de C.V., 39 230
Induban, II 196

Indura SA Industria Y Commercio, 25 82
Indus International Inc., 70 127–30
Industri Kapital, 27 269; 68 125–26
Industri Kapital 2000 Ltd., 64 17
Industria de Diseño Textil S.A. (Inditex), 64 193–95
Industrial & Commercial Bank, 56 363
Industrial Air Tool, 28 387
Industrial Airsystems Inc., 56 247
Industrial Bank of Japan, Ltd., II 300–01
Industrial Chemical and Equipment, 16 271
Industrial Circuits, IV 680
Industrial Development Corp. of Zambia Ltd., see Zambia Industrial and Mining Corp. Ltd.
Industrial Development Corporation, 57 185
Industrial Devices Inc., 48 359
Industrial Exportadora Famian, S.A. de C.V., 62 353
Industrial Gases Lagos, 25 82
Industrial Instrument Company see Foxboro Co.
Industrial Light & Magic, see Lucasfilm Ltd.
Industrial Powder Coatings, Inc., 16 475
Industrial Publishing Company, see Pittway Corp.
Industrial Resources, 6 144
Industrial Services Group, Inc., 56 161
Industrial Services of America, Inc., 46 247–49
Industrial Tectonics Corp., 18 276
Industrial Tires Limited, 65 91
Industrial Trade & Consumer Shows Inc. see Maclean Hunter Publishing Ltd.
Industrias Bachoco, S.A. de C.V., 39 228–31
Industrias del Atlantico SA, 47 291
Indústrias Klabin de Papel e Celulose S.A. see Klabin S.A.
Industrias Nacobre, 21 259
Industrias Negromex, 23 170
Industrias Penoles, S.A. de C.V., 22 284–86
Industrias Resistol S.A., 23 170–71
Industrie Natuzzi S.p.A., 18 256–58
Industrie Zignago Santa Margherita S.p.A., 67 210–12
Industriförvaltnings AB Kinnevik, 26 331–33; 36 335
AB Industrivärden, 32 397
Induyco see Industrias y Confecciones, S.A.
Indy Lighting, 30 266
Indy Racing League, 37 74
Inet Technologies Inc. see Tektronix Inc.
Infineon Technologies AG, 50 269–73
Infinity Broadcasting Corporation, 11 190–92; 48 214–17 (upd.)
Infinity Enterprises, Inc., 44 4
Infinity Partners, 36 160
Inflight Sales Group Limited, 11 82; 29 511
InfoAsia, 28 241
Infocom, 32 8

Isis Distributed Systems, Inc., *see* Stratus Computer, Inc.

Island Def Jam Music, **57** 359

The Island ECN, Inc., 48 225–29

Island Equipment Co., **19** 381

Island Pictures Corp., **23** 389

Island Records, **23** 389

Isle of Capri Casinos, Inc., 41 217–19

Isokauf *see* SIG plc.

Isosceles PLC, **24** 270; **47** 367–68

Ispat Inland Inc., 30 252–54; 40 267–72 (upd.)

Israel Aircraft Industries Ltd., 69 215–17

Israel Chemicals Ltd., 55 226–29

ISS A/S, 49 221–23

ISS Securitas, **42** 165, 167

ISSI *see* Integrated Silicon Solutions Inc.

Istante Vesa s.r.l., *see* Gianni Versace SpA.

Istituto Farmacologico Serono S.p.A. *see* Serono S.A.

Istituto Mobiliare Italiano S.p.A., **50** 407, 409

Istituto per la Ricostruzione Industriale S.p.A., I 465–67; 11 203–06 (upd.)

Isuzu Motors, Ltd., 9 293–95; 23 288–91 (upd.); 57 187–91 (upd.)

IT Group, **28** 203

IT International, **V** 255

IT-Software Companies, **48** 402

Italcimenti Group, **40** 107–08

Italianni's, **22** 128

Italstate *see* Societa per la Infrastrutture e l'Assetto del Territorio.

Italtel, **V** 326–27

Itaú *see* Banco Itaú S.A.

Itaúsa *see* Investimentos Itaú S.A.

ITC Holdings Corp., 75 206–08

Itek Corp., *see* Litton Industries Inc.

Itel Corporation, 9 296–99

Items International Airwalk Inc., 17 259–61

Ithaca Gas & Electric *see* New York State Electric and Gas.

ITI Education Corporation, **29** 472

ITM Entreprises SA, 36 294–97

Ito Gofuku Co. Ltd. *see* Matsuzakaya Company Ltd.

Ito-Yokado Co., Ltd., V 88–89; 42 189–92 (upd.)

Itochu and Renown, Inc., **12** 281

ITOCHU Corporation, 32 283–87 (upd.)

Itochu Housing, **38** 415

Itoh *see* C. Itoh & Co.

Itoham Foods Inc., II 518–19; 61 138–40 (upd.)

Itoman & Co., **26** 456

Itron, Inc., 64 202–05

The Itsy Bitsy Entertainment Company, **51** 309

ITT *see* International Telephone and Telegraph Corp.

ITT Aerospace, **33** 48

ITT Automotive Inc. *see* Valeo.

ITT Educational Services, Inc., 33 215–17; 76 200–03 (upd.)

ITT Sheraton Corporation, III 98–101 *see also* Starwood Hotels & Resorts Worldwide, Inc.

iTurf Inc., **29** 142–43

ITV PLC, **71** 368

ITW *see* Illinois Tool Works Inc.

i2 Technologies, Inc., 87 252–257

IU International, **23** 40

IURA Edition, **14** 556

IV Therapy Associates, **16** 440

IVACO Industries Inc., *see* IVAX Corp.

Ivanhoe, Inc., *see* Steinberg Inc.

Ivar's, Inc., 86 216–19

IVAX Corporation, 11 207–09; 55 230–33 (upd.)

IVC Industries, Inc., 45 208–11

iVillage Inc., 46 253–56

Ivy and Mader Philatelic Auctions, Inc., **60** 146

Ivy Mortgage Corp., **39** 380, 382

Iwerks Entertainment, Inc., 34 228–30

IXC Communications, Inc., 29 250–52

IXI Ltd., **38** 418–19

Ixos Software AG *see* Open Text Corporation

IYG Holding Company of Japan, *see* 7-Eleven, Inc.

The IZOD Gant Corporation, *see* Phillips-Van Heusen Corp

Izod Lacoste, *see* Crystal Brands, Inc.

Izukyu Corporation, **47** 408

Izumi Fudosan *see* Sumitomo Reality & Development Co., Ltd.

J

J & J Snack Foods Corporation, 24 240–42

J&L Industrial Supply, *see* Kennametal, Inc.

J&L Steel *see* Jones & Laughlin Steel Corp.

J & M Laboratories, **48** 299

J&R Electronics Inc., 26 224–26

J&W Hardie Ltd., **62** 347

J. & W. Seligman & Co. Inc., 61 141–43

J.A. Jones, Inc., 16 284–86

J. Alexander's Corporation, 65 177–79

J.B. Hunt Transport Services Inc., 12 277–79

J.B. Ivey & Company *see* Dillard's Inc.

J.B. Lippincott & Company, *see* Wolters Kluwer NV.

J.B. McLean Publishing Co., Ltd. *see* Maclean Hunter Publishing Ltd.

J.B. Wolters Publishing Company, *see* Wolters Kluwer NV.

J. Baker, Inc., 31 270–73

J Bibby & Sons, *see* Barlow Rand Ltd.

J. Boag & Son Limited, **57** 306

J. Bulova Company *see* Bulova Corp.

J C Bamford Excavators Ltd., 83 216–222

J.C. Baxter Co., **15** 501

J.C. Hillary's, **20** 54

J.C. McCormic, Inc., **58** 334

J.C. Penney Company, Inc., V 90–92; 18 269–73 (upd.); 43 245–50 (upd.)

J.C. Potter Sausage Company, **57** 56–57

J. Crew Group Inc., 12 280–82; 34 231–34 (upd.)

J.D. Bassett Manufacturing Co. *see* Bassett Furniture Industries, Inc.

J.D. Edwards & Company, 14 268–70 *see also* Oracle Corp.

J.D. Power and Associates, 32 297–301

J. D'Addario & Company, Inc., 48 230–33

J.E. Sirrine *see* CRSS Inc.

J.F. Corporation *see* Isetan Company Ltd.

J.F. Shea Co., Inc., 55 234–36

J.H. Findorff and Son, Inc., 60 175–78

J.H. Heafner Co., **20** 263

J.H. Westerbeke Corp. *see* Westerbeke Corp.

J.H. Whitney & Company, **32** 100

J. Homestock *see* R.H. Macy & Co.

J. Horner's, **48** 415

J.I.C. Group Limited, **61** 233

J.I. Case Company, 10 377–81 *see also* CNH Global N.V.

J.J. Farmer Clothing Inc., **51** 320–21

J.J. Keller & Associates, Inc., 81 2180–21

J.J. Kenney Company, Inc., **51** 244

The J. Jill Group, Inc., 35 239–41

J.K. Starley and Company Ltd, *see* Rover Group Ltd.

J.L. Clark, Inc. *see* Clarcor Inc.

J.L. French Automotive Castings, Inc. *see* Onex Corp.

J.L. Hammett Company, 72 196–99

J.L. Hudson Company *see* Target Corp.

J.L. Shiely Co. *see* English China Clays Ltd.

J.M. Huber Corporation, **40** 68

The J. M. Smucker Company, 11 210–12; 87 258–265 (upd.)

J.M. Tull Metals Co., Inc., *see* Inland Steel Industries, Inc.

J.M. Voith AG, 33 222–25

J-Mar Associates, **31** 435–36

J.P. Morgan Chase & Co., II 329–32; 30 261–65 (upd.); 38 253–59 (upd.)

J.P. Stevens Inc., *see* WestPoint Stevens Inc.

J.R. Brown & Sharpe *see* Brown & Sharpe Manufacturing Co.

J.R. Simplot Company, 16 287–89; 60 179–82 (upd.)

J Sainsbury plc, II 657–59; 13 282–84 (upd.); 38 260–65 (upd.)

J. Sears & Company *see* Sears plc.

J. Spiegel and Company *see* Spiegel, Inc.

J.U. Dickson Sawmill Inc. *see* Dickson Forest Products, Inc.

J.W. Bateson, *see* Centex Corp.

J.W. Charles Financial Services Inc., 25 542

J.W. Childs Associates, L.P., **46** 220; **64** 119

J.W. Childs Equity Partners LP, **40** 274

J.W. Foster and Sons, Inc. *see* Reebok International Ltd.

J. W. Pepper and Son Inc., 86 220–23

J.W. Spear, **25** 314

Knogo Corp., **11** 444; **39** 78
Knoll, Inc., 14 299–301; **80** 184–88 **(upd.)**
Knorr-Bremse AG, 84 226–231
Knorr Co. *see* C.H. Knorr Co.
Knorr Foods Co., Ltd., **28** 10
The Knot, Inc., 74 168–71
Knott's Berry Farm, 18 288–90
Knowledge Learning Corporation, 51 197–99; **54** 191
Knowledge Systems Concepts, **11** 469
Knowledge Universe, Inc., 54 191–94
KnowledgeWare Inc., 9 309–11; **31** 296–98 **(upd.)**
Knox County Insurance, **41** 178
Knoxville Glove Co., **34** 159
KNP BT *see* Buhrmann NV.
KNP Leykam, **49** 352, 354
KNSM *see* Koninklijke Nederlandsche Stoomboot Maatschappij.
Knudsen & Sons, Inc., *see* The J.M. Smucker Co.
KOA *see* Kampgrounds of America, Inc.
Koala Corporation, 44 260–62
Kobe Hankyu Company Ltd., **62** 170
Kobe Steel, Ltd., IV 129–31; **19** 238–41 **(upd.)**
Kobold *see* Vorwerk & Co.
Kobrand Corporation, 82 191–94
Koç Holding A.S., I 478–80; **54** 195–98 **(upd.)**
Koch Enterprises, Inc., 29 215–17
Koch Industries, Inc., IV 448–49; **20** 330–32 **(upd.); 77** 224–30 **(upd.)**
Kodak *see* Eastman Kodak Co.
Kodansha Ltd., IV 631–33; **38** 273–76 **(upd.)**
Koehring Cranes & Excavators, *see* Terex Corp.
Koei Real Estate Ltd. *see* Takashimaya Co., Ltd.
Koenig & Bauer AG, 64 222–26
Kogaku Co., Ltd., **48** 295
Kohl's Corporation, 9 312–13; **30** 273–75 **(upd.); 77** 231–35 **(upd.)**
Kohlberg Kravis Roberts & Co., 24 272–74; **56** 190–94 **(upd.)**
Kohler Company, 7 269–71; **32** 308–12 **(upd.)**
Kohler Mix Specialties, Inc. *see*Dean Foods.
Kohn Pedersen Fox Associates P.C., 57 213–16
Kokkola Chemicals Oy, *see* OM Group, Inc.
Kokomo Gas and Fuel Company, **6** 533
Kokudo Corporation, **74** 301
Kokusai Kigyo Co. Ltd., **60** 301
Kolb-Lena, **25** 85
The Koll Company, 8 300–02
Kollmorgen Corporation, 18 291–94
Kölnische Rückversicherungs- Gesellschaft AG, *see* General Re Corp.
Komag, Inc., 11 234–35
Komatsu Ltd., III 545–46; **16** 309–11 **(upd.); 52** 213–17 **(upd.)**
Kompass Allgemeine Vermögensberatung, **51** 23

KONE Corporation, 27 267–70; **76** 225–28 **(upd.)**
Kongl. Elektriska Telegraf-Verket *see* Swedish Telecom.
Konica Corporation, III 547–50; **30** 276–81 **(upd.)**
König Brauerei GmbH & Co. KG, 35 256–58 **(upd.)**
Koninklijke Ahold N.V., II 641–42; **16** 312–14 **(upd.)**
Koninklijke Bols Wessanen, N.V., **29** 480–81; **57** 105
Koninklijke Grolsch BV *see* Royal Grolsch NV.
Koninklijke Hoogovens NV *see* Koninklijke Nederlandsche Hoogovens en Staalfabrieken NV.
Koninklijke Java-China Paketvaart Lijnen *see* Royal Interocean Lines.
NV Koninklijke KNP BT *see* Buhrmann NV.
Koninklijke KPN N.V. *see* Royal KPN N.V.
Koninklijke Luchtvaart Maatschappij N.V., I 107–09; **28** 224–27 **(upd.)**
Koninklijke Nederlandsche Hoogovens en Staalfabrieken NV, IV 132–34
Koninklijke Nederlandsche Stoomboot Maatschappij, **26** 241
N.V. Koninklijke Nederlandse Vliegtuigenfabriek Fokker, I 54–56; **28** 327–30 **(upd.)**
Koninklijke Nedlloyd N.V., 6 403–05; **26** 241–44 **(upd.)**
Koninklijke Numico N.V. *see* Royal Numico N.V.
Koninklijke Paketvaart Maatschappij, **26** 242
Koninklijke Philips Electronics N.V., 50 297–302 **(upd.)**
Koninklijke PTT Nederland NV, V 299–301 *see also* Royal KPN NV.
Koninklijke Vendex KBB N.V. (Royal Vendex KBB N.V.), 62 206–09 **(upd.)**
Koninklijke Wessanen nv, II 527–29; **54** 199–204 **(upd.)**
Koninklijke West-Indische Maildienst, **26** 242
Konishiroku Honten Co., Ltd., *see* Konica Corp.
Konrad Hornschuch AG, **31** 161–62
Koo Koo Roo, Inc., 25 263–65
Kookmin Bank, 58 206–08
Koop Nautic Holland, **41** 412
Koor Industries Ltd., II 47–49; **25** 266–68 **(upd.); 68** 222–25 **(upd.)**
Kopin Corporation, 80 189–92
Köpings Mekaniska Verkstad, **26** 10
Koppel Steel, **26** 407
Koppers Industries, Inc., I 354–56; **26** 245–48 **(upd.)**
Koramic Roofing Products N.V., **70** 363
Korbel Champagne Cellers *see* F. Korbel & Bros. Inc.
Körber AG, 60 190–94
Korea Automotive Motor Corp., *see* Robert Bosch GmbH.

Korea Electric Power Corporation (Kepco), 56 195–98
Korea Ginseng Corporation *see* KT&G Corp.
Korea Independent Energy Corporation, **62** 175
Korea Tobacco & Ginseng Corporation *see* KT&G Corp.
Korean Air Lines Co. Ltd., 6 98–99; **27** 271–73 **(upd.)**
Korean Life Insurance Company, Ltd., **62** 175
Koret of California, Inc., 62 210–13
Kori Kollo Corp., **23** 41
Korn/Ferry International, 34 247–49
Korrekt Gebäudereinigung, *see* Randstad Holding n.v.
Kortbetalning Servo A.B., *see* Skandinaviska Enskilda Banken AB.
Kos Pharmaceuticals, Inc., 63 232–35
Koss Corporation, 38 277–79
Kosset Carpets, Ltd., *see* Shaw Industries.
Koszegi Industries Inc. *see* Forward Industries, Inc.
Kotobukiya Co., Ltd., V 113–14; **56** 199–202 **(upd.)**
Koyland Ltd., **64** 217
KP Corporation, **74** 163
KPM *see* Koninklijke Paketvaart Maatschappij.
KPMG International, 10 385–87; **33** 234–38 **(upd.)**
KPN *see* Koninklijke PTT Nederland N.V.
KPR Holdings Inc., **23** 203
KPS Special Situations Fund, L.P., 69 360–62
Kraft Foods Inc., II 530–34; **7** 272–77 **(upd.); 45** 235–44 **(upd.)**
Kraft Foodservice, **26** 504; **31** 359–60
Kraft Jacobs Suchard AG, 26 249–52 **(upd.)**
KraftMaid Cabinetry, Inc., 72 208–10
Kragen Auto Supply Co. *see* CSK Auto Corp.
Kramer Guitar, **29** 222
Kramer Machine and Engineering Company, **26** 117
Krames Communications Co., **22** 441, 443
Kransco, **25** 314; **61** 392
Krasnapolsky Restaurant and Wintergarden Company Ltd., **23** 228
Kraus-Anderson Companies, Inc., 36 317–20; **83** 243-248 **(upd.)**
Krause Publications, Inc., 35 259–61
Krause's Furniture, Inc., 27 274–77
Krauss-Maffei AG, *see* Mannesmann AG
Kredietbank N.V., II 304–056
Kreditanstalt für Wiederaufbau, 29 268–72
Kreher Steel Co., **25** 8
Krelitz Industries, Inc., *see* D&K Wholesale Drug, Inc.
Kresge Foundation *see* Kmart Corp.
Kreymborg, *see*Koninklijke Vendex KBB N.V. (Royal Vendex KBB N.V.)

Lacks Enterprises Inc., **61** 158–60
Laclede Steel Company, 15 271–73
Lacombe Electric *see* Public Service
Company of Colorado.
LaCrosse Footwear, Inc., 18 298–301;
61 161–65 (upd.)
Lacto Ibérica, **23** 219
Lactos, **25** 85
Ladbroke Group PLC, II 141–42; **21**
333–36 (upd.) *see also* Hilton Group
plc.
LADD Furniture, Inc., 12 299–301 *see
also* La-Z-Boy Inc.
Ladd Petroleum Corp., *see* General
Electric Co.
LADECO *see* Iberia.
Ladenburg, Thalmann & Co. Inc., *see*
New Valley Corp.
Ladish Co., Inc., 30 282–84
Lady Foot Locker, **V** 226
Lafarge Cement UK, 54 208–11 (upd.)
Lafarge Coppée S.A., III 703–05
Lafarge Corporation, 28 228–31
Lafayette Manufacturing Co., *see* Kimball
International, Inc.
Lafuma S.A., 39 248–50
LAG&E *see* Los Angeles Gas and Electric
Co.
LaGard Inc., **20** 363
Lagardère Groupe SCA, **16** 254; **34** 83
Laidlaw International, Inc., 80 205–08
Laing's Properties Ltd. *see* John Laing plc.
L'Air Liquide SA, I 357–59; **47** 217–20
(upd.)
Lake Erie Screw Corp., *see* TriMas Corp.
Lake Pacific Partners, LLC, **55** 124
Lake Superior & Ishpeming Railroad
Company, **62** 74
Lake Superior Paper Industries, **26** 363
Lakehead Pipe Line Partners, L.P., **43** 155
Lakeland Industries, Inc., 45 245–48
Lakes Entertainment, Inc., 51 205–07
The Lakeside Publishing and Printing Co.
see R.R. Donnelley & Sons Co.
Lakestone Systems, Inc., **11** 469
Lakewood Animal Hospital, Inc., **58** 354
Lala *see* Grupo Industrial Lala, S.A. de
C.V.
Lalique, **55** 309
Lam Research Corporation, 11 245–47;
31 299–302 (upd.)
**Lam Son Sugar Joint Stock Corporation
(Lasuco), 60** 195–97
Lamar Advertising Company, 27
278–80; **70** 150–53 (upd.)
The Lamaur Corporation, 41 227–29
Lamb Technicon Corp., *see* Litton
Industries Inc.
Lamb Weston, Inc., 23 319–21
Lambda Electronics Inc., **32** 411
Lambert Brussels Financial Corporation
see Drexel Burnham Lambert Inc.
Lambert Frères, **33** 339
Lambert Rivière, **41** 340
Lamborghini *see* Automobili Lamborghini
S.p.A.
Lamkin Brothers, Inc., *see* NCH Corp.

Lamons Metal Gasket Co., *see* TriMas
Corp.
Lamonts Apparel, Inc., 15 274–76
Lampadaires Feralux, Inc., *see* Valmont
Industries, Inc.
Lamplight Farms Inc. *see* W.C. Bradley
Co.
The Lamson & Sessions Co., 13
304–06; **61** 166–70 (upd.)
Lan Chile S.A., 31 303–06
Lancair International, Inc., 67 224–26
Lancaster Colony Corporation, 8
307–09; **61** 171–74 (upd.)
Lancaster Press, **23** 102
Lance, Inc., 14 305–07; **41** 230–33
(upd.)
Lancel, *see* Vendôme Luxury Group plc.
Lancer Corporation, 21 337–39
Lancey Investissement SAS, **58** 221
Land Group, **74** 283
Land O'Lakes, Inc., II 535–37; **21**
340–43 (upd.); **81** 222–27 (upd.)
Land-O-Sun Dairies, L.L.C., **26** 449
Land Securities PLC, IV 704–06; **49**
246–50 (upd.)
Landair Corporation, **75** 148
LandAmerica Financial Group, Inc., 85
213–16
Landauer, Inc., 51 208–10
Lander Company, **21** 54
Landmark Business Products, Inc., **61** 254
Landmark Communications, Inc., 12
302–05; **55** 244–49 (upd.)
Landmark Financial Services Inc., **11** 447
Landmark Theatre Corporation, 70
154–56
Landoll, Inc., *see* Tribune Co.
Landor Associates, 81 228–31
Landry's Restaurants, Inc., 15 277–79;
65 203–07 (upd.)
Lands' End, Inc., 9 314–16; **29** 276–79
(upd.); **82** 195–200 (upd.)
Landsbanki Islands hf, 81 232–35
Landstar System, Inc., 63 236–38
Lane Bryant, Inc., 64 231–33
The Lane Co., Inc., 12 306–08
Lane Industries Inc., **73** 160
Lane, Piper, and Jaffray, Inc. *see* Piper
Jaffray Companies.
Lane Publishing Co., **IV** 676; **7** 529
Laneco, Inc., *see* Wetterau Inc.
Lang Exploratory Drilling, **26** 42
Langdon Rieder Corp., **21** 97
Lange International S.A., **15** 462; **43**
375–76
Langen Packaging Inc., **51** 249, 251
Langenpac NV, **51** 249–50
Langenscheidt KG, **74** 33
Lanier Worldwide, Inc., 75 235–38
Lanman Companies, Inc., **23** 101
Lannet Data Communications Ltd., **26**
275–77
Lanoga Corporation, 62 222–24
LAPE *see* Líneas Aéreas Postales Españolas.
Lapeyre S.A. *see* Groupe Lapeyre S.A.
LaPine Technology, **II** 51; **21** 331
Lara, **19** 192
Lareco, **26** 22

Largardère Groupe, 43 210
Largo Entertainment, **25** 329
Largo Music Publishing, **55** 250
Lariat Petroleum, 65 262
Larousse Group *see* Groupe de la Cité.
Larry Flynt Publishing Inc., 31 307–10
Larry H. Miller Group, 29 280–83
Larry's Food Products, **36** 163
Larsen Company, *see* Dean Foods Co.
Larson Boats *see* Genmar Holdings, Inc.
Las Vegas Sands, Inc., 50 306–08
LaSalle Investment Management, Inc., **49**
238
LaSalle Partners, **49** 28
LaSalle Steel Corporation, **28** 314
Laser Tech Color, **21** 60
Laserscope, 67 227–29
LaSiDo Inc., 58 209–11
Lasik*Plus* *see* LCA-Vision, Inc.
Lasmo, **IV** 455, 499; **65** 316–17
Lason, Inc., 31 311–13
Lassonde Industries Inc., 68 229–31
Lasuco *see* Lam Son Sugar Joint Stock
Corp.
Latasa SA *see* Rexam PLC.
Latcom, Inc., **55** 302
Latham & Watkins, 33 252–54
Latin Communications Group Inc., **41**
151
Latin Percussion, Inc. *see* Kaman Music
Corp.
Latitude Communications, **22** 52
Latrobe Brewing Company, 54 212–14
Lattice Semiconductor Corp., 16
315–17
Lauda Air Luftfahrt AG, 48 258–60
Laura Ashley Holdings plc, 13 307–09;
37 226–29 (upd.)
Laura Scudders, **44** 348
Laureate Enterprises Inc., **64** 190
Laurel Glen, **34** 3, 5
Laurel Pipe Line Company *see* Buckeye
Partners, L.P.
The Laurel Pub Company Limited, 59
255–57
Laurel Technologies Partnership, **58** 101
Laurent-Perrier SA, 42 221–23
Laurentian Group, **48** 290
Laurus N.V., 65 208–11
LaVista Equipment Supply Co., **14** 545;
60 326
Lavold, *see* Randstad Holding n.v.
Lavoro Bank AG *see* Banca Nazionale del
Lavoro SpA.
Lawn Boy Inc., *see* Toro Co.
Lawrenceburg Gas Company *see*
Cincinnati Gas & Electric Co.
Lawson Inc., **41** 113, 115
Lawson Software, 38 284–88
Lawter International Inc., 14 308–10 *see
also* Eastman Chemical Co.
Lawyers Cooperative Publishing, *see* The
Thomson Corp.
Lawyers Title Insurance Corporation *see*
LandAmerica Financial Group, Inc.
Layer Five, **43** 252
Layne Christensen Company, 19
245–47

M.T.G.I. Textile Manufacturers Group, **25** 121

M.W. Carr, **14** 245

M.W. Kellogg Co., **34** 81; **62** 204

MAAG Gear Wheel, **72** 138, 140

Maatschappij tot Exploitatie van de Onderneming Krasnapolsky *see* Grand Hotel Krasnapolsky N.V.

Mabe *see* Controladora Mabe, S.A. de C.V.

Mabuchi Motor Co. Ltd., 68 241–43

Mabuhay Vinyl Corporation *see* Tosoh Corp.

MAC Aviation Services LLC *see* Air T, Inc.

Mac Frugal's Bargains - Closeouts Inc., 17 297–99 *see also* Big Lots, Inc.

Mac-Gray Corporation, 44 271–73

Mac Publications LLC, **25** 240

The Macallan Distillers Ltd., 63 246–48

MacAndrews & Forbes Holdings Inc., 28 246–49; **86** 253–59 **(upd.)**

MacArthur Foundation *see* The John D. and Catherine T. MacArthur Foundation.

Macauley & Co. *see* Greif Inc.

MacDermid Incorporated, 32 318–21

MacDonald Companies, **15** 87

MacDonald Dettwiler and Associates, **32** 436

Mace Security International, Inc., 57 230–32

The Macerich Company, 57 233–35

MacFrugal's Bargains Close-Outs Inc., **29** 312; **50** 98

MacGregor Golf Company, 68 244–46

MacGregor Sporting Goods Inc., **23** 449

Mach Performance, Inc., **28** 147

Macintosh *see* Apple Computer, Inc.

Mack-Cali Realty Corporation, 42 239–41

Mack Trucks, Inc., I 177–79; **22** 329–32 **(upd.); 61** 179–83 **(upd.)**

Mack-Wayne Plastics, **42** 439

Mackay Envelope Corporation, 45 256–59

Mackie Designs Inc., 30 406; **33** 278–81

Maclean Hunter Publishing Limited, IV 638–40; **26** 270–74 **(upd.)** *see also* Rogers Communications Inc.

Macluan Capital Corporation, **49** 196

The MacManus Group, **32** 140; **40** 140

MacMark Corp., **22** 459

Macmillan & Co. Ltd., **35** 452

MacMillan Bloedel Limited, IV 306–09 *see also* Weyerhaeuser Co.

Macmillan, Inc., 7 284–86

The MacNeal-Schwendler Corporation, 25 303–05

MacNeil/Lehrer Productions, 87 296–299

Macquarie Bank Ltd., 69 246–49

Macromedia, Inc., 50 328–31

MACSTEEL Monroe, Inc., **62** 289

Macy's *see* R.H. Macy & Co., Inc.

Macy's California, **21** 129

Mad Dog Athletics, **19** 385

Mad River Canoe *see* Confluence Holdings Corp.

MADD *see* Mothers Against Drunk Driving.

Madden's on Gull Lake, 52 231–34

Madeco S.A., 71 210–12

Madeira Wine Company, S.A., 49 255–57

Maderin ECO S.A., **51** 6

Madge Networks N.V., 26 275–77

Madison Dearborn Partners LLC, **46** 289; **49** 197; **51** 131, 282, 284; **69** 197

Madison Furniture Industries, *see* Shelby Williams Industries, Inc.

Madison Gas and Electric Company, 39 259–62

Madison-Kipp Corporation, 58 213–16

Madison Park Press *see* Bookspan.

Madrange SA, 58 217–19

Maersk Oile, **22** 167; **65** 316–17

Maersk Sealand *see* A.P. Møller - Maersk A/S.

Maes Group Breweries, **II** 475

Maeva Group *see* Club Mediterranee SA.

Mafco Holdings, Inc., **28** 248; **38** 293–95

Mag Instrument, Inc., 67 240–42

MagCorp, **28** 198

Magee Company, **31** 435–36

Magella Healthcare Corporation, **61** 284

Magellan Aerospace Corporation, 48 274–76

Magellan Corporation, **22** 403; **60** 137

Magellan et Bergerat., **72** 159

Magic Chef Co. *see* Maytag Corp.

Magic City Food Products Company *see* Golden Enterprises, Inc.

Magic Marker, **29** 372

Magic Years Child Care, **51** 198

Magicsilk, Inc., *see* Celebrity, Inc.

Maglificio di Ponzano Veneto dei Fratelli Benetton *see* Benetton.

Magma Copper Company, 7 287–90 *see also* BHP Billiton.

Magma Design Automation Inc., 78 203–27

Magma Power Company, 11 270–72

Magna Computer Corporation, *see* EMC Corp.

Magna Distribuidora Ltda., **43** 368

Magnaflux, *see* Illinois Tool Works Inc.

Magnavox Co., *see* Philips Electronics.

MagneTek, Inc., 15 287–89; **41** 241–44 **(upd.)**

Magnetic Peripherals Inc., **19** 513–14

Magnivision, Inc., *see* American Greetings Corp.

Magnum Hunter Resources, Inc. *see* Cimarex Energy Co.

Magro, **48** 63

Magyar Telekom Rt, 78 208–11

Magyar Viscosa, **37** 428

Mahalo Air, **22** 252

Mahir & Numan A.S., **48** 154

MAI PLC, **28** 504

MAI Systems Corporation, 11 273–76

Maid-Rite Corporation, 62 235–38

Maidenform, Inc., 20 352–55; **59** 265–69 **(upd.)**

Mail Boxes Etc., **18** 315–17; **41** 245–48 **(upd.)** *see also* U.S. Office Products Co.

Mail.com Inc., **38** 271

Mail Coups, Inc., **53** 13

Mail Finance, **53** 239

Mail Marketing Systems Inc., **53** 13

Mail-Well, Inc., 28 250–52 *see also* Cenveo Inc.

MailCoups, Inc., **53** 9

Mailtek, Inc., *see* Total System Services, Inc.

MAIN *see* Makhteshim-Agan Industries Ltd.; Mid-American Interpool Network.

Main Plaza Corporation, **25** 115

Main Street Advertising USA, **IV** 597

Maine & Maritimes Corporation, 56 210–13

Maine Central Railroad Company, 16 348–50

Maines Paper & Food Service Inc., 71 213–15

Mainline Industrial Distributors, Inc., *see* Bearings, Inc.

Maison Blanche Department Stores Group, **35** 129

Maison de Valérie, **19** 309

Maison Louis Jadot, 24 307–09

Majesco Entertainment Company, 85 225–29

Majestic Industries, Inc., **43** 459

The Major Automotive Companies, Inc., 45 260–62

Major SA, **53** 179

Major Video Concepts, **6** 410

Major Video Corporation, *see* Blockbuster Inc.

Makhteshim-Agan Industries Ltd., 85 230–34

Makita Corporation, 22 333–35; **59** 270–73 **(upd.)**

Makivik Corporation, **56** 38–39

Makoff R&D Laboratories, **56** 375

Malapai Resources, **6** 546

Malayan Banking Berhad, 72 215–18

Malaysian Airlines System Berhad, 6 100–02; **29** 300–03 **(upd.)**

Malcolm Pirnie, Inc., 42 242–44

Malden Mills Industries, Inc., 16 351–53

Malév Plc, 24 310–12

Malew Engineering, **51** 354

Malibu, **25** 141

Mall.com, **38** 271

Mallard Bay Drilling, **28** 347–48

Mallinckrodt Group Inc., 19 251–53

Malmö Aviation, **47** 61

Malmö Woodworking Factory *see* Tarkett Sommer AG.

Malone & Hyde, Inc., **14** 147 *see also* AutoZone, Inc.; Fleming Companies, Inc.

Malt-O-Meal Company, 22 336–38; **63** 249–53 **(upd.)**

Malterie Soufflet *see* Groupe Soufflet SA

Mama Fu's Noodle House, Inc., **64** 327–28

Mama's Concept, Inc., **51** 229

Mameco International, *see* RPM Inc.

Mammoet Transport B.V., 26 278–80
Man Aktiengesellschaft, III 561–63
MAN Gutehoffnungshütte AG, **15** 226
**Management and Training Corporation,
28** 253–56
Management By Information Inc., **48** 307
Management Recruiters International *see*
CDI Corp.
Manatron, Inc., 86 260–63
**Manchester United Football Club plc,
30** 296–98
Manco, Inc. *see* Henkel Manco Inc.
Mancuso & Co., **22** 116
Mandabach & Simms, **6** 40
Mandalay Pictures, **35** 278–80
Mandalay Resort Group, 32 322–26
(upd.)
Mandarin, Inc., **33** 128
Mandarin Oriental International Limited,
47 177
Mandom Corporation, 82 205–08
Manetta Home Fashions, Inc., *see*
Pillowtex Corp.
Manhattan Associates, Inc., 67 243–45
Manhattan Bagel Inc., **63** 80
Manhattan Construction Company *see*
Rooney Brothers Co.
Manhattan Drug Company *see* Integrated
BioPharma, Inc.
Manhattan Group, LLC, 80 228–31
Manhattan International Limousine
Network Ltd., **26** 62
Manheim Auctions, Inc. *see* Cox
Enterprises, Inc.
Manila Electric Company (Meralco), 56
214–16
Manischewitz Company *see* B.
Manischewitz Co.
Manitoba Telecom Services, Inc., 61
184–87
Manitou BF S.A., 27 294–96
The Manitowoc Company, Inc., 18
318–21; **59** 274–79 **(upd.)**
Mann's Wine Company, Ltd., *see*
Kikkoman Corp.
Mannatech Inc., 33 282–85
Mannesmann AG, III 564–67; **14**
326–29 **(upd.)**; **38** 296–301 **(upd.)** *see
also* Vodafone Group PLC.
Mannheim Steamroller *see* American
Gramophone LLC.
Manning Selvage & Lee (MS&L), 76
252–54
MannKind Corporation, 87 300–303
Manor AG, **48** 279
Manor Care, Inc., 6 187–90; **25** 306–10
(upd.)
Manor Healthcare Corporation, **26** 459
Manos Enterprises, **14** 87
Manpower Inc., 9 326–27; **30** 299–302
(upd.); **73** 215–18 **(upd.)**
Mantrec S.A., *see* Manitou BF S.A.
Mantua Metal Products *see* Tyco Toys, Inc.
**Manufactured Home Communities,
Inc., 22** 339–41
Manufacturera Mexicana de Partes de
Automoviles S.A., **56** 247

Manufacturers and Traders Trust
Company, *see* First Empire State Corp.
Manufacturers Casualty Insurance Co., **26**
486
Manufacturers Fire Insurance Co., **26** 486
Manufacturers Hanover Corporation, II
312–14 *see also* Chemical Bank.
Manufacturers National Bank of Detroit,
40 116
Manufacturing Management Inc., **19** 381
Manulife Financial Corporation, 85
235–38
Manutan International S.A., 72 219–21
Manville Corporation, III 706–09; **7**
291–95 **(upd.)** *see also* Johns Manville
Corp.
Manweb plc, *see* Scottish Power plc.
Manzotin S.r.l *see* Bolton Group B.V.
Maola Milk and Ice Cream *see* Maryland
& Virginia Milk Producers Cooperative
Association, Inc.
MAP *see* Marathon Ashland Petroleum
LLC.
MAPCO Inc., IV 458–59
MAPICS, Inc., 55 256–58
Maple Grove Farms of Vermont, Inc., **40**
51–52
Maple Leaf Foods Inc., 41 249–53
Maple Leaf Heritage Investments
Acquisition Corporation *see* Hudson's
Bay Co.
Maple Leaf Mills, **41** 252
**Maple Leaf Sports & Entertainment
Ltd., 61** 188–90
Maples Industries, Inc., 83 260-263
MAPP *see* Mid-Continent Area Power
Planner.
Mapra Industria e Comercio Ltda., **32** 40
MAR Associates, **48** 54
Mar-O-Bar Company, *see* Mars, Inc.
Marantha! Music, *see* Thomas Nelson Inc.
Marathon Ashland Petroleum LLC, **49**
329–30; **50** 49
Marathon Insurance Co., **26** 486
Marathon Oil Co., **49** 328, 330 *see also*
United States Steel Corp.
Marauder Company, **26** 433
Marble Slab Creamery, Inc., 87
304–307
Marblehead Communications, Inc., **23**
101
Marbodal, **12** 464
Marc's Big Boy *see* The Marcus Corp.
Marcade Group *see* Aris Industries, Inc.
Marcam Coporation *see* MAPICS, Inc.
Marceau Investments, **II** 356
March of Dimes, 31 322–25
March Plasma Systems, Inc., **48** 299
Marchands Ro-Na Inc. *see* RONA, Inc.
Marchesi Antinori SRL, 42 245–48
Marchex, Inc., 72 222–24
marchFIRST, Inc., 34 261–64
Marco Acquisition Corporation, **62** 268
Marco Business Products, Inc., 75
244–46
Marco's Franchising LLC, 86 264–67
Marcolin S.p.A., 61 191–94
Marcon Coating, Inc., **22** 347

Marconi plc, 33 286–90 **(upd.)**
Marcopolo S.A., 79 247–50
The Marcus Corporation, 21 359–63
Marcy Fitness Products, Inc., *see* Escalade,
Inc.
Maremont Corporation, *see* Arvin
Industries Inc.
Margarete Steiff GmbH, 23 334–37
Marian LLC *see* Charisma Brands LLC.
**Marie Brizard & Roger International
S.A., 22** 342–44
**Marie Callender's Restaurant & Bakery,
Inc., 28** 257–59
Marina Mortgage Company, **46** 25
Marine Computer Systems, **6** 242
Marine Harvest, **56** 257
Marine Manufacturing Corporation, **52**
406
Marine Products Corporation, 75
247–49
Marine Transport Lines, Inc., **59** 323
Marine United Inc., **42** 361
Marinela, **19** 192–93
MarineMax, Inc., 30 303–05
Marinette Marine Corporation, **59** 274,
278
Marion Foods, Inc., *see* Seneca Foods
Corp.
Marion Laboratories Inc., I 648–49
Marion Manufacturing, **9** 72
Marion Merrell Dow, Inc., 9 328–29
(upd.)
Marionet Corp., **IV** 680–81
Marionnaud Parfumeries SA, 51 233–35
Marisa Christina, Inc., 15 290–92
Maritime Electric Company, Limited, **15**
182; **47** 136–37
Maritz Inc., 38 302–05
Mark Controls Corporation, **30** 157
Mark Cross, Inc., **17** 4–5
Mark IV Industries, Inc., 7 296–98; **28**
260–64 **(upd.)**
The Mark Travel Corporation, 80
232–35
Mark's Work Wearhouse Ltd. *see*
Canadian Tire Corporation, Ltd.
Market Development Corporation *see*
Spartan Stores Inc.
Market Growth Resources, **23** 480
Marketing Data Systems, Inc., **18** 24
Marketing Equities International, **26** 136
MarketSpan Corp. *see* KeySpan Energy
Co.
Märklin Holding GmbH, 70 163–66
Marks and Spencer p.l.c., V 124–26; **24**
313–17 **(upd.)**; **85** 239–47 **(upd.)**
Marks-Baer Inc., *see* CTG, Inc.
Marks Brothers Jewelers, Inc., 24
318–20 *see also* Whitehall Jewellers,
Inc.
Marlene Industries Corp., **16** 36–37
Marley Co., **19** 360
Marley Holdings, L.P., **19** 246
Oy Marli Ab, **56** 103
The Marmon Group, Inc., IV 135–38;
16 354–57 **(upd.)**; **70** 167–72 **(upd.)**
Marmon-Perry Light Company, **6** 508
Marolf Dakota Farms, Inc., **18** 14–15

Meridian Oil Inc., **10** 190–91

Meridian Publishing, Inc., **28** 254

Merillat Industries, LLC, 13 338–39; 69 253–55 (upd.)

Merisant Worldwide, Inc., 70 184–86

Merisel, Inc., 12 334–36

Merit Distribution Services, *see* McLane Company, Inc.

Merit Medical Systems, Inc., 29 320–22

Merit Tank Testing, Inc., **IV** 411

Merita/Cotton's Bakeries, **38** 251

Meritage Corporation, 26 289–92

MeritaNordbanken, **40** 336

Meritor Automotive Inc. *see* ArvinMeritor Inc.

Merix Corporation, 36 329–31; 75 257–60 (upd.)

Merkur Direktwerbegesellschaft, **29** 152

Merpati Nusantara Airlines *see* Garuda Indonesia.

Merriam-Webster Inc., 70 187–91

Merrill Corporation, 18 331–34; 47 241–44 (upd.)

Merrill Lynch & Co., Inc., II 424–26; 13 340–43 (upd.); 40 310–15 (upd.)

Merrill Lynch Capital Partners, **47** 363

Merrill Lynch Investment Managers *see* BlackRock, Inc.

Merrill, Pickard, Anderson & Eyre IV, **11** 490

Merrill Publishing, **29** 57

Merrimack Services Corp., **37** 303

Merry-Go-Round Enterprises, Inc., 8 362–64

Merry Group *see* Boral Ltd.

Merry Maids *see* ServiceMaster Inc.

Merryhill Schools, Inc., **37** 279

The Mersey Docks and Harbour Company, 30 318–20

Mervyn's California, 10 409–10; 39 269–71 (upd.) *see also* Target Corp.

Merz Group, 81 253–56

Mesa Air Group, Inc., 11 298–300; 32 334–37 (upd.); 77 265–70 (upd.)

Mesaba Holdings, Inc., 28 265–67

Messerschmitt-Bölkow-Blohm GmbH., I 73–75 *see also* European Aeronautic Defence and Space Company EADS N.V.

Mestek, Inc., 10 411–13

Met Food Corp. *see* White Rose Food Corp.

Met-Mex Penoles *see* Industrias Penoles, S.A. de C.V.

META Group, Inc., **37** 147

Metal Box plc, I 604–06 *see also* Novar plc.

Metal-Cal *see* Avery Dennison Corp.

Metal Casting Technology, Inc., **23** 267, 269

AB Metal Pty Ltd, **62** 331

Metalcorp Ltd, **62** 331

Metales y Contactos, **29** 461–62

Metaleurop S.A., 21 368–71

MetalExchange, **26** 530

Metallgesellschaft AG, IV 139–42; 16 361–66 (upd.)

MetalOptics Inc., **19** 212

Metalúrgica Gerdau *see* Gerdau S.A.

Metalurgica Mexicana Penoles, S.A. *see* Industrias Penoles, S.A. de C.V.

Metaphase Technology, Inc., *see* Control Data Systems, Inc.

Metatec International, Inc., 47 245–48

Metcalf & Eddy Companies, Inc., **6** 441; **32** 52

Metcash Trading Ltd., 58 226–28

Meteor Film Productions, **23** 391

Meteor Industries Inc., 33 295–97

Methane Development Corporation, **6** 457

Methanex Corporation, 40 316–19

Methode Electronics, Inc., 13 344–46

MetLife *see* Metropolitan Life Insurance Co.

MetPath, Inc., *see* Corning Inc.

Metra Corporation *see* Wärtsilä Corp.

Metra Steel, **19** 381

Metragaz, **69** 191

Metrastock Ltd., **34** 5

Metric Constructors, Inc., **16** 286

Metric Systems Corporation, *see* Tech-Sym Corp.

Metris Companies Inc., 56 224–27

Metro AG, 50 335–39

Metro Distributors Inc., **14** 545

Metro-Goldwyn-Mayer Inc., 25 326–30 (upd.); 84 263–270 (upd.)

Metro Holding AG, **38** 266

Métro Inc., 77 271–75

Metro Information Services, Inc., 36 332–34

Metro International SA, **36** 335

Metro-Mark Integrated Systems Inc., **11** 469

Metro-North Commuter Railroad Company, **35** 292

Metro Pacific, *see* First Pacific Co. Ltd.

Metro Southwest Construction *see* CRSS Inc.

Metro Support Services, Inc., **48** 171

Metrocall, Inc., 41 265–68

Metrol Security Services, Inc., **32** 373

Metroland Printing, Publishing and Distributing Ltd., **29** 471

Metromail Corp., **IV** 661; **18** 170; **38** 370

Metromedia Company, 7 335–37; 14 298–300 (upd.); 61 210–14 (upd.)

Metronic AG, **64** 226

Metroplex, LLC, **51** 206

Métropole Télévision S.A., 76 272–74 (upd.)

Metropolis Intercom, **67** 137–38

Metropolitan Baseball Club Inc., 39 272–75

Metropolitan Clothing Co., **19** 362

Metropolitan Edison Company, *see* GPU, Inc.

Metropolitan Financial Corporation, 13 347–49

Metropolitan Life Insurance Company, III 290–94; 52 235–41 (upd.)

The Metropolitan Museum of Art, 55 267–70

Metropolitan Opera Association, Inc., 40 320–23

Metropolitan Reference Laboratories Inc., **26** 391

Metropolitan Tobacco Co., **15** 138

Metropolitan Transportation Authority, 35 290–92

MetroRed, **57** 67, 69

Metrostar Management, **59** 199

METSA, Inc., **15** 363

Metsä-Serla Oy, IV 314–16 *see also* M-real Oyj.

Metsec plc, **57** 402

Metso Corporation, 30 321–25 (upd.); 85 269–77 (upd.)

Mettler-Toledo International Inc., 30 326–28

Metwest, **26** 391

Metz Baking Company, **36** 164

Metzdorf Advertising Agency, **30** 80

Metzeler Kautschuk, **15** 354

Mexican Metal Co. *see* Industrias Penoles, S.A. de C.V.

Mexican Restaurants, Inc., 41 269–71

Meyer International Holdings, Ltd., 87 312–315

Meyerland Company, **19** 366

Meyers Motor Supply, **26** 347

Meyers Parking, *see* Central Parking Corp.

The Meyne Company, **55** 74

Meyr Melnhof Karton AG, **41** 325–27

M4 Data (Holdings) Ltd., **62** 293

M40 Trains Ltd., **51** 173

MFS Communications Company, Inc., 11 301–03 *see also* MCI WorldCom, Inc.

MG&E *see* Madison Gas & Electric.

MG Holdings *see* Mayflower Group Inc.

MGD Graphics Systems *see* Goss Holdings, Inc.

MGIC Investment Corp., 52 242–44

MGM *see* McKesson General Medical.

MGM Grand Inc., 17 316–19

MGM Mirage *see* Mirage Resorts, Inc.

MGM Studios, **50** 125

MGM/UA Communications Company, II 146–50 *see also* Metro-Goldwyn-Mayer Inc.

MGN *see* Mirror Group Newspapers Ltd.

MGT Services Inc. *see* The Midland Co.

MH Alshaya Group, **28** 96

MH Media Monitoring Limited, **26** 270

MHI Group, Inc., **16** 344

MHS Holding Corp., **26** 101

MHT *see* Manufacturers Hanover Trust Co.

MI *see* Masco Corp.

MI S.A., **66** 244

Mi-Tech Steel Inc., **63** 359–60

Miami Computer Supply Corporation *see* MCSi, Inc.

Miami Power Corporation *see* Cincinnati Gas & Electric Co.

Miami Subs Corp., **29** 342, 344

Mich-Wis *see* Michigan Wisconsin Pipe Line.

Michael Anthony Jewelers, Inc., 24 334–36

Michael Baker Corporation, 14 333–35;
51 245–48 **(upd.)**
MICHAEL Business Systems Plc, *see*
Control Data Systems, Inc.
Michael C. Fina Co., Inc., 52 245–47
Michael Foods, Inc., 25 331–34
Michael Joseph, **IV** 659
Michael Page International plc, 45
272–74
Michaels Stores, Inc., 17 320–22; **71**
226–30 **(upd.)**
MichCon *see* MCN Corp.
Michelin *see* Compagnie Générale des
Établissements Michelin.
Michie Co., **33** 264–65
Michigan Automotive Compressor, Inc.,
see Toyoda Automatic Loom Works,
Ltd.
Michigan Automotive Research
Corporation, **23** 183
Michigan Bell Telephone Co., 14
336–38
Michigan Consolidated Gas Company *see*
MCN Corp.
Michigan International Speedway *see*
Penske Corp.
Michigan Livestock Exchange, **36** 442
Michigan National Corporation, 11
304–06 *see also* ABN AMRO Holding,
N.V.
Michigan Packaging Company *see* Greif
Inc.
Michigan Seamless Tube Company *see*
Quanex Corp.
Michigan Shoe Makers *see* Wolverine
World Wide Inc.
Michigan Sporting Goods Distributors,
Inc., 72 228–30
Michigan Wisconsin Pipe Line, **39** 260
Mick's Inc., **30** 329
Mickey Shorr Mobile Electronics, *see* ABC
Appliance, Inc.
Micrel, Incorporated, 77 276–79
Micro-Aire Surgical Instruments Corp., *see*
Marmon Group, Inc.
Micro Contract Manufacturing Inc., **44**
441
Micro-Controle, **71** 248
Micro Decisionware, Inc., *see* Sybase, Inc.
Micro Focus Inc., *see* Viasoft Inc.
Micro Magic, Inc., **43** 254
Micro Metallics Corporation, **64** 297
Micro Power Systems Inc., *see* Exar Corp.
Micro Warehouse, Inc., 16 371–73
MicroAge, Inc., 16 367–70
MicroBilt Corporation, *see* First Financial
Management Corp.
Microcar SA, **55** 54, 56
MicroClean Inc, **50** 49
Microcom, Inc., **26** 93; **50** 227
Microdot Inc., 8 365–68
MicroFridge, **44** 273
Micromass Ltd., **43** 455
Micromedex, **19** 268
Micron Technology, Inc., 11 307–09; **29**
323–26 **(upd.)**
MicroPro International Corp. *see* The
Learning Company Inc.

Microprose Inc., **24** 538
Micros Systems, Inc., 18 335–38
Microsensor Systems Inc., **43** 366
Microsoft Corporation, 6 257–60; **27**
319–23 **(upd.); 63** 293–97 **(upd.)**
MicroStrategy Incorporated, 87
316–320
Microtek, Inc., **22** 413
MicroUnity Systems Engineering Inc., **50**
53
Microwave Communications, Inc. *see*
MCI Telecom.
Mid-America Apartment Communities,
Inc., 85 278–81
Mid-America Capital Resources, Inc., **6**
508
Mid-America Dairymen, Inc., 7 338–40
Mid-America Interpool Network, **6** 602
Mid-America Packaging, Inc., *see* Gaylord
Container Corp.
Mid Bus Inc., **33** 107
Mid-Continent Life Insurance Co., **23**
200
Mid-Continent Telephone Corporation *see*
Alltel Corp.
Mid-Georgia Gas Company, **6** 448
Mid-Illinois Gas Co., **6** 529
Mid-Michigan Music Co., **60** 84
Mid-Pacific Airlines, **24** 21–22
Mid-Packaging Group Inc., **19** 78
Mid-South Towing, **6** 583
Mid-States Development, Inc., *see* Otter
Tail Power Co.
Midas Inc., 10 414–15; **56** 228–31
(upd.)
Middle East Airlines - Air Liban S.A.L.,
79 251–54
Middle East Broadcasting Centre, Ltd., *see*
United Press International, Inc.
Middle South Utilities *see* Entergy Corp.
Middle Wisconsin Power, **6** 604
The Middleby Corporation, 22 352–55
Middlesex Water Company, 45 275–78
Middleton Aerospace, **48** 275
The Middleton Doll Company, 53
222–25
Middleton Packaging, **12** 377
Midland Advertising & Design, Inc., **56**
332
Midland Bank plc, II 318–20; **17**
323–26 **(upd.)** *see also* HSBC Holdings
plc.
Midland Brick, **14** 250
The Midland Company, 65 233–35
Midland Enterprises Inc. *see* Eastern
Enterprises.
Midland Group *see* Regency Centers
Corp.
Midland Independent Newspaper plc, **23**
351
Midland United, **6** 556
Midland Utilities Company, **6** 532
Midlantic Hotels Ltd., **41** 83
Midway Airlines Corporation, 33
301–03
Midway Games, Inc., 25 335–38
Midway Manufacturing Company, **15** 539

Midwest Air Group, Inc., 35 293–95;
85 282–86 **(upd.)**
Midwest Agri-Commodities Company, **11**
15; **32** 29
Midwest Biscuit Company, *see* Lance, Inc.
Midwest Grain Products, Inc., 49
261–63
Midwest Realty Exchange, Inc., **21** 257
Midwest Resources Inc., 6 523–25
Midwest Staffing Systems, *see* AHL
Services, Inc.
Midwest Suburban Publishing Inc., **62**
188
Miele & Cie. KG, 56 232–35
MiG *see* Russian Aircraft Corporation
(MiG).
MIG Realty Advisors, Inc., **25** 23, 25
Migros-Genossenschafts-Bund, 68
252–55
MIH Limited, 31 329–32
Mikasa, Inc., 28 268–70
Mike-Sell's Inc., 15 298–300
Mikohn Gaming Corporation, 39
276–79
Milacron, Inc., 53 226–30 **(upd.)**
Milan AC S.p.A., 79 255–58
Milbank, Tweed, Hadley & McCloy, 27
324–27
Milchem, Inc., **63** 306
Mile-Hi Distributing, **64** 180
Miles Inc., **22** 148
Miles Laboratories, I 653–55 *see also*
Bayer A.G.
Milgram Food Stores Inc., *see* Wetterau
Inc.
Milgray Electronics Inc., **47** 41
Milk Specialties Co., **12** 199
Millea Holdings Inc., 64 276–81 **(upd.)**
Millennium & Copthorne Hotels plc,
71 231–33
Millennium Chemicals Inc., **30** 231; **45**
252, 254; **71** 149–50
Millennium Materials Inc. *see* Dyson
Group PLC.
Millennium Pharmaceuticals, Inc., 47
249–52
Miller Automotive Group, **52** 146
Miller Brewing Company, I 269–70; **12**
337–39 **(upd.)** *see also* SABMiller plc.
Miller Companies, **17** 182
Miller Exploration Company *see* Edge
Petroleum Corp.
Miller Freeman, Inc., **IV** 687; **28** 501,
504
Miller Group Ltd., **22** 282
Miller Industries, Inc., 26 293–95
Miller-Meteor Company *see* Accubuilt,
Inc.
Miller, Morris & Brooker (Holdings) Ltd.
see Gibbs and Dandy plc.
Miller Plant Farms, Inc., **51** 61
Miller Publishing Group, LLC, 57
242–44
Miller, Tabak, Hirsch & Co., **28** 164
Millet, **39** 250
Millet's Leisure *see* Sears plc.
Milliken & Co., V 366–68; **17** 327–30
(upd.); 82 235–39 **(upd.)**

Milliman USA, 66 223–26

Millipore Corporation, 25 339–43; 84 271–276 (upd.)

Mills Clothing, Inc. *see* The Buckle, Inc.

The Mills Corporation, 77 280–83

Millway Foods, 25 85

Milne & Craighead, 48 113

Milne Fruit Products, Inc., 25 366

Milnot Company, 46 289–91

Milpark Drilling Fluids, Inc., 63 306

Milsco Manufacturing Co., 23 299, 300

Milton Bradley Company, 21 372–75

Milton CAT, Inc., 86 268–71

Milupa S.A., 37 341

Milwaukee Brewers Baseball Club, 37 247–49

Milwaukee Electric Railway and Light Company, 6 601–02, 604–05

Milwaukee Electric Tool, 28 40

MIM Holdings, 73 392

Mimi's Cafés *see* SWH Corp.

Minatome, IV 560

Mindpearl, 48 381

Mindport, 31 329

Mindset Corp., 42 424–25

Mindspring Enterprises, Inc., 36 168

Mine Safety Appliances Company, 31 333–35

The Miner Group International, 22 356–58

Minera Loma Blanca S.A., 56 127

Mineral Point Public Service Company, 6 604

Minerales y Metales, S.A. *see* Industrias Penoles, S.A. de C.V.

Minerals & Metals Trading Corporation of India Ltd., IV 143–44

Minerals and Resources Corporation Limited *see* Minorco.

Minerals Technologies Inc., 11 310–12; 52 248–51 (upd.)

Minerva SA, 72 289

Minerve, 6 208

Minitel, 21 233

Minneapolis Children's Medical Center, 54 65

Minneapolis Steel and Machinery Company, 21 502

Minnehoma Insurance Company, 58 260

Minnesota Brewing Company *see* MBC Holding Co.

Minnesota Mining & Manufacturing Company, I 499–501; 8 369–71 (upd.); 26 296–99 (upd.) *see also* 3M Co.

Minnesota Power, Inc., 11 313–16; 34 286–91 (upd.)

Minntech Corporation, 22 359–61

Minn-Dak Farmers Cooperative, 32 29

Minolta Co., Ltd., III 574–76; 18 339–42 (upd.); 43 281–85 (upd.)

Minorco, IV 97; 16 28, 293

Minstar Inc., 15 49; 45 174

Minton China, 38 401

The Minute Maid Company, 28 271–74

Minuteman International Inc., 46 292–95

Minyard Food Stores, Inc., 33 304–07; 86 272–77 (upd.)

Mippon Paper, 21 546; 50 58

Miquel y Costas Miquel S.A., 68 256–58

Miracle Food Mart, *see* The Great Atlantic & Pacific Tea Co., Inc.

Miracle-Gro Products, Inc., *see* Scotts Co.

Mirage Resorts, Incorporated, 6 209–12; 28 275–79 (upd.)

Miraglia Inc., 57 139

Miramax Film Corporation, 64 282–85

Mirant, 39 54, 57

MIRAX Corporation *see* JSP Corp.

Mircor Inc., 12 413

Miroglio SpA, 86 278–81

Mirror Group Newspapers plc, 7 341–43; 23 348–51 (upd.)

Misonix, Inc., 80 248–51

Misr Airwork *see* EgyptAir.

Misrair *see* AirEgypt.

Miss Erika, Inc., *see* Norton McNaughton, Inc.

Miss Selfridge *see* Sears plc.

Misset Publishers, IV 611

Mission Group *see* SCEcorp.

Mission Jewelers, 30 408

Mission Valley Fabrics, 57 285

Mississippi Chemical Corporation, 39 280–83

Mississippi Gas Company, 6 577

Mississippi Power Company, 38 446–47

Mississippi River Recycling, 31 47, 49

Mississippi Valley Title Insurance Company, 58 259–60

Missoula Bancshares, Inc., 35 198–99

Missouri Gaming Company, 21 39

Missouri Gas & Electric Service Company, 6 593

Missouri Public Service Company *see* UtiliCorp United Inc.

Missouri Utilities Company, 6 580

Mist Assist, Inc. *see* Ballard Medical Products.

Misys PLC, 45 279–81; 46 296–99

Mitchell Energy and Development Corporation, 7 344–46 *see also* Devon Energy Corp.

Mitchells & Butlers PLC, 59 296–99

MiTek Industries Inc., *see* Rexam PLC.

Mitel Corporation, 18 343–46

MITRE Corporation, 26 300–02

MITROPA AG, 37 250–53

Mitsubishi Bank, Ltd., II 321–22 *see also* Bank of Tokyo-Mitsubishi Ltd.

Mitsubishi Chemical Corporation, I 363–64; 56 236–38 (upd.)

Mitsubishi Corporation, I 502–04; 12 340–43 (upd.)

Mitsubishi Electric Corporation, II 57–59; 44 283–87 (upd.)

Mitsubishi Estate Company, Limited, IV 713–14; 61 215–18 (upd.)

Mitsubishi Group, 21 390

Mitsubishi Heavy Industries, Ltd., III 577–79; 7 347–50 (upd.); 40 324–28 (upd.)

Mitsubishi Kasei Corp., 14 535

Mitsubishi Kasei Vinyl Company, 49 5

Mitsubishi Materials Corporation, III 712–13

Mitsubishi Motors Corporation, 9 349–51; 23 352–55 (upd.); 57 245–49 (upd.)

Mitsubishi Oil Co., Ltd., IV 460–62

Mitsubishi Rayon Co. Ltd., V 369–71

Mitsubishi Trust & Banking Corporation, II 323–24

Mitsui & Co., Ltd., I 505–08; 28 280–85 (upd.)

Mitsui Bank, Ltd., II 325–27 *see also* Sumitomo Mitsui Banking Corp.

Mitsui Group, 20 310; 21 72

Mitsui Marine and Fire Insurance Company, Limited, III 295–96

Mitsui Mining & Smelting Co., Ltd., IV 145–46

Mitsui Mining Company, Limited, IV 147–49

Mitsui Mutual Life Insurance Company, III 297–98; 39 284–86 (upd.)

Mitsui-no-Mori Co., Ltd., IV 716

Mitsui O.S.K. Lines, Ltd., V 473–76

Mitsui Petrochemical Industries, Ltd., 9 352–54

Mitsui Real Estate Development Co., Ltd., IV 715–16

Mitsui Trust & Banking Company, Ltd., II 328

Mitsukoshi Ltd., V 142–44; 56 239–42 (upd.)

Mity Enterprises, Inc., 38 310–12

MIVA, Inc., 83 271–275

Mizuho Financial Group Inc., 25 344–46; 58 229–36 (upd.)

MJ Pharmaceuticals Ltd., 57 346

MK-Ferguson Company, *see* Morrison Knudsen Corp.

MLC *see* Medical Learning Co.

MLC Ltd., IV 709; 52 221–22

MLH&P *see* Montreal Light, Heat & Power Co.

MLT Vacations Inc., 30 446

MM Merchandising Munich, 54 296–97

MMAR Group Inc., 19 131

MMC Networks Inc., 38 53, 55

MML Investors Services, *see* Massachusetts Mutual Life Insurance Co.

MMS America Corp., 26 317

MNC Financial *see* MBNA Corp.

MNC Financial Corp., 11 447

MND Drilling, *see* Mitchell Energy and Development Corp.

MNet, *see* First USA, Inc.

MNS, Ltd., 65 236–38

Mo och Domsjö AB, IV 317–19 *see also* Holmen AB

MOB, 56 335

Mobil Corporation, IV 463–65; 7 351–54 (upd.); 21 376–80 (upd.) *see also* Exxon Mobil Corp.

Mobil Oil Indonesia, 56 273

Mobile America Housing Corporation *see* American Homestar Corp.

Mobile Corporation, 25 232

Mobile Mini, Inc., 58 237–39

Nasu Nikon Co., Ltd., **48** 295
Nat Robbins, **37** 269–70
NaTec Ltd. *see* CRSS Inc.
Nathan's Famous, Inc., 29 342–44
The National Academy of Television Arts
& Sciences, **55** 3
National Acme Company *see*
Acme-Cleveland Corp.
National Aeronautics and Space
Administration, **11** 201, 408; **37**
364–65
National Allied Publications *see* DC
Comics Inc.
National American Corporation, **33** 399
National Amusements Inc., 28 295–97
**National Aquarium in Baltimore, Inc.,
74 198–200**
**National Association for Stock Car Auto
Racing, 32 342–44**
**National Association of Securities
Dealers, Inc., 10 416–18** *see also*
NASD.
National Audubon Society, 26 320–23
National Auto Credit, Inc., 16 379–81
National Automotive Fibers, Inc. *see*
Chris- Craft Industries, Inc.
National Automotive Parts Association, **26**
348
National Bancard Corporation, *see* First
Financial Management Corp.
National Bank of Arizona, *see* Zions
Bancorporation.
National Bank of Canada, 85 291–94
National Bank of Commerce Trust &
Savings Association, **15** 161
National Bank of Greece, 41 277–79
National Bank of New Zealand, *see* Lloyds
TSB Group plc.
**The National Bank of South Carolina,
76 278–80**
National BankAmericard Inc. *see* Visa
International.
National Beverage Corp., 26 324–26 *see
also* Faygo Beverages Inc.
National BioSystems, **47** 37
**National Broadcasting Company, Inc.,
II 151–53; 6 164–66 (upd.); 28
298–301 (upd.)** *see also* General
Electric Co.
National Building Society, *see* Abbey
National PLC.
National Can Corp., I 607–08
**National Car Rental System, Inc., 10
419–20** *see also* Republic Industries,
Inc.
National Carriers Ltd *see* Exel plc.
National Cash Register Company *see*
NCR Corp.
National Cement Co., **35** 419; **70** 343
National Cheerleaders Association, **15**
516–18
National Chemsearch Corp. *see* NCH
Corp.
National City Bancorporation, **56** 219
National City Corp., 15 313–16
National Coach, **56** 223
National Comics Publications *see* DC
Comics Inc.

**National Convenience Stores
Incorporated, 7 372–75**
National Cranberry Association *see* Ocean
Spray Cranberries, Inc.
**National Discount Brokers Group, Inc.,
28 302–04** *see also* Deutsche Bank
A.G.
National Disinfectant Company *see* NCH
Corp.
**National Distillers and Chemical
Corporation, I 376–78** *see also*
Quantum Chemical Corp.
National Economic Research Associates,
see Marsh & McLennan Companies,
Inc.
National Educational Corporation, **26** 95
**National Educational Music Co. Ltd.,
47 256–58**
National Endowment for the Arts, **52** 15
National Enquirer, see American Media,
Inc.
**National Envelope Corporation, 32
345–47**
**National Equipment Services, Inc., 57
258–60**
National Executive Service *see* Carey
International, Inc.
**National Express Group PLC, 50
340–42**
National Express Laboratories, Inc., **10**
107
National Family Opinion *see* NFO
Worldwide, Inc.
National Farmers Organization, **53** 260
National Fence Manufacturing Co., Inc.,
45 327
National Fidelity Life Insurance Co., *see*
Conseco, Inc.
**National Financial Partners Corp., 65
254–56**
National Fire & Marine Insurance Co., *see*
Berkshire Hathaway Inc.
National Football League, 29 345–47 *see
also* NFL.
National Freight Consortium plc *see* Exel
plc.
National Fuel Gas Company, 6 526–28
**National Geographic Society, 9 366–68;
30 332–35 (upd.); 79 263–69 (upd.)**
National Golf Properties, Inc. *see*
American Golf Corporation
**National Grape Co-operative
Association, Inc., 20 383–85**
National Grid Group plc, **11** 399–400;
13 484; **45** 298–99; **47** 122
National Grid Transco plc, **66** 283
National Grid USA, 51 262–66 (upd.)
National Grocers Co Ltd., *see* George
Weston Ltd.
National Gypsum Company, 10 421–24
**National Health Laboratories
Incorporated, 11 333–35** *see also*
Laboratory Corporation of America
Holdings.
National Healthcare Resources, Inc. *see*
Concentra Inc.
**National Heritage Academies, Inc., 60
211–13**

National Hockey League, 35 300–03
**National Home Centers, Inc., 44
299–301**
National ICEE Corporation, *see* J & J
Snack Foods Corp.
National Indemnity Co., *see* Berkshire
Hathaway Inc.
National Inking Appliance Company, *see*
Beckman Instruments, Inc.
**National Instruments Corporation, 22
372–74**
National Intergroup, Inc., V 152–53 *see
also* FoxMeyer Health Corp.
**National Iranian Oil Company, IV
466–68; 61 235–38 (upd.)**
National Journal Group Inc., 67 256–58
National Key Company *see* Cole National
Corp.
National Law Publishing Company, Inc.,
32 35
National Lead Co., **21** 489
National Leisure Group, **47** 421
National Liability and Fire Insurance Co.,
see Berkshire Hathaway Inc.
National Liberty Corp., *see* Capital
Holding Corp.
National Life Assurance Co. of Canada,
see Continental Corp.
National Linen Service, **54** 251, 254
National Lumber Co. *see* National Home
Centers, Inc.
National Magazine Company Limited, *see*
The Hearst Corp.
National Marine Service, **6** 530
**National Media Corporation, 27
336–40**
National Medical Care, **22** 360
**National Medical Enterprises, Inc., III
87–88** *see also* Tenet Healthcare Corp.
**National Medical Health Card Systems,
Inc., 79 270–73**
National Mobility Corp., **30** 436
The National Motor Bearing Company *see*
Federal-Mogul Corp.
The National Motor Club of America,
Inc., **33** 418
National Office Furniture, *see* Kimball
International, Inc.
**National Oil Corporation, 66 233–37
(upd.)**
National Oilwell, Inc., 54 247–50
**National Organization for Women, Inc.,
55 274–76**
National Parks Transportation Company,
see SkyWest, Inc.
**National Patent Development
Corporation, 13 365–68** *see also* GP
Strategies Corp.
National Periodical Publications *see* DC
Comics Inc.
National Petroleum Refiners of South
Africa, **47** 340
**National Picture & Frame Company, 24
345–47**
National Pig Development Co., **46** 84
National Power Corporation, **56** 214–15
National Power PLC, 12 349–51 *see also*
International Power PLC.

Portland General Electric, **45** 313; **50** 103

Portland Plastics, **25** 430–31

Portland Shipyard LLC *see* Cascade General Inc.

Portland Trail Blazers, 50 356–60

Portland-Zementwerke Heidelberg A.G., **23** 326

Portnet, **6** 435

Portsmouth & Sunderland, **35** 242, 244

Portucel *see* Grupo Portucel Soporcel.

Portugal Telecom SGPS S.A., 69 304–07

Portugalia, **46** 398

Posadas *see* Grupo Posadas, S.A. de C.V.

POSCO, 57 287–91 **(upd.)**

Posful Corporation, **68** 9

Positive Response Television, Inc., *see* National Media Corp.

Post Office Group, V 498–501

Post Properties, Inc., 26 377–79

Postabank és Takarékpénztár Rt., **69** 155, 157

La Poste, V 470–72

Posterscope Worldwide, 70 230–32

Posti- Ja Telelaitos, 6 329–31

PostScript, *see* Fay's Inc.

Potain SAS, **59** 274, 278

Potash Corporation of Saskatchewan Inc., 18 431–33

Potbelly Sandwich Works, Inc., 83 307–310

Potelco, Inc. *see* Quanta Services, Inc.

Potlatch Corporation, 8 428–30; **34** 355–59 **(upd.); 87** 396–403 **(upd.)**

Potomac Edison Company, **38** 39–40

Potomac Electric Power Company, 6 552–54

Potter & Brumfield Inc., 11 396–98

Pottery Barn, *see* Williams-Sonoma, Inc.

Pottsville Behavioral Counseling Group, **64** 311

Pou Chen Corporation, 81 309–12

Poul Due Jensen Foundation *see* Grundfos Group

Poulan/Weed Eater *see* White Consolidated Industries Inc.

Powell Duffryn plc, 31 367–70

Powell Group, **33** 32

Powell's Books, Inc., 40 360–63

Power Applications & Manufacturing Company, Inc., **6** 441

Power Corporation of Canada, 36 370–74 **(upd.); 85** 332–39 **(upd.)**

Power-One, Inc., 79 334–37

Power Parts Co., **7** 358

Power Team, *see* SPX Corp.

PowerBar Inc., 44 351–53

Powercor *see* PacifiCorp.

POWEREDCOM Inc., **74** 348

Powergen PLC, 11 399–401; **50** 361–64 **(upd.)**

Powerhouse Technologies, Inc., 27 379–81

PowerSoft Corp., **15** 374

Powerteam Electrical Services Ltd., **64** 404

Powertel Inc., **48** 130

Powerware Corporation *see* Eaton Corp.

POZEN Inc., 81 313–16

PP&L *see* Pennsylvania Power & Light Co.

PPB Group Berhad, 57 292–95

PPG Industries, Inc., III 731–33; **22** 434–37 **(upd.); 81** 317–23 **(upd.)**

PPI *see* Precision Pattern Inc.

PPI Two Corporation, **64** 334

PPL Corporation, 41 314–17 **(upd.)**

PPR S.A., 74 244–48 **(upd.)**

PR Holdings, **23** 382

PR Newswire, 35 354–56

Practical Business Solutions, Inc., **18** 112

PracticeWorks.com, **69** 33–34

Prada Holding B.V., 45 342–45

Prairie Farms Dairy, Inc., 47 304–07

Prairielands Energy Marketing, Inc., *see* MDU Resources Group, Inc.

Prakla Seismos, **17** 419

Pranda Jewelry plc, 70 233–35

Prandium Inc., **51** 70

Pratt & Whitney, 9 416–18

Pratt Hotel Corporation, **21** 275

Pratta Electronic Materials, Inc., **26** 425

Praxair, Inc., 11 402–04; **48** 321–24 **(upd.)**

Praxis Corporation, **30** 499

Pre Finish Metals Incorporated, **63** 270–71

Pre-Paid Legal Services, Inc., 20 434–37

PreAnalytiX, **39** 335

Precept Foods, LLC, **54** 168

Precise Fabrication Corporation, **33** 257

Precise Imports Corp., **21** 516

Precision Castparts Corp., 15 365–67

Precision Engineered Products, Inc., **70** 142

Precision Husky Corporation, **26** 494

Precision IBC, Inc., **64** 20–21

Precision Interconnect Corporation, *see* AMP Inc.

Precision Moulds, Ltd., *see* Mattel, Inc.

Precision Optical Industry Company, Ltd. *see* Canon Inc.

Precision Pattern Inc., **36** 159

Precision Power, Inc., **21** 514

Precision Response Corporation, **47** 420

Precision Software Corp., **14** 319

Precision Spring of Canada, Ltd., **55** 305

Precision Stainless Inc., **65** 289

Precision Standard Inc. *see* Pemco Aviation Group Inc.

Precision Tool, Die & Machine Company Inc., **51** 116–17

Precisionaire *see* Flanders Corp.

Precoat Metals, **54** 331

Predica, **II** 266

Prefco Corporation, **57** 56–57

Preferred Medical Products *see* Ballard Medical Products.

Preferred Products, Inc., *see* Supervalu Inc.

PREINCO Holdings, Inc., *see* Transatlantic Holdings, Inc.

PREL&P *see* Portland Railway Electric Light & Power Co.

Premark International, Inc., III 610–12 *see also* Illinois Tool Works Inc.

Premcor Inc., 37 309–11

Premier Cement Ltd., **64** 98

Premier Industrial Corporation, 9 419–21

Premier Insurance Co., **26** 487

Premier Medical Services, **31** 357

Premier Milk Pte Ltd., **54** 117

Premier One Products, Inc., **37** 285

Premier Parks, Inc., 27 382–84 *see also* Six Flags, Inc.

Premier Radio Networks, Inc., **23** 292, 294

Premier Rehabilitation Centers, **29** 400

Premier Sport Group Inc., **23** 66

Premiere Labels Inc., **53** 236

Premium Standard Farms, Inc., 30 353–55

PremiumWear, Inc., 30 356–59

Premix-Marbletite Manufacturing Co. Inc. *see* Imperial Industries, Inc.

Prentice Hall Inc., **I** 453; **IV** 672; **19** 405; **23** 503

Prescott Investors, **14** 303; **50** 311

Preserver Group, Inc., 44 354–56

President Baking Co., **36** 313

President Casinos, Inc., 22 438–40

President Riverboat Casino-Mississippi Inc., **21** 300

Presidents Island Steel & Wire Company *see* Laclede Steel Co.

Presley Cos., **59** 422

Presses de la Cité *see* Groupe de la Cité.

Pressman Toy Corporation, 56 280–82

Presstar Printing, **25** 183

Presstek, Inc., 33 345–48

Pressware International, **12** 377

Prestage Farms, **46** 83

Prestel Verlag, **66** 123

Prestige Fragrance & Cosmetics, Inc., **22** 158

The Prestige Group plc., *see* Gallaher Group Plc.

Prestige International, **33** 284

Prestige Leather Creations, **31** 435–36

Prestige Properties, **23** 388

Presto Products, Inc., *see* Reynolds and Reynolds Co.; Reynolds Metals Co.

Preston Corporation, 6 421–23

Prestone Products Corp., **22** 32; **26** 349

Prestwick Mortgage Group, **25** 187

Pret A Manger, **63** 280, 284–85

Pretty Good Privacy, Inc., **25** 349

Pretty Neat Corp., *see* Goody Products, Inc.

Pretty Paper Inc., *see* Thomas Nelson Inc.

Pretzel Time *see* Mrs. Fields' Original Cookies, Inc.

Pretzelmaker *see* Mrs. Fields' Original Cookies, Inc.

Pretzels Inc., *see* J & J Snack Foods Corp.

Preussag AG, 17 378–82; **42** 279–83 **(upd.)**

PreussenElektra Aktiengesellschaft, V 698–700 *see also* E.On AG.

Preval, **19** 49–50

Previews, Inc., **21** 96

PreVision Marketing LLC *see* Valassis Communications Inc.

PRG-Schultz International, Inc., 73 264–67

Sabine Transportation Company *see* Kirby Corp.
SABMiller plc, 59 352–58 (upd.)
SABO Maschinenfabrik AG, 21 175
Sabratek Corporation, 29 410–12
Sabre Holdings Corporation, 26 427–30; 74 286–90 (upd.)
Sabre Interactive, 46 434
Sacer, 31 127–28
Sach Bicycle Components *see* SRAM Corp.
Sachs-Dolmer G.m.b.H., *see* Makita Corp.
Sacilor *see* Usinor S.A.
OY Saco AB, 23 268
SACOR, **IV** 504–06
Saddlebag Lake Resorts, Inc., 63 23
SADE Ingenieria y Construcciones S.A., 38 435, 437
Sadia S.A., 59 359–62
Saf-T-Hammer Corporation *see* Smith & Wesson Corp.
Safe Flight Instrument Corporation, 71 321–23
SAFECO Corporation, III 352–54
Safeguard Scientifics, Inc., 10 473–75
Safelite Glass Corp., 19 371–73
Safer, Inc., 21 385–86
Safeskin Corporation, 18 467–70 *see also* Kimberly-Clark Corp.
Safety Components International, Inc., 63 342–44
Safety 1st, Inc., 24 412–15
Safety-Kleen Systems Inc., 8 462–65; 82 314–20 (upd.)
Safeway Inc., II 654–56; 24 416–19 (upd.); 85 362–69 (upd.)
Safeway PLC, 50 401–06 (upd.)
Saffa SpA, 41 325–26
Saffery Champness, 80 324–27
Saffil Ltd. *see* Dyson Group PLC.
Safilo SpA, 40 155–56; 54 319–21
SAFR *see* Société Anonyme des Fermiers Réunis.
Saga *see* Sociedad Andina de Grandes Almeneces.
Saga Communications, Inc., 27 392–94
Saga Petroleum ASA, 35 318
Sagami Optical Co., Ltd., 48 295
Sagamore Insurance Company, 51 37–39
The Sage Group, 43 343–46
Sagebrush Sales, Inc., *see* Ply Gem Industries Inc.
Sagebrush Steakhouse, 29 201
SAGEM S.A., 37 346–48
Saginaw Mining Co., *see* Oglebay Norton Co.
Sagitta Arzneimittel, 18 51; 50 90
Sahara Casino Partners L.P., 19 379
Sahara Las Vegas Corp. *see* Archon Corp.
SAI *see* Stamos Associates Inc.
Saia Motor Freight Line, Inc., 6 421–23; 45 448
Saibu Gas, **IV** 518–19
SAIC *see* Science Applications International Corp.
SAIC Velcorex, *see* Groupe DMC (Dollfus Mieg & Cie).
Saiccor, **IV** 92; 49 353

SalesLink Corporation *see* CMGI, Inc.
Sainco *see* Sociedad Anonima de Instalaciones de Control.
Sainsbury's *see* J Sainsbury PLC.
St. Alban Boissons S.A., 22 515
Saint-Gobain *see* Compagnie de Saint Gobain S.A.
Saint-Gobain Weber *see* Weber et Broutin France.
St. Ives Laboratories Inc., 36 26
St Ives plc, 34 393–95
St. James Associates, 32 362–63
St. James's Place Capital, plc, 71 324–26
The St. Joe Company, 31 422–25
St. Joe Corporation, 59 185
St. Joe Gold, 23 40
St. Joe Minerals Corp., *see* Flour Corp.
St. Joe Paper Company, 8 485–88
St. John Knits, Inc., 14 466–68
St. JON Laboratories, Inc., 74 381
St. Jude Medical, Inc., 11 458–61; 43 347–52 (upd.)
St. Laurent Paperboard Inc., 30 119
St. Lawrence Cement Inc., *see* Holnam Inc.
Saint Louis Bread Company, 18 35, 37; 44 327
St. Louis Concessions Inc., 21 39
St. Louis Music, Inc., 48 351–54
St. Louis Post-Dispatch LLC, 58 283
St. Luke's-Roosevelt Hospital Center *see* Continuum Health Partners, Inc.
St. Martin's Press, 25 484–85; 35 452
St. Mary Land & Exploration Company, 63 345–47
St. Michel-Grellier S.A., 44 40
St. Paul Bank for Cooperatives, 8 489–90
St. Paul Book and Stationery, Inc., 47 90
St. Paul Fire and Marine Insurance Co. *see* The St. Paul Companies, Inc.
The St. Paul Travelers Companies, Inc., III 355–57; 22 492–95 (upd.); 79 362–69 (upd.)
St. Paul Venture Capital Inc., 34 405–06
St. Regis Paper Co., 12 377
salesforce.com, Inc., 79 370–73
Saipem S.p.A. *see* ENI S.p.A.
SAirGroup, 29 376; 33 268, 271; 37 241; 46 398; 47 287
SAirLogistics, 49 80–81
Saison Group, **V** 184–85, 187–89; 36 417–18, 420; 42 340–41
Sakae Printing Co., Ltd., 64 261
Sako Ltd., 39 151
Saks Inc., 24 420–23; 41 342–45 (upd.)
Sakura Bank *see* Sumitomo Mitsui Banking Corp.
Salant Corporation, 12 430–32; 51 318–21 (upd.)
Sale Knitting Company *see* Tultex Corp.
Salem Broadcasting, 25 508
Salem Sportswear, 25 167
Salick Health Care, Inc., 53 290–92
Salient Partners & Pinnacle Trust Co., 70 287

Salinas Equipment Distributors, Inc., 33 364
Sallie Mae *see* SLM Holding Corp.; Student Loan Marketing Association.
Sally Beauty Company, Inc., 60 258–60
Salomon Inc., II 447–49; 13 447–50 (upd.) *see also* Citigroup Inc.
Salomon Worldwide, 20 458–60 *see also* adidas-Salomon AG.
Salon Cielo and Spa *see* Ratner Companies.
Salon Plaza *see* Ratner Companies.
Salt River Project, 19 374–76
Salton, Inc., 30 402–04
Salvagnini Company, 22 6
The Salvation Army USA, 32 390–93
Salvatore Ferragamo Italia S.p.A., 62 311–13
Salzgitter AG, IV 200–01
SAM *see* Sociedad Aeronáutica de Medellín, S.A.
Sam & Libby Inc., 30 311
Sam Ash Music Corporation, 30 405–07
Sam Goody, 63 65
Sam Levin Inc., 80 328–31
Sam's Club, 40 385–87
Samancor Ltd., IV 92–93
Samaritan Senior Services Inc., 25 503
Samas-Groep N.V., 47 91
Samcor Glass *see* Corning Inc.
Samedan Oil Corporation, *see* Noble Affiliates, Inc.
Sames, S.A., 21 65–66
Samick Musical Instruments Co., Ltd., 56 297–300
Samim, IV 422
Sammy Corp., 54 16; 73 291
Samna Corp., 6 256; 25 300
Sampoerna PT, 62 96–97
Sampson Supermarkets, Inc., *see* Hannaford Bros. Co.
Samson Technologies Corp., 30 406
Samsonite Corporation, 13 451–53; 43 353–57 (upd.)
Samsung Display Co., Ltd., 59 81
Samsung Electronics Co., Ltd., 14 416–18; 41 346–49 (upd.)
Samsung Group, I 515–17
Samuel Austin & Son Company, *see* The Austin Co.
Samuel Cabot Inc., 53 293–95
Samuel Meisel & Company, Inc., *see* Duty Free International, Inc.
Samuels Jewelers Incorporated, 30 408–10
San Antonio Public Service Company *see* City Public Service.
San Diego Gas & Electric Company, V 711–14 *see also* Sempra Energy.
San Diego Padres Baseball Club L.P., 78 324–27
San Francisco Baseball Associates, L.P., 55 340–43
San Francisco Maillots, 62 228
San Giorgio Macaroni Inc., 53 242
San Jose Water Company *see* SJW Corp.
San Miguel Corporation, 15 428–30; 57 303–08 (upd.)

Service Merchandise Company, Inc., V 190–92; 19 395–99 (upd.)

Service Products Buildings, Inc. *see* Turner Construction Co.

Service Q. General Service Co., *see* Koninklijke Luchtvaart Maatschappij N.V.

The ServiceMaster Company, 6 44–46; 23 428–31 (upd.); 68 338–42 (upd.)

Services Maritimes des Messageries Impériales *see* Compagnie des Messageries Maritimes.

ServiceWare, Inc., 25 118

Servicios de Corte y Confeccion, S.A. de C.V., 64 142

Servicios Financieros Quadrum S.A., 14 156; 76 129

Servisair Plc, 49 320

ServiStar Coast to Coast Corporation *see* TruServ Corp.

ServoChem A.B., I 387

Servomation Wilbur *see* Service America Corp.

Servoplan, S.A., 8 272

Servpro Industries, Inc., 85 383–86

SES Staffing Solutions, *see* AHL Services, Inc.

Sesamee Mexicana, 48 142

Sessler Inc., 19 381

Setagaya Industry Co., Ltd., 48 295

Seton Scholl *see* SSL International plc.

7-Eleven, Inc., 32 414–18 (upd.)

Seven-Eleven Japan Co. *see* Ito-Yokado Co., Ltd.

Seven Generation, Inc., 41 177

Seven Hills Paperboard, LLC, 59 350

Seven Network Limited, 25 329

SevenOne Media, 54 297

Sevenson Environmental Services, Inc., 42 344–46

Seventh Generation, Inc., 73 294–96

Seventh Street Corporation, 60 130

Severn Trent PLC, 12 441–43; 38 425–29 (upd.)

Severonickel Combine, 48 300

Severstal Joint Stock Company, 65 309–12

Sextant In-Flight Systems, LLC, 30 74

Seymour International Press Distributor Ltd., IV 619

Seymour Press, IV 619

SF Bio, 52 51

SF Recycling & Disposal, Inc., 60 224

SFI Group plc, 51 334–36

SFIC Holdings (Cayman) Inc., 38 422

SFIM Industries, 37 348

SFNGR *see* Nouvelles Galeries Réunies.

SFS Bancorp Inc., 41 212

SFX Broadcasting Inc., 24 107

SFX Entertainment, Inc., 36 422–25

SG Cowen Securities Corporation, 75 186–87

SG Racing, Inc., 64 346

SGC *see* Supermarkets General Corp.

SGE *see* Vinci.

SGI, 29 438–41 (upd.)

SGL Carbon Group, 40 83; 46 14

SGS-Thomson Microelectronics, 54 269–70

Shakespeare Company, 22 481–84

Shakey's Pizza, *see* Jacmar Companies.

Shaklee Corporation, 12 444–46; 39 361–64 (upd.)

Shampaine Industries, Inc., 37 399

Shamrock Broadcasting Inc., 24 107

Shamrock Holdings, 25 268

Shan-Chih Business Association, 23 469

Shana Corporation, 62 142

Shandong Nichirei Foods Company Ltd. *see* Nichirei Corp.

Shandwick International, 47 97

Shanggong Co. Ltd., 65 134

Shanghai Asia Pacific Co., 59 59

Shanghai Autobacs Paian Auto Service Co., 76 38

Shanghai Baosteel Group Corporation, 71 327–30

Shanghai Dajiang, 62 63

Shanghai General Bearing Co., Ltd., 45 170

Shanghai International Finance Company Limited, 15 433

Shanghai Kyocera Electronics Co., Ltd., 21 331

Shanghai Petrochemical Co., Ltd., 18 483–85

Shanghai Shesuo UNF Medical Diagnostic Reagents Co., 61 229

Shanghai Tobacco, 49 150, 153

Shangri-La Asia Ltd., 71 331–33

Shanks Group plc, 45 384–87

Shannon Aerospace Ltd., 36 426–28

Shannon Group, Inc., *see* Manitowoc Co., Inc.

Shansby Group, 27 197; 43 218; 64 265

Shanshin Engineering Company Ltd., 60 236

Shared Financial Systems, Inc., 10 501

Shared Medical Systems Corporation, 14 432–34 *see also* Siemens AG.

ShareWave Inc., 48 92

Shari Lewis Enterprises, Inc., 28 160

Sharmoon, 63 151

Sharp Corporation, II 95–96; 12 447–49 (upd.); 40 391–95 (upd.)

Sharp Water, Inc., 56 62

The Sharper Image Corporation, 10 486–88; 62 321–24 (upd.)

Sharples Separator Company, 64 17

Shasta Beverages *see* National Beverage Corp.

Shato Holdings, Ltd., 60 357

Shaw Communications Inc., 26 274; 35 69

The Shaw Group, Inc., 50 427–30

Shaw Industries, Inc., 9 465–67; 40 396–99 (upd.)

Shaw's Supermarkets, Inc., 56 315–18

Shea Homes *see* J.F. Shea Co., Inc.

Sheaffer Group, 23 54, 57

Sheaffer Pen Corporation, 82 340–43

Shearer's Foods, Inc., 72 323–25

Shearman & Sterling, 32 419–22

Shearson Lehman Brothers Holdings Inc., II 450–52; 9 468–70 (upd.)

Shedd Aquarium Society, 73 297–99

Sheetz, Inc., 85 387–90

Sheffield Exploration Company, 28 470

Sheffield Forgemasters Group Ltd., 39 32

Sheffield Silver Company, 67 322–23

Shekou Container Terminal, 16 481; 38 345

Shelby Steel Processing Co., 51 238

Shelby Williams Industries, Inc., 14 435–37

Sheldahl Inc., 23 432–35

Shelf Life Inc. *see* King Kullen Grocery Co., Inc.

Shell *see* Royal Dutch/Shell Group; Shell Oil Company; Shell Transport and Trading Company p.l.c.

Shell Canada Limited, 32 45

Shell Chemical Corporation, IV 531–32, 540

Shell Forestry, 21 546; 50 58

Shell France, 12 153

Shell Oil Company, IV 540–41; 14 438–40 (upd.); 41 356–60 (upd.)

Shell Transport and Trading Company p.l.c., IV 530–32 *see also* Royal Dutch Petroleum Company; Royal Dutch/Shell.

Sheller-Globe Corporation, I 201–02 *see also* Lear Corp.

Shells Seafood Restaurants, Inc., 43 370–72

Shelly Brothers, Inc., 15 65

Shenhua Group *see* China Shenhua Energy Company Limited

Shenzhen Namtek Co., Ltd., 61 232–33

Shepherd Neame Limited, 30 414–16

Shepherd Products Ltd., *see* The Marmon Group, Inc.

Sheraton Corp. of America, *see* ITT Sheraton Corp.

The Sheridan Group, Inc., 86 357–60

Sherr-Gold, 23 40

The Sherwin-Williams Company, III 744–46; 13 469–71 (upd.)

Sherwood Brands, Inc., 53 302–04

Sherwood Equity Group Ltd. *see* National Discount Brokers Group, Inc.

Sherwood Medical Group, *see* American Home Porducts.

Sherwood Securities, 66 308

Shiara Holdings, Inc., 53 88

Shidler Group *see* First Industrial Realty Trust, Inc.

Shihen Technical Corporation, 60 272

Shihlin Electric & Engineering Group, 49 460

Shikoku Electric Power Company, Inc., V 718–20; 60 269–72 (upd.)

Shiley, Inc., 38 361

Shillito's, 31 192

Shimano Inc., 64 347–49

Shimizu Construction Company Ltd., 44 153

Shin-Nihon Glass Co., *see* Asahi Breweries, Ltd.

Shinko Rayon Ltd. *see* Mitsubishi Rayon Co., Ltd.

Shinko Securities Co. Ltd., 58 235

Territory Ahead, Inc., 29 279
Terumo Corporation, 48 393–95
Tesa, S.A., 23 82
TESC *see* The European Software Co.
Tesco plc, II 677–78; 24 473–76 (upd.);
68 366–70 (upd.)
Tesoro Petroleum Corporation, 7
516–19; 45 408–13 (upd.)
Tessenderlo Group, 76 345–48
Tesseract Inc., 33 331
The Testor Corporation, 51 367–70
Tetley Group *see* Tata Tea Ltd.
Tetra Pak International SA, 53 327–29
Tetra Plastics Inc. *see* NIKE, Inc.
Tetra Tech, Inc., 29 463–65
Tettemer & Associates *see* The Keith
Companies.
Teva Pharmaceutical Industries Ltd., 22
500–03; 54 362–65 (upd.)
Tex-Mex Partners L.C., 41 270
Texaco Canada Inc., 25 232
Texaco Inc., IV 551–53; 14 491–94
(upd.); 41 391–96 (upd.) *see also*
ChevronTexaco Corp.
Texas Air Corporation, I 123–24
Texas Bus Lines, *see* Coach USA, Inc.
Texas Coffee Traders, 60 210
Texas Eastern Transmission Company, 11
28
Texas Farm LLC *see* Nippon Meat Packers
Inc.
Texas Homecare, 21 335
Texas Industries, Inc., 8 522–24
Texas Instruments Incorporated, II
112–15; 11 505–08 (upd.); 46
418–23 (upd.)
Texas International Airlines, 21 142
Texas-New Mexico Utilities Company, 6
580
Texas Pacific Group Inc., 36 472–74
Texas Rangers Baseball, 51 371–74
Texas Roadhouse, Inc., 69 347–49
Texas Timberjack, Inc., 51 279–81
Texas Utilities Company, V 724–25; 25
472–74 (upd.)
Texasgulf Inc., *see* Potash Corporation of
Saskatchewan Inc.
Têxtil Santa Catarina Ltda., 72 68
Textile Diffusion, 25 466
Textile Rubber and Chemical Company,
15 490
Textron Inc., I 529–30; 34 431–34
(upd.)
Textron Lycoming Turbine Engine, 9
497–99
Texwood Industries, Inc., 20 363
TFC *see* Times Fiber Communications,
Inc.
TFH Publications, Inc., 58 60
TFM *see* Grupo Transportación Ferroviaria
Mexicana, S.A. de C.V.
TF1 *see* Télévision Française 1
TFP, Inc., 44 358–59
TFS *see* Total Filtration Services, Inc.
TG Credit Service Co. Ltd., 55 375
TGEL&PCo *see* Tucson Gas, Electric
Light & Power Co.
TH:s Group, *see* Arrow Electronics, Inc.

Tha Row Records, 69 350–52 (upd.)
**Thai Airways International Public
Company Limited**, 6 122–24; 27
463–66 (upd.)
Thai Lube Blending Co., 56 290
Thai Nylon Co. Ltd., 53 344
Thai Union Frozen Products PCL, 75
370–72
Thales S.A., 42 373–76
Thames Trains, 28 157
Thames Water plc, 11 509–11
Thameslink, 28 157
Thane International, Inc., 84 394–397
Thanulux Public Company Limited, 86
393–96
THAW *see* Recreational Equipment, Inc.
Thelem SA, 54 267
Therm-o-Disc, *see* Emerson.
Thermacore International Inc., 56 247
Thermador Corporation, 67 82
Thermadyne Holding Corporation, 19
440–43
Thermal Dynamics, *see* Thermadyne
Holding Corp.
Thermal Energies, Inc., 21 514
Thermal Snowboards, Inc., 22 462
Thermal Transfer Ltd., *see* Southern
Electric PLC.
ThermaStor Technologies, Ltd., 44 366
Thermo BioAnalysis Corp., 25 475–78
Thermo Electron Corporation, 7
520–22
Thermo Fibertek, Inc., 24 477–79
Thermo Instrument Systems Inc., 11
512–14
Thermo King Corporation, 13 505–07
see also Ingersoll-Rand Company Ltd.
Thermoform Plastics, Inc., 56 378–79
Thermogas Co., 35 175
Thermolase Corporation, 22 410
Thermos Company, 16 486–88
TheStreet.com, 34 125
THHK Womenswear Limited, 53 333
ThiemeMeulenhoff BV, 53 273
Thiess Dampier Mitsui, IV 47
Things Remembered, Inc., 84 398–401
Thiokol Corporation, 9 500–02 (upd.);
22 504–07 (upd.)
Third Age Inc., 71 137
Third Coast Capital, Inc., 51 109
Third National Bank *see* Fifth Third
Bancorp.
Third Wave Publishing Corp. *see* Acer Inc.
ThirdAge.com, 49 290
Thirteen/WNET *see* Educational
Broadcasting Corp.
Thistle Hotels PLC, 54 366–69
THM Biomedical Inc. *see* Kensey Nash
Corp.
Thom McAn *see* Melville Corp.
Thomas & Betts Corporation, 11
515–17; 54 370–74 (upd.)
Thomas Borthwick & Sons (Australia)
Pty. Ltd. *see* Nippon Meat Packers Inc.
Thomas Bros. Maps, 28 380
Thomas Cook Group Ltd., 57 195
Thomas Cook Travel Inc., 9 503–05; 33
394–96 (upd.)

Thomas Crosbie Holdings Limited, 81
384–87
Thomas De La Rue and Company, Ltd.,
44 357–58
Thomas H. Lee Co., 24 480–83
Thomas Industries Inc., 29 466–69
Thomas J. Lipton Company, 14 495–97
Thomas Jefferson Life Insurance Co., *see*
St. Paul Cos.
Thomas Kinkade Galleries *see* Media Arts
Group, Inc.
Thomas Nationwide Transport *see* TNT.
Thomas Nationwide Transport Limited *see*
TNT Post Group N.V.
Thomas Nelson Inc., 14 498–99; 38
454–57 (upd.)
Thomas Publishing Company, 26
482–85
Thomas Y. Crowell, IV 605
Thomaston Mills, Inc., 27 467–70
Thomasville Furniture Industries, Inc.,
12 474–76; 74 339–42 (upd.)
Thompson and Formby, 16 44
Thompson Medical Company *see*
Slim-Fast Nutritional Foods
International Inc.
Thompson Nutritional Products, 37 286
**Thomsen Greenhouses and Garden
Center, Incorporated**, 65 338–40
Thomson-Brandt, II 13, 116–17
The Thomson Corporation, 8 525–28;
34 435–40 (upd.); 77 433–39 (upd.)
Thomson International, 37 143
THOMSON multimedia S.A., II
116–17; 42 377–80 (upd.)
Thomson-Ramo-Woolridge *see* TRW Inc.
Thona Group *see* Hexagon AB
Thonet Industries Inc., *see* Shelby
Williams Industries, Inc.
Thor Industries, Inc., 39 391–94
Thorn Apple Valley, Inc., 7 523–25; 22
508–11 (upd.)
Thorn EMI plc, I 531–32 *see also* EMI
plc; Thorn plc.
Thorn plc, 24 484–87
Thornhill Inc., 64 217
Thornton Baker *see* Grant Thornton
International.
Thorntons plc, 46 424–26
Thorpe Park, 55 378
Thorsen Realtors, 21 96
Thos. & Wm. Molson & Company *see*
The Molson Companies Ltd.
Thousand Trails, Inc., 33 397–99
THQ, Inc., 39 395–97
Threads for Life, 49 244
Threadz, 25 300
Three-Diamond Company *see* Mitsubishi
Shokai.
The 3DO Company, 43 426–30
3 Guys, V 35
Three Ring Asia Pacific Beer Co., Ltd., 49
418
Three Score, 23 100
3 Suisses International, 12 281
3Com Corporation, 11 518–21; 34
441–45 (upd.) *see also* Palm, Inc.
3D Planet SpA, 41 409

Tokyo Gas Co., Ltd., V 734–36; 55 372–75 (upd.)

Tokyo Maritime Agency Ltd., 56 181

Tokyo Motors *see* Isuzu Motors, Ltd.

Tokyo Stock Exchange, 34 254

Tokyo Telecommunications Engineering Corp *see* Tokyo Tsushin Kogyo K.K.

TOKYOPOP Inc., 79 415–18

Tokyu Corporation, V 526–28; 47 407–10 (upd.)

Tokyu Department Store Co., Ltd., V 199–202; 32 453–57 (upd.)

Tokyu Land Corporation, IV 728–29

Toledo Edison Company *see* Centerior Energy Corp.

Toledo Milk Processing, Inc., 15 449

Toledo Scale Corp., 30 327

Toll Brothers Inc., 15 497–99; 70 323–26 (upd.)

Tollgrade Communications, Inc., 44 424–27

Tom Brown, Inc., 37 389–91

Tom Doherty Associates Inc., 25 483–86

Tom Snyder Productions, 29 470, 472

Tom Thumb, 40 365–66

Tom's Foods Inc., 66 325–27

Tom's of Maine, Inc., 45 414–16

Toman Corporation, 19 390

The Tomatin Distillery Co., Ltd., 62 347

Tombstone Pizza Corporation, 13 515–17 *see also* Kraft Foods Inc.

Tomcan Investments Inc., 53 333

Tomen Corporation, IV 224–25; 24 488–91 (upd.)

Tomkins plc, 11 525–27; 44 428–31 (upd.)

Tommy Armour Golf Co., 32 446–47

Tommy Bahama *see* Viewpoint International, Inc.

Tommy Hilfiger Corporation, 20 488–90; 53 330–33 (upd.)

TomTom N.V., 81 388–91

Tomy Company Ltd., 65 341–44

Tone Brothers, Inc., 21 496–98; 74 349–52 (upd.)

Tone Coca-Cola Bottling Company, Ltd., *see* Kikkoman Corp.

Tonen Corporation, IV 554–56; 16 489–92 (upd.)

TonenGeneral Sekiyu K.K., 54 380–86 (upd.)

Tong Yang Cement Corporation, 62 366–68

Tonka Corporation, 25 487–89

Tonkin, Inc., 19 114

Tony Lama Company Inc., 19 233

Tony Roma's, A Place for Ribs Inc. *see* Romacorp, Inc.

Tony Stone Images, 31 216–17

Too, Inc., 61 371–73

Toolex International N.V., 26 489–91

Tootsie Roll Industries, Inc., 12 480–82; 82 392–96 (upd.)

Top End Wheelchair Sports, 11 202

Top Glory International Group Company, 76 89–90

Top Tool Company, Inc., 25 75

Topack Verpackungstechnik, 60 193

The Topaz Group, Inc., 62 369–71

Topco Associates LLC, 60 302–04

Topcon Corporation, 84 406–409

Topkapi, *see* Claire's Stores, Inc.

Toppan Printing Co., Ltd., IV 679–81; 58 340–44 (upd.)

The Topps Company, Inc., 13 518–20; 34 446–49 (upd.); 83 400-406 (upd.)

Topps Markets, 16 314

Tops Appliance City, Inc., 17 487–89

Tops Markets LLC, 60 305–07

TopTip, 48 116

Tor Books *see* Tom Doherty Associates Inc.

Toray Industries, Inc., V 383–86; 51 375–79 (upd.)

Torchmark Corporation, 9 506–08; 33 405–08 (upd.)

Toresco Enterprises, Inc., 84 410–413

Torfeaco Industries Limited, *see* Pillowtex Corp.

The Toro Company, 7 534–36; 26 492–95 (upd.); 77 440–45 (upd.)

Toromont Industries, Ltd., 21 499–501

The Toronto-Dominion Bank, II 375–77; 49 395–99 (upd.)

Toronto Maple Leafs *see* Maple Leaf Sports & Entertainment Ltd.

Toronto Raptors *see* Maple Leaf Sports & Entertainment Ltd.

Toronto Sun Publishing Company *see* Sun Media.

Torrent Systems, Inc., 59 56

The Torrington Company, 13 521–24 *see also* Timken Co.

Torstar Corporation, 29 470–73 *see also* Harlequin Enterprises Ltd.

Tosco Corporation, 7 537–39 *see also* ConocoPhillips.

Toshiba Corporation, I 533–35; 12 483–86 (upd.); 40 435–40 (upd.)

Toshin Building Co. Ltd., 74 348

Toshin Kaihatsu Ltd. *see* Takashimaya Co., Ltd.

Tosoh Corporation, 70 327–30

Tostem *see* Toyo Sash Co., Ltd.

Total Beverage Corporation, *see* Dart Group PLC.

Total Compagnie Française des Pétroles S.A., IV 557–61 *see also* Total Fina Elf S.A.

Total Entertainment Restaurant Corporation, 46 427–29

Total Filtration Services, Inc., 61 66

Total Fina Elf S.A., 50 478–86 (upd.)

Total Global Sourcing, Inc., *see* Staples, Inc.

Total Home Entertainment (THE), 39 240, 242

Total Petroleum Corporation, 21 500

TOTAL S.A., 24 492–97 (upd.)

Total System Services, Inc., 18 516–18

Totem Resources Corporation, 9 509–11

Totino's Finer Foods, 26 436

TOTO LTD., III 755–56; 28 464–66 (upd.)

Tottenham Hotspur PLC, 81 392–95

Touch America Inc., 37 127; 44 288

Touch-It Corp., 22 413

Touche Remnant Holdings Ltd., II 356

Touche Ross *see* Deloitte Touche Tohmatsu International.

Touchstone Films *see* The Walt Disney Co.

Toupargel-Agrigel S.A., 76 354–56

Le Touquet's, SA, 48 197

Touristik Union International GmbH. and Company K.G., II 163–65 *see also* Preussag AG.

Tourtime America, 56 223

TOUSA *see* Technical Olympic USA, Inc.

Toval Japon, IV 680

Towa Optical Manufacturing Company, 41 261–63

Tower Air, Inc., 28 467–69

Tower Automotive, Inc., 24 498–500

Tower Records *see* MTS Inc.

Towers Department Stores, *see* Oshawa Group Ltd.

Towers Perrin, 32 458–60

Towle Manufacturing Co., *see* Syratech Corp.

Town & Country Corporation, 19 451–53

Town Sports International, Inc., 46 430–33

Towngas *see* Hong Kong and China Gas Company Ltd.

Townsend Hook, IV 650, 652

Townsends, Inc., 64 385–87

Toxicol Laboratories, Ltd., 21 424

The Toxicology Group, LLC *see* NOF Corp.

Toy Biz, Inc., 18 519–21 *see also* Marvel Entertainment, Inc.

Toy Liquidators, 50 99

Toymax International, Inc., 29 474–76

Toyo Ink Manufacturing, 26 213

Toyo Microsystems Corporation, 11 464

Toyo Rayon *see* Toray Industries, Inc.

Toyo Sash Co., Ltd., III 757–58

Toyo Seikan Kaisha Ltd., I 615–16

Toyo Soda Manufacturing Co *see* Tosoh Corp.

Toyo Tire & Rubber Co., V 255–56

Toyo Toki Co., Ltd. *see* Toto.

Toyoda Automatic Loom Works, Ltd., III 636–39

Toyota Industrial Equipment, *see* Manitou BF S.A.

Toyota Motor Corporation, I 203–05; 11 528–31 (upd.); 38 458–62 (upd.)

Toys 'R Us, Inc., V 203–06; 18 522–25 (upd.); 57 370–75 (upd.)

TP Transportation, 39 377

TPA *see* Aloha Airlines Inc.

TPCR Corporation *see* The Price Co.

TPG N.V., 64 388–91 (upd.)

TPS SNC, 76 274

Trac Inc., 44 355

Trace International Holdings, Inc., 17 182–83; 26 502

Tracinda Corporation, 25 329–30

Tracker Marine *see* Bass Pro Shops, Inc.

Ullrich Copper, Inc. *see* Foster Wheeler Corp.

Ullstein Langen Müller, **IV** 591

ULN *see* Union Laitière Normande.

Ulstein Holding ASA, *see* Vickers plc.

Ulster Television PLC, 71 366–68

Ultimate Electronics, Inc., 18 532–34; **69** 356–59 **(upd.)**

Ultimate Leisure Group PLC, 75 383–85

Ultra Mart, **16** 250

Ultra Pac, Inc., 24 512–14

Ultra Petroleum Corporation, 71 369–71

UltraCam *see* Ultrak Inc.

UltraCare Products, *see* Drypers Corp.

Ultrak Inc., 24 508–11

Ultralife Batteries, Inc., 58 345–48

Ultramar Diamond Shamrock Corporation, IV 565–68; **31** 453–57 **(upd.)**

ULVAC, Inc., 80 388–91

Umberto's of New Hyde Park Pizzeria, **16** 447

Umbro Holdings Ltd. *see* Stone Manufacturing Co.

UMC *see* United Microelectronics Corp.

UMG *see* Universal Music Group.

UMI Company, **29** 58

NV Umicore SA, 47 411–13

Umpqua Holdings Corporation, 87 443–446

Unadulterated Food Products, Inc., *see* Snapple Beverage Corp.

Unbrako Socket Screw Company Ltd., **30** 429

UNCF *see* United Negro College Fund, Inc.

Uncle Ben's Inc., 22 528–30

Under Armour Performance Apparel, 61 381–83

Underwriter for the Professions Insurance Company, **55** 128

Underwriters Laboratories, Inc., 30 467–70

Underwriters Reinsurance Co., *see* Alleghany Corp.

Unefon, S.A., **39** 194, 196

UNELCO *see* Union Electrica de Canarias S.A.

UNG *see* United National Group, Ltd.

Ungaro SA, **62** 313

Uni-Cast *see* Sturm, Ruger & Company, Inc.

Uni-Marts, Inc., 17 499–502

Uni-President Group, **49** 460

Unibail SA, 40 444–46

Unibanco Holdings S.A., 73 350–53

Unibank, **40** 336; **50** 149–50

Unic *see* GIB Group.

Unica Corporation, 77 450–54

Unicapital, Inc., **15** 281

UNICARE, *see* WellPoint Health Networks Inc.

Unicco Security Services, **27** 22

Unice, **56** 335

UNICEF *see* United Nations International Children's Emergency Fund (UNICEF).

Unicel *see* Rural Cellular Corp.

Unicer, *see* Carlsberg A/S.

Unicharm Corporation, 84 414–417

Unicom Corporation, 29 486–90 **(upd.)** *see also* Exelon Corp.

Unicoolait, **19** 51

UNICOR *see* Federal Prison Industries, Inc.

Unicord Company, **64** 60

UniCredito Italiano, **50** 410

Unidrive, **47** 280

Uniface Holding B.V., *see* Compuware Corp.

Unifi, Inc., 12 501–03; **62** 372–76 **(upd.)**

Unified Energy System of Russia *see* RAO Unified Energy System of Russia.

Unified Western Grocers, **31** 25

UniFirst Corporation, 21 505–07

Uniflex Corporation, **53** 236

Uniforce Services Inc., **40** 119

Unigate PLC, II 586–87; **28** 488–91 **(upd.)** *see also* Uniq Plc.

Uniglory, **13** 211

Unigro *see* Laurus N.V.

Unigroup, **15** 50

UniHealth America, **11** 378–79

Unijoh Sdn, Bhd, **47** 255

Unik S.A., **23** 170–171

Unilab Corp., **26** 391

Unilever PLC/Unilever N.V., II 588–91; **7** 542–45 **(upd.)**; **32** 472–78 **(upd.)**

UniLife Insurance Co., *see* CompDent Corp.

Unilog SA, 42 401–03

Uniloy Milacron Inc., **53** 230

UniMac Companies, **11** 413

Unimetal, **30** 252

Union Aéromaritime de Transport *see* UTA.

Union Bag–Camp Paper Corp. *see* Union Camp Corp.

Union Bank *see* State Street Boston Corp.

Union Bank of California, 16 496–98 *see also* UnionBanCal Corp.

Union Bank of Switzerland, II 378–79 *see also* UBS AG.

Union Biscuits *see* Leroux S.A.S.

Union Camp Corporation, IV 344–46

Union Carbide Corporation, I 399–401; **9** 516–20 **(upd.)**; **74** 358–63 **(upd.)**

Union Colliery Company *see* Union Electric Co.

Union Commerciale, **19** 98

Union Corporation *see* Gencor Ltd.

Union des Assurances de Paris, III 391–94

Union des Coopératives Bressor, **25** 85

Union des Cooperatives Laitières *see* Unicoolait.

Union des Mines, **52** 362

Union des Transports Aériens *see* UTA.

Union Electric Company, V 741–43 *see also* Ameren Corp.

Unión Electrica Fenosa *see* Unión Fenosa S.A.

Unión Fenosa, S.A., 51 387–90

Union Financière de France Banque SA, 52 360–62

Union Fork & Hoe Company *see* Acorn Products, Inc.

Union Gas & Electric Co., **6** 529

l'Union Générale des Pétroles, **IV** 560

Union Laitière Normande *see* Compagnie Laitière Européenne.

Union Light, Heat & Power Company *see* Cincinnati Gas & Electric Co.

Union Minière *see* NV Umicore SA.

Union Mutual Life Insurance Company *see* UNUM Corp.

Union Oil Co. of California *see* Unocal Corp.

Union Pacific Corporation, V 529–32; **28** 492–500 **(upd.)**; **79** 435–46 **(upd.)**

Union Pacific Resources Group, **52** 30

Union Paper & Co. AS, **63** 315

Union Planters Corporation, 54 387–90

Union Power Construction Co. *see* Quanta Services, Inc.

Union Pub Company, **57** 411, 413

Union Savings and Loan Association of Phoenix, **19** 412

Union Suisse des Coopératives de Consommation *see* Coop Schweiz.

Union Tank Car Co., *see* Marmon Group, Inc.

Union Telecard Alliance, LLC, **34** 223

Union Texas Petroleum Holdings, Inc., 9 521–23

The Union Underwear Company, *see* Fruit of the Loom, Inc.

Union Verwaltungsgesellschaft mbH, **66** 123

UnionBanCal Corporation, 50 496–99 **(upd.)**

Unione Manifatture, S.p.A., **19** 338

Uniphase Corporation *see* JDS Uniphase Corp.

Uniplex Business Software, **41** 281

Uniq plc, 83 428–433 **(upd.)**

Unique Casual Restaurants, Inc., 27 480–82

Unique Pub Company, **59** 182

Uniroy of Hempstead, Inc. *see* Aris Industries, Inc.

Uniroyal Chemical Corporation, **36** 145

Uniroyal Corp., **20** 262

Uniroyal Goodrich, **42** 88

Uniroyal Holdings Ltd., **21** 73

Unishops, Inc. *see* Aris Industries, Inc.

Unison HealthCare Corporation, 25 503–05

Unisource Worldwide, Inc., **47** 149

Unistar Radio Networks, **23** 510

Unisys Corporation, III 165–67; **6** 281–83 **(upd.)**; **36** 479–84 **(upd.)**

Unit Corporation, 63 407–09

Unitech plc, *see* Invensys PLC.

United AgriSeeds, Inc., **21** 387

United Air Express *see* United Parcel Service of America Inc.

United Air Fleet, **23** 408

W.R. Berkley Corporation, 15 525–27; 74 385–88 (upd.)

W.R. Case & Sons Cutlery Company *see* Zippo Manufacturing Co.

W.R. Grace & Company, I 547–50; 50 522–29 (upd.)

W.S. Barstow & Company, 6 575

W.W. Grainger, Inc., V 214–15; 26 537–39 (upd.); 68 392–95 (upd.)

W.W. Norton & Company, Inc., 28 518–20

Waban Inc., 13 547–49 *see also* HomeBase, Inc.

Wabash National Corp., 13 550–52

Wabash Valley Power Association, 6 556

Wabtec Corporation, 40 451–54

Wachbrit Insurance Agency, 21 96

Wachovia Bank of Georgia, N.A., 16 521–23

Wachovia Bank of South Carolina, N.A., 16 524–26

Wachovia Corporation, 12 516–20; 46 442–49 (upd.)

Wachtell, Lipton, Rosen & Katz, 47 435–38

The Wackenhut Corporation, 14 541–43; 63 423–26 (upd.)

Wacker-Chemie GmbH, 35 454–58

Wacker Oil Inc., *see* Seagull Energy Corp.

Wacoal Corp., 25 520–24

Waddell & Reed, Inc., 22 540–43

Wade Smith, 28 27, 30

Wadsworth Inc., *see* The Thompsn Corp.

WaferTech, 18 20; 43 17; 47 385

Waffle House Inc., 14 544–45; 60 325–27 (upd.)

Wagers Inc. (Idaho Candy Company), 86 416–19

Waggener Edstrom, 42 424–26

Wagner Castings Company, 16 474–75

Wagonlit Travel, *see* Carlson Wagonlit Travel.

Wagons-Lits, 27 11; 29 443; 37 250–52

Wah Chang, 82 415–18

Waha Oil Company *see* National Oil Corp.

Wahl Clipper Corporation, 86 420–23

AB Wahlbecks, 25 464

Waitrose Ltd. *see* John Lewis Partnership plc.

Wakefern Food Corporation, 33 434–37

Wako Shoji Co. Ltd. *see* Wacoal Corp.

Wal-Mart de Mexico, S.A. de C.V., 35 459–61 (upd.)

Wal-Mart Stores, Inc., V 216–17; 8 555–57 (upd.); 26 522–26 (upd.); 63 427–32 (upd.)

Walbridge Aldinger Co., 38 480–82

Walbro Corporation, 13 553–55

Walchenseewerk AG, 23 44

Waldbaum, Inc., 19 479–81

Waldenbooks, 17 522–24; 86 424–28 (upd.)

Waldorf Corporation, 59 350

Walgreen Co., V 218–20; 20 511–13 (upd.); 65 352–56 (upd.)

Walk Haydel & Associates, Inc., 25 130

Walk Softly, Inc., 25 118

Walker Dickson Group Limited, 26 363

Walker Digital, 57 296–98

Walker Manufacturing Company, 19 482–84

Walkers Shortbread Ltd., 79 464–67

Walkers Snack Foods Ltd., 70 350–52

Wall Drug Store, Inc., 40 455–57

Wall Street Deli, Inc., 33 438–41

Wallace & Tiernan Group, 11 361; 52 374

The Wallace Berrie Company *see* Applause Inc.

Wallace Computer Services, Inc., 36 507–10

Wallace International Silversmiths, *see* Syratech Corp.

Wallin & Nordstrom *see* Nordstrom, Inc.

Wallis *see* Sears plc.

Wallis Arnold Enterprises, Inc., 21 483

Wallis Tractor Company, 21 502

Walnut Capital Partners, 62 46–47

Walrus, Inc., *see* Recreational Equipment, Inc.

Walsworth Publishing Company, Inc., 78 445–48

The Walt Disney Company, II 172–74; 6 174–77 (upd.); 30 487–91 (upd.); 63 433–38 (upd.)

Walter Bau, *see* Eiffage.

Walter Herzog GmbH, *see* Varlen Corp.

Walter Industries, Inc., III 765–67; 22 544–47 (upd.); 72 368–73 (upd.)

Walter Kidde & Co., 73 208

Walter Wilson, 49 18

Walter Wright Mammoet, 26 280

Walton Monroe Mills, Inc., 8 558–60 *see also* Avondale Industries.

Wanadoo S.A., 75 400–02

Wang Global, 39 176–78

Wang Laboratories, Inc., III 168–70; 6 284–87 (upd.) *see also* Getronics NV.

WAP, 26 420

Warbasse-Cogeneration Technologies Partnership, 35 479

Warburg Pincus, 14 42; 61 403; 73 138

Warburg USB, 38 291

Ward's Communications, 22 441

Wards *see* Circuit City Stores, Inc.

Waremart *see* WinCo Foods.

WARF *see* Wisconsin Alumni Research Foundation.

Warman International *see* Weir Group PLC.

The Warnaco Group Inc., 12 521–23; 46 450–54 (upd.) *see also* Authentic Fitness Corp.

Warner Chilcott Limited, 85 446–49

Warner Communications Inc., II 175–77 *see also* AOL Time Warner Inc.

Warner Electric, 58 67

Warner-Lambert Co., I 710–12; 10 549–52 (upd.) *see also* Pfizer Inc.

Warner Roadshow Film Distributors Greece SA, 58 359

Warners' Stellian Inc., 67 384–87

Warrantech Corporation, 53 357–59

Warrell Corporation, 68 396–98

Warren Apparel Group Ltd., 39 257

Warren Bancorp Inc., 55 52

Warren Frozen Foods, Inc., 61 174

Warren, Gorham & Lamont, *see* The Thomson Corp.

Warren Petroleum, *see* Dynegy Inc.

Warrick Industries, 31 338

Warrington Products Ltd. *see* Canstar Sports Inc.

Warwick International Ltd., *see* Sequa Corp.

Warwick Valley Telephone Company, 55 382–84

Wasatch Gas Co., 6 568

Wascana Energy Inc., 13 556–58

Washburn Graphics Inc., 23 100

The Washington Companies, 33 442–45

Washington Federal, Inc., 17 525–27

Washington Football, Inc., 35 462–65

Washington Gas Light Company, 19 485–88

Washington Inventory Service, 30 239

Washington Mutual, Inc., 17 528–31

Washington National Corporation, 12 524–26

Washington Natural Gas Company, 9 539–41 *see also* Puget Sound Energy Inc.

The Washington Post Company, IV 688–90; 20 515–18 (upd.)

Washington Public Power Supply System, 50 102

Washington Railway and Electric Company, 6 552–53

Washington Scientific Industries, Inc., 17 532–34

Washington Sports Clubs *see* Town Sports International, Inc.

Washington Steel Corp., *see* Lukens Inc.

Washington Water Power Company, 6 595–98 *see also* Avista Corp.

Washtenaw Gas Company *see* MCN Corp.

Wassall Plc, 18 548–50

Waste Connections, Inc., 46 455–57

Waste Control Specialists LLC, *see* alhi, Inc.

Waste Holdings, Inc., 41 413–15

Waste Management, Inc., V 752–54

Water Pik Technologies, Inc., 34 498–501; 83 450-453 (upd.)

The Waterbury Companies, *see* Talley Industries, Inc.

Waterford Foods Plc, 59 206

Waterford Wedgwood plc, 12 527–29; 34 493–97 (upd.)

Waterhouse Investor Services, Inc., 18 551–53

Waterman Marine Corporation, *see* International Shipholding Corporation, Inc.

The Waterman Pen Company *see* BIC Corp.

Watermark Paddlesports Inc., 76 119

Waterpark Management Inc., 73 231

WaterPro Supplies Corporation *see* Eastern Enterprises.

Waters Corporation, 43 453–57

Index to Industries

Rewards Network Inc., 70 (upd.)
The Richards Group, Inc., 58
Right Management Consultants, Inc., 42
Ritchie Bros. Auctioneers Inc., 41
Robert Half International Inc., 18
Roland Berger & Partner GmbH, 37
Ronco Corporation, 15; 80 (upd.)
Russell Reynolds Associates, Inc., 38
Saatchi & Saatchi, I; 42 (upd.)
Securitas AB, 42
ServiceMaster Limited Partnership, 6
Servpro Industries, Inc., 85
Shared Medical Systems Corporation, 14
Sir Speedy, Inc., 16
Skidmore, Owings & Merrill LLP, 13; 69
    (upd.)
SmartForce PLC, 43
SOS Staffing Services, 25
Sotheby's Holdings, Inc., 11; 29 (upd.);
    84 (upd.)
Source Interlink Companies, Inc., 75
Spencer Stuart and Associates, Inc., 14
Spherion Corporation, 52
Steiner Corporation (Alsco), 53
Strayer Education, Inc., 53
Superior Uniform Group, Inc., 30
Sykes Enterprises, Inc., 45
Sylvan Learning Systems, Inc., 35
TA Triumph-Adler AG, 48
Taylor Nelson Sofres plc, 34
TBWA/Chiat/Day, 6; 43 (upd.)
Thomas Cook Travel Inc., 33 (upd.)
Ticketmaster, 76 (upd.)
Ticketmaster Group, Inc., 13; 37 (upd.)
TMP Worldwide Inc., 30
TNT Post Group N.V., 30
Towers Perrin, 32
Trader Classified Media N.V., 57
Traffix, Inc., 61
Transmedia Network Inc., 20
Treasure Chest Advertising Company, Inc.,
    32
TRM Copy Centers Corporation, 18
True North Communications Inc., 23
24/7 Real Media, Inc., 49
Tyler Corporation, 23
U.S. Office Products Company, 25
Unica Corporation, 77
UniFirst Corporation, 21
United Business Media plc, 52 (upd.)
United News & Media plc, 28 (upd.)
Unitog Co., 19
Valassis Communications, Inc., 37 (upd.);
    76 (upd.)
ValleyCrest Companies, 81 (upd.)
ValueClick, Inc., 49
Vebego International BV, 49
Vedior NV, 35
Vertis Communications, 84
Vertrue Inc., 77
Viad Corp., 73
W.B Doner & Co., 56
The Wackenhut Corporation, 14; 63
    (upd.)
Waggener Edstrom, 42
Warrantech Corporation, 53
WebEx Communications, Inc., 81
Welcome Wagon International Inc., 82

Wells Rich Greene BDDP, 6
Westaff Inc., 33
Whitman Education Group, Inc., 41
Wieden + Kennedy, 75
William Morris Agency, Inc., 23
Williams Scotsman, Inc., 65
Workflow Management, Inc., 65
WPP Group plc, 6; 48 (upd.)
Wunderman, 86
Xerox Corporation, 69 (upd.)
Young & Rubicam, Inc., I; 22 (upd.); 66
    (upd.)

Aerospace

A.S. Yakovlev Design Bureau, 15
Aerojet-General Corp., 63
Aeronca Inc., 46
Aerosonic Corporation, 69
The Aerospatiale Group, 7; 21 (upd.)
AgustaWestland N.V., 75
Alliant Techsystems Inc., 30 (upd.)
Antonov Design Bureau, 53
Aviacionny Nauchno-Tehnicheskii
    Komplex im. A.N. Tupoleva, 24
Aviall, Inc., 73
Avions Marcel Dassault-Breguet Aviation,
    I
B/E Aerospace, Inc., 30
Ballistic Recovery Systems, Inc., 87
Banner Aerospace, Inc., 14
Beech Aircraft Corporation, 8
Bell Helicopter Textron Inc., 46
The Boeing Company, I; 10 (upd.); 32
    (upd.)
Bombardier Inc., 42 (upd.); 87 (upd.)
British Aerospace plc, I; 24 (upd.)
CAE USA Inc., 48
Canadair, Inc., 16
Cessna Aircraft Company, 8
Cirrus Design Corporation, 44
Cobham plc, 30
CPI Aerostructures, Inc., 75
Daimler-Benz Aerospace AG, 16
DeCrane Aircraft Holdings Inc., 36
Diehl Stiftung & Co. KG, 79
Ducommun Incorporated, 30
EADS SOCATA, 54
Eclipse Aviation Corporation, 87
EGL, Inc., 59
Empresa Brasileira de Aeronáutica S.A.
    (Embraer), 36
European Aeronautic Defence and Space
    Company EADS N.V., 52 (upd.)
Fairchild Aircraft, Inc., 9
Fairchild Dornier GmbH, 48 (upd.)
Finmeccanica S.p.A., 84
First Aviation Services Inc., 49
G.I.E. Airbus Industrie, I; 12 (upd.)
General Dynamics Corporation, I; 10
    (upd.); 40 (upd.)
GKN plc, 38 (upd.)
Goodrich Corporation, 46 (upd.)
Groupe Dassault Aviation SA, 26 (upd.)
Grumman Corporation, I; 11 (upd.)
Grupo Aeropuerto del Sureste, S.A. de
    C.V., 48
Gulfstream Aerospace Corporation, 7; 28
    (upd.)

HEICO Corporation, 30
International Lease Finance Corporation,
    48
Irkut Corporation, 68
Israel Aircraft Industries Ltd., 69
N.V. Koninklijke Nederlandse
    Vliegtuigenfabriek Fokker, I; 28 (upd.)
Lancair International, Inc., 67
Learjet Inc., 8; 27 (upd.)
Lockheed Martin Corporation, I; 11
    (upd.); 15 (upd.)
Loral Space & Communications Ltd., 54
    (upd.)
Magellan Aerospace Corporation, 48
Martin Marietta Corporation, I
Martin-Baker Aircraft Company Limited,
    61
McDonnell Douglas Corporation, I; 11
    (upd.)
Meggitt PLC, 34
Messerschmitt-Bölkow-Blohm GmbH., I
Moog Inc., 13
Mooney Aerospace Group Ltd., 52
The New Piper Aircraft, Inc., 44
Northrop Grumman Corporation, I; 11
    (upd.); 45 (upd.)
Orbital Sciences Corporation, 22
Pemco Aviation Group Inc., 54
Pratt & Whitney, 9
Raytheon Aircraft Holdings Inc., 46
Robinson Helicopter Company, 51
Rockwell International Corporation, I; 11
    (upd.)
Rolls-Royce Allison, 29 (upd.)
Rolls-Royce plc, I; 7 (upd.); 21 (upd.)
Rostvertol plc, 62
Russian Aircraft Corporation (MiG), 86
Safe Flight Instrument Corporation, 71
Sequa Corp., 13
Shannon Aerospace Ltd., 36
Sikorsky Aircraft Corporation, 24
Smiths Industries PLC, 25
Snecma Group, 46
Société Air France, 27 (upd.)
Spacehab, Inc., 37
Spar Aerospace Limited, 32
Sukhoi Design Bureau Aviation
    Scientific-Industrial Complex, 24
Sundstrand Corporation, 7; 21 (upd.)
Surrey Satellite Technology Limited, 83
Swales & Associates, Inc., 69
Teledyne Technologies Inc., 62 (upd.)
Textron Lycoming Turbine Engine, 9
Thales S.A., 42
Thiokol Corporation, 9; 22 (upd.)
United Technologies Corporation, I; 10
    (upd.)
Van's Aircraft, Inc., 65
Vought Aircraft Industries, Inc., 49
Whittaker Corporation, 48 (upd.)
Woodward Governor Company, 49 (upd.)
Zodiac S.A., 36

Airlines

Aer Lingus Group plc, 34
Aeroflot—Russian International Airlines,
    6; 29 (upd.)
Aerolíneas Argentinas S.A., 33; 69 (upd.)

Automotive

San Miguel Corporation, 57 (upd.)
Sapporo Breweries Limited, I; 13 (upd.); 36 (upd.)
Scheid Vineyards Inc., 66
Schieffelin & Somerset Co., 61
Scottish & Newcastle plc, 15; 35 (upd.)
The Seagram Company Ltd., I; 25 (upd.)
Sebastiani Vineyards, Inc., 28
Shepherd Neame Limited, 30
Sidney Frank Importing Co., Inc., 69
Sierra Nevada Brewing Company, 70
Skalli Group, 67
Skyy Spirits LLC 78
Sleeman Breweries Ltd., 74
Snapple Beverage Corporation, 11
The South African Breweries Limited, I; 24 (upd.)
South Beach Beverage Company, Inc., 73
Southcorp Limited, 54
Southern Wine and Spirits of America, Inc., 84
Starbucks Corporation, 13; 34 (upd.); 77 (upd.)
The Stash Tea Company, 50
Stewart's Beverages, 39
The Stroh Brewery Company, I; 18 (upd.)
Suntory Ltd., 65
Sutter Home Winery Inc., 16
Taittinger S.A., 43
Taiwan Tobacco & Liquor Corporation, 75
Takara Holdings Inc., 62
Tata Tea Ltd., 76
The Terlato Wine Group, 48
Todhunter International, Inc., 27
Triarc Companies, Inc., 34 (upd.)
Tropicana Products, Inc., 73 (upd.)
Tsingtao Brewery Group, 49
Tully's Coffee Corporation, 51
Van Houtte Inc., 39
Vermont Pure Holdings, Ltd., 51
Vin & Spirit AB, 31
Viña Concha y Toro S.A., 45
Vincor International Inc., 50
Whitbread and Company PLC, I
Widmer Brothers Brewing Company, 76
Willamette Valley Vineyards, Inc., 85
William Grant & Sons Ltd., 60
The Wine Group, Inc., 39
The Wolverhampton & Dudley Breweries, PLC, 57
Young & Co.'s Brewery, P.L.C., 38

Bio-Technology

Actelion Ltd., 83
Amersham PLC, 50
Amgen, Inc., 10; 30 (upd.)
ArQule, Inc., 68
Biogen Idec Inc., 71 (upd.)
Biogen Inc., 14; 36 (upd.)
bioMérieux S.A., 75
BTG Plc, 87
Caliper Life Sciences, Inc., 70
Cambrex Corporation, 44 (upd.)
Celera Genomics, 74
Centocor Inc., 14
Charles River Laboratories International, Inc., 42

Chiron Corporation, 10; 36 (upd.)
Covance Inc., 30
CryoLife, Inc., 46
Cytyc Corporation, 69
Delta and Pine Land Company, 33
Dionex Corporation, 46
Embrex, Inc., 72
Enzo Biochem, Inc., 41
Eurofins Scientific S.A., 70
Gen-Probe Incorporated, 79
Genentech, Inc., 32 (upd.)
Genzyme Corporation, 38 (upd.)
Gilead Sciences, Inc., 54
Howard Hughes Medical Institute, 39
Huntingdon Life Sciences Group plc, 42
IDEXX Laboratories, Inc., 23
ImClone Systems Inc., 58
Immunex Corporation, 14; 50 (upd.)
IMPATH Inc., 45
Incyte Genomics, Inc., 52
Inverness Medical Innovations, Inc., 63
Invitrogen Corporation, 52
The Judge Group, Inc., 51
Kendle International Inc., 87
Life Technologies, Inc., 17
LifeCell Corporation, 77
Lonza Group Ltd., 73
Martek Biosciences Corporation, 65
Medarex, Inc., 85
Medtronic, Inc., 30 (upd.)
Millipore Corporation, 25; 84 (upd.)
Minntech Corporation, 22
Mycogen Corporation, 21
New Brunswick Scientific Co., Inc., 45
Pacific Ethanol, Inc., 81
Qiagen N.V., 39
Quintiles Transnational Corporation, 21
Seminis, Inc., 29
Senomyx, Inc., 83
Serologicals Corporation, 63
Sigma-Aldrich Corporation, 36 (upd.)
Starkey Laboratories, Inc., 52
STERIS Corporation, 29
Stratagene Corporation, 70
Tanox, Inc., 77
TECHNE Corporation, 52
TriPath Imaging, Inc., 77
Waters Corporation, 43
Whatman plc, 46
Wisconsin Alumni Research Foundation, 65
Wyeth, 50 (upd.)

Chemicals

A. Schulman, Inc., 8
Aceto Corp., 38
Air Products and Chemicals, Inc., I; 10 (upd.); 74 (upd.)
Airgas, Inc., 54
Akzo Nobel N.V., 13; 41 (upd.)
Albemarle Corporation, 59
AlliedSignal Inc., 22 (upd.)
ALTANA AG, 87
American Cyanamid, I; 8 (upd.)
American Vanguard Corporation, 47
Arab Potash Company, 85
Arch Chemicals Inc. 78
ARCO Chemical Company, 10

Asahi Denka Kogyo KK, 64
Atanor S.A., 62
Atochem S.A., I
Avantium Technologies BV, 79
Avecia Group PLC, 63
Baker Hughes Incorporated, 22 (upd.); 57 (upd.)
Balchem Corporation, 42
BASF Aktiengesellschaft, I; 18 (upd.); 50 (upd.)
Bayer A.G., I; 13 (upd.); 41 (upd.)
Betz Laboratories, Inc., I; 10 (upd.)
The BFGoodrich Company, 19 (upd.)
BOC Group plc, I; 25 (upd.); 78 (upd.)
Brenntag AG, 8; 23 (upd.)
Burmah Castrol PLC, 30 (upd.)
Cabot Corporation, 8; 29 (upd.)
Calgon Carbon Corporation, 73
Caliper Life Sciences, Inc., 70
Cambrex Corporation, 16
Catalytica Energy Systems, Inc., 44
Celanese Corporation, I
Celanese Mexicana, S.A. de C.V., 54
Chemcentral Corporation, 8
Chemi-Trol Chemical Co., 16
Church & Dwight Co., Inc., 29
Ciba-Geigy Ltd., I; 8 (upd.)
The Clorox Company, III; 22 (upd.); 81 (upd.)
Croda International Plc, 45
Crompton Corporation, 9; 36 (upd.)
Cytec Industries Inc., 27
Degussa-Hüls AG, 32 (upd.)
DeKalb Genetics Corporation, 17
The Dexter Corporation, I; 12 (upd.)
Dionex Corporation, 46
The Dow Chemical Company, I; 8 (upd.); 50 (upd.)
DSM N.V., I; 56 (upd.)
Dynaction S.A., 67
E.I. du Pont de Nemours & Company, I; 8 (upd.); 26 (upd.)
Eastman Chemical Company, 14; 38 (upd.)
Ecolab Inc., I; 13 (upd.); 34 (upd.); 85 (upd.)
Elementis plc, 40 (upd.)
Engelhard Corporation, 72 (upd.)
English China Clays Ltd., 15 (upd.); 40 (upd.)
Enterprise Rent-A-Car Company, 69 (upd.)
Equistar Chemicals, LP, 71
Ercros S.A., 80
ERLY Industries Inc., 17
Ethyl Corporation, I; 10 (upd.)
Ferro Corporation, 8; 56 (upd.)
Firmenich International S.A., 60
First Mississippi Corporation, 8
Formosa Plastics Corporation, 14; 58 (upd.)
Fort James Corporation, 22 (upd.)
G.A.F., I
The General Chemical Group Inc., 37
Georgia Gulf Corporation, 9; 61 (upd.)
Givaudan SA, 43
Great Lakes Chemical Corporation, I; 14 (upd.)

The Turner Corporation, 8; 23 (upd.)
U.S. Aggregates, Inc., 42
U.S. Home Corporation, 8; 78 (upd.)
Urbi Desarrollos Urbanos, S.A. de C.V., 81
VA TECH ELIN EBG GmbH, 49
Veit Companies, 43
Walbridge Aldinger Co., 38
Walter Industries, Inc., 22 (upd.)
The Weitz Company, Inc., 42
Willbros Group, Inc., 56
William Lyon Homes, 59
Wilson Bowden Plc, 45
Wood Hall Trust PLC, I
The Yates Companies, Inc., 62

Containers

Ball Corporation, I; 10 (upd.); 78 (upd.)
BWAY Corporation, 24
Clarcor Inc., 17
Continental Can Co., Inc., 15
Continental Group Company, I
Crown Cork & Seal Company, Inc., I; 13 (upd.); 32 (upd.)
Crown Holdings, Inc., 83 (upd.)
Gaylord Container Corporation, 8
Golden Belt Manufacturing Co., 16
Graham Packaging Holdings Company, 87
Greif Inc., 15; 66 (upd.)
Grupo Industrial Durango, S.A. de C.V., 37
Hanjin Shipping Co., Ltd., 50
Inland Container Corporation, 8
Kerr Group Inc., 24
Keyes Fibre Company, 9
Libbey Inc., 49
Liqui-Box Corporation, 16
The Longaberger Company, 12
Longview Fibre Company, 8
The Mead Corporation, 19 (upd.)
Metal Box PLC, I
Molins plc, 51
National Can Corporation, I
Owens-Illinois, Inc., I; 26 (upd.); 85 (upd.)
Packaging Corporation of America, 51 (upd.)
Primerica Corporation, I
PVC Container Corporation, 67
Rexam PLC, 32 (upd.); 85 (upd.)
Reynolds Metals Company, 19 (upd.)
Royal Packaging Industries Van Leer N.V., 30
RPC Group PLC, 81
Sealright Co., Inc., 17
Shurgard Storage Centers, Inc., 52
Smurfit-Stone Container Corporation, 26 (upd.); 83 (upd.)
Sonoco Products Company, 8
Thermos Company, 16
Toyo Seikan Kaisha, Ltd., I
U.S. Can Corporation, 30
Ultra Pac, Inc., 24
Viatech Continental Can Company, Inc., 25 (upd.)
Vidrala S.A., 67

Vitro Corporativo S.A. de C.V., 34

Drugs & Pharmaceuticals

A. Nelson & Co. Ltd., 75
A.L. Pharma Inc., 12
Abbott Laboratories, I; 11 (upd.); 40 (upd.)
Actelion Ltd., 83
Akorn, Inc., 32
Albany Molecular Research, Inc., 77
Allergan, Inc., 77 (upd.)
Alpharma Inc., 35 (upd.)
ALZA Corporation, 10; 36 (upd.)
American Home Products, I; 10 (upd.)
American Pharmaceutical Partners, Inc., 69
AmerisourceBergen Corporation, 64 (upd.)
Amersham PLC, 50
Amgen, Inc., 10
Amylin Pharmaceuticals, Inc., 67
Andrx Corporation, 55
AstraZeneca PLC, I; 20 (upd.); 50 (upd.)
Axcan Pharma Inc., 85
Barr Pharmaceuticals, Inc., 26; 68 (upd.)
Bayer A.G., I; 13 (upd.)
Berlex Laboratories, Inc., 66
Biovail Corporation, 47
Block Drug Company, Inc., 8
Boiron S.A., 73
Bristol-Myers Squibb Company, III; 9 (upd.); 37 (upd.)
BTG Plc, 87
C.H. Boehringer Sohn, 39
Caremark Rx, Inc., 10; 54 (upd.)
Carter-Wallace, Inc., 8; 38 (upd.)
Celgene Corporation, 67
Cephalon, Inc., 45
Chiron Corporation, 10
Chugai Pharmaceutical Co., Ltd., 50
Ciba-Geigy Ltd., I; 8 (upd.)
D&K Wholesale Drug, Inc., 14
Discovery Partners International, Inc., 58
Dr. Reddy's Laboratories Ltd., 59
Elan Corporation PLC, 63
Eli Lilly and Company, I; 11 (upd.); 47 (upd.)
Endo Pharmaceuticals Holdings Inc., 71
Eon Labs, Inc., 67
Express Scripts Inc., 44 (upd.)
F. Hoffmann-La Roche Ltd., I; 50 (upd.)
Fisons plc, 9; 23 (upd.)
Forest Laboratories, Inc., 52 (upd.)
FoxMeyer Health Corporation, 16
Fujisawa Pharmaceutical Company Ltd., I
G.D. Searle & Co., I; 12 (upd.); 34 (upd.)
Galenica AG, 84
GEHE AG, 27
Genentech, Inc., I; 8 (upd.); 75 (upd.)
Genetics Institute, Inc., 8
Genzyme Corporation, 13, 77 (upd.)
Glaxo Holdings PLC, I; 9 (upd.)
GlaxoSmithKline plc, 46 (upd.)
Groupe Fournier SA, 44
H. Lundbeck A/S, 44
Hauser, Inc., 46
Heska Corporation, 39

Hexal AG, 69
Hospira, Inc., 71
Huntingdon Life Sciences Group plc, 42
ICN Pharmaceuticals, Inc., 52
Immucor, Inc., 81
Integrated BioPharma, Inc., 83
IVAX Corporation, 55 (upd.)
Janssen Pharmaceutica N.V., 80
Johnson & Johnson, III; 8 (upd.)
Jones Medical Industries, Inc., 24
The Judge Group, Inc., 51
King Pharmaceuticals, Inc., 54
Kinray Inc., 85
Kos Pharmaceuticals, Inc., 63
Kyowa Hakko Kogyo Co., Ltd., 48 (upd.)
Laboratoires Arkopharma S.A., 75
Leiner Health Products Inc., 34
Ligand Pharmaceuticals Incorporated, 47
MannKind Corporation, 87
Marion Merrell Dow, Inc., I; 9 (upd.)
Matrixx Initiatives, Inc., 74
McKesson Corporation, 12; 47 (upd.)
Medicis Pharmaceutical Corporation, 59
MedImmune, Inc., 35
Merck & Co., Inc., I; 11 (upd.); 34 (upd.)
Merz Group, 81
Miles Laboratories, I
Millennium Pharmaceuticals, Inc., 47
Monsanto Company, 29 (upd.), 77 (upd.)
Moore Medical Corp., 17
Murdock Madaus Schwabe, 26
Mylan Laboratories Inc., I; 20 (upd.); 59 (upd.)
Nadro S.A. de C.V., 86
Nastech Pharmaceutical Company Inc., 79
National Patent Development Corporation, 13
Natrol, Inc., 49
Natural Alternatives International, Inc., 49
Novartis AG, 39 (upd.)
Noven Pharmaceuticals, Inc., 55
Novo Nordisk A/S, I; 61 (upd.)
Omnicare, Inc., 49
Par Pharmaceutical Companies, Inc., 65
Perrigo Company, 59 (upd.)
Pfizer Inc., I; 9 (upd.); 38 (upd.); 79 (upd.)
Pharmacia & Upjohn Inc., I; 25 (upd.)
PLIVA d.d., 70
PolyMedica Corporation, 77
POZEN Inc., 81
QLT Inc., 71
The Quigley Corporation, 62
Quintiles Transnational Corporation, 21
R.P. Scherer, I
Ranbaxy Laboratories Ltd., 70
ratiopharm Group, 84
Roberts Pharmaceutical Corporation, 16
Roche Bioscience, 14 (upd.)
Rorer Group, I
Roussel Uclaf, I; 8 (upd.)
Sandoz Ltd., I
Sankyo Company, Ltd., I; 56 (upd.)
The Sanofi-Synthélabo Group, I; 49 (upd.)
Schering AG, I; 50 (upd.)

Electrical & Electronics

Engineering & Management Services

Entertainment & Leisure

Financial Services: Excluding Banks

Food Products

Food Services & Retailers

Health & Personal Care Products

Health Care Services

Hotels

Information Technology

Insurance

Legal Services

Manufacturing

Ameron International Corporation, 67
AMETEK, Inc., 9
AMF Bowling, Inc., 40
Ampacet Corporation, 67
Ampco-Pittsburgh Corporation, 79
Ampex Corporation, 17
Amway Corporation, 30 (upd.)
Analogic Corporation, 23
Anchor Hocking Glassware, 13
Andersen Corporation, 10
The Andersons, Inc., 31
Andis Company, Inc., 85
Andreas Stihl AG & Co. KG, 16; 59 (upd.)
Andritz AG, 51
Ansell Ltd., 60 (upd.)
Anthem Electronics, Inc., 13
Apasco S.A. de C.V., 51
Apex Digital, Inc., 63
Applica Incorporated, 43 (upd.)
Applied Films Corporation, 48
Applied Materials, Inc., 10; 46 (upd.)
Applied Micro Circuits Corporation, 38
Applied Power Inc., 9; 32 (upd.)
AptarGroup, Inc., 69
ARBED S.A., 22 (upd.)
Arc International, 76
Arctco, Inc., 16
Arctic Cat Inc., 40 (upd.)
Ariens Company, 48
The Aristotle Corporation, 62
Armor All Products Corp., 16
Armstrong Holdings, Inc., III; 22 (upd.); 81 (upd.)
Artesyn Technologies Inc., 46 (upd.)
ArthroCare Corporation, 73
ArvinMeritor, Inc., 54 (upd.)
Asahi Glass Company, Ltd., 48 (upd.)
Ashley Furniture Industries, Inc., 35
ASICS Corporation, 57
ASML Holding N.V., 50
Astec Industries, Inc., 79
Astronics Corporation, 35
ASV, Inc., 34; 66 (upd.)
Atlantis Plastics, Inc., 85
Atlas Copco AB, III; 28 (upd.); 85 (upd.)
Atwood Mobil Products, 53
AU Optronics Corporation, 67
Aurora Casket Company, Inc., 56
Austin Limited, 75
Austin Powder Company, 76
Avedis Zildjian Co., 38
Avery Dennison Corporation, 17 (upd.); 49 (upd.)
Avocent Corporation, 65
Avondale Industries, 7; 41 (upd.)
AVX Corporation, 67
B.J. Alan Co., Inc., 67
The Babcock & Wilcox Company, 82
Badger Meter, Inc., 22
BAE Systems Ship Repair, 73
Baker Hughes Incorporated, III
Baldor Electric Company, 21
Baldwin Piano & Organ Company, 18
Baldwin Technology Company, Inc., 25
Balfour Beatty plc, 36 (upd.)
Ballantyne of Omaha, Inc., 27
Ballard Medical Products, 21

Ballard Power Systems Inc., 73
Bally Manufacturing Corporation, III
Baltek Corporation, 34
Baltimore Aircoil Company, Inc., 66
Bandai Co., Ltd., 55
Barmag AG, 39
Barnes Group Inc., 13; 69 (upd.)
Barry Callebaut AG, 29
Bassett Furniture Industries, Inc., 18
Bath Iron Works, 12; 36 (upd.)
Beckman Coulter, Inc., 22
Beckman Instruments, Inc., 14
Becton, Dickinson & Company, 36 (upd.)
Behr GmbH & Co. KG, 72
BEI Technologies, Inc., 65
Beiersdorf AG, 29
Bel Fuse, Inc., 53
Belden CDT Inc., 76 (upd.)
Belden Inc., 19
Bell Sports Corporation, 16; 44 (upd.)
Belleek Pottery Ltd., 71
Beloit Corporation, 14
Bénéteau SA, 55
Benjamin Moore & Co., 13; 38 (upd.)
BenQ Corporation, 67
Berger Bros Company, 62
Bernina Holding AG, 47
Berry Plastics Corporation, 21
Berwick Offray, LLC, 70
Bianchi International (d/b/a Gregory Mountain Products), 76
BIC Corporation, 8; 23 (upd.)
BICC PLC, III
Billabong International Ltd., 44
The Bing Group, 60
Binks Sames Corporation, 21
Binney & Smith Inc., 25
bioMérieux S.A., 75
Biomet, Inc., 10
Biosite Incorporated, 73
BISSELL Inc., 9; 30 (upd.)
The Black & Decker Corporation, III; 20 (upd.); 67 (upd.)
Black Diamond Equipment, Ltd., 62
Blodgett Holdings, Inc., 61 (upd.)
Blount International, Inc., 12; 48 (upd.)
Blue Nile Inc., 61
Blundstone Pty Ltd., 76
Blyth Industries, Inc., 18
Blyth, Inc., 74 (upd.)
BMC Industries, Inc., 17; 59 (upd.)
Bodum Design Group AG, 47
BÖHLER-UDDEHOLM AG, 73
Bombardier Inc., 42 (upd.); 87 (upd.)
Boral Limited, 43 (upd.)
Borden, Inc., 22 (upd.)
Borg-Warner Corporation, III
BorgWarner Inc., 14; 32 (upd.); 85 (upd.)
Boston Scientific Corporation, 37; 77 (upd.)
Bou-Matic, 62
The Boyds Collection, Ltd., 29
BPB plc, 83
Brach's Confections, Inc., 74 (upd.)
Brady Corporation 78 (upd.)
Brammer PLC, 77
Brannock Device Company, 48
Brass Eagle Inc., 34

Bridgeport Machines, Inc., 17
Briggs & Stratton Corporation, 8; 27 (upd.)
BRIO AB, 24
British Vita plc, 33 (upd.)
Brose Fahrzeugteile GmbH & Company KG, 84
Brother Industries, Ltd., 14
Brown & Sharpe Manufacturing Co., 23
Brown Jordan International Inc., 74 (upd.)
Brown-Forman Corporation, 38 (upd.)
Broyhill Furniture Industries, Inc., 10
Brunswick Corporation, III; 22 (upd.); 77 (upd.)
BSH Bosch und Siemens Hausgeräte GmbH, 67
BTR Siebe plc, 27
Buck Knives Inc., 48
Buckeye Technologies, Inc., 42
Bucyrus International, Inc., 17
Bugle Boy Industries, Inc., 18
Building Materials Holding Corporation, 52
Bulgari S.p.A., 20
Bulova Corporation, 13; 41 (upd.)
Bundy Corporation, 17
Burelle S.A., 23
Burton Snowboards Inc., 22
Bush Boake Allen Inc., 30
Bush Industries, Inc., 20
Butler Manufacturing Company, 12; 62 (upd.)
C&J Clark International Ltd., 52
C.F. Martin & Co., Inc., 42
C.R. Bard, Inc., 65 (upd.)
California Cedar Products Company, 58
California Steel Industries, Inc., 67
Callaway Golf Company, 15; 45 (upd.)
Campbell Scientific, Inc., 51
Cannondale Corporation, 21
Canon Inc., 79 (upd.)
Capstone Turbine Corporation, 75
Caradon plc, 20 (upd.)
The Carbide/Graphite Group, Inc., 40
Carbo PLC, 67 (upd.)
Carbone Lorraine S.A., 33
Cardo AB, 53
Carhartt, Inc., 77 (upd.)
Carl-Zeiss-Stiftung, III; 34 (upd.)
Carma Laboratories, Inc., 60
Carrier Corporation, 7; 69 (upd.)
Carter Holt Harvey Ltd., 70
Cascade Corporation, 65
Cascade General, Inc., 65
CASIO Computer Co., Ltd., III; 40 (upd.)
Catalina Lighting, Inc., 43 (upd.)
Caterpillar Inc., III; 15 (upd.); 63 (upd.)
Cavco Industries, Inc., 65
CEMEX S.A. de C.V., 59 (upd.)
Central Garden & Pet Company, 58 (upd.)
Central Sprinkler Corporation, 29
Centuri Corporation, 54
Century Aluminum Company, 52
Cenveo Inc., 71 (upd.)
Cepheid, 77

Materials

Paper & Forestry

Personal Services

Petroleum

Publishing & Printing

Rubber & Tires

Textiles & Apparel

Tobacco

Transport Services

DP World, 81

East Japan Railway Company, V; 66 (upd.)

EGL, Inc., 59

Emery Air Freight Corporation, 6

Emery Worldwide Airlines, Inc., 25 (upd.)

Enterprise Rent-A-Car Company, 6

Estes Express Lines, Inc., 86

Eurotunnel Group, 37 (upd.)

EVA Airways Corporation, 51

Evergreen International Aviation, Inc., 53

Evergreen Marine Corporation (Taiwan) Ltd., 13; 50 (upd.)

Executive Jet, Inc., 36

Exel plc, 51 (upd.)

Expeditors International of Washington Inc., 17; 78 (upd.)

Federal Express Corporation, V

FedEx Corporation, 18 (upd.); 42 (upd.)

Forward Air Corporation, 75

Fritz Companies, Inc., 12

Frontline Ltd., 45

Frozen Food Express Industries, Inc., 20

Garuda Indonesia, 58 (upd.)

GATX Corporation, 6; 25 (upd.)

GE Capital Aviation Services, 36

Gefco SA, 54

General Maritime Corporation, 59

Genesee & Wyoming Inc., 27

Geodis S.A., 67

The Go-Ahead Group Plc, 28

The Greenbrier Companies, 19

Greyhound Lines, Inc., 32 (upd.)

Groupe Bourbon S.A., 60

Grupo Aeroportuario del Pacífico, S.A. de C.V., 85

Grupo TMM, S.A. de C.V., 50

Grupo Transportación Ferroviaria Mexicana, S.A. de C.V., 47

Gulf Agency Company Ltd. 78

GulfMark Offshore, Inc., 49

Hanjin Shipping Co., Ltd., 50

Hankyu Corporation, V; 23 (upd.)

Hapag-Lloyd AG, 6

Harland and Wolff Holdings plc, 19

Harper Group Inc., 17

Heartland Express, Inc., 18

The Hertz Corporation, 9

Holberg Industries, Inc., 36

Hospitality Worldwide Services, Inc., 26

Hub Group, Inc., 38

Hvide Marine Incorporated, 22

Illinois Central Corporation, 11

International Shipholding Corporation, Inc., 27

J.B. Hunt Transport Services Inc., 12

John Menzies plc, 39

Kansas City Southern Industries, Inc., 6; 26 (upd.)

Kawasaki Kisen Kaisha, Ltd., V; 56 (upd.)

Keio Teito Electric Railway Company, V

Keolis SA, 51

Kinki Nippon Railway Company Ltd., V

Kirby Corporation, 18; 66 (upd.)

Knight Transportation, Inc., 64

Koninklijke Nedlloyd Groep N.V., 6

Kuehne & Nagel International AG, V; 53 (upd.)

La Poste, V; 47 (upd.)

Laidlaw International, Inc., 80

Landstar System, Inc., 63

Leaseway Transportation Corp., 12

London Regional Transport, 6

The Long Island Rail Road Company, 68

Maine Central Railroad Company, 16

Mammoet Transport B.V., 26

Marten Transport, Ltd., 84

Martz Group, 56

Mayflower Group Inc., 6

Mercury Air Group, Inc., 20

The Mersey Docks and Harbour Company, 30

Metropolitan Transportation Authority, 35

Miller Industries, Inc., 26

Mitsui O.S.K. Lines, Ltd., V

Moran Towing Corporation, Inc., 15

The Morgan Group, Inc., 46

Morris Travel Services L.L.C., 26

Motor Cargo Industries, Inc., 35

National Car Rental System, Inc., 10

National Express Group PLC, 50

National Railroad Passenger Corporation (Amtrak), 22; 66 (upd.)

Neptune Orient Lines Limited, 47

NFC plc, 6

Nippon Express Company, Ltd., V; 64 (upd.)

Nippon Yusen Kabushiki Kaisha (NYK), V; 72 (upd.)

Norfolk Southern Corporation, V; 29 (upd.); 75 (upd.)

Oak Harbor Freight Lines, Inc., 53

Ocean Group plc, 6

Odakyu Electric Railway Co., Ltd., V; 68 (upd.)

Oglebay Norton Company, 17

Old Dominion Freight Line, Inc., 57

OMI Corporation, 59

The Oppenheimer Group, 76

Österreichische Bundesbahnen GmbH, 6

OTR Express, Inc., 25

Overnite Corporation, 14; 58 (upd.)

Overseas Shipholding Group, Inc., 11

Pacer International, Inc., 54

Pacific Basin Shipping Ltd., 86

The Peninsular and Oriental Steam Navigation Company, V; 38 (upd.)

Penske Corporation, V; 19 (upd.); 84 (upd.)

PHH Arval, V; 53 (upd.)

Pilot Air Freight Corp., 67

Plantation Pipe Line Company, 68

Polar Air Cargo Inc., 60

The Port Authority of New York and New Jersey, 48

Port Imperial Ferry Corporation, 70

Post Office Group, V

Preston Corporation, 6

RailTex, Inc., 20

Railtrack Group PLC, 50

Réseau Ferré de France, 66

Roadway Express, Inc., V; 25 (upd.)

Rock-It Cargo USA, Inc., 86

Royal Olympic Cruise Lines Inc., 52

Royal Vopak NV, 41

Ryder System, Inc., V; 24 (upd.)

Santa Fe Pacific Corporation, V

Schenker-Rhenus AG, 6

Schneider National, Inc., 36; 77 (upd.)

Seaboard Corporation, 36; 85 (upd.)

SEACOR Holdings Inc., 83

Securicor Plc, 45

Seibu Railway Company Ltd., V; 74 (upd.)

Seino Transportation Company, Ltd., 6

Simon Transportation Services Inc., 27

Smithway Motor Xpress Corporation, 39

Société Nationale des Chemins de Fer Français, V; 57 (upd.)

Société Norbert Dentressangle S.A., 67

Southern Pacific Transportation Company, V

Stagecoach Holdings plc, 30

Stelmar Shipping Ltd., 52

Stevedoring Services of America Inc., 28

Stinnes AG, 8; 59 (upd.)

Stolt-Nielsen S.A., 42

Sunoco, Inc., 28 (upd.); 83 (upd.)

Swift Transportation Co., Inc., 42

The Swiss Federal Railways (Schweizerische Bundesbahnen), V

Swissport International Ltd., 70

Teekay Shipping Corporation, 25; 82 (upd.)

Tibbett & Britten Group plc, 32

Tidewater Inc., 11; 37 (upd.)

TNT Freightways Corporation, 14

TNT Post Group N.V., V; 27 (upd.); 30 (upd.)

Tobu Railway Co Ltd, 6

Tokyu Corporation, V

Totem Resources Corporation, 9

TPG N.V., 64 (upd.)

Trailer Bridge, Inc., 41

Transnet Ltd., 6

Transport Corporation of America, Inc., 49

TTX Company, 6; 66 (upd.)

U.S. Delivery Systems, Inc., 22

Union Pacific Corporation, V; 28 (upd.); 79 (upd.)

United Parcel Service of America Inc., V; 17 (upd.)

United Parcel Service, Inc., 63

United Road Services, Inc., 69

United States Postal Service, 14; 34 (upd.)

USA Truck, Inc., 42

Velocity Express Corporation, 49

Werner Enterprises, Inc., 26

Wincanton plc, 52

Wisconsin Central Transportation Corporation, 24

Wright Express Corporation, 80

Yamato Transport Co. Ltd., V; 49 (upd.)

Yellow Corporation, 14; 45 (upd.)

Yellow Freight System, Inc. of Delaware, V

Utilities

AES Corporation, 10; 13 (upd.); 53 (upd.)

Aggreko Plc, 45

Air & Water Technologies Corporation, 6

Alberta Energy Company Ltd., 16; 43 (upd.)
Allegheny Energy, Inc., V; 38 (upd.)
Ameren Corporation, 60 (upd.)
American Electric Power Company, Inc., V; 45 (upd.)
American States Water Company, 46
American Water Works Company, Inc., 6; 38 (upd.)
Aquarion Company, 84
Aquila, Inc., 50 (upd.)
Arkla, Inc., V
Associated Natural Gas Corporation, 11
Atlanta Gas Light Company, 6; 23 (upd.)
Atlantic Energy, Inc., 6
Atmos Energy Corporation, 43
Avista Corporation, 69 (upd.)
Baltimore Gas and Electric Company, V; 25 (upd.)
Bay State Gas Company, 38
Bayernwerk AG, V; 23 (upd.)
Bewag AG, 39
Big Rivers Electric Corporation, 11
Black Hills Corporation, 20
Bonneville Power Administration, 50
Boston Edison Company, 12
Bouygues S.A., 24 (upd.)
British Energy Plc, 49
British Gas plc, V
British Nuclear Fuels plc, 6
Brooklyn Union Gas, 6
California Water Service Group, 79
Calpine Corporation, 36
Canadian Utilities Limited, 13; 56 (upd.)
Cap Rock Energy Corporation, 46
Carolina Power & Light Company, V; 23 (upd.)
Cascade Natural Gas Corporation, 9
Centerior Energy Corporation, V
Central and South West Corporation, V
Central Hudson Gas and Electricity Corporation, 6
Central Maine Power, 6
Central Vermont Public Service Corporation, 54
Centrica plc, 29 (upd.)
Chesapeake Utilities Corporation, 56
China Shenhua Energy Company Limited, 83
Chubu Electric Power Company, Inc., V; 46 (upd.)
Chugoku Electric Power Company Inc., V; 53 (upd.)
Cincinnati Gas & Electric Company, 6
CIPSCO Inc., 6
Citizens Utilities Company, 7
City Public Service, 6
Cleco Corporation, 37
CMS Energy Corporation, V, 14
The Coastal Corporation, 31 (upd.)
Cogentrix Energy, Inc., 10
The Coleman Company, Inc., 9
The Columbia Gas System, Inc., V; 16 (upd.)
Commonwealth Edison Company, V
Commonwealth Energy System, 14
Companhia Energética de Minas Gerais S.A. CEMIG, 65

Connecticut Light and Power Co., 13
Consolidated Edison, Inc., V; 45 (upd.)
Consolidated Natural Gas Company, V; 19 (upd.)
Consumers Power Co., 14
Consumers Water Company, 14
Consumers' Gas Company Ltd., 6
Covanta Energy Corporation, 64 (upd.)
Dalkia Holding, 66
Destec Energy, Inc., 12
The Detroit Edison Company, V
Dominion Resources, Inc., V; 54 (upd.)
DPL Inc., 6
DQE, Inc., 6
DTE Energy Company, 20 (upd.)
Duke Energy Corporation, V; 27 (upd.)
E.On AG, 50 (upd.)
Eastern Enterprises, 6
Edison International, 56 (upd.)
El Paso Electric Company, 21
El Paso Natural Gas Company, 12
Electrabel N.V., 67
Electricidade de Portugal, S.A., 47
Electricité de France, V; 41 (upd.)
Electricity Generating Authority of Thailand (EGAT), 56
Elektrowatt AG, 6
The Empire District Electric Company, 77
Enbridge Inc., 43
ENDESA S.A., V; 46 (upd.)
Enersis S.A., 73
ENMAX Corporation, 83
Enron Corporation, V; 46 (upd.)
Enserch Corporation, V
Ente Nazionale per L'Energia Elettrica, V
Entergy Corporation, V; 45 (upd.)
Environmental Power Corporation, 68
EPCOR Utilities Inc., 81
Equitable Resources, Inc., 6; 54 (upd.)
Exelon Corporation, 48 (upd.)
Florida Progress Corporation, V; 23 (upd.)
Florida Public Utilities Company, 69
Fortis, Inc., 15; 47 (upd.)
Fortum Corporation, 30 (upd.)
FPL Group, Inc., V; 49 (upd.)
Gas Natural SDG S.A., 69
Gaz de France, V; 40 (upd.)
General Public Utilities Corporation, V
Générale des Eaux Group, V
GPU, Inc., 27 (upd.)
Great Plains Energy Incorporated, 65 (upd.)
Gulf States Utilities Company, 6
Hawaiian Electric Industries, Inc., 9
Hokkaido Electric Power Company Inc. (HEPCO), V; 58 (upd.)
Hokuriku Electric Power Company, V
Hong Kong and China Gas Company Ltd., 73
Hongkong Electric Holdings Ltd., 6; 23 (upd.)
Houston Industries Incorporated, V
Hyder plc, 34
Hydro-Québec, 6; 32 (upd.)
Iberdrola, S.A., 49
Idaho Power Company, 12
Illinois Bell Telephone Company, 14

Illinois Power Company, 6
Indiana Energy, Inc., 27
International Power PLC, 50 (upd.)
IPALCO Enterprises, Inc., 6
ITC Holdings Corp., 75
The Kansai Electric Power Company, Inc., V; 62 (upd.)
Kansas City Power & Light Company, 6
Kelda Group plc, 45
Kenetech Corporation, 11
Kentucky Utilities Company, 6
KeySpan Energy Co., 27
Korea Electric Power Corporation (Kepco), 56
KU Energy Corporation, 11
Kyushu Electric Power Company Inc., V
LG&E Energy Corporation, 6; 51 (upd.)
Long Island Lighting Company, V
Lyonnaise des Eaux-Dumez, V
Madison Gas and Electric Company, 39
Magma Power Company, 11
Maine & Maritimes Corporation, 56
Manila Electric Company (Meralco), 56
MCN Corporation, 6
MDU Resources Group, Inc., 7; 42 (upd.)
Middlesex Water Company, 45
Midwest Resources Inc., 6
Minnesota Power, Inc., 11; 34 (upd.)
The Montana Power Company, 11; 44 (upd.)
National Fuel Gas Company, 6
National Grid USA, 51 (upd.)
National Power PLC, 12
Nebraska Public Power District, 29
N.V. Nederlandse Gasunie, V
Nevada Power Company, 11
New England Electric System, V
New Jersey Resources Corporation, 54
New York State Electric and Gas, 6
Neyveli Lignite Corporation Ltd., 65
Niagara Mohawk Holdings Inc., V; 45 (upd.)
Nicor Inc., 6; 86 (upd.)
NIPSCO Industries, Inc., 6
North West Water Group plc, 11
Northeast Utilities, V; 48 (upd.)
Northern States Power Company, V; 20 (upd.)
Northwest Natural Gas Company, 45
NorthWestern Corporation, 37
Nova Corporation of Alberta, V
NRG Energy, Inc., 79
Oglethorpe Power Corporation, 6
Ohio Edison Company, V
Oklahoma Gas and Electric Company, 6
ONEOK Inc., 7
Ontario Hydro Services Company, 6; 32 (upd.)
Osaka Gas Company, Ltd., V; 60 (upd.)
Österreichische Elektrizitätswirtschafts-AG, 85
Otter Tail Power Company, 18
Pacific Enterprises, V
Pacific Gas and Electric Company, V
PacifiCorp, V; 26 (upd.)
Panhandle Eastern Corporation, V
PECO Energy Company, 11
Pennon Group Plc, 45

Waste Services

Geographic Index

Germany

Tokyu Department Store Co., Ltd., V; 32 (upd.)
Tokyu Land Corporation, IV
Tomen Corporation, IV; 24 (upd.)
Tomy Company Ltd., 65
TonenGeneral Sekiyu K.K., IV; 16 (upd.); 54 (upd.)
Topcon Corporation, 84
Toppan Printing Co., Ltd., IV; 58 (upd.)
Toray Industries, Inc., V; 51 (upd.)
Toshiba Corporation, I; 12 (upd.); 40 (upd.)
Tosoh Corporation, 70
TOTO LTD., III; 28 (upd.)
Toyo Sash Co., Ltd., III
Toyo Seikan Kaisha, Ltd., I
Toyoda Automatic Loom Works, Ltd., III
Toyota Motor Corporation, I; 11 (upd.); 38 (upd.)
Ube Industries, Ltd., III; 38 (upd.)
ULVAC, Inc., 80
Unicharm Corporation, 84
Unitika Ltd., V; 53 (upd.)
Uny Co., Ltd., V; 49 (upd.)
Victor Company of Japan, Limited, II; 26 (upd.); 83 (upd.)
Wacoal Corp., 25
Yamada Denki Co., Ltd., 85
Yamaha Corporation, III; 16 (upd.); 40 (upd.)
Yamaichi Securities Company, Limited, II
Yamato Transport Co. Ltd., V; 49 (upd.)
Yamazaki Baking Co., Ltd., 58
The Yasuda Fire and Marine Insurance Company, Limited, III
The Yasuda Mutual Life Insurance Company, III; 39 (upd.)
The Yasuda Trust and Banking Company, Ltd., II; 17 (upd.)
The Yokohama Rubber Co., Ltd., V; 19 (upd.)

Jordan
Arab Potash Company, 85

Kuwait
Kuwait Airways Corporation, 68
Kuwait Flour Mills & Bakeries Company, 84
Kuwait Petroleum Corporation, IV; 55 (upd.)

Latvia
A/S Air Baltic Corporation, 71

Lebanon
Middle East Airlines - Air Liban S.A.L. 79

Libya
National Oil Corporation, IV; 66 (upd.)

Liechtenstein
Hilti AG, 53

Luxembourg
ARBED S.A., IV; 22 (upd.)
Cargolux Airlines International S.A., 49

Espírito Santo Financial Group S.A. 79 (upd.)
Gemplus International S.A., 64
RTL Group SA, 44
Société Luxembourgeoise de Navigation Aérienne S.A., 64
Tenaris SA, 63

Malaysia
Berjaya Group Bhd., 67
Genting Bhd., 65
Malayan Banking Berhad, 72
Malaysian Airlines System Berhad, 6; 29 (upd.)
Perusahaan Otomobil Nasional Bhd., 62
Petroliam Nasional Bhd (Petronas), IV; 56 (upd.)
PPB Group Berhad, 57
Sime Darby Berhad, 14; 36 (upd.)
Telekom Malaysia Bhd, 76
Yeo Hiap Seng Malaysia Bhd., 75

Mauritius
Air Mauritius Ltd., 63

Mexico
Alfa, S.A. de C.V., 19
Altos Hornos de México, S.A. de C.V., 42
América Móvil, S.A. de C.V., 80
Apasco S.A. de C.V., 51
Bolsa Mexicana de Valores, S.A. de C.V., 80
Bufete Industrial, S.A. de C.V., 34
Casa Cuervo, S.A. de C.V., 31
Celanese Mexicana, S.A. de C.V., 54
CEMEX S.A. de C.V., 20; 59 (upd.)
Cifra, S.A. de C.V., 12
Cinemas de la República, S.A. de C.V., 83
Compañia Industrial de Parras, S.A. de C.V. (CIPSA), 84
Consorcio ARA, S.A. de C.V. 79
Consorcio Aviacsa, S.A. de C.V., 85
Consorcio G Grupo Dina, S.A. de C.V., 36
Controladora Comercial Mexicana, S.A. de C.V., 36
Controladora Mabe, S.A. de C.V., 82
Coppel, S.A. de C.V., 82
Corporación Geo, S.A. de C.V., 81
Corporación Interamericana de Entretenimiento, S.A. de C.V., 83
Corporación Internacional de Aviación, S.A. de C.V. (Cintra), 20
Desarrolladora Homex, S.A. de C.V., 87
Desc, S.A. de C.V., 23
Editorial Televisa, S.A. de C.V., 57
Empresas ICA Sociedad Controladora, S.A. de C.V., 41
Ford Motor Company, S.A. de C.V., 20
Gruma, S.A. de C.V., 31
Grupo Aeroportuario del Pacífico, S.A. de C.V., 85
Grupo Aeropuerto del Sureste, S.A. de C.V., 48
Grupo Ángeles Servicios de Salud, S.A. de C.V., 84
Grupo Carso, S.A. de C.V., 21

Grupo Casa Saba, S.A. de C.V., 39
Grupo Comercial Chedraui S.A. de C.V., 86
Grupo Corvi S.A. de C.V., 86
Grupo Cydsa, S.A. de C.V., 39
Grupo Elektra, S.A. de C.V., 39
Grupo Financiero Banamex S.A., 54
Grupo Financiero Banorte, S.A. de C.V., 51
Grupo Financiero BBVA Bancomer S.A., 54
Grupo Financiero Serfin, S.A., 19
Grupo Gigante, S.A. de C.V., 34
Grupo Herdez, S.A. de C.V., 35
Grupo IMSA, S.A. de C.V., 44
Grupo Industrial Bimbo, 19
Grupo Industrial Durango, S.A. de C.V., 37
Grupo Industrial Herradura, S.A. de C.V., 83
Grupo Industrial Lala, S.A. de C.V., 82
Grupo Industrial Saltillo, S.A. de C.V., 54
Grupo Mexico, S.A. de C.V., 40
Grupo Modelo, S.A. de C.V., 29
Grupo Posadas, S.A. de C.V., 57
Grupo Televisa, S.A., 18; 54 (upd.)
Grupo TMM, S.A. de C.V., 50
Grupo Transportación Ferroviaria Mexicana, S.A. de C.V., 47
Grupo Viz, S.A. de C.V., 84
Hylsamex, S.A. de C.V., 39
Industrias Bachoco, S.A. de C.V., 39
Industrias Penoles, S.A. de C.V., 22
Internacional de Ceramica, S.A. de C.V., 53
Jugos del Valle, S.A. de C.V., 85
Kimberly-Clark de México, S.A. de C.V., 54
Nadro S.A. de C.V., 86
Organización Soriana, S.A. de C.V., 35
Petróleos Mexicanos, IV; 19 (upd.)
Proeza S.A. de C.V., 82
Pulsar Internacional S.A., 21
Real Turismo, S.A. de C.V., 50
Sanborn Hermanos, S.A., 20
Sears Roebuck de México, S.A. de C.V., 20
Telefonos de Mexico S.A. de C.V., 14; 63 (upd.)
Tubos de Acero de Mexico, S.A. (TAMSA), 41
TV Azteca, S.A. de C.V., 39
Urbi Desarrollos Urbanos, S.A. de C.V., 81
Valores Industriales S.A., 19
Vitro Corporativo S.A. de C.V., 34
Wal-Mart de Mexico, S.A. de C.V., 35 (upd.)

Nepal
Royal Nepal Airline Corporation, 41

Netherlands
ABN AMRO Holding, N.V., 50
AEGON N.V., III; 50 (upd.)
Akzo Nobel N.V., 13; 41 (upd.)
Algemene Bank Nederland N.V., II
Amsterdam-Rotterdam Bank N.V., II

United States

Rockefeller Group International Inc., 58
Rockford Corporation, 43
Rockford Products Corporation, 55
RockShox, Inc., 26
Rockwell Automation, 43 (upd.)
Rockwell International Corporation, I; 11 (upd.)
Rocky Mountain Chocolate Factory, Inc., 73
Rocky Shoes & Boots, Inc., 26
Rodale, Inc., 23; 47 (upd.)
ROFIN-SINAR Technologies Inc., 81
Rogers Corporation, 61; 80 (upd.)
Rohm and Haas Company, I; 26 (upd.); 77 (upd.)
ROHN Industries, Inc., 22
Rohr Incorporated, 9
Roll International Corporation, 37
Rollerblade, Inc., 15; 34 (upd.)
Rollins, Inc., 11
Rolls-Royce Allison, 29 (upd.)
Roly Poly Franchise Systems LLC, 83
Romacorp, Inc., 58
Roman Meal Company, 84
Ron Tonkin Chevrolet Company, 55
Ronco Corporation, 15; 80 (upd.)
Rooms To Go Inc., 28
Rooney Brothers Co., 25
Roper Industries, Inc., 15; 50 (upd.)
Ropes & Gray, 40
Rorer Group, I
Rose Acre Farms, Inc., 60
Rose Art Industries, 58
Rose's Stores, Inc., 13
Roseburg Forest Products Company, 58
Rosemount Inc., 15
Rosenbluth International Inc., 14
Ross Stores, Inc., 17; 43 (upd.)
Rotary International, 31
Roto-Rooter, Inc., 15; 61 (upd.)
The Rottlund Company, Inc., 28
Rouge Steel Company, 8
Rounder Records Corporation 79
Roundy's Inc., 14; 58 (upd.)
The Rouse Company, 15; 63 (upd.)
Rowan Companies, Inc., 43
Roy Anderson Corporation, 75
Roy F. Weston, Inc., 33
Royal Appliance Manufacturing Company, 15
Royal Caribbean Cruises Ltd., 22; 74 (upd.)
Royal Crown Company, Inc., 23
RPM, Inc., 8; 36 (upd.)
RSA Security Inc., 46
RTM Restaurant Group, 58
Rubbermaid Incorporated, III; 20 (upd.)
Rubio's Restaurants, Inc., 35
Ruby Tuesday, Inc., 18; 71 (upd.)
Ruiz Food Products, Inc., 53
Rural Cellular Corporation, 43
Rural/Metro Corporation, 28
Rush Communications, 33
Rush Enterprises, Inc., 64
Russ Berrie and Company, Inc., 12; 82 (upd.)
Russell Corporation, 8; 30 (upd.); 82 (upd.)

Russell Reynolds Associates Inc., 38
Russell Stover Candies Inc., 12
Rust International Inc., 11
Ruth's Chris Steak House, 28
RWD Technologies, Inc., 76
Ryan Beck & Co., Inc., 66
Ryan's Restaurant Group, Inc., 15; 68 (upd.)
Ryder System, Inc., V; 24 (upd.)
Ryerson Tull, Inc., 40 (upd.)
Ryko Corporation, 83
The Ryland Group, Inc., 8; 37 (upd.)
S&C Electric Company, 15
S&D Coffee, Inc., 84
S&K Famous Brands, Inc., 23
S-K-I Limited, 15
S.C. Johnson & Son, Inc., III; 28 (upd.)
Saatchi & Saatchi, 42 (upd.)
Sabratek Corporation, 29
SABRE Group Holdings, Inc., 26
Sabre Holdings Corporation, 74 (upd.)
Safe Flight Instrument Corporation, 71
SAFECO Corporaton, III
Safeguard Scientifics, Inc., 10
Safelite Glass Corp., 19
Safeskin Corporation, 18
Safety Components International, Inc., 63
Safety 1st, Inc., 24
Safety-Kleen Systems Inc., 8; 82 (upd.)
Safeway Inc., II; 24 (upd.); 85 (upd.)
Saga Communications, Inc., 27
The St. Joe Company, 31
St. Joe Paper Company, 8
St. John Knits, Inc., 14
St. Jude Medical, Inc., 11; 43 (upd.)
St. Louis Music, Inc., 48
St. Mary Land & Exploration Company, 63
St. Paul Bank for Cooperatives, 8
The St. Paul Travelers Companies, Inc. III; 22 (upd.); 79 (upd.)
Saks Inc., 24; 41 (upd.)
Salant Corporation, 12; 51 (upd.)
salesforce.com, Inc. 79
Salick Health Care, Inc., 53
Sally Beauty Company, Inc., 60
Salomon Inc., II; 13 (upd.)
Salt River Project, 19
Salton, Inc., 30
The Salvation Army USA, 32
Sam Ash Music Corporation, 30
Sam Levin Inc., 80
Sam's Club, 40
Samsonite Corporation, 13; 43 (upd.)
Samuel Cabot Inc., 53
Samuels Jewelers Incorporated, 30
San Diego Gas & Electric Company, V
San Diego Padres Baseball Club LP 78
Sanborn Map Company Inc., 82
Sandals Resorts International, 65
Sanders Morris Harris Group Inc., 70
Sanderson Farms, Inc., 15
Sandia National Laboratories, 49
Sanford L.P., 82
Santa Barbara Restaurant Group, Inc., 37
The Santa Cruz Operation, Inc., 38
Santa Fe Gaming Corporation, 19
Santa Fe International Corporation, 38

Santa Fe Pacific Corporation, V
Sara Lee Corporation, II; 15 (upd.); 54 (upd.)
Sarnoff Corporation, 57
Sarris Candies Inc., 86
SAS Institute Inc., 10; 78 (upd.)
Saturn Corporation, 7; 21 (upd.); 80 (upd.)
Saucony Inc., 35; 86 (upd.)
Sauder Woodworking Company, 12; 35 (upd.)
Sauer-Danfoss Inc., 61
Saul Ewing LLP, 74
Savannah Foods & Industries, Inc., 7
Sawtek Inc., 43 (upd.)
Sbarro, Inc., 16; 64 (upd.)
SBC Communications Inc., 32 (upd.)
SBS Technologies, Inc., 25
SCANA Corporation, 6; 56 (upd.)
ScanSource, Inc., 29; 74 (upd.)
SCB Computer Technology, Inc., 29
SCEcorp, V
Schawk, Inc., 24
Scheels All Sports Inc., 63
Scheid Vineyards Inc., 66
Schering-Plough Corporation, I; 14 (upd.); 49 (upd.)
Schieffelin & Somerset Co., 61
Schlage Lock Company, 82
Schlotzsky's, Inc., 36
Schlumberger Limited, III; 17 (upd.); 59 (upd.)
Schmitt Music Company, 40
Schneider National, Inc., 36; 77 (upd.)
Schneiderman's Furniture Inc., 28
Schnitzer Steel Industries, Inc., 19
Scholastic Corporation, 10; 29 (upd.)
School Specialty, Inc., 68
School-Tech, Inc., 62
Schott Brothers, Inc., 67
Schott Corporation, 53
Schottenstein Stores Corp., 14
Schreiber Foods, Inc., 72
Schuff Steel Company, 26
Schultz Sav-O Stores, Inc., 21; 31 (upd.)
The Schwan Food Company, 83 (upd.)
Schwan's Sales Enterprises, Inc., 7; 26 (upd.)
Schwebel Baking Company, 72
Schweitzer-Mauduit International, Inc., 52
Schwinn Cycle and Fitness L.P., 19
SCI Systems, Inc., 9
Science Applications International Corporation, 15
Scientific Games Corporation, 64 (upd.)
Scientific-Atlanta, Inc., 6; 45 (upd.)
The SCO Group Inc. 78
The Score Board, Inc., 19
Scotsman Industries, Inc., 20
Scott Fetzer Company, 12; 80 (upd.)
Scott Paper Company, IV; 31 (upd.)
The Scotts Company, 22
Scottrade, Inc., 85
Scotty's, Inc., 22
The Scoular Company, 77
Scovill Fasteners Inc., 24
SCP Pool Corporation, 39
Screen Actors Guild, 72

Wales
Hyder plc, 34
Iceland Group plc, 33
Kwik Save Group plc, 11

Zambia
Zambia Industrial and Mining
Corporation Ltd., IV